USA TODAY

Sports Atlas

by Will Balliett & f-stop Fitzgerald

Associate Editor: Duncan Bock
Assistant Editor: Elizabeth Mitchell
Book Design: High Falls Design
Cover Design: Designed to Print
Production Manager: John Jordan

Acknowledgements:
Our thanks to our editor Rosemarie Robotham; also to Lisa Volpe, Karen Novian, Kate Smith and the entire cartographic staff at Gousha. We would also like to thank Susan Leopold, Liz Barrett, Chris Raymond, Jeanette Christopher and Donna Jordan. And at USA TODAY, it was a pleasure and a privilege to work with managing editor/sports Gene Policinski, Barbara Geehan, Scott Kauffman, Carol Herwig, Stephanie Hart, the entire USA TODAY sports staff, and, especially, Susan Bokern and Silvia Molina.

Printed in America. First Edition.
ISBN 0-13-835570-3
Published by H.M. Gousha
15 Columbus Circle, New York, NY 10023

A Division of Simon & Schuster
A Paramount Communications Company
GOUSHA—AMERICA'S MAPMAKER SINCE 1926

Table of Contents

The Maps

Tip Offs

The States

How to Use the Sports Atlas 128-129. Information for each state includes an introductory overview; the complete listing of every major and minor Spectator Venue from baseball to yachting, with map page numbers and grid coordinates; selected Outdoor Venues, including national parks, sports-oriented state parks and top alpine and nordic ski areas, also with map grid coordinates; relevant local contacts for dozens of Active Sports, from aerobics to whitewater; plus Tip Off sidebars (see left column), celebrity quotes and USA TODAY Snapshots.

State-by-State Information

The Sports

Map Directory

CANADA SEE PAGES 126-127
PACIFIC STANDARD TIME
MOUNTAIN STANDARD
PACIFIC OCEAN
MEXICO
ALASKA
MILES
KILOMETERS
NORTHWEST TERRITORIES
YUKON
BRITISH COLUMBIA
ALBERTA
CANADA SEE PAGES 126-127
MEXICO SEE PAGES 138-139
HAWAIIAN ISLANDS
OAHU
HONOLULU
ALASKA-HAWAII STANDARD TIME
Gulf of Alaska
Bering Sea
Beaufort Sea
ALEUTIAN ISLANDS
VANCOUVER
VICTORIA
SEATTLE
TACOMA
OLYMPIA
SPOKANE
PORTLAND
SALEM
EUGENE
BOISE
SALT LAKE CITY
RENO
CARSON CITY
SACRAMENTO
SAN FRANCISCO
LOS ANGELES
SAN DIEGO
LAS VEGAS
PHOENIX
TUCSON
EL PASO
ALBUQUERQUE
SANTA FE
DENVER
COLORADO SPRINGS
PUEBLO
CHEYENNE
CASPER
BILLINGS
HELENA
GREAT FALLS
BUTTE
CALGARY
REGINA
SASKATOON
BISMARCK
RAPID CITY
AMARILLO
LUBBOCK
SAN ANTONIO
NUEVO LAREDO
MONTERREY
CIUDAD JUÁREZ
ANCHORAGE
FAIRBANKS
JUNEAU
WHITEHORSE
EDMONTON
YELLOWKNIFE
WASHINGTON
M-S-UH-623-J

CANADA SEE PAGES 126-127

Tourist Regulations for Visitors to Canada

U.S. citizens or permanent residents do not require passports or visas to visit Canada but should carry some identification papers showing their citizenship. Naturalized U.S. citizens should carry a naturalization certificate. Alien residents in the U.S. must carry their Alien Registration Receipt Card. Persons under 18, not traveling with an adult, should bring a letter giving them permission to travel to Canada.

Vehicles and trailers will be admitted for touring in Canada temporarily for periods up to 12 months without customs' assessment. Motorists are advised to obtain a "Canadian Non-Resident Inter-Provincial Motor Vehicle Liability Insurance Card" for proof of financial responsibility, available only through U.S. Insurance companies.

Radio Transmitting Equipment Operators who have been issued an amateur station license by the government of the United States or citizens of the United States who operate C.B. radios are authorized to operate their stations while in Canada. Amateur radio operators must comply with the terms and conditions of their licenses as well as Canadian radio regulations when operating in Canada. C.B. radio operators must comply with the Canadian General Radio Service (G.R.S.) regulations when operating in Canada. American operators of mobile telephone radio units are authorized to use their mobile telephones while in Canada. American operators of any other type of radio equipment and all radio operators from any country other than the United States must obtain prior authorization from District Manager, Department of Communications, 473 Albert Street, Room 100B, Ottawa, Ontario, Canada K1R 5B4 to operate such equipment in Canada. Unauthorized use of any radio transmitting equipment may result in penalties and forfeiture.

Personal effects, tourists' outfits and sportsmen's equipment are admitted into Canada temporarily. However, entry of firearms and offensive weapons into Canada is rigidly controlled and they must be declared to customs. Failure to do so will result in seizure, forfeiture and possible criminal charges. Non-restricted firearms (long guns) may be brought into Canada, without permit, by persons who are 16 years of age or older, with the excepton of British Columbia where age requirement is 18. The long gun must be essential to the purpose of the person's visit, such as, legitimate sporting or competition use, personal protection against wildlife in remote wilderness areas, excluding national parks, or the visitor must be traveling in-transit through Canada. Restricted firearms can only be imported for the purpose of attending an approved shooting competition or gun show. For information governing hunting and fishing in Canada, contact the proper authorities at the capitals of the provinces in which you are interested. For information regarding travel on the Alaska Highway, write to the Canadian Government Office of Tourism, 235 Queen Street, 4th Floor East, Ottawa, Ontario, Canada K1A OH6.

Pet dogs or cats may be brought into Canada when accompanied by a certificate from a licensed veterinarian, which clearly identifies the animal and certifies that the dog or cat has been vaccinated against rabies during the last 36 months.

Each U.S. resident who has been in Canada 48 hours may bring into the United States, duty free, articles purchased for personal or household use and not intended for resale based on fair retail value of $400 if he has not claimed the exemption during the preceding 30 days. A flat rate of duty (10%) will be applied to the next $600 worth (fair retail value) of merchandise if this benefit has not been claimed within the 30 day period preceding arrival. Persons not eligible for the $400 exemption may be entitled to a $25 exemption for gifts of articles for personal or household use. Consult customs officials about special regulations governing the importation of alcoholic beverages and tobacco.

Correct at date of publication, but subject to change. TR2B

Tourist Regulations for Visitors to Mexico

U.S. citizens are not required to have passports to visit Mexico, but must have proof of citizenship (such as birth certificates, voter's registration, passport, etc.) Naturalized U.S. citizens must carry naturalization certificates or U.S. passports. Alien residents in the U.S. should consult nearest Mexican Consulate or Mexican Government Tourist Office. Consult nearest Mexican Consulate or Mexican Government Tourist Office in the U.S. or Canada for information on the following: how to obtain the (free) Tourist Card, which must be carried by persons of all ages, and additional documentation required by persons under 18, not traveling with both parents.

It is recommended that dollars be exchanged for pesos only at airport exchange booths (in the U.S. and Mexico) and banks. Banks are open only Monday thru Friday and are also closed on holidays. Be sure credit card charges are in pesos, not dollars.

A smallpox vaccination certificate is no longer required when entering Mexico or returning to the U.S. unless you have traveled to other continents or to Central or South America.

Car permits are obtainable at the border upon presentation of driver's license, registration, current license plates and proof of ownership, which can be either certificate of title or a notorized affidavit that the applicant is the owner or drives with the owner's permission. These permits must be turned in to the Mexican Customs at the border on returning to the U.S. Canadian and American insurance is not valid in Mexico. Short term tourist insurance is available at most ports of entry. Citizens of U.S. and Canada are not required to have the Tourist Card, passport or car permit if visits to border towns are less than 72 hours.

Gasoline is readily available on main highways. On other roads fill tank often.

Citizens band radios may be used in Mexico. It is recommended that you inquire locally as to useable channels.

It is against the law to take firearms into Mexico, except on trips exclusively for hunting, in which case the interested party should contact in advance the nearest Mexican Consulate for details.

Each U.S. resident may bring into the U.S. free of duty articles purchased in Mexico for personal or household use and not intended for resale to an aggregate fair retail value of $300 if he has not claimed the exemption during the preceding 30 days. Make local inquiry for further exemptions.

Correct at date of publication, but subject to change. TR46

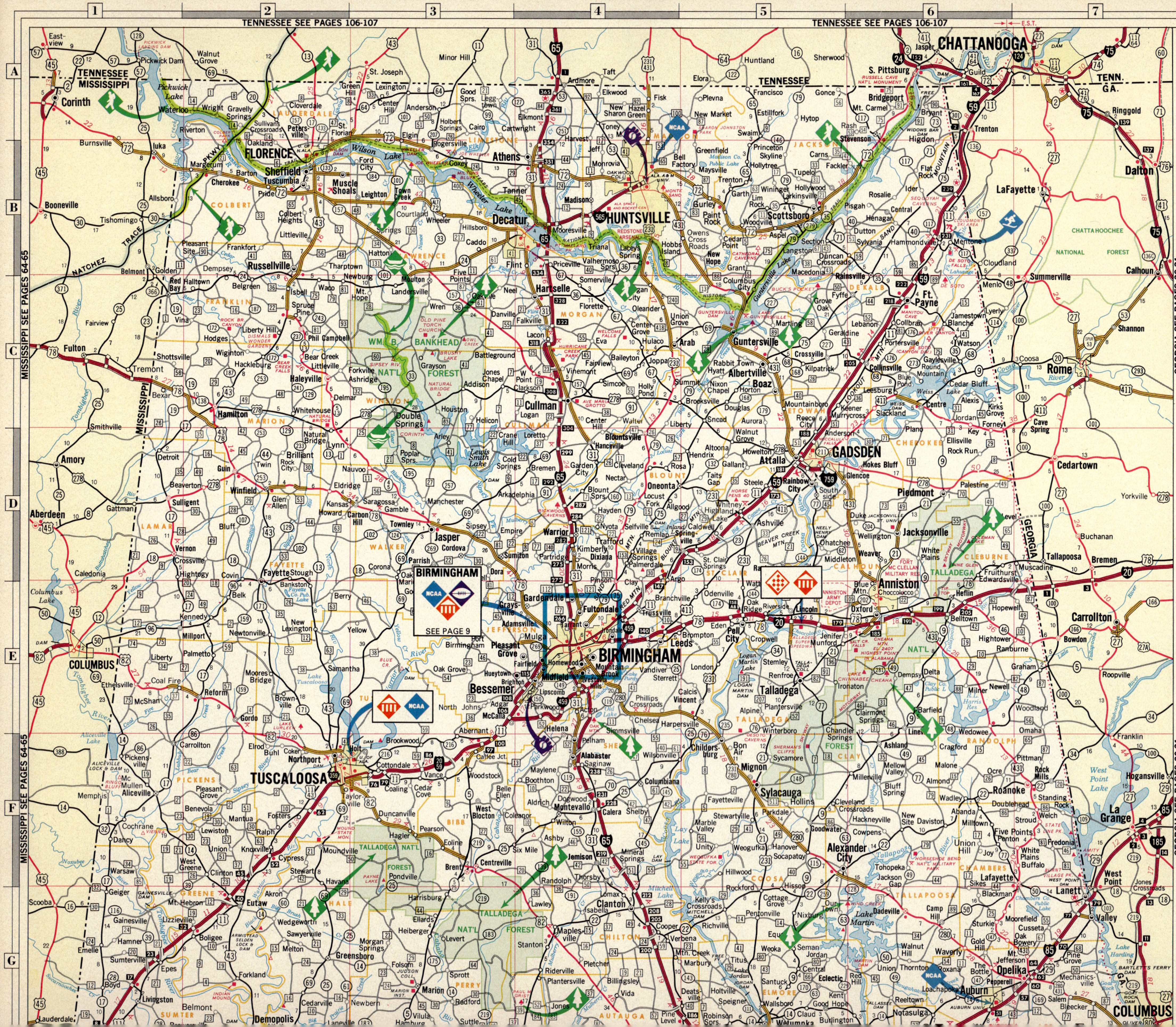

ALABAMA

Pop. (1990) 4,062,608
Area 51,609 Sq. Mi.

COUNTIES

PARTIAL LIST OF

CITIES AND TOWNS

• County Seats

ALABAMA
© H.M. GOUSHA
MONTGOMERY
ALABAMA
GULF OF MEXICO
MISSISSIPPI SEE PAGES 64-65
GEORGIA SEE PAGES 30-31
FLORIDA SEE PAGES 26-27
EXPLANATION OF ACTIVITIES
SPECIAL FEATURES
HIGHWAY MARKERS
ROAD CLASSIFICATIONS
POPULATION SYMBOLS
EGLIN AIR FORCE BASE
CONECUH NATL FOREST
Lithographed in U.S.A.

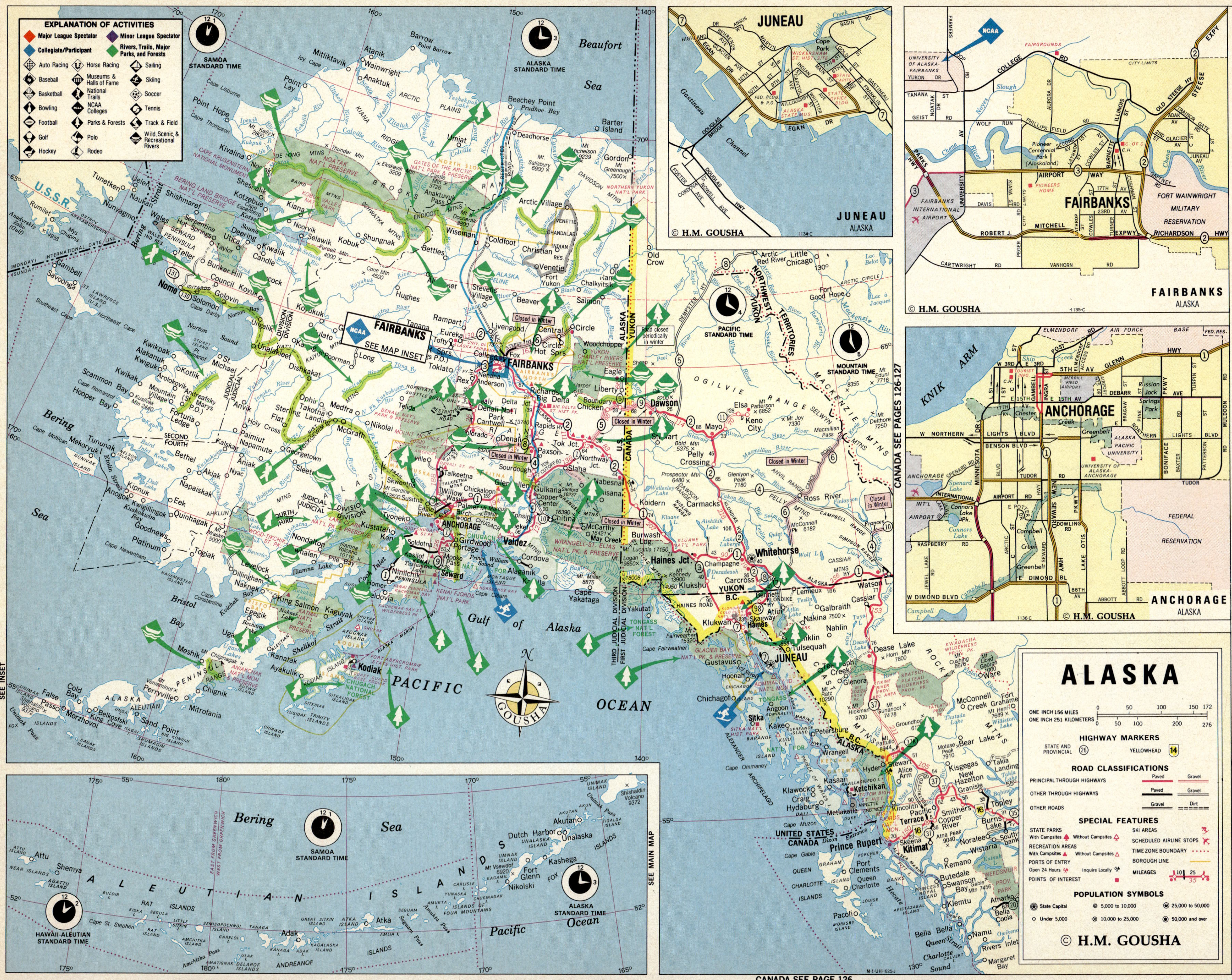

ALASKA

Pop. 551,947

PARTIAL LIST OF

CITIES AND TOWNS

Akiak	D-2
Anchorage	D-3
Anderson	C-3
Aniak	D-2
Anogok	D-1
Ayakulik	E-2
Big Delta	C-4
Cantwell	D-3
Cape Yakataga	E-4
Central	C-4
Chichagof	E-5
Chickaloon	D-3
Chignik	E-2
Chisana	D-4
Chitina	D-4
Circle	C-4
Circle Hot Springs	C-4
Colorado	D-3
Copper Center	D-4
Cordova	D-4
Craig	F-5
Delta Junction	C-4
Denali National Park	C-3
Dillingham	E-2
Eek	D-2
Egegik	E-2
Eureka	C-3
Fairbanks	C-4
Flat	D-2
Fortuna (Ledge P.O.)	D-2
Fox	C-4
Georgetown	D-2
Glennallen	D-4
Goodnews	D-1
Gulkana	D-4
Gustavus	E-5
Haines	E-5
Healy	C-3
Holy Cross	D-2
Homer	E-3
Hoonah	E-5
Hydaburg	F-5
Hyder	F-6
Juneau	E-5
Kaguyak	E-2
Kake	F-5
Kalskag	D-2
Kanatak	E-2
Kasaan	F-5
Kasilof	D-3
Katalla	E-4
Kenai	D-3
Ketchikan	F-6
Kipnuk	D-1
Klawock	F-5
Klukwan	E-5
Kodiak	E-3
Kustatan	D-3
Kwigillingok	D-1
Levelock	E-2
Livengood	C-3
Manley Hot Springs (Hot Springs P.O.)	C-3
May Creek	D-4
McCarthy	D-4
McGrath	D-3
Medfra	C-3
Mekoryuk	D-1
Meshik	E-2
Metlakatla	F-5
Mitrofania	E-2
Moose Pass	D-3
Nabesna	D-4
Naknek	E-2
Napaiskak	D-2
Napamute	D-2
Nenana	C-3
Newhalen	D-2
Nikolai	D-3
Ninilchik	E-3
Nome	C-2
Nondalton	D-2
Northway Junction	D-4
Nyac	D-2
Ophir	C-2
Paimiut	D-2
Palmer	D-3
Paxson	D-4
Petersburg	F-5
Petersville	D-3
Pile Bay	D-2
Platinum	D-1
Portage	C-4
Quinhagak	D-2
Rapids	D-4
Richardson	C-4
Seidovia	E-3
Seward	E-3
Sitka	F-5
Skagway	E-5
Skwentna	D-3
Slana	D-4
Sleetmute	D-2
Soldotna	D-3
Sourdough	D-4
Sterling Landing	D-2
Susitna	D-3
Takotna	C-2
Talkeetna	D-3
Tiekel	D-4
Tofty	C-3
Togiak	D-2
Tok Junction	D-4
Tonsina	D-4
Tununak	D-1
Tyonek	D-3
Ugashik	E-2
Valdez	D-4
Willow	D-3
Wrangell	F-5
Yakutat	E-4

SF-625-J

BIRMINGHAM AND VICINITY
MOBILE ALABAMA
TUCSON AND VICINITY
PHOENIX AND VICINITY
BIRMINGHAM
MOBILE
TUCSON
SOUTH TUCSON
PHOENIX
SCOTTSDALE
GLENDALE
PEORIA
TEMPE
MESA
CHANDLER
GILBERT
Mobile Bay
DAVIS-MONTHAN AIR FORCE BASE
SAN XAVIER INDIAN RESERVATION
SALT RIVER INDIAN RESERVATION
GILA RIVER INDIAN RESERVATION
PHOENIX SOUTH MOUNTAIN PARK
© H.M. GOUSHA
Lithographed in U.S.A.

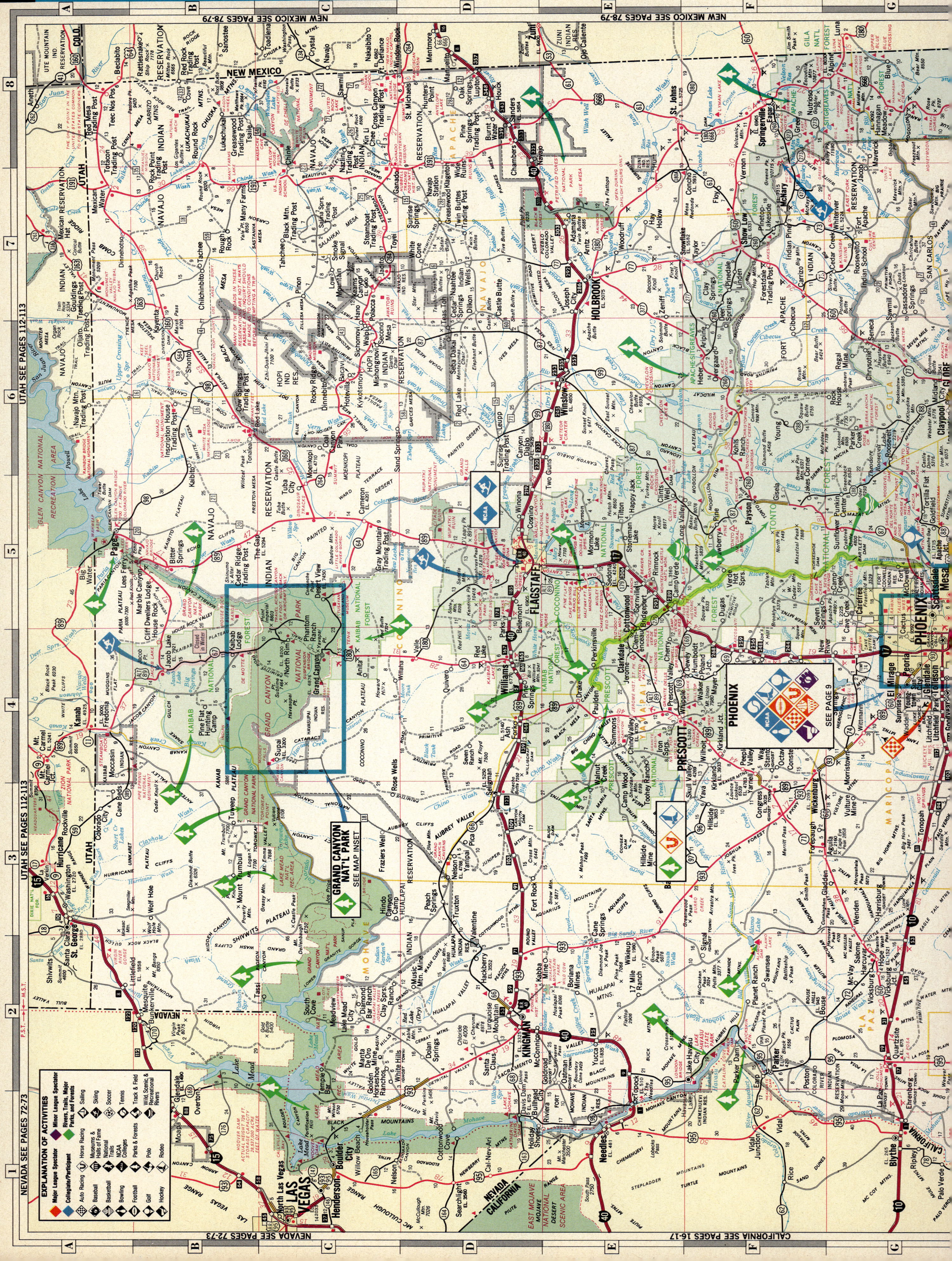
NEW MEXICO SEE PAGES 78-79
UTAH SEE PAGES 112-113
NEVADA SEE PAGES 72-73
CALIFORNIA SEE PAGES 16-17
GRAND CANYON NAT'L PARK SEE MAP INSET
PHOENIX SEE PAGE 9
EXPLANATION OF ACTIVITIES
FLAGSTAFF
PHOENIX
PRESCOTT
KINGMAN
HOLBROOK
LAS VEGAS
NEW MEXICO
UTAH
NEVADA
CALIFORNIA

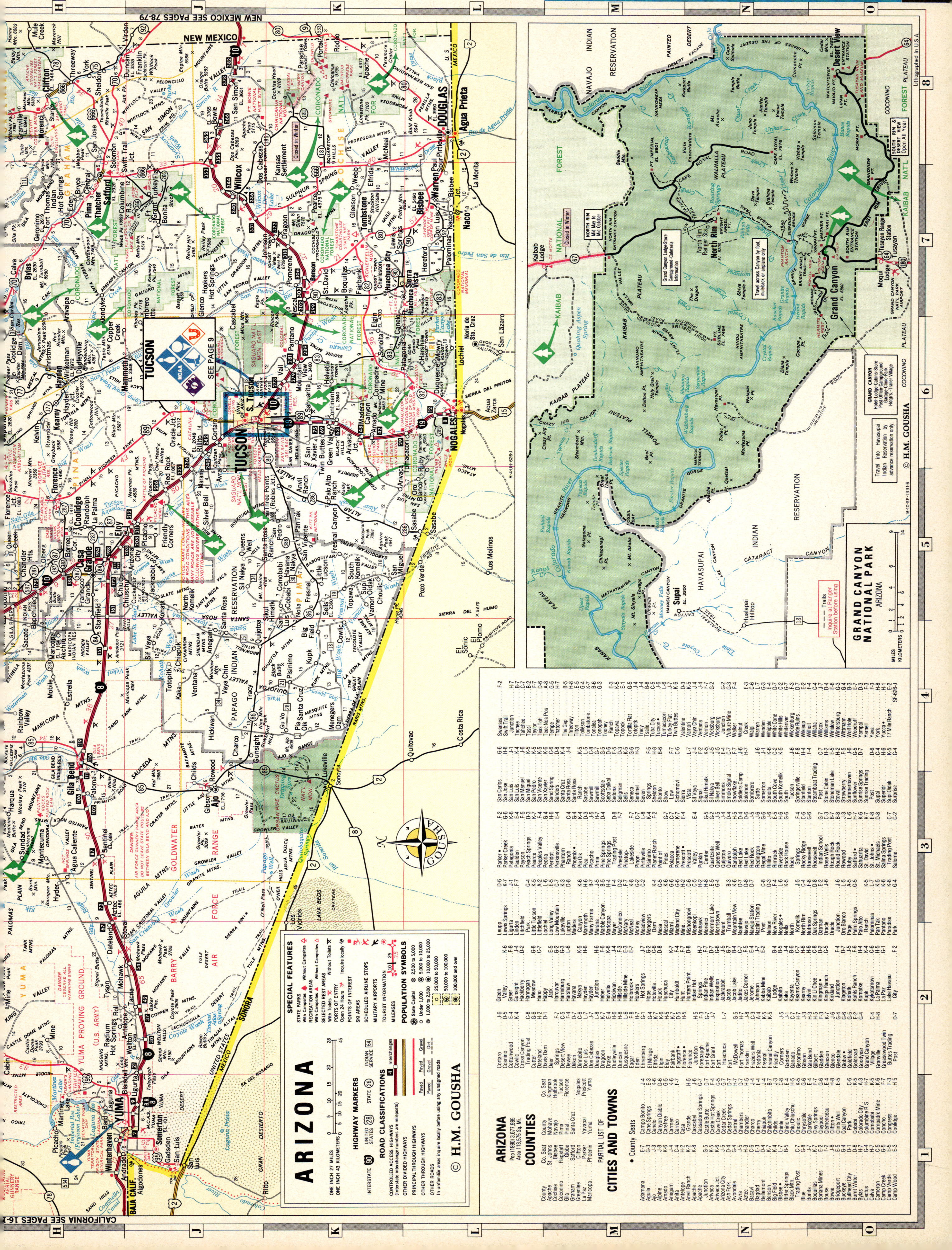
ARIZONA
© H.M. GOUSHA
GRAND CANYON NATIONAL PARK
ARIZONA
NEW MEXICO SEE PAGES 78-79
TUCSON
SEE PAGE 9
PARTIAL LIST OF CITIES AND TOWNS
COUNTIES
SPECIAL FEATURES
HIGHWAY MARKERS
ROAD CLASSIFICATIONS
POPULATION SYMBOLS

ARKANSAS

Pop (1990) 2,362,239
Area 53,104 Sq. Mi.

COUNTIES

County	County Seats
Arkansas	DeWitt
Arkansas	Stuttgart
Ashley	Hamburg
Baxter	Mountain Home
Benton	Bentonville
Boone	Harrison
Bradley	Warren
Calhoun	Hampton
Carroll	Berryville
Carroll	Eureka Springs
Chicot	Lake Village
Clark	Arkadelphia
Clay	Corning
Clay	Piggott
Cleburne	Heber Springs
Cleveland	Rison
Columbia	Magnolia
Conway	Morrilton
Craighead	Jonesboro
Craighead	Lake City
Crawford	Van Buren
Crittenden	Marion
Cross	Wynne
Dallas	Fordyce
Desha	Arkansas City
Drew	Monticello
Faulkner	Conway
Franklin	Charleston
Franklin	Ozark
Fulton	Salem
Garland	Hot Springs
Grant	Sheridan
Greene	Paragould
Hempstead	Hope
Hot Spring	Malvern
Howard	Nashville
Independence	Batesville
Izard	Melbourne
Jackson	Newport
Jefferson	Pine Bluff
Johnson	Clarksville
Lafayette	Lewisville
Lawrence	Powhatan
Lawrence	Walnut Ridge
Lee	Marianna
Lincoln	Star City
Little River	Ashdown
Logan	Booneville
Logan	Paris
Lonoke	Lonoke
Madison	Huntsville
Marion	Yellville
Miller	Texarkana
Mississippi	Blytheville
Mississippi	Osceola
Monroe	Clarendon
Montgomery	Mt. Ida
Nevada	Prescott
Newton	Jasper
Ouachita	Camden
Perry	Perryville
Phillips	Helena
Pike	Murfreesboro
Poinsett	Harrisburg
Polk	Mena
Pope	Russellville
Prairie	Des Arc
Prairie	DeValls Bluff
Pulaski	Little Rock
Randolph	Pocahontas
St. Francis	Forrest City
Saline	Benton
Scott	Waldron
Searcy	Marshall
Sebastian	Fort Smith
Sebastian	Greenwood
Sevier	DeQueen
Sharp	Evening Shade
Sharp	Hardy
Stone	Mountain View
Union	El Dorado
Van Buren	Clinton
Washington	Fayetteville
White	Searcy
Woodruff	Augusta
Yell	Danville
Yell	Dardanelle

PARTIAL LIST OF

CITIES AND TOWNS

• County Seats

Abbott	D-3
Acorn	E-3
Adona	D-6
Agnos	A-8
Alabam	B-4
Alco	B-7
Alicia	B-9
Alma	C-3
Almond	B-8
Alpena	A-5
Alpine	F-5
Altheimer	E-8
Aly	D-5
Amity	F-5
Amy	G-6
Aplin	D-6
Apt	B-10
Arkadelphia •	F-6
Arkansas City •	G-9
Ash Flat	A-8
Ashdown •	G-3
Ashton	H-9
Atkins	C-6
Augusta •	C-9
Austin	C-6
Avoca	A-4
Bald Knob	C-8
Banks	G-7
Barling	C-3
Bartono	E-10
Batavia	A-5
Batesville •	B-8
Bear Creek Springs	A-5
Bearden	G-6
Bee Branch	C-7
Beebe	D-8
Bella Vista	A-3
Bellefonte	A-6
Belleville	D-5
Ben	B-8
Benton	E-6
Bentonville	A-3
Berryville	A-4
Bethel	B-10
Big Fork	E-4
Birdtown	C-6
Birta	D-5
Bismarck	E-5
Black Oak	B-11
Black Rock	B-9
Bloomer	C-3
Blue Mountain	D-4
Blue Springs	E-5
Blytheville •	B-11
Boles	D-4
Bonnerdale	E-5
Bono	C-7
Bono	B-10
Bonneville •	D-4
Boothe	D-3
Botkinburg	C-7
Bowman	B-10
Boydell	G-9
Bradford	C-9
Branch	C-4
Brashears	B-4
Brentwood	B-3
Brickeys	D-10
Brinkley	D-9
Brister	H-5
Brookland	B-10
Bryant	E-7
Buckner	G-5
Burlington	A-5
Burnville	D-3
Busch	A-4
Cabot	D-7
Caddo Gap	E-4
Calico Rock	B-7
Camden •	G-6
Cammack Village	D-7
Carbon City	C-4
Carlisle	D-8
Carmi	B-11
Carolan	D-4
Carrollton	A-5
Casa	D-5
Caulksville	C-4
Cave City	B-8
Cecil	C-4
Center Hill	C-8
Center Ridge	C-6
Centerville	D-5
Charleston •	C-4
Chatfield	D-11
Cherokee Village	A-8
Cherry Hill	D-6
Cherry Valley	C-10
Chickalah	D-5
Choctaw	C-7
Clarendon •	E-9
Clarksville •	C-5
Clinton •	C-7
Conway •	D-7
Corning •	A-10
Cotton Plant	D-9
Cove	E-3
Cowell	B-5
Cross Roads	E-9
Crossett	H-8
Crossroads	B-5
Crows	E-6
Crystal Springs	E-5
Daisy	F-4
Dalark	F-6
Damascus	C-7
Danville •	D-5
Dardanelle •	D-5
Datto	A-10
De Queen •	F-3
De Witt •	E-9
Delaware	C-5
Dell	B-11
Denmark	C-8
Dermott	G-9
Dennard	B-6
Des Arc •	D-8
Desha	B-8
Dierks	F-3
Doddridge	H-4
Dogpatch	B-5
Donaldson	F-6
Dover	C-5
Drasco	C-8
Dryfork	A-5
Dumas	F-8
Eagleton	E-3
Earle	C-11
Ebb	E-7
Echo	D-3
El Dorado •	H-6
El Paso	D-7
Elaine	E-10
Elberta	B-7
Elberta	D-5
Elliott	G-6
Emerson	H-5
England	E-8
Eudora	H-9
Eureka Springs •	A-4
Evening Shade •	B-8
Fairview	F-6
Falls Chapel	F-3
Fannie	E-5
Farmington	B-3
Fayetteville •	B-3
Felton	D-10
Flippin	A-6
Fordyce •	G-7
Foreman	G-3
Formosa	C-7
Forrest City •	D-10
Fort Lynn	H-4
Fort Smith •	C-3
Fouke	H-4
Fourche Junction	D-5
Fox	B-7
Friars Point	E-10
Galion	G-6
Garfield	A-4
Garland	G-4
Garrett Bridge	F-8
Gassville	A-7
Gateway	A-4
Gentry	A-3
Gillham	F-3
Glencoe	A-8
Glenwood	E-4
Goobertown	B-10
Goshen	B-4
Gould	F-8
Grady	F-8
Grand Glaise	C-9
Grannis	F-3
Gravette	A-3
Gray	B-8
Green Forest	A-5
Greenbrier	0-7
Greenland	B-3
Greenway	A-11
Greenwood •	C-3
Gurdon	F-5
Guy	C-7
Hamburg •	H-8
Hamilton	E-5
Hamlet	D-7
Hampton •	G-7
Hardy •	A-8
Harmon	A-6
Harlow	G-6
Harrell	G-7
Harrisburg •	C-10
Harrison •	A-6
Hartwell	B-4
Hatfield	E-3
Hatton	E-3
Havana	D-5
Haynes	D-10
Hazen	D-8
Heber Spring •	C-7
Helena •	E-10
Hempwallace	E-5
Henderson	A-7
Highland	A-8
Hillsboro	H-7
Hindsville	A-4
Hollis	D-5
Holly Springs	F-6
Homewood	D-6
Hope •	G-4
Hopewell	C-7
Hot Springs •	E-6
Hoxie	B-9
Hudspeth	G-9
Huff	C-8
Hughes	D-10
Humnoke	E-8
Humphrey	E-8
Huntington	D-3
Huntsville •	B-4
Imboden	A-9
Ione	D-4
Ivan	F-7
Jacinto	F-6
Jacksonport	C-9
Jacksonville	D-7
Jasamine	D-8
Jasper •	B-5
Jerome	G-9
Jessieville	E-5
Johnson	A-3
Jonesboro •	B-10
Joplin	E-5
Judsonia	C-8
Junet	E-7
Kensett	D-8
Kiblah	H-4
Kimball	H-8
Kingsland	F-7
Kirby	F-4
Kirkland	G-6
Kokomo	D-10
Lake City •	B-11
Lake Village •	G-9
Lanieve	B-10
Leachville	B-11
Lena	E-5
Lepanto	C-11
Leslie	B-7
Levesque	C-10
Lewisville	G-4
Lincoln	B-3
Linwood	F-8
Little Dixie	D-9
Little Rock •	E-6
Lockesburg	F-3
Locust Bayou	G-6
Locust Grove	B-8
Lodi	E-4
Lono	F-6
Lonoke •	D-8
Louann	G-6
Lowell	A-3
Lumber	G-5
Lurton	B-5
Luxora	B-12
Macedonia	D-5
Macks	C-9
Macon Lake	G-9
Magnolia •	H-5
Malvern •	E-6
Manila	B-11
Manning	F-6
Mansfield	D-3
Marcella	B-8
Mariana •	D-10
Marion •	C-11
Marked Tree	C-10
Marmaduke	A-11
Marshall •	B-6
Marvell	E-10
Marysville	H-6
Mayfield	B-4
McArthur	G-9
McCrory	C-9
McDonald	C-10
McDougal	A-11
McGehee	G-9
McNeil	G-5
Melbourne •	B-8
Mena •	E-3
Melrose	B-8
Midway	A-7
Midway	C-5
Milltown	D-4
Minturn	B-9
Mist	H-8
Mitchellville	F-9
Monette	B-11
Monroe	E-9
Monticello •	G-8
Montrose	H-8
Morrilton •	D-6
Morton	C-9
Mount George	D-5
Mount Ida •	E-4
Mount Pleasant	G-4
Mountain Home •	A-7
Mountain Springs	D-7
Mountain View	B-7
Mulberry	C-4
Mud Lake	D-10
Mufreesboro •	F-4
Nance	E-6
Nashville	F-4
Needmore	D-4
New Blaine	C-5
Newhope	F-4
Newnata	B-7
Newport •	C-9
Norfolk	A-7
Norman	E-4
North Little Rock	D-7
Oakhaven	G-4
Ogden	G-3
Ogemaw	G-6
Oil Trough	C-9
Ola	D-5
Old Joe	B-7
Olyphant	C-9
Omaha	A-5
Onyx	D-5
Oppelo	D-6
Optimus	B-7
Osage	A-5
Osceola •	B-11
Ouachita	F-6
Owensville	E-6
Oxley	B-7
Ozan	F-4
Ozark •	C-4
Palestine	D-10
Paragould •	B-10
Paris •	C-4
Parkin	C-10
Paron	D-6
Pea Ridge	A-3
Pearcy	E-5
Pelsor	B-5
Pencil Bluff	E-4
Perry	D-6
Perryville •	D-6
Pfeiffer	B-8
Pickens	F-9
Piggott •	A-11
Pindall	B-6
Pine Bluff •	F-8
Pineville	A-7
Pleasant Grove	B-8
Pleasant Plains	C-8
Pocahontas •	A-9
Point Cedar	E-5
Pollard	A-11
Poplar Grove	E-10
Portia	B-9
Powhatan •	B-9
Poyen	E-6
Prairie Grove	B-3
Prattsville	E-6
Prescott •	F-5
Princeton	F-6
Quinn	H-6
Quitman	C-7
Ramsey	F-6
Ratcliff	C-4
Ravenden	A-9
Rector	A-11
Reed	G-9
Reedville	F-8
Reyno	A-10
Ridgeway	A-5
Rison •	F-7
Rogers	A-3
Rohwer	G-9
Rosboro	E-5
Rose Bud	C-7
Roseland	B-11
Rosston	G-5
Rover	D-5
Royal	E-5
Rushing	B-7
Russell	C-8
Russellville •	C-5
St. Francis	A-11
St. James	B-8
St. Joe	B-6
Salado	B-8
Salem •	A-8
Salem	E-4
Salesville	A-7
Saline	F-7
Scottsville	C-5
Searcy •	C-8
Sedgwick	B-10
Shell Lake	D-10
Sheridan •	E-7
Shearerville	D-11
Sherwood	D-7
Shiloh	C-5
Shirley	C-7
Siloam Springs	A-3
Smackover	G-6
Smead	G-6
Snow	A-6
Snyder	H-8
Solgohachia	C-6
Sonora	A-4
Soudan	D-10
Sparkman	F-6
Spirit Lake	G-4
Springdale	A-3
Stamps	G-5
Star City •	F-8
Stephens	G-5
Strong	H-7
Story	E-5
Stuttgart •	E-8
Summers	B-3
Summerville	G-7
Swifton	B-9
Sylamore	B-7
Tamo	F-8
Tate	G-6
Texarkana •	G-1
Thebes	H-8
Thornton	G-6
Thornburg	D-6
Tillar	G-9
Tilly	B-6
Tontitown	A-3
Trumann	C-10
Tuckerman	B-9
Tulip	F-6
Tumbling Shoals	C-8
Tyro	F-8
Ulm	E-9
Valley Springs	B-6
Van Buren •	C-3
Vandervoort	E-3
Vanndale	C-10
Varner	F-8
Vilonia	D-7
Viola	A-8
Wabbaseka	E-8
Waldo	G-5
Waldron •	D-3
Walnut Ridge •	B-9
Warren •	G-7
Washington	F-4
West Helena	E-10
West Memphis	D-11
Western Grove	B-6
White Hall	E-7
Whitehall	C-10
Wickes	E-3
Williams Junction	D-6
Wilmar	G-8
Wilmot	H-8
Wilson	C-11
Wilton	G-3
Wing	D-5
Worden	C-9
Wynne •	C-10
Y City	D-3
Yarbro	B-11
Yellville •	A-6
Young	G-5

SF-627-J

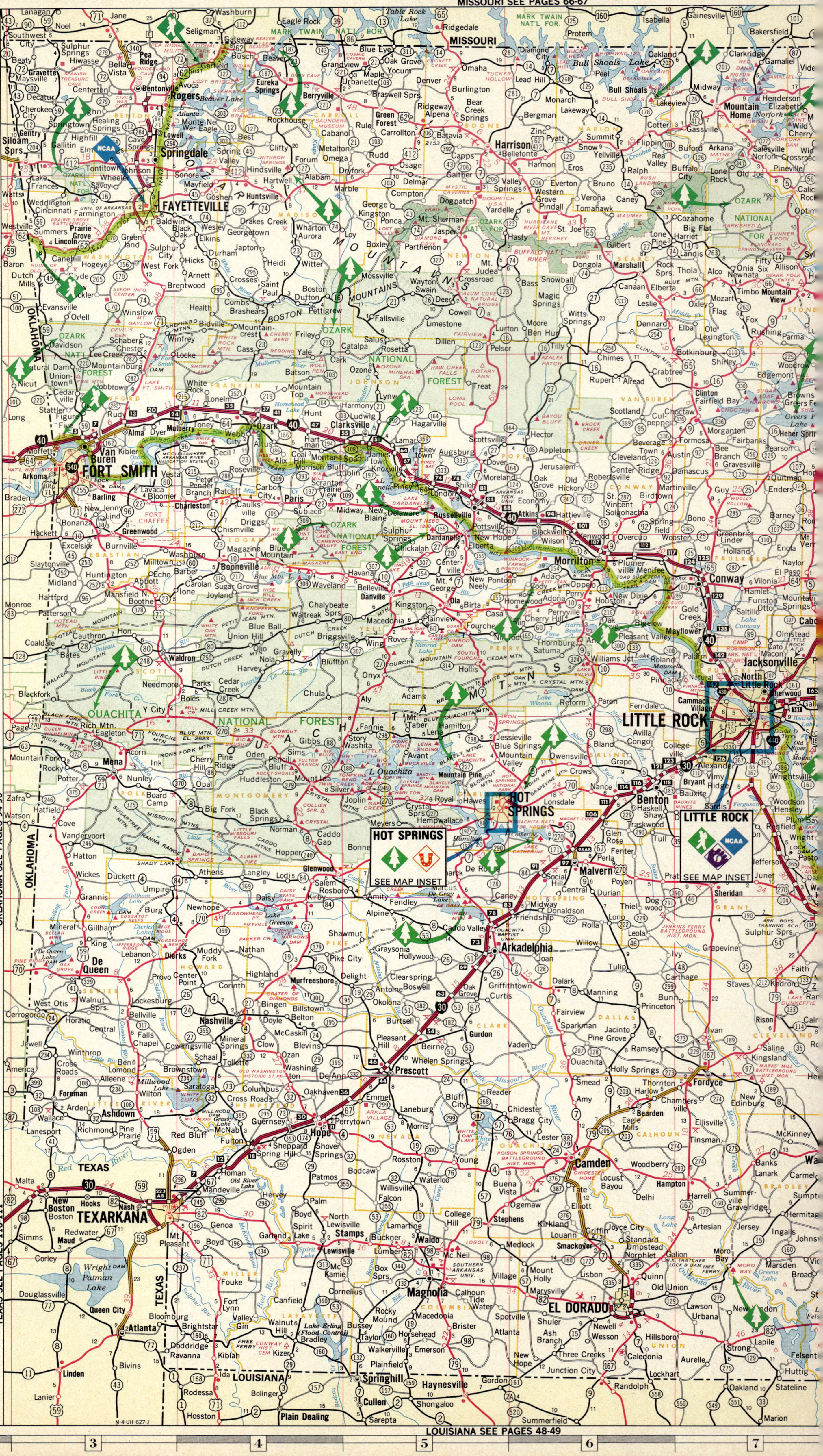

ARKANSAS
ONE INCH 19 MILES
ONE INCH 31 KILOMETERS
HIGHWAY MARKERS
INTERSTATE
UNITED STATES
STATE
GREAT RIVER ROAD
ROAD CLASSIFICATIONS
CONTROLLED ACCESS HIGHWAYS
Interchanges
OTHER DIVIDED HIGHWAYS
PRINCIPAL THROUGH HIGHWAYS
OTHER THROUGH HIGHWAYS
OTHER ROADS
Paved
Gravel
Dirt
SPECIAL FEATURES
STATE PARKS
RECREATION AREAS
SELECTED REST AREAS
POINTS OF INTEREST
SCHEDULED AIRLINE STOPS
MILITARY AIRPORTS
TOURIST INFORMATION
MILEAGES
POPULATION SYMBOLS
State Capital
Under 1,000
1,000 to 2,500
2,500 to 5,000
5,000 to 10,000
10,000 to 25,000
25,000 to 50,000
50,000 to 100,000
100,000 and over
© H.M. GOUSHA
EXPLANATION OF ACTIVITIES
Major League Spectator
Minor League Spectator
Collegiate/Participant
Rivers, Trails, Major Parks, and Forests
Auto Racing
Horse Racing
Sailing
Baseball
Museums & Halls of Fame
Skiing
Basketball
National Trails
Soccer
Bowling
NCAA Colleges
Tennis
Football
Parks & Forests
Track & Field
Golf
Polo
Wild, Scenic & Recreational Rivers
Hockey
Rodeo
MISSOURI SEE PAGES 66-67
TENNESSEE SEE PAGES 106-107
MISSISSIPPI SEE PAGES 64-65
LOUISIANA SEE PAGES 48-49
MISSISSIPPI SEE PAGES 64-65
MEMPHIS
SEE PAGE 70
JONESBORO
Batesville
Newport
Searcy
Blytheville
Osceola
Forrest City
Brinkley
Stuttgart
Helena
Dumas
McGehee
Monticello
Dermott
Lake Village
Eudora
Hamburg
Crossett
GREENVILLE
Dyersburg
MARK TWAIN NAT'L FOR.
HOT SPRINGS
HOT SPRINGS NATIONAL PARK
OAKLAWN JOCKEY CLUB RACE TRACK
HOT SPRINGS
ARKANSAS
LITTLE ROCK
NORTH LITTLE ROCK
CAMP ROBINSON ARKANSAS NATIONAL GUARD
Arkansas River
ADAMS FIELD MUNICIPAL AIRPORT
LITTLE ROCK
NORTH LITTLE ROCK
ARKANSAS
© H.M. GOUSHA
GOUSHA

OREGON SEE PAGES 96-97
OREGON
PACIFIC
OCEAN
CRESCENT CITY
EUREKA
REDDING
RED BLUFF
UKIAH
SANTA ROSA
SACRAMENTO
STOCKTON
MODESTO
MERCED
SAN FRANCISCO
OAKLAND
SAN JOSE
ALTURAS
SUSANVILLE
WEED
LASSEN VOLCANIC NAT'L PARK
SEE MAP INSET
SACRAMENTO
SEE MAP INSET
SAN FRANCISCO
SEE MAP INSET
POINT REYES NATIONAL SEASHORE
SACRAMENTO
CALIFORNIA
© H.M. GOUSHA
GOUSHA
FOR CONTINUATION OF MAP SEE PAGES 16-17

SAN FRANCISCO BAY AREA
LASSEN VOLCANIC NATIONAL PARK
CALIFORNIA
© H.M. GOUSHA
YOSEMITE NATIONAL PARK
CALIFORNIA
© H.M. GOUSHA
LAKE TAHOE
SEE PAGE 73
YOSEMITE NAT'L PARK
SEE MAP INSET
KINGS CANYON & SEQUOIA NAT'L PARKS
SEE PAGE 17
NEVADA SEE PAGES 72-73
FOR INDEX TO CITIES AND TOWNS SEE PAGE 16
FOR CONTINUATION OF MAP SEE PAGES 16-17
CALIFORNIA
NORTHERN SECTION
ONE INCH 28 MILES
ONE INCH 45 KILOMETERS
HIGHWAY MARKERS
ROAD CLASSIFICATIONS
SPECIAL FEATURES
POPULATION SYMBOLS
© H.M. GOUSHA
SAN PABLO BAY
SAN FRANCISCO BAY
PACIFIC OCEAN
SAN FRANCISCO
OAKLAND
BERKELEY
SAN JOSE
FREMONT
HAYWARD
CONCORD
VALLEJO
RICHMOND
DALY CITY
SAN MATEO
PALO ALTO
SUNNYVALE
SANTA CLARA
MILPITAS
LIVERMORE
PLEASANTON
WALNUT CREEK
SAN RAFAEL
NOVATO
FAIRFIELD
ANTIOCH
PITTSBURG
SAN LEANDRO
RENO
CARSON CITY
BISHOP
Lithographed in U.S.A.

CALIFORNIA

Pop (1990) 29,839,250
Area 158,693 Sq. Mi.

COUNTIES

County	Seat
Alameda	Oakland
Alpine	Markleeville
Amador	Jackson
Butte	Oroville
Calaveras	San Andreas
Colusa	Colusa
Contra Costa	Martinez
Del Norte	Crescent City
El Dorado	Placerville
Fresno	Fresno
Glenn	Willows
Humboldt	Eureka
Imperial	El Centro
Inyo	Independence
Kern	Bakersfield
Kings	Hanford
Lake	Lakeport
Lassen	Susanville
Los Angeles	Los Angeles
Madera	Madera
Marin	San Rafael
Mariposa	Mariposa
Mendocino	Ukiah
Merced	Merced
Modoc	Alturas
Mono	Bridgeport
Monterey	Salinas
Napa	Napa
Nevada	Nevada City
Orange	Santa Ana
Placer	Auburn
Plumas	Quincy
Riverside	Riverside
Sacramento	Sacramento
San Benito	Hollister
San Bernardino	San Bernardino
San Diego	San Diego
San Francisco	San Francisco
San Joaquin	Stockton
San Luis Obispo	San Luis Obispo
San Mateo	Redwood City
Santa Barbara	Santa Barbara
Santa Clara	San Jose
Santa Cruz	Santa Cruz
Shasta	Redding
Sierra	Downieville
Siskiyou	Yreka
Solano	Fairfield
Sonoma	Santa Rosa
Stanislaus	Modesto
Sutter	Yuba City
Tehama	Red Bluff
Trinity	Weaverville
Tulare	Visalia
Tuolumne	Sonora
Ventura	Ventura
Yolo	Woodland
Yuba	Marysville

PARTIAL LIST OF

CITIES AND TOWNS

• County Seats

Academy	K-8
Acton	N-9
Adams	E-4
Adelanto	N-10
Adin	B-6
Ager	A-4
Agoura Hills	O-9
Aqua Calinte	F-4
Aguanga	P-11
Alameda	G-4
Alamo	C-13
Albany	G-4
Albion	E-2
Alhambra	O-9
Allensworth	L-8
Almanor	C-6
Alpaugh	L-8
Alpine	Q-12
Alpine Village	L-9
Alta Sierra	L-9
Altaville	G-7
Alton	C-2
Alturas •	B-7
Amboy	N-13
Amsterdam	H-7
Anaheim	O-10
Anderson	C-5
Andrade	Q-14
Angels Camp	G-7
Angelus Oaks	O-11
Angwin	F-4
Antelope Center	N-10
Antioch	G-5
Anza	P-12
Applegate	E-6
Apple Valley	N-11
Aptos	K-5
Arbuckle	E-5
Arcadia	O-10
Arcata	B-2
Armona	L-7
Arnold	F-7
Arroyo Grande	M-6
Artois	D-5
Arvin	M-9
Ash Mountain Park	K-9
Ashford Mills	L-11
Asti	E-4
Atascadero	M-6
Atwater	H-6
Auburn •	E-6
Aukland	K-8
Avalon	P-9
Avenal	L-7
Avery	F-7
Azuca	O-10
Badger	K-8
Bagdad	N-12
Baker	M-12
Bakersfield •	M-8
Balance Rock	L-9
Banning	O-11
Barstow	N-11
Bartel	B-5
Baxter	E-6
Bealville	M-9
Bear Valley	G-7
Beaumont	O-11
Beckworth	D-7
Beegum	C-4
Belden	D-6
Bellota	G-6
Belmont	G-4
Ben Lomand	K-4
Benbow	D-3
Benicia	G-5
Benton	G-9
Benton Hot Springs	G-9
Berenda	K-7
Berkeley	G-4
Berry Creek	D-6
Beswick	A-5
Beverly Hills	O-9
Bieber	B-6
Big Bear City	O-11
Big Oak Flat	G-7
Big Pine	J-9
Big Pines	N-10
Big Sur	L-5
Big Trees	F-7
Biggs	E-5
Biola	K-7
Bishop	H-10
Black Bear	B-3
Blanchard	G-7
Blue Lake	B-2
Blythe	O-14
Bodega	F-3
Bodega Bay	F-3
Bodfish	M-9
Bombay Beach	P-13
Bonsall	P-11
Boonville	E-3
Bootjack	G-8
Borax Plants	M-10
Boron	N-10
Borrego	P-12
Borrego Springs	P-12
Bowman	E-6
Brawley	Q-13
Bray	A-5
Brea	O-10
Brentwood	G-5
Bridgehouse	F-6
Bridgeport	F-8
Bridgeville	C-3
Broderick	F-5
Brooks	F-4
Brush Creek	D-6
Bryte	F-5
Buck Meadows	G-7
Buellton	N-7
Buena Park	O-10
Burbank	O-9
Burlingame	G-4
Burney	B-5
Burnt Ranch	B-3
Burrel	K-7
Butte City	E-5
Buttonwillow	M-8
Cabazon	O-11
Cadiz	N-13
Cahuilla	P-11
Cajon	O-11
Calabasas	O-9
Calexico	Q-13
Caliente	M-9
California Hot Springs	L-9
Calipatria	P-13
Calistoga	F-4
Callahan	B-4
Calpella	E-3
Calpine	D-7
Calwa	K-7
Camarillo	O-8
Cambria	M-5
Camino	F-7
Campbell	H-5
Camp Nelson	L-9
Campo	Q-12
Campo Seco	F-6
Canby	B-6
Canyon Dam	C-6
Capay	F-5
Capistrano Beach	P-10
Capitola	K-4
Carlsbad	P-10
Carmel	K-5
Carmel Valley	K-5
Carmichael	F-6
Carpinteria	O-8
Cartago	L-10
Casitas Springs	O-8
Castaic Junction	N-9
Castella	B-5
Castro Valley	G-5
Castroville	K-5
Caswell	N-9
Cathedral City	O-12
Cayucos	M-6
Cedar Grove	K-9
Cedarville	B-7
Centerville	K-8
Central Valley	C-4
Ceres	G-6
Challenge	E-6
Chester	C-6
Chico	D-5
China Lake	M-10
Chinese Camp	G-7
Chino	O-10
Cholame	M-6
Chowchilla	H-7
Chrome	D-4
Chualar	K-5
Chula Vista	Q-11
Cima	M-13
Cisco	E-7
Citrus Heights	F-6
Clam Beach	B-2
Claremont	O-10
Clarksburg	F-5
Clay	F-6
Clear Creek (Pick-Aw-Ish)	A-3
Clearlake	E-4
Clearlake Oaks	E-4
Cloverdale	E-3
Clovis	K-7
Coachella	P-12
Coalinga	L-7
Cobb	E-4
Codora	E-5
Cohasset	D-5
Coleville	F-8
Colfax	E-6
Coloma	F-6
Colton	O-11
Colusa •	E-5
Compton	O-9
Concord	G-5
Confidence	G-7
Cool	E-6
Copperopolis	G-6
Corcoran	L-7
Cordelia	A-12
Corning	D-5
Corona	O-10
Corona del Mar	P-10
Coronado	Q-11
Costa Mesa	P-10
Cotati	F-4
Cottonwood	C-5
Coulterville	G-7
Courtland	F-5
Covelo	D-3
Coyote Well	O-12
Coyote Wells	Q-13
Crescent City	A-2
Crescent Mills	D-6
Cressey	H-6
Crestline	N-11
Creston	M-6
Cromberg	D-6
Cromir	K-6
Crows Landing	H-6
Cupertino	H-5
Cutler	K-8
Cuyama	N-7
Cuyamaca	P-12
Daggett	N-11
Dales	C-5
Daly City	G-4
Dana Point	P-10
Danby	N-13
Danville	G-5
Darwin	L-10
Davenport	H-4
Davis	F-5
Davis Creek	A-7
Day	B-6
Dayton	D-5
Death Valley Juntion	L-12
Deep Springs	H-10
Delano	L-8
Delevan	E-5
Delhi	G-6
Del Loma	B-3
Del Mar	Q-11
Del Sur	N-9
De Luz	P-11
Denair	G-6
De Sabla	D-5
Desanso	Q-12
Desert Center	O-13
Desert Hot Springs	O-12
Desert Shores	P-13
Devils Den	L-7
Devore	O-10
Diamond Springs	F-6
Dinsmore	C-3
Dinuba	K-8
Dixieland	Q-13
Dixon	F-5
Dorrington	F-7
Dorris	A-5
Dos Palos	K-6
Dos Rios	D-3
Douglas City	C-4
Douglas Flat	G-7
Downieville	D-6
Doyle	D-7
Drytown	F-6
Dublin	J-4
Ducor	L-8
Dulzura	Q-12
Duncan's Mills	F-3
Dunlap	K-8
Dunnigan	E-5
Dunsmuir	B-5
Durham	D-5
Eagle Mountain	O-13
Earlimart	L-8
Earp	O-15
East Bakersfield	M-9
Easton	K-7
Edgewood	B-4
Edison	M-9
Edna	M-6
Edwards	N-10
El Cajon	Q-11
El Centro •	Q-13
El Cerrito	G-4
El Dorado Hills	F-6
El Granada	G-4
Elizabeth Lake	N-9
Elk Creek	D-4
Elk Creek	E-3
El Portal	G-8
El Rio	O-8
El Segundo	O-9
El Toro	P-10
Empire	G-6
Encinitas	P-11
Escalon	G-6
Escondido	P-11
Esparto	F-5
Essex	N-14
Estrella	M-6
Etna	B-4
Eureka •	B-2
Exeter	L-8
Fairfax	G-4
Fairfield •	F-5
Fairmead	K-7
Fairmont	N-9
Fairview	L-9
Fall River Mills	B-6
Fallbrook	P-11
Fallon	F-4
Famoso	M-8
Farmersville	L-8
Farmington	G-6
Feather Falls	D-6
Felton	K-4
Ferndale	C-2
Fields Landing	C-2
Fillmore	N-8
Firebaugh	K-6
Fish Camp	G-8
Five Points	K-7
Florin	F-5
Floriston	E-7
Flournoy	D-4
Folsom	F-6
Fontana	O-10
Ford City	M-8
Forest Glen	C-3
Forestville	F-4
Forks of Salmon	B-3
Fort Bragg	D-2
Fort Irwin	M-11
Fort Jones	A-4
Fortuna	C-2
Foster Park	O-8
Fowler	K-8
Franklin	F-5
Frazier Park	N-8
Freedom	K-5
Freeport	F-5
Fremont	G-5
French Camp	G-6
Fresno •	K-7
Fruto	D-4
Fullerton	O-10
Furnace Creek	K-11
Furnace Creek Inn	K-11
Galt	F-6
Garberville	C-3
Garden Farms	M-6
Garey	N-7
Gasquet	A-2
Gaviota	N-7
Gazelle	A-4
Georgetown	E-6
Geyserville	F-4
Giant Forest	K-9
Gilman Hot Springs	O-11
Gilroy	K-5
Glamis	P-14
Glenbrook	E-7
Glenburn	B-5
Glencoe	F-7
Glendale	O-9
Glendora	O-10
Glenn	D-5
Glennville	L-9
Goffs	N-14
Gold Run	E-6
Goleta	N-7
Gonzales	K-5
Goodyear's Bar	D-6
Gorda	L-5
Gorman	N-9
Goshen	L-8
Graeagle	D-6
Grass Valley	E-6
Graton	F-4
Green Valley	N-9
Greenfield	L-5
Greenview	A-4
Greenville	D-6
Grenada	A-4
Gridley	E-5
Grimes	E-5
Groveland	G-7
Grover City	M-6
Guadalupe	N-6
Gualala	E-3
Guatay	Q-12
Guinda	E-5
Gustine	J-6
Half Moon Bay	G-4
Halloran Spring	M-13
Hambone	B-5
Hamburg	A-3
Hamilton City	D-5
Hammond	K-9
Hanford •	L-8
Happy Camp	A-3
Harmony	M-6
Harvard	N-12
Hat Creek	C-5
Hawkinsville	A-4
Hayfork	C-3
Hayward	G-5
Healdsburg	F-3
Helena	C-3
Helm	K-7
Hemet	O-11
Herald	F-6
Herlong	D-7
Hermosa Beach	O-9
Hesperia	N-11
Hickman	G-6
Highland	O-11
Hinkley	N-11
Hi Vista	N-10
Hollister •	K-5
Hollywood by the Sea	O-8
Holmes	C-2
Holtville	Q-13
Homewood	E-7
Hood	F-5
Hoopa	B-3
Hopeland	E-3
Hornbrook	A-4
Horse Creek	A-4
Howell Camp	D-4
Humphreys	K-8
Huntington Beach	P-9
Huron	L-7
Idyllwild	O-11
Imperial	Q-13
Imperial Beach	Q-11
Independence	K-9
Indian Falls	D-6
Indian Wells	O-12
Indio	O-12
Inglewood	O-9
Inyokern	M-10
Ione	F-6
Isleton	F-5
Ivanhoe	L-8
Ivanpah	M-13
Jackson	F-6
Jamul	Q-11
Janesville	C-7
Jasmin	M-8
Jenner	F-3
Johannesburg	M-10
Johnsondale	L-9
Johnsons	B-3
Johnstonville	C-6
Jolon	L-5
Joshua Tree	O-12
Julian	P-12
Junction City	C-3
June Lake	G-9
Keddie	D-6
Keeler	K-10
Kellogg	F-4
Kelseyville	E-4
Kelso	M-13
Kenwood	F-4
Kerman	K-7
Kernville	L-9
Kettleman City	L-7
Keyes	G-6
King City	L-6
Kingsburg	K-7
Klamath	A-2
Klamath Glen	A-2
Klamath River	A-4
Knights Landing	F-5
Kramer Junction	N-10
Kyburz	F-7
Lafayette	C-12
La Grange	G-7
Laguna Beach	P-10
Lake Alpine	F-7
Lake Arrowhead	O-11
Lake Elsinore	P-11
Lakehead	B-4
Lake Isabella	M-9
Lakeside	Q-11
Lakeview	O-11
La Mesa	Q-11
Lamont	M-9
Lancaster	N-10
Landers	O-12
La Porte	D-6
Laton	K-7
Laws	H-10
Laytonville	D-3
Lebec	N-9
Leesville	E-4
Lee Vining	G-8
Leggett	D-2
Leliter	M-10
Lemon Grove	L-8
Lemon Grove	Q-11
Lemoore	L-7
Lenwood	N-11
Likely	B-7
Lincoln	E-6
Lindcove	L-8
Linden	G-6
Lindsay	L-8
Litchfield	C-7
Little Lake	L-10
Little Norway	E-7
Little River	E-2
Littlerock	N-10
Live Oak	E-5
Livermore	G-5
Livingston	H-6
Lockeford	G-6
Lockwood	L-6
Lodi	F-6
Lodoga	E-4
Loleta	C-2
Lompoc	N-6
Lone Pine	K-9
Long Beach	O-9
Longvale	D-3
Lookout	B-6
Loraine	M-9
Los Alamos	N-7
Los Angeles •	O-9
Los Banos	K-6
Los Gatos	J-5
Los Molinos	D-5
Los Olivos	N-7
Lost Hills	M-7
Lovelock	D-5
Lower Lake	E-4
Loyalton	D-7
Lucerne	E-4
Lucerne Valley	N-11
Lucia	L-5
Ludlow	N-12
Lytton	F-4
Macdoel	A-5
Madeline	B-7
Madera •	K-7
Madison	E-5
Magalia	D-5
Malaga	K-7
Malibu	O-9
Manchester	E-3
Manix	N-12
Manteca	G-6
Maricopa	N-8
Marina	K-5
Mariposa	H-7
Marsh	O-13
Marshall	F-3
Martinez •	G-5
Martins Ferry	B-2
Marysville •	E-5
Maxwell	E-4
McArthur	B-6
McCann	C-3
McCloud	B-5
McFarland	M-8
McKittrick	M-8
Meadow	E-6
Meeks Bay	E-7
Meiners Oaks	N-8
Meloland	Q-13
Mendocino	E-2
Mendota	K-7
Menlo Park	G-5
Mentone	O-11
Merced	H-6
Meridian	E-5
Michigan Bar	F-6
Middletown	F-4
Midpines	G-7
Midway Well	P-14
Milford	D-7
Mill Valley	G-4
Milo	L-9
Milpitas	G-5
Mineral	C-5
Minkler	K-8
Minneola	N-11
Minter Field	M-8
Mira Loma	O-10
Mira Monte	N-8
Miramonte	K-8
Miranda	C-3
Modesto	J-6
Modesto •	G-6
Modjeska	O-10
Mojave	N-9
Mokelumne Hill	F-6
Monrovia	O-10
Montague	A-4
Montalvo	O-8
Montara	G-4
Montebello	O-10
Montecito	O-7
Monterey	K-4
Monte Vista	E-6
Montgomery Creek	B-5
Moorpark	O-9
Moreno Valley	O-11
Morgan Hill	J-5
Morongo Valley	O-12
Morro Bay	M-6
Mountain View	H-5
Mount Baldy	O-10
Mount Bullion	G-7
Mount Laguna	Q-12
Mount Shasta	B-5
Murrieta	P-11
Napa •	F-4
Naples	N-7
Navarro	E-3
Needles	N-14
Nelson	D-5
Nevada City	E-6
New Cuyama	N-7
Newark	G-5
Newberry Springs	N-11
Newbury Park	O-8
Newcastle	E-6
Newell	A-6
Newhall	O-9
Newman	H-6
Newport Beach	P-10
Nice	E-4
Nicholls Warm Springs	P-14
Niland	P-13
Nipinnawasee	H-8
Nipomo	M-6
Nipton	M-13
Norco	O-10
Norman	E-5
North Edwards	N-10
North San Juan	E-6
North Shore	P-13
Norwalk	O-10
Novata	G-4
Noyo	E-3
Nubieber	B-6
Oakdale	G-6
Oak Grove	P-11
Oakhurst	H-8
Oakland •	G-5
Oakley	G-5
Oak View	N-8
Oakville	F-4
Oasis	P-12
O'Brien	C-4
Oceano	M-6
Oceanside	P-10
Ocean View	F-3
Ocotillo	Q-12
Ocotillo Wells	P-12
Oildale	M-8
Ojai	N-8
Olancha	L-10
Old River	M-8
Olivehurst	E-5
Ono	C-4
Ontario	O-10
Onyx	M-9
Ora Loma	K-6
Orange	O-10
Orange Cove	K-8
Orcutt	N-6
Ordbend	D-5
Orick	B-2
Orinda	C-12
Orland	D-4
Orleans	B-3
Orosi	K-8
Oroville •	D-5
Oxnard	O-8
Paicines	K-5
Pala	P-11
Palermo	E-5
Palm Desert	O-12
Palm Springs	O-11
Palm Wells	O-12
Palmdale	N-10
Palo Alto	G-5
Palo Verde	P-14
Palomar Mountain	P-11
Panamint Springs	L-10
Paradise	D-5
Parkfield	L-7
Parlier	K-8
Pasadena	O-10
Paskenta	D-4
Paso Robles	M-6
Patterson	G-6
Pauma Valley	P-11
Paynes Creek	C-5
Pearblossom	N-10
Pepperwood	C-2
Perris	O-11
Petaluma	F-4
Phelan	N-10
Phillipsville	C-3
Philo	E-3
Piedmont	G-4
Piercy	D-3
Pilot Hill	E-6
Pine Creek	A-7
Pine Flat	L-9
Pine Grove	F-7
Pine Ridge	K-8
Pine Valley	Q-12
Pinehurst	K-8
Pinon Hills	N-10
Pioneer	F-7
Pioneertown	O-12
Pinole	G-4
Piru	N-9
Pismo Beach	M-6
Pittsburg	G-5
Pittville	B-6
Pixley	L-8
Placerville •	F-6
Plainview	L-8
Plasse	F-7
Platina	C-4
Pleasant Hill	G-5
Pleasanton	G-5
Plymouth	F-6
Point Arena	E-2
Pomona	O-10
Pond	M-8
Poplar	L-8
Port Hueneme	O-8
Porterville	L-8
Portola	D-7
Posey	L-9
Poway	Q-11
Prattville	C-6
Princeton	E-5
Project City	C-5
Prunedale	K-5
Pumpkin Center	M-8
Quartz Hill	N-9
Quincy •	N-9
Rainbow	P-11
Raisin	K-7
Ramona	P-11
Rancho California	P-11
Rancho Cordova	F-6
Rancho Mirage	O-12
Ravendale	C-7
Ravena	N-9
Red Bluff •	C-4
Red Mountain	M-10
Red Rock	B-7
Redcrest	C-2
Redding •	C-4
Redlands	O-11
Redondo Beach	O-9
Redway	D-2
Redwood City •	G-4
Reedley	K-8
Requa	A-2
Rialto	O-11
Rice	O-14
Richardson Grove	D-2
Richgrove	L-8
Richmond	G-4
Ridgecrest	M-10
Rincon	P-11
Rio Bravo	M-8
Rio Dell	C-2
Rio Linda	F-5
Rio Oso	E-5
Rio Vista	F-5
Ripley	P-14
Ripon	G-6
Riverbank	G-6
Riverdale	K-7
Riverside •	O-11
Robbins	E-5
Rodeo	G-4
Rohnert Park	F-4
Rolinda	K-7
Rosamond	N-10
Rosedale	M-8
Roseville	F-6
Round Mountain	C-5
Rumsey	E-5
Running Springs	O-11
Rutherford	F-4
Ryan	L-11
Ryde	F-5
Sacramento •	F-5
Sage •	P-11
Saint Helena •	F-4
Salida	G-6
Salinas • 80,479	K-5
Salton City •	P-13
Salton Sea Beach	P-13
Salyer	B-3
San Andreas	F-7
San Anselmo	G-4
San Ardo	L-6
San Bernardino •	O-10
San Bruno	G-4
San Carlos	G-4
San Clemente	P-10
Sandberg	N-9
San Diego •	Q-10
San Fernando	O-9
San Francisco •	G-4
Sanger	K-8
San Jacinto	O-11
San Joaquin	K-7
San Jose •	J-5
San Juan Bautista	K-5
San Juan Capistrano	P-10
San Leandro	G-4
San Lorenzo	D-12
San Lucas	L-6
San Luis Obispo •	M-6
San Marcos	P-11
San Martin	K-5
San Mateo	G-4
San Miguel	L-6
San Onofre	P-10
San Pablo	G-4
San Pasqual	P-11
San Rafael •	G-4
San Ramon	C-13
San Simeon	M-5
Santa Ana •	O-10
Santa Barbara •	O-7
Santa Clara	H-5
Santa Cruz •	K-4
Santa Margarita	M-6
Santa Maria	N-7
Santa Monica	O-9
Santa Paula	O-8
Santa Rosa •	F-4
Santa Ynez	N-7
Santa Ysabel	P-12
Santee	Q-11
Saticoy	O-8
Sattley	D-7
Sausalito	G-4
Schellville	F-4
Scotia	C-2
Scott Bar	A-4
Sea Cliff	O-8
Seal Beach •	O-10
Sebastopol	F-4
Seeley	Q-13
Seiad Valley	A-3
Selma	K-8
Sequoia Crest	L-9
Shafter	M-8
Shandon	M-7
Shasta	C-4
Shasta Retreat	B-4
Shasta Springs	B-5
Shell Beach	M-6
Sheridan	E-6
Shingletown	C-5
Shingle Springs	F-6
Shively	C-2
Shoshone	L-12
Sierra City	D-7
Sierraville	D-7
Silverado	O-10
Simi Valley	O-9
Simmler	M-7
Sisquoc	N-7
Sites	E-4
Skidoo	K-11
Sloughhouse	F-6
Smartville	F-6
Snelling	G-7
Soda Springs	E-7
Solana Beach	O-11
Soledad	K-5
Solemint	N-9
Solvang	N-7
Somes Bar	B-3
Sonoma	F-4
Sonora •	G-7
Soquel	K-4
South Dos Palos	K-6
South Fork	C-3
South Gate	O-9
South Lake Tahoe	E-7
South San Francisco	G-4
Spring Garden	D-6
Spring Valley	Q-11
Springville	L-9
Standard	G-7
Standish	C-7
Stateline	E-7
Stockton •	G-5
Stonyford	E-4
Storrie	D-6
Stratford	L-7
Strathmore	L-8
Stronghold	A-6
Suisun City	F-5
Sun City	O-11
Sunnyvale	H-5
Surf	N-6
Susanville •	C-6
Sutter	E-5
Sutter Creek	F-6
Sycamore	E-5
Taft	M-8
Tagus	L-8
Tahoe City	E-7
Tahoe Vista	E-7
Tajiguas	N-7
Tamarack	F-7
Tancred	F-4
Tecnor	A-5
Tecopa	L-12
Tehachapi	M-9
Temecula	P-11
Templeton	M-6
Tennant	A-5
Terminous	G-5
Termo	C-7
Terra Bella	L-8
Thermal	P-12
Thousand Oaks	O-9
Thousand Palms	O-12
Three Point	N-9
Three Rivers	K-8
Three Rocks	K-7
Tierra del Sol	Q-12
Tipton	L-8
Tobin	D-6
Tomales	F-4
Tom's Place	G-9
Topanga	O-9
Topanga Beach	O-9
Topaz	F-8
Torrance	O-9
Tracy	G-5
Tranquility	K-7
Traver	K-8
Tres Pinos	K-5
Trinidad	B-2
Trona	L-10
Truckee	E-7
Tudor	E-5
Tulare	L-8
Tulelake	A-6
Tuolomne	G-7
Tuolomne Meadows	G-8
Turlock	G-6
Turner	G-6
Tustin	O-10
Tuttle	H-7
Twain Harte	G-7
Twentynine Palms	O-12
Ukiah •	E-3
Union City	G-5
Upland	O-10
Upper Lake	E-4
Vacaville	F-5
Valencia	O-9
Valerie Jean	P-12
Valle Vista	O-11
Vallejo	G-4
Valley Acres	M-8
Valley Center	P-11
Valley Ford	F-4
Valley Springs	F-6
Valley Wells	M-13
Valverde Park	N-9
Valyermo	N-10
Ventura •	O-8
Vernails	G-6
Victorville	N-11
Vidal	O-15
Vidal Junction	O-14
Vinton	D-7
Viola	C-5
Virgilia	D-6
Visalia •	L-8
Vista	P-11
Walker	F-8
Wallace	F-6
Walnut Creek	G-5
Warner Springs	P-12
Wasco	M-8
Washington	E-6
Waterford	G-6
Waterloo	G-6
Watsonville	K-5
Waukena	L-8
Wawona	G-8
Weaverville	C-4
Weed	B-4
Weitchpec	B-3
Weldon	M-9
Weott	C-2
West Covina	O-10
Westend	M-10
Westley	G-6
Westmoreland	P-13
West Point	F-7
Westport	D-2
West Sacramento	F-5
Westwood	C-6
Wheatland	E-5
Wheeler Ridge	N-9
Wheeler Springs	N-8
Whitehall	F-7
White River	L-9
Whitewater	O-12
Whitley Gardens	M-6
Whittier	O-10
Wilbur Springs	E-4
Wildomar	P-11
Wildwood	C-3
Williams	E-4
Willits	E-3
Willow Creek	B-3
Willows •	D-5
Willow Springs	N-9
Wilseyville	F-7
Winchester	P-11
Windsor	F-4
Winterhaven	Q-14
Winters	F-5
Winton	H-7
Wister	P-13
Witter Springs	E-4
Wolford Heights	M-9
Woodford	M-9
Woodlake	K-8
Woodland	F-5
Woodside	H-4
Woodville	L-8
Woody	M-9
Wrightwood	O-10
Yermo	N-11
Yettem	K-8
Yorba Linda	O-14
Yorkville	E-3
Yosemite Village	G-8
Yreka •	A-4
Yuba City •	E-5
Yucaipa	O-11
Yucca Valley	O-12
Zamora	E-5

SF-628-J-X1

FOR CONTINUATION OF MAP SEE PAGES 14-15

FRESNO
CALIFORNIA

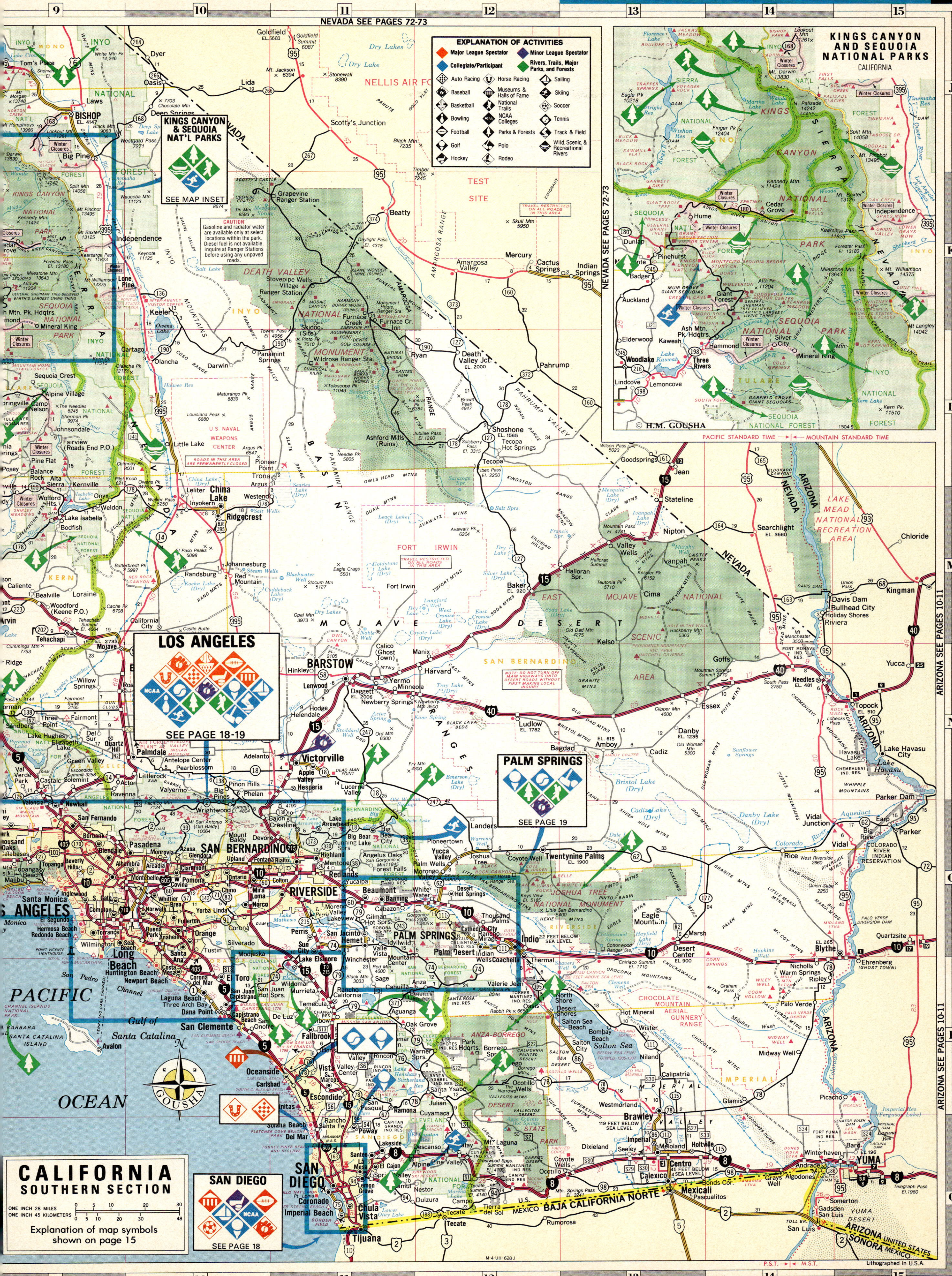
NEVADA SEE PAGES 72-73
EXPLANATION OF ACTIVITIES
Major League Spectator
Minor League Spectator
Collegiate/Participant
Rivers, Trails, Major Parks, and Forests
Auto Racing
Horse Racing
Sailing
Baseball
Museums & Halls of Fame
Skiing
Basketball
National Trails
Soccer
Bowling
NCAA Colleges
Tennis
Football
Parks & Forests
Track & Field
Golf
Polo
Wild, Scenic, & Recreational Rivers
Hockey
Rodeo
KINGS CANYON & SEQUOIA NAT'L PARKS
SEE MAP INSET
KINGS CANYON AND SEQUOIA NATIONAL PARKS
CALIFORNIA
NEVADA SEE PAGES 72-73
© H.M. GOUSHA
PACIFIC STANDARD TIME
MOUNTAIN STANDARD TIME
LOS ANGELES
SEE PAGE 18-19
PALM SPRINGS
SEE PAGE 19
SAN DIEGO
SEE PAGE 18
CALIFORNIA
SOUTHERN SECTION
ONE INCH 28 MILES
ONE INCH 45 KILOMETERS
Explanation of map symbols shown on page 15
ARIZONA SEE PAGES 10-11
PACIFIC
OCEAN
GOUSHA
DEATH VALLEY
MOJAVE
DESERT
EAST MOJAVE NATIONAL SCENIC AREA
JOSHUA TREE NATIONAL MONUMENT
ANZA-BORREGO
BAJA CALIFORNIA NORTE
MEXICO
ARIZONA UNITED STATES
SONORA MEXICO
Lithographed in U.S.A.
M-4-UH-628-J

LOS ANGELES AND VICINITY
SAN DIEGO AND VICINITY
MILES
KILOMETERS
Golf Courses
© H.M. GOUSHA
GOUSHA
SANTA MONICA BAY
PACIFIC OCEAN
Pacific Ocean
LOS ANGELES
PASADENA
GLENDALE
BURBANK
LONG BEACH
SANTA MONICA
INGLEWOOD
TORRANCE
SAN DIEGO
National City
Chula Vista
La Mesa
Tijuana
SIMI VALLEY
Thousand Oaks
SAN FERNANDO VALLEY
ANGELES

SAN BERNARDINO NATIONAL FOREST
ANGELES NATIONAL FOREST
SAN GABRIEL MOUNTAINS
CLEVELAND NATIONAL FOREST
SAN BERNARDINO
RIVERSIDE
POMONA
ONTARIO
Rancho Cucamonga
Upland
Claremont
San Dimas
Glendora
Azusa
Covina
W. COVINA
La Verne
Montclair
Chino
Corona
Norco
Fontana
Rialto
Colton
Loma Linda
REDLANDS
Highland
East Highland
Grand Terrace
Highgrove
Moreno Valley
Perris
Lake Perris
Lake Mathews
El Cerrito
Home Gardens
Mira Loma
Pedley
Sunnyslope
Bloomington
Devore
Verdemont
Arrowhead Springs
Running Springs
Lake Arrowhead
Crestline
Camp Seeley
Lake Silverwood
Cajon
Cajon Pass
Summit
Lytle Creek
Wrightwood
Big Pines
Mount Baldy
Mt. San Antonio (Old Baldy) 10064
CUCAMONGA WILDERNESS
SHEEP MOUNTAIN WILDERNESS
Crystal Lake Recreation Area
La Cienega
Walnut
Diamond Bar
Brea
Fullerton
Placentia
Yorba Linda
Anaheim Hills
Villa Park
ORANGE
SANTA ANA
Tustin
IRVINE
El Toro
Mission Viejo
Laguna Beach
South Laguna
San Juan Capistrano
Dana Point
Capistrano Beach
Three Arch Bay
Corona Del Mar
Balboa
Silverado
March Air Force Base
Woodcrest
Nuevo
Lakeview
Homeland
Romoland
CHINO HILLS
SANTA ANA MOUNTAINS
FOR CONTINUATION SEE INSET BELOW
PALM SPRINGS AREA
FOR CONTINUATION SEE MAP ABOVE
PALM SPRINGS
Banning
Beaumont
Calimesa
Cherry Valley
Cabazon
White Water
North Palm Springs
Desert Hot Springs
Cathedral City
Rancho Mirage
Palm Desert
Indian Wells
Indio
La Quinta
Thousand Palms
Idyllwild
Mountain Center
San Jacinto
Hemet
Valle Vista
Soboba Hot Sprs.
Gilman Hot Sprs.
San Jacinto Peak 10805
MOUNT SAN JACINTO STATE PARK
AGUA CALIENTE INDIAN RES.
SANTA ROSA INDIAN RES.
SANTA ROSA WILDERNESS
JOSHUA TREE NATIONAL MONUMENT
MORONGO INDIAN RES.
To Blythe
To Brawley
© H.M. GOUSHA
Lithographed in U.S.A.

© H.M. GOUSHA

COLORADO

Pop (1990) 3,307,912
Area 104,247 Sq. Mi.

COUNTIES

County	Co. Seat
Adams	Brighton
Alamosa	Alamosa
Arapahoe	Littleton
Archuleta	Pagosa Springs
Baca	Springfield
Bent	Las Animas
Boulder	Boulder
Chaffee	Salida
Cheyenne	Cheyenne Wells
Clear Creek	Georgetown
Conejos	Conejos
Costilla	San Luis
Crowley	Ordway
Custer	Westcliffe
Delta	Delta
Denver	Denver
Dolores	Dove Creek
Douglas	Castle Creek
Eagle	Eagle
El Paso	Colorado Springs
Elbert	Kiowa
Fremont	Canon City
Garfield	Glenwood Springs
Gilpin	Central City
Grand	Hot Sulphur Springs
Gunnison	Gunnison
Hinsdale	Lake City
Huerfano	Walsenburg
Jackson	Walden
Jefferson	Golden
Kiowa	Eads
Kit Carson	Burlington
La Plata	Durango
Lake	Leadville
Larimer	Fort Collins
Las Animas	Trinidad
Lincoln	Hugo
Logan	Sterling
Mesa	Grand Junction
Mineral	Creede
Moffat	Craig
Montezuma	Cortez
Montrose	Montrose
Morgan	Fort Morgan
Otero	La Junta
Ouray	Ouray
Park	Fairplay
Phillips	Holyoke
Pitkin	Aspen
Prowers	Lamar
Pueblo	Pueblo
Rio Blanco	Meeker
Rio Grande	Del Norte
Routt	Steamboat Springs
Saguache	Saguache
San Juan	Silverton
San Miguel	Telluride
Sedgewick	Julesburg
Summit	Breckenridge
Teller	Cripple Creek
Washington	Akron
Weld	Greeley
Yuma	Wray

PARTIAL LIST OF

CITIES AND TOWNS

• County Seats

Abarr	C-13
Akron •	B-12
Alamosa •	G-8
Alder	F-8
Alma	D-8
Almont	E-6
Amherst	A-14
Antero Junction	E-8
Anton	C-12
Antonito	H-8
Arlington	F-12
Aroya	E-12
Arriba	D-12
Arriola	G-3
Arvada	C-9
Aspen	D-7
Atwood	B-12
Ault	B-10
Aurora	C-10
Avondale	F-10
Axial	B-5
Bailey	D-9
Barnesville	B-10
Basalt	D-6
Bedrock	F-3
Bennett	C-10
Berthound	B-9
Blanca	G-8
Blue Mountain	B-3
Blue River	D-8
Bond	C-7
Boone	F-10
Boulder •	C-9
Bovina	D-12
Bowie	E-5
Brandon	E-13
Breckenridge •	D-8
Briggsdale	B-10
Brighton •	C-9
Bristol	F-14
Broadmoor	E-9
Broomfield	C-9
Brown	F-4
Brush	B-11
Buckingham	B-11
Buena Vista	E-7
Burlington •	D-13
Cahone	G-3
Calhan	D-10
Campion	B-9
Canon City •	E-9
Carbondale	D-6
Carlton	F-13
Cascade	E-9
Castle Rock •	D-10
Catherine	D-6
Cattle Creek	D-6
Cedaredge	E-5
Center	G-8
Cheraw	F-12
Chivington	E-13
Cimarron	E-5
Clarkville	B-13
Clifton	D-4
Climax	D-7
Coaldale	F-8
Collbran	D-5
Colona	F-5
Colorado City	F-9
Colorado Springs •	E-10
Como	D-8
Conifer	D-9
Cope	C-12
Cortez	G-3
Cotopaxi	F-8
Cowdrey	A-7
Craig •	B-5
Crawford	E-5
Creede •	G-6
Crested Butte	E-6
Cripple Creek •	E-9
Crook	A-12
Cross Mountain	B-4
Crowley	F-11
Cuchara	G-9
Dacono	C-9
Dailey	B-13
Del Norte •	G-7
Delta •	E-4
Denver •	C-9
Devine	F-10
Divide	E-9
Dolores	G-4
Dotsero	C-6
Dove Creek •	G-3
Dowd	C-7
Doyleville	E-7
Drake	B-9
Durango •	H-5
Eagle •	C-6
Eaton	B-10
Eckley	C-13
Egnar	F-3
Elizabeth	D-10
Elk Springs	B-4
Elkton	E-9
Ellicot	E-10
Empire	C-8
Englewood	C-9
Estes Park	B-8
Evans	B-10
Evergreen	C-9
Fairplay •	D-8
Falcon	E-10
Fall Creek	F-4
Farisita	G-9
Firstview	E-13
Fleming	B-12
Florence	F-9
Florissant	E-9
Fort Garland	G-9
Fort Collins •	B-9
Fort Lupton •	C-10
Fort Lyon	F-12
Ft. Morgan •	B-11
Fortification Hall	A-5
Fountain	E-10
Fowler	F-11
Franktown	D-10
Fraser	C-8
Frisco	C-8
Fruita	D-4
Galatea	E-12
Gardner	G-9
Garfield	E-7
Garo Park	D-8
Gateview	F-6
Gateway	E-3
Genoa	D-12
Georgetown •	C-8
Gilcrest	B-10
Gillett	E-9
Gilman	D-7
Gladel (Slick Rock P.O.)	F-3
Glenisle	D-8
Glentivar	D-8
Glenwood Springs •	D-5
Golden •	C-9
Goodrich	B-10
Gould	B-8
Granada	F-13
Granby	C-8
Grand Junction •	D-4
Grand Lake	B-8
Granite	D-7
Grant	D-8
Greeley •	B-9
Greenwood	F-9
Gunnison •	E-6
Gypsum	C-6
Hall Station	E-11
Hamilton	B-5
Hartsel	D-8
Hasty	F-12
Haswell	E-12
Haxtun	B-13
Hayden	B-6
Hermosa	G-5
Hillrose	B-12
Hillside	F-8
Holly	F-14
Holyoke •	B-13
Hooper	G-8
Hotchkiss	E-5
Hot Sulphur Springs •	B-8
Hudson	C-10
Hugo •	D-12
Idaho Springs	C-8
Idalia	C-13
Idlewild	A-8
Iliff	A-12
Ione	B-10
Jefferson	D-8
Joes	C-13
Johnson Village	E-8
Johnstown	B-9
Julesburg •	A-13
Kersey	B-10
Kings Canyon	A-7
Kiowa •	D-10
Kit Carson	E-13
Kornman	F-13
Kremmling	C-7
Kuhn's Crossing	D-10
Kuner	B-10
La Junta •	F-12
La Salle	B-10
La Veta	G-9
Lafayette	C-9
Laird	C-14
Lake City •	F-5
Lake George	D-9
Lakewood	C-9
Lamar •	F-13
Laporte	B-9
Las Animas •	F-12
Last Chance	C-11
Lay	B-5
Leadville •	D-7
Lewis	G-3
Limon	D-11
Lincoln Park	F-9
Lindon	C-12
Littleton •	C-9
Log Lane Village	B-11
Loma	D-3
Longmont	B-9
Louisville	C-9
Loveland	B-9
Lucerne	B-10
Lyons	B-9
Mack	D-3
Maher	E-5
Malta	D-7
Mancos	G-4
Manitou Springs	F-9
Manzanola	F-11
Masonic	G-7
Massadona	B-4
Matheson	D-11
Maybell	B-5
McClave	F-12
McCoy	C-7
Meeker •	C-5
Merino	B-12
Mesa	D-4
Milner	B-6
Minturn	D-7
Model	G-10
Moffat	F-8
Molina	D-5
Monarch	E-7
Monte Vista	G-7
Montrose •	E-5
Morley	H-10
Mosca	G-8
Narrows	B-9
Nathrop	E-8
Naturita	F-4
Nederland	C-8
New Castle	C-5
New Raymer	B-11
Nine Mile Gap	B-5
North Avondale	F-10
Northglenn	C-9
Norwood	F-4
Nucla	F-4
Nunn	A-9
Oak Creek	B-6
Oak Grove	E-5
Olathe	E-5
Oliver	E-5
Olney Springs	F-11
Ophir	F-5
Orchard	B-10
Orchard City	E-5
Ordway •	F-11
Otis	B-12
Ouray •	F-5
Ovid	A-13
Owl Canyon	A-9
Pagosa Springs •	H-6
Palisade	D-4
Palmer Lake	D-9
Paoli	B-13
Paonia	E-5
Parkdale	E-8
Parlin	E-7
Parshall	C-7
Peckham	B-10
Peetz	A-12
Penrose	F-9
Peyton	D-10
Phippsburg	B-6
Pierce	B-9
Pine Junction	D-9
Pinewood Springs	B-8
Placerville	F-4
Plateau City	D-4
Platner	B-12
Platteville	B-10
Pleasant View	G-3
Poncha Springs	E-8
Portland	F-9
Proctor	A-12
Prospect Valley	C-10
Pueblo •	F-10
Punkin Center	E-11
Ramah	D-11
Rand	B-7
Rangely	C-3
Raymond	B-9
Red Lion	A-13
Red Mountain	F-5
Redstone	D-6
Redvale	F-4
Rico	G-4
Ridgeway	F-5
Rifle	D-5
Rio Blanco	C-5
River Bend	D-11
Rockport	A-10
Rocky Ford	F-11
Rollinsville	C-8
Rulison	D-5
Rustic	A-8
Rye	F-9
Saguache •	F-7
Salida •	E-8
Santa Maria	D-8
Sapinero	E-6
Sargent School	G-8
Sargents	F-7
Security	E-10
Sedalia	D-9
Sedgwick	A-13
Shawnee	D-8
Sheridan Lake	E-13
Shramm	B-13
Siloam	F-9
Silt	C-5
Silver Plume	C-8
Silverthorne	C-8
Silverton •	G-5
Simla	D-11
Simpson	G-11
Slater	A-6
Snowmass Village	D-6
Snyder	B-11
South Fork	G-7
Springfield •	G-13
Starkville	H-10
State Bridge	C-7
Steamboat Springs •	B-7
Sterling •	B-12
Stoneham	B-11
Stoner	G-4
Streeter	B-5
Sugar City	F-11
Sunbeam	B-4
Swink	F-11
Tabernash	C-8
Teds Place	B-9
Telluride •	F-5
Texas Creek	F-8
The Forks	A-9
Thornton	C-9
Toponas	C-6
Towner	E-14
Trinidad •	H-10
Twin Lakes	D-7
Tyrone	G-11
Vail	C-7
Victor	E-9
Villa Grove	F-8
Vineland	F-10
Virginia Dale	A-8
Vulcan	F-6
Wagon Wheel Gap	G-6
Walden •	A-7
Walsenburg •	G-10
Ward	C-9
Watkins	C-10
Weldona	B-11
Wellington	A-9
Wellsville	E-8
Westcliff •	F-8
Westminster	C-9
Wetmore	F-9
Whitewater	D-4
Wild Horse	E-12
Wiley	F-13
Windsor	B-9
Winter Park	C-8
Wolcott	C-7
Wondervu	C-9
Woodland Park	D-9
Woodrow	C-11
Wray •	C-13
Yampa	B-6
Yellow Jacket	G-3
Yoder	E-10
Yuma	B-13
Zinzer	G-8

SF-629-J

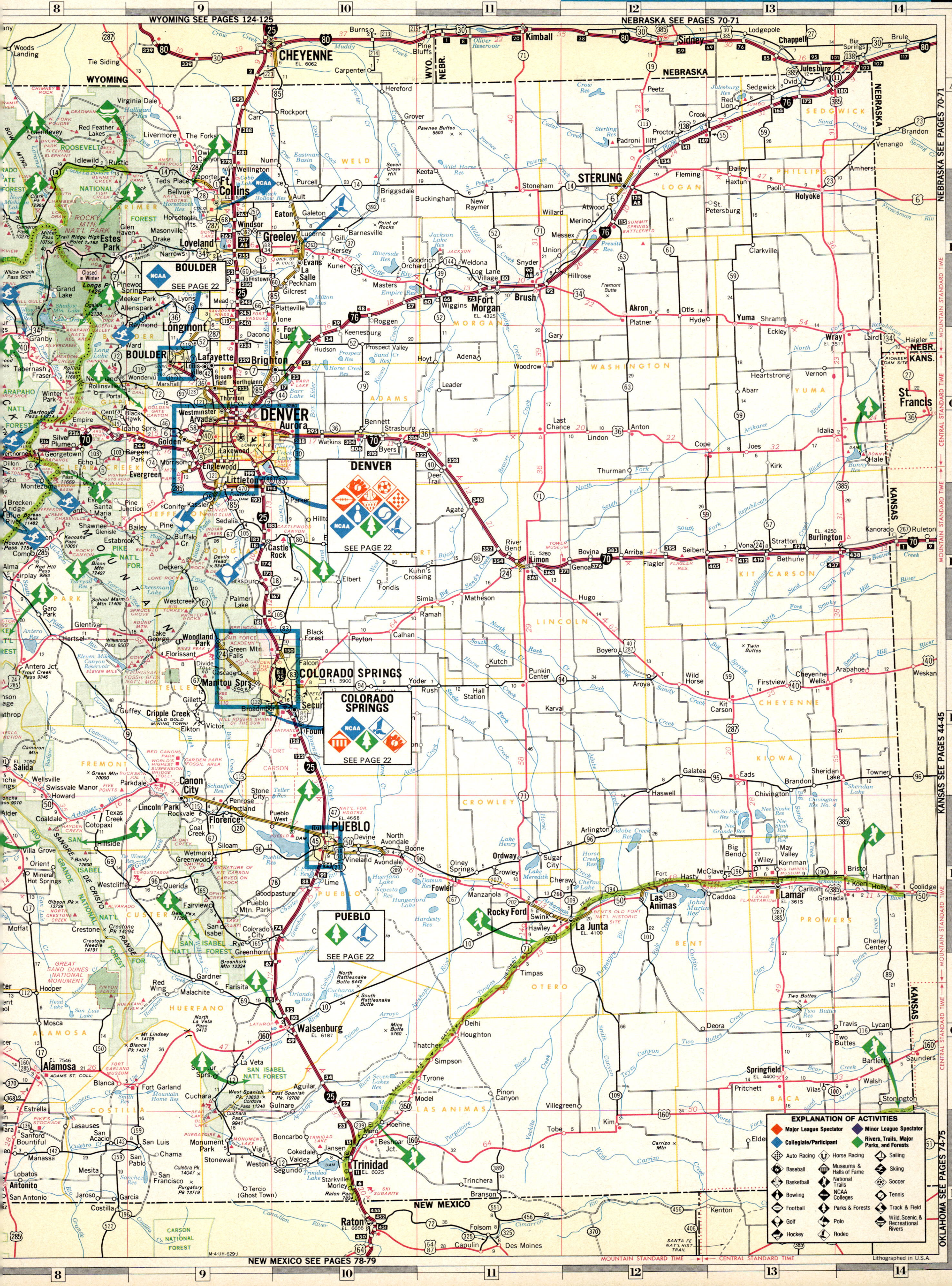
WYOMING SEE PAGES 124-125
NEBRASKA SEE PAGES 70-71
NEBRASKA SEE PAGES 70-71
KANSAS SEE PAGES 44-45
OKLAHOMA SEE PAGES 74-75
NEW MEXICO SEE PAGES 78-79
WYOMING
NEBRASKA
KANSAS
NEW MEXICO
CHEYENNE
STERLING
Fort Collins
Greeley
Loveland
Longmont
BOULDER
SEE PAGE 22
Brighton
DENVER
Aurora
Lakewood
Englewood
Littleton
DENVER
SEE PAGE 22
Castle Rock
COLORADO SPRINGS
COLORADO SPRINGS
SEE PAGE 22
Manitou Sprs.
Cripple Creek
Canon City
Florence
PUEBLO
PUEBLO
SEE PAGE 22
Walsenburg
Trinidad
Raton
Alamosa
Salida
Leadville
Fort Morgan
Brush
Akron
Yuma
Wray
Holyoke
Julesburg
Limon
Burlington
La Junta
Rocky Ford
Las Animas
Lamar
Springfield
Kimball
Sidney
Chappell
St. Francis
Eads
Kit Carson
Hugo
WELD
LOGAN
SEDGWICK
PHILLIPS
MORGAN
WASHINGTON
YUMA
ADAMS
ELBERT
LINCOLN
KIT CARSON
CHEYENNE
KIOWA
CROWLEY
OTERO
BENT
PROWERS
BACA
LAS ANIMAS
PUEBLO
HUERFANO
COSTILLA
ALAMOSA
FREMONT
PARK
ROCKY MTN. NAT'L PARK
PIKE NAT'L FOREST
SAN ISABEL NAT'L FOREST
GREAT SAND DUNES NATIONAL MONUMENT
MOUNTAIN STANDARD TIME
CENTRAL STANDARD TIME
EXPLANATION OF ACTIVITIES
Major League Spectator
Minor League Spectator
Collegiate/Participant
Rivers, Trails, Major Parks, and Forests
Auto Racing
Horse Racing
Sailing
Baseball
Museums & Halls of Fame
Skiing
Basketball
National Trails
Soccer
Bowling
NCAA Colleges
Tennis
Football
Parks & Forests
Track & Field
Golf
Polo
Wild Scenic & Recreational Rivers
Hockey
Rodeo
Lithographed in U.S.A.

DENVER AND VICINITY
MILES
KILOMETERS
Golf Courses
COLORADO SPRINGS PIKES PEAK REGION
BOULDER COLORADO
PUEBLO COLORADO
© H.M. GOUSHA
WESTMINSTER
ARVADA
COMMERCE CITY
WHEAT RIDGE
GOLDEN
LAKEWOOD
DENVER
AURORA
EDGEWATER
Glendale
ENGLEWOOD
SHERIDAN
CHERRY HILLS VILLAGE
GREENWOOD VILLAGE
LITTLETON
Morrison
Stapleton International Airport
ROCKY MOUNTAIN ARSENAL (Restricted Area)
Lowry Air Force Base
Buckley Air National Guard Base
Cherry Creek Lake
Marston Lake
Chatfield
Tinytown
Idledale
Indian Hills
Fenders
Sky Ranch Airport
To Boulder
To Cheyenne
To Fort Morgan
To Int. Hwy. 76
To Glenwood Springs
To Idaho Springs
To Colorado Springs
U.S. AIR FORCE ACADEMY
Woodland Park
Crystola
Green Mountain Falls
Chipita Park
Cascade
PIKE NATIONAL FOREST
RAMPART RANGE
PIKES PEAK 14,110
Summit House
Manitou Springs
Garden of the Gods
COLORADO SPRINGS
Briargate
Pikeview
Vista Grande
Park Vista Estates
Glen Eyrie
Cragmor
Broadmoor
Stratmoor Hills
Skyway
Ivywild
Windy Point
To Buena Vista
To Alamosa
To Denver
To Franktown
To Falcon
To Canon City
To Pueblo
BOULDER
Valmont
Chautauqua Park
Boulder Mountain Park
DENVER-BOULDER TPK
PUEBLO
City Park
Arkansas River
Blende
Salt Creek
Lake Minnequa
THATCHER
To Colorado Springs

HARTFORD AND VICINITY
MILES
KILOMETERS
Golf Courses
WEST HARTFORD
HARTFORD
WINDSOR
Bloomfield
EAST HARTFORD
NEW BRITAIN
NEWINGTON
WETHERSFIELD
MIDDLETOWN
MERIDEN
Berlin
Kensington
Cromwell
Brainard Airport
Rentschler Field
Farmington
© H.M. GOUSHA
To Springfield
To Wallingford
NEWPORT
RHODE ISLAND
NEWPORT
Jamestown
NEWPORT BRIDGE (TOLL)
NARRAGANSETT BAY
ATLANTIC OCEAN
Rhode Island Sound
Middletown
© H.M. GOUSHA
NEW LONDON GROTON
CONNECTICUT
NEW LONDON
GROTON
Thames River
GOLD STAR MEMORIAL BRIDGE
© H.M. GOUSHA
PROVIDENCE AND VICINITY
MILES
KILOMETERS
Golf Courses
PROVIDENCE
PAWTUCKET
NORTH PROVIDENCE
EAST PROVIDENCE
CRANSTON
WARWICK
ATTLEBORO
Seekonk
Barrington
Manville
Albion
Lonsdale
Valley Falls
Saylesville
Central Falls
Greenville
Esmond
PROVIDENCE RIVER
To Taunton
To Fall River
To New London
To East Greenwich
© H.M. GOUSHA

CONNECTICUT

Pop (1990) 3,295,669
Area 5,009 Sq. Mi.

COUNTIES

Fairfield	D-3
Hartford	B-6
Litchfield	A-4
Middlesex	C-6
New Haven	D-4
New London	C-7
Tolland	B-6
Windham	B-8

PARTIAL LIST OF

CITIES AND TOWNS

• County Seats

Abington	B-8
Almyville	B-9
Amston	C-7
Andover	B-6
Ansonia	D-4
Ashford	B-8
Aspetuck	D-3
Attawaugan	B-9
Augerville	D-5
Avon	B-5
Bakersville	B-4
Ballouville	B-9
Baltic	C-8
Bantam	B-3
Beacon Falls	D-4
Beckley	C-5
Berlin	C-5
Bethel	D-3
Bethlehem	C-3
Black Point	D-7
Bloomfield	B-5
Bolton Notch	B-6
Branchville	D-3
Branford	D-5
Bridgeport	E-4
Bridgewater	C-3
Bristol	B-5
Broad Brook	A-6
Brookfield	C-3
Brookfield Center	C-3
Brooklyn	B-8
Buckingham	B-6
Burlington	B-5
Canaan	A-3
Canterbury	B-8
Canton	B-5
Centerbrook	D-6
Chapin	B-8
Cheshire	C-5
Chester	D-6
Chesterfield	D-7
Chestnut Hill	C-7
Clarks Corner	B-8
Clinton	D-6
Cobalt	C-6
Colchester	C-7
Colebrook	A-4
Colebrook River	A-4
Collinsville	B-5
Columbia	B-7
Cornwall Bridge	B-3
Coventry	B-7
Cromwell	C-6
Crystal Lake	A-7
Danbury	D-3
Danielson	B-8
Darien	E-2
Dayville	B-8
Deep River	D-6
Derby	D-4
Dodgingtown	D-3
Durham	C-6
Eagleville	B-7
East Glastonbury	B-6
East Granby	A-5
East Hampton	C-6
East Hartford	B-6
East Hartland	A-5
East Haven	D-5
East Killingly	B-9
East Litchfield	B-4
East Lyme	D-7
East Morris	B-4
East Willington	B-7
Eastford	B-8
Easton	D-3
Ellington	B-6
Ellithorpe	A-7
Enfield	A-6
Essex	D-7
Fairfield	E-3
Falls Village	A-3
Farmington	B-5
Flanders	B-3
Foxon	D-5
Gardner Lake	C-7
Gaylordsville	C-3
Georgetown	D-3
Gildersleeve	C-6
Gilead	B-7
Gilman	C-7
Glasgo	C-8
Glastonbury	B-6
Goshen	B-4
Granby	A-5
Greene	B-9
Greenwich	E-2
Grosvenor Dale	A-8
Groton	D-8
Grove Beach	D-6
Guilford	D-5
Hadlyme	D-7
Hale	C-8
Hamburg	D-7
Hamden	D-4
Hampton	B-8
Hartford	B-5
Hartland	A-5
Harwinton	B-4
Hebron	C-7
Higganum	C-6
Hop River	B-7
Hoskins	B-5
Ivoryton	D-6
Jewett City	C-8
Killingworth	D-6
Lakeville	A-3
Lebanon	C-7
Ledyard Center	D-8
Leetes Island	D-5
Lime Rock	A-3
Litchfield	B-4
Macedonia	B-2
Madison	D-6
Manchester	B-6
Mansfield	B-7
Mansfield Center	B-7

INDEX CONTINUED AT RIGHT

MASSACHUSETTS SEE PAGES 56-57

RHODE ISLAND

Pop (1990) 1,005,984
Area 1,214 Sq. Mi.

COUNTIES

Name	Co. Seat
Bristol	Bristol
Kent	E. Greenwich
Newport	Newport
Providence	Providence
Washington	W. Kingston

PARTIAL LIST OF

CITIES AND TOWNS

• County Seats

UH-686-J

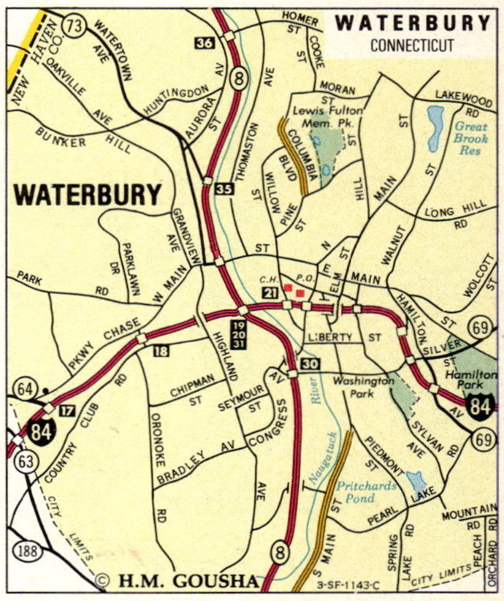

FOR DELAWARE SEE PAGES 52-53

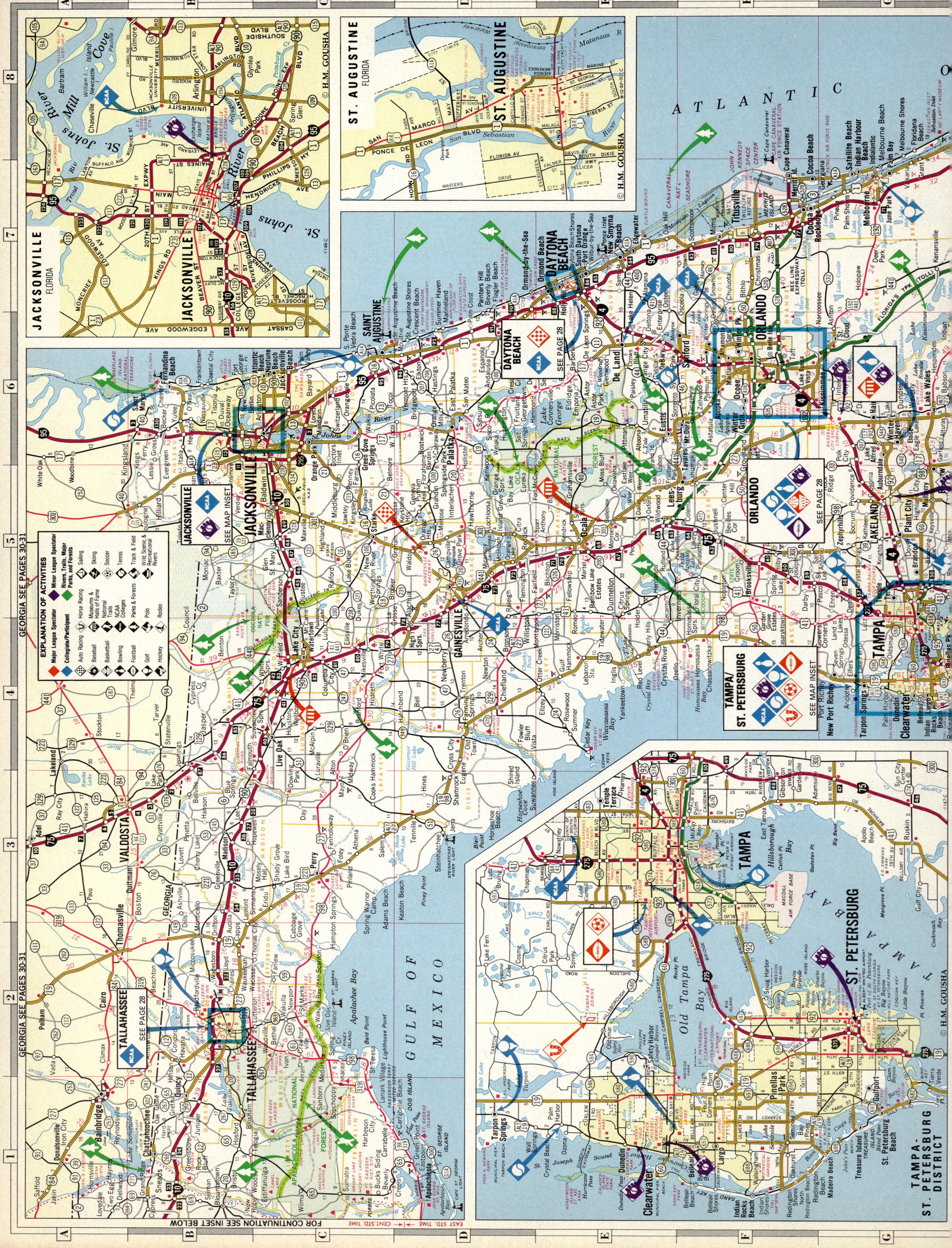

FLORIDA
HIGHWAY MARKERS
ROAD CLASSIFICATIONS
SPECIAL FEATURES
POPULATION SYMBOLS
© H.M. GOUSHA
MIAMI SEE PAGE 29
FLORIDA EAST COAST SEE PAGE 28-29
SARASOTA SEE PAGE 28
PENSACOLA SEE PAGE 28
ALABAMA SEE PAGES 6-7
FOR CONTINUATION SEE MAIN MAP
WESTERN FLORIDA
Scale: Same as Main Map
GULF OF MEXICO
ATLANTIC OCEAN
CITIES AND TOWNS
COUNTIES
FLORIDA TOLL ROADS
FLORIDA'S TURNPIKE & HOMESTEAD EXT.
EVERGLADES PARKWAY
HOLLAND EAST-WEST EXPRESSWAY
AIRPORT EXPRESSWAY
MIAMI EAST-WEST EXPRESSWAY
BEE LINE EXPRESSWAY & EXTS.
SAWGRASS EXPRESSWAY
EASTERN BELTWAY
TAMPA SOUTH CROSSTOWN
Lithographed in U.S.A.

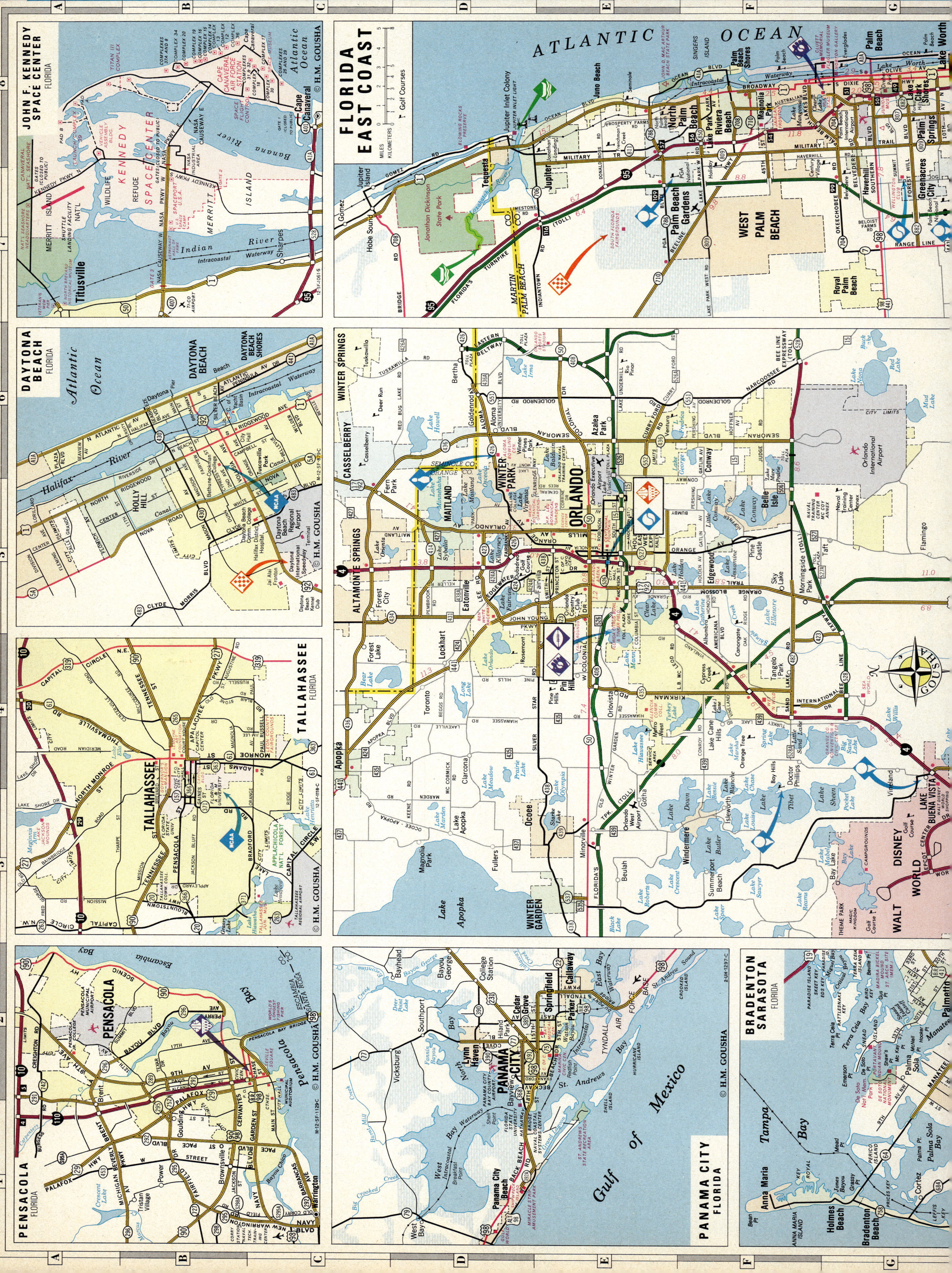

JOHN F. KENNEDY SPACE CENTER
FLORIDA
FLORIDA EAST COAST
DAYTONA BEACH
FLORIDA
TALLAHASSEE
FLORIDA
PENSACOLA
FLORIDA
PANAMA CITY
FLORIDA
BRADENTON SARASOTA
FLORIDA
ORLANDO
ATLANTIC OCEAN
Gulf of Mexico
© H.M. GOUSHA

ORLANDO AND VICINITY
MIAMI AND VICINITY
CAPE CORAL FORT MYERS FLORIDA
ATLANTIC OCEAN
BISCAYNE BAY
Gulf of Mexico
GULF OF MEXICO
Sarasota Bay
FORT LAUDERDALE
POMPANO BEACH
Boca Raton
Delray Beach
Boynton Beach
HOLLYWOOD
Hallandale
Dania
Deerfield Beach
Coral Springs
Margate
Tamarac
Sunrise
Plantation
Davie
Pembroke Pines
Miami Beach
North Miami Beach
North Miami
MIAMI
Hialeah
Miami Springs
Coral Gables
West Miami
Opa-Locka
Miramar
KISSIMMEE
SARASOTA
Bradenton
FORT MYERS
CAPE CORAL
ARTHUR R. MARSHALL LOXAHATCHEE NATIONAL WILDLIFE REFUGE
© H.M. GOUSHA

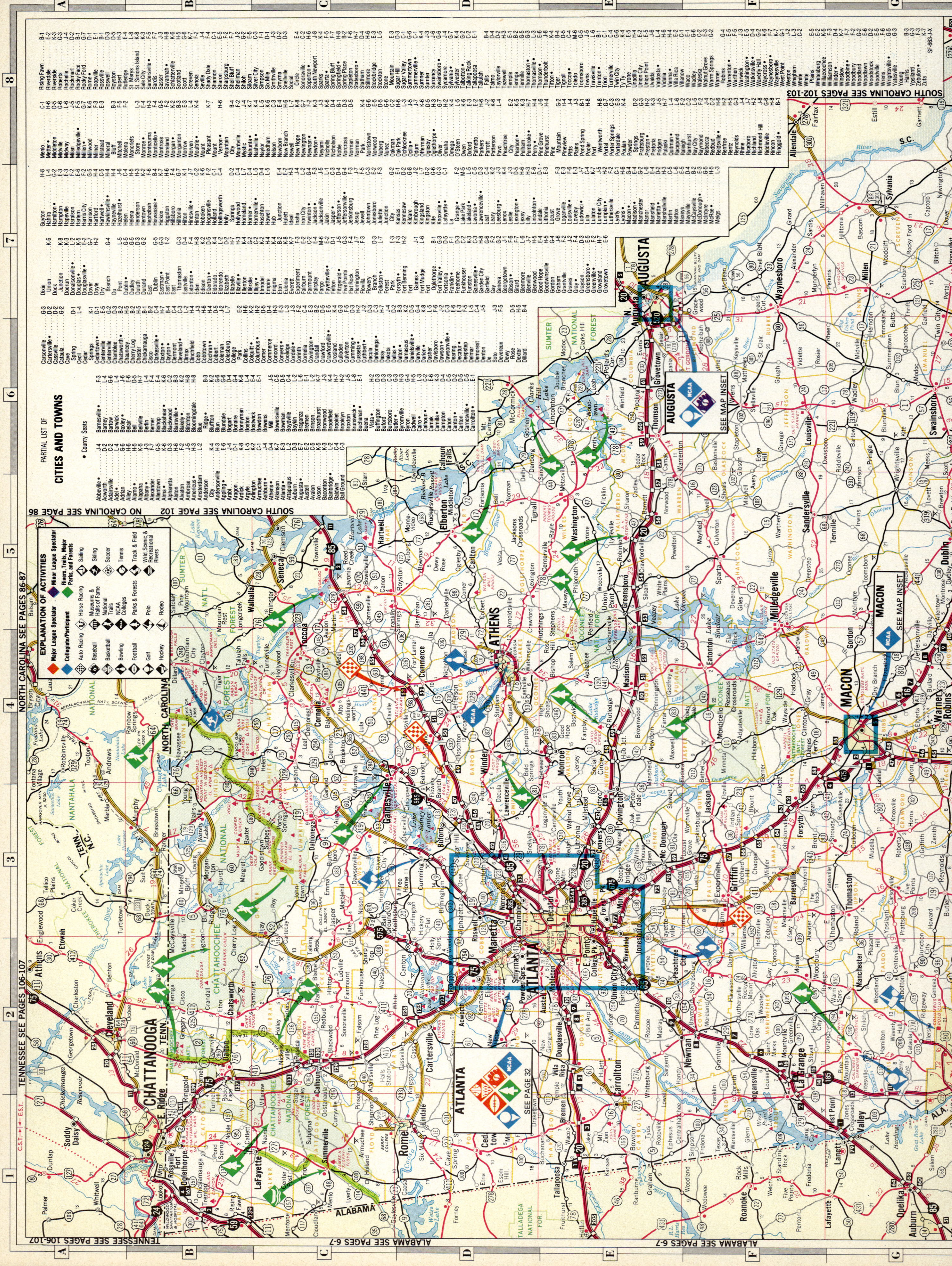
PARTIAL LIST OF CITIES AND TOWNS
EXPLANATION OF ACTIVITIES
NORTH CAROLINA SEE PAGES 86-87
NO CAROLINA SEE PAGE 86
SOUTH CAROLINA SEE PAGE 102
SOUTH CAROLINA SEE PAGES 102-103
TENNESSEE SEE PAGES 106-107
ALABAMA SEE PAGES 6-7
ATLANTA SEE PAGE 32
AUGUSTA SEE MAP INSET
MACON SEE MAP INSET
ATLANTA
ATHENS
AUGUSTA
MACON
CHATTANOOGA
ROME
GAINESVILLE
MILLEDGEVILLE

GEORGIA
SAVANNAH
JACKSONVILLE
ATLANTIC OCEAN
SAVANNAH GEORGIA
MACON GEORGIA
AUGUSTA GEORGIA
H.M. GOUSHA
FLORIDA SEE PAGES 26-27
ALABAMA SEE PAGES 6-7
Okefenokee Swamp
TALLAHASSEE
ALBANY
VALDOSTA
WAYCROSS
BRUNSWICK
TIFTON
DOTHAN
GEORGIA COUNTIES

ATLANTA
AND VICINITY
MILES
KILOMETERS
Golf Courses
GOUSHA
MARIETTA
KENNESAW
WOODSTOCK
ROSWELL
ALPHARETTA
DULUTH
NORCROSS
DORAVILLE
CHAMBLEE
SANDY SPRS
SMYRNA
AUSTELL
MABLETON
DECATUR
CLARKSTON
STONE MOUNTAIN
LILBURN
ATLANTA
EAST POINT
COLLEGE PARK
HAPEVILLE
FOREST PARK
LAKE CITY
MORROW
RIVERDALE
JONESBORO
UNION CITY
FAIRBURN
AVONDALE ESTATES
PINE LAKE
HARTSFIELD ATLANTA INTERNATIONAL AIRPORT
CHATTAHOOCHEE RIVER NAT'L RECREATION AREA
Some of the land within the authorized boundary of the Chattahoochee Riv. Nat'l Rec. Area is under private ownership. Please respect property rights
COLUMBUS
GEORGIA
Phenix City
ALABAMA
CENTRAL STANDARD TIME
EASTERN STANDARD TIME
© H.M. GOUSHA

PARTIAL LIST OF
CITIES AND TOWNS

Pop (1990) 1,115,274
Area 6,450 Sq. Mi.

HAWAII

Captain Cook F-6
Hawi D-6
Hilo E-8
Honokaa D-7
Honokohau E-6
Honomu E-8
Honuapo G-7
Kailua E-6
Kapaau D-6
Kawaihae D-6
Keaau E-8
Keokea F-6
Kukuihaele D-7
Mahukona D-6
Makapala D-6
Mountain View E-8
Naalehu G-7
Ninole E-7
Ookala D-7
Paauilo D-7
Pahala F-7
Pahoa F-8
Papaaloa D-7
Papaikou E-8
Waimea D-7

KAUAI

Anahola F-3
Haena E-2
Hanalei E-2
Hanamaulu F-3
Hanapepe G-2
Kalililaau Junction! . . F-2
Kalaheo G-2
Kalihiwai E-2
Kapaa F-3
Kaumakani G-2
Kekaha F-2
Kilauea E-3
Koloa G-2
Kukuiula G-2
Lihue F-3
Nawiliwili F-3
Wailua F-3
Waimea F-2
Wainiha E-2

MAUI

Haiku B-7
Hana B-8
Honokahua A-6
Kahakuloa A-6
Kahului B-7
Kailua B-7
Keanae B-8
Keokea B-7
Lahaina B-6
Lower Paia B-7
Makawao B-7
Olowalu B-6
Paia B-7
Puunene B-7
Waiakoa B-7
Waikapu B-6
Wailuku B-6

MOLOKAI

Halawa E-5
Halena E-4
Hoolehua E-4
Kalae E-4
Kalaupapa E-4
Kamalo E-5
Kamiloloa E-5
Kaunakakai E-4
Kawela E-5
Kepuhi E-4
Kualapuu E-4
Mahana E-4
Maunaloa E-4
Pukoo E-5
Umipaa E-4
Waialua E-5

OAHU

Aiea D-3
Ewa D-3
Haleiwa B-2
Hauula B-3
Honolulu D-4
Kaaawa B-4
Kahana B-4
Kahuku A-3
Kailua C-5
Kaneohe C-4
Laie B-4
Lanikai D-5
Maili C-2
Makaha C-2
Mokuleia B-2
Nanakuli D-2
Pearl City C-3
Wahiawa C-3
Waialee A-3
Waialua B-2
Waianae C-2
Waikane C-4
Waimanalo D-5
Waimanalo Beach D-5
Waimea B-3
Waipahu D-3
Whitmore Village C-3

SF-634-J

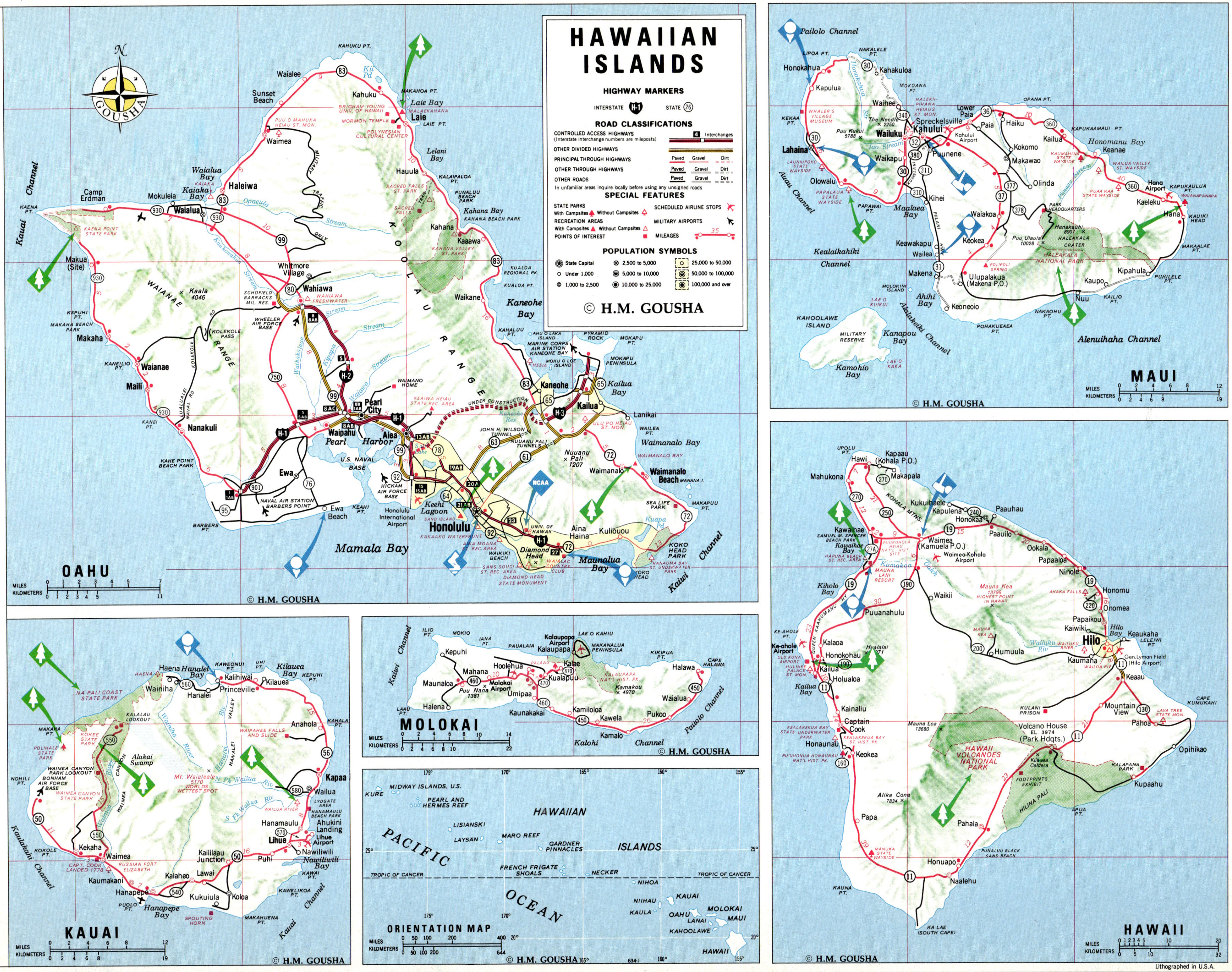

IDAHO
H.M. GOUSHA
TWIN FALLS
IDAHO
BOISE
IDAHO
POCATELLO
IDAHO
IDAHO FALLS
IDAHO
CANADA SEE PAGES 126-127
MONTANA SEE PAGES 68-69
WASHINGTON SEE PAGES 118-119
OREGON SEE PAGES 96-97
PARTIAL LIST OF CITIES AND TOWNS
COUNTIES
SPOKANE
COEUR D'ALENE
LEWISTON
MOSCOW
Bozeman

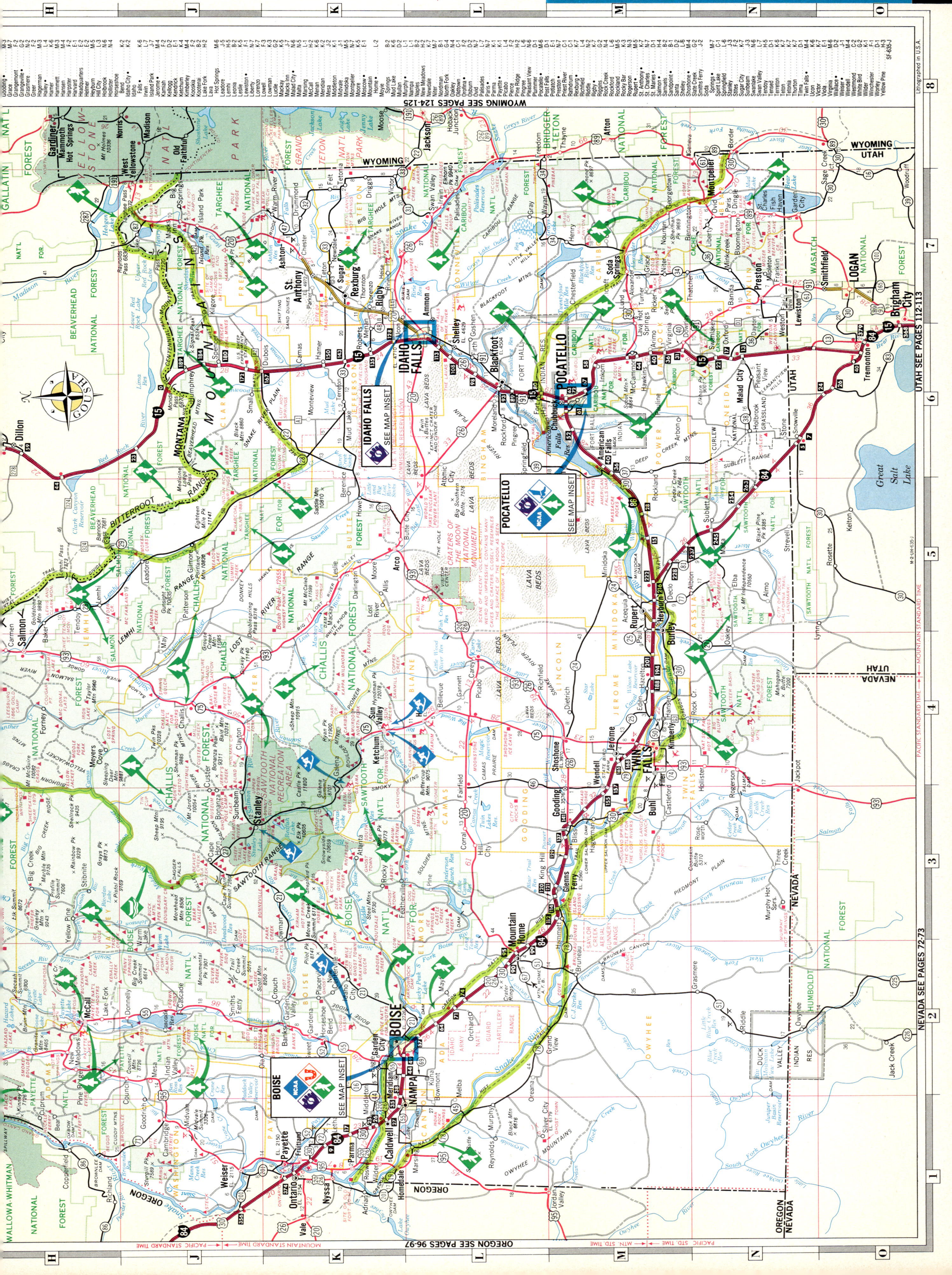
WYOMING SEE PAGES 124-125
UTAH SEE PAGES 112-113
NEVADA SEE PAGES 72-73
OREGON SEE PAGES 96-97

ILLINOIS

Pop (1990) 11,466,682
Area 56,400 Sq. Mi.

COUNTIES

Couty	County Seat	Couty	County Seat
Adams	Quincy	Lee	Dixon
Alexander	Cairo	Livingston	Pontiac
Bond	Greenville	Logan	Lincoln
Boone	Belvidere	Macon	Decatur
Brown	Mount Sterling	Macoupin	Carlinville
Bureau	Princeton	Madison	Edwardsville
Calhoun	:Hardin	Marion	Salem
Carroll	Mount Carroll	Marshall	Lacon
Cass	Virginia	Mason	Havana
Champaign	Urbana	Massac	Metropolis
Christian	Taylorville	McDonough	Macomb
Clark	Marshall	McHenry	Woodstock
Clay	Louisville	McLean	Bloomington
Clinton	Carlyle	Menard	Petersburg
Coles	Charleston	Mercer	Aledo
Cook	Chicago	Monroe	Waterloo
Crawford	Robinson	Montgomery	Hillsboro
Cumberland	Toledo	Morgan	Jacksonville
De Kalb	Sycamore	Moultrie	Sullivan
De Witt	Clinton	Ogle	Oregon
Douglas	Tuscola	Peoria	Peoria
Du Page	Wheaton	Perry	Pinckneyville
Edgar	Paris	Piatt	Monticello
Edwards	Albion	Pike	Pittsfield
Effingham	Effingham	Pope	Golconda
Fayette	Vandalia	Pulaski	Mound City
Ford	Paxton	Putnam	Hennepin
Franklin	Benton	Randolph	Chester
Fulton	Lewistown	Richland	Olney
Gallatin	Shawneetown	Rock Island	Rock Island
Greene	Carrollton	St. Clair	Belleville
Grundy	Morris	Saline	Harrisburg
Hamilton	McLeansboro	Sagamon	Springfield
Hancock	Carthage	Schuyler	Rushville
Hardin	Elizabethtown	Scott	Winchester
Henderson	Oquawka	Shelby	Shelbyville
Henry	Cambridge	Stark	Toulon
Iroquois	Watseka	Stephenson	Freeport
Jackson	Murphysboro	Tazewell	Pekin
Jasper	Newton	Union	Jonesboro
Jefferson	Mount Vernon	Vermilion	Danville
Jersey	Jerseyville	Wabash	Mount Carmel
Jo Daviess	Galena	Warren	Monmouth
Johnson	Vienna	Washington	Nashville
Kane	Geneva	Wayne	Fairfield
Kankakee	Kankakee	White	Carmi
Kendall	Yorkville	Whiteside	Morrison
Knox	Galesburg	Will	Joliet
La Salle	Ottawa	Williamson	Marion
Lake	Waukegan	Winnebago	Rockford
Lawrence	Lawrenceville	Woodford	Eureka

PARTIAL LIST OF

CITIES AND TOWNS

• County Seats

Abingdon	E-4	De Land	G-6
Adair	F-3	Decatur •	G-6
Addieville	L-5	Deer Grove	C-5
Albers	K-5	Delafield	L-6
Albion •	L-7	Delavan	F-5
Alden	A-6	Delrey	E-7
Aledo •	D-3	Delwood	N-7
Alexander	H-4	Denrock	C-4
Alonquin	B-7	Des Plaines	B-8
Allen	F-5	Detroit	H-3
Allendale	K-8	Diamond	D-7
Allenville	H-7	Dieterich	J-7
Allerton	G-8	Dillsburg	F-7
Alma	K-6	Diona	H-7
Alpha	D-4	Divernon	H-5
Altamont	J-6	Dix	L-6
Alto Pass	N-5	Dixon •	C-5
Alton	J-4	Dolton	C-8
Altona	D-4	Dongola	N-6
Amboy	C-5	Donnellson	J-5
Anchor	F-7	Donovan	E-8
Andalusia	D-3	Dorans	H-7
Andover	D-4	Dover	D-5
Andres	D-8	Du Quoin	M-6
Anna	N-5	Duncans Mills	F-4
Annawan	D-4	Dundas	K-7
Antioch	A-7	Dunfermline	F-4
Arcola	H-7	Dunlap	E-5
Argenta	G-6	Dupo	K-4
Arlington Heights	B-7	Dwight	D-7
Armstrong	F-8	Earlville	C-6
Arthur	H-7	East Alton	K-4
Ashland	G-4	East Dubuque	A-3
Ashley	L-5	East Dundee	B-7
Ashmore	H-7	East Moline	C-3
Ashton	C-5	East Newbern	J-4
Assumption	H-6	Easton	F-4
Astoria	F-4	East Peoria	E-5
Athens	G-5	East St. Louis	K-4
Atkinson	D-4	Eddyville	N-6
Atlanta	F-5	Eden	L-5
Atlas	H-3	Edgewood	J-6
Atterberry	G-4	Edington	D-3
Atwood	G-7	Edinburg	H-5
Auburn	H-5	Edwardsville	K-4
Augusta	F-3	Effingham	J-6
Aurora	C-7	Elburn	C-7
Aviston	K-5	Eldorado	M-7
Avon	E-4	Elgin	B-7
Baldwin	L-4	Elizabeth	A-4
Banner	F-4	Elizabethtown •	N-7
Barrington	B-7	Elk Grove Village	B-7
Barry	H-2	Elkville	M-5
Bartelso	K-5	Elliott	F-7
Bartonville	E-5	Ellis Grove	M-4
Batavia	C-7	Elmira	D-4
Bath	F-4	Elmwood	E-4
Beardstown	G-3	El Paso	E-6
Beason	G-5	Elsah	J-4
Beaucoup	L-5	Elvaston	F-2
Beaver Creek	K-5	Elwood	D-7
Beckemeyer	K-5	Emery	G-6
Beecher	D-8	Enfield	L-7
Beecher City	J-6	Enion	F-4
Beecreek	H-3	Equality	M-7
Belle Rive	L-6	Erie	C-4
Belleview	H-3	Ernst	H-8
Belleville •	K-4	Etherton	M-5
Bellevue	E-5	Eureka •	E-5
Bellflower	F-7	Evanston	B-8
Belvidere •	B-6	Evansville	L-4
Bement	G-6	Fairbury	E-7
Benld	J-4	Fairfield •	L-7
Bentley	F-2	Fairman	K-6
Benton •	M-6		
Bethalto	J-4		
Bethany	H-6		
Biggsville	E-3		
Bigneck	G-2		

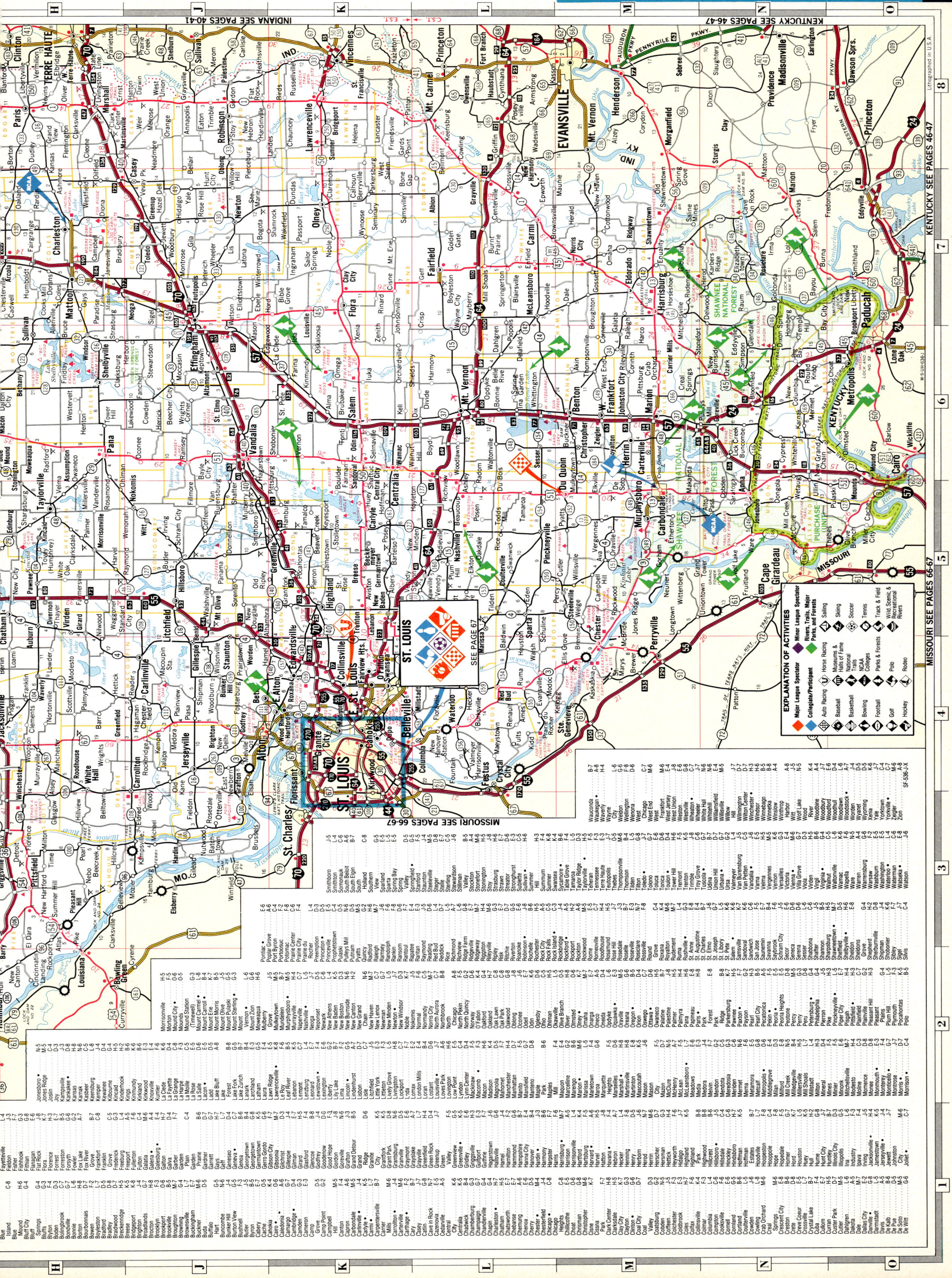
INDIANA SEE PAGES 40-41
KENTUCKY SEE PAGES 46-47
MISSOURI SEE PAGES 66-67
ST. LOUIS
SEE PAGE 67
EVANSVILLE
EXPLANATION OF ACTIVITIES
Lithographed in U.S.A.

CHICAGO AND VICINITY
INDIANAPOLIS INDIANA
EVANSVILLE INDIANA
FORT WAYNE INDIANA
SOUTH BEND INDIANA
TERRE HAUTE INDIANA
© H.M. GOUSHA

TOLL HIGHWAYS
INTERCHANGES
ILLINOIS-MICHIGAN CANAL NATIONAL HERITAGE CORRIDOR
LAKE MICHIGAN
EAST CHICAGO
GARY
HAMMOND
AURORA
JOLIET
DECATUR ILLINOIS
PEORIA ILLINOIS
SPRINGFIELD ILLINOIS
ROCKFORD ILLINOIS
© H.M. GOUSHA

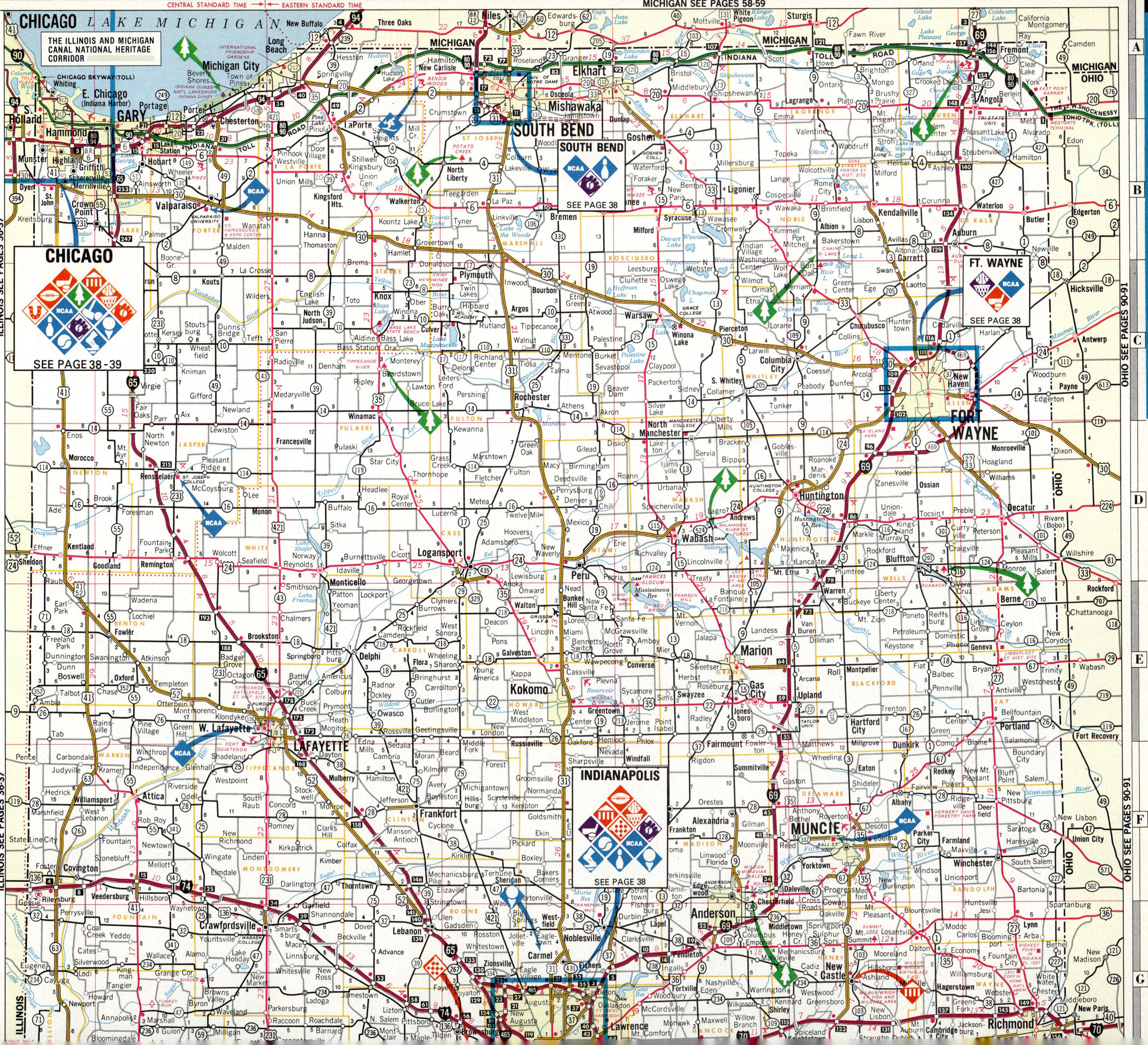

INDIANA

Pop (1990) 5,564,228
Area 36,291 Sq. Mi.

COUNTIES

County	Co. Seat
Adams	Decatur
Allen	Fort Wayne
Bartholomew	Columbus
Benton	Fowler
Blackford	Hartford City
Boone	Lebanon
Brown	Nashville
Carroll	Delphi
Cass	Logansport
Clark	Jeffersonville
Clay	Brazil
Clinton	Frankfort
Crawford	English
Daviess	Washington
De Kalb	Auburn
Dearborn	Lawrenceburg
Decatur	Greensburg
Delaware	Muncie
Dubois	Jasper
Elkhart	Goshen
Fayette	Connersville
Floyd	New Albany
Fountain	Covington
Franklin	Brookville
Fulton	Rochester
Gibson	Princeton
Grant	Marion
Greene	Bloomfield
Hamilton	Noblesville
Hancock	Greenfield
Harrison	Corydon
Hendricks	Danville
Henry	New Castle
Howard	Kokomo
Huntington	Huntington
Jackson	Brownstown
Jasper	Rensselaer
Jay	Portland
Jefferson	Madison
Jennings	Vernon
Johnson	Franklin
Knox	Vicennes
Kosciusko	Warsaw
La Porte	La Porte
Lagrange	Lagrange
Lake	Crown Point
Lawrence	Bedford
Madison	Anderson
Marion	Indianapolis
Marshall	Plymouth
Martin	Shoals
Miami	Peru
Monroe	Bloomington
Montgomery	Crawfordsville
Morgan	Martinsville
Newton	Kentland
Noble	Albion
Ohio	Rising Sun
Orange	Paoli
Owen	Spencer
Parke	Rockville
Perry	Cannelton
Pike	Petersburg
Porter	Valparaiso
Posey	Mount Vernon
Pulaski	Winamac
Putnam	Greencastle
Randolph	Winchester
Ripley	Versailles
Rush	Rushville
St. Joseph	South Bend
Scott	Scottsburg
Shelby	Shelbyville
Spencer	Rockport
Starke	Knox
Steuben	Angola
Sullivan	Sullivan
Switzerland	Vevay
Tippecanoe	Lafayette
Tipton	Tipton
Union	Liberty
Vanderburgh	Evansville
Vermillion	Newport
Vigo	Terre Haute
Wabash	Wabash
Warren	Williamsport
Warrick	Booneville
Washington	Salem
Wayne	Richmond
Wells	Bluffton
White	Monticello
Whitley	Columbia City

PARTIAL LIST OF

CITIES AND TOWNS

• County Seats

Albany F-7
Albion B-7
Alert J-6
Alexandria F-6
Allendale J-2
Ambia E-2
Amboy E-6
Anderson • G-6
Andrews D-6
Angola • A-8
Arcadia F-5
Argos C-5
Athens C-5
Attica F-3
Auburn • B-8
Augusta M-3
Aurora K-8
Austin L-6
Bass Lake C-4
Bass Station C-4
Batesville J-7
Beardstown C-4
Bedford • K-4
Beech Grove H-5
Belleville H-4
Bennettsville M-6
Benton B-6
Berne E-8
Beverly Shores A-3
Bicknell L-3
Billtown H-3
Birdseye M-4
Bloomfield • K-3
Bloomington • J-4
Blountsville G-7
Bluffton D-7
Boonville • N-3
Boston H-8
Boswell E-2
Bourbon C-5
Brazil • H-3
Bremen B-5
Bretzville M-4
Brick Chapel H-4
Bridgeport H-5
Brimfield B-7
Brook D-3
Brookston E-3
Brookville J-8
Brownsburg G-5
Brownstown • K-5
Bruceville L-2
Bryant F-8
Buckskin M-2
Bunker Hill E-5
Burnettsville D-4
Burrows E-4
Butler B-8
Butlerville K-7
Cadiz G-7
Cambridge City G-7
Campbellsburg L-5
Cannelburg L-3
Cannelton • N-4
Carlisle K-2
Carmel G-5
Carp J-4
Carwood M-6
Cayuga G-2
Cedar Lake B-2
Cedarville C-7
Centerville G-8
Chalmers E-4
Chandler N-2
Charlestown M-6
Charlottesville G-6
Chase E-3
Chester G-8

Gwynnesville H-6
Hagerstown G-7
Hamilton B-8
Hammond B-2
Hanover L-7
Harmony H-3
Hartford City • E-7
Hartsville J-6
Hubstadt M-2
Hebron C-3
Hemlock E-5
Henryville L-6
Highland B-2
Hobart B-3
Hope J-6
Huntingburg M-3
Huntington • D-7
Huron L-4
Indianapolis • G-4
Jamestown G-4
Jasonville J-3
Jasper • M-3
Jeffersonville • M-3
Jonesboro E-6
Kendallville E-6
Kentland D-2
Kimmell B-5
Kingsford Heights B-4
Kingsland D-7
Kirklin F-4
Knightstown G-7
Knightsville H-3
Knox • C-4
Kokomo • E-5
Kouts C-3
Kyana M-4
La Crosse C-3
La Fontaine E-6
La Porte • B-4
Lafayette • E-4
Lagrange A-7
Largo D-6
Lake Station B-3
Lapel G-6
Lawrence G-6
Lawrenceburg K-8
Lebanon G-4
Leesburg C-6
Lewisville G-7
Liberty • H-8
Ligonier B-6
Linden F-3
Linton K-3
Lizton G-4
Logansport • D-5
Long Beach A-4
Loogootee L-3
Losantville G-7
Lowell C-2
Lydick A-5
Lynn C-8
Lyons K-3
Mackey M-2
Madison • L-7
Manhattan H-3
Marengo M-5
Marion • E-6
Markie D-7
Markieville G-6
Martinsville • J-4
Maysville L-3
McCordsville G-6
Mechanicsburg G-6
Medaryville C-4
Memphis M-6
Merltone C-5
Merrillville B-2
Metea D-5
Michigantown F-5
Middlebury A-6
Middletown G-6

Petersburg • M-2
Pierceton C-6
Pikeville M-3
Pine Village E-3
Pittsboro G-4
Pittsburg E-4
Plainfield H-5
Plainville L-3
Plymouth • C-5
Portage A-3
Porter A-3
Portland • E-8
Princeton • M-2
Putnamville H-4
Queensville K-6
Raccoon G-4
Radioville C-4
Ramsey M-5
Raub D-2
Redkey F-7
Remington D-3
Renssalaer • D-3
Reynolds D-4
Richmond • G-8
Rising Sun • K-8
Roachdale G-4
Rob Roy F-3
Rochester • C-5
Rockfield E-4
Rockport • C-3
Rockville • H-3
Roll E-7
Rome City B-7
Romney F-4
Rossville E-4
Royal Center D-4
Rushville • H-7
Russiaville E-5
St. Joe C-8
Salem • L-5
San Pierre C-4
Sandborn K-3
Sandusky J-7
Schererville B-2
Scipio K-6
Scottsburg • L-6
Seafield D-3
Seelyville H-3
Sellersburg M-6
Seymour K-6
Shannodale G-4
Sharon E-5
Shelburn J-2
Shelbyville • H-6
Sheridan F-5
Shipshewana A-6
Shoals L-4
Sidney C-6
Silver Lake C-6
Smartsburg G-4
Smedley L-5
Somerville M-2
South Bend • B-5
South Milford B-7
South Whitley C-6
Speed M-6
Speedway G-5
Spelcherville D-6
Spencer • J-4
Spencerville C-8
Spraytown K-5
State Line City F-2
Stendal M-3
Stilesville H-4
Straughn G-7
Sullivan • K-2
Sulphur Springs G-7
Summitville F-6
Swayzee E-6
Switz City K-8
Syracuse B-6
Tell City N-4
Terre Haute • J-3
Thornhope D-4
Thorntown F-4
Tippecanoe C-5
Tipton • F-5
Town of Pines A-3
Treaty D-6
Trinity E-8
Underwood L-6
Unon City F-8
Uniondale D-7
Upland E-7
Urbana D-6
Valparaiso • B-3
Van Buren E-7
Veedersburg F-3
Vernon • K-6
Versailles • K-7
Vevay • L-8
Vienna L-6
Vincennes • L-2
Wabash • D-6
Wakarusa B-5
Walkerton B-4
Walton E-5
Warren E-7
Warrington G-6
Warsaw • C-6
Washington L-3
Waterford B-6
Waterloo B-8
Wawaka B-6
Waymansville K-5
Webster G-8
West Lafayette E-3
West Sonora E-5
Westfield G-5
Wheatland L-3
Wheeling E-4
Whitaker J-4
Whiteland H-5
Whiting A-2
Williamsburg G-7
Williamsport • F-2
Winamac • C-4
Winchester F-8
Windfall F-6
Wingate F-3
Winona Lake C-6
Winslow M-3
Wolcott D-3
Woodbury G-6
Worthington K-3
Wyatt B-5
Yorktown F-7

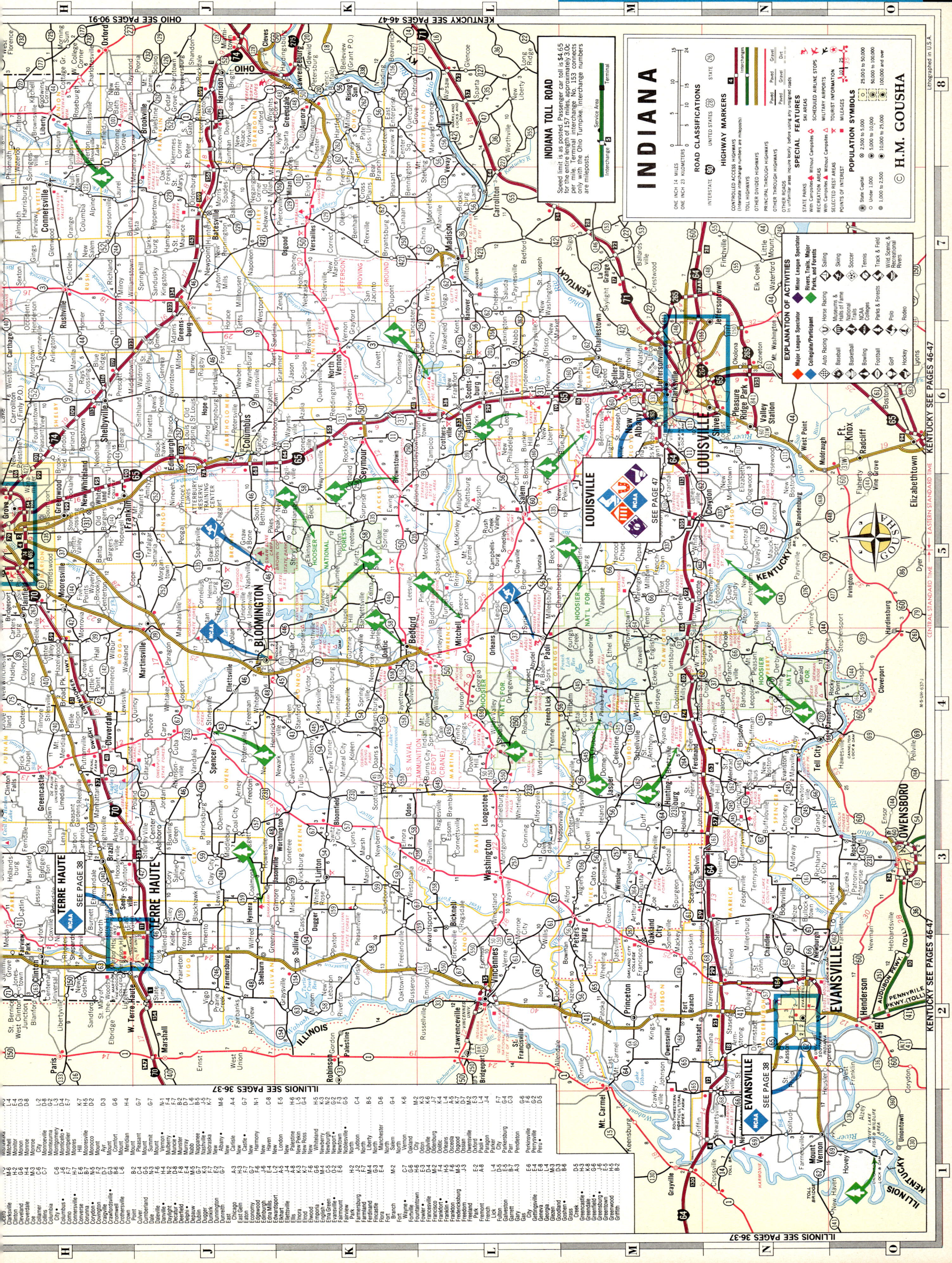
INDIANA
© H.M. GOUSHA
INDIANA TOLL ROAD
ROAD CLASSIFICATIONS
HIGHWAY MARKERS
SPECIAL FEATURES
POPULATION SYMBOLS
EXPLANATION OF ACTIVITIES
LOUISVILLE
SEE PAGE 47
TERRE HAUTE
SEE PAGE 38
EVANSVILLE
SEE PAGE 38
OHIO SEE PAGES 90-91
KENTUCKY SEE PAGES 46-47
ILLINOIS SEE PAGES 36-37
Lithographed in U.S.A.

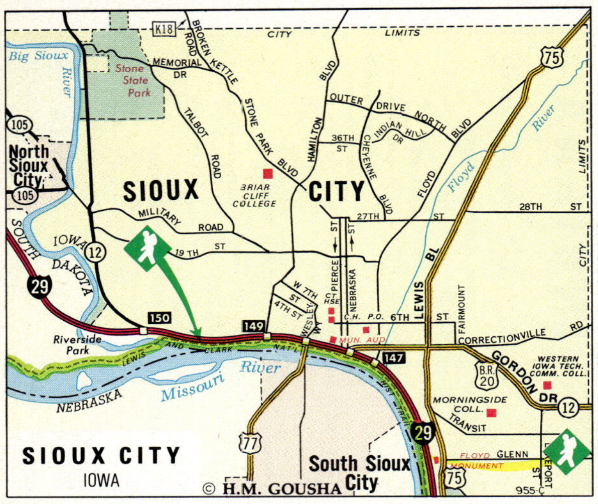

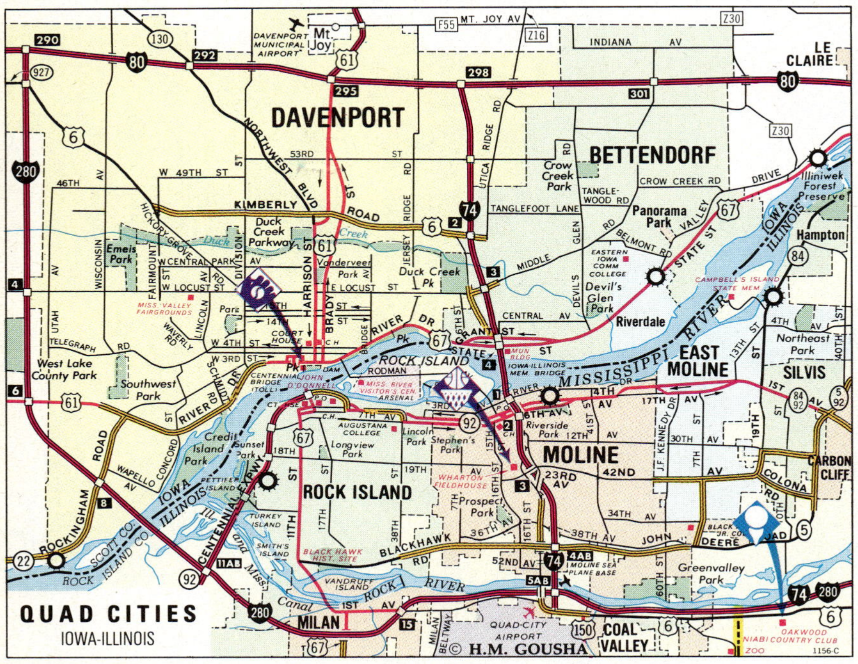

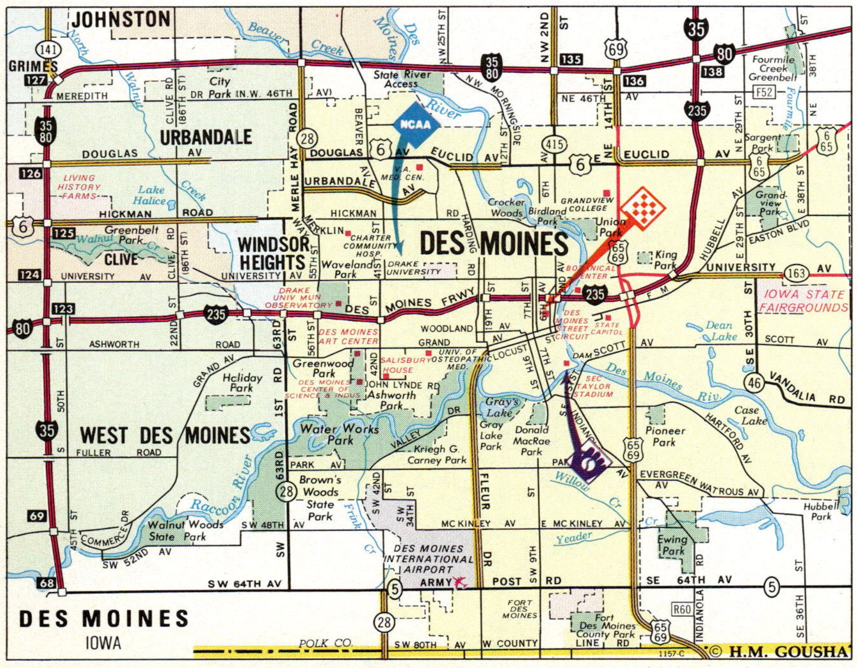

IOWA

Pop (1990) 2,787,424
Area 56,290 Sq. Mi.

COUNTIES

County	Co. Seat
Adair	Greenfield
Adams	Corning
Allamakee	Waukon
Appanoose	Centerville
Audubon	Audubon
Benton	Vinton
Black Hawk	Waterloo
Boone	Boone
Bremer	Waverly
Buchanan	Independence
Buena Vista	Storm Lake
Butler	Allison
Calhoun	Rockwell City
Carroll	Carroll
Cass	Atlantic
Cedar	Tipton
Cerro Gordo	Mason City
Cherokee	Cherokee
Chickasaw	New Hampton
Clarke	Osceola
Clay	Spencer
Clayton	Elkader
Clinton	Clinton
Crawford	Dension
Dallas	Adel
Davis	Bloomfield
Decatur	Leon
Delaware	Manchester
Des Moines	Burlington
Dickinson	Spirit Lake
Dubuque	Dubuque
Emmet	Estherville
Fayette	West Union
Floyd	Charles City
Franklin	Hampton
Fremont	Sidney
Greene	Jefferson
Grundy	Grundy Center
Guthrie	Guthrie Center
Hamilton	Webster City
Hancock	Garner
Hardin	Eldora
Harrison	Logan
Henry	Mount Pleasant
Howard	Cresco
Humboldt	Dakota City
Ida	Ida Grove
Iowa	Marengo
Jackson	Maquoketa
Jasper	Newton
Jefferson	Fairfield
Johnson	Iowa City
Jones	Anamosa
Keokuk	Sigourney
Kossuth	Algona
Lee	Fort Madison & Keokuk
Linn	Cedar Rapids
Louisa	Wapello
Lucas	Chariton
Lyon	Rock Rapids
Madison	Winterset
Mahaska	Oskaloosa
Marion	Knoxville
Marshall	Marshalltown
Mills	Glenwood
Mitchell	Osage
Monona	Onawa
Monroe	Albia
Montgomery	Red Oak
Muscatine	Muscatine
O'Brien	Primghar
Osceola	Sibley
Page	Clarinda
Palo Alto	Emmetsburg
Plymouth	Le Mars
Pocahontas	Pocahontas
Polk	Des Moines
Pottawattamie	Council Bluffs
Poweshiek	Montezuma
Ringgold	Mount Ayr
Sac	Sac City
Scott	Davenport
Shelby	Harlan
Sioux	Orange City
Story	Nevada
Tama	Toledo
Taylor	Bedford
Union	Creston
Van Buren	Keosauqua
Wapello	Ottumwa
Warren	Indianola
Washington	Washington
Wayne	Corydon
Webster	Fort Dodge
Winnebago	Forest City
Winneshiek	Decorah
Woodbury	Sioux City
Worth	Northwood
Wright	Clarion

MISSOURI SEE PAGES 66-67

PARTIAL LIST OF
CITIES AND TOWNS

• County Seats

Ackley	C-9
Adel •	E-8
Agency	F-10
Ainsworth	E-12
Akron	B-3
Albia •	F-10
Alden	C-9
Alexander	B-8
Algona •	B-7
Allison •	B-10
Alta	C-5
Alton	B-4
Altoona	E-8
Ames	D-8
Anamosa •	D-12
Andrew	D-13
Anita	E-6
Ankeny	D-8
Aplington	C-9
Arlington	B-11
Armstrong	A-7
Arnolds Park	A-6
Ashton	A-5
Atkins	D-11
Atlantic •	E-6
Auburn	C-6
Audubon •	E-6
Aurelia	C-5
Austinville	C-9
Avoca	E-5
Bancroft	A-7
Bassett	B-10
Batavia	F-11
Bedford •	G-6
Belle Plaine	D-10
Bellevue	C-14
Belmond	B-8
Bennett	D-13
Bettendorf	E-14
Birmingham	F-11
Blairstown	D-11
Bloomfield •	F-10
Blue Grass	E-13
Bode	B-7
Boone •	D-8
Boyden	B
Brighton	F-
Britt	E
Brooklyn	D-
Buffalo	E-
Buffalo Center	A
Burlington •	F-
Burr Oak	A
Bussey	F
Calamus	D-
Calmar	B-
Camanche	D
Carlisle	E
Carpenter	A
Carroll •	D
Cascade	C-
Castalia	B-
Cedar	F-
Cedar Falls	C-
Cedar Rapids •	D-
Center Grove	C-
Center Point	C-
Centerville	G-
Central City	C-
Chariton •	F

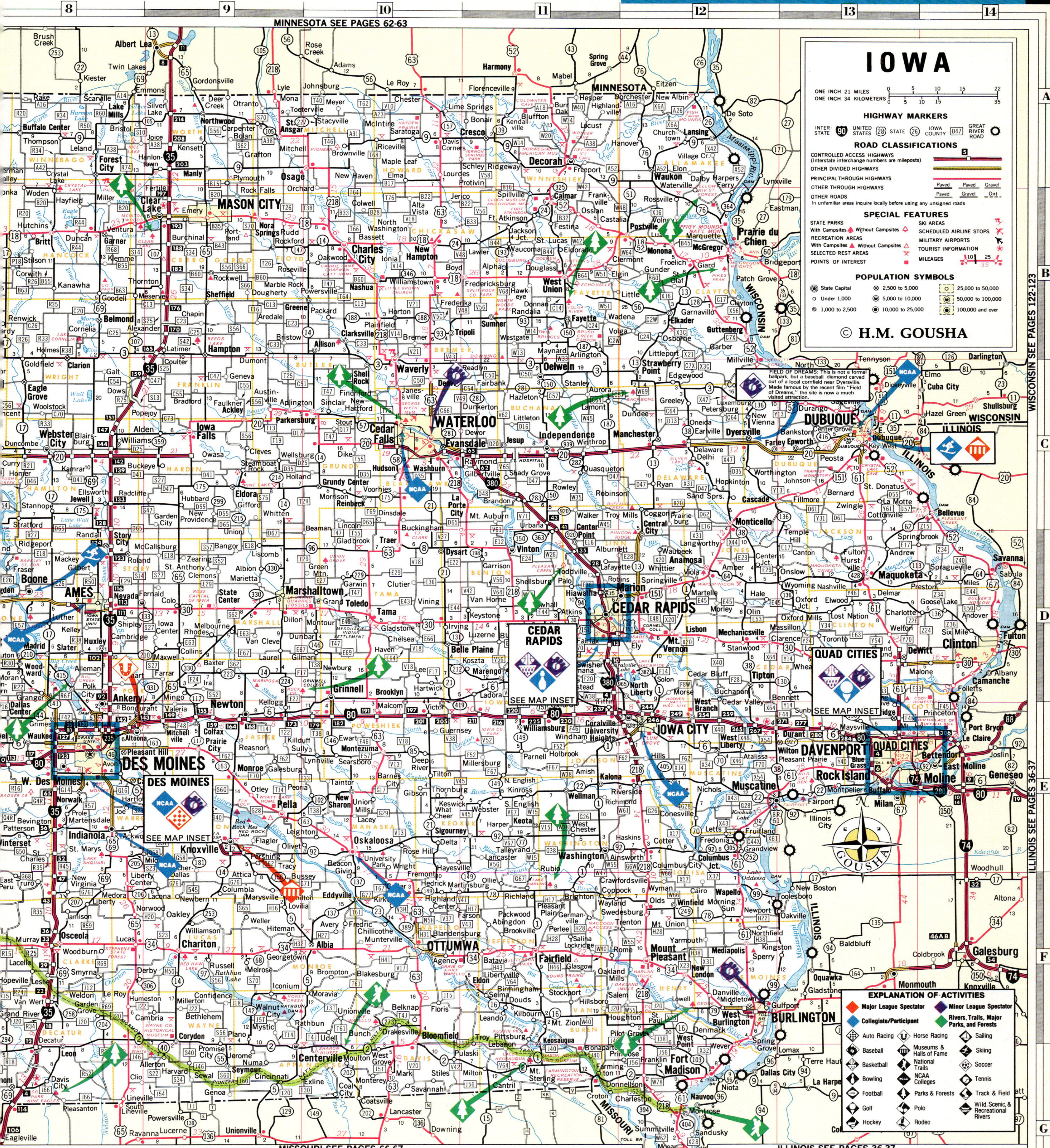

MISSOURI SEE PAGES 66-67

ILLINOIS SEE PAGES 36-37

harles City •	B-10
harlotte	D-13
herokee •	B-5
larence	D-13
larinda •	G-6
larion •	C-8
larksville	B-10
lear Lake	B-9
eghorn	B-5
linton •	D-14
olfax	E-9
olo	D-9
olumbus City	E-12
olumbus Junction	E-12
oon Rapids	D-7
oppock	F-11
oralville	E-11
orning •	F-6
orrectionville	C-5
orydon •	F-9
ouncil Bluffs •	E-5
resco •	A-11
reston •	F-7
ylinder	B-7
akota City •	B-8
Dallas Center	E-8
Danville	F-12
Davenport •	E-13
Davis Corners	A-10
Dayton	D-7
De Witt	D-13
Decorah •	A-11
Delhi	C-12
Delmar	D-13
Dension •	D-5
Denver	C-10
Des Moines •	E-8
Donnellson	G-12
Doon	A-4
Drakesville	F-10
Dubuque •	C-13
Duncan	B-8
Duncombe	C-8
Dunlap	D-5
Durant	E-13
Durango	C-13
Dyersville	C-12
Dysart	D-10
Eagle Grove	C-8
Early	C-6
Eddyville	F-10
Eldon	F-11
Eldora •	C-9
Eldridge	E-13
Elkader •	B-12
Ellsworth	C-8
Emmetsburg •	B-6
Epworth	C-13
Estherville •	A-6
Evansdale	C-10
Fairfax	D-11
Fairfield •	F-11
Farley	C-12
Farmersburg	B-12
Farnhamville	C-7
Fayette	B-11
Fenton	B-7
Forest City •	A-8
Fort Atkinson	B-11
Fort Dodge •	C-7
Fort Madison •	G-12
Fostoria	A-6
Fremont	F-10
Froelich	B-12
Garnavillo	B-12
Garner •	B-8
Garrison	D-11
George	A-4
Georgetown	F-9
Giard	B-12
Gladstone	D-10
Glenwood •	F-5
Gowrie	C-7
Grand Mound	D-13
Granville	B-4
Greene	B-9
Greenfield •	E-7
Grinnell	D-10
Griswold	F-6
Grundy Center •	C-10
Guthrie Center •	E-7
Guttenberg	B-12
Hamburg	G-5
Hampton	B-9
Harcourt	C-7
Harlan •	E-5
Hartley	B-5
Hawarden	B-4
Hedrick	F-10
Hiawatha	D-11
Holstein	C-5
Hopkinton	C-12
Hudson	C-10
Hull	B-4
Humboldt	C-7
Humeston	F-8
Hurstville	D-13
Hutchins	B-8
Ida Grove •	C-5
Independence •	C-11
Indianola •	E-8
Inwood	A-4
Iowa City •	E-12
Iowa Falls	C-9
Jackson Junction	B-11
Janesville	C-10
Jefferson •	D-7
Jesup	C-11
Jewell	C-8
Kalona	E-11
Kensett	A-9
Keokuk •	G-12
Keosauqua •	F-11
Keota	E-11
Kingsley	C-4
Knoxville •	E-9
La Porte City	C-10
Lake City	C-6
Lake Mills	A-8
Lake View	C-6
Lamoni	G-8
Lamont	C-11
Langworthy	D-12
Lansing	A-12
Launa	B-12
Laurens	B-6
Le Claire	E-14
Le Mars •	B-4
Lenox	F-7
Leon •	G-8
Liberty Center	F-8
Lisbon	D-12
Livermore	B-7
Logan •	E-5
Lohrville	C-7
Lourdes	A-10
Lowden	D-13
Lucas	F-8
Luxemburg	C-12
Lytton	C-6
Madrid	D-8
Malcom	E-10
Malvern	F-5
Manchester •	C-12
Manly	A-9
Manning	D-6
Manson	C-7
Mapleton	D-5
Maquoketa •	D-13
Marcus	B-5
Marengo	D-11
Marion	D-12
Mark	G-10
Marshalltown •	D-9
Martinsburg	F-10
Mason City •	B-9
Maynard	B-11
Maysville	E-13
McGregor	B-12
Mechanicsville	D-12
Mediapolis	F-12
Meriden	B-5
Merservey	B-8
Middletown	F-12
Milford	A-6
Millville	C-12
Missouri Valley	E-5
Mitchellville	E-9
Mooar	G-12
Mona	A-9
Mondamin	D-4
Monona	B-12
Monroe	E-9
Montezuma	E-10
Monticello	C-12
Montour	D-10
Montrose	G-12
Moorland	C-7
Morning Sun	F-12
Moulton	G-10
Mount Ayr •	G-7
Mount Pleasant •	F-12
Mount Vernon	D-12
Mount Zion	F-11
Moville	C-4
Muscatine •	E-12
Nashua	B-10
Nevada •	D-8
New Hampton •	B-10
New London	F-12
New Sharon	E-10
Newport	F-12
Newton •	E-9
Nichols	E-12
Nora Springs	B-9
North English	E-11
North Liberty	D-12
Northwood •	A-9
Norwalk	E-8
Norwood	F-8
Oakland	E-5
Odebolt	C-6
Oelwein	C-11
Ogden	D-8
Okoboji	A-6
Olds	F-12
Olin	D-12
Onawa •	D-4
Orange City •	B-4
Osage •	A-9
Osceola	F-8
Oskaloosa •	E-10
Ossian	B-11
Otley	E-9
Ottosen	B-7
Ottumwa •	F-10
Oxford Junction	D-13
Parkersburg	C-9
Paullina	B-5
Pella	E-9
Perry	D-7
Plainfield	B-10
Pleasant Hill	E-8
Pleasantville	E-9
Pocahontas •	C-6
Postville	B-12
Prairie City	E-9
Preston	D-14
Primghar •	B-5
Princeton	E-14
Protivin	A-11
Quimby	C-5
Red Oak •	F-6
Reinbeck	C-10
Remsen	B-4
Richland	F-11
Rickardsville	C-13
Riverside	E-12
Rock Rapids •	A-4
Rock Valley	B-4
Rockford	B-9
Rockwell City •	C-7
Rome	F-11
Ruthven	B-6
Sac City •	C-6
Sageville	C-13
St. Ansgar	A-9
Sanborn	B-5
Saratoga	A-10
Selma	F-11
Seney	B-4
Sergeant Bluff	C-4
Sexton	B-7
Sheffield	B-9
Sheldon	B-5
Shell Rock	C-10
Shenandoah	F-5
Sibley •	A-5
Sidney •	F-5
Sigourney •	E-10
Sioux Center	B-4
Sioux City •	C-4
Sioux Rapids	B-6
Slater	D-8
Solon	D-12
Smithland	C-4
Sloan	D-12
South Amana	D-11
Spencer •	B-6
Spillville	B-11
Spirit Lake •	A-6
Sprageville	D-14
Springville	D-12
Stanwood	D-12
State Center	D-9
Storm Lake •	C-6
Stratford	C-8
Strawberry Point	C-12
Stuart	E-7
Summitville	G-12
Sumner	B-11
Swedesburg	F-11
Talleyrand	E-11
Tama	D-10
Tenville	F-6
Thayer	F-7
Thornton	B-8
Tipton •	D-12
Toledo	D-10
Traer	D-10
Tripoli	B-11
University Heights	E-11
Urbana	C-11
Ventura	B-8
Villisca	F-6
Vinton •	D-11
Wahpeton	A-6
Walford	D-11
Wapello •	F-12
Washburn	C-10
Washington •	E-11
Waterloo •	C-10
Waukee	E-8
Waukon •	A-12
Waverly •	C-10
Wayland	F-11
Webster	E-11
Webster City •	C-8
Wellman	E-11
Welton	D-13
West Branch	E-12
West Burlington	F-12
West Chester	E-11
West Des Moines	E-8
West Grove	G-10
West Liberty	E-12
West Point	F-12
West Union	B-11
Wever	G-12
Whittemore	B-7
Williams	C-8
Williamsburg	E-11
Williamstown	B-10
Wilton	E-13
Winterset •	E-8
Winthrop	C-11
Woodbine	D-5
Woodward	D-8
Wyoming	D-13

SF-638-J

Lithographed in U.S.A.

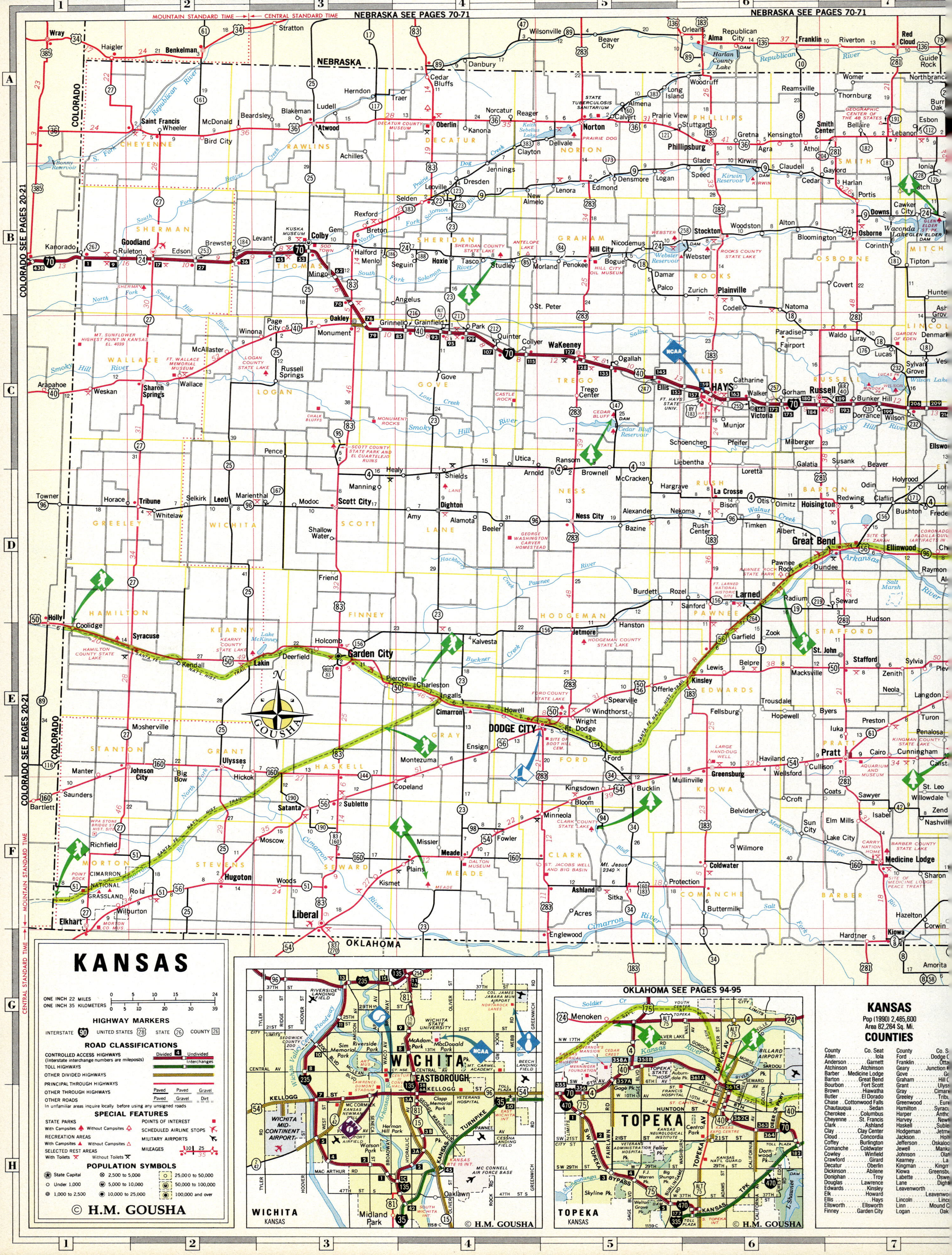

KANSAS

Pop (1990) 2,485,600
Area 82,264 Sq. Mi.

COUNTIES

County	Co. Seat	County	Co. S
Allen	Iola	Ford	Dodge C
Anderson	Garnett	Franklin	Otta
Atchinson	Atchinson	Geary	Junction
Barber	Medicine Lodge	Gove	G
Barton	Great Bend	Graham	Hill C
Bourbon	Fort Scott	Grant	Ulyss
Brown	Hiawatha	Gray	Cimar
Butler	El Dorado	Greeley	Tribu
Chase	Cottonwood Falls	Greenwood	Eur
Chautauqua	Sedan	Hamilton	Syracu
Cherokee	Columbus	Harper	Antho
Cheyenne	St. Francis	Harvey	New
Clark	Ashland	Haskell	Suble
Clay	Clay Center	Hodgeman	Jetm
Cloud	Concordia	Jackson	Hol
Coffey	Burlington	Jefferson	Oskaloo
Comanche	Coldwater	Jewell	Mank
Cowley	Winfield	Johnson	Ola
Crawford	Girard	Kearney	La
Decatur	Oberlin	Kingman	Kingm
Dickinson	Abilene	Kiowa	Greensbu
Doniphan	Troy	Labette	Oswe
Douglas	Lawrence	Lane	Dight
Edwards	Kinsley	Leavenworth	Leavenwo
Elk	Howard	Lincoln	Linc
Ellis	Hays	Linn	Mound C
Ellsworth	Ellsworth	Logan	Oak
Finney	Garden City		

Lyon	Emporia
Marion	Marion
Marshall	Marysville
McPherson	McPherson
Meade	Meade
Miami	Paola
Mitchell	Beloit
Montgomery	Independence
Morris	Council Grove
Morton	Elkhart
Nemaha	Seneca
Neosho	Erie
Ness	Ness City
Norton	Norton
Osage	Lyndon
Osborne	Osborne
Ottawa	Minneapolis
Pawnee	Larned
Philips	Philipsburg
Pottawatomie	Westmoreland
Pratt	Pratt
Rawlins	Atwood
Reno	Hutchinson
Republic	Belleville
Rice	Lyons
Riley	Manhattan
Rooks	Stockton
Rush	La Crosse
Russell	Russell
Saline	Salina
Scott	Scott City
Sedgwick	Wichita
Seward	Liberal
Shawnee	Topeka
Sheridan	Hoxie
Sherman	Goodland
Smith	Smith Center
Stafford	St. John
Stanton	Johnson City
Stevens	Hugoton
Sumner	Wellington
Thomas	Colby
Trego	WaKeeney
Wabaunsee	Alma
Wallace	Sharon Springs
Washington	Washington
Wichita	Leoti
Wilson	Fredonia
Woodson	Yates Center
Wyandotte	Kansas City

PARTIAL LIST OF

CITIES AND TOWNS

• County Seats

Abbyville	E-8
Abilene •	C-9
Alma •	C-11
Altamont	F-12
Andover	E-9
Anthony •	F-8
Argonia	F-8
Arkansas City	F-10
Arlington	E-8
Arma	E-13
Ashland •	F-5
Atchison •	B-12
Attica	F-8
Atwood •	A-3
Augusta	E-10
Axtell	A-11
Baldwin City	C-12
Barnes	A-10
Baxter Springs	F-14
Beattie	A-10
Belle Plaine	F-9
Belleville •	A-9
Beloit •	B-8
Belvue	B-11
Bennington	C-9
Bird City	A-2
Blue Mound	D-13
Blue Rapids	B-10
Bogue	B-5
Bonner Springs	C-13
Bronson	E-13
Brownell	D-5
Bucklin	F-5
Buhler	D-8
Burden	F-10
Burlingame	C-11
Burlington •	D-12
Burr Oak	A-7
Bushton	D-7
Caldwell	G-8
Cambridge	F-10
Caney	G-11
Carbondale	C-12
Cassoday	E-10
Cawker City	B-7
Cedar Vale	F-10
Chanute	E-12
Chapman	C-10
Chase	D-7
Cheney	E-8
Cherokee	F-13
Cherryvale	F-12
Chetopa	F-13
Cimarron •	E-4
Claflin	D-7
Clay Center •	B-9
Clayton	A-4
Clearwater	F-9
Clifton	B-9
Clyde	B-9
Coffeyville	G-12
Colby •	B-3
Coldwater •	F-6
Colony	E-12
Columbus	F-13
Colwich	E-9
Concordia •	B-8
Conway Springs	F-9
Coolidge	E-1
Copeland	F-4
Cottonwood Falls •	D-10
Council Grove •	C-10
Cuba	A-9
Cummings	B-12
Cunningham	E-7
Damar	B-5
De Soto	C-13
Derby	F-9
Dighton •	D-4
Dodge City •	E-4
Douglass	F-9
Downs	B-7
Dwight	C-10
Earlton	E-12
Edgerton	C-13
Edmond	B-5
Edna	F-12
Effingham	B-12
El Dorado •	E-10
Elk City	F-11
Elkhart •	F-1
Ellinwood	D-7
Ellis	C-5
Ellsworth •	C-7
Elwood	A-13
Emporia •	D-11
Ensign	E-4
Erie •	E-13
Eskridge	C-11
Eudora	C-13
Eureka •	E-11
Fairview	A-12
Florence	D-10
Ford	E-5
Fort Riley	C-10
Fort Scott •	E-13
Fowler	F-4
Frankfort	A-10
Fredonia •	F-11
Frontenac	F-14
Fulton	E-14
Galena	F-14
Galva	D-9
Garden City •	E-3
Gardner	C-13
Garfield	E-6
Garnett •	D-12
Gas	E-12
Geneseo	D-8
Girard •	F-13
Glade	B-6
Glasco	B-8
Goessel	D-9
Goodland •	B-2
Gorham	C-6
Gove •	C-4
Grainfield	C-4
Great Bend •	D-6
Greeley	D-13
Greenleaf	A-10
Greensburg •	E-6
Gridley	E-11
Grinnell	C-4
Gypsum	C-9
Haddam	A-9
Halstead	E-9
Hamilton	E-11
Hanover	A-10
Hardtner	G-7
Harper	F-8
Harris	D-12
Hartford	D-11
Haven	E-8
Havensville	B-11
Haviland	E-6
Hays •	C-6
Haysville	F-9
Herington	C-9
Herndon	A-3
Hesston	D-9
Hiawatha •	A-12
Highland	A-12
Hill City •	B-5
Hillsboro	D-9
Hoisington	D-6
Holcomb	E-3
Holton •	B-11
Holyrood	D-7
Hope	C-9
Horton	B-12
Hoxie •	B-4
Hugoton •	F-2
Humboldt	E-12
Hunter	B-7
Hutchinson •	E-8
Independence •	F-12
Ingalls	E-4
Inman	D-8
Iola •	E-12
Jennings	B-4
Jetmore •	E-5
Jewell	B-8
Johnson City •	E-2
Junction City •	C-10
Kanopolis	C-8
Kanorado	B-1
Kansas City •	B-13
Kechi	E-9
Kensington	A-6
Kincaid	E-13
Kingman •	E-8
Kinsley •	E-6
Kiowa	G-7
La Crosse •	D-6
La Cygne	D-13
La Harpe	E-12
Lakin •	E-3
Lancaster	B-12
Lane	D-13
Lansing	B-13
Larned •	D-6
Lawrence •	C-12
Le Roy	D-12
Leavenworth •	B-13
Lebanon	A-7
Lenexa	C-13
Leonardville	B-10
Leoti •	D-2
Lewis	E-6
Liberal •	F-3
Liebenthal	C-6
Lincoln •	C-8
Lincolnville	D-10
Lindsborg	D-8
Lone Elm	D-12
Long Island	A-5
Louisburg	C-13
Louisville	B-11
Lucas	C-7
Luray	C-7
Lyndon •	D-12
Lyons •	D-8
Macksville	E-6
Madison	D-11
Manhattan •	B-10
Mankato •	A-8
Mapleton	E-13
Marion •	D-9
Marysville •	A-10
Matfield Green	D-10
Mayetta	B-12
McCracken	D-5
McDonald	A-2
McFarland	C-11
McLouth	B-12
McPherson •	D-9
Meade •	F-4
Medicine Lodge •	F-7
Merriam	C-13
Milan	F-8
Miltonvale	B-9
Minneapolis •	C-8
Minneola	F-5
Mission •	C-14
Moline	F-11
Montezuma	E-4
Moran	E-13
Morrowville	A-9
Moscow	F-3
Mound City •	D-13
Mound Valley	F-12
Moundridge	D-9
Mount Hope	E-8
Mullinville	F-5
Mulvane	F-9
Natoma	B-6
Neodesha	F-12
Nesho Rapids	D-11
Ness City •	D-5
Newton •	E-9
Nickerson	D-8
Niotaze	F-11
Norcatur	A-4
North Newton	E-9
Norton •	A-5
Nortonville	B-12
Oakley	C-3
Oberlin •	A-4
Offerle	E-5
Ogden	C-10
Oketo	A-10
Olathe •	C-13
Olpe	D-11
Onaga	B-11
Osage City	C-12
Osawatomie	D-13
Osborne •	B-7
Oskaloosa •	B-12
Oswego •	F-13
Ottawa •	C-12
Overland Park	C-13
Oxford	F-9
Ozawkie	B-12
Palmer	B-9
Paola •	D-13
Paradise	C-6
Park	C-4
Park City	E-9
Parkerville	C-10
Parsons	F-12
Partridge	E-8
Pawnee Rock	D-6
Peabody	D-9
Perry	C-12
Peru	F-11
Phillipsburg •	A-6
Pittsburg	F-14
Plains	F-4
Plainville	B-6
Pleasanton	D-14
Plevna	E-7
Portis	B-7
Potwin	E-10
Prairie View	A-5
Prairie Village	C-14
Pratt •	E-7
Preston	E-7
Princeton	D-12
Quinter	C-4
Ransom	C-5
Raymond	D-7
Reading	D-11
Reserve	A-12
Rexford	B-3
Richmond	D-13
Riley	B-10
Roeland Park	C-14
Rolla	F-2
Roseland	F-13
Rossville	C-11
Rozel	D-6
Rush Center	D-6
Russell •	C-6
Russell Springs •	C-3
Sabetha	A-11
St. Francis •	A-2
St. John •	E-7
St. Marys	B-11
St. Paul	F-13
Salina •	C-9
Satanta	F-3
Savonburg	E-12
Sawyer	F-7
Scandia	A-8
Scott City •	D-3
Sedan •	F-11
Sedgwick	E-9
Selden	B-4
Seneca •	A-11
Seward	D-7
Sharon Springs •	C-2
Shawnee	C-13
Silver Lake	C-11
Smith Center •	A-7
South Haven	F-9
Spearville	E-5
Spivey	F-8
Spring Hill	C-13
Stafford	E-7
Stark	E-13
Sterling	D-8
Stockton •	B-6
Strong City	D-10
Sublette •	F-3
Summerfield	A-10
Sun City	F-6
Sylvan Grove	C-7
Sylvia	E-7
Syracuse •	E-2
Thayer	F-12
Tipton	B-7
Tonganoxie	B-13
Topeka •	C-12
Towanda	E-9
Tribune •	D-2
Troy •	A-13
Turon	E-7
Tyro	G-12
Ulysses •	E-2
Uniontown	E-13
Utica	C-4
Valley Center	E-9
Valley Falls	B-12
Victoria	C-6
Viola	F-8
Virgil	E-11
WaKeeney •	C-5
Wakefield	B-9
Waldo	C-7
Waldron	G-8
Wallace	C-2
Walnut	E-13
Walton	D-9
Wamego	B-11
Washington •	A-9
Waterville	B-10
Wathena	A-13
Waverly	D-12
Webber	A-8
Weir	F-13
Wellington •	F-9
Wellsford	E-6
Wellsville	C-13
Wheaton	B-11
White City	C-10
Whitewater	E-9
Wichita •	E-9
Wilson	C-7
Winfield •	F-10
Winona	C-3
Yates Center •	E-12

SF-639-J
Lithographed in U.S.A.

KENTUCKY

Pop (1990) 3,698,969
Area 40,395 Sq. Mi.

COUNTIES

County	Co. Seat
Adair	Columbia
Allen	Scottsville
Anderson	Lawrenceburg
Ballard	Wickliffe
Barren	Glasgow
Bath	Owingsville
Bell	Pineville
Boone	Burlington
Bourbon	Paris
Boyd	Catlettsburg
Boyle	Danville
Bracken	Brooksville
Breathitt	Jackson
Breckinridge	Hardinsburg
Bullitt	Shepherdsville
Butler	Morgantown
Caldwell	Princeton
Calloway	Murray
Campbell	Alexandria
Carlisle	Bardwell
Carroll	Carrollton
Carter	Grayson
Casey	Liberty
Christian	Hopkinsville
Clark	Winchester
Clay	Manchester
Clinton	Albany
Crittenden	Marion
Cumberland	Burkesville
Daviess	Owensboro
Edmonson	Brownsville
Elliott	Sandy Hook
Estill	Irvine
Fayette	Lexington
Fleming	Flemingsburg
Floyd	Prestonsburg
Franklin	Frankfort
Fulton	Hickman
Gallatin	Warsaw
Garrard	Lancaster
Grant	Williamstown
Graves	Mayfield
Grayson	Litchfield
Green	Greensburg
Greenup	Greenup
Hancock	Hawesville
Hardin	Elizabethtown
Harlan	Harlan
Harrison	Cynthiana
Hart	Munfordville
Henderson	Henderson
Henry	New Castle
Hickman	Clinton
Hopkins	Madisonville
Jackson	McKee
Jefferson	Louisville
Jessamine	Nicholasville
Johnson	Paintsville
Kenton	Independence
Knott	Hindman
Knox	Barbourville
Larue	Hodgenville
Laurel	London
Lawrence	Louisa
Lee	Beattyville
Leslie	Hyden
Letcher	Whitesburg
Lewis	Vanceburg
Lincoln	Stanford
Livingston	Smithland
Logan	Russellville
Lyon	Eddyville
Madison	Richmond
Magoffin	Salyersville
Marion	Lebanon
Marshall	Benton
Martin	Inez
Mason	Maysville
McCracken	Paducah
McCreary	Whitley City
McLean	Calhoun
Meade	Brandenburg
Menifee	Frenchburg
Mercer	Harrodsburg
Metcalfe	Edmonton
Monroe	Tompkinsville
Montgomery	Mt. Sterling
Morgan	West Liberty
Muhlenberg	Greenville
Nelson	Bardstown
Nicholas	Carlisle
Ohio	Hartford
Oldham	La Grange
Owen	Owenton
Owsley	Booneville
Pendleton	Falmouth
Perry	Hazard
Pike	Pikeville
Powell	Stanton
Pulaski	Somerset
Robertson	Mt. Olivet
Rockcastle	Mt. Vernon
Rowan	Morehead
Russell	Jamestown
Scott	Georgetown
Shelby	Shelbyville
Simpson	Franklin
Spencer	Taylorsville
Taylor	Campbellsville
Todd	Elkton
Trigg	Cadiz
Trimble	Bedford
Union	Morganfield
Warren	Bowling Green
Washington	Springfield
Wayne	Monticello
Webster	Dixon
Whitley	Williamsburg
Wolfe	Campton
Woodford	Versailles

PARTIAL LIST OF

CITIES AND TOWNS

• County Seats

Adairville	F-6
Albany •	F-9
Alexandria •	A-10
Allen	D-13
Allen Springs	E-7
Allensville	E-5
Alvaton	E-7
Anchorage	B-8
Annville	D-11
Arlington	E-2
Ashland	B-13
Auburn	E-6
Augusta	B-11
Bagdad	B-9
Bandy	D-10
Barbourville •	E-11
Bardstown •	C-8
Bardwell •	E-2
Barlow	E-2
Bear Wallow	E-8
Beattyille •	D-11
Beaver Dam	D-6
Bedford •	B-8
Beechwood	B-9
Benham	E-12
Benton •	E-3
Berea	D-10
Berry	B-10
Blaine	C-13
Bloomfield	C-8
Bon Ayr	E-7
Bonnieville	D-7
Booneville •	D-11
Boston	C-8
Bowling Green •	E-6
Bradfordsville	D-9
Brandenburg •	C-7
Brodhead	D-10
Bromley	B-9
Brooksville •	B-11
Brownsville •	E-7
Buffalo	D-8
Bulan	D-12
Burgin	C-9
Burkesville •	E-8
Burlington •	A-9
Burning Springs	D-11
Burnside	E-10
Burton	D-13
Butler	B-10
Cadiz •	E-4
Calhoun •	D-5
California	A-10
Campbellsburg	B-9
Campbellsville •	D-8
Campton •	D-11
Caneyville	D-6
Carlisle •	B-11
Carrollton •	B-8
Carter	B-12
Catlettsburg •	B-13
Cave City	E-7
Cawood	E-12
Cecilia	D-7
Central City	D-5
Clarkson	D-7
Clay	D-4
Clifty	E-5
Clinton •	E-2
Columbia •	E-8
Columbus	E-2
Concord	B-11
Corbin	E-11
Corinth	B-10
Corydon	C-4
Covington	A-10
Crab Orchard	D-10
Crofton	E-5
Cumberland	E-12
Cynthiana •	B-10
Danville •	D-9
Dawson Springs	E-4
Dixon •	D-4
Dizney	E-12
Donaldson	E-4
Dover	B-11
Dry Ridge	B-10
Earlington	D-5
Eddyville •	E-4
Edmonton •	E-8
Eighty Eight	E-8
Ekron	C-7
Elizabethtown •	D-8
Elkhorn City	D-14
Elkton •	E-5
Emmence	B-9
Erlanger	A-9
Eubank	D-9
Evarts	E-12
Ewing	B-11
Fairfield	C-8
Fairview	E-5
Falmouth •	B-10
Fancy Farm	E-3
Flemingsburg •	B-11
Florence	A-10
Fordsville	D-6
Forks of Elkhorn	C-9
Fort Knox	C-7
Fort Thomas	A-10
Foster	B-10
Fountain Run	E-7
Frankfort •	C-9
Franklin •	E-6
Fredericktown	D-8
Fredonia	D-4
Freedom	E-9
Frenchburg •	C-11
Fulton	F-2
Gamaliel	F-8
Georgetown •	C-9
Glasgow •	E-7
Golden Pond	E-4
Gordon	E-12
Gracey	E-4
Grand Rivers	E-4
Grassy Creek	C-12
Gratz	B-9
Gray	E-11
Grays Knob	E-12
Graysbranch	B-12
Grayson •	B-12
Grayson Springs	D-7
Greenmount	D-11
Greensburg •	D-8
Greenup •	B-12
Greenville •	E-5
Greenwood	E-10
Gregory	E-9
Grethel	D-13
Gulnare	D-13
Gunningham	E-2
Guthrie	F-5
Haddix	D-12
Hadley	E-6
Halifax	E-7
Hanson	D-5
Hardin	E-3
Hardinsburg •	C-7
Harlan •	E-12
Harold	D-13
Harris	B-12
Harrodsburg •	C-9
Hartford •	D-6
Hawesville •	C-6
Hays Crossing	C-12
Haywood	E-7
Hazard •	D-12
Hazel	F-3
Hedgeville	D-9
Hellier	D-13
Henderson •	C-4
Hickman •	F-2
Hindman •	D-12
Hiseville	E-8
Hodgenville •	D-8
Hollyhill	F-9
Hope	C-11
Hopewell	B-12
Hopkinsville •	E-5
Horse Branch	D-6
Horse Cave	E-7
Hosea	E-12
Howe Valley	D-7
Huntsville	E-6
Hustonville	D-9
Hyden •	E-12
Independence •	A-10
Index	C-12
Inez •	C-13
Irma	D-4
Irvine •	D-11
Irvington	C-7
Island	D-5
Isom	D-12
Isonville	C-12
Iuka	E-3
Ivyton	C-12
Jabez	E-9
Jackson •	D-12
Jacktown	D-9
Jamestown •	E-9
Jean	C-13
Jeffersontown	C-8
Jeffersonville	C-11
Jenkins	D-13
Jenson	E-11
Jeremiah	E-12
Jewel City	D-5
Johnsonville	C-8
Jonesville	B-9
Jordan	F-2
Josephine	B-9
Joy	D-3
Judy	C-11
Junction City	D-9
Kayjay	E-11
Keaton	C-12
Keavy	E-10
Keene	C-9
Kehoe	B-12
Kelat	B-10
Kelly	E-5
Kentontown	B-10
Kermit	C-13
Kevil	E-2
Keysburg	E-5
Kimper	D-13
Kings Mountain	D-9
Kingston	D-10
Kinniconick	B-11
Kirbyton	E-2
Kirkmansville	E-5
Kirksey	E-3
Kirksville	D-10
Kite	D-13
Knifley	D-9
Knob Creek	D-8
Knob Lick	E-8
Knottsville	C-6
Kuttawa	E-4
La Center	E-2
La Fayette	F-5
La Grange •	B-8
Lackey	D-12
Lancaster •	D-10
Lawrenceburg •	C-9
Layne	D-13
Leatherwood	E-12
Lebanon •	D-9
Lebanon Junction	C-8
Ledbetter	E-3
Lee City	C-12
Lees Lick	B-10
Leesburg	C-10
Leitchfield •	D-7
Leon	B-12
Level Green	D-10
Levi	D-11
Lewisburg	E-6
Lewisport	C-6
Lexington •	C-10
Liberty •	D-9
Lily	E-11
Little Mount	C-9
Little Sandy	C-12
Livermore	D-5
Livingston	D-10
Locust Grove	B-10
Lola	D-3
London •	E-10
Lone Oak	E-3
Long Ridge	B-9
Lookout	D-13
Loretto	D-8
Lost Creek	D-12
Lothair	D-12
Louellen	E-12
Louisa •	C-13
Louisville •	C-7
Lovely	C-13
Lowes	E-2
Lowmansville	C-12
Loyall	E-12
Lucas	E-7
Ludlow	A-10
Lynch	E-13
Lynn	B-12
Lynn Grove	F-3
Lynnville	F-3
Lyonia	D-6
Macedonia	E-4
Mackville	D-9
Madisonville •	D-4
Majestic	D-14
Mammoth Cave	E-7
Manchester •	E-11
Manitou	D-4
Marion •	D-4
Martha	C-12
Martin	D-13
Mary	D-11
Mason	B-10
Maud	C-8
Maxon	E-3
Mayfield •	E-3
Mayflower	D-13
Maysville •	B-11
Mazie	C-12
McDaniels	D-6
McHenry	D-6
McKee •	D-11
McRoberts	D-13
McVeigh	D-14
Meredith	D-7
Merrimac	D-9
Mexico	D-4
Middlesboro	F-11
Middletown	C-8
Midway	C-9
Millersburg	B-10
Millerstown	D-7
Millwood	D-6
Milton	B-8
Monterey	B-9
Monticello •	E-9
Montpelier	E-9
Morehead •	C-12
Moreland	D-9
Morganfield •	D-4
Morgantown •	D-6
Mortons Gap	D-5
Moscow	F-2
Mount Aerial	E-7
Mount Carmel	B-11
Mount Eden	C-9
Mount Hermon	E-8
Mount Olivet •	B-10
Mount Pisgah	F-9
Mount Pleasant	B-8
Mount Salem	D-9
Mount Sherman	D-8
Mount Sterling •	C-11
Mount Union	F-7
Mount Vernon •	D-10
Mount Victory	E-10
Mount Washington	C-8
Mount Zion	E-9
Mountain Valley	D-12
Muldraugh	C-7
Mummie	D-11
Munfordville •	D-7
Murray •	F-3
Nancy	E-9
Nebo	D-5
Nevada	D-9
New Castle •	B-9
New Columbus	B-9
New Concord	F-4
New Haven	D-8
New Hope	D-8
New Market	D-8
New Zion	D-11
Newfoundland	C-12
Newman	C-5
Newport •	A-10
Niagara	D-5
Nicholasville •	C-9
North Middletown	C-10
Nortonville	E-5
Oak Grove	F-5
Oakdale	D-11
Oakland	E-7
Oakley	C-11
Oaks	E-3
Okolona	C-8
Old Pine Grove	C-10
Oldtown	B-12
Olive Branch	C-8
Olive Hill	B-12
Olmstead	E-6
Olympia	C-11
Oneida	D-11
Oscar	E-2
Oven Fork	E-13
Owensboro •	C-5
Owenton •	B-9
Owingsville •	C-11
Paducah •	E-3
Paintsville •	C-12
Paris •	C-10
Park City	E-7
Parkers Lake	E-10
Parksville	D-9
Parnell	E-9
Partridge	E-12
Pellville	C-6
Pembroke	E-5
Perryville	D-9
Petersville	B-11
Phelps	D-14
Pierce	E-8
Pikeville •	D-13
Pilot Oak	F-3
Pine Knot	F-10
Piner	A-10
Pineville •	E-11
Pittsburg	E-11
Pleasant Hill	C-9
Pleasant Ridge	D-6
Pleasure Ridge Park	C-7
Plummers Landing	B-11
Poole	D-4
Port Royal	B-9
Powersburg	E-9
Preachersville	D-10
Preston	C-11
Prestonsburg •	D-13
Pride	D-4
Princeton •	E-4
Proctor	D-11
Providence	C-10
Providence	D-4
Providence	F-6
Quail	D-10
Quicksand	D-12
Quincy	B-12
Raceland	B-13
Radcliff	C-7
Ravenna	D-11
Raywick	D-8
Redbush	C-12
Reed	C-5
Richardson	C-13
Richarsville	E-7
Richmond •	C-10
Roaring Springs	E-4
Rochester	D-6
Rockport	D-5
Rowland	D-10
Rowletts	D-7
Rumsey	D-5
Russell	B-13
Russell Springs	E-9
Russellville •	E-6
Sacramento	D-5
Sadieville	B-10
St. Elmo	E-5
St. Helens	D-11
St. Joseph	D-5
St. Mary	D-8
Salem	D-3
Salt Lick	C-11
Salyersville •	C-12
Sanders	B-9
Sandy Hook •	C-12
Sardis	B-11
Science Hill	E-10
Scottsville •	E-7
Sebree	D-5
Seco	E-13
Sharpsburg	C-10
Shelbyville •	C-9
Shepherdsville •	C-8
Shively	C-7
Sidney	D-14
Simpsonville	C-8
Slaughters	D-5
Smithfield	B-8
Smithland •	E-3
Smiths Grove	E-7
Somerset •	E-10
Sonora	D-7
South Bee Spring	D-7
South Carrollton	D-5
South Elkhorn	C-9
South Shore	B-12
South Union	E-6
South Williamson	D-13
Springfield •	D-8
Stamping Ground	B-9
Stanford •	D-9
Stanton •	C-11
Stearns	F-10
Sturgis	D-4
Sullivan	D-4
Tar Hill	D-7
Taylorsville •	C-8
Texas	D-9
Thompsonville	C-9
Three Springs	E-8
Threeforks	E-7
Tilden	D-4
Tiline	E-3
Tillie	E-13
Tilton	B-11
Tinsley	E-11
Tiptop	D-12
Tobacco	F-3
Tollesboro	B-11
Tomahawk	C-13
Thompkinsville •	E-8
Trenton	E-5
Trinity	B-11
Triplett	B-12
Twila	E-12
Union	A-9
Union City	C-10
Union Star	C-7
Uniontown	C-4
Upton	D-7
Utica	D-5
Utility	C-6
Valley Station	C-8
Valley View	C-10
Van Lear	C-13
Vanceburg •	B-11
Vancleve	D-12
Versailles •	C-9
Vertrees	D-7
Vest	D-12
Vester	E-8
Vicco	D-12
Victory	D-10
Vine Grove	C-7
Virgie	D-13

INDIANA SEE PAGES 40-41

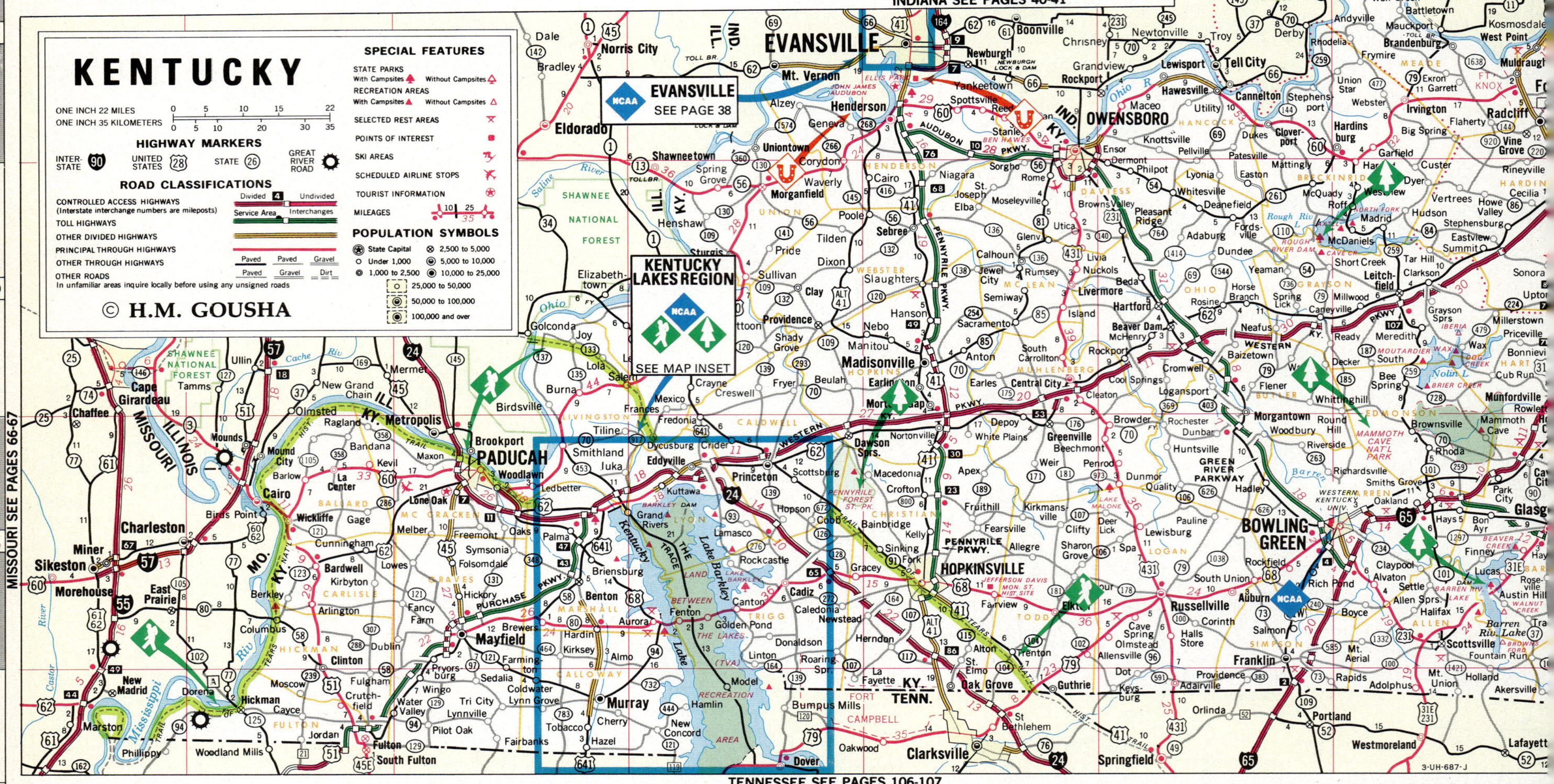

TENNESSEE SEE PAGES 106-107

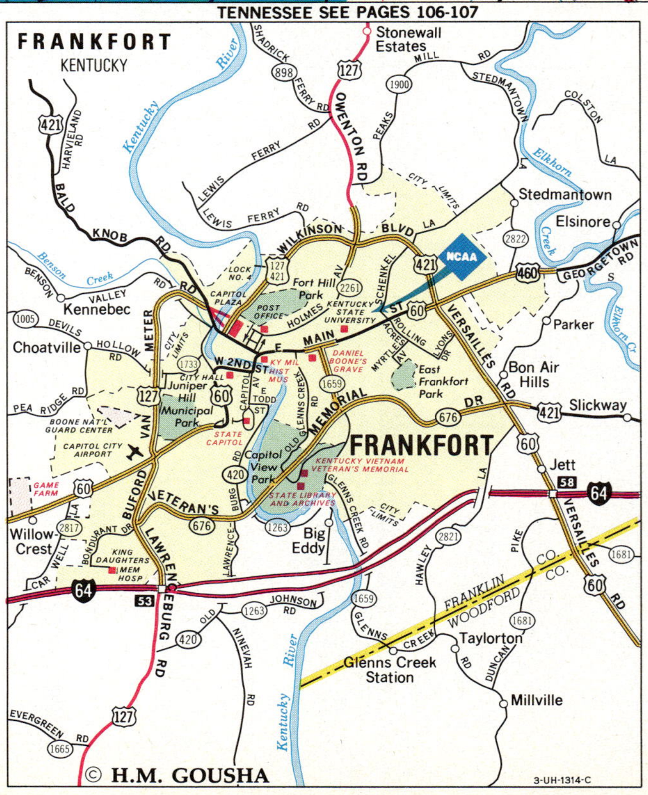

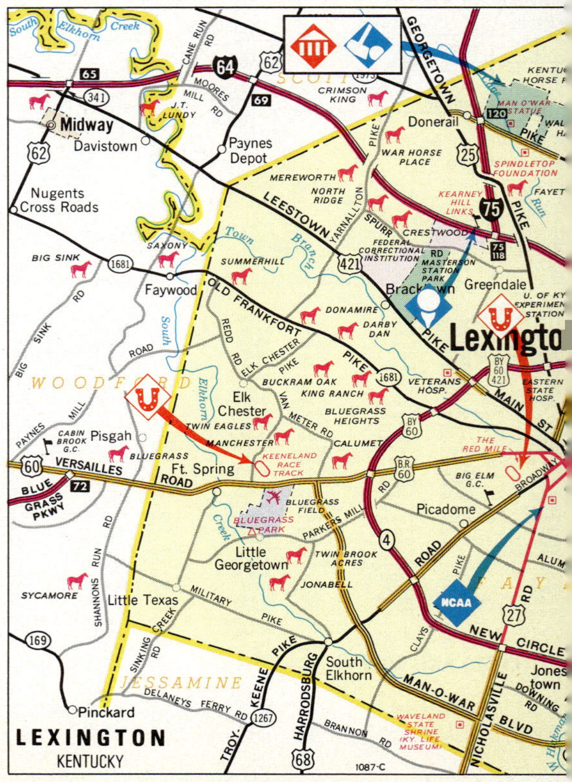

SF-687-J-X

INDIANA SEE PAGES 40-41
OHIO SEE PAGES 90-91
WEST VIRGINIA SEE PAGES 116-117
VIRGINIA SEE PAGES 114-115
TENNESSEE SEE PAGES 106-107
KENTUCKY TOLL ROADS
Entrance or exit only at interchanges, shown thus:
Service Area
Interchange
AUDUBON PARKWAY
Passenger car toll is 50c for the entire length of 23 miles, approximately 2.2c per mile.
CUMBERLAND PARKWAY
Passenger car toll is $2.00 for the entire length of 91 miles, approximately 2.3c per mile.
DANIEL BOONE PARKWAY
Passenger car toll is $1.40 for the entire length of 59 miles; approximately 2.4c per mile.
GREEN RIVER PARKWAY
Passenger car toll is $1.50 for the entire length of 70 miles, approximately 2.1c per mile.
PENNYRILE PARKWAY
Passenger car toll is $1.00 for the entire length of 57 miles, approximately 1.8c per mile.
PURCHASE PARKWAY
Passenger car toll is 90c for the entire length of 51 miles, approximately 1.7c per mile.
CINCINNATI
SEE PAGE 92
FRANKFORT
SEE MAP INSET
LOUISVILLE
SEE MAP INSET
LEXINGTON
SEE MAP INSET
EXPLANATION OF ACTIVITIES
Major League Spectator
Minor League Spectator
Collegiate/Participant
Rivers, Trails, Major Parks, and Forests
Auto Racing
Horse Racing
Sailing
Baseball
Museums & Halls of Fame
Skiing
Basketball
National Trails
Soccer
Bowling
NCAA Colleges
Tennis
Football
Parks & Forests
Track & Field
Golf
Polo
Wild, Scenic, & Recreational Rivers
Hockey
Rodeo
GOUSHA
CENTRAL STANDARD TIME
EASTERN STANDARD TIME
LOUISVILLE AND VICINITY
MILES
KILOMETERS
Golf Courses
© H.M. GOUSHA
H.M. GOUSHA
3-UH-1033-C
Lithographed in U.S.A.

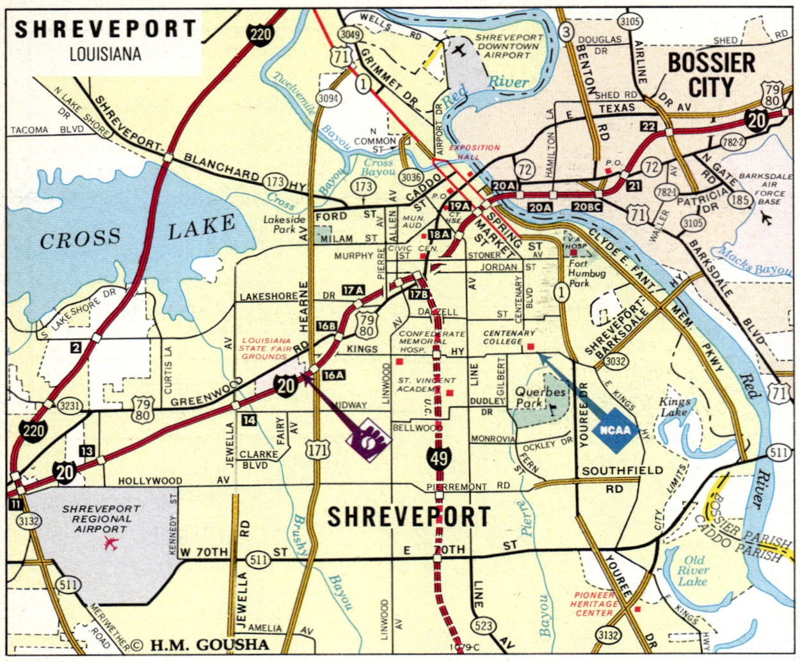

LOUISIANA

Pop (1990) 4,238,216
Area 48,523 Sq. Mi.

PARISHES

Parish	Parish Seat
Acadia	Crowley
Allen	Oberlin
Ascension	Donaldsonville
Assumption	Napoleonville
Avoyelles	Marksville
Beauregard	De Ridder
Bienville	Arcadia
Bossier	Benton
Caddo	Shreveport
Calcasieu	Lake Charles
Caldwell	Columbia
Cameron	Cameron
Catahoula	Harrisonburg
Claiborne	Homer
Concordia	Vidalia
De Soto	Mansfield
East Baton Rouge	Baton Rouge
East Carroll	Lake Providence
East Feliciana	Clinton
Evangeline	Ville Platte
Franklin	Winnsboro
Grant	Colfax
Iberia	New Iberia
Iberville	Plaquemine
Jackson	Jonesboro
Jefferson	Gretna
Jefferson Davis	Jennings
La Salle	Jena
Lafayette	Lafayette
Lafourche	Thibodaux
Lincoln	Ruston
Livingston	Livingston
Madison	Tallulah
Morehouse	Bastrop
Natchitoches	Natchitoches
Orleans	New Orleans
Ouachita	Monroe
Plaquemines	Pointe a la Hache
Point Coupee	New Roads
Rapides	Alexandria
Red River	Coushatta
Richland	Rayville
Sabine	Many
St. Bernard	Chalmette
St. Charles	Hahnville
St. Helena	Greensburg
St. James	Convent
St. John the Baptist	Edgard
St. Landry	Opelousas
St. Martin	St. Martinville
St. Mary	Franklin
St. Tammany	Covington
Tangipahoa	Amite
Tensas	St. Joseph
Terrebonne	Houma
Union	Farmerville
Vermillion	Abbeville
Vernon	Leesville
Washington	Franklinton
Webster	Minden
West Baton Rouge	Port Allen
West Carroll	Oak Grove
West Feliciana	St. Francisville
Winn	Winnfield

PARTIAL LIST OF

CITIES AND TOWNS

• PARISH SEATS

Abbeville •	J-7
Acme	D-8
Addis	F-9
Airline Park	B-10
Akers	F-11
Albany	F-10
Alden Bridge	A-5
Alexandria •	D-7
Alsatia	A-9
Alsen	E-9
Alto	B-8
Amite •	E-11
Anacoco	D-5
Anandale	D-7
Ansley	B-6
Antioch	A-6
Arabi	B-13
Arcadia •	B-6
Archibald	B-8
Archie	D-8
Arnaudville	F-8
Atheps	A-6
Azucena	C-9
Bains	E-9
Baker	E-9
Baldwin	G-9
Ball	D-7
Banks Springs	C-8
Barataria	G-11
Barber	E-7
Basile	F-7
Baskin	B-8
Bastrop •	A-8
Batchelor	E-8
Baton Rouge •	F-10
Bayou Cane	G-10
Bayou Chicot	E-7
Bayou Current	E-8
Beekman	A-8
Beggs	E-8
Bel	F-6
Belle Chasse	G-12
Belle Rose	F-10
Belmont	C-5
Benson	C-5
Bentley	D-7
Benton •	A-5
Bernice	A-6
Bertrandville	G-12
Berwick	G-9
Bienville	B-6
Bogalusa	E-12
Bolinger	A-5
Bonita	A-8
Boothville	H-13
Bossier City	B-5
Boutte	G-11
Boyce	D-6
Braithwaite	C-14
Breaux Bridge	F-8
Broussard	F-8
Brule	G-10
Brusly	F-9
Bunkie	E-7
Buras	H-12
Burr Ferry	E-5
Bush	E-12
Cameron •	C-5
Campti	C-6
Caney	D-5
Carencro	F-8
Carlisle	G-12
Carterville	A-5
Caspiana	B-5
Centerville	G-9
Chacahoula	G-10
Chalmette •	G-12
Chambers	D-7
Chase	B-8
Chatham	B-7
Cheneyville	E-7
Chestnut	C-6
Church Point	F-7
Clarence	C-6
Clay	B-7
Clayton	C-9
Clifton	E-11
Clinton •	E-10
Colfax •	D-6
Columbia •	B-8
Convent •	G-10
Converse	C-5
Conway	A-7
Coon	E-8
Corey	B-8
Cottonport	E-8
Cotton Valley	A-5
Couchwood	A-5
Coushatta •	C-5
Covington •	F-11
Crews	C-6
Crowley •	F-7
Crowville	B-9
Cullen	A-5
Cut Off	H-11
Cypress	C-6
Dalcour	G-12
D'Arbonne	A-7
Darnell	A-9
Davant	G-12
Delcambre	G-8
Delhi	B-9
Denham Springs	F-10
De Qunicy	F-5
De Ridder •	E-5
Derry	D-6
Des Allemands	G-11
Dido	E-6
Dodson	C-6
Donaldsonville •	F-10
Doyline	B-5
Dry Prong	C-7
Dubach	A-7
Duson	F-7
Easton	E-7
Echo	D-7
Edgard •	G-11
Edna	F-6
Elba	E-8
Elizabeth	E-6
Elton	F-6
Empire	H-12
Epps	B-9
Erath	G-8
Eros	B-7
Erwinville	F-9
Ethel	E-9
Eunice	F-7
Eva	D-8
Farmerville •	A-7
Felps	E-10
Fenton	F-6
Ferriday	C-8
Fillmore	B-5
Fisher	D-5
Fishville	D-7
Flatwoods	D-6
Flora	C-6
Florien	D-5
Folsom	E-11
Fondale	B-8
Forbing	B-4
Forest	A-9
Forest Hill	E-7
Fort Jesup	C-5
Fort St. Leon	C-13
Foules	C-8
Franklin •	G-9
Franklinton •	E-11
Friendship	B-6
Frost	F-10
Gahagan	C-5
Galbraith	D-6
Galion	A-8
Galliano	H-11
Gardner	D-6
Garyville	F-10
Gassoway	A-9
Georgetown	C-7
Gibsland	B-6
Gibson	G-10
Gilbert	C-8
Gillis	F-5
Glenmora	E-7
Golden Meadow	H-11
Gonzales	F-10
Goosport	F-6
Gordon	A-6
Grambling	B-6
Gramercy	G-10
Grand Bayou	B-5
Grand Cane	B-4
Grand Coteau	F-8
Grand Encore	C-6
Grand Isle	H-12
Grangeville	E-10
Gray	G-10
Grayson	C-8
Greensburg •	E-10
Greenwood	B-4
Gretna •	G-12
Gueydan	G-7
Hagewood	C-5
Hahnville •	G-11
Haile	A-7
Halmwood	G-6
Hamburg	E-8
Hammond	F-11
Hanna	C-5
Harahan	G-11
Harrisonburg •	C-8
Harvey	G-11
Hathaway	F-6
Haynesville	A-6
Hickory	F-12
Highland	A-9
Hineston	D-6
Hodge	B-6
Holloway	D-7
Homer •	A-6
Hornbeck	D-5
Hosston	A-4
Houma •	G-10
Humphreys	G-10
Ida	A-4
Independence	E-11
Innis	E-8
Iota	F-7
Iowa	F-6
Jackson	E-9
Jamestown	B-6
Jeanerette	G-8
Jean •	C-8
Jennings •	F-6
Jesuit Bend	G-12
Jones	A-8
Jonesboro •	B-6
Jonesville	C-8
Joyce	C-7
Juanita	E-5
Junction City	A-6
Kaplan	G-7
Keatchie	B-4
Keithville	B-4
Kenner	F-11
Kentwood	E-11
Kilbourne	A-9
Kinder	F-6
Krotz Springs	F-8
LaPlace	G-11
Labadieville	G-10
Lafayette •	F-8
Lake Arthur	F-7
Lake Charles •	F-6
Lake End	C-5
Lake Providence •	A-9
Lamar	B-9
Larose	G-11
Latanier	D-7
Lawtell	F-7
Le Blanc	F-6
Leander	D-6
Lebeau	E-8
Lecompte	D-7
Lee Bayou	C-9
Leesville •	D-5
Leeville	H-11
Le Moyan	E-8
Lena	D-6
Leton	A-5
Lettsworth	E-8
Lillie	A-6
Liverpool	E-10
Livingston •	F-10
Livonia	E-9
Lockport	G-10
Logansport	C-4
Log Cabin	A-8
Longstreet	B-4
Longville	E-5
Lottie	F-8
Louisa	G-8
Lucky	B-6
Ludington	E-5
Luling	G-11
Lutcher	G-10
Madisonville	E-11
Mamou	E-7
Mandeville	F-11
Mangham	B-8
Manifest	C-8
Mansfield •	C-4
Mansura	E-8
Many •	D-5
Maple Woods	F-5
Maringouin	F-9
Marion	A-7
Marksville •	D-8
Marrero	G-11
Maurice	F-8
Maxie	F-7
McCall	F-10
McDade	B-5
McManus	E-9
Meeker	E-7
Melville	E-8
Meraux	B-14
Mer Rouge	A-8
Merryville	E-5
Messick	C-5
Metairie	G-11
Minden •	A-5
Mire	F-7
Mittie	E-6
Monroe •	B-8
Montegut	H-11
Montgomery	C-6
Montpelier	E-10
Montrose	D-6
Morgan City	G-9
Morganza	E-8
Morrow	E-8
Moss Bluff	F-6
Myrtle Grove	G-12
Myrtis	A-4
Naomi	G-12
Napoleonville •	G-10
Natalbany	F-11
Natchez	C-6
Natchitoches •	C-6
Newellton	C-9
New Iberia •	G-8
New Llano	D-5
New Orleans •	F-12
New Roads •	E-9
New Sarpy	G-11
Noble	C-5
Norco	G-11
North Hodge	B-6
Oakdale	E-7
Oak Grove	A-9
Oak Grove •	G-6
Oak Ridge	A-8
Oasplana	B-5
Oberlin •	E-6
Oil City	A-4
Olla	C-7
Opelousas •	F-8
Oscar	E-9
Packton	C-7
Paincourtville	G-10
Paradis	G-11
Parks	F-8
Patterson	G-9
Pearl River	F-12
Peck	C-8
Perryville	A-8
Phoenix	G-12
Pickering	E-5
Pine Grove	E-10
Pine Island	F-6
Pineville	D-7
Pioneer	A-9
Pitkin	E-6
Plain Dealing	A-5
Plaquemine •	F-9
Pleasant Hill	C-5
Point a la Hache •	G-12
Pollock	D-7
Ponchatoula	F-11
Port Allen •	F-9
Port Barre	E-8
Port Hudson	E-9
Port Sulphur	H-12
Powhatan	C-5
Poydras	G-12
Prairieville	F-10
Prong	C-7
Quitman	B-6
Raceland	G-10
Ragley	F-5
Ramsey	E-11
Rapides	D-7
Rayne	F-7
Rayville •	B-8
Reeves	F-6
Remy	G-10
Reserve	F-11
Ridgecrest	C-9
Rilla	B-8
Ringgold	B-5
Riverton	B-8
Robeline	C-5
Robert	F-11
Rodessa	A-4
Roseland	E-11
Rosepine	E-5
Ruston •	B-6
St. Francisville •	E-9
St. Genevieve	D-9
St. Joseph •	C-9
St. Martinville •	F-8
St. Maurice	C-6
St. Rose	G-11
Sandel	D-5
Sarepta	A-4
Scarsdale	G-12
Scott	F-8
Sheridan	E-12
Shiloh	A-7
Shriever	G-10
Shongaloo	A-5
Shreveport •	B-4
Sibley	B-5
Sicily Island	C-8
Simmesport	E-8
Slaughter	E-9
Slidell	F-12
Somerset	B-9
Sondheimer	B-9
Sorrento	F-10
South Mansfield	C-4
Southport	B-11
Spencer	A-7
Springhill	A-5
Stacy	C-8
Stanley	C-4
Starhill	E-9
Starks	F-5
Start	B-8
Sterlington	A-8
Stonewall	B-4
Sugartown	E-6
Sulphur	F-5
Summerfield	A-6
Summerville	C-7
Sun	E-12
Sunset	F-8
Supreme	G-10
Talisheek	F-12
Tallulah •	B-9
Tannehill	C-6
Taylortown	B-5
Thibodaux •	G-10
Ticktaw	E-11
Tioga	D-7
Torbert	E-9
Transylvania	A-9
Trees	A-4
Triumph	H-13
Trout	C-7
Truxno	A-7
Tullos	C-7
Tunica	E-9
Turkey Creek	E-7
Unionville	A-6
Utility	D-8
Urania	C-7
Vacherie	G-10
Vanceville	A-5
Varnado	E-12
Venice	H-13
Verda	C-6
Vidalia •	D-9
Ville Platte	E-7
Vinton	F-5
Violet	G-12
Vivian	A-4
Wakefield	E-9
Waldheim	E-12
Walker	F-10
Walters	D-8
Warden	B-9
Warnerton	E-11
Washington	E-8
Waterproof	C-9
Watson	E-10
Waverly	B-9
Weeks	G-8
Weiss	E-10
Welsh	F-6
Westdale	B-5
Westlake	F-5
West Monroe	B-7
West Pointe a la Hache	G-12
Westwego	G-11
White Castle	F-9
Whitehall	C-8
Wildsville	C-8
Williana	C-7
Wilson	E-9
Winnfield •	C-6
Winnsboro •	B-8
Wisner	C-8
Woodlawn	F-6
Woodworth	D-7
Wright	G-7
Wyandote	G-9
Wyatt	B-6
Youngsville	F-8
Zachary	E-9
Zwolle	C-5

SF-641-J-X1

ARKANSAS SEE PAGES 12-13
MISSISSIPPI SEE PAGES 64-65
MONROE
SEE MAP INSET
VICKSBURG
NATCHEZ
Vidalia
Ferriday
Tallulah
Bastrop
Winnsboro
Port Gibson
LAKE PONTCHARTRAIN
NEW ORLEANS AND VICINITY
MILES
KILOMETERS
Golf Courses
© H.M. GOUSHA
NEW ORLEANS
Metairie
Kenner
Harahan
Westwego
Gretna
Harvey
Arabi
Chalmette
Marrero
Mississippi River
West Monroe
MONROE
LOUISIANA
LAKE CHARLES
LOUISIANA
Lake Charles
Westlake
Sulphur
EXPLANATION OF ACTIVITIES
Major League Spectator
Minor League Spectator
Collegiate/Participant
Rivers, Trails, Major Parks, and Forests
Auto Racing
Horse Racing
Sailing
Baseball
Museums & Halls of Fame
Skiing
Basketball
National Trails
Soccer
Bowling
NCAA Colleges
Tennis
Football
Parks & Forests
Track & Field
Golf
Polo
Wild, Scenic, & Recreational Rivers
Hockey
Rodeo
MISSISSIPPI
BATON ROUGE
SEE MAP INSET
LAFAYETTE
New Iberia
Opelousas
Hammond
Slidell
Bogalusa
Houma
Thibodaux
Morgan City
Donaldsonville
Plaquemine
Franklin
Jeanerette
Abbeville
St. Martinville
Picayune
GULFPORT
BILOXI
Ocean Springs
Long Beach
Pass Christian
Bay St. Louis
Mississippi Sound
Lake Borgne
Chandeleur Sound
Breton Sound
Lake Pontchartrain
Lake Maurepas
NEW ORLEANS
SEE MAP INSET
GULF ISLANDS NATIONAL SEASHORE
Vermilion Bay
Atchafalaya Bay
Barataria Bay
Timbalier Bay
Terrebonne Bay
Caminada Pass
Grand Isle
Golden Meadow
Venice
Empire
Port Sulphur
MEXICO
GOUSHA
Lithographed in U.S.A.
A
B
C
D
E
F
G
H
8
9
10
11
12
13
14

MAINE
CITIES AND TOWNS
COUNTIES
EXPLANATION OF ACTIVITIES
ACADIA NATIONAL PARK
MAINE
H.M. GOUSHA
CANADA SEE PAGE 127
QUEBEC
NEW BRUNSWICK
HIGHWAY MARKERS
ROAD CLASSIFICATIONS
SPECIAL FEATURES
POPULATION SYMBOLS

MAINE TURNPIKE
Speed limit is as posted. Passenger car toll is $2.70 for the entire length of 100 miles, approximately 2.7c per mile. Entrance or exit only at interchanges, shown thus:
Interchange
Service Area
ACADIA NAT'L PARK SEE MAP INSET
BANGOR SEE MAP INSET
PORTLAND SEE MAP INSET
A permit is required on most private roads and many are subject to toll.
NEW HAMPSHIRE SEE PAGES 74-75
NEW HAMPSHIRE
PORTLAND MAINE
BANGOR MAINE
© H.M. GOUSHA
Lithographed in U.S.A.
EASTERN STANDARD TIME
ATLANTIC STANDARD TIME
ATLANTIC OCEAN

INDEX TO COUNTIES

PARTIAL LIST OF

CITIES AND TOWNS

• County Seats

UH-688-S-X

PENNSYLVANIA SEE PAGES 98-99
TOLL ROADS
Entrance or exit only at interchanges, shown thus:
Interchange
Service Area
FORT MC HENRY TUNNEL
Passenger car toll is $1.00 for the entire length of 2.6 miles, approximately 38.5c per mile.
FRANCIS SCOTT KEY BRIDGE
Passenger car toll is $1.00 for the entire length of 10.3 miles, approximately 9.7c per mile.
HARBOR TUNNEL THRUWAY
Passenger car toll is $1.00 for the entire length of 13.5 miles, approximately 7.4c per mile.
JOHN F. KENNEDY MEM. HIGHWAY (Delaware)
Passenger car toll is $1.00 for the entire length of 11 miles, approximately 9.0c per mile.
JOHN F. KENNEDY MEM. HIGHWAY (Maryland)
Passenger car toll is $1.00 for the entire length of 42 miles, approximately 2.4c per mile.
PHILADELPHIA
WILMINGTON
WILMINGTON SEE MAP INSET
BALTIMORE
BALTIMORE SEE PAGE 54
ANNAPOLIS
ANNAPOLIS SEE PAGE 54
WASHINGTON
Alexandria
DOVER
DOVER SEE MAP INSET
NEW JERSEY SEE PAGES 76-77
DELAWARE BAY
ATLANTIC OCEAN
CHESAPEAKE BAY
MARYLAND
DELAWARE
VIRGINIA SEE PAGES 114-115
Lithographed in U.S.A.

BALTIMORE AND VICINITY
© H.M. GOUSHA
BALTIMORE
Towson
Lutherville
Pikesville
Randallstown
Catonsville
Dundalk
Essex
Middle River
White Marsh
Glen Burnie
Linthicum
Ferndale
Baltimore-Washington International Airport
Harmans
Severn
Jessup
Elkridge
Arbutus
Halethorpe
Lansdowne
Woodlawn
Owings Mills
Perry Hall
Joppatown
Edgemere
Sparrows Point
Fort Howard
CHESAPEAKE BAY
Riviera Beach
Green Haven
Bayside Beach
5-UH-1319-C

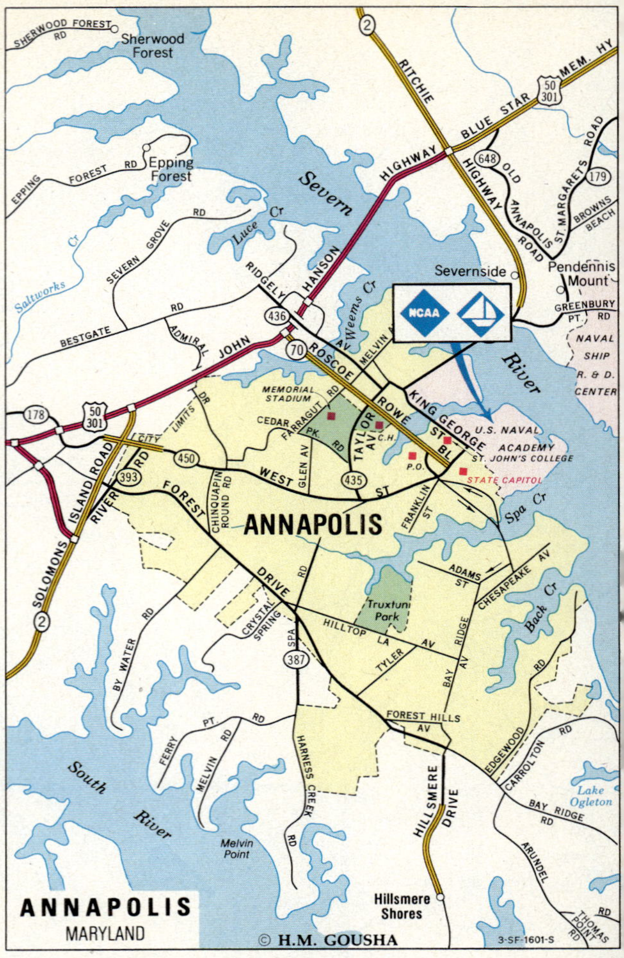
ANNAPOLIS MARYLAND
© H.M. GOUSHA
ANNAPOLIS
Severn River
South River
U.S. NAVAL ACADEMY
Sherwood Forest
Epping Forest
Severnside
Pendennis Mount
Melvin Point
Hillsmere Shores
3-SF-1601-S

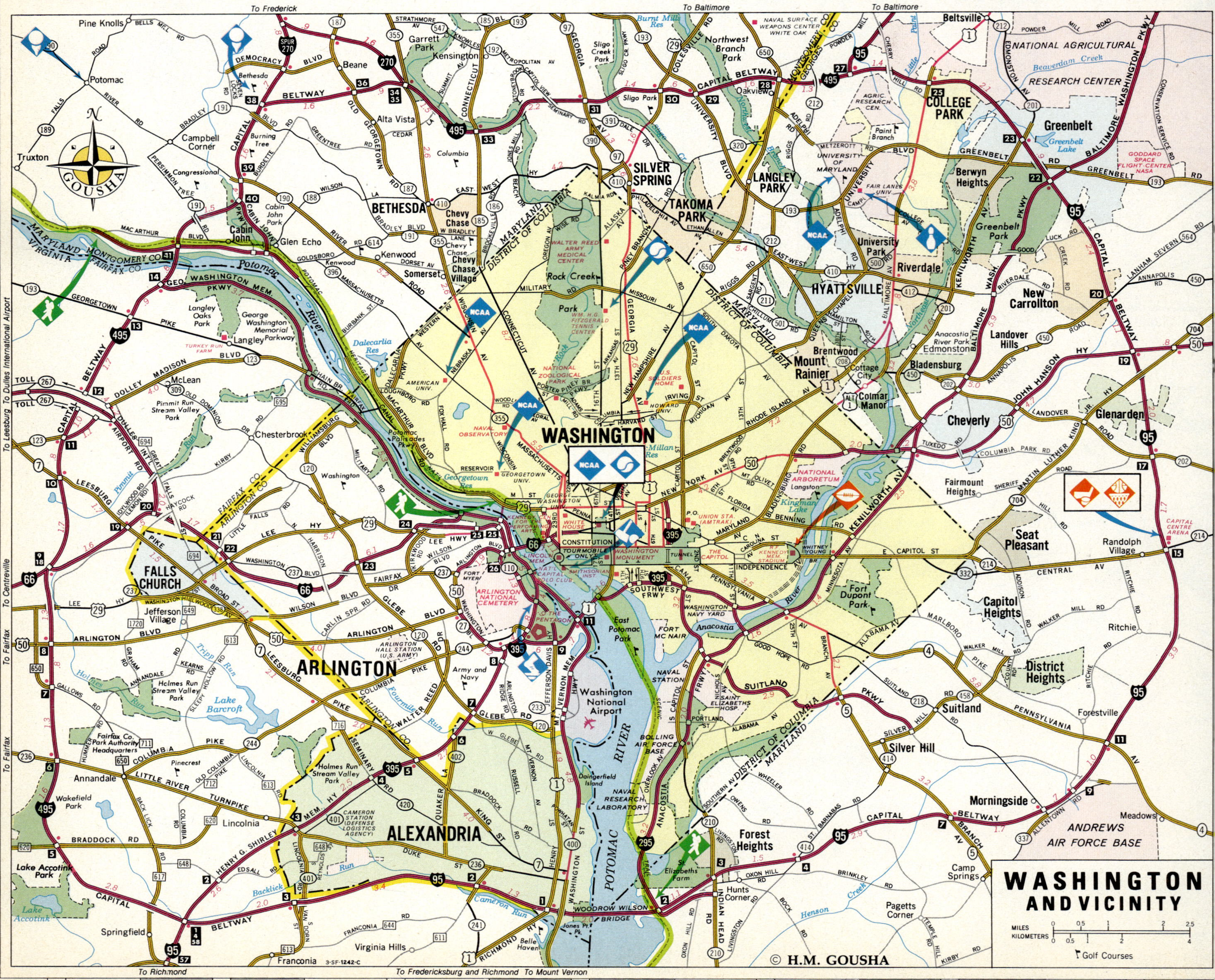
WASHINGTON AND VICINITY
© H.M. GOUSHA
GOUSHA
To Frederick
To Baltimore
To Richmond
To Fredericksburg and Richmond
To Mount Vernon
To Leesburg
To Dulles International Airport
To Centreville
To Fairfax
WASHINGTON
ARLINGTON
ALEXANDRIA
BETHESDA
SILVER SPRING
TAKOMA PARK
HYATTSVILLE
COLLEGE PARK
LANGLEY PARK
FALLS CHURCH
Greenbelt
Riverdale
Cheverly
Glenarden
Seat Pleasant
Capitol Heights
District Heights
Suitland
Silver Hill
Forestville
Morningside
ANDREWS AIR FORCE BASE
Forest Heights
Camp Springs
Springfield
Annandale
Lincolnia
McLean
Potomac
Chevy Chase
Kensington
Wheaton
Beltsville
NATIONAL AGRICULTURAL RESEARCH CENTER
Washington National Airport
Potomac River
Anacostia
3-SF-1242-C
MILES
KILOMETERS
Golf Courses

BOSTON AND VICINITY
MILES
KILOMETERS
Golf Courses
To Tewksbury
To Methuen
To Lawrence
To Portsmouth
To Gloucester
BILLERICA
Burlington
Bedford
LEXINGTON
WALTHAM
BELMONT
ARLINGTON
WOBURN
Wilmington
Reading
Lynnfield
Wakefield
Stoneham
Winchester
MELROSE
MEDFORD
MALDEN
EVERETT
REVERE
Saugus
LYNN
PEABODY
SALEM
Danvers
BEVERLY
Swampscott
Nahant
NAHANT BAY
BROAD SOUND
MASSACHUSETTS
BAY
SOMERVILLE
CAMBRIDGE
CHELSEA
Winthrop
WATERTOWN
NEWTON
BROOKLINE
BOSTON
BOSTON HARBOR
Logan International Airport
Dorchester Bay
QUINCY BAY
HINGHAM BAY
QUINCY
MILTON
BRAINTREE
WEYMOUTH
WELLESLEY
NEEDHAM
DEDHAM
Westwood
NORWOOD
RANDOLPH
BLUE HILLS RESERVATION
FELLS RESERVATION
GOUSHA
© H.M. GOUSHA
To Providence
To Taunton
To Bridgewater
To Kingston and Plymouth
To Marshfield

MASSACHUSETTS

Pop (1990) 6,029,051

Area 8,257 Sq. Mi.

COUNTIES

County	Co. Seat	County	Co. Seat
Barnstable	Barnstable	Hampshire	Northampton
Berkshire	Pittsfield	Middlesex	Cambridge
Bristol	Taunton	Nantucket	Nantucket
Dukes	Edgartown	Norfolk	Dedham
Essex	Salem	Plymouth	Plymouth
Franklin	Greenfield	Suffolk	Boston
Hampden	Springfield	Worcester	Worcester

PARTIAL LIST OF

CITIES AND TOWNS

• County Seats

NEW HAMPSHIRE SEE PAGES 74-75
MASSACHUSETTS
ONE INCH 10 MILES
ONE INCH 16 KILOMETERS
HIGHWAY MARKERS
INTERSTATE
UNITED STATES
STATE
ROAD CLASSIFICATIONS
CONTROLLED ACCESS HIGHWAYS (Interstate interchange numbers are mileposts)
Divided
Undivided
Interchanges
TOLL HIGHWAYS
OTHER DIVIDED HIGHWAYS
PRINCIPAL THROUGH HIGHWAYS
OTHER THROUGH HIGHWAYS
OTHER ROADS
Paved
Gravel
Dirt
In unfamiliar areas inquire locally before using any unsigned roads
© H.M. GOUSHA
SPECIAL FEATURES
STATE PARKS
With Campsites
Without Campsites
RECREATION AREAS
SELECTED REST AREAS
POINTS OF INTEREST
SKI AREAS
SCHEDULED AIRLINE STOPS
MILITARY AIRPORTS
MILEAGES
POPULATION SYMBOLS
State Capital
Under 1,000
1,000 to 2,500
2,500 to 5,000
5,000 to 10,000
10,000 to 25,000
25,000 to 50,000
50,000 to 100,000
100,000 and over
MASSACHUSETTS TURNPIKE
Speed limit as posted.
Passenger car toll is $5.60 for the entire length of 135 miles, approximately 4.1c per mile.
TURNPIKE INTERCHANGES
Entrance or exit only at interchanges, shown thus:
Service Area
Interchange
EXPLANATION OF ACTIVITIES
Major League Spectator
Minor League Spectator
Collegiate/Participant
Rivers, Trails, Major Parks, and Forests
Auto Racing
Horse Racing
Sailing
Baseball
Museums & Halls of Fame
Skiing
Basketball
National Trails
Soccer
Bowling
NCAA Colleges
Tennis
Football
Parks & Forests
Track & Field
Golf
Polo
Wild, Scenic & Recreational Rivers
Hockey
Rodeo
BOSTON
SEE PAGE 55
WORCESTER
SEE MAP INSET
CAPE COD NATIONAL SEASHORE
Much of the land within the authorized boundary of Cape Cod Nat'l Seashore is under private ownership. Please respect property rights.
ODE ISLAND SEE PAGES 24-25
Massachusetts Bay
Cape Cod Bay
Nantucket Sound
ATLANTIC OCEAN
BOSTON
PROVIDENCE
NEW BEDFORD
FALL RIVER
NEWPORT
GLOUCESTER
PLYMOUTH
PROVINCETOWN
CAPE COD
NANTUCKET ISLAND
MARTHA'S VINEYARD
GOUSHA
Lithographed in U.S.A.

MICHIGAN
© H.M. GOUSHA
HIGHWAY MARKERS
ROAD CLASSIFICATIONS
SPECIAL FEATURES
POPULATION SYMBOLS
WESTERN MICHIGAN
ISLE ROYALE NATIONAL PARK MICHIGAN
LAKE SUPERIOR
LAKE HURON
LAKE MICHIGAN
GREEN BAY
Index to Counties
MICHIGAN
PARTIAL LIST OF CITIES AND TOWNS
FOR CONTINUATION SEE MAIN MAP
FOR CONTINUATION SEE INSET AT RIGHT
WISCONSIN SEE PAGES 122-123
Sault Ste. Marie
Marquette
Escanaba
Menominee
Traverse City
Petoskey
Cheboygan
Alpena
Manistique
Munising
Gladstone
Ironwood
Iron Mountain
Mackinaw City
St. Ignace
Straits of Mackinac
North Channel
Mackinac Id.
Beaver Island
Drummond Island
Grand Island
ONTARIO
WISCONSIN

EXPLANATION OF ACTIVITIES
CANADA SEE PAGE 127
LAKE ST. CLAIR
DETROIT
SEE PAGE 60
TOLEDO
OHIO SEE PAGES 90-91
INDIANA SEE PAGES 40-41
SOUTH BEND
FLINT
Pontiac
Ypsilanti
Ann Arbor
Jackson
LANSING
Saginaw
Bay City
SAGINAW BAY
Midland
GRAND RAPIDS
KALAMAZOO
Battle Creek
MUSKEGON
LUDINGTON
Big Rapids
Cadillac
Port Huron
Mishawaka
Elkhart

DETROIT
AND VICINITY
MILES
KILOMETERS
Golf Courses
GOUSHA
© H.M. GOUSHA
To Flint, Saginaw and Bay City
To Flint
To Imlay City and Bad Axe
To Lansing and Grand Rapids
To Jackson and Lansing
To South Bend and Chicago
To Jackson
To Toledo
To Tilbury
To Essex
Bloomfield Hills
Birmingham
Troy
Clawson
Sterling Heights
Fraser
Franklin
Bingham Farms
Beverly Hills
ROYAL OAK
MADISON HEIGHTS
ROSEVILLE
Lathrup Village
Berkley
Huntington Woods
WARREN
ST. CLAIR SHORES
SOUTHFIELD
FARMINGTON HILLS
Pleasant Ridge
Hazel Park
Center Line
EAST DETROIT
FERNDALE
OAK PARK
Harper Woods
Grosse Pointe Woods
HIGHLAND PARK
Hamtramck
Grosse Pointe Shores
Grosse Pointe Farms
LIVONIA
Redford Township
DETROIT
Grosse Pointe
Grosse Pointe Park
DEARBORN HEIGHTS
GARDEN CITY
DEARBORN
Westland
INKSTER
WINDSOR
Melvindale
River Rouge
Ecorse
ROMULUS
ALLEN PARK
TAYLOR
LINCOLN PARK
SOUTHGATE
WYANDOTTE
MICHIGAN
ONTARIO
UNITED STATES
CANADA
Belle Isle Park
FLINT
Burton
FLINT MICHIGAN
GRAND RAPIDS
East Grand Rapids
Walker
Wyoming
Kentwood
Grandville
GRAND RAPIDS MICHIGAN
East Lansing
LANSING
Millett
LANSING MICHIGAN
Parchment
KALAMAZOO
Portage
KALAMAZOO MICHIGAN

MINNEAPOLIS ST. PAUL AND VICINITY
ROCHESTER MINNESOTA
MINNEAPOLIS
ST. PAUL
STILLWATER
WHITE BEAR LAKE
ROSEVILLE
RICHFIELD
BLOOMINGTON
EDINA
ST. LOUIS PARK
MINNETONKA
EDEN PRAIRIE
BURNSVILLE
APPLE VALLEY
EAGAN
INVER GROVE HEIGHTS
WOODBURY
PLYMOUTH
GOLDEN VALLEY
BROOKLYN CENTER
BROOKLYN PARK
FRIDLEY
SHAKOPEE
© H.M. GOUSHA
Lithographed in U.S.A.
8 9 10 11 12 13 14
A B C D E F G H

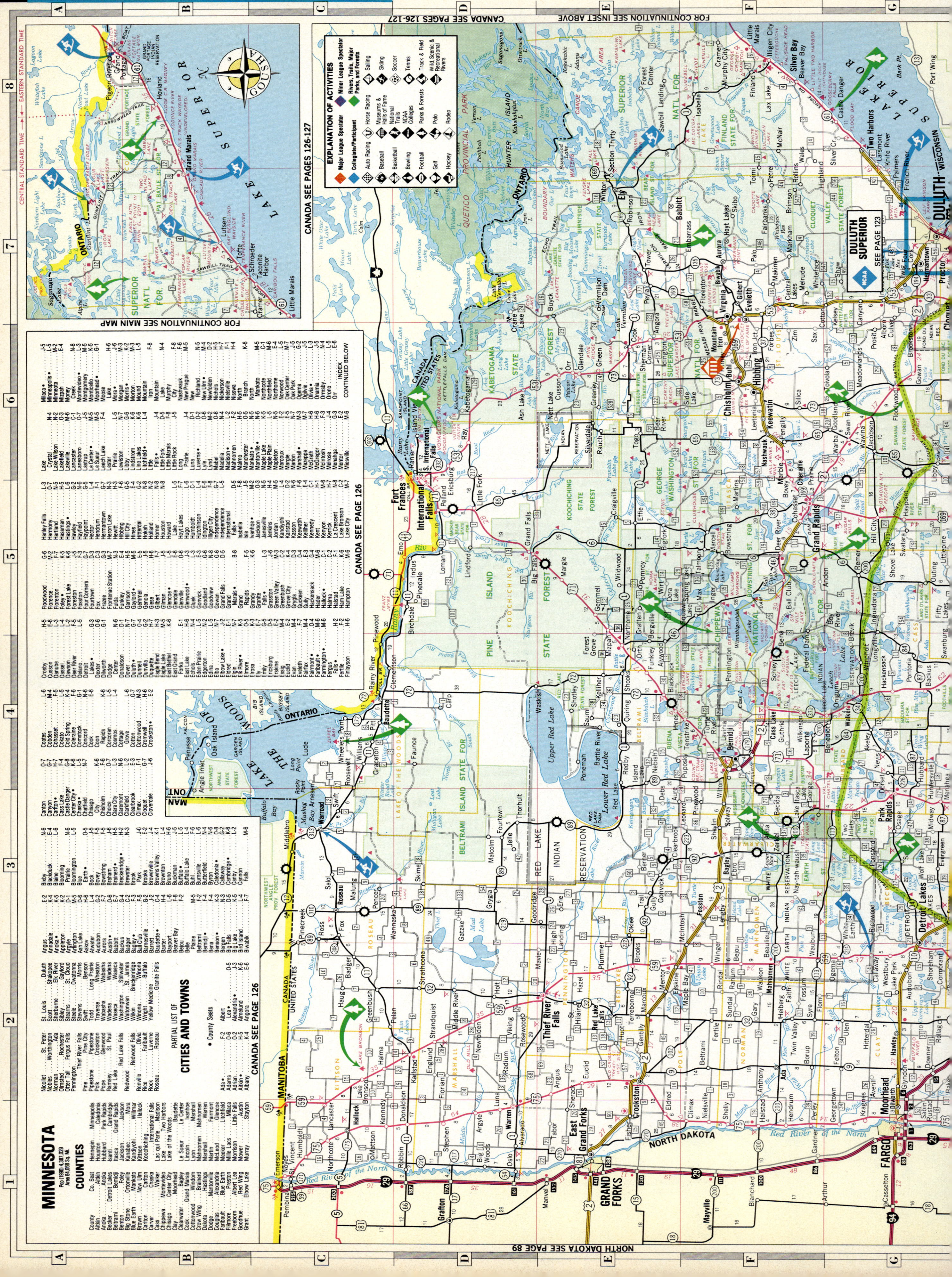
MINNESOTA
COUNTIES
PARTIAL LIST OF CITIES AND TOWNS
CANADA SEE PAGE 126
CANADA SEE PAGES 126-127
FOR CONTINUATION SEE MAIN MAP
FOR CONTINUATION SEE INSET ABOVE
NORTH DAKOTA SEE PAGE 89
EXPLANATION OF ACTIVITIES
DULUTH SUPERIOR SEE PAGE 123
LAKE SUPERIOR
LAKE OF THE WOODS
MANITOBA
ONTARIO
NORTH DAKOTA
WISCONSIN
UNITED STATES
CANADA
GRAND FORKS
FARGO
MOORHEAD
DULUTH

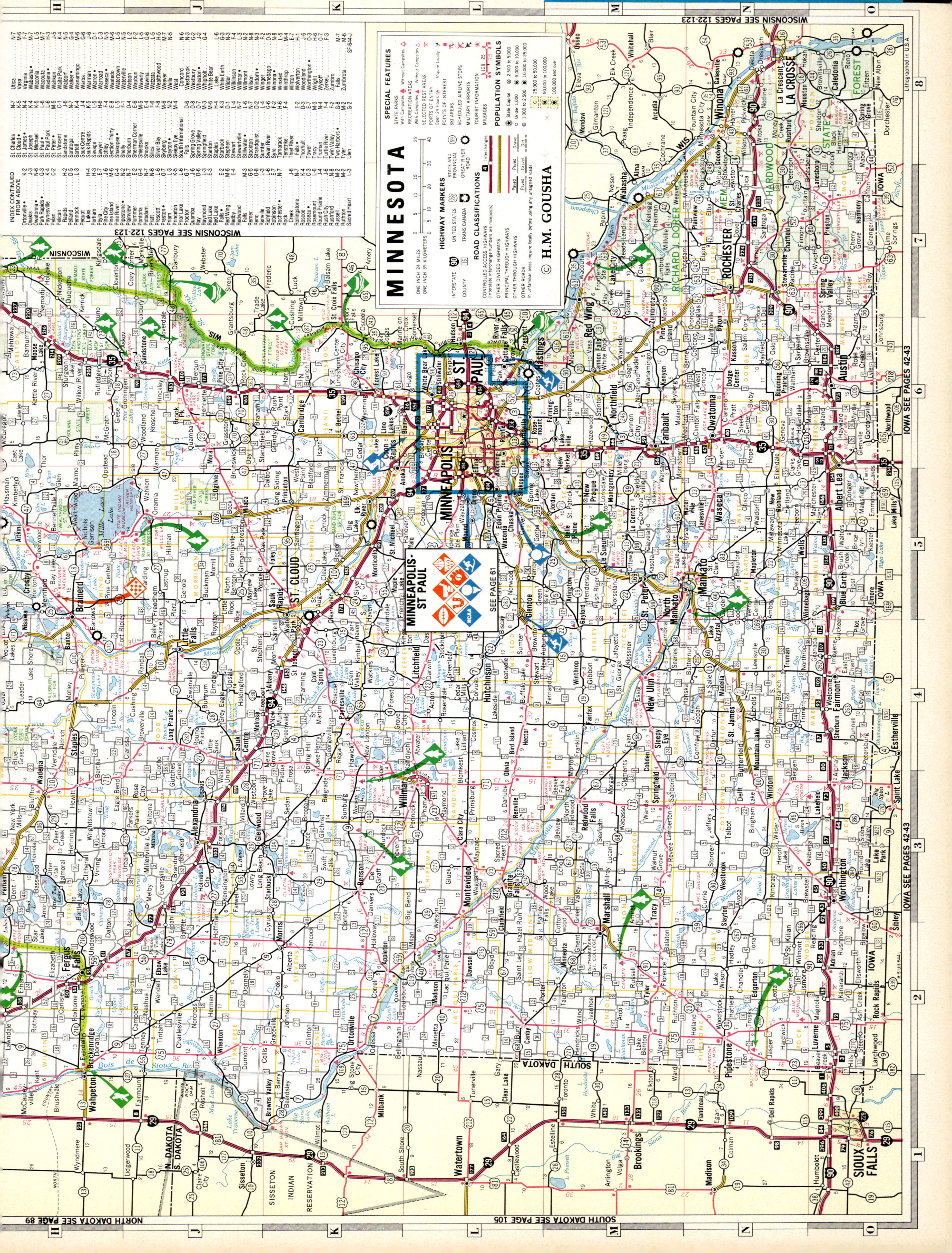
MINNESOTA
© H.M. GOUSHA
MINNEAPOLIS-ST PAUL
SEE PAGE 61
WISCONSIN SEE PAGES 122-123
IOWA SEE PAGES 42-43
SOUTH DAKOTA SEE PAGE 105
NORTH DAKOTA SEE PAGE 89

TENNESSEE SEE PAGES 106-107
ALABAMA SEE PAGES 6-7
ARKANSAS SEE PAGES 12-13
LOUISIANA SEE PAGES 48-49
MEMPHIS
COLUMBUS
GREENVILLE
GREENWOOD
MERIDIAN
MISSISSIPPI
VICKSBURG
MISSISSIPPI
NATCHEZ
MISSISSIPPI
© H.M. GOUSHA
MISSISSIPPI
COUNTIES
PARTIAL LIST OF
CITIES AND TOWNS

MISSISSIPPI
ALABAMA SEE PAGES 6-7
LOUISIANA SEE PAGES 48-49
SEE MAP INSET
EXPLANATION OF ACTIVITIES
HIGHWAY MARKERS
ROAD CLASSIFICATIONS
SPECIAL FEATURES
POPULATION SYMBOLS
© H.M. GOUSHA
JACKSON
MERIDIAN
HATTIESBURG
VICKSBURG
NATCHEZ
MOBILE
GULFPORT
BILOXI
PASCAGOULA
NEW ORLEANS
GULF OF MEXICO
Chandeleur Sound
Lake Pontchartrain
Lake Borgne
Mississippi Sound
JACKSON MISSISSIPPI
Lithographed in U.S.A.

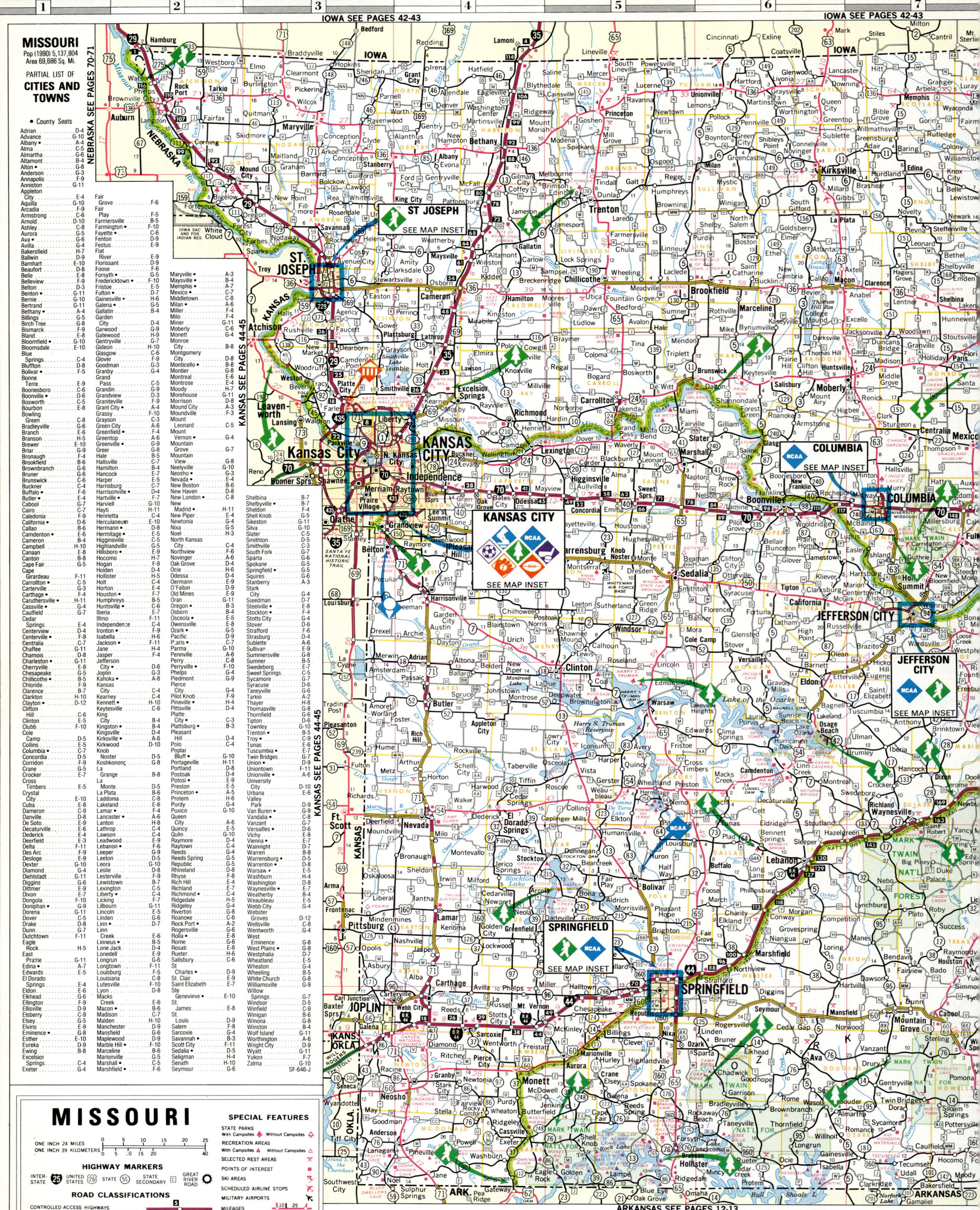

MISSOURI

Pop (1990) 5,137,804
Area 69,686 Sq. Mi.

PARTIAL LIST OF

CITIES AND TOWNS

• County Seats

SF-646-J

Index to Counties

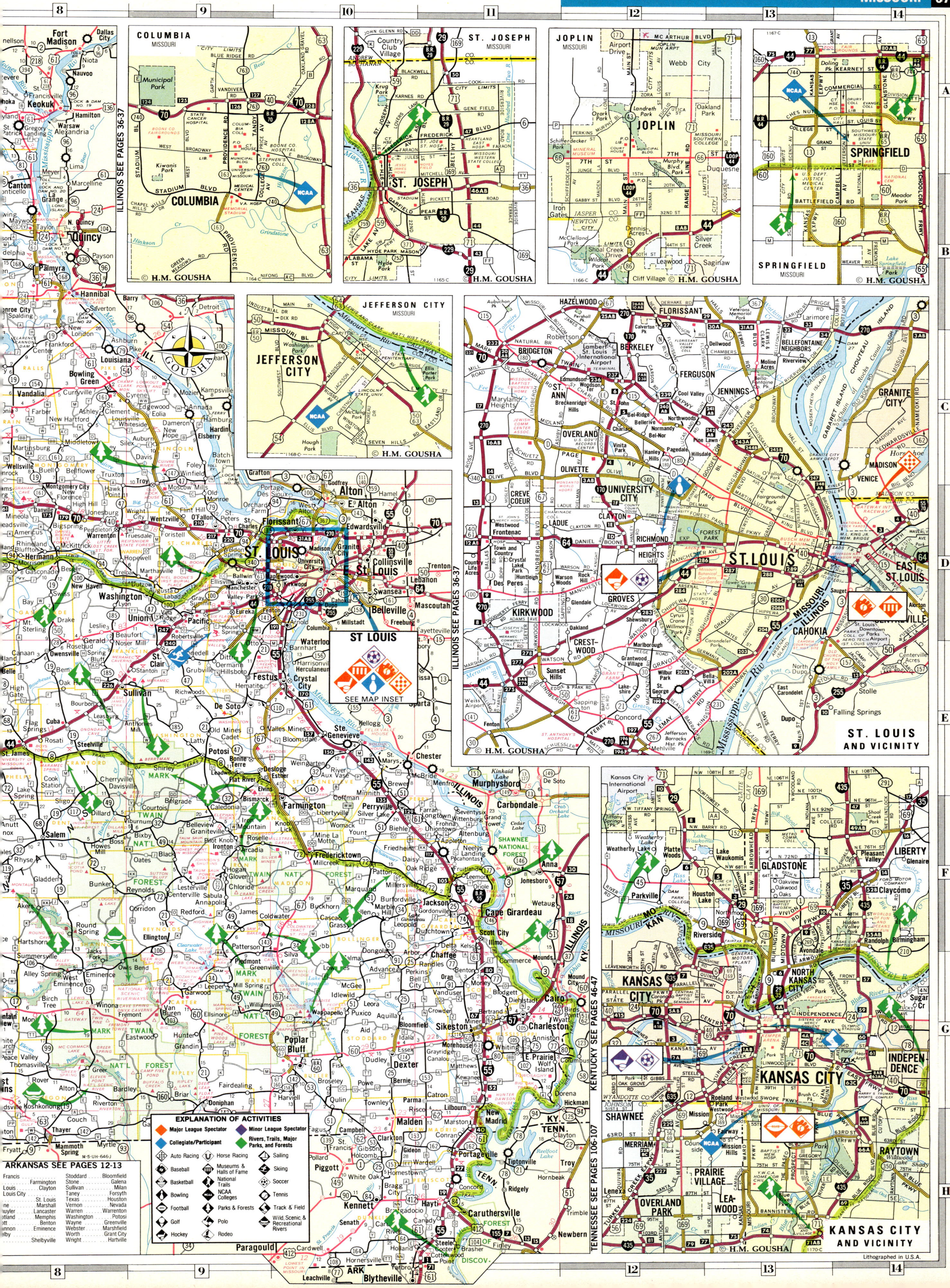
COLUMBIA
MISSOURI
© H.M. GOUSHA
ST. JOSEPH
MISSOURI
© H.M. GOUSHA
JOPLIN
MISSOURI
© H.M. GOUSHA
SPRINGFIELD
MISSOURI
© H.M. GOUSHA
JEFFERSON CITY
MISSOURI
© H.M. GOUSHA
ST. LOUIS AND VICINITY
© H.M. GOUSHA
KANSAS CITY AND VICINITY
© H.M. GOUSHA
ST LOUIS
SEE MAP INSET
ILLINOIS SEE PAGES 36-37
KENTUCKY SEE PAGES 46-47
TENNESSEE SEE PAGES 106-107
ARKANSAS SEE PAGES 12-13
EXPLANATION OF ACTIVITIES
Major League Spectator
Minor League Spectator
Collegiate/Participant
Rivers, Trails, Major Parks, and Forests
Auto Racing
Horse Racing
Sailing
Baseball
Museums & Halls of Fame
Skiing
Basketball
National Trails
Soccer
Bowling
NCAA Colleges
Tennis
Football
Parks & Forests
Track & Field
Golf
Polo
Wild, Scenic, & Recreational Rivers
Hockey
Rodeo
Lithographed in U.S.A.

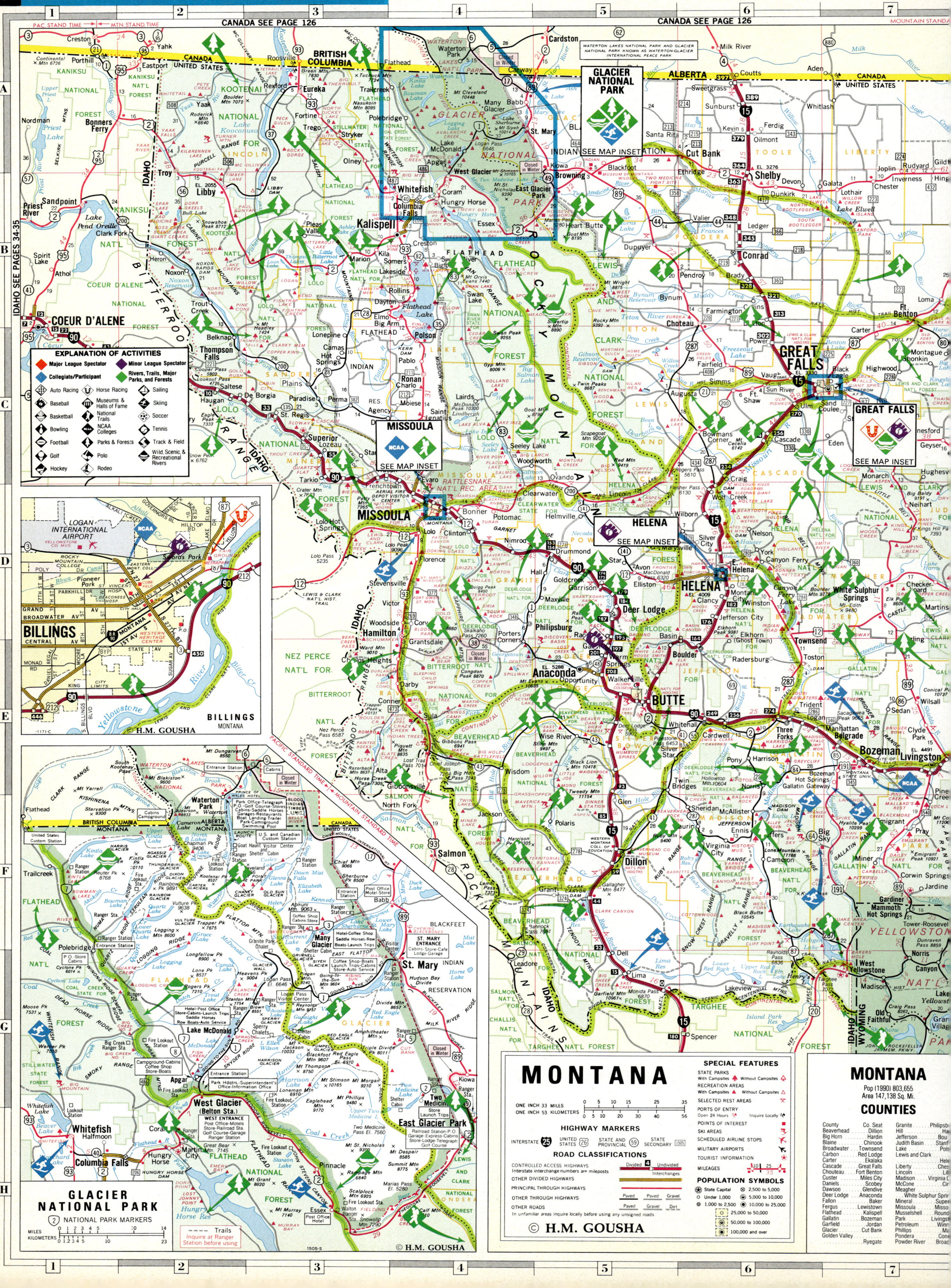
CANADA SEE PAGE 126
BRITISH COLUMBIA
ALBERTA
CANADA
UNITED STATES
IDAHO SEE PAGES 34-35
GLACIER NATIONAL PARK
SEE MAP INSET
GREAT FALLS
SEE MAP INSET
MISSOULA
SEE MAP INSET
HELENA
SEE MAP INSET
EXPLANATION OF ACTIVITIES
Major League Spectator
Minor League Spectator
Collegiate/Participant
Rivers, Trails, Major Parks, and Forests
Auto Racing
Horse Racing
Sailing
Baseball
Museums & Halls of Fame
Skiing
Basketball
National Trails
Soccer
Bowling
NCAA Colleges
Tennis
Football
Parks & Forests
Track & Field
Golf
Polo
Wild, Scenic & Recreational Rivers
Hockey
Rodeo
LOGAN INTERNATIONAL AIRPORT
BILLINGS
BILLINGS
MONTANA
© H.M. GOUSHA
GLACIER NATIONAL PARK
NATIONAL PARK MARKERS
Trails
Inquire at Ranger Station before using
© H.M. GOUSHA
MONTANA
ONE INCH 33 MILLES
ONE INCH 53 KILOMETERS
HIGHWAY MARKERS
INTERSTATE
UNITED STATES
STATE AND PROVINCIAL
STATE SECONDARY
ROAD CLASSIFICATIONS
CONTROLLED ACCESS HIGHWAYS
OTHER DIVIDED HIGHWAYS
PRINCIPAL THROUGH HIGHWAYS
OTHER THROUGH HIGHWAYS
OTHER ROADS
© H.M. GOUSHA
SPECIAL FEATURES
STATE PARKS
RECREATION AREAS
SELECTED REST AREAS
PORTS OF ENTRY
POINTS OF INTEREST
SKI AREAS
SCHEDULED AIRLINE STOPS
MILITARY AIRPORTS
TOURIST INFORMATION
MILEAGES
POPULATION SYMBOLS
MONTANA
Pop (1990) 803,655
Area 147,138 Sq. Mi.
COUNTIES
County Co. Seat
Beaverhead Dillion
Big Horn Hardin
Blaine Chinook
Broadwater Townsend
Carbon Red Lodge
Carter Ekalaka
Cascade Great Falls
Chouteau Fort Benton
Custer Miles City
Daniels Scobey
Dawson Glendive
Deer Lodge Anaconda
Fallon Baker
Fergus Lewistown
Flathead Kalispell
Gallatin Bozeman
Garfield Jordan
Glacier Cut Bank
Golden Valley Ryegate
Granite
Hill
Jefferson
Judith Basin
Lake
Lewis and Clark
Liberty
Lincoln
Madison
McCone
Meagher
White Sulphur
Mineral
Missoula
Musselshell
Park
Petroleum
Phillips
Pondera
Powder River

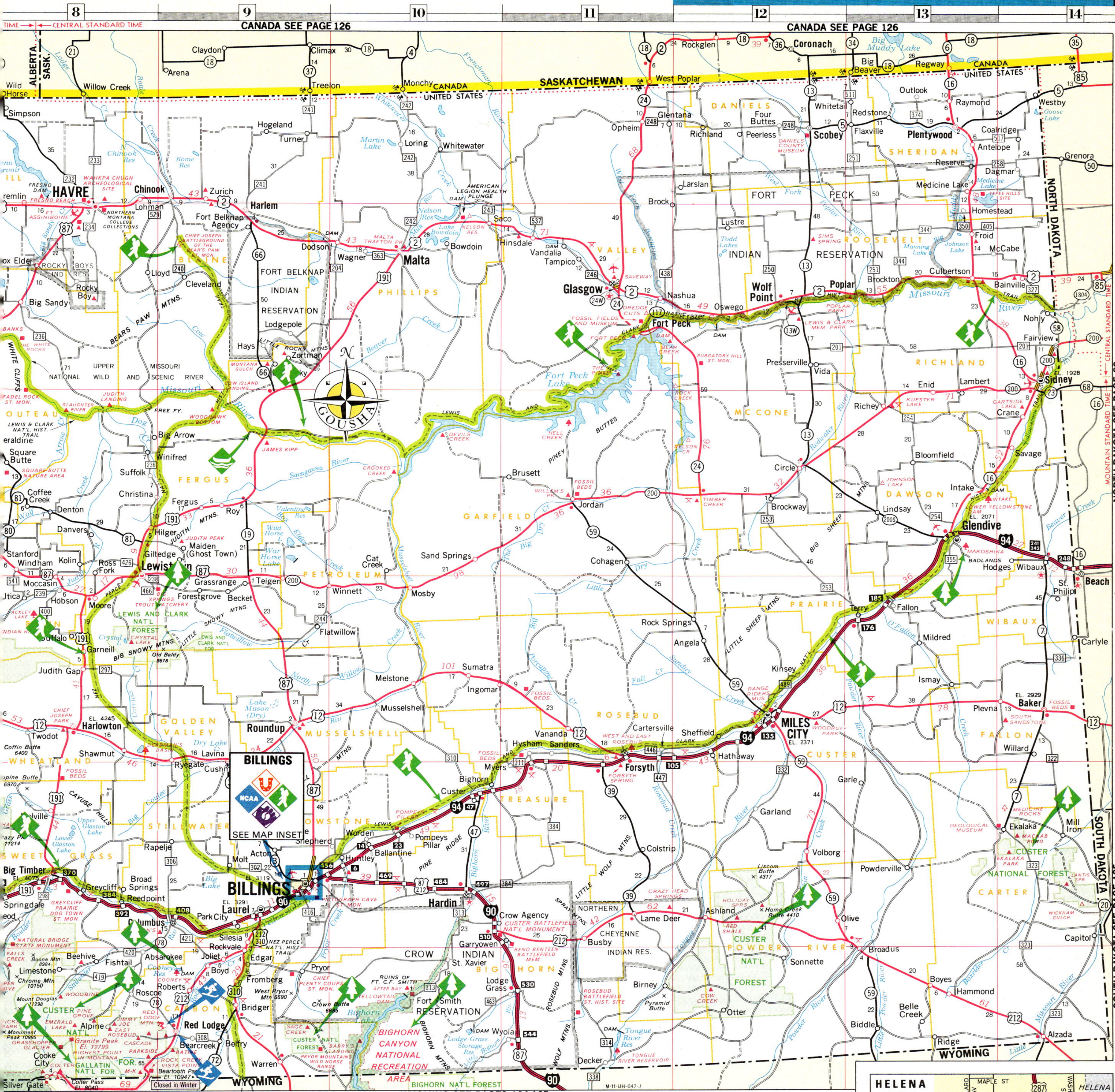

WYOMING SEE PAGES 124-125

Powell ... Deer Lodge
Prairie ... Terry
Ravalli ... Hamilton
Richland ... Sidney
Roosevelt ... Wolf Point
Rosebud ... Forsyth
Sanders ... Thompson Falls
Sheridan ... Plentywood
Silver Bow ... Butte
Stillwater ... Columbus
Sweet Grass ... Big Timber
Teton ... Choteau
Toole ... Shelby
Treasure ... Hysham
Valley ... Glasgow
Wheatland ... Harlowton
Wibaux ... Wibaux
Yellowstone ... Billings

PARTIAL LIST OF
CITIES AND TOWNS

• County Seats

Acton ... E-9
Alder ... F-6
Alzada ... F-14
Anaconda • ... E-5
Antelope ... A-13
Apgar ... A-4
Arlee ... C-4
Ashland ... E-12
Augusta ... C-5
Avon ... D-5
Babb ... A-4
Bainville ... B-14
Baker • ... D-14
Basin ... D-5
Belgrade ... E-7
Belknap ... C-2
Big Arm ... B-3
Big Sandy ... B-8
Big Timber • ... E-8
Bigfork ... B-4
Billings • ... E-9
Birney ... F-11
Blackfoot ... A-5
Bonner ... D-4
Boulder • ... E-6
Bowdoin ... B-10
Bowmans Corner ... C-6
Box Elder ... B-8
Boyd ... F-9
Boyes ... F-13
Bozeman • ... E-7
Bozeman Hot Springs ... E-6
Brady ... B-6
Bridger ... F-9
Broadus • ... F-13
Broadview ... E-9
Brockton ... B-13
Browning ... B-5
Buffalo ... D-8
Busby ... E-11
Butte • ... E-5
Bynum ... B-5
Cameron ... F-6
Canyon Creek ... D-5
Cardwell ... E-6
Charlos Heights ... E-3
Checkerboard ... D-7
Chester • ... B-7
Chinook • ... A-8
Choteau • ... B-5
Circle • ... C-12
Clancy ... D-6
Clearwater ... D-4
Cleveland ... B-9
Clinton ... D-4
Clyde Park ... E-7
Coalridge ... A-13
Coffee Creek ... C-8
Collins ... B-6
Columbia Falls ... B-4
Columbus • ... E-8
Conner ... E-3
Conrad • ... B-6
Cooke City ... F-8
Coram ... B-4
Corwin Springs ... F-7
Craig ... C-6
Crane ... C-14
Culbertson ... B-13
Custer ... E-10
Cut Bank • ... A-6
Dagmar ... A-13
Darby ... E-4
Dayton ... B-3
De Borgia ... C-3
Deer Lodge • ... D-5
Denton ... C-8
Devon ... B-6
Dillon ... F-5
Dixon ... C-3
Dodson ... B-9
Dunkirk ... B-6
Dupuyer ... B-5
Dutton ... B-6
East Glacier Park ... B-4
East Helena ... D-6
Ekalaka ... E-14
Elliston ... D-5
Elmo ... B-3
Emigrant ... F-7
Enid ... B-13
Ennis ... F-6
Essex ... B-4
Ethridge ... B-6
Eureka ... A-3
Evaro ... C-4
Fairfield ... C-6
Ferdig ... A-6
Fergus ... C-9
Flaxville ... A-13
Florence ... D-4
Forestgrove ... D-9
Forsyth ... E-11
Fort Belknap Agency ... B-9
Fort Benton ... B-7
Fort Peck ... B-11
Fort Shaw ... C-6
Fortine ... A-3
Four Buttes ... A-12
Frazer ... B-12
Frenchtown ... D-3
Froid ... B-13
Fromberg ... F-9
Galata ... B-7
Galen ... E-5
Gallatin Gateway ... E-6
Gardiner ... F-7
Garneill ... D-8
Garrison ... D-5
Geraldine ... C-8
Geyser ... C-7
Gildford ... A-7
Glasgow • ... B-11
Glendive • ... C-13
Glentana ... A-11
Great Falls ... C-6
Hall ... D-5
Hamilton • ... D-3
Hammond ... F-13
Hardin ... E-10
Harlem • ... B-9
Harlowton • ... D-8
Harrison ... E-6
Havre • ... A-8
Hays ... B-9
Helena • ... D-6
Hilger ... C-9
Hingham ... B-7
Hinsdale ... B-11
Hogeland ... A-9
Hot Springs ... C-3
Hungry Horse ... B-4
Huson ... C-3
ingomar ... D-10
Inverness ... B-7
Jackson ... F-4
Jefferson City ... D-6
Joliet ... F-9
Joplin ... B-7
Jordan • ... C-11
Judith Gap ... D-8
Kalispell • ... B-3
Kevin ... A-6
Kila ... B-3
Kiowa ... A-5
Kolin ... C-8
Kremlin ... A-8
Lake McDonald ... A-4
Lakeside ... B-3
Lambert ... B-13
Lame Deer ... E-11
Larslan ... A-12
Laurel ... E-9
Laurin ... F-6
Lavina ... D-9
Ledger ... B-6
Lewiston • ... C-8
Libby • ... B-2
Lincoln ... D-5
Lindsay ... C-13
Livingston • ... E-7
Lloyd ... B-8
Lodge Grass ... F-10
Logan ... E-6
Lohman ... B-8
Lolo ... D-4
Lolo Hot Springs ... D-3
Loma ... B-7
Lonepine ... C-3
Loring ... A-10
Lothair ... B-7
Malta • ... B-10
Manhattan ... E-7
Marion ... B-3
Marysville ... D-5
Maxville ... D-5
McAllister ... F-6
Medicine Lake ... A-13
Melstone ... D-10
Melville ... E-8
Miles City • ... D-12
Mill Iron ... E-14
Missoula • ... D-3
Moccasin ... D-8
Monarch ... C-7
Moore ... D-8
Mosby ... D-10
Nashua ... B-11
Neihart ... D-7
Nohly ... B-14
Norris ... E-6
Oilmont ... A-6
Olive ... E-12
Olney ... A-3
Opheim ... A-11
Opporunity ... E-5
Oswego ... B-12
Outlook ... A-13
Pablo ... C-4
Paradise ... C-3
Park City ... E-9
Peerless ... A-12
Pendroy ... B-6
Perma ... C-3
Philipsburg • ... D-5
Plains ... C-3
Pleasant Valley ... B-3
Plentywood • ... A-13
Plevna ... D-13
Polebridge ... A-3
Polson • ... C-4
Poplar ... B-12
Porters Corners ... D-4
Potomac ... D-4
Powderville ... E-13
Presserville ... B-12
Racetrack ... D-5
Ravalli ... C-3
Raymond ... A-13
Raynesford ... C-7
Red Lodge • ... F-9
Redstone ... A-13
Reedpoint ... E-8
Reserve ... A-13
Rexford ... A-4
Richey ... C-13
Richland ... A-12
Ringling ... E-7
Roberts ... F-9
Rockvale ... F-9
Rocky Boy ... B-8
Rollins ... B-4
Ronan ... C-4
Roundup • ... D-9
Roy ... C-9
Rudyard ... A-7
Ryegate • ... E-9
Saco ... B-10
St. Ignatius ... C-4
St. Mary ... A-4
St. Regis ... C-3
Saltese ... C-2
Sand Springs ... C-10
Santa Rita ... A-5
Scobey • ... A-12
Shawmut ... D-8
Shelby • ... B-6
Sheridan ... F-6
Sidney • ... B-14
Silesia ... E-9
Silver Gate ... F-8
Silver Star ... E-5
Simms ... C-6
Simpson ... A-8
Somers ... B-4
Springdale ... E-8
Square Butte ... C-8
Stanford • ... C-8
Star ... D-5
Stryker ... A-3
Sula ... E-4
Sumatra ... D-10
Sun River ... C-6
Sunburst ... A-6
Superior • ... C-3
Swan Lake ... B-4
Swan River ... B-4
Sweetgrass ... A-6
Tarkio ... C-3
Teigen ... D-9
Thompson Falls • ... C-2
Three Forks ... E-6
Toston ... E-6
Townsend • ... E-6
Trailcreek ... A-3
Trego ... A-3
Trout Creek ... B-2
Troy ... A-2
Turner ... A-9
Twin Bridges ... E-5
Valier ... B-6
Vananda ... D-11
Vaughn ... C-6
Victor ... D-4
Virginia City • ... F-6
Volborg ... E-12
Walkerville ... E-5
Warren ... F-9
West Glacier ... B-4
Westby ... A-14
White Sulphur Springs • ... D-7
Whitefish ... B-4
Whitehall ... E-6
Whitetail ... A-12
Whitewater ... A-10
Whitlash ... A-6
Wilsall ... E-7
Windham ... C-8
Winifred ... C-9
Winnett • ... D-10
Winston ... D-6
Wisdom ... E-4
Wise River ... E-5
Wolf Point • ... B-12
Woodside ... D-3
Wyola ... F-11
Zortman ... B-9
Zurich ... A-9

SF-647-J

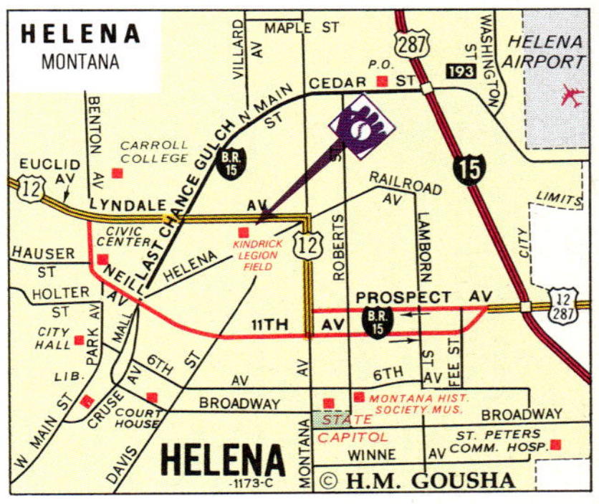

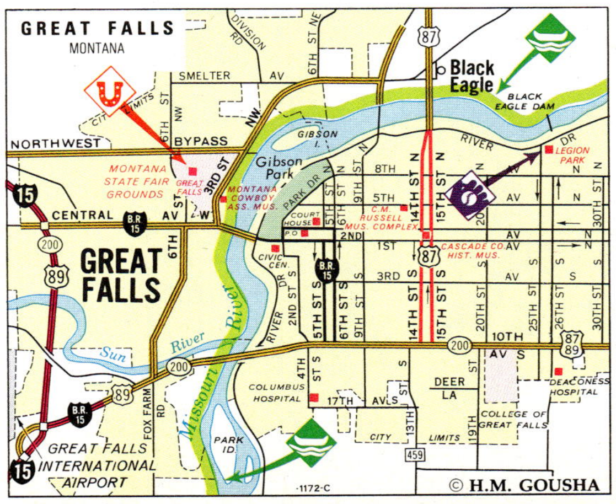

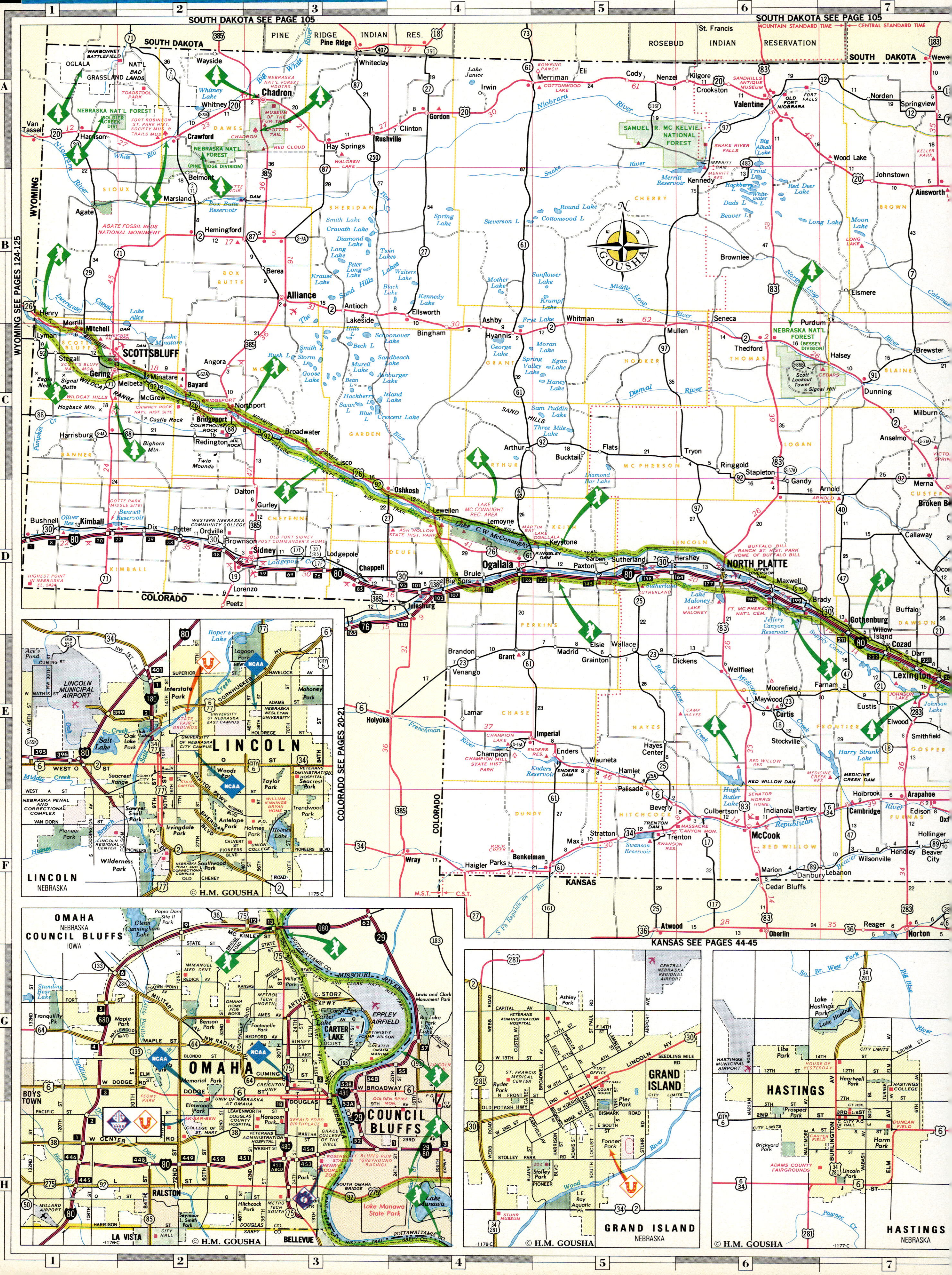
SOUTH DAKOTA SEE PAGE 105
SOUTH DAKOTA SEE PAGE 105
PINE RIDGE INDIAN RES.
ROSEBUD INDIAN RESERVATION
MOUNTAIN STANDARD TIME
CENTRAL STANDARD TIME
SOUTH DAKOTA
WYOMING
WYOMING SEE PAGES 124-125
COLORADO
COLORADO SEE PAGES 20-21
KANSAS
KANSAS SEE PAGES 44-45
Chadron
Crawford
Harrison
Alliance
SCOTTSBLUFF
Gering
Bridgeport
Sidney
Kimball
Ogallala
NORTH PLATTE
Valentine
Ainsworth
Lexington
McCook
Imperial
Gothenburg
Cozad
Julesburg
Rushville
Gordon
Hay Springs
Mullen
Thedford
Broken Bow
Holdrege
Atwood
Oberlin
Norton
SAMUEL R. MC KELVIE NATIONAL FOREST
NEBRASKA NAT'L FOREST
NEBRASKA NAT'L FOREST (BESSEY DIVISION)
LAKE MC CONAUGHT REC. AREA
Lake C.W. McConaughy
GOUSHA
LINCOLN
NEBRASKA
© H.M. GOUSHA
OMAHA NEBRASKA
COUNCIL BLUFFS IOWA
OMAHA
COUNCIL BLUFFS
© H.M. GOUSHA
GRAND ISLAND
NEBRASKA
© H.M. GOUSHA
HASTINGS
NEBRASKA
© H.M. GOUSHA

NEBRASKA

Pop (1990) 1,584,617
Area 77,227 Sq. Mi.

COUNTIES

County	Co. Seat
Adams	Hastings
Antelope	Neligh
Arthur	Arthur
Banner	Harrisburg
Blaine	Brewster
Boone	Albion
Box Butte	Alliance
Boyd	Butte
Brown	Ainsworth
Buffalo	Kearney
Burt	Tekamah
Butler	David City
Cass	Plattsmouth
Cedar	Hartington
Chase	Imperial
Cherry	Valentine
Cheyenne	Sidney
Clay	Clay Center
Colfax	Schuyler
Cuming	West Point
Custer	Broken Bow
Dakota	Dakota City
Dawes	Chadron
Dawson	Lexington
Deuel	Chappell
Dixon	Ponca
Dodge	Fremont
Douglas	Omaha
Dundy	Benkelman
Fillmore	Geneva
Franklin	Franklin
Frontier	Stockville
Furnas	Beaver City
Gage	Beatrice
Garden	Oshkosh
Garfield	Burwell
Gosper	Elwood
Grant	Hyannis
Greeley	Greeley
Hall	Grand Island
Hamilton	Aurora
Harlan	Alma
Hayes	Hayes Center
Hitchcock	Trenton
Holt	O'Neill
Hooker	Mullen
Howard	St. Paul
Jefferson	Fairbury
Johnson	Tecumseh
Kearney	Minden
Keith	Ogallala
Keya Paha	Springview
Kimball	Kimball
Knox	Center
Lancaster	Lincoln
Lincoln	North Platte
Logan	Stapleton
Loup	Taylor
Madison	Madison
McPherson	Tryon
Merrick	Central City
Morrill	Bridgeport
Nance	Fullerton
Nemaha	Auburn
Nuckolls	Nelson
Otoe	Nebraska City
Pawnee	Pawnee City
Perkins	Grant
Phelps	Holdrege
Pierce	Pierce
Platte	Columbus
Polk	Osceola
Red Willow	McCook
Richardson	Falls City
Rock	Bassett
Saline	Wilbur
Sarpy	Papillion
Saunders	Wahoo
Scotts Bluff	Gering
Seward	Seward
Sheridan	Rushville
Sherman	Loup City
Sioux	Harrison
Stanton	Stanton
Thayer	Hebron
Thomas	Thedford
Thurston	Pender
Valley	Ord
Washington	Blair
Wayne	Wayne
Webster	Red Cloud
Wheeler	Bartlett
York	York

PARTIAL LIST OF

CITIES AND TOWNS

• County Seats

Adams	E-12
Ainsworth •	B-7
Albion •	C-10
Allen	B-12
Alliance •	B-3
Alma •	F-8
Altona	B-11
Alvo	D-12
Ames	C-12
Amherst	E-8
Angora	C-2
Anselmo	C-7
Ansley	D-8
Antioch	B-3
Arapahoe	F-7
Arcadia	D-8
Arlington	C-12
Arnold	D-7
Arthur •	C-4
Ashby	B-4
Ashland	D-12
Ashton	D-9
Atkinson	B-8
Atlanta	E-8
Auburn •	E-13
Aurora •	E-10
Axteil	E-8
Ayr	E-9
Bancroft	B-12
Barneston	F-12
Bartlett •	C-9
Bartley	F-6
Bassett •	B-8
Battle Creek	C-11
Bayard	C-2
Bazile Mills	B-10
Beatrice •	F-12
Beaver City	F-7
Belden	B-11
Belgrade	D-10
Bellevue	D-13
Bellwood	D-11
Benedict	D-10
Benkelman •	F-5
Bennet	E-12
Bennington	D-13
Berea	B-3
Bertrand	E-8
Berwyn	D-8
Beverly	F-5
Big Springs	D-4
Bingham	C-4
Blair •	C-13
Bloomfield	B-10
Bloomington	F-8
Blue Hill	F-9
Boelus	D-9
Bow Valley	A-11
Boys Town	D-13
Bradshaw	D-10
Brady	D-6
Brandon	E-4
Brewster •	C-7
Bridgeport •	C-2
Bristow	A-9
Broadwater	C-3
Brock	E-13
Broken Bow •	D-7
Brownson	D-2
Brownville	E-14
Brule	D-4
Burchard	F-12
Burton	A-8
Burwell •	C-8
Bushnell	D-1
Butte •	A-9
Cairo	D-9
Callaway	D-7
Cambridge	F-7
Campbell	F-9
Carroll	B-11
Cedar Bluffs	D-12
Cedar Creek	D-13
Center •	A-10
Central City	D-10
Ceresco	D-12
Chadron •	A-3
Chambers	B-9
Chapman	D-10
Chappell •	D-3
Chester	F-11
Clarks	D-10
Clarkson	C-11
Clatonia	E-12
Clay Center •	E-10
Clearwater	B-9
Cody	A-5
Coleridge	B-11
Colon	D-12
Columbus •	D-11
Concord	B-11
Cortland	E-12
Cotesfield	D-9
Cozad	E-7
Craig	C-12
Crawford	A-2
Creighton	B-10
Creston	C-11
Crete	E-11
Crofton	A-10
Crookston	A-6
Crowell	C-12
Culbertson	F-6
Curtis	E-6
Dakota City	B-12
Dalton	D-2
Danbury	F-6
Dannebrog	D-9
Darr	E-7
Davenport	F-10
David City •	D-11
Dawson	F-13
Daykin	E-11
De Witt	E-12
Decatur	C-12
Denman	E-9
Deweese	E-10
Dickens	E-6
Diller	F-12
Dix	D-2
Dixon	B-11
Dodge	C-12
Doniphan	E-9
Dorchester	E-11
Du Bois	F-13
Dunbar	E-13
Duncan	D-11
Dunning	C-7
Eagle	E-12
Eddyville	D-8
Edison	F-7
Elba	D-9
Eldorado	E-10
Elgin	C-10
Elk City	D-12
Ellis	F-12
Ellsworth	B-4
Elm Creek	E-8
Elmwood	D-12
Elsie	E-5
Elwood •	E-7
Emerson	B-12
Emmet	B-9
Enders	E-5
Endicott	F-11
Ericson	C-9
Eustis	E-7
Ewing	B-9
Exeter	E-11
Fairbury •	F-11
Fairfield	E-10
Fairmont	E-11
Falls City •	F-14
Farnam	E-7
Farwell	D-9
Filley	E-12
Flats	C-5
Fontanelle	C-12
Friend	E-11
Fordyce	A-11
Fort Calhoun	C-13
Foster	B-10
Franklin •	F-9
Fremont •	D-12
Fullerton •	D-10
Funk	E-8
Gandy	C-6
Geneva •	E-11
Genoa	D-10
Gering •	C-1
Gibbon	E-9
Gilead	F-11
Gordon	A-4
Gothenburg	D-7
Grafton	E-10
Grainton	E-5
Grand Island •	D-9
Grant •	E-4
Greeley •	C-9
Greenwood	D-12
Gretna	D-12
Guide Rock	F-10
Gurley	D-3
Hadar	B-11
Haigler	F-4
Halsey	C-7
Hamlet	E-5
Hampton	D-10
Harbine	F-11
Harrison •	A-1
Hartington •	A-11
Harvard	E-10
Hastings •	E-9
Havens	D-10
Hay Springs	A-3
Hayes Center	E-5
Hazard	D-8
Heartwell	E-9
Hebron •	F-11
Hemingford	B-2
Hendley	F-7
Henry	B-1
Herman	C-12
Hershey	D-6
Hildreth	F-8
Holbrook	F-7
Holdrege •	E-8
Holland	E-12
Hollinger	F-7
Holstein	E-9
Homer	B-12
Hooper	C-12
Hordville	D-10
Hoskins	B-11
Howells	C-11
Hubbard	B-12
Humboldt	F-13
Humphrey	C-10
Hyannis •	C-4
Imperial •	E-5
Inavale	F-9
Indianola	F-6
Inman	B-9
Jamison	A-8
Jansen	F-11
Johnson	E-13
Johnstown	B-7
Kearney •	E-8
Kennard	C-13
Keystone	D-5
Kilgore	A-6
Kimball •	D-1
Lakeside	B-3
Lanham	F-12
Laurel	B-11
Lawrence	F-10
Lebanon	F-7
Leigh	C-11
Lemoyne	D-4
Lewellen	D-4
Lewiston	F-12
Lexington •	E-7
Lincoln •	E-12
Lindsay	C-10
Lindy	A-10
Lisco	C-3
Litchfield	D-8
Lodgepole	D-3
Loomis	E-8
Loretto	C-10
Lorton	E-13
Louisville	D-13
Loup City	D-8
Lynch	A-9
Lyons	C-12
Macy	B-12
Madison •	C-11
Madrid	E-5
Manley	D-13
Marion	F-6
Marsland	B-2
Martinsburg	B-11
Maskell	A-11
Mason City	D-8
Max	F-5
Maxwell	D-6
Maywood	E-6
McCock •	F-6
McCool Jct.	E-11
McGrew	C-2
McLean	B-11
Mead	D-12
Meadow	D-13
Meadow Grove	C-10
Melbeta	C-2
Memphis	D-12
Merna	D-7
Merriman	A-5
Milford	E-11
Miller	D-8
Minatare	C-2
Minden •	E-8
Mitchell	C-1
Monowl	A-9
Monroe	C-11
Moorefield	E-6
Morrill	C-1
Morse Bluff	D-12
Mullen •	C-5
Murray	D-13
Naper	A-8
Nebraska City	E-13
Neligh •	B-10
Nelson •	F-10
Nemaha	E-13
Nenzel	A-5
Newcastle	A-11
Newport	B-8
Nickerson	C-12
Niobrara	A-10
Norden	A-7
Norfolk	B-11
Norman	E-9
North Bend	C-12
North Loup	C-9
North Platte •	D-6
Northport	C-2
Oakdale	B-10
Oakland	C-12
Obert	A-11
Oconto	D-7
Octavia	D-11
Odell	F-12
Odessa	E-8
Ogallala •	D-4
Omaha •	D-13
O'Neill	B-9
Orchard	B-9
Ord •	C-8
Oreapolis	D-13
Orleans	F-8
Osceola •	D-11
Oshkosh •	D-4
Osmond	B-11
Overton	E-8
Oxford	F-7
Palisade	E-5
Panama	E-12
Papillion •	D-13
Pawnee City •	F-13
Paxton	D-5
Pender •	B-12
Peru	E-13
Petersburg	C-10
Pickrell	E-12
Pierce •	B-11
Pilger	C-11
Plainview	B-10
Plattsmouth	D-13
Pleasanton	D-8
Polk	D-10
Ponca •	B-12
Potter	D-2
Prague	D-12
Princeton	E-12
Ragan	F-8
Randolph	B-11
Ravenna	D-9
Red Cloud •	F-9
Redington	C-2
Republican City	F-8
Reynolds	F-11
Ringgold	C-6
Rising City	D-11
Riverdale	E-8
Riverton	F-9
Rockville	D-9
Rogers	C-12
Rohrs	E-13
Royal	B-10
Rulo	F-14
Rushville •	A-3
Ruskin	F-10
St. Mary	E-13
St. Paul	D-9
Sargent	C-8
Saronville	E-10
Schuyler •	C-11
Scotia	D-9
Scottsbluff	C-2
Scribner	C-12
Seward •	D-11
Shelby	D-11
Shelton	E-9
Sholes	B-11
Shubert	F-14
Sidney •	D-3
Silver Creek	D-10
Smithfield	E-7
Snyder	C-12
South Sioux City	B-12
Spencer	A-9
Springfield	D-13
Springview •	A-7
Stamford	F-8
Stanton •	C-11
Stapleton •	C-6
Steele City	F-11
Stella	F-13
Sterling	E-12
Stockville •	E-6
Stratton	F-5
Stromsburg	D-11
Stuart	B-8
Sumner	D-8
Superior	F-10
Sutherland	D-5
Sutton	E-10
Swan Lake	B-8
Swedeburg	D-12
Swedehome	D-10
Sweetwater	D-8
Syracuse	E-13
Table Rock	F-13
Tamora	D-11
Taylor •	C-8
Tecumseh •	E-13
Tekamah •	C-13
Thedford •	C-6
Thompson	F-11
Tilden	C-10
Tobias	E-11
Touhy	D-12
Trenton •	F-5
Trumbull	E-10
Tryon •	C-6
Uehling	C-12
Unadilla	E-13
Union	E-13
Upland	F-9
Utica	D-11
Valentine •	A-6
Valley	D-12
Valparaiso	D-12
Venango	E-4
Verdel	A-9
Verdigre	B-10
Verdon	F-13
Vesta	E-12
Virginia	F-12
Waco	E-11
Wahoo •	D-12
Wakefield	B-11
Wallace	E-5
Walthill	B-12
Waterloo	D-12
Wauneta	E-5
Wausa	B-10
Waverly	D-12
Wayne •	B-11
Wayside	A-2
Weeping Water	D-13
Wellfleet	E-6
West Point	C-12
Western	E-11
Westerville	D-8
Whiteclay	A-3
Whitman	B-5
Wilber •	E-11
Wilcox	E-8
Willis	B-12
Willow Island	D-7
Wilsonville	F-7
Winnebago	B-12
Winside	B-11
Winslow	C-12
Wisner	C-12
Wolbach	D-9
Wood Lake	A-7
Wood River	E-9
Wymore	F-12
Wynot	A-11
York •	E-11

SF-648-J

Lithographed in U.S.A.

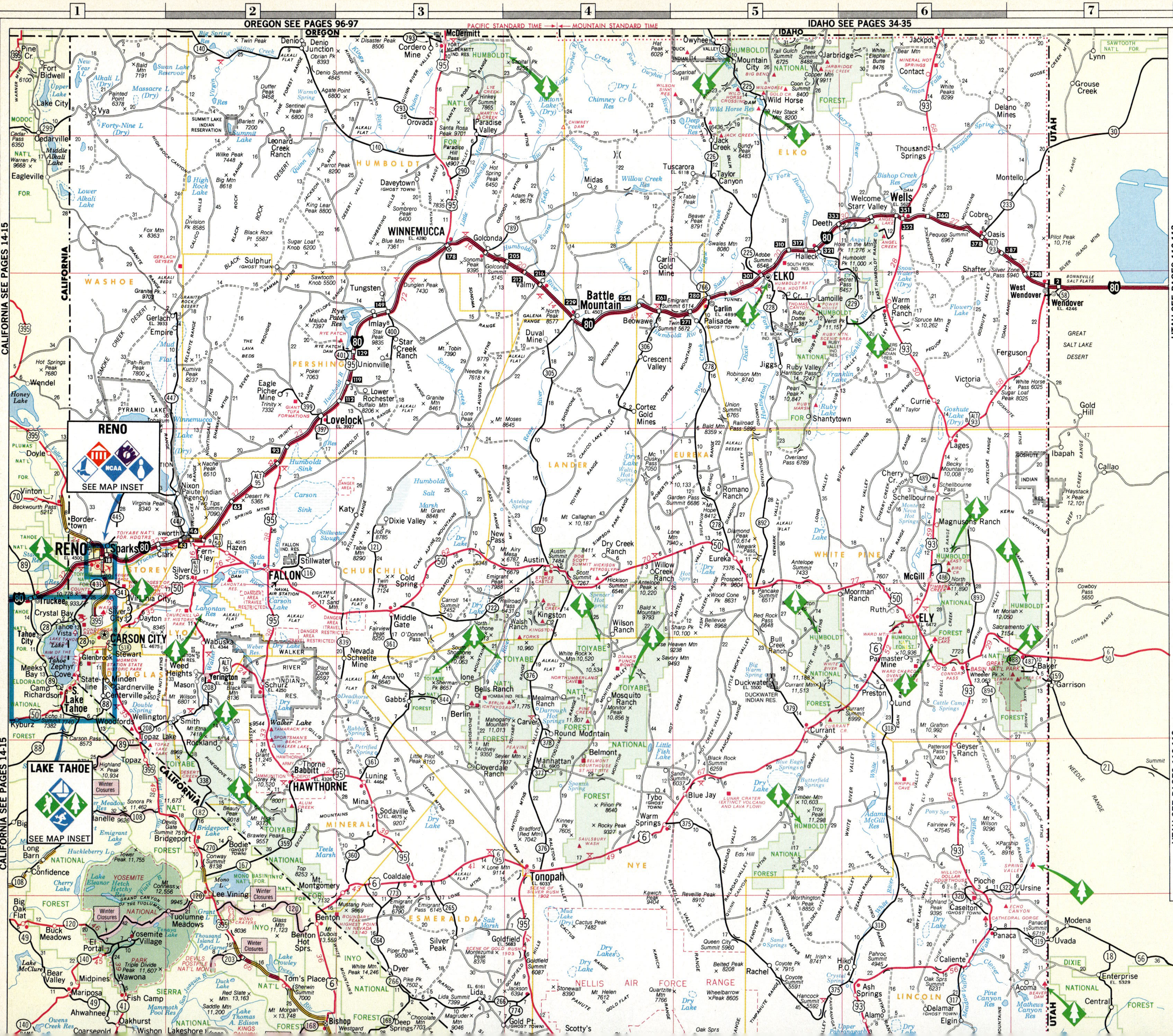

NEVADA

Pop (1990) 1,206,152
Area 110,540 Sq. Mi.

COUNTIES

County	Co. Seat
Churchill	Fallon
Clark	Las Vegas
Douglas	Minden
Elko	Elko
Esmeralda	Goldfield
Eureka	Eureka
Humboldt	Winnemucca
Lander	Austin
Lincoln	Pioche
Lyon	Yerington
Mineral	Hawthorne
Nye	Tonopah
Pershing	Lovelock
Storey	Virginia City
Washoe	Reno
White Pine	Ely

PARTIAL LIST OF

CITIES AND TOWNS

• County Seats

Acoma	G-7
Alamo	G-6
Amargosa Valley	H-4
Ash Meadows Rancho	J-5
Ash Springs	G-6
Austin •	D-4
Babbitt	F-2
Baker	E-7
Battle Mountain	C-4
Beatty	H-4
Belmont	F-4
Beowawe	C-4
Berlin	E-3
Blue Jay	F-5
Boulder Beach	J-6
Boulder City	J-6
Bull Creek Ranch	E-5
Bunkerville	H-7
Cactus Springs	H-5
Caliente	G-6
Carlin	C-5
Carlin Gold Mine	B-4
Carp	H-6
Carson City	E-1
Carver	E-4
Caselton	G-6
Centerville	E-1
Cherry Creek	D-6
Clark	D-1
Cloverdale Ranch	F-3
Coaldale	F-3
Cobre	B-6
Cold Spring	D-3
Contact	A-6
Cordero Mine	A-3
Cortez Gold Mines	C-4
Crescent Valley	C-4
Crystal Bay	E-1
Currant	E-5
Currie	C-6
Daveytown	B-3
Dayton	E-1
Deeth	B-5
Delamar	G-6
Denio	A-2
Denio Junction	A-2
Dixie Valley	D-3
Dry Creek Ranch	D-4
Duckwater	E-5
Duval Mine	C-4
Dyer	G-3
Eagle Picher Mine	C-2
Elgin	G-6
Elko •	C-5
Ely •	E-6
Empire	C-1
Eureka •	D-5
Fallon •	D-2
Ferguson	C-6
Fernley	D-2
Gabbs	E-3
Gardnerville	E-1
Gerlach	C-1
Geyser Ranch	F-6
Glenbrook	E-1
Glendale	H-6
Golconda	B-3
Gold Point	G-4
Goldfield •	G-4
Goodsprings	J-5
Halleck	B-5
Hawthorne •	F-2
Hazen	D-2
Henderson	J-6
Hiko P.O.	G-6
Imlay	C-3
Indian Springs	H-5
Ione	E-3
Jack Creek	B-5
Jackpot	A-6
Jarbridge	A-5
Jean	J-6
Jiggs	C-5
Kingston	E-4
Lamoille	C-5
Las Vegas •	J-5
Laughlin	K-6
Lee	C-5
Leonard Creek Ranch	B-2
Lida	G-3
Logandale	H-6
Lovelock •	C-2
Lower Rochester	C-3
Lund	E-6
Luning	F-3
Magnusons Ranch	D-6
Manhattan	F-4
Mason	E-2
McDermitt	A-3
McGill	D-6
Mealman Ranch	E-4
Mercury	H-5
Mesquite	H-7
Midas	B-4
Middle Gate	E-3
Mina	F-3
Minden •	E-1
Moapa	H-6
Montello	B-6
Moorman Ranch	E-6
Mosquito Ranch	E-4
Mount Charleston	J-5
Mount Montgomery	F-2
Mountain City	A-5
Mountain Springs	J-5
Nelson	K-6
Nevada Scheelite Mine	E-3
New Pass	D-3
Nixon	D-2
North Las Vegas	J-6
Oasis	B-6
Orovada	A-3
Overton	H-6
Owyhee	A-5
Pahrump	J-5
Palisade	C-5
Panaca	G-6
Paymaster Mine	E-6
Pioche •	F-6
Preston	E-6
Rachel	G-5
Reno •	D-1
Rhyolite	H-4
Rockland	F-2
Romano Ranch	D-5
Round Mountain	E-4
Ruby Valley	C-5
Ruth	E-6
Schellbourne	D-6
Schurz	E-2
Scotty's Junction	G-4
Searchlight	K-6
Shafter	B-6
Silver City	E-1
Silver Peak	G-3
Silver Springs	D-2
Sloan	J-6
Smith	E-2
Sparks	D-1
Spring Creek	C-5
Stage Stop	D-6
Star Creek Ranch	C-3
Stateline	E-1
Stateline	K-5
Stewart	E-1
Stillwater	D-2
Sulphur	B-2
Sutcliffe	D-1
Taylor Canyon	B-5
Thorne	F-2
Thousand Springs	B-6
Tonopah •	F-4
Topaz Lake	E-1
Tungsten	C-3
Tuscarora	B-5
Tybo	F-4
Unionville	C-3
Ursine	F-7
Valmy	C-4
Virginia City •	E-1
Vya	A-1
Wabuska	E-2
Wadsworth	D-1
Walsh Ranch	E-4
Warm Creek Ranch	C-6
Warm Springs	F-4
Weed Heights	E-2
Welcome Starr Valley	B-6
Wellington	E-1
Wells	B-6
Wild Horse	A-5
Willow Creek Ranch	D-6
Wilson Ranch	E-4
Winnemucca	B-3
Yerington •	E-2
Zephyr Cove	E-1

SF-649-J

NEVADA
H.M. GOUSHA
LAS VEGAS NEVADA
RENO NEVADA
LAKE TAHOE REGION
LAKE MEAD NATIONAL RECREATION AREA
ARIZONA SEE PAGES 10-11
CALIFORNIA SEE PAGES 16-17
PACIFIC STANDARD TIME
MOUNTAIN STANDARD TIME

NEW HAMPSHIRE
PARTIAL LIST OF
CITIES AND TOWNS
• County Seats
VERMONT
NEW HAMPSHIRE
COUNTIES
VERMONT
COUNTIES
MANCHESTER
NEW HAMPSHIRE
CONCORD
NEW HAMPSHIRE
BURLINGTON
VERMONT
© H.M. GOUSHA
CANADA SEE PAGE 127
MAINE SEE PAGES 50-51
NEW YORK SEE PAGE 83
BURLINGTON SEE MAP INSET
LAKE CHAMPLAIN
MONTPELIER
BARRE
NEWPORT
ST. JOHNSBURY
BERLIN
LITTLETON
MIDDLEBURY
PLATTSBURGH

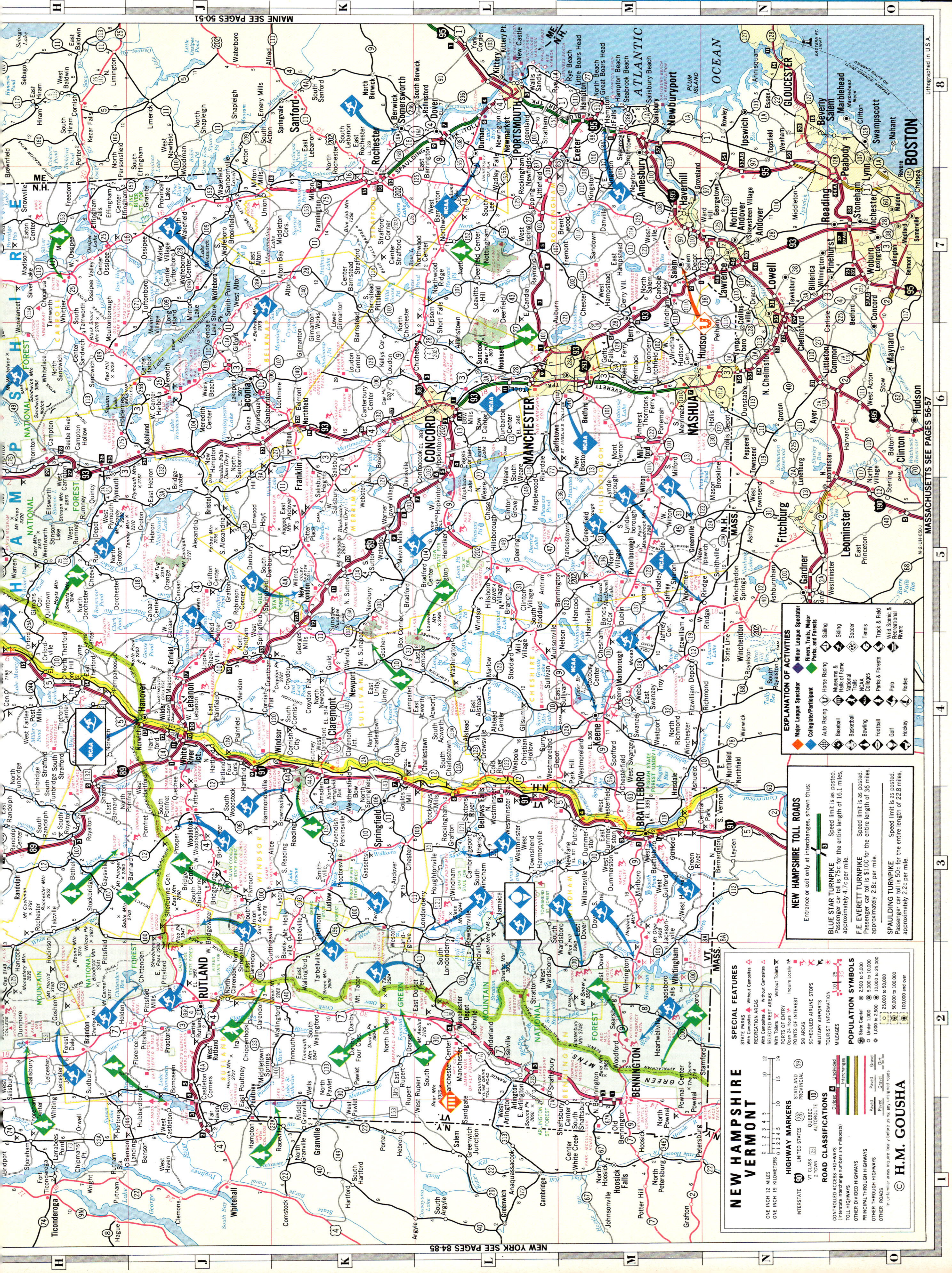
MAINE SEE PAGES 50-51
NEW YORK SEE PAGES 84-85
MASSACHUSETTS SEE PAGES 56-57
NEW HAMPSHIRE VERMONT
© H.M. GOUSHA
ATLANTIC OCEAN
NEW HAMPSHIRE TOLL ROADS
BLUE STAR TURNPIKE Passenger car toll is 75¢ for the entire length of 16.1 miles, approximately 4.7¢ per mile.
F.E. EVERETT TURNPIKE Passenger car toll is $1.00 for the entire length of 36 miles, approximately 2.8¢ per mile.
SPAULDING TURNPIKE Passenger car toll is 50¢ for the entire length of 22.8 miles, approximately 2.2¢ per mile.
EXPLANATION OF ACTIVITIES
SPECIAL FEATURES
HIGHWAY MARKERS
ROAD CLASSIFICATIONS
POPULATION SYMBOLS
CONCORD
MANCHESTER
NASHUA
PORTSMOUTH
BOSTON
RUTLAND
BENNINGTON
BRATTLEBORO
KEENE
LACONIA
Lithographed in U.S.A.

NEW JERSEY

Pop (1990) 7,748,634
Area 7,836 Sq. Mi.

COUNTIES

County	Co. Seat
Atlantic	Mays Landing
Bergen	Hackensack
Burlington	Mount Holly
Camden	Camden
Cape May	Cape May C.H.
Cumberland	Bridgeton
Essex	Newark
Cloucester	Woodbury
Hudson	Jersey City
Hunterdon	Flemington
Mercer	Trenton
Middlesex	New Brunswick
Monmouth	Freehold
Morris	Morristown
Ocean	Toms River
Passaic	Paterson
Salem	Salem
Somerset	Somerville
Sussex	Newton
Union	Elizabeth
Warren	Belvidere

CITIES AND TOWNS

• County Seats

Absecon L-6
Albion J-4
Aldine L-3
Allamuchy C-5
Allendale C-7
Allentown G-6
Allerton E-5
Alloway K-3
Alpha E-4
Anderson D-5
Andover C-5
Ardena G-7
Arneytown H-6
Asbury D-4
Asbury Park G-8
Atco J-5
Atlantic City M-6
Atlantic Highlands F-8
Atsion K-5
Auburn K-3
Audubon J-4
Augusta B-5
Avalon N-5
Avon by the Sea G-8
Awosting B-7
Bakersville G-5
Balesville B-5
Baptistown E-4
Barbertown F-4
Bargaintown L-6
Barnegat K-7
Barnegat Beach J-7
Barnegat Light J-8
Barnsboro J-4
Bartley D-5
Basking Ridge D-6
Bay Head H-8
Bay Point M-3
Bay Side K-7
Bayonne E-7
Bayside L-3
Bayville J-7
Beach Haven L-7
Beach Haven Crest K-7
Beach Haven Park K-7
Beach Haven Terrace K-7
Beachwood J-7
Beattystown D-5
Beaver Lake B-6
Beaver Run B-6
Bedminster E-5
Beemerville B-5
Belcoville L-5
Belle Mead F-6
Belleplain M-5
Belleville D-7
Bellmawr J-4
Belmar G-8
Belvedere • D-4
Bergenfield C-8
Berkeley Heights E-6
Berkshire Valley C-6
Berlin J-4
Bernardsville D-6
Beverly H-4
Bivalve M-4
Blackwood J-4
Blairstown C-4
Blawenburg F-5
Bloomfield D-7
Bloomingdale C-7
Bloomsbury E-4
Blue Anchor K-5
Bogota D-8
Bonhamtown F-7
Boonton C-6
Bordentown G-5
Bound Brook E-6
Bradevelt F-7
Bradley Beach G-8
Branchville B-5
Brant Beach K-7
Brass Castle D-4
Breton Woods H-8
Bricktown H-7
Bricksboro M-4
Bridgeboro H-5
Bridgeport J-3
Bridgeton • L-3
Bridgeville D-4
Brielle H-8
Brigantine L-7
Brighton C-5
Brighton Beach K-7
Broadway D-4
Brookside D-6
Brookville J-7
Brotmanville L-4
Browns B-6
Browns Mills H-6
Browntown F-7
Buck Hill M-5
Buckshutem M-4
Budd Lake D-5
Buddtown J-5
Buena L-4
Bunnvale E-5
Burlington H-5
Burrs Mills J-6
Butler C-7
Buttzville D-4
Byram F-4
Caldwell D-7

Everittstown E-4
Evesboro J-5
Ewan K-4
Ewanville H-5
Ewingville G-5
Fair Haven F-8
Fair Lawn C-7
Fairfield D-7
Fairmount D-5
Fairton L-3
Fairview H-4
Fairview J-5
Fanwood E-7
Far Hills D-6
Farmingdale G-7
Five Points B-5
Flanders D-5
Flatbrookville B-4
Flemington • F-5
Florence H-5
Florham Park D-6
Folsom K-5
Forked River J-7
Fort Dix H-6
Fort Lee D-8
Fort Plains G-7
Fortescue M-3
Four Mile J-6
Franklin B-6
Franklin Lakes C-7
Franklin Park F-6
Franklinville K-4
Fredon C-5
Freehold • G-7
Freewood Acres G-7
Frenchtown E-4
Fries Mill K-4
Gandys Beach M-3
Garfield D-8
Garwood E-7
Georgia G-7
Gibbsboro J-4
Gibbstown J-3
Gilford Park H-7
Gillette E-6
Gladstone D-5
Glassboro K-4
Glasser C-5
Glen Gardner E-4
Glen Rock C-7
Glenwood A-6
Gloucester City J-4
Gordons Corner G-7
Goshen N-5
Gouldtown L-4
Gravelly Run L-5
Great Meadows D-5
Green Bank K-6
Green Creek N-5
Green Village D-6
Greendell C-5
Greenville H-7
Greenwich L-3
Griggstown F-6
Gum Tree Corner L-3
Hackensack • C-8
Hackettstown D-5
Haddon Heights J-4
Haddonfield J-4
Hagerville L-2
Hainesburg C-4
Hainesport H-5
Hainesville A-5
Haledon C-7
Halsey B-5
Hamburg B-6
Hamden E-5
Hammonton K-5
Hampton D-4
Hampton Furnace J-5
Hampton Lakes J-5
Hancocks Bridge L-2
Haneys Mill B-5
Hanover Furnace H-6
Harbourton F-5
Hardistonville B-6
Harlingen F-6
Harmersville L-3
Harmony D-4
Harrington Park C-8
Harris Station J-6
Harrisonville K-2
Harrisonville K-3
Hartford H-5
Harvey Cedars K-7
Haskell C-7
Hawthorne C-7
Hazen D-4
Hazlet F-7
Headquarters F-5
Hedger House J-6
Helslerville M-4
Helmetta F-6
Herbertsville H-8
Hermon K-6
Hermon C-4
Hesstown M-4
Hewitt B-7
Hibernia C-6
High Bridge E-5
Highland Lake B-6
Highland Park F-6

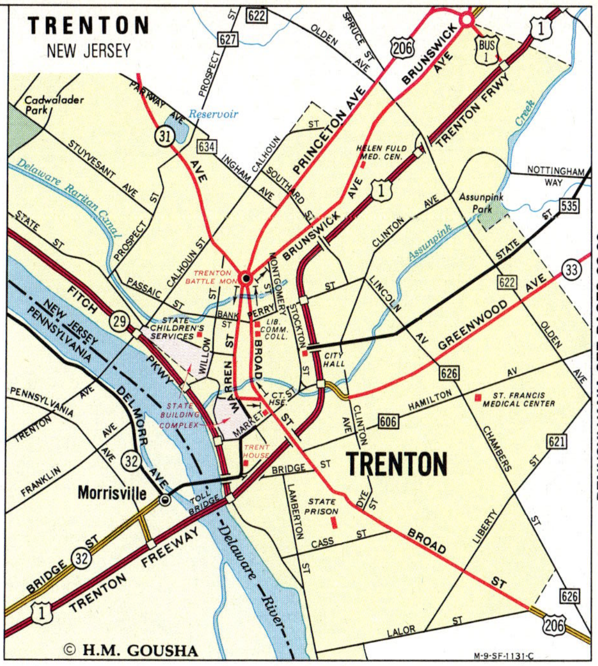

Cape May	O-5
Cape May C.H. •	N-5
Cape May Point	O-4
Cardiff	L-6
Carlls Corner	L-3
Carlstadt	D-7
Carmel	L-4
Carneys Point	K-2
Carrs Corners	G-7
Carteret	E-7
Cedar Brook	K-5
Cedar Run	K-7
Cedarville	M-4
Cedarwood Park	H-7
Centerton	H-4
Centerton	L-4
Centerville	E-5
Center Grove	M-4
Chairville	J-5
Chambers Corners	H-5
Chatham	D-6
Chatsworth	J-6
Cherry Hill	J-4
Cherryville	E-5
Chesilhurst	K-5
Chester	D-5
Chesterfield	H-6
Churchtown	K-2
Cinnaminson	H-4
Clarksburg	G-6
Clarksville	G-5
Clayton	K-4
Clementon	J-4
Clermont	N-5
Clinton	E-4
Closter	C-8
Clover Hill	F-5
Cohansey	L-3
Cold Springs	O-4
Colesville	A-6
Colliers Mills	H-6
Collingswood	J-4
Cologne	L-6
Colts Neck	G-7
Columbus	H-5
Conovertown	L-6
Convent Station	D-6
Cookstown	H-6
Copper Hill	F-5
Corbin City	M-5
Cornish	D-4
Country Lakes	J-6
Cranvury	G-6
Cranbury Station	G-6
Cresskill	C-8
Cross Keys	K-4
Crosswicks	G-6
Crystal Lake	C-7
Culvers Inlet	B-5
Cumberland	M-4
Daretown	K-3
Dayton	F-6
Deacons	H-5
Deal	G-8
Deans	F-6
Deerfield	L-3
Delair	H-4
Delaware	C-4
Delmont	M-4
Dennisville	M-5
Dividing Creek	M-4
Dorchester	M-4
Dorthy	L-5
Double Trouble	J-7
Dover	D-6
Downstown	L-4
Dukes Bridge	J-6
Dumont	C-8
Dunbarton	K-5
Dunellen	E-6
Dutch Neck	G-6
East Brunswick	F-6
East Keansburg	F-8
East Millstone	E-6
East Vineland	L-4
East Windsor	G-6
Eatontown	G-8
Edgewater Park	H-5
Edinburg	G-6
Edison	E-6
Egg Harbor City	L-5
Eldora	M-5
Elizabeth •	E-7
Elm	K-5
Elmer	K-4
Elwood	K-5
Emerson	C-8
Englewood	C-8
Englewood Cliffs	D-8
Englishtown	G-6
Erma	O-5
Erskine	B-7
Espanong	C-5
Essex Fells	D-7
Estell Manor	L-5
Estellville	L-5
Holgate	L-7
Holiday City	H-7
Holly Park	J-7
Holmdel	F-7
Holmeson	G-6
Hopatcong	C-5
Hope	C-4
Hopewell	F-5
Hornerstown	H-6
Howardsville	J-7
Howell	G-7
Huntsville	C-5
Hurdtown	C-6
Hurffville	J-4
Hutchinson	D-4
Indian Mills	J-5
Interlaken	G-8
Ironia	D-5
Irvington	D-7
Island Heights	J-7
Jackson	H-7
Jacksonburg	C-4
Jacksonville	H-5
Jacobstown	H-6
Jamesburg	F-6
Jefferson	K-4
Jenkins Neck	K-6
Jersey City •	D-8
Jerseyville	G-7
Jobstown	H-5
Johnsonburg	C-5
Juliustown	H-5
Jutland	E-4
Keansburg	F-7
Kearny	D-7
Kendall Park	F-6
Kenilworth	E-7
Kenvil	D-6
Keswick Grove	H-7
Keyport	F-7
Kings Grant	J-5
Kingston	F-6
Kinnelon	C-6
Kirby's Mill	J-5
Kresson	J-5
Lafayette	B-5
Lake Hiawatha	D-6
Lake Mohawk	C-5
Lake Pine	J-5
Lakehurst	H-7
Lakewood	H-7
Lambertville	F-5
Lamington	E-5
Lanoka Harbor	J-7
Larisons Corner	F-5
Laurence Harbor	F-7
Lavallette	H-8
Lawrenceville	G-5
Layton	B-5
Lebanon	E-5
Ledgewood	D-5
Leeds Point	L-6
Leektown	K-6
Leesburg	M-4
Leonardo	F-8
Liberty Corner	E-6
Libertyville	B-6
Lincoln Park	C-7
Lincroft	F-7
Linden	E-7
Lindenwold	J-4
Linvale	F-5
Linwood	M-6
Little Silver	F-8
Little York	E-4
Littleton	D-6
Livingston	D-7
Locktown	F-4
Lockwood	C-5
Lodi	D-7
Long Branch	G-8
Long Valley	D-5
Longport	M-6
Loveladies	K-8
Lower Bank	K-6
Lower Harmony	D-4
Lumberton	H-5
Lyons	E-6
Macopin	C-6
Madison	D-6
Magnolia	J-4
Malaga	K-4
Manahawkin	K-7
Manalapan	G-6
Manasquan	H-8
Mansfield Square	H-5
Mantoloking	H-8
Mantua	J-4
Manunkachunk	D-4
Manville	E-6
Maplewood	D-7
Marcella	C-6
Margate City	M-6
Marksboro	C-5
Marlboro	G-7
Marlton	J-5
Marmora	M-5
Marshalls Corner	F-5
Martinsville	E-6
New Shrewsbury	G-7
New Vernon	D-6
New Village	D-4
Newark	D-7
Newfield	L-4
Newfoundland	C-6
Newport	M-3
Newton •	C-5
Newtonville	L-5
Norburys Landing	N-4
Norma	L-4
Normandy Beach	H-8
Normanock	B-5
North Arlington	D-7
North Beach	K-7
North Beach Haven	K-7
North Branch	E-5
North Branch Station	E-5
North Brunswick	F-6
North Cape May	O-4
North Haledon	C-7
North Highlands Beach	N-4
North Plainfield	E-6
North Wildwood	O-5
Northfield	D-7
Northfield	M-6
Northvale	C-8
Nutley	D-7
Oak Grove	E-4
Oak Ridge	C-6
Oak Tree	E-6
Oakhurst	G-8
Oakland	C-7
Oaklyn	J-4
Oakville	M-5
Ocean City	M-6
Ocean Gate	J-7
Ocean View	N-5
Oceanport	G-8
Oceanville	L-6
Ogdensburg	C-6
Old Bridge	F-7
Oldwick	E-5
Olivet	L-4
Ongs Hat	J-5
Oradell	C-8
Orange	D-7
Othello	L-3
Oxford	D-4
Paisley	J-6
Palatine	L-3
Palmyra	H-4
Panther Valley	C-5
Paramus	C-8
Parkertown	K-7
Parsippany-Troy Hills	D-6
Passaic	D-7
Paterson •	C-7
Pattenburg	E-4
Paulina	C-4
Paulsboro	J-3
Peaback	E-5
Pecks Corner	L-3
Pedricktown	J-3
Pellettown	B-5
Pemberton	H-5
Penn Beach	K-2
Pennington	F-5
Pennsauken	H-4
Penns Grove	K-2
Penns Neck	F-5
Pennsville	K-2
Penny Pot	K-5
Penton	K-3
Penwell	D-5
Pequannock	C-7
Pequest	D-4
Perrineville	G-6
Perth Amboy	F-7
Petersburg	D-5
Petersburg	M-5
Phillipsburg	E-4
Pine Hill	J-4
Pinewald	J-7
Piscataway	E-6
Pitman	K-4
Pittstown	E-4
Plainfield	E-6
Plainsboro	F-6
Pleasant Grove	D-5
Pleasant Mills	K-5
Pleasant Plains	H-7
Pleasant Run	E-5
Pleasant Valley	D-4
Pleasantville	L-6
Pluckemin	E-6
Plumbsock	B-5
Point Pleasant	H-8
Point Pleasant Beach	H-8
Pole Tavern	K-3
Polkville	C-4
Pomona	L-6
South Branch	E-5
South Brunswick	F-6
South Dennis	N-5
South Orange	D-7
South Plainfield	E-6
South River	F-7
South Seaville	N-5
Southard	G-7
Sparta	C-5
Speedwell	J-6
Spotswood	F-6
Spray Beach	K-7
Spring Lake	G-8
Spring Lake Heights	G-8
Springdale	C-5
Springtown	E-4
Stafford Forge	K-7
Staffordville	K-7
Stanhope	C-5
Stanton	E-5
Stanton Ste.	E-5
Wildwood	O-5
Wildwood Crest	O-5
Williamstown	K-4
Willingboro	H-5
Windsor	G-6
Winslow	K-5
Woodbine	M-5
Woodbury •	J-4
Woodbury Heights	J-4
Woodcliff Lake	C-8
Woodlane	H-5
Woodmansie	J-6
Woodport	C-6
Woodruffs Gap	C-5
Woods Tavern	E-5
Woodstock	C-6
Woodstown	K-3
Wrightstown	H-5
Yellow Frame	C-5
Yorketown	K-3
Zion	F-5

SF-651-J

NEW JERSEY TOLL ROADS

Entrance or exit only at interchanges, shown thus: [5 Interchange — Service Area]

Space limitations prevent showing all interchanges on this map.

NEW JERSEY TURNPIKE

Speed limit is as posted. Passenger car toll is $2.70 for the main route of 118 miles, approximately 2.3c per mile. Interchange No. 6 connects only with the Pennsylvania Turnpike. No. 10 connects with Interstate 287. No. 11 connects with the Garden State Parkway. No. 14C connects with the Holland Tunnel, and 16E with the Lincoln Tunnel. No. 15W connects with Interstate 280. No's. 18E and 18W connect with the George Washington Bridge and Interstate 80.

GARDEN STATE PARKWAY

Speed limit is as posted. Passenger car toll is $3.85 for the entire length of 173 miles, approximately 2.2c per mile. 35c is collected at each toll area.
Interchange numbers shown on map along the Garden State Parkway also indicates the mileage from the southern terminus at Cape May.

ATLANTIC CITY EXPRESSWAY

Speed limit is as posted. Passenger car toll is $1.25 for the entire length of 44 miles, approximately 2.8c per mile. 10c, 25c or $1.00 is collected at each toll area. Access is limited as indicated below:

28 Complete Interchange — 14W Westbound Entrance-Eastbound Exit

31E Eastbound Entrance-Westbound Exit

Interchange numbers shown on map also indicate the mileage from Atlantic City.

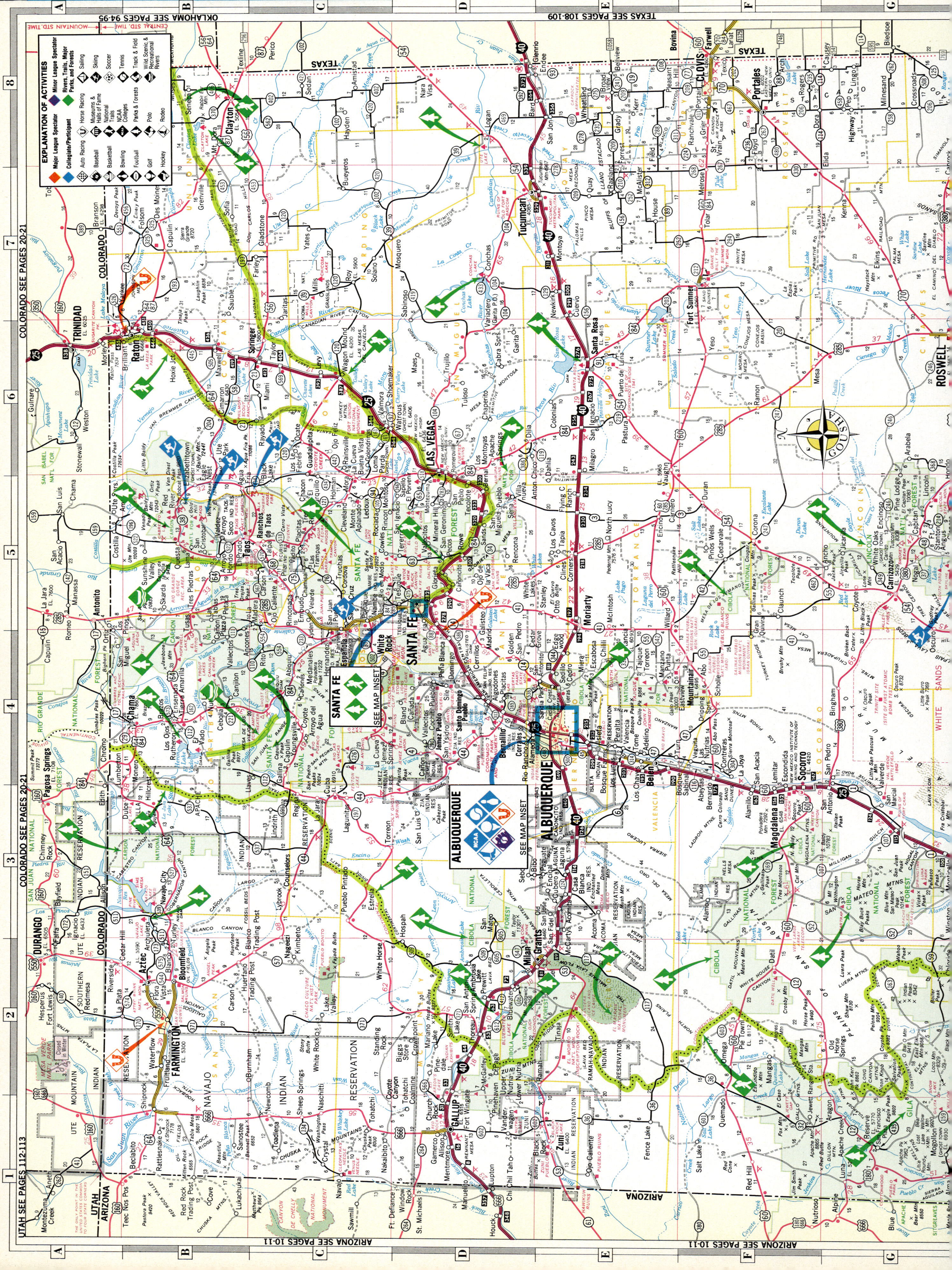
EXPLANATION OF ACTIVITIES
Major League Spectator
Minor League Spectator
Collegiate/Participant
Rivers, Trails, Major Parks, and Forests
Auto Racing
Baseball
Basketball
Bowling
Football
Golf
Hockey
Horse Racing
Museums & Halls of Fame
National Trails
NCAA Colleges
Parks & Forests
Polo
Rodeo
Sailing
Skiing
Soccer
Tennis
Track & Field
Wild, Scenic & Recreational Rivers
COLORADO SEE PAGES 20-21
OKLAHOMA SEE PAGES 94-95
TEXAS SEE PAGES 108-109
ARIZONA SEE PAGES 10-11
UTAH SEE PAGES 112-113
ALBUQUERQUE
SEE MAP INSET
SANTA FE
SEE MAP INSET
SANTA FE
ALBUQUERQUE
LAS VEGAS
ROSWELL
FARMINGTON
GALLUP
CLOVIS
TUCUMCARI
RATON
SOCORRO
TRINIDAD
DURANGO
Santa Rosa
Portales
Grants
Belen
Moriarty
Taos
Española
Carrizozo
Magdalena

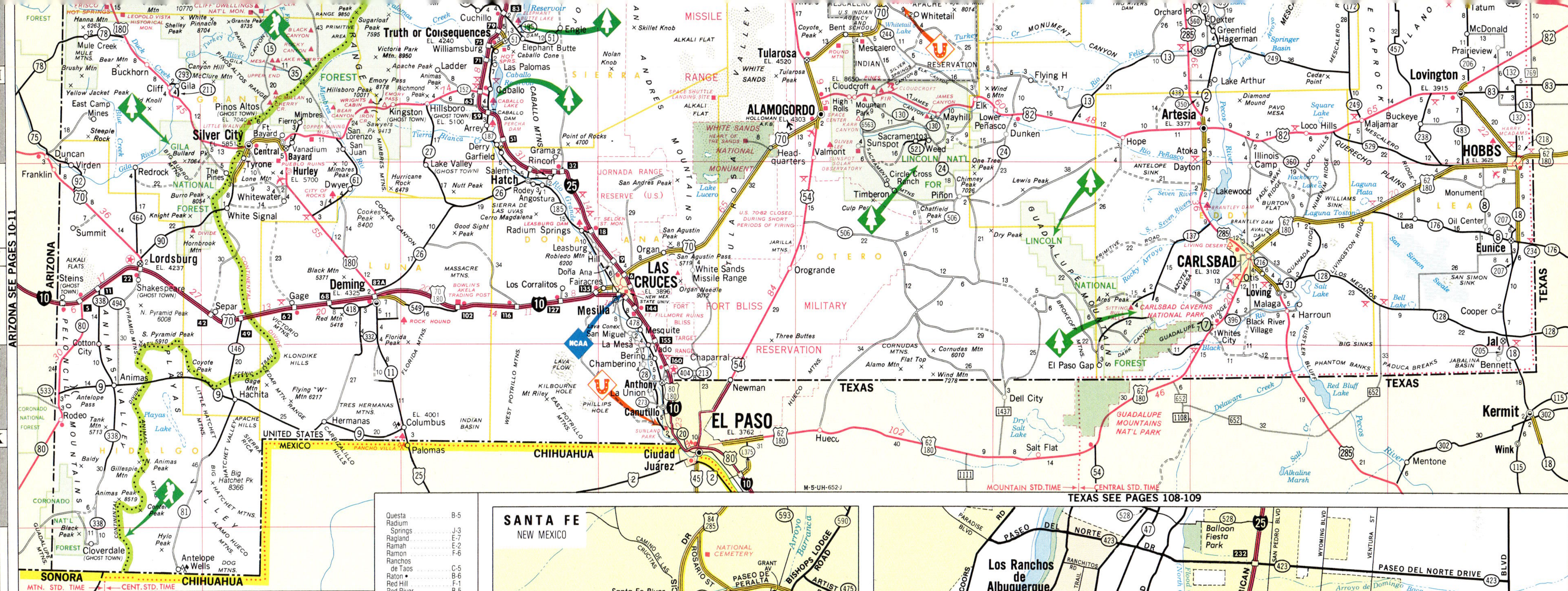

NEW MEXICO

Pop (1990) 1,521,779
Area 121,510 Sq. Mi.

COUNTIES

County	Co. Seat
Bernalillo	Albuquerque
Catron	Reserve
Chaves	Roswell
Cibola	Grants
Colfax	Raton
Curry	Clovis
De Baca	Fort Sumner
Dona Ana	Las Cruces
Eddy	Carlsbad
Grant	Silver City
Guadalupe	Santa Rosa
Harding	Mosquero
Hidalgo	Lordsburg
Lea	Lovington
Lincoln	Carrizozo
Los Alamos	Los Alamos
Luna	Deming
McKinley	Gallup
Mora	Mora
Otero	Alamogordo
Quay	Tucumcari
Rio Arriba	Tierra Amarilla
Roosevelt	Portales
Sandoval	Bernalillo
San Juan	Aztec
San Miguel	Las Vegas
Santa Fe	Santa Fe
Sierra	Truth or Consequences
Socorro	Socorro
Taos	Taos
Torrance	Estancia
Union	Clayton
Valencia	Los Lunas

PARTIAL LIST OF

CITIES AND TOWNS

• County Seats

Abiquiu	C-4
Abo	F-4
Adelino	E-4
Agua Fria	B-5
Alameda	D-4
Alamogordo •	H-4
Albuquerque •	E-3
Alma	G-1
Amistad	C-8
Angostura	J-3
Animas	K-1
Anthony	K-4
Apache Creek	G-1
Apache Springs	D-6
Aplanado	C-5
Arabela	G-6
Aragon	G-1
Arch	F-8
Archuleta	B-2
Arroyo Hondo	B-5
Artesia	H-6
Aztec •	B-2
Bayard	H-2
Beclabito	B-1
Belen	E-4
Bent	H-5
Bernalillo •	D-4
Bibo	D-3
Bingham	G-4
Black Lake	C-5
Black Rock	E-1
Blanco	B-2
Bloomfield	B-2
Bluewater	D-2
Bosque Farms	E-4
Brazos	B-4
Broadview	E-8
Buckeye	H-8
Buckhorn	H-1
Buena Vista	C-6
Bueyeros	C-7
Caballo	H-3
Canon	D-4
Canoncito	D-5
Capitan	G-5
Caprock	G-7
Capulin	B-7
Capulin	C-4
Carlsbad •	J-7
Carrizozo •	G-5
Carson	C-5
Causey	G-8
Cebolla	B-4
Cedar Crest	E-4
Cedar Hill	A-2
Cedarvale	F-5
Central	H-2
Chacon	C-5
Chama	B-4
Chamisal	C-5
Cimarron	B-6
Clayton •	B-8
Cliff	H-1
Clines Corners	E-5
Cloudcroft	H-5
Clovis • 31,194	F-8
Columbus	K-3
Conchas	D-7
Contreras	F-4
Costilla	A-5
Counselors	C-3
Coyote	C-4
Crossroads	G-8
Crystal	C-1
Cuba	C-3
Cuchillo	H-3
Cuervo	E-7
Datil	F-2
Deming •	J-2
Derry	H-3
Des Moines	B-7
Dilia	D-6
Dora	F-8
Dulce	B-3
Duran	F-5
Dwyer	J-2
Eagle Nest	B-5
Edgewood	E-4
El Porvenir	D-5
El Prado	B-5
El Rito	C-4
El Turquillo	C-5
Elephant Butte	H-3
Elida	G-8
Elizabethtown	B-5
Elk	H-5
Elkins	G-7
Embudo	C-5
Encino	E-5
Espanola	C-4
Estancia •	E-4
Eunice	J-8
Fairacres	J-3
Farley	C-7
Farmington	B-2
Folsom	B-7
Fort Bayard	H-2
Fort Sumner •	F-7
Fruitland	B-2
Galisteo	D-5
Gallina	C-4
Gallup •	D-1
Garfield	H-3
Gila	H-1
Glencoe	G-5
Glenwood	G-1
Golden	D-4
Grady	E-8
Grants	E-2
Greenfield	H-7
Grenville	B-7
Grier	F-8
Hagerman	H-7
Hatch	J-3
Headquarters	H-4
Hernandez	C-4
High Rolls	H-5
Highway	G-8
Hillsboro	H-3
Hobbs	H-8
Holman	C-5
Hondo	G-5
Hope	H-6
House	E-7
Hoxie Junction	B-6
Huerfano Trading Post	B-2
Hurley	J-2
Isleta	E-4
Jal	J-8
Jemez Pueblo	D-4
Jemez Springs	C-4
Kenna	G-7
Kingston	H-2
La Cueva	C-6
La Jara	C-3
La Joya	F-4
La Mesilla	J-4
La Plata	A-2
Las Cruces	J-4
Las Nutrias	F-4
Las Trampas	C-5
Las Vegas	D-6
Lea	J-8
Levy	C-6
Lincoln	G-5
Lingo	G-8
Loco Hills	H-7
Logan	D-8
Lordsburg •	J-1
Los Alamos •	C-4
Los Lunas •	E-4
Los Montoyas	D-6
Los Ojos	B-4
Loving	J-7
Lovington •	H-8
Lower Penasco	H-5
Lumberton	A-4
Luna	G-1
Madrid	D-4
Magdalena	F-3
Malaga	J-7
Maljamar	H-7
Mayhill	H-5
Medanales	C-4
Melrose	F-7
Mentmore	D-1
Mescalero	H-5
Milan	D-2
Monero	B-4
Mora •	C-5
Moriarty	E-5
Mosquero •	C-7
Mountain Park	H-5
Mountainair	F-4
Nageezi	C-2
Naschitti	C-1
Navajo City	B-3
Newcomb	C-1
Newkirk	E-7
Old Horse Springs	G-2
Omega	F-2
Orogrande	J-5
Oscuro	G-4
Otis	J-7
Paguate	E-3
Pastura	E-6
Pena Blanca	D-4
Picacho	H-6
Pie Town	F-2
Pilar	C-5
Placitas	C-5
Pleasanton	H-1
Pojoaque	C-5
Portair	F-8
Portales •	F-8
Quay	E-7
Quemado	F-1
Questa	B-5
Radium Springs	J-3
Ragland	E-7
Ramah	E-2
Ramon	F-6
Ranchos de Taos	C-5
Raton •	B-6
Red Hill	F-1
Red River	B-5
Regina	C-3
Reserve •	G-1
Rinconada	C-5
Riverside	A-2
Rodeo	K-1
Roswell •	G-6
Rowe	D-5
Roy	C-7
Ruidoso	H-5
St. Vrain	F-8
Salem	J-3
San Antonio	G-3
San Jon	E-8
San Mateo	D-3
San Patricio	G-5
San Pedro	G-4
San Rafael	E-2
San Ysidro	D-4
Sandia Park	E-4
Santa Cruz	C-5
Santa Fe •	D-4
Santa Rita	H-2
Santa Rosa	E-6
Santo Domingo Pueblo	D-4
Scholle	F-4
Sheep Springs	C-1
Shiprock	B-1
Silver City •	H-2
Smith Lake	D-2
Socorro •	F-4
Springer	C-6
Stanley	E-5
Sunset	H-6
Taos •	B-5
Tatum	H-8
Taylor	C-6
Thoreau	D-2
Three Rivers	H-5
Tierra Amarilla •	B-4
Tinaja	E-2
Tinnie	G-6
Tolar	F-7
Torreon	C-3
Tres Piedras	B-5
Tres Ritos	C-5
Trujillo	D-6
Truth or Consequences •	H-3
Tucumcari •	D-7
Tularosa	H-4
Tusas	B-5
Tyrone	J-2
Valmont	H-5
Vanadium	H-2
Variadero	D-6
Vaughn	E-5
Velarde	C-5
Virden	J-1
Wagon Mound	C-6
White Horse	C-2
White Lakes	D-5
White Rock	C-4
Whites City	J-7
Willard	E-5
Williamsburg	H-3
Winston	G-3
Yeso	F-6
Youngsville	C-4
Zuni	E-1

SF-652-J

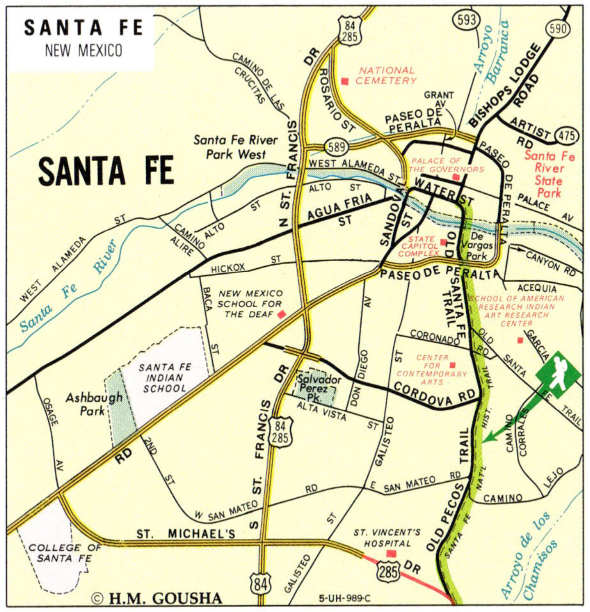

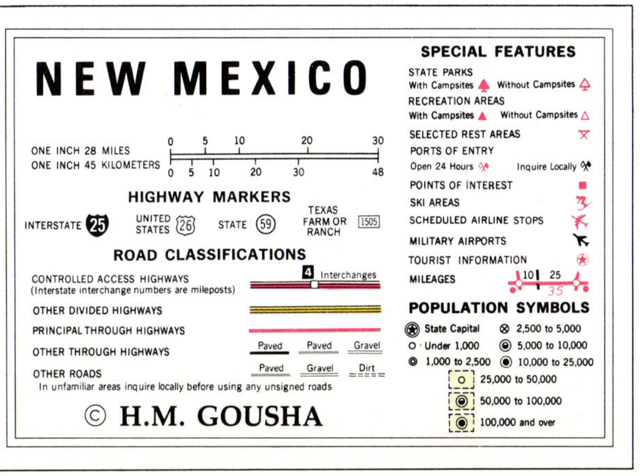

Lithographed in U.S.A.

WHITE PLAINS
NEW ROCHELLE
MOUNT VERNON
YONKERS
BRONX
Hudson River
Tappan Zee
SLEEPY HOLLOW
Tarrytown
Nyack
Hastings-on-Hudson
Dobbs Ferry
Scarsdale
Bronxville
Pelham
Mamaroneck
Larchmont
HACKENSACK
PATERSON
PASSAIC
CLIFTON
GARFIELD
BERGENFIELD
NUTLEY
BLOOMFIELD
MONTCLAIR
Paramus
Ridgewood
Englewood
FORT LEE
Teaneck
Mahwah
Suffern
Spring Valley
Hawthorne
Wayne
Oakland
Wanaque
Pompton Lakes
Eastchester Bay
Pelham Bay
RAMAPO MOUNTAINS
Wanaque Reservoir
Kensico Reservoir
TEANECK
TETERBORO AIRPORT
ROCKLAND LAKE STATE PARK
HOOK MTN. STATE PARK
BLAUVELT STATE PARK
TALLMAN MTN. STATE PARK
ROCKEFELLER PRESERVE
NEW JERSEY
NEW YORK

METROPOLITAN NEW YORK CITY
GARDEN STATE PARKWAY
INTERCHANGES
Full Interchange
Northbound On Southbound Off
Southbound On Northbound Off
Interchange numbers indicate distance in miles from terminus in southern New Jersey
Interchange or Exit Numbers
Seaplanes or Heliports
Golf Courses
Yacht Clubs
QUEENS
BROOKLYN
STATEN ISLAND
JERSEY CITY
NEWARK
ELIZABETH
BAYONNE
LINDEN
KEARNY
HARRISON
EAST ORANGE
IRVINGTON
UNION CITY
PERTH AMBOY
JOHN F. KENNEDY INTERNATIONAL AIRPORT
NEWARK INT'L AIRPORT
Jamaica Bay
GATEWAY NATIONAL REC. AREA
Upper New York Bay
Lower Bay
Raritan Bay
ATLANTIC OCEAN
Coney Island
© H.M. GOUSHA
Lithographed in U.S.A.

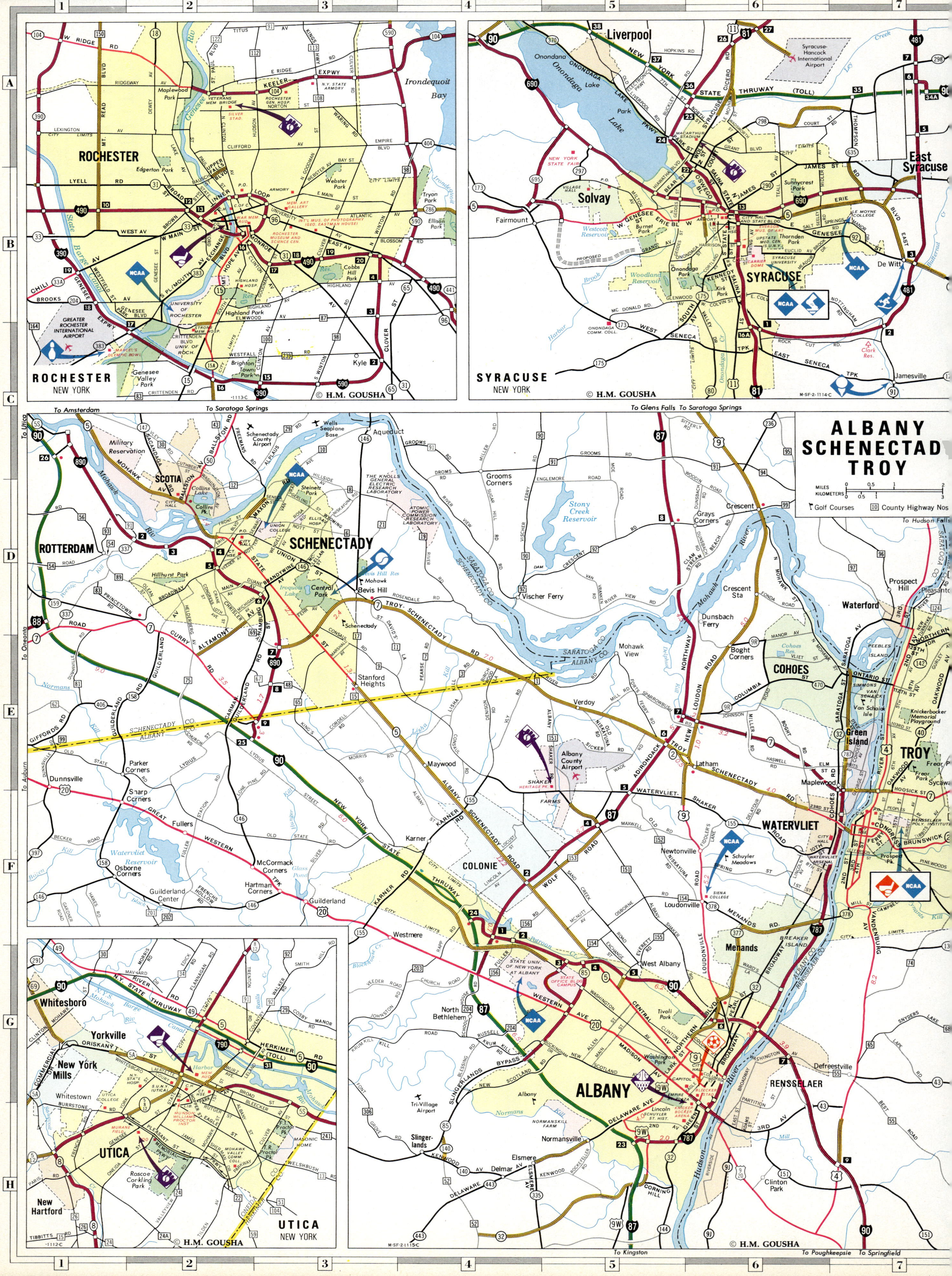
ROCHESTER
NEW YORK
© H.M. GOUSHA
Irondequoit Bay
Edgerton Park
Genesee Valley Park
Highland Park
Brighton Town Park
Cobbs Hill Park
Kyle
GREATER ROCHESTER INTERNATIONAL AIRPORT
UNIVERSITY OF ROCHESTER
SYRACUSE
NEW YORK
© H.M. GOUSHA
Liverpool
Onondaga Lake
Solvay
Fairmount
East Syracuse
De Witt
Jamesville
Syracuse-Hancock International Airport
Westcott Reservoir
Woodland Reservoir
Onondaga Park
Thornden Park
SYRACUSE UNIVERSITY
NEW YORK STATE FAIR
LE MOYNE COLLEGE
Clark Res.
ALBANY SCHENECTADY TROY
MILES
KILOMETERS
Golf Courses
County Highway Nos.
To Amsterdam
To Saratoga Springs
To Glens Falls
To Saratoga Springs
To Hudson Falls
To Utica
To Oneonta
To Auburn
To Kingston
To Poughkeepsie
To Springfield
SCOTIA
ROTTERDAM
SCHENECTADY
Military Reservation
Schenectady County Airport
Wells Seaplane Base
Aqueduct
Grooms Corners
Stony Creek Reservoir
Vischer Ferry
Crescent
Grays Corners
Crescent Sta
Dunsbach Ferry
Boght Corners
Mohawk View
Waterford
Prospect Hill
Pleasantdale
COHOES
Green Island
TROY
Van Schaick Isle
Stanford Heights
Verdoy
Latham
Maplewood
Albany County Airport
Maywood
Parker Corners
Sharp Corners
Dunnsville
Fullers
Watervliet Reservoir
Osborne Corners
McCormack Corners
Hartman Corners
Guilderland Center
Guilderland
Karner
COLONIE
WATERVLIET
Newtonville
Loudonville
Schuyler Meadows
SIENA COLLEGE
Menands
West Albany
Westmere
North Bethlehem
STATE UNIV. OF NEW YORK AT ALBANY
Tivoli Park
Washington Park
ALBANY
Lincoln Park
RENSSELAER
Defreestville
Tri-Village Airport
Slingerlands
Normansville
Elsmere
Delmar
Clinton Park
Hudson River
© H.M. GOUSHA
Whitesboro
Yorkville
New York Mills
Whitestown
UTICA
Roscoe Conkling Park
New Hartford
UTICA
NEW YORK
© H.M. GOUSHA

NEW YORK

Pop (1990) 18,044,505
Area 49,576 Sq. Mi.

COUNTIES

County	County Seat
Albany	Alabny
Allegany	Belmont
Bronx	Bronx
Broome	Binghamton
Cattaraugus	Little Valley
Cayuga	Auburn
Chautauqua	Mayville
Chemung	Elmira
Chenango	Norwich
Clinton	Plattsburg
Columbia	Hudson
Cortland	Cortland
Delaware	Delhi
Dutchess	Poughkeepsie
Erie	Buffalo
Essex	Elizabethtown
Franklin	Malone
Fulton	Johnstown
Genesee	Batavia
Greene	Catskill
Hamilton	Lake Pleasant
Herkimer	Herkimer
Jefferson	Watertown
Kings	Brooklyn
Lewis	Lowville
Livingston	Geneseo
Madison	Wampsville
Monroe	Rochester
Montgomery	Fonda
Nassau	Mineola
New York	New York
Niagara	Lockport
Oneida	Utica
Onondaga	Syracuse
Ontario	Canandaigua
Orange	Goshen
Orleans	Albion
Oswego	Oswego
Ostego	Cooperstown
Putnam	Carmel
Queens	Jamaica
Rensselaer	Troy
Richmond	St. George
Rockland	New City
St. Lawrence	Canton
Saratoga	Ballston Spa
Schenectady	Schenectady
Schoharie	Schoharie
Schuyler	Watkins Glen
Seneca	Waterloo
Steuben	Bath
Suffolk	Riverhead
Sullivan	Monticello
Tioga	Owego
Tompkins	Ithaca
Ulster	Kingston
Warren	Lake George
Washington	Hudson Falls
Wayne	Lyons
Westchester	White Plains
Wyoming	Warsaw
Yates	Penn Yan

PARTIAL LIST OF

CITIES AND TOWNS

• County Seats

Accord	K-12
Adams	D-9
Addison	J-7
Afton	J-9
Aiden Lair	E-12
Akron	G-4
Alabama	G-4
Albany •	H-12
Albion •	F-5
Alden	G-4
Alder Creek	F-10
Alexander	G-5
Alexandria Bay	C-9
Alfred	J-5
Allaben	J-12
Allegany	J-4
Almond	H-6
Altamont	H-12
Alton	G-7
Amagansett	L-7
Amboy Center	F-9
Ames	G-11
Amityville	M4,M14
Amsterdam	G-12
Andes	J-11
Andover	J-6
Angelica	H-5
Angola	H-3
Angus	H-7
Antwerp	C-9
Apulia	G-9
Aquebogue	L-6
Arcade	H-4
Ardsley	L-2
Argyle	E-13
Arieta	F-11
Arkville	J-11
Arkwright	H-3
Arlington	K-13
Ashford	H-4
Ashland	H-12
Ashville	J-2
Athens	H-13
Attica	G-4
Auburn •	G-8
Aurora	H-7
Au Sable Forks	C-13
Ava	F-10
Avoca	H-6
Avon	G-6
Babylon	M4,M14
Baggs Corners	D-8
Bainbridge	J-9
Bakers Mills	F-12
Balcoms Corners	H-3
Baldwin	M-3
Baldwinsville	G-8
Ballston Spa •	G-12
Balmat	C-10
Bangor	B-12
Barbourville	J-10
Bardonia	K-2
Barneveld	F-10
Barryville	K-11
Barton	J-8
Basom	G-4
Batavia •	G-5
Bath •	H-7
Bay Shore	M4,M14
Bayville	L3,L13
Beacon	K-12
Beans	H-6
Bedell	J-11
Bedford	K3
Bedford Center	K-3
Beekmantown	B-113
Belfast	H-5
Bellport	M-5
Bellport Station	M-5
Bellwood	E-9
Belmont •	J-5
Bennettsville	J-10
Benson Mines	C-11
Bergen	G-5
Berne	H-12
Bethany	G-5
Bethel	K-11
Bethpage	M-3
Bettsburg	J-10
Billings	K-13
Billsboro Station	G-7
Binghamton •	J-9
Black River	E-9
Blasdell	G-3
Bliss	H-5
Blockville	J-2
Bloomerville	H-6
Bloomingdale	C-12
Bloomville	H-11
Blue Mountain	E-11
Blue Stores	J-13
Boice	B-10
Bolivar	J-5
Bolton	F-13
Bolton Lodge	F-13
Bombay	B-11
Bonney	H-9
Boonville	F-10
Boquet	C-13
Boston	H-4
Brainardsville	B-12
Brant Lake	E-13
Brasher Falls	B-11
Brasie Corners	C-9
Breakabeen	H-11
Brentwood	M-4
Briarcliff Manor	K-2
Bridgehampton	L-7
Bridgewater	G-10
Brier Hill	G-9
Brightwaters	M-4
Bristol Center	G-6
Broadalbin	G-12
Brockport	G-5
Brocton	H-3
Bronx • (Part of N. Y. C.)	M-13
Bronxville	L-2
Brooklyn • (Part of N. Y. C.)	M2,M12
Brooksburg	H-12
Brown Corners	C-9
Brownville	E-9
Brunswick Center	G-13
Bucks Bridge	B-10
Buffalo •	G-3
Burdett	H-7
Burke Center	B-12
Burnt Hills	G-12
Burrs Mills	E-9
Cadiz	H-4
Cadyville	B-13
Cairo	H-12
Calcium	D-9
Caledonia	G-5
Callicoon	K-10
Cambridge	G-14
Camden	F-9
Camillus	G-8
Canada Lake	G-11
Canajoharie	G-11
Canadaigua •	G-6
Canastota	G-9
Candor	J-8
Caneadea	H-5
Canisteo	J-6
Cannon Corners	B-13
Canoga	G-7
Canton	C-10
Cape Vincent	D-8
Cardiff	G-8
Carlisle	G-12
Caroline	H-8
Carthage	E-9
Cassadaga	H-3
Castile	H-5
Castle Creek	J-9
Castleton-on-Hudson	H-13
Catatonk	J-8
Catawba	H-6
Cato	G-8
Catskill •	J-12
Cattaraugus	H-3
Cayuta	J-7
Caywood	H-7
Cazenovia	G-9
Cedarhurst	M3,M13
Celoron	J-3
Centereach	L-4
Center Moriches	M-5
Centerville	J-10
Central Islip	M-4
Chaffee	H-6
Chambers	J-7
Champlain	B-13
Chappaqua	K-3
Chateaugay	B-12
Chatham	H-13
Chaumont	D-8
Chaz	B-13
Chazy Lake	B-12
Cherry Creek	H-3
Cherry Valley	G-11
Chester	K-12
Childs	F-5
Childwold	C-11
Chilson	E-13
Chippewa Bay	C-9
Chittenango	G-9
Cincinnatus	H-9
Clarence	G-4
Clarkson	F-5
Clarksville	H-12
Clayton	C-9
Clear Creek	J-3
Clermont	J-13
Cleveland	F-9
Clifton Springs	G-7
Climax	H-12
Clinton	G-10
Clintonville	C-13
Clyde	G-7
Clymer	J-2
Clymer Center	J-2
Cobleskill	H-11
Cochecton Center	K-4
Cohocton	H-6
Cohoes	G-13
Cold Brook	F-10
Cold Brook	J-12
Cold Spring	K-13
Cold Spring Harbor	L3,M13
Collins Lodge	C-9
Colosse	F-8
Colton	C-11
Columbus	H-10
Commack	L4,M14
Comstock	F-13
Constableville	F-10
Constantia	F-9
Conewango	J-3
Cooksburg	H-12
Coonrod	F-9
Cooperstown •	H-11
Cooperstown Junction	H-11
Coopersville	B-13
Copenhagen	E-9
Copes Corner	H-10
Coplague	M-4
Coram	L-5
Corinth	F-12
Corning	J-7
Cortland •	H-8
Coventryville	H-9
Covert	H-7
Coveville	G-13
Coxsackie	H-13
Cranberry Creek	G-12
Cranberry Lake	C-11
Craryville	J-13
Crosby	H-7
Cross	C-13
Croton-on-Hudson	L-13
Crown Point	D-13
Cuba	J-5
Cuddebackville	K-11
Curry	J-11
Cutchogue	L-6
Cuyler	H-9
Dairyland	K-11
Dale	G-5
Damascus	J-9
Danby	H-8
Dannemora	B-12
Dansville	H-6
Darien Center	G-4
Davenport	H-11
Dayton	H-3
Debruce	J-11
Deer Park	M-4
Deer River	D-10
Deferiet	E-9
De Kalb	C-10
Delhi •	J-11
Denmark	E-9
Denver	J-11
Depew	G-4
Deposit	J-10
Dewittville	J-3
Dexter	D-9
Diamond Point	F-13
Diana	D-10
Dickinson	B-11
Dobbs Ferry	L-2
Dolgeville	G-11
Dorloo	H-11
Downsville	J-11
Dresden	H-7
Dryden	H-8
Duane Center	B-12
Duanesburg	G-12
Dugway	F-9
Dundee	H-7
Dunkirk	H-3
Dunraven	J-11
Durham	H-12
Eagle	H-5
Eagle Bay	E-11
East Aurora	G-4
East Greenbush	H-13
East Hampton	L-7
East Hills	M-3
East Islip	M-4
East Marion	K-7
East Martinsburg	F-10
East Meadow	M-3
East Moriches	L-5
East Northport	L-4
East Norwich	L-3
Easton	G-13
East Patchogue	M-5
Eastport	L-5
East Quoque	L-6
East Rochester	G-6
East Setauket	L-4
East Worcester	H-11
Eddy	C-10
Eden	H-3
Edwardsville	C-9
Elba	G-5
Eldkale	J-4
Elizabethtown •	C-13
Ellenburg	B-12
Ellenville	K-12
Ellicottville	J-4
Ellington	J-3
Ellis	H-8
Elmira •	J-7
Elmira Heights	J-7
Elmsford	L-2
Elmwood	G-8
Endicott	J-8
Endwell	J-9
Essex	C-13
Fair Haven	F-7
Fairmount	G-8
Fairport	G-6
Fairview	H-5
Fairview	K-13
Falconer	J-3
Fancher	F-5
Fargo	D-9
Farmersville	H-4
Farmingdale	M-3
Farmingville	L-5
Fayetteville	G-9
Fillmore	H-5
Fine	C-10
Flackville	B-10
Flanders	L-6
Fleming	G-8
Flint	G-7
Floral Park	M-3
Florida	L-12
Flower Hill	L-3
Floyd	G-10
Fonda •	G-11
Forestport	F-10
Fort Ann	F-13
Fort Covington	B-11
Fort Edward	F-13
Fort Johnson	G-12
Fort Miller	G-13
Fort Plain	G-11
Forestdale	K-11
Fowler	C-10
Fowlerville	H-4
Frankfort	G-10
Franklin	H-10
Franklin Square	M3,M13
Franklington	H-12
Franklinville	H-4
Fraser	J-11
Fredonia	H-3
Freehold	H-12
Freeport	M3,M13
Freetown	L-7
French Mountain	F-13
Friendship	J-5
Fulton	F-8
Fultonham	H-12
Gabriels	C-12
Gaines	F-5
Gale	C-11
Garland	G-5
Garoga	G-11
Garratsville	H-11
Gee Brook	H-9
Genegantslet	H-9
Geneseo	G-5
Geneva	G-7
Genoa	H-8
Georgetown	G-9
Gerry	J-3
Glasco	J-12
Glen	G-12
Glen Aubrey	J-9
Glen Castle	J-9
Glen Cove	L-3
Glenfield	E-10
Glenpark	D-9
Glens Falls	F-13
Gloversville	G-11
Goshen •	K-12
Gouverneur	C-10
Gowanda	H-3
Grahamsville	J-11
Grand Gorge	H-11
Grant Mills	J-11
Granville	F-14
Graphite	E-13
Great Bend	D-9
Great Neck	L3,M13
Great Valley	J-4
Greene	H-9
Greenlawn	L-4
Greenport	K-7
Greenville	H-12
Greenwich	G-13
Greenwood	J-5
Greenwood Lake	L-12
Griffin	F-12
Groton	H-8
Gunn Corners	D-9
Hagaman	G-12
Hague	E-13
Hailesboro	C-10
Haines Falls	J-12
Halesite	L-4
Half Hollows	M-4
Hallsport	J-5
Hamburg	H-4
Hamden	J-10
Hamilton	G-10
Hamlet	H-3
Hammond	C-9
Hammondsport	H-6
Hampton Bays	L-6
Hancock	J-10
Hannawa Falls	B-10
Hardscrabble	L-7
Harford	H-8
Harpersfield	H-11
Harris Corners	G-4
Harrisburg	E-9
Harrison	L-3
Harrisville	D-10
Hartford	F-13
Hartsdale	L-2
Hartwick	H-10
Haven	K-11
Hayground	L-7
Hebron	F-14
Hempstead	M-3
Herkimer •	G-11
Heuvelton	B-10
Hicksville	M-3
Highland	K-12
Highland Falls	K-12
Highmount	J-11
Hilton	F-6
Hoag Corners	H-13
Hobart	H-11
Hoffmans	G-12
Hoffmeister	F-11
Hogansburg	B-11
Holbrook	L-5
Holland	H-4
Holley	F-5
Holmesville	H-10
Homer	H-8
Honeoye	G-6
Honeoye Falls	G-6
Hoosick Falls	G-13
Hope	F-12
Hopkinton	B-11
Hornell	H-6
Horseheads	J-7
Hoghton	H-5
Houseville	E-9
Hudson •	J-13
Hudson Falls •	F-13
Huguenot	K-11
Hume	H-5
Hunter	J-12
Huntington	L3,M14
Huntington Bay	L-4
Huntington Station	L-4
Hyde Park	K-13
Ilion	G-10
Indian Lake	E-12
Indian River	D-10
Ingleside	H-6
Inlet	E-11
Interlaken	H-7
Inwood	M-2
Irvine Mills	J-4
Irvington	L2,L12
Island Park	M3,M13
Islip	M4,M14
Itaska	J-9
Ithaca •	H-8
Jamaica • (N.Y. City)	M2,M13
Jamesport	L-6
Jamestown	J-3
Jasper	J-5
Jay	C-13
Jeddo	F-4
Jefferson	H-11
Jericho	L3,M13
Jewell	G-9
Johnson City	J-9
Johnstown •	G-12
Johnsville	G-11
Jordan	G-8
Jordanville	G-11
Katrine	J-12
Kattelville	J-9
Keene Valley	C-12
Keeseville	C-13
Kenmore	G-4
Kennedy	J-3
Kenoza Lake	K-11
Keuka	H-7
Kidders	H-7
Killawog	H-9
Kinderhook	H-13
Kindrews Corners	C-10
Kings	G-13
Kingsbury	F-13
Kings Corner	C-10
Kings Park	L4,L14
Kings Point	L-2
Kingston •	J-12
Kirkwood	J-9
Knox	H-12
Kossuth	J-5
Kuckville	F-5
Kysorville	H-5
Lackawanna	G-3
Lacona	F-9
Ladentown	K-1
La Fargeville	C-9
La Fayette	G-9
Lake Carmel	K-13
Lake Clear Junction	C-12
Lake Delaware	J-11
Lake George •	F-13
Lake Minnewaska	K-12
Lake Placid	C-12
Lake Pleasant •	F-12
Lake Ronkonkoma	L-4
Lakewood	J-3
Lamberton	H-3
Lancaster	G-4
Langdon Corners	B-10
Laona	H-3
Larchmont	L-3
Lattingtown	L-3
Lava	K-11
Lawrence	M3,M13
Lawrenceville	B-11
Ledger Corners	B-13
Lee	F-9
Leicester	G-5
Leon	J-3
Leonardsville	G-10
Leonta	H-10
Le Roy	G-5
Levant	J-3
Levittown	M3,M13
Lewis	C-13
Lexington	J-12
Liberty	K-11
Lima	G-6
Lime Lake	H-4
Limestone	J-4
Lincklaen	H-9
Lisbon	B-10
Lisle	H-9
Little Falls	G-11
Little Valley •	J-4
Liverpool	G-8
Livingston Manor	J-11
Livingstonville	H-12
Livonia	G-6
Lloyd Harbor	L-3
Lock Berlin	G-7
Locke	H-8
Lockport •	G-4
Locust Valley	L-3
Long Beach	M3,M13
Long Lake	E-12
Loomis	J-10
Lorraine	E-9
Lowville •	E-10
Lynbrook	M3,M13
Lyon Mountain	B-12
Lyons •	G-7
Lyons Falls	F-10
Macedon	G-6
Machias	H-4
Madison	G-10
Madrid	B-10
Madrid Springs	B-10
Mahopac	K-13
Malone •	B-12
Malta	G-13
Mamaroneck	L3,L13
Manchester	G-6
Manhasset	M3,M13
Manhattan (Part N.Y.C.)	M-2
Manlius	G-9
Mannsville	E-9
Maplehurst	J-4
Mapleview	F-8
Marathon	H-9
Markham	H-3
Marlboro	K-12
Maryland	H-11
Masonville	J-10
Mastic Beach	M-5
Martinsburg	E-9
Massepequa Park	M-3
Massena	B-11
Mattituck	L-6
Maybrook	K-12
Mayfield	G-12
Mayville •	J-2
McCollums	C-12
McDonough	H-9
McGraw	H-9
McKeever	F-10
Meacham Lake	B-12
Mechanicville	G-13
Medford	L-5
Medina	F-4
Menands	H-13
Meridale	H-11
Merrick	M-3
Mexico	F-8
Middleburgh	H-12
Middle Island	L-5
Middletown	K-11
Middleville	G-10
Mileses	K-10
Milford	H-11
Milford Center	H-10
Millbrook	K-13
Millen's Bay	D-8
Millersport	G-4
Millerton	J-13
Millport	J-7
Millwood	K-2
Minaville	G-12
Mineola •	M-3
Minerva	E-12
Minetto	F-8
Modena	K-12
Moffittsville	B-12
Mohawk	G-10
Mohawk Hill	F-10
Moira	B-11
Monroe	L-12
Montauk	L-8
Monticello	K-11
Montour Falls	H-7
Moody	C-11
Mooers	B-13
Montgomery	K-12
Moons	H-3
Morris	H-10
Moravia	H-8
Morehouseville	F-11
Morley	B-10
Morristown	C-9
Morrisville	G-9
Mount Ivy	K-2
Mount Kisco	L-13
Mount Morris	H-5
Mount Vernon	L2,L13
Mount Vison	H-10
Murray	F-5
Nanuet	K-2
Napanoch	K-12
Naples	H-6
Nassau	H-13
Natural Bridge	D-10
Natural Dam	C-10
Navarino	G-8
Nedrow	G-8
Nesconset	L-4
Newark Valley	J-8
New Berlin	H-10
New Boston	E-9
New Bremen	E-10
Newburgh	K-12
New City •	K-2
Newcomb	E-12
Newfane	F-4
New London	G-9
New Paltz	K-12
Newport	G-10
New Rochelle	L-3
New Russia	C-13
New York •	M-2
Niagara Falls	G-3
Nicholville	B-11
Nile	J-5
Noblesboro	F-11
Norfolk	B-10
North Bangor	B-11
North Bay	F-9
North Creek	E-12
North Colesville	J-9
North Collins	H-3
North Elba	C-12
North Franklin	H-10
North Hudson	E-13
North Norwich	H-10
Northport	L4,L14
North Ridge	F-4
North River	E-12
Northrup Corners	B-10
North Syracuse	G-8
North Tonawanda	G-3
Northville	F-12
Norwich	H-9
Norwood	B-10
Nunda	H-5
Nyack	L-12
Oakdale	M-4
Oakfield	G-5
Oak Hill	H-12
Oak Orchard	F-4
Oak Point	C-9
Oceanside	M-3
Odessa	H-7
Ogdensburg	B-10
Ohio	F-11
Olcott	F-4
Old Forge	E-10
Olean	J-4
Olivebridge	J-12
Omar	C-9
Oneida	G-9
Oneonta	H-10
Oramel	H-5
Orchard Park	G-4
Orient Point	K-7
Oriskany	G-10
Ossining	L-13
Oswegatchie Corners	D-10
Oswego	F-8
Otego	H-10
Otter Lake	F-10
Otto	H-3
Ovid •	H-7
Owego	J-8
Oxford	H-9
Oyster Bay	L-3
Paradox	A-13
Painted Post	J-7
Palermo	F-8
Palmyra	G-6
Panama	J-2
Pantigo	L-7
Parish	F-9
Parishville Center	B-11
Parma Center	B-11
Patchin	H-4
Patchogue	M-5
Paul Smiths	C-12
Pavillion	G-5
Pea Brook	J-10
Peconic	L-6
Peekskill	L-13
Pelham Manor	L-2
Penn Yan •	H-7
Peoria	G-5
Perch River	D-9
Perkinsville	H-6
Perry	H-5
Perry City	H-7
Perth	G-12
Peruville	H-8
Phelps	G-7
Philadelphia	C-9
Philmont	J-13
Phoenicia	J-12
Phoenix	F-8
Picketts Corners	B-13
Piercefield	C-11
Piermont	L-2
Pierrepont	C-10
Pike	H-5
Pinelawn	M-4
Pine Valley	J-7
Pine Woods	G-9
Pitcairn	C-10
Pitcher	H-9
Pittsfield	H-10
Plainview	M-3
Plainville	G-8
Plattsburg	B-13
Pleasantville	K-3
Plessis	C-9
Plymouth	H-9
Point Rock	F-10
Poland	F-10
Pompey	G-9
Pope Mills	C-9
Portageville	H-5
Port Byron	G-8
Port Chester	L3,L13
Porter	F-13
Port Ewen	J-12
Port Henry	D-13
Port Jefferson	L-5
Port Jefferson Station	L-5
Port Jervis	K-11
Port Leyden	F-10
Port Ontario	F-8
Portville	J-4
Port Washington	L3,M13
Post Creek	J-7
Potsdam	B-10
Potters Corners	F-10
Pottersville	E-12
Poughkeepsie •	K-13
Pound Ridge	K-3
Prattsburg	H-6
Prattsville	H-12
Preble	H-8
Prospect	F-10
Pulaski •	F-8
Pulteney	H-6
Quaker Street	H-12
Randolph	J-3
Ransomville	F-3
Raquette Lake	E-11
Ravena	H-13
Ray Brook	C-12
Raymondville	B-10
Red Creek	F-7
Red Falls	H-12
Red Hook	J-13
Red Mills	B-10
Redwood	C-9
Remington Corners	D-10
Rensselaer	H-13
Rensselaerville	H-12
Rexville	J-6
Rhinebeck	J-13
Richfield Springs	G-11
Richford	H-8
Richmondville	H-11
Richville	C-10
Ridge	L-5
Ridgewood	F-4
Rio	K-11
Riparius	E-12
Riverdale	H-11
Riverhead	L-6
Rochester •	F-6
Rockdale	H-10
Rock Glen	H-5
Rock Hill	K-11
Rock Rift	J-10
Rockville Centre	M3,M13
Rocky Point	L-5
Rodman	E-9
Rogers	C-13
Rome •	G-10
Ronkonkoma	L-4
Rooseveltown	B-11
Romulus	H-7
Roseboom	H-11
Rotterdam	G-12
Round Lake	G-13
Rushford	H-4
Rye	L3,L13
Sabael	E-12
Sabbath Day Point	E-13
Sacandaga	F-12
Sackets Harbor	D-8
Sag Harbor	L-7
St. George (Part of N.Y.C.)	M-1
St. Huberts	C-12
St. James	L-4
Salamanca	J-4
Salem	G-13
Samfordville	B-11
San Remo	L4,L14
Sands Point	L-3
Sandusky	H-4
Sanford	J-10
Santa Clara	B-11
Saranac	B-13
Saranac Inn	C-12
Saranac Lake	C-12
Saratoga Springs	G-12
Sardinia	H-4
Saugerties	J-13
Savannah	G-7
Saxton	J-12
Sayville	M-2
Scarsdale	L-2
Schenectady •	G-13
Schenevus	H-11
Schroon Lake	E-13
Schuylerville	G-13
Scio	J-5
Sciota	B-13
Scotia	G-12
Scottsville	G-5
Scriba	F-8
Sea Cliff	L-3
Selden	L-5
Seneca Falls	G-7
Setauket	L-4
Severence	E-13
Sevey	C-11
Shady	J-12
Shandaken	J-12
Sharon Springs	G-11
Sheds	G-9
Sherburne	H-10
Sherrill	G-9
Shinhopple	J-10
Shortsville	G-6
Shrub Oak	L-13
Sidney	J-10
Silver Bay	E-13
Silver Creek	H-3
Skaneateles	G-8
Sloan	G-4
Sloansville	G-12
Sloatsburg	L-12
Smithtown	L-4
Smyrna	H-9
Sodom	E-12
Sodus	F-7
Sodus Point	F-7
Solvay	G-8
Somerville	C-10
Sonyea	H-5
Sound Beach	L-5
South Bombay	B-11
South Butler	G-7
South Colton	C-11
South Corning	J-7
South Cortland	H-8
South Edmeston	H-10
South Fallsburg	K-11
South Glens Falls	F-13
South Hammond	C-9
Southampton	L-7
South Haven	M-5
South Huntington	L3,M14
South Schroon	E-12
Southville	B-11
Southwest Oswego	F-8
Speculator	F-12
Spencer	J-8
Spencerport	G-5
Spring Valley	K-2
Springfield Center	G-11
Springville	H-4
Springwater	H-6
Spy Lake	F-11
Stamford	H-11
Stannards	J-5
Star Lake	C-10
Stark	C-11
Stetsonville	H-10
Stillwater	G-13
Stocton	H-3
Stokes	F-10
Stoney Brook	L-4
Stony Point	L-12
Stratford •	G-11
Street Road	E-13
Sugartown	J-4
Sullivanville	J-7
Summit	H-11
Surprise	H-12
Syosset	L-3
Syracuse •	G-8
Tallman	K-1
Tarrytown	L-13
Taylor	H-9
Termaines Corners	E-9
Terrace Park	C-9
Thayer Corners	B-12
The Forge	B-12
The Glen	F-12
Thendara	E-10
Three Mile Bay	D-8
Ticonderoga	D-13
Tilden	B-10
Tonawanda	G-4
Towahloondah	E-12
Town Line	G-4
Triangle	H-9
Trout Creek	J-10
Trout River	B-12
Troy •	H-13
Trumansburg	H-7
Trudeau	C-12
Truxton	H-9
Tuckahoe	L-2
Tuckahoe	L-6
Tupper Lake	C-11
Turin	F-10
Turners Corners	G-4
Unadilla	H-10
Union Springs	G-7
Upper Lisle	H-9
Upper St. Regis	C-12
Urbana	H-6
Utica	G-10
Valatie	H-13
Valcour	B-13
Valley Stream	M2,M13
Vandalia	J-4
Van Etten	J-8
Vega	J-11
Vernon	G-10
Vernon Valley	L-4
Verona	G-9
Vestal	J-9
Victor	G-6
Vincent	G-6
Volney	F-8
Vrooman	H-12
Waddington	B-10
Wadhams	C-13
Walden	K-12
Wales Center	G-4
Wallkill	K-12
Walton	J-10
Wampsville	G-9
Wantagh	M-3
Wappingers Falls	K-13
Warrens Corners	F-4
Warrensburg	F-13
Warsaw •	H-5
Warwick	L-12
Washington Mills	G-10
Washingtonville	K-12
Water Mill	L-7
Waterford	G-13
Waterloo	G-7
Watertown •	E-9
Waterville	G-10
Watervliet	H-13
Watkins Glen •	H-7
Waverly	J-8
Wawbeek	C-11
Wayland	H-6
Webster	G-6
Weedsport	G-8
Wells	F-12
Wellsville	J-5
Wesley	H-3
Westbrookville	K-11
Westbury	F-9
West Carthage	E-9
West Chazy	B-13
Westdale	F-9
West End	H-10
Westernville	F-10
Westfield	H-2
Westhampton Beach	M-6
West Haverstraw	L-12
West Kill	J-12
West Leyden	F-10
West Lowville	E-9
West Monroe	F-9
West Plattsburgh	B-13
West Point	K-13
Westport	C-13
West Schuyler	G-10
West Seneca	G-4
Westview	H-5
Westville	B-11
Westville Center	B-12
West Winfield	G-10
Wevertown	F-12
Whallonsburg	C-13
Wheeler	H-6
White Plains	L3,L13
Whitehall	F-13
Whitney Point	H-9
Willard	H-7
Willet	H-9
Williamson	F-7
Williamsville	G-4
Williston Park	M-3
Willow	J-12
Willsboro	C-13
Willseyville	J-8
Wilson	F-4
Wilton	G-13
Wilmington	C-12
Wilmurt	F-11
Windham	H-12
Windsor	J-9
Winthrop	B-11
Wolcott	F-7
Woodburne	K-11
Woodgate	F-10
Woodhull	J-6
Woodmere	M-3
Woodridge	K-11
Woodstock	J-12
Worcester	H-11
Worth	E-9
Wurtsboro	K-11
Wyandanch	M-4
Yaphank Station	L-5
Yonkers	L2,L13
Yorkshire	H-4
Yorktown	L-13
Yorktown Heights	L-13
Yorkville	G-10
Yosts	G-11
Youngstown	F-3
Youngsville	K-11
Yulan	K-11

SF-653-J

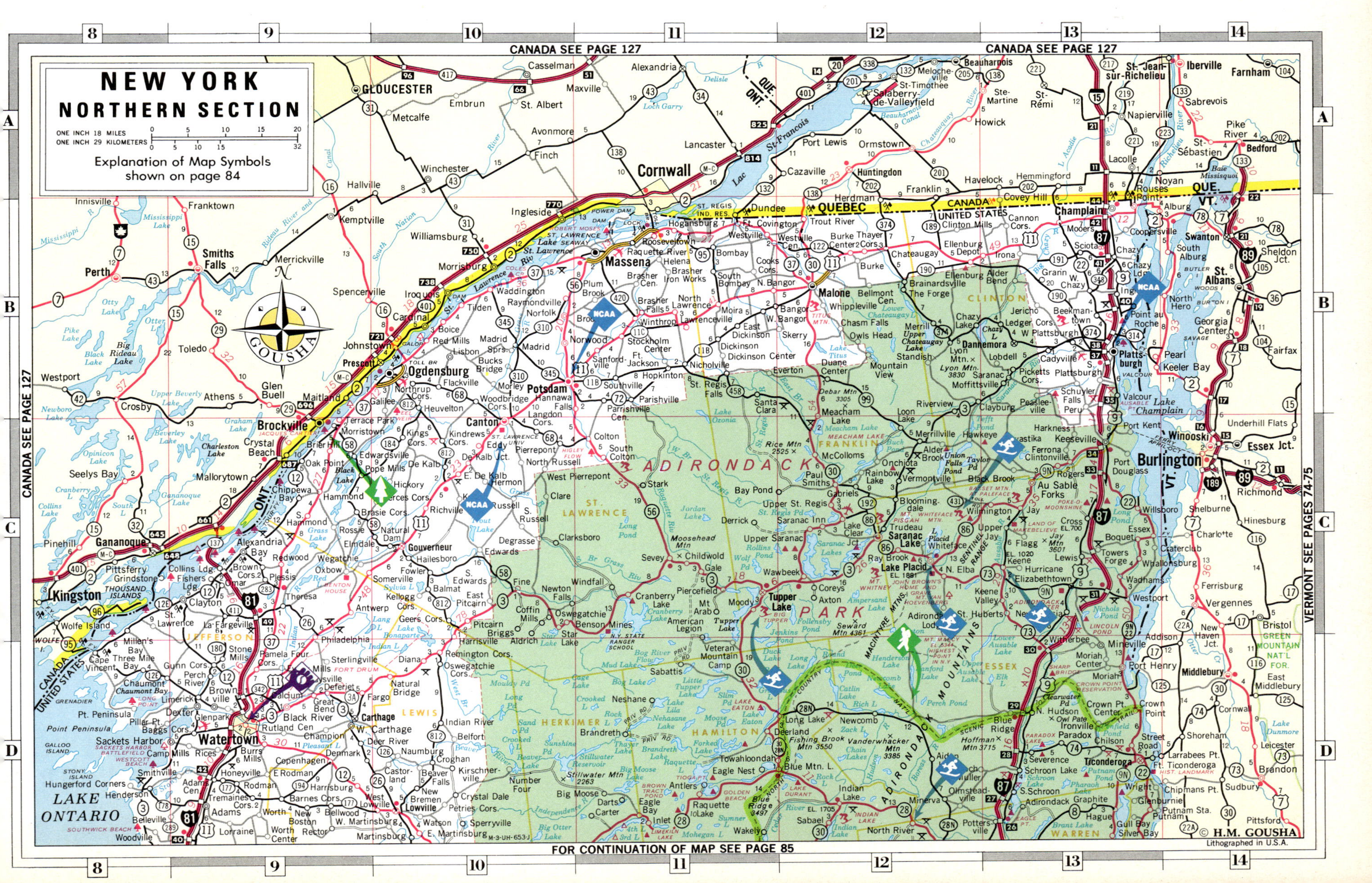

NEW YORK
SOUTHERN SECTION
ONE INCH 18 MILES
ONE INCH 29 KILOMETERS
HIGHWAY MARKERS
INTERSTATE
UNITED STATES
STATE AND PROVINCIAL
TRANS CANADA
QUEBEC AUTOROUTE
ROAD CLASSIFICATIONS
CONTROLLED ACCESS HIGHWAYS (Interstate interchange numbers are mileposts)
TOLL HIGHWAYS
OTHER DIVIDED HIGHWAYS
PRINCIPAL THROUGH HIGHWAYS
OTHER THROUGH HIGHWAYS
OTHER ROADS
In unfamiliar areas inquire locally before using any unsigned roads
SPECIAL FEATURES
STATE PARKS
RECREATION AREAS
SELECTED REST AREAS
PORTS OF ENTRY
POINTS OF INTEREST
SKI AREAS
SCHEDULED AIRLINE STOPS
MILITARY AIRPORTS
MILEAGES
POPULATION SYMBOLS
State Capital
Under 1,000
1,000 to 2,500
2,500 to 5,000
5,000 to 10,000
10,000 to 25,000
25,000 to 50,000
50,000 to 100,000
100,000 and over
© H.M. GOUSHA
FOR INDEX TO CITIES AND TOWNS SEE PAGE 83
NIAGARA FALLS
NEW YORK
BUFFALO
NEW YORK
ROCHESTER
SEE PAGE 82
SEE MAP INSET
ONTARIO SEE PAGES 132-133
LAKE ONTARIO
LAKE ERIE
GOUSHA
23
1306
1347
NEW YORK STATE
HIGHWAY REFERENCE MARKERS
MOTORISTS RECORD NEAREST REFERENCE MARKER NUMERALS ON ACCIDENT REPORT
Eight-inch square green signs have been installed at every one-tenth mile along the New York State Highway network. These provide the basis for a sound systematic accident location and prevention program, and may also be used by motorists to report disabled vehicles, flooding, obstructions and other highway hazards.
PENNSYLVANIA SEE PAGES 98-99
PENNSYLVANIA SEE PAGES 98-99
PENNSYLVANIA
ALLEGHENY NATIONAL FOREST
ALLEGANY STATE PARK
LONG ISLAND SOUND
FIRE ISLAND NATIONAL SEASHORE
Much of the land within the authorized boundary of Fire Island Nat'l Seashore is under private ownership. Please respect property rights.
FERRIES TO FIRE ISLAND DO NOT CARRY AUTOMOBILES
LONG ISLAND
NEW YORK
FOR CONTINUATION SEE MAIN MAP AT RIGHT
ATLANTIC OCEAN
Buffalo
Rochester
Jamestown
Olean
Elmira
Batavia
Dunkirk
Bridgeport
Stamford
White Plains
Riverhead
Lackawanna
Kenmore
Tonawanda
Niagara Falls

FOR CONTINUATION OF MAP SEE PAGE 83
LAKE ONTARIO
SYRACUSE
SEE PAGE 82
UTICA
SEE PAGE 82
ADIRONDACK PARK
ALBANY SCHENECTDY TROY
SEE PAGE 82
BINGHAMTON
SEE MAP INSET
LONG ISLAND
SEE MAP INSET
NEW YORK CITY
SEE PAGE 80-81
VERMONT SEE PAGES 74-75
MASSACHUSETTS SEE PAGES 56-57
CONNECTICUT SEE PAGES 24-25
FOR CONTINUATION SEE INSET AT LEFT
PENNSYLVANIA SEE PAGES 98-99
EXPLANATION OF ACTIVITIES
Major League Spectator
Minor League Spectator
Collegiate/Participant
Rivers, Trails, Major Parks, and Forests
Auto Racing
Horse Racing
Sailing
Baseball
Museums & Halls of Fame
Skiing
Basketball
National Trails
Soccer
Bowling
NCAA Colleges
Tennis
Football
Parks & Forests
Track & Field
Golf
Polo
Wild, Scenic, & Recreational Rivers
Hockey
Rodeo
FISHERS ISLAND
JOHNSON CITY
PORT DICKINSON
BINGHAMTON
NEW YORK
© H.M. GOUSHA
NEW YORK (DEWEY) THRUWAY
Entrance or exit only at interchanges, shown thus:
Toll Station
Service Area
Interchange
MAIN LINE SECTION (New York City to Buffalo)
Passenger car toll is $11.55 eastbound and $10.05 westbound, for the entire length of 426 miles.
BERKSHIRE SECTION
Passenger car toll is 95c for the entire length of 24 miles approximately 4.0c per mile.
NEW ENGLAND SECTION
Passenger car toll is 40c for the entire length of 15 miles, approximately 2.7c per mile.
ERIE SECTION
Passenger car toll is $1.65 for the entire length of 70 miles, approximately 2.4c per mile.
NIAGARA SECTION
Passenger car toll is 85c for the entire length of 21 miles, approximately 4.0c per mile.
NEW JERSEY SEE PAGES 76-77
NEW YORK
ATLANTIC OCEAN
Lithographed in U.S.A.

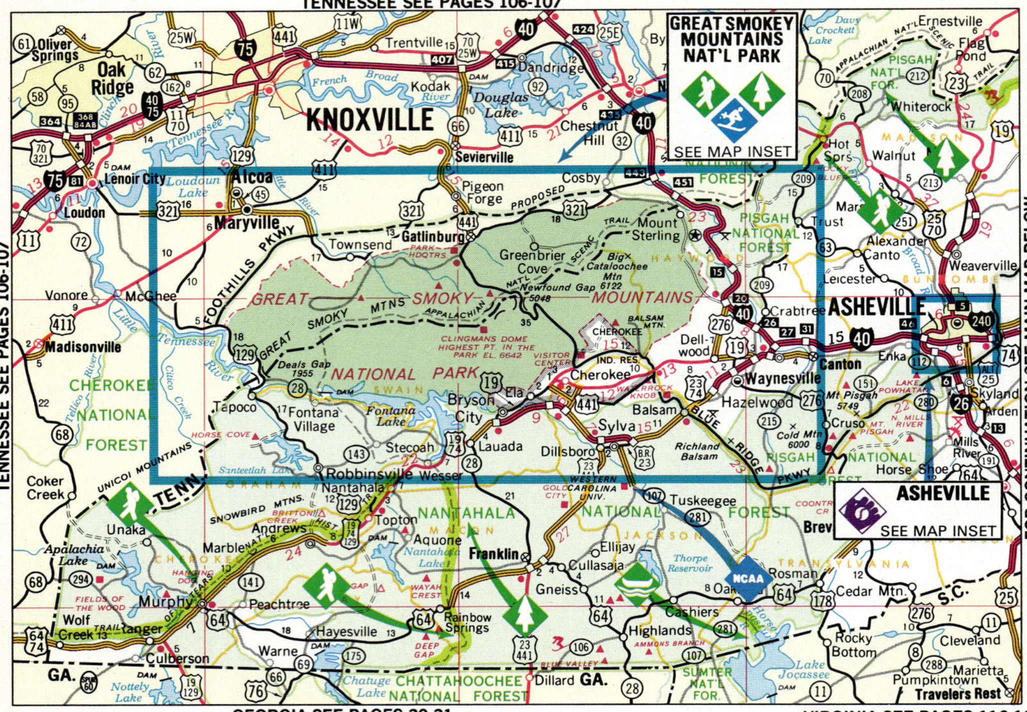

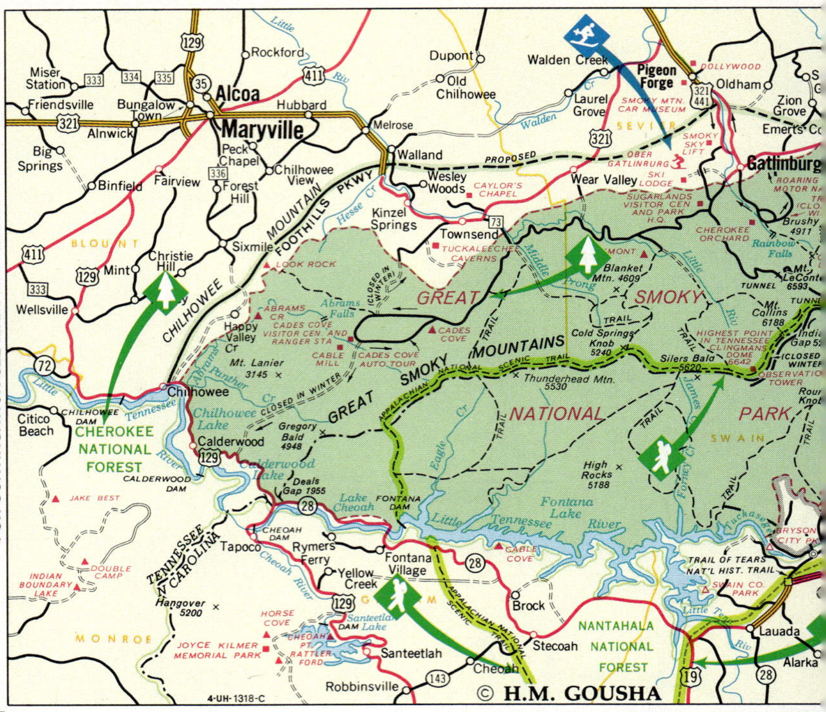

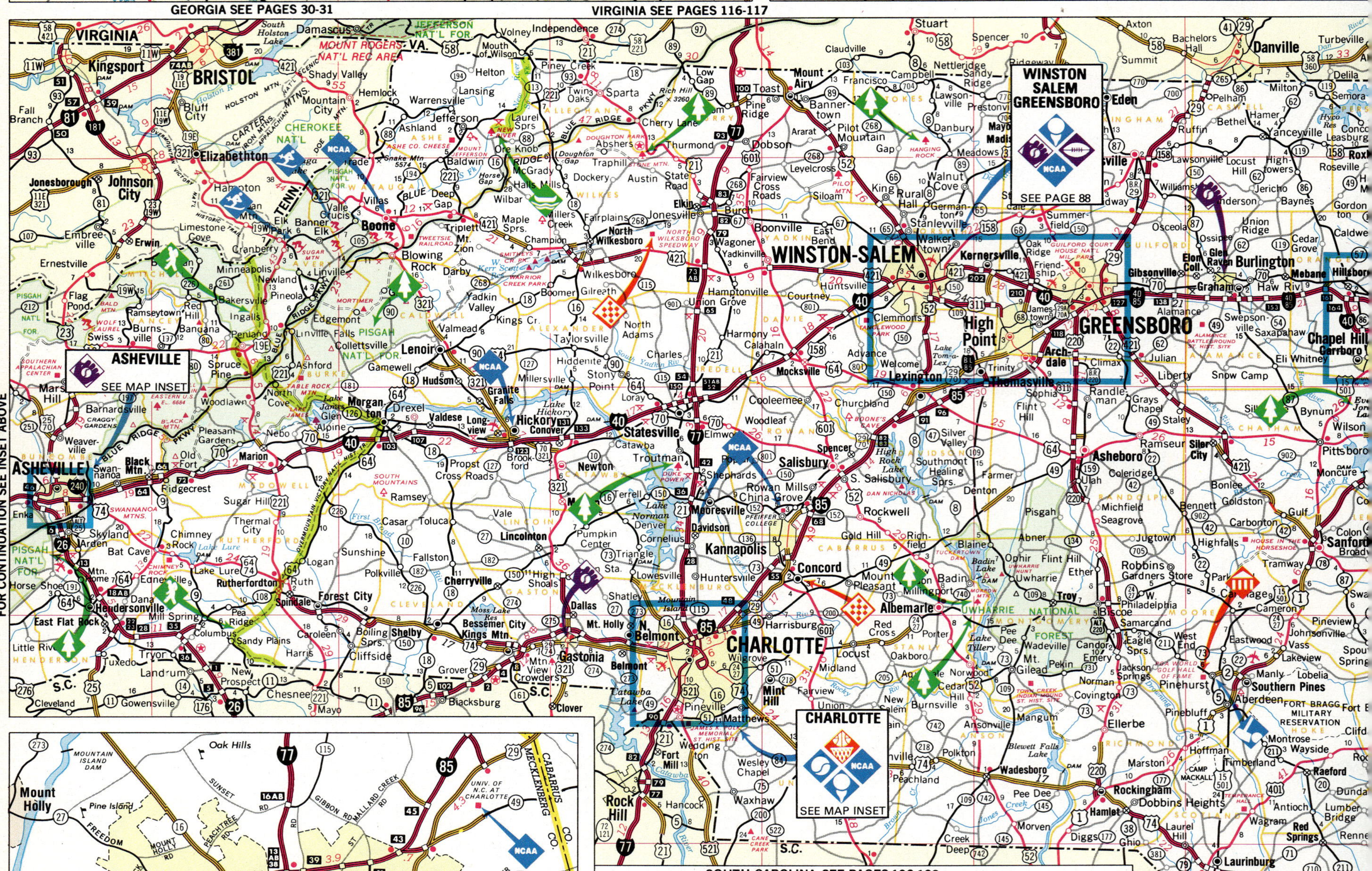

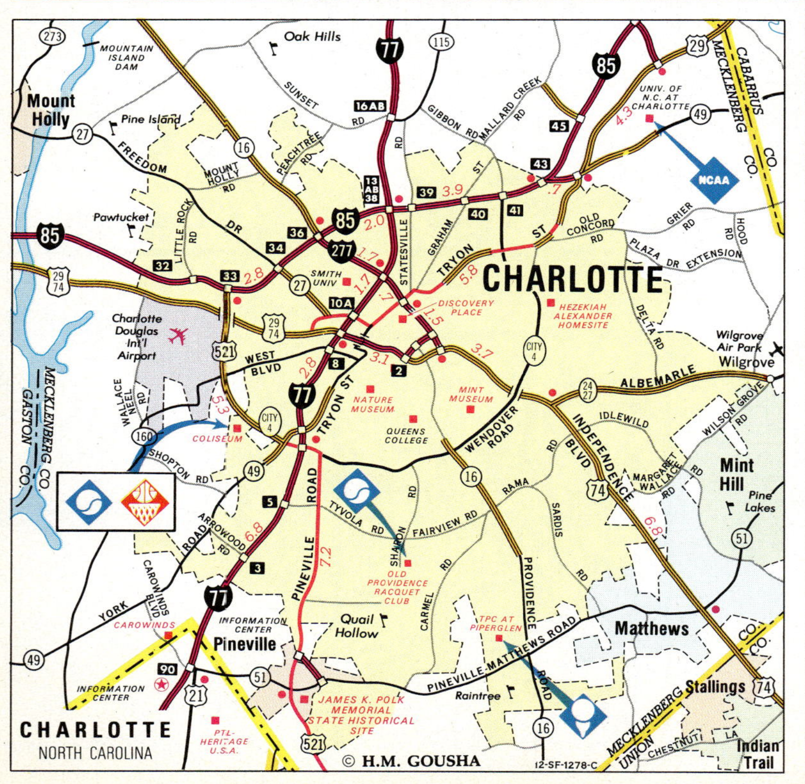

SOUTH CAROLINA SEE PAGES 102-103

NORTH CAROLINA

Pop (1990) 6,657,630
Area 52,712 Sq. Mi.

COUNTIES

County	Co. Seat
Alamance	Graham
Alexander	Taylorsville
Alleghany	Sparta
Anson	Wadesboro
Ashe	Jefferson
Avery	Newland
Beaufort	Washington
Bertie	Windsor
Bladen	Elizabethtown
Brunswick	Southport
Buncombe	Asheville
Burke	Morganton
Cabarrus	Concord
Caldwell	Lenoir
Camden	Camden
Carteret	Beaufort
Caswell	Yanceyville
Catawba	Newton
Chatham	Pittsboro
Cherokee	Murphy
Chowan	Edenton
Clay	Hayesville
Cleveland	Shelby
Columbus	Whiteville
Craven	New Bern
Cumberland	Fayetteville
Currituck	Currituck
Dare	Manteo
Davidson	Lexington
Davie	Mocksville
Duplin	Kenansville
Durham	Durham
Edgecombe	Tarboro
Forsyth	Winston-Salem
Franklin	Louisburg
Gaston	Gastonia
Gates	Gatesville
Graham	Robbinsville
Granville	Oxford
Greene	Snow Hill
Guilford	Greensboro
Halifax	Halifax
Harnett	Lillington
Haywood	Waynesville
Henderson	Hendersonville
Hertford	Winton
Hoke	Raeford
Hyde	Swan Quarter
Iredell	Statesville
Jackson	Sylva
Johnston	Smithfield
Jones	Trenton
Lee	Sanford
Lenoir	Kinston
Lincoln	Lincolnton
Macon	Franklin
Madison	Marshall
Martin	Williamston
McDowell	Marion
Mecklenburg	Charlotte
Mitchell	Bakersville
Montgomery	Troy
Moore	Carthage
Nash	Nashville
New Hanover	Wilmington
Northampton	Jackson
Onslow	Jacksonville
Orange	Hillsborough
Pamlico	Bayboro
Pasquotank	Elizabeth City
Pender	Burgaw
Perquimans	Hertford
Person	Roxboro
Pitt	Greenville
Polk	Columbus
Randolph	Asheboro
Richmond	Rockingham
Robeson	Lumberton
Rockingham	Wentworth
Rowan	Salisbury
Rutherford	Rutherfordton
Sampson	Clinton
Scotland	Laurinburg
Stanly	Albemarle
Stokes	Danbury
Surry	Dodson
Swain	Bryson City
Transylvania	Brevard
Tyrrell	Columbia
Union	Monroe
Vance	Henderson
Wake	Raleigh
Warren	Warrenton
Washington	Plymouth
Watauga	Boone
Wayne	Goldsboro
Wilkes	Wilkesboro
Wilson	Wilson
Yadkin	Yadkinville
Yancey	Burnsville

PARTIAL LIST OF

CITIES AND TOWNS

• County Seats

Aberdeen	F-7
Ahoskie	D-11
Alamance	D-6
Albemarle •	E-5
Andrews	B-2
Ansonville	F-6
Apex	E-8
Arapahoe	F-11
Archdale	D-6
Archers Lodge	E-9
Arcola	D-9
Arden	E-1
Arlington	D-4
Ash	H-8
Asheboro •	E-6
Asheville •	B-4
Ashford	D-2
Ashland	D-11
Askewville	D-11
Atkinson	G-9
Atlantic	F-12
Atlantic Beach	G-11
Aulander	D-11
Aurelian Springs	C-10
Austin	D-4
Autryville	F-8
Aventon	D-9
Avon	E-14
Ayden	E-10
Aydlett	C-13
Bailey	E-9
Bakersville •	D-2
Banner Elk	D-2
Bannertown	C-5
Barco	C-13
Bath	E-11
Battleboro	D-10
Bayboro •	F-11
Beaufort •	G-12
Belgrade	F-10
Belhaven	E-12
Belmont	F-4
Benson	E-8
Bessemer City	E-3
Bethel	E-10
Beulaville	F-10
Biscoe	E-6
Black Mountain	E-1
Bladenboro	G-8
Blowing Rock	D-3
Bogue	G-11
Boiling Springs	F-3
Bolivia	H-9
Bonnie Doon	F-7
Boone •	D-3
Boonville	D-4
Brevard •	B-4
Bridgeton	F-11
Broad Creek	G-11
Broadway	E-7
Brookford	E-3
Brunswick	G-8
Bryantown	D-10
Bryson City •	B-3
Buckhorn Cross Roads	E-9
Buies Creek	E-8
Bunn	D-9
Burgaw •	G-9
Burlington	D-7
Burnsville •	F-5
Buxton	E-14
Bynum	E-7
Calabash	H-8
Calypso	F-9
Camden •	C-12
Cameron	E-7
Candor	F-6
Canton	B-4
Caroleen	F-2
Carolina Beach	H-9
Carrboro	D-7
Carthage	E-7
Carvers	G-9
Cary	E-8
Casar	E-3
Castle Hayne	G-9
Catawba	E-4
Centerville	D-9
Cerro Gordo	G-8
Chadbourn	G-8
Chapel Hill	D-7
Charlotte •	F-4
Cherryville	E-3
China Grove	E-4
Chocowinity	E-11
Clarkton	G-8
Clayton	E-8
Clemmons	D-5
Cliffside	F-3
Clinton •	F-9
Coats	E-8
Cofield	C-11
Coinjock	C-13
Colerain	D-11
Columbia •	D-12
Columbus	F-2
Como	C-11
Concord •	E-5
Conetoe	D-10
Conover	E-3
Conway	C-10
Cooleemee	E-5
Cornelius	E-4
Costin	G-9
Council	G-8
Cove City	F-10
Cramerton	F-4
Creedmoor	D-8
Creswell	D-12
Crisp	E-10
Croatan	F-11
Currituck •	C-13
Dallas	E-4
Dana	E-1
Danbury •	C-5
Darby	D-3
Davidson	E-4
Delco	G-9
Delway	G-9
Denton	E-5
Dillsboro	B-3
Dixon	G-10
Dobbersville	F-9
Dobbins Heights	F-6
Dobson •	C-4
Dover	F-10
Drexel	E-3
Dublin	G-8
Dunn	E-8
Durham •	D-8
East Flat Rock	F-1
East Lake	D-13
Eden	C-6
Edenton •	D-12
Edgecombe	G-10
Eli Whitney	D-7
Elizabeth City	C-12
Elizabethtown •	G-8
Elk Park	D-2
Elkin	D-4
Ellerbe	F-6
Elliott	F-9
Elm City	D-9
Elon College	D-6
Emerald Isle	G-11
Enfield	D-10
Engelhard	E-13
Erwin	E-8
Ether	E-6
Eureka	E-9
Everetts	D-11
Fair Bluff	G-7
Fairfield	E-12
Fairmont	G-7
Faison	F-9
Falcon	F-8
Falkland	E-10
Falling Creek	F-10
Fallston	E-3
Fayetteville •	F-8
Folkstone	G-10
Forest City	E-2
Four Oaks	E-8
Franklin •	B-3
Franklinton	D-8
Freeland	H-8
Freeman	G-9
Frisco	F-13
Fuquay-Varina	E-8
Gamewell	D-3
Garland	G-9
Garner	E-8
Garysburg	C-10
Gaston	C-10
Gastonia •	F-4
Gates	C-11
Gatesville •	C-11

CONTINUED AT RIGHT

Lithographed in U.S.A.

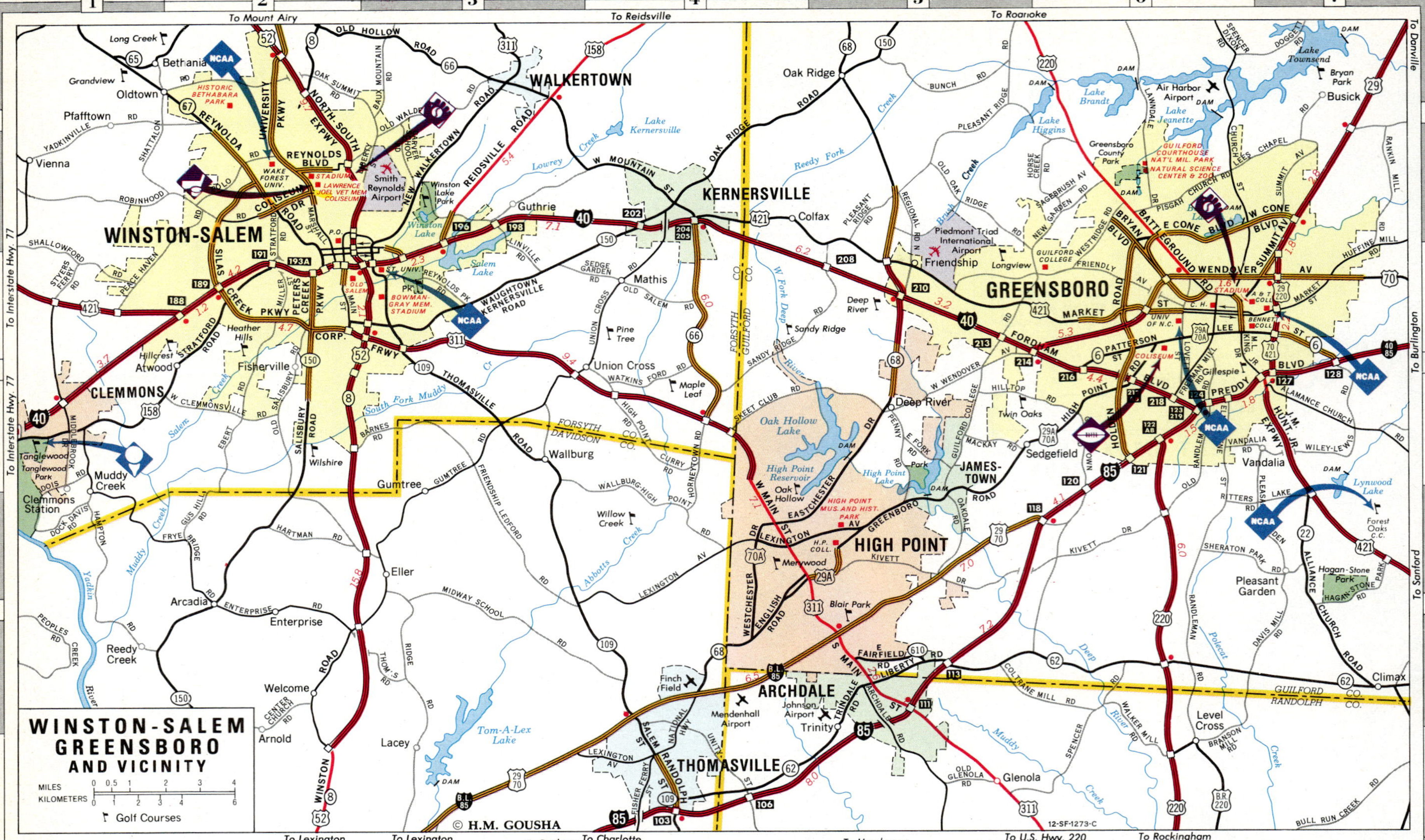

1 2 3 4 5 6 7
A B C D
To Mount Airy
To Reidsville
To Roanoke
To Danville
To Interstate Hwy. 77
To Burlington
To Sanford
WALKERTOWN
KERNERSVILLE
WINSTON-SALEM
GREENSBORO
CLEMMONS
HIGH POINT
JAMESTOWN
ARCHDALE
THOMASVILLE
Bethania
Oldtown
Pfafftown
Vienna
Lewisville
Walkertown
Oak Ridge
Colfax
Friendship
Guthrie
Mathis
Union Cross
Deep River
Sedgefield
Vandalia
Pleasant Garden
Climax
Level Cross
Glenola
Trinity
Wallburg
Gumtree
Ellen
Enterprise
Arcadia
Reedy Creek
Welcome
Arnold
Lacey
Muddy Creek
Tanglewood Park
Clemmons Station
Tom-A-Lex Lake
Oak Hollow Lake
High Point Reservoir
Lake Brandt
Lake Higgins
Lake Jeanette
Lake Townsend
Busick
Piedmont Triad International Airport
Smith Reynolds Airport
WINSTON-SALEM GREENSBORO AND VICINITY
MILES
KILOMETERS
Golf Courses
© H.M. GOUSHA
To Lexington
To Lexington
To Charlotte
To Rockingham
12-SF-1273-C

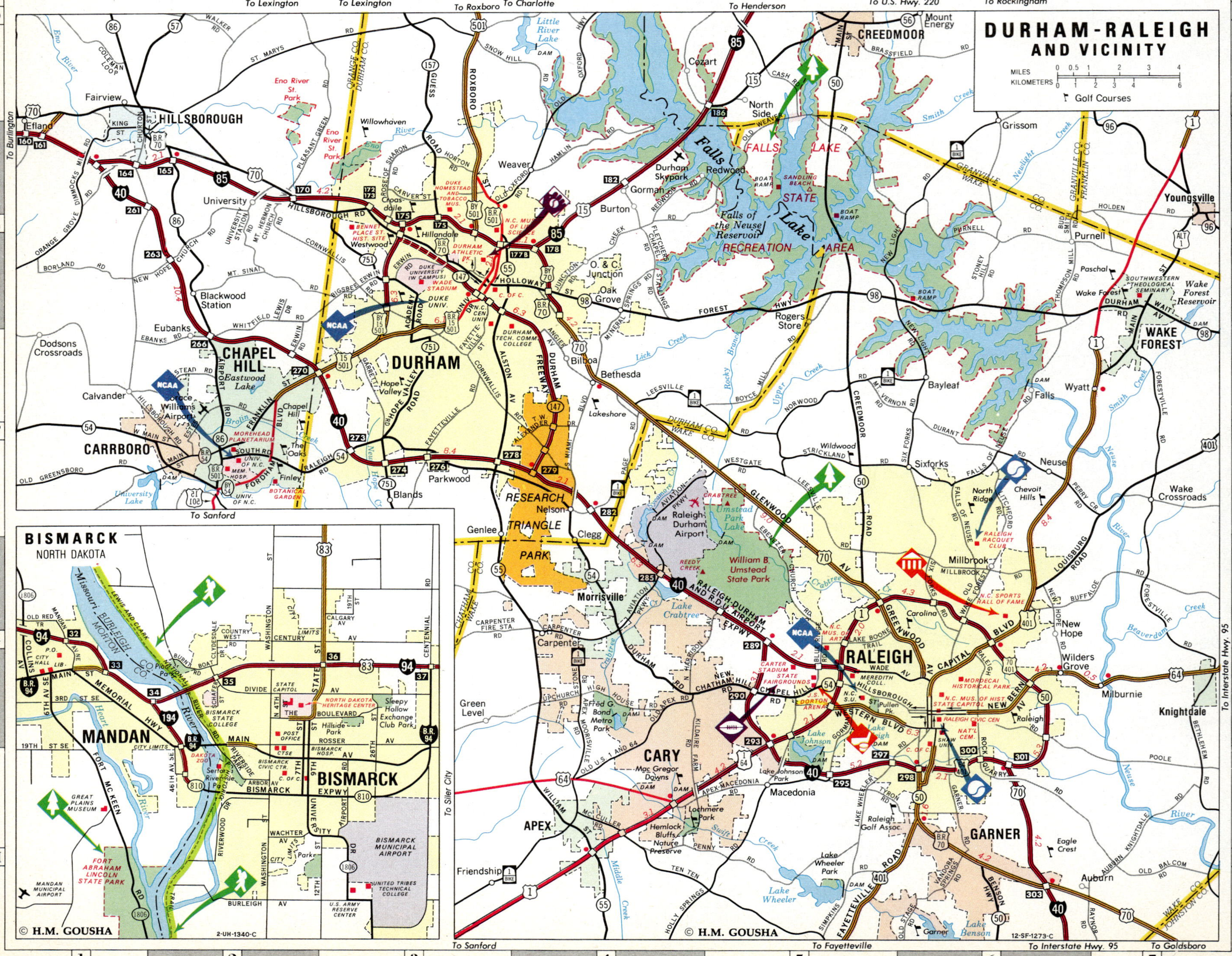

To Roxboro
To Henderson
To U.S. Hwy. 220
To Burlington
To Sanford
To Fayetteville
To Interstate Hwy. 95
To Goldsboro
To Siler City
DURHAM-RALEIGH AND VICINITY
MILES
KILOMETERS
Golf Courses
HILLSBOROUGH
Efland
Fairview
University
CHAPEL HILL
CARRBORO
DURHAM
Creedmoor
Cozart
North Side
Falls Lake
Falls of the Neuse Reservoir
FALLS LAKE STATE RECREATION AREA
Grissom
Youngsville
Wake Forest
WAKE FOREST
Purnell
Bayleaf
Falls
Wyatt
Neuse
Sixforks
Durham Skypark
Gorman
Burton
Weaver
Oak Grove
Bethesda
Lakeshore
Rogers Store
Bilboa
Parkwood
Blands
Genlee
Nelson
Clegg
RESEARCH TRIANGLE PARK
Raleigh Durham Airport
William B. Umstead State Park
Morrisville
Carpenter
Green Level
CARY
APEX
Friendship
RALEIGH
GARNER
Macedonia
Millbrook
North Ridge
Wake Crossroads
New Hope
Wilders Grove
Milburnie
Knightdale
Auburn
Eagle Crest
Lake Wheeler
Lake Benson
Blackwood Station
Eubanks
Dodsons Crossroads
Calvander
University Lake
Eno River St. Park
Little River Lake
© H.M. GOUSHA
12-SF-1273-C
BISMARCK NORTH DAKOTA
MANDAN
BISMARCK
Missouri River
Fort Abraham Lincoln State Park
Great Plains Museum
Mandan Municipal Airport
Bismarck Municipal Airport
United Tribes Technical College
U.S. Army Reserve Center
Sleepy Hollow Exchange Club Park
Hillside Park
State Capitol
North Dakota Heritage Center
© H.M. GOUSHA
2-UH-1340-C

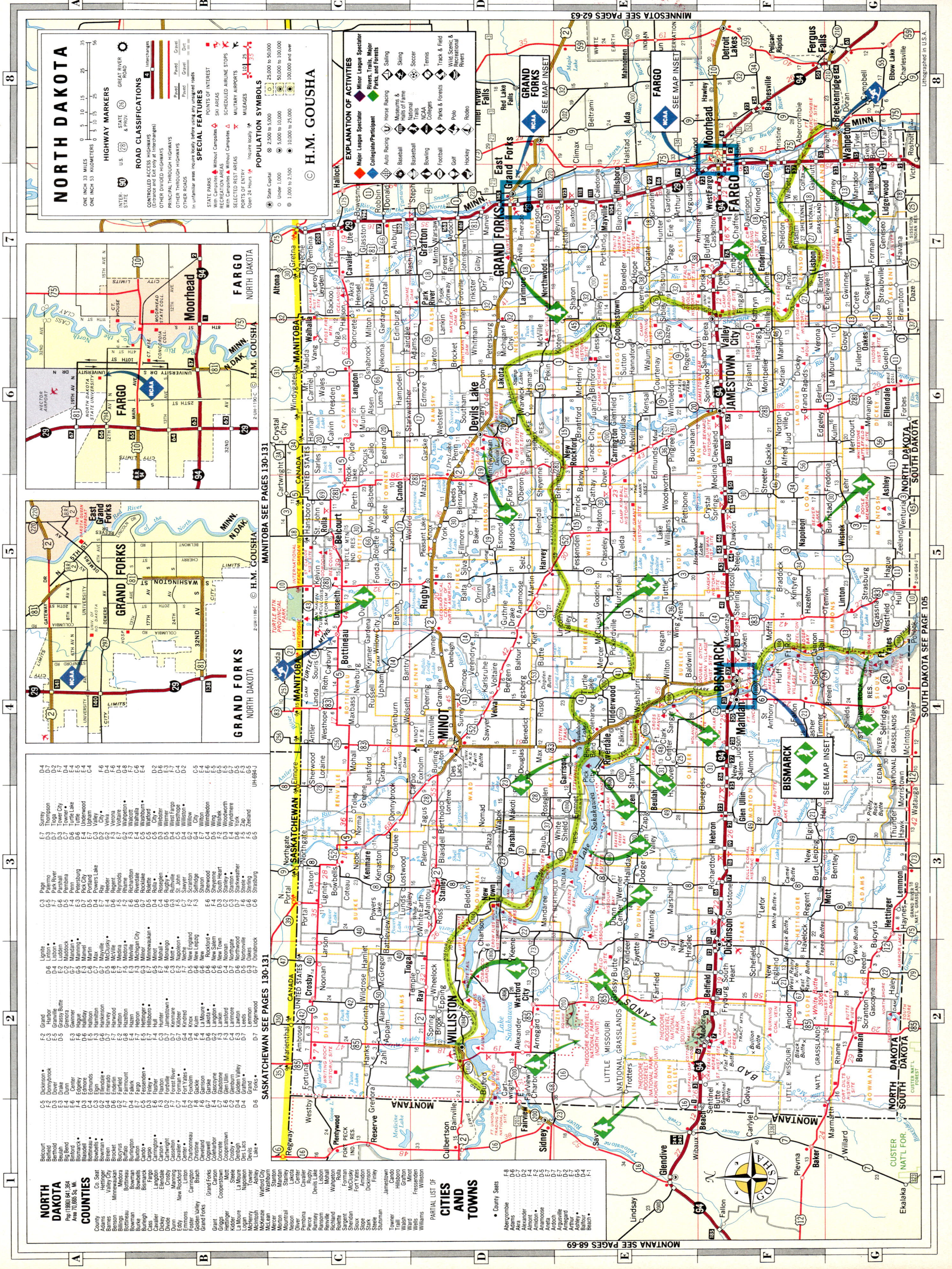
NORTH DAKOTA
ONE INCH 33 MILES
ONE INCH 53 KILOMETERS
HIGHWAY MARKERS
ROAD CLASSIFICATIONS
SPECIAL FEATURES
POPULATION SYMBOLS
© H.M. GOUSHA
EXPLANATION OF ACTIVITIES
MINNESOTA SEE PAGES 62-63
MONTANA SEE PAGES 68-69
SOUTH DAKOTA SEE PAGE 105
MANITOBA SEE PAGES 130-131
SASKATCHEWAN SEE PAGES 130-131
GRAND FORKS NORTH DAKOTA
FARGO NORTH DAKOTA
GRAND FORKS SEE MAP INSET
FARGO SEE MAP INSET
BISMARCK SEE MAP INSET
NORTH DAKOTA COUNTIES
PARTIAL LIST OF CITIES AND TOWNS
BISMARCK
FARGO
GRAND FORKS
MINOT
JAMESTOWN
WILLISTON
DICKINSON
Lithographed in U.S.A.

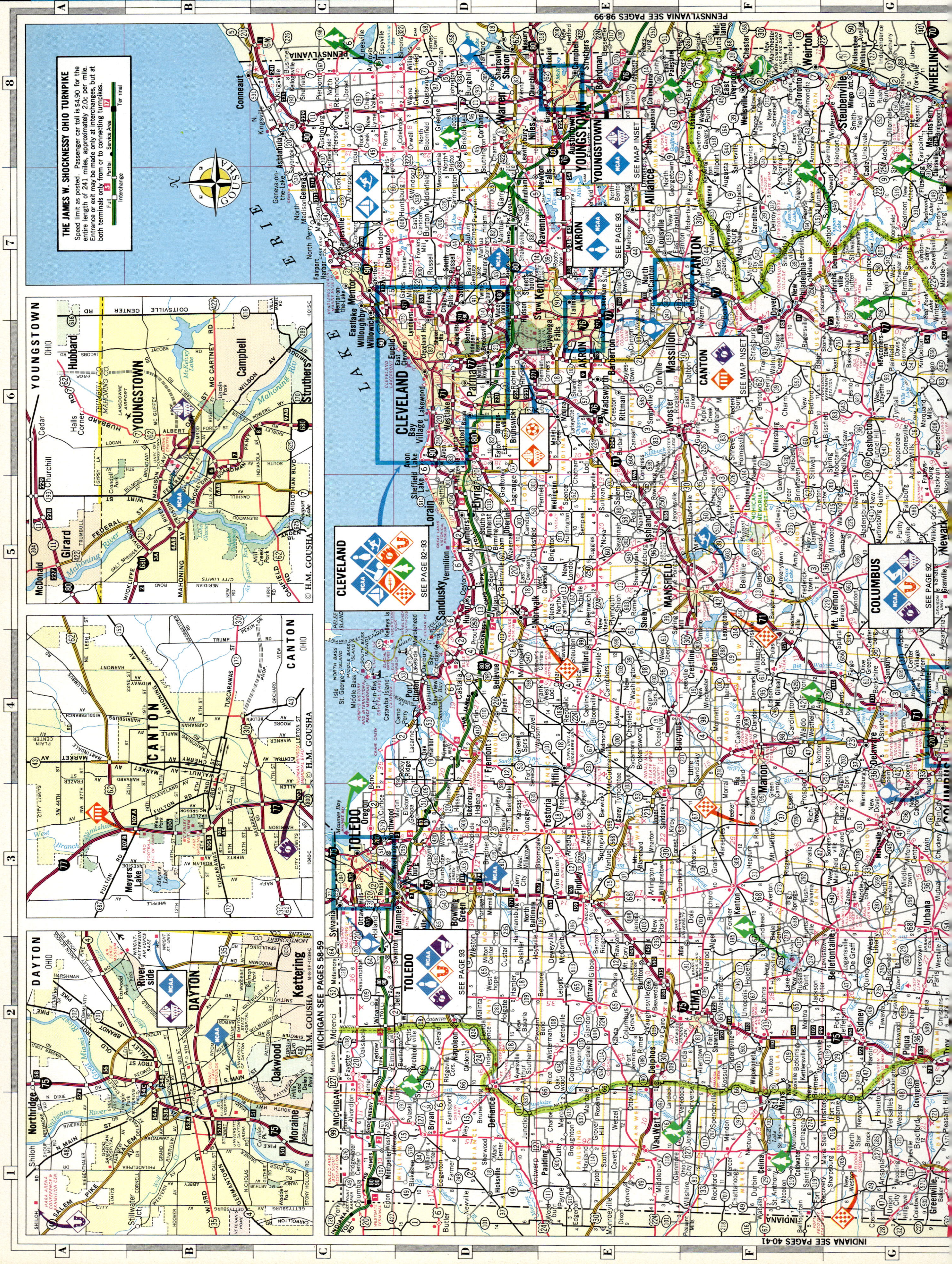
THE JAMES W. SHOCKNESSY OHIO TURNPIKE
Speed limit as posted. Passenger car toll is $4.90 for the entire length of 241 miles, approximately 2.0¢ per mile. Entrance or exit may be made only at interchanges, but at both terminals only from or to connecting turnpikes.
LAKE ERIE
PENNSYLVANIA SEE PAGES 98-99
MICHIGAN SEE PAGES 58-59
INDIANA SEE PAGES 40-41
YOUNGSTOWN OHIO
CANTON OHIO
DAYTON OHIO
© H.M. GOUSHA
CLEVELAND SEE PAGE 92-93
TOLEDO SEE PAGE 93
COLUMBUS SEE PAGE 92
AKRON SEE PAGE 93
CANTON SEE MAP INSET
YOUNGSTOWN SEE MAP INSET

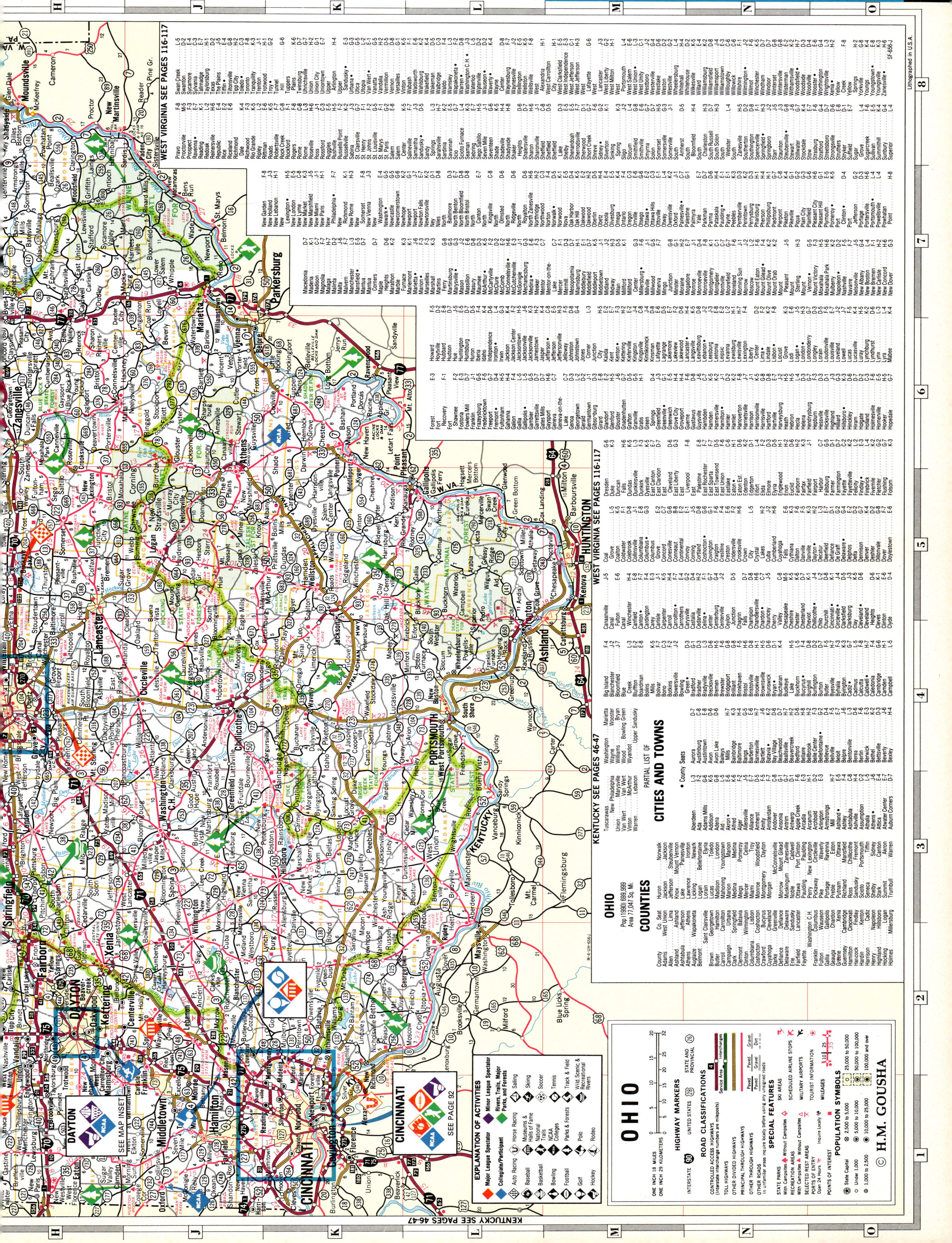
OHIO
H.M. GOUSHA
HIGHWAY MARKERS
ROAD CLASSIFICATIONS
SPECIAL FEATURES
POPULATION SYMBOLS
EXPLANATION OF ACTIVITIES
DAYTON
SEE MAP INSET
CINCINNATI
SEE PAGE 92
KENTUCKY SEE PAGES 46-47
WEST VIRGINIA SEE PAGES 116-117
COUNTIES
PARTIAL LIST OF
CITIES AND TOWNS
Springfield
Xenia
Kettering
Middletown
Hamilton
Zanesville
Lancaster
Circleville
Chillicothe
Athens
Marietta
Parkersburg
Portsmouth
Huntington
Ashland
Gallipolis
Lithographed in U.S.A.

COLUMBUS AND VICINITY
MILES
KILOMETERS
Golf Courses
CLEVELAND AND VICINITY
MILES
KILOMETERS
Golf Courses
CINCINNATI AND VICINITY
MILES
KILOMETERS
Golf Courses
Dublin
WORTHINGTON
Westerville
Riverlea
Minerva Park
HILLIARD
UPPER ARLINGTON
GRANDVIEW HEIGHTS
COLUMBUS
Gahanna
WHITEHALL
BEXLEY
REYNOLDSBURG
Valleyview
New Rome
Urbancrest
GROVE CITY
Obetz
Groveport
Canal Winchester
Brice
AVON LAKE
BAY VILLAGE
WESTLAKE
AVON
NORTH OLMSTED
NORTH RIDGEVILLE
OLMSTED FALLS
FOREST PARK
SPRINGDALE
SHARONVILLE
GREENHILLS
GLENDALE
BLUE ASH
MOUNT HEALTHY
NORTH COLLEGE HILL
WOODLAWN
LINCOLN HTS.
EVENDALE
MONTGOMERY
LOVELAND
WYOMING
LOCKLAND
READING
AMBERLEY
DEER PARK
MADEIRA
ELMWOOD PLACE
GOLF MANOR
SILVERTON
ST. BERNARD
NORWOOD
CHEVIOT
INDIAN HILL
MILFORD
TERRACE PARK
MARIEMONT
FAIRFAX
NEWTOWN
CINCINNATI
ADDYSTON
DAYTON
BELLEVUE
FORT THOMAS
NEWPORT
COVINGTON
Ludlow
Park Hills
Villa Hills
Greater Cincinnati International Airport
© H.M. GOUSHA

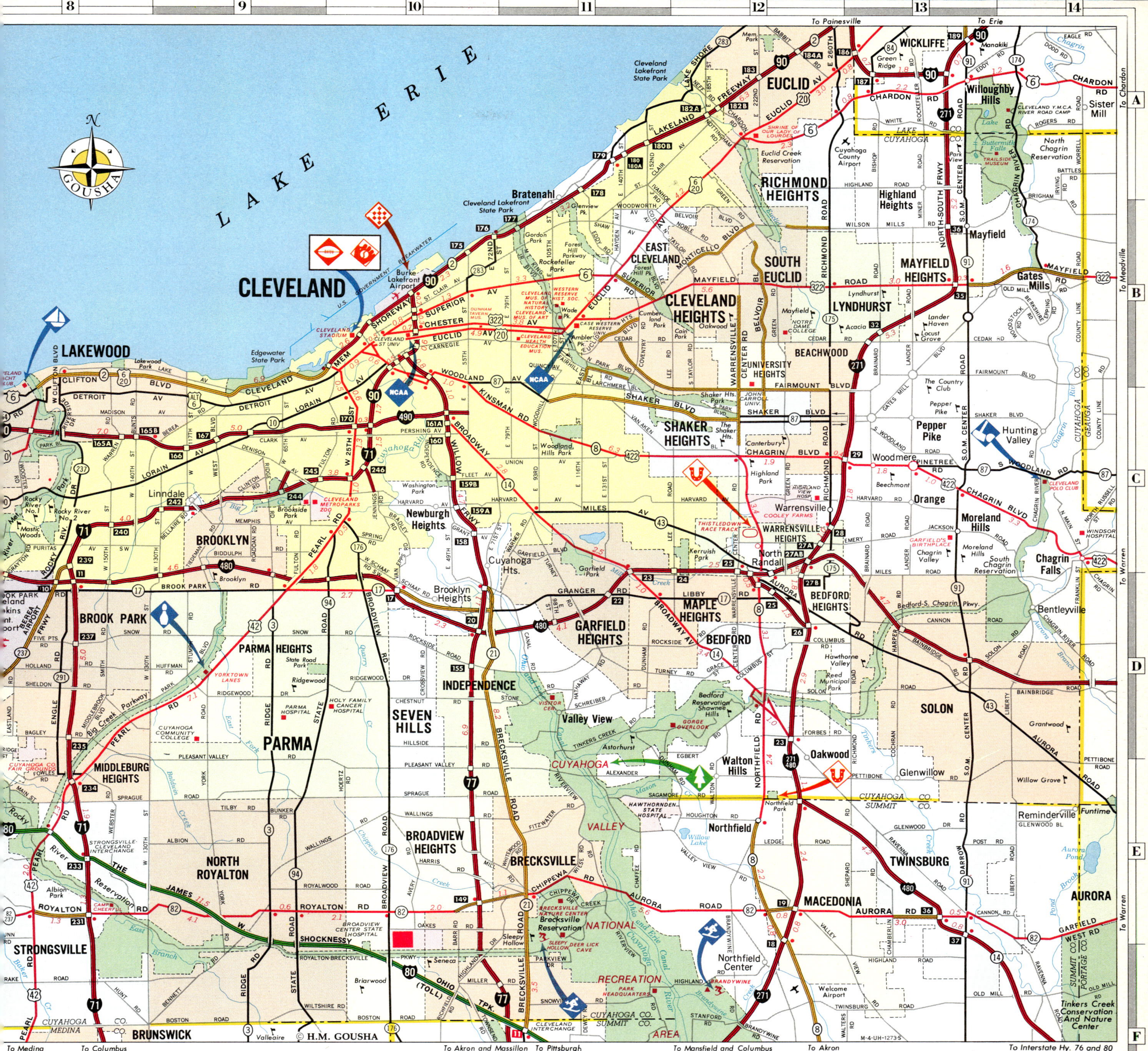
LAKE ERIE
CLEVELAND
LAKEWOOD
EUCLID
WICKLIFFE
Willoughby Hills
RICHMOND HEIGHTS
Highland Heights
Mayfield
SOUTH EUCLID
MAYFIELD HEIGHTS
Gates Mills
LYNDHURST
EAST CLEVELAND
CLEVELAND HEIGHTS
UNIVERSITY HEIGHTS
BEACHWOOD
SHAKER HEIGHTS
Pepper Pike
Hunting Valley
Bratenahl
Linndale
BROOKLYN
Newburgh Heights
Cuyahoga Hts.
Brooklyn Heights
Warrensville
WARRENSVILLE HEIGHTS
Orange
Moreland Hills
Chagrin Falls
Bentleyville
North Randall
BEDFORD HEIGHTS
MAPLE HEIGHTS
GARFIELD HEIGHTS
BEDFORD
BROOK PARK
PARMA HEIGHTS
PARMA
SEVEN HILLS
INDEPENDENCE
Valley View
Walton Hills
Oakwood
Glenwillow
SOLON
MIDDLEBURG HEIGHTS
NORTH ROYALTON
BROADVIEW HEIGHTS
BRECKSVILLE
Northfield
TWINSBURG
MACEDONIA
AURORA
Reminderville
STRONGSVILLE
BRUNSWICK
CUYAHOGA VALLEY NATIONAL RECREATION AREA
© H.M. GOUSHA
To Painesville
To Erie
To Chardon
To Meadville
To Warren
To Medina
To Columbus
To Akron and Massillon
To Pittsburgh
To Mansfield and Columbus
To Akron
To Interstate Hy. 76 and 80

AKRON OHIO
FAIRLAWN
CUYAHOGA FALLS
MUNROE FALLS
TALLMADGE
NORTON
BARBERTON
LAKEMORE
AKRON FULTON INTERNATIONAL AIRPORT
© H.M. GOUSHA

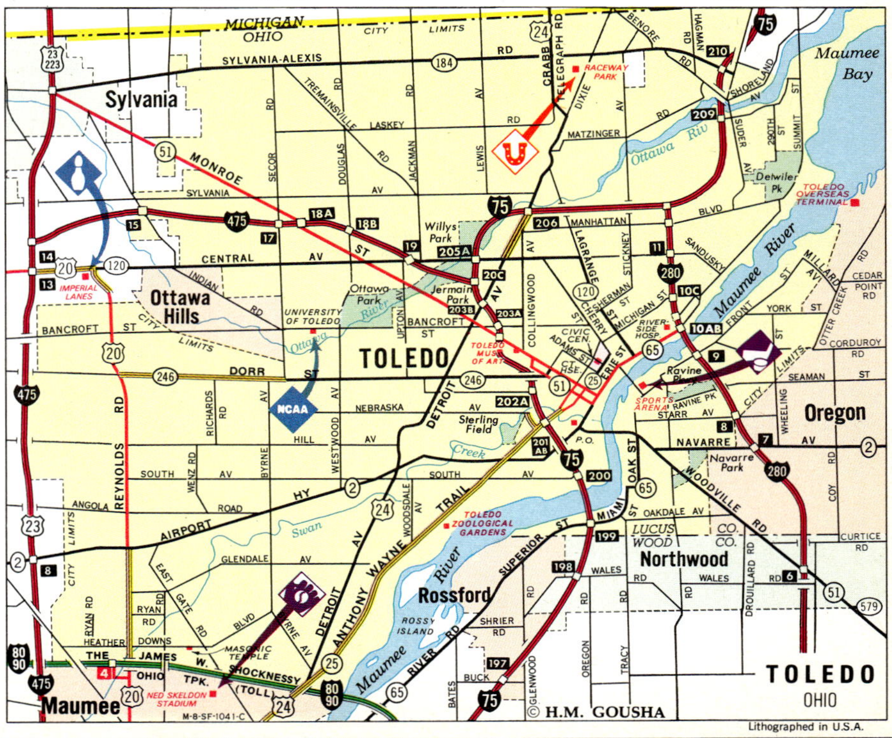
TOLEDO OHIO
MICHIGAN
OHIO
Sylvania
Ottawa Hills
TOLEDO
Oregon
Northwood
Rossford
Maumee
Maumee Bay
Maumee River
© H.M. GOUSHA
Lithographed in U.S.A.

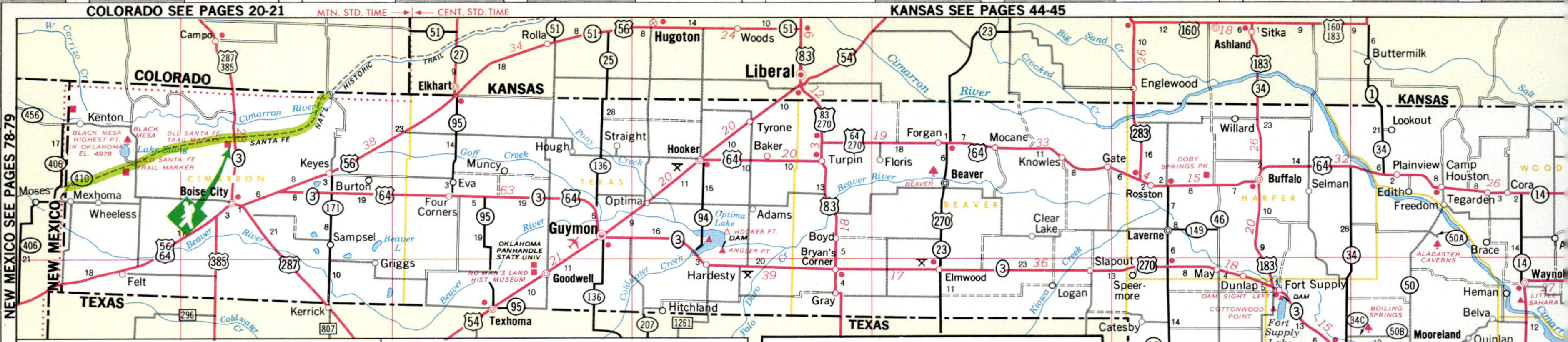

OKLAHOMA

Pop (1990) 3,157,604
Area 69,919 Sq. Mi.

COUNTIES

County	Co. Seat	County	Co. Seat
Adair	Stilwell	Le Flore	Poteau
Alfalfa	Cherokee	Lincoln	Chandler
Atoka	Atoka	Logan	Guthrie
Beaver	Beaver	Love	Marietta
Bockham	Sayre	Major	Fairview
Blaine	Watonga	Marshall	Madill
Bryan	Durant	Mayes	Pryor
Caddo	Anadarko	McClain	Purcell
Canadian	El Reno	McCurtain	Idabel
Carter	Ardmore	McIntosh	Eufaula
Cherokee	Tahlequah	Murray	Sulphur
Choctaw	Hugo	Muskogee	Muskogee
Cimarron	Boise City	Noble	Perry
Cleveland	Norman	Nowata	Nowata
Coal	Coalgate	Okfuskee	Okemah
Comanche	Lawton	Oklahoma	Oklahoma City
Cotton	Walters	Okmulgee	Okmulgee
Craig	Vinita	Osage	Pawhuska
Creek	Sapulpa	Ottawa	Miami
Custer	Arapaho	Pawnee	Pawnee
Delaware	Jay	Payne	Stillwater
Dewey	Taloga	Pittsburg	McAlester
Ellis	Arnett	Pontotoc	Ada
Garfield	Enid	Pottawatomie	Shawnee
Garvin	Pauls Valley	Pushmataha	Anters
Grady	Chickasha	Roger Mills	Cheyenne
Grant	Medford	Rogers	Claremore
Greer	Mangum	Seminole	Wewoka
Harmon	Hollis	Sequoyah	Sallisaw
Harper	Buffalo	Stephens	Duncan
Haskell	Stigler	Texas	Guymon
Hughes	Holdenville	Tillman	Frederick
Jackson	Altus	Tulsa	Tulsa
Jefferson	Waurika	Wagoner	Wagoner
Johnston	Tishomingo	Washington	Bartlesville
Kay	Newkirk	Washita	Cordell
Kingfisher	Kingfisher	Woods	Alva
Kiowa	Hobart	Woodward	Woodward
Latimer	Wilburton		

PARTIAL LIST OF

CITIES AND TOWNS

• County Seats

Ada •	E-10
Adair	B-13
Addington	E-9
Afton	A-13
Ahloso	E-11
Albion	E-13
Alderson	D-12
Aledo	C-7
Alfalfa	D-8
Allen	D-11
Alpers	E-9
Altus •	E-7
Alva •	A-8
Anadarko •	D-8
Antlers •	E-12
Apache	D-8
Arapaho	C-7
Ardmore •	F-10
Armstrong	F-11
Arnett	B-6
Arpetar	D-12
Atoka •	E-11
Atwood	D-11
Babbs	D-7
Bado	B-7
Baker	A-4
Bald Hill	C-12
Ballard	B-14
Barnsdall	B-11
Bartlesville •	A-11
Baum	E-10
Beaver •	A-5
Beggs	C-11
Bellvue	C-11
Bennington	F-12
Bethany	C-9
Big Cabin	B-13
Big Cedar	E-14
Binger	D-8
Bison	B-9
Bixby	C-12
Blackwell	A-10
Blair	E-6
Blanchard	D-9
Blue	F-11
Boise City •	A-2
Bokchito	F-11
Boswell	F-12
Boyd	A-4
Braithwaite	D-7
Brewer	D-12
Bridgeport	C-8
Bristow	C-11
Broken Arrow	B-12
Broken Bow	F-14
Brushy	C-14
Bryan's Corner	B-4
Buckhorn	E-10
Buffalo •	A-6
Burbank	A-10
Bushyhead	B-12
Butler	C-7
Cabaniss	D-11
Cache	E-8
Caddo	F-11
Calera	F-11
Calumet	C-8
Calvin	D-11
Camp Houston	A-7
Caney	E-11
Canute	D-7
Carnegie	D-8
Caston	D-13
Cedar Springs	B-8
Cestos	B-7
Chandler •	C-10
Checotah	C-12
Chelsea	B-12
Cherokee •	A-8
Chester	B-7
Chickasha •	D-8
Chockie	E-11
Choctaw	C-10
Chouteau	B-12
Claremore •	B-12
Clayton	E-12
Cleveland	B-11
Clinton	C-7
Coalgate •	E-11
Collinsville	B-12
Colony	D-8
Comanche	E-8
Commerce	A-13
Concho	C-8
Cora	A-7
Cordell •	D-7
Countyline	E-9
Covington	B-9
Coweta	C-12
Crescent	C-9
Cushing	C-10
Custer City	C-7
Cyril	D-8
Dale	D-10
Dane	B-8
Darwin	E-12
Davidson	E-7
Davis	E-10
Del City	D-9
Delaware	A-12
Devol	F-8
Dewey	A-12
Dickson	E-10
Dill City	D-7
Drumright	C-11
Ducan •	E-8
Dunlap	B-6
Durant •	F-11
Eagletown	F-14
Edmond	C-9
El Reno •	C-9
Eldon	C-13
Elk City	C-6
Elmwood	B-5
Enid	B-9
Erick	D-6
Eufaula •	D-12
Eva	A-3
Fairfax	B-10
Fairview •	B-8
Fittstown	E-10
Fitzhugh	E-10
Forgan	A-5
Fort Gibson	C-13
Fort Supply	B-6
Fort Towson	F-13
Four Corners	A-3
Foyil	B-12
Frederick	E-7
Garber	B-9
Garvin	F-13
Gate	A-5
Geary	C-8
Goodwell	B-3
Gracemont	D-8
Grandfield	F-8
Granite	D-6
Gray	B-4
Greenfield	C-8
Grove	B-13
Guthrie •	C-9
Guymon •	A-3
Haileyville	D-12
Hallett	B-11
Hammon	C-7
Harden City	E-11
Hardesty	B-4
Harrah	C-10
Hartshorne	D-12
Haskell	C-12
Haywood	D-12
Healdton	E-9
Heavener	D-14
Hennepin	E-10
Hennessey	B-9
Henryetta	C-11
Hext	D-6
Heyburn	C-11
Hinton	C-8
Hobart •	D-7
Hodgen	D-14
Holdenville •	D-11
Hollis •	E-6
Hollow	A-12
Hominy	B-11
Hooker	A-4
Hopeton	A-8
Howe	D-14
Hucmac	B-7
Hughes	D-13
Hugo •	F-12
Hydro	C-8
Idabel •	F-13
Ingersoll	A-8
Jacktown	C-10
Jamesville	C-12
Jay •	B-13
Jefferson	A-9
Jenks	B-12
Jet	B-8
Jones	C-10
Kansas	B-13
Kent	F-12
Keyes	A-2
Kiamichi	E-13
Kingfisher •	C-8
Kingston	F-10
Kinta	D-13
Kiowa	E-12
Knowles	A-5
Konawa	D-10
Krebs	D-12
Lahoma	B-8
Lamont	A-9
Laverne	A-6
Lawrence	E-10
Lawton	E-8
Lehigh	E-11
Lela	B-10
Lenapah	A-12
Lexington	D-10
Lindsay	D-9
Locust Grove	B-13
Lone Grove	F-10
Lookeba	D-8
Lucien	B-9
Lugert	D-7
Madill •	F-10
Mangum	D-6
Manitou	E-7
Mannsville	F-10
Marietta •	F-10
Marlow	E-9
Marshall	B-9
Maud	D-10
May	B-6
Maysville	E-9
McAlester •	D-12
McLoud	C-10
Medford •	A-9
Meno	B-8
Miami •	A-13
Midwest City	C-9
Minco	D-9
Mocane	A-5
Moore	D-9
Mooreland	B-7
Morrison	B-10
Mountain View	D-7
Muldrow	C-14
Mulhall	B-9
Muskogee •	C-13
Nardin	A-9
Nash	A-8
Nebo	E-10
Newkirk •	A-10
Noble	D-10
Norman •	D-9
Nowata •	A-12
Oilton	B-11
Okarche	C-8
Okeene	B-8
Okemah •	C-11
Oklahoma City •	C-9
Okmulgee •	C-12
Oleta	E-13
Oologah	B-12
Optima	A-3
Orienta	B-8
Orlando	B-9
Owasso	B-12
Page	E-14
Panama	D-14
Panola	D-13
Pauls Valley •	E-10
Pawhuska •	A-11
Pawnee •	B-10
Pensacola	B-13
Perkins	C-10
Perry •	B-10
Phillips	E-11
Picher	A-13
Pittsburg	E-12
Pocola	D-14
Ponca City	A-10
Pond Creek	B-9
Poteau •	D-14
Prague	C-11
Proctor	C-14
Pryor •	B-12
Purcell •	D-9
Putnam	C-7
Quapaw	A-13
Quinton	D-13
Randlett	F-8
Ratliff City	E-9
Red Oak	D-13
Renfrow	A-9
Ringling	F-9
Ringwood	B-8
Rocky	D-7
Roff	E-10
Roosevelt	D-7
Rose	B-13
Rosston	A-6
Rush Springs	E-9
Ryan	F-9
Salina	B-13
Sallisaw •	C-14
Sampsel	A-2
Sand Creek	A-9
Sand Springs	B-11
Sapulpa •	B-11
Savanna	D-12
Sayre •	D-6
Scullin	E-10
Selling	B-7
Seminole	D-11
Shady Point	D-14
Sharon	B-7
Shattuck	B-6
Shawnee	D-10
Skiatook	B-11
Slapout	B-5
Slick	C-11
Smithville	E-14
Snow	E-13
Snyder	E-7
South Coffeyville	A-12
Spavinaw	B-13
Speermore	B-6
Sperry	B-11
Spiro	D-14
Stapp	D-14
Stigler •	D-13
Stillwater •	B-10
Stilwell •	C-14
Stratford	D-10
Stringtown	E-12
Stroud	C-11
Stuart	D-11
Sugden	F-8
Sulphur •	E-10
Sunray	E-9
Tabler	D-9
Tahlequah •	C-13
Talala	B-12
Talihina	E-13
Taloga •	C-7
Tatums	E-9
Taylor	F-8
Tecumseh	D-10
Tegarden	A-7
Temple	E-8
Terral	F-9
Texota	D-6
The Village	C-9
Thomas	C-7
Tipton	E-7
Tishomingo •	E-11
Tonkawa	A-10
Tulsa •	B-11
Tupelo	E-11
Turpin	A-4
Tushka	E-11
Tuttle	D-9
Tyrone	A-4
Unger	F-12
Valliant	F-13
Velma	E-9
Vian	C-13
Vici	B-7
Vinita	A-13
Wagoner •	C-12
Walters •	E-8
Warner	C-13
Warwick	C-10
Watonga •	C-8
Watts	B-14
Waukomis	B-9
Waurika •	F-8
Waynoka	B-7
Weatherford	C-7
Welch	A-13
Weleetka	D-11
Wellston	C-10
Westville	B-14
Wetumka	D-11
Wewoka •	D-11
Whitefield	D-13
Wilburton •	D-13
Wilson	F-9
Woodward •	B-7
Wright City	F-13
Wynnewood	E-10
Yale	B-11
Yukon	C-9

657-J

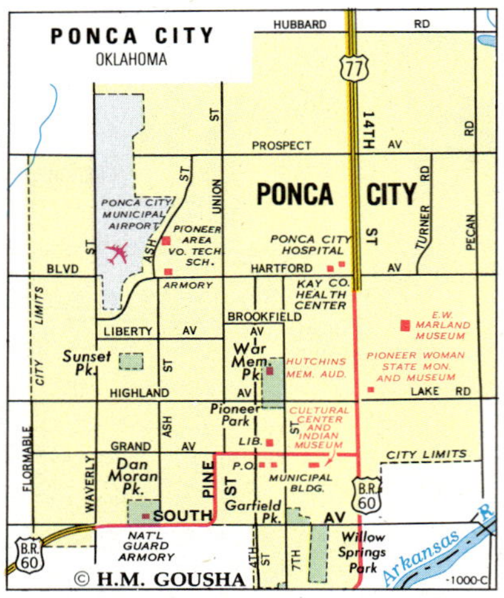

OKLAHOMA TOLL ROADS

Entrance or exit only at interchanges, shown thus:

Interchange — Concession Area

H.E. BAILEY TURNPIKE
Passenger car toll is $2.75 for the entire length of 86 miles, approximately 3.2c per mile.

TURNER TURNPIKE
Passenger car toll is $2.50 for the entire length of 86 miles, approximately 2.9c per mile.

WILL ROGERS TURNPIKE
Passenger car toll is $2.50 for the entire length of 88 miles, approximately 2.8c per mile.

INDIAN NATION TURNPIKE
Passenger car toll is $3.50 for the entire length of 105 miles approximately 3.3c per mile.

MUSKOGEE TURNPIKE
Passenger car toll is $1.75 for the entire length of 54 miles, approximately 3.3c per mile.

CIMARRON TURNPIKE
Passenger car toll is $1.75 for the entire length of 60 miles, approximately 3.0c per mile.

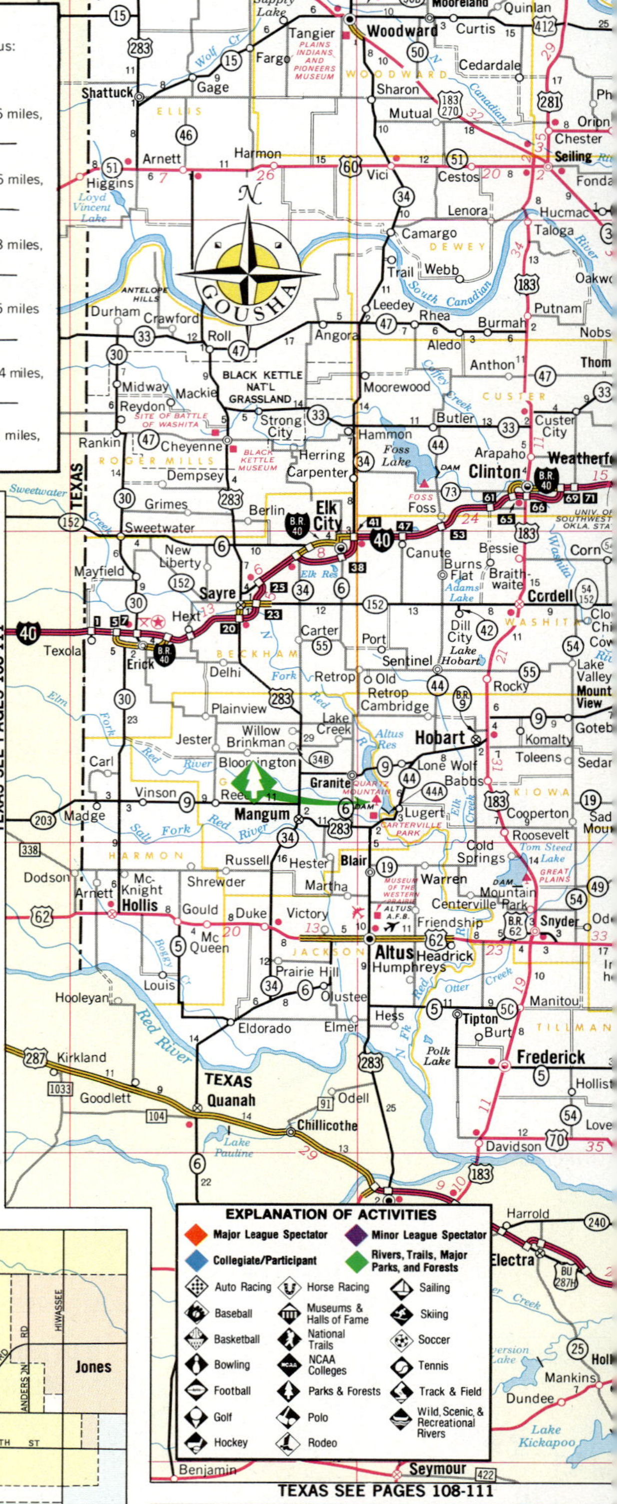

KANSAS SEE PAGES 44-45
MISSOURI SEE PAGES 66-67
ARKANSAS SEE PAGES 12-13
TEXAS SEE PAGES 108-111
TULSA
SEE MAP INSET
OKLAHOMA CITY
SEE MAP INSET
OKLAHOMA CITY
TULSA
ENID
PONCA CITY
BARTLESVILLE
MUSKOGEE
LAWTON
WICHITA FALLS
FORT SMITH
MC ALESTER
JOPLIN
Arkansas City
Coffeyville
Stillwater
Norman
Shawnee
Ada
Ardmore
Durant
Denison
Sherman
Paris
Okmulgee
Henryetta
Sapulpa
Broken Arrow
Claremore
Pryor
Miami
Vinita
Tahlequah
Chickasha
Duncan
Guthrie
El Reno
Edmond
Seminole
Sulphur
Hugo
Idabel
Broken Bow
Antlers
Atoka
Eufaula
Kingfisher
Anadarko
Perry
Blackwell
Tonkawa
Pawhuska
North Enid
Crosslin Park
ENID
OKLAHOMA
Dewey
BARTLESVILLE
OKLAHOMA
MUSKOGEE
OKLAHOMA
Honor Heights Park
Spaulding Park
Hatbox Downtown Airfield
OKLAHOMA
ONE INCH 24 MILES
ONE INCH 39 KILOMETERS
HIGHWAY MARKERS
INTERSTATE
UNITED STATES
TEXAS FARM OR RANCH
ROAD CLASSIFICATIONS
CONTROLLED ACCESS HIGHWAYS
(Interstate interchange numbers are mileposts)
Interchanges
TOLL HIGHWAYS
OTHER DIVIDED HIGHWAYS
PRINCIPAL THROUGH HIGHWAYS
OTHER THROUGH HIGHWAYS
OTHER ROADS
In unfamiliar areas inquire locally before using any unsigned roads
Paved
Gravel
Dirt
SPECIAL FEATURES
STATE PARKS
With Campsites
Without Campsites
RECREATION AREAS
With Campsites
Without Campsites
SELECTED REST AREAS
With Toilets
Without Toilets
POINTS OF INTEREST
SCHEDULED AIRLINE STOPS
MILITARY AIRPORTS
TOURIST INFORMATION
MILEAGES
POPULATION SYMBOLS
State Capital
Under 1,000
1,000 to 2,500
2,500 to 5,000
5,000 to 10,000
10,000 to 25,000
25,000 to 50,000
50,000 to 100,000
100,000 and over
© H.M. GOUSHA
© H.M. GOUSHA
© H.M. GOUSHA
© H.M. GOUSHA
Lithographed in U.S.A.

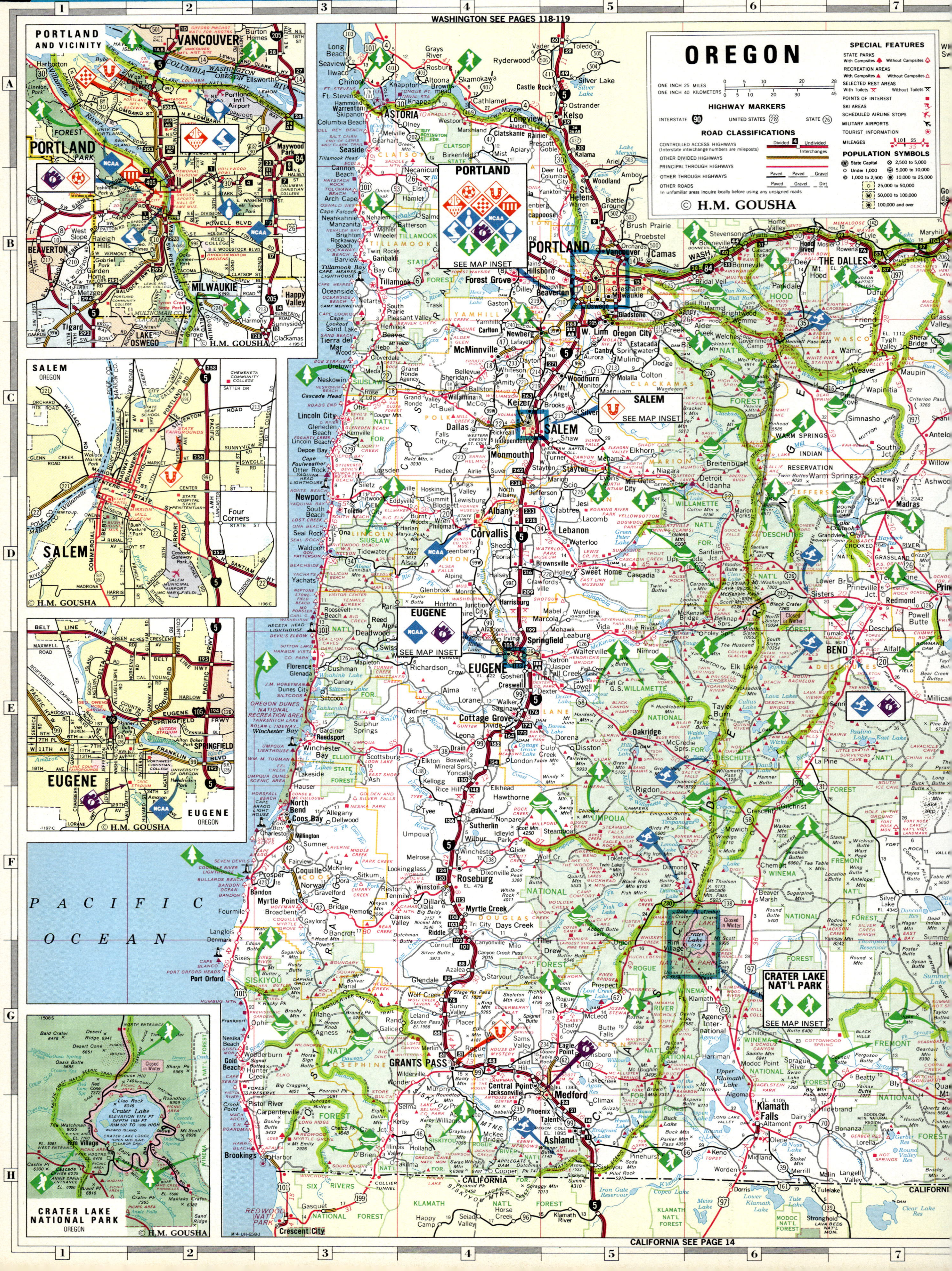

WASHINGTON SEE PAGES 118-119
OREGON
ONE INCH 25 MILES
ONE INCH 40 KILOMETERS
HIGHWAY MARKERS
INTERSTATE
UNITED STATES
STATE
ROAD CLASSIFICATIONS
CONTROLLED ACCESS HIGHWAYS
OTHER DIVIDED HIGHWAYS
PRINCIPAL THROUGH HIGHWAYS
OTHER THROUGH HIGHWAYS
OTHER ROADS
SPECIAL FEATURES
STATE PARKS
RECREATION AREAS
SELECTED REST AREAS
POINTS OF INTEREST
SKI AREAS
SCHEDULED AIRLINE STOPS
MILITARY AIRPORTS
TOURIST INFORMATION
MILEAGES
POPULATION SYMBOLS
State Capital
© H.M. GOUSHA
PORTLAND AND VICINITY
SALEM OREGON
EUGENE OREGON
CRATER LAKE NATIONAL PARK OREGON
PORTLAND SEE MAP INSET
SALEM SEE MAP INSET
EUGENE SEE MAP INSET
CRATER LAKE NAT'L PARK SEE MAP INSET
PACIFIC OCEAN
CALIFORNIA SEE PAGE 14
PORTLAND
SALEM
EUGENE
ASTORIA
THE DALLES
BEND
MEDFORD
KLAMATH FALLS
GRANTS PASS
ROSEBURG
CORVALLIS
ALBANY

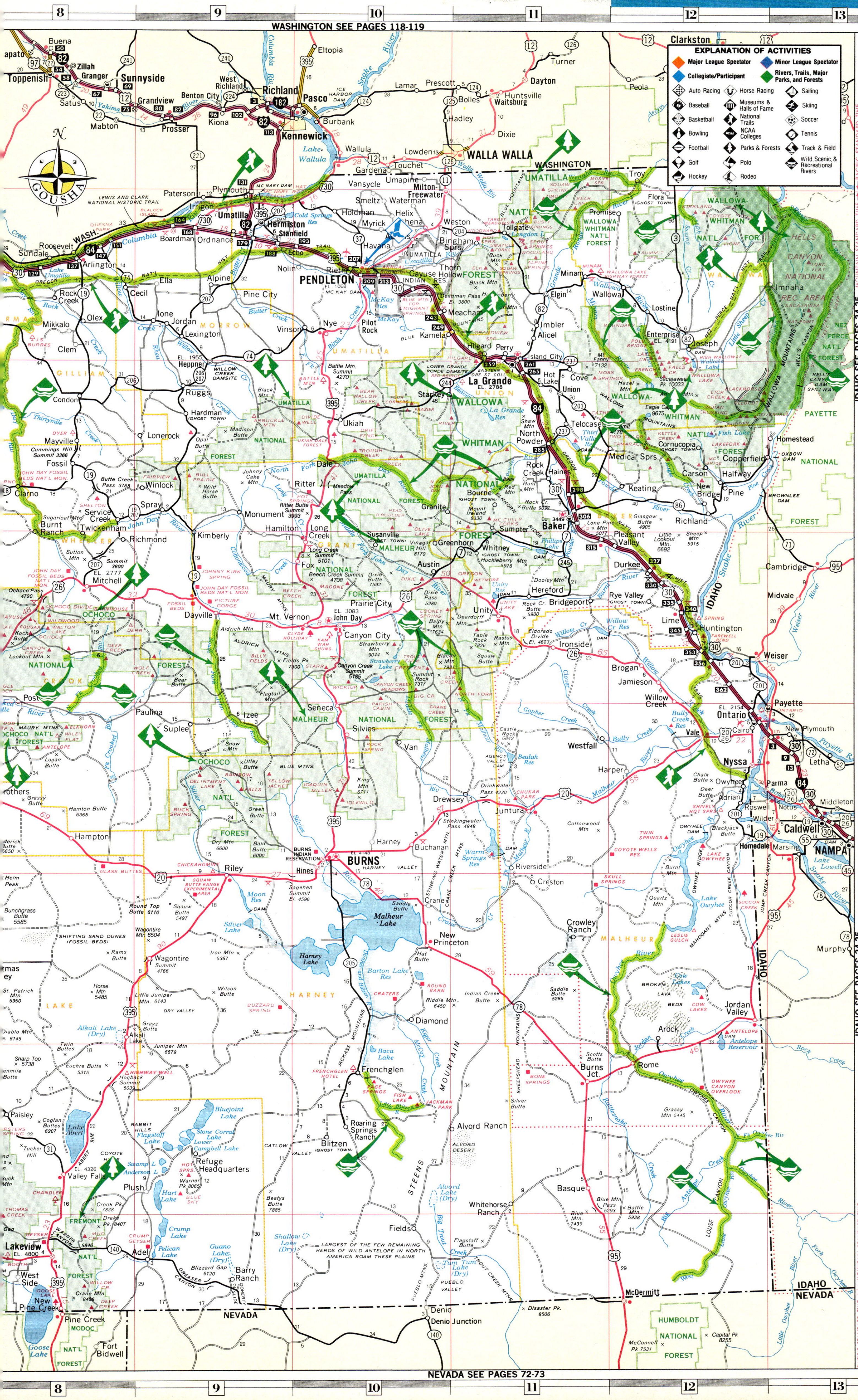

IDAHO SEE PAGES 34-35

PACIFIC STANDARD TIME → | ← MOUNTAIN STANDARD TIME

OREGON

Pop (1990) 2,853,733
Area 96,981 Sq. Mi.

COUNTIES

County	Co. Seat	County	Co. Seat
Baker	Baker	Klamath	Klamath Falls
Benton	Corvallis	Lake	Lakeview
Clackamas	Oregon City	Lane	Eugene
Clatsop	Astoria	Lincoln	Newport
Columbia	St. Helens	Linn	Albany
Coos	Coquille	Malheur	Vale
Crook	Prineville	Marion	Salem
Curry	Gold Beach	Morrow	Heppner
Deschutes	Bend	Multnomah	Portland
Douglas	Roseburg	Polk	Dallas
Gilliam	Condon	Sherman	Moro
Grant	Canyon City	Tillamook	Tillamook
Harney	Burns	Umatilla	Pendleton
Hood River	Hood River	Union	La Grande
Jackson	Medford	Wallowa	Enterprise
Jefferson	Madras	Wasco	The Dalles
Josephine	Grants Pass	Washington	Hillsboro
		Wheeler	Fossil
		Yamhill	McMinnville

PARTIAL LIST OF

CITIES AND TOWNS

• County Seats

Adams	B-10
Adrian	E-12
Agency International	G-6
Albany•	D-4
Alder Creek	C-6
Alicel	B-11
Altamont	H-6
Amity	C-4
Arago	F-3
Arch Cape	B-3
Ashland	H-5
Astoria•	C-1
Athena	B-10
Baker•	C-11
Bandon	F-2
Barview	B-3
Basque	G-11
Bay City	B-3
Beatty	G-7
Beaver	C-3
Beaver	F-6
Beaverton	B-5
Belknap Springs	D-6
Bend•	E-7
Blodgett	D-4
Blue River	D-5
Bly	G-7
Bridge	F-3
Brighton	B-3
Brightwood	B-6
Brogan	D-12
Brookings	H-2
Brothers	E-8
Brownsboro	G-5
Brownsville	D-5
Buchanan	E-10
Burns•	E-10
Burns Jct.	G-11
Burnt Woods	D-4
Buxton	B-4
Cairo	E-12
Camas Valley	F-3
Canby	C-5
Cannon Beach	B-3
Canyon City•	D-10
Carlton	C-4
Cascade Locks	B-6
Cascadia	D-5
Cave Jct.	H-3
Central Point	G-4
Chemult	F-6
Chitwood	D-3
Clatskanie	A-4
Cloverdale	C-3
Columbia Beach	A-3
Condon•	C-8
Coos Bay	F-3
Coquille•	F-3
Corvallis	D-4
Cottage Grove	E-4
Crabtree	D-5
Crescent	F-6
Creswell	E-4
Dairy	H-6
Dale	C-10
Dallas•	C-4
Days Creek	F-4
Dayton	C-4
Dayville	D-9
Denmark	G-2
Depoe Bay	C-3
Detroit	D-6
Dexter	E-5
Dillard	F-4
Drain	E-4
Drew	G-5
Dufur	B-7
Eagle Point	G-5
Eddyville	D-3
Elgin	B-11
Elkton	E-4
Elsie	B-4
Enterprise•	B-12
Estacada	C-5
Eugene•	E-4
Fall Creek	E-5
Florence	E-3
Forest Grove	B-4
Fort Klamath	G-6
Fossil	C-8
Fourmile	F-2
Fox	D-10
Gales Creek	B-4
Gardiner	E-3
Gearhart	A-3
Gilchrist	F-6
Gladstone	B-5
Glenada	E-3
Gleneden Beach	C-3
Glenwood	B-4
Glide	F-4
Goble	A-5
Gold Beach	G-2
Goverment Camp	C-6
Grants Pass•	G-4
Grass Valley	B-7
Gresham	B-5
Hampton	E-8
Harbor	H-3
Harrisburg	D-4
Hauser	F-3
Hebo	C-3
Hemlock	C-3
Heppner•	C-9
Hermiston	B-9
Hildebrand	H-6
Hillsboro•	B-4
Hines	E-10
Hood River•	B-6
Hot Lake	C-11
Idanha	D-6
Illinois Valley	H-3
Independence	C-4
Ironside	D-11
Jacksonville	G-4
Jamieson	D-12
Jefferson	D-4
John Day	D-10
Jordan Valley	F-12
Junction City	D-4
Juntura	E-11
Keizer	C-4
Kent	C-7
Kerby	H-3
Kernville	C-3
Kimberly	D-9
Kings Valley	D-4
Klamath Falls•	H-6
La Grande•	C-11
La Pine	E-6
Lafayette	C-4
Lakeside	E-3
Lake Oswego	B-5
Lakeview•	H-8
Langlois	F-2
Leaburg	E-5
Lebanon	D-5
Lee's Camp	B-4
Lexington	B-9
Lincoln Beach	C-3
Lincoln City	C-3
Long Creek	C-10
Lostine	B-12
Lyons	D-5
Madras•	D-7
Manning	B-4
Manzanita	B-3
Marion Forks	D-6
Marshland	A-4
Maupin	C-7
McKenzie Bridge	D-5
McLeod	G-5
McMinnville•	C-4
Medford•	G-5
Mehama	C-5
Midland	H-6
Mill City	D-5
Millican	E-7
Milton-Freewater	A-10
Milwaukie	B-5
Minam	B-11
Mist	A-4
Mitchell	D-8
Modoc Point	G-6
Mohler	B-3
Molalla	C-5
Monmouth	C-4
Moro•	B-7
Mount Angel	C-5
Mount Vernon	D-9
Mowich	F-6
Myrtle Creek	F-4
Myrtle Point	F-3
Natron	E-5
Neahkahnie	B-3
Nehalem	B-3
Nesika Beach	G-2
Neskowin	C-3
New Pine Creek	H-8
Newberg	C-4
Newport•	D-3
Niagara	C-5
North Bend	F-3
Nye	B-10
Nyssa	E-12
Oakland	F-4
Oakridge	E-5
O'Brien	H-3
Olalla	F-4
Olene	H-6
Ontario	E-12
Ophir	G-2
Oregon City•	C-5
Oretown	C-3
Otter Rock	C-3
Owyhee	E-12
Pedee	C-4
Pendleton•	B-10
Philomath	D-4
Phoenix	H-4
Pistol River	H-2
Pleasant Valley	B-3
Port Orford	G-2
Portland•	B-5
Prairie City	D-10
Prescott	A-4
Princeton	F-10
Prineville•	D-7
Prospect	G-5
Prosper	F-3
Quartz Mountain	G-7
Rainier	A-4
Redmond	D-7
Reedsport	E-3
Remote	F-3
Rhododendron	C-6
Riddle	F-4
Riley	E-9
Rockaway Beach	B-3
Rouge Elk	G-5
Rome	G-12
Roosevelt Beach	D-3
Roseburg•	F-4
Ruggs	C-9
St. Helens•	B-5
St. Paul	C-5
Salem•	C-5
Sandy	B-6
Santiam Junction	D-6
Scappoose	B-4
Scio	D-5
Scottsburg	E-3
Seal Rock	D-3
Seaside	A-3
Selma	H-4
Seneca	E-10
Service Creek	C-8
Shady Cove	G-5
Shaniko	C-7
Sheridan	C-4
Silverton	C-5
Sisters	D-6
Sixes	G-2
Skipanon	A-3
South Beach	D-3
South Prairie	B-3
Spray	C-9
Springfield	B-9
Stanfield	E-4
Starkey	C-10
Stayton	C-5
Steamboat	F-5
Sutherlin	F-4
Sweet Home	D-5
Talent	H-5
Tenmile	F-3
Terrebonne	D-7
The Dalles•	B-7
Tillamook•	B-3
Toledo	D-3
Trail	G-5
Tygh Valley	C-7
Twin Rocks	B-3
Union	C-11
Union Creek	G-5
Unity	D-11
Upper Soda	D-5
Vale•	E-12
Valley Falls	G-8
Valley Jct.	C-4
Veneta	E-4
Vida	D-5
Wagontire	F-9
Waldport	D-3
Wallowa	B-11
Walterville	E-5
Warm Springs	D-6
Warren	B-5
Warrenton	A-3
Wasco	B-7
Wemme	C-6
West Linn	C-5
Westport	A-4
Wheeler	B-3
Whiteson	C-4
Wilderville	G-4
Willamina	C-4
Willow Creek	E-12
Willowdale	C-7
Winchester Bay	E-3
Winston	F-4
Wonder	G-3
Woodburn	C-5
Worden	H-6
Wren	D-4
Yachats	D-3
Yamhill	C-4
Yoncalla	E-4

SF-658-J

PENNSYLVANIA

Pop (1990) 11,924,710
Area 45,333 Sq. Mi.

COUNTIES

County	Co. Seat
Adams	Gettysburg
Allegheny	Pittsburgh
Armstrong	Kittanning
Beaver	Beaver
Bedford	Bedford
Berks	Reading
Blair	Hollidaysburg
Bradford	Towanda
Bucks	Doylestown
Butler	Butler
Cambria	Ebensburg
Cameron	Emporium
Carbon	Jim Thorpe
Centre	Bellefonte
Chester	West Chester
Clarion	Clarion
Clearfield	Clearfield
Clinton	Lock Haven
Columbia	Bloomsburg
Crawford	Meadville
Cumberland	Carlisle
Dauphin	Harrisburg
Delaware	Media
Elk	Ridgway
Erie	Erie
Fayette	Uniontown
Forest	Tiomesta
Franklin	Chambersburg
Fulton	McConnellsburg
Green	Waynesburg
Huntingdon	Huntingdon
Indiana	Indiana
Jefferson	Brookville
Juniata	Mifflintown
Lackawanna	Scranton
Lancaster	Lancaster
Lawrence	New Castle
Lebanon	Lebanon
Lehigh	Allentown
Luzerne	Wilkes-Barre
Lycoming	Williamsport
McKean	Smethport
Mercer	Mercer
Mifflin	Lewistown
Monroe	Stroudsburg
Montgomery	Norristown
Montour	Danville
Northampton	Easton
Northumberland	Sunbury
Perry	New Bloomfield
Philadelphia	Philadelphia
Pike	Milford
Potter	Coudersport
Schuylkill	Pottsville
Snyder	Middleburg
Somerset	Somerset
Sullivan	Laporte
Susquehanna	Montrose
Tioga	Wellsboro
Union	Lewisburg
Venango	Franklin
Warren	Warren
Washington	Washington
Wayne	Honesdale
Westmoreland	Greensburg
Wyoming	Tunkhannock
York	York

PARTIAL LIST OF

CITIES AND TOWNS

• County Seats

Adamstown	G-11
Addison	H-4
Akron	G-10
Alba	C-9
Albion	C-1
Alburtis	F-11
Aliquippa	F-1
Allentown •	F-12
Allison	G-2
Altoona	F-6
Ambridge	F-2
Annville	G-10
Ansonia	C-8
Apollo	F-3
Archbald	D-12
Arnold	F-3
Ashland	E-10
Athens	C-9
Atlas	E-10
Avella	G-1
Avis	D-8
Avon	G-10
Avondale	H-11
Avonmore	F 3
Baden	F 2
Bald Eagle	F-6
Bangor	E-12
Barnesboro	F-5
Bath	F-12
Beallsville	G-2
Beaver •	D-1
Beaver Falls	E-1
Beaver Meadows	E-11
Bedford •	G-5
Beech Creek	E-7
Bellefonte •	E-7
Belleville	F-7
Bellevue	F-2
Bellwood	F-6
Belsano	F-5
Bentleyville	G-2
Benton	D-10
Berlin	H-4
Berwick	E-10
Bessemer	E-1
Bethlehem	F-12
Big Beaver	E-1
Bigler	E-6
Birdsboro	G-11
Black Lick	F-4
Blairsville	F-4
Blakely	D-12
Bloomsburg	E-10
Blossburg	C-8
Boiling Springs	G-8
Boswell	G-4
Boyertown	G-11
Boynton	H-4
Brackenridge	F-3
Bradford	B-5
Brandy Camp	D-5
Bridgeville	F-2
Brier Hill	G-3
Brockport	D-5
Brockway	D-5
Brodheadsville	E-12
Brookville •	E-4
Broomall	G-12
Brownsville	G-2
Buckstown	G-5
Burgettstown	F-1
Burlington	C-9
Burnham	F-7
Burnside	E-5
Burtville	C-6
Bushkill	E-13
Butler •	E-3
Cairnbrook	G-5
California	G-2
Cambridge Springs	C-2
Cameron	D-6
Camp Hill	G-9
Campbelltown	G-10
Canoe Creek	F-6
Canonsburg	G-2
Canton	C-9
Carbondale	C-12
Carlisle •	G-8
Carnegie	F-2
Carrolltown	F-5
Catasauqua	F-12
Catawissa	E-10
Cedar Ledge	C-9
Centerville	G-2
Centerville	H-5
Central City	G-5
Centralia	E-10
Centre Hall	E-7
Chadds Ford	H-12
Chalfont	G-12
Chalk Hill	H-3
Challenge	D-5
Chambersburg •	H-7
Charleroi	G-2
Charleston	D-1
Chatwood	G-12
Cherry Hill	C-1
Chester	H-12
Chicora	E-3
Christiana	G-11
Clairton	G-2
Clarendon	C-4
Clarion •	D-4
Clarks Summit	D-11
Clearfield •	E-5
Cleona	G-10
Clymer	F-4
Coaldale	E-11
Coatesville	G-11
Cochranton	D-2
Collegeville	G-12
Columbia	G-10
Colver	F-5
Conneaut Lake	C-2
Conneautville	C-1
Connellsville	G-3
Coopersburg	F-12
Coraopolis	F-2
Cornwall	G-10
Corry	C-3
Corsica	D-4
Coudersport •	C-7
Crabtree	F-3
Cranberry	D-3
Cresson	F-5
Cressona	F-10
Crucible	G-2
Cuddy	F-2
Curry Run	E-5
Curtisville	F-2
Curwensville	E-5
Daguscahonda	D-5
Dallas	D-11
Dallastown	H-9
Dalton	D-11
Danville •	E-9
Darby	H-12
Degolia	C-5
Delmont	F-3
Denver	G-10
Derry	G-4
Dillsburg	G-9
Dingmans Ferry	D-13
Donora	G-2
Dormont	F-2
Downingtown	G-11
Doylestown •	G-12
Driftwood	D-6
Du Bois	E-5
Dunbar	G-3
Duncannon	F-8
Duncansville	F-5
Dunmore	D-12
Duquesne	F-2
Duryea	D-11
Dushore	D-10
East Berlin	G-9
East Brady	E-3
East Conemaugh	G-5
East Greenville	F-12
East Hickory	C-4
East Petersburg	G-10
East Smethport	C-6
East Stroudsburg	E-13
East Troy	C-9
East Washington	G-2
Easton •	F-12
Ebensburg •	F-5
Echo Lake	E-13
Economy	F-2
Edgeworth	F-2
Edinboro	C-2
Egypt Mills	E-13
Elderton	F-4
Eldred	C-6
Elizabeth	G-3
Elizabethtown	G-9
Elizabethville	F-9
Elkland	B-8
Ellsworth	G-2
Ellwood City	E-2
Elmhurst	D-12
Elmo	D-3
Elysburg	E-10
Emmaus	F-12
Emporium •	D-6
Ephrata	G-10
Erie •	B-2
Espyville	C-1
Etna	F-2
Evans City	E-2
Everrett	G-6
Everson	G-3
Exton	G-12
Fairchance	H-3
Fairview	B-2
Falls Creek	E-5
Farmington	H-3
Farrell	D-1
Ferndale	G-4
Farrellton	G-4
Flat Rock	H-3
Fleetwood	F-11
Flemington	E-8
Florin	G-10
Ford City	E-3
Forest City	C-12
Forest Inn	E-12
Forty Fort	D-11
Fountain Hill	F-12
Frackville	E-10
Franklin •	D-3
Fredericksburg	C-2
Freedom	F-2
Freeland	E-11
Freeport	F-3
Frisco	E-2
Gaines	C-7
Gallitzin	F-5
Garden View	D-8
Geistown	G-5
Gettysburg •	H-8
Gilberton	E-10
Girard	B-2
Glen Lyon	E-11
Glen Rock	H-9
Glenolden	H-12
Glenside	G-12
Grampian	E-5
Greencastle	H-7
Greensburg •	G-3
Greenville	D-1
Grove City	D-2
Guffey	C-5
Hallstead	C-11
Hamburg	F-11
Hannah	E-6
Hanover	H-9
Harmony	E-2
Harrisburg •	G-9
Harstown	C-1
Hatboro	G-13
Hawley	D-12
Hazleton	E-11
Hershey	G-9
Highspire	G-9
Hollidaysburg •	F-6
Homer City	F-4
Honesdale •	C-12
Hopwood	H-3
Houston	G-2
Houtzdale	E-6
Howard	D-6
Hughesville	D-9
Huntingdon •	F-7
Hyndman	H-5
Hyner	D-7
Imperial	F-1
Indian Orchard	D-12
Indiana •	F-4
Industry	[illegible]
Irwin	[illegible]
Jamestown	[illegible]
Jamison	[illegible]
Jeannette	[illegible]
Jenkintown	[illegible]
Jennerstown	[illegible]
Jermyn	[illegible]
Jerome	[illegible]
Jersey Shore	[illegible]
Jim Thorpe •	[illegible]
Johnsonburg	[illegible]
Johnstown	[illegible]
Julian	[illegible]
Kane	[illegible]
Kenhorst	[illegible]
Kennett Square	[illegible]
Kingston	[illegible]
Kittanning •	[illegible]
Knox	[illegible]
Koppel	[illegible]
Kresgeville	[illegible]
Kulpmont	[illegible]
Kutztown	[illegible]
La Plume	[illegible]
Laborde	[illegible]
Laddsburg	[illegible]
Lancaster	[illegible]
Lanes Mills	[illegible]
Langhorne	[illegible]
Lansdale	[illegible]
Lansford	[illegible]
Lantz Corners	[illegible]
Latrobe	[illegible]
Laughlintown	[illegible]
Laureldale	[illegible]
Lebanon	[illegible]
Leechburg	[illegible]
Lehighton	[illegible]

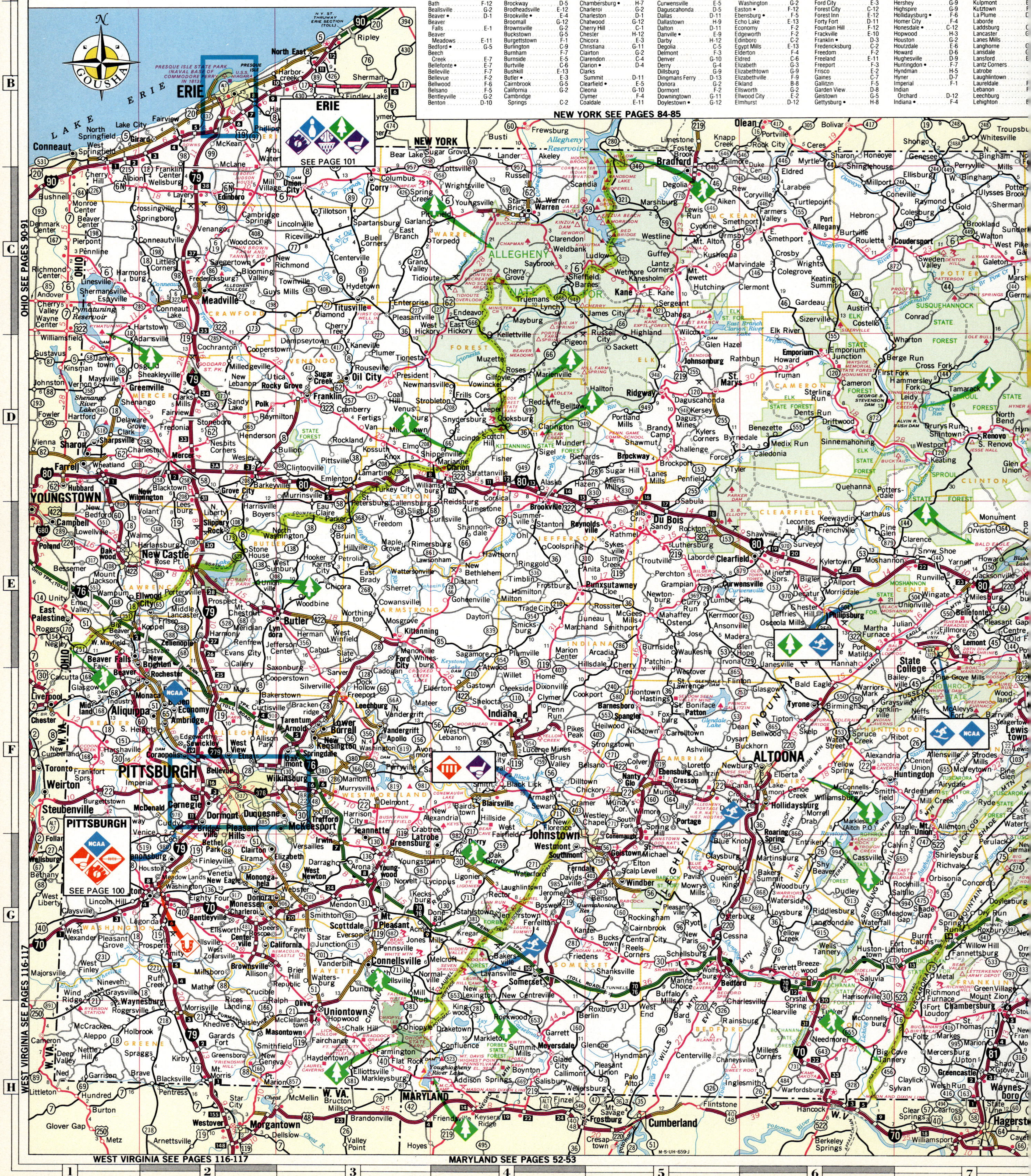

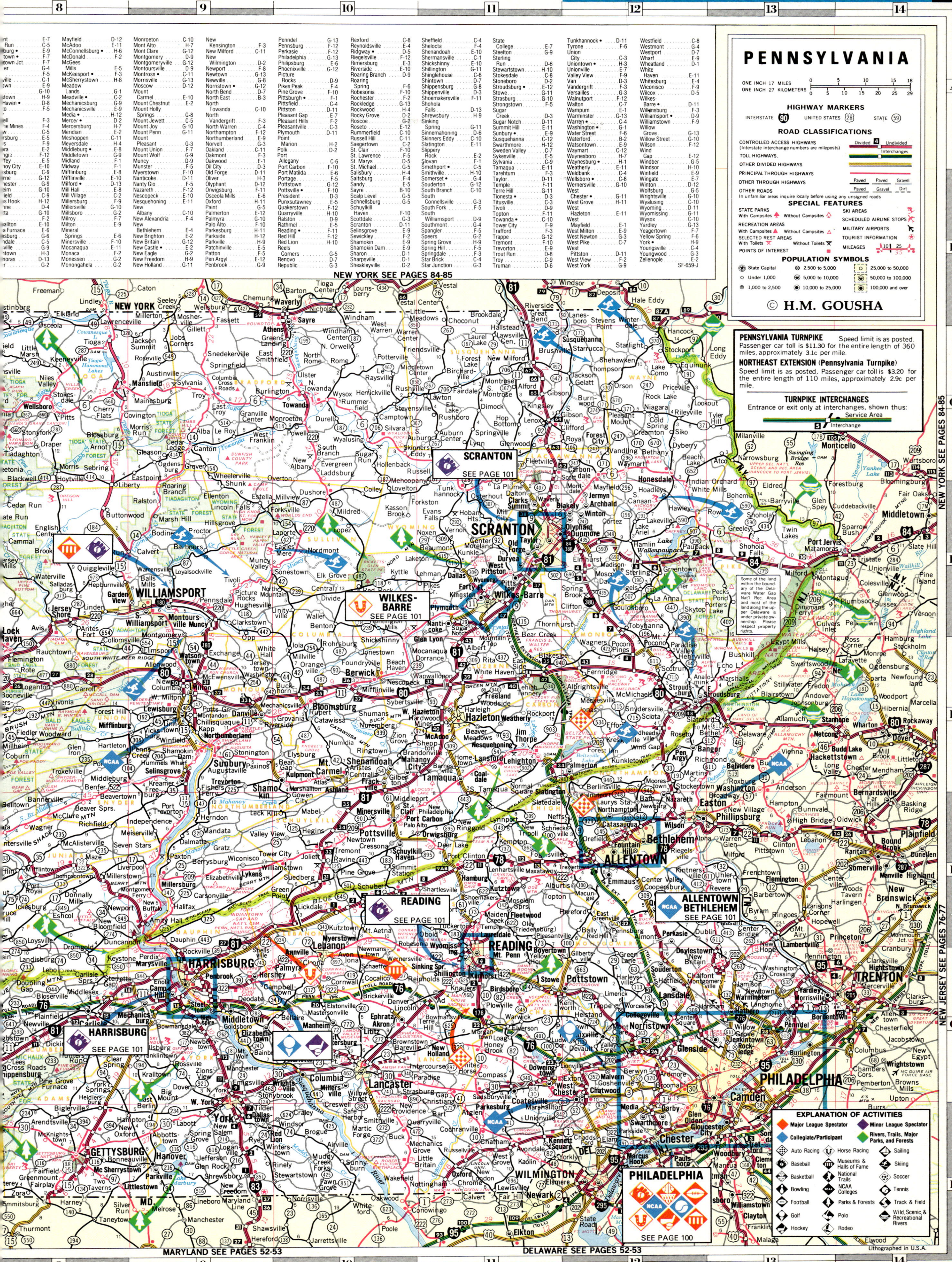
PENNSYLVANIA
ONE INCH 17 MILES
ONE INCH 27 KILOMETERS
HIGHWAY MARKERS
INTERSTATE 90 UNITED STATES 28 STATE 59
ROAD CLASSIFICATIONS
CONTROLLED ACCESS HIGHWAYS (Interstate interchange numbers are mileposts)
TOLL HIGHWAYS
OTHER DIVIDED HIGHWAYS
PRINCIPAL THROUGH HIGHWAYS
OTHER THROUGH HIGHWAYS
OTHER ROADS
In unfamiliar areas inquire locally before using any unsigned roads
SPECIAL FEATURES
STATE PARKS With Campsites Without Campsites
RECREATION AREAS With Campsites Without Campsites
SELECTED REST AREAS With Toilets Without Toilets
POINTS OF INTEREST
SKI AREAS
SCHEDULED AIRLINE STOPS
MILITARY AIRPORTS
TOURIST INFORMATION
MILEAGES
POPULATION SYMBOLS
State Capital
Under 1,000
1,000 to 2,500
2,500 to 5,000
5,000 to 10,000
10,000 to 25,000
25,000 to 50,000
50,000 to 100,000
100,000 and over
© H.M. GOUSHA
PENNSYLVANIA TURNPIKE Speed limit is as posted. Passenger car toll is $11.30 for the entire length of 360 miles, approximately 3.1c per mile.
NORTHEAST EXTENSION (Pennsylvania Turnpike) Speed limit is as posted. Passenger car toll is $3.20 for the entire length of 110 miles, approximately 2.9c per mile.
TURNPIKE INTERCHANGES
Entrance or exit only at interchanges, shown thus:
Service Area
Interchange
NEW YORK SEE PAGES 84-85
NEW JERSEY SEE PAGES 76-77
MARYLAND SEE PAGES 52-53
DELAWARE SEE PAGES 52-53
SCRANTON SEE PAGE 101
WILKES-BARRE SEE PAGE 101
READING SEE PAGE 101
HARRISBURG SEE PAGE 101
ALLENTOWN BETHLEHEM SEE PAGE 101
PHILADELPHIA SEE PAGE 100
EXPLANATION OF ACTIVITIES
Major League Spectator
Minor League Spectator
Collegiate/Participant
Rivers, Trails, Major Parks, and Forests
Auto Racing
Horse Racing
Sailing
Baseball
Museums & Halls of Fame
Skiing
Basketball
National Trails
Soccer
Bowling
NCAA Colleges
Tennis
Football
Parks & Forests
Track & Field
Golf
Polo
Wild, Scenic & Recreational Rivers
Hockey
Rodeo
Lithographed in U.S.A.
SF-659-J

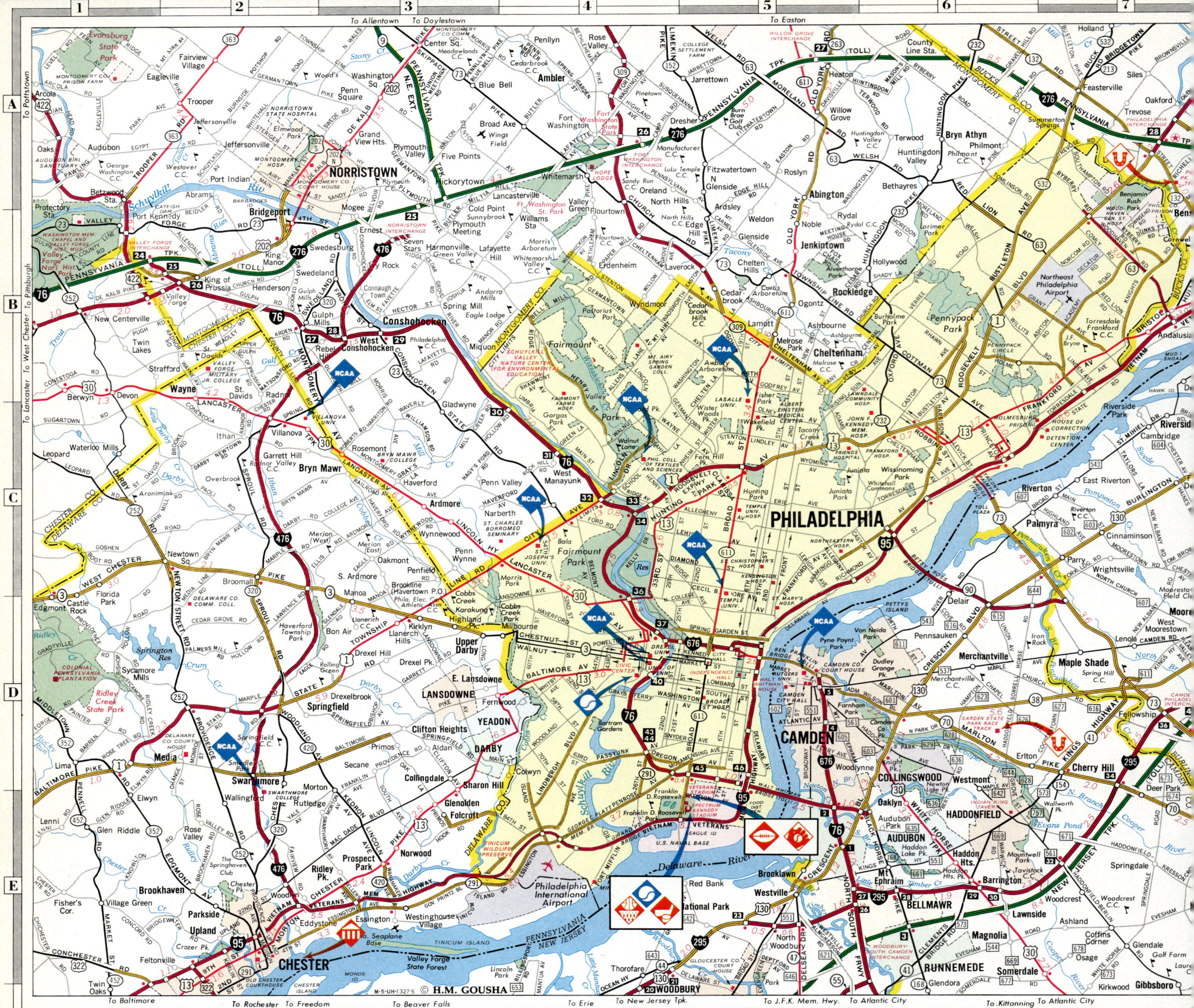
PHILADELPHIA
CAMDEN
CHESTER
NORRISTOWN
Conshohocken
Philadelphia International Airport
To Allentown
To Doylestown
To Easton
To Baltimore
To New Jersey Tpk.
To J.F.K. Mem. Hwy.
To Atlantic City
© H.M. GOUSHA

PITTSBURGH
PITTSBURGH AND VICINITY
Greater Pittsburgh International Airport
CARNEGIE
WILKINSBURG
McKEESPORT
WEST MIFFLIN
BALDWIN
BRENTWOOD
To Washington
To Waynesburg
To Uniontown
MILES
KILOMETERS
Golf Courses
© H.M. GOUSHA

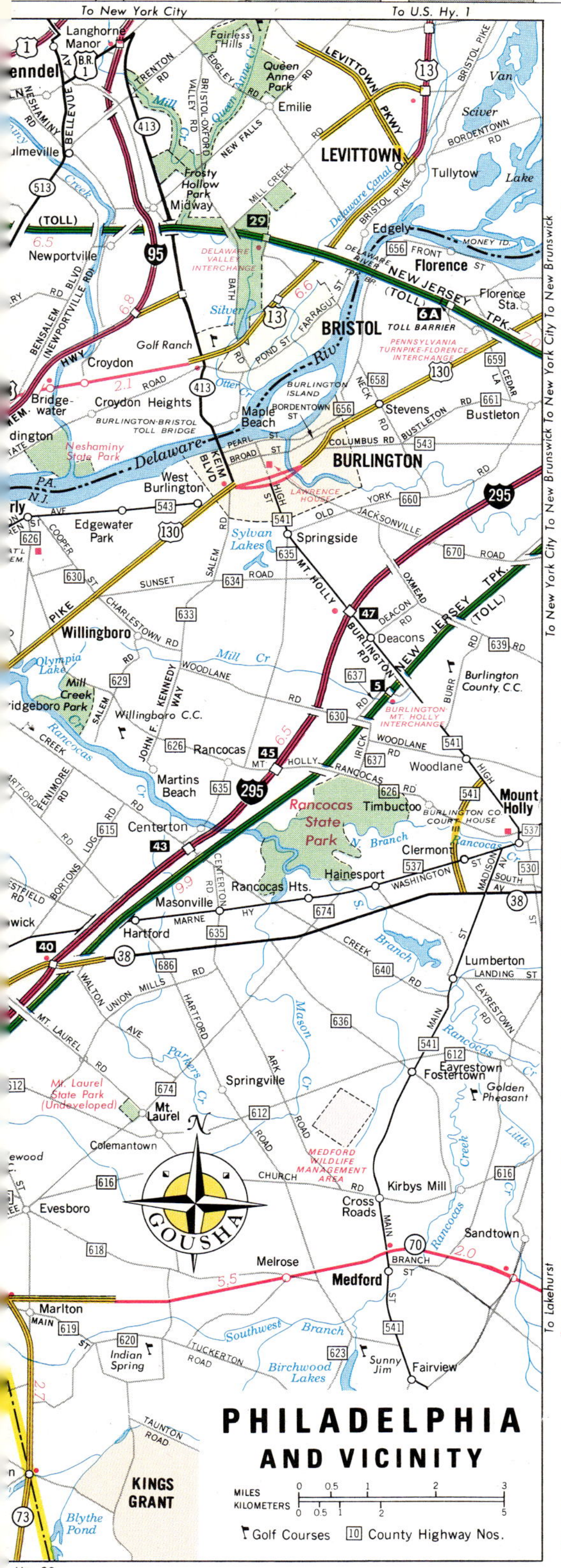
PHILADELPHIA
AND VICINITY
To New York City
To U.S. Hy. 1
LEVITTOWN
BRISTOL
BURLINGTON
Willingboro
Mount Holly
Medford
KINGS GRANT
Golf Courses
County Highway Nos.
GOUSHA

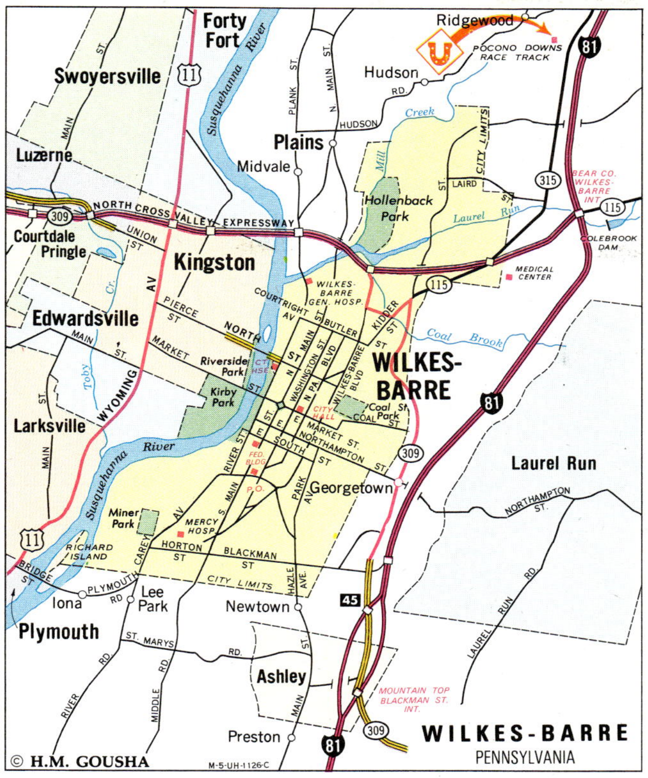
WILKES-BARRE
PENNSYLVANIA
Kingston
Plymouth
Edwardsville
Larksville
Swoyersville
Forty Fort
Plains
Hudson
Laurel Run
Georgetown
Ashley
Preston
© H.M. GOUSHA

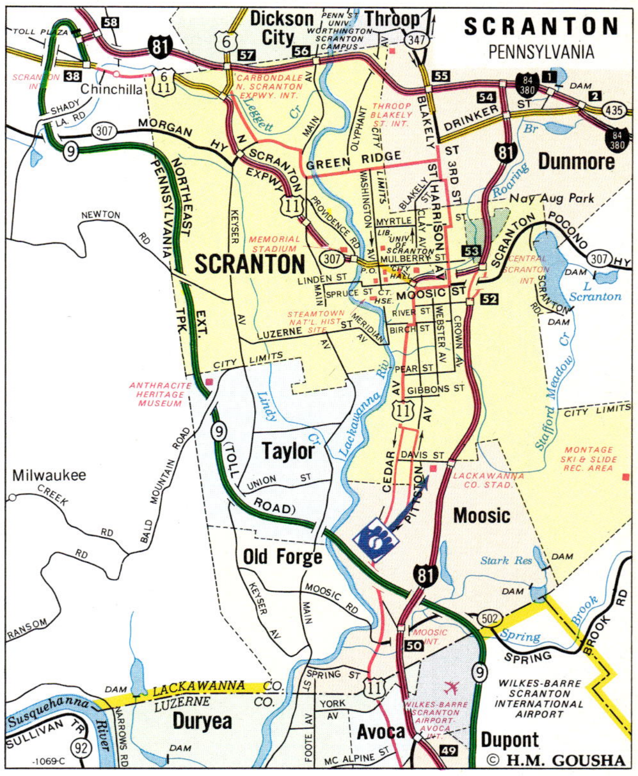
SCRANTON
PENNSYLVANIA
Dickson City
Throop
Dunmore
Chinchilla
Taylor
Old Forge
Moosic
Duryea
Avoca
Dupont
Milwaukee
© H.M. GOUSHA

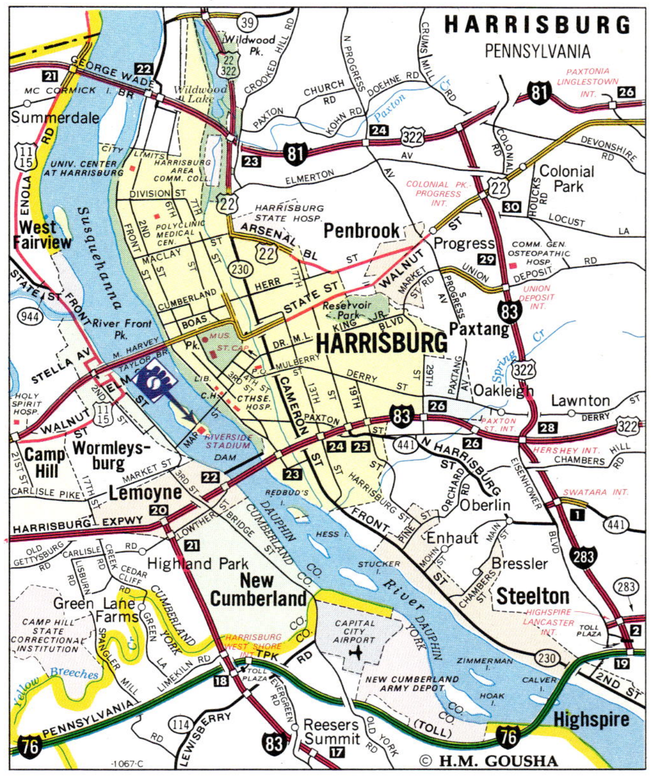
HARRISBURG
PENNSYLVANIA
Summerdale
West Fairview
Penbrook
Progress
Colonial Park
Paxtang
Camp Hill
Wormleysburg
Lemoyne
New Cumberland
Steelton
Highspire
Oberlin
Enhaut
Bressler
© H.M. GOUSHA

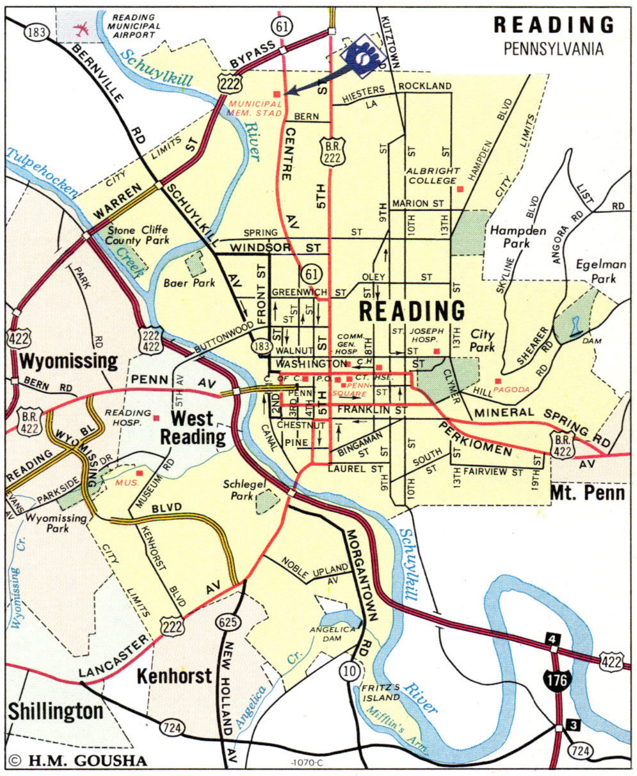
READING
PENNSYLVANIA
Wyomissing
West Reading
Mt. Penn
Kenhorst
Shillington
Hampden Park
Egelman Park
© H.M. GOUSHA

ERIE
PENNSYLVANIA
LAKE ERIE
Presque Isle
Presque Isle Bay
Lawrence Park
Wesleyville
Belle Valley
Kearsarge
Peach Glen
© H.M. GOUSHA

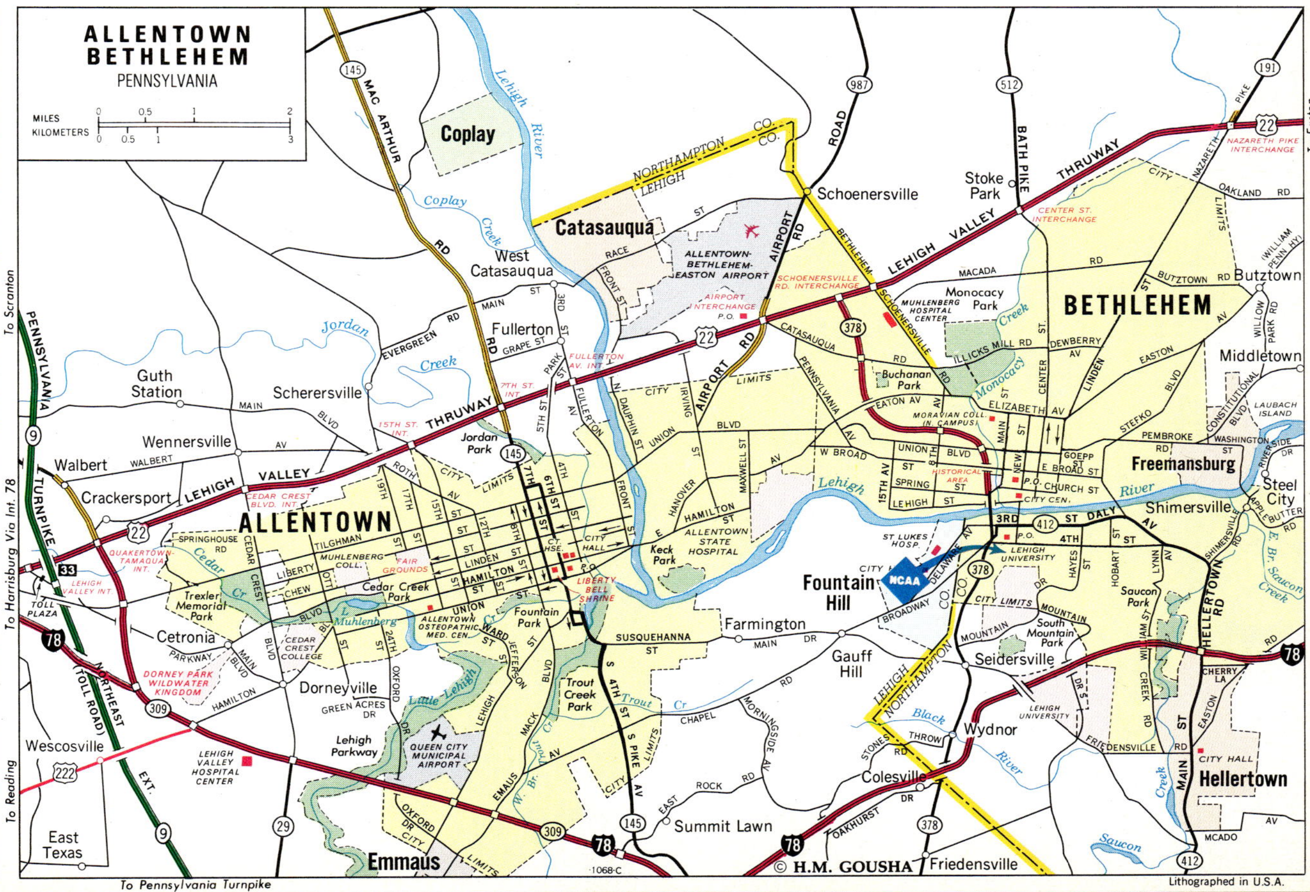
ALLENTOWN
BETHLEHEM
PENNSYLVANIA
Coplay
Catasauqua
West Catasauqua
Fullerton
Schoenersville
Stoke Park
Butztown
Middletown
Freemansburg
Steel City
Shimersville
Fountain Hill
Hellertown
Emmaus
Wescosville
East Texas
Summit Lawn
Friedensville
© H.M. GOUSHA
Lithographed in U.S.A.

FOR RHODE ISLAND SEE PAGES 24-25

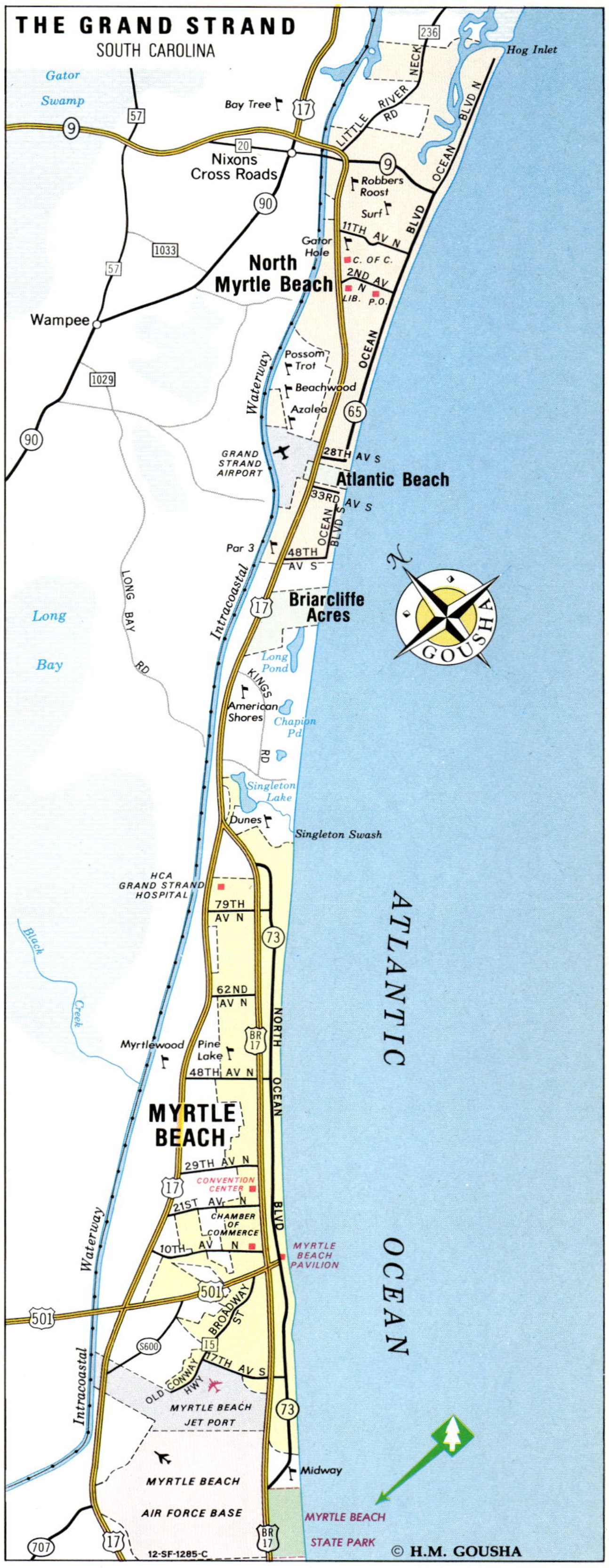

SOUTH CAROLINA

Pop (1990) 3,505,707
Area 31,055 Sq. Mi.

COUNTIES

County	Co. Seat
Abbeville	Abbeville
Aiken	Aiken
Allendale	Allendale
Anderson	Anderson
Bamberg	Bamberg
Barnwell	Barnwell
Beaufort	Beaufort
Berkeley	Moncks Corner
Calhoun	St. Matthews
Charleston	Charleston
Cherokee	Gaffney
Chester	Chester
Chesterfield	Chesterfield
Clarendon	Manning
Colleton	Walterboro
Darlington	Darlington
Dillon	Dillon
Dorchester	St. George
Edgefield	Edgefield
Fairfield	Winnsboro
Florence	Florence
Georgetown	Georgetown
Greenville	Greenville
Greenwood	Greenwood
Hampton	Hampton
Horry	Conway
Jasper	Ridgeland
Kershaw	Camden
Lancaster	Lancaster
Laurens	Laurens
Lee	Bishopville
Lexington	Lexington
Marion	Marion
Marlboro	Bennettsville
McCormick	McCormick
Newberry	Newberry
Oconee	Wahlahalla
Orangeburg	Orangeburg
Pickens	Pickens
Richland	Columbia
Saluda	Saluda
Spartanburg	Spartanburg
Sumter	Sumter
Union	Union
Williamsburg	Kingstree
York	York

CITIES AND TOWNS

• County Seats

Abbeville •	C-3
Aiken •	E-5
Allendale •	F-5
Allsbrook	C-11
Anderson •	B-2
Andrews	E-9
Atlantic Beach	D-11
Awendaw	F-9
Aynor	D-10
Bamberg •	E-6
Barnwell •	E-6
Batesburg	D-5
Beaufort •	G-7
Beech Island	E-4
Belton	B-3
Bennettsville •	B-9
Bethune	C-8
Bishopville •	C-8
Blacksburg	A-5
Blackville	E-6
Blenheim	B-9
Bonneau	E-9
Bowman	E-7
Branchville	E-7
Briarcliffe Acres	D-11
Brownsville	C-9
Calhoun Falls	C-3
Camden •	C-7
Carlisle	B-5
Cassatt	C-8
Cayce	D-6
Centenary	C-10
Chappells	C-4
Charleston •	G-9
Cheraw	B-9
Chesnee	A-4
Chester •	B-6
Chesterfield •	B-8
Chicora	E-8
Clearwater	E-4
Clemson	B-2
Clinton	C-4
Clio	B-9
Clover	A-6
Columbia •	D-6
Conway •	D-11
Cornwell	B-6
Coward	D-9
Cowpens	A-5
Cross Anchor	B-4
Dalzell	D-8
Darlington •	C-9
DeKalb	C-7
Denmark	E-6
Dillon •	C-10
Donalds	C-3
Dorchester	F-7
Due West	C-3
Easley	B-3
Edgefield •	D-4
Effingham	C-9
Elgin	C-7
Elko	E-5
Elliott	C-8
Enoree	B-4
Estill	G-6
Fair Play	B-2
Fairfax	F-6
Florence •	C-9
Floyd	C-9
Floyds	C-11
Foreston	D-8
Fork	C-10
Fort Lawn	B-7
Fort Mill	A-6
Fountain Inn	B-4
Gaffney •	A-5
Galivants Ferry	C-10
Gardens Corner	G-7
Garnett	G-6
Gaston	D-6
Georgetown •	E-10
Gifford	F-6
Gluck	B-3
Great Falls	B-6
Greeleyville	E-8
Green Sea	C-11
Greenville •	B-3
Greenwood •	C-3
Greer	A-4
Grover	F-7
Hampton •	F-6
Harleyville	E-7
Hartsville	C-8
Heath Springs	B-7
Heineman	E-9
Hemingway	D-9
Holly Hill	E-8
Homewood	D-11
Honea Path	B-3
Inman	A-4
Isle of Palms	F-9
Iva	C-3
Jackson	E-4
Jacksonboro	F-7
James Island	G-8
Jamestown	E-9
Joanna	C-5
Johnsonville	D-10
Johnston	D-4
Jordanville	D-10
Kershaw	B-7
Kingsburg	D-9
Kingstree •	D-9
Kirksey	D-4
Lake City	D-9
Lamar	C-8
Lancaster •	B-7
Landrum	A-4
Latta	C-10
Laurens •	B-4
Leesville	D-5
Lesslie	B-6
Lexington •	D-6
Liberty	B-3
Liberty Hill	B-7
Little River	D-11
Lobeco	G-7
Lockhart	B-5
Lodge	F-6
Longs	D-11
Loris	C-11
Lowrys	B-6
Lugoff	C-7
Luray	F-6
Lydia	C-8
Lynchburg	C-8
Manning •	D-8
Manville	C-8
Marion •	C-10
Mary	D-10
Mauldin	B-4
Mayson	C-4
McBee	B-8
McColl	B-9
McConnells	B-6
McCormick •	D-4
Midway	E-6
Monarch	B-5
Moncks Corner •	E-8
Mount Croghan	B-8
Mount Holly	F-8
Mount Pleasant	F-9
Mouzon	D-8
Mullins	C-10
Murrells Inlet	E-11
Myrtle Beach	D-11
Neeses	E-6
New Ellenton	E-5
Newberry •	C-5
Nichols	C-10
North	E-6
North Augusta	E-4
North Charleston	F-9
North Myrtle Beach	D-11
Norway	E-6
Oak Grove	C-9
Oakwood	E-5
Oatland	E-10
Olar	E-6
Old House	G-7
Outland	D-10
Owdoms	D-4
Pacolet	B-5
Pageland	B-8
Palmetto	C-9
Pamplico	D-9
Paris	A-3
Parkers Ferry	F-8
Patrick	B-8
Paxville	D-8
Pee Dee	C-9
Pendelton	B-3
Pickens •	A-3
Piedmont	B-3
Plantersville	E-10
Pocotaligo	G-7
Pontiac	C-7
Port Royal	G-7
Princeton	B-4
Rains	C-10
Rantowles	F-8
Rembert	C-7
Rhems	E-10
Richburg	B-6
Ridgeland •	G-6
Robertville	G-6
Rock Hill	A-6
Ruby	B-8
Ruffin	F-7
St. George •	F-7
St. Matthews •	D-7
St. Stephens	E-9
Saluda •	D-4
Sampit	E-10
Santuck	B-5
Scotia	G-6
Scranton	D-9
Seneca	B-2
Shannontown	D-7
Simpsonville	B-4
Society Hill	B-9
Spartanburg •	A-4
Sullivans Island	F-9
Summerton	D-7
Summerville	F-8
Sumter •	D-8
Swansea	D-6
Sycamore	F-6
Tarboro	G-6
Tillman	G-6
Timmonsville	C-8
Toddville	D-10
Townville	B-2
Travelers Rest	A-3
Trio	E-9
Troy	D-3
Turbeville	D-8
Ulmer	F-6
Union •	B-5
Vance	E-8
Varnville	F-6
Vaucluse	E-5
Verdery	C-3
Wagener	D-5
Walhalla	B-2
Wallace	B-9
Walterboro •	F-7
Wando	F-9
Ward	D-5
Ware Shoals	C-3
Warrenville	E-5
Warsaw	E-9
Wateree	D-7
Waterloo	C-4
Watts Mills	B-4
Wedgefield	D-7
West Columbia	D-6
West Springs	B-5
West Union	B-2
Westminster	B-1
Westville	C-7
White Rock	C-6
Whitmire	B-5
Wiggins	G-7
Wilkins	G-7
Williams	F-6
Williamston	B-3
Willington	D-3
Williston	E-5
Windsor	E-5
Winnsboro •	C-6
Wisacky	C-8
Wolfton	E-6
Woodford	D-6
Woodrow	C-8
Woodruff	B-4
Woodward	B-6
Yauhannah	D-10
Yemassee	G-7
Yenome	E-5
Yonges Island	G-8
York •	A-6

UH-691-J-X

Lithographed in U.S.A.

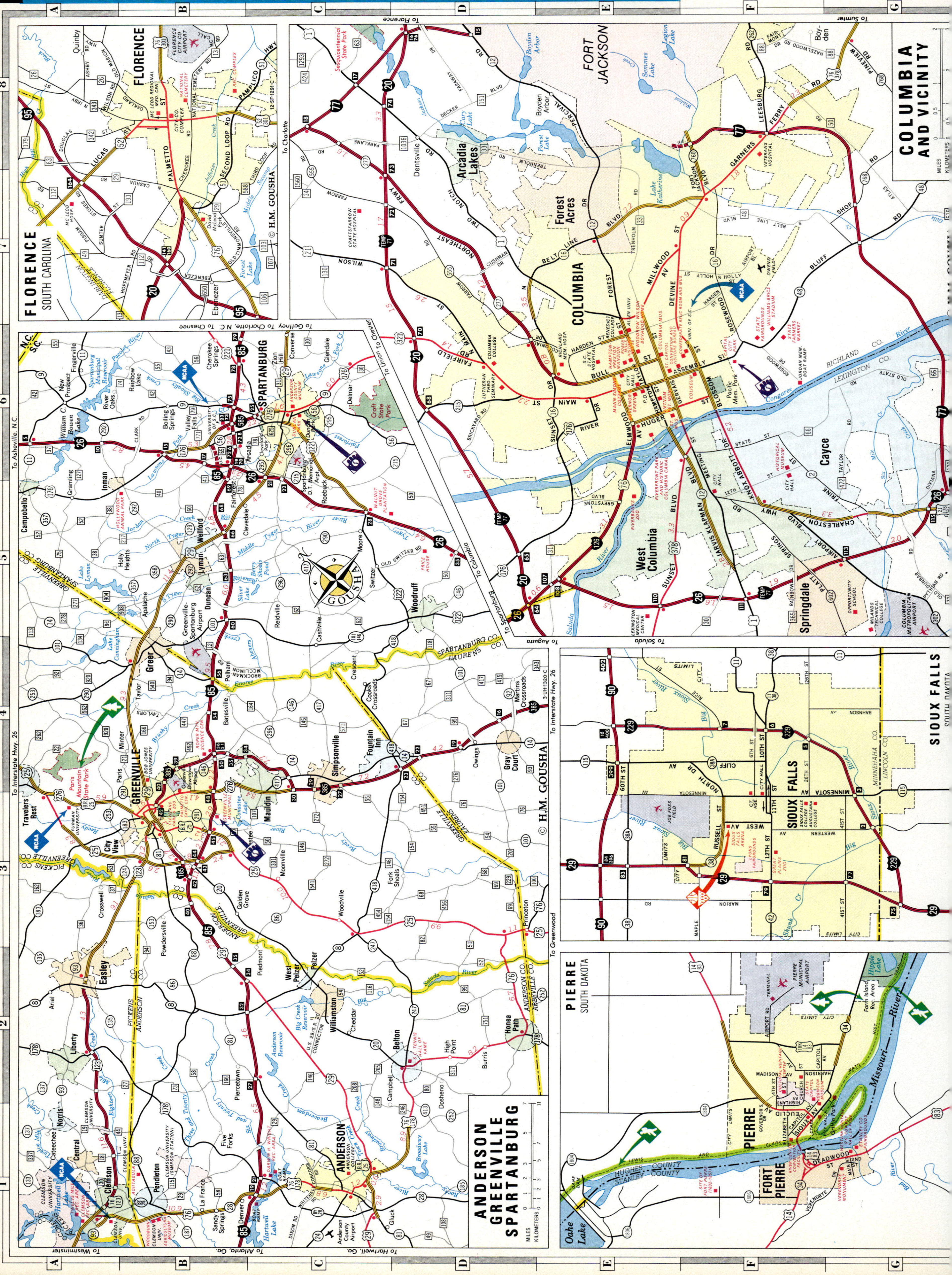
FLORENCE
SOUTH CAROLINA
ANDERSON
GREENVILLE
SPARTANBURG
COLUMBIA
AND VICINITY
SIOUX FALLS
SOUTH DAKOTA
PIERRE
SOUTH DAKOTA
© H.M. GOUSHA

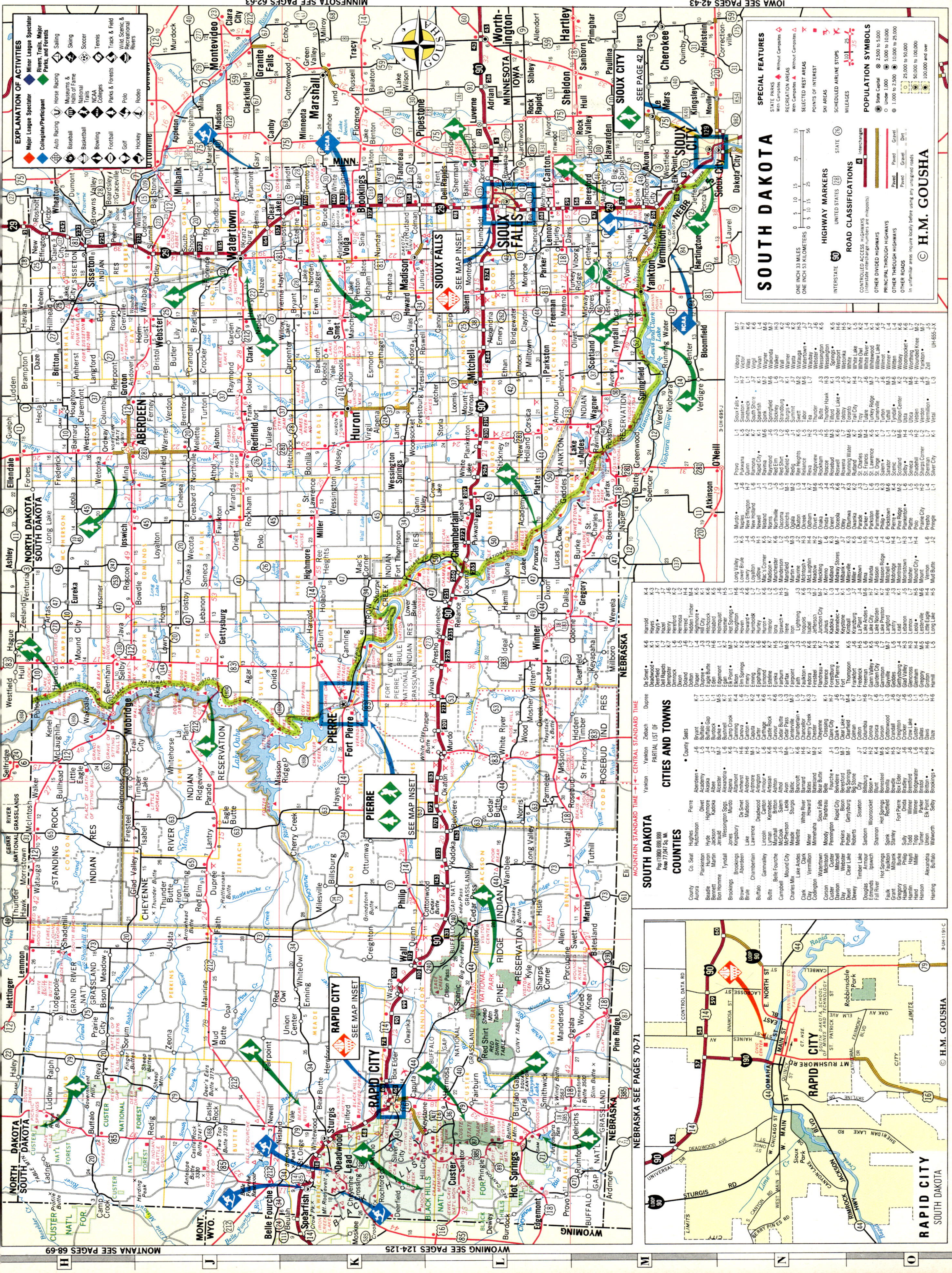
SOUTH DAKOTA
© H.M. GOUSHA
MINNESOTA SEE PAGES 62-63
IOWA SEE PAGES 42-43
NEBRASKA SEE PAGES 70-71
WYOMING SEE PAGES 124-125
MONTANA SEE PAGES 68-69
EXPLANATION OF ACTIVITIES
SPECIAL FEATURES
ROAD CLASSIFICATIONS
HIGHWAY MARKERS
POPULATION SYMBOLS
CITIES AND TOWNS
COUNTIES
RAPID CITY SEE MAP INSET
PIERRE SEE MAP INSET
SIOUX FALLS SEE MAP INSET
RAPID CITY SOUTH DAKOTA

MISSOURI SEE PAGES 66-67
KENTUCKY SEE PAGES 46-47
MISSOURI SEE PAGES 66-67
ARKANSAS SEE PAGES 12-13

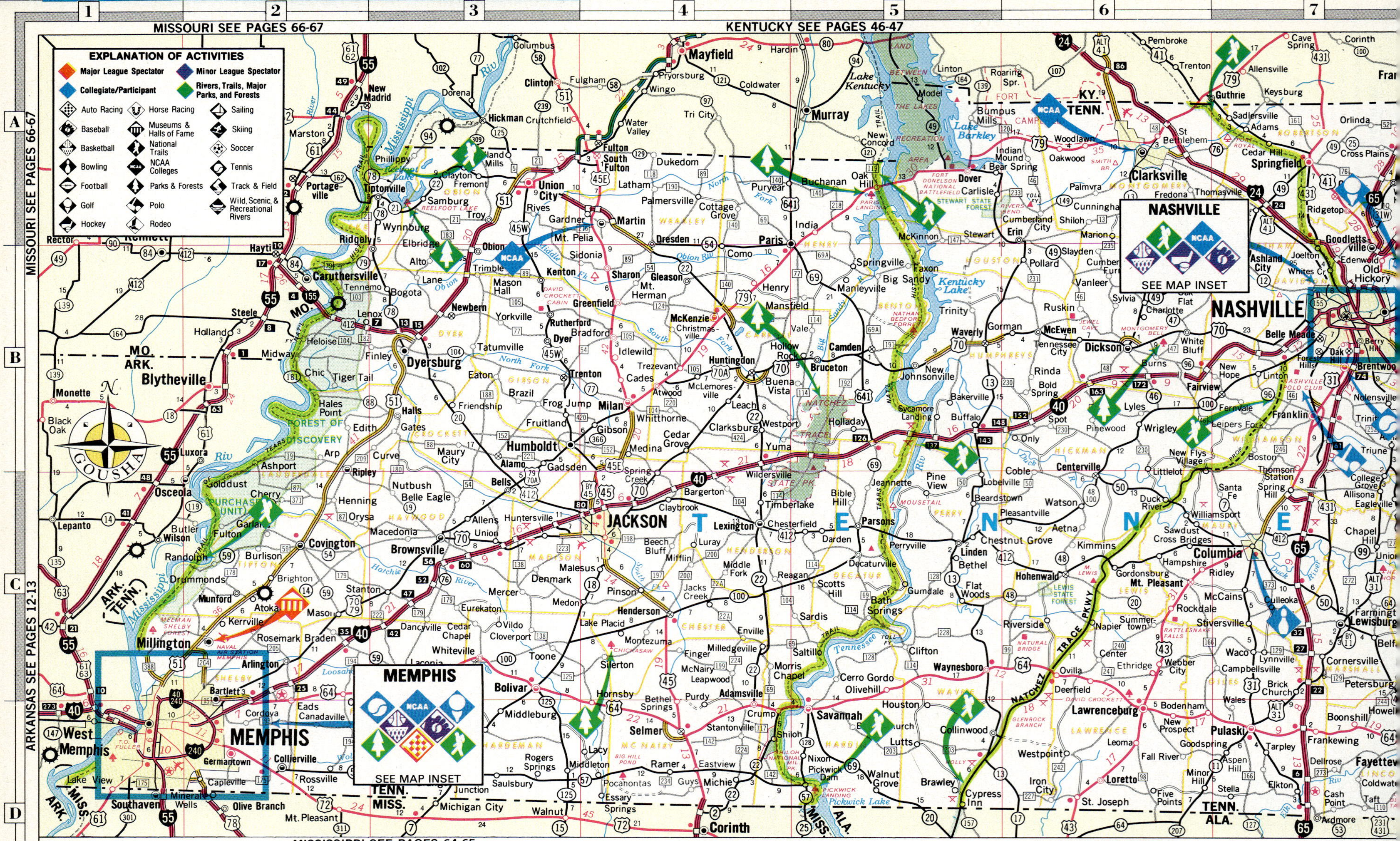

MISSISSIPPI SEE PAGES 64-65
ALABAMA SEE PAGES 6-7

TENNESSEE

ONE INCH 22 MILES
ONE INCH 35 KILOMETERS

HIGHWAY MARKERS

INTERSTATE 90 · UNITED STATES 28 · STATE 26 · STATE SECONDARY 26 · GREAT RIVER ROAD

ROAD CLASSIFICATIONS

CONTROLLED ACCESS HIGHWAYS (Interstate interchange numbers are mileposts) — Divided 4 Undivided
TOLL HIGHWAYS — Service Area, Interchanges
OTHER DIVIDED HIGHWAYS
PRINCIPAL THROUGH HIGHWAYS
OTHER THROUGH HIGHWAYS — Paved, Paved, Gravel
OTHER ROADS — Paved, Gravel, Dirt
In unfamiliar areas inquire locally before using any unsigned roads

SPECIAL FEATURES

STATE PARKS — With Campsites, Without Campsites
RECREATION AREAS — With Campsites, Without Campsites
SELECTED REST AREAS
POINTS OF INTEREST
SKI AREAS
SCHEDULED AIRLINE STOPS
MILITARY AIRPORTS
TOURIST INFORMATION
MILEAGES 10 25 35

POPULATION SYMBOLS

State Capital · 2,500 to 5,000
Under 1,000 · 5,000 to 10,000
1,000 to 2,500 · 10,000 to 25,000
25,000 to 50,000
50,000 to 100,000
100,000 and over

TENNESSEE

Pop (1990) 4,896,641

Area 42,244 Sq. Mi.

COUNTIES

County	Co. Seat
Anderson	Clinton
Bedford	Shelbyville
Benton	Camden
Bledsoe	Pikeville
Blount	Maryville
Bradley	Cleveland
Campbell	Jacksboro
Cannon	Woodbury
Carroll	Huntingdon
Carter	Elizabethton
Cheatham	Ashland City
Chester	Henderson
Claiborne	Tazewell
Clay	Celina
Cocke	Newport
Coffee	Manchester
Crockett	Alamo
Cumberland	Crossville
Davidson	Nashville
De Kalb	Smithville
Decatur	Decatursville
Dickson	Charlotte
Dyer	Dyersburg
Fayette	Somerville
Fentress	Jamestown
Franklin	Winchester
Gibson	Trenton
Giles	Pulaski
Grainger	Rutledge
Greene	Greeneville
Grundy	Altamont
Hamblen	Morristown
Hamilton	Chattanooga
Hancock	Sneedville
Hardeman	Bolivar
Hardin	Savannah
Hawkins	Rogersville
Haywood	Brownsville
Henderson	Lexington
Henry	Paris
Hickman	Centerville
Houston	Erin
Humphreys	Waverly
Jackson	Gainesboro
Jefferson	Dandridge
Johnson	Mountain City
Knox	Knoxville
Lake	Tiptonville
Lauderdale	Ripley
Lawrence	Lawrenceburg
Lewis	Hohenwald
Lincoln	Fayetteville
Loudon	Loudon
Macon	Lafayette
Madison	Jackson
Marion	Jasper
Marshall	Lewisburg
Maury	Columbia
McMinn	Athens
McNairy	Selmer
Meigs	Decatur
Monroe	Madisonville
Montgomery	Clarksville
Moore	Lynchburg
Morgan	Wartburg
Obion	Union City
Overton	Livingston
Perry	Linden
Pickett	Byrdstown
Polk	Benton
Putnam	Cookeville
Rhea	Dayton
Roane	Kingston
Robertson	Springfield
Rutherford	Mufreesboro
Scott	Huntsville
Sevier	Sevierville
Sequatchie	Dunlap
Shelby	Memphis
Smith	Carthage
Stewart	Dover
Sullivan	Blountville
Sumner	Gallatin
Tipton	Covington
Trousdale	Hartsville
Unicoi	Erwin
Union	Maynardville
Van Buren	Spencer
Warren	McMinnville
Washington	Jonesboro
Wayne	Waynesboro
Weakley	Dresden
White	Sparta
Williamson	Franklin
Wilson	Lebanon

PARTIAL LIST OF
CITIES AND TOWNS

• County Seats

Acorn	C-12
Adams	A-7
Adamsville	C-4
Aetna	C-6
Afton	E-12
Alamo •	B-3
Albany	B-14
Alcoa	C-12
Alexandria	B-8
Algood	B-9
Allardt	A-10
Allens	C-3
Allisona	C-7
Allons	A-10
Allred	A-10
Almaville	B-7
Alnwick	C-12
Alpha	B-13
Alpine	A-10
Altamont •	C-9
Anchor Mill	C-8
Anderson	D-8
Andersonville	B-12
Annadel	B-11
Ardmore	D-7
Arlington	C-2
Ashland City •	B-7
Ashport	B-2
Aspen Hill	D-7
Athens •	C-11
Atoka	C-2
Atwood	B-4
Auburntown	B-8
Avondale	B-13
Awalt	D-8
Baileytown	B-14
Bairds Mill	B-8
Bakerville	B-5
Bakewell	C-10
Banner Hill	E-12
Barnardsville	C-11
Bartlett	C-2
Bath Springs	C-5
Bean Station	A-13
Bear Spring	A-5
Beardstown	C-5
Beaver Hill	B-10
Beech Bluff	C-4
Beechgrove	C-8
Beersheba Springs	C-9
Belfast	C-7
Bell Buckle	C-8
Belle Eagle	C-3
Belle Meade	B-7
Bells	C-3
Bellsburg	B-6
Benton •	D-11
Berry Hill	B-7
Bethel	C-5
Bethel Springs	C-4
Bethpage	A-8
Bible Hill	C-5
Big Sandy	B-5
Big Spring	C-10
Birchwood	C-10
Black Oak	A-11
Blaine	B-12
Bloomington	A-10
Bloomington Springs	B-9
Blountville •	D-13
Bluff City	E-13
Bold Spring	B-6
Bolivar •	C-3
Bon Air	B-10
Boonshill	D-7
Boyds Creek	B-12
Braden	C-2
Bradford	B-3
Bradyville	C-8
Bransford	A-8
Brayton	C-10
Brazil	B-3
Brentwood	B-7
Briceville	B-11
Brick Church	C-7
Bridgeport	B-13
Brighton	C-2
Brockdell	C-9
Brownsville •	C-3
Bruceton	B-5
Brush Creek	B-8
Buchanan	A-5
Buena Vista	B-5
Buffalo	B-5
Buffalo Springs	B-13
Bulls Gap	B-14
Butler	E-13
Butlers Landing	A-9
Byrdstown	A-10
Cades	B-4
Calderwood	C-12
Camden •	B-5
Campaign	C-9
Campbellsville	C-7
Canadaville	D-2
Caney Branch	B-14
Capital Hill	A-11
Capleville	D-2
Carlisle	A-5
Carthage •	B-9
Caryville	A-11
Cash Point	D-7
Castalian Springs	A-8
Cedar Chapel	C-3
Cedar Grove	B-4
Cedar Hill	A-7
Cedar Lane	E-12
Celina •	A-9
Center Grove	B-9
Centertown	C-9
Centerville •	B-6
Chapel Hill	C-7
Charleston	C-11
Charleys Branch	B-11
Charlotte •	B-6
Chattanooga •	D-9
Cherry	C-2
Chesterfield	C-4
Chestnut Grove	C-5
Chestnut Hill	B-13
Chestnut Mound	B-9
Christiana	C-8
Christie Hill	C-12
Christmasville	B-4
Church Hill	A-14
Citico Beach	C-12
Clarkrange	B-10
Clarksburg	B-4
Clarksville •	A-6
Claxton	B-12
Claybrook	C-4
Clayton	A-3
Clearwater	C-11
Cleveland •	D-10
Clinton •	B-12
Coalfield	B-11
Coalmont	C-9
Coker Creek	C-11
College Grove	C-7
Collegedale	D-10
Collierville	D-2
Collinwood	D-5
Columbia •	C-6
Como	B-4
Conasauga	D-11
Cookeville	B-9
Cordova	D-2
Cornersville	C-7
Cottage Grove	A-4
Covington •	C-2
Cowan	D-8
Crab Orchard	B-10
Cross Bridges	C-6
Cross Plains	A-7
Crossroads	B-9
Crossville •	B-10
Cumberland City	A-5
Cumberland Furnace	B-6
Cumberland Gap	A-12
Cunningham	A-5
Cypress Inn	D-5
Dallas Hills	D-10
Dancyville	C-3
Dandridge •	B-13
Davenport	C-9
Dayton •	C-10
De Rossett	B-9
Deason	C-8
Decatur •	C-10
Decaturville •	C-5
Decherd	D-8
Deer Lodge	B-11
Deerfield	C-6
Denmark	C-3
Dibrell	B-9
Dickson	B-6
Dixon Springs	A-8
Doeville	E-13
Dossett	B-11
Dover •	A-5
Doyle	B-9
Dresden	A-4
Drummonds	C-1
Duck River	C-6
Ducktown	D-11
Dunlap •	C-9
Dyer	B-3
Dyersburg •	B-3
Eads	D-2
Eagleville	C-7
East Cleveland	D-11
East Jamestown	A-10
East Ridge	D-10
East Sweetwater	C-11
Eastland	B-10
Eastview	D-4
Eaton Crossroad	B-11
Edith	B-2
Elgin	A-11
Elizabethton •	E-13
Elk Valley	A-11
Elkton	D-7
Embreeville	E-12
Emmett	D-13
Englewood	C-11
Erin •	A-5
Ernestville	E-12
Erwin •	E-13
Essary Springs	D-4
Estill Springs	C-8
Etowah	C-11
Eulia	A-8
Eureka	D-10
Eurekaton	C-3
Evensville	C-10
Fairview	B-6
Fairview	C-11
Fall Branch	E-12
Fall River	D-6
Farmington	C-7
Fayetteville •	D-7
Fernvale	B-7
Five Points	D-6
Flag Pond	E-12
Flat Creek	C-8
Flat Woods	C-5
Flintville	D-8
Forbus	A-10
Forest Hills	B-7
Francisco	D-8
Frankewing	D-7
Franklin •	B-7
Fremont	A-3
Friendship	B-3
Fruitland	B-3
Fulton	C-2
Gadsden	B-3
Gainesboro •	A-9
Gallatin •	A-7
Garland	C-2
Gates	B-3
Gatlinburg	C-13
Genesis	B-10
Georgetown	C-10
Germantown	D-2
Gibson	B-4
Gleason	B-4
Glen Alice	B-10
Golddust	C-2
Good Hope	A-12
Goodfield	C-10
Goodlettsville	A-7
Goodspring	D-6
Gordonsburg	C-6
Gorman	B-5
Grand Junction	D-3
Graysville	C-10
Greenbrier	A-7
Greenfield	B-3
Greenville •	B-14
Greenwood	B-8
Grimsley	B-10
Gruetli	C-9
Guild	D-9
Hales Point	B-2
Halls	B-3
Halls Crossroads	B-12
Hampshire	C-6
Hampton	E-13
Happy Valley	C-12
Harriman	B-11
Harrison	D-10
Hartford	B-14
Hartsville •	
Helena	
Henderson •	
Hendersonville	
Hermitage Springs	
Hickory Star Lodge	
Hickory Valley	
High Point	
Highland	
Hilham	
Hillsboro	
Hohenwald •	
Holladay	
Hollow Rock	
Hollow Springs	
Holston Valley	
Homestead	
Hornsby	
Houston	
Howell	
Humboldt	
Huntersville	
Huntingdon •	
Huntland	
Huntsville •	
India	
Indian Mound	
Isham	
Jacks Creek	
Jacksboro •	
Jackson •	
Jamestown •	
Jasper •	
Jearoldstown	
Jefferson City	
Jellico	
Joelton	
Johnson City	
Jonesborough •	
Jonesville	
Joppa	
Kelso	
Kenton	
Kerrville	
Kingsport	

MEMPHIS
TENNESSEE

NASHVILLE
TENNESSEE

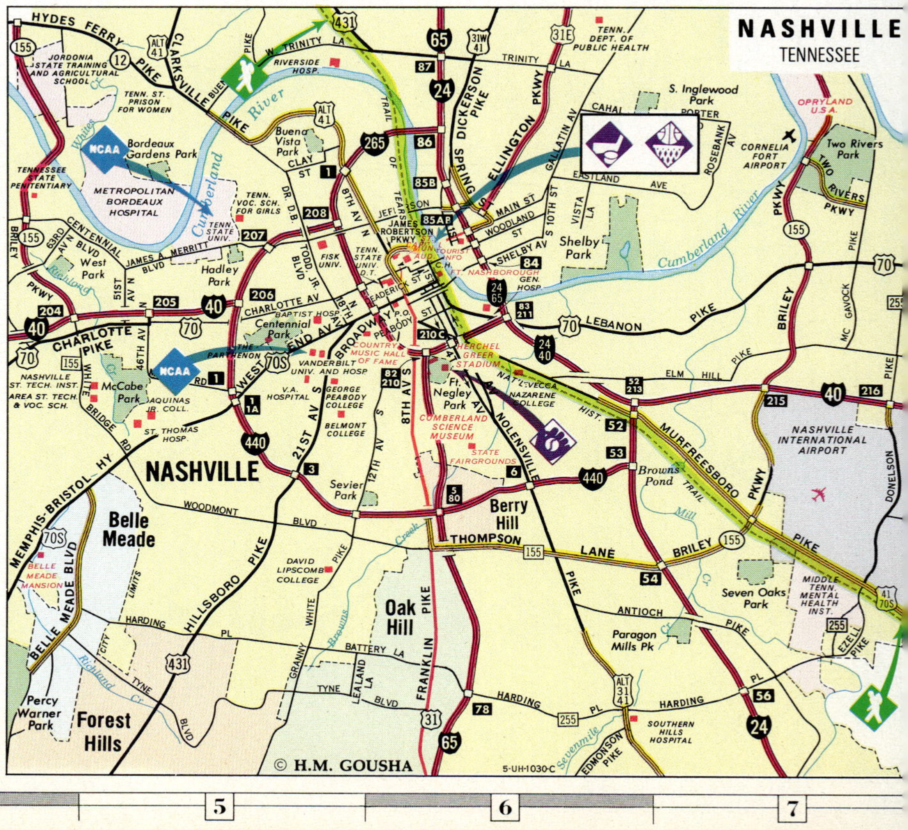

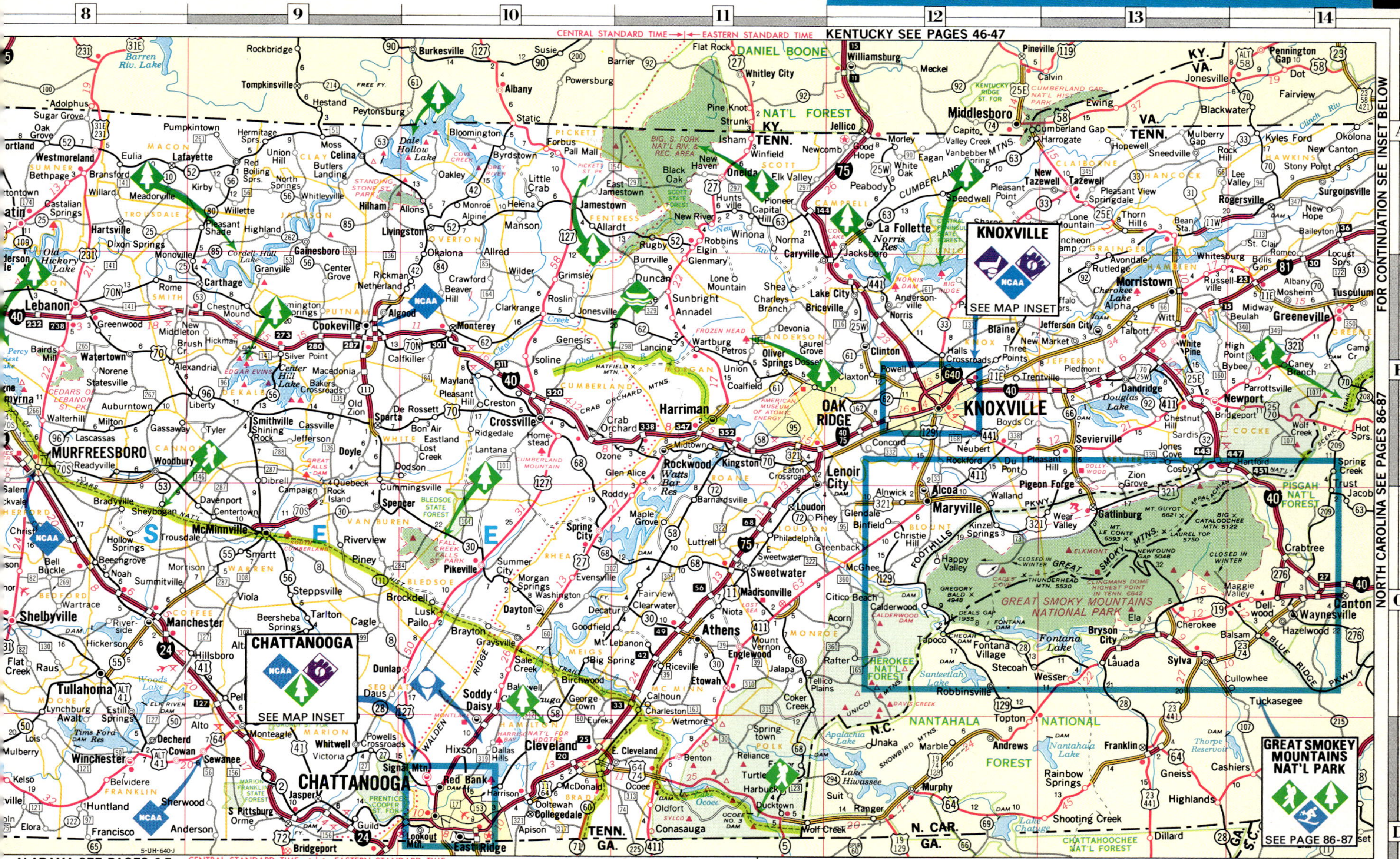

…n •	B-11	Manchester	C-8	Moss	A-9	Oliver Springs	B-11	Riceville	C-11	Shiloh	A-6	Tatumville	B-3	Walland	C-12
…Springs	C-12	Manleyville	B-5	Mount Herman	B-4	Oneida	A-11	Ridgedale	B-10	Shiloh	D-4	Tazewell •	A-13	Walnut Grove	D-5
…le •	B-12	Manson	A-10	Mount Lebanon	C-10	Ooltewah	D-10	Ridgely	A-2	Shining Rock	B-9	Telford	E-12	Walterhill	B-8
…ord	A-14	Maple Grove	C-11	Mount Pelia	A-3	Overall	B-7	Ridge Top	A-7	Shouns	E-14	Tellico Plains	C-11	Wartburg •	B-11
…ette	A-12	Marion	A-5	Mount Pleasant	C-6	Ovilla	C-6	Ridley	C-6	Sidonia	B-3	Tennemo	B-2	Wartrace	C-8
…nge	D-3	Martin	A-4	Mount Vernon	C-11	Ozone	B-10	Ripley •	B-2	Signal Mountain	D-9	Tennessee City	B-6	Washburn	B-12
…gne	B-8	Maryville •	C-12	Mountain City •	D-14	Pailo	C-10	Riverside	C-6	Silerton	C-4	Thomasville	A-6	Watertown	B-8
…a	C-3	Mason	C-2	Mulberry	D-8	Pall Mall	A-10	Riverview	C-9	Silver Point	B-9	Thomson Station	B-7	Watson	C-6
	D-4	Maury City	B-3	Mulberry Gap	A-13	Palmer	C-9	Rives Gardner	A-3	Slayden	B-6	Thorn Hill	A-13	Waverly •	B-5
…tte •	A-8	Maynardville •	B-12	Munford	C-2	Palmersville	A-4	Roan Mountain	E-13	Smartt	C-9	Three Points	B-12	Waynesboro •	C-5
…ty	B-11	McCains	C-6	Murfreesboro •	C-8	Pandora	E-14	Robbins	A-11	Smithville •	B-9	Tiger Tail	B-2	Wear Valley	C-13
…acid	C-4	McDonald	D-10	Nashville •	B-6	Paris •	A-4	Rock Island	C-9	Smyrna	B-8	Tiger Valley	E-13	Webber City	C-6
…g	B-11	McEwen	B-6	New Canton	A-14	Parrottsville	B-14	Rockdale	C-6	Sneedville •	A-13	Timberlake	C-4	Westmoreland	A-8
…a	B-10	McGhee	C-12	New Flys Village	B-6	Parsons	C-5	Rockwood	B-10	Soddy Daisy	C-10	Tiptonville •	A-2	Westpoint	D-6
…sas	B-8	McKenzie	B-4	New Haven	A-11	Paulette	B-12	Roddy	C-10	Somerville •	C-2	Toone	C-3	Westport	B-4
…Bloomery	D-14	McKinnon	A-5	New Hope	A-14	Peabody	A-12	Rogers Springs	D-3	South Fulton	A-4	Topton	D-12	Wetmore	D-11
…Grove	B-11	McLemoresville	B-4	New Hope	B-7	Pelham	C-9	Rogersville •	A-14	South Pittsburg	D-9	Tracy City	C-9	White Bluff	B-6
…ceburg •	D-6	McMinnville •	C-8	New Johnsonville	B-5	Petersburg	C-7	Rome	B-8	South Side	A-5	Trade	E-14	White House	A-7
	B-4	Meadorville	A-8	New Market	B-12	Philadelphia	C-11	Rosemark	C-2	Sparta •	B-9	Trenton •	B-3	White Oak	A-12
…n •	B-8	Medina	B-4	New Middleton	B-8	Pickwick Dam	D-5	Rossville	D-2	Speedwell	A-12	Trentville	B-12	White Oak Flat	B-6
…Fork	B-7	Medon	C-3	New Prospect	D-6	Pigeon Forge	B-12	Rugby	A-11	Spencer •	C-9	Trezevant	B-4	White Pine	B-13
…City	B-12	Memphis •	D-2	New River	A-11	Pikeville •	C-10	Ruskin	B-6	Spring City	C-10	Trimble	B-3	Whites Creek	B-7
	B-2	Michie	D-4	New Tazewell	A-12	Pinewood	B-6	Russellville	B-13	Spring Hill	C-7	Trinity	B-5	Whitesburg	A-13
	D-6	Middle Fork	C-4	Newbern	B-3	Piney	C-11	Rutherford	B-3	Springdale	A-13	Trinity	B-7	Whiteville	C-3
…urg •	C-7	Middleburg	D-3	Newcastle	D-3	Pinson	C-4	Rutledge •	B-13	Springfield •	A-7	Triune	B-7	Whitleyville	A-9
…ton •	C-4	Middleton	D-3	Newport •	B-13	Pleasant Point	A-12	Sadlersville	A-7	Springtown	D-11	Trousdale	C-8	Whitthorne	B-4
	B-9	Midtown	B-11	Niota	C-11	Pleasant Shade	A-9	St. Bethlehem	A-6	Springville	B-5	Troy	A-3	Whitwell	D-9
…one Cove	E-13	Midway	B-14	Nixon	D-5	Pleasant View	A-7	St. Clair	A-14	Stanton	C-2	Tullahoma	C-8	Wilder	B-10
… •	C-5	Mifflin	C-4	Noah	C-8	Pleasantville	C-6	St. Joseph	D-6	Stantonville	D-4	Turtletown	D-11	Wildersville	C-4
…rab	A-10	Milan	B-4	Nolensville	B-7	Pocahontas	D-4	Sale Creek	C-10	Statesville	B-8	Tusculum	E-12	Willard	A-8
…t	C-6	Milledgeville	C-4	Norris	B-12	Pollard	B-6	Samburg	A-3	Static	A-10	Unicol	E-13	Willette	A-9
…ton •	A-9	Milligan College	E-13	North Springs	A-9	Portland	A-8	Santa Fe	C-7	Steppsville	C-9	Union	B-11	Williamsport	C-6
…lle	C-5	Millington	C-1	Oak Grove	A-8	Powell	B-12	Saulsbury	D-3	Stiversville	C-6	Union	C-3	Williston	D-3
…Springs	E-12	Milton	B-8	Oak Hill	A-5	Powells Crossroads	D-9	Savannah	D-5	Stony Point	A-14	Union City •	A-3	Winchester •	D-8
…lountain	A-13	Minor Hill	D-6	Oak Hill	B-7	Pulaski •	D-7	Sawdust	C-6	Sugar Grove	A-8	Union Hill	A-9	Winfield	A-11
…lountain	B-11	Monroe	A-10	Oak Ridge	B-11	Pumpkintown	A-8	Scotts Hill	C-5	Summer City	C-10	Union Temple	E-12	Winona	A-11
…t Mountain	D-10	Monteagle	D-9	Oakland	D-2	Puryear	A-4	Selmer •	D-4	Summertown	C-6	Unionville	C-7	Wolf Creek	E-12
	D-6	Monterey	B-10	Oakwood	A-5	Quebeck	B-9	Sevierville •	B-13	Summitville	C-8	Valley Creek	A-12	Woodbury •	B-8
…n	C-11	Montezuma	C-4	Obion	B-3	Ramer	D-4	Sewanee	D-9	Sunbright	B-11	Vanbebber Spring	A-12	Woodland Mills	A-3
	C-4	Morgan Springs	C-10	Ocoee	D-11	Randolph	C-1	Shady Valley	D-14	Surgoinsville	A-14	Vanleer	B-6	Woodlawn	A-6
	C-10	Morris Chapel	C-4	Okalona	A-10	Readyville	B-8	Sharon	B-4	Sweetwater	C-11	Victoria	D-9	Wrigley	B-6
…burg •	C-8	Morrison	C-8	Okolona	A-14	Reagan	C-4	Sharps Chapel	A-12	Sycamore Landing	B-5	Vildo	C-3	Wynnburg	A-3
…onia	B-9	Morristown •	B-13	Old Zion	B-9	Red Bank	D-10	Shea	B-11	Sylvia	B-6	Viola	C-9	Yuma	B-4
…n	B-7	Moscow	D-3	Oldfort	D-11	Red Boiling Springs	A-9	Shelbyville •	B-11	Talbott	B-13	Waco	C-7		
…nville •	C-11	Mosheim	B-14	Olivehill	C-5	Reliance	D-11	Sherwood	D-8	Tarlton	C-9	Wales	D-7		
…s	C-3							Sheybogan	C-8	Tarpley	D-7				

UH-640-J-X

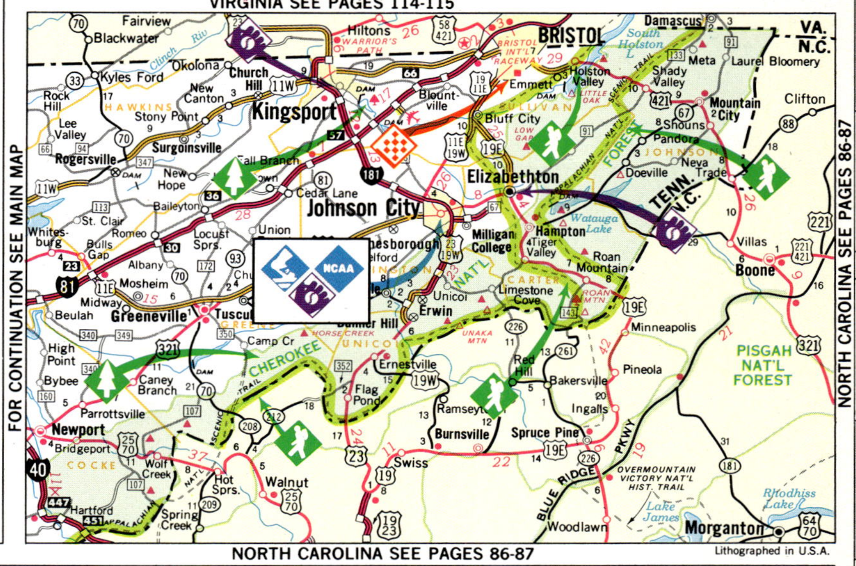

NORTH CAROLINA SEE PAGES 86-87

Lithographed in U.S.A.

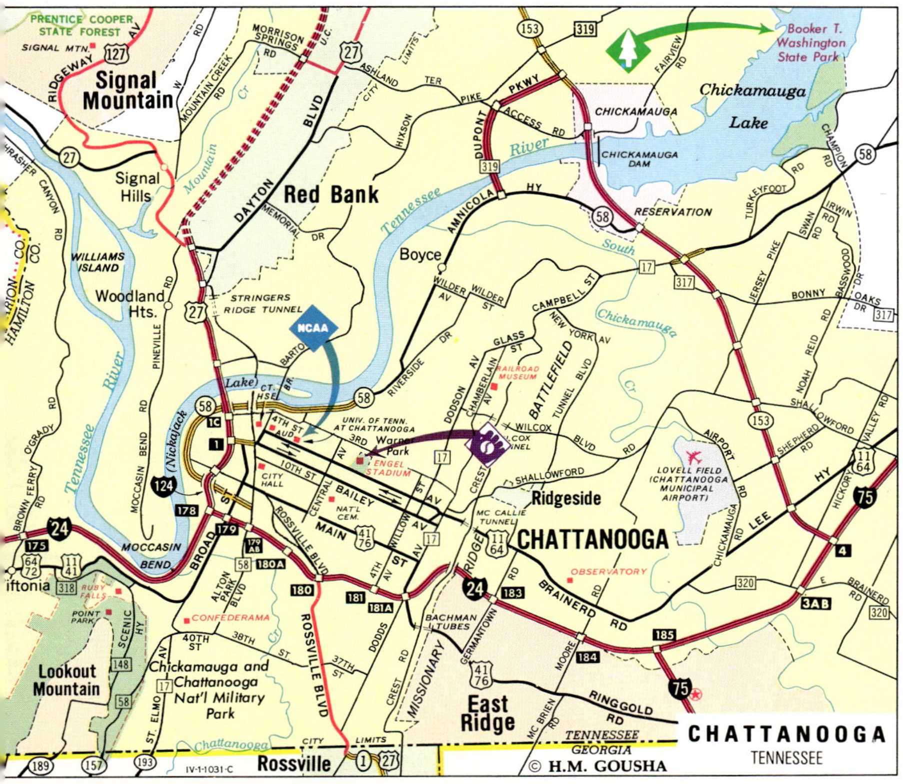

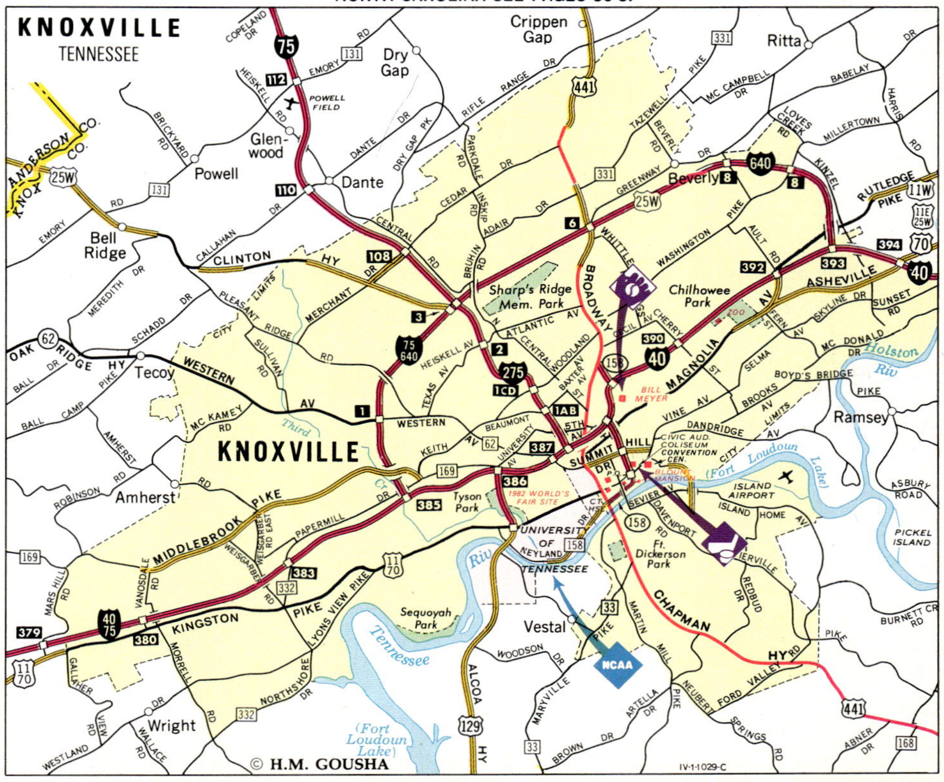

OKLAHOMA SEE PAGES 94-95
NEW MEXICO SEE PAGES 78-79
AMARILLO
LUBBOCK
MIDLAND
ABILENE
BIG SPRING
LUBBOCK SEE MAP INSET
MIDLAND SEE MAP INSET
WICHITA FALLS
AUSTIN
EL PASO
TEXAS
COUNTIES
MOUNTAIN STANDARD TIME
CENTRAL STANDARD TIME
© H.M. GOUSHA

8 9 10 11 12 13 14

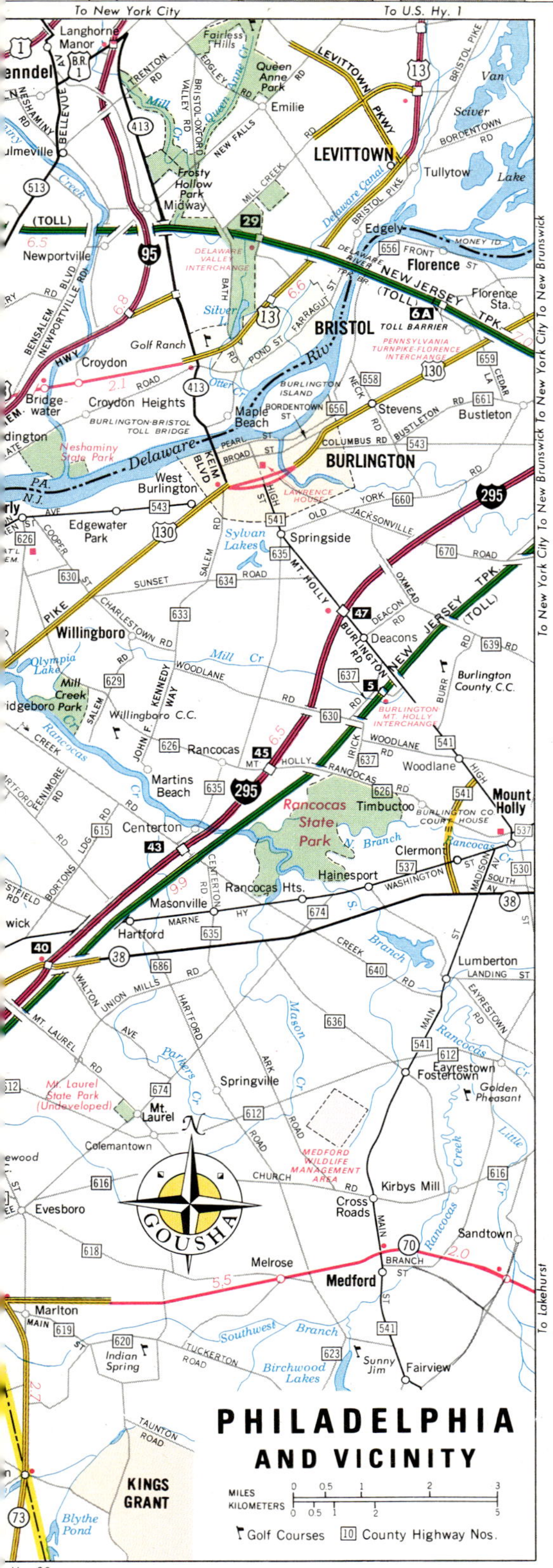

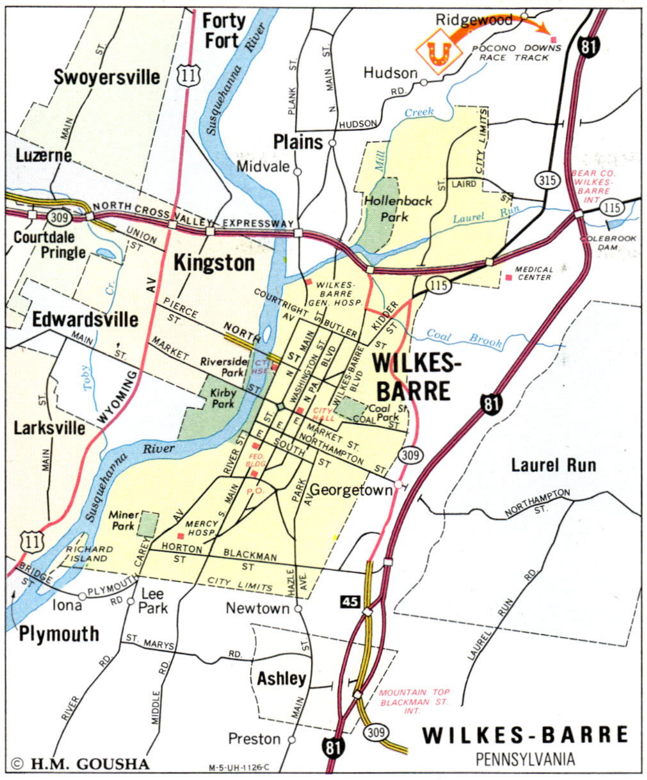

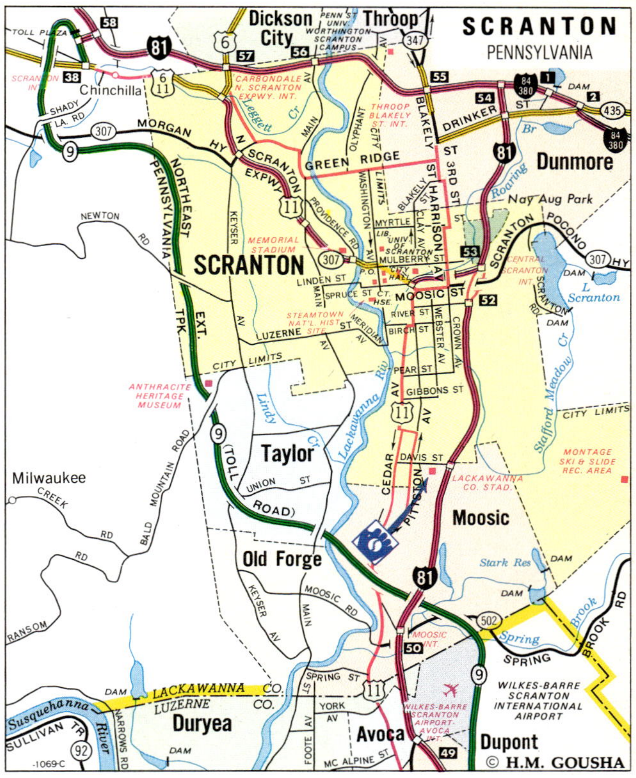

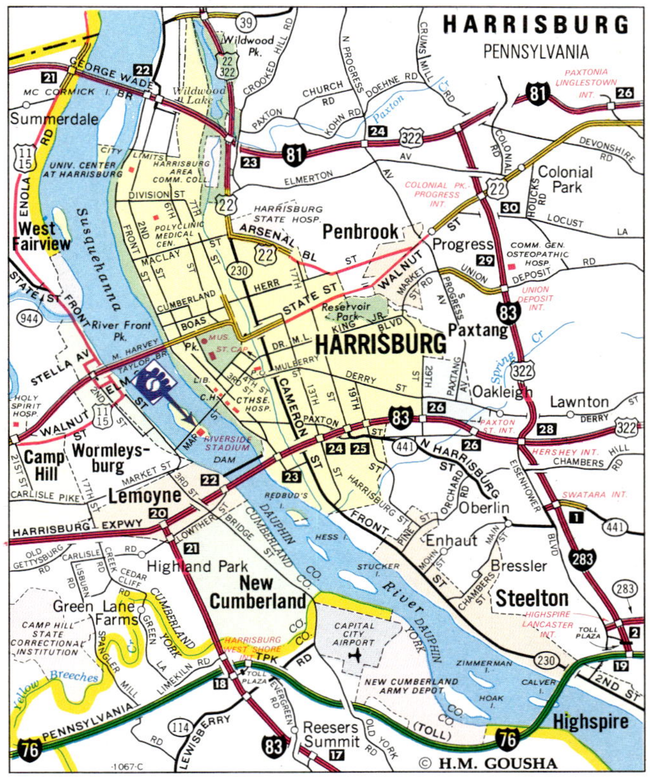

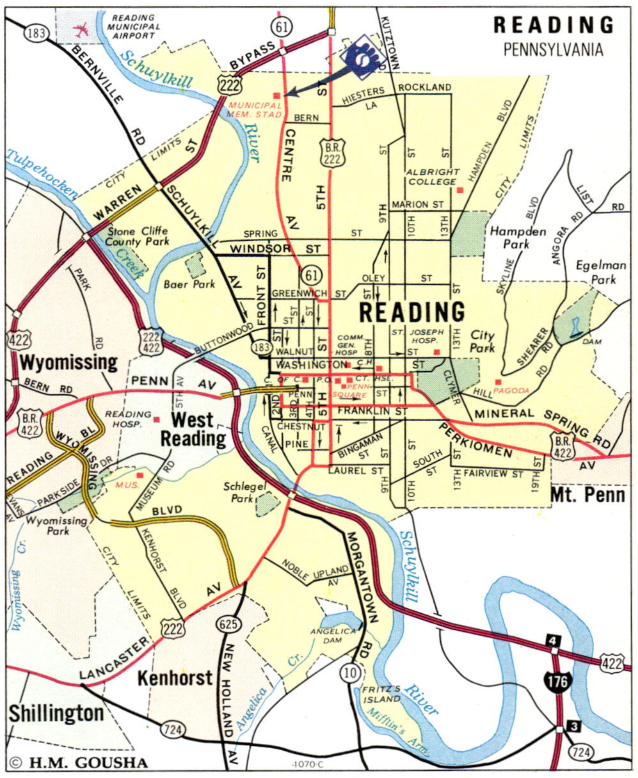

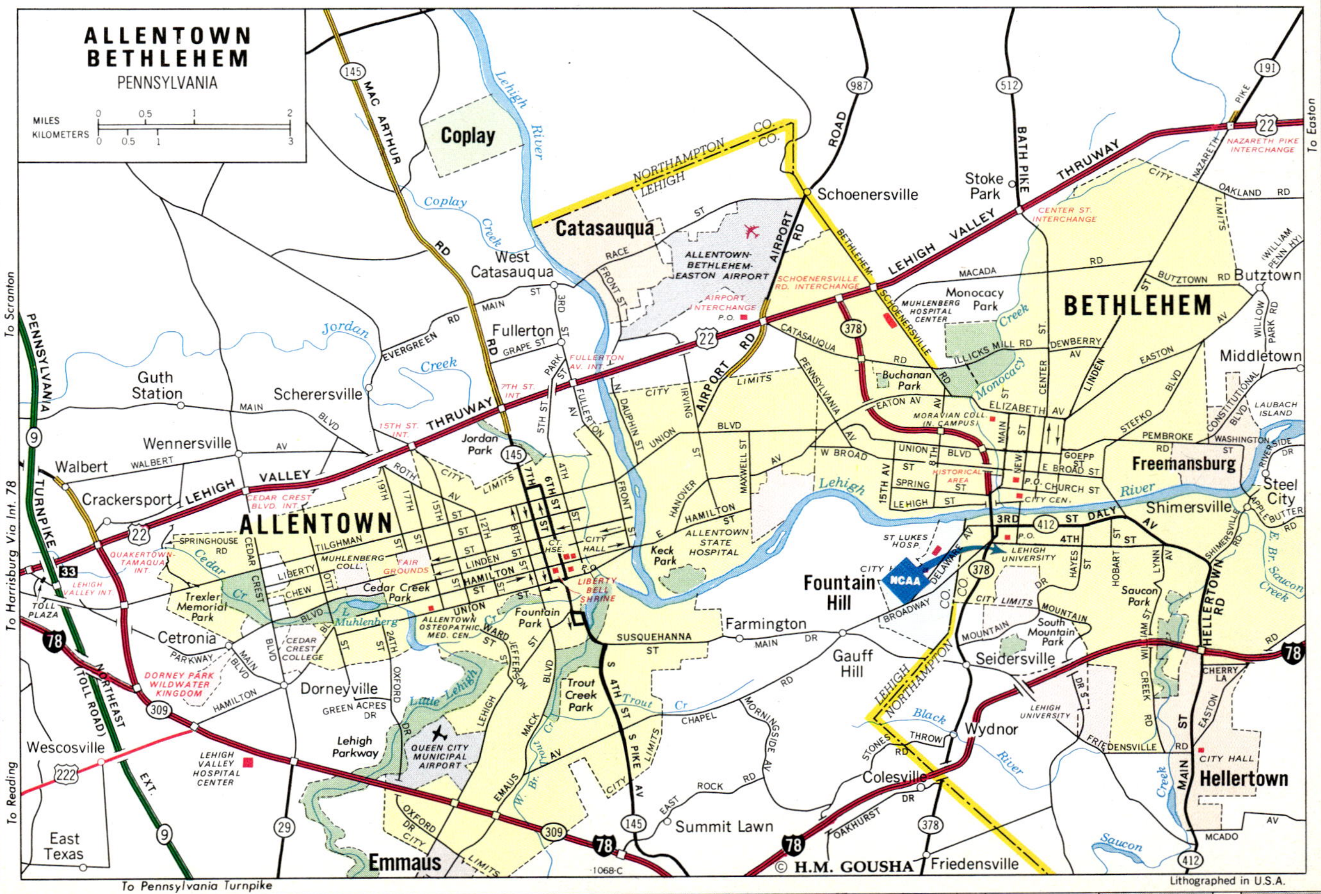

8 9 10 11 12 13 14

FOR RHODE ISLAND SEE PAGES 24-25

SF-659-J

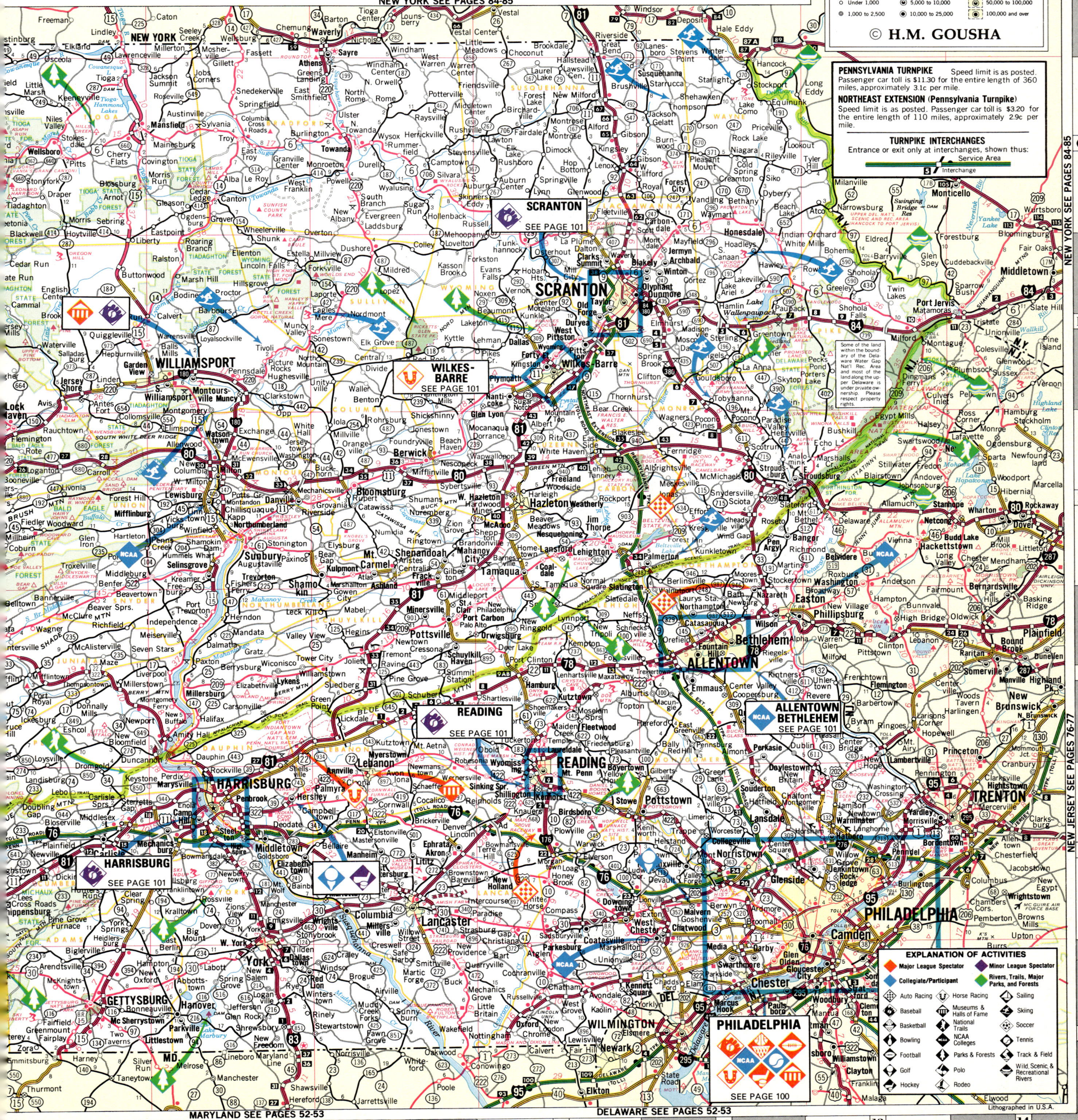

NEW YORK SEE PAGES 84-85
PENNSYLVANIA
ONE INCH 17 MILES
ONE INCH 27 KILOMETERS
HIGHWAY MARKERS
INTERSTATE
UNITED STATES
STATE
ROAD CLASSIFICATIONS
CONTROLLED ACCESS HIGHWAYS
(Interstate interchange numbers are mileposts)
TOLL HIGHWAYS
OTHER DIVIDED HIGHWAYS
PRINCIPAL THROUGH HIGHWAYS
OTHER THROUGH HIGHWAYS
OTHER ROADS
In unfamiliar areas inquire locally before using any unsigned roads
SPECIAL FEATURES
POPULATION SYMBOLS
© H.M. GOUSHA
PENNSYLVANIA TURNPIKE Speed limit is as posted. Passenger car toll is $11.30 for the entire length of 360 miles, approximately 3.1c per mile.
NORTHEAST EXTENSION (Pennsylvania Turnpike) Speed limit is as posted. Passenger car toll is $3.20 for the entire length of 110 miles, approximately 2.9c per mile.
TURNPIKE INTERCHANGES
Entrance or exit only at interchanges, shown thus:
NEW YORK SEE PAGES 84-85
NEW JERSEY SEE PAGES 76-77
SCRANTON SEE PAGE 101
WILKES-BARRE SEE PAGE 101
READING SEE PAGE 101
ALLENTOWN BETHLEHEM SEE PAGE 101
HARRISBURG SEE PAGE 101
PHILADELPHIA SEE PAGE 100
EXPLANATION OF ACTIVITIES
MARYLAND SEE PAGES 52-53
DELAWARE SEE PAGES 52-53
Lithographed in U.S.A.

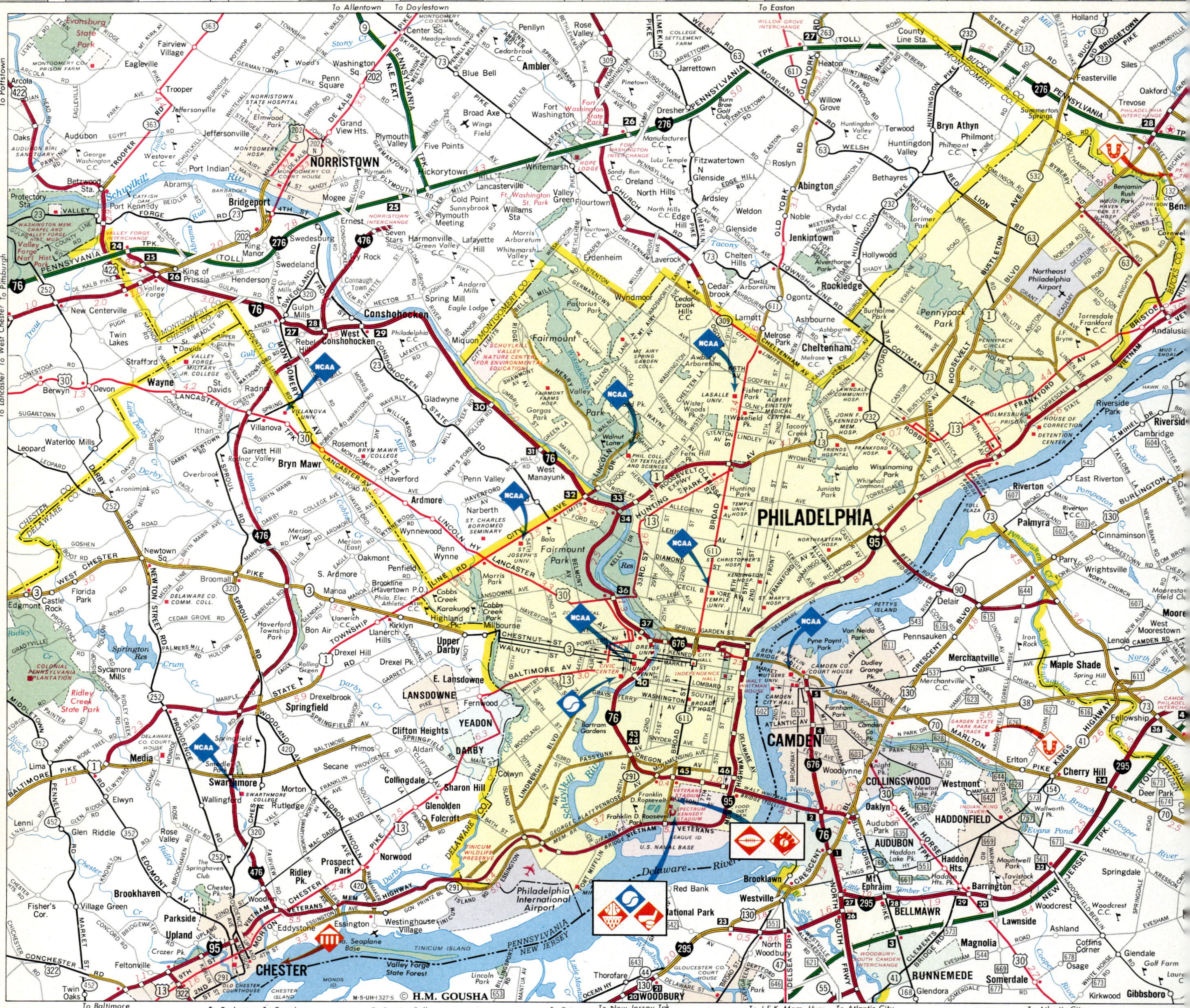
PHILADELPHIA
CAMDEN
CHESTER
NORRISTOWN
Conshohocken
Bridgeport
Wayne
Bryn Mawr
Ardmore
Media
Swarthmore
Springfield
Upper Darby
LANSDOWNE
YEADON
DARBY
Collingdale
Norwood
Ridley Pk.
Prospect Park
Brookhaven
Upland
Eddystone
Essington
Philadelphia International Airport
Woodbury
Westville
Brooklawn
Gloucester City
Audubon
Haddon Hts.
HADDONFIELD
COLLINGSWOOD
Westmont
Cherry Hill
Merchantville
Pennsauken
Palmyra
Riverton
Barrington
BELLMAWR
RUNNEMEDE
Somerdale
Magnolia
Lawnside
Cheltenham
Abington
Jenkintown
Rockledge
Willow Grove
Jarrettown
Ambler
Blue Bell
Plymouth Meeting
King of Prussia
Valley Forge
Fort Washington
Fairview Village
Eagleville
Trooper
Jeffersonville
Audubon
Northeast Philadelphia Airport
Delaware River
Schuylkill River
To Allentown
To Doylestown
To Easton
To Pottstown
To Lancaster
To West Chester
To Baltimore
To Rochester
To Freedom
To Beaver Falls
To Erie
To New Jersey Tpk.
To J.F.K. Mem. Hwy.
To Atlantic City
© H.M. GOUSHA

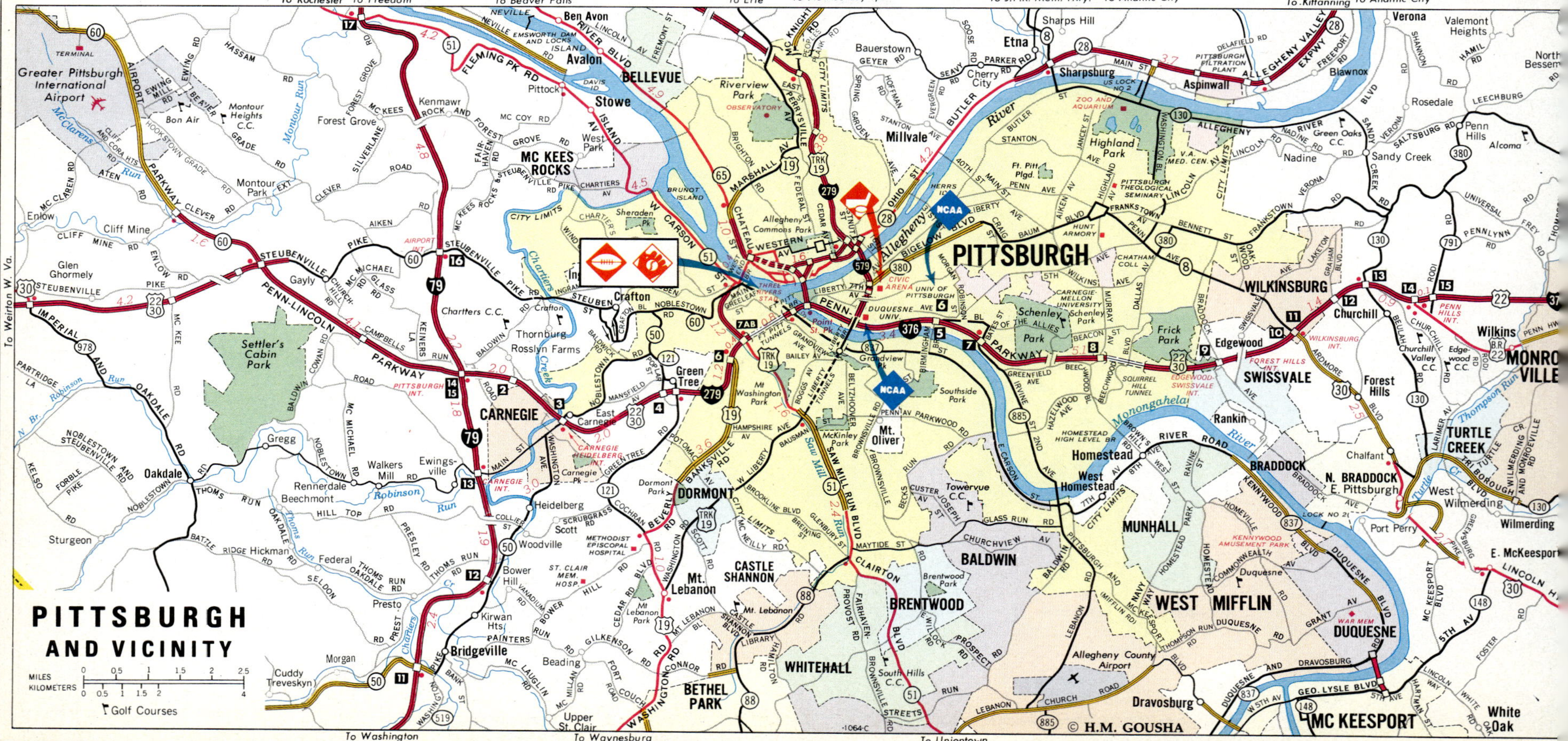
PITTSBURGH AND VICINITY
PITTSBURGH
MC KEES ROCKS
BELLEVUE
Avalon
Ben Avon
Etna
Sharpsburg
Aspinwall
Millvale
WILKINSBURG
SWISSVALE
Edgewood
Churchill
Wilkins
MONROEVILLE
TURTLE CREEK
BRADDOCK
N. BRADDOCK
Rankin
Homestead
West Homestead
MUNHALL
WEST MIFFLIN
DUQUESNE
MC KEESPORT
Dravosburg
White Oak
BALDWIN
BRENTWOOD
WHITEHALL
BETHEL PARK
CASTLE SHANNON
Mt. Lebanon
DORMONT
Mt. Oliver
Green Tree
CARNEGIE
Crafton
Heidelberg
Bridgeville
Oakdale
Coraopolis
Greater Pittsburgh International Airport
Settler's Cabin Park
Allegheny County Airport
To Weirton W. Va.
To Washington
To Waynesburg
To Uniontown
To Kittanning
MILES
KILOMETERS
Golf Courses
© H.M. GOUSHA

NORTH CAROLINA SEE PAGES 86-87
SOUTH CAROLINA
© H.M. GOUSHA
EXPLANATION OF ACTIVITIES
SPECIAL FEATURES
HIGHWAY MARKERS
ROAD CLASSIFICATIONS
POPULATION SYMBOLS
THE GRAND STRAND
SOUTH CAROLINA
North Myrtle Beach
Atlantic Beach
Briarcliffe Acres
MYRTLE BEACH
ATLANTIC OCEAN
HILTON HEAD ISLAND
SOUTH CAROLINA
CHARLESTON
SEE MAP INSET
GRAND STRAND
SEE MAP INSET
FRANCIS MARION NATIONAL FOREST
SOUTH CAROLINA
Pop (1990) 3,505,707
Area 31,055 Sq. Mi.
COUNTIES
CITIES AND TOWNS
County Seats
Lithographed in U.S.A.

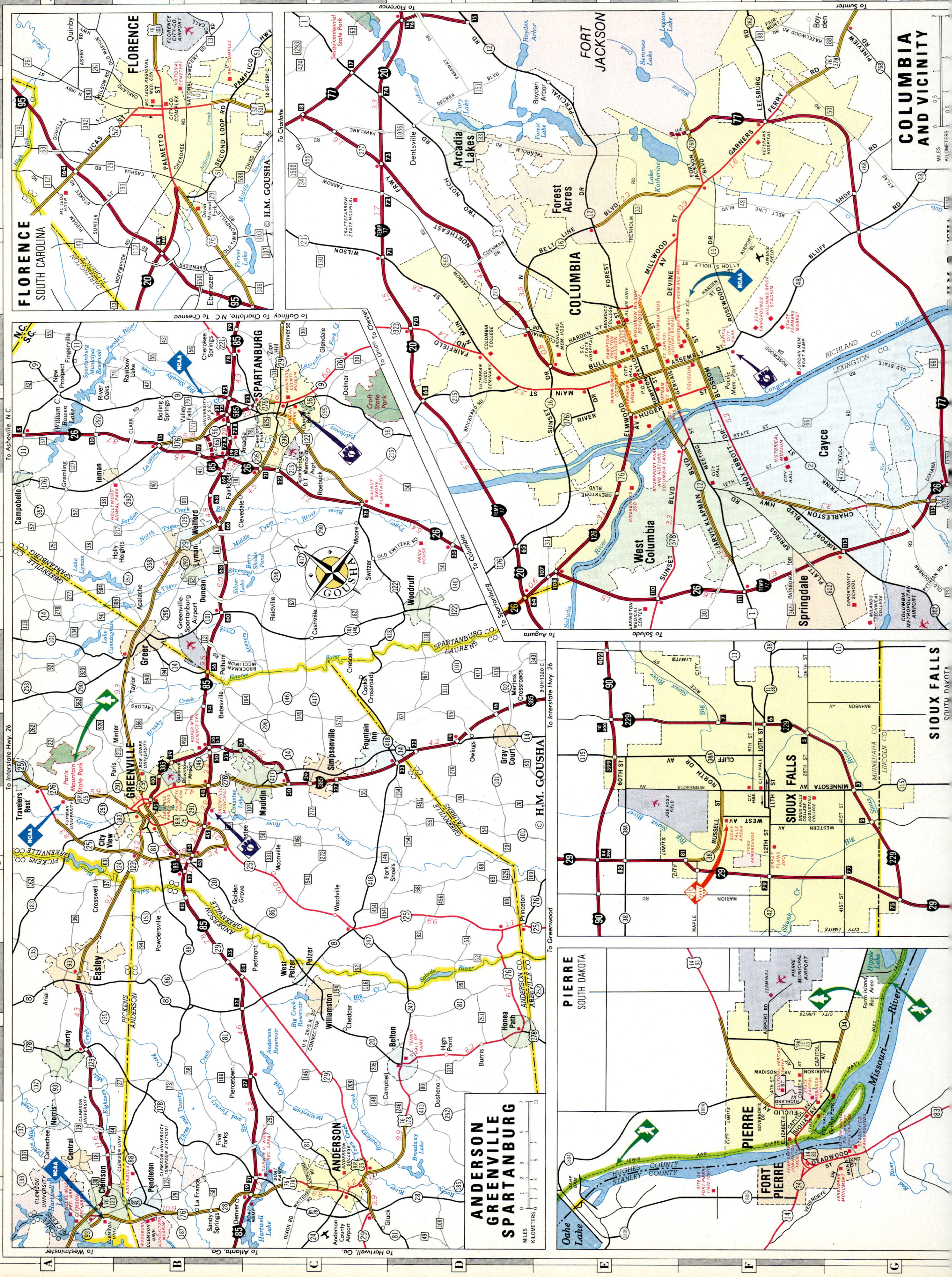

FLORENCE
SOUTH CAROLINA
COLUMBIA
AND VICINITY
ANDERSON
GREENVILLE
SPARTANBURG
SIOUX FALLS
SOUTH DAKOTA
PIERRE
SOUTH DAKOTA
© H.M. GOUSHA

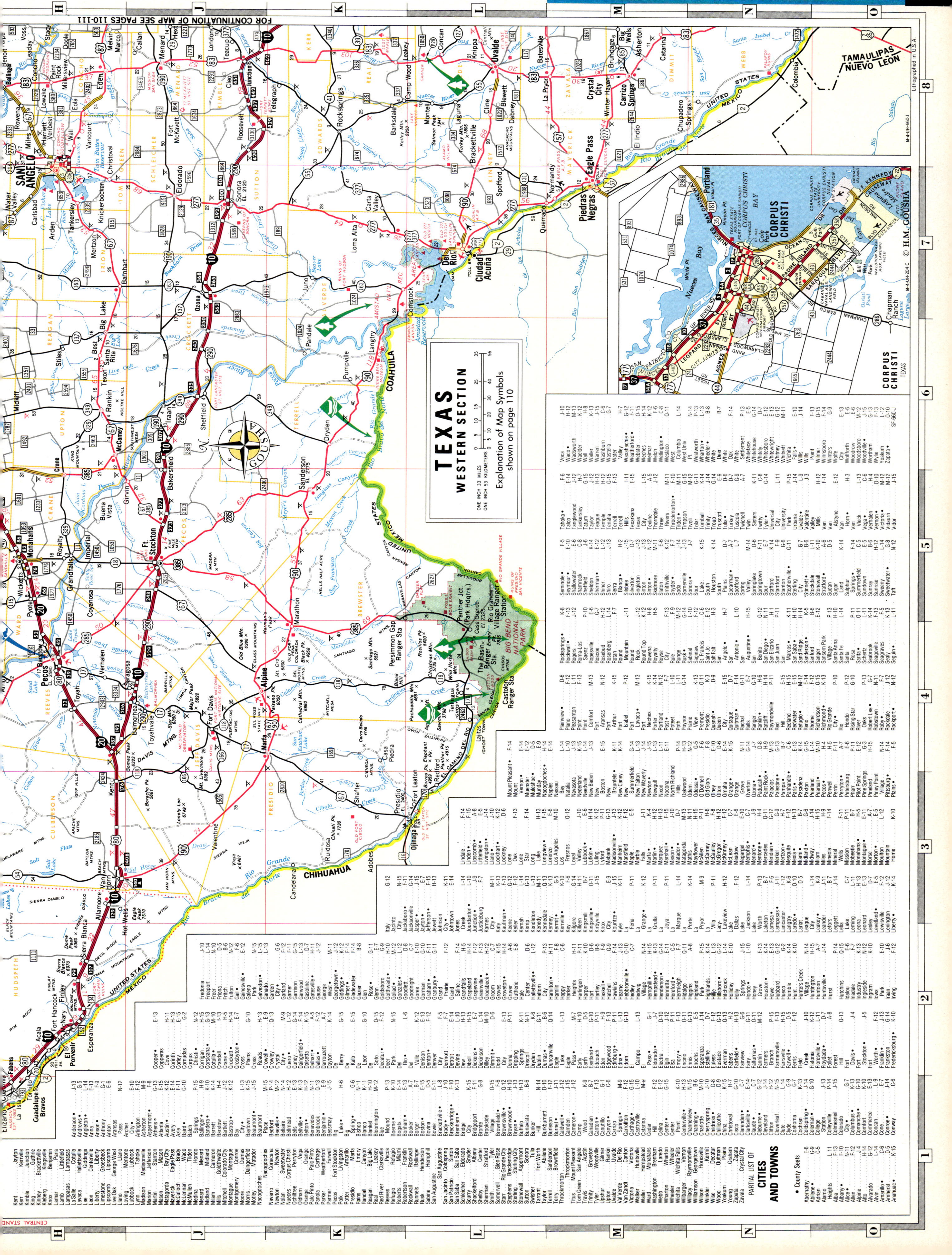
FOR CONTINUATION OF MAP SEE PAGES 110-111
TEXAS
WESTERN SECTION
Explanation of Map Symbols
shown on page 110
BIG BEND NATIONAL PARK
CORPUS CHRISTI
COAHUILA
CHIHUAHUA
TAMAULIPAS
NUEVO LEON
PARTIAL LIST OF
CITIES
AND TOWNS
© H.M. GOUSHA
Lithographed in U.S.A.

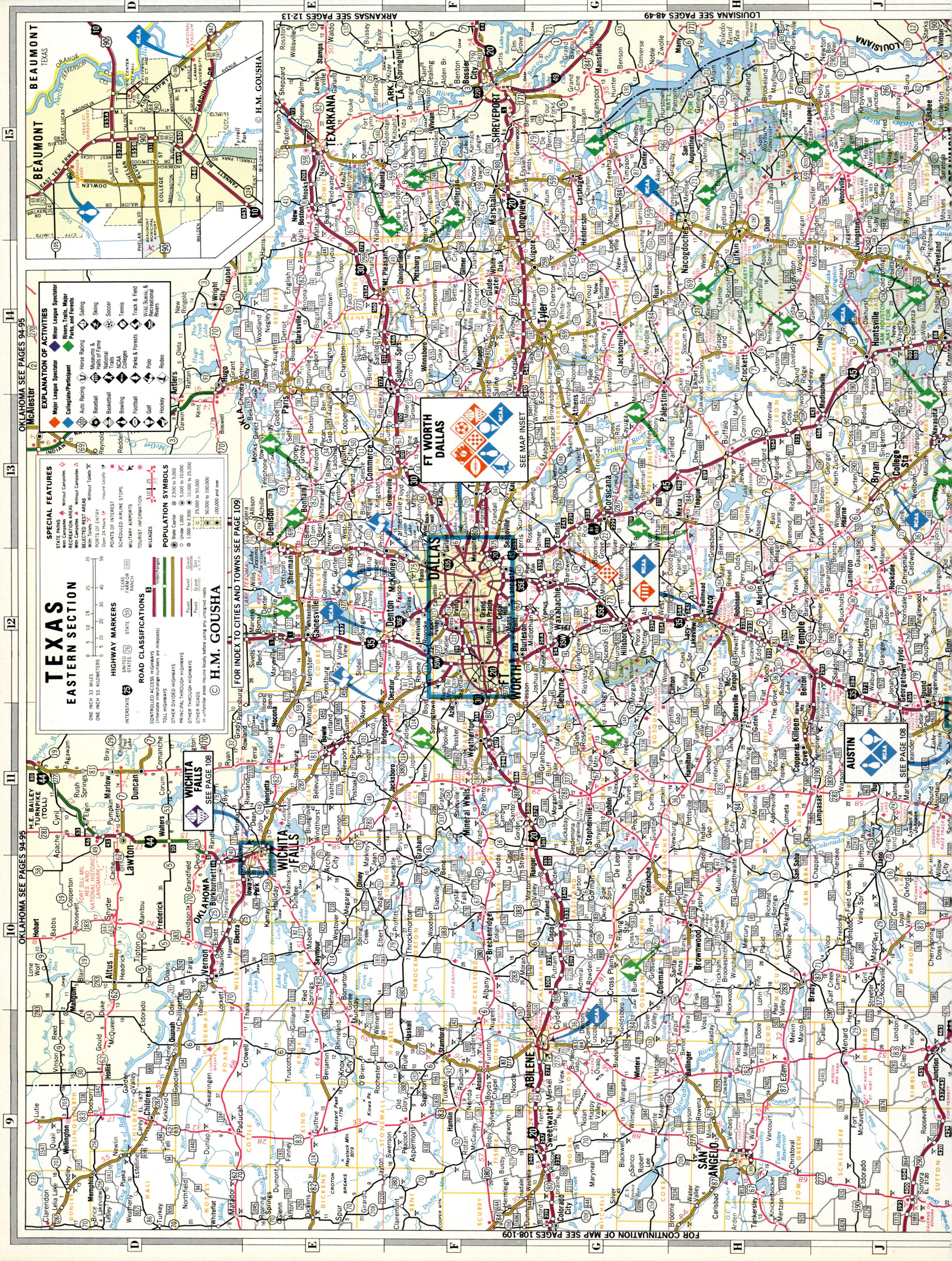
TEXAS
EASTERN SECTION
H.M. GOUSHA
BEAUMONT
EXPLANATION OF ACTIVITIES
SPECIAL FEATURES
HIGHWAY MARKERS
ROAD CLASSIFICATIONS
POPULATION SYMBOLS
FOR INDEX TO CITIES AND TOWNS SEE PAGE 109
OKLAHOMA SEE PAGES 94-95
ARKANSAS SEE PAGES 12-13
LOUISIANA SEE PAGES 48-49
FOR CONTINUATION OF MAP SEE PAGES 108-109
FT WORTH DALLAS SEE MAP INSET
WICHITA FALLS SEE PAGE 108
AUSTIN SEE PAGE 108

GULF OF MEXICO
HOUSTON
SEE MAP INSET
SAN ANTONIO
SEE MAP INSET
BEAUMONT
SEE MAP INSET
GALVESTON
CORPUS CHRISTI
BROWNSVILLE
LAREDO
DALLAS
FORT WORTH
FORT WORTH DALLAS AREA
SAN ANTONIO TEXAS
HOUSTON TEXAS
PADRE ISLAND NATIONAL SEASHORE
TAMAULIPAS
NUEVO LEON
COAHUILA
UNITED STATES
MEXICO
TEXAS TOLL ROADS
DALLAS NORTH TOLLWAY
Passenger car toll is $1.00 for the entire length of 17 miles.
HARDY TOLL ROAD
Passenger car toll is $2.00 for the entire length of 21.7 miles.
SAM HOUSTON TOLLWAY
Passenger car toll is $1.50 for the entire length of 15.1 miles.
H.M. GOUSHA

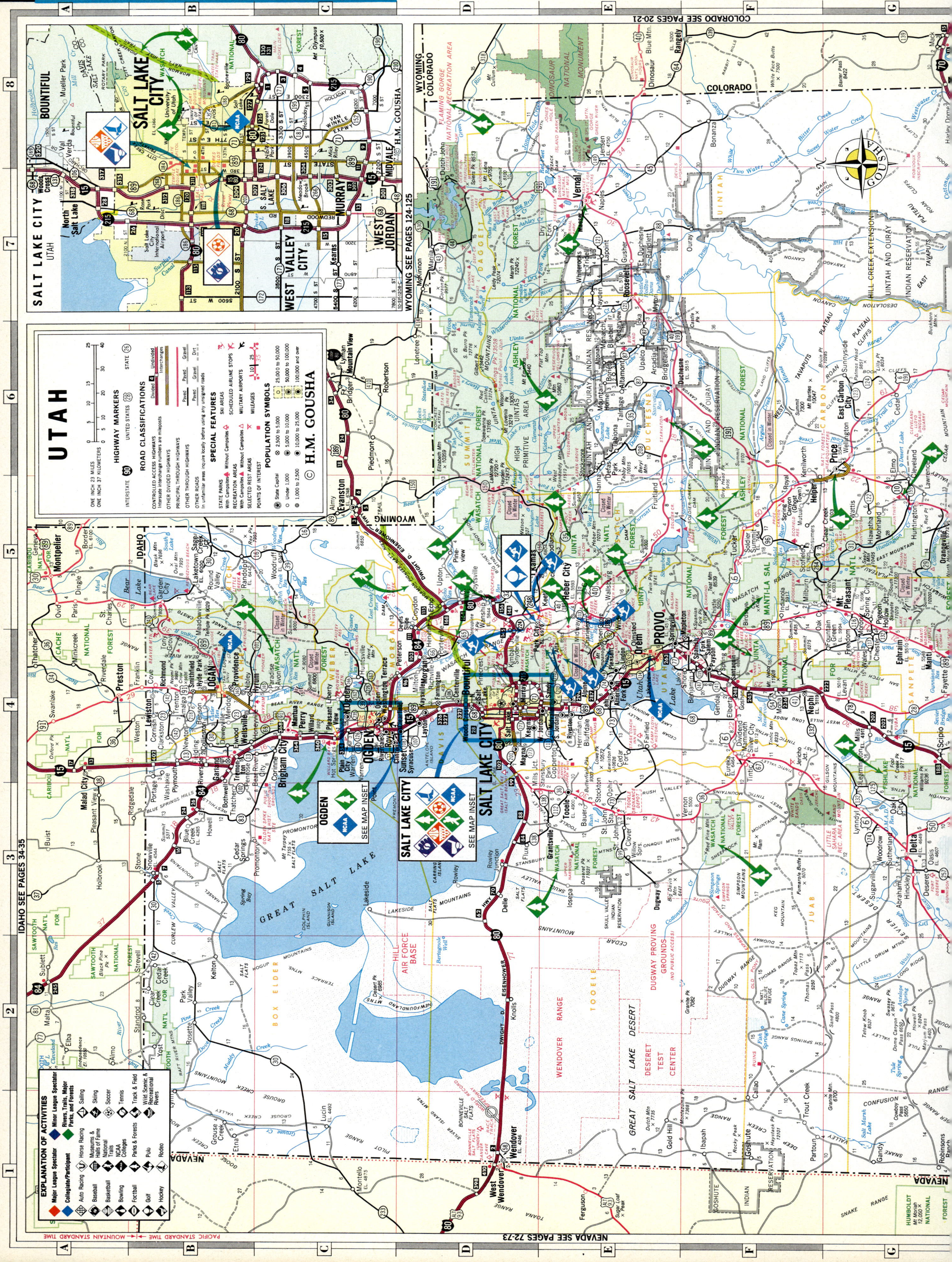
UTAH
HIGHWAY MARKERS
ROAD CLASSIFICATIONS
SPECIAL FEATURES
POPULATION SYMBOLS
© H.M. GOUSHA
SALT LAKE CITY
UTAH
SALT LAKE CITY SEE MAP INSET
OGDEN SEE MAP INSET
EXPLANATION OF ACTIVITIES
GREAT SALT LAKE
GREAT SALT LAKE DESERT
DUGWAY PROVING GROUNDS
HILL AIR FORCE BASE
DINOSAUR NATIONAL MONUMENT
FLAMING GORGE NATIONAL RECREATION AREA
IDAHO SEE PAGES 34-35
WYOMING SEE PAGES 124-125
COLORADO SEE PAGES 20-21
NEVADA SEE PAGES 72-73
PACIFIC STANDARD TIME
MOUNTAIN STANDARD TIME
PROVO
OGDEN
LOGAN
BRIGHAM CITY
TOOELE
PRICE
VERNAL
HEBER CITY
DELTA
NEPHI
WENDOVER
EVANSTON

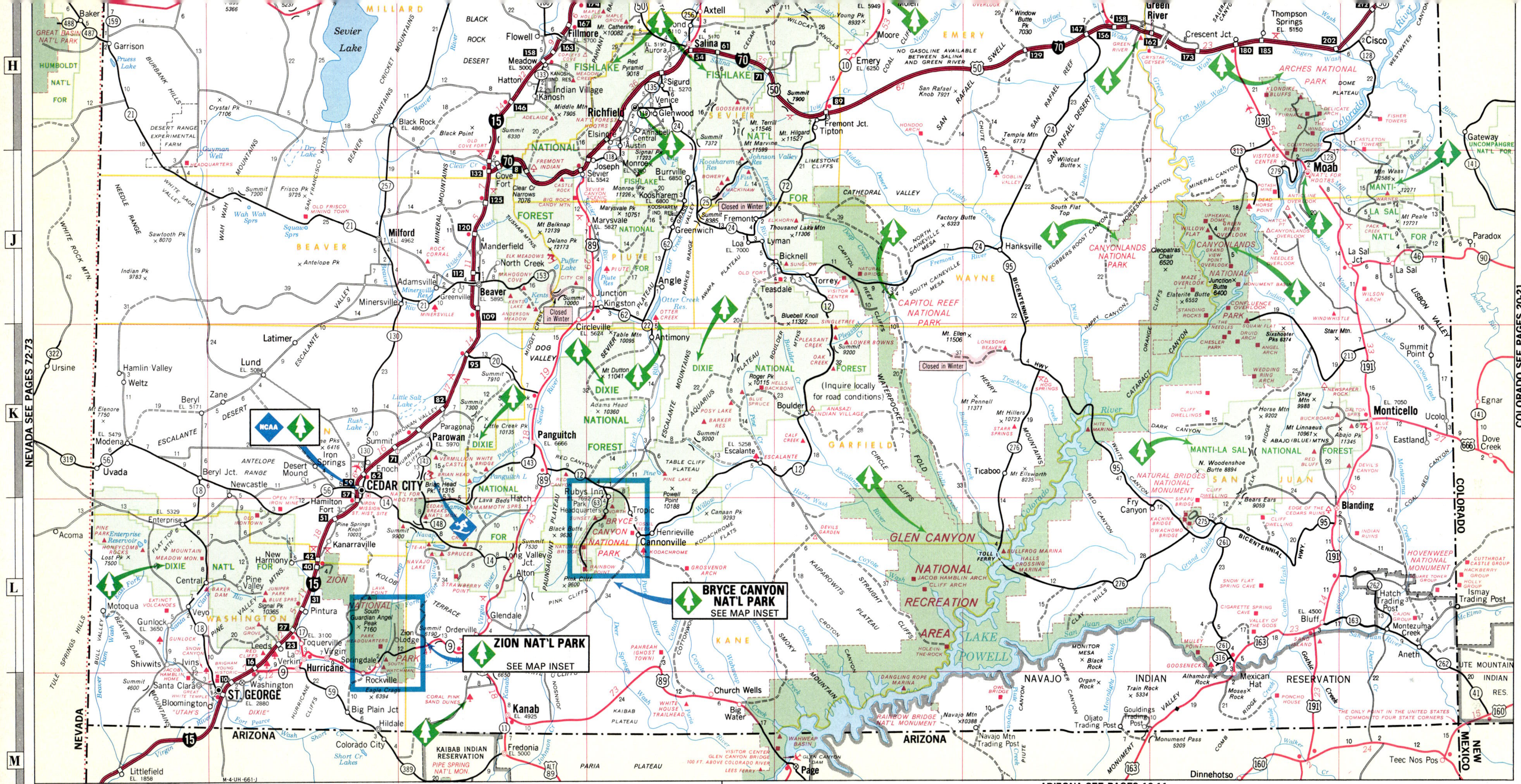

UTAH

Pop. (1990) 1,722,850
Area 84,916 Sq. Mi.

COUNTIES

Co.	Co. Seat
Beaver	Beaver
Box Elder	Brigham City
Cache	Logan
Carbon	Price
Daggett	Manila
Davis	Farmington
Duchesne	Duchesne
Emery	Castle Dale
Garfield	Panguitch
Grand	Moab
Iron	Parowan
Juab	Nephi
Kane	Kanab
Millard	Fillmore
Morgan	Morgan
Piute	Junction
Rich	Randolph
Salt Lake	Salt Lake City
San Juan	Monticello
Sanpete	Manti
Sevier	Richfield
Summit	Coalville
Tooele	Tooele
Uintah	Vernal
Utah	Provo
Wasatch	Heber City
Washington	St. George
Wayne	Loa
Weber	Ogden

PARTIAL LIST OF

CITIES AND TOWNS

• County Seats

Abraham	G-3
Adamsville	J-3
Alpine	E-4
Altamont	E-6
American Fork	E-4
Aneth	L-8
Antimony	K-4
Austin	H-4
Axtell	H-4
Beaver •	J-3
Beryl Jct.	K-1
Bicknell	J-5
Big Plain Jct	M-2
Big Water	M-4
Birdseye	F-5
Black Rock	H-3
Blanding	L-8
Bluff	L-7
Bonanza	F-8
Bothwell	B-3
Boulder	K-5
Bountiful	D-4
Brigham City •	C-4
Burrville	J-4
Cannonville	L-4
Castle Dale •	G-5
Cedar City	K-2
Cedar Fort	E-4
Centerfield	H-4
Centerville	D-4
Central	L-1
Chester	G-4
Church Wells	M-4
Circleville	K-3
Clarkston	B-4
Clawson	H-5
Clear Creek	G-5
Clear Lake	H-3
Clearfield	D-4
Cleveland	G-5
Clinton	C-4
Clover	E-3
Corinne	C-4
Cove	B-4
Cove Fort	J-3
Crescent Jct	H-7
Croydon	D-5
Defas Park	E-6
Delle	D-3
Delta	G-3
Deseret	G-3
Duchesne •	E-6
Dugway	E-3
Dutch John	D-7
E. Carbon City	G-6
Echo	D-5
Elberta	F-4
Elsinore	H-4
Emery	H-5
Enoch	K-2
Enterprise	L-1
Ephraim	G-4
Escalante	K-4
Eureka	F-4
Fairfield	E-4
Fairview	G-5
Farmington •	D-4
Fayette	G-4
Ferron	H-5
Fillmore •	H-3
Flowell	H-3
Flux	D-3
Fountain Green	G-4
Francis	E-5
Franklin	B-4
Fremont	J-4
Fruitland	E-5
Garden City	B-5
Garland	B-4
Garrison	H-1
Glendale	L-3
Goshen	F-4
Grantsville	E-3
Green River	H-6
Greenwich	J-4
Grouse Creek	B-1
Gunnison	G-4
Gusher	E-7
Hanksville	J-6
Hanna	E-5
Heber City •	E-5
Helper	F-5
Henefer	D-5
Henrieville	L-4
Herriman	E-4
Hiawatha	G-5
Hildale	M-2
Hinckley	G-3
Holden	H-3
Huntington	G-5
Hurricane	L-2
Hyde Park	B-4
Hyrum	B-4
Ioka	E-6
Iron Springs	K-2
Jensen	E-8
Jericho Jct.	F-4
Joseph	J-3
Junction •	J-4
Kamas	D-5
Kanab •	M-3
Kanosh	H-3
Kaysville	D-4
Kearns	D-4
Kimball Jct.	D-4
Kingston	J-4
Knolls	D-2
Koosharem	J-4
La Sal	J-8
La Sal Jct	J-8
La Verkin	L-2
Lapoint	E-7
Lawrence	G-5
Layton	D-4
Leamington	G-4
Leeds	L-2
Lehi	E-4
Levan	G-4
Lewiston	B-4
Lindon	E-4
Loa •	J-4
Logan	B-4
Long Valley Junction	L-3
Lynn	B-1
Lynndyl	G-3
Maeser	E-7
Magna	D-4
Manila •	D-7
Manti •	G-4
Mantua	C-4
Mapleton	F-4
Marion	D-5
Marysvale	J-4
Mayfield	H-4
Meadow	H-3
Midvale	E-4
Midway	E-5
Milford	J-2
Mills	G-4
Mills Jct	D-3
Minersville	J-2
Moab •	J-7
Modena	K-1
Mona	F-4
Monroe	J-4
Montezuma Cr	L-8
Monticello •	K-8
Morgan •	D-4
Moroni	G-4
Mt. Carmel	L-3
Mt. Carmel Jct	L-3
Mt. Pleasant	G-5
Murray	D-4
Myton	E-7
Naples	E-7
Neola	E-7
Nephi •	F-4
North Ogden	C-4
North Salt Lake	D-4
Oak City	G-3
Oakley	D-5
Ogden •	C-4
Olmsted	E-4
Orangeville	G-5
Orderville	L-3
Orem	E-4
Ouray	F-7
Panguitch •	K-3
Paragonah	K-3
Park City	D-4
Park Headquarters	L-2
Park Valley	B-2
Parowan •	K-3
Payson	F-4
Peoa	D-5
Perry	C-4
Pigeon Hollow Junction	G-5
Pintura	L-2
Plain City	C-4
Pleasant Grove	E-4
Pleasant View	C-4
Plymouth	B-3
Portage	B-3
Price •	G-6
Providence	B-4
Provo •	E-4
Randolph •	B-5
Redmond	H-4
Richfield •	H-4
Richmond	B-4
Riverdale	C-4
Riverside	B-4
Riverton	E-4
Rockville	M-2
Roosevelt	E-7
Rosette	B-2
Roy	C-4
Royal	F-5
Sage Creek Jct	B-5
St. George •	M-2
St. John Sta	E-3
Salem	F-4
Salina	H-4
Salt Lake City •	D-4
Sandy	E-4
Santaquin	F-4
Scipio	G-4
Scofield	F-5
Sevier	J-4
Sigurd	H-4
Silver City	F-4
Smithfield	B-4
Snowville	B-3
South Jordan	E-4
South Ogden	C-4
South Salt Lake	D-4
Spanish Fork	F-4
Spring City	G-5
Springdale	L-2
Springville	E-4
Stansbury Park	E-3
Sterling	G-4
Stockton	E-3
Sunnyside	G-6
Sunset	D-4
Syracuse	D-4
Tabiona	E-6
Thistle	F-5
Tintic	F-4
Tooele •	E-3
Toquerville	L-2
Torrey	J-5
Tremonton	B-4
Tropic	L-4
Tucker	F-5
Upalco	E-6
Vernal •	E-7
Vernon	F-3
Veyo	L-1
Virgin	L-2
Wales	G-4
Washington Terrace	C-4
Wellington	G-6
Wellsville	B-4
West Jordan	E-4
Whiterocks	E-7
Wildwood	E-4
Willard	C-4
Willow Sprs	E-3
Woodland	E-5
Woodruff	C-5
Woods Cross	D-4
Yost	B-2

SF-661-J

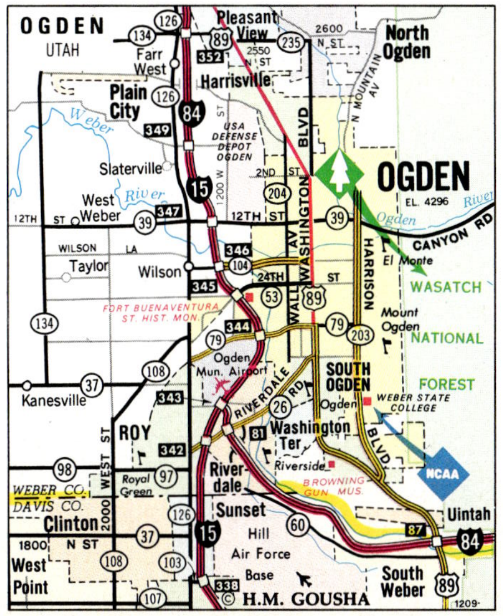

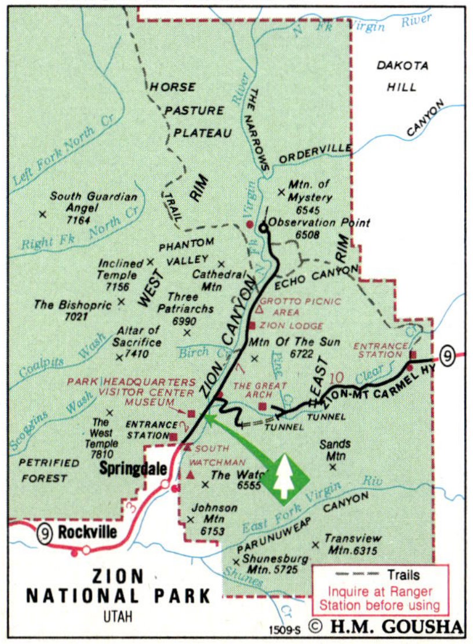

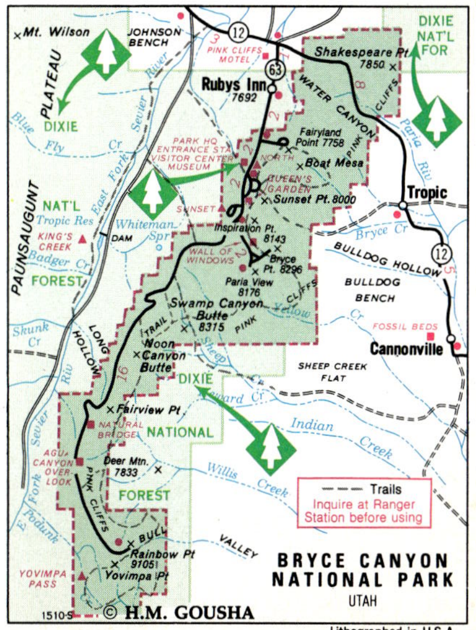

Lithographed in U.S.A.

FOR VERMONT SEE PAGES 74-75

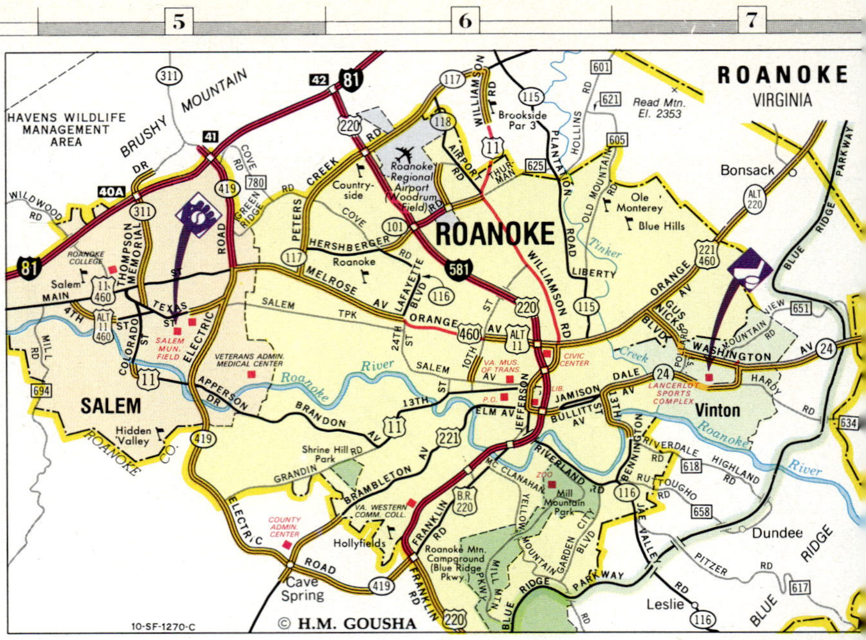

VIRGINIA

Pop (1990) 6,216,568
Area 40,815 Sq. Mi.

COUNTIES

County	County Seat
Accomack	Accomac
Albermarle	Charlottesville
Alleghany	Covington
Amelia	Amelia Court House
Amherst	Amherst
Appomattox	Appomattox
Arlington	Arlington
Augusta	Staunton
Bath	Warm Springs
Bedford	Bedford
Bland	Bland
Botetourt	Fincastle
Brunswick	Lawrenceville
Buchanan	Grundy
Buckingham	Buckingham
Campbell	Rustburg
Caroline	Bowling Green
Carroll	Hillsville
Charles City	Charles City
Charlotte	Charlotte Court House
Chesterfield	Chesterfield
Clarke	Berryville
Craig	New Castle
Culpepper	Culpepper
Cumberland	Cumberland
Dickenson	Clintwood
Dinwiddie	Dinwiddie
Essex	Tappahannock
Fairfax	Fairfax
Fauquier	Warrenton
Floyd	Floyd
Fluvanna	Palmyra
Franklin	Rocky Mount
Frederick	Winchester
Giles	Pearisburg
Gloucester	Gloucester
Goochland	Goochland
Grayson	Independence
Greene	Stanardsville
Greensville	Emporia
Halifax	Halifax
Hanover	Hanover
Henrico	Richmond
Henry	Martinsville
Highland	Monterey
Isle of Wight	Isle of Wight
James City	Williamsburg
King and Queen	King and Queen C.H.
King George	King George
King William	King William
Lancaster	Lancaster
Lee	Jonesville
Loudoun	Leesburg
Louisa	Louisa
Lunenburg	Lunenburg
Madison	Madison
Mathews	Mathews
Mecklenburg	Boydton
Middlesex	Saluda
Montgomery	Christiansburg
Nelson	Lovingston
New Kent	New Kent
Northampton	Eastville
Northumberland	Heathsville
Nottoway	Nottoway
Orange	Orange
Page	Luray
Patrick	Stuart
Pittsylvania	Chatham
Powhatan	Powhatan
Prince Edward	Farmville
Prince George	Prince George
Prince William	Manassas
Pulaski	Pulaski
Rappahannock	Washington
Richmond	Warsaw
Roanoke	Salem
Rockbridge	Lexington
Rockingham	Harrisonburg
Russell	Lebanon
Scott	Gate City
Shenandoah	Woodstock
Smyth	Marion
Southampton	Courtland
Spotsylvania	Spotsylvania
Stafford	Stafford
Surry	Surry
Sussex	Sussex
Tazewell	Tazewell
Warren	Front Royal
Washington	Abingdon
Westmoreland	Montross
Wise	Wise
Wythe	Wytheville
York	Yorktown

PARTIAL LIST OF

CITIES AND TOWNS

• County Seats

Abingdon •	H-3
Accomac	F-14
Adner	F-12
Aldie	D-11
Allmonds Wharf	G-12
Altavista	G-8
Amelia C.H. •	G-10
Amherst •	F-8
Appalachia	H-2
Appomattox	G-9
Ark	G-12
Arlington	D-11
Armstrong	E-7
Ashland	F-11
Ashleys	H-4
Augusta Springs	F-8
Avon	F-9
Axton	H-7
Bacons Castle	G-12
Barbours Creek	F-7
Barboursville	E-9
Bartonsville	D-9
Basset Forks	H-7
Bassett	H-7
Bavon	G-13
Baynesville	E-12
Bealeton	E-10
Bear Wallow	G-4
Bedford	G-8
Belle Meade	D-10
Belle Valley	F-8
Ben Venue	D-10
Bent Creek	F-9
Bent Mountain	G-7
Berea	E-11
Berryville •	D-10
Beulahville	F-11
Big Island	F-8
Big Stone Gap	H-2
Birchleaf	G-3
Blackford	G-4
Blacklick	H-5
Blacksburg	G-6
Blackstone	G-10
Blackwater	H-1
Blairs	H-8
Bluefield	G-5
Bluemont	D-10
Boones Mill	G-7
Boston	E-10
Bowling Green	E-11
Boydton •	H-9
Boykins	H-11
Branchville	H-11
Brandy Station	E-10
Brays Fork	F-12
Bridgetown	G-13
Bridgewater	E-8
Bridle Creek	H-5
Brightwood	E-10
Bristol	H-3
Bristow	D-11
Broadford	H-4
Broadway	E-8
Brookneal	G-8
Browntown	D-9
Brunswick	H-10
Bryant	F-8
Buchanan	F-7
Buckingham	F-9
Buena Vista	F-8
Buffalo Gap	E-8
Buffalo Springs	H-9
Burgess	F-12
Burgess	G-11
Burkes Garden	G-5
Burkeville	G-10
Burnsville	E-7
Burnt Chimney	G-7
Cabin Point	G-11
Callao	F-12
Calvary	D-9
Cape Charles	G-13
Capron	H-11
Caret	F-12
Carrsville	H-12
Carsonville	H-5
Cartersville	F-10
Cascade	H-7
Castle Craig	G-8
Catlett	D-10
Cave Spring	G-6
Cedar Bluff	G-4
Cedar Springs	H-5
Center Cross	F-12
Chalk Level	H-8
Champlain	F-12
Chancellorsville	E-10
Chantilly	D-11
Charles City •	G-11
Charlotte Court House •	G-9
Charlottesville •	F-9
Chase City	H-9
Chatham •	H-8
Chatham Hill	H-4
Cherry Hill	H-11
Chesapeake	H-13
Chester	G-11
Chesterfield	G-11
Chincoteague	F-14
Christiansburg •	G-6
Churchville	E-8
Clarksville	H-9
Clear Brook	C-10
Clear Fork	G-5
Clifton Forge	F-7
Clinchfield	G-3
Clinton	G-10
Clintwwod •	G-3
Clover Creek	E-7
Cluster Springs	H-8
Cobbs Creek	F-12
Cochran	H-10
Coles Point	E-12
Colleen	F-9
Colonial Beach	E-11
Colonial Heights	G-11
Columbia	D-9
Columbia	F-10
Concord	G-8
Copper Hill	G-6
Copper Valley	G-6
Courtland •	H-11
Covesville	F-9
Covington •	F-7
Craig Springs	G-6
Crandon	G-5
Crewe	G-10
Cross Junction	C-9
Crossroads	F-10
Crystal Hill	H-9
Cuckoo	F-10
Culpeper •	E-10
Cumberland •	G-9
Curdsville	G-9
Danieltown	H-10
Dante	G-3
Danville	H-7
Darlington Heights	G-9
Davenport	G-3
Dawn	F-11
Dayton	E-8
Deatonville	G-10
Deerfield	E-8
Delaplane	D-10
Deltaville	F-13
DeWitt	G-10
Dickensonville	H-3
Dillwyn	F-9
Dinwiddie •	G-11
Disputanta	G-11
Dixie	F-9
Doe Hill	E-8
Dranesville	D-11
Dugwell	G-7
Dumfries	E-11
Dunbrooke	F-11
Dundas	H-10
Dungannon	H-3
Durand	H-11
Dwight	G-4
Eagle Rock	F-7
Earlysville	E-9
Eastville	G-13
Edgerton	H-10
Edinburg	D-9
Edom	E-8
Elk Creek	H-5
Elkrun	E-10
Elkton	E-9
Ellisville	E-10
Elon	G-8
Elway	G-3
Emporia •	H-11
Endicott	H-7
Esserville	G-2
Evington	G-8
Exmore	F-14
Faber	F-9
Fair Port	F-13
Fairfax •	D-11
Fairlawn	G-6
Fairview	H-2
Falmouth	E-11
Fancy Gap	H-6
Farmville •	G-9
Farnham	F-12
Ferncliff	F-10
Fieldale	H-7
Fincastle	G-7
Finchley	H-9
Flat Rock	F-10
Flint Hill	D-10
Ford	G-10
Forks of Buffalo	F-8
Fort Blackmore	H-3
Fort Defiance	E-8
Franklin	H-12
Fredericksburg	E-11
Front Royal •	D-10
Gainesboro	C-10
Galax	H-5
Garysville	G-11
Gate City	H-2
Gaylord	D-10
Georges Tavern	F-10
Gibson Station	H-1
Gillespie	G-7
Gladehill	G-7
Gladys	G-8
Glasgow	F-8
Glenns	F-12
Gold Hill	F-9
Goldbond	G-6
Goldvein	E-10
Gordonsville	E-10
Gore	C-9
Grafton	G-12
Gratton	G-4
Gray	H-11
Green Bay	G-10
Green Springs	E-10
Green Springs	H-4
Greenfield	F-9
Gretna	H-8
Greys Point	F-12
Griffinsburg	E-10
Grottoes	E-9
Grove	G-12
Grundy •	G-3
Guinea Mills	G-9
Gwynn	G-13
Hague	E-12
Halifax •	H-8
Hallwood	F-14
Hampton •	G-13
Hanover	F-11
Hansonville	H-3
Harrisonburg •	E-8
Hartfield	F-12
Hartwood	E-10
Hayfield	C-9
Haymarket	D-10
Head Waters	E-8
Healing Springs	F-7
Heathsville •	F-12
Highland Springs	F-11
Hightown	E-7
Hillsville •	H-6
Hiltons	H-3
Hiwassee	H-6
Holly Brook	G-5
Holy Neck	H-12
Homeville	H-11
Hopewell	G-11
Horse Pasture	H-7
Hot Springs	F-7
Huddleston	G-7
Independence	H-5
Independent Hill	D-11
Index	E-11
Indian Valley	H-6
Ingram	H-8
Isle of Wight	G-12
Ivor	H-12
Jamaica	F-12
Jamestown	G-12
Jasper	H-2
Jewell Ridge	G-4
Jonesville	H-1
Jordan Mines	F-6
Keene	F-9
Keller	F-14
Kells Corner	H-9
Kenbridge	G-10
Keokee	H-2
Kerrs Creek	F-7
Keysville	G-9
King George	E-11
King William	F-12
King and Queen	F-12
Kingsville	G-9
Kiptopeke	G-13
La Crosse	H-10
Lacey Springs	E-9
Ladysmith	F-11
Lagrange	E-10
Lancaster	F-12
Laurel Fork	H-6
Lawrenceville •	H-10
Lebanon •	H-3
Leesburg •	D-11
Leesville	G-8
Leon	E-10
Leona Mills	H-2
Leslie	G-7
Letersville	G-10
Lexington •	F-7
Linden	D-10
Littleton	H-11
Locust Dale	E-10
Locust Grove	E-10
Loretto	E-11
Lottsburg	F-12
Louisa •	F-10
Love	F-8
Lovingston	F-9
Lunenburg •	G-9
Luray •	E-9
Lusters Gate	G-6
Lydia	E-9
Lyells	F-12
Lynchburg	G-8
Lynnhaven	H-13
Madison •	E-9
Madison Mills	E-10
Madisonville	G-9
Maggie	G-6
Manassas	D-11
Manassas Park	D-11
Mappsville	F-14
Marion	H-4
Markham	D-10
Marshall	D-10
Martinsville •	H-7
Massaponax	E-11
Mathews •	G-13
Mauzy	E-9
Maybrook	G-6
McDowell	E-8
Meherrin	G-9
Melfa	F-14
Middleburg	D-10
Midland	E-10
Millers Tavern	F-12
Mint Springs	F-8
Monterey •	E-7
Montross •	E-12
Morrisville	E-10
Mount Crawford	E-9
Mount Jackson	D-9
Mount Laurel	H-9
Mount Rush	G-9
Mountain Valley	H-7
Mustoe	E-7
Nain	C-9
Narrows	G-5
Naruna	G-8
Natural Bridge	F-8
Natural Well	F-7
Nelsonia	F-14
New Baltimore	D-10
New Bohemia	G-11
New Castle	G-7
New Hope	E-9
New Market	D-9
New Point	G-13
Newport	F-8
Newport News	G-12
Nickelsville	H-3
Norfolk	G-13
North Garden	F-9
North Holston	H-4
North View	H-10
Norton	G-2
Nortonsville	E-9
Nottoway •	G-10
Oak Hall	F-14
Oakville	G-9
Oakwood	G-4
Oatlands	D-10
Oilville	F-10
Onancock	F-13
Opal	E-10
Orange •	E-10
Orchid	F-10
Otterville	G-8
Owens	E-11
Paint Bank	F-6
Painter	F-14
Pamplin City	G-9
Paris	D-10
Parksley	F-14
Pastorin	F-14
Patterson	H-6
Paul	H-3
Pearisburg •	G-6
Pennington Gap	H-2
Peola Mills	E-9
Peters Creek	H-6
Petersburg	G-11
Phenix	G-9
Piney Grove	H-9
Piney River	F-8
Pleasant Gap	H-8
Pleasantview	F-8
Poages Mill	G-7
Pocahontas	G-4
Poole Siding	G-10
Poplar Hill	G-6
Poquoson	G-13
Port Royal	E-11
Portsmouth	H-12
Potts Creek	F-7
Powhatan •	G-10
Pulaski •	G-5
Purcell	H-3
Purcellville	D-10
Purdy	H-11
Quinque	E-9
Radford	G-6
Rawley Springs	E-8
Rawlings	H-10
Red Oak	H-9
Redbank	H-9
Redwood	G-7
Rehoboth	H-9
Remington	E-10
Reston	D-11
Return	E-11
Rhoadesville	E-10
Rich Creek	G-5
Richlands	G-4
Richmond •	F-11
Riverdale	H-9
Riverton	D-9
Roanoke	G-6
Rockbridge Baths	F-7
Rockdell	H-4
Rocky Mount •	G-7
Rose Garden	F-12
Rose Hill	H-1
Rosedale	H-4
Roxbury	G-11
Ruckersville	E-9
Rugby	H-4
Rumford	F-11
Rustburg •	G-8
St. Clair Bottom	H-4
Salem •	G-7
Saltville	H-4
Saluda •	F-12
Sandy Ford	G-7
Sandy Point	E-12
Sandy River	H-7
Scotland	G-12
Scottsburg	H-9
Scottsville	F-9
Sebrell	H-11
Seven Pines	G-11
Shacklefords	F-12
Sheppards	G-9
Silver Beach	F-13
Singers Glen	E-8
Skinquarter	G-10
Skippers	H-11
Sliders	G-9
Smithfield	G-12
Snowville	G-6
South Boston	H-8
South Hill	H-10
Southanna	F-10
Sperryville	E-9
Spotsylvania	E-10
Spring Garden	H-8
Spring Grove	G-12
Springville	G-5
Staffordsville	G-5
Stanardsville •	E-9
Stanley	E-9
Staunton •	E-8
Steeles Tavern	F-8
Stephens City	D-9
Stephenson	C-10
Stewartsville	G-7
Stone Creek	H-2
Stony Creek	G-11
Strasburg	D-9
Suffolk •	H-12
Sugar Grove	H-5
Surry •	G-12
Sussex •	H-11
Sutherland	G-11
Swansonville	H-7
Sweet Springs	F-6
Sycamore	G-8
Tabb	G-12
Tappahannock •	F-11
Tasley	F-14
Tazewell •	G-4
Templeman	F-12
The Falls	G-10
Thornburg	E-11
Timberville	D-9
Toano	G-12
Tobaccoville	G-10
Townsend	G-13
Trammel	G-3
Triangle	E-11
Trinity	G-7
Upperville	D-10
Valentines	H-10
Vanderpool	E-7
Vernon Hill	H-8
Vicksville	H-11
Victoria	G-10
Vienna	D-11
Villamont	G-7
Vinton	G-7
Virgilina	H-9
Virginia Beach	H-13
Volney	H-4
Wakefield	G-12
Walters	H-12
Wares	F-10
Warm Springs •	F-7
Warrenton •	D-10
Warsaw •	F-12
Washington	D-9
Wattsville	F-14
Waverly	G-11
Waynesboro	E-8
Weber City	H-3
West Augusta	E-8
West Point	F-12
Westland	F-13
Wharf	F-14
White Gate	G-5
White Hall	E-9
White Marsh	G-12
White Post	D-10
White Stone	F-13
Whiteville	F-10
Wicomico Church	F-13
Wide Water	E-11
Wilderness Corner	E-10
Williamsburg •	G-12
Williamsville	E-7
Willis	H-6
Wilson	G-10
Winchester •	D-9
Windsor	H-12
Winston	E-10
Wise •	G-3
Woodlawn	H-5
Woods Mill	F-9
Woodstock •	D-9
Woodville	E-10
Worsham	G-9
Wylliesburg	H-9
Wytheville •	H-5
Yale	H-11
Yancey Mill	F-9
Yorktown	G-12
Zion Crossroads	F-10
Zuni	H-12

UH-696-J

WEST VIRGINIA SEE PAGES 116-117
KENTUCKY SEE PAGES 46-47

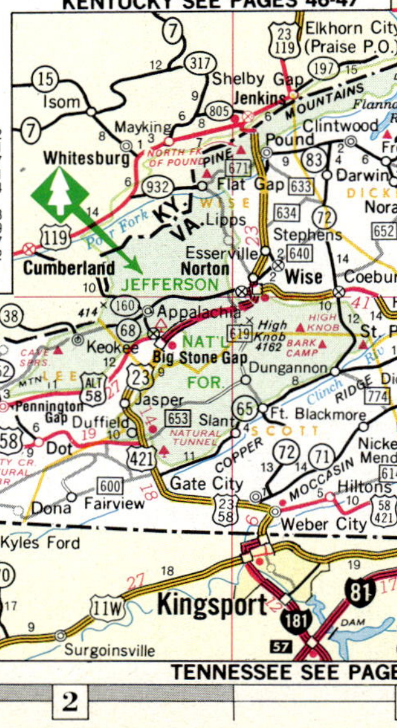

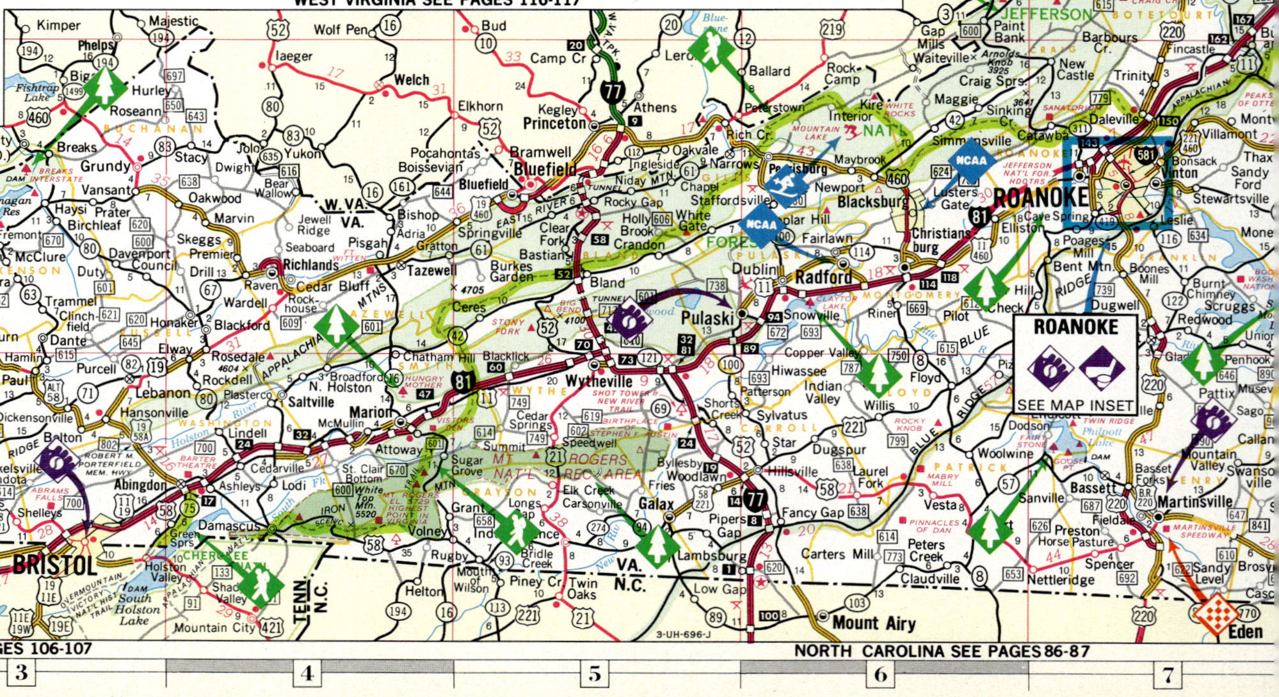

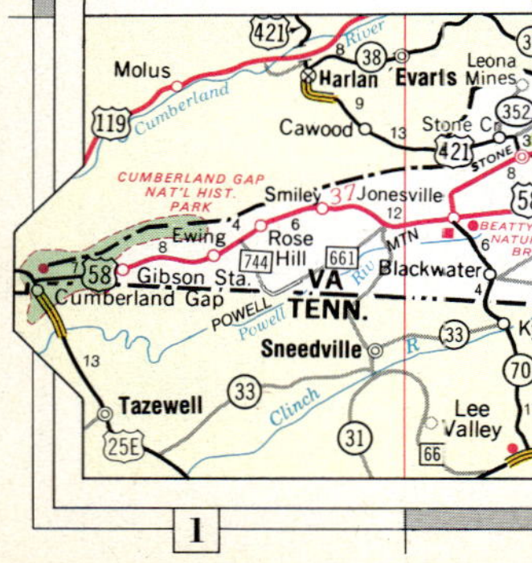

TENNESSEE SEE PAGES 106-107
NORTH CAROLINA SEE PAGES 86-87

GULF OF MEXICO
HOUSTON TEXAS
FORT WORTH DALLAS AREA
SAN ANTONIO TEXAS
TEXAS TOLL ROADS
DALLAS NORTH TOLLWAY Passenger car toll is $1.00 for the entire length of 17 miles.
HARDY TOLL ROAD Passenger car toll is $2.00 for the entire length of 21.7 miles.
SAM HOUSTON TOLLWAY Passenger car toll is $1.50 for the entire length of 15.1 miles.
© H.M. GOUSHA

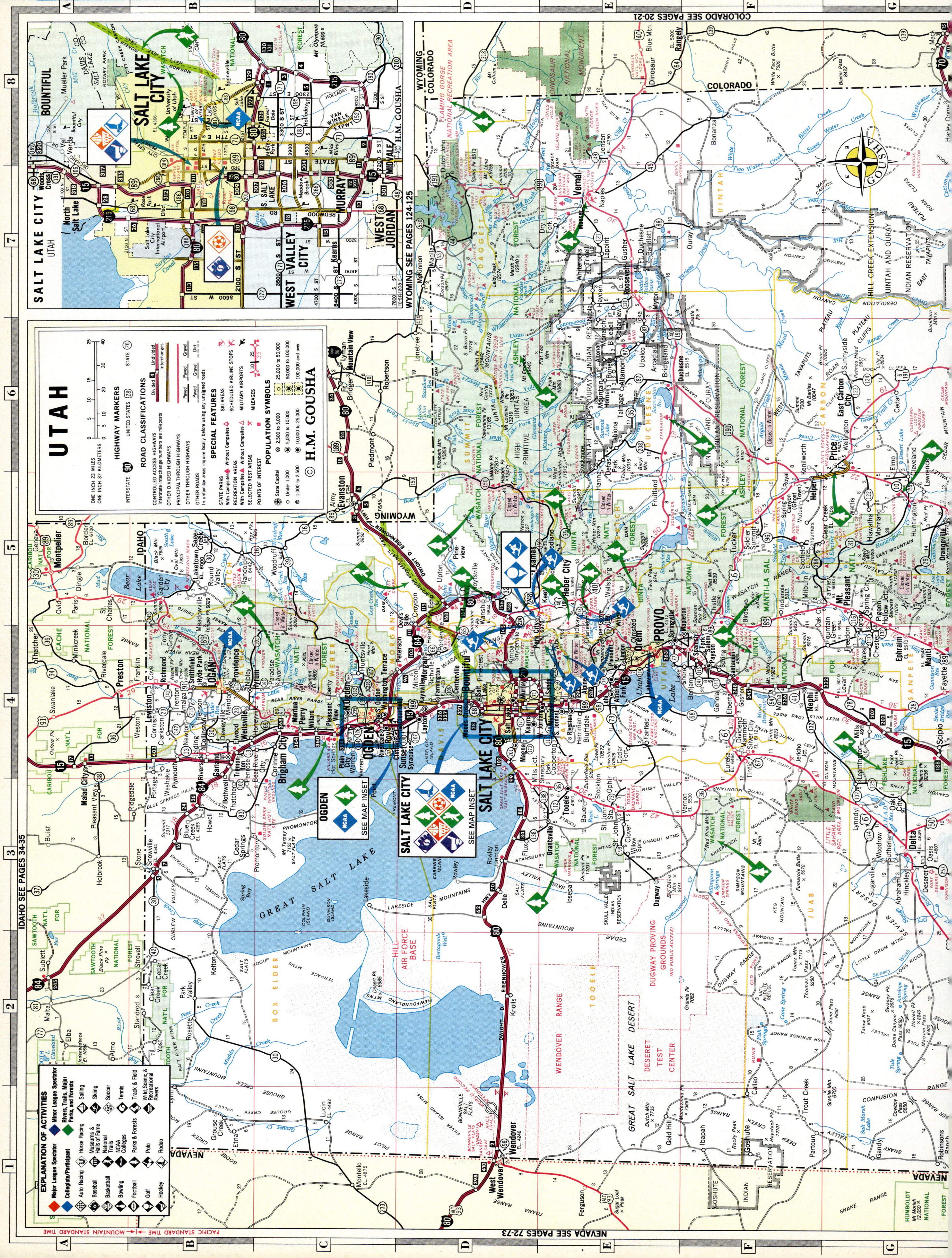

UTAH
SALT LAKE CITY UTAH
HIGHWAY MARKERS
ROAD CLASSIFICATIONS
SPECIAL FEATURES
POPULATION SYMBOLS
© H.M. GOUSHA
EXPLANATION OF ACTIVITIES
GREAT SALT LAKE
GREAT SALT LAKE DESERT
SALT LAKE CITY
OGDEN
PROVO
LOGAN
WYOMING
COLORADO
IDAHO SEE PAGES 34-35
WYOMING SEE PAGES 124-125
COLORADO SEE PAGES 20-21
NEVADA SEE PAGES 72-73
PACIFIC STANDARD TIME
MOUNTAIN STANDARD TIME
SEE MAP INSET
HILL AIR FORCE BASE
DUGWAY PROVING GROUNDS
WENDOVER RANGE
DESERET TEST CENTER

SOUTH CAROLINA

Pop (1990) 3,505,707
Area 31,055 Sq. Mi.

COUNTIES

County	Co. Seat
Abbeville	Abbeville
Aiken	Aiken
Allendale	Allendale
Anderson	Anderson
Bamberg	Bamberg
Barnwell	Barnwell
Beaufort	Beaufort
Berkeley	Moncks Corner
Calhoun	St. Matthews
Charleston	Charleston
Cherokee	Gaffney
Chester	Chester
Chesterfield	Chesterfield
Clarendon	Manning
Colleton	Walterboro
Darlington	Darlington
Dillon	Dillon
Dorchester	St. George
Edgefield	Edgefield
Fairfield	Winnsboro
Florence	Florence
Georgetown	Georgetown
Greenville	Greenville
Greenwood	Greenwood
Hampton	Hampton
Horry	Conway
Jasper	Ridgeland
Kershaw	Camden
Lancaster	Lancaster
Laurens	Laurens
Lee	Bishopville
Lexington	Lexington
Marion	Marion
Marlboro	Bennettsville
McCormick	McCormick
Newberry	Newberry
Oconee	Wahlahalla
Orangeburg	Orangeburg
Pickens	Pickens
Richland	Columbia
Saluda	Saluda
Spartanburg	Spartanburg
Sumter	Sumter
Union	Union
Williamsburg	Kingstree
York	York

CITIES AND TOWNS

• County Seats

Abbeville •	C-3
Aiken •	E-5
Allendale •	F-5
Allsbrook	C-11
Anderson •	B-2
Andrews	E-9
Atlantic Beach	D-11
Awendaw	F-9
Aynor	D-10
Bamberg •	E-6
Barnwell •	E-6
Batesburg	D-5
Beaufort •	G-7
Beech Island	E-4
Belton	B-3
Bennettsville •	B-9
Bethune	C-8
Bishopville •	C-8
Blacksburg	A-5
Blackville	E-6
Blenheim	B-9
Bonneau	E-9
Bowman	E-7
Branchville	E-7
Briarcliffe Acres	D-11
Brownsville	C-9
Calhoun Falls	C-3
Camden •	C-7
Carlisle	B-5
Cassatt	C-8
Cayce	D-6
Centenary	C-10
Chappells	C-4
Charleston •	G-9
Cheraw	B-9
Chesnee	A-4
Chester •	B-6
Chesterfield •	B-8
Chicora	E-8
Clearwater	E-4
Clemson	B-2
Clinton	C-4
Clio	B-9
Clover	A-6
Columbia •	D-6
Conway •	D-11
Cornwell	B-6
Coward	D-9
Cowpens	A-5
Cross Anchor	B-4
Dalzell	D-8
Darlington •	C-9
DeKalb	C-7
Denmark	E-6
Dillon •	C-10
Donalds	C-3
Dorchester	F-7
Due West	C-3
Easley	B-3
Edgefield •	D-4
Effingham	C-9
Elgin	C-7
Elko	E-5
Elliott	C-8
Enoree	B-4
Estill	G-6
Fair Play	B-2
Fairfax	F-6
Florence •	C-9
Floyd	C-9
Floyds	C-11
Foreston	D-8
Fork	C-10
Fort Lawn	B-7
Fort Mill	A-6
Fountain Inn	B-4
Gaffney •	A-5
Galivants Ferry	C-10
Gardens Corner	G-7
Garnett	G-6
Gaston	D-6
Georgetown •	E-10
Gifford	F-6
Gluck	B-3
Great Falls	B-6
Greeleyville	E-8
Green Sea	C-11
Greenville •	B-3
Greenwood •	C-3
Greer	A-4
Grover	F-7
Hampton •	F-6
Harleyville	E-7
Hartsville	C-8
Heath Springs	B-7
Heineman	E-9
Hemingway	D-9
Holly Hill	E-8
Homewood	D-11
Honea Path	B-3
Inman	A-4
Isle of Palms	F-9
Iva	C-3
Jackson	E-4
Jacksonboro	F-7
James Island	G-8
Jamestown	E-9
Joanna	C-5
Johnsonville	D-10
Johnston	D-4
Jordanville	D-10
Kershaw	B-7
Kingsburg	D-9
Kingstree •	D-9
Kirksey	D-4
Lake City	D-9
Lamar	C-8
Lancaster •	B-7
Landrum	A-4
Latta	C-10
Laurens •	B-4
Leesville	D-5
Lesslie	B-6
Lexington •	D-6
Liberty	B-3
Liberty Hill	B-7
Little River	D-11
Lobeco	G-7
Lockhart	B-5
Lodge	F-6
Longs	D-11
Loris	C-11
Lowrys	B-6
Lugoff	C-7
Luray	F-6
Lydia	C-8
Lynchburg	C-8
Manning •	D-8
Manville	C-8
Marion •	C-10
Mary	D-10
Mauldin	B-4
Mayson	C-4
McBee	B-8
McColl	B-9
McConnells	B-6
McCormick •	D-4
Midway	E-6
Monarch	B-5
Moncks Corner •	E-8
Mount Croghan	B-8
Mount Holly	F-8
Mount Pleasant	F-9
Mouzon	D-8
Mullins	C-10
Murrells Inlet	E-11
Myrtle Beach	D-11
Neeses	E-6
New Ellenton	E-5
Newberry •	C-5
Nichols	C-10
North	E-6
North Augusta	E-4
North Charleston	F-9
North Myrtle Beach	D-11
Norway	E-6
Oak Grove	C-9
Oakwood	E-5
Oatland	E-10
Olar	E-6
Old House	G-7
Outland	D-10
Owdoms	D-4
Pacolet	B-5
Pageland	B-8
Palmetto	C-9
Pamplico	D-9
Paris	A-3
Parkers Ferry	F-8
Patrick	B-8
Paxville	D-8
Pee Dee	C-9
Pendelton	B-3
Pickens •	A-3
Piedmont	B-3
Plantersville	E-10
Pocotaligo	G-7
Pontiac	C-7
Port Royal	G-7
Princeton	B-4
Rains	C-10
Rantowles	F-8
Rembert	C-7
Rhems	E-10
Richburg	B-6
Ridgeland •	G-6
Robertville	G-6
Rock Hill	A-6
Ruby	B-8
Ruffin	F-7
St. George •	F-7
St. Matthews •	D-7
St. Stephens	E-9
Saluda •	D-4
Sampit	E-10
Santuck	B-5
Scotia	G-6
Scranton	D-9
Seneca	B-2
Shannontown	D-7
Simpsonville	B-4
Society Hill	B-9
Spartanburg •	A-4
Sullivans Island	F-9
Summerton	D-7
Summerville	F-8
Sumter •	D-8
Swansea	D-6
Sycamore	F-6
Tarboro	G-6
Tillman	G-6
Timmonsville	C-8
Toddville	D-10
Townville	B-2
Travelers Rest	A-3
Trio	E-9
Troy	D-3
Turbeville	D-8
Ulmer	F-6
Union •	B-5
Vance	E-8
Varnville	F-6
Vaucluse	E-5
Verdery	C-3
Wagener	D-5
Walhalla	B-2
Wallace	B-9
Walterboro •	F-7
Wando	F-9
Ward	D-5
Ware Shoals	C-3
Warrenville	E-5
Warsaw	E-9
Wateree	D-7
Waterloo	C-4
Watts Mills	B-4
Wedgefield	D-7
West Columbia	D-6
West Springs	B-5
West Union	B-2
Westminster	B-1
Westville	C-7
White Rock	C-6
Whitmire	B-5
Wiggins	G-7
Wilkins	G-7
Williams	F-6
Williamston	B-3
Willington	D-3
Williston	E-5
Windsor	E-5
Winnsboro •	C-6
Wisacky	C-8
Wolfton	E-6
Woodford	D-6
Woodrow	C-8
Woodruff	B-4
Woodward	B-6
Yauhannah	D-10
Yemassee	G-7
Yenome	E-5
Yonges Island	G-8
York •	A-6

UH-691-J-X

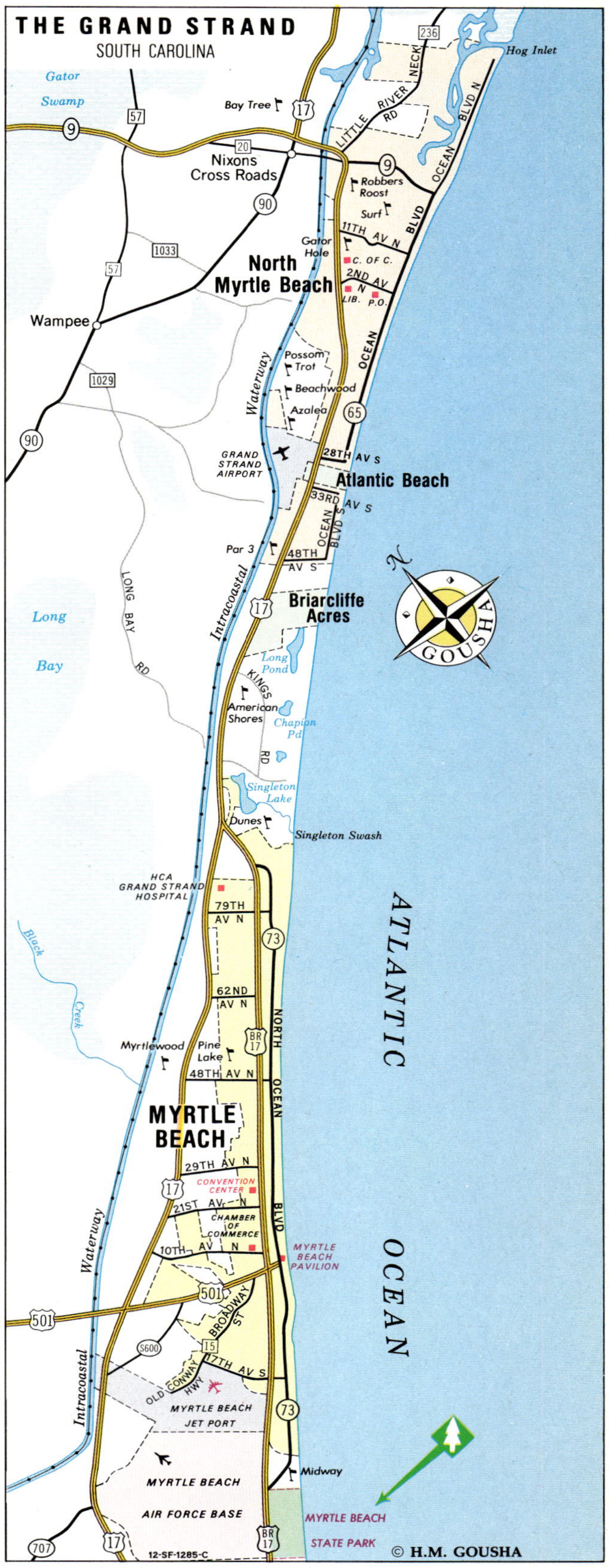

Lithographed in U.S.A.

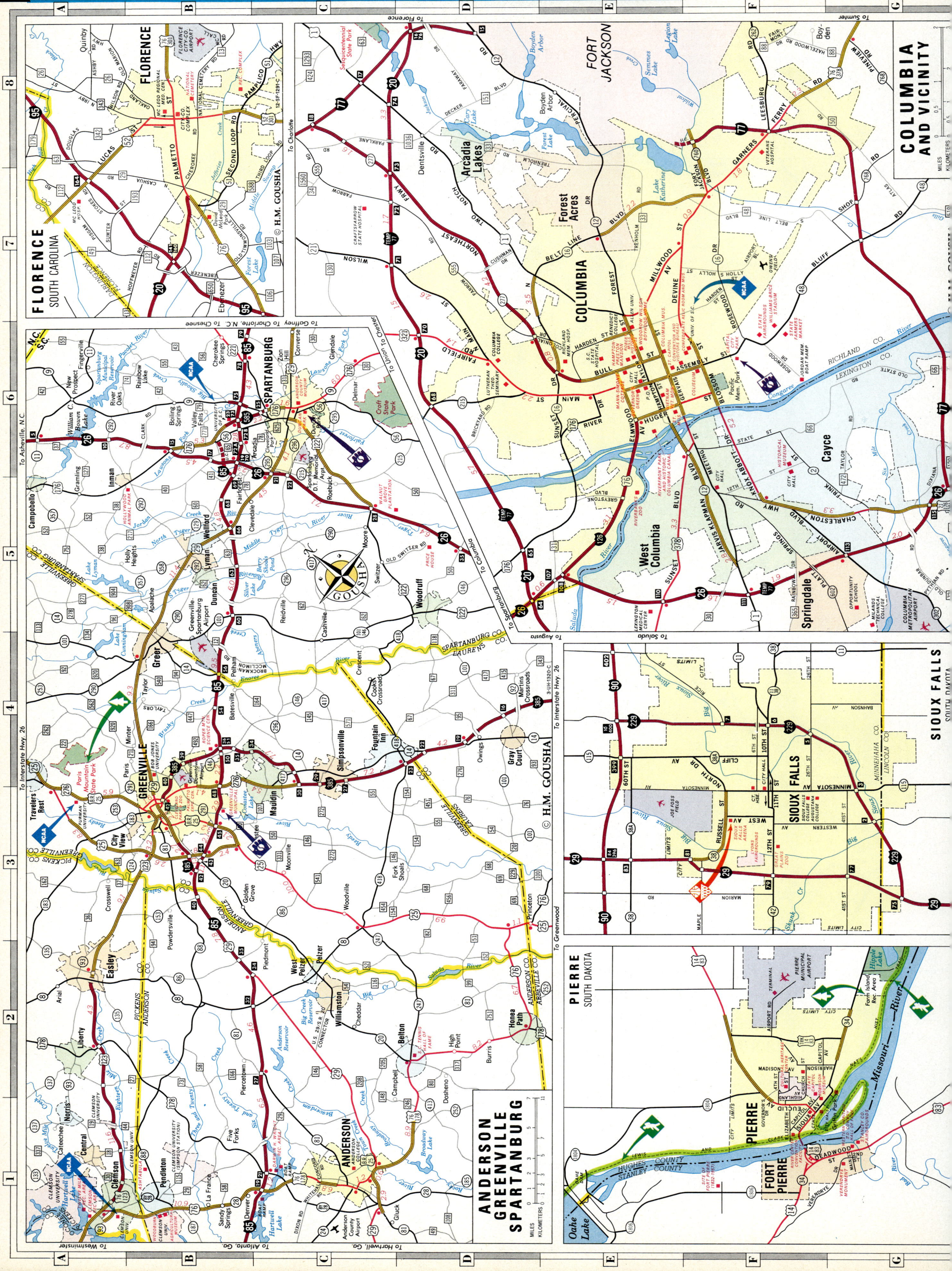
FLORENCE
SOUTH CAROLINA
COLUMBIA
AND VICINITY
ANDERSON
GREENVILLE
SPARTANBURG
SIOUX FALLS
SOUTH DAKOTA
PIERRE
SOUTH DAKOTA
© H.M. GOUSHA

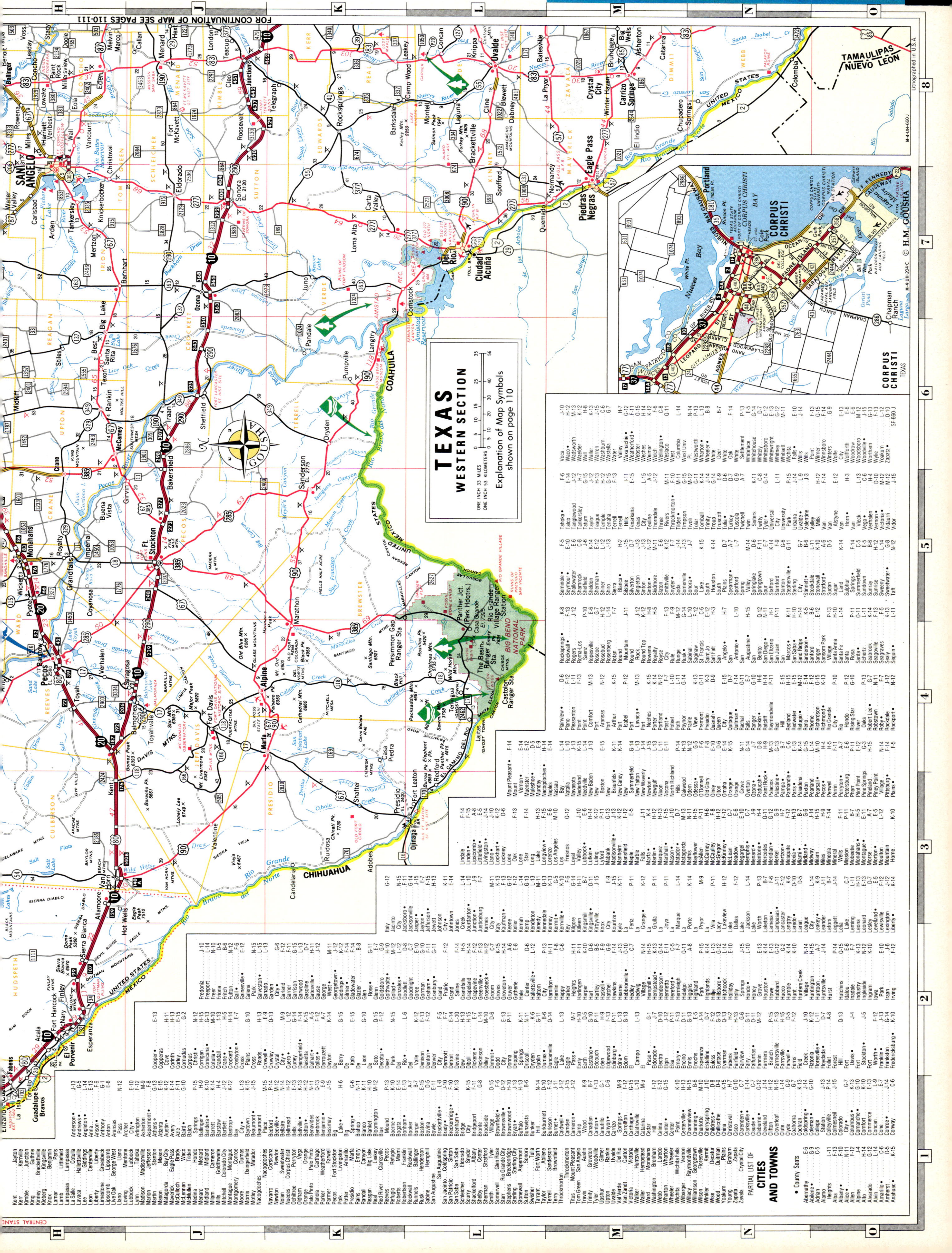
FOR CONTINUATION OF MAP SEE PAGES 110-111
TEXAS
WESTERN SECTION
Explanation of Map Symbols shown on page 110
BIG BEND NATIONAL PARK
COAHUILA
CHIHUAHUA
TAMAULIPAS
NUEVO LEON
CORPUS CHRISTI
PARTIAL LIST OF CITIES AND TOWNS
© H.M. GOUSHA
Lithographed in U.S.A.

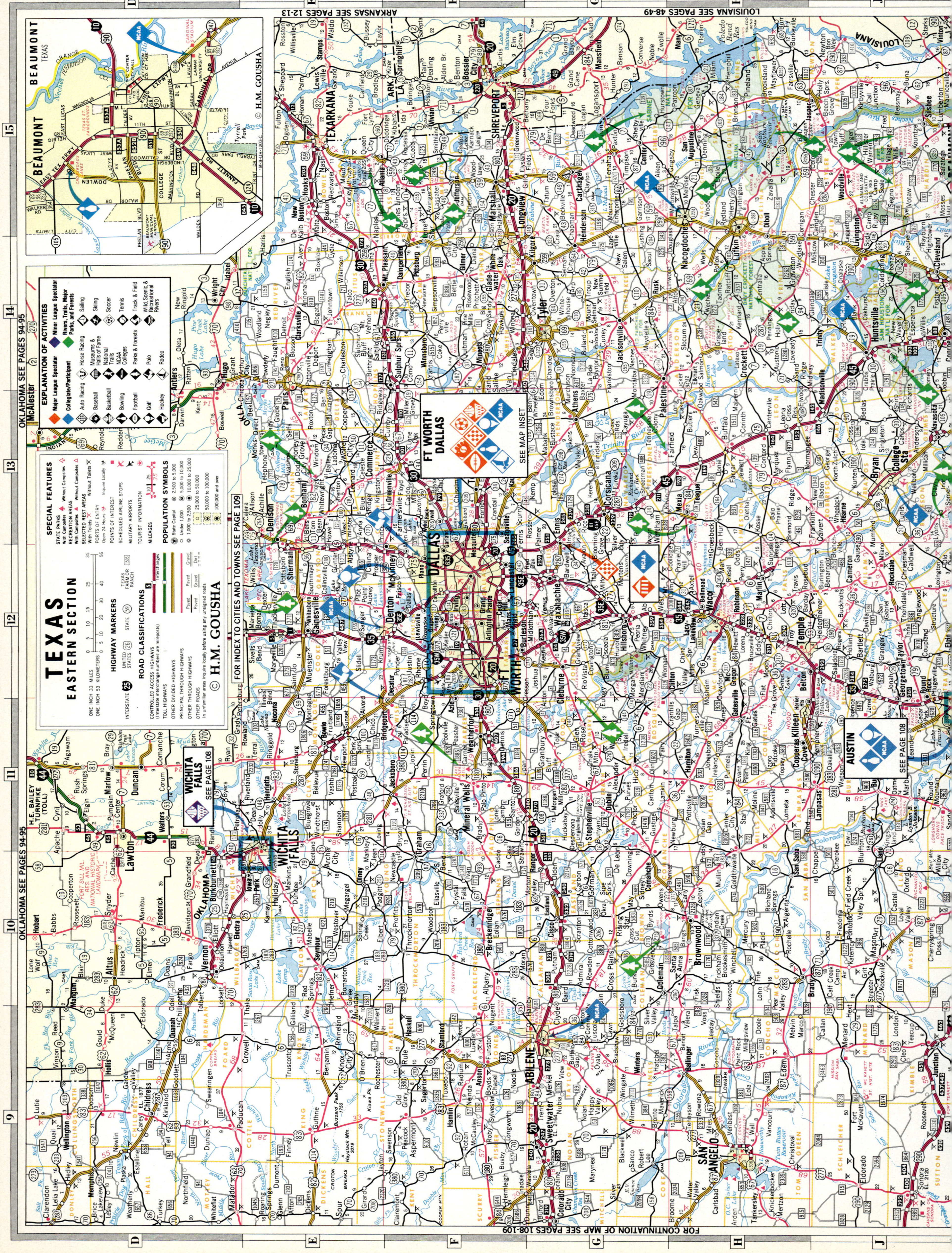
TEXAS
EASTERN SECTION
© H.M. GOUSHA
BEAUMONT
© H.M. GOUSHA
EXPLANATION OF ACTIVITIES
SPECIAL FEATURES
HIGHWAY MARKERS
ROAD CLASSIFICATIONS
POPULATION SYMBOLS
FOR INDEX TO CITIES AND TOWNS SEE PAGE 109
FT WORTH DALLAS
SEE MAP INSET
AUSTIN
SEE PAGE 108
WICHITA FALLS
SEE PAGE 108
OKLAHOMA SEE PAGES 94-95
ARKANSAS SEE PAGES 12-13
LOUISIANA SEE PAGES 48-49
FOR CONTINUATION OF MAP SEE PAGES 108-109

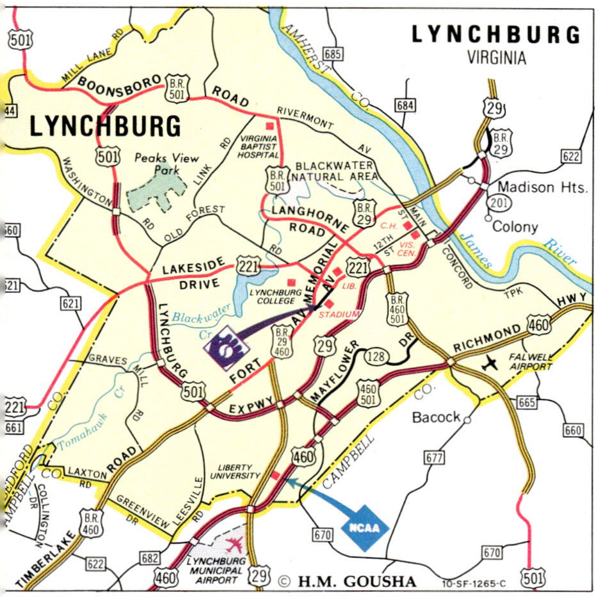

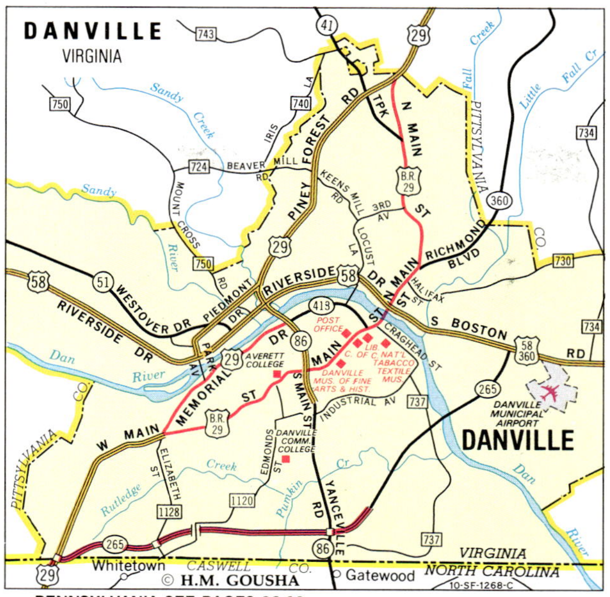

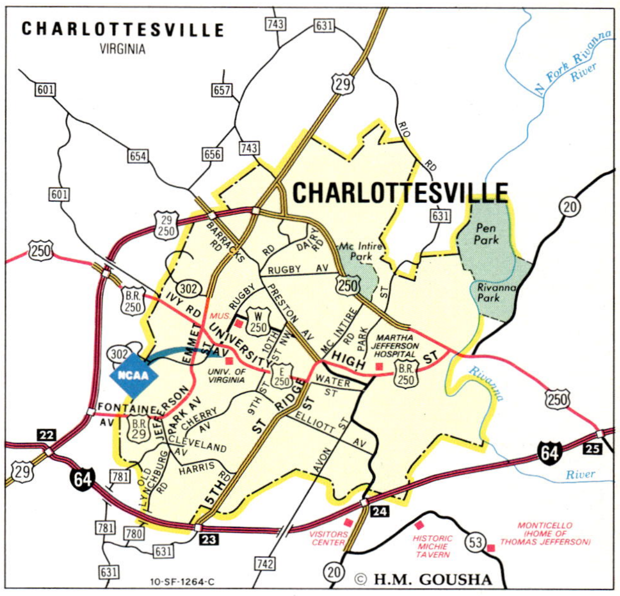

PENNSYLVANIA SEE PAGES 98-99

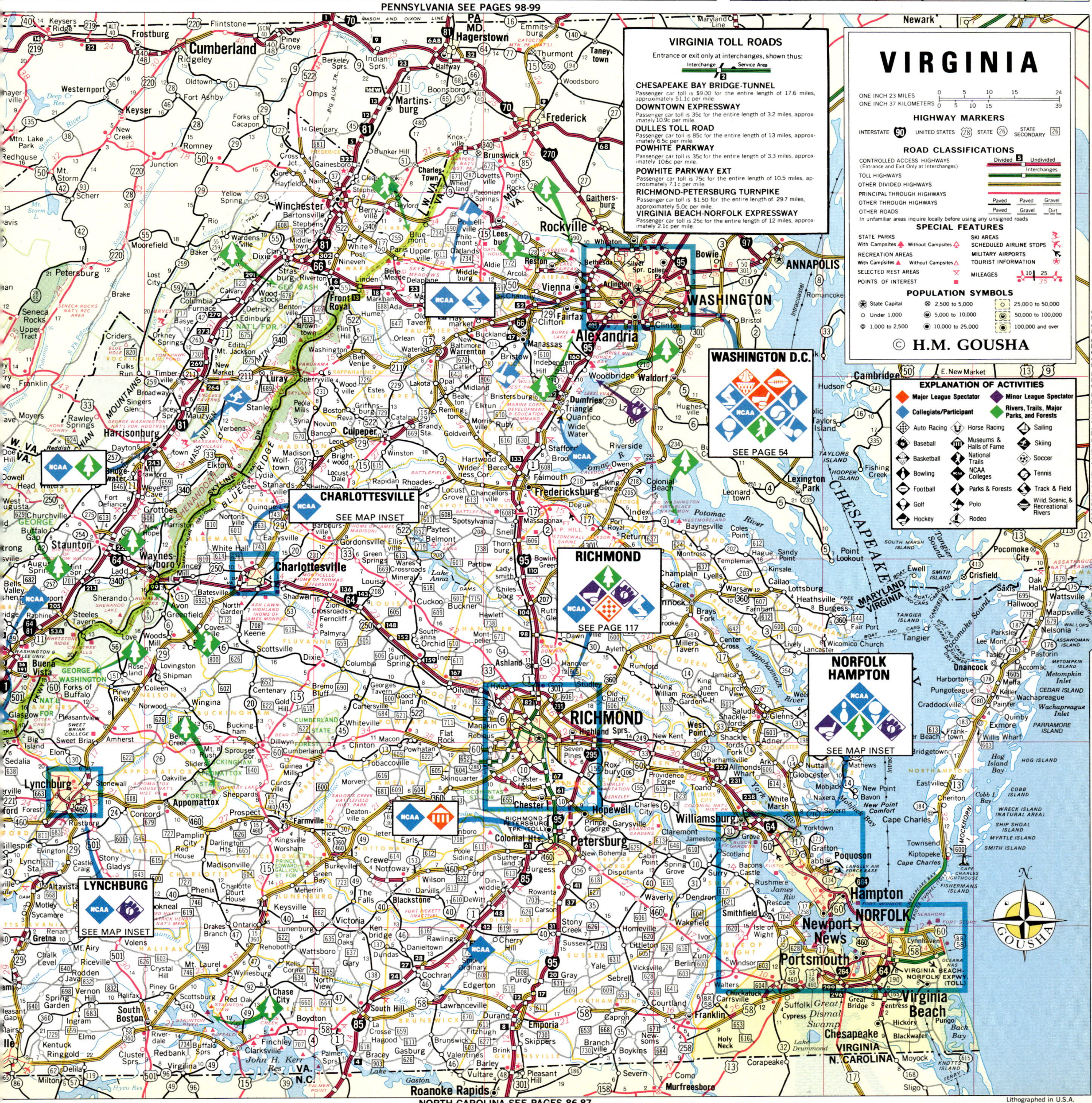

MARYLAND AND DELAWARE SEE PAGES 52-53

NORTH CAROLINA SEE PAGES 86-87

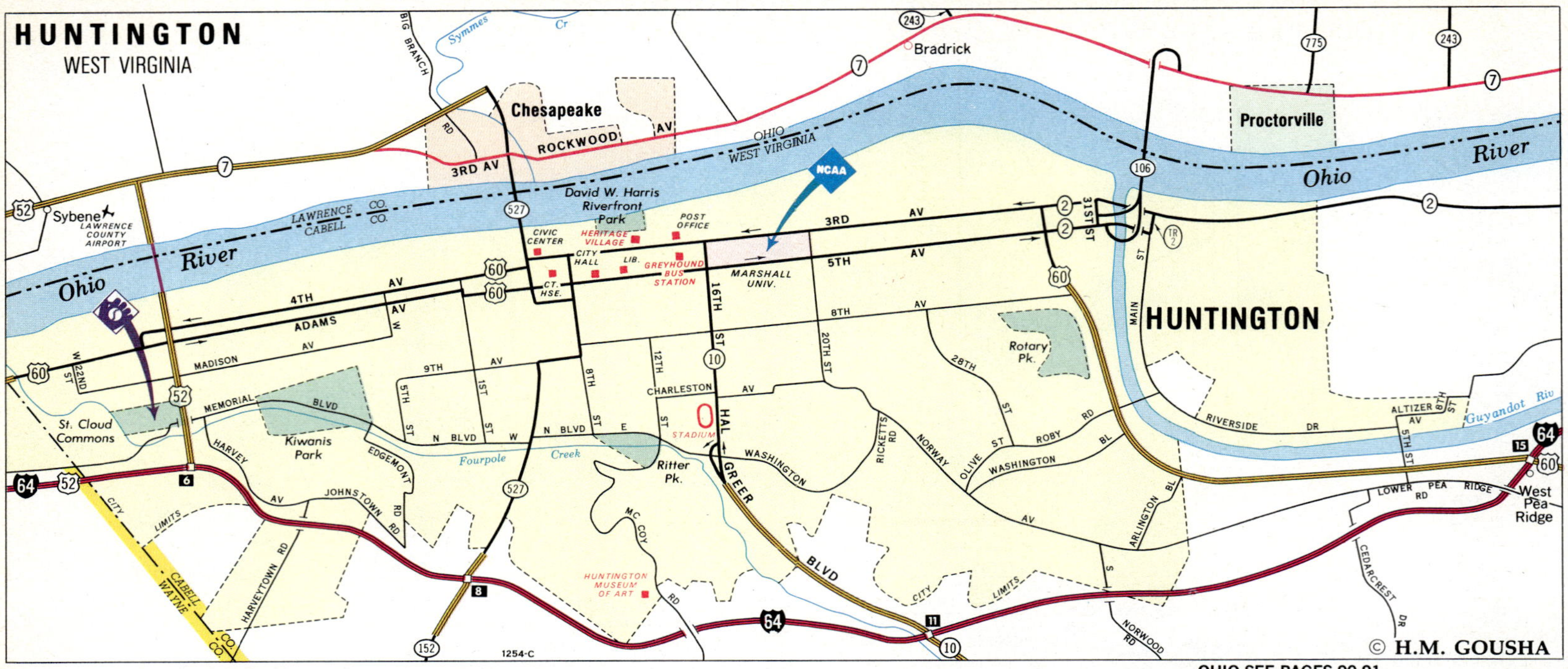

OHIO SEE PAGES 90-91

WEST VIRGINIA

Pop (1990) 1,801,625
Area 24,181 Sq. Mi.

COUNTIES

County	County Seat
Barbour	Phillippi
Berkeley	Martinsburg
Boone	Madison
Braxton	Sutton
Brooke	Wellsburg
Cabell	Huntington
Calhoun	Grantsville
Clay	Clay
Doddridge	West Union
Fayette	Fayetteville
Gilmer	Glenville
Grant	Petersburg
Greenbrier	Lewisburg
Hampshire	Romney
Hancock	New Cumberland
Hardy	Moorefield
Harrison	Clarksburg
Jackson	Ripley
Jefferson	Charles Town
Kanawha	Charleston
Lewis	Weston
Lincoln	Hamlin
Logan	Logan
Marion	Fairmount
Marshall	Moundsville
Mason	Point Pleasant
McDowell	Welch
Mercer	Princeton
Mineral	Keyser
Mingo	Williamson
Monongalia	Morgantown
Monroe	Union
Morgan	Berkeley Springs
Nicholas	Summersville
Ohio	Wheeling
Pendleton	Franklin
Pleasants	Saint Marys
Pocahontas	Marlinton
Preston	Kingwood
Putnam	Winfield
Raleigh	Beckley
Randolph	Elkins
Ritchie	Harrisville
Roane	Spencer
Summers	Hinton
Taylor	Grafton
Tucker	Parsons
Tyler	Middlebourne
Upshur	Buckhannon
Wayne	Wayne
Webster	Webster Springs
Wetzel	New Martinsville
Wirt	Elizabeth
Wood	Parkersburg
Wyoming	Pineville

PARTIAL LIST OF

CITIES AND TOWNS

• County Seats

Albright	C-9
Alderson	G-7
Amherstdale	G-5
Anawalt	F-6
Ansted	F-6
Athens	H-6
Auburn	D-7
Barboursville	F-4
Beckley •	G-6
Belington	D-8
Belle	F-5
Belmont	C-6
Benwood	B-7
Berkeley Springs •	C-12
Bethany	B-7
Beverly	E-9
Big Run Creek	C-7
Bigbend	D-6
Birch River	E-7
Blacksville	C-8
Blandville	D-7
Bloomingrose	F-5
Bluefield	H-6
Bradshaw	H-5
Brake	E-10
Bramwell	H-6
Brandonville	C-9
Brandywine	E-10
Bridgeport	D-8
Brooks	G-7
Brookside	D-9
Buckhannon •	D-8
Buffalo	E-4
Bunker Hill	D-12
Burlington	D-10
Burning Springs	D-6
Burnsville	E-7
Burnt House	D-6
Burton	C-7
Cairo	D-6
Camden	D-7
Cameron	B-7
Capon Bridge	D-11
Caretta	H-5
Cedar Grove	F-6
Ceredo	F-3
Chapmanville	G-4
Charles Town •	D-13
Charleston •	F-5
Chelyan	F-5
Chester	A-7
Christian	G-5
Clarksburg •	D-7
Clay •	F-6
Clendenin	F-6
Cowen	F-7
Danville	F-4
Davis	D-9
Davy	H-5
Dunbar	F-5
East Bank	F-6
Eccles	G-6
Eleanor	E-5
Elizabeth •	D-5
Elkhorn	H-6
Elkins •	D-8
Elkview	F-5
Elkwater	E-8
Fairmont •	C-8
Fairview	C-8
Falling Spring	G-8
Farmington	C-8
Fayetteville •	F-6
Follansbee	A-7
Forest Hill	G-7
Forks of Cacapon	C-11
Fort Gay	F-3
Franklin •	E-10
Friendly	C-6
Gallipolis Ferry	E-4
Garretts Bend	F-4
Gary	H-5
Gassaway	E-7
Gauley Bridge	F-6
Gilbert	G-5
Glen Daniel	G-6
Glen Fork	G-5
Glenville •	E-7
Grafton •	D-8
Grantsville •	E-6
Guardian	E-7
Gum Spring	C-9
Hacker Valley	E-8
Hamlin •	F-4
Harman	D-9
Harrisville •	D-6
Hartland	F-6
Hedgesville	C-12
Hereford	E-5
Hernshaw	F-5
Hilbert	E-6
Hillsboro	F-8
Hinton •	G-6
Hodgesville	D-8
Hominy Falls	F-7
Howesville	C-9
Hundred	C-7
Huntersville	F-8
Huntington •	F-4
Hurricane	F-4
Huttonsville	E-8
Iaeger	H-5
Ivydale	E-6
Jacksonburg	C-7
Jane Lew	D-8
Jesse	G-5
Jetsville	F-7
Job	E-9
Jolo	H-5
Jones Springs	C-12
Jordan Run	D-10
Josephs Mills	C-7
Judy Gap	E-9
Junior	D-8
Justice	G-5
Kanawha Head	E-8
Kayford	G-5
Kearneysville	C-12
Kenova	F-3
Kentuck	E-5
Kermit	G-4
Kester	E-6
Kettle	E-5
Keyser •	C-10
Keystone	H-5
Kidwell	C-7
Killarney	G-6
Kingwood •	C-9
Kistle	G-5
Kopperston	G-5
Lakin	D-4
Landes	E-10
Landisburg	G-6
Laneville	D-9
Larew	C-9
Largent	C-11
Lavalette	F-3
Lead Mine	D-9
Left Hand	E-6
Leon	E-5
Leopold	D-7
Lerona	H-6
Letart	E-5
Lewisburg •	G-7
Liberty	E-5
Lindside	H-7
Linwood	F-8
Little Birch	E-7
Littleton	C-7
Logan •	G-4
Lone Valley	D-6
Lorentz	D-8
Lost City	D-11
Lubeck	D-5
Lyburn	G-5
Maben	G-5
Mace	F-8
Macomber	D-9
Madison •	F-5
Mallory	G-5
Mammoth	F-6
Man	G-4
Mannington	C-8
Market	D-7
Marlinton •	F-8
Marmet	F-5
Martinsburg •	C-12
Mason	D-4
Masontown	C-9
Matewan	G-4
Matoaka	H-6
Maxwelton	G-8
Maybeury	H-6
Maysville	D-10
McMechen	B-7
Meadow Bridge	G-6
Mercers Bottom	E-4
Middlebourne •	C-7
Mill Creek	E-8
Mill Point	F-8
Millard	E-6
Millstone	E-6
Milton	F-4
Mingo	E-8
Minnehaha Springs	F-8
Monterville	E-8
Montgomery	F-5
Montrose	D-9
Moorefield •	D-10
Morgansville	D-7
Morgantown •	C-9
Moundsville •	B-7
Mount Alto	E-5
Mount Gay	G-4
Mount Hope	G-6
Mount Nebo	F-7
Mount Olive	E-4
Mount Storm	D-10
Mount Zion	E-6
Mountain View	G-4
Mullens	G-5
Murphytown	D-5
Nallen	F-7
Naoma	G-5
Napier	E-7
Natrium	C-7
Neola	G-8
Nestorville	D-9
Nettie	F-7
New Creek	C-10
New Cumberland •	A-7
New Haven	D-4
New Martinsville •	C-7
Newdale	C-7
Newhall	H-5
Newton	E-6
Nolan	G-4
Normantown	E-7
Norton	D-8
Nutter Fort	D-7
Oak Flat	E-10
Oak Hill	G-6
Oakvale	H-6
Oceana	G-5
Odaville	D-5
Okonoko	C-11
Old Fields	D-10
Paden City	C-7
Palestine	D-5
Pansy	E-10
Panther	H-5
Parkersburg •	D-5
Parsons •	D-9
Paw Paw	C-11
Pecks Mill	G-4
Peeltree	D-8
Peewee	D-5
Pennsboro	D-6
Petersburg •	D-10
Peterstown	H-7
Pettry	H-6
Philippi •	D-8
Pickaway	G-7
Pickens	E-8
Pike	D-6
Pineville •	G-5
Pipestem	H-6
Poca	E-5
Pocatalico	E-5
Point Plesant •	E-4
Points	C-11
Port Amherst	F-5
Prenter	G-5
Prichard	F-3
Prince	G-6
Princeton •	H-6
Procious	E-6
Proctor	C-7
Pruntytown	D-8
Pullman	D-6
Pumpkintown	E-8
Purgitsville	D-10
Putney	F-6
Queens	E-8
Quinnimont	G-6
Quniwood	F-7
Racine	F-5
Rainelle	G-7
Rainelle Junction	G-7
Ramage	G-5
Ramp	G-7
Raven Rock	C-6
Ravencliff	G-5
Ravenswood	D-5
Reader	C-7
Reedsville	C-9
Reedy	E-5
Richwood	F-7
Ridge	C-12
Ridgeley	C-11
Ridgeville	D-10
Ridgeway	D-12
Rimel	F-8
Ripley •	E-5
Rivesville	C-8
Robertsburg	E-5
Rock Camp	H-7
Rock Cave	E-8
Rock Creek	F-5
Rock Oak	D-11
Rocklick	B-7
Rockport	D-5
Romney •	D-11
Ronceverte	G-7
Rosedale	E-7
Roxalana	E-6
Ruddle	E-9
Rupert	G-7
St. Albans	F-4
St. Joseph	C-7
St. Marys	C-6
Salem	D-7
Salineville	A-7
Sand Fork	D-7
Sandstone	G-7
Sandyville	E-5
Sanoma	D-6
Saulsbury	D-5
Sedalia	C-7
Seneca Rocks	E-10
Shady Spring	G-6
Shepherstown	C-13
Shinnston	C-7
Shirley	C-7
Silver Lake	D-9
Sinks Grove	G-7
Sistersville	C-6
Slanesville	C-11
Slate	D-6
Smithers	F-6
Smithfield	C-7
Smithville	D-6
Sophia	G-6
South Charleston	F-5
Spencer •	E-6
Sprague	G-6
Star City	C-8
Stonewood	D-8
Summersville •	F-7
Sutton •	E-7
Switzer	G-4
Sylvester	F-5
Terra Alta	C-9
Thomas	D-9
Thorpe	H-5
Three Forks of Williams River	F-7
Tunnelton	C-9
Union •	G-7
Verdunville	G-4
Vienna	D-5
War	H-5
Wardensville	D-11
Wayne •	F-4
Webster Springs •	E-7
Weirton	A-7
Welch •	H-5
Wellsburg	A-7
West Hamlin	F-4
West Union •	D-7
Weston •	D-7
Westover	C-8
Wheeling •	B-7
White Sulphur Springs	G-8
Whitesville	G-5
Williamson •	G-4
Williamstown	C-5
Winfield •	E-4
Worthington	C-8

UH-693-J-X

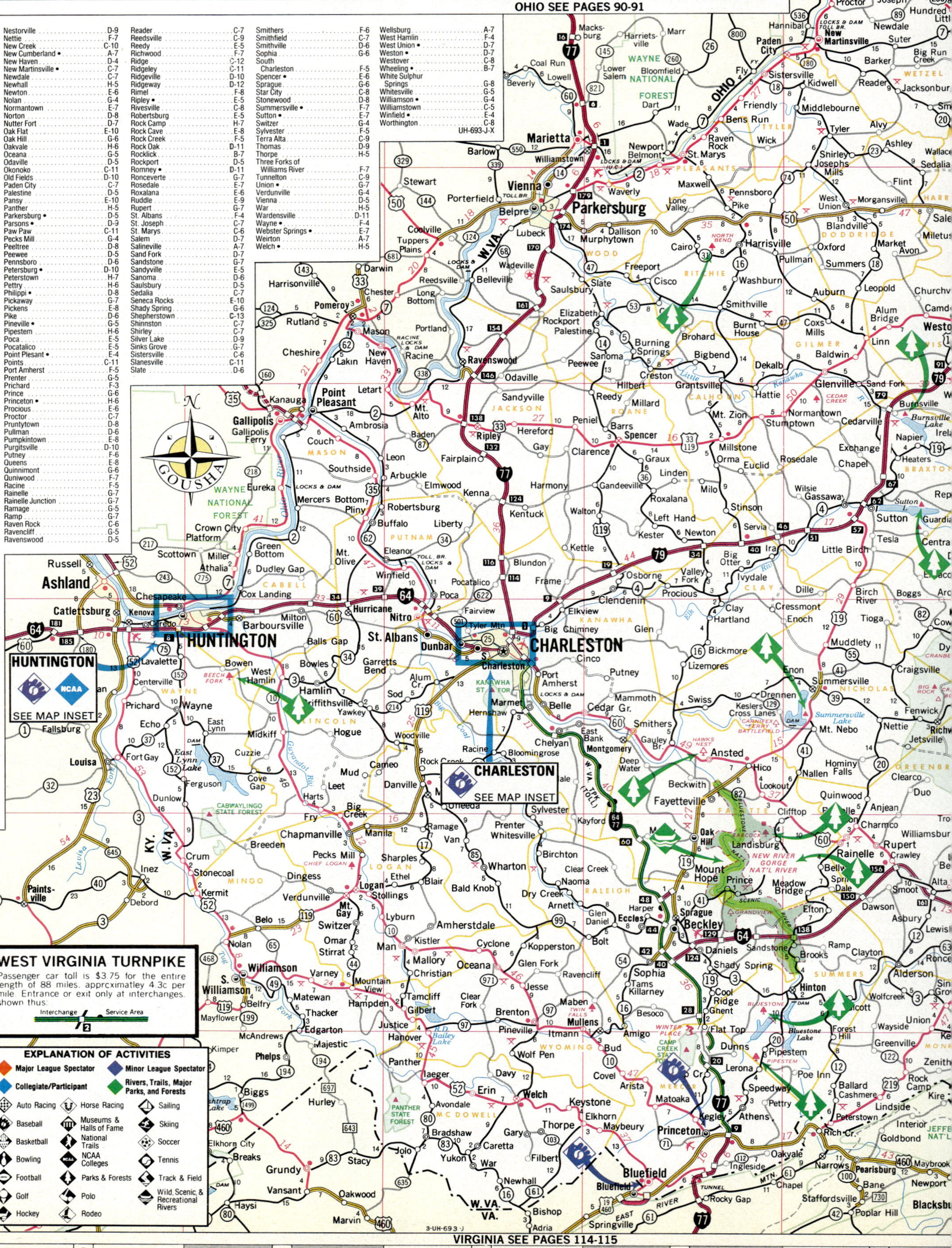

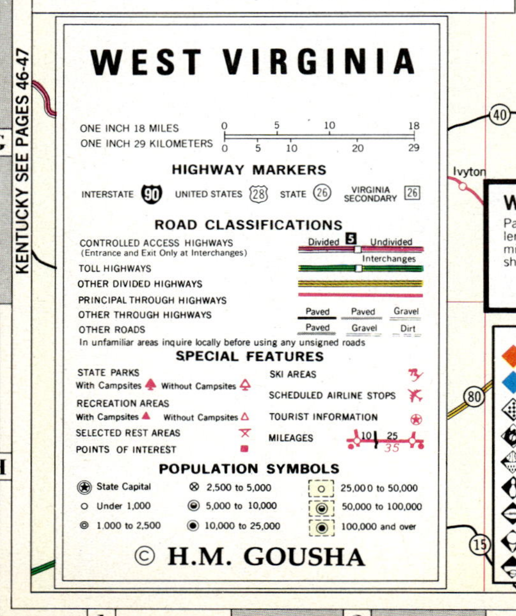

KENTUCKY SEE PAGES 46-47

VIRGINIA SEE PAGES 114-115

CHARLESTON
WEST VIRGINIA
© H.M. GOUSHA
WHEELING
WEST VIRGINIA
© H.M. GOUSHA
PENNSYLVANIA SEE PAGES 98-99
MARYLAND SEE PAGES 52-53
VIRGINIA SEE PAGES 114-115
RICHMOND
VIRGINIA
© H.M. GOUSHA
Lithographed in U.S.A.

WASHINGTON

Pop (1990) 4,887,941
Area 68,192 Sq. Mi.

COUNTIES

County	County Seat
Adams	Ritzville
Asotin	Asotin
Benton	Prosser
Chelan	Wenatchee
Clallam	Port Angeles
Clark	Vancouver
Columbia	Dayton
Cowlitz	Kelso
Douglas	Waterville
Ferry	Republic
Franklin	Pasco
Garfield	Pomeroy
Grant	Ephrata
Grays Harbor	Montesano
Island	Coupeville
Jefferson	Port Townsend
King	Seattle
Kitsap	Port Orchard
Kittitas	Ellensburg
Klickitat	Goldendale
Lewis	Chehalis
Lincoln	Davenport
Mason	Shelton
Okanogan	Okanogan
Pacific	South Bend
Pend Oreille	Newport
Pierce	Tacoma
San Juan	Friday Harbor
Skagit	Mount Vernon
Skamania	Stevenson
Snohomish	Everett
Spokane	Spokane
Stevens	Colville
Thurston	Olympia
Wahkiakum	Cathlamet
Walla Walla	Walla Walla
Whatcom	Bellingham
Whitman	Colfax
Yakima	Yakima

PARTIAL LIST OF

CITIES AND TOWNS

• County Seats

Aberdeen E-4
Acme B-7
Addy B-13
Adna F-5
Agate E-5
Albion E-14
Alder E-6
Allyn D-6
Almira D-11
Alpowa F-13
Amanda Park D-4
Amboy G-6
American River E-8
Anacortes B-6
Arctic E-4
Arden B-12
Arlington C-7
Ashford E-7
Asotin • F-14
Auburn D-6
Ayer F-12
Azwell C-10
Baring D-7
Barstow B-12
Battle Ground G-6
Batum E-11
Belfair D-6
Bellevue D-7
Bellingham • B-6
Belmont E-14
Belvedere C-11
Benge E-12
Benton City F-10
Beverly E-10
Big Lake B-6
Birch Bay A-6
Black Diamond E-7
Blaine A-6
Blewett D-9
Bluecreek C-13
Blueslide B-13
Bluestem D-12
Blyn C-5
Bogachiel C-3
Boistfort F-5
Bolles F-12
Bossburg B-12
Bothell D-6
Boyds B-12
Bremerton D-6
Brewster C-10
Bridgeport C-10
Brinnon D-5
Brook F-5
Brooklyn E-5
Brownstown F-9
Brownsville D-6
Buckley E-7
Bucoda E-6
Buena F-9
Burbank G-11
Burlington B-6
Burnett E-7
Camas H-6
Canby D-12
Carlton C-9
Carson G-7
Cascade Tunnel D-8
Cashmere D-9
Castle Rock F-5
Cathlamet • F-5
Cedarville E-5
Cedonia C-12
Centerville G-8
Central Ferry F-13
Centralia F-5
Chambers F-14
Chattaroy C-13
Chehalis • F-5
Chelan C-10
Cheney D-13
Chesaw A-11
Chewelah C-13
Chinook F-4
Chuckanut Bay B-6
Cinebar F-6
Claquato F-5
Clarkston F-14
Clayton C-13
Cle Elum E-8
Cliffdel E-8
Clyde F-12
Coal Canyon F-6
Cohasset E-4
Colbert C-13
Colfax • E-13
College Place G-12
Colton F-14
Columbia Beach C-6
Columbia Center F-13
Colville • B-12
Colville Indian Agency C-11
Concrete B-7
Connell F-11
Cook G-7
Cordell B-10
Cosmopolis E-4
Coulee City D-11
Coulee Dam C-11
Crescent Bar E-9
Creston D-12
Cunningham E-11
Curlew B-12
Curtis F-5
Cusick B-13
Dalkena C-13
Darrington C-7
Davenport • D-12
Dayton • F-13
Deep Creek D-13
Deer Park C-13
Delaney F-13
Delphi E-5
Deming B-6
Denison C-13
Des Moines D-6
Discovery Bay C-5
Dishman D-13
Dixie G-12
Dodge F-13
Donald F-9
Doty F-5
Douglas D-10
Dryad F-5
Duluth G-6
Dusty E-13
Duvall D-7
East Wenatchee D-9
Easton E-8
Eden E-14
Edmonds D-6
Edwall D-12
Egypt C-12
Elbe E-6
Eldon D-5
Electric City C-11
Ellensburg • E-9
Ellisforde B-10
Elma E-5
Eltopia F-11
Endicott E-13
Entiat D-9
Enumclaw E-7
Ephrata • D-10
Eureka F-12
Evans B-12
Everett • C-6
Ewan E-13
Fairfield D-14
Fairholm C-4
Fallon E-14
Farmer D-10
Ferndale B-6
Fishtrap D-13
Forks C-3
Fortson C-7
Frances F-5
Freeland C-6
Friutland C-12
Galvin F-5
Garfield E-14
George E-10
Gifford C-12
Gig Harbor D-6
Gilbert B-9
Glacier B-7
Gleed F-9
Glenoma F-7
Glenwood G-8
Gold Bar C-7
Goldendale • G-9
Grand Coulee C-11
Grandview F-10
Granger F-9
Grayland E-4
Grays River F-4
Greenwater E-7
Grotto D-8
Hadley G-12
Harrington D-12
Hartline D-11
Hatton E-11
Hazel C-7
Hoodsport D-5
Hoquiam E-4
Humptulips E-4
Hunters C-12
Huntsville F-12
Husum G-7
Ilwaco F-4
Ingalls Creek D-9
Ione B-13
Issaquah D-7
Jared B-13
Joyce C-4
Kahlotus F-12
Kalaloch D-3
Kalama G-6
Keller C-11
Kelso • G-5
Kendall B-6
Kennewick G-11
Kent D-6
Kettle Falls B-12
Key Center D-6
Kiona F-10
Kirkland D-6
Klickitat G-8
La Center G-6
La Crosse E-13
La Grande E-6
Lacey E-6
Lamar F-12
Lamona D-12
Latah D-14
Laurel B-6
Lawrence B-6
Leahy C-10
Leavenworth D-9
Lester E-7
Lilliwaup D-5
Lincoln C-12
Lind E-12
Little Falls C-12
Little Rock E-5
Locke B-13
Lofall D-6
Long Lake C-13
Longmire E-7
Longview G-5
Loomis B-10
Loon Lake C-13
Loveland E-6
Lowden G-12
Lyle G-8
Lynden A-6
Lynnwood D-6
Malaga D-9
Malone E-5
Mansfield D-10
Manson C-9
Maple Falls A-7
Maple Valley D-7
Marble B-12
Marcellus E-12
Marcus B-12
Marengo F-13
Maryhill G-8
Marys Corner F-6
Marysville C-7
Matlock E-5
Mattawa F-10
Maytown E-5
Mazama B-9
McCleary E-5
McKenna E-6
Medical Lake D-13
Megler F-4
Menlo F-4
Merritt D-8
Mesa F-11
Metaline B-13
Metaline Falls A-13
Methow C-10
Miles C-12
Millwood D-13
Milton E-6
Mineral F-6
Mockonema E-13
Molson A-11
Mondovi D-12
Monroe C-7
Monse C-10
Montborne C-7
Montesano • E-5
Moody E-11
Morton F-6
Moses Lake E-11
Mossyrock F-6
Mount Baker Lodge B-7
Mount Vernon • B-6
Mountain View B-6
Mountlake Terrace D-6
Moxee City F-9
Mukilteo C-6
Murdock H-8
Naches F-9
Nahcotta F-4
Naselle F-4
Neah Bay B-3
Neilton D-4
Nemah F-4
Nespelem C-11
New London E-4
Newhalem B-8
Newport • C-14
Nighthawk A-10
Northport A-13
Oak Harbor C 6
Oakesdale E-13
Oakville E-5
Odessa D-11
Ohanapecosh F-7
Okanogan • C-10
Olympia • E-5
Omak B-10
Opportunity D-14
Orchards G-6
Orient B-12
Orondo D-9
Oroville A-10
Orting E-6
Oso C-7
Othello E-11
Packwood F-7
Paddock F-12
Paha E-12
Palouse E-14
Paradise E-7
Park Rapids B-13
Pasco • F-11
Pataha F-13
Pateros C-10
Paterson G-10
Pe Ell F-5
Penawawa F-13
Peola F-13
Pine City E-13
Pleasant View F-12
Pomeroy • F-13
Port Angeles C-5
Port Gamble C-6
Port Orchard • D-6
Port Townsend • C-6
Porter E-5
Potlatch D-5
Poulsbo D-6
Prairie B-6
Prescott F-12
Prosser • G-10
Providence E-11
Pullman E-14
Purdy D-6
Puyallup E-6
Pysht C-4
Queets D-3
Quilcene D-5
Quincy E-10
Rainier E-6
Ralston E-12
Randle F-7
Raymond F-4
Reardan D-13
Redmond D-7
Renton D-7
Republic • B-11
Rice B-12
Richland F-11
Ridgefield G-6
Rimrock F-8
Ringold F-11
Ritzville • E-12
Riverside B-10
Rochester E-5
Rock Island D-9
Rockford D-14
Rocklyn D-12
Rockport B-7
Rodna D-13
Roosevelt G-9
Rosalia E-13
Rosburg F-4
Roslyn E-8
Roxboro E-11
Roy E-6
Royal Camp E-10
Royal City E-10
Ruby B-13
Ryderwood F-5
St. Andrews D-10
St. John E-13
Salkum F-6
Sappho C-3
Satsop E-5
Sauk B-7
Schwana E-10
Schoonover E-11
Schrag E-11
Seattle • D-6
Seaview F-4
Sedro Woolley B-6
Selah F-9
Seltice E-14
Sequim C-5
Shelton • E-5
Shuksan A-7
Silcott F-14
Silverdale D-6
Skamokawa F-5
Smyrna E-10
Snohomish C-7
Snoqualmie D-7
Soap Lake D-10
South Bend F-4
South Cle Elum E-8
Spokane • D-13
Sprague D-12
Springdale C-13
Stanwood C-6
Starbuck F-12
Steilacoom E-6
Steptoe E-13
Stillwater D-7
Stratford D-11
Sultan C-7
Sumas A-6
Sumner E-7
Sunnyside F-10
Tacoma • E-6
Taunton E-11
Tekoa E-14
Thornton E-13
Thrall E-9
Tiger B-13
Toledo F-6
Tonasket B-10
Toppenish F-9
Torbcy B-11
Toroda A-11
Touchet G-11
Trafton C-7
Trout Lake G-7
Tumwater E-5
Turner F-13
Twisp C-9
Union Gap F-9
Uniontown F-14
Usk C-13
Vader F-5
Valley C-13
Van Horn B-7
Vancouver • H-6
Vesta E-4
Wahkiacus G-8
Waitsburg F-12
Walla Walla G-12
Wallula G-11
Wapato F-9
Warden E-11
Washougal H-6
Washtucna E-12
Waterville • D-9
Wauconda B-11
Waverly D-13
Wawawai F-13
Weikswood E-5
Wenatchee • D-9
West Fork B-11
West Richland F-10
White Salmon G-7
White Swan F-9
Whites E-5
Wickersham B-7
Wilbur D-11
Wilcox E-13
Wildwood F-5
Wilkeson E-7
Willapa F-4
Winchester E-10
Winesap D-9
Winlock F-5
Winona E-13
Winslow D-6
Winthrop B-9
Withrow D-10
Woodland G-6
Wymer E-9
Yakima • F-9
Yale G-5
Zillah F-9

SF-662-J

CANADA SEE PAGE 126
OREGON SEE PAGES 96-97
IDAHO SEE PAGES 34-35
BRITISH COLUMBIA
IDAHO
OREGON
CANADA
UNITED STATES
GOUSHA
CASCADE PROV. REC. AREA
MANNING PROVINCIAL PARK
OKANOGAN NATIONAL FOREST
COLVILLE NATIONAL FOREST
KANIKSU NATIONAL FOREST
WENATCHEE NATIONAL FOREST
SNOQUALMIE
COLVILLE INDIAN RES
SPOKANE INDIAN RESERVATION
YAKIMA INDIAN RESERVATION
UMATILLA NATIONAL FOREST
YAKIMA FIRING CENTER
SPOKANE
SEE PAGE 120
YAKIMA
SEE PAGE 118
Wenatchee
Ellensburg
Moses Lake
Ephrata
Richland
Pasco
Kennewick
Walla Walla
Pullman
Moscow
Lewiston
Clarkston
Pendleton
The Dalles
Goldendale
Toppenish
Sunnyside
Cheney
Omak
Okanogan
Colville
Republic
Oroville
WASHINGTON
ONE INCH 22 MILES
ONE INCH 35 KILOMETERS
HIGHWAY MARKERS
INTERSTATE
UNITED STATES
STATE AND PROVINCIAL
TRANS CANADA
ROAD CLASSIFICATIONS
CONTROLLED ACCESS HIGHWAYS (Interstate interchange numbers are mileposts)
Divided
Undivided
Interchanges
OTHER DIVIDED HIGHWAYS
PRINCIPAL THROUGH HIGHWAYS
OTHER THROUGH HIGHWAYS
OTHER ROADS
Paved
Gravel
Dirt
In unfamiliar areas inquire locally before using any unsigned roads
© H.M. GOUSHA
SPECIAL FEATURES
STATE PARKS
With Campsites
Without Campsites
RECREATION AREAS
SELECTED REST AREAS
PORTS OF ENTRY
Open 24 Hours
Inquire Locally
POINTS OF INTEREST
SKI AREAS
SCHEDULED AIRLINE STOPS
MILITARY AIRPORTS
TOURIST INFORMATION
MILEAGES
POPULATION SYMBOLS
State Capital
Under 1,000
1,000 to 2,500
2,500 to 5,000
5,000 to 10,000
10,000 to 25,000
25,000 to 50,000
50,000 to 100,000
100,000 and over
EXPLANATION OF ACTIVITIES
Major League Spectator
Minor League Spectator
Collegiate/Participant
Rivers, Trails, Major Parks, and Forests
Auto Racing
Horse Racing
Sailing
Baseball
Museums & Halls of Fame
Skiing
Basketball
National Trails
Soccer
Bowling
NCAA Colleges
Tennis
Football
Parks & Forests
Track & Field
Golf
Polo
Wild, Scenic & Recreational Rivers
Hockey
Rodeo
Lithographed in U.S.A.

SEATTLE TACOMA AND VICINITY
MILES
KILOMETERS
Golf Courses
SEATTLE
TACOMA
BELLEVUE
KIRKLAND
REDMOND
RENTON
KENT
AUBURN
PUYALLUP
DES MOINES
MERCER ISLAND
EDMONDS
PUGET SOUND
Lake Washington
VASHON ISLAND
MAURY ISLAND
BAINBRIDGE ISLAND
To Everett and Bellingham
To Olympia
To Mount Rainier Nat'l Park
To Ellensburg and Yakima
© H.M. GOUSHA
SPOKANE WASHINGTON
SPOKANE
Spokane International Airport
OLYMPIA WASHINGTON
OLYMPIA
TUMWATER
Budd Inlet
MOUNT RAINIER NATIONAL PARK WASHINGTON
Mt Rainier 14410
GIFFORD PINCHOT NATIONAL FOREST
MT. BAKER-SNOQUALMIE NATIONAL FOREST
OLYMPIC NATIONAL PARK WASHINGTON
Strait of Juan de Fuca
Port Angeles
Mt Olympus 7965
OLYMPIC NATIONAL PARK
OLYMPIC NATIONAL FOREST
Trails
Inquire at Ranger Station before using

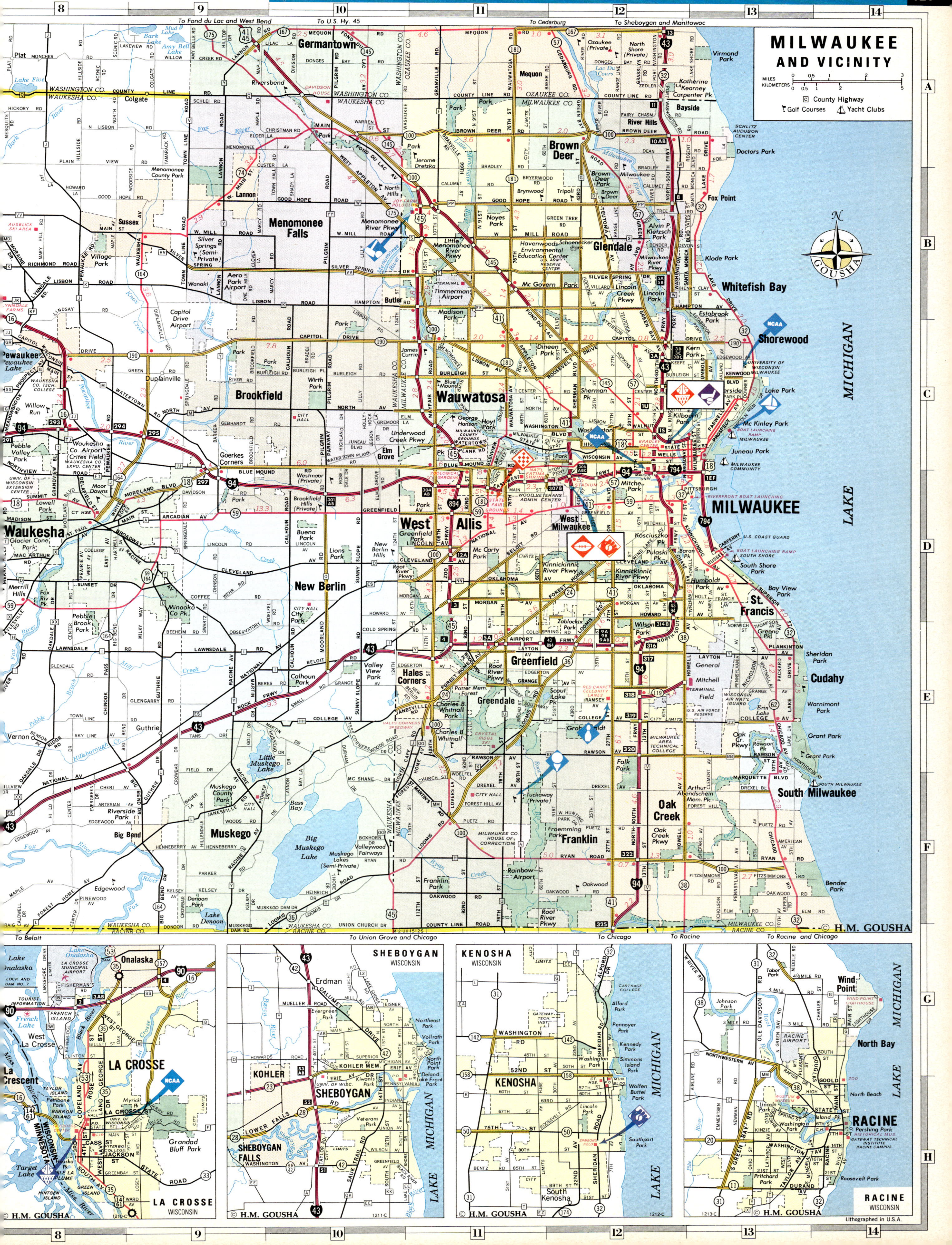
MILWAUKEE AND VICINITY
MILES
KILOMETERS
County Highway
Golf Courses
Yacht Clubs
To Fond du Lac and West Bend
To U.S. Hy. 45
To Cedarburg
To Sheboygan and Manitowoc
Germantown
Mequon
Brown Deer
River Hills
Bayside
Fox Point
Glendale
Whitefish Bay
Shorewood
Menomonee Falls
Lannon
Sussex
Colgate
Brookfield
Wauwatosa
Elm Grove
Pewaukee
Waukesha
West Allis
West Milwaukee
MILWAUKEE
New Berlin
St. Francis
Cudahy
South Milwaukee
Greenfield
Hales Corners
Greendale
Oak Creek
Franklin
Muskego
Big Bend
Vernon
Guthrie
LAKE MICHIGAN
GOUSHA
N.
© H.M. GOUSHA
To Beloit
To Union Grove and Chicago
To Chicago
To Racine
To Racine and Chicago
LA CROSSE
WISCONSIN
Onalaska
La Crescent
MINNESOTA
WISCONSIN
SHEBOYGAN
WISCONSIN
KOHLER
SHEBOYGAN FALLS
KENOSHA
WISCONSIN
RACINE
WISCONSIN
North Bay
Wind Point
Lithographed in U.S.A.

WISCONSIN
ONE INCH 21 MILES
ONE INCH 34 KILOMETERS
HIGHWAY MARKERS
ROAD CLASSIFICATIONS
SPECIAL FEATURES
POPULATION SYMBOLS
© H.M. GOUSHA
EXPLANATION OF ACTIVITIES
FOR CONTINUATION SEE MAIN MAP
MICHIGAN SEE PAGES 58-59
FOR CONTINUATION SEE INSET ABOVE
MINNESOTA SEE PAGES 62-63
DULUTH-SUPERIOR SEE MAP INSET
GREEN BAY SEE MAP INSET
CENTRAL STANDARD TIME
EASTERN STANDARD TIME
LAKE SUPERIOR
GREEN BAY
MICHIGAN
MINNESOTA
DULUTH
Superior
Ashland
Hayward
Spooner
Rhinelander
Merrill
WAUSAU
Stevens Point
Marshfield
Medford
EAU CLAIRE
Chippewa Falls
Menomonie
ST. PAUL
Hudson
Red Wing
MARINETTE
Menominee
Green Bay
Oconto
Shawano
Antigo
Ironwood
Sturgeon Bay
APOSTLE ISLANDS
CHEQUAMEGON NATIONAL FOREST
NICOLET NATIONAL FOREST

WISCONSIN

Pop (1990) 4,906,745
Area 56,154 Sq. Mi.

COUNTIES

County	Co. Seat	County	Co. Seat
Adams	Friendship	Manitowac	Manitowoc
Ashland	Ashland	Marathon	Wausau
Barron	Barron	Marinette	Marinette
Bayfield	Washburn	Marquette	Montello
Brown	Green Bay	Menominee	Keshena
Buffalo	Alma	Milwaukee	Milwaukee
Burnett	Grantsburg	Monroe	Sparta
Calumet	Chilton	Oconto	Oconto
Chippewa	Chippewa Falls	Oneida	Rhinelander
Clark	Neillsville	Outagamie	Appleton
Columbia	Portage	Ozaukee	Port Washington
Crawford	Prairie du Chien	Pepin	Durand
Dane	Madison	Pierce	Ellsworth
Dodge	Juneau	Polk	Balsam Lake
Door	Sturgeon Bay	Portage	Stevens Point
Douglas	Superior	Price	Philips
Dunn	Menomonie	Racine	Racine
Eau Claire	Eau Claire	Richland	Richland Center
Florence	Florence	Rock	Janesville
Fond du Lac	Fond du Lac	Rusk	Ladysmith
Forest	Crandon	St. Croix	Hudson
Grant	Lancaster	Sauk	Baraboo
Green	Monroe	Sawyer	Hayward
Green Lake	Green Lake	Shawano	Shawano
Iowa	Dogville	Sheboygan	Sheboygan
Iron	Hurley	Taylor	Medford
Jackson	Black River Falls	Trempealeau	Whitehall
Jefferson	Jefferson	Vernon	Viroqua
Juneau	Mauston	Vilas	Eagle River
Kenosha	Kenosha	Walworth	Elkhorn
Kewaunee	Kewaunee	Washburn	Shell Lake
LaCrosse	LaCrosse	Washington	West Bend
Lafayette	Darlington	Waukesha	Waukesha
Langlade	Antigo	Waupaca	Waupaca
Lincoln	Merrill	Waushara	Wautoma
		Winnebago	Oshkosh
		Wood	Wisconsin Rapids

PARTIAL LIST OF

CITIES AND TOWNS

• County Seats

Abbotsford	F-4
Adams	H-5
Algoma	G-8
Alma •	G-2
Altoona	F-3
Amery	E-2
Amherst Jct.	G-6
Aniwa	F-6
Antigo •	E-6
Appleton •	G-7
Arbor Vitae	D-5
Arcadia	G-3
Arena	K-5
Armstrong Creek	D-7
Ashland •	B-4
Auburndale	G-5
Augusta	F-3
Auroraville	H-6
Baraboo •	J-5
Barron •	E-2
Barronett	D-2
Barton	J-7
Beaver Dam	J-6
Beetown	L-3
Bell Center	K-4
Belleville •	L-5
Belmont	L-4
Beloit	L-6
Berlin	H-6
Big Bend	K-7
Birnamwood	F-6
Black Earth	K-5
Black River Falls •	G-3
Blair	G-3
Blenker	G-5
Bloomer	E-3
Bloomington	K-3
Bloomville	E-5
Bonduel	F-7
Boscobel	K-4
Bosstown	J-4
Bradley	E-5
Bridgeport	K-3
Brillion	H-8
Brodhead	L-6
Brookside	F-8
Brooklyn	L-6
Brown Deer	K-8
Browntown	L-5
Bruce	E-3
Brule	B-3
Burlington	L-7
Butternut	D-4
Cable	C-3
Campbellsport	J-7
Carlsville	B-8
Carter	E-7
Cassville	L-3
Catawba	E-4
Cayuga	C-4
Cazenovia	J-4
Cedar	B-4
Cedar Grove	J-8
Cedarburg	K-8
Chelsea	E-4
Chetek	E-3
Chilton •	H-7
Chippewa Falls	F-3
Clayton	E-2
Clear Lake	E-2
Clifford	E-5
Clinton	L-6
Clintonville	G-7
Cobb	K-4
Colby	F-4
Coleman	F-8
Colfax	F-2
Columbus	J-6
Connorsville	E-2
Coral City	G-3
Cornell	E-3
Cottage Grove	K-6
Couderay	D-3
Crandon •	D-6
Cross Plains	K-5
Cuba City	L-4
Cudahy	K-8
Cumberland	E-2
Danbury	C-2
Darlington •	L-5
De Pere	G-7
Delavan	L-7
Denmark	G-8
Dexterville	G-5
Dickeyville	L-4
Dodgeville •	K-5
Downsville	F-2
Draper	D-4
Drummond	C-3
Dudley	E-6
Dunbar	D-7
Durand •	G-2
Dyckesville	G-8
Eagle River •	D-6
East Troy	L-7
Easton	H-5
Eau Claire •	F-3
Edgerton	L-6
Edmund	K-4
Egg Harbor	B-8
Eland	F-6
Eleva	G-3
Elk Mound	F-2
Elkhorn •	L-7
Ellison Bay	A-8
Ellsworth •	F-1
Elmo	L-4
Elroy	J-4
Ephraim	B-8
Evansville	L-6
Falun	D-1
Fennimore	K-4
Fifield	D-4
Finley	H-4
Fish Creek	B-8
Fond du Lac •	H-7
Forest	E-2
Forest Jct.	G-7
Fort Atkinson	K-6
Fox Lake	J-6
Fox Point	K-8
Frederic	D-1
Fredonia	J-8
Fremont	G-6
Friendship •	H-5
Galesville	H-3
Genoa City	L-7
Gillett	F-7
Gills Rock	A-8
Gilman	E-4
Gleason	E-6
Glen Flora	E-4
Glidden	C-4
Goodman	D-7
Gordon	C-2
Gotham	K-4
Grafton	K-8
Grandview	C-3
Gratiot	L-5
Green Bay •	G-8
Green Lake •	H-6
Greenwood	F-4
Hammond	F-1
Hartford	K-7
Haugen	D-2
Hawkins	E-4
Hayton	H-7
Hayward •	C-3
Hazel Green	L-4
Heafford Jct.	E-5
Hillsboro	J-4
Hillsdale	E-2
Hilltop	J-5
Hollister	E-6
Holmen	H-3
Horicon	J-7
Hortonville	G-7
Howard	G-7
Hudson	F-1
Hurley •	B-4
Independence	G-3
Ingram	E-4
Ino	B-3
Iron River	B-3
Ironton	J-5
Ithaca	J-4
Janesville •	L-6
Jefferson •	K-7
Jordan	L-5
Jump River	E-4
Junction City	G-5
Juneau •	J-7
Kaukauna	G-7
Kennan	E-4
Kenosha •	L-8
Keshena •	F-7
Kewaskum	J-7
Kewaunee •	G-8
Kiel	H-8
Kimberly	G-7
Knapp	F-2
La Crosse •	H-3
La Farge	J-4
La Valle	J-5
Lac du Flambeau	D-5
Ladysmith •	E-3
Lake Geneva	L-7
Lake Mills	K-6
Lancaster •	L-4
Langes Corners	G-8
Langlade	E-6
Laona	E-7
Leadmine	L-4
Lena	F-8
Lewis	D-1
Lily	E-6
Little Chute	G-7
Lodi	K-5
Loganville	J-5
Lomira	J-7
Loretta	D-4
Loyal	F-4
Loyd	J-2
Luck	D-1
Lynn	G-4
Madison •	K-5
Manawa	G-6
Manitowish	C-5
Manitowoc •	H-8
Mann	F-4
Maple Bluff	F-8
Marathon City	F-5
Marengo	C-4
Marinette •	F-8
Marion	F-6
Markesan	J-6
Marshfield	F-4
Mather	H-4
Mauston •	H-5
Mayville	J-7
Mazomanie	K-5
McCord	E-5
McKinley	D-2
Medford •	E-4
Medina	G-7
Meehan	G-5
Mellen	C-4
Menasha	H-7
Menomonee Falls	K-7
Menomonie •	F-2
Mercer	C-5
Merrill •	E-5
Merrillan	G-4
Middle Inlet	E-8
Middleton	K-5
Milladore	G-5
Milton	L-6
Milwaukee •	K-8
Minong	C-2
Mondovi	G-2
Monico	E-6
Monona	K-6
Monroe •	L-5
Montello •	H-6
Montfort	K-4
Monticello	L-5
Mosinee	F-5
Mount Horeb	K-5
Mount Ida	K-4
Mount Vernon	K-5
Mukwonago	L-7
Muscoda	K-4
Muskego	K-8
Necedah	H-5
Neenah	H-7
Neillsville •	G-4
Nekoosa	G-5
Nelson	G-2
Neopit	F-6
Neshkoro	H-6
New Berlin	K-8
New Glarus	L-5
New Holestein	H-8
New Lisbon	H-5
New London	G-7
New Richmond	E-1
North Andover	L-3
North Fond du Lac	H-7
North Hudson	F-1
Oak Creek	K-8
Oconcmowoc	K-7
Oconto •	F-8
Oconto Falls	F-7
Ojibwa	D-3
Okauchee	K-7
Onalaska	H-3
Ontario	J-4
Oostburg	J-8
Oregon	K-6
Osceola	E-1
Oshkosh •	H-7
Osseo	G-3
Ostego	J-6
Owen	F-4
Oxbow	D-4
Palmyra	L-7
Pardeeville	J-6
Park Falls	D-4
Parrish	E-6
Patch Grove	K-3
Pembine	D-8
Peshtigo	F-8
Petersburg	K-4
Phillips •	D-4
Pickerel	E-6
Pigeon Falls	G-3
Pittsville	G-5
Plain	K-5
Plainville	J-5
Platteville	L-4
Plover	G-5
Plymouth	H-8
Polar	E-6
Poplar	B-2
Port Edwards	G-5
Port Washington •	J-8
Portage •	J-6
Poskin	E-2
Potosi	L-4
Pound	F-8
Poy Sippi	H-6
Poynette	J-6
Prairie du Chien	K-3
Prairie du Sac	K-5
Prentice	E-4
Princeton	H-6
Pulaski	F-7
Racine •	L-8
Radisson	D-3
Randolph	J-6
Random Lake	J-8
Readfield	G-7
Readstown	J-4
Reedsburg	J-5
Reedsville	H-8
Rhinelander •	D-6
Rice Lake	E-2
Richland Center •	J-4
Ridgeland	E-2
Ringle	F-6
Ripon	H-6
River Falls	F-1
Rockton	J-4
Rockville	L-4
Rothschild	F-5
St. Frances	K-8
St. Germain	D-5
Sarona	D-2
Sauk City	K-5
Saukville	J-8
Saxon	B-4
Schofield	F-5
Seeley	C-3
Seymour	G-7
Sharon	L-7
Shawano •	F-7
Sheboygan •	J-8
Sheboygan Falls	J-8
Sheridan	G-6
Shorewood	K-8
Shullsburg	L-4
Siren	D-1
Sister Bay	A-8
Slinger	J-7
Soldiers Grove	J-4
Solon Springs	C-2
South Milwaukee	K-8
South Wayne	L-5
Sparta •	H-4
Spencer	F-4
Spooner	D-2
Sprague	H-5
Spring Green	K-5
Stanley	F-3
Stetsonville	F-4
Stevens Point	G-5
Stiles	F-7
Stiles Jct.	F-7
Stoughton	K-6
Stratford	F-5
Sturgeon Bay •	B-8
Sturtevant	L-8
Summit Lake	E-6
Sun Prairie	K-6
Superior •	B-2
Sussex	K-7
Tennyson	L-4
Thiensville	K-8
Thorp	F-4
Three Lakes	D-6
Tigerton	F-6
Tomah	H-4
Tomahawk	E-5
Tony	E-3
Trade Lake	D-1
Trego	D-2
Tripoli	E-5
Twin Lakes	L-7
Two Rivers	H-8
Union Grove	L-8
Unity	F-4
Valders	H-8
Verona	K-5
Viola	J-4
Viroqua •	J-4
Walworth	L-7
Wascott	C-2
Waterford	L-7
Waterloo	K-6
Watertown	K-7
Waukesha •	K-7
Waunakee	K-6
Waupaca •	G-6
Waupun •	J-7
Wausau •	F-5
Wausaukee	E-8
Wautoma •	H-6
Webster	D-2
Wentworth	B-2
West Bend •	J-7
Westboro	E-4
Westby	J-4
Weyauwega	G-6
Weyerhaeuser	E-3
Whitefish Bay	K-8
Whitehall •	G-3
Whitewater	L-7
Wilson	F-2
Wilton	H-4
Wind Point	L-8
Winneconne	H-7
Winter	D-3
Wisconsin Dells	J-5
Wisconsin Rapids •	G-5
Wittenberg	F-6
Wonewoc	J-4
Woodboro	D-5
Woodruff	D-5

SF-663-J

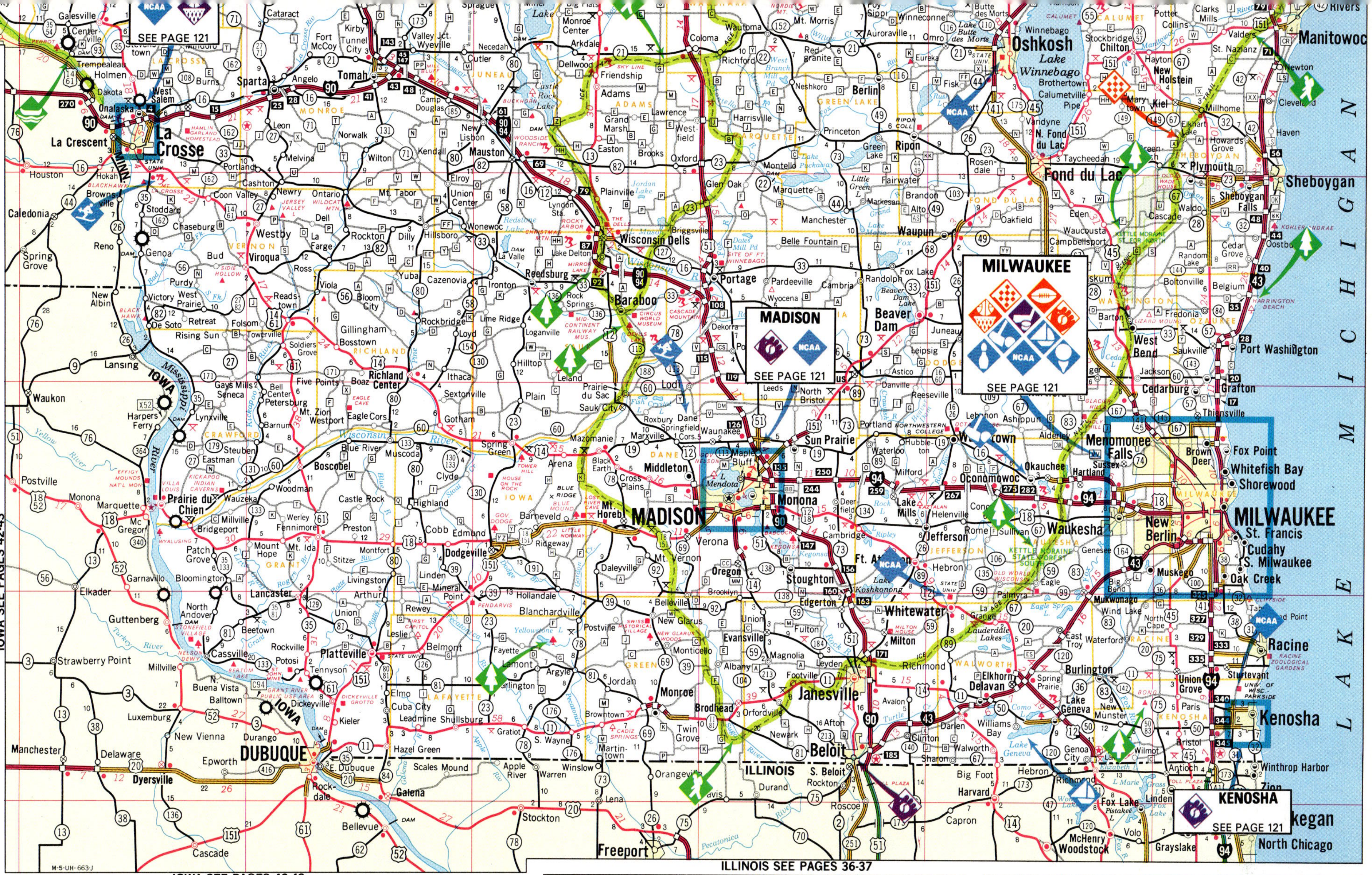

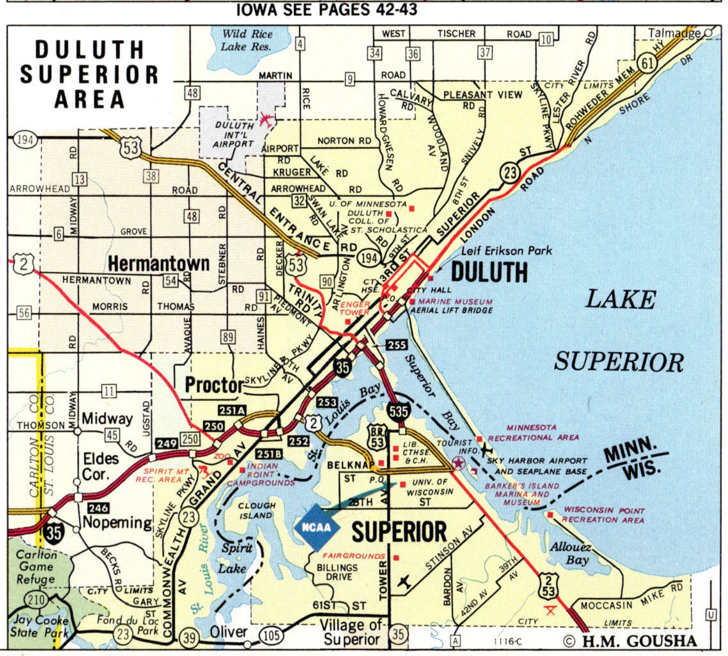

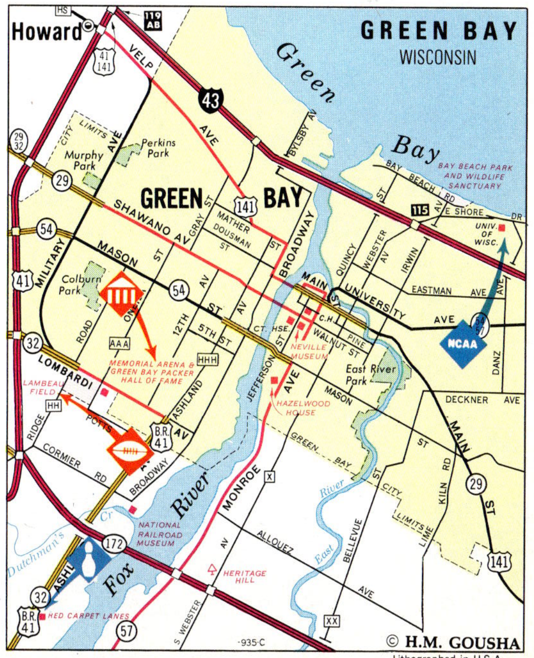

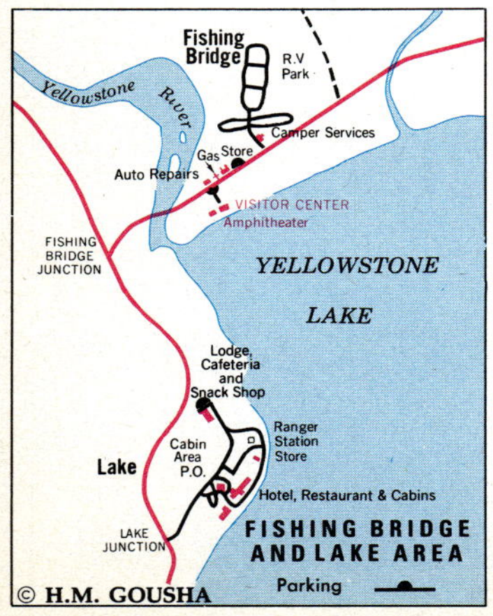

UTAH SEE PAGES 112-113

WYOMING

Pop (1990) 455,975
Area 94,914 Sq. Mi.

COUNTIES

County	County Seat
Albany	Laramie
Big Horn	Basin
Campbell	Gillette
Carbon	Rawlins
Converse	Douglas
Crook	Sundance
Fremont	Lander
Goshen	Torrington
Hot Springs	Thermopolis
Johnson	Buffalo
Laramie	Cheyenne
Lincoln	Kemmerer
Natrona	Casper
Niobrara	Lusk
Park	Cody
Platte	Wheatland
Sheridan	Sheridan
Sublette	Pinedale
Sweetwater	Green River
Teton	Jackson
Uinta	Evanston
Washakie	Worland
Weston	Newcastle

PARTIAL LIST OF

CITIES AND TOWNS

• County Seats

Acme A-9
Afton D-4
Aladdin A-12
Albany F-9
Albin F-12
Alcova D-9
Almy F-4
Alva A-11
Anchor C-6
Arapahoe D-7
Arlington F-10
Arminto C-8
Arrowhead Lodge A-8
Arvada A-9
Atlantic City D-7
Auburn D-4
Baggs F-8
Bairoil E-8
Banner A-8
Barnum C-8
Basin• B-7
Bear Lodge A-8
Beckton A-8
Bedford D-4
Beulah A-12
Big Piney D-5
Big Sandy D-6
Bighorn A-8
Bill C-11
Bitter Creek F-7
Bondurant C-5
Border E-4
Bosler F-10
Boulder D-5
Buffalo• B-9
Buford F-11
Burlington B-7
Burns F-12
Burntfork F-5
Burris C-6
Calpet E-5
Canyon A-5
Carliie A-11
Carpenter F-11
Carter F-4
Casper• D-9
Centennial F-10
Cheyenne F-11
Chugwater E-11
Clareton C-11
Clark A-6
Clearmont A-9
Cody• A-6
Colten Bay B-4
Cora D-5
Cow Creek C-11
Cowley A-7
Crowheart C-6
Daniel D-5
Dayton A-8
Deaver A-7
Devils Tower A-11
Devils Tower Junction B-11
Diamondville E-4
Dixon F-8
Douglas• D-10
Dubois C-5
East Thermopolis C-7
Eden E-6
Edgerton C-9
Egbert F-12
Elk Mountain E-9
Elmo E-9
Emblem A-7
Encampment F-9
Ervay D-8
Esterbrook D-10
Ethete D-6
Etna D-4
Evanston• F-4
Evansville D-9
Fairview D-4
Farson E-6
Federal F-11
Fishing Bridge A-5
Fletcher Park E-10
Fontenelle E-5
Fort Bridger F-4
Fort Laramie E-11
Fort Washakie D-6
Four Corners B-12
Frannie A-7
Freedom D-4
Garland A-7
Garrett E-10
Gillette• B-10
Glendo D-11
Glenrock D-10
Granger F-5
Grant Village B-4
Grass Creek B-7
Green River• F-5
Greybull B-7
Grover D-4
Guernsey E-11
Hamilton Dome C-6
Hampshire C-11
Hanna E-9
Hartville E-11
Hat Creek D-12
Hawk Springs E-11
Hiland D-8
Hillsdale F-11
Hoback Jct. C-4
Horse Creek F-11
Hudson D-7
Hulett A-11
Huntley E-12
Hyattville B-8
Iron Mountain F-11
Jackson• C-4
Jay Em D-11
Jeffrey City D-8
Kaycee C-9
Kearny A-9
Keeline D-11
Kelly C-4
Kemmerer• E-4
Keystone F-9
Kinnear C-6
Kirby C-7
La Barge E-5
La Grange F-12
Lake A-5
Lamont E-8
Lance Creek D-11
Lander• D-6
Laramie• F-10
Leiter A-9
Linch C-9
Lingle E-12
Lindbergh F-12
Little America F-5
Lonetree F-5
Lost Cabin C-8
Lost Springs D-11
Lovell A-7
Lucerne C-7
Lusk D-12
Lyman F-5
Lysite C-8
Madison A-4
Mammoth Hot Springs (Yellowstone Park P.O.) A-4
Manderson B-7
Manville D-11
Marbleton D-5
Mayoworth B-9
McFadden F-10
McKinley D-11
McKinnon F-5
Medicine Bow E-9
Meeteetse B-6
Meriden F-12
Merna D-5
Midwest C-9
Mills D-9
Moneta C-8
Moorcroft B-11
Moran B-4
Moskee B-12
Mountain Home F-9
Mountain View F-5
Mule Creek Jct C-12
Natrona D-9
New Haven A-11
Newcastle• B-12
Node D-12
Norris A-4
Old Faithful B-4
Opal E-5
Orchard Valley F-11
Orin D-11
Osage B-11
Oshoto A-11
Otto B-7
Painter A-5
Parkerton D-10
Parkman A-8
Pavillion C-7
Piedmont F-4
Pine Bluffs F-12
Pinedale• D-5
Point of Rocks E-6
Powder River D-9
Powell A-6
Quealy F-6
Ralston A-6
Ranchester A-8
Rawlins• E-8
Recluse A-10
Red Bird C-11
Red Desert F-7
Riverside F-9
Riverton D-7
Robertson F-4
Rock River E-10
Rock Springs F-6
Rockypoint A-10
Rozet B-11
Ryan Park F-9
Saddlestring B-8
St. Stephens D-7
Sand Draw D-7
Saratoga F-9
Savery F-8
Seely A-11
Seminoe Dam E-8
Shawnee D-11
Shell B-8
Sheridan• A-9
Shirley Basin D-9
Shoshoni C-7
Sinclair E-8
Slater E-11
Smoot D-4
Soda Well A-10
South Superior E-6
Spotted Horse A-10
Story A-8
Sundance• B-12
Sunrise E-11
Superior E-6
Sussex C-9
Sweetwater Station D-7
Ten Sleep B-8
Teton Village C-4
Thayne D-4
Thermopolis• C-7
Thornton B-11
Tie Siding F-10
Torrington E-12
Tower-Roosevelt A-5
Turnercrest C-10
Ucross A-9
Ulm A-9
Upton B-11
Valley B-5
Van Tassell D-12
Veteran E-11
Walcott E-9
Waltman D-8
Wamsutter E-7
Wapiti B-6
West Thumb B-4
Weston A-10
Wheatland• E-11
Willwood A-7
Wilson C-4
Wind River D-6
Woods Landing F-10
Worland• B-7
Wyarno A-9
Yoder E-12

SF-664-J

MONTANA SEE PAGES 68-69
COLORADO SEE PAGES 20-21
SOUTH DAKOTA SEE PAGE 105
NEBRASKA SEE PAGES 70-71
COLORADO SEE PAGES 20-21
SHERIDAN
Buffalo
Gillette
Sundance
Newcastle
Casper
Douglas
Lusk
Torrington
Wheatland
Rawlins
Laramie
CHEYENNE
Ft. Collins
Loveland
Greeley
DENVER
Aurora
THUNDER BASIN NATIONAL GRASSLAND
MEDICINE BOW NATIONAL FOREST
ROOSEVELT NATIONAL FOREST
ROUTT NATIONAL FOREST
BLACK HILLS NATIONAL FOREST
CASPER SEE MAP INSET
LARAMIE SEE MAP INSET
CHEYENNE SEE MAP INSET
SHERIDAN WYOMING
CASPER WYOMING
LARAMIE WYOMING
CHEYENNE WYOMING
WYOMING
ONE INCH 30 MILES
ONE INCH 48 KILOMETERS
HIGHWAY MARKERS
INTERSTATE
UNITED STATES
STATE
STATE SECONDARY
ROAD CLASSIFICATIONS
CONTROLLED ACCESS HIGHWAYS (Entrance and Exit only at Interchanges)
OTHER DIVIDED HIGHWAYS
PRINCIPAL THROUGH HIGHWAYS
OTHER THROUGH HIGHWAYS
OTHER ROADS
In unfamiliar areas inquire locally before using any unsigned roads
SPECIAL FEATURES
STATE PARKS
RECREATION AREAS
SELECTED REST AREAS
POINTS OF INTEREST
SKI AREAS
SCHEDULED AIRLINE STOPS
MILITARY AIRPORTS
TOURIST INFORMATION
MILEAGES
POPULATION SYMBOLS
State Capital
EXPLANATION OF ACTIVITIES
Major League Spectator
Minor League Spectator
Collegiate/Participant
Rivers, Trails, Major Parks, and Forests
© H.M. GOUSHA
Lithographed in U.S.A.

Tourist Regulations for Visitors to the United States

LEAVING CANADA-Citizens of Canada and of Commonwealth countries with permanent resident status in Canada may travel in the United States without passport or visa. However, it is advisable that visitors carry proof of their permanent resident status, or some other identifying document, such as birth or baptismal certificate, driver's license, or similar papers bearing the owner's signature and photograph. Although there is no limitation on funds taken into or out of the United States, if you import or export an amount of $10,000 or more you must file a report of the transaction with U.S. Customs.

A Canadian visitor may take back to Canada in his personal baggage, duty free goods up to a value of $20.00, excluding tobacco and alcohol, providing the visitor has been away at least 24 hours, and $100.00 if away at least 48 hours. Also, after an absence of seven days or more (not counting the day of departure) he may take back duty free goods up to the value of $300.00, once in each calendar year. At no time may alcoholic beverages exceed 40 ounces (1.1 liters) per person. All values stated are in Canadian funds.

ENTERING THE UNITED STATES-Report to the U.S. Customs and Immigration Offices at the point of entry into the U.S. for clearance. A non-resident of the U.S. may enter free of duty or internal revenue tax, an automobile, trailer, motorcycle or boat to be used for his personal transportation, to be exported upon his departure. Every 6-month period a $100 exemption is allowed on gifts accompanying non-residents who will remain in the U.S. at least 72 hours. Persons not eligible may be entitled to a $25 exemption for gifts or articles for personal or household use. Consult Customs Officer for special regulations governing the importation of alcoholic beverages and tobacco.

Correct at date of publication, but subject to change. TR9

DISTANCES IN MILES AND KILOMETERS

Miles are in red; kilometers in black

	Charlottetown, P.E.I.	Edmonton, Alta.	Fredericton, N.B	Halifax, N.S.	Medicine Hat, Alta.	Montreal, Que.	Ottawa, Ont.	Prince Rupert, B.C.	Quebec, Que.	Regina, Sask.	St. John's, N.F.	Saskatoon, Sask.	Sault-Ste. Marie, Ont.	Thunder Bay, Ont.	Toronto, Ont.	Vancouver, B.C.	Victoria, B.C.	Whitehorse, Yukon	Windsor, Ont.	Winnipeg, Man.	Yellowknife, N.W.T.
CALGARY, ALTA.	4964 / 3085	294 / 183	4586 / 2850	5059 / 3144	293 / 182	3739 / 2324	3540 / 2200	1508 / 937	3998 / 2485	763 / 474	6245 / 3881	623 / 386	2742 / 1704	2051 / 1275	3471 / 2157	1061 / 659	1080 / 671	2314 / 1483	3857 / 2387	1371 / 852	1915 / 1190
CHARLOTTETOWN, P.E.I.		4983 / 3097	378 / 235	426 / 265	4581 / 2847	1218 / 757	1418 / 881	6471 / 4022	965 / 600	4154 / 2582	1253 / 779	4413 / 2743	2222 / 1381	2912 / 1810	1986 / 1234	6080 / 3779	6161 / 3829	7332 / 4557	2122 / 1319	3593 / 2233	6698 / 4163
EDMONTON, ALTA.			4605 / 2862	5078 / 3156	524 / 326	3829 / 2380	3720 / 2312	1464 / 910	4088 / 2541	843 / 524	6264 / 3893	526 / 326	2922 / 1816	2232 / 1387	3651 / 2269	1289 / 801	4755 / 870	2048 / 1273	4021 / 2499	1350 / 839	1757 / 1091
FREDERICTON, N.B				473 / 294	3944 / 2451	899 / 559	1099 / 683	6093 / 3787	634 / 394	3776 / 2347	1659 / 1031	4035 / 2508	1844 / 1146	2534 / 1575	1667 / 1036	5702 / 3544	5783 / 3594	6954 / 4322	1744 / 1084	3215 / 1998	6320 / 3928
HALIFAX, N.S.					4624 / 2874	1372 / 853	1512 / 940	6468 / 4020	962 / 598	4151 / 2580	1347 / 837	4410 / 2741	2212 / 1375	2903 / 1804	2080 / 1293	6071 / 3773	6151 / 3823	7329 / 4555	2119 / 1317	3590 / 2231	6436 / 4000
MEDICINE HAT, ALTA.						3356 / 2086	3157 / 1962	1891 / 1175	3615 / 2247	515 / 320	5810 / 3611	462 / 287	2447 / 1521	1757 / 1092	3176 / 1974	1352 / 840	1463 / 909	2751 / 1710	3546 / 2204	988 / 614	2460 / 1528
MONTREAL, QUE.							182 / 113	5247 / 3261	257 / 160	2930 / 1821	2499 / 1553	3189 / 1982	998 / 620	1688 / 1049	523 / 325	4856 / 3018	4936 / 3068	5767 / 3584	904 / 562	2368 / 1472	5474 / 3402
OTTAWA, ONT.								5047 / 3137	459 / 285	2730 / 1697	2698 / 1677	2935 / 1824	798 / 496	1488 / 925	396 / 246	4656 / 2894	4737 / 2944	5908 / 3672	901 / 560	2169 / 1348	5274 / 3278
PRINCE RUPERT, B.C.									5506 / 3422	2317 / 1440	7752 / 4818	2048 / 1273	4249 / 2641	3559 / 2212	4978 / 3094	1509 / 938	1590 / 988	1408 / 875	5284 / 3284	2814 / 1749	2722 / 1692
QUEBEC, QUE.										3189 / 1982	2246 / 1396	3448 / 2143	1257 / 781	1947 / 1210	787 / 489	5115 / 3179	5195 / 3229	6367 / 3957	1157 / 719	2627 / 1633	5733 / 3563
REGINA, SASK.											5435 / 3378	254 / 157	1932 / 1201	1242 / 772	2661 / 1654	1790 / 1114	1889 / 1174	2892 / 1797	3035 / 1884	572 / 356	2601 / 1615
ST. JOHN'S, N.F.												5701 / 3543	3503 / 2177	4053 / 2519	3266 / 2030	7073 / 4396	7184 / 4465	8370 / 5202	3617 / 2248	4737 / 2942	8051 / 5004
SASKATOON, SASK.													2338 / 1453	1648 / 1024	3067 / 1906	1699 / 1056	1810 / 1125	2632 / 1636	3418 / 2124	777 / 483	2339 / 1454
SAULT-STE. MARIE, ONT.														704 / 438	729 / 453	3710 / 2306	3821 / 2375	4769 / 2964	1099 / 683	1370 / 852	4476 / 2782
THUNDER BAY, ONT.															1419 / 882	3020 / 1877	3131 / 1946	4079 / 2535	1789 / 1112	692 / 430	3786 / 2353
TORONTO, ONT.																4439 / 2759	4550 / 2828	5498 / 3417	371 / 230	2100 / 1305	5207 / 3235
VANCOUVER, B.C.																	111 / 69	2434 / 1513	5557 / 3454	2339 / 1454	2784 / 1730
VICTORIA, B.C.																		2515 / 1563	4920 / 3058	2451 / 1523	2895 / 1799
WHITEHORSE, YUKON																			5645 / 3317	3398 / 2112	3050 / 1895
WINDSOR, ONT.																				2470 / 1535	5575 / 3465
WINNIPEG, MAN.																					3109 / 1930

The figure given in the space where columns intersect is approximate distance between the two points, computed over main traveled roads.

IV-665-J-X

How to Use the Sports Atlas

Gousha's **USA TODAY Sports Atlas** is the first comprehensive, hands-on, geographical guide to sports venues, events and activities ever published. From every baseball stadium in the country to sports-oriented national parks and forests, from ski resorts to 10K races, the USA offers a seemingly infinite supply of sports resources. We have created a structure to make all this information readily accessible, both on our state maps and in our accompanying state chapters. This introduction explains that structure by carefully following the sequence you will find in each chapter.

The text for each state covers two primary categories: **where to find sports activities to watch, and and where to find sports activities to do.**

The first category—sports to watch—is covered by our comprehensive **Spectator Venues** section. This includes all the primary professional venues for 16 sports, from auto racing to yachting. In addition to other useful information (see below), each venue is accompanied by a grid coordinate—e.g. [P.50, G-6]—so that readers may easily locate the venue on the corresponding state or city map, identifying its sport specific icon (see How to Read these Maps, inside front cover).

In the case where a venue is used by several different sports, it is listed under each separate sport subheading, with the appropriate information for that sport's tenant team or event. For instance, New York's Madison Square Garden, host to the Knicks, Rangers, and major tennis and track events, is listed separately in the New York chapter under Basketball, Hockey, Tennis and Track & Field. On the maps, that venue also carries the icons for all four sports.

In addition, listings for certain spectator (and outdoor) venues are marked by a blue diamond with extra text. These are venue notes, supplying added background or trivia information about select locales of the editors' choosing.

When a spectator venue category (e.g. Baseball) is not included in a chapter, the state has no teams, events or spectator facilities in that sport which meet our criteria.

Participant sports—sports to do—are represented in every state by two sections: **Outdoor Venues** and **Active Sports**.

Outdoor Venues include federal and state parks and recreation areas, and alpine and nordic ski facilities, all with map grid coordinates and all pinpointed on the state maps with specialized icons.

The **Active Sports** listing provides local contacts in each state for dozens of activities from aerobics to volleyball.

Each sport subheading in each section has its own explanation below, specifically detailing what information we have provided.

Each chapter begins with a brief **introduction** which characterizes sporting life in that state, and a **Stat Box**, with available vital statistics, from square miles to park acreage to the number of major league teams. In cases such as football's New York Giants—a squad which actually plays in New Jersey—the team would be credited to the stat boxes of both states.

Complementing and setting off the listings are **Snapshot** graphics from the pages of USA TODAY, **Tip Off** sidebars featuring editorial extras not found elsewhere in the Atlas (see Table of Contents on page 2), and quotes by well-known sports figures.

SPECTATOR VENUES

Auto Racing

We list the tracks for the top road series of the seven major auto racing circuits, (with every event listed under a particular venue accompanied by one of the following parenthetical abbreviations): the PPG Indy Car World Series of Championship Auto Racing Teams (CART); the Camel GT series of The International Motor Sports Association (IMSA); The Trans-Am Championships of the Sports Car Club of America (SCCA); The Winston Cup Series of The National Association of Stock Car Auto Racing (NASCAR); The national event schedule for the International Hot Rod Association (IHRA); the national events schedule of the National Hot Rod Association (NHRA); and the Silver Crown Series of the United States Automobile Club (USAC).

For each auto racing venue, we list the address, telephone, track length (choosing the longest where there are two circuits at the same venue), surface and type where applicable, and the name, month and circuit(s) of the race or races involved.

Baseball and Football

For Major League Baseball (MLB) and the National Football League (NFL) we list the name of the venue, address, year built, capacity, name of resident team, league, division or conference (in football, NFC indicates National Football Conference and AFC, American Football Conference), telephone number, year franchise began, local television and radio broadcast outlets, and all minor league affiliates (by city and class level, so they may be easily cross-referenced to other states).

For the baseball minor leagues we list the name of the venue, the address, the capacity, the name of the team, the league and class (e.g. International League, Class AAA), the telephone number, the year they entered the league, local broadcast outlets and their MLB affiliation. We have included the Pacific Coast, International, Eastern, Southern, Texas, California, Carolina, Florida State, Midwest, South Atlantic, New York-Penn, Northwest and Appalachian Leagues.

We list the World League of American Football as a minor league, with the same basic information, except that there are no team affiliations.

Basketball and Hockey

For the National Basketball Association (NBA) and the National Hockey League (NHL), we list the name of the arena, the address, when built, capacity, the name of the team, telephone, when the franchise began (with geographic history where applicable), league, conference and division, local broadcast outlets, and affiliates, where applicable.

For the two basketball minor leagues and the three hockey minor leagues, we list the name of each venue, the address, the capacity, the name of the team, the league, telephone, the year the franchise began or entered the league, local broadcasts and major league affiliation, where applicable.

Bowling, PGA/LPGA (golf), Rodeo, Tennis, Track & Field, Yachting

For these six event-oriented sports we list the name of the venue, the address, the phone number, the name of the event, and the month in which it takes place. We also include certain bowling and golf venues which have hosted major events, but do not necessarily do so every year. In those cases, we indicate the year the event was last held.

For bowling we also list whether the event is for men (PBA) or women (LPBA). For golf we indicate men, women or senior men (PGA, LPGA, Senior PGA), and list the number of holes in the event (divide by 18 for the number of days of the tournament). For rodeo, we chose the top 25 events in the USA as selected by the Professional Rodeo Cowboy's Association. For tennis, we indicate whether the event is sanctioned by the men's, women's or TeamTennis circuits (ATP, WTA, TT) as well as the court surface. For Track & Field we have primarily chosen national championships, annual invitationals and major marathons. For Yachting, we provide the base club for a variety of major events, sanctioned by the United States Yacht Racing Union.

College

For college, we list NCAA-sanctioned division 1 schools (football and/or basketball), with selected additions from lower divisions where an athletic program seemed to merit it from a spectator's standpoint.

For each school, we list the name of the school and its team, then the campus address, phone, name of stadium and capacity (if applicable), and name of fieldhouse and capacity (also if applicable.)

Horse Racing

For horse racing, we list the name of the track, the address, telephone number, when it opened, separate clubhouse and grandstand capacities where applicable, whether the track hosts thoroughbred or harness racing or both, and the months of the season(s).

Museums & Halls of Fame

For the institutions we have included, we list address and telephone number. Many of these have venue notes with further explanations.

Polo

For polo, in most cases we list polo clubs (sanctioned by the US Polo Association) which either host major events, or are ongoing, year round operations with a full-time clubhouse.

Soccer

For soccer, treated as a minor league in our listings and on our maps, we include the name of the stadium, the address, the capacity, the resident team, its league (American Professional Soccer League, or World Soccer League) and team telephone.

OUTDOOR VENUES

A range of recreational activities, (e.g. bike trails, boating, camping, etc.), indicated by our own letter code, are available in the federal and state parks system. The key to this code is included in every state. Call the local state tourism office (see Tip Off on p. 178) for a telephone contact to any individual park. Each of the listings in this section include a map page and grid coordinate indicating the corresponding map marking.

National Parks

In each state we list all major national parks, forests and recreation areas (with the exception, in some cases, of national historic sites and monuments), and the address or locale, the park acreage, and major available recreational activities indicated by the letter code.

State Parks

For every state, we note the most sports-relevant parks and recreation areas, as recommended by the state authorities. An (ac) after a park name indicates that it is under the jurisdiction of the Army Corps of Engineers. For each park we list address or locale with directions where available, acreage, and the recreational activity codes.

Skiing

We list top alpine and nordic resorts (under separate subheadings). For alpine, or downhill, resorts, we include the name of the resort, the address, the telephone, the vertical drop of the slopes in feet, and the number and type of lifts. For nordic, or cross-country, resorts, we list the address, and telephone.

ACTIVE SPORTS

Nearly every state lists one or more contact organizations for each of the following 31 activities, along with an address and telephone number. In a few cases, the listed contact is in a nearby state, which means that there is one regional contact for several states in that area. For states where you find no listing at all for a particular sport, check the listings of contiguous states, which may have a regional contact, or turn to the National Contacts Tip Off on p. 164. In the case of one or two organizations, there is just one national number (repeated in every state); this contact will refer you to a current local number.

Using these organizational contacts as a starting point will enable you to find everything in your area from the right Little League or hunting license to the right foot race or triathlon club. In many cases, the local contacts are volunteers who are participants themselves. In the rare case that a provided contact is unable to refer you to the new number, see the National Contacts Tip Off on p. 164 for the national headquarters.

In addition to using the parks, skiing facilities and active organization contacts, active readers can find resources between the lines. All of the colleges listed have sports facilities, some available to local residents, alumnae or visitors. And many of the facilities listed in Spectator Venues for bowling, tennis, yachting, and even polo and rodeo are available for use by the active sports enthusiast as well.

Listed below are the 31 active sports and their contact organizations, with any provisos necessary. Acronyms used in the listings are included here in parentheses.

Adventure

We list one of the five Outward Bound USA wilderness schools in each of the states in which there are programs, with regional numbers.

Aerobics

In nearly every state, we list a local contact for the Aerobics and Fitness Association of America (AFAA), a national certification body, which can steer you toward instructor classes or certified studios in your area.

Baseball

In each state we list a regional number for Little League, local and/or regional numbers for Pony Baseball/Softball, a local number for American Legion Baseball, and a regional number for Babe Ruth Baseball. In states which have no such listings, look under baseball in a contiguous state for a regional listing. In some states we list a local number for the Men's Senior Baseball League (MSBL), which is hardball for men over 30.

Billiards

We list a small range of well-known, local billiards or pool halls, with recommendations from (and thanks to) Billiards Digest.

Boardsailing

We list American Windsurfing Industries Association (AWIA, formerly ABIA) certified dealers with schools. We also list United States Windsurfing Association (USWA) regional directors.

Bowling

In every state, we list the American Bowling Congress' national number. They, in turn, can refer you to local leagues and events.

Canoeing and Kayaking

We list an American Canoe Association (ACA) regional vice-commodore, who can refer you to local clubs, events and schools.

Cycling

In most states we list three separate cycling organizations: regional contacts for the American Youth Hostel Councils (AYH), which can provide touring information; regional representatives for the United States Cycling Federation (USCF), which deals with competitive cycling, and the categorization of licensed riders; and regional directors for the League of American Wheelmen (LAW), an organization which can provide touring and club information.

Fitness

We list local contacts for the National Strength and Conditioning Association in the states which have one; otherwise we list their national office. We also list state branches of the National Association of Governors' Council on Physical Fitness and Sports.

Football

For Pop Warner Football (a juniors program) we list a national number which can refer you to the nearest league. For the United States Flag Football League (geared toward adults), we have a regional listing for some Eastern states.

Golf

We list state PGA sections, the participant arm of the Professional Golfer's Association, as well as local golf associations in most states. In addition to supporting amateur competition, the latter may be helpful in supplying specific public course information.

Hiking and Climbing

We list regional contacts for the Sierra Club and their affiliates, plus numerous state affiliates of the American Hiking Society (AHS), and other independent local organizations.

Hockey

Most states have a regional listing for a USA Hockey registrar who can help to connect you to amateur hockey for all ages.

Hunting & Fishing

We supply state fish & game numbers for licensing and season information. Where space allows, we also include certified Orvis dealerships, and regional contacts for Trout Unlimited.

Lacrosse

In most states, we list regional chapters of the Lacrosse Foundation.

Racquetball

We list regional contacts for The American Amateur Racquetball Association (AARA).

Riding

Most states have a local contact for American Horse Councils, a starting point in looking for schools and competition.

Rodeo

We list the regional circuits of the Professional Rodeo Cowboy's Association (PRCA), the organization's semi-amateur arm.

Running

The Road Runner's Club of America (RRCA) representatives in nearly all states should be able to direct you to regional clubs and local events.

Scuba

We list as many Professional Association of Diving Instructors (PADI)-sanctioned five star dive centers in each state as space allows.

Shooting

Most states have listings for National Sporting Clays Association (NSCA) affiliated ranges and clubs, as well as independent local clubs.

Skating

We list a national contact of the United States Figure Skating Association. (USFSA) in every state, as well as both state and regional branches of speedskating's National Skating Union.

Soccer

Nearly every state lists the local association affiliated with the United States Soccer Federation (USSF), the state association(s) affiliated with the United States Youth Soccer Association (YSA), and regional directors, or a national contact, for the American Youth Soccer Organization (AYSO).

Softball

We list one or more state contacts for the American Softball Association (ASA), where applicable.

Squash

Courtesy of the United States Squash Racquets Association (USSRA), we list certain local clubs open to non-members, some affiliated with the USSRA. Where there is no listing, see the number in the National Contacts Tip Off on p. 164.

Swimming

We list Local Masters Swimming Committee (LMSC) registrars for the state and regional subdivisions of United States Masters Swimming.

Table Tennis

Most states provide a contact for a local US Table Tennis Association state coordinator.

Tennis

We list the regional program coordinators for TEAMTENNIS (the recreational division of the professional league), plus state and/or regional sections of the United States Tennis Association (USTA), which administer numerous youth and masters programs.

Triathlon

Courtesy of the Triathlon Federation/USA, we list local clubs, where applicable.

Volleyball

We list the state United States Volleyball Association (USVBA) commissioners, where applicable.

Whitewater Rafting

In most states we list local touring companies who are member outfitters of the industry's trade organization, America Outdoors.

Dedications:

To my coach Frank, and his coach Cy.
— f-stop fitzgerald

To all the B's who've had to listen to the game.
— W.B.

Alabama

Bring your rods and reels to this state: Lake Eufala (in the southeast) is a great spot for big bass, Lake Weiss (northeast) is a haven for crappie fishing, and deep sea fishing in the Gulf of Mexico is a drawing card for Mobile. ◆ Alabama's most famous bear, late football coach Paul "Bear" Bryant, is commemorated in his own museum at the University of Alabama's Tuscaloosa campus. Yes, his famous houndstooth hat is on display. ◆ The 70,000-seat Talladega Superspeedway (with room for 70,000 more in the infield), hosts two annual NASCAR Winston Cup stock car races: the Winston 500 and Talledega Diehard 500. ◆ And you can catch future baseball millionaires at Class AA games in Birmingham (Chicago White Sox) and Huntsville (Oakland Athletics).

SPECTATOR VENUES

Auto Racing

TALLADEGA SUPERSPEEDWAY
Off I-20, adjacent to airport, Talladega **[P. 6, E-5]**; (205) 362-2261. Track is 2.66 miles.
◆The biggest speedway in the world. In 1989, Bill Elliott set a world record for stock car racing by qualifying for the Winston 500 at the amazing speed of 212.809 miles per hour.
Winston 500 (NASCAR Winston Cup), May. Diehard 500 (NASCAR Winston Cup), July.

Baseball

HOOVER METROPOLITAN STADIUM
100 Ben Chapman Drive, Bessemer **[P. 6, E-4]**. Capacity: 10,000
Birmingham Barons (Southern League, Class AA); (205) 988-3200. Entered League in 1981. Broadcasts by WERC 960 AM. MLB affiliation, Chicago White Sox.

JOE W. DAVIS STADIUM
3125 Leeman Ferry Rd., Huntsville **[P. 6, A-4]**. Capacity: 10,250
Huntsville Stars (Southern League, Class AA); (205) 882-2562. Entered League in 1985. Broadcasts by WKGL 1450 AM. MLB affiliation, Oakland Athletics (1985).

College Sports

ALABAMA A&M UNIVERSITY BULLDOGS
Normal **[P. 6, B-4]**; (205) 851-5365. Joe Davis, capacity 11,000. Health Building, capacity 7,000.

ALABAMA STATE UNIVERSITY HORNETS
915 S. Jackson Street, Montgomery **[P. 7, N-7]**; (205) 293-4444. Cramton Bowl, capacity 24,600. C.J. Dunn Arena, capacity 3,600.

AUBURN UNIVERSITY TIGERS
Auburn **[P. 6, G-6]**; (205) 844-4750. Jordan Hare, capacity 85,187. Memorial, capacity 13,500.

SAMFORD UNIVERSITY BULLDOGS
800 Lakeshore Drive, Birmingham **[P. 9, D-3]**; (205) 870-2966. Seibert, capacity 6,000. Bashinsky Field House, capacity not available.

TROY STATE UNIVERSITY TROJANS
University Avenue, Troy **[P. 7, J-6]**; (205) 566-8112. Memorial, capacity 12,000. Sartain, capacity 3,500.

TUSKEGEE UNIVERSITY GOLDEN TIGERS
Tuskegee Institute **[P. 7, H-6]**; (205) 727-8849. Alumni Bowl, capacity 10,000. James Center Arena, capacity 5,000.

UNIVERSITY OF ALABAMA BLAZERS
UAB Station, Birmingham **[P. 9, C-3]**; (205) 934-3402. Civic Center, capacity 17,000.

UNIVERSITY OF ALABAMA CRIMSON TIDE
Tuscaloosa **[P. 6, F-3]**; (205) 348-3600. Bryant-Denny, capacity 70,000. Coleman Coliseum, capacity 15,043.
◆Football country. Fans love to yell, "Roll Tide" — loud and often. Check out the museum dedicated to late football legend Paul "Bear" Bryant. Not so easy on the eyes are the plaid jackets favored by basketball coach Wimp Sanderson. The basketball pep band also dresses in the trademark jackets. The football team plays half its home games at Legion Field (Birmingham, AL), capacity 77,000.

UNIVERSITY OF SOUTH ALABAMA JAGUARS
Mobile **[P. 7, M-1]**; (205) 460-7121. Stanky Field, capacity 5,000. Municipal Auditorium, capacity 10,200.

Football

LEGION FIELD
401 8th Avenue West, Birmingham. **[P. 9, C-2]** Capacity: 72,000.
Birmingham Fire (World League of American Football, North American West Division); (205) 324-FIRE. Franchise began in 1991. Broadcasts by WERC AM, 960 AM.

Museums & Halls of Fame

ALABAMA SPORTS HALL OF FAME
1 Civic Center Plaza, Birmingham **[P. 9, C-3]**; (205) 323-6665.

INTERNATIONAL MOTORSPORTS HALL OF FAME
4000 Speedway Blvd., Talladega **[P. 6, E-5]**; (205) 362-5002.

PAUL W. BRYANT MUSEUM
300 Paul Bryant Drive, Tuscaloosa **[P. 6, F-3]**; (205) 348-4668.

UNITED STATES SPORTS ACADEMY/ AMERICAN SPORT ART MUSEUM
One Academy Dr., Daphne **[P. 7, M-2]**; (205) 626-3303.

OUTDOOR VENUES

National Parks

CONECUH NATIONAL FOREST
Andalusia **[P. 7, L-4]**. Contains 84,000 acres. **C HK F S**

TALLADEGA NATIONAL FOREST
Central Alabama **[P. 6, D-6 & F-3]**. Contains 371,272 acres. **C HK BT F S**

TUSKEGEE NATIONAL FOREST
NE of Tuskegee **[P. 6-7, H-6]**. Contains 10,791 acres. **C HK F S**

WILLIAM B. BANKHEAD NATIONAL FOREST
NW Alabama **[P. 6, C-3]**. Contains 181,237 acres. **C HK BT F S BK**

Bike Trails:BK
Boating: BT
Camping: C
Climbing: CL
Diving: DV
Fishing: F
Golfing: G
Hiking: HK
Hunting: HT
Riding: R
Surfing: SU
Swimming: S
Tennis: TE
Whitewater: WW
Winter Sports: W

STATBOX

POPULATION: 4,204,000
SQUARE MILES: 51,998
TIME ZONE: Central
MOTTO: Audemus Jura Nostra Defendre (We Dare Defend Our Rights)
BIRD: Yellowhammer
TREE: Southern Pine
CAPITAL: Montgomery
AVERAGE ANNUAL RAINFALL: 52"
MEAN TEMP: 47 (Jan.); 82 (July)
MAJOR LEAGUE TEAMS: 0
NATIONAL PARK/FOREST ACREAGE: 651,000
STATE PARK ACREAGE: 49,123
HIGHEST ELEVATION: 2,407'
LOWEST ELEVATION: sea level
WATERWAYS: 500,000 acres of lakes, rivers, and streams

State Parks

BUCK'S POCKET STATE PARK
2 mi. N of Groveoak **[P. 6, C-5]**. Contains 2,000 acres. **C HK BT F**

CHEAHA STATE PARK
29 mi. S of Anniston **[P. 6, E-6]**. Contains 2,799 acres. **C HK BT S BK**

CLAUDE D. KELLY STATE PARK
17 mi. N of I-65 at Atmore **[P. 7, L-3]**. Contains 960 acres. **C BT F S**

GULF STATE PARK
10 mi. S of Foley off AL 59 **[P. 7, N-2]**. Contains 6,000 acres. **C HK BT F S BK G**

JOE WHEELER STATE PARK - FIRST CREEK
2 mi. W of Rogersville via US 72 **[P. 6, B-3]**. Contains 2,550 acres. **C HK BT F S BK G**

LAKE GUNTERSVILLE STATE PARK
6 mi. NE of Guntersville off AL 227 **[P. 6, C-5]**. Contains 5,909 acres. **C HK BT F S BK G**

LAKEPOINT RESORT STATE PARK
7 mi. N of Eufaula, off US 431. **[P. 7, J-7]** Contains 1,220 acres. **C HK BT F S BK W G**

OAK MOUNTAIN STATE PARK
15 mi. S of Birmingham and 3 mi. E of US 31 from Pelham **[P. 6, E-4]**. Contains 9,940 acres. **C HK BT F S BK G**

PAUL M. GRIST STATE PARK
15 mi. N of Selma off AL 22 **[P. 6, G-4]**. Contains 1,080 acres. **C HK BT F S**

WIND CREEK STATE PARK
7 mi. SE of Alexander City off AL 63 **[P. 6, G-6]**. Contains 1,445 acres. **C HK BT F S**

Skiing

ALPINE SKIING

CLOUDMONT SKI RESORT
Lookout Mountain Parkway, Mentone **[P. 6, B-6]**; (205) 634-3841.
Vertical drop is 150 feet. Has two tows.

ACTIVE SPORTS

AEROBICS: AFAA, 250 Michigan Ave., #6, Mobil; (205) 433-1771.

BASEBALL: Little League Baseball Southern Region HQ, PO Box 13366, St. Petersburg, FL; (813) 344-2661. • **American Legion Baseball,** 2107 Maysville Rd., Huntsville; (205) 534-6316. • **Babe Ruth Baseball,** William E. Whitehurst, Rt. 2, Box 56, Grifton, NC; (919) 524-5525. • **Men's Senior Baseball League - Birmingham,** 5581 Cheryl Drive, Pinson; (205) 681-9504.

CONTINUED ON PAGE 131

USA SNAPSHOTS®

A look at statistics that shape the sports world

Ballpark benchmarks

Source: USA TODAY research

By Bob Laird, USA TODAY

Alabama

CONTINUED FROM PAGE 130

BOARDSAILING: USWA Regional Director, 2580 Prosperity Oaks Ct., Palm Beach Gdns., FL; (407) 881-0001.

BOWLING: American Bowling Congress, 5301 S. 76th St., Greendale, WI; (414) 421-6400.

CANOEING & KAYAKING: ACA Dixie Vice Commodore, 2320 Salcedo Street, Savannah, GA; (912) 352-0717.

CYCLING: LAW Southeastern Regional Director, 201 1st Ave., PO Box 2549, High Springs, FL; (904) 454-5000. • **USCF Alabama Representative,** PO Box 94520, Birmingham; (205) 854-2171.

FITNESS: Governor's Commission on Physical Fitness, 560 S. McDonough Street, Montgomery; (205) 242-4496.

FOOTBALL: Pop Warner Football, 1315 Walnut Street, Suite 1632, Philadelphia, PA; (215) 735-1450.

GOLF: Alabama Golf Association, 1025 Montgomery Highway, Suite 210, PO Box 20149, Birmingham; (205) 979-1234. • **PGA Dixie Section,** 601 Vestavis Parkway, Suite 142, Birmingham; (205) 822-0321.

HIKING & CLIMBING: Alabama Sierra Club Chapter, PO Box 55591, Birmingham; (205) 592-9233. • **Vulcan Trail Association (AHS),** PO Box 19116, Birmingham; (205) 991-7762.

HOCKEY: USA Hockey Southeastern Registrar, PO Box 5208, Takoma Park, MD; (301) 622-0032.

HUNTING & FISHING: Department of Conservation and Natural Resources, 64 N. Union St., Room 728, Montgomery; (205) 242-3465. • **Trout Unlimited,** 508 Sharpsburg Cir., Birmingham; (205) 956-9590.

RACQUETBALL: AARA, 3410 Chisholm Rd. #1212J, Florence; (205) 760-1121.

RODEO: PRCA Southeastern Circuit, 1111 S. McGee Rd., Bonifay, FL; (904) 547-2534.

SCUBA: Southeastern Divers, Inc., 908-A Bob Wallace Ave., Huntsville; (205) 536-8404. • **Southeastern Divers, Inc.,** 325 South Court Street, Florence; (205) 766-3483. • **The Dive Site, Inc.,** 191-G West Valley Avenue, Homewood; (205) 495-9111.

SKATING: USFSA, 20 First Street, Colorado Springs, CO; (719) 635-5200.

SOCCER: Alabama Soccer Ass'n, 2111 Woodledge Street, Birmingham; (205) 823-1464. • **Alabama YSA,** 3176 Cahaba Heights Road, Birmingham; (205) 967-8652. • **AYSO Regional Director,** 1405 Inman Drive, Huntsville; (205) 881-3138.

SOFTBALL: Alabama ASA, PO Box 227, Gadsden; (205) 442-1754. • **Jefferson County ASA,** 436 Cumberland Dr., Birmingham; (205) 833-4585.

TABLE TENNIS: USTTA State Coordinator, 2607 Sherwood Oaks Ct., Decatur; (205) 350-1182.

TENNIS: Recreational TEAMTENNIS Midwest-Southeast Region, National Program Coordinator, 445 N. Wells Street, Suite #404, Chicago, IL ; (800) TEAMTEN. • **Southern USTA,** 200 Sandy Springs Place, Suite 200, Atlanta, GA; (404) 257-1297.

TRIATHLON: War Eagle Triathletes, 272 Woodfield Dr., Auburn; (205) 844-9473

VOLLEYBALL: USVBA Southern Commissioner, PO Box 1799, Gadsden; (205) 442-5224.

Tip Offs

The Field of Dreams and other Sports Fantasy Trips

What better way to use the Sports Atlas, than to create your own sports fantasy vacation? These getaways have been popularized over the last few years by fans who wish to visit a series of personal sports shrines (and maybe discover some new ones) in the course of one trip. Time often necessitates creative juggling of team schedules, routes and preference to come up with the optimal itinerary.

There are two givens in this process: a) One of the best aspects of the trip is the fun and challenge of planning and b) the other highlights will be probably be all the surprises you never could have planned for in the first place. An early practitioner of this increasingly popular new road sport may have been W. P. Kinsella, the author of *Shoeless Joe,* a novel which was eventually made into the movie *Field of Dreams.* According to Kinsella, "In 1982, when we were promoting the book, we drove in our Datsun from Toronto to New York, and then back over to Los Angeles, and in the process saw games in those cities plus Detroit, Philadelphia, Pittsburgh, Kansas City and a few others." If you have similar dreams but less time, a sample tour, in honor of fantasy-pioneer Kinsella, might be the ***Field of Dreams* Midwest Meander**, (otherwise known as the Corn Field Cruise). Taking in Illinois, neighboring Iowa and Missouri, there are infinite possible versions of just this one trip, but the basic structure will give you an idea of the potential. In addition to Kinsella's superb *Shoeless Joe*, add a copy of Eliot Asinov's *Eight Men Out* (about Joe Jackson's 1919 'Black Sox') to your pre-trip reading list for historical context and local lore. Then throw in another Kinsella novel, *The Iowa Baseball Conspiracy* for the proper overall flavor.

Let the Trip Begin

Beginning in Chicago, any self-respecting fantasy-tripper should take time to preface the journey at the accepted local mecca, Wrigley Field. You may want to stop in at one of the adjacent Cubbie-oriented watering holes before the game to check out the atmosphere. Day games are preferable.

After the last out, travel northwest sixty miles, and back several years in the maturity of baseball talent, to start at the beginning. Having arrived in Rockford, head over to catch the Class A Expos of the Midwest League at cozy **Marinelli Field.** (For those with extra-baseball interests, the Rockford Polo Club, and the championship-level Don Carter bowling lanes are also in this neigborhood).

Having purified yourself in the cleansing waters of the low minor leagues, you are ready to proceed northwest to Iowa and then to the small town of Dyersville (pop. 3,825). Three-and-one-third miles northeast of town, you will drive right into your screen fantasies, the **Field of Dreams**, [P. 43, C-12] carved out of a cornfield.

"If you build it, he will come," the film promised. He did, and they do, year round and by the thousands. According to Katie Olberding of the local Chamber of Commerce (319-875-2311), there are always people out there on farmer **Don Lansing's field**, pitching, playing pickup games and generally soaking up the Lourdes-like atmosphere. The field has become Dyersville's most-visited attraction, and, of course, there is a souvenir shop at the site which sells t-shirts, baseball bats and other memorabilia. The only motel in town is the Colonial Inn, but there are camp-grounds which the chamber can direct you to. Farmer Lansing himself isn't around before 4:30 every afternoon, when he comes in from his fields.

Ball in the Corn Belt

Following the route of all true baseball dreamers, you will now have a tremendous urge to head back up the minor league ladder toward the bigs. (A regional fantasy trip for another time might be to visit all six minor league parks in this heartland state). Veer southwest through the corn fields to Des Moines (half-a-day's drive) and watch the competition heat up to near Major-League levels as the Iowa Cubs play class AAA ball at **Sec Taylor Stadium.** Then head a few miles further west to the small town of Adel, where at **Kinnick-Feller park** you can gaze upon the spot where the legendary school boy hurler and eventual Hall-of-Famer Bob Feller used to whiff his childhood playmates.

From this point follow the Des Moines River down to the Mississippi and then south to St. Louis, for a long-awaited reimmersion in The Show (make sure to consult and coordinate team schedules here). Catch the Cardinals at **Busch Stadium** in St. Louis, the city where Feller peers Dizzy Dean, Stan Musial and a host of other Hall-of-Famers have excelled since since 1876. (For that bowling fan in the backseat, the National Bowling Hall of Fame is here as well, plus the St. Louis Sports Hall of Fame).

When you have had your fill of blues clubs and the Redbirds, you can begin the trip back to Chicago. (Horse fanciers might have a hard time not veering east to Kentucky for a detour through thoroughbred tracks and farms). You might want to break the trip in Peoria and catch the next Ryne Sandberg playing for the Chiefs at **Meinen Field**, a class A Cubbie's affiliate. Or to change speeds, show up for some top-notch softball at the **Decatur Shootout** in June (217-423-2400).

Home Again

Try to time your return to Chicago to coincide with a White Sox game on the South Side. Even if the Sox are out of town, a proper postscript to this particular pilgrimage is a trip to the empty lot next to the new **Comiskey**, to pay homage to where Shoeless Joe Jackson and the infamous 1919 Black Sox actually labored. A game at the new Comiskey next door will bring you back to the future.

A glance at the state maps or text of the Atlas, will inspire countless fantasy trips, detours and simply... fantasies. Movie themes are not a bad place to start. For instance there is the *Slapshot* tour of minor league hockey (starting in Erie, PA and ideally travelling by Greyhound bus), or the *Bull Durham* tour of the Carolina League (starting where else but in **Durham Athletic Park** in Durham, NC, home of the Durham Bulls). Accompanying activities for either of these trips will be left up to the imagination and resources of the travellers. In no way should this be interpreted to mean that the editors endorse midnight mudsliding under the sprinklers in empty minor league ball parks.

On a final note, for those who want a sports vacation to be more than sitting and watching, the second and third sections of every state chapter (Outdoor Venues and Active Sports) are an ideal planner. As you wind your way toward your final destination, infinite possibilities present themselves. The sport key for national and state parks is your pass to hundreds of outdoor activities in each state, while the Active Sports section is entree to local activities from aerobics to whitewater. Swim one day, hike the next, ride a rented horse the day after, and top off your quadrathlon by arriving somewhere in time for a 5 or 10K run. The challenge is to stay on the road, yet still get your daily workout. It's a great way to see the country.

—Will Balliett

(Note: See Illinois, Iowa, Missouri, Pennsylvania and North Carolina listings for details on all of the venues mentioned.)

Alaska

With a coastline longer than that of the entire lower 48 states, and two of the USA's largest state parks, Alaska is a haven for outdoor sports. Nearly 400,000 recreational anglers harvest some 3.2 million fish each year. ◆ The Silver Salmon Derby every August in Seward—one of many such contests around the state—features a purse of over $40,000 (907-224-8051). ◆ In March, intrepid mushers cover 1,049 miles between Anchorage and Nome in the Iditarod, Alaska's famous sled dog race. (Course record, set in 1986 by Susan Butcher: 11 days, 15 hours.) ◆ The Fairbanks Goldpanners of Alaska League baseball—whose graduates include Tom Seaver and Mark McGwire—play a Midnight Sun Game every June 21. The game starts at 11 p.m. and has never needed lights in its 85-year history.

STATBOX

POPULATION: 525,000
SQUARE MILES: 586,412
TIME ZONE: Alaskan
MOTTO: North to the Future
BIRD: Willow Ptarmigan
TREE: Sitka Spruce
CAPITAL: Juneau
AVERAGE ANNUAL RAINFALL: 200" (southeast panhandle); 6-12" (arctic desert)
MEAN TEMP: 21 (Jan.); 55 (July)
MAJOR LEAGUE TEAMS: 0
NATIONAL PARK/FOREST ACREAGE: 54,750,000
STATE PARK ACREAGE: 3,200,000
HIGHEST ELEVATION: 20,320'
LOWEST ELEVATION: sea level
WATERWAYS: 3,000 rivers; 3,000,000 bodies of 20 acres or more

▶ SPECTATOR VENUES

College Sports

UNIVERSITY OF ALASKA FAIRBANKS NANOOKS
Fairbanks **[P. 8, A-6]**; (907) 474-7205. Carlson Center, capacity 4,700. Patty Center, capacity 2,000.

▶ OUTDOOR VENUES

National Parks

Bike Trails: BK
Boating: BT
Camping: C
Climbing: CL
Diving: DV
Fishing: F
Golfing: G
Hiking: HK
Hunting: HT
Riding: R
Surfing: SU
Swimming: S
Tennis: TE
Whitewater: WW
Winter Sports: W

CHUGACH NATIONAL FOREST
SE of Anchorage, surrounds Prince William Sound **[P. 8, D-3]**. Contains 5,936,000 acres.
C HK BT F W HT

DENALI NATIONAL PARK & PRESERVE
George Parks Hwy., near Healy **[P. 8, C-3]**. Contains 6,000,000 acres. **C HK F W CL**

GATES OF THE ARCTIC NATIONAL PARK & PRESERVE
N of Arctic Circle **[P. 8, B-3]**. Contains 8,500,000 acres. **C HK**

GLACIER BAY NATIONAL PARK & PRESERVE
Gustavus **[P. 8, E-5]**. Contains 3,280,000 acres. **C HK BT F**

KATMAI NATIONAL PARK & PRESERVE
Near King Salmon **[P. 8, E-2]**. Contains 4,159,000 acres. **C HK BT F**

KENAI FJORDS NATIONAL PARK
SE side of Kenai Peninsula **[P. 8, E-3]**. Contains 670,000 acres. **C HK BT F W**

KLONDIKE GOLDRUSH NATIONAL HISTORICAL PARK
Skagway **[P. 8, E-5]**. Contains 13,000 acres.**C HK**

KOBUK VALLEY NATIONAL PARK
100 mi. E of Kotzebue **[P. 8, B-2]**. Contains 1,750,421 acres. **HK BT F W**

LAKE CLARK NATIONAL PARK & PRESERVE
Port Alsworth **[P. 8, D-3]**. Contains 4,000,000 acres. **C BT F W WW**

TONGASS NATIONAL FOREST
Southeastern AK panhandle **[P. 8, E-4, F-6]**. Contains 17,000,000 acres. **C HK BT F W HT**

WRANGELL-ST. ELIAS NATIONAL PARK & PRESERVE
Glennallen **[P. 8, D-4]**. Contains 13,000,000 acres. **C HK BT F CL**

YUKON-CHARLEY RIVERS NATIONAL PRESERVE
Taylor and Steese Hwys. to Eagle and Circle **[P. 8, C-4]**. Contains 2,500,000 acres.
C BT F WW

State Parks

BIG LAKE NORTH STATE RECREATION SITE
5 North Big Lake Road **[P. 8, D-3]**. Contains 19 acres. **C BT F S W**

BIG LAKE SOUTH STATE RECREATION SITE
5.2 South Big Lake Road. Contains 16 acres **[P. 8, D-3]**. **C BT F S W**

CAPTAIN COOK STATE RECREATION AREA
24 mi. N of Kenai on N. Kenai Rd **[P. 8, D-3]**. Contains 3,466 acres. **C HK BT F S**

CHENA RIVER STATE RECREATION AREA
27 mi. W of Fairbanks on Chena Hot Springs Road **[P. 8, C-4]**. Contains 254,080 acres.
C HK BT F W

CHILKAT STATE PARK
7 mi. S of Haines on AK 7 **[P. 8, E-5]**. Contains 6,045 acres. **C HK BT F**

CHILKOOT LAKE STATE RECREATION SITE
10 Lutak Rd., N of Haines **[P. 8, E-5]**. Contains 80 acres. **C BT F S**

CHUGACH STATE PARK
E of Anchorage, Chugach Mountains **[P. 8, D-3]**. Contains 495,204 acres.
C HK BT F R BK W CL

DENALI STATE PARK
N of Talkeetna on Parks Hwy., Milepost 135-164 **[P. 8, D-3]**. Contains 324,240 acres.
C HK BT F

FINGER LAKE STATE RECREATION SITE
Bogart Rd., Palmer **[P. 8, D-3]**. Contains 47 acres. **C HK BT F S W**

FORT ABERCROMBIE STATE HISTORIC PARK
Kodiak **[P. 8, E-3]**. Contains 183 acres.
C HK BT F

HARDING LAKE STATE RECREATION AREA
W of Delta Junction **[P. 8, C-4]**. Contains 169 acres. **C BT F S W**

KACHEMAK BAY STATE PARK
Near Homer **[P. 8, E-3]**. Contains 328,290 acres. **C BT F**

NANCY LAKE STATE RECREATION AREA
Mile 67.2 Parks Hwy., S of Willow **[P. 8, D-3]**. Contains 22,685 acres. **C HK BT F W**

QUARTZ LAKE STATE RECREATION AREA
NW of Delta Junction on Richardson Hwy **[P. 8, C-4]**. Contains 600 acres. **C BT F S W**

TOK RIVER STATE RECREATION SITE
5 mi. E of Tok Junction on Alaska Hwy., Milepost 1309 **[P. 8, D-4]**. Contains 38 acres.
C BT F S

Skiing

ALPINE SKIING

ALYESKA RESORT
Girdwood **[P. 8, D-3]**; (907) 783-2222.
Vertical drop is 3,100 feet. Has two tows and five chairs.

EAGLECREST
Douglas Island, Juneau **[P. 8, E-5]**; (907) 586-5284.
Vertical drop is 1,400 feet. Has two chairs and one poma.

NORDIC SKIING

EAGLECREST SKI RESORT
155 S. Seward Street, Juneau **[P. 8, E-5]**; (907) 586-5284.

▶ ACTIVE SPORTS

ADVENTURE: Colorado Outward Bound School, 945 Pennsylvania Street, Denver, CO; (800) 477-2627.

AEROBICS: AFAA, General Delivery, Elmendorf AFB; (901) 753-3329. Attn: Colleen Anne Franks.

BASEBALL: Pony Baseball-Softball, 908 Redbird Drive, San Jose, CA; (408) 265-3309. • **American Legion Baseball,** 1200 W. Dimond #1472, Anchorage; (907) 344-4852. •**Babe Ruth Baseball,** Jim Lemp, 1911 Oxford Drive, Cheyenne, WY; (307) 638-6023.

BILLIARDS: Anchorage Billiard Palace, 4848 Old Sewards Hwy., Anchorage; (907) 562-4251 • **Son of River City Billiards,** 322 E. Fireweed, Anchorage.

BOARDSAILING: USWA Regional Director, 9889 N.W. Hoge, Portland, OR; (503) 286-6100.

BOWLING: American Bowling Congress, 5301 S. 76th St., Greendale, WI; (414) 421-6400.

CANOEING & KAYAKING: ACA Central Vice Commodore, 3410 Ridge Rd., N. Little Rock, AR; (501) 758-4716.

CYCLING: Alaska AYH Council, PO Box 24037, Anchorage; (907) 562-7772. • **USCF Alaska Representative,** PO Box 111095, Anchorage; (907) 344-1436.

FOOTBALL: Pop Warner Football, 1315 Walnut Street, Suite 1632, Philadelphia, PA; (215) 735-1450.

GOLF: Alaska Golf Association, PO Box 112210, Anchorage; (907) 349-4653. • **PGA Pacific Northwest Section,** 1201 M St. Southeast, Auburn, WA; (503) 222-1139.

HIKING & CLIMBING: Alaska Sierra Club Chapter, PO Box 103-441, Anchorage; (907) 276-8768. • **Taku Conservation Society (AHS),** 1700 Branta Rd., Juneau; (907) 789-7504.

HOCKEY: USA Hockey Alaska Registrar, 3301 W. 79th, Anchorage; (907) 243-1924. • **USA Hockey Pacific Registrar,** 5703 Sun Ridge Ct., Castro Valley, CA; (415) 886-0706.

HUNTING & FISHING: Department of Fish and Game, PO Box 3-200, Juneau; (907) 465-4100. • **Trout Unlimited,** HC 32, Box 6525Z5, Wasilla; (907) 746-1666.

SCUBA: Alaska Diving Service, 1601 Tongass, Ketchikan; (907) 225-4667.

SKATING: USFSA, 20 First Street, Colorado Springs, CO; (719) 635-5200.

SOCCER: Alaska Soccer Ass'n, 4103 Minnesota Dr., Anchorage; (907) 561-1653. • **Alaska State YSA,** PO Box 71879, Anchorage; (907) 345-2539. • **AYSO National Office,** 5403 W. 138th Street, Hawthorne, CA; (800) 421-5700.

SOFTBALL: Alaska ASA, 2950 Drake Dr., Anchorage; (907) 272-7683.

SQUASH: Elmendorf Air Force Base, Anchorage; (907) 552-1110.

SWIMMING: LMSC Alaska Registrar, 3051 Lois Drive, #507, Anchorage; (907) 274-3072.

TENNIS: Recreational TEAMTENNIS Central-West Region, National Program Coordinator, 2105 Grant Ave., #4, Redondo Beach, CA; (800) 992-9042. • **Pacific Northwest USTA,** 10175 SW Barbur Blvd., 306B, Portland, OR; (503) 245-3048.

VOLLEYBALL: USVBA Alaska Commissioner, 4165 Horizon, Anchorage; (907) 248-9052.

Tip Offs: Alaska Baseball

Alaska League

Fairbanks Goldpanners
Growden Park, Fairbanks, (907) 452-4456

Anchorage Bucs
Mulcahy Stadium, Anchorage
(907) 272-2827

Washington State Palouse Cougars
Washington State University Stadium, Pullman
(509) 332-3000

Hawaii Island Movers
Rainbow Stadium, Honolulu
(808) 948-6247

Alaska Central Baseball League

Anchorage Glacier Pilots
Mulcahy Stadium, Anchorage
(907) 274-3627

Mat-Su Miners
Herman Brothers Field, Palmer
(907) 745-6401

Kenai Peninsula Oilers
Oiler Field, Kenai
(907) 283-7133

Arizona

Though it is better known as the Grand Canyon State, Arizona is the baseball mecca of the West come February and March. Eight major league teams conduct spring training in the Cactus League, with six based in the Phoenix area. ◆ Other major spectator sports: NFL Cardinals, NBA Suns, college football's Fiesta Bowl (all in Phoenix), and the Copper Bowl and La Fiesta De Los Vaqueros rodeo (Tucson). ◆ Golf is a big draw with more than 200 facilities. And for those who'd rather watch the pros tee off, the PGA and LPGA Tours make annual stops (see below). ◆ Fast-car fans will thrill to the Phoenix Grand Prix in March. ◆ Saguaro Lake and Lake Powell are great for fishing and boating. And while it's tough to match the spectacular views at the Grand Canyon, Four Peaks and Organ Pipe National Monument are also beautiful hikes.

▶ SPECTATOR VENUES

Auto Racing

FIREBIRD RACEWAY
Gila River Indian Reservation, I-10 at Mariposa Exit, 10 mi. S of Phoenix, Chandler **[P. 9, H-1]**; (602) 268-0200. Track is quarter-mile strip (for NHRA races).
Motorcraft-Ford Arizona Nationals (NHRA), mid-February.

PHOENIX INTERNATIONAL RACEWAY
S of I-10, 115th Avenue & Baseline, Phoenix **[P. 10, G-4]**; (602) 252-3833. Track is 1-mile oval.
Skoal Bandit Copper World Classic (USAC Silver Crown), February.
Valvoline 200 (CART PPG Indy Car World Series), April.
Pyroil 500 (NASCAR Winston Cup), November.

PHOENIX STREET CIRCUIT
Btwn. Washington & Jefferson Sts. and 6th Ave. & 6th St., Phoenix **[P. 9, G-3]**; (602) 253-RACE. Track is 2.35-mile, 13-turn street course.
◆The country's one truly "foreign" sports event now takes place here; Formula One's USA Grand Prix has settled in downtown Phoenix for the past three years. Of the 100,000 spectators who turned up for the three-day festivities in 1991, most were from out of town. With strong followings in Southern California (from the race's Long Beach years) and in Japan, 50% of the crowd came from out of state and more than 16% from out of the country. Formula One's pit stops include Japan, Australia, Brazil, Mexico and Canada, as well its nine European countries. Former raceways in the USA have included Watkins Glen and Detroit. From 1976 to 1984, it ran in two US cities each year, adding Long Beach, Dallas and Las Vegas in the west.
United States Formula One Grand Prix, March.

Baseball

HI CORBETT FIELD
3400 E. Camino Campestre St., Tucson **[P. 9, D-7]**. Capacity: 9,500
◆Much of the movie *Major League* was filmed here. Scrambling to find a new spring tenant because Indians are leaving after 1992.
Tucson Toros (Pacific Coast League, Class AAA); (602) 325-2621. Entered League in 1969. Broadcasts by KTKT 990-AM. MLB affiliation, Houston Astros.

PHOENIX MUNICIPAL STADIUM
5999 E. Van Buren St., Phoenix **[P. 9, G-4]**. Capacity: 7,983
◆Spring training home of the Oakland Athletics.
Phoenix Firebirds (Pacific Coast League, Class AAA); (602) 275-0500. Entered League in 1958. Broadcasts by KTAR 620 AM. MLB affiliation, San Francisco Giants.

Basketball

ARIZONA VETERANS MEMORIAL COLISEUM
1826 West McDowell Road, Phoenix **[P. 9, G-2]**. Built in 1965. Capacity: 14,487.
Phoenix Suns (NBA Western Conf., Pacific Division); (602) 266-5753. Franchise began in 1968. Broadcasts by KTAR 620 AM, KUTP Channel 45, Dimension Cable (ASPN).

Bowling

GOLDEN PIN LANES
1010 W. Miracle Mile, Tucson **[P. 9, C-6]**; (602) 888-4272.
Tucson Open (PBA), July.

INCA LANES
1250 W. 16th St., Yuma **[P. 11, H-1]**; (602) 782-1814.
Yuma Open (LPBT), February.

TEMPE BOWL
1100 E. Apache Blvd., Tempe **[P. 9, G-4]**; (602) 967-1656.
Hammer Western Open (LPBT), May.

College Sports

ARIZONA STATE UNIVERSITY SUN DEVILS
Tempe **[P. 9, G-4]**; (602) 965-3482. Sun Devil, capacity 74,500. University Activity Center, capacity 14,287.

GRAND CANYON UNIVERSITY ANTELOPES
3300 West Camelback Boulevard, Phoenix **[P. 9, F-2]**; (602) 589-2806. Brazell Field, capacity 2,500. Antelope Gym, capacity 800.

NORTHERN ARIZONA UNIVERSITY LUMBERJACKS
Flagstaff **[P. 10, D-5]**; (602) 523-5353. Sky Dome, capacity 15,000. Sky Dome, capacity 6,500.

UNIVERSITY OF ARIZONA WILDCATS
Tucson **[P. 9, D-6]**; (602) 621-2681. Arizona, capacity 56,136. McKale Center, capacity 13,477.
◆McKale Center has become one of the toughest places to play since Coach Lute Olson built the team into a national power. Don't even think about tickets. The Wildcats are always sold out. The fans don't sit down until the opposing team scores its first basket. If you catch Olson with a hair out of place, you've seen something special.

Football

SUN DEVIL STADIUM
Fifth Street, Tempe **[P. 9, G-4]**. Built in 1958. Capacity: 72,000.
Phoenix Cardinals (NFC Eastern Division); (602) 379-0101. Franchise began in 1920. Broadcasts by KTAR.

Hockey

VETERANS MEMORIAL COLISEUM
Arizona State Fairgrounds, 1826 W. McDowell Road, Phoenix **[P. 9, G-2]**. Capacity: 13,737.
Phoenix Roadrunners (International Hockey League); (602) 252-6771. Franchise began in 1989. Broadcasts by KAMJ 1230 AM.

USA SNAPSHOTS®

A look at statistics that shape the sports world

Most-traded NBA players

Active players who have played on the most teams:

Source: National Basketball Association — By Julie Stacey, USA TODAY

STATBOX

POPULATION: 3,600,000
SQUARE MILES: 113,909
TIME ZONE: Mountain Standard (no daylight savings)
MOTTO: Ditat Deus (God enriches)
BIRD: Cactus Wren
TREE: Palo Verde
CAPITAL: Phoenix
AVERAGE ANNUAL RAINFALL: 7.5"
MEAN TEMP: Flagstaff 14/40 (Jan.), 50/80 (July); Phoenix 37/64 (Jan.), 77/104 (July)
MAJOR LEAGUE TEAMS: 2
NATIONAL PARK/FOREST ACREAGE: 1,307,000
STATE PARK ACREAGE: 39,773
HIGHEST ELEVATION: 12,670'
LOWEST ELEVATION: 70'
WATERWAYS: 492 square miles of inland water

Horse Racing

PRESCOTT DOWNS
Off Miller Valley Road, 828 Rodeo Drive, Prescott **[P. 10, E-4]**; (602) 445-0220. Opened in 1964. Total capacity: 4,800.
Thoroughbred season from May to Sep.
◆Before the track opened, races had been held on the fair grounds since 1913.

RILLITO RACE TRACK
4502 N. First Avenue, Tucson **[P. 9, C-6]**; (602) 293-5011. Opened in 1953. Clubhouse capacity: 650. Grandstand capacity: 3000.
Thoroughbred season from Nov. to Mar.

TURF PARADISE
1501 W. Bell Road, Phoenix **[P. 9, E-2]**; (602) 942-1101. Opened in 1956. Clubhouse capacity: 2,084. Grandstand capacity: 5,200.
Thoroughbred season from Oct. to May.

PGA/LPGA

DESERT MOUNTAIN
38580 N. Desert Mountain Parkway, Scottsdale **[P. 10, G-5]**; (602) 258-4084.
The Tradition at Desert Mountain (Senior PGA), Mar. Number of holes: 72.

MOON VALLEY COUNTRY CLUB
151 W. Moon Valley Dr., Phoenix **[P. 9, E-3]**; (602) 942-0000.
Standard Register Ping (LPGA), March. Number of holes: 72.

RANDOLPH PARK NORTH GOLF COURSE
602 North Alveron, Tucson **[P. 9, D-7]**; (602) 325-2811.
Ping/Welch's Championship (LPGA), Feb. Number of holes: 72.

TPC AT STARPASS
3645 W. 22nd Street, Tucson **[P. 9, D-5]**; (602) 325-2811.
Northern Telecom Open (PGA), Feb. Number of holes: 72.

TPC OF SCOTTSDALE
17020 N. Hayden Rd., Scottsdale **[P. 10, G-5]**; (602) 585-4334. Phoenix Open (PGA), Jan. Number of holes: 72.

Rodeo

TUCSON RODEO GROUNDS
4823 S. 6th Ave., Tucson **[P. 9, E-6]**; (602) 741-4703.
La Fiesta De Los Vaqueros, Feb.

VETERANS MEMORIAL COLISEUM
1826 W. McDowell Road, Phoenix **[P. 9, G-2]**; (602) 258-6711.
Phoenix Jaycees Rodeo of Rodeos, March.

YAVAPAI COUNTY FAIRGROUNDS
Rodeo Drive & Fairgrounds Ave., Prescott **[P. 10, E-4]**; (602) 445-3103.
Prescott Frontier Days, July.

CONTINUED ON PAGE 134

Arizona

CONTINUED FROM PAGE 133

Tennis

SCOTTSDALE PRINCESS
7575 E. Princess Dr., Phoenix **[P. 9, E-4]**; (602) 585-2733. Surface is hard.
◆Has previously hosted the Arizona Classic (WTA).

OUTDOOR VENUES

National Parks

Bike Trails: BK
Boating: BT
Camping: C
Climbing: CL
Diving: DV
Fishing: F
Golfing: G
Hiking: HK
Hunting: HT
Riding: R
Surfing: SU
Swimming: S
Tennis: TE
Whitewater: WW
Winter Sports: W

APACHE-SITGREAVES NATIONAL FOREST
Clifton & N **[P. 10, E-6]**. Contains 2,112,986 acres. **C HK BT F R W**

COCONINO NATIONAL FOREST
Flagstaff **[P. 10, E-5]**. Contains 1,827,435 acres. **C HK BT F R W**

CORONADO NATIONAL FOREST
Near Tucson **[P. 11, H-7, J-6, K-6, K-8]**. Contains 1,800,000 acres. **C HK BT F S R W**

GLEN CANYON NATIONAL RECREATION AREA
Page **[P. 10, A-5]**. Contains 1,236,880 acres. **C HK BT F S**

GRAND CANYON NATIONAL PARK
Grand Canyon **[P. 10, C-2, B-5]**. Contains 1,218,175 acres. **C HK F R**

KAIBAB NATIONAL FOREST
Williams **[P. 10, B-4]**. Contains 1,534,453 acres. **C HK BT F R W**

LAKE MEAD NATIONAL RECREATION AREA
Boulder City **[P. 10, C-1]**. Contains 1,495,666 acres. **C BT F S**

PETRIFIED FOREST NATIONAL PARK
I-40, E of Holbrook **[P. 10, E-7]**. Contains 93,533 acres. **HK**

PRESCOTT NATIONAL FOREST
Prescott **[P. 10, E-4]**. Contains 1,250,613 acres. **C HK BT F R**

TONTO NATIONAL FOREST
NE of Phoenix **[P. 10, F-5]**. Contains 2,900,000 acres. **C HK BT F S R**

STATE PARKS

ALAMO LAKE STATE PARK
38 mi. N of Wenden **[P. 10, F-2]**. Contains 5,642 acres. C HK BT F S

BUCKSKIN MOUNTAIN STATE PARK
11 mi. N of Parker on AZ 95 **[P. 10, F-2]**. Contains 1,676 acres. **C HK BT F S**

LAKE HAVASU STATE PARK
Lake Havasu City **[P. 10, F-2]**. Contains 11,839 acres. **C HK BT F S**

PAINTED ROCKS STATE PARK
27 mi. NW of Gila Bend **[P. 11, H-3]**. Contains 2,690 acres. **C HK BT F S**

PATAGONIA LAKE STATE PARK
12 mi. E of Nogales on AZ 82, 4 mi. N on gravel road **[P. 10, L-6]**. Contains 640 acres. **C HK BT F S**

PICACHO PEAK STATE PARK
40 mi. N of Tucson on I-10 **[P. 11, J-5]**. Contains 3,400 acres. **C HK**

> **"Arizona has snowskiing, a lot of hiking and a lot of golf throughout the state. I play golf, four to five times a week. . . all around the area of Tucson."**
>
> **Oakland Athletics pitching coach *Dave Duncan***

ROPER LAKE STATE PARK
6 mi. S of Safford **[P. 11, H-7]**. Contains 319 acres. **C HK BT F S**

SLIDE ROCK
8 mi. N of Sedona off US 89A **[P. 10, E-5]**. Contains 54 acres. **HK F S**

Skiing

ALPINE SKIING

FAIRFIELD SNOWBOWL
Highway 180 & Snowbowl Road, Flagstaff **[P. 10, D-4]** (602) 779-1951.
Vertical drop is 2,300 feet. Has four chairs.

SUNRISE SKI RESORT
Highway 273, E of McNary **[P. 10, F-8]**; (602) 735-7676.
Vertical drop is 1,800 feet. Has two tows, one bar and eight chairs.

NORDIC SKIING

FLAGSTAFF NORDIC CENTER
Route 4, Flagstaff **[P. 10, D-5]**; (602) 774-6216.

NORTH RIM NORDIC/CANYONEERS
Junction US 89A & AZ 67, Jacob Lake **[P. 10, B-4]**; (800) 525-0924.

ACTIVE SPORTS

ADVENTURE: Colorado Outward Bound School, 945 Pennsylvania Street, Denver, CO; (800) 477-2627.

AEROBICS: AFAA, 3448 N. Apache Circle, Chandler; (602) 527-0999.

BASEBALL: Little League Baseball Western Region HQ, 6707 Little League Dr., San Bernadino, CA; (714) 887-6444. • **Pony Baseball-Softball,** 1922 Goldboro Street, San Diego, CA; (619) 276-3094. • **American Legion Baseball,** 3702 W. Hearn Rd., Phoenix; (602) 938-1267. • **Babe Ruth Baseball,** Dennis R. Poarch, 809 W. Gibson Rd., Woodland, CA; (415) 581-6879. • **Men's Senior Baseball League - Tucson,** 4702 W. Placita de Suerte, Tucson; (602) 743-0604.

BILLIARDS: Golden Eight Ball Billiards, 2740 W. Indian School Rd., Phoenix; (602) 264-6068. • **Lucky Cue,** 1612 E. McDowell, Phoenix; (602) 256-0892.

BOARDSAILING: Alpine Ski Keller , Phoenix; (602) 968-9056. • **Sailboards & More ,** Tucson; (602) 327-0088. • **USWA Regional Director,** PO Box 6272, Laguna Niguel, CA; (714) 495-0368.

BOWLING: American Bowling Congress, 5301 S. 76th St., Greendale, WI; (414) 421-6400.

CANOEING & KAYAKING: ACA Pacific Vice Commodore, 3008 Blossom Ln., Redondo Beach, CA; (213) 542-8757.

CYCLING: Arizona-Southern Nevada AYH Council, 1046 E. Lemon St., Tempe; (602) 894-5128. • **USCF Arizona Representative,** PO Box ABC, Bisbee; (602) 432-5795.

FITNESS: Governor's Council on Health, Physical Fitness and Sports, 1740 W. Adams St., Room 409, Phoenix; (602) 542-6396. • **National Strength and Conditioning Ass'n State Director,** Glendale Community College, 6000 W. Olive, Glendale; (602) 435-3787.

Tip Offs: Hiking with the Baby

For those active parents who want to introduce their baby to the joys of the outdoors, author and hiker Cindy Ross (*Journey on the Crest: Walking 2,600 miles from Mexico to Canada*) has some tips.

- Invest in a high-performance quality backpack made especially to carry babies, preferably one with a high back and front supports for the neck, to allow for comfortable napping.
- Tie rattles, teething rings and small, soft, plush toys within baby's reach.
- Include a fast-acting fever reducer recommended by your pediatrician; also an insect repellent that won't irritate baby's skin.
- Include a hat in your baby's wardrobe, whether it is hot or cold. Like the rest of us, babies lose the majority of their body heat from their head and necks.
- Hike a trail you are familiar with, especially if you don't have a lot of backpacking experience. And perhaps most important of all: set out with no predetermined goals in terms of pace or daily mileage. In fact, put aside all expectations whatsoever. Be prepared to break about every hour, or when baby lets you know he or she wants out.
- Amongst the other provisions Ross and her husband brought on a multi-day hike with their four-month daughter were: a foam pad for changing; about a dozen washable diapers for each day on the trails; a line on which to air them out at night; and a plastic bag to carry them in until they arrived at an environmentally sound washing opportunity (e.g. home). For longer hikes, such a diaper bag can be stashed, and then retrieved on the return trip.

FOOTBALL: Pop Warner Football, 1315 Walnut Street, Suite 1632, Philadelphia, PA; (215) 735-1450.

GOLF: Arizona Golf Association, 11801 North Tatum Blvd., Suite 247, Phoenix; (602) 953-5990. • **PGA Southwest Section,** 11801 North Tatum Blvd., Suite 247, Phoenix; (602) 953-5990.

HIKING & CLIMBING: Central AZ Backpackers Assoc. (AHS), 5 South Pueblo Street, Gilbert; (617) 256-9184. • **Grand Canyon Sierra Club Chapter,** Route 4, Box 886, Flagstaff; (602) 774-1571. • **Green Valley Hiking Club (AHS),** 2481 South Avenida Loma Linda, Green Valley; (602) 648-0727. • **Huachuca Hiking Club (AHS),** 3705 Shawnee Drive, Sierra Vista; (602) 378-2517.

HOCKEY: USA Hockey Rocky Mountain Registrar, 7335 S. Garfield Ct., Littleton, CO; (303) 721-0936.

HUNTING & FISHING: Game and Fish Department, 2221 W. Greenway Rd., Phoenix; (602) 942-3000. • **Lee's Ferry Lodge (Orvis),** HC 67, Box 2, Marble Canyon; (602) 355-2261. • **Trout Unlimited,** c/o Bosco & DiMatteo, PC, 700 SW Financial Plaza, 3101 N. Central Ave., Phoenix; (602) 279-7460.

RACQUETBALL: AARA, 10424 S. 46th Way, Phoenix; (602) 893-7655.

RIDING: Arizona State Horsemen's Association, 8707 W. Northern Ave., Glendale; (602) 872-1272.

RODEO: PRCA Turquoise Circuit, 4010 W. Palo Seco, Tucson; (602) 744-2304.

RUNNING: RRCA AZ State Rep., PO Box 40728, Tucson; (602) 298-6833.

SCUBA: Arizona Scuba, 1632 Fourth Avenue, Yuma; (602) 783-1177. • **Desert Divers,** 3550 North 1st Avenue, Suite 260, Tucson; (602) 888-7300. • **El Mar Diving Center,** 2245 West Broadway, Mesa; (602) 833-2971. • **Scuba Ventures,** 2813 East McDowell Road, Phoenix; (602) 952-9307.

SKATING: USFSA, 20 First Street, Colorado Springs, CO; (719) 635-5200.

SOCCER: Arizona Soccer Ass'n, 4401 West Wagoner Road, Glendale; (602) 938-7396. • **Arizona YSA,** 4250 East Havasu, Tucson; (602) 299-9416. • **AYSO Regional Director,** 2971 N. Coronado St., Chandler; (602) 839-2114.

SOFTBALL: Arizona ASA, PO Box 1850, Prescott; (602) 445-5725. • **Phoenix ASA,** 6611 North 7th Drive, Phoenix; (602) 246-0183.

SQUASH: Crescent Hotel of Phoenix (USSRA), Phoenix; (602) 253-6181. • **Phoenix Downtown YMCA,** Phoenix; (602) 253-6181.

SWIMMING: LMSC Arizona Registrar, 3329 North Valencia Lane, Phoenix; (602) 946-5805.

TENNIS: Recreational TEAMTENNIS Central-West Region, National Program Coordinator, 2105 Grant Ave., #4, Redondo Beach, CA; (800) 992-9042. • **Southwestern USTA,** 2164 E. Broadway Rd., Suite 235, Tempe; (602) 921-8964.

VOLLEYBALL: USVBA Cactus Commissioner, 502 Oak, Prescott; (602) 776-9297.

WHITEWATER RAFTING: Adventure/Discovery Tours , 319 N. Humphrey, Flagstaff; (602) 774-1926. • **Arizona Raft Adventures ,** 4050 E. Huntington Dr., Dept. G, Flagstaff; (602) 526-8200. • **Arizona River Runners ,** Box 47788, Phoenix; (602) 867-4866. • **Expeditions, Inc.,** Rt. 4, Box 755, Flagstaff; (602) 774-8176. • **Worldwide Explorations, Inc. ,** Box 686, Flagstaff; (602) 774-6462.

Arkansas

Arkansas may be the only state in the union that holds a National Mule Jumping Contest (October, 501-451-1350). There's also a golf tournament designed by a former U.S. Open champ (Jack Fleck) and hosted by a rancher who "is kind enough every year to remove his cows" so that the 12-hole Booneville Open Cow Pasture Pool can take place (501-675-2666) ◆ With 500,000 acres of lakes, 9,700 miles of streams and rivers, 45 state parks and 60 percent of the state covered by timberland, it's no surprise that camping, fishing, canoeing, hiking and every conceivable outdoor activity are abundant here. ◆ And who needs major pro sports when you've got the University of Arkansas Razorbacks football and basketball teams, Double-A baseball (see below), and a thoroughbred race track (Oaklawn) that hosts a Kentucky Derby prep race?

► SPECTATOR VENUES

Baseball

RAY WINDER FIELD
War Memorial Park, off I-630, Little Rock **[P. 13, G-12]**. Capacity: 6,100
Arkansas Travelers (Texas League, Class AA); (501) 664-1555. Entered League in 1966. Broadcasts by KARN 920AM. MLB affiliation, St. Louis Cardinals.

College Sports

ARKANSAS STATE UNIVERSITY INDIANS
State University; (501) 972-3880 **[P. 13, B-10]**. Indian, capacity 18,709. Convocation Center, capacity 10,563.

UNIVERSITY OF ARKANSAS AT FAYETTEVILLE RAZORBACKS
Broyles Athletic Complex, Fayetteville **[P. 12, B-3]** (501) 575-2751. Razorbacks, capacity 55,000. Barnhill Arena, capacity 10,000.

UNIVERSITY OF ARKANSAS AT LITTLE ROCK TROJANS
2801 South University, Little Rock **[P. 12, G-12]**; (501) 569-3304. Barton Coliseum, capacity 8,303.

Horse Racing

OAKLAWN
Hot Springs National Park, Hot Springs **[P. 13, E-13]**; (501) 623-4411. Opened in 1905. Clubhouse capacity: 1,200. Grandstand capacity: 25,000.
Thoroughbred season from Feb. to Apr.

► OUTDOOR VENUES

National Parks

HOT SPRINGS NATIONAL PARK
US 270, US 70 or AR 7, Hot Springs **[P. 13, C-13]**. Contains 5,839 acres. **C HK S R**

OUACHITA NATIONAL FOREST
West central AR, extending into OK **[P. 12, D-3, E-6]**. Contains 1,591,849 acres. **C HK BT F S R BK HT**

OZARK NATIONAL FOREST
North central Arkansas **[P. 12, A-3, B-3, B-5, B-7, C-4]**. Contains 1,119,801 acres.
C HK BT F S R BK CL

ST. FRANCIS NATIONAL FOREST
East central Arkansas **[P. 13, E-10]**. Contains 20,977 acres. **C HK BT F S HT**

State Parks

- Bike Trails: BK
- Boating: BT
- Camping: C
- Climbing: CL
- Diving: DV
- Fishing: F
- Golfing: G
- Hiking: HK
- Hunting: HT
- Riding: R
- Surfing: SU
- Swimming: S
- Tennis: TE
- Whitewater: WW
- Winter Sports: W

BEAVER LAKE (AC)
Eureka Springs and Rogers **[P. 12, A-4]**. Contains 28,220 acres.
C HK BT F S DV

BULL SHOALS STATE PARK
14 mi. NW of Mountain Home via AR 5 & AR 178 **[P. 12, A-6]**. Contains 663 acres. **C HK BT F**

DE GRAY LAKE RESORT STATE PARK
7 mi. N of Arkadelphia on AR 7 **[P. 12, F-5]**. Contains 939 acres. **C HK BT F S BK W G**

GREERS FERRY LAKE (AC)
Heber Springs **[P. 12, C-7]**. Contains 40,000 acres. **C HK BT F S DV**

LAKE CATHERINE STATE PARK
AR 171, 15 mi. NW of Malvern **[P. 12, C-7]**. Contains 2,180 acres. **C HK BT F S**

LAKE DARDANELLE
Dardanelle **[P. 12, C-5]**. Contains 294 acres.
C HK BT F S BK

LAKE OUACHITA STATE PARK
6 mi. N of Mountain Pine or 15 mi. NW of Hot Springs **[P. 12, E-5]**. Contains 370 acres.
C HK BT F S

MORO BAY STATE PARK
SR 15, 21 mi. NE of El Dorado **[P. 12, H-7]**. Contains 117 acres. **C HK BT F S**

MOUNT NEBO STATE PARK
AR 155, 7 mi. W of Dardanelle **[P. 12, C-5]**. Contains 3,362 acres. **C HK F BK**

NORFORK LAKE (AC)
Norfork **[P. 12, A-7]**. Contains 45,480 acres.
C HK BT F S

PETIT JEAN STATE PARK
Morrilton **[P. 12, D-6]**. Contains 3,637 acres.
C HK BT F S

VILLAGE CREEK STATE PARK
AR 284, 13 mi. N of Forrest City **[P. 13, D-10]**. Contains 7,018 acres. **C HK BT F S BK**

WITHROW SPRINGS STATE PARK
AR 23, 5 mi. N of Huntsville **[P. 12, A-4]**. Contains 774 acres. **C HK BT F S**

► ACTIVE SPORTS

BASEBALL: Little League Baseball Southern Region HQ, PO Box 13366, St. Petersburg, FL; (813) 344-2661. • **Pony Baseball-Softball,** 7820 Pebbleford Dr., Ft. Worth, TX; (817) 293-1664. • **American Legion Baseball,** 1007 Wisconsin, Pine Bluff; (501) 534-7403. • **Babe Ruth Baseball,** James Wagoner, 2930 Jenny Lind, Fort Smith; (501) 646-3065. • **Men's Senior Baseball League - Central Arkansas,** 4606 N. Locust St., Little Rock; (501) 758-4613.

BILLIARDS: Slick Willie's, Markham & Victory, Little Rock; (501) 372-5505.

BOARDSAILING: USWA Regional Director, 18354 W. 58th Pl. #62, Golden, CO; (303) 279-3185.

BOWLING: American Bowling Congress, 5301 S. 76th St., Greendale, WI; (414) 421-6400.

CANOEING & KAYAKING: ACA Central Vice Commodore, 3410 Ridge Rd., North Little Rock; (501) 758-4716.

CYCLING: LAW South Central Regional Director, 1618 7th S., New Orleans, LA; (504) 899-8575. • **USCF Arkansas Representative,** 2720 Charter Oak Rd., Little Rock; (501) 225-6077.

FITNESS: National Strength and Conditioning Ass'n State Director, c/o Arkansas Sports Fitness, 15 Laurel Plaza, Conway; (501) 327-4229.

FOOTBALL: Pop Warner Football, 1315 Walnut Street, Suite 1632, Philadelphia, PA; (215) 735-1450.

GOLF: Arkansas Seniors Golf Association, 7002 Lucerne Dr., Little Rock; (501) 666-0951. • **Arkansas State Golf Association,** 2311 Biscayne Dr., Suite 308, Little Rock; (501) 277-8555. • **PGA South Central Section,** 2745 E. Skelly Dr., Ste. 103, Tulsa, OK; (918) 742-5672.

HIKING & CLIMBING: Arkansas Sierra Club Chapter, 1669 Carolyn Dr., Fayetteville; (501) 521-9794. • **Ozark Highlands Trail Ass'n (AHS),** 411 Patricia Lane, Fayetteville; (501) 442-2799.

HOCKEY: USA Hockey Southeastern Registrar, PO Box 5208, Takoma Park, MD; (301) 622-0032.

HUNTING & FISHING: Angler's Den (Orvis), 19 South Block St., Fayetteville; (501) 442-2193. • **Game & Fish Commission,** #2 Natural Resources Dr., Little Rock; (501) 223-6300. • **Trout Unlimited,** 2525 Country Way, Fayetteville; (501) 452-5703.

RACQUETBALL: AARA, 10119 Garrison Rd., Little Rock; (501) 868-9609.

RIDING: Arkansas Horse Council, 17501 Colonel Glenn Rd., Little Rock; (501) 851-3366.

RODEO: PRCA Southeastern Circuit, 1111 S. McGee Rd., Bonifay, FL; (904) 547-2534.

RUNNING: RRCA AR State Rep., 416 N. Maddox Rd., Pearcy; (501) 767-1591.

SCUBA: Arkansas Sport Divers, 500 South Locust, Pine Bluff; (501) 536-3483. • **Ricks Pro Dive 'N Ski Shop,** 2323 North Poplar, North Little Rock; (501) 753-6004. • **Scuba Services Company,** 37th and Grand, PO Box 2828, Station A, Fort Smith; (501) 785-4525. • **Sports Co,** 2007 West Sunset, Springdale; (501) 751-0636. • **Sportsco,** 824 West Walnut, Rogers; (501) 636-5346.

SHOOTING: Crowley Ridge Shooting Resort, Rt. 1, Box 350, Forrest City; (501) 633-3352. • **Sugar Creek Sporting Clays,** Rt. 4, Box 326, Bentonville; (501) 273-0848.

SKATING: USFSA, 20 First Street, Colorado Springs, CO; (719) 635-5200.

SOCCER: Arkansas State YSA, PO Box 1699, Springdale; (501) 751-7200. • **AYSO Regional Director,** 1405 Inman Dr., Huntsville; (205) 881-3138.

SOFTBALL: Arkansas ASA, 5110 Candlewick Ln., North Little Rock; (501) 753-8794.

SQUASH: Central YMCA, Little Rock; (501) 372-5421.

SWIMMING: LMSC Arkansas Registrar, 46 Alicante Way, Hot Springs; (501) 922-0683.

TABLE TENNIS: USTTA State Coordinator, 13 Chaparral Ln., Little Rock; (501) 225-9598.

TENNIS: Recreational TEAMTENNIS Midwest-Southeast Region, National Program Coordinator, 445 N. Wells, Ste. #404, Chicago, IL; (800) TEAMTEN. • **Southern USTA,** 200 Sandy Springs Place, Suite 200, Atlanta, GA; (404) 257-1297.

TRIATHLON: Little Rock Athletic Club Tri, PO Box 24856, Little Rock; (501) 225-3600.

VOLLEYBALL: USVBA Delta Commissioner, 305 Stonewall Dr., Jacksonville; (501) 982-1269.

STATBOX

POPULATION: 2,500,000
SQUARE MILES: 53,187
TIME ZONE: Central
MOTTO: The Natural State
BIRD: Mockingbird
TREE: Pine
CAPITAL: Little Rock
AVERAGE ANNUAL RAINFALL: 45" in the mountains; 50-55" in the delta
MEAN TEMP: 58-65
MAJOR LEAGUE TEAMS: 0
NATIONAL PARK/FOREST ACREAGE: 104,821
STATE PARK ACREAGE: 44,073
HIGHEST ELEVATION: 2,753'
LOWEST ELEVATION: 54'
WATERWAYS: 9,740 miles of streams; 35 large lakes (plus many small lakes)

"The thing that appeals to me is the wide variety of outdoors activities, including hunting and fishing. My favorite place is my own duck farm, the Double Deuce Duck Hunting Club outside of DeWitt."

New York Mets baseball star *Kevin McReynolds*

California

Pro sports fans have their choice of four NBA teams, five Major League Baseball teams, four NFL teams and the Gretzky franchise in the NHL (with a new NHL expansion team to come in San Jose). ◆ Water recreation, from fishing to surfing, boardsailing to whale watching, abounds along 1,100 miles of Pacific coastline. ◆ A pack of 100,000 runs in San Francisco's annual Bay to Breaker race (May), one of a continuous, statewide cycle of competitive events for athletes ranging from body builders to triathletes. ◆ Alpine and nordic skiing is plentiful, from Mammoth and Mt. Shasta to Royal Gorge and the world-class powder at Lake Tahoe. ◆ Joshua Tree is a climber's mecca, Yosemite is among the most sublime hiking high countries in the USA and the Pacific Crest Trail snakes along the spine of the Sierra Nevada, and can be bitten off in day-hike-size chunks.

STATBOX

- **POPULATION:** 29,063,000
- **SQUARE MILES:** 158,706
- **TIME ZONE:** Pacific
- **MOTTO:** Eureka (I have found it)
- **BIRD:** California Valley Quail
- **TREE:** California Redwood
- **CAPITAL:** Sacramento
- **AVERAGE ANNUAL RAINFALL:** 17" (no.); 12" (so.)
- **MEAN TEMP:** 45/75 (no.); 56/70 (so.)
- **MAJOR LEAGUE TEAMS:** 15
- **NATIONAL PARK ACREAGE:** 5,225,000
- **STATE PARK ACREAGE:** 1,306,780
- **HIGHEST ELEVATION:** 14,494'
- **LOWEST ELEVATION:** 282' below sea level
- **WATERWAYS:** 2,407 square miles of inland water

▶ SPECTATOR VENUES

Auto Racing

LEXPO STATE FAIRGROUNDS
Arden Way, Sacramento **[P. 14, G-2]**; (916) 446-7223. Track is 1-mile dirt oval.
Golden State 100 (USAC Silver Crown), June.

DEL MAR FAIRGROUNDS CIRCUIT
I-5 Via de La Valle exit, Del Mar **[P. 17, Q-11]**; (213) 437-0341. Track is 1.6 miles.
Camel Grand Prix of Greater San Diego Presented by Nissan (IMSA Camel GT), October.

LAGUNA SECA RACEWAY
1021 Monterey Highway 68, Salinas **[P. 16, K-5]**; (408) 648-5100. Track is 2.214-mile road.
Toyota Monterey Grand Prix (CART PPG Indy Car World Series), Oct.

LONG BEACH STREET CIRCUIT
100 W. Broadway, Long Beach **[P. 18, F-6]**; (213) 437-0341. Track is 1.67-mile temporary road
Toyota Grand Prix of Long Beach (CART PPG Indy Car Grand Prix), April.

LOS ANGELES FAIRPLEX
I-10, north of Fairplex Drive or White Ave. exits, Pomona **[P. 19, C-9]**; (818) 914-4761. Track is quarter-mile strip (for NHRA races).
Chief Auto Parts Winternationals (NHRA), early February.
Winston Finals (NHRA), late Oct.

SEARS POINT INTERNATIONAL RACEWAY
Highways 37 and 121, Sonoma **[P. 15, A-11]**; (707) 938-8448. Track is 2.52 miles.
The Banquet Frozen Foods 300 (NASCAR Winston Cup), June.
Autolite Motorcraft California Nationals (NHRA), late July.

Baseball

ANAHEIM STADIUM
2000 Gene Autry Way, Anaheim **[P. 19, E-8]**. Built in 1966. Capacity: 64,593
◆Nicknamed "The Big A."
California Angels (AL West); (714) 937-7200. Franchise began in 1961. Broadcasts by KMPC 710 AM, XPRS 1090 AM (Spanish), KTLA Channel 5, SportsChannel. Affiliates: Edmonton, Alberta (AAA); Midland, TX (AA); Palm Springs, CA (A); Quad City, Davenport, IA (A); Boise, ID (A); Mesa, AZ (rookie). Spring training held in Mesa, AZ and Palm Springs, CA.

BILLY HEBERT FIELD
Sutter and Alpine, Stockton **[P. 14, G-6]**. Capacity: 3,500
Stockton Ports (California League, Class A); (209) 944-5943. Entered League in 1941. Broadcasts by Community Access, Channel 30. MLB affiliation, Milwaukee Brewers.

CANDLESTICK PARK
Jamestown Ave. and Harney Way, San Francisco **[P. 15, D-11]**. Built in 1960. Capacity: 62,000
◆San Francisco is a popular stop with ballplayers, but not for the ballpark. It gets colder here in July than some parts of Alaska. Isolated on the beautiful Candlestick Point on the SF Bay, the park is warm and wonderful by day, but can get nasty at night.
San Francisco Giants (NL West); (415) 468-3700. Franchise began in 1876. Broadcasts by KNBR 680 AM, KTVU Channel 2. Affiliates: Phoenix, AZ (AAA); Shreveport, LA (AA); San Jose, CA (A); Clinton, IA (A); Everett, WA (Rookie). Spring training held in Scottsdale, AZ.

DODGER STADIUM
1000 Elysian Park Avenue, Los Angeles **[P. 18, C-5]**. Built in 1962. Capacity: 56,000
◆When the smog lifts, the walkways offer a spectacular view of Downtown L.A. and the San Bernardino mountains. Nattily attired ushers wear old-fashioned boaters. The valuable Chavez Ravine real estate is owned by the Dodgers, who are considered among the best corporations in the nation to work for. Always a celeb or two in the deluxe seats (and in manager Tom Lasorda's office). The Skipper owns a pasta-and-ribs place under his own name in nearby Pasadena. No tail gate parties in the parking lot.
Los Angeles Dodgers (NL West); (213) 224-1500. Franchise began in 1890. Broadcasts by KABC 790 AM, KWKW 1330 AM (Spanish), KTTV Channel 11. Affiliates: Albuquerque, NM (AAA); San Antonio, TX (AA); Bakersfield, CA (A); Vero Beach, FL (A); Great Falls, MT (Rookie); Kissimmee, FL (Rookie); Yakima, WA (A). Spring training held in Vero Beach, FL.

FISCALINI FIELD
1007 E. Highland, San Bernardino **[P. 19, C-12]**. Capacity: 3,500
San Bernardino Spirit (California League, Class A); (714) 881-1836. Entered League in 1987. Broadcasts by KCKC 1350 AM. MLB affiliation, Seattle Mariners.

JOHN THURMAN FIELD
501 Neece Drive, Modesto **[P. 14, G-6]**. Capacity: 2,500
Modesto A's (California League, Class A); (209) 529-7368. Entered League in 1966. MLB affiliation, Oakland A's.

MAVERICK STADIUM
1200 Stadium Road, Adelanto **[P. 17, N-11]**. Capacity: 3,500
High Desert Mavericks (California League, Class A); (619) 246-2687. Entered League in 1988. Broadcasts by KVVQ 910 AM, Q103 FM. MLB affiliation, San Diego Padres.

OAKLAND COLISEUM
Nimitz Freeway & Hegenberger Rd., Oakland **[P. 15, D-12]**. Built in 1968. Capacity: 47,313
◆Once called the "Mausoleum" in the low-attendance days with Charlie Finley as the A's owner, it now caters to fans with a family section, a great variety of food concessions (including the superlative Louisiana hot links) and is the first outdoor stadium to have a non-smoking policy.
Oakland Athletics (AL West); (415) 638-4900. Franchise began in 1901. Broadcasts by KSFO 560 AM, KPIX Channel 5, KICU-TV Channel 36, SportsChannel. Affiliates: Tacoma, WA (AAA); Huntsville, AL (AA); Modesto, CA (A); Madison, WI (A); Southern Oregon (A); Scottsdale, AZ (Rookie). Spring training held in Phoenix, Az.

PALM SPRINGS ANGEL STADIUM
1900 Baristo Road, Palm Springs **[P. 19, G-3]**. Capacity: 5,185
Palm Springs Angels (California League, Class A); (619) 325-4487. Entered League in 1986. MLB affiliation, California Angels.

USA SNAPSHOTS®

A look at statistics that shape the sports world

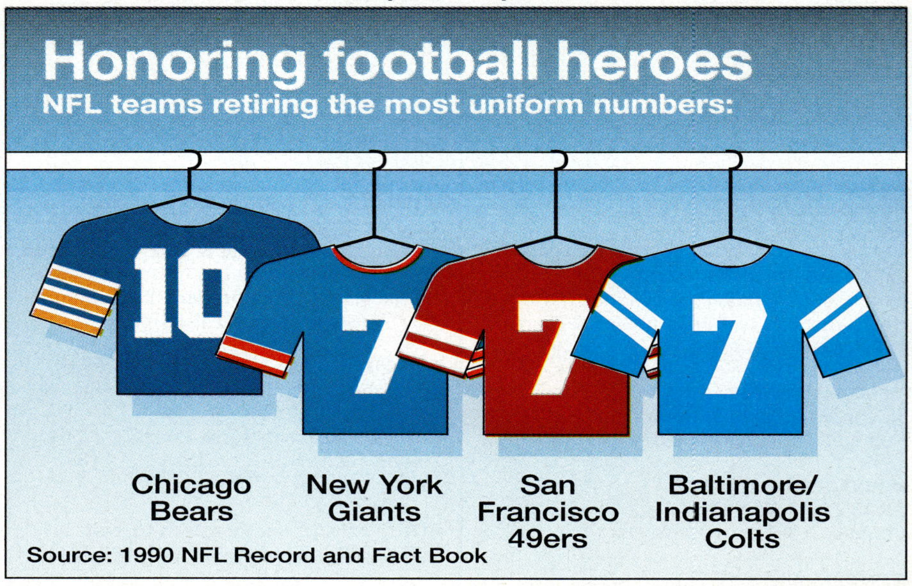

By Marty Baumann, USA TODAY

RECREATION PARK
440 Giddings Ave., Visalia **[P. 16, L-8]**. Capacity: 2,000
Visalia Oaks (California League, Class A); (209) 625-0480. Entered League in 1977. Broadcasts by KTIP 100 FM. MLB affiliation, Minnesota Twins.

SALINAS MUNICIPAL STADIUM/ CHET CHESHOLM FIELD
175 Maryal Dr., Salinas **[P. 16, K-5]**. Capacity: 3,000
Salinas Spurs (California League, Class A); (408) 422-3812. Entered League in 1989. Broadcasts by KSPB 91.9 FM. MLB affiliation, Independent.

SAM LYNN BALLPARK
4009 Chester Ave., Bakersfield **[P. 16, M-8]**. Capacity: 3,300
◆When injured L.A. Dodgers' pitcher Orel Hershiser threw five innings here during a rehabilitation assignment in May, 1991, fans camped out the night before to get seats, the stadium sold out and three thousand people were turned away. GM Rick Smith said, "This is the biggest thing to happen in Bakersfield — ever."
Bakersfield Dodgers (California League, Class A); (805) 322-1363. Entered League in 1941. MLB affiliation, Los Angeles Dodgers.

SAN DIEGO JACK MURPHY STADIUM
9449 Friars Rd., San Diego **[P. 18, F-2]**. Built in 1967. Capacity: 59,022
◆In 1990 became the first and only major-league park to sell sushi. Also became first (and no doubt, last) to have Roseanne Barr sing the national anthem. Look for sections of nothing but sailors in uniform from nearby bases on weekend games. The Padres were formed as a Pacific Coast League team in the 1930's, and gave Ted Williams his start in pro baseball as a pitcher and part-time outfielder.
San Diego Padres (NL West); (619) 283-7294. Franchise began in 1969. Broadcasts by KFMB 760 AM, XEXX AM, KUSI Channel 51, Cox Cable. Affiliates: Las Vegas, NV (AAA); Wichita, KS (AA); Victorville, CA (A); Waterloo, IA (A); Charleston, SC (A); Scottsdale, AZ (Rookie); Spokane, WA (Rookie). Spring training held in Yuma, AZ.

SAN JOSE MUNICIPAL STADIUM
10th & Alma St., San Jose **[P. 15, F-14]**. Capacity: 5,200
San Jose Giants (California League, Class A); (408) 297-1435. Entered League in 1948. Broadcasts by KSJS 90.7 FM. MLB affiliation, San Francisco Giants.

Basketball

ARCO ARENA
1 Sports Parkway, I-5 N to Del Paso exit, Sacramento **[P. 14, F-1]**. Built in 1988. Capacity: 17,014.
◆The Kings have gradually migrated across the continent, starting off in Rochester, New York in 1948, moving west to Cincinnati for fourteen years in 1958, stopping off in Kansas City from 1972 to 1978, and finally ending up in Sacramento.
Sacramento Kings (NBA Western Conf., Pacific Div.); (916) 928-0000. Franchise

CONTINUED ON PAGE 137

California

CONTINUED FROM PAGE 136

began in 1948. Broadcasts by KFBK 1530 AM, KRBK Channel 31, Pacific West.

L.A. MEMORIAL SPORTS ARENA
3939 South Figueroa Street, Los Angeles **[P. 18, D-5]**. Built in 1959. Capacity: 15,350.
◆Played in Buffalo 1970-78, then in San Diego until 1984. A nice, family atmosphere at the Sports Arena.
Los Angeles Clippers (NBA Western Conference, Pacific Division); (213) 748-8000. Franchise began in 1970. Broadcasts by KRLA 1110 AM, KTLA Channel 5.

OAKLAND COLISEUM ARENA
Nimitz Freeway & Hegenberger Road, Oakland **[P. 15, D-12]**. Built in 1966. Capacity: 15,025.
◆The Philadelphia Warriors moved west to San Francisco in 1952.
Golden State Warriors (NBA Western Conference, Pacific Division); (415) 638-6300. Franchise began in 1946. Broadcasts by KNBR 680 AM, KPIX Channel 5, KICU Channel 36, Pacific Sports Network.

SAN JOSE STATE ARENA
One Washington Square, 7th and San Carlos Streets, San Jose **[P. 15, F-13]**. Capacity: 5,000.
San Jose Jammers (Continental Basketball Association, National Conference, Western Division); (408) 272-3865. Entered League in 1989. Broadcasts by KSJ 1500 AM; KSJS 90.7 FM; KFJC 89.7 FM.

THE GREAT WESTERN FORUM
3900 West Manchester Boulevard, Inglewood **[P. 18, D-5]**. Built in 1967. Capacity: 17,505.
◆The Lakers moved from Minneapolis in 1960. What you hear is true; on any given night you are guaranteed to see at least one of the following: Jack Nicholson, John McEnroe, Michael Douglas, Dyan Cannon, super agent Michael Ovitz, Rob Lowe, Arsenio Hall. While the Hollywood celebs, their agents and other season ticket holders arrive for the second quarter (after paying up to $450 per seat), schmooze each other and scan the crowd with opera glasses, seats are beginning to open up in the upper levels. Although the Lakers still hold the edge by a longshot in regular season attendance, theirs has dropped by 15,000 since the 1988 championship season and the Kings', meanwhile, with the stellar presence of superstar Wayne Gretzky, has risen by 30,000. Still, the Laker Girls provide some of the best time out dancing in the business — even without Paula Abdul — who got her start as one.
Los Angeles Lakers (NBA Western Conference, Pacific Division); (213) 419-3100. Franchise began in 1948. Broadcasts by KLAC 570 AM, KCAL Channel 9, Prime Ticket.

Bowling

ACTIVE WEST TOWN SQUARE LANES
4135 Chicago Ave., Riverside **[P. 19, D-12]**; (714) 683-3800.
Kessler Classic (PBA), June.

CEDAR LANES
3131 N. Cedar, Fresno **[P. 16, P-7]**; (209) 222-4424.
Fresno Open (PBA), June.

EARL ANTHONY'S DUBLIN BOWL
6750 Regional St., Dublin **[P. 15, D-13]**; (415) 828-7550.
Kessler Open (PBA), June.

GABLE HOUSE BOWL
22501 Hawthorne Ave., Torrance **[P. 18, E-4]**; (213) 378-2265.
AC-Delco Classic (PBA), January.

PINOLE VALLEY LANES
1580 Pinole Valley Road, Pinole **[P. 15, B-11]**; (415) 724-9130.
ARC Pinole Open (PBA), January.

College Sports

CALIFORNIA POLY STATE UNIVERSITY MUSTANGS
San Luis Obispo **[P. 16, M-6]**; (805) 756-5802. Mustang, capacity 7,000. Robert A. Mott, capacity 4,000.

CALIFORNIA STATE POLY UNIVERSITY BRONCOS
3801 W. Temple Avenue, Pomona **[P. 19, C-9]**; (714) 869-2809. Kellogg Field, capacity 6,000. Kellogg Gym, capacity 5,000.

CALIFORNIA STATE UNIVERSITY TOROS
1000 E. Victoria, Carson **[P. 18, E-5]**; (213) 516-3893. Gym, capacity 4,200.

CALIFORNIA STATE UNIVERSITY TITANS
Fullerton **[P. 19, E-8]**; (714) 773-2677. Santa Ana, capacity 12,000. Titan Gym, capacity 4,000.

CALIFORNIA STATE UNIVERSITY 49ERS
1250 Bellflower Blvd., Long Beach **[P. 18, F-6]**; (213) 985-4655. Veterans Memorial, capacity 12,450. Long Beach Arena, capacity 12,000.

CALIFORNIA STATE UNIVERSITY MATADORS
18111 Nordhoff Street, Northridge **[P. 18, B-3]**; (818) 885-3208.

CALIFORNIA STATE UNIVERSITY HORNETS
6000 J Street, Sacramento **[P. 14, G-3]**; (916) 278-6481. Hornet, capacity 7,500.

CALIFORNIA STATE UNIVERSITY-FRESNO BULLDOGS
Fresno **[P. 16, P-7]**; (209) 268-2643. Bulldog, capacity 30,000. Selland, capacity 10,132.

LOYOLA MARYMOUNT UNIVERSITY LIONS
7101 West 80th Street, Los Angeles **[P. 18, D-4]**; (213) 338-2765. Gersten Pavilion, capacity 4,156.

PEPPERDINE UNIVERSITY WAVES
24255 Pacific Coast Highway, Malibu **[P. 18, C-2]**; (213) 456-4150. Firestone, capacity 3,104.

SAN DIEGO STATE UNIVERSITY AZTECS
San Diego **[P. 18, F-3]**; (619) 594-5163. San Diego Jack Murphy, capacity 60,500. San Diego Sports Arena, capacity 13,000.

SAN JOSE STATE UNIVERSITY SPARTANS
One Washington Square, San Jose **[P. 15, F-13]**; (408) 924-1200. Spartan, capacity 30,000. Civic Auditorium, capacity 2,700..

SANTA CLARA UNIVERSITY BRONCOS
Santa Clara **[P. 15, F-13]**; (408) 554-4063. Buck Shaw, capacity 10,000. Leavey Activity, capacity 5,000.

ST. MARY'S COLLEGE GAELS
Moraga **[P. 15, C-12]**; (415) 631-4390. St. Mary's, capacity 3,500. McKeon Pavilion, capacity 3,500.

STANFORD UNIVERSITY CARDINAL
Stanford **[P. 15, E,F-12]**; (415) 723-4591. Stanford, capacity 84,892. Maples Pavilion, capacity 7,800.

UNIVERSITY OF CALIFORNIA GOLDEN BEARS
Berkeley **[P. 15, C-12]**; (415) 642-0580. Memorial, capacity 76,780. Harmon Gym, capacity 6,600.

UNIVERSITY OF CALIFORNIA AGGIES
Davis **[P. 14, F-5]**; (916) 752-1111. Toomey Field, capacity 9,000. Recreation Hall, capacity 7,600.

UNIVERSITY OF CALIFORNIA ANTEATERS
Irvine **[P. 19, G-8]**; (714) 856-6931. Bren Events Center, capacity 5,000.

UNIVERSITY OF CALIFORNIA BRUINS
405 Hilgard Avenue, Los Angeles **[P. 18, C-4]**; (213) 825-8699. Rose Bowl, capacity 104,091. Pauley Pavilion, capacity 12,543.

UNIVERSITY OF CALIFORNIA GAUCHOS
Santa Barbara **[P. 16, N-7]**; (805) 893-3291. Harder, capacity 17,500. Events Center, capacity 6,000.

UNIVERSITY OF THE PACIFIC TIGERS
Pacific Avenue, Stockton **[P. 14, G-6]**; (209) 946-2472. Amos Alonzo Stagg Memorial Stadium, capacity 30,000. Spanos Center, capacity 6,000.

UNIVERSITY OF SAN DIEGO TOREROS
Alcala Park, San Diego **[P. 18, F-2]**; (619) 260-4803. USD, capacity 4,000. USD Sports Center, capacity 2,500.

UNIVERSITY OF SAN FRANCISCO DONS
San Francisco **[P. 15, D-10]**; (415) 666-6891. Negoesco, capacity 3,000. Memorial, capacity 4,500.

UNIVERSITY OF SOUTHERN CALIFORNIA TROJANS
University Park, Los Angeles **[P. 18, D-5]**; (213) 743-2222. L.A. Coliseum, capacity 92,500. L.A. Memorial Sports Arena, capacity 15,509.
◆Perhaps the most famous mascot in college football — a white stallion. The cheerleader dressed in Trojan garb gets the horse prancing when USC puts the ball in the end zone.

Football

ANAHEIM STADIUM
1900 S. State College Blvd., Anaheim **[P. 19, E-8]**. Built in 1966. Capacity: 69,008.
Los Angeles Rams (NFC Western Division); (714) 937-6767. Franchise began in 1937. Broadcasts by KMPC AM.

CANDLESTICK PARK
Jamestown Ave. and Harney Way, San Francisco **[P. 15, D-11]**. Built in 1960. Capacity: 65,729.
◆Not as windy in fall and winter. Beautiful setting, off the bay.
San Francisco 49ers (NFC Western Division); (408) 562-4949. Franchise began in 1946. Broadcasts by KGO.

HUGHES STADIUM
3835 Freeport Blvd., Sacramento City College, Sacramento **[P. 14, H-2]**. Capacity: 23,000.
Sacramento Surge (World League of American Football, North American West Division); (916) 354-1000. Franchise began in 1991. Broadcasts by KRAK 1140 AM.

LOS ANGELES MEMORIAL COLISEUM
3911 South Figueroa Street, Los Angeles **[P. 18, D-5]**. Built in 1923. Capacity: 92,488.
Los Angeles Raiders (AFC Western Division); (213) 322-3451. Franchise began in 1960. Broadcasts by KFI-AM, KWKW AM (Spanish).

SAN DIEGO JACK MURPHY STADIUM
9449 Friars Road, San Diego **[P. 18, F-3]**. Built in 1967. Capacity: 60,750.
◆No mass transit. Near the beautiful San Diego zoo.
San Diego Chargers (AFC Western Division); (619) 280-2111. Franchise began in 1960. Broadcasts by XTRA.

Hockey

COW PALACE
Geneva & Santos Streets, Daly City **[P. 15, D-10]**. Built in 1941. Capacity: 10,800.
◆Temporary home of the NHL expansion team San Jose Sharks, who will move to the new San Jose Arena (temporary name) at I-280 and Guadalupe Pkwy. in Fall, 1993. Projected seating capacity 19,000.
San Jose Sharks (NHL, Campbell Conference, Smythe Division); (408) 287-4275. Franchise began in 1991. Broadcasts by KICU Channel 36.

SAN DIEGO SPORTS ARENA
3500 Sports Arena Blvd., San Diego **[P. 18, F-2]**. Capacity: 13,200.
San Diego Gulls (International Hockey League); (619) 224-4171. Franchise began in 1990. Broadcasts by KCEO 1000 AM.

THE GREAT WESTERN FORUM
3900 West Manchester Blvd., Inglewood **[P. 18, D-5]**. Built in 1967. Capacity: 16,005.
Los Angeles Kings (NHL, Campbell Conference, Smythe Divsion); (213) 419-3160. Franchise began in 1967. Broadcasts by XTRA (690 AM), Prime Ticket Cable Network.

Horse Racing

ALAMEDA COUNTY FAIRGROUNDS
4501 Pleasanton Avenue, Pleasanton **[P. 15, D-13]**; (415) 846-2881. Opened in 1939. Grandstand capacity: 6,608.
Thoroughbred season from June to July.
◆Thirteen days of racing. Mixed meet, includes quarterhorses.

BAY MEADOWS
2600 S. Delaware Street, San Mateo **[P. 15, E-11]**; (415) 574-RACE. Opened in 1934. Clubhouse capacity: 4,000. Grandstand capacity: 20,000.
Thoroughbred season from Aug. to Jan.

CAL-EXPO RACE TRACK
1600 Exposition Blvd., Sacramento **[P. 14, G-3]**; (916) 924-2000. Opened in 1971. Clubhouse capacity: 634. Grandstand capacity: 6,200.
Harness season from Apr. to Aug.

DEL MAR THOROUGHBRED CLUB
Via de la Valle exit off I-5, Jimmy Durante Blvd., Del Mar Fairgrounds, Del Mar **[P. 17, Q-11]**; (619) 755-1141. Opened in 1937. Clubhouse capacity: 3,100. Grandstand capacity: 5,600. Total capacity: 15,300.
Thoroughbred season from July to Sep.
◆The best marriage of Surf & Turf. They say when the weather changes one degree the residents take notice. San Diego is only 30 minutes away.

FAIRPLEX PARK
1101 W. McKinley Ave., Pomona **[P. 19, C-9]**; (714) 623-3111. Opened in 1922. Grandstand capacity: 10,000.
Thoroughbred season from July to Sep.
◆Went parimutuel in 1933.

HOLLYWOOD PARK
1050 S. Prairie, Inglewood; (213) 419-1500 **[P. 18, D-5]**. Opened in 1938. Total capacity: 80,348.
Thoroughbred season from Apr. to July and in Nov. & Dec.
◆The prestigious and lucrative end-of-the-year race day, the Breeder's Cup, was inaugurated here in 1984 and returned in 1987. Watch the races during the day, then cross the street and see the Lakers or Kings play at the Great Western Forum at night.

LADBROKE AT GOLDEN GATE FIELDS
1100 East Shore Hwy., Albany **[P. 15, C-11]**; (415) 526-3020. Opened in 1947. Clubhouse capacity: 5,230. Grandstand capacity: 7,960. Total capacity: 18,000.
Thoroughbred season from Jan. to June.

LOS ALAMITOS RACE COURSE
4961 Katella Avenue, Los Alamitos **[P. 18, E-7]**; (714) 995-1234. Opened in 1951. Clubhouse capacity: 3,000. Grandstand capacity: 18,000.
Harness season from Dec. to Apr and Aug. to Oct. Thoroughbred season from July to Aug.

SAN JOAQUIN FAIRGROUNDS
1658 S. Airport Way, Stockton **[P. 14, G-6]**; (209) 466-5041. Opened in 1933. Grandstand capacity: 4,160. Total capacity: 5,660.
Thoroughbred season from June to Nov.
◆Thirteen days only of live racing.

SANTA ANITA PARK
Huntington Drive & Colorado Place, Arcadia **[P. 18, B-7]**; (818) 574-7223. Opened in 1934. Clubhouse capacity: 2,660. Grandstand capacity: 15,589. Total capacity: 85,000.
Thoroughbred season from Dec. to Apr.
◆No vista is as impressive as the San Gabriel Mountains seen from the track here. Santa Anita stunned the racing world in 1935 by offering a $100,000 purse for the Santa Anita Handicap, a race which (now at $1,000,000) has become the oldest, continually-run hundred grand stakes in the nation. A half-century later, the third

CONTINUED ON PAGE 138

California

CONTINUED FROM PAGE 137

Breeder's Cup would become the richest day in sports when $15,410,409 were wagered here in a single day (a record since topped by the 1988 Kentucky Derby).

SOLANO COUNTY FAIRGROUNDS
900 Fairgrounds Drive, Vallejo **[P. 15, A-12]**; (707) 644-4401. Opened in 1951. Total capacity: 4,000.
Thoroughbred season in July.
◆Thirteen days of racing.

SONOMA COUNTY FAIRGROUND
1350 Bennett Valley Road, Santa Rosa **[P. 14, F-4]**; (707) 545-4200. Opened in 1936. Grandstand capacity: 5,181. Total capacity: 8,181.
Thoroughbred season from July to Aug.
◆Thirteen days of racing.

THE HUMBOLDT COUNTY FAIRGROUNDS
5th & Arlington, Ferndale **[P. 14, C-2]**; (707) 786-9511. Opened in 1896. Grandstand capacity: 2,700.
Thoroughbred season in August.
◆Ten days of racing.

Museums & Halls of Fame

AMATEUR ATHLETIC FOUNDATION OF LOS ANGELES
2141 W. Adams Blvd., Los Angeles **[P. 18, D-5]**; (213) 730-9600.
◆Houses the best sports library around.

INTERNATIONAL GYMNASTICS HALL OF FAME
227 Brooks Street, Oceanside **[P. 17, P-10]**; (619) 722-0606.

RALPH W. MILLER GOLF LIBRARY AND MUSEUM
1 Industry Hills Parkway, City of Industry **[P. 19, D-9]**; (818) 853-3453.

ROSE BOWL ROOM
Pasadena Tournament of Roses, 391 S. Orange Grove Blvd., Pasadena **[P. 18, C-6]**; (818) 449-4100.

SAN DIEGO HALL OF CHAMPIONS SPORTS MUSEUM
1649 El Prado, Balboa Park, San Diego **[P. 18, F-2]**; (619) 234-2544.
◆Includes the International Surfing Hall of Fame.

PGA/LPGA

BERMUDA DUNES COUNTRY CLUB
42-360 Adams St., Bermuda Dunes **[P. 19, G-13]**; (619) 345-2771.
Bob Hope Chrysler Classic (PGA), Jan. Number of holes: 90.

INDIAN WELLS COUNTRY CLUB
4600 Club Dr., Indian Wells **[P. 19, H-14]**; (619) 345-2561.
Bob Hope Chrysler Classic (PGA), Jan. Number of holes: 90.

LA COSTA RESORT & SPA
Costa del Mar Rd., Carlsbad **[P. 17, P-11]**; (619) 438-9111.
Infiniti Tournament of Champions (PGA) and Infiniti Senior Tournament of Champions (Senior PGA), Jan. Number of holes: 72.

LOS COYOTES COUNTRY CLUB
8888 Los Coyotes Dr., Buena Park **[P. 18, E-7]**; (714) 521-6171.
MBS LPGA Classic, Sep. Number of holes: 72.

MISSION HILLS COUNTRY CLUB
34-600 Mission Hills Dr., Rancho Mirage **[P. 19, G-14]**; (619) 321-8400.
Nabisco Dinah Shore (LPGA), March. Number of holes: 72.

OJAI VALLEY INN & COUNTRY CLUB
Country Club Dr., Ojai **[P. 16, N-8]**; (805) 646-5796.
GTE West Classic (Senior PGA), March. Number of holes: 54.

PEBBLE BEACH GOLF LINKS
17-Mile Dr., Pebble Beach **[P. 16, K-5]**; (408) 624-3811.
AT&T Pebble Beach National Pro-Am (PGA), Feb. Number of holes: 72.

PGA WEST
55955 PGA Blvd., La Quinta **[P. 19, H-13]**; (619) 564-8100.
◆Gorgeous, desert setting.
Skins Game (PGA), Nov. Number of holes: 36.

RANCHO MURIETA COUNTRY CLUB
14813 Jackson Rd., Rancho Murieta **[P. 14, F-6]**; (916) 985-7200.
Raley's Senior Gold Rush (Senior PGA), Oct. Number of holes: 54.

RANCHO PARK GOLF COURSE
10460 W. Pico Blvd., Los Angeles **[P. 18, D-4]**; (213) 838-7373.
Security Pacific Senior Classic (Senior PGA), Oct. Number of holes: 54.

RIVIERA COUNTRY CLUB
1250 Capri Dr., Pacific Palisades **[P. 18, C-3]**; (213) 454-6591.
Nissan Los Angeles Open (PGA), Feb. Number of holes: 72.

SHERWOOD COUNTRY CLUB
320 West Stafford Road, Thousand Oaks **[P. 18, B-2]**; (805) 496-3036.
RMCC Invitational (PGA), Nov. Number of holes: 54.

SILVERADO COUNTRY CLUB
1600 Atlas Peak Rd., Napa **[P. 14, F-4]**; (707) 257-0200.
Transamerica Senior Golf Championship (Senior PGA), Oct. Number of holes: 54.

SPYGLASS HILL GOLF COURSE
Spyglass Hill Rd. & Stevenson Dr., Pebble Beach **[P. 16, K-5]**; (408) 625-8563.
AT&T Pebble Beach National Pro-Am (PGA), Feb. Number of holes: 72.

STONERIDGE COUNTRY CLUB
17166 StoneRidge Country Club Lane, Poway **[P. 17, Q-11]**; (619) 487-2138.
Inamori Classic (LPGA), April. Number of holes: 72.

THE VINTAGE CLUB
75001 Vintage Drive West, Indian Wells **[P. 19, G-14]**; (619) 340-0500.
Vintage Arco Invitational (Senior PGA), Mar. Number of holes: 54.

TORREY PINES MUNICIPAL GOLF COURSES
11480 N. Torrey Pines Rd., La Jolla **[P. 18, E-1]**; (619) 452-3226.
Shearson Lehman Hutton Open (PGA), Feb. Number of holes: 72.

Polo

ELDORADO POLO CLUB
50950 Madison, Indio **[P. 19, H-14]**; (619) 342-2223.

EMPIRE POLO CLUB
81-800 Ave. 51, Indio **[P. 19, H-14]**; (619) 342-3321.

FAIR HILLS POLO CLUB
2735 Santa Maria Rd., Topanga **[P. 18, C-3]**; (818) 347-5049.

GREENBRIAR POLO CLUB
3648 E. Lincoln, Sacramento **[P. 14, H-1]**; (209) 632-8546.

HORSE PARK POLO CLUB
Whiskey Hill Rd. & Sand Hill Rd., Woodside **[P. 15, E-11]**; (415) 854-0251.

SANTA BARBARA POLO CLUB
3375 Foothill Rd., Santa Barbara **[P. 16, N-7]**; (805) 684-6683.

VENTURA POLO CLUB
Ventura **[P. 16, O-8]**; (805) 684-5879.

WILL ROGERS POLO CLUB
Will Rogers State Park, Los Angeles **[P. 18, C-3]**; (213) 566-8284.

Rodeo

SALINAS RODEO GROUNDS
1034 N. Main St., Salinas **[P. 16, K-5]**; (408) 424-1375.
California Rodeo, July.

Soccer

NEWARK MEMORIAL STADIUM
39375 Cedar Blvd., Newark **[P. 15, E-12]**. Capacity: 4,000.
San Francisco Bay Blackhawks (American Professional Soccer League, Western Conference); (415) 736-1571.

SAN DIEGO SPORTS ARENA
3500 Sports Arena Blvd., San Diego **[P. 18, F-2]**. Capacity: 12,884.
San Diego Sockers (Major Soccer League); (619) 224-4625.

VENUE TO BE ANNOUNCED
Real California (American Professional Soccer League).
◆Formerly Real Santa Barbara. Relocating. To resume league play in 1992.

Tennis

BONO RESTAURANT
1700 N. Indian Canyon, Palm Springs **[P. 19, B-14]**; (619) 322-6200. Surface is hard.
Virginia Slims of Palm Springs (WTA), Feb.

CIVIC AUDITORIUM
99 Grove Street, San Francisco **[P. 15, C-11]**; (415) 239-4800. Surface is Supreme.
Volvo Tennis/San Francisco (ATP), February.

GOLD RIVER RACQUET CLUB
2201 Gold Rush Dr., Gold River **[P. 14, F-6]**; (916) 638-7001. Surface is Extol (hard).
Sacramento Capitals (TT), July to August.

GREAT WESTERN FORUM
3900 W. Manchester Blvd., Inglewood **[P. 18, D-5]**; (213) 419-3257. Surface is Taraflex.
Los Angeles Strings (TT), July to August.

HYATT GRAND CHAMPIONS RESORT
44-600 Indian Wells Lane, Indian Wells **[P. 19, H-14]**; (619) 340-3166. Surface is Plexi-Pave.
Newsweek Champions Cup (ATP), March.

JOHN WAYNE CLUB
1171 Jamboree Rd., Newport Beach **[P. 19, F-8]**; (714) 644-6900. Surface is hard.
◆An Orange County tennis mecca.
Newport Beach Dukes (TT), July to August.

LA COSTA RESORT AND SPA
El Camino Real & Costa del Mar Road, Carlsbad **[P. 17, P-11]**; (619) 438-5683. Surface is hard.
Mazda Tennis Classic (WTA), July and Aug.

LOS ANGELES TENNIS CENTER-UCLA
420 Circle Drive West, Los Angeles **[P. 18, C-4]**; (213) 208-3838. Surface is hard.
Volvo Tennis/Los Angeles (ATP), July to August.

MANHATTAN COUNTRY CLUB
1330 Park View Ave., Manhattan Beach **[P. 18, E-4]**; (213) 546-7753. Surface is hard.
Virginia Slims of Los Angeles (WTA), August.

OAKLAND-ALAMEDA COUNTY COLISEUM ARENA
Nimitz Freeway and Hegenberger Rd., Oakland **[P. 15, D-12]**; (415) 569-2121. Surface is Supreme.
Virginia Slims of California (WTA), November.

Track & Field

LOS ANGELES SPORTS ARENA
3939 S. Figueroa St., Los Angeles **[P. 18, C-5]**; (213) 278-2030.
Sunkist Invitational (TAC Grand Prix Event), Feb.

STREETS OF LONG BEACH
Ocean Blvd., Long Beach **[P. 18, E-6]**; (213) 494-2664.
Long Beach Marathon (US Women's National Championship),May.

STREETS OF SAN FRANCISCO
San Francisco **[P. 15, C-10]**; (415) 681-2323.
San Francisco Marathon, June.

STREETS OF LOS ANGELES
L.A. Memorial Coliseum, Los Angeles **[P. 18, D-5]**; (213) 444-5544.
Los Angeles Marathon, March.

THE GREAT WESTERN FORUM
3900 W. Manchester Blvd., Inglewood **[P. 18, D-4]**; (800) LAT-IMES, ext. 75771.
Times Indoor Games (TAC Grand Prix Event), Feb.

Yachting

CORINTHIAN YACHT CLUB OF SAN FRANCISCO
Foot of Main St., Tiburon **[P. 15, C-11]**; (415) 435-4771.
Adams Cup (U.S. Women's Sailing Championship/USYRU), Sept.

KING HARBOR YACHT CLUB
280 Yacht Club Way, Redondo Beach **[P. 18, E-4]**; (213) 376-2559.
◆Host of Mallory Cup (US Men's Sailing Championship) in 1990.

LONG BEACH YACHT CLUB
6201 Appian Way, Long Beach **[P. 18, F-6]**; (213) 598-9401.
◆Host of U.S. Multihull Championship (Alter Cup) in 1990.

NEWPORT HARBOR YACHT CLUB
720 W. Bay Ave., Balboa **[P. 19, G-8]**; (714) 673-7730.
◆Host of USYRU/Rolex Jr. Sailing Championship in 1990.

SAN DIEGO YACHT CLUB
1011 Anchorage Ln., San Diego **[P. 18, F-1]**; (619) 221-8400.
U.S. Women's Singlehanded, Doublehanded and Boardsailing Championships, March, 1991.

SAUSALITO YACHT CLUB
Sausalito **[P. 15, C-10]**; (415) 332-7400.
Leiter Trophy (USYRU/Rolex Junior Women's Sailing Championships), Aug.

ST. FRANCIS YACHT CLUB
On The Marina, San Francisco **[P. 15, C-11]**; (415) 563-6364.
St. Francis International Masters Regatta, Oct.

TAHOE YACHT CLUB
at 5190 West Lake Blvd., Homewood **[P. 73, J-1]**; (702) 329-9084.
◆The Concourse d'Elegance, August. Offices are in Reno, NV.

► OUTDOOR VENUES

National Parks

ANGELES NATIONAL FOREST
E of I-5 & W of San Bernadino County **[P. 17, N-9 & P. 18, B-7]**. Contains 691,000 acres.
C HK BT F S R BK W

CHANNEL ISLANDS NATIONAL PARK
US 101 to Ventura **[P. 16, O-7 & P. 17, P-9]**. Contains 249,353 acres. **C HK BT F S DV**

CLEVELAND NATIONAL FOREST
Laguna, Palomar, & Santa Ana Mountains, near San Diego **[P. 19, E-10 & P. 17, P-10 & Q-12]**. Contains 420,630 acres. **C HK BT R W**

CONTINUED ON PAGE 139

California

CONTINUED FROM PAGE 138

Bike Trails: BK
Boating: BT
Camping: C
Climbing: CL
Diving: DV
Fishing: F
Golfing: G
Hiking: HK
Hunting: HT
Riding: R
Surfing: SU
Swimming: S
Tennis: TE
Whitewater: WW
Winter Sports: W

ELDORADO NATIONAL FOREST
US 50 & Hwy. 88 to Echo Summit **[P. 14, F-7]**. Contains 586,724 acres. **C HK BT F S R W**

GOLDEN GATE NATIONAL RECREATION AREA
San Francisco **[P. 15, B & C-10]**. Contains 73,000 acres. **HK F S R BK**

INYO NATIONAL FOREST
On CA 395 btwn. Lone Pine and Lee Vining **[P. 15, G-10 & P. 17, J-15 & P. 17, L-15]**. Contains 1,931,115 acres. **C HK BT F S R BK W**

JOSHUA TREE NATIONAL MONUMENT
Off CA 10 & CA 62, S of Twentynine Palms **[P. 17, O-13 & P. 19, F-13]**. Contains 558,000 acres. **C HK R BK CL**

KLAMATH NATIONAL FOREST
Off I-5 **[P. 14, A-3 & 5]**. Contains 1,726,000 acres. **C HK BT F S R BK W WW**

LASSEN VOLCANIC NATIONAL PARK
Off Hwy. 89 or CA 36 & 44 **[P. 15, A & B-8 & 9]**. Contains 1,006,000 acres. **C HK BT F S R BK W**

LASSEN NATIONAL FOREST
I-5 to Red Bluff, then CA 36, or CA 44 from Redding, or I-395 to CA 36 **[P. 14 C-5 & 6 & P. 15, A & B-8 & 9]**. Contains 1,100,000 acres. **C HK BT F S R BK W HT**

LOS PADRES NATIONAL FOREST
Btwn. Monterey & Morro Bay **[P. 16, L-5, M-7, N-7]**. Contains 1,752,539 acres. **C HK F S R BK W HT**

MENDOCINO NATIONAL FOREST
N of San Francisco **[P. 14, D-4]**. Contains 884,231 acres. **C HK BT F S R**

MODOC NATIONAL FOREST
Northeastern corner of CA **[P. 14, A & B-6 & 7]**. Contains 1,663,320 acres. **C HK BT F S R BK W HT**

PINNACLES NATIONAL MONUMENT
Via CA 25 & 146 **[P. 16, K-5]**. Contains 16,250 acres. **HK CL**

PLUMAS NATIONAL FOREST
Off CA 70, or CA 89, or CA 49 **[P. 14, D-7]**. Contains 1,146,900 acres. **C HK BT F S R BK W CL**

POINT REYES NATIONAL SEASHORE
40 minutes N of San Francisco **[P. 14, G-3]**. Contains 74,000 acres. **C HK F R BK**

REDWOOD NATIONAL PARK
US 101, between Crescent City & Orick **[P. 14, A-2]**. Contains 106,000 acres. **C HK F S R BK WW**

SAN BERNARDINO NATIONAL FOREST
San Bernardino & Riverside Counties **[P. 19, B & G-11]**. Contains 670,284 acres. **C HK BT F S R BK W CL**

SANTA MONICA MOUNTAINS NATIONAL RECREATION AREA
Btwn. Griffith Park & Los Posas Rd. and btwn. Pacific Coast Highway & 101 **[P. 18, C-2 & 3]**. Contains 150,050 acres. **C HK F S R BK**

SEQUOIA & KINGS CANYON NATIONAL PARKS
On CA 198 from US 99 or off US 99 to CA 180 **[P. 17, K & L-14]**. Contains 864,500 acres. **C HK F R W CL**

SEQUOIA NATIONAL FOREST
S of Fresno & N of Bakersfield **[P. 17, L-9 & 14]**. Contains 1,100,000 acres. **C HK BT F R W WW**

SHASTA NATIONAL FOREST
Northern CA **[P. 14, B & C-4]**. **C HK BT F S R W WW**

> **"When I'm at home in Bakersfield, and I want to relax, I drive over to Oxnard, take my boat out to the Channel Islands and down around Catalina to go sport fishing. I usually have good luck there catching bonito, tuna, marlin, dorado and barracuda."**
>
> **Indy car driver *Rick Mears***

SIERRA NATIONAL FOREST
NE of Fresno-Clovis area, off CA 168, CA 41 **[P. 15, D-9, H-9]**. Contains 1,303,047 acres. **C HK BT F S R W WW**

SIX RIVERS NATIONAL FOREST
NW corner of state, via US 199, CA 299, CA 36, or CA 96 **[P. 14, A-3]**. Contains 958,543 acres. **C HK BT F R W WW**

SMITH RIVER NATIONAL RECREATION AREA
Northern district of Six Rivers National Forest **[P. 14, A-2]**. Contains 305,337 acres. **C HK F S R BK WW**

STANISLAUS NATIONAL FOREST
Off CA 120, CA 108, CA 4 **[P. 15, C-8]**. Contains 898,902 acres. **C HK BT F S R BK W CL**

TAHOE NATIONAL FOREST
W of Lake Tahoe, 60 mi. N of Sacramento **[P. 14, D-7]**. Contains 794,000 acres. **C HK BT F S R BK W WW**

TRINITY NATIONAL FOREST
Northern CA **[P. 14, B & C-3]**. **C HK BT F S R W CL**

WHISKEYTOWN-SHASTA-TRINITY NATIONAL RECREATION AREA
On CA 299, 8 mi. N of Redding **[P. 14, B-4]**. Contains 42,503 acres. **C HK BT F S R BK DV**

YOSEMITE NATIONAL PARK
CA 140 & 120 eastbound from Merced and Manteca **[P. 15, C & D-8 & 9]**. Contains 761,170 acres. **C HK BT F S R BK W CL**

State Parks

ANNADEL STATE PARK
Channel Dr., E off Montgomery Dr. **[P. 14, F-4]**. Contains 4,913 acres. **HK F R**

ANZA-BORREGO DESERT STATE PARK
85 mi. NE of San Diego via I-8, Hwys 79 & 78 **[P. 17, P-12]**. Contains 600,000 acres. **C HK R**

AUBURN STATE RECREATION AREA
State Route 49, 1 mi. S of Auburn **[P. 14, E-6]**. Contains 42,000 acres. **C HK BT F S R HT**

BENBOW LAKE STATE RECREATION AREA
2 mi. S of Garberville on US 101 **[P. 14, D-3]**. Contains 786 acres. **C HK BT F S BK**

BOLSA CHICA STATE BEACH
Route 1, 3 mi. W of Huntington Beach **[P. 18, F-7]**. Contains 164 acres. **F S BK**

CASTLE CRAGS STATE PARK
6 mi. S of Dunsmuir on I-5 **[P. 14, B-4]**. Contains 6,218 acres. **C HK F S R BK CL**

CHINA CAMP STATE PARK
NE of San Rafael via US 101 & N. San Pedro Rd. **[P. 19, B-11]**. Contains 1,640 acres. **C HK BT F R**

DOHENY STATE BEACH
Dana Point, near jct. of I-5 & Hwy. 1 **[P. 19, H-10]**. Contains 62 acres. **C F S SU**

FOLSOM LAKE STATE RECREATION AREA
US 50, 2 mi. NW of Folsom **[P. 14, F-6]**. Contains 17,718 acres. **C HK BT F S R BK**

GAVIOTA STATE PARK
33 mi. W of Santa Barbara on US 101 **[P. 16, N-7]**. Contains 2,776 acres. **C HK BT F S R SU**

HENDY WOODS STATE PARK
Route 128, 8 mi. NW of Boonville **[P. 14, E-3]**. Contains 693 acres. **C HK F S R BK**

HENRY W. COE STATE PARK
14 mi. E of Morgan Hill on E. Dunne Ave. **[P. 16, I-5]**. Contains 67,655 acres. **C F R**

HUMBOLDT REDWOODS STATE PARK
45 mi. S of Eureka on US 101 **[P. 14, C-2]**. Contains 51,000 acres. **C HK BT F S R BK**

HUNTINGTON BEACH
Huntington Beach, SE edge, Hwy. 1 at Hwy. 39 **[P. 18, G-7]**. Contains 78 acres. **F S BK SU**

LAKE CASITAS RECREATION AREA
Off CA 150, 5 mi. SW of Ojai **[P. 16, 0-8]**. Contains 6,000 acres. **C HK BT F**

LAKE ELSINORE STATE RECREATION AREA
22 mi. SE of Corona, via I-15 **[P. 17, P-11]**. Contains 2,954 acres. **C BT F S**

LAKE OROVILLE STATE RECREATION AREA
Hwy. 16, 7 mi. E of Oroville **[P. 14, D-5]**. Contains 31,600 acres. **C HK BT F S R BK**

LAKE PERRIS STATE RECREATION AREA
11 mi. SE of Riverside on CA 60 or I-215 **[P. 19, E-13]**. Contains 8,800 acres. **C HK BT F S R BK CL**

LAKE SAN ANTONIO
Off US 101, 40 mi. S of King City **[P. 16, L-6]**. Contains 5,000 acres. **C HK BT F S R**

MCARTHUR-BURNEY FALLS MEMORIAL STATE PARK
11 mi. NE of Burney on Hwy. 89 **[P. 14, C-5]**. Contains 768 acres. **C HK BT F S R**

MILLERTON LAKE STATE RECREATION AREA
CA 41, 20 mi. NE of Fresno **[P. 16, K-7]**. Contains 6,553 acres. **C HK BT F S R BK**

MORRO BAY STATE PARK
Morro Bay, 3 mi. S **[P. 16, M-6]**. Contains 2,435 acres. **C HK BT F S BK**

MOUNT DIABLO STATE PARK
5 mi. E of I-680, Danville, on Diablo Road **[P. 15, C-14]**. Contains 18,000 acres. **C HK R BK**

PFEIFFER BIG SUR STATE PARK
Big Sur, 26 mi. S of Carmel on Hwy. 1 **[P. 16, L-5]**. Contains 821 acres. **C HK F S BK**

PISMO DUNES STATE VEHICULAR RECREATION AREA
CA 1, 3 mi. S of Pismo Beach **[P. 16, N-6]**. Contains 2,500 acres. **C HK F S R**

PISMO STATE BEACH
CA 1, 3 mi. S of City of Pismo Beach **[P. 16, M-6]**. Contains 1,051 acres. **C HK F S BK**

REFUGIO STATE BEACH
23 mi. NW of Santa Barbara on US 101 **[P. 16, N-7]**. Contains 155 acres. **C HK F S BK SU**

SALT POINT STATE PARK
CA 1, 24 m. N of Jenner **[P. 14, F-3]**. Contains 5,970 acres. **C HK F R**

SAMUEL P. TAYLOR STATE PARK
15 mi. W of San Rafael on Sir Francis Drake Blvd. **[P. 14, G-4]** Contains 2,708 acres. **C HK F S R BK**

SILVERWOOD LAKE STATE RECREATION AREA
CA 138, 30 mi. N of San Bernadino **[P. 19, A-12]**. Contains 2,200 acres. **C HK BT F S**

SUGAR PINE POINT STATE PARK
10 mi. S of Tahoe City on Hwy. 89 **[P. 73, J-1]**. Contains 2,011 acres. **C HK F S BK W TE**

SUGARLOAF RIDGE STATE PARK
CA 12, 7 mi. E of Santa Rosa **[P. 14, F-4]**. Contains 2,500 acres. **C HK R BK**

SUNSET STATE BEACH
16 mi. S of Santa Cruz via Hwy. 1 & San Andreas Rd. **[P. 16, K-4] Contains 324 acres. C F S SU**

TAHOE STATE RECREATION AREA
Tahoe City, 1/4 mi. E **[P. 73, J-1]**. Contains 57 acres. **C BT F S**

TURLOCK LAKE STATE RECREATION AREA
CA 132, 22 mi. E of Modesto **[P. 14, H-7]**. Contains 228 acres. **C HK BT F S BK**

VAN DAMME STATE PARK
CA 1, 3 mi. S of Mendocino **[P. 14, E-3]**. Contains 2,163 acres. **C HK F**

WILLIAM RANDOLPH HEARST MEMORIAL STATE BEACH
San Simeon **[P. 16, M-5]**. Contains 8 acres. **BT F S**

Skiing

ALPINE SKIING

ALPINE MEADOWS SKI AREA
Alpine Meadows Road, Tahoe City **[P. 73, J-1]**; (916) 583-4232.
Vertical drop is 1,797 feet. Has two bars and eleven chairs.

BADGER PASS SKI AREA
Glacier Point Rd., off Hwy. 41, Yosemite **[P. 15, D-8]**; (209) 372-1330.
Vertical drop is 800 feet. Has one tow, one bar and four chairs.

BEAR MOUNTAIN SKI RESORT
Hwy. 18, off Big Bear Blvd., Big Bear Lake **[P. 17, O-11]**; (714) 585-2519.
Vertical drop is 1,700 feet. Has 3 bars and nine chairs.

HEAVENLY SKI RESORT
Off Highway 50, South Lake Tahoe **[P. 73, K-2]**; (916) 541-1330.
Vertical drop is 3,600 feet. Has 17 chairs, one tram and 6 surface lifts.
◆You can see Lake Tahoe from the chair lifts. Located at the state line, with casino gambling a prime nighttime activity.

JUNE MOUNTAIN SKI RESORT
On Highway 158, June Lake Scenic Route, June Lake **[P. 15, D-9]**; (619) 648-7733.
Vertical drop is 2,590 feet. Has seven chairs and one tram.

KIRKWOOD SKI RESORT
Kirkwood Meadows Drive, Kirkwood **[P. 17, Q-12]**; (209) 258-6000.
Vertical drop is 2,000 feet. Has one bar and ten chairs.

MAMMOTH MOUNTAIN SKI AREA
1 Minaret Road, Mammoth **[P. 15, D-9]**; (619) 934-2571.
Vertical drop is 3,100 feet. Has three bars, 26 chairs and two gondolas.
◆Big with the Southern California ski crowd. The snow here often lasts into late June.

MT. BALDY SKI LIFTS
End of Mt. Baldy Road, Mt. Baldy **[P. 19, B-10]**; (714) 981-3344.
Vertical drop is 2,100 feet. Has four chairs.

MT. REBA/BEAR VALLEY
Off Highway 4, Bear Valley **[P. 14, F-7]**; (209) 753-2301.
Vertical drop is 2,100 feet. Has nine chairs.

NORTHSTAR-AT-TAHOE
Hwy. 267 & Northstar Drive, Truckee **[P. 73,**

CONTINUED ON PAGE 140

California

CONTINUED FROM PAGE 139

H-1]; (916) 562-1010.
Vertical drop is 2,200 feet. Has two tows, eight chairs and one gondola.

SIERRA SKI RANCH
Twin Bridges **[P. 14, F-7]**; (916) 659-7453.
Vertical drop is 2,212 feet. Has nine chairs.

SNOW SUMMIT SKI AREA
880 Summit Blvd., off CA 18, Big Bear Lake **[P. 17, O-11]**; (714) 866-5766.
Vertical drop is 1,200 feet. Has eleven chairs.

SQUAW VALLEY USA
Off CA 89, Squaw Valley Road, Squaw Valley **[P. 73, H-1]**; (916) 583-6985.
Vertical drop is 2,850 feet. Has four tows, 26 chairs, one tram and one gondola.
◆Just inland from Lake Tahoe. Most diverse and best for all levels of skiing in the area. 1960 Winter Olympics were held here.

NORDIC SKIING

BEAR VALLEY CROSS COUNTRY
#1 Bear Valley Road, Bear Valley **[P. 14, F-7]**; (209) 752-2834.

MONTECITO-SEQUOIA RESORT
King's Canyon National Park, Grant Grove **[P. 17, K-13]**; (800) 227-9900.

NORTHSTAR-AT-TAHOE
Highway 267 & Northstar Drive, Truckee **[P. 73, H-1]**; (916) 562-1010.

RIM NORDIC SKI AREA
Running Springs **[P. 19, B-14]**; (714) 337-3182.

ROCK CREEK LODGE XC SKI
Rock Creek Road, Mammoth Lakes **[P. 15, D-9]**; (619) 935-4452.

ROYAL GORGE XC SKI RESORT
Pahatsi Road, Soda Springs **[P. 14, E-7]**; (916) 426-3871.
◆Considered the nation's foremost touring center, with over 125 miles of groomed trails.

TAHOE DONNER XC
15275 Alder Creek Road, Truckee **[P. 73, H-1]**; (916) 587-9484.

TAHOE NORDIC SKI CENTER
925 Country Club Drive, Tahoe City **[P. 73, J-1]**; (916) 583-0484.

TAMARACK XC SKI CENTER
Twin Lakes Road, Mammoth Lakes **[P. 15, G-9]**; (609) 934-2442.

YOSEMITE XC SKI SCHOOL
At Badger Pass, Yosemite **[P. 15, D-8]**; (209) 372-1244.

ACTIVE SPORTS

ADVENTURE: Colorado Outward Bound School, 945 Pennsylvania Street, Denver, CO; (800) 477-2627. • **Pacific Crest Outward Bound School,** 0110 SW Bancroft Street, Portland, OR; (800) 547-3312.

AEROBICS: AFAA, 533 W. Gainsborough Ave., #103, Thousand Oaks; (818) 905-0040.

BASEBALL: Little League Baseball Western Region HQ, 6707 Little League Dr., San Bernadino, CA; (714) 887-6444. • **Pony Baseball-Softball (Southern California),** 1123 W. Second Street, San Pedro; (213) 833-4239. • **Pony Baseball-Softball (Southern California),** 1922 Goldboro Street, San Diego; (619) 276-3094. • **Pony Baseball-Softball (Northern California),** 908 Redbird Dr., San Jose; (408) 265-3309. • **American Legion Baseball,** 4319 Rocky Point Rd., Anaheim; (714) 921-2318. • **Babe Ruth Baseball,** Dennis R. Poarch, 809 W. Gibson Rd., Woodland; (415) 581-6879. • **Men's Senior Baseball League - Sacramento,** 8772 Aquarius Ave., Elk Grove; (916) 685-5358. • **Men's Senior Baseball League - Southern California,** 1708 Langing Dr., Vista; (619) 598-7220. • **Men's Senior Baseball League - San Francisco,** 1571 Hawes Ct., Redwood City; (415) 365-1383. • **Men's Senior Baseball League - Los Angeles,** 15226 Lassen Street, Mission Hills; (818) 785-7011.

BILLIARDS: Chino's Pool Hall, 2301 Telegraph Ave., Oakland; (415) 893-0884. • **College Billiard Center,** 5303 El Cajon, San Diego; (619) 583-6361. • **Hollywood Billiards,** 5504 Hollywood Blvd., Hollywood; (213) 465-0115. • **Q's Billiards,** 11835 Wilshire Blvd., Santa Monica; (213) 477-7550.

BOARDSAILING: C.A.R.R. Watersports , San Diego; (619) 544-0133. • **Hobie Sports ,** Dana Point; (714) 496-1251. • **Long Beach Windsurf Center ,** Long Beach; (213) 433-1014. • **San Diego Sailing Center ,** San Diego; (619) 488-0651. • **San Francisco School of Windsurfing ,** San Francisco; (415) 750-0412. • **Sundance Windsurfing ,** Santa Barbara; (805) 966-4400. • **USWA Regional Director,** PO Box 6272, Laguna Niguel; (714) 495-0368.

BOWLING: American Bowling Congress, 5301 S. 76th St., Greendale, WI; (414) 421-6400.

CANOEING & KAYAKING: ACA Pacific Vice Commodore, 3008 Blossom Ln., Redondo Beach; (213) 542-8757.

CYCLING: Central California AYH Council, PO Box 3645, Merced; (209) 383-0686. • **Golden Gate AYH Council,** 425 Divisadero St. #307, San Francisco; (415) 863-1444. • **Los Angeles AYH Council,** 1434 Second St., Santa Monica; (213) 393-6991. • **San Diego AYH Council,** 355 West Beech St., San Diego; (619) 239-2644. • **USCF California/Nevada North Representative,** 1153 Delaware Street, Berkeley; (415) 526-5983. • **USCF California Central/Southwest Representative,** 438 Dolores Street, Wilmington; (213) 835-8388. • **USCF California/Nevada Southeast Representative,** 5221 E. Fern Haven Ln., Anaheim; (714) 637-9171.

FITNESS: National Strength and Conditioning Ass'n Northern CA State Director, Human Performance Lab, San Jose State Univ., One Washington Square, San Jose; (408) 277-3537.

FOOTBALL: Pop Warner Football, 1315 Walnut Street, Suite 1632, Philadelphia, PA; (215) 735-1450.

GOLF: Northern California Golf Association, PO Box NCGA, Pebble Beach; (408) 625-4653. • **PGA Northern California Section,** 2133 Las Positas Ct., Suite A, Livermore; (415) 449-5700. • **PGA Southern California Section,** 2323 W. Lincoln Ave., Suite 229, Anaheim; (714) 776-4653. • **San Diego County Junior Golf Association,** San Diego Jack Murphy Stadium, 9449 Friars Rd., San Diego; (619) 280-8505. • **San Diego County Women's Golf Association,** 15949 Arena Dr., Ramona; (619) 789-3627. • **Southern California Golf Association,** 48/125 Via Hermosa, La Quinta; (818) 980-3630. • **Women's Southern California Golf Association,** 402 W. Arrow Highway, Suite 10, San Dimas; (714) 592-1281.

HIKING & CLIMBING: Angeles Sierra Club Chapter, 3550 W. 6th St., Suite 321, Los Angeles; (213) 387-4287. • **Berkeley Hiking Club (AHS),** PO Box 147, Berkeley; (415) 834-5917. • **Contra Costa Hills Club (AHS),** c/o YWCA, 1515 Webster, #434, Oakland; (415) 232-7475. • **Diablo Hiking Club/A B Barton (AHS),** 3424 Sentinel, Martinez; (415) 228-5732. • **Hayward Hiking Club (AHS),** PO Box 367, Hayward; (415) 582-0942. • **Kern-Kaweah Sierra Club Chapter,** 1013 Hogan Way, Bakersfield; (805) 834-8035. • **La Canada Flint Ridge Trail Council (AHS),** PO Box 852, La Canada-Flint; (818) 790-2679. • **Loma Prieta Sierra Club Chapter,** 2448 Watson Ct., Palo Alto; (415) 494-9901. • **Los Padres Sierra Club Chapter,** 1411 Ramona Dr., Newbury Park; (805) 498-1736. • **Mother Lode Sierra Club Chapter,** PO Box 1335, Sacramento; (916) 444-2180. • **Redwood Sierra Club Chapter,** POBox 466, Santa Rosa; (707) 544-7651. • **San Diego Sierra Club Chapter,** 3820 Ray St., San Diego; (619) 299-1743. • **San Francisco Bay Sierra Club Chapter,** 6014 College Ave., Oakland; (415) 653-6127. • **San Gorgonio Sierra Club Chapter,** 568 N. Mountain View Ave., Suite 130, San Bernardino; (714) 381-5015. • **Santa Lucia Sierra Club Chapter,** PO Box 15755, San Luis Obispo; (805) 549-5059. • **Tehipite Sierra Club Chapter,** PO Box 5396, Fresno; (209) 233-1820. • **Trails Club of Rossmoor (AHS),** 3324 Ptarmigan Dr., #2C, Walnut Creek; (415) 934-8251. • **Ventana Sierra Club Chapter,** PO Box 5667, Carmel; (408) 624-8032.

HOCKEY: USA Hockey Pacific Registrar, 5703 Sun Ridge Ct., Castro Valley; (415) 886-0706.

HUNTING & FISHING: Bob Marriotts Fly Fishing Store (Orvis), 2700 W. Orangethorpe Ave., Fullerton; (714) 525-1827. • **Feather River Ltd. (Orvis),** 2580 Fair Oaks Blvd., Sacramento; (916) 483-8711. • **Department of Fish & Game,** 1416 9th St., 12th Floor, Sacramento; (916) 445-3531. • **Huebner Sports (Orvis),** 1021 E. Herndon, Fresno; (916) 483-0555. • **Orvis San Francisco,** 300 Grant Ave., San Francisco; (415) 392-1600. • **T.O. Littlestone Wilderness Shoppe (Orvis),** 820 E. Thousand Oaks Blvd., Thousand Oaks; (805) 497-0040. • **Trout Unlimited,** 16712 Bolero Lane, Huntington Beach; (714) 778-1164.

LACROSSE: Lacrosse Foundation Chapter, c/o Knapp, Peterson & Clarke, 4000 MacArthur Blvd., Suite 900, Newport Beach; (714) 851-8600. • **Lacrosse Foundation Chapter,** 531 Country Club Ln., Coronado; (619) 435-8084. • **Lacrosse Foundation Chapter,** 8434 Chenin Blanc Ln., San Jose; (408) 238-4298.

RACQUETBALL: AARA, 411 Picadilly Pl. #12, San Bruno; (415) 873-1354.

RIDING: California State Horsemen's Association, 897 Third St., Santa Rosa; (707) 544-2250.

RODEO: PRCA Sierra Circuit, 9831 Shadow Rd., La Mesa; (619) 469-6364.

RUNNING: RRCA CA State Rep., 1561 Hillcrest Pl., San Luis Obis; (805) 544-9320.

SCUBA: Aqua Ventures Diving School, 2172 Pickwick Drive, Camarillo; (805) 484-1594. • **Black Bart's Aquatics,** 24882 Muirlands Blvd., El Toro; (714) 855-2323. • **Channel Islands Scuba,** 1495 Palma Drive, Unit C, Ventura; (805) 644-3483. • **Dolphin Smim School & Scuba Center,** 1530 El Camino Avenue, Sacramento; (916) 929-8188. • **Guccione's Scuba Habitat,** 2843-A Diamond Bar Blvd., Diamond Bar; (714) 594-7927. • **Innerspace Divers,** 1305 North Chester Avenue, Bakersfield; (805) 399-1425. • **Malibu Divers,** 21231 Pacific Coast Highway, Malibu; (213) 456-2396. • **Marina Del Rey Divers, Inc.,** 2539 Lincoln Blvd., Marina Del Rey; (213) 827-1131. • **Mother Lode Dive Shop,** 2020 "H" Street, Sacramento; (916) 446-4041. • **Ocean Enterprises,** 7710 Balboa Avenue, San Diego; (619) 565-6054. • **Pacific Offshore Divers, Inc.,** 1195 Branham Lane, San Jose; (408) 265-3483. • **Pinnacles Dive Center,** 875 Grant Avenue, Novato; (415) 897-9962. • **Scuba Discoveries,** 651 Howard Street, San Francisco; (415) 777-3483. • **Scuba Unlimited,** 4000 Pimlico Drive, #114, Pleasanton; (415) 734-9343. • **The Dive Shop of Santa Maria,** 1975-B South Broadway, Santa Maria; (805) 922-0076. • **Underwater Diversions,** 1802 East Katella Avenue, Orange; (714) 633-1880. • **Wallin Dive Store,** 517 East Bayshore Road, Redwood; (415) 369-2131.

SHOOTING: Birds Landing Sporting Clays, PO Box 5, Birds Landing; (707) 374-5092. • **Raahauge's Shotgun Sports,** 5800 Bluff St., Norco; (714) 735-7981. • **River Road. Sporting Clays,** PO Box 3016, Gonzales; (408) 675-2473. • **Timbuctoo Sporting Estate,** PO Box 357, Smartville; (916) 639-2200.

SKATING: Southern California Skating Association, 10700 Woodley Ave., #7, Granada Hills; (818) 895-0963. • **USFSA,** 20 First Street, Colorado Springs, CO; (719) 635-5200.

SOCCER: California Soccer Ass'n, 1438 Silver Ave., San Francisco; (415) 467-1881. • **California YSA, Inc.,** 5673 W. Las Positas Blvd., Suite 202, Pleasanton; (415) 847-9111. • **California YSA - South,** 1440 S. State College Blvd., No. 2-B, Anaheim; (714) 778-2972. • **AYSO Regional Director (Southern CA),** 1433 W. Princeton, Ontario; (714) 988-6947. • **AYSO Regional Director (Northern CA),** 4119 East Ave., Hayward; (415) 886-4119.

SOFTBALL: Central California ASA, 6155 Conejo Rd., Atascadero; (805) 466-8505. • **Greater San Joaquin County ASA,** Room 301. City Hall, Stockton; (209) 464-6964. • **Northern California ASA,** 1400 Roosevelt Ave., Redwood City; (415) 366-5450. • **Oakland ASA,** 2177 Corte Hornitos, San Lorenzo; (415) 278-8970. • **Sacramento ASA,** 4623 T Street, Sacramento; (916) 485-2023. • **San Francisco ASA,** San Francisco Rec./Park Dept., Fell & Stanyan Streets, San Francisco; (415) 382-0968. • **Santa Clara ASA,** 1500 Warburton Ave., Santa Clara; (408) 243-8616. • **Southern California ASA,** 17200 Raymer Street, Northridge; (818) 349-8399.

SQUASH: Center Courts (USSRA), West Los Angeles; (213) 826-6648. • **Naval Training Center,** San Diego; (714) 225-5211. • **University of California at Berkeley,** Berkeley; (415) 642-8342. • **University Club of Los Angeles (USSRA),** Los Angeles; (213) 627-8651. • **University Club of San Francisco (USSRA),** San Francisco; (415) 781-0900.

SWIMMING: LMSC Pacific Registrar, 580 Sunset Parkway, Novato; (415) 892-0771. • **LMSC San Diego Registrar,** 1135 Garnet Ave. #K, San Diego; (619) 435-2953. • **LMSC SPMA Registrar,** PO Box 204, El Toro; (714) 581-1135.

TABLE TENNIS: USTTA State Coordinator (Northern CA), 1900 Vine Street, Berkeley; (415) 527-1309. • **USTTA State Coordinator (Southern CA),** 2052 Linden, Apt. S, Riverside; (714) 682-0085

TENNIS: Recreational TEAMTENNIS Central-West Region, National Program Coordinator, 2105 Grant Ave., #4, Redondo Beach, CA ; (800) 992-9042. • **Northern California USTA,** 1350 South Loop Rd., Suite 200, Alameda; (415) 748-7373. • **Southern California USTA,** PO Box 240015, Los Angeles; (213) 208-3838.

TRIATHLON: Attorney for Athletes, 400 S. Melrose, Suite 104, Vista; (619) 724-0500. • **Davis Scott Tri Club,** 3113 Evening Bay Place, Davis; (916) 758-3542. • **Team Malibu,** 25816 Cold Springs Street, Calabases Hills; (213) 456-6649. • **Team NTTC,** 1015 Bayley Avenue, Suite 217, Los Angeles; (213) 478-8304. • **Triathlon Club of San Diego,** PO Box 84211, San Diego; (619) 789-3986.

VOLLEYBALL: USVBA Northern Calif. Commissioner, 611 North Claremont Street, San Mateo; (415) 347-3554. • **USVBA Southern California Commissioner,** PO Box 3036, Torrance; (213) 377-0778.

WHITEWATER RAFTING: Adventure Connection , Box 475, Coloma; (916) 626-7385. • **American River Recreation, Inc. ,** 11257 South Bridge Street, Rancho Cordova; (916) 635-4516. • **American River Touring Association ,** Star Rt. 73, Groveland; (209) 962-7873. • **Cal Adventures/U.C. Berkeley ,** 2301 Bancroft Way, Berkeley; (415) 642-4000. • **Sierra Mac River Trips ,** Box 366, Sonora; (209) 532-1327. • **Turtle River Rafting Company ,** PO Box 313, Mt. Shasta; (916) 926-3223.

Colorado

If Colorado's towering peaks were flattened out, the state could well be the largest in the Lower 48—but it wouldn't be half as much fun. The Centennial State's 27 ski areas are world-famous for their steep runs, dry powder, and in the case of Aspen and Vail, celebrities. ◆ The Rocky Mountains also provide thousands of miles of breathtaking hiking and biking, icy cold trout-fishing, hair-raising rafting and high-altitude lake sailing. ◆ Home of the United States Olympic Committee, the Rocky Mountain State is also home base to many of the world's best cyclists and endurance athletes, who thrive in the challenging terrain. ◆ Pro sports fans can take in the NFL Broncos, the NBA Nuggets, or Triple-A baseball (see below). ◆ And the state's weather can be wacky: It's not unusual to be able to play golf and ski every month of the year.

STATBOX

POPULATION: 3,500,000
SQUARE MILES: 104,147
TIME ZONE: Mountain
MOTTO: Nil Sine Numine (Nothing without providence)
BIRD: Lark Bunting
TREE: Blue Spruce
CAPITAL: Denver
AVERAGE ANNUAL RAINFALL: 15"
MEAN TEMP: 50
MAJOR LEAGUE TEAMS: 2
NATIONAL PARK/FOREST ACREAGE: 602,867
STATE PARK ACREAGE: 152,666
HIGHEST ELEVATION: 14,431'
LOWEST ELEVATION: 3,350'
WATERWAYS: 8,000 miles of rivers and streams; 2,000 lakes

▶ SPECTATOR VENUES

Auto Racing

BANDIMERE SPEEDWAY
3051 South Rooney Rd., Morrison **[P. 22, C-2]**; (303) 697-6001. Track is quarter-mile strip (for NHRA races).
Mopar Parts Mile-High Nationals (NHRA), mid-July.

DENVER STREET CIRCUIT
14th & Lincoln Avenues, Denver **[P. 22, B-4]**; (303) 623-7773. Track is 1.9-mile temporary street course.
Liquid Tide Trans-Am Tour (SCCA Trans Am Championship), Aug.
Texaco/Havoline Grand Prix of Denver (CART PPG Indy Car World Series), August.

Baseball

MILE HIGH STADIUM
2850 West 20th Ave., Denver **[P. 22, B-4]**. Capacity: 76,000
Denver Zephyrs (American Association, Class AAA); (303) 433-2032. Entered League in 1969. Broadcasts by KQXI 1550 AM. MLB affiliation, Milwaukee Brewers.
(See p. 165 for info on MLB expansion.)

SKY SOX STADIUM
4385 Tutt Blvd., Colorado Springs **[P. 22, G-5]**. Capacity: 6,130
Colorado Springs Sky Sox (Pacific Coast League, Class AAA); (719) 597-1449. Entered League in 1988. Broadcasts by KSSS 740-AM. MLB affiliation, Cleveland Indians.

Basketball

MCNICHOLS SPORTS ARENA
1635 Clay Street, Denver **[P. 22, B-4]**. Built in 1975. Capacity: 17,022.
◆Jumped from ABA to NBA in 1976.
Denver Nuggets (NBA Western Conf., Midwest Div.); (303) 893-6700. Franchise began in 1967. Broadcasts by KOA 850 AM, PSN.

College Sports

COLORADO COLLEGE TIGERS
14 E. Cache La Poudre, Colorado Springs **[P. 22, G-4]**; (719) 389-6475. Washburn Field, capacity 2,500. E. Pomar Center, capacity 1,500.

COLORADO SCHOOL OF MINES MINERS
Golden **[P. 22, B-1]**; (303) 273-3360. Brooks Field, capacity 5,000. Steinhauer, capacity 1,000.

COLORADO STATE UNIVERSITY RAMS
Fort Collins **[P. 21, B-9]**; (303) 491-5300. Hughes, capacity 30,000 . Moby Arena, capacity 10,000.

U.S. AIR FORCE ACADEMY FALCONS
Air Force Academy **[P. 22, E-3]**; (719) 472-4140. Falcon, capacity 52,153. Cadet, capacity 6,007.

UNIVERSITY OF COLORADO BUFFALOES
Boulder **[P. 22, E-6]**; (303) 492-7931. Folson, capacity 51,463. Conference Center, capacity 11,199.

UNIVERSITY OF DENVER PIONEERS
Denver **[P. 22, C-4]**; (303) 871-2275. Arena capacity 4,727. Gym, capacity 2,000.

Bowling

CELEBRITY SPORTS CENTER
888 S. Colorado Blvd., Denver **[P. 22, C-5]**; (303) 757-3322.
Celebrity Denver Open (PBA), May.

Football

DENVER MILE HIGH STADIUM
1900 West Eliot, Denver **[P. 22, B-4]**. Built in 1948. Capacity: 76,273.
Denver Broncos (AFC Western Division); (303) 649-9000. Franchise began in 1960. Broadcasts by KOA, Denver.

Museums & Halls of Fame

MOUNTAIN BIKE HALL OF FAME AND MUSEUM
Behind Mountain Earth Natural Foods, 425 Elk Ave., Crested Butte **[P. 20, E-6]**; (303) 349-7382.
◆Hosts the annual Pearl Pass Tour, a tradition stretching back to 1976, when a group of locals decided to ride their proto-mountain bike "klunkers" over the 12,700-foot pass to Aspen.

PRORODEO HALL OF FAME AND MUSEUM OF THE AMERICAN COWBOY
101 ProRodeo Dr., Colorado Springs **[P. 22, F-4]**; (719) 593-8840.

UNITED STATES FIGURE SKATING HALL OF FAME AND MUSEUM
20 First St., Colorado Springs **[P. 22, H-3]**; (719) 635-5200.

PGA/LPGA

CASTLE PINES GOLF CLUB
1000 Hummingbird Dr., Castle Rock **[P. 21, D-10]**; (303) 688-6000.
The International (PGA), Aug. Number of holes: 72.

Polo

DENVER POLO CLUB
10415 Roxborough Park Road, Littleton **[P. 21, C-9]**; (303) 792-7656.

Rodeo

COLORADO STATE FAIRGROUNDS
Beulah Avenue at Small St., Pueblo **[P. 22, G-6]**; (719) 561-8484.
Colorado State Fair & Rodeo, Aug.

DENVER COLISEUM
46th St. at I-70, Denver **[P. 22, B-4]**; (302) 297-1166.
National Western Stock Show, Jan.

ISLAND GROVE PARK
14th Avenue North, Greeley **[P. 21, B-9]**; (303) 352-1543, ext. 225.
Greeley Independence Stampede, June.

PENROSE STADIUM & EQUESTRIAN CENTER
1045 W. Rio Grande, Colorado Springs **[P. 22, H-3]**; (719) 633-6641.
Pikes Peak or Bust Rodeo, August.

Soccer

JEFFERSON COUNTY STADIUM
Sixth Ave. and Kipling St., Denver **[P. 22, B-3]**. Capacity: 10,000.
Colorado Foxes (American Professional Soccer League, Western Conference); (303) 840-1111.

Tennis

HEATHER RIDGE COUNTRY CLUB
13521 E. Iliff Street, Aurora; (303) 755-3440. **[P.22, C-6]** Surface is hard.
Colorado Tennis Classic (WTA), Feb.

USA SNAPSHOTS®

A look at statistics that shape the sports world

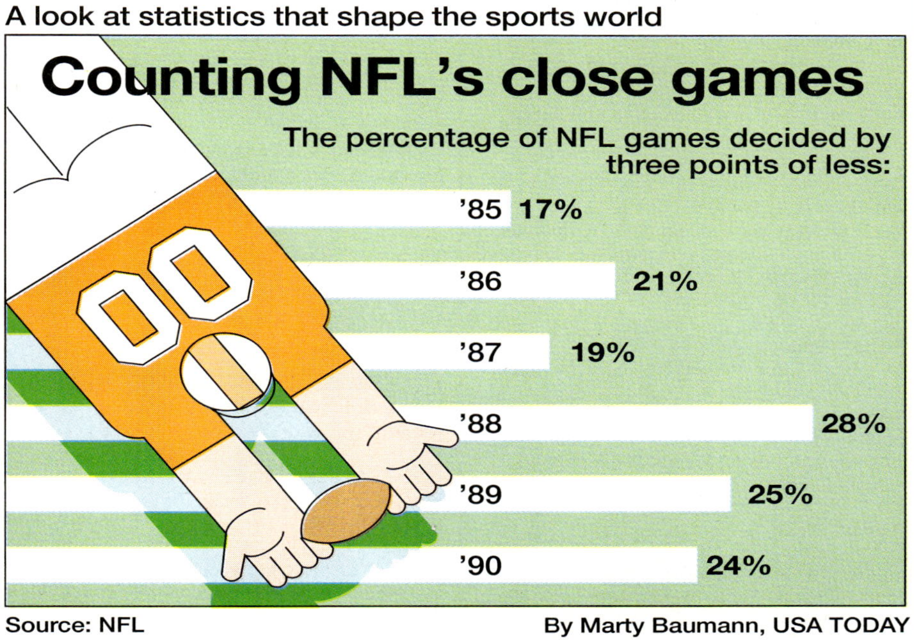

Source: NFL — By Marty Baumann, USA TODAY

▶ OUTDOOR VENUES

National Parks

Bike Trails:BK
Boating: BT
Camping: C
Climbing: CL
Diving: DV
Fishing: F
Golfing: G
Hiking: HK
Hunting: HT
Riding: R
Surfing: SU
Swimming: S
Tennis: TE
Whitewater: WW
Winter Sports: W

ARAPAHO NATIONAL FOREST
SW of Fort Collins **[P. 20, B-7]** & **[P. 21, C-8]**. Contains 1,022,000 acres. **C HK BT F S W**

ARAPAHO NATIONAL RECREATION AREA
North central Colorado, near Denver **[P. 21, C-8]**. Contains 36,000 acres.
C HK BT F S W HT

BLACK CANYON OF THE GUNNISON NATIONAL MONUMENT
Montrose **[P. 20, E-5]**. Contains 20,766 acres.
C HK F W CL

COLORADO NATIONAL MONUMENT
Fruita **[P. 20, D-3]**. Contains 20,454 acres.
C HK R BK W CL

CURECANTI NATIONAL RECREATION AREA
Gunnison.**[P. 20, F-6]** Contains 41,971 acres.
C HK BT F S R W

DINOSAUR NATIONAL MONUMENT
NW state **[P. 20, B-3]**. Contains 211,141 acres.
C HK F WW

GRAND MESA NATIONAL FOREST
W of Grand Junction. Contains 346,000 acres. **C HK BT F S R W HT**

GUNNISON NATIONAL FOREST
S of Grand Junction & W of Mt. Rose **[P. 20, E & F-6]**. Contains 944,000 acres.
C HK BT F S R BK W HT

PIKE NATIONAL FOREST
W of Colorado Springs **[P. 21, D-8]**. Contains 1,111,000 acres. **C HK BT F S R W HT**

RIO GRANDE NATIONAL FOREST
San Luis Valley, surrounding Alamosa **[P. 20, F-6 & 7]** & **[P. 21, F-8]**. Contains 1,852,000 acres. **C HK BT F S R W HT**

ROCKY MOUNTAIN NATIONAL PARK
Estes Park **[P. 21, B-8]**. Contains 265,200

CONTINUED ON PAGE 142

Colorado

CONTINUED FROM PAGE 141

acres. C HK F R W CL

ROOSEVELT NATIONAL FOREST
W of Denver [P. 21, A-8]. Contains 789,000 acres. C HK BT F S R W WW

ROUTT NATIONAL FOREST
Steamboat Springs [P. 20, A-7, B-7]. Contains 1,127,000 acres. C HK BT F S R W HT

SAN ISABEL NATIONAL FOREST
Pueblo, S of Leadville [P. 21, F-8, G-9]. Contains 1,119,000 acres. C HK BT F S R W HT

SAN JUAN NATIONAL FOREST
SW state, near Durango [P. 20, G-4]. Contains 1,871,000 acres. C HK BT F S R W HT

UNCOMPAHGRE NATIONAL FOREST
Near Gunnison. Contains 1,662,000 acres. C HK BT F S R BK W HT

WHITE RIVER NATIONAL FOREST
Glenwood Springs [P. 20, C-5, D-5, D-7]. Contains 1,960,000 acres. C HK BT F S R W HT

State Parks

BARR LAKE STATE PARK
Off I-76, NE of Denver [P. 21, C-10]. Contains 2,609 acres. HK BT F R W

BONNY STATE RECREATION AREA
1.5 mi. off US 385, 33 mi. N of Burlington [P. 21, C-14]. Contains 6,940 acres. C HK BT F S R W

CASTLEWOOD CANYON STATE PARK
CO 83, 3 mi. SW of Franktown [P. 21, D-10]. Contains 873 acres. C HK R W

CHATFIELD STATE RECREATION AREA
US 85, 8 mi. SW of Denver via CO 121 [P. 22, E-3]. Contains 6,750 acres. C HK BT F S R BK

CHERRY CREEK STATE RECREATION AREA
1 mi. S of I-225 on Parker Road, S of Denver [P. 22, C-7]. Contains 4,795 acres. C HK BT F S R BK

GOLDEN GATE CANYON STATE PARK
Off CO 46, 4 mi. E of Blackhawk [P. 21, C-9]. Contains 10,020 acres. C HK F R BK W

HIGHLINE STATE RECREATION AREA
Off CO 139, 14 mi. W of Grand Junction [P. 20, D-4]. Contains 824 acres. C BT F S

LATHROP STATE PARK
US 160, 3 mi. W of Walsenburg [P. 21, G-10]. Contains 1,274 acres. C HK BT F S

PAONIA STATE RECREATION AREA
CO 133, 14 mi. n. of Paonia [P. 20, D-6]. Contains 1,816 acres. C BT F W

PUEBLO STATE RECREATION AREA
On Pueblo Reservoir, off US 50, W of Pueblo [P. 21, F-10]. Contains 17,155 acres. C HK BT F S R BK

RIFLE GAP STATE RECREATION AREA & RIFLE FALLS STATE PARK
CO 325, 10 mi. N of Rifle [P. 20, C-5]. Contains 2,535 acres. C HK BT F S W

STATE FOREST
75 mi. W of Ft. Collins on CO 14, over Cameron Pass [P. 21, B-8]. Contains 72,130 acres. C HK BT R W

STEAMBOAT LAKE STATE RECREATION AREA
25 mi. N of Steamboat Springs via County Road 129 [P. 20, A-6]. Contains 2,773 acres C HK BT F W

VEGA STATE RECREATION AREA
8 mi. E of Collbran via CO 330 [P. 20, D-5]. Contains 2,730 acres. C HK BT F S R W

Skiing

ALPINE SKIING

ARAPAHOE BASIN
1252 County Road 8, Keystone [P. 21, C-8]; (303) 468-2316.
Vertical drop is 1,670 feet. Has five chairs.

ASPEN HIGHLANDS
1600 Maroon Creek Road, Aspen [P. 20, D-6]; (303) 925-5300.
Vertical drop is 3,800 feet. Has two pomas and nine chairs.

ASPEN MOUNTAIN
East Durant St., Aspen [P. 20, D-6]; (303) 925-1220.
Vertical drop is 3,267 feet. Has seven chairs and one gondola.
◆ The classic glitzy and ritzy resort. One of the first developed and most popular. The powder doesn't last very long these days. A favorite of Gerald Ford.

BEAVER CREEK
Village Road, Beaver Creek Resort, Avon [P. 20, C-7]; (303) 949-5750.
Vertical drop is 3,340 feet. Has eleven chairs.

BRECKENRIDGE SKI AREA
Highway 9, Breckenridge [P. 21, D-8]; (303) 453-5000.
Vertical drop is 3,398 feet. Has two tows, one bar and thirteen chairs.

BUTTERMILK MOUNTAIN
38700 West Highway 82, Aspen [P. 20, D-6]; (303) 925-1220.
Vertical drop is 2,030 feet. Has six chairs.
◆ A noted learners' spot.

COPPER MOUNTAIN RESORT
I-70, exit 195, Copper Mountain [P. 20, D-7]; (800) 458-8386.
Vertical drop is 2,760 feet. Has two tows, two pomas and sixteen chairs.

CRESTED BUTTE MOUNTAIN RESORT
Gothic Road, Crested Butte [P. 20, E-6]; (303) 349-2333.
Vertical drop is 3,062 feet. Has one bar, one poma and ten chairs.

KEYSTONE RESORT
1252 County Road 8, Keystone [P. 21, C-8]; (303) 468-2316.
Vertical drop is 2,340 feet. Has two pomas, sixteen chairs and two gondolas.

PURGATORY/DURANGO SKI RESORT
175 Beatrice Drive, Durango [P. 20, G-5]; (303) 247-9000.
Vertical drop is 2,029 feet. Has nine chairs.

SNOWMASS AT ASPEN
40 Carriage Way, Snowmass Village [P. 20, D-6]; (303) 923-1220.
Vertical drop is 3,615 feet. Has two bars and fourteen chairs.
◆ An excellent intermediate mountain; don't miss the Big Burn.

STEAMBOAT SKI AREA
2305 Mt. Werner Circle, Steamboat Springs [P. 20, B-7]; (303) 879-6111.
Vertical drop is 3,600 feet. Has one tow, seventeen chairs and one gondola.

TELLURIDE SKI RESORT
562 Mt. Village Road, Telluride [P. 20, F-5]; (303) 728-3856.
Vertical drop is 3,522 feet. Has one bar and nine chairs.

VAIL
Vail [P. 20, C-7]; (303) 476-5601.
Vertical drop is 3,250 feet. Has two pomas, seventeen chairs and one gondola.
◆ Large, diverse mountain, with famous back bowls for powder skiing.

WINTER PARK
677 Grand County Road 70, US 40, Winter Park [P. 21, C-8]; (303) 726-5514.
Vertical drop is 2,220 feet. Has nineteen chairs.
◆ Long, open trails. Where the locals go to avoid fanfare.

NORDIC SKIING

ASHCROFT CROSS COUNTRY
Historic Ghost Town, Ashcroft [P. 20, D-6]; (303) 925-1971.

BLUE RIDGE TOURING/DEVIL'S THUMB
850 Lion's Lane, Granby [P. 21, C-8]; (303) 887-2806.

BRECKENRIDGE NORDIC CENTER
1200 Ski Hill Road, Breckenridge [P. 21, D-8]; (303) 453-6855.

CORDILLERA
2205 Cordillera, Edwards [P. 20, C-7]; (303) 926-2200.

FRISCO NORDIC CENTER
18454 Highway 9, Frisco [P. 21, C-8]; (303) 668-0866.

GRAND LAKE XC
Golf Course Road, Grand Lake [P. 21, B-8]; (303) 627-8008.

PEACEFUL VALLEY LODGE
Star Route, Lyons [P. 21, B-9]; (303) 747-2881.

SKI COOPER NORDIC CENTER
Ski Cooper Ski Area, Leadville [P. 20, D-7]; (719) 486-2277.

SPRUCE LODGE
Northshore Word Lake, Cedaredge [P. 20, E-5]; (303) 856-3210.

STEAMBOAT
200 Club House Drive, Steamboat Springs [P. 20, B-6]; (303) 879-8180.

THE HOME RANCH
Highway 129, Clark [P. 20, A-6]; (303) 879-1780.

VISTA VERDE RANCH
Seedhaus Road, Clark [P. 20, A-6]; (800) 526-7433.

► ACTIVE SPORTS

ADVENTURE: Colorado Outward Bound School, 945 Pennsylvania Street, Denver; (800) 477-2627.

AEROBICS: AFAA, 12 Manzanita, Littleton; (303) 979-5582.

BASEBALL: Little League Baseball Western Region HQ, 6707 Little League Dr., San Bernadino, CA; (714) 887-6444. • **American Legion Baseball,** 5613 Pioneer Rd., Boulder; (303) 530-1714. • **Babe Ruth Baseball,** Norman Travis, Box 339, Burlington; (719) 346-8803. • **Men's Senior Baseball League - Denver,** 768 S. Fairplay Ct., Aurora; (303) 755-4619.

BILLIARDS: Sheridan Billiards, 1132 S. Sheridan, Denver; (303) 936-6699.

BOARDSAILING: Colorado Windsurfing , Colorado Springs; (719) 594-6868. • **Rocky Mountain Marine ,** Denver; (303) 399-2824. • **USWA Regional Director,** 18354 W. 58th Pl. #62, Golden; (303) 279-3185.

BOWLING: American Bowling Congress, 5301 S. 76th St., Greendale, WI; (414) 421-6400.

CANOEING & KAYAKING: ACA Rocky Mountain Vice Commodore, c/o Four Corners Marine, Box 379, Durango; (303) 259-3893.

CYCLING: Rocky Mountain AYH Council, PO Box 2370, Boulder; (303) 442-1166. • **USCF Colorado Representative,** 1135 A S. Oneida, Denver; (303) 757-1892.

FITNESS: Governor's Council on Health Promotion and Physical Fitness, 6th & McWelthy, Leadville; (303) 778-3888.

FOOTBALL: Pop Warner Football, 1315 Walnut Street, Suite 1632, Philadelphia, PA; (215) 735-1450.

GOLF: Colorado Golf Association, 5655 S. Yosemite, Suite 101, Englewood; (303) 779-4653. • **PGA Colorado Section,** 12323 E. Cornell, Suite 21, Aurora; (303) 745-3697.

HIKING & CLIMBING: Rocky Mountain Sierra Club Chapter, 777 Grant St., Suite 606, Denver; (303) 861-8819. • **The Colorado Mountain Club (AHS),** 2530 W. Alameda Ave., Denver; (303) 922-8976.

HOCKEY: USA Hockey Rocky Mountain Registrar, 7335 S. Garfield Ct., Littleton; (303) 721-0936.

HUNTING & FISHING: Department of Natural Resources, 6060 Broadway, Denver; (303) 297-1192. • **Olympic Sports (Orvis),** 101 W. Colorado Ave., Telluride; (800) 828-7547. • **The Flyfisher Ltd. (Orvis),** 252 Clayton St., Denver; (303) 322-5014. • **Trout Unlimited,** 2119 South Brentwood Ct., Lakewood; (303) 987-1249.

LACROSSE: Lacrosse Foundation Chapter, 893 Tari Dr., Colorado Springs; (719) 597-6222.

RACQUETBALL: AARA, 4633-B South Frazer, Aurora; (303) 699-8121.

RIDING: Colorado Horsemen's Council, 242 Laurel St., Broomfield; (303) 469-5863.

RODEO: PRCA Mountain States Circuit, 23459 WCR 58, Greeley; (303) 352-6638.

RUNNING: RRCA CO State Rep., PO Box 38235, Colorado Springs; (719) 473-2625.

SCUBA: A-1 Scuba Center, 1800 West Oxford, Suite B, Englewood; (303) 789-2450. • **Divers Reef, Inc.,** 3014 North Nevada, Colorado Springs; (719) 634-3366. • **High Plains Scuba,** 1605 South College, Fort Collins; (303) 493-8562. • **Weaver's Dive Center,** 637-L South Broadway, Boulder; (303) 499-8500.

SHOOTING: High Country Game Birds, 33300 Road 25, Elizabeth; (303) 646-3315. • **Mt. Blanca Game Bird & Trout,** PO Box 236, Blanca; (719) 379-3825. • **Western Colorado Sporting Clays,** 3172 Glendam Dr., Grand Junction; (303) 434-0906.

SKATING: Colorado Skating Association, 1534 Zaiger Pl., Colorado Springs; (719) 596-2778. • **USFSA,** 20 First Street, Colorado Springs; (719) 635-5200.

SOCCER: Colorado Soccer Ass'n, 1780 S. Bellaire, Suite 120, Denver; (303) 692-0211. • **Colorado State YSA,** 7375 E. Orchard Rd., No. 200, Englewood; (303) 770-6440. • **AYSO Regional Director,** 2971 N. Coronado St., Chandler; (602) 839-2114. • **AYSO Regional Director,** 5403 W. 138th Street, Hawthorne, CA; (800) 421-5700.

SOFTBALL: Colorado ASA, 2273 S. Eagle St., Aurora; (303) 751-7299.

SQUASH: Racquet World, Ltd. (USSRA), Denver; (303) 758-7080. • **University of Colorado,** Boulder; (303) 499-2731.

SWIMMING: LMSC Colorado Registrar, PO Box 599, Kittredge; (303) 674-7212.

TENNIS: Recreational TEAMTENNIS Central-West Region, National Program Coordinator, 2105 Grant Ave., #4, Redondo Beach, CA; (800) 992-9042. • **Intermountain USTA,** 1201 South Parker Rd., #102, Denver; (303) 695-4117.

TRIATHLON: CSU Tri Club, Student Recreation Center, Fort Collins; (303) 491-6539. • **Triathlon Club of Colorado,** 11446 Hilary Ct., Parker; (303) 290-7913.

VOLLEYBALL: USVBA Rocky Mountain Commissioner, 985 Wuthering H eights, Colorado Springs; (719) 488-3870.

WHITEWATER RAFTING: Adrift Adventures, 1816 Orchard Pl., Fort Collins; (303) 493-4005. • **Adventure Bound River Expeditions,** 2392 H Rd., Grand Junction; (303) 241-5633. • **Telluride Outside,** 666 W. Colorado Ave., Telluride; (303) 728-3895. • **Wilderness Aware Rafting,** Box 1550, Buena Vista; (719) 395-2112.

Connecticut

Hikers will find more than 100 parks and forests ablaze with color during the fall in Connecticut; more adventurous types can view the foliage from above while hang gliding at Talcott Mountain or West Rock Park (New Haven). ◆ With the NHL Whalers in Hartford, it's no surprise that hockey has a following. Meanwhile, the Big East Conference Connecticut Huskies are a big draw for basketball. ◆ Berensen's Hartford Jai Alai is one of the few places in the USA that features the sport. ◆ The Connecticut and Housatonic rivers are great for sailing and other water sports. ◆ And baseball is not forgotten here; New York Mets pitching ace Ron Darling is a Yale alumnus, and the Red Sox have Double-A talent in New Britain playing all summer long, one eye on the ball and the other on Fenway.

► SPECTATOR VENUES

Auto Racing

LIME ROCK PARK
Route 112, Lakeville **[P. 24, A-2]**; (203) 435-2571. Track is 1.53-mile, 7-turn road course.
◆USA's oldest continually operated road course, Lime Rock opened in 1957. Tucked in the Berkshire foothills, its proximity to New York City has attracted weekend racers like Paul Newman, Tom Cruise and football great Walter Payton. Fans take in the rural scenery and the racing from their own picnic blankets and lawn chairs.
Toyota Trucks' Lime Rock Camel Grand Prix (IMSA Camel GT), May.

Baseball

BEEHIVE FIELD
Willowbrook Park Complex, South Main St., New Britain **[P. 23, D-1]**. Capacity: 4,200
New Britain Red Sox (Eastern League, Class AA); (203) 224-8383. Entered League in 1983. Broadcasts by WBIS 1120 AM. MLB affiliation, Boston Red Sox.

Bowling

BRADLEY BOWL
129 Turnpike Road, Windsor Locks **[P. 24, A-5]**; (203) 623-2597.
Tums Classic (PBA), April.

College Sports

CENTRAL CONNECTICUT STATE BLUE DEVILS
1615 Stanley Street, New Britain **[P. 23, C-1]**; (203) 827-7635. Arute Field, capacity 4,500. Kaiser Hall, capacity 4,500.

FAIRFIELD UNIVERSITY STAGS
N. Benson Road, Fairfield **[P. 24, G-5]**; (203) 254-3000. Alumni Hall, capacity 3,000.

SACRED HEART UNIVERSITY PIONEERS
5151 Park Avenue, Fairfield **[P. 24, F-5]**; (203) 371-7827. Fieldhouse capacity 1,100.

SOUTHERN CONNECTICUT STATE UNIVERSITY OWLS
501 Crescent Street, New Haven **[P. 25, F-11]**; (203) 397-4378. Jess Dow Field. J.W. Moore, capacity 2,700.

TRINITY COLLEGE
Summit Street, Hartford **[P. 23, B-3]**; (203) 297-2057. Jessee Field, capacity 6,500. Memorial, capacity 2,500.

U.S. COAST GUARD ACADEMY
New London **[P. 23, F-2]**; (203) 444-8600. Cadet Memorial, capacity 4,000. Roland, capacity 2,000.

UNIVERSITY OF BRIDGEPORT PURPLE KNIGHTS
120 Waldemere Avenue, Bridgeport **[P. 24, H-5]**; (203) 576-4735. Hubbell, capacity 2,000.

UNIVERSITY OF CONNECTICUT HUSKIES
2111 Hillside Road, Storrs **[P. 24, B-6]**; (203) 486-5786. Memorial, capacity 16,200. Gym, capacity 4,460.

UNIVERSITY OF HARTFORD HAWKS
200 Bloomfield Avenue, West Hartford **[P. 23, A-3]**; (203) 243-4658. Yousuf Al-Marzook, capacity 2,000. Sports Center, capacity 4,475.

UNIVERSITY OF NEW HAVEN CHARGERS
300 Orange Avenue, West Haven **[P. 25, F-10]**; (203) 932-7017. Robert Dodds Field, capacity 3,000. North Campus Gym, capacity 1,400.

WESLEYAN UNIVERSITY CARDINALS
Middletown **[P. 24, C-5]**; (203) 347-9411. Andrus Field, capacity 5,200. Alumni, capacity 1,200.

YALE UNIVERSITY BULLDOGS
New Haven **[P. 11, F-11]**; (203) 432-4747. Yale Bowl, capacity 70,896. Payne Whitney, capacity 3,100.

Hockey

HARTFORD CIVIC CENTER COLISEUM
One Civic Center Plaza, Hartford **[P. 23, B-4]**. Built in 1975. Capacity: 15,485.
◆A World Hockey Association team in 1975, the Whalers joined the National Hockey League in 1979.
Hartford Whalers (NHL, Wales Conference, Adams Division); (203) 728-3366. Franchise began in 1979. Broadcasts by WTIC-AM (1080), WTXX (Channel 20), SportsChannel.

NEW HAVEN VETERANS MEMORIAL COLISEUM
275 S. Orange St., New Haven **[P. 25, G-11]**. Capacity: 5,933.
New Haven Nighthawks (American Hockey League); (203) 787-0101. Franchise began in 1972. Broadcasts by WAVZ 1300 AM.

PGA/LPGA

TPC AT RIVER HIGHLANDS
Golf Club Road, off Rt. 99, Cromwell **[P. 23, F-3]**; (203) 635-5000. Canon Greater Hartford Open (PGA), July. Number of holes: 72.

Polo

SHALLOWBROOK POLO CLUB
247 Hall Hill Rd., Somers **[P. 24, A-5]**; (203) 749-0749.

Tennis

CONNECTICUT TENNIS CENTER AT YALE UNIVERSITY
Lapham Field House, West Haven **[P. 25, F-11]**; (203) 776-7331. Surface is Deco Turf II. Volvo International Tennis Tournament (ATP), August.

Track & Field

ALUMNI ARENA
Wesleyan University, Middletown **[P. 24, C-5]**; (203) 347-9411.
National Collegiate Athletic Association III (Collegiate National Championship), March, 1991.

USA SNAPSHOTS®

A look at statistics that shape the sports world

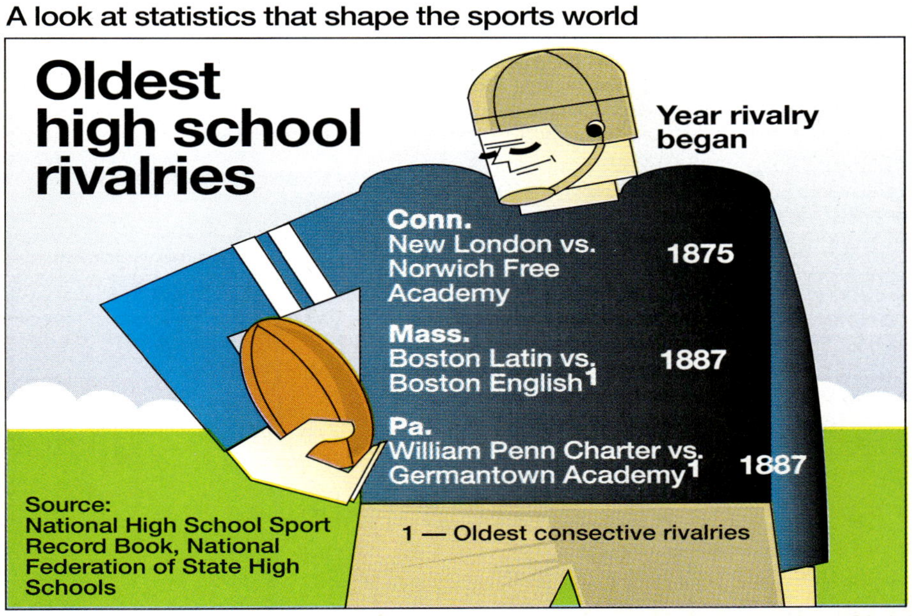

Oldest high school rivalries
Year rivalry began
Conn.
New London vs. Norwich Free Academy
1875
Mass.
Boston Latin vs. Boston English[1]
1887
Pa.
William Penn Charter vs. Germantown Academy[1]
1887
1 — Oldest consective rivalries
Source: National High School Sport Record Book, National Federation of State High Schools

By Rod Little, USA TODAY

STATBOX

POPULATION: 3,277,980
SQUARE MILES: 5,009
TIME ZONE: Eastern
MOTTO: Qui Transtulit Sustinet (He who transplanted still sustains)
BIRD: American Robin
TREE: White Oak
CAPITAL: Hartford
AVERAGE ANNUAL RAINFALL: 42.85"
MEAN TEMP: 25 (Jan.); 73 (July)
MAJOR LEAGUE TEAMS: 1
STATE PARK ACREAGE: 29,856
HIGHEST ELEVATION: 2,380'
LOWEST ELEVATION: sea level
WATERWAYS: 8,400 miles of rivers and streams; 6,000 lakes and ponds

► OUTDOOR VENUES

State Parks

Bike Trails: BK
Boating: BT
Camping: C
Climbing: CL
Diving: DV
Fishing: F
Golfing: G
Hiking: HK
Hunting: HT
Riding: R
Surfing: SU
Swimming: S
Tennis: TE
Whitewater: WW
Winter Sports: W

COCKAPONSEET STATE FOREST
3 mi. W of Chester on CT 148 **[P. 24, D-5]**. Contains 15,652 acres. C HK F S BK W HT

HAMMONASSET BEACH STATE PARK
7 mi. S of I-95, exit 62 **[P. 24, D-5]**. Contains 919 acres.
C HK BT F S BK DV

HOPEVILLE POND STATE PARK
3 mi. E of Jewett City on Route 201 **[P. 25, C-7]**. Contains 554 acres. C HK BT F S

MACEDONIA BROOK STATE PARK
4 mi. NW of Kent off CT 341 **[P. 24, B-2]**. Contains 2,300 acres.
C HK F W

MANSFIELD HOLLOW STATE PARK
1 mi. E of Mansfield Center off CT 89 **[P. 24, B-6]**. Contains 2,328 acres. HK BT F

MOHAWK MOUNTAIN STATE PARK
6 mi. W of Goshen off CT 4 **[P. 24, B-2]**. Contains 260 acres. HK W

NATCHAUG STATE FOREST
4 mi. S of Phoenixville on CT 198 **[P. 25, B-7]**. Contains 12,935 acres. C HK F R W HT

OSBORNEDALE STATE PARK
1 mi. NW of Derby off US 34 **[P. 24, D-3]**. Contains 350 acres. HK F W

PACHAUG STATE FOREST
1 mi. N of Voluntown off Route 49 **[P. 25, C-7]**. Contains 22,938 acres. C HK BT F R W DV

QUADDICK STATE PARK
7 mi. NE of Putnam off Route 44 **[P. 25, A-8]**. Contains 116 acres. BT F S W

ROCKY NECK STATE PARK
7 mi. W of Waterford, CT Turnpike exit 72 **[P. 24, D-6]**. C HK F S BK W DV

SHERWOOD ISLAND STATE PARK
2 mi. S of Westport, CT Turnpike exit 18 **[P. 24, H-3]**. Contains 234 acres. F S BK DV

WHARTON BROOK STATE PARK
2 mi. S of Wallingford on Route 5 **[P. 24, C-4]**. Contains 96 acres. HK F S W

CONTINUED ON PAGE 144

Connecticut

CONTINUED FROM PAGE 143

Skiing

ALPINE SKIING

MOHAWK MOUNTAIN SKI AREA
43 Great Hollow Road, off CT 4, Cornwall **[P. 24, B-2]**; (203) 672-6100.
Vertical drop is 640 feet. Has one tow and five chairs.

POWDER RIDGE SKI AREA
Route 147, Middlefield **[P. 24, C-5]**; (203) 349-3454.
Vertical drop is 500 feet. Has one tow and four chairs.

NORDIC SKIING

CEDAR BROOK FARMS
1481 Ratley, West Suffield **[P. 24, A-5]**; (203) 668-5026.

PINE MOUNTAIN XC SKI TOURING CENTER
Route 179, East Hartland **[P. 24, A-4]**; (203) 653-4279.

QUINEBAUG CROSS COUNTRY
Roosevelt Avenue, Preston **[P. 25, C-7]**; (203) 886-2284.

WINDING TRAILS XC
50 Winding Trails Drive, Farmington **[P. 24, C-4]**; (203) 678-9582.

ACTIVE SPORTS

AEROBICS: AFAA, 202 Mamanasco Rd., #20, Ridgefield; (203) 431-8562.

BASEBALL: Little League Baseball Eastern Region HQ, PO Box 3485, Williamsport, PA; (717) 326-1921. • **Pony Baseball-Softball,** 86 Park Street, Stratford; (203) 378-5013. • **American Legion Baseball,** 161 Allen St., Groton; (203) 449-8293. • **Babe Ruth Baseball,** Ernest P. Papazoglou, 71 Tracy Ave., Lynn, MA; (617) 595-7603. • **Men's Senior Baseball League - Connecticut,** 23-3 Arthur Dr., S. Windsor; (203) 644-1396.

BOARDSAILING: Gone With The Wind Surf Club , Georgetown; (203) 852-1857. • **Longshore Sailing School ,** Westport; (203) 226-4646. • **USWA Regional Director,** Bayview Bus Park Unit 10, Gilford, NH; (603) 293-2727.

BOWLING: American Bowling Congress, 5301 S. 76th St., Greendale, WI; (414) 421-6400.

CANOEING & KAYAKING: ACA New England Vice Commodore, 785 Bow Ln., Middleton.

CYCLING: LAW New England Regional Director, PO Box 305, Atkinson, NH,; (603) 362-4572. • **USCF Connecticut Representative,** 58 Littlefield Rd., New Milford; (203) 354-4879. • **Yankee AYH Council,** 118 Oak Street, Hartford; (203) 247-6356

FITNESS: Governor's Committee on Physical Fitness, Center for Health Fitness, University of Connecticut, 359 Mansfield Rd., Storrs; (203) 486-2763.

FOOTBALL: Pop Warner Football, 1315 Walnut Street, Suite 1632, Philadelphia, PA; (215) 735-1450.

GOLF: Connecticut State Golf Association, 35 Cold Spring Rd., Suite 212, Rocky Hill; (203) 257-4171. • **Connecticut Women's Golf Association,** 567 Nut Plains Rd., Guilford. • **PGA Connecticut Section,** 35 Cold Spring Rd., Suite 212, Rocky Hill; (203) 257-4653.

HIKING & CLIMBING: Adirondack Mountain Club , RR #3, Box 3055, Lake George, NY; (518) 668-4447. • **Connecticut Sierra Club Chapter,** 118 Oak St., Hartford; (203) 527-9788. • **The Appalachian Mountain Club ,** 5 Joy St., Boston, MA; (617) 523-0636.

HOCKEY: USA Hockey New England Registrar, 15 Orange Street, Rumford, RI; (401) 438-2954.

HUNTING & FISHING: Department of Environmental Protection, State Office Building, 165 Capitol Ave., Hartford; (203) 566-4522. • **Trout Unlimited,** 18E Weaver's Hill, Greenwich; (203) 531-7939.

RACQUETBALL: AARA, 345 Main Street, Suite 202, Newington; (203) 667-7633.

RIDING: Connecticut Horse Council, 1185 Main St., S. Windsor; (203) 289-8823.

RODEO: PRCA First Frontier Circuit, 5982 Summit Bridge Rd., Townsend, DE; (302) 378-4551.

RUNNING: RRCA CT State Rep., 61 Hope St., Stamford; (203) 325-4688.

SCUBA: Scuba Shack of Connecticut, Ltd., 1765 Silas Deane Highway, Rocky Hill; (203) 563-0119. • **The Diving Bell, Ltd.,** 461 Federal Road, Route 7, Brookfield; (203) 775-3573.

SKATING: Middle Atlantic Skating Association, 3419 Irwin Ave., Bronx, NY; (212) 549-4290. • **USFSA,** 20 First Street, Colorado Springs, CO; (719) 635-5200.

SOCCER: Connecticut Soccer Ass'n, 18 Fox Rd., Plainville; (203) 747-9202. • **Connecticut Junior Soccer Ass'n,** 32 Avonridge, Avon; (203) 673-4371. • **AYSO Regional Director,** 4014 Oneida St., New Hartford, NY; (315) 737-5610.

SOFTBALL: Connecticut ASA, Parson's Complex, 70 W. River Street, Milford; (203) 874-4036.

SQUASH: Downtown Racquet Club, New Haven; (203) 787-6501. • **Hartford YMCA (USSRA),** Hartford; (203) 522-4183.

SWIMMING: LMSC Connecticut Registrar, 251 Race Hill Rd., Madison; (203) 421-3370.

TENNIS: Recreational TEAMTENNIS East Region, National Program Coordinator, 246 N. Reservoir St., Lancaster, PA; (800) 633-6122. • **Eastern USTA,** 550 Mamaroneck Ave., Suite 505, Harrison, NY; (914) 698-0414. • **New England USTA,** PO Box 587, Needham Heights, MA; (617) 964-2030.

Tip Offs

Sports Bars - Part I

As singles bars died out after the disco era, and the sports industry boomed, a new sort of socializing came to the fore. Sports bars and restaurants became after-work spots where mutual interest made for a non-threatening hangout. These often, highly profitable establishments range from big-city investments for sports celebrities to multi-state chains, to local hangouts. They offer everything from big-screen televisions with interactive video (QB1) to boxing rings. The following is a list of some of the sturdier entries from around the USA.

ARIZONA

Chicago Sports Bar, 2730 No. Scottsdale Rd., Scottsdale 602-947-9707
Max's, 6727 No. 47th Avenue, Glendale 602-937-1671
Sports Page, 7730 E. McDowell Rd., Scottsdale 602-949-9705

CALIFORNIA

B.B. O'Brien's Sports Cafe, 72185 Painters Pass, Palm Desert 619-346-5576
Bunz & Co., 311 Judah St., Roseville 916-969-0142
Cask 'n Cleaver, 9584 Micron Ave., Sacramento 916-364-1231
Champions, 18000 Von Karman Ave., Irvine 714-975-1508
Champions, 5855 W. Century Blvd., Los Angeles 213-641-5700
Champions Bar & Grill, 7492 Ettinger Ave., Huntington Beach 714-848-2929
C.J. Brett's, 2701 Pacific Coast Highway, Hermosa Beach 213-374-0953
Drinker's Hall of Fame, 151 E. Huntington Dr., Arcadia 818-447-3947
Foggy's Notion, 3655 Sports Arena Blvd., San Diego 619-222-2791
Harry C's, 1414 University Ave., Riverside 714-686-2212
King's X, 4401 Piedmont Ave., Oakland 415-653-4200
Lefty O'Douls, 333 Geary Blvd., San Francisco 415-982-8900
Legends, 5236 East Second St., Long Beach 213-433-5743
Limelight, 1014 Alhambra Blvd., Sacramento 916-446-2236
McGee's, 1645 Park St., Alameda 415-522-3470
Pat O'Shea's, 3848 Geary Blvd., San Francisco 415-752-3148
Rickey's Sports Lounge, 15028 Hesperian Blvd., San Leandro 415-352-0200
Silky Sullivan's, 10201 Slater Ave., Fountain Valley 714-963-2718
Sports Bar & Grill, 4060 Sunrise Blvd., Fair Oaks 916-967-8492
Sports Deli, 2040 Ave. of the Stars, Century City 213-553-5800
Yankee Doodle's, 4100 E. Ocean Blvd., Long Beach 213-439-9777

COLORADO

Brooklyn's, 2644 W. Colfax, Denver 303-572-3999
Friendly Confines, 15350 Smokey Hill Rd., Aurora 303-693-4500
Jackson's Hole, 990 S. Oneida, Denver 303-388-2883
Jackson's Hole, 675 Kipling, Lakewood 303-238-3000
Jackson's Hole, Thorton Town Center, Thorton 303-457-2100
Zang Brewing Co., 2301 Seventh St., Denver 303-455-2500

CONNECTICUT

Bobby Valentine's Sports Gallery Cafe, 304 Old Gate Lane, Milford 203-878-5262
Bobby Valentine's Sports Gallery Cafe, 225 Main Street, Stamford 203-348-0010
Bobby Valentine's Sports Gallery Cafe, 280 Connecticut Ave., Norwalk 203-854-9300

DISTRICT OF COLUMBIA

Champions, 1206 Wisconsin Ave., N.W., Georgetown 202-965-4005

FLORIDA

Champions, 1001 No. Westshore Blvd., Tampa 813-287-2555
Penalty Box Bar/Coral Plaza Motel, 2701 No. Federal, Fort Lauderdale 305-565-6658
Players Sports Pub, 4432 Curry Ford Rd., Orlando 407-273-9696
Scores, 843 Lee Rd., Orlando 407-628-0774
Sneakers, 4880 So. Kirkman Rd., Orlando 407-293-8881
Sports Hut, 11865 S.W. 26th St., Miami 305-227-9210

GEORGIA

Champions, 265 Peachtree Center Ave., Atlanta 404-521-0000
P.J. Haley's Pub, 1799 Briarcliff Rd., Atlanta 404-874-3116
Rupert's, 3330 Piedmont Rd., Atlanta 404-266-9834
Stooge's, 2020 Collier Rd., Atlanta 404-355-5445

ILLINOIS

Champions, 8535 W. Higgins Rd., Chicago 312-380-8888
The Cubby Bear, 1059 W. Addison, Chicago, 312-327-1662
Ditka's, 223 W. Ontario St., Chicago 312-280-1790
Harry Caray's, 33 W. Kinsey, Chicago 312-465-9265
Miller's Pub, 134 S. Wabash, Chicago 312-645-5377

INDIANA

Sports, 231 So. Meridian, Indianapolis 317-631-5838

KENTUCKY

Jock's Sports Bar & Grill, 3423 Breckenridge Lane, Louisville 502-491-1199
Players, 2427 Bardstown Rd., Louisville 502-451-5888

LOUISIANA

Champions of New Orleans Lakeside Shopping Center 3301 Veterans Memorial Blvd. Metorie, LA 504-834-0600

MARYLAND

Balls, 200 W. Pratt St., Baltimore 301-659-5844
Champions, 1748 W. Nursery Rd., Baltimore 301-859-5555

CONTINUED ON PAGE 159

Delaware

The state's popular beaches feature contests such as Reheboth's Best Body on the Beach (July, 302-227-9466), and Dewey Beach's East Coast Skim Boarding Championships. ◆ In early May, the 10-day Tour Du Pont bicycle race shows off the top cyclists in the world (in a blur) to road-side spectators. ◆ During the first full week of June, the LPGA stops in Wilmington for the McDonald's Championship LPGA Tournament (302-428-1681).◆ Fishing is permitted year-round, except for freshwater trout. A state hunting license is required for any game, and water-fowl hunters must also buy state and federal stamps. ◆ NASCAR Winston Cup racing visits the Dover Downs International Speedway in June and September, and the Georgetown and Delmar Speedways are popular for dirt track racing.

POPULATION: 666,168	**STATBOX**
SQUARE MILES: 1,982	
TIME ZONE: Eastern	
MOTTO: Liberty and Independence	
BIRD: Blue Hen Chicken	
TREE: American Holly	
CAPITAL: Dover	
AVERAGE ANNUAL RAINFALL: 41"	
MEAN TEMP: 54	
MAJOR LEAGUE TEAMS: 0	
NATIONAL PARK/FOREST ACREAGE: 7,433	
STATE PARK ACREAGE: 11,597	
HIGHEST ELEVATION: 442	
LOWEST ELEVATION: sea level	
WATERWAYS: 112 square miles of inland water	

Bike Trails: BK
Boating: BT
Camping: C
Climbing: CL
Diving: DV
Fishing: F
Golfing: G
Hiking: HK
Hunting: HT
Riding: R
Surfing: SU
Swimming: S
Tennis: TE
Whitewater: WW
Winter Sports: W

▶ SPECTATOR VENUES

Auto Racing

DOVER DOWNS INTERNATIONAL SPEEDWAY
US Route 13, north of Dover **[P. 52, G-4]**; (302) 674-4600. Track is 1 mile.
◆"The Monster Mile" is a high-banked oval.
Budweiser 500 (NASCAR Winston Cup), June.
PEAK Antifreeze 500 (NASCAR Winston Cup), September.

Bowling

HOLIDAY LANES
2105 Philadelphia Pike, Claymont **[P. 53, B-12]**; (302) 798-6656.
Columbia 300 Delaware Open (LPBT), September.

College Sports

DELAWARE STATE COLLEGE HORNETS
Dupont Highway, Dover **[P. 52, G-4]**; (302) 736-4928. Alumni Field, capacity 4,000.

UNIVERSITY OF DELAWARE FIGHTIN' BLUE HENS
Newark **[P. 53, B-12]**; (302) 451-6564. Delaware, capacity 23,000. University of Delaware, capacity 3,000.

Horse Racing

DELAWARE PARK RACE TRACK
Route 7, S of Wilmington, off I-95, exit 4B, Stanton **[P. 53, B-12]**; (302) 994-2521. Opened in 1937. Total capacity: 17,500. Thoroughbred season from Mar. to Nov.

DOVER DOWNS RACEWAY
1131 N. DuPont Highway, Dover **[P. 52, G-4]**; (302) 674-4600. Opened in 1969. Clubhouse capacity: 5000. Grandstand capacity: 4,200. Harness season from Nov. to Mar.
◆Horse drawn buggies meet high tech race cars here at the Dover Downs International Speedway.

HARRINGTON RACEWAY
US Route 13, Harrington **[P. 53, E-12]**; (302) 398-3269. Opened in 1946. Clubhouse capacity: 400. Grandstand capacity: 4,500. Harness season from Sep. to Nov.
◆Additional 1991 meet March to November; may become permanent.

PGA/LPGA

DU PONT COUNTRY CLUB
Black Gates & Rockland Rd., Wilmington **[P. 52, F-2]**; (302) 654-4435.
McDonald's Championship (LPGA), June.
Number of holes: 72.

▶ OUTDOOR VENUES

State Parks

BELLEVUE STATE PARK
Exit 9 off I-95 **[P. 53, B-12]**. Contains 271 acres. **HK F R BK W**

BRANDYWINE CREEK STATE PARK
3 mi. N of Wilmington at jct. of DE 100 & DE 92 **[P. 53, B-12]**. Contains 795 acres. **HK BT F W**

CAPE HENLOPEN STATE PARK
1 mi. E of Lewes **[P. 53, E-14]**. Contains 6,120 acres. **C HK F S TE**

DELAWARE SEASHORE STATE PARK
1 mi. S of Dewey Beach **[P. 53, E-14]**. Contains 3,102 acres. **C BT F S SU**

FENWICK ISLAND STATE PARK
Just S of South Bethany Beach on DE 1 **[P. 53, F-14]**. Contains 208 acres. **BT F S SU**

FORT DELAWARE STATE PARK
Delaware City, N of C & D Canal off Route 9 **[P. 53, B-12]**. Contains 288 acres. **HK**

HOLTS LANDING STATE PARK
5 mi. NW of Bethany Beach on Indian River Bay **[P. 53, F-14]**. Contains 203 acres. **BT F**

KILLENS POND STATE PARK
12 mi. S of Dover off US 13 **[P. 53, D-13]**. Contains 878 acres. **C HK BT F S W**

LUMS POND STATE PARK
3 mi. S of Glasgow on DE 896 **[P. 53, C-12]**. Contains 1,748 acres. **C HK BT F S W**

TRAP POND STATE PARK
4 mi. E of Laurel off DE 24 **[P. 53, F-12]**. Contains 965 acres. **C HK BT F S**

WALTER S. CARPENTER STATE PARK
3 mi. N of Newark via DE 896 **[P. 53, B-12]**. Contains 594 acres. **C HK F W HT**

▶ ACTIVE SPORTS

BASEBALL: Little League Baseball Eastern Region HQ, PO Box 3485, Williamsport, PA; (717) 326-1921 • **American Legion Baseball,** 1017 Faun Road, Wilmington; (302) 478-7591. • **Babe Ruth Baseball,** Raymond P. Jones, 300 Lodge St., Piscataway, NJ; (201) 469-5841.

BOARDSAILING: East of Maui , Dewey Bch.; (302) 227-4703. • **USWA Regional Director,** 1912 MacCumber Ln., Wilmington, NC; (919) 256-3553.

BOWLING: American Bowling Congress, 5301 S. 76th St., Greendale, WI; (414) 421-6400.

CANOEING & KAYAKING: ACA Middle States Vice Commodore, 10236 Raider Ln., Fairfax, VA; (703) 359-2594.

CYCLING: LAW Eastern Regional Director, 303 South Washington, Gettysburg, PA; (717) 334-0742. • **USCF Maryland/Delaware Representative,** PO Box 131, Riva, MD; (301) 956-2767.

FITNESS: Governor's Council on Lifestyle and Fitness, c/o Division of Public Health, Health Education Office, Jesse Cooper Building, Federal & Water St.s; (302) 739-4724.

FOOTBALL: Pop Warner Football, 1315 Walnut Street, Suite 1632, Philadelphia, PA; (215) 735-1450.

GOLF: Delaware State Golf Association, 2800 Lancaster Ave., Suite 8, Wilmington; (302) 656-5515.

HIKING & CLIMBING: The Appalachian Mountain Club , 5 Joy Street, Boston, MA; (617) 523-0636. • **Wilmington Trail Club (AHS),** PO Box 1184, Wilmington; (302) 656-1155.

HOCKEY: USA Hockey Atlantic Registrar, 3 Pendleton Dr., Cherry Hill, NJ; (609) 424-8343.

HUNTING & FISHING: Department of Natural Resources & Environmental Control, 89 Kings Highway, Dover; (302) 736-5295.

RACQUETBALL: AARA, 706 Kilburn Rd., Wilmington; (302) 478-7919.

RODEO: PRCA First Frontier Circuit, 5982 Summit Bridge Rd., Townsend; (302) 378-4551.

RUNNING: RRCA DE State Rep., PO Box 226, Wilmington; (302) 772-2222.

SCUBA: Scuba World, Inc., 4004-B South Dupont Highway, Dover; (302) 697-2882.

SKATING: USFSA, 20 First Street, Colorado Springs, CO; (719) 635-5200.

SOCCER: Delaware Soccer Ass'n, 2116-F Haven Rd., Wilmington; (302) 798-4204. • **Delaware YSA,** PO Box 5325, Wilmington; (302) 575-0800. • **AYSO Regional Director,** 4014 Oneida St., New Hartford, NY; (315) 737-5610.

SOFTBALL: Delaware ASA, Sheridan Square, 2122 Nicholby Dr., Wilmington; (302) 998-6124.

SQUASH: Wilmington YMCA, Wilmington; (302) 571-6900.

SWIMMING: LMSC Delaware Valley Registrar, 1024 Elkton Rd., Newark; (302) 368-5176.

TENNIS: Recreational TEAMTENNIS East Region, National Program Coordinator, 246 North Reservoir Street, Lancaster, PA; (800) 633-6122. • **Middle States USTA,** 580 Shoemaker Road, King of Prussia, PA; (215) 768-4040.

TRIATHLON: Brandywine Valley Tri Club, PO Box 344, Montchanin; (215) 793-1930.

USA SNAPSHOTS®

A look at statistics that shape the sports world

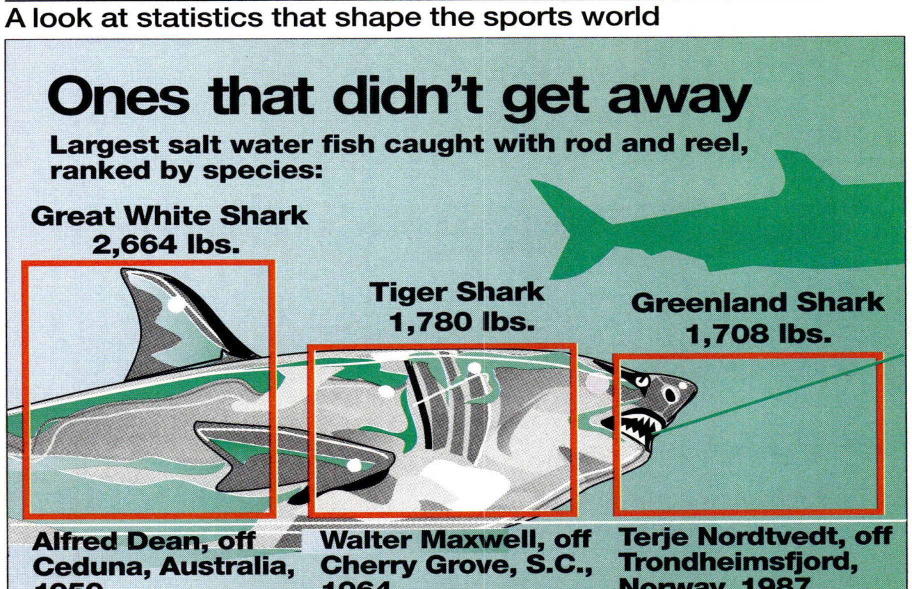

Source: International Game Fish Association

By Suzy Parker, USA TODAY

Florida

In Florida, sport is more than a lifestyle—it's big business, with $16 billion in annual revenues. ◆ The state is the most popular place in the world for both fresh and saltwater angling, as well as the world's No. 1 scuba and skin diving destination, with a million divers visiting one destination alone: North America's only live coral reef near Key Largo. ◆ Placed end-to-end, all the fairways on Florida's 1,000-plus golf courses would stretch from Miami to British Columbia. ◆ Tennis enthusiasts can choose from 7,000 court complexes and training facilities. ◆ The Sunshine State has two NFL teams, two NBA teams, and a new NHL franchise (see below). Plus 18 of the 26 Major League Baseball teams hold spring training here, making up the Grapefruit League. It's a tradition that started with the Washington Statesmen (now the Minnesota Twins) in 1888.

STATBOX

POPULATION: 12,937,926
SQUARE MILES: 54,153
TIME ZONE: Eastern and Central
MOTTO: In God We Trust
BIRD: Mockingbird
TREE: Sabal Palm
CAPITAL: Tallahassee
AVERAGE ANNUAL RAINFALL: 50-65"
MEAN TEMP: 73
MAJOR LEAGUE TEAMS: 4
NATIONAL PARK ACREAGE: 2,511,570
STATE PARK ACREAGE: 366,423
HIGHEST ELEVATION: 345
LOWEST ELEVATION: sea level
WATERWAYS: 4,500 sq. miles inland water

▶ SPECTATOR VENUES

Auto Racing

DAYTONA INTERNATIONAL SPEEDWAY
U.S. 92, east of I-95, Daytona **[P. 28, B-6]**; (904) 254-2700. Track is 3.56 miles (Camel GT)/ 2.5 miles (NASCAR Winston Cup).
◆Home of the NASCAR headquarters and the Daytona 500 — which attracts the largest crowd in the southeast — the speedway is called "the world center of racing."
SunBank 24 at Daytona (IMSA Camel GT), February 1991.
Daytona 500 by STP (NASCAR Winston Cup), February.
Pepsi 400 (NASCAR Winston Cup), July.

GAINESVILLE RACEWAY
FL 225, Gainesville **[P. 26, D-5]**; (904) 377-0046. Track is quarter-mile strip (for NHRA races).
Motorcraft Gatornationals (NHRA), mid-March.

MIAMI STREET CIRCUIT
Biscayne Blvd. & Bicentennial Park, Miami **[P. 29, N-5]**; (305) 662-5660. Track is 1.873 miles
Nissan Grand Prix of Miami (IMSA Camel GT), April.

SEBRING INTERNATIONAL RACEWAY
US 98, Sebring **[P. 27, H-6]**; (813) 655-1442. Track is 3.7 miles.
◆In 1959, the first USA Formula One Grand Prix was run here. Sebring is called "the scene of the rip-roaringest hell-on-wheels auto race in the whole United States," in T.D. Allman's book, *Miami: City of the Future*. Races here inspired Ralph Sanchez, the man who would create the Miami Grand Prix. "I saw the Grand Canyon at dusk, and that was lovely. I saw the leaning tower of Pisa at midnight, and it was beautiful. But there was nothing like my first Sebring," Allman quotes him as saying.
12 Hours of Sebring Grand Prix of Endurance (IMSA Camel GT), March.

SOUTH FLORIDA FAIRGROUNDS
9069 Southern Blvd., West Palm Beach **[P. 28, E-7]**; (407) 793-7223. Track is 1.6 miles.
Toyota Grand Prix of Palm Beach (IMSA Camel Grand Prix), March.

Baseball

AL LANG STADIUM
180 Second Avenue SE, St. Petersburg **[P. 26, G-2]**. Capacity: 7,004
St. Petersburg Cardinals (Florida State League, Class A); (813) 822-3384. Entered League in 1955. MLB affiliation, St. Louis Cardinals.

BASEBALL CITY SPORTS COMPLEX
Intersection of I-4 and US 27, 300 Stadium Way, Davenport **[P. 26, G-6]**. Capacity: 8,000
Baseball City Royals (Florida State League, Class A); (813) 424-7130. Entered League in 1987. MLB affiliation, Kansas City Royals.

CHAIN O'LAKES PARK
Winter Haven **[P. 26, G-6]**. Capacity: 4,545
Winter Haven Red Sox (Florida State League, Class A); (813) 293-3900. Entered League in 1969. MLB affiliation, Boston Red Sox.

CHARLOTTE COUNTY STADIUM
2300 El Jobean Road, Pt. Charlotte **[P. 27, J-5]**. Capacity: 6,026
Charlotte Rangers (Florida State League, Class A); (813) 625-9500. Entered League in 1987. MLB affiliation, Texas Rangers.

CITY OF FT. LAUDERDALE YANKEE STADIUM
5301 NW 12th Ave., Ft. Lauderdale **[P. 29, L-8]**. Capacity: 8,340
Ft. Lauderdale Yankees (Florida State League, Class A); (305) 776-1921. Entered League in 1962. MLB affiliation, New York Yankees.

DUNEDIN STADIUM AT GRANT FIELD
311 Douglas Ave., Dunedin **[P. 26, E-1]**. Capacity: 6,218
Dunedin Blue Jays (Florida State League, Class A); (813) 733-9302. Entered League in 1987. MLB affiliation, Toronto Blue Jays.

ED SMITH STADIUM
12th St. & Tuttle Ave., Sarasota **[P. 29, L-2]**. Capacity: 7,500
Sarasota White Sox (Florida State League, Class A); (813) 954-7699. Entered League in 1989. Broadcasts by WCTQ 92.1 FM. MLB affiliation, Chicago White Sox.

HOLMAN STADIUM
401 26th Street, Vero Beach **[P. 27, H-8]**. Capacity: 6,500
◆A part of Dodgertown, the parent club's sprawling and deluxe spring complex.
Vero Beach Dodgers (Florida State League, Class A); (407) 569-4900. Entered League in 1980. Broadcasts by WAXE 1370-AM. MLB affiliation, Los Angeles Dodgers.

JACK RUSSELL MEMORIAL STADIUM
800 Phillies Drive, Clearwater **[P. 26, E-1]**. Capacity: 7,385
Clearwater Phillies (Florida State League, Class A); (813) 441-8638. Entered League in 1985. Broadcasts by 760 AM WEND. MLB affiliation, Philadelphia Phillies.

JOKER MARCHANT STADIUM
Lakeland Hills Blvd., Lakeland **[P. 26, G-5]**. Capacity: 7,500
Lakeland Tigers (Florida State League, Class A); (813) 686-1133. Entered League in 1960. MLB affiliation, Detroit Tigers.

OSCEOLA COUNTY STADIUM
1000 Osceola Blvd., Kissimmee **[P. 29, H-5]**. Capacity: 5,100
Osceola Astros (Florida State League, Class A); (407) 933-5500. Entered League in 1985. Broadcasts by WMJK 1220 AM. MLB affiliation, Houston Astros.

POMPANO BEACH MUNICIPAL STADIUM
1799 N.E. 8th St., Pompano Beach **[P. 29, L-8]**. Capacity: 5,000
Miami Miracle (Florida State League, Class A); (305) 783-2111. Entered League in 1962. Broadcasts by WSBR 740 AM. MLB affiliation, Independent.

THOMAS J. WHITE STADIUM
525 NW Peacock Blvd., Port St. Lucie **[P. 27, H-8]**. Capacity: 7,400
St. Lucie Mets (Florida State League, Class A); (407) 871-2100. Entered League in 1988. Broadcasts by WPSL 1590 AM. MLB affiliation, New York Mets.

TINKER FIELD
287 Tampa Ave. South, Orlando **[P. 28, E-4]**. Capacity: 5,104
Orlando SunRays (Southern League, Class AA); (407) 872-7593. Entered League in 1973. Broadcasts by WWNZ 740AM. MLB affiliation, Minnesota Twins (1973).

WEST PALM BEACH MUNICIPAL STADIUM
715 Hank Aaron Drive, West Palm Beach **[P. 28, F-8]**. Capacity: 4,300
West Palm Beach Expos (Florida State League, Class A); (407) 684-6801. Entered League in 1969. MLB affiliation, Montreal Expos.

WOLFSON PARK
1201 E. Duval St., Jacksonville **[P. 26, B-8]**. Capacity: 8,200
Jacksonville Suns (Southern League, Class AA); (904) 358-2846. Entered League in 1970. Broadcasts by WQIK 1320 AM, 92.1 FM. MLB affiliation, Seattle Mariners.

Basketball

FLORIDA ATLANTIC UNIVERSITY GYMNASIUM
38 Volusia Street, Boca Raton **[P. 29, K-8]**. Capacity: 4,439.
Florida Jades (World Basketball League); (407) 241-3731. Entered League in 1991. Broadcasts by WRBD 1470 AM.

ORLANDO ARENA
600 West Amelia St., Orlando **[P. 28, E-5]**. Built in 1989. Capacity: 15,077.
Orlando Magic (NBA Eastern Conf., Atlantic Div.); (407) 649-3200. Franchise began in 1989. Broadcasts by WWNZ 740 AM, WKCF-TV Channel 68, Sunshine Network Cable.

PENSACOLA CIVIC CENTER
201 East Gregory Street, Pensacola **[P. 28, B-2]**. Capacity: 9,856.
Pensacola Tornados (Continental Basketball Association, American Conference, Eastern Division); (904) 432-8326. Entered League in 1978. Broadcasts by WCOA, 1370 AM.

THE MIAMI ARENA
721 N.W. First Ave., Miami **[P. 29, N-4]**. Built in 1988. Capacity: 15,008.
◆Great view from any seat.
Miami Heat (NBA Eastern Conf., Atlantic Div.); (305) 577-4328. Franchise began in 1988. Broadcasts by WQAM 560 AM, WRFM 830 AM, SportsChannel Florida/WBFS Channel 33.

Bowling

ALOMA BOWLING CENTER
2530 Aloma Avenue, Winter Park **[P. 28, D-6]**; (407) 671-8675.
Ebonite Thunderbolt Classic (LPBT), April.

CYPRESS LANES
2010 Dundee Road, Winter Haven **[P. 26, G-6]**; (813) 294-3295.
Florida Open (PBA), February.

CONTINUED ON PAGE 147

USA SNAPSHOTS®

A look at statistics that shape the sports world

Driving for the PGA

More golfers than ever are trying to qualify for the PGA tour.

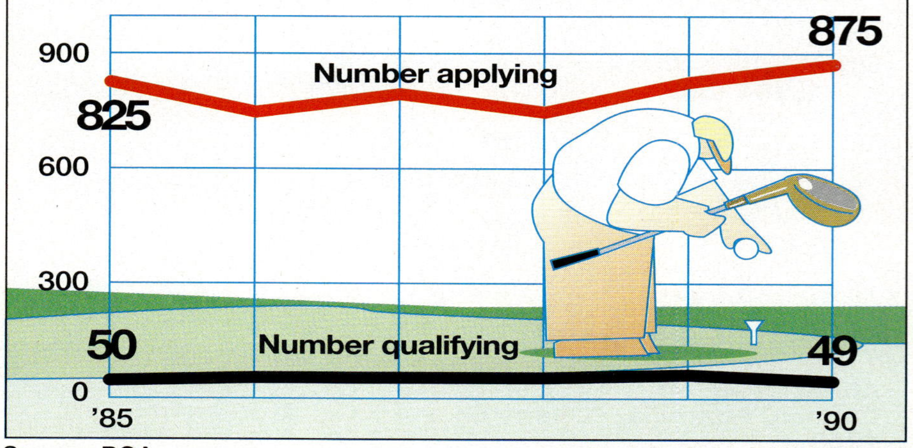

Source: PGA
By Julie Stacey, USA TODAY

Florida

CONTINUED FROM PAGE 146

DON CARTER'S ALL STAR LANES-SAWGRASS
1391 N.W. 136th Avenue, Sunrise **[P. 27, L-8]**; (305) 846-8088.
Bud Light Classic (PBA), February.

FORT PIERCE BOWL
2500 North Federal Highway, Fort Pierce **[P. 27, H-8]**; (407) 464-3343.
Treasure Coast PBA Senior Open, October.

RAINBOW LANES
1225 S. Highland Ave., Clearwater **[P. 26, E-1]**; (813) 442-8167.
Clearwater Classic (LPBT), May.

REGAL LANES
4847 N. Armenia Ave, Tampa **[P. 26, E-3]**; (813) 877-7418.
WIBC Queens (LPBT), May.

STARDUST LANES
1465 US 441 SE, Okeechobee **[P. 27, A-7]**; (813) 467-1800.
Okeechobee Classic (LPBT), Feb.

College Sports

BETHUNE-COOKMAN COLLEGE WILDCATS
640 Second Avenue, Daytona Beach **[P. 28, B-6]**; (904) 255-1401. Memorial, Jacksonville Gator Bowl, or Tampa Stadium. Moore Gym.

FLORIDA A&M UNIVERSITY RATTLERS
Martin Luther King Jr. Boulevard, Tallahassee **[P. 28, B-4]**; (904) 599-3868. Bragg Memorial, capacity 25,500. Gaither Center, capacity 5,000.

FLORIDA INTERNATIONAL UNIVERSITY GOLDEN PANTHERS
Tamiami Trail, Miami **[P. 27, M-8]**; (305) 348-2756.

JACKSONVILLE UNIVERSITY DOLPHINS
University Boulevard North, Jacksonville **[P. 26, B-8]**; (904) 744-3950. Veterans Memorial, capacity 10,000.

STETSON UNIVERSITY HATTERS
De Land **[P. 26, E-6]**; (904) 822-8120.
Edmunds Center, capacity 5,000.

UNIVERSITY OF CENTRAL FLORIDA KNIGHTS
Orlando **[P. 26, F-6]**; (407) 823-2256. Orlando, capacity 55,000. Gym, capacity 3,000.

UNIVERSITY OF FLORIDA GATORS
Gainesville **[P. 26, D-4]**; (904) 375-4683. Florida Field, capacity 72,000. O'Connell Center, capacity 12,000.
◆The annual Georgia game is played off-campus in Jacksonville. A tailgater's special, it's billed as the world's largest outdoor cocktail party.

UNIVERSITY OF MIAMI HURRICANES
#1 Hurricane Drive, Coral Gables **[P. 29, O-3]**; (305) 284-3822. Orange Bowl, capacity 74,000. Miami Arena, capacity 16,500.
◆One of the top football programs in the country. And here's the good news. The Hurricanes rarely sell out at home, so tickets are available.

UNIVERSITY OF SOUTH FLORIDA BULLS
4202 E. Fowler Avenue, Tampa **[P. 26, E-3]**; (813) 974-2125.

Football

FLORIDA CITRUS BOWL
1610 W. Church Street, Orlando **[P. 28, E-5]**.
Capacity: 70,000.
Orlando Thunder (World League of American Football, North American East Division); (407) 422-1616. Franchise began in 1991. Broadcasts by WDBO 580 AM.

JOE ROBBIE STADIUM
2269 N.W. 199th Street, Miami **[P. 29, J-5]**.
Built in 1987. Capacity: 73,000.
◆Great sight lines. Can be hot. No protection from rain.
Miami Dolphins (AFC Eastern Division); (305) 620-5000. Franchise began in 1966. Broadcasts by WIOD-AM, WQBA-AM.

TAMPA STADIUM
North Dale Mabry, Tampa **[P. 26, E-3]**. Built in 1967. Capacity: 74,315.
◆Great sight lines. Near a ritzy shopping mall.
Tampa Bay Buccaneers (NFC Central Division); (813) 870-2700. Franchise began in 1976. Broadcasts by WRBQ.

> **"From a water skier's perspective, Florida is paradise. There's a countless number of small, calm lakes. . . just about enough for every skier to have their own private lake."**
>
> Water skier *Camille Duvall*

Hockey

VENUE TO BE ANNOUNCED
Tampa.
Tampa Bay Lightning (NHL, Conference & Division TBA); (813) 229-2658. Franchise to begin in 1992.

Horse Racing

CALDER RACE COURSE
21001 N.W. 27th Avenue, Miami **[P. 29, J-4]**; (305) 625-1311. Opened in 1971. Clubhouse capacity: 5,273. Grandstand capacity: 8,192.
Thoroughbred season from May to Nov.

GULFSTREAM PARK
901 South Federal Highway, Hallandale **[P. 29, M-8]**; (305) 944-1242. Opened in 1939.
Total capacity: 22,500.
Thoroughbred season from Jan. to May.
◆Located between Ft. Lauderdale and Miami. You can spend the morning on the beach and the day at the track. Gulfstream offers an early look at the Triple Crown contenders. In an area brimming with four-star restaurants, the track crowd favors Manero's, which serves one of the greatest steaks found anywhere. A favorite hangout of some of the nation's top trainers, owners and jockeys. Gulfstream originally opened in 1939 but lasted only four days before going bankrupt. Reopened in 1944 under the ownership of Jimmy Donn, Sr., whose grandson, Doug Donn, is the park's current president. The 1989 Breeder's Cup took place here, and will come south again in October, 1992.

POMPANO PARK HARNESS TRACK
1800 S.W. 3rd Street, Pompano Beach **[P. 29, L-8]**; (305) 972-2000. Opened in 1964.
Clubhouse capacity: 2,250. Grandstand capacity: 7,500.
Harness season from Oct. to Apr.

TAMPA BAY DOWNS
Off Hillsborough Ave., Race Track Road, Oldsmar **[P. 26, E-2]**; (813) 855-4401. Opened in 1926. Clubhouse capacity: 1,000.
Grandstand capacity: 2,900.
Thoroughbred season from Dec. to late spring.
◆Dates vary slightly year to year.

Museums & Halls of Fame

DON GARLITS MUSEUM OF DRAG RACING
13700 S.W. 16th Avenue, Belleview **[P. 26, E-5]**; (904) 245-8661.
◆More than 120 drag racers and antique cars.

FLORIDA SPORTS HALL OF FAME
601 Hall of Fame Drive, Lake City **[P. 26, C-4]**; (904) 755-5666.

INTERNATIONAL REFERENCE LIBRARY OF FISHES AND MUSEUM
3000 E. Las Olas Blvd., Fort Lauderdale **[P. 29, M-8]**; (305) 467-0161.

INTERNATIONAL SWIMMING HALL OF FAME
1 Hall of Fame Dr., Fort Lauderdale **[P. 29, M-8]**; (305) 462-6536.

WATER SKI HALL OF FAME
799 Overlook Drive S.E., Winter Haven **[P. 26, G-6]**; (813) 324-2472

PGA/LPGA

BAY HILL CLUB & LODGE
9000 Bay Hill Blvd., Orlando **[P. 28, F-3]**; (407) 876-2429.
The Nestle Invitational (PGA), March.
Number of holes: 72.

BINKS FOREST COUNTRY CLUB
400 Binks Forest Dr., Wellington, in West Palm Beach **[P. 27, K-8]**; (407) 795-0595.
Sazale Classic (PGA), Dec. Number of holes: 72.

DORAL RESORT & COUNTRY CLUB
4400 N.W. 87th Ave., Miami **[P. 27, L-8]**; (305) 592-2000.
Doral Ryder Open (PGA), Feb. Number of holes: 72.

INNISBROOK RESORT
U.S. Highway 19 South, Tarpon Springs **[P. 26, D-1]**; (813) 942-2000.
JCPenney Classic (PGA, LPGA), Nov. and Dec. Number of holes: 72.

INVERRARY COUNTRY CLUB & RESORT
3501 Inverrary Blvd., Lauderhill **[P. 29, M-7]**; (305) 485-0500.
The Phar-Mor at Inverrary (LPGA), Feb.
Number of holes: 54.

KILLEARN COUNTRY CLUB & INN
100 Tyron Circle, Tallahassee **[P. 26, B-2]**; (904) 893-2186.
Centel Classic (LPGA), May. Number of holes: 72.

MAGNOLIA, PALM & LAKE BUENA VISTA GOLF COURSES
Walt Disney World, Lake Buena Vista **[P. 28, G-3]**; (407) 824-2250.
Walt Disney World/Oldsmobile Golf Classic (PGA), Oct. Number of holes: 72.

PGA NATIONAL GOLF CLUB
1000 Ave. of the Champions, Palm Beach Gardens **[P. 28, F-7]**; (407) 627-1800.
PGA Seniors Championship (Senior PGA), April. Number of holes: 72.

SUNTREE COUNTRY CLUB
1 Country Club Dr., Melbourne **[P. 26, G-7]**; (407) 242-6260.
Fairfield Barnett Space Coast Classic (Senior PGA), Sept. Number of holes: 54.

TAMPA PALMS GOLF & COUNTRY CLUB
5811 Tampa Palms Blvd., Tampa **[P. 26, G-4]**; (813) 972-1991.
GTE Suncoast Classic (Senior PGA), Feb.
Number of holes: 54.

THE LINKS AT KEY BISCAYNE
6700 Crandon Blvd., Key Biscayne **[P. 29, O-5]**; (305) 361-9139.
Royal Caribbean Classic (Senior PGA), Jan. to Feb. Number of holes: 54.

THE VINEYARDS
400 Vineyards Blvd., Naples **[P. 27, L-6]**; (813) 353-1500.
Aetna Challenge (Senior PGA), Feb. Number of holes: 54.

TPC AT PRESTANCIA
4409 TPC Dr., Sarasota **[P. 29, L-1]**; (813) 922-2800.
Chrysler Cup (Senior PGA), Feb. Number of holes: 72.

TPC AT SAWGRASS
110 TPC Blvd., Ponte Vedra **[P. 26, C-6]**; (904) 285-3700.
The Players Championship (PGA), March.
Number of holes: 72.

WYCLIFFE GOLF & COUNTRY CLUB
4150 Wycliffe Country Club Blvd., Lake Worth **[P. 28, G-7]**; (407) 642-6644.
Oldsmobile LPGA Classic, Feb. Number of holes: 72.

Polo

GULFSTREAM POLO CLUB
4550 Polo Rd., Lake Worth **[P. 29, H-7]**; (407) 965-2057.

ROYAL PALM POLO CLUB
6300 Old Clint Moore Rd., Boca Raton **[P. 29, J-7]**; (407) 994-1876.

TAMPA BAY POLO CLUB
Walden Lake Polo & Country Club Community, Plant City **[P. 26, G-5]**; (813) 754-1894.

Soccer

LOCKHART STADIUM
5301 N.W. 12th Avenue, Ft. Lauderdale **[P. 29, L-8]**. Capacity: 9,500.
Ft. Lauderdale Strikers (American Professional Soccer League, American Conference); (305) 776-1991.
◆Until Lockhart was renovated in 1990, the Strikers found themselves playing some games on local polo and baseball fields.

MIAMI ORANGE BOWL
1501 NW Third Street, Miami **[P. 26, N-4]**.
Capacity: 70,000.
Miami Freedom (American Professional Soccer League, American Conference); (305) 858-7477.
◆The Orange Bowl is one of the venues contending to host 1994 World Cup games.

TAMPA STADIUM
4201 North Dale Mabry, Tampa **[P. 26, E-3]**.
Capacity: 72,000.
Tampa Bay Rowdies (American Professional Soccer League, American Conference); (813) 877-7800.

Tennis

AMELIA ISLAND PLANTATION
Fernandina Beach **[P. 26, B-6]**; (904) 261-6161. Surface is Clay.
Bausch & Lomb Championships (WTA), April.

HARBOUR ISLAND ATHLETIC CLUB
900 S. Harbour Island Blvd., Tampa **[P. 26, F-3]**; (813) 229-5062. Surface is Har-Tru.
USTA Men's Clay Courts of Tampa, April and May.

INNISBROOK RESORT
36750 US Highway 19 North, Palm Harbor **[P. 26, E-1]**; (813) 942-2000. Surface is Clay.
Light N' Lively Doubles (WTA), March.

INTERNATIONAL TENNIS CENTER - KEY BISCAYNE
7800 Crandon Boulevard, Key Biscayne **[P. 29, O-5]**; (305) 361-9725. Surface is Laykold (hard).
Lipton International Players Championships (ATP, WTA), March.

ORLANDO ARENA
600 W. Amelia St., Orlando **[P. 28, E-5]**; (407) 849-2000. Surface is hard.
World Doubles (WTA), September.

THE POLO CLUB OF BOCA RATON
5400 Champion Blvd., Boca Raton **[P. 29, J-8]**; (407) 997-2002. Surface is hard.

CONTINUED ON PAGE 148

Florida

CONTINUED FROM PAGE 147

Virginia Slims of Florida (WTA), March.

THE RACQUET CLUB AT HEATHROW
1550 Lake Mary Boulevard, N of Orlando, Lake Mary [P. 26, F-6]; (407) 333-1475. Surface is Plexi-Cushion. Prudential-Bache Securities Classic (ATP), April.

TURNBERRY ISLE RESORT & CLUB
19999 W. Country Club Drive, Aventura [P. 29, J-6]; (305) 932-6200. Surface is hard. Miami Beach Breakers (TT), July to August.

WELLINGTON CLUB
1900 Aero Club Drive, Wellington, in West Palm Beach [P. 28, G-7]; (407) 795-3512. Surface is Har-Tru (clay). Wellington Aces (TT), July to August.

OUTDOOR VENUES

National Parks

Bike Trails: BK
Boating: BT
Camping: C
Climbing: CL
Diving: DV
Fishing: F
Golfing: G
Hiking: HK
Hunting: HT
Riding: R
Surfing: SU
Swimming: S
Tennis: TE
Whitewater: WW
Winter Sports: W

APALACHICOLA NATIONAL FOREST
Crawfordville and Bristol, SW of Tallahassee [P. 26, C-1]. Contains 563,668 acres. C HK BT F S R HT

BISCAYNE NATIONAL PARK
E of Homestead on S.W. 328th St. to Convoy Point [P. 27, M-8]. Contains 181,500 acres. C HK BT F S DV

CANAVERAL NATIONAL SEASHORE
E of Titusville via US 1 & I-95 [P. 26, E-7]. Contains 57,000 acres. F S

EVERGLADES NATIONAL PARK
11 mi. from Florida City on FL 9336 [P. 27, M-7]. Contains 1,400,000 acres. C HK BT F BK

GULF ISLANDS NATIONAL SEASHORE
8 mi. on US 98 from Pensacola [P. 27, M-2]. Contains 65,800 acres. C HK BT F S

OCALA NATIONAL FOREST
E of Ocala on FL 40 & N of Umatilla on FL 19 [P. 26, D-5]. Contains 383,049 acres. C HK BT F S HT

OSCEOLA NATIONAL FOREST
NE of Lake City, along I-10 or US 441 [P. 26, C-4]. Contains 179,732 acres. C HK BT F S HT

State Parks

ANASTASIA STATE RECREATION AREA
St. Augustine Beach on FL A1A [P. 26, C-6]. Contains 1,308 acres. C HK BT F S BK SU

BAHIA HONDA STATE RECREATION AREA
Bahia Honda Key off US 1 [P. 27, O-6]. Contains 325 acres. C HK BT F S

BLUE SPRINGS STATE PARK
Orange City [P. 26, E-6]. Contains 2,192 acres. C HK BT F S

COLLIER-SEMINOLE STATE PARK
17 mi. SE of Naples on US 41 [P. 27, L-6]. Contains 6,423 acres. C HK BT F

FLORIDA CAVERNS STATE PARK
Marianna, off FL 167 [P. 27, M-4]. Contains 1,279 acres. C HK BT F S R

> **"Coming back from a race, the most relaxing thing I can do is go out on my boat. Being on Biscayne Bay, with the sun setting, and just being with nature . . . provides me with an atmosphere where I can focus and recharge my batteries."**
>
> **Racecar champion *Emerson Fittipaldi***

FORT CLINCH STATE PARK
Fernandina Beach, off A1A [P. 26, B-6]. Contains 1,118 acres. C HK BT F S

FORT PIERCE INLET STATE RECREATION AREA
Fort Pierce [P. 26, H-8]. Contains 340 acres. HK BT F S SU

ICHETUCKNEE SPRINGS STATE PARK
Off FL 47, near Fort White [P. 26, C-4]. Contains 2,241 acres. HK S DV

JOHN PENNEKAMP CORAL REEF STATE PARK
Key Largo [P. 29, N-8]. Contains 56,011 acres. C HK BT F S DV

LAKE KISSIMMEE STATE PARK
Lake Wales [P. 26, G-6]. Contains 5,030 acres. C HK BT F

MYAKKA RIVER STATE PARK
12 mi E of Sarasota on FL 72 [P. 26, J-5]. Contains 28,875 acres. C HK BT F R

THREE RIVERS STATE RECREATION AREA
1 mi. N of Sneads off FL 271 or I-10 [P. 26, B-1]. Contains 686 acres. C HK BT F

TOMOKA STATE PARK
3 mi. N of Ormond Beach [P. 26, D-7]. Contains 998 acres. C HK BT F

WEKIWA SPRINGS STATE PARK
Off FL 434 [P. 26, F-6]. Contains 6,397 acres. C HK BT F S

WITHLACOOCHEE STATE FOREST
Central Florida, W of Orlando [P. 26, F-5]. Contains 123,241 acres. C HK BT F S R BK HT

ACTIVE SPORTS

ADVENTURE: Hurricane Island Outward Bound School, PO Box 429, Rocklane, ME; (800) 341-1744. • **North Carolina Outward Bound School,** 121 N. Sterling Street, Morganton, NC; (800) 627-5971.

AEROBICS: AFAA, 10455 SW 78th Street, Miami; (305) 595-5302.

BASEBALL: Little League Baseball Southern Region HQ, PO Box 13366, St Petersburg, FL; (813) 344-2661. • **American Legion Baseball,** PO Box 449, Deland; (904) 734-3750. • **Babe Ruth Baseball,** William E. Whitehurst, Rt. 2, Box 56, Grifton, NC; (919) 524-5525. • **Men's Senior Baseball League - St. Petersburg,** 517 39th Ave., St. Petersburg; (813) 360-5223. • **Men's Senior Baseball League - Tampa,** 7311 Canal Blvd., Tampa; (813) 885-6968. • **Men's Senior Baseball League - Palm Beach,** 1809 Hill Crest Ave., Lake Worth; (407) 585-2140. • **Men's Senior Baseball League - Jacksonville,** 1306 Monticello Rd., Jacksonville; (904) 399-3942.

BILLIARDS: Boca Billiards, 8221 Glades Rd., Boca Raton; (407) 451-9200. • **Jillian's,** 12070 N. Kendall, Kendall; (305) 595-0070. • **Society Billiards,** 2895 McFarland Rd., Miami; (305) 441-8787.

BOARDSAILING: Windsurfing of Melbourne , Melbourne; (407) 984-3766. • **Sailing Store ,** Orlando; (407) 291-2345. • **USWA Regional Director,** 2580 Prosperity Oaks Ct., Palm Beach Gardens; (407) 881-0001. • **A Windsurfing Place ,** Key Biscayne; (305) 361-1225.

BOWLING: American Bowling Congress, 5301 S. 76th St., Greendale, WI; (414) 421-6400.

CANOEING & KAYAKING: ACA Dixie Vice Commodore, 2320 Salcedo Street, Savannah, GA; (912) 352-0717.

CYCLING: Florida AYH Council, PO Box 333097, Orlando; (407) 649-8761. • **LAW Southeastern Regional Director,** 201 1st Ave., PO Box 2549, High Springs; (904) 454-5000. • **USCF Florida Representative,** 8900 L S.W. 97th Lane Rd., Ocala; (904) 854-9559.

FITNESS: Governor's Council on Physical Fitness & Sports, 1330 NW 6th Street, Ste. A, Gainesville; (904) 336-2120. • **National Strength and Conditioning Ass'n Northern FL State Director,** Florida State University, Football Office, Moore Athletic Center, Tallahassee; (904) 644-2549.

FOOTBALL: Pop Warner Football, 1315 Walnut Street, Suite 1632, Philadelphia, PA; (215) 735-1450. • **U.S. Flag Football League,** 5834 Pine Tree Drive, Sanibel; (813) 472-0544.

GOLF: Florida Golf Rep. Association, PO Box 2280, Boca Raton; (407) 391-3292. • **Florida State Golf Association,** 5710 Clark Rd., PO Box 21177, Sarasota; (813) 921-5695. • **Pensacola Sports Association,** 201 E. Gregory Street, Pensacola; (904) 434-2800 • **PGA Dixie Section,** 601 Vestavia Parkway, Suite 142, Birmingham, AL; (205) 822-0321. • **PGA North Florida Section,** Daytona Beach Country Club, 1 North Florida PGA Ln., Daytona Beach; (904) 252-0557. • **PGA South Florida Section,** PO Box 8372, Coral Springs; (305) 752-9299.

HIKING & CLIMBING: Florida Sierra Club Chapter, 462 Fernwood, Key Biscane; (305) 361-1292. • **Florida Trail Association (AHS),** Box 13708, Gainesville; (904) 378-8823. • **Loxahatchee Chapter FTA (AHS),** PO Box 19393, W. Palm Beach; (407) 588-1595.

HOCKEY: USA Hockey Southeastern Registrar, PO Box 5208, Takoma Park, MD; (301) 622-0032.

HUNTING & FISHING: Florida Game and Fresh Water Fish Commission, 620 South Meridian Street, Tallahassee; (904) 488-1960. • **East Coast Outdoors, Inc. (Orvis),** 385 South Yonge St., Ormond Beach; (904) 672-5063. • **Down East Sporting Classics (Orvis),** 538 Park Ave. South, Winter Park; (407) 645-5100. • **Kleiser's Sport Shop, Inc. (Orvis),** 125 Datura St., West Palm Beach; (407) 655-4434. • **Outdoor Outfitters (Orvis),** 355 W. Oakland Park Blvd., Ft. Lauderdale; (305) 564-6408. • **Sarasota Outfitters, Inc. (Orvis),** 3540 S. Osprey Ave., Sarasota; (813) 953-9591. • **Southern Sporting Outfitters (Orvis),** 9834 Baymeadows Rd., Jacksonville; (904) 646-4000. • **Treasure Coast Outfitters, Inc. (Orvis),** 3758 S.E. Ocean Blvd., Stuart; (407) 220-6602. • **Trout Unlimited,** 4006 S. Florida Ave., Lakeland; (813) 646-1476.

LACROSSE: Lacrosse Foundation Chapter, 7410 Sunset Dr., Miami; (305) 667-1144.

RACQUETBALL: AARA, 3390 Kori Road, Jacksonville; (904) 268-8888.

RODEO: PRCA Southeastern Circuit, 1111 S. McGee Rd., Bonifay; (904) 547-2534.

RUNNING: RRCA FL State Rep., PO Box 226, Deland; (904) 736-0002.

SCUBA: Adventures Underwater, Inc., 415 South Dale Mabry Highway, Tampa; (813) 875-2376. • **Coral Reef Park Co./REEF TIX,** PO Box 1560, Key Largo; (305) 451-1621. • **Coral Reef Scuba,** 4984 North University, Lauderhill; (305) 748-5105. • **Divers Unlimited,** 6023 Hollywood Blvd., Hollywood; (305) 981-0156. • **Dixie Divers, Inc.,** 1717 South US Highway 1, Fort Pierce; (407) 461-4488. • **Fantasea Scuba Headquarters,** PO Box 5498, #1 Highway 98, Destin; (904) 837-0732. • **Florida Down Under, Inc.,** 5714 Clark Road, Sarasota, (813) 922-3483. • **Florida Keys Dive Center,** PO Box 391, Mile Marker 90.5, Plantation Key; (305) 852-4599. • **Force-E,** 2104 West Oakland Park Blvd., Ft. Lauderdale; (305) 735-6227. • **Lady Cyana Divers,** Mile Marker 85.9 US Highway 1, PO Box 1157, Islamorada; (305) 664-8717. • **Ocean Divers, Inc.,** 522 Caribbean Drive, Key Largo; (305) 451-1113. • **Professional Diving Schools of Florida,** 801 Seabreeze Blvd., Fort Lauderdale; (305) 761-3413. • **Reef Raiders Dive Shop,** 109 Duval Street, Key West; (305) 294-3635. • **The Dive Station,** 3465 Edgewater Drive, Orlando; (407) 843-3483.

SHOOTING: Big D Sporting Clays, 2160 S. Marion St., Lake City; (904) 752-0594. • **Indian River Trap & Skeet Club,** 389 Island Creek Dr., Vero Beach; (407) 231-1783.

SKATING: USFSA, 20 First Street, Colorado Springs, CO; (719) 635-5200.

SOCCER: Florida Soccer Ass'n, 1455-B NW 80th Ave., Margate; (305) 974-5313. • **Florida YSA,** 207 Hillcrest Street, Orlando; (407) 423-0613. • **AYSO Regional Director,** 1405 Inman Dr., Huntsville, AL; (205) 881-3138.

SOFTBALL: Florida ASA, 180 Governmental Center, 5th Floor, PO Box 12910, Pensacola; (904) 432-6287. • **Jacksonville ASA,** 7413 Tahiti Rd., Jacksonville; (904) 724-3510. • **Orlando ASA,** 649 W. Livingston Street, Orlando; (407) 898-7855. • **South Florida ASA,** PO Box 40, Hialeah; (305) 435-4128. • **St. Petersburg ASA,** 1408 Douglas Dr., Clearwater; (813) 447-2449. • **Tampa ASA,** 3104 South Kings Ave., Brandon; (813) 684-0083.

SQUASH: Downtown Athletic Club, Miami; (305) 358-9988. • **Forestmeadows Racquet Club (USSRA),** Tallahassee; (904) 893-1907. • **Harbour Island Athletic Club (USSRA),** Tampa; (813) 229-5062.

SWIMMING: LMSC Florida Registrar, 2601 NE 23 Blvd. #104, Gainesville; (904) 373-0049. • **LMSC Florida Gold Coast Registrar,** 2308 NE 19th Ave., Ft. Lauderdale; (305) 654-6185.

TABLE TENNIS: USTTA State Coordinator, 1300 Plum Ave., Merritt Island; (407) 452-8990.

TENNIS: Recreational TEAMTENNIS Midwest-Southeast Region, National Program Coordinator, 445 N. Wells, Ste. #404, Chicago, IL; (800) TEAMTEN. • **Florida USTA,** 801 NE 167th Street, Suite 301, N. Miami Beach; (305) 652-2866.

TRIATHLON: Broward Endurance Sports, PO Box 2343, Ft. Lauderdale; (305) 742-3193. • **Team Tampa,** PO Box 273167, Tampa; (813) 681-3555.

VOLLEYBALL: USVBA Florida Commissioner, 11781 109th Street N., Largo; (813) 398-6833.

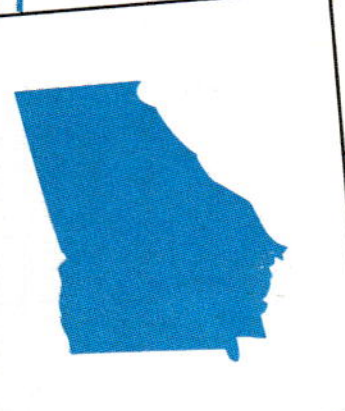

Georgia

Every Fourth of July, 40,000 runners from all over the country converge upon Atlanta for some Southern hospitality and the Peachtree 10K footrace. ◆ Other major sports in and around the future home of the 1996 summer Olympics include the Masters golf tournament, the NFL Falcons, the NBA Hawks, Major League Baseball's Atlanta Braves, NASCAR Winston Cup races (mid-March, mid-November), and college football's Peach Bowl. ◆ At Callaway Gardens in Western Georgia, the Masters Water Ski Tournament, is held every Memorial Day weekend. ◆ The Appalachian Mountains offer prime hiking, while outside of Atlanta, the ideal conditions at the Chattahoochee River play host to the Head of the Chattahoochee, a rowing regatta that features some 1,400 participants in early November. ◆ For equestrian fans, the Atlanta Steeplechase is held every year in April.

▶ SPECTATOR VENUES

Auto Racing

ATLANTA MOTOR SPEEDWAY
US Highways 19 & 41, Hampton **[P. 30, E-3]**; (404) 946-4211. Track is 1.522 miles.
◆A true superspeedway oval, with turns twice as long as the straightaways.
Hardee's 500 (NASCAR Winston Cup), November.
Motorcraft Quality Parts 500 (NASCAR Winston Cup), March.

ATLANTA DRAGWAY
Interstate 85 & US 441, Commerce **[P. 30, D-4]**; (404) 335-2301. Track is quarter-mile strip (for NHRA races).
AC-Delco Southern Nationals (NHRA), late April.

ROAD ATLANTA
GA 53 between I-85 & GA 365, near Gainesville, Braselton **[P. 30, D-4]**; (404) 967-6143. Track is 2.52-mile, 12-turn road course.
Nissan Grand Prix of Atlanta (IMSA Camel GT), April.
SCCA Road Atlanta Trans-Am, July.

Baseball

ATLANTA-FULTON COUNTY STADIUM
521 Capitol Avenue, SW, Atlanta **[P. 32, E-4]**. Built in 1965. Capacity: 52,007
◆Will be used in '96 Summer Olympics.
Atlanta Braves (NL West); (404) 522-7630. Franchise began in 1876. Broadcasts by WSB 750-AM, WTBS Channel 17.
Affiliates:Richmond, VA (AAA); Greenville, SC (AA); Durham, NC (A); Macon, GA (A); Pulaski, VA (Rookie); Bradenton, FL (Rookie); Idaho Falls, ID (Rookie). Spring training held in West Palm Beach, FL.

GRAYSON STADIUM
1401 Victory Drive, Savannah **[P. 31, N-6]**. Capacity: 8,500
Savannah Cardinals (South Atlantic League, Class A); (912) 351-9150. Entered League in 1984. MLB affiliation, St. Louis Cardinals.

HEATON STADIUM
78 Milledge Road, Augusta **[P. 31, N-3]**. Capacity: 4,000
Augusta Pirates (South Atlantic League, Class A); (404) 736-7889. Entered League in 1984. Broadcasts by WGUS 1380 AM. MLB affiliation, Pittsburgh Pirates.

Basketball

THE OMNI
100 Techwood Drive N.W., Atlanta **[P. 32, E-4]**. Built in 1972. Capacity: 16,371.
◆The Hawks originally played in Moline, IL before moving to Milwaukee in 1951, then to St. Louis in 1955, before arriving in Atlanta in 1968.
Atlanta Hawks (NBA Eastern Conf., Central Div.); (404) 827-3800. Franchise began in 1949. Broadcasts by WGST 640-AM, TBS Superstation, SportSouth, WGNX-TV.

Bowling

FAYETTEVILLE LANES
124 N. 85 Parkway, Fayetteville **[P. 30, E-3]**; (404) 461-8822.
Greater Atlanta Open (LPBT), April.

SHOWTIME BOWL
555 Macon Hwy., Athens; **[P. 30, D-4]**; (404) 548-1028.
Athens Open.

College Sports

AUGUSTA COLLEGE JAGUARS
2500 Walton Way, Augusta **[P. 31, N-2]**; (404) 737-1626. Augusta Civic Center, capacity 7,200.

EMORY UNIVERSITY
Woodruff Physical Education Center, Atlanta **[P. 32, E-5]**; (404) 727-6547. Emory Field, capacity 2,000. Emory Gym, capacity 3,000.

GEORGIA SOUTHERN COLLEGE EAGLES
Statesboro **[P. 31, H-7]**; (912) 681-5376. Allen E. Paulson, capacity 17,000. W.S. Hanner, capacity 5,500.

GEORGIA STATE UNIVERSITY CRIMSON PANTHERS
University Plaza, Atlanta **[P. 32, E-4]**; (404) 651-2772. GSU Spirts Arena, capacity 5,500.

GEORGIA TECH YELLOW JACKETS
Atlanta **[P. 32, E-4]**; (404) 894-5400. Grant Field, capacity 46,000. Alexander Memorial Coliseum, capacity 10,000.
◆Renovated Thriller Dome is a loud place to watch the game. Inventive students at least once a season dress up as Coach Bobby Cremins look-alikes, including silver-haired wigs.

MERCER UNIVERSITY BEARS
1400 Coleman Avenue, Macon **[P. 31, N-4]**; (912) 744-2994. Macon Coliseum, capacity 9,000.

MORRIS BROWN COLLEGE WOLVERINES
643 Martin Luther King Jr. Dr., NW, Atlanta **[P. 32, E-4]**; (404) 525-7831. Herndon, capacity 13,000. John Lewis, capacity 3,200.

UNIVERSITY OF GEORGIA BULLDOGS
Athens **[P. 30, D-4]**; (404) 542-1306. Sanford, capacity 82,122. Coliseum, capacity 10,512.
◆One of college football's prettiest locations; you play football between the hedges.

Football

ATLANTA-FULTON COUNTY STADIUM
521 Capitol Avenue, S.W., Atlanta **[P. 32, E-4]**. Built in 1966. Capacity: 59,643.
Atlanta Falcons (NFC Western Division); (404) 945-1111. Franchise began in 1966. Broadcasts by WSB.

PGA/LPGA

ATLANTA COUNTRY CLUB
500 Atlanta Country Club Dr., Marietta **[P. 32, C-3]**; (404) 953-2100.
Bellsouth Atlanta Classic (PGA), May. Number of holes: 72.

USA SNAPSHOTS®

A look at statistics that shape the sports world

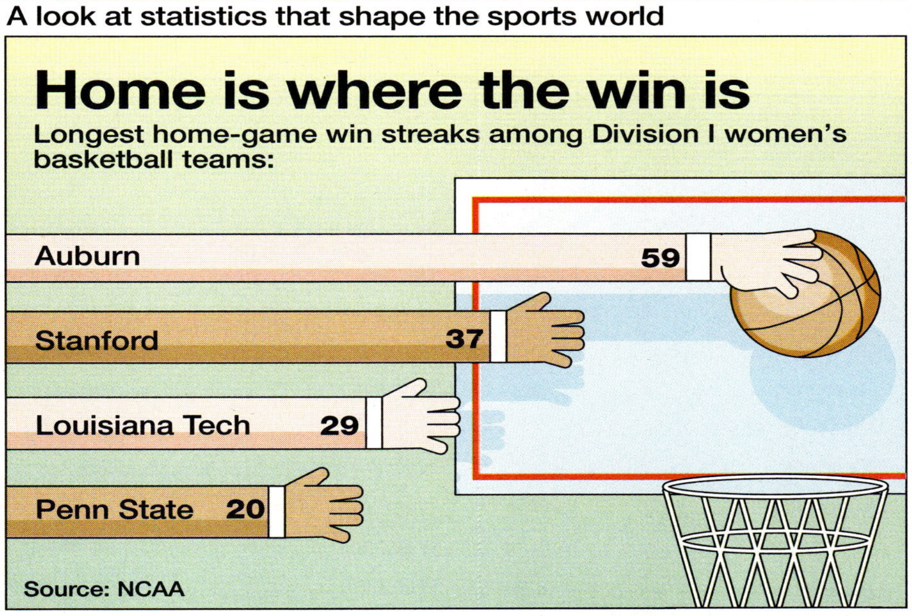

By Marty Baumann, USA TODAY

POPULATION: 6,436,000	**STATBOX**
SQUARE MILES: 58,910	
TIME ZONE: Eastern	
MOTTO: Wisdom, Justice, Moderation	
BIRD: Brown Thrasher	
TREE: Live Oak	
CAPITAL: Atlanta	
AVERAGE ANNUAL RAINFALL: 48"	
MEAN TEMP: 65	
MAJOR LEAGUE TEAMS: 3	
NATIONAL PARK/FOREST ACREAGE: 54,953	
STATE PARK ACREAGE: 61,000	
HIGHEST ELEVATION: 4,784'	
LOWEST ELEVATION: sea level	
WATERWAYS: 21,252 miles of streams; 300,000 acres of lakes	

AUGUSTA NATIONAL GOLF CLUB
2604 Washington Rd., Augusta **[P. 31, N-2]**; (404) 738-7761.
◆The Masters is probably the toughest ticket to acquire in all of US sports.
The Masters Tournament (PGA), April. Number of holes: 72.

CALLAWAY GARDENS RESORT
Highway 27, Pine Mountain; **[P. 30, G-2]**; (404) 324-2184.
Buick Southern Open (PGA), Sept. Number of holes: 72.

COUNTRY CLUB OF THE SOUTH
4100 Old Alabama Road, Alpharetta; **[P. 32, B-6]**;(404) 475-1803.
Nationwide Championship (Senior PGA), September. Number of holes: 54.

Polo

COLUMBUS POLO CLUB
7600 Fulton Rd., Columbus **[P. 30, G-2]**; (404) 568-3095.

SOUTHEASTERN POLO CLUB
6300 Polo Club Dr., Cumming **[P. 30, D-3]**; (404) 394-9100.

Tennis

SPORTING CLUB AT WINDY HILL
135 Interstate North Pkwy, NW, Atlanta; **[P. 32, C-3]**; (404) 953-1100. Surface is hard.
Atlanta Thunder (TT), July to Aug.

▶ OUTDOOR VENUES

National Parks

CHATTAHOOCHEE NATIONAL FOREST
Off I-75 & US 76 in Gainesville **[P. 30, B-2, C-1, C-3]**. Contains 748,608 acres.
C HK BT F S R BK

CHATTAHOOCHEE RIVER NATIONAL RECREATION AREA
Dunwoody **[P. 32, B-4, B-7, C-3]**. Contains 4,200 acres.
HK BT F S BK WW

CUMBERLAND ISLAND NATIONAL SEASHORE
10 mi. SE of St. Mary's **[P. 31, L-8]**. Contains 37,000 acres. **C HK BT F S**

Bike Trails: BK
Boating: BT
Camping: C
Climbing: CL
Diving: DV
Fishing: F
Golfing: G
Hiking: HK
Hunting: HT
Riding: R
Surfing: SU
Swimming: S
Tennis: TE
Whitewater: WW
Winter Sports: W

CONTINUED ON PAGE 150

Georgia

CONTINUED FROM PAGE 149

State Parks

ALEXANDER H. STEPHENS MEMORIAL PARK
Crawfordville, on US 278 and GA 22 [**P. 30, E-5**]. Contains 1,189 acres. **C HK BT F S**

BOBBY BROWN STATE PARK
21 mi. SE of Elberton, off GA 72 [**P. 30, D-6**]. Contains 665 acres.

ELIJAH CLARK STATE PARK
7 mi. NE of Lincolnton, on US 378 [**P. 30, D-6**]. Contains 447 acres. **HK BT F S**

FORT YARGO STATE PARK
1 mi. S of Winder on GA 81 [**P. 30, D-4**]. Contains 1,850 acres. **C HK BT F S**

FRANKLIN D. ROOSEVELT STATE PARK
5 mi. SE of Pine Mountain [**P. 30, G-2**]. Contains 10,000 acres. **C HK BT F S**

GEORGE T. BAGBY STATE PARK
3 mi. N of Fort Gaines off GA 39 [**P. 31, J-1**]. Contains 289 acres. **HK BT F S**

HARD LABOR CREEK STATE PARK
2 mi. N of Rutledge off I-20 [**P. 30, E-4**]. Contains 5,805 acres. **C HK BT F S X**

KOLOMOKI MOUNDS STATE PARK
Blakely [**P. 31, K-2**]. Contains 1,293 acres. **C HK BT F S**

LITTLE OCMULGEE STATE PARK
2 mi. N of McRae on US 441 [**P. 31, H-5**]. Contains 1,397 acres. **C HK BT F S G**

MISTLETOE STATE PARK
10 mi. N of Appling, off GA 150 [**P. 30, E-6**]. Contains 1,924 acres. **C HK BT F S**

TUGALOO STATE PARK
6 mi. N of Lavonia, off GA 328 [**P. 30, C-5**]. Contains 393 acres. **C HK BT F S R BK**

Skiing

ALPINE SKIING

SKY VALLEY
Highlands Road, Dillard [**P. 30, B-4**]; (404) 746-5301.
Vertical drop is 250 feet. Has one tow and one chair.

ACTIVE SPORTS

ADVENTURE: North Carolina Outward Bound School, 121 N. Sterling Street, Morganton, NC; (800) 627-5971.

AEROBICS: AFAA, 1381 Wessynton Rd., Atlanta; (404) 876-9393.

BASEBALL: Little League Baseball Southern Region HQ, PO Box 13366, St. Petersburg, FL; (813) 344-2661. • **American Legion Baseball,** 2191 Lyle Rd., College Park; (404) 766-1816. • **Babe Ruth Baseball,** William E. Whitehurst, Rt. 2, Box 56, Grifton, NC; (919) 524-5525. • **Men's Senior Baseball League - Atlanta,** 4541 Woodlawn Lake Dr., Marietta; (404) 973-5188. • **Men's Senior Baseball League - Northwest Georgia,** 1532 Erwin Hole Road, Adarsville; (404) 629-0016.

BILLIARDS: Barley's Billiards, 6259 Peachtree Blvd., Doraville; (404) 455-1124. • **Barley's Billiards,** 2000 Powers Ferry Rd. SE, Marietta; (404) 988-8200. • **Johnny's Poolroom,** 430 Broadway, Macon; (912) 746-3648.

BOARDSAILING: Go With the Flow , Roswell; (404) 992-3200. • **USWA Regional Director,** 2580 Prosperity Oaks Ct., Palm Beach Gdns, FL; (407) 881-0001.

> **"For people who like that, there's the Speedway south of Atlanta, and. . . a lot of good dirt tracks that I grew up following. Georgia, to me, covers so much territory. You can go to the southeast and be on the ocean front, or go north and be in the mountains. They have designated trails for mountain bikes and dirt bikes. There are a lot of good areas to ride up in this part of the country."**
>
> **Race car driver *Bill Elliott***

BOWLING: American Bowling Congress, 5301 S. 76th St., Greendale, WI; (414) 421-6400.

CANOEING & KAYAKING: ACA Dixie Vice Commodore, 2320 Salcedo Street, Savannah; (912) 352-0717.

CYCLING: LAW Southeastern Regional Director, 201 1st Ave., PO Box 2549, High Springs, FL; (904) 454-5000. • **USCF Georgia Representative,** PO Box 2562, Atlanta; (404) 377-6621.

FOOTBALL: Pop Warner Football, 1315 Walnut Street, Suite 1632, Philadelphia, PA; (215) 735-1450. • **U.S. Flag Football League,** 5834 Pine Tree Drive, Sanibel, FL; (813) 472-0544.

Tip Offs

The Top Active Sports

Skiing is tops in California and Colorado. And everybody knows Kentucky loves basketball. But water skiing in Texas?

The National Sporting Goods Association surveys the popularity of recreational sports in 49 states based on participation. Some might be surprised to learn that dart throwing is number three in Massachusetts and billiards ranks second with West Virginians.

The number one recreational sports — according to the NSGA — are:

Alabama	fishing (saltwater)	Nebraska	football
Alaska	fishing	Nevada	water skiing
Arizona	racquetball	New Hampshire	skiing (alpine)
Arkansas	hunting	New Jersey	fishing (saltwater)
California	skiing (alpine)	New Mexico	backpacking
Colorado	skiing (alpine)	New York	canoeing
Connecticut	skiing (alpine)	North Carolina	fishing (saltwater)
Delaware	canoeing	North Dakota	hunting
Florida	fishing (saltwater)	Ohio	canoeing
Georgia	fishing(saltwater)	Oklahoma	fishing (freshwater)
Idaho	hunting	Oregon	backpacking
Illinois	golf	Pennsylvania	hunting
Indiana	fishing (freshwater)	Rhode Island	skiing (alpine)
Iowa	camping	South Carolina	water skiing
Kansas	fishing (fresh water)	South Dakota.	hunting
Kentucky	basketball	Tennessee.	basketball
Louisiana	fishing (saltwater)	Texas	water skiing
Maine	canoeing	Utah	backpacking
Maryland	soccer	Vermont	backpacking
Massachusetts	skiing (alpine)	Virginia	fishing
Michigan	golf	Washington.	backpacking
Minnesota	canoeing	West Virginia	hunting
Mississippi	hunting	Wisconsin	hunting
Missouri	water skiing	Wyoming	backpacking
Montana	hunting		

GOLF: Georgia State Golf Association, 4200 Northside Parkway, Building 9, Suite 100, Atlanta; (404) 233-4742. • **PGA Georgia Section,** 1640 Powers Ferry Rd., Building 18, Suite 300, Marietta; (404) 952-9063.

HIKING & CLIMBING: Georgia Sierra Club Chapter, PO Box 467151, Atlanta; (404) 921-5389.

HOCKEY: USA Hockey Southeastern Registrar, PO Box 5208, Takoma Park, MD; (301) 622-0032.

HUNTING & FISHING: Department of Natural Resources, Floyd Towers East, 205 Butler St., SE, Suite 1362, Atlanta; (404) 656-3530. • **The Fish Hawk (Orvis),** 283 Buckhead Ave., Atlanta; (404) 237-3473. • **Trout Unlimited,** 5074 Odins Way, Marietta; (404) 992-8789.

RACQUETBALL: AARA, 1590 N. Roberts Rd., Suite 202, Kennesaw; (404) 988-9130.

RIDING: Georgia Horse Foundation, Box 52903, Atlanta; (404) 347-0506.

RODEO: PRCA Southeastern Circuit, 1111 S. McGee Rd., Bonifay, FL; (904) 547-2534.

RUNNING: RRCA GA State Rep., 1803 Jackson Creek Dr., Marietta; (404) 992-0808. • **RRCA TN State Rep.,** 42 Dailey Hill Road, Ringold; (404) 861-4570.

SCUBA: Atlanta Diving & Aquatic Center, 732 Johnson Ferry Road, Suite 106, Marietta; (404) 973-3120. • **Diving Locker-Ski Chalet,** 74 West Montgomery Crossroads, Savannah; (912) 927-6603. • **Island Dive Center,** 1610-1/2 Frederica Road, St. Simons Island; (800) 940-3483. • **Sandy Springs Divers,** 6445 Roswell Road, Atlanta; (404) 252-9372. • **The Outdoors Shop,** 416 Northside Drive, Valdosta; (912) 244-1024. • **Venture Out Sports & Travel,** 7050 Jimmy Carter Blvd., Norcross; (404) 263-8796.

SHOOTING: Cat Creek Sporting Clays, Inc., PO Box 2475, Valdosta; (912) 686-7700. • **Cherokee Rose Shooting Resort,** PO Drawer 509, Griffin; (404) 228-CLAY. • **Little Pachitla Sporting Clays,** PO Box 421, Newton; (912) 835-3044. • **Myrtlewood Championship Sporting Clays,** PO Box 32, Thomasville; (912) 228-6232. • **Northeast Georgia Sporting Clays,** Rt. 1, Box 348, Winterville; (404) 742-7719. • **Pigeon Mountain Sporting Clays,** 197 Camp Rd., Chickamauga; (404) 539-2287. • **South River Gun Club,** 157 N. Salem Rd. NE, Conyers; (404) 786-9456. • **Southern Game & Fish Sporting,** 101 S. Circle Drive, Swainsboro; (912) 237-4155. • **Valley Brook Sporting Clays,** Rt. 1, Box 570, Lyerly; (404) 441-2092. • **Wolf Creek,** 3070 Merk Rd. S.W., Atlanta; (404) 346-1545.

SKATING: USFSA, 20 First Street, Colorado Springs, CO; (719) 635-5200.

SOCCER: Georgia State Soccer Ass'n, Inc., 3584 Stewart Rd., B1, Atlanta; (404) 452-0505. • **AYSO Regional Director,** 5403 W. 138th Street, Hawthorne, CA; (800) 421-5700.

SOFTBALL: Georgia ASA, PO Box 447, 1301 N. Monroe, Albany; (912) 435-4273. • **Atlanta ASA,** 7574 Carlisle Dr., Jonesboro; (404) 478-2305.

SQUASH: Atlanta Health & Racquet Club (USSRA), Atlanta; (404) 952-3200.

SWIMMING: LMSC Georgia Registrar, 1968 Lebanon Dr. NE, Atlanta; (404) 875-3178.

TENNIS: Recreational TEAMTENNIS Midwest-Southeast Region, National Program Coordinator, 445 N. Wells, Ste. #404, Chicago, IL; (800) TEAMTEN. • **Southern USTA,** 200 Sandy Springs Place, Suite 200, Atlanta; (404) 257-1297.

TRIATHLON: Spectrum Racing Team, 10305 Brixworth Place, Atlanta; (404) 633-0183. • **Team Race Monsters Tri Club,** PO Box 8084, Fort Gordon; (404) 791-5874. • **Tri Atlanta,** 222 Lucky Dr., Atlanta; (404) 578-1063.

WHITEWATER RAFTING: Southeastern Expeditions, 2936-4 Druid Hills Rd., NE, Atlanta; (404) 329-0433.

Hawaii

Naturally, the Hawaiian Islands play host to an assortment of international ocean events, including the annual 40.8-mile Bankoh Molokai-Hoe in October, a six-person outrigger canoe race from Molokai to Oahu; professional surfing's Triple Crown, a trio of events held every winter on Oahu's north shore ; and professional windsurfing every April and May at Ho'okipa Beach on Maui, the Aspen of windsurfing. ◆ On the Big Island (Hawaii), the International Hawaiian Billfish Tournament lures the world's top anglers every August, while October's Ironman Triathlon annually attracts some of the fittest athletes. ◆ In Honolulu, Aloha Stadium (adjacent to Pearl Harbor) is the site of college football's Aloha and Hula Bowls, and the NFL Pro Bowl. Honolulu is also home of the Honolulu Marathon and the PGA's Hawaiian Open.

► SPECTATOR VENUES

College Sports

UNIVERSITY OF HAWAII RAINBOWS
1337 Lower Campus Road, Honolulu **[P. 33, D-4]**; (808) 956-7301. Aloha, capacity 50,000. Blaisdell Arena, capacity 7575.

PGA/LPGA

KAPALUA GOLF CLUB
Plantation Course, 300 Kapalua Drive, Kapalua, Maui **[P. 33, A-6]**; (808) 669-8044.
Kapalua International (PGA), Nov.
Number of holes: 72.

KO OLINA RESORT
92-1220 Alii Nui Dr., Ewa Beach **[P. 33, D-3]**; (808) 676-5300.
Orix Hawaiian Ladies Open (LPGA), Feb.
Number of holes: 54.

MAUNA LANI RESORT
Kohala Coast **[P. 33, D-6]**; (808) 885-6622.
Senior Skins Game (Senior PGA), Jan.
Number of holes: 36.

PRINCEVILLE MAKAI GOLF CLUB
Princeville, Kauai **[P. 33, E-2]**; (808) 826-3585.
Itoman LPGA Match Play Championship of the World, Decmeber. Number of holes: 72.

ROYAL KAANAPALI GOLF COURSE (NORTH)
Kaanapali Parkway, Lahaina **[P. 33, B-6]**; (808) 661-3691.
First Development Kaanapali Classic, Dec. Number of holes: 54.

STOUFFER'S WAILEA BEACH RESORT
120 Kauaahi St., Wailea, Maui **[P. 33, B-7]**; (808) 879-2922.
Women's Kemper Open (LPGA), March.
Number of holes: 72.

WAIALAE COUNTRY CLUB
4997 Kahala Ave., Honolulu **[P. 33, D-4]**; (808) 734-2151.
Hawaiian Open (PGA), Feb. Number of holes: 72.

Polo

MAUI POLO CLUB, INC.
Kahului **[P. 33, B-7]**; (808) 885-4445.

MAUNA KEA POLO CLUB
Kamuela **[P. 33, D-7]**; (808) 885-4445.

Track & Field

STREETS OF HONOLULU
ALOHA Tower, Honolulu **[P. 33, D-4]**; (808) 734-7200.
Honolulu Marathon, December.

► OUTDOOR VENUES

National Parks

HALEAKALA NATIONAL PARK
From Kahului, HI 36, 37, 377 and 378, Maui **[P. 33, B-7]**. Contains 28,000 acres. **C HK S R**

HAWAII VOLCANOES NATIONAL PARK
SW of Hilo and E of Kailua via HI 11, Hawaii **[P. 33, F-7]**. Contains 229,998 acres. **C HK BT**

State Parks

Bike Trails: BK
Boating: BT
Camping: C
Climbing: CL
Diving: DV
Fishing: F
Golfing: G
Hiking: HK
Hunting: HT
Riding: R
Surfing: SU
Swimming: S
Tennis: TE
Whitewater: WW
Winter Sports: W

HAPUNA BEACH STATE RECREATION AREA
2.3 mi. S of Kawaihae on HI 19 (Queen Kaahumanu Hwy.), Hawaii **[P. 33, D-6]**. Contains 61 acres. **F S**

KAENA POINT STATE PARK
Makua, off HI 930 (Farrington Hwy.), Oahu **[P. 33, B-1]**. Contains 853 acres. **HK F S SU**

KOKEE STATE PARK
15 mi. N of Kekaha on HI 550 (Kokee Rd.), Kauai **[P. 33, F-2]**. Contains 4,345 acres. **C HK F HT**

MALAEKAHANA STATE RECREATION AREA
Off Kamehameha Hwy. (HI 83); Kalanai Point Section; 6 mi. N of Laie Town, Kahuku Section; 1.3 mi. N of Laie Town, Oahu **[P. 33, B-3]**. Contains 110 acres. **C F S**

NA PALI COAST STATE PARK
Trail at end of Kuhio Hwy. (HI 56), Haeha State Park, Kauai **[P. 33, E-2]**. Contains 6,175 acres. **C HK BT F HT**

OLD KONA AIRPORT STATE RECREATION AREA
End of Kuakini Hwy. (HI 11), Kailua-Kona, Hawaii **[P. 33, E-6]**. Contains 118 acres. **F SU**

PAPALAUA STATE WAYSIDE
14 mi. SW of Kahului Airport, on Honoapiilani Hwy. (HI 30), Maui **[P. 33, B-6]**. Contains 7 acres. **F S DV**

POLIHALE STATE PARK
5 mi. N of Mana Village, off Kaumualii Hwy. (HI 30), Kauai **[P. 33, F-1]**. Contains 137 acres. **C F S**

SAND ISLAND STATE RECREATION AREA
End of Sand Island Access Road, off HI 92, Oahu **[P. 33, D-4]**. Contains 140 acres.
C HK BT F S SU

WAIANAPANAPA STATE RECREATION AREA
Off Hana Hwy. (HI 360), 53 mi. E of Kahului Airport, Maui **[P. 33, B-8]**. Contains 120 acres. **C HK F S**

WAILUA RIVER STATE PARK
Wailua, Kauai **[P. 33, F-3]**. Contains 1,126 acres. **BT F S BK SU**

WAIMANALO BAY STATE RECREATION AREA
Kamehameha Hwy. (HI 83), between Bellows Air Force Base and Aloiloi St., Waimanalo, Oahu **[P. 33, D-5]**. Contains 74.8 acres
C HK S R SU

► ACTIVE SPORTS

AEROBICS: AFAA, 5750 A. Erne Ave., Ewa Beach; (808) 499-1747.

BASEBALL: American Legion Baseball, 3038 Hiehie St., Honolulu; (808) 988-4772. • **Babe Ruth Baseball,** Dennis R. Poarch, 809 W. Gibson Rd., Woodland, CA; (415) 581-6879.

BILLIARDS: Hawaiian Brian's, 1680 Kapiolani Blvd., Honolulu; (808) 946-1343.

BOARDSAILING: Aloha Windsurfing Hawaii , Honolulu; (808) 926-1185. • **Hawaiian Sailboarding ,** Paia; (808) 871-5423. • **USWA Regional Director,** Hi-Tech, 444 Hana Hwy., Kahului; (808) 877-2111.

BOWLING: American Bowling Congress, 5301 S. 76th St., Greendale, WI; (414) 421-6400.

CANOEING & KAYAKING: ACA Hawaii Vice Commodore, 47-401 Lulani Street, Kaneohe; (808) 239-9143.

CYCLING: USCF Hawaii Representative, 523 Pavlele Street, Kailua; (808) 263-3435.

FITNESS: Governor's Council on Physical Fitness and Sports, PO Box 3378, Honolulu; (808) 735-8582.

FOOTBALL: Pop Warner Football, 1315 Walnut Street, Suite 1632, Philadelphia, PA; (215) 735-1450.

GOLF: Hawaii Golf Association, 1859 Alaweo Street, Honolulu; (808) 521-6622. • **PGA Aloha Section,** 770 Kapiolani Blvd., Room 513, Honolulu; (808) 528-3700.

HIKING & CLIMBING: Hawaii Sierra Club Chapter, P.O. Box 2577, Honolulu; (808) 538-6616.

HUNTING & FISHING: Department of Land & Natural Resources, 1151 Punchbowl St., Room 330, Honolulu; (808) 548-4000.

LACROSSE: Lacrosse Foundation Chapter, 1600 Pauahi Tower, 1001 Bishop St., Honolulu; (808) 395-3803.

RACQUETBALL: AARA, 4370 Kukui Grove Street, Lihue; (808) 245-5381.

STATBOX

POPULATION: 1,112,110
SQUARE MILES: 6,471
TIME ZONE: Hawaiian (no daylight savings)
MOTTO: Ua mau ke ea o ka aina i ka pono. (The life of the land is perpetuated in righteousness.)
BIRD: Nene
TREE: Candlenut
CAPITAL: Honolulu, Oahu
AVERAGE ANNUAL RAINFALL: 9" (Kawaihae); 444" (Waialeale)
MEAN TEMP: 77-82
MAJOR LEAGUE TEAMS: 0
NATIONAL PARK/FOREST ACREAGE: 247,349
STATE PARK ACREAGE: 24,857
HIGHEST ELEVATION: 13,795
LOWEST ELEVATION: sea level
WATERWAYS: 45 square miles of inland water; surrounded by Pacific Ocean

RUNNING: RRCA HI State Rep., PO Box 698, Wailuku; (808) 242-8298.

SCUBA: A Sea Paradise, PO Box 580, Kailua-Kona; (808) 322-2500. • **Aaron's Dive Shop,** 602 Kailua Road, Kailua, Oahu; (808) 262-2333. • **Aloha Dive Shop,** Koko Marine Shopping Center, Honolulu; (808) 395-5922. • **Breeze Hawaii Diving Adventures,** 735 Sheridan Street, #26, Honolulu; (808) 955-4541. • **Dive Kauai,** 4-976 Kuhio Highway, Kapaa, Kauai; (808) 822-0452. • **Fathom Five Pro Divers,** Poipu Road, Box 907, Koloa, Kauai; (808) 742-6991. • **King Kamehameha Divers,** 75-5660 Palani Road, #P-1, Kailua-Kona; (808) 329-5662. • **Kona Coast Skin Divers,** 75-5614 Palani Road, Kailua-Kona; (808) 329-8802. • **Lahaina Divers, Inc.,** 162 Lahainaluna Road, Lahaina, Maui; (808) 667-6280. • **Maui Dive Shop,** PO Box 1018, Azeka Place, Azeka, Kihei; (808) 871-2111. • **Ocean Adventures, Inc.,** 98-406 Kam Highway, Pearl City; (808) 487-9060. • **South Seas Aquatics,** 870 Kapahulu Avenue, #109, Honolulu; (808) 735-0437.

SKATING: USFSA, 20 First Street, Colorado Springs, CO; (719) 635-5200.

SOCCER: Hawaii Soccer Ass'n, 265 Kealahou Street, Honolulu; (808) 396-0027. • **Hawaii YSA,** PO Box 7159, Honolulu; (808) 527-4901. • **AYSO Regional Director,** 86-148 Puhawai Rd., Waianae; (808) 696-3341.

SOFTBALL: Hawaii ASA, PO Box 22001, Honolulu; (808) 545-5043.

SQUASH: Honolulu Club (USSRA), Honolulu; (808) 543-3900.

SWIMMING: LMSC Hawaii Registrar, 46-459 Hololio Street, Kaneohe; (808) 247-6909.

TENNIS: Recreational TEAMTENNIS Central-West Region, National Program Coordinator, 2105 Grant Ave., #4, Redondo Beach, CA; (800) 992-9042. • **Hawaii Pacific USTA,** 2615 South King Street, Suite 2A, Honolulu; (808) 955-6696.

VOLLEYBALL: USVBA Aloha Commissioner, 1546 Hanai Loop, Honolulu; (808) 847-3196. • **USVBA Moku O Keawe Commissioner,** PO Box 1317, Hilo; (808) 961-6276.

"One of my favorite landmarks on Oahu, and one of my regular runs. . . is Mount Leahi or Diamond Head."

Beach volleyball player/coach *Janice Opalinski-Harrier*

Idaho

Idaho is known as the whitewater capital of the U.S., with some of the best rafting at the Payette River, Salmon River and in Hell's Canyon. The Whitewater Rodeo (mid-May) features kayaking and jet boating. ◆ Silver Creek is a world-class fly fishing stream, while the McCall Cascades area is known for its great trophy lakes. ◆ One of Idaho's top ski resorts is historic and posh Sun Valley. ◆ Rock climbers from all over the world visit the City of Rocks, southeast of Twin Falls. ◆ Boise's ORE-IDA Women's Challenge (mid-June) is the longest women's cycling event in the world—600 miles. ◆ Rodeos are popular throughout the state, highlighted by the Dodge National Circuit Finals in Pocatello (late March). ◆ And for runners, the 13-mile Race to Robie Creek in late April has over 2,000 entrants.

▶ SPECTATOR VENUES

Baseball

HALLIWELL PARK
1100 W. Alameda Rd., Pocatello **[P. 34, E-6]**. Capacity: 2,580
Pocatella Pioneers (Pioneer League, Advanced Rookie Class); (208) 238-1200. Entered League in 1987. Broadcasts by KWIK 1240-AM. MLB affiliation, Co-op.
◆The Pioneers have been in and out of the league since 1946. Under the current arrangement with Major League Baseball, big league teams supply Pocatello with players contracted to them, while no single team actually owns the club.The Pioneers could conceivably field a team owned by twenty different major league clubs.

MCDERMOTT FIELD
500 West Elva Street, Idaho Falls **[P. 34, E-5]**. Capacity: 3,800
Idaho Falls Braves (Pioneer League, Advanced Rookie Class); (208) 522-8363. Entered League in 1943. Broadcasts by KID 590 AM. MLB affiliation, Atlanta Braves.

MEMORIAL STADIUM
5600 N. Glenwood, Boise **[P. 34, A-4]**. Capacity: 4,500
Boise Hawks (Northwest League, Class A, short season); (208) 322-5000. Entered League in 1987. Broadcasts by KSGR 1340 AM. MLB affiliation, California Angels

College Sports

BOISE STATE UNIVERSITY BRONCOS
1910 University Drive, Boise **[P. 34, B-6]**; (208) 385-1288. Bronco, capacity 22,600. Boise State University Pavilion, capacity 12,200.

IDAHO STATE UNIVERSITY BENGALS
Pocatello **[P. 34, F-7]**; (208) 236-2771. Holt Arena, capacity 12,000. Holt Arena, capacity 7,938.

UNIVERSITY OF IDAHO VANDALS
Moscow **[P. 34, E-1]**; (208) 885-0200. Kibbie-ASUI, capacity 16,000.

Horse Racing

LES BOIS PARK
5610 Glenwood Road, Boise **[P. 34, A-4]**; (208) 376-3991. Opened in 1970. Clubhouse capacity: 300. Grandstand capacity: 3,000. Thoroughbred season from May to Aug.

Rodeo

ISU HOLT ARENA
Idaho State University Campus, Pocatello **[P. 34, F-7]**; (208) 233-1771.
Dodge National Circuit Finals, March.

▶ OUTDOOR VENUES

National Parks

BOISE NATIONAL FOREST
Boise **[P. 35, J-2]**. Contains 2,648,380 acres. C HK BT F S R BK W

CARIBOU NATIONAL FOREST
Pocatello, SE Idaho **[P.34, F-7, P. 35, M-6 & N-7,]**. Contains 987,191 acres. C HK F S W

CHALLIS NATIONAL FOREST
Challis **[P. 35, J-4 & J-5]**. Contains 2,464,674 acres. C HK BT F S R W WW

CLEARWATER NATIONAL FOREST
US 12, Orofino **[P. 34, E-3]**. Contains 1,700,000 acres. C HK BT F S R W HT

COEUR D'ALENE NATIONAL FOREST
N Idaho, Panhandle area **[P. 34, C-2]**. Contains 804,000 acres. C HK BT F S W HT

HELLS CANYON NATIONAL RECREATION AREA
ID 71, NW from Cambridge (to dam) **[P. 34, G-1]**. Contains 662,000 acres.
C HK BT F R WW

KANISKU NATIONAL FOREST
N Idaho, Panhandle area **[P. 34, A-2, B1 & C-2]**. Contains 1,510,000 acres. C HK BT F S R W HT

NEZ PERCE NATIONAL FOREST
Grangeville **[P. 34, G-2 & 3]**. Contains 2,200,000 acres. C HK BT F S R BK W WW

PAYETTE NATIONAL FOREST
McCall **[P. 35, H-2]**. Contains 2,324,466 acres. C HK BT F S R W

SALMON NATIONAL FOREST
US 93, Salmon **[P. 35, H-4 & 5]**. Contains 1,772,125 acres. C HK BT F S R W WW

SAWTOOTH NATIONAL RECREATION AREA
N of Ketchum, in Sawtooth National Forest **[P. 35, J-4]**. Contains 758,533 acres.
C HK BT F S R BK W

SAWTOOTH NATIONAL FOREST
Ketchum, adjacent to Sun Valley, Twin Falls **[P. 35, K-3, M-5, N-4 & 5]**. Contains 1,801,530 acres. C HK BT F S R BK W

ST. JOE NATIONAL FOREST
N Idaho, Panhandle area **[P. 34, D-2]**. Contains 1,710,000 acres. C HK BT F S W HT

TARGHEE NATIONAL FOREST
N & E of St. Anthony, in Teton Range **[P. 35, J-5, K-7]**. Contains 642,944 acres.
C HK BT F S R BK

Bike Trails: BK
Boating: BT
Camping: C
Climbing: CL
Diving: DV
Fishing: F
Golfing: G
Hiking: HK
Hunting: HT
Riding: R
Surfing: SU
Swimming: S
Tennis: TE
Whitewater: WW
Winter Sports: W

State Parks

BEAR LAKE STATE PARK
6 mi. E of St. Charles off US 89 **[P. 35, N-7]**. Contains 52 acres. C HK BT F S

DWORSHAK STATE PARK
26 mi. NW of Orofino **[P. 34, E-2]**. Contains 1,000 acres. C HK BT F S

FARRAGUT STATE PARK
4 mi. E of Athol on ID 54 (on Lake Pend Oreille) **[P. 34, C-2]**. Contains 4,733 acres.
C HK BT F S BK W

HARRIMAN STATE PARK
18 mi. N of Ashton on US 20 **[P. 35, A-7]**. Contains 4,700 acres. F

HELLS GATE STATE PARK
4 mi S of Lewiston on Snake River **[P. 34, F-1]**. Contains 960 acres. C HK BT F S R BK WW

HEYBURN STATE PARK
5 mi. E of Plummer on ID 5 **[P. 34, D-1]**. Contains 7,825 acres. C HK BT F S R W

LAKE PEND OREILLE
Sandpoint **[P. 34, C-2]**. Contains 94,600 acres.
C BT F S

MASSACRE ROCKS STATE PARK
12 mi. SW of American Falls off I-86 **[P. 35, M-5]**. Contains 565 acres. C HK BT F S

PONDEROSA STATE PARK
2 mi. E of McCall on E. Lake Dr. **[P. 35, H-2]**. Contains 1,280 acres. C HK BT F S W

WINCHESTER LAKE STATE PARK
1 mi. SW of Winchester on US 95 **[P. 34, F-1]**. Contains 418 acres. C HK F W

USA SNAPSHOTS®

A look at statistics that shape the sports world

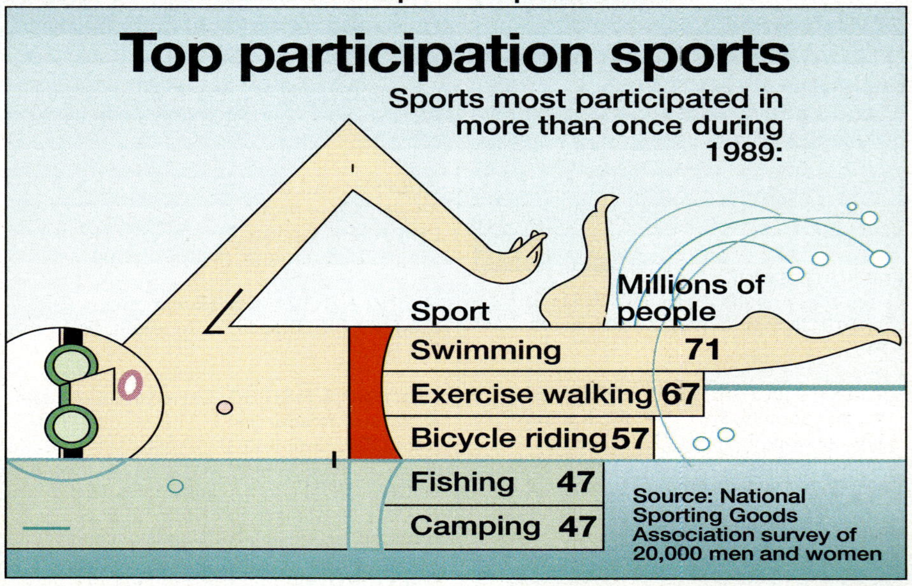

By Marcia Staimer, USA TODAY

STATBOX

POPULATION: 1,006,000
SQUARE MILES: 83,557
TIME ZONE: Pacific and Mountain
MOTTO: Esto Perpetua
BIRD: Mountain Bluebird
TREE: Western White Pine
CAPITAL: Boise
AVERAGE ANNUAL RAINFALL: 12"
MEAN TEMP: 48-51
MAJOR LEAGUE TEAMS: 0
STATE PARK ACREAGE: 41,670
HIGHEST ELEVATION: 12,662'
LOWEST ELEVATION: 738'
WATERWAYS: 2,000 lakes

Skiing

ALPINE SKIING

BOGUS BASIN
Bogus Basin Road, 16 mi. N of Boise **[P. 35, K-2]**; (208) 336-4500.
Vertical drop is 1,800 feet. Has four tows and six chairs.

SCHWEITZER MOUNTAIN RESORT
10,000 Schweitzer Mountain Road, Sandpoint **[P. 34, B-2]**; (208) 263-9555.
Vertical drop is 2,489 feet. Has one bar and seven chairs.

SUN VALLEY RESORT
Sun Valley **[P. 35, K-4]**; (208) 622-4111.
Vertical drop is 3,400 feet. Has fifteen chairs.
◆One of the oldest resorts in the West has maintained some of the intimate, elegant feel.

NORDIC SKIING

BOGUS BASIN SKI RESORT
2405 Bogus Basin Road, Boise **[P. 35, K-2]**; (208) 336-4500.

BUSTERBACK RANCH
ID 75, Ketchum **[P. 35, K-4]**; (208) 774-2217.
◆Gateway to rugged back country skiing near the the Salmon River headwaters.

GALENA LODGE
ID 75, Star Route, Ketchum **[P. 35, K-3]**; (208) 726-4010.
◆The Ketchum area boasts excellent views and all levels of difficulty, and Galena Lodge is an old favorite.

IDAHO ROCKY MOUNTAIN RANCH
ID 75, Stanley **[P. 35, J-3]**; (208) 774-3544.

CONTINUED ON PAGE 153

Illinois

Chicago (with L.A.) is one of two American cities with five "big four" major league teams inside its borders. And where there are sports fanatics, there are sports bars. The Windy City's include Ditka's City Lights ("Iron Mike" cologne is named after the same coach), Harry Caray's, Champions, and the Cubby Bear. ◆ The nation's best fast-pitch softball takes place at the Decatur Shootout Tournament in June (217-423-2400). ◆ And in Adam's County, if you look up, you might see as many as 2,000 falling parachutes at the World Free Fall competition (August, 217-AAA-JUMP). ◆ Those who would rather keep their feet on the ground race on one of the world's fastest 26-mile courses at the Chicago Marathon in October (312-951-0660). For athletes not after a world record, there are beautiful running and cycling trails along the city's Lakefront.

STATBOX

POPULATION: 11,544,100
SQUARE MILES: 56,400
TIME ZONE: Central
MOTTO: State Sovereignty, National Union
BIRD: Cardinal
TREE: White Oak
CAPITAL: Springfield
AVERAGE ANNUAL RAINFALL: 32-48" (no.); 48-64" (so.)
MEAN TEMP: 22/77(no.); 37/70 (so.)
MAJOR LEAGUE TEAMS: 5
NATIONAL PARK/FOREST ACREAGE: 265,147
STATE PARK ACREAGE: 400,644
HIGHEST ELEVATION: 1,241'
LOWEST ELEVATION: 269'
WATERWAYS: 13,200 miles of rivers and streams; 86,000 lakes and ponds

▶ SPECTATOR VENUES

Auto Racing

DUQUOIN STATE FAIRGROUNDS
US 51, DuQuoin **[P. 37, M-6]**; (618) 542-9373. Track is 1-mile dirt oval.
USAC Silver Crown, September.

GATEWAY INTERNATIONAL RACEWAY
558 N Highway 203, I-55 to IL 203, then 1/2 mi. N to light, then W, Fairmont City **[P. 67, D-14]**; (618) 482-5501. Track is 1/4-mile asphalt-concrete pad.
Gateway Nitrous Nationals (IHRA), June.

ILLINOIS STATE FAIRGROUNDS
Sangamon Ave. & Peoria Rd., Springfield **[P. 39, M-4]**; (217) 782-0777. Track is 1-mile dirt oval.
Tony Bettenhausen 100 (USAC Silver Crown), August.

Baseball

COMISKEY PARK
333 West 35th St., Chicago **[P. 39, H-6]**. Built in 1990. Capacity: 44,177
◆An attempt at a more human-scale, less sterile modern stadium, the new Comiskey, built adjacent to the 1910 version in South Chicago, replaces the nation's oldest existing ballpark. Designed by the same architects responsible for the new Baltimore Orioles park, in Camden Yards(name not yet settled), to open in 1992.
Chicago White Sox (AL West); (312) 924-1000. Franchise began in 1901. Broadcasts by WMAQ 670 AM, WGN TV-9, SportsChannel America. Affiliates: Vancouver, British Columbia (AAA); Birmingham, AL (AA); Sarasota, FL (A); South Bend, IN (A); Utica, NY (A); Sarasota, FL (Rookie). Spring training held in Sarasota, FL.

KANE COUNTY EVENTS CENTER
34W002 Cherry Lane, Geneva **[P. 38, G-1]**. Capacity: 3,600
Kane County Cougars (Midwest League, Class A); (708) 232-8811. Entered League in 1991. Broadcasts by WAUR 930 AM. MLB affiliation, Baltimore Orioles.

LANPHIER PARK
1351 N. Grand Avenue East, Springfield **[P. 39, M-4]**. Capacity: 5,000
Springfield Cardinals (Midwest League, Class A); (217) 525-6570. Entered League in 1982. Broadcasts by WCVS 1450 AM, WBBA 1580 AM/97.5 FM, WKXQ 96.7 FM. MLB affiliation, St. Louis Cardinals.

MARINELLI FIELD
101 15th Avenue, Rockford **[P. 39, N-1]**. Capacity: 4,200
Rockford Expos (Midwest League, Class A); (815) 964-5400. Entered League in 1988. Broadcasts by WROK 1440-AM. MLB affiliation, Montreal Expos.

MEINEN FIELD
1524 W. Nebraska Ave., Peoria **[P. 39, N-5]**. Capacity: 5,000
Peoria Chiefs (Midwest League, Class A); (309) 688-1622. Entered League in 1983. Broadcasts by WTAZ 102 FM. MLB affiliation, Chicago Cubs.

WRIGLEY FIELD
Clark and Addison Streets, Chicago **[P. 38, G-6]**. Built in 1914. Capacity: 38,710
◆Cubs have played on this historic field since 1916. Irrepressible baseball maverick Bill Veeck planted the outfield wall ivy in 1938; the scoreboard dates to 1937, and night game lights were finally installed only in 1988. Many people say this is the best ballpark experience in baseball. Be sure to stop at any neighborhood bar for a post-game libation. You can't beat the atmosphere. Try an Italian beef sandwich, a Chicago specialty. Legendary announcer Harry Caray owns an eatery, "Harry Caray's" that is quite good.
Chicago Cubs (NL East); (312) 404-CUBS. Franchise began in 1876. Broadcasts by WGN 720 AM, WGN Channel 9. Affiliates: Iowa (AAA); Charlotte, SC (AA); Winston-Salem, NC (A); Peoria, IL (A); Geneva, NY (A); Hunington, WV (Rookie). Spring training held in Mesa, AZ.

Basketball

CHICAGO STADIUM
1800 West Madison Street, Chicago **[P. 38, G-5]**. Built in 1929. Capacity: 17,339.
◆Most noisy, fan-involved arena in USA. Visiting teams say the din during time outs can make hearing one another difficult.
Chicago Bulls (NBA Eastern Conf., Central Division); (312) 943-5800. Franchise began in 1966. Broadcasts by WLUP 1000 AM, WGN Channel 9, Sportschannel.

ROCKFORD METROCENTRE
300 Elm Street, Rockford **[P. 39, N-1]**. Capacity: 8,900.
Rockford Lightning (Continental Basketball Association, American Conference, Central Division); (815) 968-5666. Entered League in 1978. Broadcasts by "WROK 1440 AM".

WHARTON FIELDHOUSE
1800 20th Avenue, Moline **[P. 42, F-3]**. Capacity: 5,872.
Quad City Thunder (Continental Basketball Association, American Conference, Central Division); (309) 788-2255. Entered League in 1987. Broadcasts by WLLR, 1230 AM.

Bowling

BRUNSWICK NORTHERN BOWL
558 East North Avenue, Glendale Hts. **[P. 38, G-3]**; (708) 858-1300.
Brunswick Memorial World Open (PBA), Nov.

DON CARTER LANES
4007 E. State St., Rockford **[P. 39, N-2]**; (815) 399-0314.
Hammer Midwest Open (LPBT), October.

HOFFMAN LANES
80 W. Higgins Rd, Hoffman Estates **[P. 38, F-3]**; (708) 885-2500.
Hoffman/Schaumburg Open (LPBT), April.

LANDMARK RECREATION CENTER
3225 North Dries Lane, Peoria **[P. 39, N-5]**; (309) 685-7000.
True Value Open (PBA), March.

CONTINUED ON PAGE 154

Idaho

CONTINUED FROM PAGE 152

SUN VALLEY NORDIC CENTER
Sun Valley Village, Sun Valley **[P. 35, K-4]**; (208) 622-2251.

▶ ACTIVE SPORTS

AEROBICS: AFAA, 3601 Gekeler Ln., #83, Boise; (208) 336-6384.

BASEBALL: Little League Baseball Western Region HQ, 6707 Little League Dr., San Bernadino, CA; (714) 887-6444. • **Pony Baseball-Softball,** 908 Redbird Dr., San Jose, CA; (408) 265-3309 • **American Legion Baseball,** 2605 Sunset Dr., Lewiston; (208) 743-7574. • **Babe Ruth Baseball,** Jim Lemp, 1911 Oxford Dr., Cheyenne, WY; (307) 638-6023. • **Men's Senior Baseball League - Boise,** 6110 Emerald, Boise; (208) 345-8977.

BOARDSAILING: Boise Marine Center , Boise; (208) 342-8985. • **Sawtooth Windsurfing ,** Boise; (208) 342-0548. • **USWA Regional Director,** 9889 N.W. Hoge, Portland, OR; (503) 286-6100.

BOWLING: American Bowling Congress, 5301 S. 76th St., Greendale, WI; (414) 421-6400.

CANOEING & KAYAKING: ACA Northwest Vice Commodore, 550 Shoup Avenue, Idaho Falls; (208) 524-0282.

CYCLING: USCF Idaho Representative, 1099 Redwood Cir., Twin Falls; (208) 733-4110.

FITNESS: National Strength and Conditioning Ass'n State Director, Boise State University, Varsity Center, 1910 U. Dr., Boise; (208) 385-1980.

FOOTBALL: Pop Warner Football, 1315 Walnut Street, Suite 1632, Philadelphia, PA; (215) 735-1450.

GOLF: Idaho Golf Association, PO Box 3025, Boise; (208) 342-4442. • **PGA Rocky Mountain Section,** 595 E. State St., Eagle; (208) 939-6028.

HIKING & CLIMBING: Northern Rockies Sierra Club Chapter, 1408 Joyce St., Boise; (208) 344-4565.

HOCKEY: USA Hockey Pacific Registrar, 5703 Sun Ridge Ct., Castro Valley, CA; (415) 886-0706. • **USA Hockey Rocky Mountain Registrar,** 7335 S. Garfield Ct., Littleton, CO; (303) 721-0936.

HUNTING & FISHING: Fish & Game Department, 600 S. Walnut, Boise; (208) 334-3700.

RACQUETBALL: AARA, 7211 Colonial, Boise; (208) 342-0899.

RIDING: Idaho Horse Council, Box 84, Castleford; (208) 537-6664.

RODEO: PRCA Columbia River Circuit, Rt. 2, Box 286, Walla Walla, WA; (509) 529-0819. • **PRCA Wilderness Circuit,** 254 Clinton Drive, Twin Falls; (208) 536-2772.

SCUBA: Boise Water Sports, 3204 Overland Road, Boise; (208) 342-1378.

SHOOTING: Buz Fawcett's Shooting Grounds, 2090 S. Meridian Rd., Meridian; (208) 888-3415.

SKATING: USFSA, 20 First Street, Colorado Springs, CO; (719) 635-5200.

SOCCER: Idaho Soccer Ass'n, 6219 Tahoe Dr., Boise; (208) 375-2612. • **Idaho YSA,** 106 N. 6th St., #220, Boise; (208) 336-5256. • **AYSO Regional Director,** 1720 Carmel Dr., Idaho Falls; (208) 529-2649.

SOFTBALL: Idaho ASA, 1202 Mountain Ave., PO Box 336, Coeur D'Alene; (208) 664-8067.

SQUASH: Boise Family YMCA, Boise; (208) 344-5501.

SWIMMING: LMSC Snake River Registrar, 1431 Cottonwood Ct., Boise; (208) 345-5407.

TENNIS: Recreational TEAMTENNIS Central-West Region, National Program Coordinator, 2105 Grant Ave., #4, Redondo Beach, CA; (800) 992-9042. • **Intermountain USTA,** 1201 South Parker Rd., #102, Denver, CO; (303) 695-4117. • **Pacific Northwest USTA,** 10175 SW Barber Blvd., 306B, Portland, OR; (503) 245-3048.

WHITEWATER RAFTING: Middle Fork River Company , PO Box 54, Sun Valley; (208) 726-8888. • **Northwest River Company,** Box 403, Boise; (208) 344-7119. • **River Odysseys West (ROW),** Box 579-WG, Coeur D'Alene; (208) 765-0841. • **Rocky Mountain River Tours - Middlefork ,** Box 2552-AO, Boise; (208) 344-6668.

Illinois

CONTINUED FROM PAGE 153

College Sports

BRADLEY UNIVERSITY BRAVES
1501 W. Bradley Avenue, Peoria **[P. 39, N-5]**; (309) 677-2670. Peoria Civic Center, capacity 10,300.

CHICAGO STATE UNIVERSITY COUGARS
95th & King Drive, Chicago **[P. 39, J-6]**; (312) 995-2295. Phys Ed & Rec Athletics Dept Gymnasium, capacity 2,500.

DE PAUL UNIVERSITY BLUE DEMONS
1011 W. Belden Avenue, Chicago **[P. 38, G-6]**; (312) 341-8010. Alumni Hall, capacity 5,308.
◆Home of basketball's most legendary coaching family. Former coach Ray Meyer now does the radio commentary while son Joey coaches.

EASTERN ILLINOIS UNIVERSITY PANTHERS
Grant Street, Charleston **[P. 37, H-7]**; (217) 581-2319. O'Brien, capacity 10,000. Lantz, capacity 6,465.

ILLINOIS STATE UNIVERSITY REDBIRDS
West College at Delaine Drive, Normal **[P. 36, F-6]**; (309) 438-3633. Hancock, capacity 15,000. Redbird Arena, capacity 10,500.

LAKE FOREST COLLEGE FORESTERS
College and Sheridan Roads, Lake Forest **[P. 38, C-4]**; (312) 234-3100. Farwell, capacity 3,000. Sports Center, capacity 2,000.

LOYOLA UNIVERSITY RAMBLERS
6525 North Sheridan Road, Chicago **[P. 38, F-6]**; (312) 508-2560. Rosemont Horizon, capacity 17,500. Alumni Gym, capacity 2,500.

NORTHEASTERN ILLINOIS GOLDEN EAGLES
5500 N. St. Louis Avenue, Chicago **[P. 38, F-5]**; (312) 583-4050.

NORTHWESTERN UNIVERSITY WILDCATS
1501 Central Street, Evanston **[P. 38, F-6]**; (708) 491-3205. Dyche, capacity 49,256. McGaw Hall, capacity 8,117.

ROCKFORD COLLEGE REGENTS
5050 East State Street, Rockford **[P. 39, N-2]**; (815) 226-4085. Smith Field, capacity 2,100. Seaver Gym, capacity 1,700.

SOUTHERN ILLINOIS UNIVERSITY SALUKIS
Carbondale **[P. 37, M-5]**; (618) 453-5311. McAndrew, capacity 17,324. SIU Arena, capacity 10,014.

TRINITY CHRISTIAN COLLEGE TROLLS
6601 W. College Drive, Palos Heights **[P. 39, K-5]**; (708) 597-3000. Mitchell Memorial.

UNIVERSITY OF CHICAGO MAROONS
5640 S. University Avenue, Chicago **[P. 39, H-6]**; (312) 702-7681. Stagg Field, capacity 1,200. Henry Crown, capacity 1,400.

UNIVERSITY OF ILLINOIS FIGHING ILLINI
112 Assembly Hall, 1800 S. First Street, Champaign **[P. 36, G-7]**; (217) 333-3678. Memorial, capacity 71,227. Assembly Hall, capacity 16,100.
◆Lou Henson coaches the basketball team. His haircut, the worst in the sport, has a nickname — "the Lou Do."

UNIVERSITY OF ILLINOIS FLAMES
Chicago **[P. 39, H-6]**; (312) 996-2772., capacity. UIC Pavilion, capacity 12,000.

WESTERN ILLINOIS UNIVERSITY LEATHERNECKS
Macomb **[P. 36, F-3]**; (309) 298-1106. Hanson Field, capacity 12,000. Western Hall, capacity 5,200.

Football

SOLDIER FIELD
425 McFetridge Place, Chicago **[P. 39, H-6]**. Built in 1924. Capacity: 66,946.
◆A wonderful, distinct field, with unforgettable architecture. On the lake and very cold. The Bears moved into Soldier in 1971, having played at Wrigley for the previous half-century. Artificial turf replaced by natural grass in 1988.
Chicago Bears (NFC Central Division); (708) 295-6600. Franchise began in 1920. Broadcasts by WGN-AM.

Hockey

CHICAGO STADIUM
1800 W. Madison St., Chicago **[P. 38, G-5]**. Built in 1929. Capacity: 17,337.
◆Noisy, frenetic crowds.
Chicago Blackhawks (NHL, Campbell Conference, Norris Division); (312) 733-5300. Franchise began in 1926. Broadcasts by WBBM (AM 780), SportsChannel.

PEORIA CIVIC CENTER
201 S.W. Jefferson St., Peoria **[P. 39, N-6]**. Capacity: 9,074.
Peoria Rivermen (International Hockey League); (309) 673-8900. Franchise began in 1984. Broadcasts by WTAX 102.3 FM. Louis.

Horse Racing

ARLINGTON INTERNATIONAL RACECOURSE
Euclid Avenue and Wilke Road, Arlington Heights **[P. 38, E-3]**; (708) 255-4300. Opened in 1927. Total capacity: 30,000.
Thoroughbred season from May to Oct.
◆The new facility opened in 1989 after a 1985 fire. Has set Illinois records in total amount wagered at a single meeting. Pat Day won eight of nine races on September 13, 1989. Home since 1981 to the Arlington Million.

BALMORAL PARK
Route 1 & Elms Court Lane, Crete **[P. 36, D-8]**; (708) 568-5700. Opened in 1926. Clubhouse capacity: 2,000. Grandstand capacity: 8,281.
Harness season from Oct. to May.
Thoroughbred season from May to Oct.
◆Originally opened as Lincoln Fields, a thoroughbred track. One mile track added in 1989. Thoroughbred racing may not continue here, as of April, 1991. The Illinois Racing Board has ruled that harness racing continue year round, but the final decision has been appealed to the Supreme Court.

FAIRMOUNT PARK
I-55/70 N at I-255, Collinsville **[P. 37, K-4]**; (618) 345-4300 or (314) 436-1516 in Missouri. Opened in 1925. Clubhouse capacity: 1,200. Grandstand capacity: 2,400.
Harness season from Dec. to Apr.
Thoroughbred season from Apr. to Dec.

HAWTHORNE RACE COURSE
3501 S. Laramie Avenue, Cicero **[P. 39, H-5]**; (708) 780-3700. Opened in 1891. Clubhouse capacity: 12,000. Grandstand capacity: 18,000.
Harness season from Jan. to Feb.
Thoroughbred season from Oct. to Dec.
◆First harness race held in 1969.

MAYWOOD PARK
8600 W. North Avenue, Maywood **[P. 38, G-4]**; (708) 343-4800. Opened in 1946. Clubhouse capacity: 16,000. Grandstand capacity: 10,847.
Harness season from Feb. to May and Oct. to Dec.

QUAD CITY DOWNS
5005 Morton Drive, East Moline **[P. 36, C-4]**; (800) 747-3696. Opened in 1973. Clubhouse capacity: 1,780. Grandstand capacity: 4,000.
Harness season from Apr. to Oct.
◆Racing dates will vary year to year. Illinois phone, (309) 792-0202.

SPORTSMAN'S PARK
3301 South Laramie Avenue, Cicero **[P. 39, H-5]**; (312) 242-1121. Opened in 1932. Clubhouse capacity: 10,000. Grandstand capacity: 20,000. Total capacity: 35,000.
Harness season from May to Oct.
Thoroughbred season from Feb. to May.
◆Added harness racing in 1949. Free grandstand admission. Every spring hosts the Illinois Derby, area's richest race for 3-year-olds.

Museums & Halls of Fame

CHICAGO SPORTS HALL OF FAME
227 W. Ontario, Chicago **[P. 38, G-6]**; (312) 915-4500.
◆Moved in 1989 from Soldier Field to a space adjacent to Mike Ditka's restaurant. Inductees include Bronco Nagurski, Johnny Weismuller, and Cubs infielders Tinkers, Evers and Chance.

NATIONAL ITALIAN AMERICAN SPORTS HALL OF FAME
2625 Clearbrook Dr., Arlington Heights **[P. 38, F-3]**; (708) 437-3077.
◆Features mementos such as driver Mario Andretti's 1970 Formula One car and boxer Rocky Marciano's title belt.

PGA/LPGA

COG HILL GOLF AND COUNTRY CLUB
119th St. & Archer Ave., Lemont **[P. 39, K-3]**; (708) 257-5872.
Centel Western Open (PGA), June. Number of holes: 72.

OAK BROOK GOLF CLUB
700 Oak Brook Road, Oak Brook **[P. 39, H-4]**; (708) 990-3020.
LPGA Chicago Shoot Out, August. Number of holes: 72.

OAKWOOD COUNTRY CLUB
Route 6, Coal Valley **[P. 42, F-4]**; (309) 799-5558.
Hardee's Golf Classic (PGA), Sept. Number of holes: 72.

RAIL GOLF CLUB
R.R. 5, Route 124N, Springfield **[P. 39, M-4]**; (217) 525-0365.
Rail Charity Golf Classic (LPGA), Sep. Number of holes: 54.

STONE BRIDGE COUNTRY CLUB
2705 Stone Bridge Blvd., Aurora; (708) 820-8887.
Ameritech Senior Open (Senior PGA), July. Number of holes: 54.

Polo

CHAUTAUQUA POLO CLUB
Ponce Field, Route 2, NE of Carbondale **[P. 37, M-5]**; (618) 549-3952.

NAPERVILLE POLO CLUB
23700 W. 119th St., Naperville **[P. 38]**; (708) 355-1503.

OAK BROOK POLO CLUB
3N541 Bloomingdale Road, Glendale Heights **[P. 38, G-3]**; (708) 574-0442.

ROCKFORD POLO CLUB
Atwood Rd. in the Olsen Forest Preserve, Rockford **[P. 36, A-6]**; (815) 623-6760.

Tennis

UNIVERSITY OF ILLINOIS AT CHICAGO PAVILLION
1150 West Houston, Chicago **[P. 39, H-6]**; (312) 413-5770. Surface is Supreme.
Volvo Chicago (ATP), Feb. to March
Virginia Slims of Chicago (WTA), February.

Track & Field

NORTH CENTRAL COLLEGE STADIUM
North Central College, Naperville **[P. 39, J-2]**; (815) 332-4743.
U.S. National Outdoor Masters Track & Field Championships, July, 1991.

STREETS OF CHICAGO
Daley Plaza, Chicago **[P. 39, G-6]**; (312) 951-0660.
Chicago Marathon, October.

OUTDOOR VENUES

National Parks

SHAWNEE NATIONAL FOREST
S of IL 13 & N of IL 146 **[P. 37, M-5, 7]**. Contains 265,135 acres. **C HK BT F S R BK HT**

State Parks

ANDERSON LAKE CONSERVATION AREA
12 mi. SW of Havana **[P. 36, F-4]**. Contains 2,135 acres.
C BT F W HT

ARGYLE LAKE STATE PARK
8 mi. SW of Macomb on US 136, then 1.5 mi. N **[P. 36, F-3]**. Contains 1,184 acres.
C HK BT F R W HT

CARLYLE-ELDON HAZLET STATE PARK
5 mi. N & 3 mi. E of Carlyle, off Route 127, on Lake Carlyle **[P. 37, K-5]**. Contains 3,000 acres. **C HK BT F W HT**

- Bike Trails: BK
- Boating: BT
- Camping: C
- Climbing: CL
- Diving: DV
- Fishing: F
- Golfing: G
- Hiking: HK
- Hunting: HT
- Riding: R
- Surfing: SU
- Swimming: S
- Tennis: TE
- Whitewater: WW
- Winter Sports: W

CONTINUED ON PAGE 155

USA SNAPSHOTS®

A look at statistics that shape the sports world

Source: NCAA

By Bob Laird, USA TODAY

Illinois

CONTINUED FROM PAGE 154

CHAIN O'LAKES STATE PARK
3 mi. E of Spring Grove off US 12 **[P. 38, A-2]**. Contains 6,063 acres. **C HK BT F R W HT**

CLINTON LAKE STATE PARK
8 mi. E of Clinton on IL 54 **[P. 36, G-6]**. Contains 9,907 acres. **C HK BT F S W**

CRAB ORCHARD NATIONAL WILDLIFE REFUGE
On IL 148, S of IL 13 **[P. 37, M-6]**. Contains 44,000 acres. **C HK BT F S HT**

DIXON SPRINGS STATE PARK
Dixon Springs nr. jct. of IL 145 and 146 **[P. 37, N-7]**. Contains 496 acres. **C HK S**

ILLINOIS BEACH STATE PARK
4 mi. N of Waukegan on IL 131 **[P. 38, A-5]**. Contains 3,000 acres. **C F S BK W**

KANKAKEE RIVER STATE PARK
8 mi. NW of Kankakee on IL 102 **[P. 36, D-7]**. Contains 4,000 acres. **C HK BT F R BK W HT**

LAKE LE-AQUA-NA STATE PARK
4 mi. N of Lena off IL 73 **[P. 36, A-4]**. Contains 715 acres. **C HK BT F S R W HT**

REND LAKE FISH AND WILDLIFE AREA (AC)
1 mi. N of Benton **[P. 37, L-6]**. Contains 39,819 acres. **HK BT F S BK W HT**

RICE LAKE CONSERVATION AREA
3 1/2 mi. S of Banner **[P. 36, F-4]**. Contains 5,608 acres. **C BT F HT**

ROCK CUT STATE PARK
5 mi. NE of Rockford on IL 51 **[P. 39, M-2]**. Contains 3,092 acres. **C HK BT F R BK W HT**

STARVED ROCK STATE PARK
2 mi. off Route 71 from La Salle **[P. 36, D-6]**. Contains 2,630 acres. **C HK BT F R W HT**

STEPHEN A. FORBES STATE PARK
15 mi. from Salem on I-57 & Route 50 **[P. 37, K-6]**. Contains 3,100 acres. **C HK BT F S R W**

WASHINGTON CONSERVATION AREA
5 mi. S of Nashville off IL 127 **[P. 37, L-5]**. Contains 1,417 acres. **C HK BT F HT**

Skiing

ALPINE SKIING

CHESTNUT MOUNTAIN RESORT
Blackjack Rd., Galena **[P. 36, A-4]**; (800) 397-1320.
Vertical drop is 465 feet. Has five tows and three chairs.

PLUMTREE SKI AREA
200 Plumtree Drive, Lanark **[P. 36, B-4]**; (815) 493-2881.
Vertical drop is 210 feet. Has one bar and one chair.

SNOWSTAR
4500 126th Street West, Taylor Ridge **[P. 36, D-3]**; (309) 798-2666.
Vertical drop is 208 feet. Has two tows and two chairs.

NORDIC SKIING

LAKE LE-AQUA-NA STATE PARK
Route 2, Lena **[P. 36, A-4]**; (815) 369-4282.

ACTIVE SPORTS

ADVENTURE: Voyageur Outward Bound School, 10900 Cedar Lake Rd., Minnetonka, MN; (800) 328-2943.

AEROBICS: AFAA, 12916 S. Commercial Ave., Chicago; (312) 646-2751.

BASEBALL: Little League Baseball Central Region HQ, 4360 N. Mitthoeffer Rd., Indianapolis, IN; (317) 897-6127. • **Pony Baseball-Softball,** 110 N. 5th Street, Auburn; (217) 438-3130. • **Pony Baseball-Softball,** 531 Parkshore Dr., Shorewood; (815) 725-3047. • **American Legion Baseball,** 416 Madison St., Joilet; (815) 725-2318. • **Babe Ruth Baseball,** Robert Dickson, RR 4, Box 332F, Alexandria, IN; (317) 724-4883. • **Men's Senior Baseball League - Central Chicago,** 7555 W. Belmont, Chicago; (312) 804-0637

BILLIARDS: Chicago Billiard Cafe, 5949 W. Irving Park, Chicago; (312) 545-5102. • **Chris's Billiards,** 4637 N. Milwaukee, Chicago; (312) 286-4714. • **Muddler's Pool Room,** 1800 N. Clybourne Ave., Chicago; (312) 944-7665. • **Oak Park Billiards,** 1019 South Blvd., Oak Park; (708) 848-9085. • **River Stix,** 820 North Orleans, Chicago; (312) 642-1948. • **St. Paul Billiards,** 1415 W. Fullerton, Chicago; (312) 472-9494.

BOARDSAILING: Adventure Sports , Springfield; (217) 753-2807. • **Offshore Marine ,** Vernon Hills; (708) 362-4880. • **USWA Regional Director,** N7315 Winnebago Dr., Fond du Lac, WI; (414) 922-2550.

BOWLING: American Bowling Congress, 5301 S. 76th St., Greendale, WI; (414) 421-6400.

CANOEING & KAYAKING: ACA Midwest Vice Commodore, 1343 N. Portage, Palatine; (708) 359-4057.

CYCLING: LAW Illinois Regional Director, 450 Checker Dr., Buffalo Grove; (708) 459-8242. • **Metro Chicago AYH Council,** 3036 N. Ashland Ave., Chicago; (312) 327-8114. • **USCF Illinois Representative,** 419 Linden Ave., Wilmette; (708) 251-6021.

FITNESS: Governor's Council on Health & Physical Fitness, 525 W. Jefferson Street, Springfield; (217) 785-8216.

FOOTBALL: Pop Warner Football, 1315 Walnut Street, Suite 1632, Philadelphia, PA; (215) 735-1450.

GOLF: Central Illinois Golf Course Superintendents Association, 1601 Illini Rd., Springfield; (217) 546-8735. • **Chicago District Golf Association,** 619 Enterprise Dr., Suite 101, Oak Brook; (708) 954-2180. • **Illinois Junior Golf Association,** P.O. Box 162, Golf; (708) 724-1906. • **PGA Gateway Section,** 2333 Grissom Dr., Suite 109, Maryland Heights,MO; (205) 822-0321. • **PGA Illinois Section,** 2100 Clearwater Dr., Suite 206, Oak Brook; (708) 990-7864. • **PGA Nebraska Section,** 9301 Firethorn Ln., Lincoln, NE; (402) 489-7760. • **Western Golf Association,** 1 Briar Rd., Golf; (708) 724-4600. • **Women's Western Golf Association,** 200 Forest Street, Winnetka; (708) 446-7915.

HIKING & CLIMBING: Illinois Sierra Club Chapter, 506 S. Wabash, Room 525, Chicago; (312) 431-0158.

HOCKEY: USA Hockey Central Registrar, P.O. Box 1738, Lisle; (708) 963-1098.

HUNTING & FISHING: Department of Conservation, Lincoln Tower Plaza, 524 S. 2nd St., Springfield; (217) 782-6302. • **Fly 'N Field (Orvis),** 550 Crescent Blvd., Glen Ellyn; (708) 858-7844. • **Trout Unlimited,** 2580 Forest View Ave., River Grove; (708) 453-8102.

RACQUETBALL: AARA, 931 Taylor Dr., Gurnee; (312) 816-3894.

RIDING: Horsemen's Council of Illinois, 1402 W. Pennsylvania Dr., Urbana; (217) 333-1784.

RODEO: PRCA Great Lakes Circuit, Rt. 1, Box 54, Clayton, IN; (317) 539-5039.

RUNNING: RRCA IL State Rep., 1408 Noble Ave., Springfield; (217) 698-8600.

SCUBA: Black Magic Dive Shop, 334 Peterson Road, Libertyville; (708) 362-3483. • **Do Dive In, Inc. Scuba Supply,** 9011 North University, Suite A, Peoria; (309) 692-7600. • **Goose's Scuba Shack, Inc.,** 18143 Torrence Avenue, Lansing; (708) 474-7380. • **Neptune's Locker, Inc.,** 538 East 147th Street, Sibley Blvd., South Holland; (708) 331-3372. • **Scuba Emporium,** 12003 South Cicero, Alsip; (708) 389-9410. • **Scuba Systems, Ltd.,** 3919 Oakton Street, Skokie; (708) 674-0222. • **Underwater Safaris,** 620 North LaSalle, Chicago; (312) 337-7730.

SHOOTING: Diamond S. Sporting Clays, Inc., Rt. 1, Tremont; (309) 449-5500. • **Seneca Hunt Club Limited,** P.O. Box 824, Seneca; (815) 357-8080.

SKATING: Amateur Skating Association of Illinois, 721 Duane St., Glen Ellyn; (708) 858-4358. • **USFSA,** 20 First Street, Colorado Springs, CO; (719) 635-5200.

SOCCER: Illinois Soccer Ass'n, 3403 W. Lawrence Ave., Chicago; (312) 463-0653. • **Illinois YSA,** 800 E. Northwest Hwy. #700, Palatine; (708) 253-5292. • **AYSO Regional Director,** 1918 Sringside Dr., Naperville; (807) 416-8520.

SOFTBALL: Illinois ASA, 218 W. Elm, Chillicothe; (309) 274-3936. • **Chicago ASA,** 8137 Hillcrest Ln., Tinley Park; (708) 429-2008.

SQUASH: Downtown Sports Club (USSRA), 441 N. Wabash, Chicago; (312) 644-4884.

SWIMMING: LMSC Central Registrar, 923 Sunset Rd., Wheaton; (708) 653-7079.

TENNIS: Recreational TEAMTENNIS Midwest-Southeast Region, National Program Coordinator, 445 N. Wells, Ste. #404, Chicago; (800) TEAMTEN. • **Missouri Valley USTA,** 722 Walnut St., Suite #1, Kansas City, MO; (816) 556-0777 • **Western USTA,** 8720 Castle Creek Parkway, Ste. 329, Indianapolis, IN; (513) 390-2740.

TRIATHLON: Chicago Tri-Club, 1735 W. School Street, Chicago; (312) 644-4880. • **Tri-Masters Chicago,** 7458 S. Coles Street, Chicago; (312) 989-3960.

VOLLEYBALL: USVBA Great Lakes Commissioner, 1635 Greenleaf, Des Plaines; (708) 297-3419.

Tip Offs

Where to Bike Off-Road

Off-road or fat-tire biking was one of the fastest growing sports in the USA over the latter half of the 1980s, with some 7.5 million Americans regularly on mountain bikes. What began as an eccentric hobby in the hills north of San Francisco has grown into an international industry.

The International Mountain Bike Association (IMBA, Route 2, Box 303, Bishop, CA 93514, 619-387-2757) is a participant's clearinghouse and policy group, with affiliated clubs all across the USA. An abbreviated version of their Rules of the Trail follows:

1) Ride on open trails only—Respect trail and road closures, avoid possible trespass, obtain permits and authorization as may be required. Federal and State wilderness areas are closed to cycling.
2) Leave no trace.
3) Control your bicycle!—Inattention for even a second can cause disaster.
4) Always yield the trail.
5) Never spook animals.
6) Plan ahead—Know your equipment, your ability, and the area in which you are riding—and prepare accordingly. Be self-sufficient at all times. Wear a helmet.

The following is a partial listing of IMBA-afiliated clubs:

Adirondack Region Bike Club, NY, (518) 523-4339.
Almanac/Burlington Bicycle Club, NC, (919) 226-3566
Backcountry Bicycle Trails Club, Issaquah WA, (206) 643-8672
Bicycle Trails Council of Marin, CA (415) 456-7512
Capital Bicycling Club, WA, (206) 956-3321
California Association of Bicycling Organizations, CA, (415) 828-5299
Central California Off-Road Cyclists, CA, (209) 252-1335
Coalition of Connecticut Bicyclists, Storrs, CT, (203) 429-5957
Colorado Plateau Mtn. Bike Trail Association, CO, (303) 241-9561
Dallas Off Road Bicycling Association, TX, (214) 424-1066
Desert Ratz Mt. Bike Club, El Paso, TX, (915) 581-4399
Eastern Virginia Mountain Bike Association, VA, (804) 877-9389
Fat Trackin' Homies, Carmel, IN, (317) 848-9300
Great Plains Bicycle Club, Box 81564, Lincoln, NE, 68501
Memphis Hightailers Bicycle Club, TN, (615) 726-5153
Michigan Mountain Biking Association, Detroit, MI, (616) 784-9327
Morris Velo Sports, NJ, (201) 984-5313
Mountain Bike Association of Arizona, AZ, (702) 832-7675
Nebraska Ruff Riders, NE, (402) 551-9354
New England Mountain Bike Association, MA, (617) 497-6891
North Carolina State Univ. Mtn. Bike Club, NC, (919) 832-3635
Ontario Cycling Association, Canada, (416) 495-4141
Portland United Mountain Pedalers, OR, (502) 223-3954
Santa Cruz County Cycle Club, CA, (408) 423-0829
Southern Connecticut Cycle Club, CT, (203) 562-9502
Southern Maine Off-Road Bicycling Association, ME, (207) 797-5124
Southern Off-Road Bicycling Association, GA, (404) 373-3058
Southern Wisconsin Trail Biking Club, WI, (414) 862-6502
Suwannee Bicycle Tours, White Springs, FL, (904) 878-2042
Tarheel Cyclists, NC, (704) 537-7985
West Virginia Mountain Bike Ass'n, WV, (304) 259-5286

Indiana

Although the state is best known for the Indianapolis 500 (the Sunday before Memorial Day), John Feinstein, author of *A Season on the Brink* points out that for Hoosiers, their local high school and college basketball "ranks in importance only slightly ahead of the fate of the free world." ◆ Indianapolis also is one of the largest amateur sports centers, having hosted events such as the National Sports Festival, the Pan American Games, and NCAA Men's Division I Basketball. The city is also home to The Athletics Congress, six Olympic governing bodies, and two national masters championships. ◆ The southern mountains are ideal for skiers, hikers, canoeists and whitewater rafters. ◆ If the Indy 500 starts the summer, the NHRA U.S. Nationals end it. The world's largest drag racing event is held at Indianapolis Raceway Park on Labor Day weekend.

▶ SPECTATOR VENUES

Auto Racing

INDIANAPOLIS MOTOR SPEEDWAY
4790 W. 16th St., Speedway **[P. 38, F-7]**; (317) 241-2501. Track is 2.5-mile oval.
◆The Indianapolis 500 begins on the first Saturday of May, with qualifying laps and practice leading to the nation's premiere race on the final Sunday in the month. Race is sanctioned by the USAC, although points are awarded for the CART series.
Indianapolis 500 (USAC Gold Crown & CART PPG Indy Car World Series), May.

INDIANAPOLIS RACEWAY PARK
Highway 136, Exit 16, Clermont **[P. 40, G-5]**; (317) 291-4090. Track is 0.686-mile paved oval.
Pepsi-Cola 100 (USAC Silver Crown), June.
US Nationals (NHRA), late August.

INDIANA STATE FAIRGROUNDS
E. 38th St. at Fall Creek Parkway, Indianapolis **[P. 38, E-7]**; (317) 923-3431. Track is 1-mile dirt oval.
Hulman Hundred (USAC Silver Crown), May.
Hoosier Hundred (USAC Silver Crown), August.

Baseball

OWEN J. BUSH STADIUM
1501 West 16th St., Indianapolis **[P. 38, F-7]**. Capacity: 12,500
Indianapolis Indians (American Association, Class AAA); (317) 269-3545. Entered League in 1902. Broadcasts by WIRE 100.9 FM. MLB affiliation, Montreal Expos.

STANLEY COVELESKI REGIONAL STADIUM
501 W. South Street, South Bend **[P. 38, A-6]**. Capacity: 5,000
South Bend White Sox (Midwest League, Class A); (219) 284-9988. Entered League in 1988. Broadcasts by WHME 103.1-FM. MLB affiliation, Chicago White Sox.

Basketball

ALLEN COUNTY WAR MEMORIAL COLISEUM
400 Parnell Avenue, Fort Wayne. **[P. 38, A-8]** Capacity: 10,000.
Fort Wayne Fury (Continental Basketball Association, Conference & Division TBA); (219) 424-6233. Entered League in 1991. Broadcasts by WQHK, 1380 AM.

MARKET SQUARE ARENA
300 E. Market Street, Indianapolis **[P. 38, F-7]**. Built in 1974. Capacity: 16,912.
◆Moved from ABA to NBA in 1976.
Indiana Pacers (NBA Eastern Conf., Central Div.); (317) 263-2100. Franchise began in 1967. Broadcasts by WNDE 1260 AM, WXIN Channel 59, Prime Sports Network-Midwest.

Bowling

CHIPPEWA BOWL
225 Chippewa, South Bend **[P. 38, B-6]**; (219) 291-5093.
Ebonite Open (LPBT), May.

OLYMPIA LANES
4150 Calumet Ave., Hammond **[P. 39, K-7]**; (219) 933-6677.
Hammond Open (LPBT), October.

WOODLAND BOWL
3421 E. 96th Street, Indianapolis **[P. 38, D-7]**; (317) 844-4099.
BPAA U.S. Open (PBA), April.

College Sports

BALL STATE UNIVERSITY CARDINALS
2000 University Avenue, Muncie **[P. 40, F-7]**; (317) 285-8225. Ball State University, capacity 16,319. Gym, capacity 7,000.

BUTLER UNIVERSITY BULLDOGS
4600 Sunset Avenue, Indianapolis **[P. 38, F-7]**; (317) 283-9375. Butler Bowl, capacity 20,000. Hinkle Fieldhouse, capacity 11,000.
◆When first built in 1928, Hinkle was the largest on-campus basketball facility in the nation, seating 11,000. Scenes from the movie Hoosiers were filmed here.

INDIANA STATE UNIVERSITY SYCAMORES
Terre Haute **[P. 38, C-5]**; (812) 237-4040. Memorial, capacity 20,500. Hulman Civic Center, capacity 10,220.

INDIANA UNIVERSITY FIGHTIN' HOOSIERS
Assembly Hall, Bloomington **[P. 41, J-4]**; (812) 855-2794. IU Memorial, capacity 52,354. Assembly Hall, capacity 17,500.
◆Home of Bob Knight and Hoosier hysteria. The volatile Knight can be worth the price of admission himself some nights. His teams always play hard and almost never play zone defenses.

INDIANA UNIVERSITY-PURDUE UNIVERSITY MASTODONS
2101 Coliseum Boulevard East, Fort Wayne **[P. 38, A-8]**; (219) 481-6643. Multipurpose Building, capacity 3,200.

PURDUE UNIVERSITY BOILERMAKERS
W. Lafayette **[P. 40, E-3]**; (317) 494-3189. Ross-Ade, capacity 67,861. Mackey Arena, capacity 14,123.

ST. JOSEPH'S COLLEGE PUMAS
Rensselaer **[P. 40, D-3]**; (219) 866-6338. Alumni Field, capacity 4,000. Alumni Gym, capacity 2,500.

UNIVERSITY OF EVANSVILLE ACES
1800 Lincoln Avenue, Evansville **[P. 38, D-8]**; (812) 479-2237. Arad McCutchan, capacity 3,500. Roberts, capacity 11,096.

UNIVERSITY OF NOTRE DAME FIGHTING IRISH
Notre Dame **[P. 38, A-6]**; (219) 239-6107. Notre Dame, capacity 59,075. A&C Center, capacity 11,418.
◆The most storied campus in college sports. And, by the way, in Irish tradition, the booze pours freely among the parking lot tailgaters before the game.

VALPARAISO UNIVERSITY CRUSADERS
Valparaiso **[P. 40, B-3]**; (219) 464-5230. Brown Field, capacity 4,500. Athletics-Recreation Center, capacity 4,300.

USA SNAPSHOTS®

A look at statistics that shape the sports world

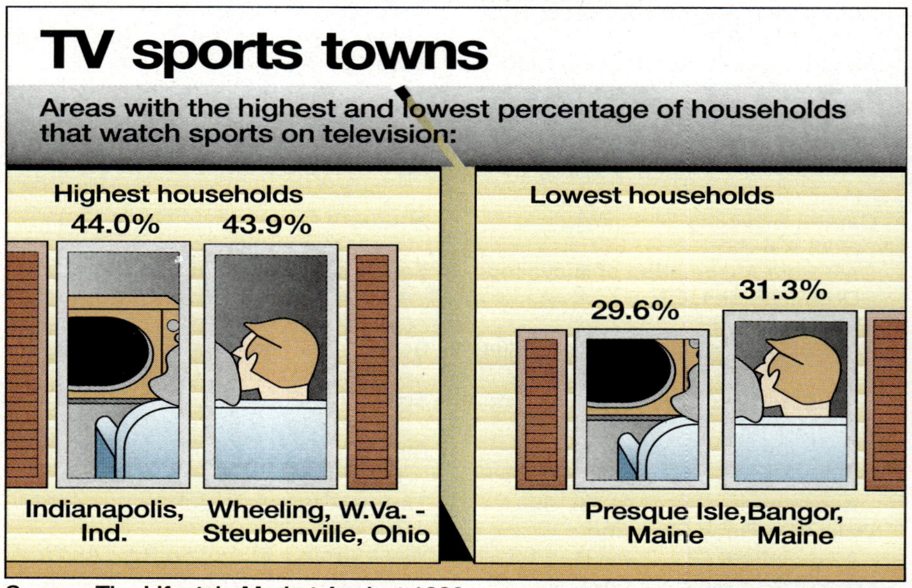

Source: The Lifestyle Market Analyst 1990

By Marcy E. Mullins, USA TODAY

STATBOX

POPULATION: 5,593,000
SQUARE MILES: 36,185
TIME ZONE: Eastern and Central
MOTTO: The Crossroads of America
BIRD: Cardinal
TREE: Tulip Poplar
CAPITAL: Indianapolis
AVERAGE ANNUAL RAINFALL: 39"
MEAN TEMP: 26 (Jan.); 75 (July)
MAJOR LEAGUE TEAMS: 2
NATIONAL PARK ACREAGE: 9,810
STATE PARK ACREAGE: 56,767
HIGHEST ELEVATION: 1,257'
LOWEST ELEVATION: 320'
WATERWAYS: 253 square miles of inland water

Football

HOOSIER DOME
100 South Capitol Avenue, Indianapolis **[P. 38, F-7]**. Built in 1983. Capacity: 60,127.
◆The Dome housed the largest audience ever to attend an indoor basketball game (67,596) in 1984 when the US Olympic team played the NBA All-Stars. It also hosted the 1991 NCAA Final Four and will do so again in 1997.
Indianapolis Colts (AFC Eastern Division); (317) 297-2658. Franchise began in 1953. Broadcasts by WIBC.

Hockey

ALLEN COUNTY MEMORIAL COLISEUM
4000 Parnell Avenue, Fort Wayne **[P. 38, A-8]**. Capacity: 8,004.
Fort Wayne Komets (International Hockey League); (219) 482-9502. Franchise began in 1952. Broadcasts by WOWO 1190 AM.

INDIANA STATE FAIRGROUNDS
1202 E. 38th Street, Indianapolis **[P. 38, E-7]**. Capacity: 8,233.
Indianapolis Ice (International Hockey League); (317) 927-7622. Franchise began in 1988. Broadcasts by WNDE 1260 AM.

Museums & Halls of Fame

INDIANA MUSEUM OF SPORTS
202 N. Alabama Street, Indianapolis **[P. 38, F-7]**; (317) 232-1637.

INDIANAPOLIS MOTOR SPEEDWAY HALL OF FAME MUSEUM
4790 W. 16th Street, Indianapolis **[P. 38, F-6]**; (317) 248-6747.
◆The museum is open year-round except on Christmas Day.

INDIANA BASKETBALL HALL OF FAME
1 Hall of Fame Court, New Castle **[P. 40, G-7]**; (317) 529-1891.

NATIONAL ART MUSEUM OF SPORT
111 Monument Circle, Bank-One Center, Mezzanine Level, Indianapolis **[P. 38, F-7]**; (317) 687-1715.

NATIONAL TRACK AND FIELD HALL OF FAME
1 Hoosier Dome, Ste. 1400, Indianapolis **[P. 38, F-7]**; (317) 261-0483.

PGA/LPGA

BROADMOOR COUNTRY CLUB
2155 Kessler Blvd., West Dr., Indianapolis **[P. 38, E-7]**; (317) 253-3114.
GTE North Classic (Senior PGA), Aug.
Number of holes: 54.

CROOKED STICK GOLF CLUB
1964 Burning Tree Lane, Carmel; **[P. 40, G-5]**; (317) 844-9938.
1991 PGA Championship (PGA), Aug.
Number of holes: 72.

CONTINUED ON PAGE 157

Indiana

CONTINUED FROM PAGE 156

Tennis

INDIANAPOLIS SPORTS CENTER
815 W. New York Street, Indianapolis **[P. 38, F-7]**; (317) 632-4100. Surface is Deco Turf II. GTE U.S. Men's hard Championships (ATP), August.

INDIANAPOLIS INDOOR SPORTS CENTER
755 University Blvd., Indianapolis **[P. 38, F-8]**; (317) 636-7719. Surface is hard. Jello Tennis Classic (WTA), November.

Track & Field

HOOSIER DOME
100 S. Capital Ave., Indianapolis **[P. 38, F-7]**; (317) 261-0500. NCAA I (Collegiate National Championship, 1991), March.

OUTDOOR VENUES

National Parks

INDIANA DUNES NATIONAL LAKESHORE
3 mi. E of IN 49 on US 12 at Kemil Rd. **[P. 40, A-3]**. Contains 12,857 acres. **HK BT F S R BK W**

WAYNE-HOOSIER NATIONAL FOREST
Southern **[P. 41, K-5, N-4]**. Contains 188,000 acres. **C HK BT F S R HT**

State Parks

- Bike Trails: BK
- Boating: BT
- Camping: C
- Climbing: CL
- Diving: DV
- Fishing: F
- Golfing: G
- Hiking: HK
- Hunting: HT
- Riding: R
- Surfing: SU
- Swimming: S
- Tennis: TE
- Whitewater: WW
- Winter Sports: W

CHAIN O'LAKES STATE PARK
6 mi. S of Albion on IN 9 **[P. 40, B-7]**. Contains 2,678 acres. **C HK BT F S BK W**

CLARK STATE FOREST
1 mi. N of Henryville off US 31 **[P. 41, L-6]**. Contains 23,979 acres. **C HK BT F R HT**

DEAM LAKE STATE RECREATION AREA
5 mi. E of Borden on IN 60 **[P. 41, M-6]**. Contains 1,300 acres. **C HK BT F S HT**

FERDINAND STATE FOREST
6 mi. E of Ferdinand on IN 264 **[P. 41, M-4]**. Contains 7,657 acres. **C HK BT F S HT**

HARDY LAKE STATE RESERVOIR
8 mi. NE of Austin off IN 256 **[P. 41, L-6]**. Contains 2,062 acres. **C HK BT F S HT**

HARRISON-CRAWFORD STATE FOREST
10 mi. SW of Corydon on SR 462 **[P. 41, N-5]**. Contains 25,619 acres. **C HK F S R BK W HT**

HOVEY LAKE FISH AND WILDLIFE AREA
S of Mount Vernon on IN 69 **[P. 41, O-1]**. Contains 4,298 acres. **C HK BT F HT**

INDIANA DUNES STATE PARK
Along Lake Michigan, 3 mi. N of Chesterton on IN 49 **[P. 40, A-3]**. Contains 2,182 acres. **C HK S W**

JACKSON-WASHINGTON STATE FOREST
3 mi. SE of Brownstown on IN 39 **[P. 41, K-5]**. Contains 15,330 acres. **C HK BT F HT**

MCCORMICK'S CREEK STATE PARK
3 mi. E of Spencer on IN 46 **[P. 41, J-4]**. Contains 1,833 acres. **C HK F S R TE**

> **"The best thing about Indiana sports? The University of Evansville's Purple Aces, my hometown team. I love college basketball, and I've been following them for years."**
>
> **Yankee baseball star *Don Mattingly***

MONROE RESERVOIR (AC)
10 mi. s. of Bloomington on SR 446 **[P. 41, K-5]**. Contains 23,952 acres. **C BT F S HT**

MOUNDS STATE PARK
3 mi. E of Anderson on IN 32 **[P. 40, F-6]**. Contains 254 acres. **C HK F S R W**

PATOKA LAKE STATE RESERVOIR
18 mi. E of Jasper on IN 164 **[P. 41, M-4]**. Contains 25,583 acres. **C HK BT F S BK HT**

POKAGON STATE PARK
5 mi. N of Angola on IN 727 **[P. 40, A-8]**. Contains 1,203 acres. **C HK BT F S R W TE**

POTATO CREEK STATE PARK
2 mi. E of North Liberty on IN 4 **[P. 40, B-5]**. Contains 3,840 acres. **C HK BT F S R BK W**

QUABACHE STATE PARK
4 mi. E of Bluffton on IN 216 **[P. 40, D-7]**. Contains 1,065 acres. **C HK BT F S R W TE**

SALAMONIE RESERVOIR
2 mi. S of Lagro on IN 524 **[P. 40, D-6]**. Contains 11,506 acres. **C HK BT F R W HT**

SHAKAMAK STATE PARK
4 mi. W of Jasonville on IN 48 **[P. 41, J-3]**. Contains 1,766 acres. **C HK BT F S R TE**

SPRING MILL STATE PARK
Mitchell **[P. 41, L-5]**. Contains 1,319 acres. **C HK BT F S R TE**

TIPPECANOE RIVER STATE PARK
6 mi. N of Winamac on US 35 **[P. 40, C-4]**. Contains 2,761 acres. **C HK BT F R W**

WHITEWATER MEMORIAL STATE PARK
3 mi. S of Liberty off IN 101 **[P. 41, H-8]**. Contains 1,710 acres. **C HK BT F S R BK**

Skiing

ALPINE SKIING

SKI PAOLI PEAKS
Route 3 or Willow Creek Road, Paoli **[P. 41, L-4]**; (812) 723-4696.
Vertical drop is 300 feet. Has four tows and four chairs.

NORDIC SKIING

BENDIX WOODS SKI AREA
32132 State Road 2, New Carlisle **[P. 40, A-4]**; (219) 654-3155.

GNAW BONE CAMP
RR 2, Nashville **[P. 41, J-5]**; (812) 988-4852.

ACTIVE SPORTS

AEROBICS: AFAA, 731 S. Sherman, Crown Point; (219) 662-0928.

BASEBALL: Little League Baseball Central Region HQ, 4360 N. Mitthoeffer Rd., Indianapolis, IN; (317) 897-6127. • **Pony Baseball-Softball,** 1729 Arrowhead Dr., Booneville; • **American Legion Baseball,** 1059 E. Boone, Frankfort; (317) 654-8135. • **Babe Ruth Baseball,** Robert Dickson, RR 4, Box 332F, Alexandria, IN; (317) 724-4883. • **Men's Senior Baseball League - Indianapolis,** 6181 N. Meriden West Dr., Indianapolis; (317) 257-9523.

BOARDSAILING: USWA Regional Director, N7315 Winnebago Dr., Fond du Lac, WI; (414) 922-2550.

Tip Offs: Where to Find Dirt Tracks

The bumper stickers say "Dirt's for Racing, Pavement's for Getting There." It's the motto of auto racing fans who regularly venture into a dirt cyclone to watch the oldest and, they say, purest form of auto racing: the slam-bang action at dirt oval speedways. Fans often have favorite tracks, but part of the fun is finding new ones because each is different. A few names are hallowed:

Atomic Speedway:
Oak Ridge, Tenn.: At 25 and 29 degrees, the banked corners are so steep you can't walk up them when the track is moist and fast.

Brownstown (Ind.) Speedway:
A short track, a quarter-mile plus 62 feet, that claims the best "racing surface" in the Midwest.

Devil's Bowl Speedway:
Mesquite, Texas: Great name, great half-mile.

Eldora Speedway:
Rossburg, Ohio: In 1955, Earl Baltes built the Taj Mahal of half-mile dirt ovals in a cornfield behind a roadside ballroom named Eldora. One fan willed that his ashes be spread on the front straight of Baltes.

Hagerstown (Md.) Speedway:
This is the speedway historian Allen E. Brown rates the USA's best overall.

Knoxville (Iowa) Raceway:
For one week in August, it's sprint-car capital of the universe. The rest of the time, it's the sprint capital of the world.

Manzanita Speedway:
Phoenix: Twelve classes of dirt cars run here - sprints, midgets, late models, even something called dwarf cars.

New York State Fairgrounds:
Syracuse, N.Y.: A classic fairgrounds mile, home in October of Super Dirt Week - the richest and best-attended dirt event in the USA.

Pennsboro (W.Va.) Speedway:
A cantankerous D-shaped half-mile in a beautiful mountain valley. Home of the Hillbilly 100 and the Dirt Track World Championship for late models.

Williams Grove (Pa.) Speedway:
Hallowed ground in sprint car-crazy central Pennsylvania.

BOWLING: American Bowling Congress, 5301 S. 76th St., Greendale, WI; (414) 421-6400.

CANOEING & KAYAKING: ACA Midwest Vice Commodore, 1343 N. Portage, Palatine, IL; (708) 359-5047.

CYCLING: LAW Great Lakes Regional Director, 2310 Queens Way, Bloomington; (812) 334-4058. • **Northwest Indiana AYH Council,** 8231 Lake Shore Drive, Gary. • **USCF Indiana/Kentucky Representative,** 305 McConnell Drive, New Albany; (812) 949-2125 or (502) 491-8201.

FITNESS: Governor's Council on Physical Fitness & Sports, Indiana State Board of Health, 1330 W. Michigan, PO Box 1964, Indianapolis; (317) 633-0299. • **National Strength and Conditioning Ass'n State Director,** Assembly Hall, Indiana University, Bloomington; (812) 855-4419.

FOOTBALL: Pop Warner Football, 1315 Walnut Street, Suite 1632, Philadelphia, PA; (215) 735-1450. • **U.S. Flag Football League,** 5834 Pine Tree Drive, Sanibel, FL; (813) 472-0544.

GOLF: Indiana Golf Association, 111 E. Main Street, Carmel; (317) 844-7271. • **Indiana Junior Golf Association,** PO Box 4454, Lafayette; (317) 447-1992. • **PGA Indiana Section,** 111 E. Main Street, Carmel; (317) 844-7271.

HIKING & CLIMBING: Hoosier Sierra Club Chapter, PO Box 40275, Indianapolis; (317) 253-2687.

HOCKEY: USA Hockey Mid-American Registrar, 647 Stacey Ln., Maumee, OH; (419) 893-9665.

HUNTING & FISHING: Department of Natural Resources, 608 State Office Building, Indianapolis; (317) 232-4080.

RACQUETBALL: AARA, 6090 Orchard Hill Ln., Indianapolis; (317) 255-7730.

RIDING: Indiana Horse Council, 5240 Elmwood Ave., Indianapolis; (317) 786-6646.

RODEO: PRCA Great Lakes Circuit, Rt. 1, Box 54, Clayton; (317) 539-5039.

RUNNING: RRCA IN State Rep., 1109 West Wayne, Ft. Wayne; (219) 424-6723.

SCUBA: DNP Diving, Inc., 604 East Main Street, Logansport; (219) 735-3483. • **Midwest Scuba Center, Inc.,** 4306 West 96th Street, Indianapolis; (317) 872-2522.

SHOOTING: Shotgun Hollow, RR 1, Box 105, Cloverdale; (317) 795-3999. • **West Creek Shooting Preserve,** 15547 W. 169th Avenue, Cedar Lake; (219) 696-6101.

SKATING: USFSA, 20 First Street, Colorado Springs, CO; (719) 635-5200.

SOCCER: Indiana Soccer Ass'n, 3573 DeCamp Dr., Indianapolis; (317) 897-3197. • **AYSO Regional Director,** 5403 W. 138th Street, Hawthorne, CA; (800) 421-5700.

SOFTBALL: Indiana ASA, 330 South 5th Street, Terre Haute; (812) 234-0339. • **Indianapolis ASA,** 218 David Ln., Indianapolis; (317) 881-5170.

SQUASH: Indianapolis Athletic Club (USSRA), Indianapolis; (317) 634-4331.

SWIMMING: LMSC Indiana Registrar, 5223 N. Pennsylvania Ave., Indianapolis; (317) 257-1988.

TENNIS: Recreational TEAMTENNIS Midwest-Southeast Region, National Program Coordinator, 445 N. Wells, Ste. #404, Chicago, IL; (800) TEAMTEN. • **Western USTA,** 8720 Castle Creek Parkway, Ste. 329, Indianapolis; (513) 390-2740.

VOLLEYBALL: USVBA Michiana Commissioner, c/o Oak Manor Offices, Suite A10, 29089 US 20 W., Elkhart; (219) 264-3424.

Iowa

Whether it's the Big Ten Hawkeyes, Big Eight Iowa State, or January's National Catholic Basketball Tournament luring small college teams from across the USA to Dubuque, Iowans love their college sports. ◆ For roaring engines there are the Ruan Greater Des Moines Grand Prix in early July and the National Sprint Car Championship in mid-August (Knoxville Speedway). ◆ If peace and quiet are more to your liking, take a hike, bike or ski along the Cedar Valley Nature Trail (northeast Iowa) or the Wabash Trace Nature Trail (western Iowa). ◆ More ambitious cyclists can join the the RAGBRAI race, a week-long ride across the state (mid-July). ◆ The Iowa Great Lakes (East and West Okoboji and Spirit Lake) are best bets for fishing, along with the Clear Lake, Red Rock, and Saylorville reservoirs in central Iowa. Rathbun Lake is one of the best crappie lakes in the state.

▶ SPECTATOR VENUES

Auto Racing

DES MOINES STREET CIRCUIT
Abuts Veteran's Auditorium, 4th St. & Crocker, Des Moines **[P. 42, G3]**; (515) 243-5515. Track is 1.8 mile street course. Greater Des Moines Grand Prix (SCCA Trans-Am Championship), July.

Baseball

COMMUNITY FIELD
2712 Mt. Pleasant St., Burlington **[P. 43, F-12]**. Capacity: 3,500
Burlington Astros (Midwest League, Class A); (319) 754-5705. Entered League in 1960. MLB affiliation, Houston Astros.

JOHN O'DONNELL STADIUM
209 S. Gaines Street, Davenport **[P. 42, E-2]**. Capacity: 5,000
◆Former IBF Middleweight Champion Michael Nunn did a lot for his population 100,000 hometown, Davenport, but not much for himself when he took on undefeated contender James Toney here at John O'Donnell stadium. With the Mississippi River just beyond the outfield fence and a temporary ring set up over the pitcher's mound, the prize fight spoke of economic revival for the farming-based Quad City area; but, leading in points in the final round, Nunn was knocked cold.
Quad City Angels (Midwest League, Class A); (319) 324-2032. Entered League in 1960. Broadcasts by KSTT 1170-AM. MLB affiliation, California Angels.

MUNICIPAL STADIUM
850 Park Road, Waterloo **[P. 43, C-10]**. Capacity: 5,400
Waterloo Diamonds (Midwest League, Class A); (319) 233-8146. Entered League in 1958. Broadcasts by KOUR 95.3 FM/1220 AM. MLB affiliation, San Diego Padres.

RIVERVIEW STADIUM
6th Ave. North & 1st St., Clinton **[P. 43, D-14]**. Capacity: 3,600
Clinton Giants (Midwest League, Class A); (319) 242-0727. Entered League in 1954. Broadcasts by KROS 1340-AM. MLB affiliation, San Francisco Giants.

SEC TAYLOR STADIUM
2nd and Riverside Dr., Des Moines **[P. 42, H-3]**. Capacity: 7,600
Iowa Cubs (American Association, Class AAA); (515) 243-6111. Entered League in 1969. Broadcasts by KKSO 1390 AM. MLB affiliation, Chicago Cubs.

VETERANS MEMORIAL BALLPARK
950 Rockford Road SW, Cedar Rapids **[P. 42, C-2]**. Capacity: 6,000
Cedar Rapids Reds (Midwest League, Class A); (319) 363-3887. Entered League in 1963. Broadcasts by KHAK 1360 AM. MLB affiliation, Cincinnati Reds.

Basketball

FIVE SEASONS CENTER
370 First Avenue, NE, Cedar Rapids **[P. 42, C-2]**. Capacity: 7,247.
Cedar Rapids Silver Bullets (Continental Basketball Association, American Conference, Central Division); (319) 362-7000. Entered League in 1982. Broadcasts by KCRG 1600 AM.

Bowling

WESTDALE BOWLING CENTER
2020 Scotty Drive SE, Cedar Rapids **[P. 42, D-1]**; (319) 396-2500.
WIBC Queens (LPBT), May.

College Sports

DRAKE UNIVERSITY BULLDOGS
25th & University, Des Moines **[P. 42, G-2]**; (515) 271-2102. Drake, capacity 18,000. Veterans Auditorium, capacity 13,500.

IOWA STATE UNIVERSITY CYCLONES
Ames **[P. 43, D-8]**; (515) 294-3662. Cyclone, Jack Trice Field, capacity 50,000. Hilton Coliseum, capacity 14,020.

SIMPSON COLLEGE FLAMES
Indianola **[P. 43, E-8]**; (515) 961-1617. Simpson-Indianola Field, capacity 3,500. Cowles, capacity 2,000.

UNIVERSITY OF DUBUQUE SPARTANS
2050 University Avenue, Dubuque **[P. 43, C-13]**; (319) 589-3225. Chalmers Field, capacity 5,000. McCormick, capacity 2,000.

UNIVERSITY OF IOWA HAWKEYES
Iowa City **[P. 43, E-12]**; (319) 335-9327. Kinnick, capacity 70,000. Carver Hawkeye Arena, capacity 15,502.
◆Football coach Hayden Fry is king in Iowa, a state mad about the Hawkeyes. How to recognize him? He's the one in the dark-tinted glasses.

UNIVERSITY OF NORTHERN IOWA PANTHERS
23rd & College, Cedar Falls **[P. 43, C-10]**; (319) 273-2470. UNI-Dome, capacity 16,400. UNI-Dome, capacity 11,000.

WILLIAM PENN COLLEGE STATESMEN
Trueblood Avenue, Oskaloosa **[P. 43, E-10]**; (515) 673-1001. Oskaloosa, capacity 10,000. Wm. Penn Gym, capacity 1,800.

Horse Racing

PRAIRIE MEADOWS
One Prairie Meadows Drive, Altoona **[P. 43, E-8]**; (515) 967-1000. Opened in 1989. Grandstand capacity: 2,100. Total capacity: 5,000.
Thoroughbred season from Mar. to Sep.
◆Combined thoroughbred and quarter-horse season.

Museums & Halls of Fame

NATIONAL RIVERS HALL OF FAME
3rd Street Ice Harbor, Dubuque **[P. 43, C-13]**; (319) 557-9545.

NATIONAL SPRINT CAR HALL OF FAME AND MUSEUM
1402 N. Lincoln Ave., Knoxville **[P. 43, E-9]**; (800) 874-4488.
◆To open August, 1991.

USA SNAPSHOTS®

A look at statistics that shape the sports world

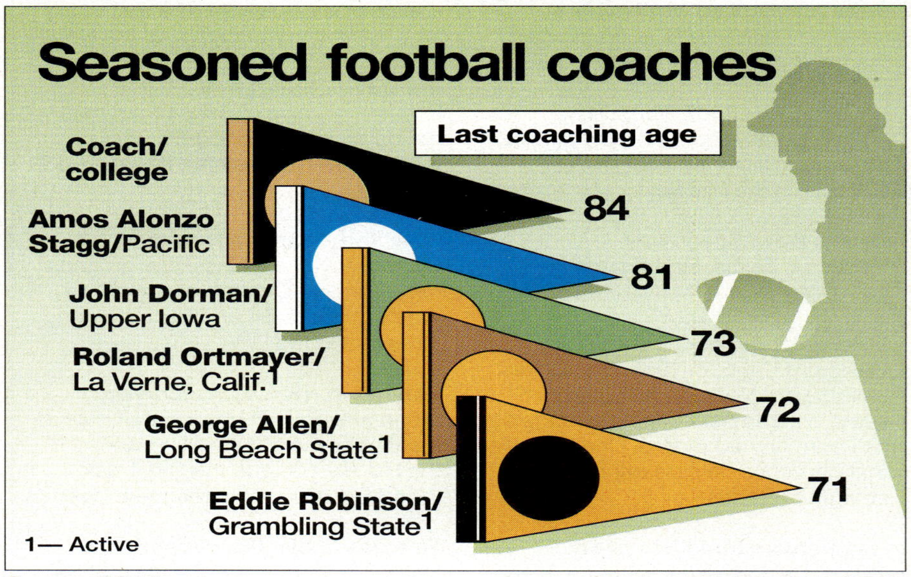

Source: NCAA

By Suzy Parker, USA TODAY

STATBOX

POPULATION: 2,840,000
SQUARE MILES: 56,275
TIME ZONE: Central
MOTTO: Our liberties we prize and our rights we will maintain.
BIRD: Eastern Goldfinch
TREE: Oak
CAPITAL: Des Moines
AVERAGE ANNUAL RAINFALL: 32"
MEAN TEMP: 48
MAJOR LEAGUE TEAMS: 0
NATIONAL PARK/FOREST ACREAGE: 1,661
STATE PARK ACREAGE: 100,000
HIGHEST ELEVATION: 1,600'
LOWEST ELEVATION: 500'
WATERWAYS: 310 square miles of inland water

▶ OUTDOOR VENUES

State Parks

Bike Trails: BK
Boating: BT
Camping: C
Climbing: CL
Diving: DV
Fishing: F
Golfing: G
Hiking: HK
Hunting: HT
Riding: R
Surfing: SU
Swimming: S
Tennis: TE
Whitewater: WW
Winter Sports: W

BACKBONE STATE PARK
Strawberry Point, 4 mi. SW of IA 410 **[P. 43, C-12]**. Contains 1,780 acres. **C HK BT F S BK W**

BIG CREEK STATE PARK
2 mi. N of Polk City on IA 415 **[P. 43, D-8]**. Contains 1,536 acres. **HK BT F S BK W HT**

CLEAR LAKE STATE PARK
2 mi. S of Clear Lake **[P. 43, B-9]**. Contains 55 acres. **C BT F S BK W**

GEODE STATE PARK
4 mi. SW of Danville **[P. 43, F-12]**. Contains 1,640 acres. **C HK BT F S**

GEORGE WYTH MEMORIAL STATE PARK
Cedar Falls, on the N shore of the Cedar River **[P. 43, C-10]**. Contains 494 acres. **C HK BT F S BK W**

GULL POINT STATE PARK
IA 32, 3 mi. N of Milford **[P. 42, A-6]**. Contains 165 acres. **C HK BT F S**

LACEY-KEOSAUQUA STATE PARK
Keosauqua **[P. 43, G-11]**. Contains 1,653 acres. **C HK BT F S**

LAKE DARLING STATE PARK
3 mi. W of Brighton on IA 78 **[P. 43, F-11]**. Contains 1,387 acres. **C HK BT F S**

LAKE OF THREE FIRES STATE PARK
3 mi. NE of Bedford **[P. 42, G-6]**. Contains 694 acres. **C HK BT F S R**

LEWIS AND CLARK STATE PARK
3 mi. NW of Onawa **[P. 42, D-4]**. Contains 176 acres. **C HK BT F S HT**

NINE EAGLES STATE PARK
6 mi. SE of Davis City **[P. 43, G-8]**. Contains 1,119 acres. **C HK BT F S R**

PIKES PEAK STATE PARK
McGregor **[P. 43, B-12]**. Contains 970 acres. **C HK W**

PLEASANT CREEK STATE RECREATION AREA
5 mi. NW of Palo **[P. 43, D-11]**. Contains 1,927 acres. **C HK BT F S R W**

ROCK CREEK STATE PARK
6 mi. NE of Kellogg **[P. 43, D-10]**. Contains 1,697 acres. **C HK BT F S**

VOLGA RIVER STATE RECREATION AREA
4 mi. N of Fayette **[P. 43, B-11]**. Contains 5,422 acres. **C HK BT F R W**

CONTINUED ON PAGE 159

Iowa

CONTINUED FROM PAGE 158

YELLOW RIVER STATE FOREST
14 mi. SE of Waukon via IA 76 **[P. 43, B-12]**. Contains 7,649 acres. C HK F R W HT

Skiing

ALPINE SKIING

SUNDOWN
17017 Asbury Road, Dubuque **[P. 43, C-13]**; (319) 556-6676.
Vertical drop is 475 feet. Has three tows and four chairs.

NORDIC SKIING

RIVERSIDE HILLS SKI AREA
RR 3, Estherville **[P. 42, A-6]**; (712) 362-5376.

SKI VALLEY
RFD 4, Boone **[P. 43, D-8]**; (515) 432-2423.

SUNSET SKI AREA
East Main, Cherokee **[P. 42, B-5]**; (712) 225-9970.

ACTIVE SPORTS

AEROBICS: AFAA, 115 Brentwood Heights, Council Bluffs; (712) 328-0117.

BASEBALL: Little League Baseball Central Region HQ, 4360 N. Mitthoeffer Rd., Indianapolis, IN; (317) 897-6127. • **American Legion Baseball,** 641 28th St. Ct., Cedar Rapids; (319) 364-2355. • **Babe Ruth Baseball,** Norman Travis, Box 339, Burlington, CO; (719) 346-8803. • **Men's Senior Baseball League - Quad City,** PO Box 4515, Davenport; (319) 332-4673.

BOARDSAILING: USWA Regional Director, 2625 S. 46th, Lincoln, NE; (402)489-1002 • **Wind & Water, Inc.,** Johnston; (515) 270-1591.

BOWLING: American Bowling Congress, 5301 S. 76th St., Greendale, WI; (414) 421-6400.

CANOEING & KAYAKING: ACA Midwest Vice Commodore, 1343 N. Portage, Palatine, IL; (708) 359-5047.

CYCLING: LAW North Central Regional Director, Route 1, Box 99, Cushing, WI; (715) 648-5519. • **Northeast Iowa AYH Council,** PO Box 10, Postville; (319) 864-3923. • **USCF Iowa Representative,** 117 E. 9th Street, Ames; (515) 232-6346.

FITNESS: Governor's Council on Physical Fitness & Sports, 4120 72nd Street, Urbandale; (515) 242-7814. • **National Strength and Conditioning Ass'n State Director,** University of Iowa, Football Office, Iowa City; (319) 335-8931.

FOOTBALL: Pop Warner Football, 1315 Walnut Street, Suite 1632, Philadelphia, PA; (215) 735-1450.

GOLF: Iowa Golf Association, 1930 Saint Andrews Ct. NE, Cedar Rapids; (319) 378-9142. • **PGA Iowa Section,** 1930 Saint Andrews NE, Cedar Rapids; (319) 378-9142.

HIKING & CLIMBING: Iowa Sierra Club Chapter, The Thoreau Center, 3500 Kingman Blvd., Des Moines; (515) 277-8868. • **Iowa Trails Council (AHS),** 1201 Central, Center Point; (319) 849-6944.

HOCKEY: USA Hockey Central Registrar, PO Box 1738, Lisle, IL; (708) 963-1098.

HUNTING & FISHING: Department of Natural Resource, East 9th & Grand Ave., Wallace Building, Des Moines; (515) 281-5145.

RACQUETBALL: AARA, 808 Oregon Street, Waterloo; (319) 236-2668. • **AARA,** 808 Oregon Street, Waterloo; (319) 236-2668.

RIDING: Iowa Horse Industry Council, 5426 Skyline Dr. NW, Cedar Rapids; (319) 396-9366.

RODEO: PRCA Great Lakes Circuit, Rt. 1, Box 54, Clayton, IN; (317) 539-5039.

RUNNING: RRCA IA State Rep., 921 West 16th St., Davenport; (319) 324-1513.

SHOOTING: Black Hawk Sporting Clays, RR 1, Janesville; (319) 987-2625. • **Flood Creek Hunting Preserve,** RR 2, Box 58, Nora Springs; (515) 395-2725. • **Hunter's Knob Gun Club,** 623 Pershing St., St. Charles; (515) 297-2250. • **Lazy H Hunting Club,** RR 2, Woodbine; (712) 647-2877. • **River Valley Sporting Clays,** PO Box 117, Sioux Rapids; (712) 283-2342. • **Spring Run Sportsman's Club,** Box 8364A, Spirit Lake; (712) 336-5595. • **Triple H Hunting Preserve & Sporting Clays,** Rt. 2, Box 165, Burlington; (319) 985-2253.

SKATING: Iowa Skating Association, 1631 Elaine Dr. NW, Cedar Rapids; (319) 396-2880. • **USFSA,** 20 First Street, Colorado Springs, CO; (719) 635-5200.

SOCCER: Iowa Youth Soccer Ass'n, 1445 NW 106th St., Des Moines; (515) 225-9597. • **AYSO Regional Director,** 2971 N. Coronado St., Chandler; (602) 839-2114. • **AYSO Regional Director,** 1918 Springside Dr., Naperville, IL; (807) 416-8520.

SOFTBALL: Iowa ASA, 210 South Quadrangle, University of Iowa, Iowa City; (319) 337-7097.

SQUASH: Racquet Club West, Des Moines; (515) 278-0461.

SWIMMING: LMSC Iowa Registrar, 1008 S. 14th Ave. West, Newton; (515) 792-5039.

TABLE TENNIS: USTTA State Coordinator, 2626 East Ct., Iowa City; (319) 337-5952.

TENNIS: Recreational TEAMTENNIS Midwest-Southeast Region, National Program Coordinator, 445 N. Wells, Ste. #404, Chicago, IL; (800) TEAMTEN. • **Missouri Valley USTA,** 722 Walnut St., Suite #1, Kansas City, MO; (816) 556-0777.

VOLLEYBALL: USVBA Corn Belt Commissioner, 6770 NW Trail Ridge Dr., Johnston; (515) 278-1912.

Tip Offs

CONTINUED FROM PAGE 144

Sports Bars: Part II

MARYLAND

Original Sports Bar, 34 Market Place, Baltimore 301-244-0135

MASSACHUSETTS

Challenges, 5 Stearns Square, Springfield 413-739-8501
Champions, 110 Huntington Ave., Boston 617-262-5776
Champions, 574 Iyanough Road, Rt. 132, Hyannis 508-226-7171
Cheers, 84 Beacon St., Boston 617-227-9605
Dockside, 183 State St., Boston 617-723-7050
Elliot Lounge, 370 Commonwealth Ave., Boston 617-262-1078
Sports Page, 600 Squire Rd., Revere 617-289-9594

MICHIGAN

Nemo's, 1384 Michigan Ave., Detroit 313-965-3180

MINNESOTA

Champions, 105 W. Lake St., Minneapolis 612-827-4765
Champps, 790 W. 66th St., Richfield 612-861-3333
Champps, 2431 W. Seventh St., St. Paul 612-698-5050
Hubert's, 601 Chicago, Minneapolis 612-332-6062
Joe Senser's, 2350 Cleveland Ave., St. Paul 612-631-1781
Joe Senser's, 4217 W. 80th St., Bloomington 612-835-1191
Juke Box Saturday Night, 14 N. Fifth St., Minneapolis 612-339-5890
Ray Scott's, 418 So. Fourth St., Minneapolis 612-642-1110
Rupert's, 5410 Wayzata Blvd., Golden Valley 612-544-3550

MISSOURI

Fuzzy's, 4113 Pennsylvania, Kansas City 816-561-9191
Fuzzy's South, 1227 W. 103rd St., Kansas City 816-941-7702
Mike Shannon's, 100 No. Seventh St., St. Louis 314-421-1540
Rupert's, 5130 Oakland Ave., St. Louis 314-652-6866
Schmiezing's, 1115 Hampton Ave., St. Louis 314-645-4780
Sportsman's Park, 9901 Clayton Ave., Ladue 314-991-3381

NEW JERSEY

Manny's, 110 Moonachie Ave., Moonachie 201-939-1244
The Sports Page, 100 Brighton Ave., W. Long Branch 201-571-4661
The Stadium, 810 The Plaza, Sea Girt 201-449-1444

NEW YORK

Canterbury Ales, 314 New York Ave., Huntington 516-549-4404
Dunne's Pub, 15 Shapham Pl., White Plains 914-684-9366
Garcia's Irish Pub, 74 Pearl St., Buffalo 716-856-0111
Genesee Sports Bar, Hyatt Hotel, 1 Fountain Plaza, Buffalo 716-856-1234
Pat McGinty's, 38 Swan St., Buffalo 716-856-0663
Mickey Mantle's, 42 Central Park South, New York City 212-688-7777
Pettibone's Grille, 275 Washington St., Buffalo 716-846-2100
Polo Grounds, 1472 Third Ave., New York City 212-570-5590
Runyon's, 932 Second Ave., New York City 212-759-7800
Runyon's, 305 E. 50th St., New York City 212-223-9592
Rusty's, 1271 Third Ave., New York City 212-861-4518
Sporting Club, 99 Hudson St., New York City 212-219-0900
Sports, 2182 Broadway, New York City 212-874-7208
Sports Page, 90 Second Ave., New York City 212-254-1562
Rockwell's, 1205 Mamaroneck Ave., White Plains 914-761-6697
Third Avenue Sports Bar, 497 Third Avenue, New York City 212-686-8422
Upper Deck, 140 Midland Ave., Port Chester 914-934-1110

NORTH CAROLINA

Champions, 4500 Marriott Dr., Raleigh 919-781-2899
Scoreboard, 2500 Crown Point Executive Drive, Charlotte 704-847-7678
Shooter's, 3217 The Plaza, Charlotte 704-343-9500

OHIO

Black Horse Cafe, 11634 Madison, Cleveland 216-226-5220
Champions of Cleveland, Reserve Square, 1701 E. 13th St., Cleveland 216-781-1000
Montgomery Inn, 9440 Montgomery Rd., Montgomery 513-791-3482
Montgomery Inn East, I-275 & Beechmont, Cherry Grove 513-528-2272
Montgomery Inn Downtown, 925 Eastern Ave., Cincinnati 513-721-7427
Scoreboard, 6150 Sunbury Rd., Westerville 614-882-7104
Scoreboard Inn, 886 E. 200th St., Cleveland 216-481-6643
The Varsity Club, 278 W. Lane Ave., Columbus 614-299-6269

OKLAHOMA

O'Connell's Irish Pub & Grille, 120 East Lindsey, Norman 405-364-8454
Varsity Sports Grill, 1140 N.W. 63rd St., Oklahoma City 405-842-0898

OREGON

Champions, 1401 S. Front Ave., Portland 503-274-2470
East Bank Saloon, 727 S.E. Grand Ave., Portland 503-231-1659

PENNSYLVANIA

Chiodo Tavern, 107 W. Eighth Ave., Homestead 412-461-3113
Silky's Saloon, 1731 Murray Ave., Pittsburgh 412-421-9222
Sportsters, 980 W. Dekalb Ave., King of Prussia 215-265-7427
Sportsters, 2520 Grant Ave., Philadelphia 215-677-0770

RHODE ISLAND

Player's Corner Pub, 194 Washington St., Providence 401-621-8738
Bobby Valentine's Sports Gallery Cafe, 68 Purgatory Road, Middletown, RI (401) 847-7678

SOUTH CAROLINA

Sports, 280 W. Coleman Blvd., Mount Pleasant 803-881-6157

TENNESSEE

Sports Bar & Grill, 3569 So. Mendenhall, Memphis 901-360-0932
Sports Page, 764 Mt. Moriah Rd., Memphis 901-683-5706

TEXAS

Bobby Valentine's Sports Gallery Cafe, 715 Ryan Plaza Dr., Arlington 817-261-1000
Bobby Valentine's Sports Gallery Cafe, 4301 So. Bowen, Arlington 817-467-9922

CONTINUED ON PAGE 174

Kansas

The National Collegiate Athletic Association makes its headquarters in Overland Park, and offers a 12,000-square foot visitor's center. The complex opened in October, 1990, with exhibits and videos of intercollegiate athletics, past and present. ◆ If you think Kansas is nothing but cornfields and yellow brick roads, you may be surprised to find out that some of the nation's best windsurfing and sailing takes place right here, especially at Cheney Lake Reservoir. ◆ For top water skiing, try Lake Afton. ◆ The National Junior College Athletic Association Basketball Tournament is held annually in Hutchinson. ◆ Auto racing is popular, particularly at Heartland Park, which features the NHRA Heartland Nationals in late September. ◆ Fishing is found throughout the state; try Tuttle Creek Lake, known for its plentiful catches of walleye and big bass.

► SPECTATOR VENUES

Auto Racing

HEARTLAND PARK TOPEKA
Highway 75, 4 mi. off S. Topeka exit of Kansas Turnpike, Topeka **[P. 45, C-12]**; (913) 862-4781. Track is 2.5-mile road course.
Camel Grand Prix of the Heartland (IMSA Camel GT), May.
AC-Delco Heartland Nationals (NHRA), Sept.

Baseball

LAWRENCE-DUMONT STADIUM
300 S. Sycamore St., Wichita **[P. 44, H-3]**. Capacity: 7,000
Wichita Wranglers (Texas League, Class AA); (316) 267-3372. Entered League in 1988. Broadcasts by KQAM 1410 AM. MLB affiliation, San Diego Padres.

Bowling

NORTHROCK LANES
3232 N. Rock Rd., Wichita **[P. 45, G-4]**; (316) 636-5444.
Wichita Open (PBA), July.

College Sports

FORT HAYS STATE UNIVERSITY TIGERS
Hays **[P. 44, C-6]**; (913) 628-4050. Lewis Field, capacity 7,000. Gross Memorial, capacity 7,000.

KANSAS STATE UNIVERSITY WILDCATS
Manhattan **[P. 45, B-10]**; (913) 532-6910. KSU, capacity 45,000. Bramlage Coliseum, capacity 13,500.
◆Another place where the students make the game fun. Watch them once a game try to break the world record mark for batting a beach ball around a basketball gym.

UNIVERSITY OF KANSAS JAYHAWKS
Lawrence **[P. 45, C-12]**; (913) 864-3143. Memorial, capacity 51,500. Allen, capacity 15,800.
◆Perhaps college basketball's birthplace. James Naismith coached here and so did Phog Allen. Wilt Chamberlain and Dean Smith played here. Chamberlain scored a few more points.

WICHITA STATE UNIVERSITY SHOCKERS
Wichita **[P. 44, G-4]**; (316) 689-3250. Cessna, capacity 31,500. Levitt Arena, capacity 10,666.

Horse Racing

THE WOODLANDS RACECOURSE
9700 Leavenworth Road, Kansas City **[P. 45, C-13]**; (913) 299-9797. Opened in 1990. Clubhouse capacity: 2,200. Grandstand capacity: 4,250. Total capacity: 22,000.
◆Thoroughbred season from May to Sept.

Museums & Halls of Fame

GREYHOUND HALL OF FAME
407 South Buckeye, Abilene **[P. 45, C-9]**; (913) 263-3000.

Rodeo

DODGE CITY ROUND-UP ARENA
Off 14th Street, Dodge City **[P. 44, E-5]**; (316) 225-2244.
Dodge City Days Round-Up Rodeo, August.

Soccer

KANSAS COLISEUM
1229 E. 85th North, Wichita **[P. 45, E-9]**. Capacity: 9,681.
Wichita Wings (Major Soccer League); (316) 262-3545.

Tennis

CENTURY III CONVENTION HALL
225 W. Douglas, Wichita; **[P. 44, A-3]**; (316) 264-9121. Surface is Courtship.
Wichita Advantage (TT), July to Aug.

Track & Field

BRAMLAGE COLISEUM
Kansas State University, Manhattan **[P. 45, B-10]**; (913) 532-6910.
NJCAA (Junior College National Championship), March.

USA SNAPSHOTS®

A look at statistics that shape the sports world

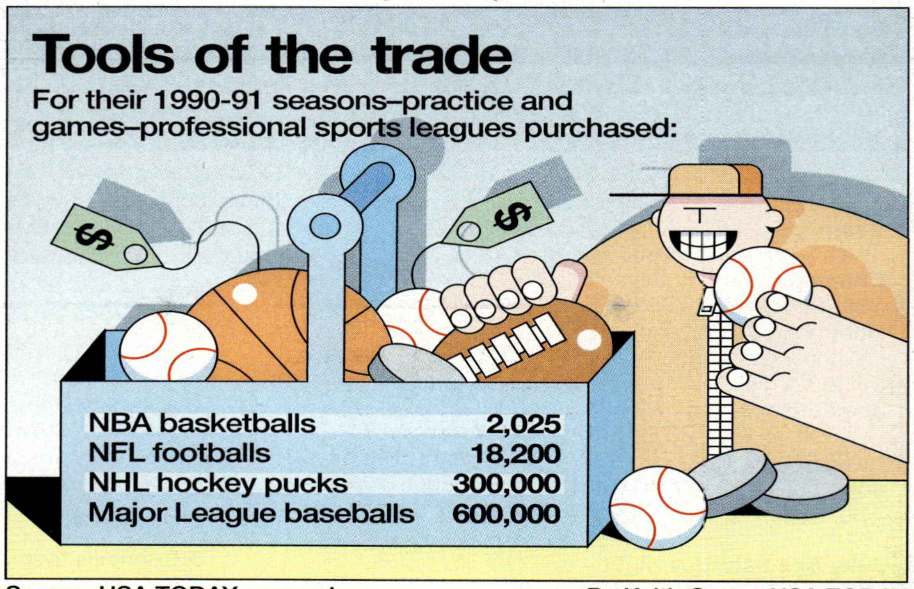

Tools of the trade
For their 1990-91 seasons–practice and games–professional sports leagues purchased:
NBA basketballs 2,025
NFL footballs 18,200
NHL hockey pucks 300,000
Major League baseballs 600,000

Source: USA TODAY research — By Keith Carter, USA TODAY

► OUTDOOR VENUES

State Parks

- Bike Trails: BK
- Boating: BT
- Camping: C
- Climbing: CL
- Diving: DV
- Fishing: F
- Golfing: G
- Hiking: HK
- Hunting: HT
- Riding: R
- Surfing: SU
- Swimming: S
- Tennis: TE
- Whitewater: WW
- Winter Sports: W

ATCHISON STATE FISHING LAKE
6 mi. NW of Atchison **[P. 45, B-12]**. Contains 179 acres. **C BT F**

CEDAR BLUFF STATE PARK
Off KS 147, 23 mi. SE of Wakeeney **[P. 44, C-5]**. Contains 1,715 acres. **C HK BT F S**

CHENEY STATE PARK
KS 251, 30 mi. NW of Wichita **[P. 45, E-8]**. Contains 2,495 acres. **C HK BT F S**

CLARK STATE FISHING LAKE
KS 94, 11 mi. SW of Kingsdown **[P. 44, F-5]**. Contains 1,243 acres. **C BT F**

CLINTON LAKE STATE PARK
Off US 40, 4 mi. W of Lawrence **[P. 45, C-12]**. Contains 1,455 acres. **C HK BT F S**

EL DORADO STATE PARK
US 77, 5 mi. NE of El Dorado **[P. 45, E-10]**. Contains 3,800 acres. **C BT F S**

STATBOX

POPULATION: 2,480,000
SQUARE MILES: 82,264
TIME ZONE: Central
MOTTO: To the stars with difficulty
BIRD: Meadowlark
TREE: Cottonwood
CAPITAL: Topeka
AVERAGE ANNUAL RAINFALL: 27"
MEAN TEMP: 55
MAJOR LEAGUE TEAMS: 0
NATIONAL PARK/FOREST ACREAGE: 108,000
STATE PARK ACREAGE: 30,200
HIGHEST ELEVATION: 4,039'
LOWEST ELEVATION: 680'
WATERWAYS: 499 square miles of inland water

ELK CITY (AC)
Off US 160 & US 75, 7 mi. NW of Independence **[P. 45, F-12]**. Contains 857 acres. **C HK BT F S**

GLEN ELDER STATE PARK
US 24, 12 mi. W of Beloit **[P. 44, B-7]**. Contains 1,250 acres. **C BT F S**

KINGMAN STATE FISHING LAKE
US 54, 7 mi. W of Kingman **[P. 44, E-7]**. Contains 4,529 acres. **C BT F**

LOVEWELL STATE PARK
Off KS 14, 15 mi. NE of Mankato **[P. 45, A-8]**. Contains 1,126 acres. **C BT F S**

MCPHERSON STATE FISHING LAKE
8 mi. NW of Canton **[P. 45, D-9]**. Contains 2,560 acres. **C BT F**

MEADE STATE PARK
Off KS 23, 12 mi. SW of Meade **[P. 44, F-4]**. Contains 1,443 acres. **C BT F S**

MILFORD (AC)
MS 57, 2 mi. NW of Junction City **[P. 45, C-10]**. Contains 1,084 acres. **C HK BT F S R**

MONTGOMERY STATE FISHING LAKE
4 mi. SE of Independence **[P. 45, F-12]**. Contains 408 acres. **C BT F**

NEOSHO STATE FISHING LAKE
7 mi. SW of St. Paul **[P. 45, F-13]**. Contains 216 acres. **C BT F**

OTTAWA STATE FISHING LAKE
6 mi. NE of Bennington **[P. 45, C-9]**. Contains 711 acres. **C BT F S**

POTTAWATOMIE STATE FISHING LAKE
Off US 24, 4 mi. N of Manhattan **[P. 45, B-10]**. Contains 248 acres. **C BT F**

SHERIDAN STATE FISHING LAKE
Off US 24, 3 mi. W of Studley, or 11 mi. E of Hoxie **[P. 44, B-4]**. Contains 335 acres. **C BT F**

WOODSON STATE FISHING LAKE
Off US 54, 10 mi. SW of Yates Center, or 5.5 mi. E of Toronto **[P. 45, E-11]**. Contains 2,885 acres. **C HK BT F**

► ACTIVE SPORTS

AEROBICS: AFAA, 5816 Minnie, Wichita; (316) 522-5493.

BASEBALL: Little League Baseball Central Region HQ, 4360 N. Mitthoeffer Rd., Indianapolis, IN; (317) 897-6127. • **American Legion Baseball,** 1210 Virginia Ln. #6, Olathe; (913) 829-1291. • **Babe Ruth Baseball,** Norman Travis, Box 339, Burlington, CO; (719) 346-8803.

BOARDSAILING: Paradise Sailboarding Co. , Wichita; (316) 265-0258. • **Surf Rider Sailboard Co. ,** Wichita; (316) 838-9069. • **USWA Regional Director,** 2625 S. 46th, Lincoln, NE; (402) 489-1002.

CONTINUED ON PAGE 161

Kentucky

Welcome to the hotbed of fast horses—and fast-break basketball. Since the Kentucky Derby was first run at Louisville's Churchill Downs in 1875, 88 Derby winners have been Kentucky-bred horses. Lexington is home to Keeneland (site of the Blue Grass Stakes and the July Selected Yearling Sale), and the Red Mile, which hosts harness racing's Kentucky Futurity in October. ◆ On the courts, Lexington's Kentucky Wildcats boast one of college basketball's winningest programs (five NCAA titles), while Louisville's Cardinals are two-time NCAA champions. ◆ Hillerich and Bradsby makes the Louisville Slugger here, near where the Louisville Redbirds (St. Louis Cardinals) play Triple-A baseball at Cardinal Stadium. ◆ And for those who like to fish, there is Crappiethon USA at Kentucky Lake and Lake Barkley, a $450,000, two-month event.

STATBOX

POPULATION: 3,728,144
SQUARE MILES: 40,395
TIME ZONE: Eastern and Central
MOTTO: United we stand, divided we fall
BIRD: Cardinal
TREE: Kentucky Coffee Tree
CAPITAL: Frankfort
AVERAGE ANNUAL RAINFALL: 45"
MEAN TEMP: 54-58
MAJOR LEAGUE TEAMS: 0
NATIONAL PARK/FOREST ACREAGE: 1,000,000
STATE PARK ACREAGE: 42,440
HIGHEST ELEVATION: 4,145'
LOWEST ELEVATION: 257'
WATERWAYS: 1,100 miles of navigable rivers and streams

▶ SPECTATOR VENUES

Baseball

CARDINAL STADIUM
at the Kentucky Fair & Exposition Center, Freedom Way and Phillips Lane, Louisville **[P. 47, H-11]**. Capacity: 33,500
Louisville Redbirds (American Association, Class AAA); (502) 367-9121. Entered League in 1982. Broadcasts by WAVG 970-AM. MLB affiliation, St. Louis Cardinals.

Bowling

BLUE RIBBON LANES
1108 Winchester Avenue, Ashland **[P. 47, B-13]**; (606) 329-2695.
LPBT, May.

College Sports

EASTERN KENTUCKY UNIVERSITY COLONELS
Lancaster Avenue, Richmond **[P. 47, D-10]**; (606) 622-1230. Begley, capacity 20,000. Alumni, capacity 6,500.

KENTUCKY STATE UNIVERSITY THOROBREDS
East Main Street, Frankfort **[P. 46, G-4]**; (502) 227-6011. Alumni Stadium, capacity 6,000. Dudgeon Civic Center, capacity 7,200.

MOREHEAD STATE UNIVERSITY EAGLES
Morehead **[P. 47, C-11]**; (606) 783-2088. Jayne, capacity 10,000. Academic-Athletic Center, capacity 6,500.

MURRAY STATE UNIVERSITY RACERS
Murray **[P. 46, H-1]**; (502) 762-6184. Roy Stewart, capacity 16,800. Racer Arena, capacity 5,550.

UNIVERSITY OF KENTUCKY WILDCATS
Lexington **[P. 46, G-7]**; (606) 257-8000. Commonwealth, capacity 56,696. Rupp Arena, capacity 23,000.
◆College basketball's most storied program has a fitting palace for its players. Half gym, half mansion, Rupp is perhaps the sport's gaudiest structure. And if you want to see athletes put up in luxury, visit the Wildcat Lodge, the school's athletic dorm.

UNIVERSITY OF LOUISVILLE CARDINALS
Louisville **[P. 47, G-11]**; (502) 588-5732. Cardinal, capacity 37,500. Freedom Hall, capacity 19,000.
◆Cardinal Stadium and Freedom Hall are located at the Kentucky Fair & Exposition Center.

WESTERN KENTUCKY UNIVERSITY HILLTOPPERS
Bowling Green **[P. 46, E-6]**; (502) 745-3542. L.T. Smith, capacity 19,250. E.A. Diddle Arena, capacity 12,500.

Hockey

BROADBENT ARENA
at the Kentucky Fair & Exposition Center, 937 Phillips Ln., Louisville **[P. 47, H-11]**. Capacity: 6,410.
Louisville IceHawks (East Coast Hockey League); (502) 367-7797. Franchise began in 1990.

Horse Racing

CHURCHILL DOWNS
700 Central Ave., Louisville **[P. 47, H-10]**; (502) 636-4400. Opened in 1875. Total capacity: 51,500.
Thoroughbred season from Apr. to June and in Oct. & Nov.
◆Home of the horse world's preeminent event, the Kentucky Derby. Mint juleps flow on the first Saturday in May, as the nation's finest three-year olds gather for the first leg of the Triple Crown. The Derby was first run in 1875. Churchill Downs' trademark twin spires are the most photographed feature of any US track. Host of the 1988 and 1991 Breeder's Cups.

ELLIS PARK
U.S. Highway 41 N., Henderson **[P. 46, C-5]**; (502) 826-0608. Opened in 1955. Clubhouse capacity: 2,200. Grandstand capacity: 7,000.
Thoroughbred season from July to Sep.

KEENELAND
U.S. Highway 60, Lexington **[P. 46, G-6]**; (606) 254-3412. Opened in 1936. Clubhouse capacity: 2,000. Grandstand capacity: 5,000.
◆ Races in April and October only. A national historic landmark, Keeneland is the home of old-style racing. There's no track announcer; they paint the winner's circle on the track after each race, and, unlike any other in the USA, the club house is located on the stretch rather than the finish line. Keeneland's stone facade and tall oaks make it one of the most beautiful in the country, and it's surrounded by the well-manicured breeding farms of central Kentucky. Morning workouts open to the public year round, daybreak to 10 a.m.

LOUISVILLE DOWNS
4520 Poplar Level Road, Louisville **[P. 47, H-12]**; (502) 964-6415. Opened in 1966. Clubhouse capacity: 3,200. Grandstand capacity: 5,500.
Harness season from Mar. to Apr., July to Sept. and in Oct.

RIVERSIDE DOWNS
3003 Sunset Lane, Henderson **[P. 46, C-5]**; (502) 826-9746. Opened in 1987. Clubhouse capacity: 600. Grandstand capacity: 2,000. Harness season from Apr. to June and Oct. to Dec.
◆The race course was remodelled and reopened in 1987 as Riverside Downs, but had previously been in operation since 1953 as the Autoban Raceway and the Midwest Harness Raceway.

THE RED MILE
1200 Red Mile Road, Lexington **[P. 46, G-7]**; (606) 255-0752. Opened in 1875. Clubhouse capacity: 500. Grandstand capacity: 6,000.
Harness season from Apr. to July.
◆Racing continues Sept. to Oct. More harness racing world records have been set at The Red Mile than at any other track. Home of the Kentucky Futurity, the Trotting Triple Crown's final race.

TURFWAY PARK
7500 Turfway Road, Florence **[P. 47, A-10]**; (606) 371-0200. Opened in 1959. Clubhouse capacity: 3,000. Grandstand capacity: 3,500.
Thoroughbred season from Dec. to Apr. and in September.

Museums & Halls of Fame

AMERICAN SADDLEHORSE MUSEUM
4093 Iron Works Pike, Lexington **[P. 47, G-8]**; (606) 259-2746.
◆Located inside the Kentucky Horse Park.

KENTUCKY DERBY MUSEUM
704 Central Ave., Louisville **[P. 47, H-11]**; (502) 637-1111.
◆A great, theater-in-the-round video gives a history of the Kentucky Derby.

KENTUCKY HORSE PARK/INTERNATIONAL MUSEUM OF THE HORSE
4089 Iron Works Pike, Lexington **[P. 46, F-7]**; (606) 233-4303.
◆A sprawling complex in Kentucky's Bluegrass country, it includes everything from an equine Hall of Champions to a

CONTINUED ON PAGE 162

Kansas

CONTINUED FROM PAGE 160

BOWLING: American Bowling Congress, 5301 S. 76th St., Greendale, WI; (414) 421-6400.

CANOEING & KAYAKING: ACA Central Vice Commodore, 3410 Ridge Rd., N. Little Rock, AR; (501) 758-4716.

CYCLING: USCF Kansas Representative, 1361 Medford, Topeka; (913) 235-0428.

FITNESS: Governor's Council on Fitness, Department of Health, Physical Education and Recreation, Pittsburg State University, Pittsburg; (316) 231-7000. • **National Strength and Conditioning Ass'n State Director,** Kansas State University, Football Office, Manhattan; (913) 532-5876.

FOOTBALL: Pop Warner Football, 1315 Walnut Street, Suite 1632, Philadelphia, PA; (215) 735-1450.

GOLF: Kansas City Golf Association, 7200 West 106th Street, Overland Park; (913) 381-5380. • **Kansas Golf Association,** 3301 Clinton Parkway Ct., Suite 4, Lawrence; (913) 842-4833. • **PGA Midwest Section,** 1703 Oak Cir., Blue Springs, MO; (816) 229-6565. • **PGA South Central Section,** 2745 E. Skelly Dr., Ste. 103, Tulsa, OK; (918) 742-5672.

HIKING & CLIMBING: Kansas Sierra Club Chapter, PO Box 47319, Wichita; (316) 683-8492.

HOCKEY: USA Hockey Central Registrar, PO Box 1738, Lisle, IL; (708) 963-1098.

HUNTING & FISHING: Department of Wildlife & Parks, 900 Jackson St., Suite 502, Topeka; (913) 296-2281. • **The Gun Shop (Orvis),** 718A S. Rogers Rd., Olathe; (913) 782-6900.

RACQUETBALL: AARA, 3806 Broadway, Great Bend; (316) 792-4445.

RODEO: PRCA Prairie Circuit, RR 2, Box 20, Abbyville; (316) 286-5319.

RUNNING: RRCA KS State Rep., 5001 Stateline, Kansas City; (816) 531-2387.

SCUBA: Midwest Aquatics, Inc., 11721 College Blvd., Overland Park; (913) 451-6238.

SHOOTING: Cimarron Sporting Clays, Box 575, Cimarron; (316) 855-7050. • **Flint Oak,** Rt. 1, Box 262, Fall River; (316) 658-4401. • **Marais Des Cygnes Sporting Park,** PO Box 811, 2201 E. 15th St., Ottawa; (913) 242-7468.

SKATING: USFSA, 20 First Street, Colorado Springs, CO; (719) 635-5200.

SOCCER: Kansas Soccer Ass'n, 7409 W. 112th St., Overland Park; (913) 451-2051. • **Kansas State YSA,** 5905 W. 100th Terrace, Overland Park; (913) 648-3097. • **AYSO Regional Director,** 2971 N. Coronado St., Chandler; (602) 839-2114.

SOFTBALL: Kansas ASA, 4145 SE Iowa, Topeka; (913) 267-2225.

SWIMMING: LMSC Missouri Valley Registrar, 5708 Outlook #301, Mission; (913) 362-2018.

TENNIS: Recreational TEAMTENNIS Midwest-Southeast Region, National Program Coordinator, 445 N. Wells, Ste. #404, Chicago, IL; (800) TEAMTEN. • **Missouri Valley USTA,** 722 Walnut St., Suite #1, Kansas City, MO; (816) 556-0777.

Kentucky

CONTINUED FROM PAGE 161

museum that follows the horse from prehistoric times to the present. There are also polo fields, jumping and dressage arenas, and an adjacent camping ground.

MUSEUM OF POLO AND HALL OF FAME
4059 Iron Works Pike, Lexington **[P. 46, F-7]**; (606) 281-6285.

PGA/LPGA

KEARNEY HILL LINKS
3403 Kearney Rd., Lexington **[P. 46, G-7]**; (606) 253-1981.
Bank One Classic (Senior PGA), September. Number of holes: 54.

Polo

KENTUCKY POLO ASSOCIATION/ LOUISVILLE CHAPTER, INC.
Hays Kennedy Park, Louisville **[P. 47, B-8]**; (502) 266-6001.

KENTUCKY POLO ASSOCIATION/ LEXINGTON CHAPTER, INC. ("LEXINGTON POLO")
4059 Iron Works Pike, Lexington **[P. 46, F-7]**; (606) 254-5667.
◆Matches played at the Kentucky Horse Park.

Track & Field

BROADBENT ARENA
937 Phillips Ln., Louisville **[P. 47, H-11]**; (502) 239-5258.
Mason-Dixon Games, Feb.

▶ OUTDOOR VENUES

National Parks

BIG SOUTH FORK NATIONAL RIVER & RECREATION AREA
15 mi. W of Oneida & 24 mi. E of Jamestown, at the Bandy Creek Campground off Leatherwood Ford Road (TN 297) **[P. 47, F-10]**. Contains 125,000 acres.
C HK BT F S R WW

> **"Throughout most of the year, you can find a sporting event worth watching in any state of the union. But on the first Saturday in May, there's only one. The Kentucky Derby, the most monumental two minutes sports has to offer."**
>
> **Retired baseball pitcher, U.S. Representative *Jim Bunning***

DANIEL BOONE NATIONAL FOREST
Between Morehead & Whitley City **[P. 47, C-10, E-10]**. Contains 666,000 acres. **C HK BT F S R BK CL**

Bike Trails: BK
Boating: BT
Camping: C
Climbing: CL
Diving: DV
Fishing: F
Golfing: G
Hiking: HK
Hunting: HT
Riding: R
Surfing: SU
Swimming: S
Tennis: TE
Whitewater: WW
Winter Sports: W

LAND BETWEEN THE LAKES NATIONAL RECREATION AREA (Tennessee Valley Authority)
Peninsula between Kentucky Lake & Lake Barkley, Golden Pond **[P. 46, G-2]**. Contains 170,000 acres. **C HK BT F S BK HT**

MAMMOTH CAVE NATIONAL PARK
10 mi. W of I-65, Mammoth Cave **[P. 46, E-7]**. Contains 51,354 acres. **C HK BT F R**

State Parks

BARREN RIVER LAKE STATE RESORT PARK
13 miles SW of Glasgow on 31 E **[P. 46, E-7]**. Contains 2,187 acres.
C HK BT F S R BK TE

BREAKS INTERSTATE PARK
Elkhorn City **[P. 47, D-14]**. Contains 4,600 acres. **C HK BT F S**

CARTER CAVES STATE RESORT PARK
Olive Hill **[P. 47, B-12]**. Contains 1,000 acres.
C HK BT F S R TE

CUMBERLAND FALLS STATE RESORT PARK
Corbin **[P. 47, E-10]**. Contains 1,794 acres.
C HK F S R TE

CUMBERLAND FALLS STATE RESORT PARK
From Corbin, I-75 to US 25 West. Contains 1,657 acres. **C HK F S WW**

DALE HOLLOW LAKE STATE PARK
S of Bow **[P. 47, F-8]**. Contains 3,497 acres.
C HK BT F S

GREEN RIVER LAKE STATE PARK
6 mi. S of Campbellsville off KY 55 **[P. 47, D-8]**. Contains 1,331 acres. **C HK BT F S**

GREENBO LAKE STATE RESORT PARK
KY 1 off US 23, 18 mi. N of I-64 **[P. 47, B-12]**. Contains 3,330 acres. **C HK BT F S G**

KENLAKE STATE RESORT PARK
KY 94, S of US 68, 16 mi. NE of Murray **[P. 46, G-2]**. Contains 1,800 acres. **C HK BT F S R TE**

KENTUCKY DAM VILLAGE STATE RESORT PARK
Near Gilbertsville on US 641, exit 27 off I-24 **[P. 46, F-1]**. Contains 1,352 acres.
C HK BT F S R G

LAKE BARKLEY STATE RESORT PARK
7 mi. W of Cadiz US 68/80 **[P. 46, G-2]**. Contains 3,700 acres. **C HK BT F S R BK G**

LAKE CUMBERLAND STATE RESORT PARK
10 mi. S of Jamestown off US 127 **[P. 47, E-9]**. Contains 3,117 acres. **C HK BT F S R G**

LAKE CUMBERLAND (AC)
US 127, 15 mi. S of Jamestown **[P. 47, E-9]**. Contains 63,000 acres. **C HK BT F S DV**

PENNYRILE FOREST STATE RESORT PARK
7 mi. S of Dawson Springs on KY 109 **[P. 46, E-4]**. Contains 863 acres. **C HK BT F S R G**

ROUGH RIVER DAM STATE RESORT PARK
15 mi. S of Harned on KY 79 off Western Kentucky Parkway **[P. 46, D-6]**. Contains 637 acres. **C HK BT F S TE**

SKIING

ALPINE SKIING

SKIBUTLER
in General Butler State Park, Carrollton **[P. 47, B-9]**; (502) 732-4231.
Vertical drop is 300 feet. Has three tows, one bar and three chairs.

▶ ACTIVE SPORTS

AEROBICS: AFAA, 1400 Mill Race Rd., Louisville.

BASEBALL: Little League Baseball Southern Region HQ, PO Box 13366, St. Petersburg, FL; (813) 344-2661. • **American Legion Baseball,** Box 23, Rt. 3, Shelbyville; (502) 633-3865. • **Babe Ruth Baseball,** Robert Dickson, RR 4, Box 332F, Alexandria, IN; (317) 724-4883.

BOARDSAILING: USWA Regional Director, N7315 Winnebago Dr., Fond du Lac, WI; (414) 922-2550.

BOWLING: American Bowling Congress, 5301 S. 76th St., Greendale, WI; (414) 421-6400.

CANOEING & KAYAKING: ACA Dixie Vice Commodore, 2320 Salcedo Street, Savannah, GA; (912) 352-0717.

CYCLING: LAW East Central Regional Director, 4724 Bokay Drive, Dayton, OH; (513) 435-9366. • **USCF Indiana/Kentucky Representative,** 305 McConnell Drive, New Albany, IN; (812) 949-2125 or (502) 491-8201.

FITNESS: National Strength and Conditioning Ass'n State Director, PO Box 1037, Cadiz; (502) 522-6072.

FOOTBALL: Pop Warner Football, 1315 Walnut Street, Suite 1632, Philadelphia, PA; (215) 735-1450.

GOLF: Kentucky Golf Assoc., 2950 Breckinridge Ln., Suite 10, PO Box 20146, Louisville; (502) 452-1584. • **PGA Kentucky Section,** PO Box 20146, Louisville; (502) 452-1584.

HIKING & CLIMBING: Cumberland Sierra Club Chapter, 2004 Writt Ct., Lexington; (606) 259-1922.

HOCKEY: USA Hockey Mid-American Registrar, 647 Stacey Ln., Maumee, OH; (419) 893-9665.

HUNTING & FISHING: Department of Fish & Wildlife Resources, #1 Game Farm Rd., Arnold Mitchell Building, Frankfort; (502) 564-3400. • **The Sporting Tradition (Orvis),** Lexington Festival Market, 325 W. Main St., Lexington; (606) 255-8652. • **The Sporting Tradition (Orvis),** The Mall at St. Matthews, 5000 Shelbyville Rd., Louisville; (502) 895-4060. • **Trout Unlimited,** 724 Oxford Dr., Huntington, WV; (304) 522-6191.

RACQUETBALL: AARA, 5312 Sherlock Way, Louisville; (502) 239-1797.

RODEO: PRCA Great Lakes Circuit, Rt. 1, Box 54, Clayton, IN; (317) 539-5039.

RUNNING: RRCA KY State Rep., 840 Ironwood Dr., Bowling Green; (502) 843-8719.

SHOOTING: Shoot-Fire Sporting Clays, 290 Koostra Rd., Bowling Green; (502) 781-9545. • **Triple S Sporting Clays,** Rt. 5, Box 46-A, Morganfield; (502) 389-3580.

SKATING: USFSA, 20 First Street, Colorado Springs, CO; (719) 635-5200.

SOCCER: Kentucky Soccer Ass'n, 10809 Oreland Mill Rd., Louisville; (502) 964-2148. • **Kentucky YSA,** 5808 Cadillac Dr., Independence; (606) 356-8383. • **AYSO Regional Director,** 1405 Inman Dr., Huntsville, AL; (205) 881-3138.

SOFTBALL: Kentucky ASA, 435 Pekin Pike, Wilmore; (606) 858-8031. • **Louisville ASA,** 2400 Keswick Boulevard, Louisville; (502) 636-2313.

SQUASH: Downtown Athletic Club, Louisville; (502) 582-2295.

SWIMMING: LMSC Kentucky Registrar, 2107 Eastview Avenue, Louisville; (502) 454-3029.

TABLE TENNIS: USTTA State Coordinator, Box 8, Middleburg; (606) 678-4023.

TENNIS: Recreational TEAMTENNIS Midwest-Southeast Region, National Program Coordinator, 445 N. Wells, Ste. #404, Chicago, IL; (800) TEAMTEN. • **Southern USTA,** 200 Sandy Springs Place, Suite 200, Atlanta, GA; (404) 257-1297. • **Western USTA,** 8720 Castle Creek Parkway, Ste. 329, Indianapolis, IN; (513) 390-2740.

TRIATHLON: Bluegrass Triathlon Club, PO Box 22161, Lexington; (606) 269-6530. • **Derby City Tri Club,** 844 Jefferson Street, Louisville; (502) 587-6651.

Tip Offs

High School Basketball Crowds

The following are some top attendance figures for high school boys basketball championship games, in the states listed.

Year	State (Venue)	Attendance
1963-72	Illinois (U. of I.)	16, 144
1965, '67	Ohio (St. John Arena)	13, 884
1971	Minnesota (U. of M.)	17, 164
1975-89	Indiana (Market Square Arena)	17, 490
1981	Kentucky (U. of K.)	20, 764
1987	Texas (U. of T.)	15, 287
1990	California (Oakland Coliseum)	14, 629

Louisiana

Mardi Gras isn't the only game in town. Louisiana State basketball and football in Baton Rouge are two of the state's biggest attractions. ◆ In New Orleans, the Superdome is home to the NFL Saints, college football's Sugar Bowl, and the Bayou Classic (Grambling and Southern). ◆ College football's Independence Bowl is played in Shreveport, which is also home to the Louisiana Marathon (September). ◆ Horse racing is available at five different tracks, including September's Super Derby at the Louisiana Downs. ◆ The Toledo Bend Reservoir, one of the largest freshwater lakes in the south, provides some of the state's best freshwater fishing, while saltwater angling can be found along the Gulf of Mexico. ◆ Whitetail deer and turkey attract hunters throughout the state's many Wildlife Management Areas, which also provide ample camping and hiking (see below).

▶ SPECTATOR VENUES

Auto Racing

NEW ORLEANS STREET CIRCUIT
315 Tchoupitoulas Street, New Orleans **[P. 49, B-12]**; (504) 592-0345.
Grand Prix du Mardi Gras (IMSA Camel GT), June.

Baseball

FAIRGROUNDS FIELD
Louisiana State Fairgrounds, Hearne Ave. & I-20, Shreveport **[P. 48, B-2]**. Capacity: 6,200
Shreveport Captains (Texas League, Class AA); (318) 636-5555. Entered League in 1968. Broadcasts by KEEL 710AM. MLB affiliation, San Francisco Giants.

Bowling

FAZZIO'S RAINBOW LANES
5555 Bullard Road, New Orleans **[P. 49, A-14]**; (504) 241-2695.
New Orleans Classic.

FOUR SEASONS BOWL
3510 North Blvd., Alexandria **[P. 48, D-7]**; (318) 445-2695.
Robby's Open (LPBT), February.

College Sports

CENTENARY COLLEGE GENTLEMEN
Shreveport **[P. 48, B-3]**; (318) 869-5275. Gold Dome, capacity 4,000.

GRAMBLING STATE UNIVERSITY TIGERS
Grambling **[P. 48, B-6]**; (318) 274-2634. Robinson, capacity 23,000. Memorial Gym, capacity 4,500.

LOUISIANA STATE UNIVERSITY FIGHTING TIGERS
Baton Rouge **[P. 48, E-1]**; (504) 388-6606. Tiger, capacity 80,148. Gym, capacity 2,500.
Pete Maravich Assembly Center, capacity 14,164.
◆The true college football fan hasn't experienced it all until he or she is in Baton Rouge for a Saturday night game. Caution: don't get too close to the tiger. He's in a cage for a reason.

LOUISIANA TECH UNIVERSITY
Ruston **[P. 48, B-17]**; (318) 257-4111. Joe Aillet, capacity 30,600. Thomas Assembly Center, capacity 8,000.

MCNEESE STATE UNIVERSITY COWBOYS
Ryan Street, Lake Charles **[P. 49, E-13]**; (318) 475-5215. Cowboy, capacity 20,000. Burton Coliseum, capacity 8,000.

NICHOLLS STATE UNIVERSITY COLONELS
Thibodaux **[P. 49, G-10]**; (504) 448-4806. John L. Guidry, capacity 12,800. Stopher Gym, capacity 3,400.

NORTHEAST LOUISIANA UNIVERSITY INDIANS
700 University Avenue, Monroe **[P. 49, C-12]**; (318) 342-3100. Malone, capacity 23,277. Ewing Coliseum, capacity 8,000.

NORTHWESTERN STATE UNIVERSITY DEMONS
Natchitoches **[P. 48, C-6]**; (318) 357-5251. Rags Turpin, capacity 16,500. Prather Coliseum, capacity 5,000.

SOUTHEASTERN LOUISIANA UNIVERSITY LIONS
Corner of North Hazel & West Dakota, Hammond **[P. 49, F-11]**; (504) 549-2253. Strawberry, capacity 8,300. University Center, capacity 7,500.

SOUTHERN UNIVERSITY & A&M JAGUARS
Baton Rouge **[P. 49, F-9]**; (504) 771-3170. A.W. Mumford, capacity 24,000. F.G. Clark Center, capacity 7,500.

TULANE UNIVERSITY GREEN WAVE
New Orleans **[P. 49, B-12]**; (504) 865-5501. Superdome, capacity 71,000. Fogelman Arena, capacity 5,000.

UNIVERSITY OF NEW ORLEANS PRIVATEERS
New Orleans **[P. 49, A-12]**; (504) 286-6239. Lakefront Arena, capacity 10,000.

UNIVERSITY OF SOUTHWESTERN LOUISIANA RAGIN' CAJUNS
201 Reinhardt Drive, Lafayette **[P. 49, F-8]**; (318) 231-6310. Cajun Field, capacity 31,000. Cajundome, capacity 12,000.

Football

LOUISIANA SUPERDOME
1500 Poydras Street, New Orleans **[P. 49, B-12]**. Built in 1975. Capacity: 69,065.
◆Near the French Quarter.
New Orleans Saints (NFC Western Division); (504) 733-0255. Franchise began in 1967. Broadcasts by WWL.

Horse Racing

DELTA DOWNS
LA Route 3063, Vinton **[P. 48, F-5]**; (318) 589-7441. Opened in 1973. Clubhouse capacity: 2,500. Grandstand capacity: 500.
Thoroughbred season from Sep. to Mar.
Quarterhorse season from Easter to Labor Day.

LOUISIANA DOWNS
8000 East Texas Street, Bossier City **[P. 48, B-5]**; (318) 742-5555. Opened in 1974. Clubhouse capacity: 3,460. Grandstand capacity: 5,280. Total capacity: 17,240.
Thoroughbred season from Apr. to Nov.

NEW ORLEANS FAIR GROUNDS
1751 Gentilly Blvd., New Orleans **[P. 49, B-12]**; (504) 944-5515. Opened in 1872. Clubhouse capacity: 2,500. Grandstand capacity: 10,000.
Thoroughbred season from Nov. to Apr.
◆The third oldest existing track in the country, in operation for 119 years.

STATBOX

- **POPULATION:** 4,419,723
- **SQUARE MILES:** 47,751
- **TIME ZONE:** Central
- **MOTTO:** Union, justice, and confidence
- **BIRD:** Eastern Brown Pelican
- **TREE:** Bald Cypress
- **CAPITAL:** Baton Rouge
- **AVERAGE ANNUAL RAINFALL:** 55"
- **MEAN TEMP:** 67.4
- **MAJOR LEAGUE TEAMS:** 1
- **NATIONAL PARK/FOREST ACREAGE:** 29,000
- **STATE PARK ACREAGE:** 38,499
- **HIGHEST ELEVATION:** 535'
- **LOWEST ELEVATION:** 5' below sea level
- **WATERWAYS:** 4 million acres of naturally navigable water

THE NEW EVANGELINE DOWNS
US Highway 167 North, Carencro **[P. 49, F-8]**; (318) 896-7223. Opened in 1966. Clubhouse capacity: 1,200. Grandstand capacity: 3,000.
Thoroughbred season from Apr. to Sep.

PGA/LPGA

ENGLISH TURN GOLF & COUNTRY CLUB
1 Clubhouse Dr., New Orleans **[P. 49, B-14]**; (504) 392-2200.
USF&G Classic (PGA), March. Number of holes: 72.

Track & Field

STREETS OF NEW ORLEANS
City Park, New Orleans **[P. 49, A-12]**; (504) 482-6682.
◆In its 28th year, among the four oldest marathons in country.
Bud Lite Mardi Gras Marathon, January.

▶ OUTDOOR VENUES

National Parks

KISATCHIE NATIONAL FOREST
Separate areas near Natchitoches, Homer, Winnfield, Pollock, Leesville and Alexandria **[P. 48, A-5, C-6, E-6]**. Contains 600,000 acres.
C HK BT F S R BK HT

State Parks

BAYOU SEGNETTE STATE PARK
Westwego off US 90 **[P. 49, C-11]**. Contains 580 acres. **C HK BT F**

CHICOT STATE PARK
8 mi. N of Ville Platte off LA 3042 **[P. 48, E-7]**. Contains 6,400 acres.
C HK BT F S BK

FONTAINEBLEAU STATE PARK
3 mi. SE of Mandeville on US 190 **[P. 49, F-12]**. Contains 2,800 acres.
C HK BT F S

LAKE BISTINEAU STATE PARK
10 mi. S of Doyline on LA 163 **[P. 48, B-5]**. Contains 750 acres. **C HK BT F S**

LAKE CLAIBORNE STATE PARK
7 mi. SE of Homer on LA 146 **[P. 48, A-6]**. Contains 620 acres. **C HK BT F S**

Bike Trails: BK
Boating: BT
Camping: C
Climbing: CL
Diving: DV
Fishing: F
Golfing: G
Hiking: HK
Hunting: HT
Riding: R
Surfing: SU
Swimming: S
Tennis: TE
Whitewater: WW
Winter Sports: W

CONTINUED ON PAGE 164

USA SNAPSHOTS®

A look at statistics that shape the sports world

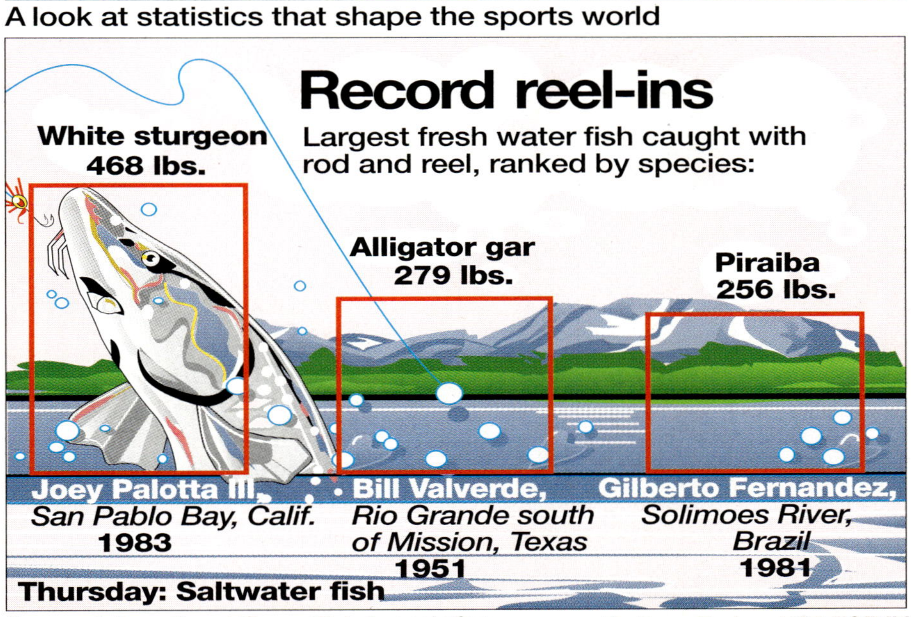

Source: International Game Fish Association

By Suzy Parker, USA TODAY

Louisiana

CONTINUED FROM PAGE 163

> **"The license plates in Louisiana call it a Sportsman's Paradise, and that's what it is. You can hardly throw out a line here without catching a fish. If hunting's your bag, just name it. If it moves and it's legal game, you'll more often than not get your limit."**
>
> **San Francisco Giants slugger *Will Clark***

LAKE FAUSSE POINTE STATE PARK
25 mi. E of St. Martinville off the West Atchafalaya protection levee road **[P. 49, G-9]**. Contains 6,000 acres. **C HK BT F**

NORTH TOLEDO BEND STATE PARK
4 mi. SW of Zwolle off LA 3229 **[P. 48, C-4]**. Contains 990 acres. **C HK BT F S**

SAM HOUSTON JONES STATE PARK
9 mi. N of Lake Charles off LA 378 **[P. 48, F-5]**. Contains 1,080 acres. **C HK BT F**

ACTIVE SPORTS

AEROBICS: AFAA, 2746 Brentwood Dr., Baton Rouge; (504) 924-8494.

BASEBALL: Little League Baseball Southern Region HQ, PO Box 13366, St. Petersburg, FL; (813) 344-2661. • **American Legion Baseball,** Rt. 4, Box 206, New Iberia; (318) 364-2970. • **Babe Ruth Baseball,** James Wagoner, 2930 Jenny Lind, Fort Smith, AR; (501) 646-3065.

BILLIARDS: Sport Palace, 1125 Jefferson Hwy., New Orleans; (504) 835-9117.

BOARDSAILING: USWA Regional Director, 244 Spring Rd., Argyle TX;(817)455-2819

BOWLING: American Bowling Contress, 5301 S. 76th St., Greendale, WI; (414) 421-6400.

CANOEING & KAYAKING: ACA Central Vice Commodore, 3410 Ridge Rd., N. Little Rock, AR; (501) 758-4716.

CYCLING: LAW South Central Regional Director, 1618 7th S., New Orleans; (504) 899-8575. • **USCF Louisiana Representative,** 605 Parkview Dr., New Iberia; (318) 367-6226.

FITNESS: Governor's Council on Physical Fitness & Sports, Louisiana Orthopedic and Sports Rehabilitation Institute, 175 Physicians Park Drive, Baton Rouge; (504) 751-6666.

FOOTBALL: Pop Warner Football, 1315 Walnut Street, Suite 1632, Philadelphia, PA; (215) 735-1450.

GOLF: Louisiana State Golf Association, 1305 Emerson Street, Monroe; (318) 342-4140. • **PGA Gulf States Section,** PO Box 29426, New Orleans; (504) 245-7333.

HIKING & CLIMBING: Delta Sierra Club Chapter, PO Box 19469, Bienville St., New Orleans; (504) 482-9566.

HOCKEY: USA Hockey Southeastern Registrar, PO Box 5208, Takoma Park, MD; (301) 622-0032.

HUNTING & FISHING: Department of Wildlife & Fisheries, PO Box 98000, Baton Rouge; (504) 765-2803.

RACQUETBALL: AARA, 8964 Audrey Dr., Baton Rouge; (504) 924-2109.

RODEO: PRCA Southeastern Circuit, 1111 S. McGee Rd., Bonifay, FL; (904) 547-2534.

RUNNING: RRCA LA State Rep., 23353 Elberta Lane, Zachary; (504) 654-8570.

SCUBA: Adventure Sports, Inc., 1817 Texas Avenue, Shreveport; (318) 425-5870. • **Dive Odyssey,** 12330 Florida Blvd., Baton Rouge; (504) 272-3483. • **Sea Horse Diving Academy,** 8726 Chef Menteur Highway, New Orleans; (504) 246-6523. • **The Water Habitat of Alexandria, Inc.,** 1602 Jackson Street, PO Box 4442, Alexandria; (318) 443-5075. • **Venture Sports, Inc.,** 1409 Ryan Street, Lake Charles; (318) 433-4444.

SHOOTING: Wild Wings Sporting Clays, Rt. 2, Box 356, Worthington; (812) 875-2789.

SKATING: USFSA, 20 First Street, Colorado Springs, CO; (719) 635-5200.

SOCCER: Louisiana Soccer Ass'n, 241 Maxmillian Street, Baton Rouge; (504) 383-8100. • **AYSO Regional Director,** 1405 Inman Dr., Huntsville, AL; (205) 881-3138.

SOFTBALL: Louisiana ASA, 4540 Young Ln., Lake Charles; (318) 477-4027.

SQUASH: Rivercenter Tennis Club (USSRA), New Orleans; (504) 587-7242.

SWIMMING: LMSC Southern Registrar, 2700 Lavender, New Orleans; (504) 949-7338.

TENNIS: Recreational TEAMTENNIS Midwest-Southeast Region, National Program Coordinator, 445 N. Wells, Ste. #404, Chicago, IL; (800) TEAMTEN. • **Southern USTA,** 200 Sandy Springs Place, Suite 200, Atlanta, GA; (404) 257-1297.

◆ ◆ ◆

Tip Offs

Active Sports National Contact List

The following are the names, addresses and contacts of the national headquarters of all the active organizations listed in the Active Sports section of each state chapter.

Aerobics and Fitness Association of America (AFAA), 15250 Ventura Blvd., Suite 310, Sherman Oaks, CA; (800) 445-5950, or, in CA, (800) 343-2584.

Amateur Skating Union, National Office, 1033 Shady Lane, Glen Ellyn, IL 60137; (708) 790-3230.

Amateur Softball Association (ASA), 2801 N.E. 50th Street, Oklahoma City, OK 73111-7203; (405) 424-5266.

America Outdoors (merger of Western River Guides Association and Eastern Professional River Operators Association), PO Box 1348, Knoxville, TN 37901; (615) 524-1045

American Amateur Racquetball Association, 815 North Weber, Suite 101, Colorado Springs, CO 80903; (719) 635-5396.

American Bowling Congress, 5301 S. 76th St., Greendale, WI; (414) 421-6400.

American Canoe Association, Inc. (ACA), National Office, 8580 Cinderbed Road, Suite 1900, PO Box 1190, Newington, VA 22122-1190; (703) 550-7495 or 550-7523.

American Horse Council, Inc., 1700 K Street, Suite 300, Washington, DC 20006; (202) 296-4031.

American Legion Baseball, National Headquarters, 700 N. Pennsylvania, Indianapolis, IN 46204; (317) 635-8411.

American Windsurfing Industries Association (AWIA), 99 East Blithedale, Mill Valley, CA 94941; (800) 333-2242.

American Youth Hostels, Inc. (AYH), National Office, PO Box 37613, Washington, DC 20013-7613; (202) 783-6161.

American Youth Soccer Organization (AYSO), PO Box 5045, Hawthorne, CA 90251-5045; (800) USA-AYSO

Babe Ruth Baseball, International Headquarters, 1770 Brunswick Ave., PO Box 5000, Trenton, NJ 08638; (609) 695-1434.

League of American Wheelmen (LAW), 6707 Whitestone Road, Suite 209, Baltimore, MD 21207; (301) 944-3399.

Little League Baseball, PO Box 3485, Williamsport, PA 17701; (717) 326-1921.

Men's Senior Baseball League (MSBL), 8 Sutton Terrace, Jericho, NY; (516) 931-2615.

National Association of Governors' Councils on Physical Fitness and Sports, Pan American Plaza, Suite 440, 201 S. Capitol Ave., Indianapolis, IN 46225; (317) 237-5630.

National Sporting Clays Association, PO Box 680007, San Antonio, TX 78268-0007; (800) 877-5338.

National Strength and Conditioning Association, PO Box 81410, Lincoln, NE 68501; (402) 472-3000.

Outward Bound USA, 384 Field Point Road, Greenwich, CT 06830; (800) 243-8520.

PADI Headquarters, 1251 E. Dyer Road, #100, Santa Ana, CA 92705-5605; (714) 540-7234.

Pony Baseball/Softball, PO Box 225, Washington, PA 15301-0225; (412) 225-1060.

Pop Warner Football, 1315 Walnut Street, Suite 1632, Philadelphia, PA; (215) 735-1450.

Professional Golfers' Association of America (PGA), 100 Avenue of the Champions, Palm Beach Gardens, FL 33418; (407) 624-8400.

Professional Rodeo Cowboys Association (PRCA), 101 Pro Rodeo Drive, Colorado Springs, CO 80919-9989; (719) 593-8840.

Road Runners Club of America, 629 S. Washington Street, Alexandria, VA 22314; (703) 836-0558.

Recreational Team Tennis, National Headquarters, 445 N. Wells, Suite #404, Chicago, IL 60610; (312) 245-5300 or (800) TEAMTEN.

Sierra Club, 730 Polk Street, San Francisco, CA 94109; (415) 923-5576.

The American Hiking Society, 1015 31st Street, NW, Washington, DC 20007-4990; (703) 385-3252.

The Lacrosse Foundation National Headquarters and Hall of Fame Museum, 113 West University Parkway, Baltimore, MD 21210; (301) 235-6882.

Triathlon Federation/USA, PO Box 15820, Colorado Springs, CO 80935; (719) 597-9090.

Trout Unlimited, 501 Church Street, NE, Vienna, VA 22180; (703) 281-1100.

United States Cycling Federation, 1750 East Boulder St., Colorado Springs, CO 80909; (719) 578-4581.

United States Figure Skating Association (USFSA), 20 First Street, Colorado Springs, CO; (719) 635-5200.

United States Flag Football League, 5834 Pine Tree Drive, Sanibel, FL; (813) 472-0544.

United States Masters Swimming National Office, 2 Peter Avenue, Rutland, MA 01543; (508) 886-6631. Note: "LMSC" denotes Local Masters Swimming Committee.

United States Soccer Federation, Federation Headquarters, 1750 East Boulder St., Colorado Springs, CO 80909; (719) 578-4678.

United States Squash Racquets Association (USSRA), PO Box 1216, Bala-Cynwyd, PA 19004; (215) 667-4006.

United States Table Tennis Association (USTTA), 1750 E. Boulder St., Colorado Springs, CO 80909-5769; (719) 578-4583.

United States Tennis Association, Inc. (USTA), 707 Alexander Road, Princeton, NJ 08540-6399; (609) 452-2580.

United States Youth Soccer Association (YSA), 1835 Union Ave., Suite 190, Memphis, TN 38104-3943.

United States Volleyball Association (USVBA), 3595 E. Fountain Blvd., Colorado Springs, CO 80910-1740; (719) 637-8300.

United States Windsurfing Association, PO Box 978, Hood River, OR 97031; (503) 386-8708.

USA Hockey, Inc., 2997 Broadmoor Valley Road, Colorado Springs, CO 80906; (719) 576-4990.

Maine

Look for lots of Quebecers who come to vacation in the natural beauty "down east." There are 6,000 lakes in Maine; the Allagash Wilderness Waterway—a 92-mile chain of lakes and river—is a popular canoe wilderness trip, and the Penobscot River Corridor is great for canoeing and fishing. ◆ Winter brings snow, snow, and more snow—and some of the best snowmobiling in the country, primarily in the western mountains. Groomed, maintained, and marked trail networks take riders as far north as the Canadian maritime, or over to neighboring states. ◆ Alpine skiing is the top winter sport, with 13 ski areas, including Sunday River and Sugarloaf/USA. Among the most popular skiing events is the Bust And Burn and Legends of Freestyle on White Heat (April at Sunday River). ◆ And the Rangeley Lakes Sled Dog Race draws nearly 130 teams each March.

▶ SPECTATOR VENUES

College Sports

UNIVERSITY OF MAINE BLACK BEARS
Orono **[P. 51, H-5]**; (207) 581-1058. Alumni, capacity 10,000. Bangor Audi, capacity 6,500.

Hockey

CUMBERLAND COUNTY CIVIC CENTER
1 Civic Center Plaza, Portland **[P. 51, N-5]**. Capacity: 6,726.
Maine Mariners (American Hockey League); (207) 775-3411. Franchise began in 1977. Broadcasts by WGAN AM-Portland, ME, WSME AM-Sanford, ME, WIDE AM-Biddeford, ME, WJTO AM-Bath, ME, WXGL AM-Lewiston, ME, WFAU AM-Augusta, ME, WGME TV 13, WCSH TV6, WMTW TV 8, WPXT TV 51.

Horse Racing

BANGOR RACEWAY
100 Dutton Street, Bangor **[P. 51, N-7]**; (207) 947-3313. Opened in 1849. Clubhouse capacity: 100. Grandstand capacity: 3,750. Total capacity: 5,350.
Harness season from May to July and in Oct.

SCARBOROUGH DOWNS
U.S. Route One, Scarborough **[P. 51, M-2]**; (207) 883-4331. Opened in 1950. Clubhouse capacity: 1,050. Grandstand capacity: 10,000.
Harness season from Mar. to Dec.

Museums & Halls of Fame

MAINE SPORTS HALL OF FAME
295 Fore Street, Portland **[P. 51, N-5]**; (207) 799-4555.
◆Exhibits also at Legends Sports Bar, 16 Union Street, Bangor, (207) 941-1181.

▶ OUTDOOR VENUES

National Parks

ACADIA NATIONAL PARK
Bar Harbor **[P. 50, C-2; P. 51, K-6, L-5]**. Contains 42,000 acres. **C HK BT F S R BK W SU**

State Parks

Bike Trails: BK
Boating: BT
Camping: C
Climbing: CL
Diving: DV
Fishing: F
Golfing: G
Hiking: HK
Hunting: HT
Riding: R
Surfing: SU
Swimming: S
Tennis: TE
Whitewater: WW
Winter Sports: W

ALLAGASH WILDERNESS WATERWAY
92 mile corridor of rivers and lakes in northwestern Maine **[P. 50, B-4, E-4]**. Contains NA acres. **C BT F S W**

AROOSTOOK STATE PARK
Presque Isle off US 1 **[P. 50, C-6]**. Contains 577 acres. **C HK BT F S W x**

BAXTER STATE PARK
N of Millinocket and W of Patten in north-central Maine **[P. 50, E-5]**. Contains 201,018 acres. **C HK F S W CL**

CRESCENT BEACH STATE PARK
Cape Elizabeth, S of Portland, off ME 77 **[P. 51, M-2]**. Contains 243 acres. **S W**

LAKE ST. GEORGE STATE PARK
2 mi. W of Liberty on ME 3 **[P. 51, K-4]**. Contains 360 acres. **C BT F S W**

MOUNT BLUE STATE PARK
Near Weld **[P. 51, K-4]**. Contains 4,398 acres. **C HK BT F S W**

PEAKS-KENNY STATE PARK
6 mi. N of Dover-Foxcroft on ME 153 **[P. 50, G-4]**. Contains 839 acres. **C HK BT F S**

SEBAGO LAKE STATE PARK
3 mi. S of Naples on US 302 **[P. 51, L-2]**. Contains 1,300 acres. **C HK BT F S**

WARREN ISLAND STATE PARK
Penobscot Bay **[P. 51, K-5]**. Contains 70 acres. **C HK F**

Skiing

ALPINE SKIING

SADDLEBACK SKI & SUMMER LAKE PRESERVE
Saddleback Mountain Road, Rangeley **[P. 51, H-2]**; (207) 864-5671.
Vertical drop is 1,830 feet. Has three bars and two chairs.

SHAWNEE PEAK AT PLEASANT MOUNTAIN
Mountain Road, Bridgton **[P. 51, L-1]**; (207) 647-8444.
Vertical drop is 1,300 feet. Has one bar and four chairs.

SUGARLOAF/USA
Route 27, Carrabassett Valley **[P. 51, H-2]**; (207) 237-2000.
Vertical drop is 2,637 feet. Has two bars and eleven chairs.

SUNDAY RIVER SKI RESORT
Sunday River Road, Bethel **[P. 51, K-1]**; (207) 824-3000.
Vertical drop is 1,865 feet. Has ten chairs.

NORDIC SKIING

BEN-LOCH FARM XC CENTER
North Road, Dixmont **[P. 51, J-4]**; (207) 257-4768.

HARRIS FARM XC SKI CENTER
Buzzell Road, Biddeford **[P. 51, M-2]**; (207) 499-2678.

SKI NORDIC AT SADDLEBACK
Saddleback Mountain, Rangley **[P. 51, H-2]**; (207) 864-5671.

SUNDAY RIVER XC CENTER
Sunday River Skiway Road, Bethel **[P. 51, K-1]**; (207) 824-2410.

TROLL VALLEY LODGE
Red School House Road, Farmington **[P. 51, J-2]**; (207) 778-2830.

▶ ACTIVE SPORTS

ADVENTURE: Hurricane Island Outward Bound School, PO Box 429, Rockland; (800) 341-1744.

AEROBICS: AFAA, 16 Knowlton Street, Camden; (207) 236-6531.

BASEBALL: Little League Baseball Eastern Region HQ, PO Box 3485, Williamsport, PA; (717) 326-1921. • **Pony Baseball-Softball,** 2 Byrnes Ln. E., Sayreville, NJ; (718) 692-0444. • **American Legion Baseball,** 6 Hunton Pl., Auburn; (207) 783-6396. • **Babe Ruth Baseball,** Ernest P. Papazoglou, 71 Tracy Ave., Lynn, MA; (617) 595-7603.

BOARDSAILING: Port Sports , Portland; (207) 775-6080. • **USWA Regional Director,** Bayview Bus Park Unit 10, Gilford, NH; (603) 293-2727.

BOWLING: American Bowling Congress, 5301 S. 76th St., Greendale, WI; (414) 421-6400.

CANOEING & KAYAKING: ACA New England Vice Commodore, 785 Bow Ln., Middleton, CT.

CYCLING: LAW New England Regional Director, PO Box 305, Atkinson, NH; (603) 362-4572. • **USCF Maine/New Hampshire Representative,** 34 Taschereau Blvd, Nashua, NH; (603) 888-8657.

FITNESS: National Strength and Conditioning Ass'n State Director, c/o Sports Medicine East, 45 Leavitt Street, Skowhegan; (207) 474-8847.

FOOTBALL: Pop Warner Football, 1315 Walnut Street, Suite 1632, Philadelphia, PA; (215) 735-1450.

GOLF: Maine State Golf Association, 40 Pierce Street, Gardiner; (207) 548-7130. • **PGA New England Section,** 1 Audubon Rd., Wakefield, MA; (617) 246-4653.

HIKING & CLIMBING: The Appalachian Mountain Club , 5 Joy St., Boston, MA; (617) 523-0636.

STATBOX

POPULATION: 1,200,000
SQUARE MILES: 33,215
TIME ZONE: Eastern
MOTTO: Dirigo (I lead)
BIRD: Chickadee
TREE: White Pine
CAPITAL: Augusta
AVERAGE ANNUAL RAINFALL: 40" (no.); 42 (so.); 46 (coastal)
MEAN TEMP: 20 (winter); 70 (summer)
MAJOR LEAGUE TEAMS: 0
NATIONAL PARK ACREAGE: 205,896
STATE PARK ACREAGE: 81,917
HIGHEST ELEVATION: 5,268'
LOWEST ELEVATION: sea level
WATERWAYS: 32,000 miles of rivers and streams; 6,000 lakes and ponds

HOCKEY: USA Hockey New England Registrar, 15 Orange Street, Rumford, RI; (401) 438-2954.

HUNTING & FISHING: Department of Inland Fisheries & Wildlife, 284 State St., State House #41, Augusta; (207) 289-2766. • **Trout Unlimited,** 540 Duck Pond Dr., Westbrook; (207) 854-6191.

LACROSSE: Lacrosse Foundation Chapter, PO Box 753, Portland; (207) 772-1315.

RACQUETBALL: AARA, 25 High Street, Yarmouth; (207) 846-4236.

RODEO: PRCA First Frontier Circuit, 5982 Summit Bridge Rd., Townsend, DE; (302) 378-4551.

RUNNING: RRCA ME State Rep., 172 Bradley St., Portland; (207) 772-5781.

SKATING: Northeastern Skating Association, 1477 Beacon Street, #69, Brookline, MA; (617) 731-9411. • **USFSA,** 20 First Street, Colorado Springs, CO; (719) 635-5200.

SOCCER: Maine State YSA, 23 Barrel Lane, York; (207) 363-3268. • **AYSO Regional Director,** 5403 W. 138th Street, Hawthorne, CA; (800) 421-5700.

SOFTBALL: Portland ASA, 21 Nelson Rd., South Portland; (207) 767-2971.

SQUASH: Bowdoin College (USSRA), Brunswick; (207) 725-3000. • **Portland YMCA,** Portland; (207) 874-1111.

TENNIS: Recreational TEAMTENNIS East Region, National Program Coordinator, 246 N. Reservoir St., Lancaster, PA; (800) 633-6122. • **New England USTA,** PO Box 587, Needham Heights, MA; (617) 964-2030.

WHITEWATER RAFTING: Eastern River Expeditions , Moosehead Lake, PO Box 1173, Greenville; (207) 695-2411. • **Wilderness Expeditions, Inc. ,** PO Box 41-EP, on Moosehead Lake, Rockwood; (207) 534-2242.

Tip Offs — Two New MLB Teams

As the Sports Atlas went to press, two new National League baseball franchises were provisionally approved, to begin play in 1993.

Denver Mile High Stadium, 1990 West Eliot, Denver. Built in 1948. Total capacity: 76,000. **Denver franchise,** (NL West), (303) 866-0428. Franchise begins in 1993. Broadcast outlets and affiliates TBA.

Joe Robbie Stadium, 2269 N.W. 199th Street, Miami. Built in 1987. Capacity: 50,000 for baseball. **Miami franchise** (NL East), (305) 623-6100. Franchise begins in 1993. Broadcast outlets and affiliates TBA.

Maryland

Short-centerfield in the Baltimore Orioles' new ballpark (opening 1992) occupies the spot on which Babe Ruth's grandfather operated a saloon, where the Bambino purportedly spent a good part of his childhood; his nearby birthplace is the site of the Babe Ruth Museum. ◆ The Maryland Jockey Club, which operates Baltimore's Pimlico track, is the nation's oldest sporting association, formed in 1743. George Washington frequented its races at Annapolis. These days, Pimlico hosts the Preakness Stakes in June. ◆ Some of the country's best fishing, sailing, crabbing, and clamming is available on Chesapeake Bay. ◆ The University of Maryland at College Park fields respectable football and basketball teams in the powerful Atlantic Coast Conference; Annapolis is home to the U.S. Naval Academy, another hotbed for football and basketball.

▶ SPECTATOR VENUES

Baseball

HARRY GROVE STADIUM
6201 New Design Road, Frederick **[P. 52, C-7]**. Capacity: 4,500
Frederick Keys (Carolina League, Class A); (301) 662-0013. Entered League in 1989. Broadcasts by WQSI 820AM. MLB affiliation, Baltimore Orioles.

MEMORIAL STADIUM
100 E. 33rd St., Baltimore **[P. 54, B-3]**. Built in 1954. Capacity: 53,371
◆Has the best crab cake in the majors. The Orioles will abandon this home after the '91 season. New stadium under construction for 1992, designed to recapture old-style, intimate ball yard feel.
Baltimore Orioles (AL East); (301) 243-9800. Franchise began in 1901. Broadcasts by WBAL 1090 AM, WMAR Channel 2, Home Team Sports Cable. Affiliates: Rochester, NY (AAA); Hagerstown, MD (AA); Frederick, MD (A); Geneva, IL (A); Bluefield, WV (Rookie). Spring training held in Sarasota, FL.

MUNICIPAL STADIUM
274 East Memorial Blvd., Hagerstown **[P. 52, E-2]**. Capacity: 6,000
Hagerstown Suns (Eastern League, Class AA); (301) 791-6266. Entered League in 1988. Broadcasts by WJEJ 1240AM. MLB affiliation, Baltimore Orioles.

Basketball

CAPITAL CENTRE
1 Harry S. Truman Drive, Landover **[P. 54, F-7]**. Built in 1973. Capacity: 18,756.
◆The Bullets previously played in Chicago (1961-63) and Baltimore (1963-73).
Washington Bullets (NBA Eastern Conf., Atlantic Div.); (301) 773-2255. Franchise began in 1961. Broadcasts by WTOP 1500 AM, WDCA Channel 20, Home Team Sports.

Bowling

COUNTRY CLUB LANES
9020 Pulaski Hwy., Baltimore **[P. 54, B-3]**; (301) 686-2556.
Hammer Eastern Open (LPBT), October.

FAIR LANES KINGS POINT
4111 Deer Park Road, Randallstown **[P. 54, A-1]**; (301) 521-3000.
Fair Lanes Open (PBA), March.

FAIR LANES SHADY GROVE
1520 Shady Grove Rd, Gaithersburg **[P. 53, D-8]**; (301) 948-1390.
Lady Fair Lanes Open (LPBT), April.

FAIR LANES UNIVERSITY
2031 University Blvd., Adelphi **[P. 54, E-5]**; (301) 439-1660.
Lady Fair Lanes Open, April.

College Sports

COPPIN STATE COLLEGE
2500 W. North Avenue, Baltimore **[P. 54, B-2]**; (301) 333-5488. Coppin Center, capacity 2,500.

JOHNS HOPKINS UNIVERSITY BLUE JAYS
Charles & 34th Streets, Baltimore **[P. 54, A-3]**; (301) 338-7490. Homewood, capacity 4,000. Newton H. White, Jr., capacity 1,200.

LOYOLA COLLEGE GREYHOUNDS
4501 N. Charles Street, Baltimore **[P. 54, A-3]**; (301) 532-5013. Reitz Arena, capacity 3,000.

MORGAN STATE UNIVERSITY GOLDEN BEARS
Coldspring Lane & Hillen Road, Baltimore **[P. 54, A-3]**; (301) 444-3050. Hughes, capacity 10,000. Hill, capacity 8,000.

MOUNT ST. MARY'S COLLEGE MOUNTAINEERS
Route 15, Emmitsburg **[P. 52, B-7]**; (301) 447-5296. Knott Arena, capacity 3,500.

TOWSON STATE UNIVERSITY TIGERS
Towson **[P. 54, A-3]**; (301) 830-2758. Minnegan, capacity 5,000. Towson Center, capacity 5,200.

U.S. NAVAL ACADEMY MIDS
Annapolis **[P. 54, B-7]**; (301) 268-6220. Navy M.C. Memorial, capacity 30,000. Halsey, capacity 5,000.

UNIVERSITY OF MARYLAND RETRIEVERS
5401 Wilkens Avenue, Baltimore **[P. 54, B-2]**; (301) 455-2126. UMBC, capacity 4,500. UMBC, capacity 4,000.

UNIVERSITY OF MARYLAND TERRAPINS
College Park **[P. 54, D-5]**; (301) 454-4705. Byrd, capacity 45,000. Cole, capacity 14,500.
◆Cole Fieldhouse is old, with a very homey feeling. Students get into it.

UNIVERSITY OF MARYLAND HAWKS
Princess Anne **[P. 53, G-12]**; (301) 651-2200. Hawks, capacity 4,500. Tawes, capacity 3,500.

WESTERN MARYLAND COLLEGE TERRORS
Westminster **[P. 53, B-8]**; (301) 857-2580. Bair, capacity 3,000. PE Center, capacity 2,000.

Hockey

BALTIMORE ARENA
201 W. Baltimore Street, Suite 412, Baltimore **[P. 54, B-3]**. Capacity: 11,025.
Baltimore SkipJacks (American Hockey League); (301) 727-0703. Franchise began in 1982. Broadcasts by WLIF 1300 AM.

CAPITAL CENTRE
1 Harry S. Truman Dr., Landover **[P. 54, F-7]**. Built in 1973. Capacity: 18,130.
◆A tough ticket to get with the Caps' recent success. No metro rail.
Washington Capitals (NHL, Wales Conference, Patrick Division); (301) 386-7000. Franchise began in 1974. Broadcasts by WMAL (630 AM), WCAO (600 AM), WDCA-TV (Channel 20), Home Team Sports (Cable).

USA SNAPSHOTS®

A look at statistics that shape the sports world

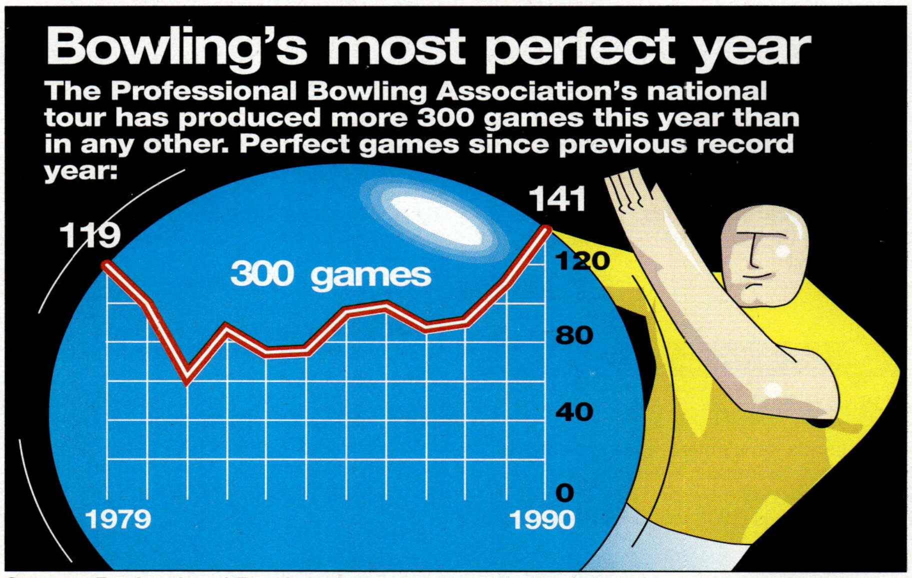

Bowling's most perfect year
The Professional Bowling Association's national tour has produced more 300 games this year than in any other. Perfect games since previous record year:
119
141
300 games
120
80
40
0
1979
1990

Source: Professional Bowlers Association — By Elys McLean-Ibrahim, USA TODAY

STATBOX

POPULATION: 4,216,975
SQUARE MILES: 10,460
TIME ZONE: Eastern
MOTTO: Fatti maschi parole femine (Manly deeds, womanly words)
BIRD: Baltimore Oriole
TREE: White Oak
CAPITAL: Annapolis
AVERAGE ANNUAL RAINFALL: 43"
MEAN TEMP: 55
MAJOR LEAGUE TEAMS: 3
NATIONAL PARK/FOREST ACREAGE: 47,000
STATE PARK ACREAGE: 73,159
HIGHEST ELEVATION: 3,360'
LOWEST ELEVATION: sea level
WATERWAYS: 623 square miles of inland water

Horse Racing

DELMARVA DOWNS
Routes 50 & 589, 4 mi. W of Ocean City, Berlin **[P. 53, G-14]**; (301) 641-0600. Opened in 1949. Clubhouse capacity: 400. Grandstand capacity: 4,650.
Harness season from May to Sep.
◆Simulcast year-round; live racing Memorial Day to Labor Day.

LAUREL RACE COURSE
Route 198 & Race Track Road, Laurel **[P. 53, D-9]**; (301) 725-0400. Opened in 1911. Clubhouse capacity: 2,500. Grandstand capacity: 12,000. Total capacity: 19,400. Thoroughbred season from Oct. to Mar. and July & August.

PIMLICO RACE COURSE
Hayward & Winner Ave. S, Baltimore **[P. 54, A-2]**; (301) 542-9400. Opened in 1870. Clubhouse capacity: 2,778. Grandstand capacity: 17,257.
Thoroughbred season from Mar. to July and Sep. to Oct.
◆The nation's oldest thoroughbred track after Saratoga, Pimlico is home of the Triple Crown's second race, the Preakness Stakes, held annually in May since 1873 (with the exception of nineteen years from 1890 to 1909, when the race moved to New York). The track is operated by the nation's oldest sporting association, the Maryland Jockey Club, formed in 1743 and issued a charter by congress in 1830.

ROSECROFT RACEWAY
6336 Rosecroft Drive, Fort Washington **[P. 53, E-8]**; (301) 567-4000. Opened in 1949. Clubhouse capacity: 9,000. Grandstand capacity: 6,000.
Harness season from Oct. to Sep.

TIMONIUM
2200 York Road, Timonium **[P. 53, C-9]**; (301) 252-0200. Opened in 1887. Grandstand capacity: 4,500.
Thoroughbred season from Aug. to Sep.

Museums & Halls of Fame

BABE RUTH BIRTHPLACE/BALTIMORE ORIOLES MUSEUM
216 Emory Street, Baltimore **[P. 54, B-3]**; (301) 727-1539.
◆The second largest baseball museum in America, after Cooperstown.

LACROSSE FOUNDATION NATIONAL HEADQUARTERS AND HALL OF FAME MUSEUM
113 W. University Parkway, Baltimore **[P. 54, B-3]**; (301) 235-6882.

PGA/LPGA

BETHESDA COUNTRY CLUB
7601 Bradley Blvd., Bethesda **[P. 54, D-2]**; (301) 365-1700.
◆Course was first built for women.
Mazda LPGA Championship, July. Number of holes: 72.

CONTINUED ON PAGE 167

Maryland

CONTINUED FROM PAGE 166

TOURNAMENT PLAYERS CLUB AT AVENEL
10000 Oaklyn Dr., Potomac **[P. 54, D-1]**; (301) 469-3700.
Kemper Open (PGA), May and June. Number of holes: 72.

Soccer

BALTIMORE ARENA
201 W. Baltimore Street, Baltimore **[P. 54, B-3]**. Capacity: 12,510.
Baltimore Blast (Major Soccer League); (301) 327-2100.

CEDAR LANE PARK
5081 Cedar Lane, Colombia **[P. 53, D-9]**. Capacity: 3,000.
Maryland Bays (American Professional Soccer League, Western Conference); (301) 880-0047.
◆The Bays play four of their eleven home games at RFK Stadium, which happens to be one of the venues bidding to host 1994 World Cup matches.

Yachting

U.S. NAVAL ACADEMY
Robert Crown Center, Annapolis **[P. 54, B-7]**; (301) 267-3746.
Lloyd Phoenix Trophy (USYRU Offshore Championship), Nov.

► OUTDOOR VENUES

National Parks

ASSATEAGUE ISLAND NATIONAL SEASHORE
Parallel to the Maryland coast, MD 611 off MD 50 **[P. 53, H-13]**. Contains 39,630 acres. **C HK BT F S R BK SU**

State Parks

Bike Trails: BK
Boating: BT
Camping: C
Climbing: CL
Diving: DV
Fishing: F
Golfing: G
Hiking: HK
Hunting: HT
Riding: R
Surfing: SU
Swimming: S
Tennis: TE
Whitewater: WW
Winter Sports: W

ASSATEAGUE STATE PARK
6 mi. S of Ocean City via MD 611 **[P. 53, G-14]**. Contains 755 acres. **C HK BT F S BK**

CUNNINGHAM FALLS STATE PARK
Off US 15 at Thurmont **[P. 52, C-7]**. Contains 4,950 acres. **C HK BT F S W**

DEEP CREEK LAKE STATE PARK
2 mi. NE. of Thayerville **[P. 52, C-7]**. Contains 1,888 acres. **C HK BT F S W HT**

ELK NECK STATE PARK
9 mi. S of North East on SR 272 **[P. 53, C-11]**. Contains 2,188 acres. **C HK BT F S HT**

GREENBRIER STATE PARK
10 mi. E of Hagerstown on US 40 **[P. 52, C-6]**. Contains 1,288 acres. **C HK BT F S W HT**

GUNPOWDER FALLS
Along the Little and Big Gunpowder Rivers near Kingsville **[P. 53, C-10]**. Contains 13,020 acres. **HK BT F S BK W WW**

HERRINGTON MANOR
5 mi. NW of Oakland on CR 20 **[P. 52, C-1]**. Contains 365 acres. **HK BT F S R BK W**

NEW GERMANY STATE PARK
5 mi. S of Grantsville of US 48 on New Germany Road **[P. 52, B-2]**. Contains 455 acres. **C HK BT F S W**

POCOMOKE RIVER (SHAD LANDING)
4 mi. SW of Snow Hill on US 113 **[P. 53, G-13]**. Contains 370 acres. **C HK BT F S BK**

POINT LOOKOUT STATE PARK
Point Lookout **[P. 53, H-10]**. Contains 528 acres. **C HK BT F S BK**

ROCKY GAP STATE PARK
6 mi. E of Cumberland on US 40 **[P. 52, B-3]**. Contains 2,993 acres. **C HK BT F S BK W HT**

SENECA CREEK STATE PARK
2 mi. W of Gaithersburg on MD 117 **[P. 53, D-8]**. Contains 6,109 acres. **HK BT F R BK W HT**

TUCKAHOE STATE PARK
6 mi. N of Queen Anne **[P. 53, D-11]**. Contains 3,498 acres. **C HK BT F R BK W**

Skiing

ALPINE SKIING

WISP SKI RESORT
Marsh Hill Road, McHenry **[P. 52, C-1]**; (301) 387-4911.
Vertical drop is 610 feet. Has one tow, one bar and five chairs.

NORDIC SKIING

HERRINGTON MANOR STATE PARK
Route 5, Oakland **[P. 52, C-1]**; (301) 334-9180.

NEW GERMANY CROSS COUNTRY
Route 2, Grantsville **[P. 52, B-2]**; (301) 895-5453.

► ACTIVE SPORTS

ADVENTURE: Hurricane Island Outward Bound School, PO Box 429, Rockland, ME; (800) 341-1744.

AEROBICS: AFAA, 2003 Dumont Rd., Timonium; (301) 252-5280.

BASEBALL: Little League Baseball Eastern Region HQ, PO Box 3485, Williamsport, PA; (717) 326-1921. • **American Legion Baseball,** 255 Nanticoke Rd., Baltimore; (301) 686-0428. • **Babe Ruth Baseball,** Raymond P. Jones, 300 Lodge St., Piscataway, NJ; (201) 469-5841. • **Men's Senior Baseball League - Annapolis,** 9306 Hallsboro Cir., #302, Baltimore; (301) 668-0620. • **Men's Senior Baseball League - Chesapeake,** 996 Headwater Road, Annapolis; (301) 267-7417.

BILLIARDS: Gentleman's Cue, 312 Reistertown, Pikesville; (301) 653-0407.

BOARDSAILING: American Windsurfing Schools, Annapolis; (301) 757-4574. • **Baltimore Boardsailing Academy,** Timonium; (301) 666-9463. • **USWA Regional Director,** 1912 MacCumber Ln., Wilmington, NC; (919) 256-3553. • **Windsurfing Unlimited,** Bethesda; (301) 951-0705.

BOWLING: American Bowling Congress, 5301 S. 76th St., Greendale, WI; (414) 421-6400.

CANOEING & KAYAKING: ACA Middle States Vice Commodore, 10236 Raider Ln., Fairfax, VA; (703) 359-2594.

CYCLING: LAW Coastal Regional Director, 205 E. Joppa Road, Baltimore; (301) 828-8604. • **USCF Maryland/Delaware Representative,** PO Box 131, Riva; (301) 956-2767.

FITNESS: Commission on Physical Fitness, 4201 Patterson Ave., Baltimore; (301) 764-2965

FOOTBALL: Pop Warner Football, 1315 Walnut Street, Suite 1632, Philadelphia, PA; (215) 735-1450. • **U.S. Flag Football League,** 9620 Dundawn Road, Baltimore; (301) 256-2816.

GOLF: Maryland State Golf Association, PO Box 16289, Baltimore; (301) 467-8899. • **PGA Middle Atlantic Section,** 7270 Cradlerock Way, Columbia; (301) 621-8320. • **PGA Tri-State Section,** 221 Sherwood Dr., Monaca, PA; (412) 774-2224.

HIKING & CLIMBING: C & O Canal Association (AHS), Box 166, Glen Echo; (703) 356-1809. • **Center Hiking Club (AHS),** 4608 Coachway Dr., Rockville; (301) 770-1977. • **Continental Divide Trail Society (AHS),** PO Box 30002, Bethesda; (301) 493-4080. • **Mountain Club of Maryland (AHS),** 5229 Benson Ave., Baltimore. • **Potomac Appalachian Trail Club,** 1718 N St. Northwest, Washington, DC; (202) 638-5306. • **Potomac Sierra Club Chapter,** 1116 C West St., Annapolis; (301) 268-3935. • **The Appalachian Mountain Club,** 5 Joy St., Boston, MA; (617) 523-0636.

Tip Offs

Surf's Up

The sport of surfing is gaining a truly major league image, replete with television exposure, big money and bigger crowds — the annual Ocean Pacific Professional Surfing Championship at the beginning of August in Huntington Beach, California draws more than 100,000 spectators.

Surfers who manage to execute the most radical and controlled maneuvers in the most critical section of the best waves for the longest distance, stand the best chance of doing well. The maneuvers are judged with an emphasis on big, explosive moves that bring out the fullest potential of both the wave and the surfer.

The following are a few of the best spots to catch world-class action:

- **Malibu, CA**
- **Rincon Bay, Santa Barbara, CA**
- **The Ranch, Lompoc, CA**
- **Sebastian Inlet, FL**
- **Honolua Bay, Maui, HI**
- **Banzai Pipeline, Oahu, HI**
- **Cape Hatteras, NC**
- **Padang Padang, Bali, Indonesia**
- **Ragland Point, New Zealand.**

HOCKEY: USA Hockey Southeastern Registrar, PO Box 5208, Takoma Park; (301) 622-0032.

HUNTING & FISHING: Department of Natural Resources, 580 Taylor Ave., Annapolis; (301) 974-3775. • **Sporting Adventure (Orvis),** 9191 Baltimore National Pike, Ellicott City; (301) 465-1112. • **Trout Unlimited,** 9615 Parkwood Drive, Bethesda; (301) 493-8398.

LACROSSE: Lacrosse Foundation Chapter, 6011 Osceola Rd., Bethesda; (202) 382-2466. • **Lacrosse Foundation Chapter,** 1705 Porter's Hill Rd., Annapolis; (301) 859-7592.

RACQUETBALL: AARA, 2076 Lord Baltimore Dr., Baltimore; (301) 298-8700.

RIDING: Maryland Horse Council, Box 4891, Timonium; (301) 261-5507.

RODEO: PRCA First Frontier Circuit, 5982 Summit Bridge Rd., Townsend, DE; (302) 378-4551.

RUNNING: RRCA MD State Rep., 12714 Viers Mill Road, Rockville; (301) 933-3939.

SCUBA: Dynamo, Inc., 8906 Rhode Island Avenue, PO Box 1019, College Park; (301) 474-6380. • **Sea Colony Aqua Sports,** 836 Ritchie Highway, Suite 4, Severna Park; (301) 544-3607. • **The Brass Anchor-Diving,** 338 East Patrick Street, PO Box 3665, Frederick; (301) 663-9363.

SHOOTING: PG County Trap and Skeet, 10400 Good Luck Road, Glenn Dale; (301) 577-7177. • **Chesapeake Gun Club,** Rt. 1, Box 76B, Henderson; (301) 758-1824. • **Fairgale Sporting Clays,** Rt. 2, Box 742, Chestertown; (301) 778-3322. • **Hopkins Game Farm,** Rt. 298, Kennedyville; (301) 348-5287. • **J & P Sporting Clays,** PO Box 111, Benton Creek Rd., Sudlersville; (301) 438-3832.

SKATING: Maryland Speedskating Association, 106 Deep Dale Dr., Timonium; (301) 252-0319. • **USFSA,** 20 First Street, Colorado Springs, CO; (719) 635-5200.

SOCCER: Maryland Soccer Ass'n, 1 Maple Ave., Baltimore; (301) 744-5864. • **Maryland State YSA,** 14313 Barkwood Dr., Rockville; (301) 460-9318. • **AYSO Regional Director,** 4014 Oneida St., New Hartford, NY; (315) 737-5610.

SOFTBALL: Maryland ASA, 8231 Old Harford Rd., Baltimore; (301) 661-0124. • **Metropolitan Washington DC ASA,** 2410 Springlake Court W., Gambrills; (301) 621-7152.

SQUASH: Baltimore Raquet & Fitness (USSRA), Baltimore; (301) 625-6400. • **Racquet Club of Roland Park (USSRA),** Baltimore; (301) 243-7434.

SWIMMING: LMSC Maryland Registrar, 7919 Main Falls Circle, Catonsville; (301) 788-2964.

TABLE TENNIS: USTTA State Coordinator, 5134 Durham Rd., West, Columbia; (301) 730-5626.

TENNIS: Recreational TEAMTENNIS East Region, National Program Coordinator, 246 N. Reservoir St., Lancaster, PA; (800) 633-6122. • **Mid-Atlantic USTA,** PO Drawer F, Springfield, VA; (703) 321-9045.

TRIATHLON: Tri-Maryland Triathlon Club, PO Box 28477, Baltimore; (301) 882-6103.

WHITEWATER RAFTING: River and Trail Outfitters, Inc. , 604 Valley Rd., Knoxville; (301) 695-5177.

Massachusetts

Massachusetts is home to two of the best-known sports shrines in the USA: Fenway Park and the Boston Garden. Another shrine worthy of mention is "Heartbreak Hill," where even the top distance runners "hit the wall" in April's venerable Boston Marathon. ◆ The Head of the Charles Regatta is one of rowing's premier events (late October). ◆ Cape Cod, Nantucket and Martha's Vineyard offer great boating, fishing, biking, horseback riding and National Seashore. Runners of all stripes flock to the Cape to compete in the Falmouth Road Race 7-Miler (mid-August) while promising young players spend summers in the Cape Cod Baseball League. ◆ In central and western Massachusetts, the Appalachian Trail and the Berkshire Hills are popular hiking destinations; Rose Ledges attracts rock climbers; the Mohawk Trail is great for biking.

▶ SPECTATOR VENUES

Baseball

FENWAY PARK
4 Yawkey Way, Boston **[P. 55, E-3]**. Built in 1912. Capacity: 34,142
◆The ultimate, bandbox jewel, with great seats in the bleachers, the Green Monster luring right-handed batters to their doom, and the Curse of Ruth still blighting New England autumns after more than half a century.
Boston Red Sox (AL East); (617) 267-9440. Franchise began in 1901. Broadcasts by WRKO-AM, WSBK Channel 38, New England Sports Network Cable TV. Affiliates: Pawtucket, RI (AAA); New Britain, CT (AA); Lynchburg, VA (A); Winter Haven, FL (A); Elmira, NY (A); Winter Haven, FL (Rookie). Spring training held in Winter Haven, FL.

WAHCONAH PARK
105 Wahconah Street, Pittsfield **[P. 56, B-2]**. Capacity: 5,200
Pittsfield Mets (New York-Penn League, Class A); (413) 499-6387. Entered League in 1989. Broadcasts by WBEC 1420-AM. MLB affiliation, New York Mets.

Basketball

BOSTON GARDEN
150 Causeway Street, Boston **[P. 55, E-3]**. Built in 1928. Capacity: 14,890.
◆Red Auerbach denies that the Garden's famous parquet floor has any dead spots, but numerous victims of Celtic magic will tell you otherwise. Other factors add to this venerable building's mystique: the sweltering visitors' locker room — where the heat has allegedly been left on during playoff games; the electrical problems; the unexplained appearance of a pigeon on the court during a conference semifinal, after which Larry Bird decisively shifted the game's momentum in favor of the Celtics. Nonetheless, the intimate hall with the Celtic's 16 championship banners hanging from the ceiling is one of basketball's enduring images. As a farewell present during his final visit, the team gave arch-nemesis Kareem Abdul-Jabbar a piece of the parquet.
Boston Celtics (NBA Eastern Conf., Atlantic Division); (617) 523-6050. Franchise began in 1946. Broadcasts by WEEI 590 AM, WFTX Channel 25, SportsChannel.

College Sports

BOSTON COLLEGE EAGLES
Chestnut Hill **[P. 55, E-2]**; (617) 552-3000. Alumni, capacity 32,000. Silvio O. Conte Forum.

BOSTON UNIVERSITY TERRIERS
285 Babcock Street, Boston **[P. 55, E-3]**; (617) 353-4630. Nickerson Field, capacity 17,500. Brown Arena, capacity 5,000.

BRANDEIS UNIVERSITY JUDGES
415 South Street, Waltham **[P. 55, E-1]**; (617) 736-3630. Gordon Field, capacity 2,000.

HARVARD UNIVERSITY CRIMSON
60 John F. Kennedy St., Cambridge **[P. 55, E-3]**; (617) 495-2204. Harvard, capacity 37,289.

HOLY CROSS COLLEGE CRUSADERS
College Street, Worcester **[P. 56, F-4]**; (508) 793-2571. Fitton Field, capacity 25,000. Hart Recreation Center, capacity 4,000.
◆A tiny gym, Hart Center gives the Crusaders a nice homecourt advantage. The building is named after Father Hart, who ran the school's intramural sports program for more than half a century.

NICHOLS COLLEGE BISONS
Dudley Hill, Dudley **[P. 56, D-7]**; (617) 943-1560. Nichols, capacity 2,500. Chalmers, capacity 2,500.

NORTHEASTERN UNIVERSITY HUSKIES
360 Huntington Avenue, Boston **[P. 55, E-3]**; (617) 437-2672. Parsons Field, capacity 7,000. Matthews, capacity 6,000.

SPRINGFIELD COLLEGE CHIEFS
Alden Street, Springfield **[P. 56, F-2]**; (413) 788-3332. Benedum Field, capacity 6,000. Blake Arena PE Complex, capacity 2,000.

UNIVERSITY OF MASSACHUSETTS-AMHERST MINUTEMEN
Amherst **[P. 56, C-5]**; (413) 545-1556. McGuirk Alumni, capacity 17,000. Curry Hicks, capacity 4,200.

UNIVERSITY OF MASSACHUSETTS-BOSTON BEACONS
Boston **[P. 55, F-4]**; (617) 287-7800. Clark Athletic Center, capacity 3,500.

WILLIAMS COLLEGE EPHS
Williamstown **[P. 56, A-2]**; (413) 597-2366. Weston Field, capacity 7,300. Towne.

WORCESTER POLYTECHNIC INSTITUTE ENGINEERS
Worcester **[P. 56, F-4]**; (508) 831-5243. Alumni Field, capacity 2,300. Harrington, capacity 3,000.

Football

FOXBORO STADIUM
Route 1, Foxboro **[P. 57, D-9]**. Built in 1971. Capacity: 60,794.
◆A good 40-minute drive from downtown Boston. The Pats' demise means seats are usually available day of game.
New England Patriots (AFC Eastern Division); (508) 543-8200. Franchise began in 1960. Broadcasts by WHDH.

Hockey

BOSTON GARDEN
Causeway Street, off North Station, Boston **[P. 55, E-3]**. Built in 1928. Capacity: 14,448.
◆Rabid fans. Old and somewhat dirty arena.
Boston Bruins (NHL, Wales Conference, Adams Division); (617) 227-3206. Franchise began in 1924. Broadcasts by WEEI (590 AM), Bruins Radio Network, New England Sports Network, WSBK TV-3

SPRINGFIELD CIVIC CENTER
58 Dwight St., Springfield **[P. 56, F-1]**. Capacity: 7,602.
Springfield Indians(American Hockey League); (413) 736-4546. Franchise began in 1936. Broadcasts by WTCC 90.7 FM, Continental Cablevision.

USA SNAPSHOTS®

A look at statistics that shape the sports world

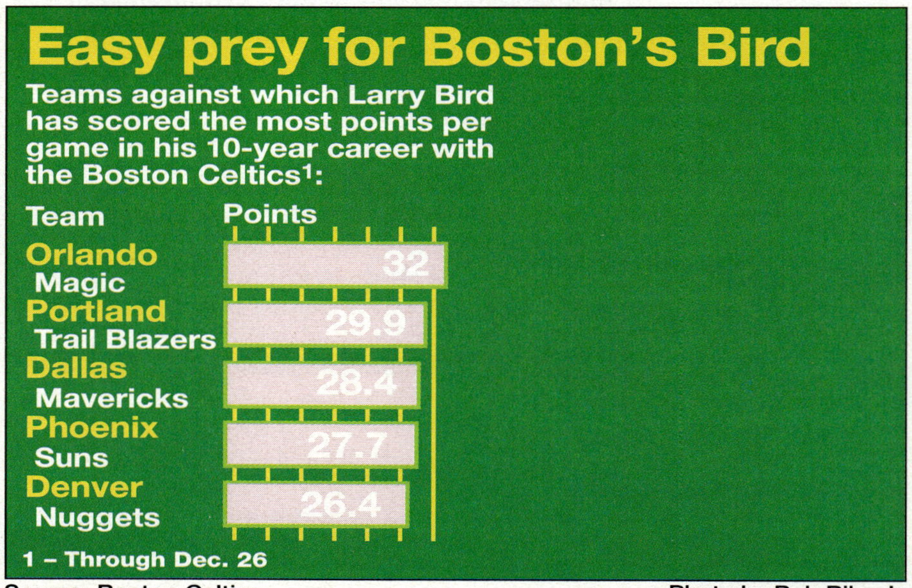

Easy prey for Boston's Bird
Teams against which Larry Bird has scored the most points per game in his 10-year career with the Boston Celtics[1]:
Team
Points
Orlando Magic
32
Portland Trail Blazers
29.9
Dallas Mavericks
28.4
Phoenix Suns
27.7
Denver Nuggets
26.4
1 – Through Dec. 26

Source: Boston Celtics — Photo by Bob Riha Jr.

STATBOX

POPULATION: 5,921,000
SQUARE MILES: 7,839
TIME ZONE: Eastern
MOTTO: By the sword we seek peace, but peace only under liberty.
BIRD: Chickadee
TREE: American Elm
CAPITAL: Boston
AVERAGE ANNUAL RAINFALL: 44"
MEAN TEMP: 29 (Jan.); 73 (June)
MAJOR LEAGUE TEAMS: 4
NATIONAL PARK/FOREST ACREAGE: 30,000
STATE PARK: 277,155 square miles
HIGHEST ELEVATION: 3,563'
LOWEST ELEVATION: sea level
WATERWAYS: 390 square miles of inland water

Horse Racing

MARSHFIELD FAIR
Main Street, Marshfield **[P. 57, D-11]**; (617) 834-6629. Opened in 1867. Grandstand capacity: 1,600.
Thoroughbred season in Aug.
◆Ten day season.

THREE COUNTY FAIRGROUNDS
Off Route 9, Northampton **[P. 56, C-4]**; (413) 584-2237. Opened in 1943. Clubhouse capacity: 250. Grandstand capacity: 1,600. Total capacity: 12,950.
Thoroughbred season from Aug. to Sep.
◆Nine days of racing.

Museums & Halls of Fame

HELLENIC SPORTS HALL OF FAME
180 Bolton Street, Marlborough **[P. 57, C-8]**; (617) 485-0736.

NAISMITH MEMORIAL BASKETBALL HALL OF FAME
1150 W. Columbus Ave., Springfield **[P. 56, F-1]**; (413) 781-6500.
◆Fun-spirited exhibits, including a tunnel decorated with hundreds of shoes, are geared for viewer participation.

SPORTS MUSEUM OF NEW ENGLAND
1175 Soldiers Field Rd., Boston **[P. 55, E-3]**; (617) 787-7678.

VOLLEYBALL HALL OF FAME AT HOLYOKE, INC.
444 Dwight St., Holyoke **[P. 56, D-4]**; (413) 536-0926.

PGA/LPGA

BLUE HILL COUNTRY CLUB
23 Pecunit Street, Canton **[P. 57, D-10]**; (508) 345-6185.
LPGA Bay State Classic, Aug. Number of holes: 72.

NASHAWTUC COUNTRY CLUB
1861 Sudbury Rd., Concord **[P. 57, B-9]**; (508) 369-6420.
Digital Seniors Classic (Senior PGA), June. Number of holes: 54.

PLEASANT VALLEY COUNTRY CLUB
Armsby Rd., Sutton **[P. 56, D-7]**; (508) 865-1491.
New England Classic (PGA), July. Number of holes: 72.

Polo

MYOPIA POLO CLUB
Off Box Rd., S. Hamilton **[P. 57, B-11]**; (508) 468-4433.

Tennis

WORCESTER CENTRUM
50 Foster St., Worcester **[P. 56, F-4]**; (508) 755-6800. Surface is Supreme.
◆Not currently hosting any major tourna-

CONTINUED ON PAGE 169

Massachusetts

CONTINUED FROM PAGE 168

ments. Previously hosted WTA's Virginia Slims of New England.

Track & Field

ALBERT GORDON TRACK & FIELD FACILITY
Harvard University, Cambridge **[P. 55, E-3]**; (617) 647-1221.
GBTC Invitational, Jan.
New England Invitational Championships, Jan.

STREETS OF BOSTON
Starting line at Route 135 in Hopkinton, Boston **[P. 57, D-8]**; (508) 435-6905.
Boston Marathon, April.

THE COMMONWEALTH ARMORY
Gaffrey Street, Boston University, Boston; (617) 353-2911.
Terrier Classic, Jan.

Yachting

EASTERN YACHT CLUB
Foster St. on Marblehead Neck, in town of Marblehead **[P. 57, B-11]**; (617) 631-1400.
◆Host of U.S. Women's Singlehanded, Doublehanded and Boardsailing Championships in 1990.

OUTDOOR VENUES

National Parks

CAPE COD NATIONAL SEASHORE
From South Wellfleet to Provincetown **[P. 57, E-14]**. Contains 43,500 acres. **HK BT F S BK SU**

State Parks

- Bike Trails:BK
- Boating: BT
- Camping: C
- Climbing: CL
- Diving: DV
- Fishing: F
- Golfing: G
- Hiking: HK
- Hunting: HT
- Riding: R
- Surfing: SU
- Swimming: S
- Tennis: TE
- Whitewater: WW
- Winter Sports: W

BRIMFIELD STATE FOREST
2 mi. S of Brimfield off US 20 **[P. 56, D-6]**. Contains 3,290 acres. **C HK F S R W**

COCHITUATE STATE PARK
3 mi. E of Framingham off MA 30 **[P. 57, C-9]**. Contains 1,012 acres. **BT F S**

DOUGLAS S. FOREST
Douglas **[P. 57, D-8]**. Contains 3,752 acres. **HK BT F S R W**

ERVING STATE PARK
2 mi. NE of Erving on MA 2A **[P. 56, B-5]**. Contains 4,779 acres. **C HK BT F S R**

HAROLD PARKER STATE PARK
2 mi. NW of Middleton off MA 114 **[P. 57, B-10]**. Contains 3,400 acres. **C HK F S R**

HOLLAND STATE PARK
2 mi. N of Holland off MA 20 **[P. 56, D-6]**. Contains 35 acres. **BT F S R**

HORSENECK BEACH STATE RESERVATION
14 mi. S of Fall River on MA 88 at Horseneck Beach **[P. 57, G-10]**. Contains 594 acres. **C Boating F S**

LAKE DENNISON STATE RECREATION AREA
Baldwinville **[P. 56, B-6]**. Contains 9,000 acres. **C HK BT F S R W**

MASSASOIT STATE PARK
Taunton **[P. 57, E-10]**. Contains 1,500 acres. **C BT F S R BK W**

MOUNT WASHINGTON STATE PARK
SW of South Egremont off MA 41 on Mount Washington Road **[P. 56, D-1]**. Contains 4,134 acres. **C HK F R HT**

MYLES STANDISH STATE PARK
6 mi. W of Plymouth off US 3 **[P. 57, E-11]**. Contains 14,000 acres. **C HK BT F S R BK W**

PITTSFIELD STATE FOREST
4 mi. NW of Pittsfield **[P. 56, B-2]**. Contains 9,695 acres. **C HK F S R W**

ROLAND C. NICKERSON STATE PARK
1 mi. E of East Brewster off MA 6A **[P. 57, E-14]**. Contains 1,779 acres. **C HK BT F S R BK W**

SALISBURY STATE PARK
Salisbury **[P. 57, A-11]**. Contains 520 acres. **C HK BT F S**

SANDISFIELD STATE PARK
1 mi. W of Sandisfield off MA 57 **[P. 56, D-2]**. Contains 4,060 acres. **C HK BT F S R**

SAVOY MOUNTAIN STATE PARK
6 mi. SE of North Adams off MA 2 **[P. 56, B-3]**. Contains 10,500 acres. **C HK BT F S R W**

TOLLAND STATE PARK
3 mi. N of New Boston off MA 8 **[P. 56, D-3]**. Contains 8,000 acres. **C HK BT F S R**

WACHUSETT MOUNTAIN STATE PARK
SW of Shirley **[P. 56, B-7]**. Contains 1,950 acres. **HK R W**

WOMPATUCK STATE PARK
off MA 228, E of Hingham **[P. 57, D-11]**. Contains 3,000 acres. **C HK F R BK W**

Skiing

ALPINE SKIING

BLUE HILLS SKI AREA
Canton **[P. 55, H-3]**; (617) 828-7490.
Vertical drop is 365 feet. Has two bars and one chair.

BOUSQUET SKI AREA
Dan Fox Drive, Pittsfield **[P. 56, C-1]**; (413) 442-8316.
Vertical drop is 750 feet. Has three tows and two chairs.

BRODIE MOUNTAIN SKI RESORT
On Route 7, New Ashford **[P. 56, B-2]**; (413) 443-4752.
Vertical drop is 1,250 feet. Has two tows and four chairs.

BUTTERNUT BASIN SKI AREA
On Route 23, Great Barrington **[P. 56, D-2]**; (413) 528-2000.
Vertical drop is 1,000 feet. Has one bar and six chairs.

JIMINY PEAK (THE MOUNTAIN RESORT)
Carey Road, Hancock **[P. 56, B-2]**; (413) 738-5500.
Vertical drop is 1,140 feet. Has one bar and four chairs.

MT. TOM SKI AREA
On Route 5, Holyoke **[P. 56, C-4]**; (413) 536-0416.
Vertical drop is 680 feet. Has two tows, three bars and three chairs.

NASHOBA VALLEY SKI AREA
Powers Road, Westford **[P. 57, B-9]**; (508) 692-3033.
Vertical drop is 240 feet. Has five tows, one bar and three chairs.

WACHUSETT MOUNTAIN
499 Mountain Road, Princeton **[P. 56, B-7]**; (508) 464-5101.
Vertical drop is 1,000 feet. Has one tow and three chairs.

NORDIC SKIING

BROOKFIELD ORCHARDS
12 Lincoln Road, North Brookfield **[P. 56, C-6]**; (508) 867-6858.

BUCKSTEEP CROSS COUNTRY
Washington Mountain Road, Washington **[P. 56, C-6]**; (413) 623-6651.

BUTTERNUT CROSS COUNTRY
Route 23, Great Barrington **[P. 56, D-2]**; (413) 528-0610.

CUMMINGTON FARM VILLAGE
South Street, Cummington **[P. 56, B-3]**; (800) 562-9666.

FRIENDS OF THE BLUE HILLS
Blue Hill Reservation, Milton **[P. 55, H-3]**; (617) 326-0079.

HICKORY HILL XC CENTER
Buffington Hill Road, Worthington **[P. 56, C-3]**; (413) 238-5813.

MAPLE CORNER FARM
Beech Hill Road, Granville **[P. 56, D-3]**; (413) 357-6697.

NORTHFIELD MOUNTAIN
Route 63, Northfield **[P. 56, A-5]**; (413) 659-3713.

ROLLING GREEN SKI CENTER
Sheraton Golf & Fitness Center, Andover **[P. 57, B-10]**; (508) 475-4066.

STOW ACRES COUNTRY CLUB
58 Randall Road, Stow **[P. 57, C-8]**; (508) 568-8690.

STUMP SPROUTS SKI & LODGE
West Hill Road, West Hawley **[P. 56, B-3]**; (413) 339-4265.

WESTON CROSS COUNTRY
Park Road, Weston **[P. 57, C-9]**; (617) 891-6575.

ACTIVE SPORTS

ADVENTURE: Hurricane Island Outward Bound School, PO Box 429, Rockland, ME; (800) 341-1744.

AEROBICS: AFAA, 120 High Street, Mansfield; (508) 460-0427.

BASEBALL: Little League Baseball Eastern Region HQ, PO Box 3485, Williamsport, PA; (717) 326-1921. • **Pony Baseball-Softball,** 2 Byrnes Ln. E., Sayreville, NJ; (718) 692-0444. • **American Legion Baseball,** 491 Warren St., Fall River; (508) 679-6042. • **Men's Senior Baseball League - Boston,** 1026 Boylston Street, Newton; (617) 244-1324.

BILLIARDS: Jillian's Billiard Club, 145 Ipswich St., Boston; (617) 437-0300. • **The Charlie Horse,** 1235 Bedford St., North Abington; (617) 871-3424.

BOARDSAILING: Community Boating, Inc., Boston; (617) 523-1038. • **Force 5 Water Sports,** Nantucket; (508) 228-0700. • **Madd Mike's Windsurfing,** Boston; (617) 451-6181. • **Ski Market,** Boston; (617) 731-6100. • **USWA Regional Director,** Bayview Bus Park Unit 10, Gilford, NH; (603) 293-2727. • **Wind's Up,** Vineyard Haven; (508) 693-4252.

BOWLING: American Bowling Congress, 5301 S. 76th St., Greendale, WI; (414) 421-6400.

CANOEING & KAYAKING: ACA New England Vice Commodore, 785 Bow Ln., Middleton, CT.

CYCLING: Greater Boston AYH Council, 1020 Commonwealth Ave., Boston; (617) 731-5430. • **LAW New England Regional Director,** PO Box 305, Atkinson, NH; (603) 362-4572. • **USCF Massachusetts/Rhode Island Representative,** 98 Franklin Ave., Wollaston; (617) 328-8704.

FITNESS: Governor's Committee on Physical Fitness & Sports, 1395 N. Main St., Randolph; (617) 963-8116.

FOOTBALL: Pop Warner Football, 1315 Walnut Street, Suite 1632, Philadelphia, PA; (215) 735-1450. • **U.S. Flag Football League,** 5834 Pine Tree Drive, Sanibel, FL; (813) 472-0544.

GOLF: Massachusetts Golf Association, 190 Park Rd., Golf House, Weston; (617) 891-4300. • **PGA New England Section,** 1 Audubon Rd., Wakefield; (617) 246-4653.

HIKING & CLIMBING: Chatham Trails Association (AHS), 36 Galloway Rd., Chelmsford; (603) 225-5797. • **New England Sierra Club Chapter,** 3 Joy St., Boston; (617) 227-5339. • **The Appalachian Mountain Club,** 5 Joy St., Boston; (617) 523-0636.

HOCKEY: USA Hockey Massachusetts Registrar, 83 Maple Street, Wenham; (508) 774-2813.

HUNTING & FISHING: Department of Fisheries, Wildlife & Environmental Law Enforcement, 100 Cambridge St., Room 1902, Boston; (617) 727-3151. • **Points North Outfitters (Orvis),** Rt. 8-Adams/Cheshire Line, The Berkshires, Adams; (413) 743-4030. • **Trout Unlimited,** 33 Jericho Path, Falmouth; (508) 548-4087. • **Wayland Orvis Shop,** 213 W. Plain St., Wayland; (508) 653-9144.

LACROSSE: Lacrosse Foundation Chapter, Dean Junior College, 99 Main Street, Franklin; (617) 528-9100.

RACQUETBALL: AARA, 58 Holden Rd., Sterling; (508) 422-8010.

RODEO: PRCA First Frontier Circuit, 5982 Summit Bridge Rd., Townsend, DE; (302) 378-4551.

RUNNING: RRCA MA State Rep., 22 Winsor Dr., Dracut; (617) 957-4230.

SCUBA: Alpine Ski Sports, Inc./Divers World, 154 Faunce Corner Road, Keystone Plaza, North Dartmouth; (508) 999-0096. • **Aquarius Dive Center,** 3239 Cranberry Highway, Buzzards Bay; (508) 759-3483. • **East Coast Divers, Inc.,** 280 Worcester Road, Route 9, Framingham; (508) 620-1176. • **Northeast Scuba,** 125 Liberty Street, Danvers; (508) 777-3483.

SHOOTING: Falmouth Skeet Club, Inc., PO Box 157W, Waquoit; (508) 540-3177.

SKATING: Northeastern Skating Association, 1477 Beacon Street, #69, Brookline; (617) 731-9411. • **Northern New York Skating Association,** 116 Shore Dr., Pittsfield; (413) 443-3466. • **USFSA,** 20 First Street, Colorado Springs, CO; (719) 635-5200.

SOCCER: Massachusetts Soccer Ass'n, 2 Exeter Way, Andover; (617) 475-1035. • **Massachusetts YSA,** 311 Great Rd., Littleton; (508) 486-0516. • **AYSO Regional Director,** 5403 W. 138th Street, Hawthorne, CA; (800) 421-5700.

SOFTBALL: Massachusetts ASA, 226 Appleton Ave., Pittsfield; (413) 442-6881. • **Boston ASA,** 11 Marmion Rd., Melrose; (617) 665-5925.

SQUASH: Boston Racquet Club (USSRA), Boston; (617) 482-8881. • **Concord Acton Squash Club (USSRA),** Concord; (617) 897-2972. • **Squash Club (USSRA),** Allston; (617) 731-4177. • **Wellesley Racquet Club (USSRA),** Wellesley Hills; (617) 235-4307.

SWIMMING: LMSC New England Registrar, 1093 Main Street, Norwell; (617) 659-4594.

TENNIS: Recreational TEAMTENNIS East Region, National Program Coordinator, 246 N. Reservoir St., Lancaster, PA; (800) 633-6122. • **New England USTA,** PO Box 587, Needham Heights; (617) 964-2030.

TRIATHLON: Spoke-n-Wheel Tri Club, 386 Main Street, #4, Hudson; (508) 841-2245.

VOLLEYBALL: USVBA New England Commissioner, 366 Main Street, Hudson; (508) 562-7757.

WHITEWATER RAFTING: Zoar Outdoor Adventure, Inc., PO Box 245, Charlemont; (413) 339-4010

Michigan

One quick trip to the Michigan Sports Hall of Fame (Detroit) will give travelers a taste of the state's thriving sports history. Detroit has teams in all of the major professional sports, plus Big Ten rivals Michigan State (East Lansing) and the University of Michigan (Ann Arbor). ◆ Summertime in Motor City brings auto racing to downtown streets in the Detroit Grand Prix (see below). ◆ For more than 70 years, thousands have packed the Detroit riverfront for the American Power Boat Association's annual unlimited hydroplane championship. ◆ Michigan has more public golf courses—over 500—than any other state. ◆ With 11,000 lakes in the state, you are never more than six miles from a body of water. ◆ Nearly half of Michigan is still wooded: 18.4 million acres. That's about 14,000 campsites, where fishing and hiking abound.

STATBOX

POPULATION: 9,200,000
SQUARE MILES: 56,818
TIME ZONE: Central and Eastern
MOTTO: If you seek a pleasant peninsula, look about you.
BIRD: Robin
TREE: White Pine
CAPITAL: Lansing
AVERAGE ANNUAL RAINFALL: 31"
MEAN TEMP: 23 (Jan.); 72 (July)
MAJOR LEAGUE TEAMS: 4
NATIONAL PARK/FOREST ACREAGE: 134,400
STATE PARK ACREAGE: 260,000
HIGHEST ELEVATION: 1,980'
LOWEST ELEVATION: 572'
WATERWAYS: 36,350 miles of rivers and streams; 11,000 inland lakes

▶ SPECTATOR VENUES

Auto Racing

DETROIT STREET CIRCUIT
Foot of St. Antoine at Atwater, Detroit **[P. 60, E-5]**; (313) 259-7749 (CART) or (313) 259-5400 (SCCA). Track is 2.5-mile temporary street course.
Valvoline Detroit Grand Prix (CART PPG Indy Car World Series and SCCA Trans-Am Championship), June.

MICHIGAN INTERNATIONAL SPEEDWAY
12626 U.S. 12, Brooklyn **[P. 59, N-6]**; (517) 592-6666. Track is 2-mile oval.
Miller Genuine Draft 500 (NASCAR Winston Cup), June.
Champion Spark Plug 400, August (NASCAR Winston Cup).
Marlboro 500 (CART PPG Indy Car World Series), August.

Baseball

TIGER STADIUM
2121 Trumbull Ave., Detroit **[P. 60, E-5]**. Built in 1912. Capacity: 52,416
◆With the White Sox vacating Comiskey Park, this is now the oldest stadium used by Major League Baseball.
Detroit Tigers (AL East); (313) 962-4000. Franchise began in 1901. Broadcasts by WJR 760 AM, WDIV Channel 4. Affiliates: Toledo, OH (AAA); London, Ontario (AA); Lakeland, FL (A); Fayetteville, NC (A); Niagra Falls, NY (A); Bristol, VA (Rookie). Spring training held in Lakeland, FL.

Basketball

THE PALACE OF AUBURN HILLS
Two Championship Drive, Auburn Hills **[P. 59, L-7]**. Built in 1988. Capacity: 21,454.
◆The Pistons played their first nine seasons in Ft. Wayne, Indiana before moving to Detroit in 1957. No mass transit.
Detroit Pistons (NBA Eastern Conf., Central Div.); (313) 377-0100. Franchise began in 1948. Broadcasts by Pistons Network WWJ 950 AM, WKBD Channel 50.

WELSH AUDITORIUM
245 Monroe Avenue, NW, Grand Rapids **[P. 60, H-2]**. Capacity: 3,600.
Grand Rapids Hoops (Continental Basketball Association, National Conference, Eastern Division); (616) 451-4667. Entered League in 1989. Broadcasts by WBRD 1140 AM; WOTV NBC, Channel 8.

Bowling

SATELLITE BOWL
25451 Michigan Ave., Dearborn Heights **[P. 60, E-2]**; (313) 278-7400.
Seagram's Coolers U.S. Open (LPBT), May.

TAYLOR LANES
24800 Eureka Avenue, Taylor **[P. 60, G-2]**; (313) 946-9092.
Budweiser Touring Players Championship (PBA), December.

College Sports

CENTRAL MICHIGAN UNIVERSITY CHIPPEWAS
Rose Center, Mt. Pleasant **[P. 59, J-5]**; (517) 774-3041. Kelly/Shorts, capacity 20,083. Rose, capacity 6,000.

EASTERN MICHIGAN UNIVERSITY HURONS
Ypsilanti **[P. 59, M-7]**; (313) 487-1050. Rynearson, capacity 25,500. Bowen, capacity 5,200.

FERRIS STATE UNIVERSITY BULLDOGS
Big Rapids **[P. 59, J-4]**; (616) 592-2860. Top Taggart Field, capacity 10,000. H&PE Building, capacity 4,175.

HILLSDALE COLLEGE CHARGERS
201 Oak Street, Hillsdale **[P. 59, N-5]**; (517) 437-7341. Frank Waters, capacity 5,500. George Roche Sports Complex.

MICHIGAN STATE UNIVERSITY SPARTANS
East Lansing **[P. 60, G-5]**; (517) 355-9710. Spartan, capacity 76,000. Breslin Students Events Center, capacity 10,004.

NORTHERN MICHIGAN UNIVERSITY WILDCATS
Presque Isle Avenue, Marquette **[P. 58, C-2]**; (906) 227-2105. Memorial, capacity 8,500. C.B. Hedgecock, capacity 6,000.

UNIVERSITY OF DETROIT TITANS
4001 W. McNichols, Detroit **[P. 60, C-4]**; (313) 927-1700. Calihan Hall.

UNIVERSITY OF MICHIGAN WOLVERINES
1000 S. State Street, Ann Arbor **[P. 59, M-7]**; (313) 747-2583. Michigan, capacity 101,701. Crisler Arena, capacity 13,608.
◆Michigan Stadium becomes a city in itself on Saturdays when it fills up with 100,000-plus, who come to watch the Wolverines take the field. It's the largest college-owned structure of its kind in the country.

WESTERN MICHIGAN UNIVERSITY BRONCOS
Kalamazoo **[P. 60, G-6]**; (616) 387-3120. Waldo, capacity 30,062. Read, capacity 8,250.

Football

PONTIAC SILVERDOME
1200 Featherston Road, Pontiac **[P. 59, M-7]**. Built in 1975. Capacity: 80,500.
◆Thirty minutes from downtown Detroit. In the snowbelt.
Detroit Lions (NFC Central Division); (313) 335-4131. Franchise began in 1930. Broadcasts by WWJ.

Hockey

JOE LOUIS SPORTS ARENA
600 Civic Center Drive, Detroit **[P. 60, E-5]**. Built in 1979. Capacity: 19,275.
Detroit Red Wings (NHL, Campbell Conference, Norris Division); (313) 567-7333. Franchise began in 1926. Broadcasts by WJR-AM 760, Pro-Am Sports System (PASS Cable), WKBD-TV (Channel 50).

L.C. WALKER SPORTS ARENA
470 Western, Muskegon **[P. 59, K-2]**. Capacity: 5,043.
◆For a minor league hockey team, this is a suprisingly nice venue.
Muskegon Lumberjacks (International Hockey League); (616) 726-2939. Franchise began in 1984. Broadcasts by WLCS 98.3 FM.

WINGS STADIUM
3600 Van Rick Drive, Kalamazoo **[P. 60, H-7]**. Capacity: 5,113.
Kalamazoo Wings (International Hockey League); (616) 345-1125. Franchise began in 1974. Broadcasts by WNWN 98.5 FM.

Horse Racing

DETROIT RACE COURSE
Schoolcraft & Middlebelt, Livonia **[P. 60, D-1]**; (313) 525-7300. Opened in 1950. Clubhouse capacity: 7,500. Grandstand capacity: 11,000.
Thoroughbred season from Mar. to Nov.

HAZEL PARK HARNESS RACEWAY
1650 East Ten Mile Road, Hazel Park **[P. 60, B-4]**; (313) 398-1000. Opened in 1949. Clubhouse capacity: 3,000. Grandstand capacity: 9,200.
Harness season from Apr. to Oct.

JACKSON HARNESS RACEWAY
200 W. Ganson Street, Jackson **[P. 59, M-5]**; (517) 788-4500. Opened in 1948. Grandstand capacity: 6,500.
Harness season from Apr. to June and Aug. to Oct.

MUSKEGON RACE COURSE
4800 Harvey Street, Fruitport **[P. 59, L-5]**; (616) 798-7123. Opened in 1989. Grandstand capacity: 7,000.
Harness season from May to Oct.

NORTHVILLE DOWNS
301 South Center Street, Northville **[P. 59, M-7]**; (313) 349-1000. Opened in 1944. Clubhouse capacity: 2,000. Grandstand capacity: 5,200.
Harness season from Oct. to Apr.

SAGINAW HARNESS RACEWAY
2701 East Genesee Street, Saginaw **[P. 59, K-6]**; (517) 755-3451. Opened in 1980. Clubhouse capacity: 250. Grandstand capacity: 2,500.
Harness season from Apr. to Aug.

SPORTS CREEK RACEWAY
4290 Morrish Road, Swartz Creek **[P. 59, L-6]**; (313) 635-3333. Opened in 1986. Clubhouse capacity: 2,000. Grandstand capacity: 4,500.
Harness season from Oct. to Mar.

Museums & Halls of Fame

DETROIT TIGERS MUSEUM
44 Frank Lloyd Wright Dr., Ann Arbor **[P. 59, M-6]**; (313) 930-3818.

INTERNATIONAL AFRO-AMERICAN SPORTS HALL OF FAME AND GALLERY
600 Randolph St., Room 458, Detroit **[P. 60, D-5]**; (313) 224-0948.

MICHIGAN JEWISH SPORTS HALL OF FAME
Jewish Community Center, 6600 W. Maple Road, W. Bloomfield **[P. 60, A-1]**; (313) 661-1000.

MICHIGAN SPORTS HALL OF FAME
Cobo Hall, 1 Washington Ave., Detroit **[P. 60, E-5]**; (313) 259-4333.

CONTINUED ON PAGE 171

USA SNAPSHOTS®

A look at statistics that shape the sports world

In the running for No. 1
Teams that have been ranked the most times in the top 10 in the USA TODAY/CNN final football poll¹:
7
6
6
1 – Poll began in 1983.
Miami
Nebraska
Michigan

Source: USA TODAY research — By Rod Little, USA TODAY

Michigan

CONTINUED FROM PAGE 170

◆Limited exhibitions open to public.

MOTORSPORTS MUSEUM AND HALL OF FAME AMERICA
45175 Ten Mile Road, Novi **[P. 59, M-7]**; (313) 349-7223.

MUSKEGON AREA SPORTS HALL OF FAME
430 W. Clay Ave., Muskegon **[P. 59, K-2]**; (616) 722-0278.

NATIONAL POLISH-AMERICAN SPORTS HALL OF FAME
Dombrowski Field House, St. Mary's College, Orchard Lake Somerset, Detroit **[P. 59, M-7]**; (313) 527-7774.
◆Must call for appointment.

U.S. NATIONAL SKI HALL OF FAME
Poplar St. & Mather Ave., Ishpeming **[P. 58, B-8]**; (906) 486-9281.

PGA/LPGA

OAKLAND HILLS COUNTRY CLUB
3951 W. Maple Road, Birmingham **[P. 59, M-7]**; (313) 644-2500.
US Senior Open (Senior PGA), July. Number of holes: 72.

THE HIGHLANDS
2715 Leonard St., N.W., Grand Rapids **[P. 60, G-1]**; (616) 453-2451.
First of America Classic (Senior PGA), September. Number of holes: 54.

TPC AT MICHIGAN
1 Nicklaus Drive, Dearborn **[P. 60, E-3]**; (313) 561-0800.
Senior Players Championship Presented by Mazda (Senior PGA), June. Number of holes: 72.

WARWICK HILLS GOLF & COUNTRY CLUB
G-9057 S. Saginaw St., Grand Blanc **[P. 59, L-7]**; (313) 694-9257. Buick Open (PGA), July. Number of holes: 72.

Polo

DETROIT POLO CLUB
2770 W. Milford Rd., Milford **[P. 59, M-7]**; (313) 559-2828.

Yachting

BAYVIEW YACHT CLUB
100 Clairpoint, Detroit **[P. 60, D-6]**; (313) 822-1853.
◆Host of U.S. Match Racing Championship (Prince of Wales Bowl) in 1990.

OUTDOOR VENUES

National Parks

Bike Trails: BK
Boating: BT
Camping: C
Climbing: CL
Diving: DV
Fishing: F
Golfing: G
Hiking: HK
Hunting: HT
Riding: R
Surfing: SU
Swimming: S
Tennis: TE
Whitewater: WW
Winter Sports: W

HIAWATHA NATIONAL FOREST
On US 41 or I-75 or US 2 **[P. 58, C-2, C-5]**. Contains 892,000 acres.
C HK BT F S R W HT

HURON NATIONAL FOREST
Between Tawas City & Grayling, off I-75 **[P. 58-59, G-6, H-4]**. Contains 436,313 acres.
C HK BT F S R W HT

ISLE ROYALE NATIONAL PARK
By boat from Haughton **[P. 58, B-3]**. Contains 57,790 acres. **C HK BT F S**

MANISTEE NATIONAL FOREST
N on US 31, or off US 27 btwn. Cadillac & Muskegon **[P. 59, H-3,4]**. Contains 531,695 acres. **C HK BT F S R W HT**

OTTAWA NATIONAL FOREST
On US 2 or MI 28 **[P. 58, C-6]**. Contains 953,000 acres. **C HK BT F S W HT**

PICTURED ROCKS NATIONAL LAKESHORE
Munising, on County Road H58 **[P. 58, C-2,3]**. Contains 72,896 acres. **C HK BT F S W**

SLEEPING BEAR DUNES NATIONAL LAKESHORE
20 mi. NW of Traverse City on US 31 or MI 22 **[P. 58, G-3]**. Contains 71,132 acres. **C HK BT F S R BK W DV**

State Parks

ALGONAC STATE PARK
MI 29, 2 mi. N of Algonac **[P. 59, M-8]**. Contains 1,375 acres. **C BT F**

BARAGA STATE PARK
US 41, 1 mi. S of Baraga **[P. 58, B-7]**. Contains 55 acres. **C HK BT F S**

BAY CITY STATE PARK
MI 247, 5 mi. N of Bay City **[P. 59, J-6]**. Contains 196 acres. **C HK BT F S**

BRIGHTON STATE RECREATION AREA
3 mi. SW of Brighton **[P. 59, M-6]**. Contains 4,909 acres. **C HK BT F S R W**

BRIMLEY STATE PARK
0.75 mi. E of Brimley **[P. 58, C-6]**. Contains 151 acres. **C HK BT F S W**

CHEBOYGAN STATE PARK
US 23, 3 mi. SE of Cheboygan **[P. 58, E-6]**. Contains 932 acres. **C HK BT F S W**

CLEAR LAKE STATE PARK
Off MI 33, 8 mi. N of Atlanta **[P. 58, F-6]**. Contains 289 acres. **C HK BT F S W**

FORT CUSTER STATE RECREATION AREA
MI 96, 8 mi. W of Battle Creek **[P. 59, M-4]**. Contains 2,962 acres. **C HK BT S R BK W**

HIGHLAND STATE RECREATION
17 mi. W of Pontiac, off MI 59 **[P. 59, M-7]**. Contains 5,699 acres. **C HK BT F S R W**

HOLLAND STATE PARK
7 mi. W of Holland **[P. 59, L-3]**. Contains 143 acres. **C BT F S**

HOLLY STATE RECREATION AREA
Off I-75, 12 mi. NW of Pontiac **[P. 59, L-7]**. Contains 7,581 acres. **C BT F S W**

IONIA STATE RECREATION AREA
MI 66, 6 mi. SW of Ionia **[P. 59, L-4]**. Contains 4,079 acres. **HK BT F R W**

ISLAND LAKE STATE RECREATION AREA
Just S of I-96, 4 mi. E of Brighton **[P. 59, M-6]**. Contains 3,978 acres. **C HK BT F S BK W**

KENSINGTON
I-96, 33 mi. NW of Detroit **[P. 59, M-7]**. Contains 4,437 acres. **HK BT F S BK W G**

LUDINGTON STATE PARK
MI 116, 8.5 mi. NW of Ludington **[P. 59, H-2]**. Contains 4,582 acres. **C HK BT F S BK W**

ORTONVILLE STATE RECREATION AREA
4 mi. NE of Ortonville, off MI 15 **[P. 59, L-7]**. Contains 4,454 acres. **C HK BT F S R W**

P.J. HOFFMASTER STATE PARK
S of Muskegon, 3 mi. W of US 31 **[P. 59, L-3]**. Contains 1,043 acres. **C HK BT F S W**

PINCKNEY STATE RECREATION AREA
Off MI 36, E of Village of Gregory **[P. 59, M-6]**. Contains 10,815 acres. **C HK BT F S R BK W**

PONTIAC LAKE STATE RECREATION AREA
MI 59, 7 mi. W of Pontiac **[P. 59, L-7]**. Contains 3,711 acres. **C HK BT F S R W**

PORCUPINE MOUNTAINS WILDERNESS STATE PARK
29 mi. W of Ontonagan, at terminus of MI 107 **[P. 58, B-6]**. Contains 59,015 acres. **C HK BT F R W**

PROUD LAKE STATE RECREATION AREA
12 mi. SW of Pontiac **[P. 59, M-7]**. Contains 3,615 acres. **C HK BT F S W**

SLEEPY HOLLOW RECREATION AREA
Off US 27, 15 mi. NE of Lansing **[P. 59, L-5]**. Contains 2,678 acres. **C HK BT F S W**

TAHQUAMENON FALLS STATE PARK
NE of Newberry **[P. 58, C-5]**. Contains 36,576 acres. **C HK BT F S W**

VAN RIPER STATE PARK
21 mi. W of Ishpeming on US 41 **[P. 58, C-8]**. Contains 1,124 acres. **C HK BT F S W**

WATERLOO STATE RECREATION AREA
Off I-94, 7 mi. W of Chelsea **[P. 59, M-6]**. Contains 19,839 acres. **C HK BT F S R W**

Skiing

ALPINE SKIING

BIG POWDERHORN MOUNTAIN
N. 11375 Powderhorn Road, Bessemer **[P. 58, B-6]**; (906) 932-4838.
Vertical drop is 622 feet. Has eight chairs.

CABERFAE SKI RESORT
Route 55 West, Cadillac **[P. 59, H-4]**; (616) 862-3301.
Vertical drop is 470 feet. Has three tows, five bars and three chairs.

INDIANHEAD MT. & BEAR CREEK RESORT
500 Indianhead Road, Wakefield **[P. 58, C-6]**; (906) 229-5181.
Vertical drop is 638 feet. Has one tow, three bars and five chairs.

MARQUETTE MOUNTAIN
County Road 553, Marquette **[P. 58, C-1]**; (906) 225-1155.
Vertical drop is 600 feet. Has one tow and two chairs.

NUB'S NOB
4021 Nub's Nob Road, Harbor Springs **[P. 58, E-5]**; (616) 526-2131.
Vertical drop is 427 feet. Has one tow and six chairs.

SKI BRULE MTN/SKI HOMESTEAD
119 Big Bear Road, Iron River **[P. 58, C-7]**; (906) 265-4957.
Vertical drop is 580 feet. Has two tows, two bars and three chairs.

SUGAR LOAF RESORT
4500 Sugar Loaf Mountain Road, Cedar **[P. 58, G-3]**; (616) 228-5461.
Vertical drop is 500 feet. Has one bar and six chairs.

NORDIC SKIING

ADDISON OAKS PARK
1480 W. Romeo Road, Oxford **[P. 59, L-7]**; (313) 693-2432.

BOYNE NORDIC CENTER
Boyne Mountain Road, Boyne Falls **[P. 58, F-5]**; (800) 462-6963.

CORSAIR SKI COUNCIL TRAILS
Monument Road, Tawas City **[P. 59, H-7]**; (517) 362-8644.

CROSS COUNTRY SKI HEADQUARTERS
9435 Road 100, Higgins Lake, Roscommon **[P. 58, G-5]**; (517) 821-6661.

GARLAND
County Road 489, Lewiston **[P. 58, G-6]**; (800) 678-4952.

INDEPENDENCE OAKS PARK
9501 Shashabaw Road, Clarkston **[P. 59, L-7]**; (313) 625-0877.

JOHNSON'S NORDIC TRAILS
Route 1, Wakefield **[P. 58, C-6]**; (906) 224-4711.

MAPLE LANE XC SKI AREA
124 Kreiger Drive, Skandia **[P. 58, C-1]**; (906) 942-7662.

OAKLAND COUNTY PARKS AND RECREATION
2800 Watkins Lake Road, Pontiac **[P. 59, M-7]**; (313) 858-0906.

R. & L. FRYE
9435 County Road 100, Roscommon **[P. 58, G-6]**; (517) 821-6661.

SHANTY CREEK-SCHUSS MT.
RR 3, Bellaire **[P. 58, F-4]**; (800) 632-7118.

TREE TOPS SYLVAN RESORT
3962 Wilkinson Road, Gaylord **[P. 58, F-5]**; (800) 444-6711.

WILDERNESS VALLEY XC
7519 Mancelona Road, Gaylord **[P. 58, G-5]**; (616) 585-7141.

ACTIVE SPORTS

AEROBICS: AFAA, 2766 Still Valley Ct., East Lansing; (517) 351-3144.

BASEBALL: Little League Baseball Central Region HQ, 4360 N. Mitthoeffer Rd., Indianapolis, IN; (317) 897-6127. • **American Legion Baseball,** 642 Cherry Creek Rd., Marquette; (906) 249-3575. • **Babe Ruth Baseball,** Robert Dickson, RR 4, Box 332F, Alexandria, IN; (317) 724-4883. • **Men's Senior Baseball League - Detroit,** 8980 Wedell, Taylor; (313) 291-8468.

BILLIARDS: Paul's Recreation Center, 9478 Conner, Detroit; (313) 521-9634.

BOARDSAILING: North Shore Aqua Sports, South Haven; (616) 637-6208. • **Sailboard Warehouse,** St. Paul; (612) 482-9995. • **USWA Regional Director,** N7315 Winnebago Dr., Fond du Lac, WI; (414) 922-2550.

BOWLING: American Bowling Congress, 5301 S. 76th St., Greendale, WI; (414) 421-6400.

CANOEING & KAYAKING: ACA Midwest Vice Commodore, 1343 N. Portage, Palatine, IL; (708) 359-5047.

CYCLING: LAW Great Lakes Regional Director, 2310 Queens Way, Bloomington, IN; (812) 334-4058. • **Michigan AYH Council,** 3024 Coolidge, Berkley; (313) 545-0511. • **Mid South AYH Council,** PO Box 242108, Memphis; (901) 324-4017. • **USCF Michigan Representative,** PO Box 28, Somerset Center; (517) 688-4860.

FITNESS: National Strength and Conditioning Ass'n State Director, Box 182, Millington; (517) 871-4462.

FOOTBALL: Pop Warner Football, 1315 Walnut Street, Suite 1632, Philadelphia, PA; (215) 735-1450. • **U.S. Flag Football League,** 5834 Pine Tree Drive, Sanibel, FL; (813) 472-0544.

GOLF: Golf Association of Michigan, 37935 Twelve Mile Rd., Suite 200, Farmington Hills; (313) 553-2148. • **Michigan Publinx Senior Golf Association,** 43525 W. 6 Mile Rd., Northville; (313) 349-2148. • **PGA Michigan Section,** 8600 PGA Dr., Walled Lake; (313) 669-4099.

HIKING & CLIMBING: Mackinac Sierra Club Chapter, 115 W. Allegan #10B, Cap Hall, Lansing; (517) 484-2372. • **Michigan Trailfinders Club (AHS),** 2680 Rockhill NE, Grand Rapids; (616) 363-6168. • **North Country Trail Association (AHS),** PO Box 311, White Cloud; (313) 280-2921.

HOCKEY: USA Hockey Michigan Registrar, 234 Tamarack Street, Laurium; (906) 487-2246.

HUNTING & FISHING: Department of Natural Resources, Box 30028, Lansing; (517) 373-2329. • **Johnston's Pere Marquette Lodge (Orvis),** Box 1290, Rt. 1, Baldwin; (616) 745-3972. • **Riverbend Sport Shop (Orvis),** 29229 Northwestern Highway,

CONTINUED ON PAGE 172

Minnesota

The 140-mile North Shore of Lake Superior, from Duluth to Grand Portage, is as scenic as any drive in North America. Stretch your legs nearby at the Gunflint Trail, which has lodge-to-lodge cross-country skiing during the winter and is the gateway to the Boundary Waters Wilderness. You could catch sight of moose, eagle, deer, or bear. ◆ If the national Hockey Hall of Fame (Eveleth) isn't unusual enough for you, stand along the shores of the Mississippi during the annual Minneapolis Aquatennial and watch milk-carton rafts racing on the Big Muddy. ◆ In February, the International 500, billed as the world's toughest snowmobile race, spans 500 miles from Thunder Bay, Ontario, to St. Paul. ◆ Minnesota has 12,000 lakes and sells 2 million fishing licenses a year. The catch includes walleye, northern pike, and bass.

▶ SPECTATOR VENUES

Auto Racing

BRAINERD RACEWAY
Highway 371, 6 miles north of Brainerd **[P. 63, H-5]**; (612) 475-1500. Track is quarter-mile strip (for NHRA races).
Quaker State NorthStar Nationals (NHRA), mid-Aug.

Baseball

HUBERT H. HUMPHREY METRODOME
501 Chicago Ave. South, Minneapolis **[P. 61, C-3]**. Built in 1982. Capacity: 55,883
Minnesota Twins (AL West); (612) 375-1366. Franchise began in 1901. Broadcasts by WCCO 830 AM, WCCO-TV Channel 4. Affiliates: Portland, OR (AAA); Orlando, FL (AA); Visalia, CA (A); Kenosha, WI (A); Elizabethton, TN (Rookie); Fort Myers, FL (Rookie). Spring training held in Fort Myers, Fl.

Basketball

TARGET CENTER
600 1st Ave. North, Minneapolis **[P. 61, C-3]**. Built in 1990. Capacity: 18,200.
Minnesota Timberwolves (NBA Western Conf., Midwest Div.); (612) 337-3865. Franchise began in 1989. Broadcasts by WDGY 1130 AM, KSTP Channel 5, KITN Channel 29, Prime Sports Network-Upper Midwest.

College Sports

BETHEL COLLEGE ROYALS
3900 Bethel Drive, St. Paul **[P. 61, A-5]**; (612) 638-6397. Bethel Field, capacity 3,000. PE Center, capacity 1,600.

UNIVERSITY OF MINNESOTA GOLDEN GOPHERS
516 15th Avenue, S.E., Minneapolis **[P. 61, C-4]**; (612) 625-4838. Hubert H. Humphrey Metrodome, capacity 62,000. Williams, capacity 16,990 (basketball)/ 7,572 (hockey).

UNIVERSITY OF ST. THOMAS TOMMIES
St. Paul **[P. 61, D-4]**; (612) 647-5356. O'Shaughnessy, capacity 4,500. Schoenecker Arena, capacity 2,300.

Football

HUBERT H. HUMPHREY METRODOME
500 11th Avenue South, Minneapolis **[P. 61, C-3]**. Built in 1982. Capacity: 63,000.
◆Located downtown, near a shopping area with enclosed walkways to protect pedestrians from the frigid Minnesota winters.
Minnesota Vikings (NFC Central Division); (612) 828-6500. Franchise began in 1961. Broadcasts by WCCO-AM.

Hockey

MET CENTER
7901 Cedar Avenue South, Bloomington **[P. 61, E-4]**. Built in 1967. Capacity: 15,093.
Minnesota North Stars (NHL, Campbell Conference, Norris Division); (612) 853-9333. Franchise began in 1967. Broadcasts by KSTP-AM 1500, KMSP-TV, Channel 9.

Horse Racing

CANTERBURY DOWNS
1100 Canterbury Road, Shakopee **[P. 61, G-1]**; (612) 445-7223. Opened in 1985. Grandstand capacity: 6,200. Total capacity: 11,200.
Thoroughbred season from Apr. to Oct.

Museums & Halls of Fame

UNITED STATES HOCKEY HALL OF FAME
801 Hat Trick Ave., Eveleth **[P. 62, F-6]**; (218) 744-5167.

PGA/LPGA

EDINBURGH USA
8700 Edinbrook Crossing, Brooklyn Park **[P. 61, A-3]**; (612) 424-7060.
Northgate Classic (LPGA), Aug. Number of holes: 72.

HAZELTINE NATIONAL GOLF CLUB
1900 Hazeltine Blvd., Chaska **[P. 63, L-5]**; (612) 448-1991.
1991 US Open Championship (USGA), June. Number of holes: 72.

Track & Field

NATIONAL SPORTS CENTER
1700 105th Ave. NE, Blaine **[P. 63, L-6]**; (612) 785-5600.
TAC National Indoor Masters Track & Field Championships,March, 1991.

▶ OUTDOOR VENUES

National Parks

CHIPPEWA NATIONAL FOREST
North central MN, 4 hours from Twin Cities on MN 2 **[P. 62, B-7]**. Contains 663,000 acres.
C HK BT F S BK W HT

SUPERIOR NATIONAL FOREST
Northeast MN, 3.5 hours from Minneapolis/St. Paul **[P. 62, E-6]**. Contains 2,145,105 acres.

STATBOX

POPULATION: 4,353,000
SQUARE MILES: 84,000
TIME ZONE: Central
MOTTO: L'Etoile du Nord (Star of the North)
BIRD: Common Loon
TREE: Norway Pine
CAPITAL: St. Paul
AVERAGE ANNUAL RAINFALL: 26"
MEAN TEMP: 11 (Jan.); 73 (July)
MAJOR LEAGUE TEAMS: 4
NATIONAL PARK/FOREST ACREAGE: 218,000
STATE PARK ACREAGE: 225,000
HIGHEST ELEVATION: 2,301'
LOWEST ELEVATION: 602'
WATERWAYS: 25,000 miles of lakes and streams

C HK BT F S R W HT

VOYAGEURS NATIONAL PARK
International Falls via MN 11 or US 53 **[P. 62, D-6]**. Contains 218,035 acres.
C HK BT F S DV

State Parks

- Bike Trails:BK
- Boating: BT
- Camping: C
- Climbing: CL
- Diving: DV
- Fishing: F
- Golfing: G
- Hiking: HK
- Hunting: HT
- Riding: R
- Surfing: SU
- Swimming: S
- Tennis: TE
- Whitewater: WW
- Winter Sports: W

BANNING STATE PARK
Off I-35, exit 195, near Askov **[P. 63, J-6]**. Contains 6,237 acres.
C HK BT F R W WW

BEAR HEAD LAKE STATE PARK
16 mi. E of Tower **[P. 62, E-7]**. Contains 4,384 acres.
C HK BT F S W

CAMDEN STATE PARK
10 mi. S of Marshall off MN 23 **[P. 63, M-2]**. Contains 1,712 acres.
C HK BT F S R BK W

FRONTENAC STATE PARK
US 61, 10 mi. SE of Red Wing **[P. 63, -7]**. Contains 1,754 acres. **C HK BT F S W**

GOOSEBERRY FALLS STATE PARK
12 mi. NE of Two Harbors on US 61 **[P. 62, G-8]**. Contains 1,662 acres. **C HK F W**

ITASCA STATE PARK
21 mi. N of Park Rapids on US 71 **[P. 62, F-3]**. Contains 32,000 acres. **C HK BT F S BK W**

JAY COOKE STATE PARK
8 mi. SW of Duluth off MN 210 **[P. 63, H-7]**. Contains 8,813 acres. **C HK F R W**

JUDGE MAGNEY STATE PARK
14 mi. NE of Grand Marais **[P. 62, B-8]**. Contains 4,514 acres. **C HK F W**

LAKE BRONSON
Near town of Lake Bronson, access via Hwy. 28 **[P. 62, C-2]**. Contains 2,983 acres.
C HK BT F S W

CONTINUED ON PAGE 173

Michigan

CONTINUED FROM PAGE 171

Southfield; (313) 350-8484. • **Riverrun (Orvis),** 6800-B South Westnedge Ave., Kalamazoo; (616) 327-7755. • **Streamside (Orvis),** 4400 Grand Traverse Village, Williamsburg; (616) 938-5337. • **Thornapple Orvis Shop,** Thornapple Village, PO Box 133, Ada; (616) 676-0177. • **Trout Unlimited,** 271 Sleights Rd., Traverse City; (616) 947-0219.

LACROSSE: Lacrosse Foundation Chapter, De La Salle Colegiate, 14600 Common Rd., Warren; (313) 778-2207.

RACQUETBALL: AARA, 38154 Seaway, Mt. Clemens; (313) 468-2787.

RIDING: Michigan Horse Council, 21600 Currie, Northville; (313) 437-1525.

RODEO: PRCA Great Lakes Circuit, Rt. 1, Box 54, Clayton, IN; (317) 539-5039.

RUNNING: RRCA MI State Rep., 10144 Lincoln, Huntington; (313) 544-9099.

SCUBA: Advanced Aquatics Diving, Inc., 25020 Jefferson, St. Clair Shores; (313) 779-8777. • **Divers Incorporated,** 3380 Washtenaw Avenue, Ann Arbor; (313) 971-7770. • **US Scuba Center,** 3260 South Rochester Road, Rochester; (313) 853-2800. • **West Michigan Dive Center, Inc.,** 2367 West Sherman Blvd., Muskegon; (616) 755-3771.

SHOOTING: Hunters Ridge Hunt Club, 3921 Barber Rd., Oxford; (313) 628-4868.

SKATING: Michigan Speedskating Association, 12546 Lake Shore Dr., Grand Haven; (616) 846-0269. • **USFSA,** 20 First Street, Colorado Springs, CO; (719) 635-5200.

SOCCER: Michigan Soccer Ass'n, 2673 Warwick Ct., Bloomfield Heights; (313) 338-2333. • **Michigan State YSA,** 8029 Menge, Center Line; (517) 351-1844. • **AYSO Regional Director,** 308 Woodside Ave., Kalamazoo; (616) 343-6040.

SOFTBALL: ASA, 123 Ashman St., Midland; (519) 631-5123. • **Detroit ASA,** 2398 Pontiac Drive, Sylvan Lake; (313) 681-7717.

SQUASH: University Club of Detroit (USSRA), Detroit; (313) 567-9280.

SWIMMING: LMSC Michigan Registrar, 1387 Albany Street, Ferndale; (313) 398-9396.

TABLE TENNIS: USTTA State Coordinator, 1784 Placio Ct., Caledonia; (616) 698-4974.

TENNIS: Recreational TEAMTENNIS Midwest-Southeast Region, National Program Coordinator, 445 N. Wells, Ste. #404, Chicago, IL; (800) TEAMTEN. • **Western USTA,** 8720 Castle Creek Parkway, Ste. 329, Indianapolis, IN; (513) 390-2740.

TRIATHLON: Down River Triathlete Team, 18269 Meridian, Grosse Ile; (313) 729-8000. • **Heart Smart Tri Club,** 2921 W. Grand Blvd., NCP-1107, Detroit; (313) 972-1919.

Minnesota

CONTINUED FROM PAGE 172

MAPLEWOOD STATE PARK
7 mi. SE of Pelican Rapids off MN 108 **[P. 63, H-2]**. Contains 9,250 acres. **C HK BT F S R W**

MILLE LACS KATHIO STATE PARK
County Road 26, 1 mi. off US 169, near Onamia **[P. 63, H-5]**. Contains 10,985 acres. **C HK BT F S R W**

MINNEOPA STATE PARK
5 mi. W of Mankato on MN 68 & US 169 **[P. 63, M-5]**. Contains 1,145 acres. **C HK BT F BK W**

MINNESOTA VALLEY
US 169, W of Jordan **[P. 63, M-5]**. Contains 8,000 acres. **C HK BT F R BK W**

MONSON LAKE STATE PARK
4 mi. SW. of Sunburg, via MN 104 **[P. 63, K-3]**. Contains 187 acres. **C HK BT F**

SCHOOLCRAFT STATE PARK
8 mi. S of Deer River **[P. 62, F-5]**. Contains 295 acres. **C HK BT F**

SIBLEY
7 mi. W of New London on US 71 **[P. 63, K-3]**. Contains 3,067 acres. **C HK BT F S R BK W**

SPLIT ROCK CREEK STATE PARK
7 mi. SW of Pipestone, off MN 23 **[P. 63, N-2]**. Contains 400 acres. **C HK BT F S W**

ST. CROIX STATE PARK
20 mi. E of Hinckley on MN 48 **[P. 63, J-7]**. Contains 34,037 acres. **C HK BT F S R BK W**

WILD RIVER
MN 95 to CR 12 **[P. 63, K-6]**. Contains 7,000 acres. **C HK BT F R W**

ZIPPEL BAY
9 mi. NE of Williams on CR 8 on Lake of the Woods **[P. 62, C-4]**. Contains 2,946 acres. **C HK BT F S R W**

Skiing

ALPINE SKIING

AFTON ALPS
6600 Peller Avenue, South, Hastings **[P. 63, L-6]**; (612) 436-5245.
Vertical drop is 350 feet. Has two tows and eighteen chairs.

SPIRIT MOUNTAIN RECREATION AREA
4500 Spirit Mountain Place, Duluth **[P. 62, G-7]**; (218) 628-2891.
Vertical drop is 700 feet. Has two tows and five chairs.

NORDIC SKIING

AAMODT'S APPLE FARM
6428 Manning Ave. S., Stillwater **[P. 61, B-8]**; (612) 439-3127.

BEARSKIN LODGE XC RESORT
Gunflint Trail, Grand Marais **[P. 62, A-7]**; (800) 338-4170.

CASCADE LODGE
HCR 3, Lutsen **[P.62,B-7]**; (218) 387-1112.

GOLDEN EAGLE LODGE
Gunflint Trail, Grand Marais **[P. 62, A-7]**; (800) 346-2203.

GRAND PORTAGE RESERVATION TRAIL SYSTEM
Grand Portage **[P. 62, A-8]**; (218) 475-2239.

GUNFLINT LODGE
750 Gunflint Trail, Grand Marais **[P. 62, B-7]**; (800) 328-3325.

HENNEPIN PARKS
12615 County Road 9, Plymouth **[P. 61, B-1]**; (612) 559-9000.

LUTSEN RESORT
MN 61, Lutsen **[P. 62, B-7]**; (218) 663-7212.

MAPLELAG
Route 1, Callaway **[P. 62, G-2]**; (218) 375-4466.

MCLEOD LANDFILL
Route 3, Glencoe **[P. 63, L-5]**; (612) 804-5504.

MINNEAPOLIS SKI CLUB
3948 W. 50th Street, Minneapolis **[P. 61, D-3]**; (612) 925-9473.

NORTHWIND LODGE
Fernberg Road, County 18, Ely **[P. 62, E-7]**; (800) 777-4402.

PINCUSHION B&B XC CENTER
Grand Marais **[P. 62, B-7]**; (218) 387-1276.

SOLBAKKEN RESORT
HCR 3, Lutsen **[P. 62, B-7]**; (218) 663-7566.

TAMAROCK OUTFITTERS
Warroad **[P. 62, C-3]**; (218) 386-2678.

ACTIVE SPORTS

ADVENTURE: Voyageur Outward Bound School, 10900 Cedar Lake Rd., Minnetonka; (800) 328-2943.

AEROBICS: AFAA, 6641 E. Shadow Lake Dr., Lino Lakes; (612) 426-7491.

BASEBALL: Little League Baseball Central Region HQ, 4360 N. Mitthoeffer Rd., Indianapolis, IN; (317) 897-6127. • **Pony Baseball-Softball,** 110 N. 5th St., Auburn, IL; (217) 438-3130. • **American Legion Baseball,** 1203-8th Ave. NE, Brainerd; (218) 829-2189. • **Babe Ruth Baseball,** Norman Travis, Box 339, Burlington, CO; (719) 346-8803. • **Men's Senior Baseball League - Minneapolis,** 5345 Williston Rd., Minnesonka; (612) 938-5331.

BOARDSAILING: USWA Regional Director, 2625 S. 46th, Lincoln, NE; (402)489-1002.

BOWLING: American Bowling Congress, 5301 S. 76th St., Greendale, WI; (414) 421-6400.

CANOEING & KAYAKING: ACA Midwest Vice Commodore, 1343 N. Portage, Palatine, IL; (708) 359-5047.

CYCLING: LAW North Central Regional Director, Route 1, Box 99, Cushing, WI; (715) 648-5519. • **Minnesota AYH Council,** 795 Raymond Ave., St. Paul; (612) 659-0407. • **USCF Minnesota/Dakota-East Representative,** 3135 Quebec Ave. S, St. Louis Park; (612) 926-2213.

FITNESS: Governor's Council on Physical Fitness and Sports, 4510 West 77th Street, Edina; (612) 831-4121.

FOOTBALL: Pop Warner Football, 1315 Walnut Street, Suite 1632, Philadelphia, PA; (215) 735-1450.

GOLF: Minnesota Golf Association, 6550 York Ave. S., Suite 405, Edina; (612) 927-4643. • **PGA Minnesota Section,** Bunker Hills Golf Club, Highway 242 & Foley Blvd., Coon Rapids; (612) 754-0820. • **Trans-Mississippi Golf Association,** 240 Minnetonka Ave. South, Box 617, Wayzata; (612) 473-3722.

HIKING & CLIMBING: Minnesota Rovers Outing Club (AHS), PO Box 14133, Minneapolis; (612) 522-2461. • **North Star Sierra Club Chapter,** 1313 Fifth St. SE, Room 323, Minneapolis; (612) 379-3853. • **Superior Hiking Trail Ass'n (AHS),** Box 4, Two Harbors; (218) 834-4436.

HOCKEY: USA Hockey Minnkota Registrar, PO Box 34340, Blaine; (612) 755-3753.

HUNTING & FISHING: Department of Natural Resources, 500 Lafayette Rd., St. Paul; (612) 296-6157. • **Trout Unlimited,** 2835 Xanthus Lane, Plymouth; (612) 473-0737.

RACQUETBALL: AARA, 2650 Bryant Ave. S., Minneapolis; (612) 377-5779.

RIDING: Minnesota Horse Council, Box 75481, St. Paul; (203) 274-2642.

RODEO: PRCA Great Lakes Circuit, Rt. 1, Box 54, Clayton, IN; (317) 539-5039.

RUNNING: RRCA MN State Rep., 2493 Orchard Lane, White Bear Lake; (612) 770-8453.

SCUBA: Fantasea Scuba, 3429 East Highway 13, Burnsville; (612) 890-3483. • **Mick's Scuba Pro Dive Shop,** 420 South 21st Street, Box 517, Moorehead; (218) 233-0448. • **Minnesota Dive Center,** 4164 18th Avenue NW, Rochester; (507) 288-8802. • **Scuba Center,** 5015 Penn Avenue South, Minneapolis; (612) 925-4818.

SHOOTING: Caribou Gun Club, RR 1, Box 26A, Le Sheur; (612) 665-3796. • **Clear Creek Outdoors Inc.,** Rt. 1, Box 53-A, Wrenshall; (218) 384-3670. • **Minnesota Horse & Hunt Club,** 2920 220th St., Prior Lake; (612) 447-2272. • **Rice Creek Hunting & Recreation,** Rt. 5, Box 213, Little Falls; (612) 745-2232. • **Royal Flush Shooting Club,** Rt. 5, Box 228, Little Falls; (612) 745-2522. • **Valhalla Hunt Club,** RR1, Box 255, Albert Lea; (507) 377-7225. • **Wild Marsh Sporting Clays, Inc.,** 13767 County Rd. 3, Clear Lake; (612) 662-2021.

SKATING: Eastern Minnesota Skating Association, 2578 N. Pascal Street, Roseville; (612) 636-4337. • **Minnesota Skating Association,** 3353 35th Ave. South, Minneapolis; (612) 729-4066. • **USFSA,** 20 First Street, Colorado Springs, CO; (719) 635-5200.

SOCCER: Minnesota Soccer Ass'n, 7676 Ivystone Ave. South, Cottage Grove; (612) 459-6872. • **Minnesota YSA, Inc.,** 3015 Ottawa, Ste. B, Minneapolis; (612) 925-5181. • **AYSO Regional Director,** 5403 W. 138th Street, Hawthorne, CA; (800) 421-5700.

SOFTBALL: Minnesota ASA, 11235 96th Ave. North, Maple Grove; (612) 425-0311. • **Minneapolis ASA,** 2643 Polk Street NE, Minneapolis; (612) 789-0024. • **St. Paul ASA,** 25 W. 4th Street, Room 175, Woodbury; (612) 738-2622.

SQUASH: Commodore Squash Club (USSRA), St. Paul; (612) 228-0501.

SWIMMING: LMSC Minnesota Registrar, 7501-118 W. 101 St., Bloomington; (612) 941-5551.

TENNIS: Recreational TEAMTENNIS Midwest-Southeast Region, National Program Coordinator, 445 N. Wells, Ste. #404, Chicago, IL; (800) TEAMTEN. • **Northwestern USTA,** 5525 Cedar Lake Rd., St. Louis Park; (612) 546-0709.

TRIATHLON: Tri Club New Mexico, 6106 Bellaman NE, Albuquerque; (505) 845-3440.

VOLLEYBALL: USVBA North Country Commissioner, 910 E. 4th Street, Northfield; (507) 663-1597.

Tip Offs

Climbing's Up

According to champion American climber Lynn Hill, her sport "has never been about getting from Point A to Point B. It's a form of vertical ballet."

Competitive climbing in the USA has picked up momentum since Europeans brought it here in the '70s. The USA now boasts summer stops on the sport's World Cup circuit, a growing following, and the use of artificial surfaces in competition.

Artificial walls have calmed two worries: potential damage to fragile mountains from competitors and spectators, and the advantage that local climbers can gain when events are held in their home regions.

For competitions on an artifical wall, expert route-setters bolt hand and foot holds onto the surface. Everyone faces the same set of choices. No one is allowed to see the route in advance or to watch a rival climb.

Says Hill: "The bottom line is that climbing on an artificial wall is exactly like a natural rock climb. You have to go with your instincts." The surfaces are currently making their way across the USA in health clubs, gyms and schools.

The next stage in competitive climbing? A moveable artificial wall, with motors and gears that can change the complexion of the "rock" like a theatrical set.

Natural surfaces are, of course, still the foundation of rock climbing–especially for those who are uninterested in competition. Among the most popular of the USA's climbing regions:

- **Yosemite Valley, CA**
- **Joshua Tree National Monument, CA**
- **The Tetons, ID,WY**
- **Boulder, CO**
- **Shawangunk Mountains, near New Paltz, NY**
- **North Conway, NH**
- **New River Gorge, WV**
- **Bend, OR**

Those who want to learn more about climbing on artificial walls, or in natural settings, should contact The American Alpine Club, 113, E. 90th St., NY, NY 10128.

Mississippi

Don't expect the bland in the home state of Elvis and B.B. King. Come in July and watch Gulfport's four-day Deep Sea Fishing Rodeo (601-863-2713, 896-2320). Visiting Presley pilgrims may fish all along Mississippi's Gulf Coast without a license; the best months are April-November. ◆ If 26 miles of uninterrupted white sand beaches aren't enough, take a ferry from Gulfport or Biloxi to Ship Island (601-864-1014, Gulfport; 601-486-6010, Biloxi). ◆ Freshwater fishing does require a license; recommended spots are Pickwick Lake near Corinth and the 33,000-acre Ross Barnett Reservoir near Jackson (also good for sailing). ◆ Hunting is available statewide; Jefferson and Adams counties (along the Mississippi River) are known for big deer. ◆ And Jackson is home to Double-A Texas League baseball (Houston Astros), as well as the Dixie National Rodeo (on dry land) in February.

STATBOX

POPULATION: 2,573,216
SQUARE MILES: 47,233
TIME ZONE: Central
MOTTO: Virtute et Armis (By valor and arms)
BIRD: Mockingbird
TREE: Magnolia
CAPITAL: Jackson
AVERAGE ANNUAL RAINFALL: 50"
MEAN TEMP: 65
MAJOR LEAGUE TEAMS: 0
NATIONAL PARK/FOREST ACREAGE: 1,100,000
STATE PARK ACREAGE: 23,751
HIGHEST ELEVATION: 806'
LOWEST ELEVATION: sea level
WATERWAYS: 456 square miles of inland water

▶ SPECTATOR VENUES

Baseball

SMITH-WILLS STADIUM
1200 Lakeland Drive, Jackson **[P. 65, N-2]**. Capacity: 5,200
Jackson Generals (Texas League, Class AA); (601) 981-4664. Entered League in 1975. Broadcasts by WJDS 620 AM. MLB affiliation, Houston Astros.

College Sports

ALCORN STATE UNIVERSITY BRAVES
Lorman **[P. 65, D-2]**; (601) 877-6500. Henderson, capacity 10,000. H&PE Building, capacity 7,000.

JACKSON STATE UNIVERSITY TIGERS
1325 West Lynch Street, Jackson **[P. 65, H-4]**; (601) 968-2291. Mississippi Memorial, capacity 62,000.

MISSISSIPPI STATE UNIVERSITY BULLDOGS
Mississippi State **[P. 64, E-7]**; (601) 325-2532. Scott Field, capacity 40,000. Humphrey Coliseum, capacity 10,000.

MISSISSIPPI VALLEY STATE UNIVERSITY DELTA DEVILS
Highway 82, Itta Bena **[P. 64, E-4]**; (601) 254-9041. Magnolia, capacity 10,000. Gym, capacity 6,500.

UNIVERSITY OF MISSISSIPPI OLE MISS REBELS
University **[P. 64, C-5]**; (601) 232-7241. Vaught-Hemingway, capacity 41,000. Smith Coliseum, capacity 8,500.

UNIVERSITY OF SOUTHERN MISSISSIPPI GOLDEN EAGLES
Hattiesburg **[P. 65, K-6]**; (601) 266-5017. Roberts, capacity 33,000. Green Coliseum, capacity 8,095.

PGA/LPGA

HATTIESBURG COUNTRY CLUB
Country Club Drive, Hattiesburg **[P. 65, K-6]**; (601) 264-5076.
Deposit Guaranty Golf Classic (PGA), April. Number of holes: 72.

Yachting

GULFPORT YACHT CLUB
East Pier, Gulfport **[P. 65, N-6]**; (601) 863-2263.
◆Host of US Youth Sailing Championship in 1990.

▶ OUTDOOR VENUES

National Parks

Bike Trails: BK
Boating: BT
Camping: C
Climbing: CL
Diving: DV
Fishing: F
Golfing: G
Hiking: HK
Hunting: HT
Riding: R
Surfing: SU
Swimming: S
Tennis: TE
Whitewater: WW
Winter Sports: W

BIENVILLE NATIONAL FOREST
Central MS **[P. 65, H-6]**. Contains 179,402 acres. **C HK BT F S R**

DE SOTO NATIONAL FOREST
Near Biloxi **[P. 65, K-7, L-6, M-7]**. Contains 500,487 acres. **C HK BT F S R BK**

DELTA NATIONAL FOREST
Rolling Fork, west central MS **[P. 64, G-3]**. Contains 59,553 acres. **C HK F**

GULF ISLANDS NATIONAL SEASHORE
Oceansprings **[P. 65, N-7, -8]**. Contains 70,400 acres. **C HK BT F S DV**

HOLLY SPRINGS NATIONAL FOREST
Holly Springs, northern MS **[P. 64, B-6]**. Contains 152,207 acres. **C HK BT F S BK**

HOMOCHITTO NATIONAL FOREST
Meadville & Gloster, southwestern MS **[P. 65, K-3]**. Contains 188,994 acres. **C HK BT F S**

TOMBIGBEE NATIONAL FOREST
Ackerman, east central MS **[P. 65, F-6, D-5,7]**. Contains 66,576 acres. **C HK BT F S R BK**

State Parks

BUCCANEER STATE PARK
Off US 90 at Waveland **[P. 65, N-6]**. Contains 365 acres. **C HK F S TE**

CLARKCO STATE PARK
6 mi. N of Quitman on US 45 **[P. 65, H-7]**. Contains 792 acres. **C HK BT F S BK TE**

GRENADA LAKE (AC)
Grenada, 6 mi. E of I-55 on MS 7 **[P. 64, D-5]**. Contains 90,000 acres. **C HK BT F S HT**

HUGH WHITE STATE PARK
5 mi. E of Grenada, MS 8 **[P. 64, D-5]**. Contains 600 acres. **C HK BT F S**

J.P. COLEMAN STATE PARK
10 mi. N of Iuka off MS 25 **[P. 64, A-8]**. Contains 1,468 acres. **C HK BT F S BK**

LE FLEUR'S BLUFFS STATE PARK
2140 Riverside Drive, exit 98B off I-55, Jackson **[P. 65, N-2]**. **C F S G**

NATCHEZ STATE PARK
10 mi. N of Natchez, off US 61 at Stanton **[P. 65, K-2]**. Contains 3,441 acres. **C HK BT F BK**

PERCY QUIN STATE PARK
5 mi. SW of McComb off I-55, exit 13 **[P. 65, L-4]**. Contains 1,620 acres. **C HK BT F S BK**

ROOSEVELT STATE PARK
I-20, exit 77 **[P. 65, H-5]**. Contains 77 acres. **C HK BT S TE**

SARDIS LAKE (AC)
8 mi. E of Sardis on MS 315 (I-55, exit 252) **[P. 64, C-5]**. Contains 98,400 acres. **C HK BT F S HT**

TISHOMINGO STATE PARK
3 mi. N of Dennis off MS 25 **[P. 64, B-8]**. Contains 1,400 acres. **C HK BT F S BK**

TOMBIGBEE STATE PARK
6 mi. SE of Tupelo off MS 6 **[P. 64, C-7]**. Contains 822 acres. **C HK BT F S BK TE**

TRACE STATE PARK
10 mi. E of Pontotoc off MS 6 **[P. 64, C-7]**. Contains 2,500 acres. **C HK BT F S BK**

WALL DOXEY STATE PARK
7 mi. S of Holly Springs off MS 7 **[P. 64, B-6]**. Contains 855 acres. **C HK BT BK**

▶ ACTIVE SPORTS

BASEBALL: Little League Baseball Southern Region HQ, PO Box 13366, St. Petersburg, FL; (813) 344-2661. • **Pony Baseball-Softball,** 7820 Pebbleford Dr., Ft. Worth, TX; (817) 293-1664. • **American Legion Baseball,** Rt. 1, Box 48-D, Saltillo; (601) 844-5039. • **Babe Ruth Baseball,** William E. Whitehurst, Rt. 2, Box 56, Grifton, NC; (919) 524-5525.

BILLIARDS: Longhorn, 1700 Terry Rd., Jackson; (601) 944-1626.

BOARDSAILING: USWA Regional Director, 2580 Prosperity Oaks St., Palm Beach Gardens, FL; (407) 881-0001.

CANOEING & KAYAKING: ACA Central Vice Commodore, 3410 Ridge Rd., N. Little Rock, AR; (501) 758-4716.

CYCLING: LAW Southeastern Regional Director, 201 1st Ave., PO Box 2549, High Springs, FL; (904) 454-5000. • **USCF Mississippi Representative,** 105 S. Long Street, #2, Starkville; (601) 325-2876.

FOOTBALL: Pop Warner Football, 1315 Walnut Street, Suite 1632, Philadelphia, PA; (215) 735-1450.

GOLF: Mississippi Golf Association, 630 Cherry Ln., PO Box 684, Laurel; (601) 649-0570. • **PGA Gulf States Section,** PO Box 29426, New Orleans, LA; (504) 245-7333.

HIKING & CLIMBING: Mississippi Sierra Club Chapter, Drawer 6249, Biloxi; (601) 388-2889.

HOCKEY: USA Hockey Southeastern Registrar, PO Box 5208, Takoma Park, MD; (301) 622-0032.

HUNTING & FISHING: Department of Wildlife Fisheries and Parks, PO Box 451, Jackson; (601) 961-5300. • **Fireside Fly and Field (Orvis),** 1060 E. Countyline Road, CENTRE PARK, Ridgeland; (601) 957-9705.

RACQUETBALL: AARA, 1765 E. Sudan, Greenville; (601) 335-3565.

RIDING: Mississippi Horse Council, Box 1609, Jackson; (601) 924-1260.

RODEO: PRCA Southeastern Circuit, 1111 S. McGee Rd., Bonifay, FL; (904) 547-2534.

RUNNING: RRCA MS State Rep., PO Box 954, Magee; (601) 849-2365.

SCUBA: Scuba World of Mississippi, 326 Courthouse Road, Gulfport; (601) 896-9490.

SKATING: USFSA, 20 First Street, Colorado Springs, CO; (719) 635-5200.

SOCCER: Mississippi YSA, PO Box 13066, Jackson; (601) 359-1448. • **AYSO Regional Director,** 1405 Inman Dr., Huntsville, AL; (205) 881-3138.

SOFTBALL: ASA, 182 Clower Street, Biloxi; (601) 432-7726.

TENNIS: Recreational TEAMTENNIS Midwest-Southeast Region, National Program Coordinator, 445 N. Wells, Ste. #404, Chicago, IL ; (800) TEAMTEN. • **Southern USTA,** 200 Sandy Springs Place, Suite 200, Atlanta, GA; (404) 257-1297

Tip Offs: Sports Bars Part III

CONTINUED FROM PAGE 174

Scoreboard, 7613 Katy Fwy, Houston 713-681-6987
Season Tickets, 3303 Richmond Ave., Houston 713-522-8585
Sports Pub, 2118 Jackson-Keller Rd., San Antonio 512-349-8055
Ultimate Sports Grille, 16101 Addison Road, Addison 214-733-1626

UTAH

Green Street, 650 E. Fifth So., Salt Lake City 801-532-4200
Vierra's, 5445 So. Ninth E., Salt Lake City 801-266-9552

VIRGINIA

Champions of Richmond, 550 E. Marshall St., Richmond 804-649-9424
Champions, 8201 Greensboro Dr., McLean 703-442-0877

WASHINGTON

F.X. McRory's, 419 Occidental South, Seattle 206-623-4800
Sneakers, 538 First Ave. So., Seattle 206-625-1340

WISCONSIN

Major Goolsby's, 340 W. Kilbourn, Milwaukee 414-271-3414

Missouri

Since their founding in 1876, the St. Louis Cardinals (Busch Stadium) have contributed 35 players to baseball's Hall of Fame, won 15 league titles and nine World Series championships, and quietly become the epitome of an American ball club. ◆ St. Louis was home to the Olympics in 1904 (the only American city other than Los Angeles to have hosted the summer games), and was the site of football's first forward pass at St. Louis University in 1906. ◆ Kansas City features the Truman Sports Complex, America's only twin-stadium facility, home to baseball's Royals and the NFL Chiefs. ◆ At 150,000 square feet, Springfield's Bass Pro Shops Outdoor World is the world's largest mall complex for the sports-minded. ◆ For those with dreams of Huckleberry Finn, over 50,000 miles of rivers and streams are liquid roadways for that old Missouri favorite: the float trip.

► SPECTATOR VENUES

Baseball

BUSCH STADIUM
250 Stadium Plaza, St. Louis **[P. 67, D-13]**. Built in 1966. Capacity: 56,227
◆Even though this is a huge ballpark, Mike Laga once hit a foul ball out of it. Famous for the late owner of the Cards, August "Gussie" Busch, riding in on a wagon drawn by Clydesdales. Budweiser theme music played at high levels. Possibly most sophisticated fans in NL. Good restaurants owned by former players abound. Try Mike Shannon's, one block from the park.
St. Louis Cardinals (NL East); (314) 421-3060. Franchise began in 1876. Broadcasts by KMOX 1120 AM, KPLR Channel 11. Affiliates: Louisville, KY (AAA); Arkansas (AA); St. Petersburg, FL (A); Savannah, GA (A); Springfield, IL (A); Johnson City, TN (Rookie); Hamilton, Ontario (A); Peoria, AZ (Rookie). Spring training held in St. Petersburg, FL.

ROYALS STADIUM
I-70 to Blue Ridge Cut Off, at the Harry S. Truman Sports Complex, 1 Royal Way, Kansas City **[P. 67, G-14]**. Built in 1973. Capacity: 40,625
Kansas City Royals (AL West); (816) 921-2200. Franchise began in 1969. Broadcasts by KMBZ 980 AM, WDAF-TV Channel 4. Affiliates: Omaha, NE (AAA); Memphis, TN (AA); Baseball City, FL (A); Appleton, WI (A); Eugene, OR (A); Baseball City, FL (Rookie). Spring training held in Baseball City, FL.

Bowling

TROPICANA LANES
7960 Clayton Road, Tichmond Hts. **[P. 67, D-12]**; (314) 781-0282.
Toyota Classic (PBA), November.

College Sports

LINCOLN STATE UNIVERSITY BLUE TIGERS
Jefferson City **[P. 67, C-10]**; (314) 681-5326. Dwight Reed, capacity 5,600. Jason Gym, capacity 2,500.

SOUTHWEST BAPTIST UNIVERSITY BEARCATS
Bolivar **[P. 66, F-5]**; (417) 326-1652. Plaster, capacity 3,000. Bearcat, capacity 3,000.

SOUTHWEST MISSOURI STATE UNIVERSITY BEARS
901 S. National, Springfield **[P. 67, A-14]**; (417) 836-5244. Briggs, capacity 9,000. Hammons Center, capacity 8,858.

UNIVERSITY OF MISSOURI TIGERS
Columbia **[P. 67, A-9]**; (314) 882-6501. Faurot Field, capacity 68,152. Hearnes, capacity 13,103.
◆One of the country's wildest student basketball sections. They occasionally have to be reprimanded for being off color. Coach Norm Stewart is a Missouri legend — a prep boy star in the state, a Missouri grad and now its most successful coach.

UNIVERSITY OF MISSOURI KANGAROOS
5100 Rockhill Road, Kansas City **[P. 67, H-13]**; (816) 276-1036. Municipal Auditorium.

Football

ARROWHEAD STADIUM
At the Harry S. Truman Sports Complex, One Arrowhead Drive, Kansas City **[P. 67, G-14]**. Built in 1972. Capacity: 78,067.
◆Cold in fall and winter, sometimes below zero.
Kansas City Chiefs (AFC Western Division); (816) 924-9300. Franchise began in 1960. Broadcasts by KCMO.

Hockey

KEMPER ARENA
1800 Genessee, Kansas City **[P. 67, G-13]**. Capacity: 15,875.
Kansas City Blades (International Hockey League); (816) 274-1900. Franchise began in 1990. Broadcasts by KCFM 107.3 FM.

ST. LOUIS ARENA
5700 Oakland Avenue, St. Louis **[P. 67, D-12]**. Built in 1929. Capacity: 17,188.
St. Louis Blues (NHL, Campbell Conference, Norris Division); (314) 781-5300. Franchise began in 1967. Broadcasts by KMOX Radio, KPLR-TV (Channel 11).

Museums & Halls of Fame

NATIONAL BOWLING HALL OF FAME
111 Stadium Plaza, St. Louis **[P. 67, D-13]**; (314) 231-6340.

NATIONAL HIGH SCHOOL SPORTS HALL OF FAME
11724 Northwest Plaza Circle, Kansas City **[P. 66, C-3]**; (816) 464-5400.

ST. LOUIS SPORTS HALL OF FAME
100 Stadium Plaza Rd., St. Louis **[P. 67, D-13]**; (314) 421-3263.

PGA/LPGA

LOCH LLOYD COUNTRY CLUB
16750 Country Club Drive, Belton **[P. 66, D-3]**; (816) 322-2117.
Southwestern Bell Classic (Senior PGA), May. Number of holes: 54.

Soccer

KEMPER ARENA
1800 Genessee Street, Kansas City **[P. 67, G-13]**. Capacity: 15,800.
Kansas City Comets (Major Soccer League); (816) 274-1900. Please call ahead to confirm team information.

ST. LOUIS ARENA
5700 Oakland Avenue, St. Louis **[P. 67, D-12]**. Capacity: 17,931.
St. Louis Storm (Major Soccer League); (314) 781-6475.

Track & Field

MUNICIPAL AUDITORIUM
13th St. & Central, Kansas City **[P. 67, G-13]**; (816) 842-5050.

USA SNAPSHOTS®

A look at statistics that shape the sports world

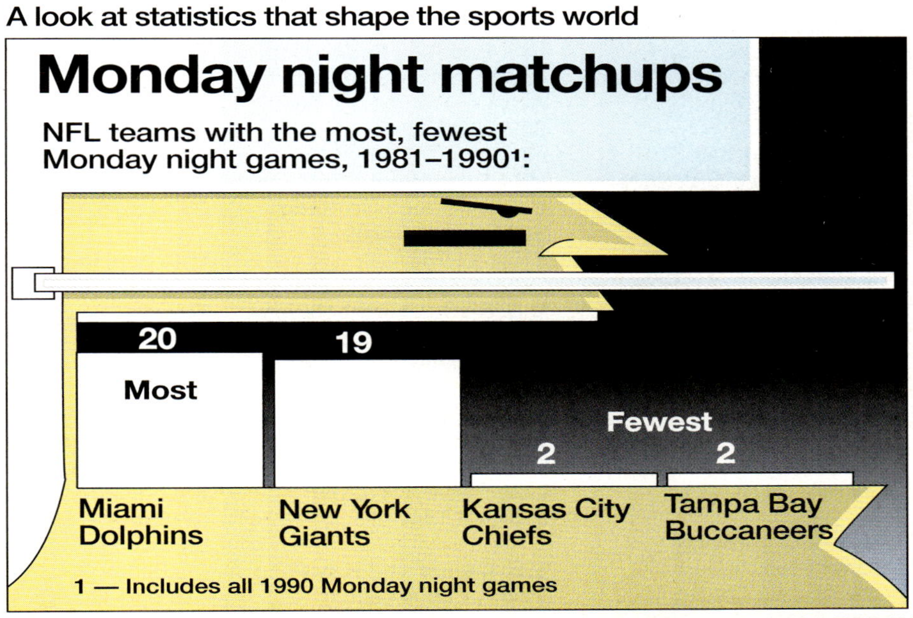

Source: 1990 NFL record and Fact Book
By Rod Little, USA TODAY

STATBOX

POPULATION: 5,141,000
SQUARE MILES: 69,674
TIME ZONE: Central
MOTTO: Salus Populi Suprema Lax Esto (Let the Good of the People Be the Supreme Law)
BIRD: Bluebird
TREE: Dogwood
CAPITAL: Jefferson City
AVERAGE ANNUAL RAINFALL: 42"
MEAN TEMP: 28 (Jan.); 91 (July)
MAJOR LEAGUE TEAMS: 4
NATIONAL PARK/FOREST ACREAGE: 2,011,673
STATE PARK ACREAGE: 107,000
HIGHEST ELEVATION: 1,772'
LOWEST ELEVATION: 230'
WATERWAYS: 50,000 miles of rivers and streams; 1,100 springs; 14 major lakes

NAIA (Collegiate National Championship), March.

► OUTDOOR VENUES

National Parks

MARK TWAIN NATIONAL FOREST
S of I-94 **[P. 66, D-7, G-5 and P. 67, E-9, G-8]**. Contains 1,472,667 acres. **C HK BT F S R BK HT**

OZARK NATIONAL SCENIC RIVERWAY
Off MO 19 **[P. 67, G-8]**. Contains 80,000 acres. **C HK BT F S R HT**

State Parks

Bike Trails: BK
Boating: BT
Camping: C
Climbing: CL
Diving: DV
Fishing: F
Golfing: G
Hiking: HK
Hunting: HT
Riding: R
Surfing: SU
Swimming: S
Tennis: TE
Whitewater: WW
Winter Sports: W

BENNETT SPRING STATE PARK
12 mi. W of Lebanon on MO 64 **[P. 66, F-6]**. Contains 3,064 acres. **C HK BT F S**

CASTLEWOOD STATE PARK
6 mi. E of New Ballwin on Kiefer Creek Rd. off MO 100 in St. Louis County **[P. 67, D-9]**. Contains 1,790 acres. **HK BT F R BK**

CROWDER STATE PARK
5 mi. NW of Trenton on MO 146 in Grundy County **[P. 66, B-5]**. Contains 673 acres. **C HK BT F S W**

CUIVRE RIVER STATE PARK
4 mi. E of Troy off MO 47 **[P. 67, C-9]**. Contains 6,250 acres. **C HK BT F S R**

DR. EDMUND A. BABLER MEMORIAL
20 mi. W of St. Louis on MO 109, btwn. I-40 & MO 10 **[P. 67, D-9]**. Contains 2,439 acres. **C HK S R BK TE**

HARRY S. TRUMAN STATE PARK
5 mi. W of Warsaw off MO 7, on County UU in Benton County **[P. 66, E-5]**. Contains 1,440 acres. **C HK BT F S**

LAKE OF THE OZARKS STATE PARK
Off MO 42 and I-54, in Camden & Miller Counties **[P. 66, E-6]**. Contains 17,152 acres. **C HK BT F S R W**

LAKE WAPPAPELLO STATE PARK
16 mi. N of Poplar Bluff on US 67 and 9 mi. E on MO 172 **[P. 67, G-10]**. Contains 1,854 acres. **C HK BT F S**

MARK TWAIN LAKE (AC)
On MO 107 in Monroe County **[P. 66, C-7]**. Contains 18,600 acres. **C HK BT F S**

MERAMEC STATE PARK
4 mi. E of Sullivan **[P. 67, E-9]**. Contains 6,734 acres. **C HK BT F S W**

CONTINUED ON PAGE 176

Missouri

CONTINUED FROM PAGE 175

MONTAUK STATE PARK
21 mi. SW of Salem via MO 119 **[P. 67, F-8]**. Contains 1,353 acres. **C HK F S W**

ONONDAGA CAVE STATE PARK
Hwy. H, 7 mi. SE of I-44 Leasburg exit **[P. 67, E-8]**. Contains 1,317 acres. **C HK BT F S**

ROCK BRIDGE STATE PARK
Near Columbia **[P. 66, D-7]**. Contains 2,238 acres. **HK**

SAM A. BAKER STATE PARK
3 mi. N of Patterson on MO 143, in Wayne County **[P. 67, F-9]**. Contains 5,168 acres. **C HK BT F S R**

ST. JOE STATE PARK
Near Flat River on US 32, in St. Francois County **[P. 67, E-9]**. Contains 8,238 acres. **C HK BT F S R BK**

STOCKTON STATE PARK
S of Stockton on MO 215, in Cedar County **[P. 66, F-4]**. Contains 2,176 acres. **C HK BT F S**

TABLE ROCK (AC)
7 mi. W of Branson via MO 165 **[P. 66, H-5]**. Contains 356 acres. **C HK BT F S DV**

TRAIL OF TEARS
10 mi. E of Fruitland on MO 177 **[P. 67, F-11]**. Contains 3,415 acres. **C HK BT F S R**

WATKINS MILL STATE PARK
Hwy. RA, 6 mi. N of Excelsior Springs off MO 92, in Clay County **[P. 66, C-4]**. Contains 1,442 acres. **C HK BT F S BK**

Skiing

ALPINE SKIING

HIDDEN VALLEY
Eureka **[P. 67, D-9]**; (314) 938-5373. Vertical drop is 300 feet. Has six tows and one chair.

> **"I think one of the major attractions. . . [is] the Ozarks: fishing, camping, canoeing — we have many wonderful streams. . . I find it very alluring. [And] St. Louis is. . . not very far away. You can drive from here. It's a very nice place to live. It puts me right smack dab in the middle of everything I do. . . "**
>
> **Golfer *Hale Irwin***

ACTIVE SPORTS

AEROBICS: AFAA, 566 McBride Point Dr., Ballwin; (314) 458-3562.

BASEBALL: Little League Baseball Central Region HQ, 4360 N. Mitthoeffer Rd., Indianapolis, IN; (317) 897-6127. • **American Legion Baseball,** 2516 Meadow Ln., Cape Girardeau; (314) 334-1017. • **Babe Ruth Baseball,** Norman Travis, Box 339, Burlington, CO; (719) 346-8803. • **Men's Senior Baseball League - Kansas City,** 9216 W. 76th Terrace, Overland Park, KS; (913) 649-2942.

BILLIARDS: Raytown Rec, 10012 1/2 E. 63rd, Raytown; (816) 358-5977.

BOARDSAILING: Missouri Sailboards , Columbia; (314) 474-6311. • **USWA Regional Director,** 2625 S. 46th, Lincoln, NE;(402)489-1002.

BOWLING: American Bowling Congress, 5301 S. 76th St., Greendale, WI; (414) 421-6400.

CANOEING & KAYAKING: ACA Midwest Vice Commodore, 1343 N. Portage, Palatine, IL; (708) 359-5047.

CYCLING: LAW North Central Regional Director, Route 1, Box 99, Cushing, WI; (715) 648-5519. • **Ozark Area AYH Council,** 7187 Manchester Rd., St. Louis; (314) 644-4660. • **USCF Missouri Representative,** 4454 Lindell Boulevard, #31, St. Louis; (314) 652-9939.

FITNESS: Governor's Council on Physical Fitness & Health, Box 809, Office of Administration, Truman State Office Building, Room 760, Jefferson City; (314) 751-0915.

FOOTBALL: Pop Warner Football, 1315 Walnut Street, Suite 1632, Philadelphia, PA; (215) 735-1450.

GOLF: Missouri Golf Association, PO Box 104164, Jefferson City; (314) 636-8994. • **PGA Gateway Section,** 2333 Grissom Dr., Suite 109, Maryland Heights; (314) 991-4994. • **PGA Midwest Section,** 1900 Corporate Centre, South Outer Rd., Ste. 1E; (816) 229-6565. • **St. Louis District Golf Association,** 537 North Clay, Kirkwood; (314) 821-1511.

HIKING & CLIMBING: Ozark Sierra Club Chapter, 1005A South Big Bend Blvd., St. Louis; (314) 645-1019.

HOCKEY: USA Hockey Central Registrar, PO Box 1738, Lisle, IL; (708) 963-1098.

HUNTING & FISHING: Department of Conservation, PO Box 180, Jefferson City; (314) 751-4115. • **Frontenac Outfitters, Ltd. (Orvis),** 751 Old Frontenac Square, St. Louis; (314) 993-4570. • **Trout Unlimited,** 4725 Nebraska, St. Louis; (314) 752-3418.

RACQUETBALL: AARA, 1900 S.W. 9th, Blue Springs; (816) 228-3279.

RIDING: Missouri Equine Council, Rt. 1, Box 215, Brookline; (417) 882-1727.

RODEO: PRCA Great Lakes Circuit, Rt. 1, Box 54, Clayton, IN; (317) 539-5039.

RUNNING: RRCA MO State Rep., c/o Mid-America Running Ass'n, 6517 New Platte Hills Rd., Parkville; (816) 741-1468.

SCUBA: Academy of Scuba Training, 437 Broadway, Cape Girardeau; (314) 335-0756. • **Captain John's Sports & Scuba,** PO Box E, M.M. Highway, Oronogo; (417) 673-2724. • **The Dive Shop,** 2526 NE Vivion, Kansas City; (816) 455-1492. • **Underwater Sports,** 7269 Watson, St. Louis; (314) 352-9200.

SHOOTING: Game Hill Hunting Club, 18480 Hwy P., Weston; (816) 431-5057. • **Hazel Creek Sporting Clays,** Rt. 2, Box 167, Greentop; (816) 949-2689. • **Malinmor Sporting Estate,** RR 4, Box 108, Eolia; (314) 324-3366. • **Pond Fort Estate Hunt Club,** 8860 Highway N., O'Fallon; (314) 327-5680. • **Shooting Academy Trail Ridge,** Rt. 1, Box 56-1, Blairstown; (816) 885-7511.

SKATING: Missouri Skating Association, 7127 Pershing, St. Louis; (314) 725-0886. • **USFSA,** 20 First Street, Colorado Springs, CO; (719) 635-5200.

SOCCER: Missouri Soccer Ass'n, 10260 Reavis Gardens Dr., St. Louis; (314) 638-9528. • **Missouri YSA,** PO Box 1328, St. Peters; (816) 464-5400. • **AYSO Regional Director,** 2971 N. Coronado St., Chandler; (602) 839-2114.

SOFTBALL: Missouri ASA, Springfield Parks & Recreation Dept., 1923 North Weller, Springfield; (417) 869-2120. • **Kansas City ASA,** 511 W. 101st Street, Kansas City; (816) 942-7972. • **St. Louis ASA,** PO Box 21627, St. Louis; (314) 752-9551.

SQUASH: Racquet Club of St. Louis (USSRA), St. Louis; (314) 361-0288.

SWIMMING: LMSC Ozark Registrar, 900 Weidmann Rd., Manchester; (314) 434-2191.

TABLE TENNIS: USTTA State Coordinator, 3321 Jamesdale Rd., Columbia; (314) 474-6450.

TENNIS: Recreational TEAMTENNIS Midwest-Southeast Region, National Program Coordinator, 445 N. Wells, Ste. #404, Chicago, IL; (800) TEAMTEN. • **Missouri Valley USTA,** 722 Walnut St., Suite #1, Kansas City; (816) 556-0777.

VOLLEYBALL: USVBA Heat of America Commissioner, 616 W. 70th Street, Kansas City; (816) 333-6691.

Tip Offs

Olympic Organizing Bodies: Part I

The following is an alphabetical list of Olympic organizing bodies and other associations affiliated with the Olympic effort.

American Amateur Racquetball Association (AARA), 815 North Weber, Colorado Springs, CO 80903
719-635-5396

USA Amateur Boxing Federation (USA/ABF), 1750 East Boulder Street, Colorado Springs, CO 80909
719-578-4506

U.S. Amateur Confederation of Roller Skating (USAC/RS), P.O. Box 6579, Lincoln, NE 68506
402-483-7551

Amateur Softball Association (ASA), 2801 N.E. 50th Street, Oklahoma City, OK 73111
405-424-5266

American Horse Shows Association (AHSA), National Equestrian Federation of the United States, 220 East 42nd Street, Suite 409, New York, NY 10017-5806
212-972-2472

Atlanta Organizing Committee, Suite 3450, One Atlantic Center, 1201 West Peachtree Street, Atlanta, GA 30309
404-874-1996

The Athletics Congress (TAC), P.O. Box 120, Indianapolis, IN 46206
317-261-0500

U.S. Badminton Association (USBA), 501 West 6th Street, Papillion, NE 68046
402-592-7309

U.S. Baseball Federation (USBF), 2160 Greenwood Avenue, Trenton, NJ 08609
609-586-2381

USA Basketball, 1750 East Boulder Street, Colorado Springs, CO 80909
719-632-7687

U.S. Biathlon Association (USBA), P.O. Box 5515, Essex Junction, VT 05453
802-655-4524

U.S. Bobsled and Skeleton Federation, P.O. Box 828, Lake Placid, NY 12946
518-523-1842

U.S. Canoe and Kayak Team, Pan American Plaza, Suite 470, 201 South Capitol Avenue, Indianapolis, IN 46225
317-237-5690

U.S. Curling Association (USCA), 1100 Center Point Drive, Box 971, Stevens Point, WI 54481
715-344-1199

U.S. Cycling Federation (USCF), 1750 East Boulder Street, Colorado Springs, CO 80909
719-578-4581

United States Diving, Inc. (USD), Pan American Plaza, Suite 430, Indianapolis, IN 46225
317-237-5252

U.S. Fencing Association (USFA), 1750 East Boulder Street, Colorado Springs, CO 80909
719-578-4511

Field Hockey Association of America (FHAA) (Men) U.S. Field Hockey Association (USFHA) (Women) 1750 East Boulder Street, Colorado Springs, CO 80909
719-578-4587 (FHAA)
719-578-4567 (USFHA)

U.S. Figure Skating Association (USFSA), 20 First Street, Colorado Springs, CO 80906
719-635-5200

U.S. Gymnastics Federation (USGF), Pan American Plaza, Suite 300, 201 South Capitol Avenue, Indianapolis, IN 46225
317-237-5050

USA Hockey, 2997 Broadmoor Valley Road, Colorado Springs, CO 80906
719-576-4990

U.S. International Speedskating Association (USISA), 1750 East Boulder Street, Colorado Springs, CO 80909
719-578-0661

United States Judo, Inc. (USJ), P.O. Box 10013, El Paso, TX 79991
915-565-8754

U.S. Karate Federation, 1300 Kenmore Boulevard, Akron, OH 44314
216-753-3114

CONTINUED ON PAGE 196

Montana

One of the state's biggest events is Butte's Winternational Sports Festival in February, a six-week, 13-sport competition that draws athletes from all over the United States and Canada. ◆ Butte also features the U.S. High Altitude Training Center, one of two training grounds for the U.S. Olympic speed skating team. The complex is open to the public; admission is free. ◆ Big Sky and Big Mountain are two of the state's largest ski areas, while great snowmobiling trails are available at Yellowstone National Park. ◆ Yellowstone, as well as Glacier National Park, are particularly popular among mountain climbers. ◆ For boating and sailing, Flathead Lake and Canyon Ferry are prime spots. ◆ Montana's Blue Ribbon trout streams in the southwest are angling havens. Big-game hunting is available in the entire state, with a special season for archers.

▶ SPECTATOR VENUES

Baseball

ALUMNI COLISEUM
Montana Tech College, West Park Street, Butte **[P. 68, E-5]**. Capacity: 5,000
Butte Copper Kings (Pioneer League, Rookie Class); (406) 723-8206. Entered League in 1987. Broadcasts by KBOW 550-AM. MLB affiliation, Texas Rangers.

COBB FIELD
27th St. & 9th Ave., Billings **[P. 68, D-2]**. Capacity: 4,500
Billings Mustangs (Pioneer League, Rookie Class); (406) 252-1241. Entered League in 1948. Broadcasts by KCTR 970-AM. MLB affiliation, Cincinnati Reds.

KINDRICK LEGION FIELD
Memorial & Warren Streets, Helena **[P. 69, G-13]**. Capacity: 2,700
Helena Brewers (Pioneer League, Rookie Class); (406) 449-7616. Entered League in 1978. Broadcasts by KMTX 950 AM. MLB affiliation, Milwaukee Brewers.

LEGION PARK
2600 River Drive North, Great Falls **[P. 69, G-12]**. Capacity: 4,000
Great Falls Dodgers (Pioneer League, Rookie Class); (406) 452-5311. Entered League in 1969. Broadcasts by KQDI 1450-AM. MLB affiliation, Los Angeles Dodgers.

College Sports

EASTERN MONTANA COLLEGE YELLOWJACKETS
1500 N. 30th, Billings **[P. 68, D-2]**; (406) 657-2369. Campus, capacity 3,200.

MONTANA STATE UNIVERSITY BOBCATS
Bozeman **[P. 68, E-7]**; (406) 994-4221. Reno H. Sales, capacity 15,197. Brick Breeden, capacity 7,848.

UNIVERSITY OF MONTANA GRIZZLIES
Missoula **[P. 69, H-14]**; (406) 243-5331. Washington Grizzly, capacity 15,000.

Horse Racing

METRAPARK
308 6th Ave., Billings **[P. 68, D-2]**; (406) 256-2400.
Thoroughbred season from Aug. to Oct.
◆Formerly Billings.

MONTANA STATE FAIR RACE MEET (GREAT FALLS)
400 3rd Street NW, Great Falls **[P. 69, G-11]**; (406) 727-8900. Opened in 1931. Grandstand capacity: 3,500.
Thoroughbred season from May to Aug.

▶ OUTDOOR VENUES

National Parks

BEAVERHEAD NATIONAL FOREST
Southwest **[P. 68, E-4, F-5,6]**. Contains 2,147,500 acres. C HK BT F S R BK W HT

BIGHORN CANYON NATIONAL RECREATION AREA
Fort Smith **[P. 69, F-10]**. Contains 119,303 acres.
C HK BT F S R BK W HT

BITTERROOT NATIONAL FOREST
Southwest **[P. 68, E-4]**. Contains 1,577,883 acres. C HK BT F S R BK W WW

CUSTER NATIONAL FOREST
South central **[P. 69, F-8,9 and E-12,14]**. Contains 1,100,000 acres. C HK F S R BK W CL

DEERLODGE NATIONAL FOREST
Butte **[P. 68, E-6, D-4,5]**. Contains 1,355,783 acres. C HK BT F S R BK W HT

FLATHEAD NATIONAL FOREST
Western Montana **[P. 68, A-3, B-3,4, F-1, H-2]**. Contains 2,330,000 acres.
C HK BT F S R BK W WW

GALLATIN NATIONAL FOREST
South central **[P. 68-9, E-7, F-7,8]**. Contains 1,735,239 acres. C HK BT F S R BK W WW

GLACIER NATIONAL PARK
N of US 2, btwn. East & West Glacier **[P. 68, A-5]**. Contains 1,012,996 acres.
C HK BT F S R BK W

HELENA NATIONAL FOREST
16 mi. N of Helena **[P. 68, D-5,6]**. Contains 976,000 acres. C HK BT F S R BK W HT

KOOTENAI NATIONAL FOREST
Northwest **[P. 68, A-2]**. Contains 1,800,000 acres. C HK BT F S R BK W HT

LEWIS AND CLARK NATIONAL FOREST
Western **[P. 68, B-5, C-7, H-4, D-7,8]** Contains 1,843,397 acres. C HK BT F S R BK W CL

LOLO NATIONAL FOREST
Southwestern **[P. 68, B-3, D-3, C-2,4]**. Contains 2,100,000 acres. C HK BT F S R BK W CL

State Parks

CANYON FERRY STATE PARK
SE of Helena off US 287 on Canyon Ferry Lake **[P. 68, D-6]**. Contains 2,787 acres.
C BT F S HT

COONEY LAKE STATE PARK
54 mi. SE of Billings at Boyd **[P. 69, F-9]**. Contains 1,000 acres.
C BT F S

FLATHEAD LAKE STATE PARK
20 mi. S of Kalispell on US 93 **[P. 68, B-4]**. Contains 343 acres. C HK BT F S R BK DV

HUNGRY HORSE RESERVOIR RECREATION AREA
24 mi. NE of Kalispell off US 2 **[P. 68, H-2]**. Contains 29,000 acres. C HK BT F S R BK W HT

Bike Trails: BK
Boating: BT
Camping: C
Climbing: CL
Diving: DV
Fishing: F
Golfing: G
Hiking: HK
Hunting: HT
Riding: R
Surfing: SU
Tennis: TE
Swimming: S
Whitewater: WW
Winter Sports: W

LEWIS AND CLARK CAVERNS STATE PARK
19 mi. W of Three Forks on MT 2 **[P. 68, E-6]**. Contains 2,735 acres. C HK

MAKOSHIKA STATE PARK
1 mi. S of Glendive **[P. 69, C-13]**. Contains 8,800 acres. C HK BK HT

THOMPSON FALLS STATE PARK
3 mi. W of Thompson Falls off MT 200 **[P. 68, C-3]**. Contains 36 acres. C HK BT F

USA SNAPSHOTS®

A look at statistics that shape the sports world

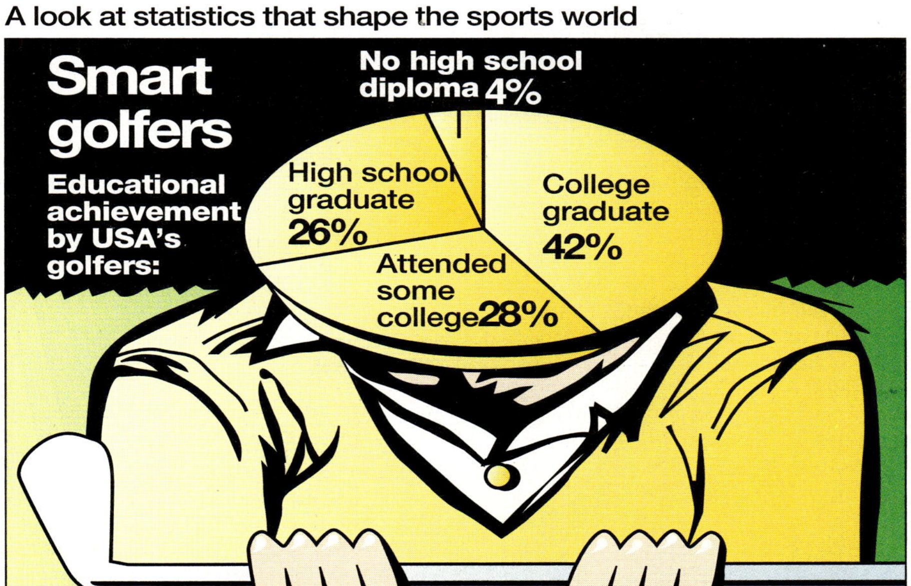

Source: National Golf Federation — By Elys McLean-Ibrahim, USA TODAY

STATBOX

POPULATION: 800,000
SQUARE MILES: 145,392
TIME ZONE: Mountain
MOTTO: The Treasure State/Unspoiled, Unforgettable
BIRD: Meadowlark
TREE: Ponderosa Pine
CAPITAL: Helena
AVERAGE ANNUAL RAINFALL: 11"
MEAN TEMP: 18 (Jan.); 68 (July)
MAJOR LEAGUE TEAMS: 0
NATIONAL PARK/FOREST ACREAGE: 2,500,000
STATE PARK AND WILDLIFE ACREAGE: 461,000
HIGHEST ELEVATION: 12,799'
LOWEST ELEVATION: 1,800'
WATERWAYS: 17,000 miles of rivers; 600 lakes

Skiing

ALPINE SKIING

BIG SKY SKI & SUMMER RESORT
1 Lone Mt. Trail, Big Sky **[P. 68, F-6]**; (800) 548-4486.
Vertical drop is 3,030 feet. Has two tows, five chairs and two gondolas.

BRIDGER BOWL SKI AREA
15 mi. N of Bozeman on MT 86, Bozeman **[P. 68, F-6]**; (406) 587-2111.
Vertical drop is 2,000 feet. Has one tow and five chairs.

RED LODGE MOUNTAIN
Ski Run Road, Red Lodge **[P. 69, F-9]**; (406) 446-2610.
Vertical drop is 2,016 feet. Has one tow and five chairs.

THE BIG MOUNTAIN SKI AND SUMMER RESORT
Off Highway 93, Whitefish **[P. 68, G-1]**; (406) 862-3511.
Vertical drop is 2,170 feet. Has one tow, one bar and six chairs.

NORDIC SKIING

BIG MOUNTAIN RESORT
Whitefish **[P. 68, H-1]**; (800) 858-5439.

GLACIER PARK SKI TOURS
Whitefish **[P. 68, H-1]**; (406) 888-5700.

GROUSE MOUNTAIN LODGE/ GLACIER NORDIC CENTER
1205 Highway 93 West, Whitefish **[P. 68, H-1]**; (800) 321-8822.

IZAAK WALTON INN
Railroad Street, Essex **[P. 68, H-3]**; (406) 888-5700.

LAKEVIEW SKI RANCH
Monida Star Route, Lima **[P. 68, G-5]**; (406) 276-3278.

LONE MOUNTAIN RANCH
Meadow Village, Big Sky **[P. 68, F-6]**; (406) 995-4644.

NIGHTINGALE NORDIC
Highway 12 West, Lolo **[P. 68, D-4]**; (406) 273-2415.

OUTER LIMITS TOURS
Gallatin Gateway **[P. 68, E-7]**; (406) 763-4629.

CONTINUED ON PAGE 178

Montana

CONTINUED FROM PAGE 177

RED LODGE NORDIC SKI AREA
Red Lodge **[P. 69, F-9]**; (406) 446-3158.

▶ ACTIVE SPORTS

ADVENTURE: Voyageur Outward Bound School, 10900 Cedar Lake Rd., Minnetonka, MN; (800) 328-2943.

AEROBICS: AFAA, 3914 Palisades, Billings; (406) 656-1968.

BASEBALL: Little League Baseball Western Region HQ, 6707 Little League Dr., San Bernadino, CA; (714) 887-6444. • **Pony Baseball-Softball,** 110 N. 5th St., Auburn, IL; (217) 438-3130. • **American Legion Baseball,** 136 Riverview 5 W., Great Falls; (406) 453-9412. • **Babe Ruth Baseball,** Jim Lemp, 1911 Oxford Dr., Cheyenne, WY; (307) 638-6023.

BOARDSAILING: Big Sky Windsurfing , Bozeman; (406) 587-5227. • **USWA Regional Director,** 18354 W. 58th Pl., #62, Golden, CO; (303)279-3185.

BOWLING: American Bowling Congress, 5301 S. 76th St., Greendale, WI; (414) 421-6400.

CANOEING & KAYAKING: ACA Rocky Mountain Vice Commodore, c/o Four Corners Marine, Box 379, Durango, CO; (303) 259-3893.

CYCLING: USCF Montana Representative, 1708 34th St., Missoula; (314) 652-9939.

FOOTBALL: Pop Warner Football, 1315 Walnut Street, Suite 1632, Philadelphia, PA; (215) 735-1450.

GOLF: Montana State Golf Association, PO Box 3389, Butte; (406) 782-9208. • **PGA Pacific Northwest Section,** 1201 M St. Southeast, Auburn, WA; (503) 222-1139. • **PGA Rocky Mountain Section,** 595 E. State St., Eagle, ID; (208) 939-6028.

HIKING & CLIMBING: Montana Sierra Club Chapter, 78 Konley Dr., Kalispell; (406) 752-8925.

HOCKEY: USA Hockey Rocky Mountain Registrar, 7335 S. Garfield Ct., Littleton, CO; (303) 721-0936.

HUNTING & FISHING: Department of Fish, Wildlife & Parks, 1420 E. 6th Ave., Helena; (406) 444-2535. • **Montana Troutfitters Orvis Shop,** 1716 West Main, Bozeman; (406) 587-4707. • **Trout Unlimited,** c/o Rocky Mountain Lab, Hamilton; (406) 363-3465.

RACQUETBALL: AARA, 3758 Mt. Rushmore Ave., Billings; (406) 656-3890.

RODEO: PRCA Montana Circuit, Rt. 1, Box 54, Geyser; (406) 735-4391.

RUNNING: RRCA MT State Rep., Civic Center, PO Box 5021, Great Falls; (406) 452-3116.

SHOOTING: Sport Montana, 9430 Pryor Rd., Billings; (406) 252-8188.

SKATING: Montana Amateur Speedskating Association, 1730 Delaware, Butte; (406) 723-6703. • **USFSA,** 20 First Street, Colorado Springs, CO; (719) 635-5200.

SOCCER: Montana Soccer Ass'n, 2200 Tipperary Way, Missoula; (406) 543-1290. • **Montana YSA,** 1309 Driftwood Dr., Bozeman; (406) 994-6315. • **AYSO Regional Director,** 1720 Carmel, Idaho Falls, ID; (208) 529-2649.

SOFTBALL: Montana ASA, 1340 Harrison Avenue., Civic Center, Butte; (406) 494-7017.

SWIMMING: LMSC Montana Registrar, PO Box 7338, Missoula; (406) 728-8917.

TENNIS: Recreational TEAMTENNIS Central-West Region, National Program Coordinator, 2105 Grant Ave., #4, Redondo Beach, CA; (800) 992-9042. • **Pacific Northwest USTA,** 10175 SW Barbur Blvd., 306B, Portland, OR; (503) 245-3048. Lincoln County.

WHITEWATER RAFTING: Glacier Raft Company , #6 Going-to-the-Sun Rd., PO Box 218, West Glacier; (406) 888-5454. • **Yellowstone Raft Co.,** Box 46, Gardiner; (406) 848-7777.

Tip Offs

State Travel Offices

From hotels and motels to seasonal event listings to general state park information contacts, these tourism offices are excellent resources for planning your vacation.

Alabama Bureau of Tourism, 532 S. Perry, Montgomery, AL; (205) 261-4169 or (800) ALABAMA.

Alaska Division of Tourism, PO Box Pouch E, Juneau, AK; (907) 465-2010.

Arizona Office of Tourism, 1480 E. Bethany Home Rd., Phoenix, AZ; (602) 542-8687.

Arkansas Department of Parks and Tourism, One Capitol Mall, Little Rock, AR; (501) 682-7777.

California Office of Tourism, 1121 L St., Suite 103, Sacramento, CA; (916) 322-1397 or (800) 862-2543.

Colorado Department of Tourism, 1625 Broadway, Denver, CO; (800) 433-2656.

Connecticut Department of Economic Development, 210 Washington St., Hartford, CT; (203) 566-3977.

Delaware Tourism Office, 99 Kings Highway, PO Box 1401, Dover, DE; (302) 736-4271 or (800) 441-8846.

Washington Convention and Visitors Bureau, 1575 Eye St., NW, Washington, DC; (202) 789-7048.

Florida Division of Tourism, 107 West Gaines St., Tallahassee, FL; (904) 487-1462.

Georgia Department of Industry and Trade, PO Box 1776, Atlanta, GA; (404) 656-3592.

Hawaii Visitors Bureau, 2270 Kalakaua Ave., Suite 801, Honolulu, HI; (808) 923-1811.

Idaho Travel Council, Room 108, State Capitol Bldg., Boise, ID; (800) 635-7820 or (208) 334-2470.

Illinois Office of Tourism, Room 108, 310 South Michigan Ave., Chicago, IL; (312) 793-2094.

Indiana Tourism Development Division, One North Capitol, Suite 700, Indianapolis, IN; (317) 232-8860.

Iowa Development Commission, Tourist Travel Division, 600 East Court Ave., Des Moines, IA; (515) 281-3100.

Kansas Department of Travel and Tourism, 503 Kansas Ave., 6th Floor, Topeka, KS; (913) 296-2009.

Kentucky Department of Travel Development, Capitol Plaza Tower, 22nd Floor, Frankfort, KY; (502) 564-4930 or (800) 225-TRIP.

Louisiana Office of Tourism, PO Box 94291, Capitol Station, Baton Rouge, LA; (504) 342-8119.

Maine State Development Office of Tourism, 189 State St., Augusta, ME; (207) 289-5710.

Maryland Office of Tourism, 45 Calvert St., Annapolis, MD; (800) 543-1036.

Massachusetts Division of Tourism, 100 Cambridge St., Boston, MA; (617) 727-3201.

Michigan Travel Bureau, PO Box, Lansing, MI; (517) 373-0670.

Minnesota Office of Tourism, 240 Bremer Bldg., 419 North Robert St., St. Paul, MN; (612) 296-5029 or (800) 328-1461.

Mississippi Division of Tourism, PO Box 849, Jackson, MS; 800) 647-2290.

Missouri Division of Tourism, Truman State Office Building, PO Box 1055, Jefferson City, MO; (314) 751-4133.

Montana Travel Promotion Division, 1424 9th Ave, Helena, MT; (406) 444-2654.

Nebraska Department of Economic Development, Division of Travel and Tourism, 301 Centennial Mall South, Box 94666, Lincoln, NE; (402) 471-3796.

Nevada Commission on Tourism, Capitol Complex, Carson City, NV; (702) 733-2323.

New Hampshire Office of Vacation Travel, Box 856, Concord, NH; (603) 271-2665.

New Jersey Division of Travel and Tourism, CN 826, Trenton, NJ; (609) 292-2470.

New Mexico Tourism and Travel, Bataan Memorial Bldg., Santa Fe, NM; (800) 545-2040 or (505) 827-6230.

New York State Division of Tourism, One Commerce Plaza, Albany, NY; (518) 474-4116.

North Carolina Travel and Tourism Division, 430 North Salisbury Street, Raleigh, NC; (919) 733-4171.

North Dakota Tourism Promotion, Liberty Memorial Building, Bismarck, ND; (701) 224-2525 or (800) 847-4862.

Ohio Department of Development, Division of Travel and Tourism, PO Box 1001, Columbus, OH; (800) 282-5393.

Oklahoma Tourism and Recreation Department, 505 Will Rogers Building, Oklahoma City, OK; (405) 521-2406.

Oregon Economic Development Department, Tourism Division, 595 Cottage St., NE, Salem, OR; (503) 378-6309 or (800) 547-7842.

Pennsylvania Bureau of Travel Development, 416 Forum Building, Harrisburg, PA; (717) 787-5453 or (800) 237-4363.

Rhode Island Department of Economic Development, Tourism Promotion, Seven Jackson Walkway, Providence, RI; (401) 277-2601.

South Carolina Department of Parks, Recreation and Tourism, Box 71, Columbia, SC; (803) 734-0122.

South Dakota Division of Tourism, 711 Wells Ave., Pierre, SD; (605) 773-3301 or (800) 843-1930.

Tennessee Department of Tourist Development, PO Box 23170, Nashville, TN; (615) 741-2158.

Texas Highways and Public Transportation Department, 11th and Brazos St., Austin, TX; (800) 888-8TEX

Utah Travel Council, Council Hall/Capitol Hill, Salt Lake City, UT; (801) 538-1030.

Vermont Travel Division, 134 State Street, Montpelier, VT; (802) 828-3236.

Virginia Division of Tourism, 202 North Ninth St., Suite 500, Richmond, VA; (804) 786-2051.

Washington State Department of Trade and Economic Development, 101 General Administration Building, Olympia, WA; (206) 753-5600.

West Virginia Tourism Information Office, State Capitol Complex, Charleston, WV; (800) 225-5982.

Wisconsin Division of Tourism, PO Box 7970, Madison, WI; (608) 266-2147.

Wyoming Travel Commission, I-25 at College Dr., Cheyenne, WY; (800) 225-5996.

Nebraska

The University of Nebraska Cornhuskers, almost always ranked among the top 10 college football teams in the nation, have drawn sellout crowds to Lincoln's Memorial Stadium since 1962—the longest streak in the USA. The weekly throng of 76,000 is a sea of red and—for three hours— is the largest community in the state after Omaha and Lincoln itself. ◆ Every June for the past 40 years, Omaha has hosted the eight-team College Baseball World Series for the NCAA championship. ◆ Omaha also has Triple-A baseball.◆ Nebraskans follow high school sports so closely that more than 100,000 fans annually attend Lincoln's March Madness, a succession of tournaments for state basketball championships. ◆ The world-class Governor's Regatta Sailboat Cup (Labor Day weekend) on 35,000 acre Lake Ogallala, is one of the largest inland regattas in the USA.

► SPECTATOR VENUES

Baseball

ROSENBLATT STADIUM
1202 Bert Murphy Ave., S. 13th St. exit off I-80, Omaha **[P. 70, H-3]**. Capacity: 17,500
Omaha Royals (American Association, Class AAA); (402) 734-2550. Entered League in 1969. Broadcasts by KKAR 1180-AM. MLB affiliation, Kansas City Royals.

Basketball

AK-SAR-BEN COLISEUM
63rd & Shirley Streets, Omaha **[P. 70, H-2]**. Capacity: 5,151.
Omaha Racers (Continental Basketball Association, American Conference, Midwest Division); (402) 551-5151. Entered League in 1982. Broadcasts by KOIL, 1290 AM.

College Sports

CREIGHTON UNIVERSITY BLUEJAYS
2500 California, Omaha **[P. 70, G-3]**; (402) 280-2720. Civic Auditorium, capacity 10,000.

NEBRASKA WESLEYAN UNIVERSITY PLAINSMEN
5000 St. Paul, Lincoln **[P. 70, E-3]**; (402) 465-2356. Able, capacity 2,500. Knight, capacity 350.

UNIVERSITY OF NEBRASKA CORNHUSKERS
Lincoln **[P. 70, E-2]**; (402) 472-3644. Memorial, capacity 73,650.
◆You better have red in your wardrobe on an autumn Saturday or you're going to feel out of place. A state without any pro sports takes its Husker football very seriously. Coach Tom Osborne may have more unpaid assistant coaches than anybody in college football. Every Nebraskan has an opinion.

UNIVERSITY OF NEBRASKA AT OMAHA MAVERICKS
Omaha **[P. 70, G-2]**; (402) 554-2305. Al F. Caniglia Field, capacity 9,500. UNO, capacity 4,000.

WAYNE STATE COLLEGE WILDCATS
Wayne **[P. 71, B-11]**; (402) 375-7520. Memorial, capacity 3,000. Rice, capacity 2,500.

Horse Racing

AK-SAR-BEN
63rd & Center, Omaha **[P. 70, H-2]**; (402) 556-2305. Opened in 1921. Clubhouse capacity: 1,250. Grandstand capacity: 11,500.
Thoroughbred season from May to Aug.

ATOKAD PARK
Highway 77 South, South Sioux City **[P. 71, B-12]**; (402) 494-4502. Opened in 1955. Grandstand capacity: 3,112.
Thoroughbred season from June to July. Also in Nov. & Dec.

COLUMBUS RACES
10th Ave. & 15th Street, Columbus **[P. 71, D-11]**; (402) 564-0133. Opened in 1941. Grandstand capacity: 4,000.
Thoroughbred season from Sep. to Nov.

FONNER PARK
East Stolley Park Road, Grand Island **[P. 70, H-5]**; (308) 382-4515. Opened in 1954. Clubhouse capacity: 1,648. Grandstand capacity: 1,863. Total capacity: 5,766.
Thoroughbred season from Feb. to Apr.

STATE FAIR PARK
1800 State Fair Park Drive, Lincoln **[P. 70, E-2]**; (402) 474-5371. Opened in 1935. Total capacity: 5,800.
Thoroughbred season from Aug. to Sep.
◆Season varies annually.

► OUTDOOR VENUES

National Parks

NEBRASKA NATIONAL FOREST (Two Units)
S of Chadron and N of I-80, N of N. Platte **[P. 70, A-1, C-6]**. Contains 142,000 acres.
C HK F S W

OGLALA NATIONAL GRASSLAND
NW corner of state **[P. 70, A-1]**. Contains 94,435 acres. C HK F R

State Parks

CALAMUS RESERVOIR STATE RECREATION AREA
6 mi. NW of Burwell **[P. 71, C-8]**. Contains 11,720 acres.
C BT F S W

CHADRON STATE PARK
Pine Ridge **[P. 70, A-3]**. Contains 972 acres.
C HK S R

DEAD TIMBER STATE RECREATION AREA
6.5 mi. NE of Scribner **[P. 71, C-12]**. Contains 200 acres. C HK BT F W

EUGENE T. MAHONEY STATE PARK
Near Ash, off I-80, exit 426 **[P. 71, D-12]**. Contains 500 acres.
C HK F R G

FORT ROBINSON STATE PARK
Crawford **[P. 70, A-2]**. Contains 22,672 acres.
C HK BT F S R BK W

INDIAN CAVE STATE PARK
15 mi. SE of Brownville **[P. 71, F-14]**. Contains 3,052 acres. C HK F R

Bike Trails: BK
Boating: BT
Camping: C
Climbing: CL
Diving: DV
Fishing: F
Golfing: G
Hiking: HK
Hunting: HT
Riding: R
Surfing: SU
Swimming: S
Tennis: TE
Whitewater: WW
Winter Sports: W

JOHNSON LAKE STATE PARK
7 mi. SW of Lexington on US 283 **[P. 70, E-7]**. Contains 2,140 acres. C HK BT F S W

LAKE MCCONAUGHY STATE RECREATION AREA
9 mi. N of Ogallala **[P. 70, D-4]**. Contains 41,651 acres. C HK BT F S W

LEWIS & CLARK LAKE STATE RECREATION AREA
N of Crofton off US 81 **[P. 71, A-10]**. Contains 8,570 acres. C HK BT F S W

NIOBRARA STATE PARK
Near Niobara **[P. 71, A-10]**. Contains 1,639 acres. C HK BT F R

PLATTE RIVER STATE PARK
2.5 mi. S of Louisville off NE 50 **[P. 71, D-13]**. Contains 418 acres. HK S R W TE

PONCA STATE PARK
2 mi. N of Ponca **[P. 71, A-12]**. Contains 859 acres. C HK BT F R

RED WILLOW STATE RECREATION AREA
11 mi. N of McCook on US 83 **[P. 70, E-6]**. Contains 5,948 acres. C HK BT F S W

TWO RIVERS
2 mi. SW of Venice **[P. 71, D-12]**. Contains 964 acres. C HK F S BK W

WILDCAT HILLS STATE RECREATION AREA
S of Gering **[P. 70, C-1]**. Contains 962 acres. C HK

Skiing

ALPINE SKIING

THE NEBRASKI AREA COMPLEX
I-80 between Omaha & Lincoln, Gretna **[P. 71, D-12]**; (402) 332-3313.
Vertical drop is 200 feet. Has three tows, one bar and one chair.

► ACTIVE SPORTS

AEROBICS: AFAA, 2524 S. 60th, #22, Omaha; (402) 558-9669.

BASEBALL: Little League Baseball Central Region HQ, 4360 N. Mitthoeffer Rd., Indianapolis, IN; (317) 897-6127. • **American Legion Baseball,** 2602 Lincoln Street, Beatrice; (402) 223-5006. • **Babe Ruth Baseball,** Norman Travis, Box 339, Burlington, CO; (719) 346-8803.

BILLIARDS: Big John's, 9819 M Street, Omaha; (402) 592-3545. • **The Break,** 500 W. 4th St., Kearney; (308) 234-4545.

BOARDSAILING: Main Sail Loft , Omaha; (402) 331-0776. • **USWA Regional Director,** 2625 S.46th, Lincoln,NE ;(402)489-1002

BOWLING: American Bowling Congress, 5301 S. 76th St., Greendale, WI; (414) 421-6400.

CANOEING & KAYAKING: ACA Midwest Vice Commodore, 1343 N. Portage, Palatine, IL; (708) 359-5047.

CYCLING: Nebraskaland AYH Council, 129 N. 10th St. #413, Lincoln; (402) 472-3265. • **USCF Nebraska Representative,** 1825 Radial Highway NW, #4, Omaha; (402) 551-7428.

FITNESS: Health Promotion and Physical Fitness Council, University of Nebraska-Lincoln, 105 Henzlik Hall, Lincoln; (402) 472-5404.

FOOTBALL: Pop Warner Football, 1315 Walnut Street, Suite 1632, Philadelphia, PA; (215) 735-1450.

GOLF: Nebraska Amateur Golf Association, 6001 South 72nd Street, Lincoln; (402) 486-1440. • **PGA Nebraska Section,** 9301 Firethorn Ln., Lincoln; (402) 489-7760.

HIKING & CLIMBING: Nebraska Sierra Club Chapter, 2036 Ranhdolph #70, Lincoln; (402) 475-9951.

HOCKEY: USA Hockey Central Registrar, PO Box 1738, Lisle, IL; (708) 963-1098.

HUNTING & FISHING: Game & Parks Commission, 2200 N. 33rd St., PO Box 30370, Lincoln; (402) 464-0641.

RACQUETBALL: AARA, 2103 N. 52nd St., Lincoln; (402) 423-2511.

RODEO: PRCA Prairie Circuit, RR 2, Box 20, Abbyville, KS; (316) 286-5319.

RUNNING: RRCA NE State Rep., 1701 C Street, Apt. 3, Lincoln; (402) 435-4642.

SCUBA: Heartland Scuba Center, 101 East 24th Street, Kearney; (308) 237-7943. • **Mid Coast Divers Supply,** 8831 Maple Street, Omaha; (402) 391-1559.

SHOOTING: Midland Sportsman's Club, 801 P Street, Lincoln; (402) 477-9249.

SKATING: USFSA, 20 First Street, Colorado Springs, CO; (719) 635-5200.

SOCCER: Nebraska Soccer Ass'n, 1114 S. 32nd Street, Omaha; (402) 345-7133. • **AYSO Regional Director,** 2971 N. Coronado St., Chandler; (602) 839-2114.

SOFTBALL: Nebraska ASA, 1840 North "C" Street, Fremont; (402) 721-1356. • **Omaha ASA,** 14504 Burdette Street, Omaha; (402) 496-3545.

SQUASH: Lincoln Central YMCA, Lincoln; (402) 475-9622.

SWIMMING: LMSC Midwestern Registrar, 1112 S. 93rd Ave., Omaha; (402) 391-4956.

TENNIS: Recreational TEAMTENNIS Central-West Region, National Program Coordinator, 2105 Grant Ave., #4, Redondo Beach, CA; (800) 992-9042. • **Missouri Valley USTA,** 722 Walnut St., Suite #1, Kansas City, MO; (816) 556-0777.

VOLLEYBALL: USVBA Great Plains Commissioner, 5610 Prescott Ave., Lincoln; (402) 486-1533.

STATBOX

POPULATION: 1,600,000
SQUARE MILES: 77,355
TIME ZONE: Central and Mountain
MOTTO: Equality Before the Law
BIRD: Meadowlark
TREE: Cottonwood
CAPITAL: Lincoln
AVERAGE ANNUAL RAINFALL: 18" (west); 27" (east)
MEAN TEMP: 23 (Jan.); 75 (July)
MAJOR LEAGUE TEAMS: 0
NATIONAL PARK/FOREST ACREAGE: 6,247
STATE PARK ACREAGE: 149,163 (land and water)
HIGHEST ELEVATION: 5,426'
LOWEST ELEVATION: 840'
WATERWAYS: 11,000 miles of rivers and streams; 3,000 lakes

Nevada

Legalized sports gambling racks up bets to the tune of 2.5 billion dollars per year in Reno and Las Vegas. ◆ The Reno-Tahoe area boasts 31 Alpine and Nordic ski areas—including some world-class slopes—all within an hour of each other. A top elevation of 10,000 feet helps bring more snow than either Colorado or the Alps. ◆ The University of Nevada-Las Vegas' Thomas and Mack Center is home to the Runnin' Rebels, one of college basketball's most exciting teams, as well as to the National Finals Rodeo in early December. ◆ Reno hosts the Great Reno Balloon Races and International Camel Races the weekend after Labor Day. ◆ The tiny town of Wendover (Nevada-Utah border) hosts Bonneville Speed Week each August, on the famed Salt Flats. The late Gary Gabelich still holds the world, land-speed record (633.47 miles per hour) set in 1970 in his "Blue Flame."

▶ SPECTATOR VENUES

Baseball

CASHMAN FIELD
850 Las Vegas Blvd. North, Las Vegas **[P. 73, M-4]**. Capacity: 9,370
Las Vegas Stars (Pacific Coast League, Class AAA); (702) 386-7200. Entered League in 1983. Broadcasts by KVEG 840-AM. MLB affiliation, San Diego Padres.

MOANA STADIUM
240 West Moana Lane, Reno **[P. 73, O-2]**. Capacity: 4,500
Reno Silver Sox (California League, Class A); (702) 825-0678. Entered League in 1958. Broadcasts by KPLY 1270 AM. MLB affiliation, Independent.

Bowling

BALLY'S RENO LANES
2500 E. Second St., Reno **[P. 73, N-2]**; (702) 789-2295.
Cambridge Mixed Doubles (PBA, LPBT), December.

SAM'S TOWN
5111 Boulder Hwy., Las Vegas **[P. 73, M-4]**; (815) 332-5756.
LPBT Gold Rush Mixed Doubles Shoot-out and LPBT National Doubles, August.
Sam's Town 9-Pin No-Tap National Pro/AM and Sam's Town Invitational (LPBT), August, November.

SHOWBOAT HOTEL, CASINO & BOWLING CENTER
2800 Fremont Street, Las Vegas **[P. 73, M-4]**; (702) 385-9123.
Showboat Senior Invitational, May to June.
Showboat Invitational (PBA), January.

College Sports

UNIVERSITY OF NEVADA REBELS
4505 Maryland Parkway, Las Vegas **[P. 73, N-4]**; (702) 739-3483. Silver Bowl, capacity 32,000. Thomas & Mack Center, capacity 18,500.

UNIVERSITY OF NEVADA WOLF PACK
Reno **[P. 73, M-1]**; (702) 784-6900. Mackay, capacity 20,000. Lawlaor Events Center, capacity 12,000.

Museums & Halls of Fame

NATIONAL AUTOMOBILE MUSEUM
10 Lake Street S, at Mill St., Reno **[P. 73, N-2]**; (702) 333-9300.

PGA/LPGA

DESERT INN COUNTRY CLUB
3145 Las Vegas Blvd., South, Las Vegas **[P. 73, M-4]**; (702) 733-4288.
Desert Inn LPGA International, March. Number of holes: 54.
Las Vegas Senior Classic (Senior PGA), May. Number of holes: 54.
Las Vegas Invitational (PGA), Oct. Number of holes: 90.

LAS VEGAS COUNTRY CLUB
3000 Joe W. Brown Dr., Las Vegas **[P. 73, M-4]**; (702) 734-1122.
Las Vegas Invitational (PGA), Oct. Number of holes: 90.

Rodeo

LIVESTOCK EVENTS CENTER
1350 N. Wells Ave., Reno **[P. 73, M-2]**; (702) 329-3877.
Reno Rodeo, June.

THOMAS & MACK ARENA
UNLV Campus, Las Vegas **[P. 73, N-4]**; (702) 731-2115.
◆Total payoff of $2.45 million. National Finals Rodeo, in Dec.

USA SNAPSHOTS®

A look at statistics that shape the sports world

Source: Gallup poll of 1,200 adults

By Jeff Dionise, USA TODAY

▶ OUTDOOR VENUES

National Parks

Bike Trails: BK
Boating: BT
Camping: C
Climbing: CL
Diving: DV
Fishing: F
Golfing: G
Hiking: HK
Hunting: HT
Riding: R
Surfing: SU
Swimming: S
Tennis: TE
Whitewater: WW
Winter Sports: W

GREAT BASIN NATIONAL PARK
5 mi. W of Baker **[P. 72, E-6]**. Contains 77,100 acres. **C HK F R W CL**

HUMBOLDT NATIONAL FOREST
Elko **[P. 72, A-3, C-5, F-5]**. Contains 2,469,395 acres. **C HK F S R W**

LAKE MEAD NATIONAL RECREATION AREA
Boulder City **[P. 73, J-6]**. Contains 157,900 acres. **C BT F S R DV**

TOIYABE NATIONAL FOREST
Sparks **[P. 72, D-1, E-4, J-5]**. Contains 3,212,545 acres. **C HK BT F S R W**

State Parks

BEAVER DAM STATE PARK
35 mi. NE of Caliente **[P. 72, G-7]**. Contains 2,218 acres. **C HK F S**

CAVE LAKE STATE RECREATION AREA
Success Summit Rd., SE of Ely **[P. 72, E-6]**. Contains 1,208 acres. **C HK BT F S W**

LAHONTAN STATE RECREATION AREA
18 mi. W of Fallon on US 50 **[P. 72, E-2]**. Contains 35,000 acres. **C BT F S**

LAKE TAHOE - NEVADA STATE PARK
NV 28, 4 mi. S of Incline Village **[P. 73, H-2]**. Contains 13,468 acres. **HK BT F S R BK W**

SPRING VALLEY STATE PARK
20 mi. E of Pioche **[P. 72, F-7]**. Contains 1,200 acres. **C HK BT F S R**

VALLEY OF FIRE STATE PARK
Overton **[P. 73, J-6]**. Contains 36,000 acres. **C HK**

WASHOE LAKE STATE PARK
E of US 395, btwn. Carson City & Reno **[P. 72, H-2]**. Contains 7,500 acres. **C HK BT F S R**

WILD HORSE STATE RECREATION AREA
NV 225, 65 mi. N of Elko **[P. 72, A-5]**. Contains 120 acres. **C BT F S W**

STATBOX

POPULATION: 1,300,000
SQUARE MILES: 109,540
TIME ZONE: Mountain
MOTTO: The Battle Born State
BIRD: Mountain Bluebird
TREE: Bristlecone Pine
CAPITAL: Carson City
AVERAGE ANNUAL RAINFALL: 7"
MEAN TEMP: 32 (Jan.); 70 (July)
MAJOR LEAGUE TEAMS: 0
NATIONAL PARK ACREAGE: 1,572,775
STATE PARK ACREAGE: 142,206
HIGHEST ELEVATION: 13,145'
LOWEST ELEVATION: 470'
WATERWAYS: 750 square miles of water

Skiing

ALPINE SKIING

DIAMOND PEAK AT SKI INCLINE
Incline Village **[P. 73, H-2]**; (702) 832-1177.
Vertical drop is 1,840 feet. Has seven chairs.

MT. ROSE SKI AREA
22222 Mt. Rose Highway, Reno **[P. 73, H-2]**; (702) 849-0704.
Vertical drop is 1,450 feet. Has five chairs.

NORDIC SKIING

SPOONER LAKE XC
Highway 28 near Highway 50, Glenbrook **[P. 73, J-2]**; (702) 749-5349.

▶ ACTIVE SPORTS

AEROBICS: AFAA, 2384 Melody Ln., Reno; (702) 673-2601.

BASEBALL: Little League Baseball Western Region HQ, 6707 Little League Dr., San Bernardino, CA; (714) 887-6444. • **Pony Baseball-Softball,** 1922 Goldboro Street, San Diego, CA; (619) 276-3094. • **American Legion Baseball,** 2436 High Vista, Henderson; (702) 451-8443. • **Babe Ruth Baseball,** Dennis R. Poarch, 809 W. Gibson Rd., Woodland, CA; (415) 581-6879.

BILLIARDS: Keystone Cue & Cushion, 935 W. Fifth, Reno; (702) 329-5718.

BOARDSAILING: McGhies Ski Chalet , Las Vegas; (702) 734-8888. • **USWA Regional Director,** PO Box 6272, Laguna Niguel, CA; (714) 495-0368.

BOWLING: American Bowling Congress, 5301 S. 76th St., Greendale, WI; (414) 421-6400.

CANOEING & KAYAKING: ACA Pacific Vice Commodore, 3008 Blossom Ln., Redondo Beach, CA; (213) 542-8757.

CYCLING: USCF California/Nevada North Representative, 1153 Delaware Street, Berkeley, CA; (415) 526-5983.

FITNESS: National Strength and Conditioning Ass'n State Director, NV Nautilus, 1802 N. Carson St., Carson City; (702) 887-8881.

FOOTBALL: Pop Warner Football, 1315 Walnut Street, Suite 1632, Philadelphia, PA; (215) 735-1450.

GOLF: Nevada State Golf Association, PO Box 5630, Sparks; (702) 673-4653. • **PGA Rocky Mountain Section,** 595 E. State St., Eagle, ID; (208) 939-6028. • **PGA Southwest Section,** 11801 N. Tatum Blvd., Suite 247, Phoenix, AZ; (602) 953-5990. • **PGA Utah**

CONTINUED ON PAGE 181

New Hampshire

New Hampshire is known for outdoor recreation, but it also features such unexpected spectator events as a NASCAR Busch Grand National circuit race at Loudon's International Speedway (mid-July) and the Loudon Classic, America's oldest continuously running motorcycle contest (mid-June). ◆ Fishing, boating, and windsurfing are popular in the Lakes Region. Prime spot: Lake Winnipesaukee, one of the Northeast's largest natural-water lakes. Fishing tournaments held there include the Great Rotary Ice Fishing Derby (February) and the Winni Derby (May). ◆ At Mount Washington, highest peak in the Northeast, some runners make the 7.6-mile Mount Washington Road Race (mid-June) one of New England's most popular. ◆ Hiking, whitewater rafting, and, of course, skiing (e.g. Bretton Woods, Loon, Waterville Valley) are all readily available in the White Mountains.

STATBOX

POPULATION: 1,107,000
SQUARE MILES: 9,304
TIME ZONE: Eastern
MOTTO: Live Free or Die
BIRD: Purple Finch
TREE: White Birch
CAPITAL: Concord
AVERAGE ANNUAL RAINFALL: 38"
MEAN TEMP: 57
MAJOR LEAGUE TEAMS: 0
NATIONAL PARK/FOREST ACREAGE: 770,000
STATE PARK ACREAGE: 150,460
HIGHEST ELEVATION: 6,288'
LOWEST ELEVATION: sea level
WATERWAYS: 15,544 miles of rivers and streams; 13,000 lakes and ponds

Bike Trails: BK
Boating: BT
Camping: C
Climbing: CL
Diving: DV
Fishing: F
Golfing: G
Hiking: HK
Hunting: HT
Riding: R
Surfing: SU
Swimming: S
Tennis: TE
Whitewater: WW
Winter Sports: W

▶ SPECTATOR VENUES

College Sports

DARTMOUTH COLLEGE BIG GREEN
Hanover **[P. 75, J-4]**; (603) 646-2465. Memorial Field, capacity 20,416. Thompson Arena, capacity 5,000.

FRANKLIN PIERCE COLLEGE RAVENS
Rindge **[P. 75, N-5]**; (603) 899-6448. FPC Gym, capacity 1,500.

KEENE STATE COLLEGE OWLS
229 Main Street, Keene **[P. 75, M-4]**; (603) 352-1909. Owl Stadium, capacity 1,500. Spaulding Gym, capacity 2,300.

NEW HAMPSHIRE COLLEGE PENMEN
2500 River Road, Manchester **[P. 75, L-6]**; (603) 645-9604. Gym, capacity 3,000.

ST. ANSELM COLLEGE HAWKS
St. Anselm Drive, Manchester **[P. 75, M-6]**; (603) 641-7800. Stoutenburgh Gym, capacity 1,200.

UNIVERSITY OF NEW HAMPSHIRE WILDCATS
Durham **[P. 75, L-8]**; (603) 862-2013. Cowell, capacity 13,500. Lundholm Gym, capacity 3,500.

Horse Racing

ROCKINGHAM PARK
Rockingham Road, Salem **[P. 75, M-7]**; (603) 898-2311. Opened in 1906. Total capacity: 5,000.
Thoroughbred season from January to December.
◆Park was rebuilt in 1984.

▶ OUTDOOR VENUES

National Parks

WHITE MOUNTAIN NATIONAL FOREST
Off I-93 North **[P. 74, E-6, G-5]**. Contains 768,962 acres. **C HK BT F S W HT**

State Parks

BEAR BROOK STATE PARK
5 mi. NE of Hooksett **[P. 75, L-6]**. Contains 9,600 acres. **C HK F S W HT**

COLEMAN STATE PARK
E of Colebrook on Route 26 **[P. 74, D-6]**. Contains 2,700 acres. **C BT F HT**

CRAWFORD NOTCH STATE PARK
12 mi. W of Bartlett on US 302 **[P. 74, G-6]**. Contains 5,950 acres.
C HK F HT

FRANCONIA NOTCH STATE PARK
5 mi. N of North Woodstock **[P. 74, G-5]**. Contains 6,440 acres.
C HK F S BK W HT

LAKE FRANCIS STATE PARK
5 mi. N of Pittsburgh **[P. 74, C-7]**. Contains 2,060 acres. **C BT F HT**

MOUNT SUNAPEE STATE PARK
Sunapee **[P. 75, K-4]**. Contains 2,174 acres.
HK BT F S W

PAWTUCKAWAY STATE PARK
4 mi. NE of Raymond off NH 156 **[P. 75, L-7]**. Contains 5,500 acres. **C HK BT F S W HT**

PILLSBURY STATE PARK
3.5 mi. N of Washington on NH 31 **[P. 75, L-5]**. Contains 3,702 acres. **C HK F HT**

WHITE LAKE STATE PARK
1 mi. N of West Ossipee on NH 16 **[P. 75, H-7]**. Contains 603 acres. **C HK F S W**

Skiing

ALPINE SKIING

ATTITASH
Route 302, Bartlett **[P. 74, G-7]**; (603) 374-2368.
Vertical drop is 1,750 feet. Has six chairs.

BRETTON WOODS SKI RESORT
Route 302, Bretton Woods **[P. 74, F-6]**; (603) 278-5000.
Vertical drop is 1,500 feet. Has one bar and four chairs.

CANNON MOUNTAIN
Route 93, Franconia **[P. 74, G-6]**; (603) 823-5563.
Vertical drop is 2,146 feet. Has one tow, three chairs and one tram.

GUNSTOCK
Area Road, Route 11A, Gilford **[P. 74, G-6]**; (603) 293-4341.
Vertical drop is 1,400 feet. Has two tows and five chairs.

LOON MOUNTAIN
Route 112, Lincoln **[P. 74, G-6]**; (603) 745-8111.
Vertical drop is 2,100 feet. Has one tow, seven chairs and one gondola.

MT. CRANMORE
Skimobile Road, North Conway **[P. 74, G-7]**; (603) 356-5543.
Vertical drop is 1,200 feet. Has five chairs.

TENNEY MOUNTAIN SKI RESORT
Plymouth **[P. 75, J-5]**; (603) 536-1717.
Vertical drop is 1,400 feet. Has two bars and two chairs.

WATERVILLE VALLEY RESORT
Waterville Valley **[P. 75, H-6]**; (603) 236-8311.
Vertical drop is 3,020 feet. Has one tow, two bars and ten chairs.

WILDCAT MOUNTAIN SKI AREA
Route 16, Pinkham Notch **[P. 74, F-7]**; (603) 466-3326.
Vertical drop is 2,100 feet. Has five chairs, one gondola.

NORDIC SKIING

APPLETOUR
Route 88, Hampton Falls **[P. 75, M-8]**; (603) 926-3721.

B.U. SARGENT SKI CENTER
Windy Road, Peterborough **[P. 75, M-5]**; (603) 525-3311.

BALSAM WILDERNESS
Route 26, Dixville Notch **[P. 74, M-5]**; (800) 255-0800.

BRETTON WOODS XC
Route 302, Bretton Woods **[P. 74, F-6]**; (603) 278-5181.

EASTMAN CROSS COUNTRY SKI
Club House Lane, Grantham **[P. 75, J-4]**; (603) 863-4500.

GUNSTOCK CROSS COUNTRY
Route 11A, Gilford **[P. 75, J-6]**; (603) 293-4341.

INN AT EAST HILL FARM
Mountain Road, Troy **[P. 75, M-4]**; (603) 242-6495.

INTERVALE NORDIC CENTER
Route 16A, Intervale **[P. 74, G-7]**; (603) 356-7340.

JACKSON SKI FOUNDATION
Jackson **[P. 74, G-7]**; (603) 383-9355.

LOON MOUNTAIN XC CENTER
Route 112, Lincoln **[P. 74, G-6]**; (603) 745-8111.

CONTINUED ON PAGE 182

Nevada

CONTINUED FROM PAGE 180

Section, 419 E., 100 South, Salt Lake City, UT; (801) 532-7421. • **Southern Nevada Golf Association,** 1434 Cottonwood, Las Vegas; (702) 794-0445.

HIKING & CLIMBING: Toiyabe Sierra Club Chapter, PO Box 8096, Reno; (702) 323-3162.

HOCKEY: USA Hockey Pacific Registrar, 5703 Sun Ridge Ct., Castro Valley, CA; (415) 886-0706.

HUNTING & FISHING: Department of Wildlife, Box 10678, Reno; (702) 789-0500.

RACQUETBALL: AARA, 880 Northwood, PO Box 7062, Incline Village; (702) 831-4214.

RODEO: PRCA Wilderness Circuit, 254 Clinton Drive, Twin Falls, ID; (208) 536-2772.

SCUBA: Blue Seas Scuba Center, Inc., 4661 Spring Mountain Road, Las Vegas; (702) 367-2822. • **Desert Divers Supply, Inc.,** 5720 East Charleston Blvd., Las Vegas; (702) 438-1000. • **Sierra Diving Center,** 104 East Grove Street, Reno; (702) 825-2147.

SHOOTING: Birdello Gun Club, Inc., 336 Thoma St., Reno; (702) 322-1006. • **Lazy Five Gun Club,** PO Box 1566, Reno; (702) 673-1370. • **Peppermill/Arvada Gun Club,** PO Box 360, Mesquite; (702) 346-5232. • **Sage Hill Clay Sports,** 11500 Mira Loma Rd., Reno; (702) 851-1123. • **Topaz Sportsman's Club,** 3851 Hwy. 208, Wellington; (702) 266-3381.

SKATING: USFSA, 20 First Street, Colorado Springs, CO; (719) 635-5200.

SOCCER: Nevada Soccer Ass'n, 1250 Laguna Ave., Las Vegas; (702) 735-4093. • **AYSO Regional Director,** 4119 East Ave., Hayward, CA; (415) 886-4119.

SOFTBALL: Nevada ASA, 1104 California Ave., Reno; (702) 673-3033.

SQUASH: Reno YMCA, Reno; (702) 329-1311.

TABLE TENNIS: USTTA State Coordinator, PO Box 157, Mercury; (702) 295-6459.

TENNIS: Recreational TEAMTENNIS Central-West Region, National Program Coordinator, 2105 Grant Ave., #4, Redondo Beach, CA; (800) 992-9042. • **Intermountain USTA,** 1201 South Parker Rd., #102, Denver, CO; (503) 245-3048. • **Northern California USTA,** 1350 South Loop Rd., Suite 200, Alameda, CA; (415) 748-7373. (Washoe & Carson City Counties.)

TRIATHLON: Las Vegas Triathlon Club, 8916 Signal Terrace Dr., Las Vegas; (702) 254-4370.

New Hampshire

CONTINUED FROM PAGE 181

MT. CUBE CROSS COUNTRY
Route 25A, Orford **[P. 75, H-4]**; (603) 353-4709.

MT. WASHINGTON VALLEY SKI TOURING FOUNDATION
Intervale **[P. 74, G-7]**; (800) 282-5220 or (603) 356-9304.

NORSK CROSS COUNTRY
Exit 11, off I-84, New London **[P. 75, K-5]**; (603) 526-4685.

OCCUM SKI CENTER
Dartmouth College Outing Club, Hanover **[P. 75, H-4]**; (603) 646-2440.

QUAKER HOLLOW FARM
14 Huntington Road, Henniker **[P. 75, L-5]**; (603) 428-7639.

RIVER BEND
171 Central Street, Woodsville **[P. 74, G-5]**; (603) 747-3581.

SHATTUCK INN NORDIC CENTER
28 Dublin Road, Jaffrey **[P. 75, M-5]**; (603) 532-6619.

SUNNINGDALE GOLF CLUB
301 Green Street, Somersworth **[P. 75, K-8]**; (603) 742-8056.

TEMPLE MOUNTAIN XC
Route 101, Peterborough **[P. 75, M-5]**; (603) 924-9376.

THE NORDIC SKIER XC CENTER
19 N. Main Street, Wolfeboro **[P. 75, J-7]**; (603) 569-3151.

WATERVILLE VALLEY
Waterville Company Inc., Waterville Valley **[P. 75, H-6]**; (603) 236-4666.

WINDBLOWN
Route 124, New Ipswich **[P. 75, M-5]**; (603) 878-2869.

▶ ACTIVE SPORTS

ADVENTURE: Hurricane Island Outward Bound School, PO Box 429, Rockland, ME; (800) 341-1744.

AEROBICS: AFAA, 46 Route 27, #24, Raymond; (603) 595-2384.

BASEBALL: Little League Baseball Eastern Region HQ, PO Box 3485, Williamsport, PA; (717) 326-1921. • **Pony Baseball-Softball,** 2 Byrnes Lane E., Sayreville, NJ; (718) 692-0444. • **American Legion Baseball,** 84 Cameron St., Manchester; (603) 625-6833. • **Babe Ruth Baseball,** Ernest P. Papazoglou, 71 Tracy Ave., Lynn, MA; (617) 595-7603.

BILLIARDS: Snooker's, 150 Congress, Portsmouth; (603) 433-7301.

BOARDSAILING: North Country Scuba & Windsurfing , Laconia; (603) 524-8606. • **USWA Regional Director,** Bayview Bus Pk Unit 10, Gilford; (603) 293-2727.

BOWLING: American Bowling Congress, 5301 S. 76th St., Greendale, WI; (414) 421-6400.

CANOEING & KAYAKING: ACA New England Vice Commodore, 785 Bow Ln., Middleton, CT.

CYCLING: LAW New England Regional Director, PO Box 305, Atkinson; (603) 362-4572. • **USCF Maine/New Hampshire Representative,** 34 Taschereau Blvd, Nashua; (603) 888-8657.

FOOTBALL: Pop Warner Football, 1315 Walnut Street, Suite 1632, Philadelphia, PA; (215) 735-1450.

GOLF: New Hampshire Golf Association, 45 Kearney Street, Manchester; (603) 623-0396. • **PGA New England Section,** 1 Audubon Rd., Wakefield, MA; (617) 246-4653.

HIKING & CLIMBING: New Hampshire Outing Club (AHS), Univ. of NH/MUB Room 129, Durham; (603) 862-2145. • **The Appalachian Mountain Club,** 5 Joy St., Boston, MA; (617) 523-0636.

HOCKEY: USA Hockey New England Registrar, 15 Orange Street, Rumford, RI; (401) 438-2954.

HUNTING & FISHING: Fish & Game Department, 2 Hazen Dr., Concord; (603) 271-3421. • **Trout Unlimited,** 10 Holstein Ave., Londondarry; (603) 434-9779.

RACQUETBALL: AARA, 23 Cliff Ave., Boars Head, Hampton Beach; (603) 926-3223.

RIDING: New Hampshire Horse Council, Box 261, Wakefield; (603) 522-9218.

RODEO: PRCA First Frontier Circuit, 5982 Summit Bridge Rd., Townsend, DE; (302) 378-4551.

RUNNING: RRCA NH State Rep., 90 Linwood St., Nashua; (201) 290-1182.

SCUBA: Divers Den Dive Shop, 730 Mammoth Road, Manchester; (603) 627-2536. • **Underwater Sports of New Hampshire, Inc.,** 334 Park Avenue, Keene; (603) 357-4430.

SHOOTING: Major Waldron Sportsmen's Association, PO Box 314, Barrington; (603) 742-6866. • **Skat Sporting Clays,** PO Box 137, Temple Rd., New Ipswich; (603) 878-1257.

SKATING: Northeastern Skating Association, 1477 Beacon Street, #69, Brookline, MA; (617) 731-9411. • **USFSA,** 20 First Street, Colorado Springs, CO; (719) 635-5200.

SOFTBALL: ASA, 32 Court Street, PO Box 1008, Exeter; (603) 778-1183.

SQUASH: Mountain Club on Loon (USSRA), Lincoln; (603) 745-8111.

TENNIS: Recreational TEAMTENNIS East Region, National Program Coordinator, 246 N. Reservoir St., Lancaster, PA; (800) 633-6122. • **New England USTA,** PO Box 587, Needham Heights, MA; (617) 964-2030.

WHITEWATER RAFTING: Downeast Whitewater Rafting, Inc. , Box 119, Rt. 302, Center Conway; (603) 447-3002.

Tip Offs: College Conferences Part I

The following is an alphabetical list of the major, NCAA-associated college athletic conferences.

American South Athletic Conference,
One Galeria Blvd., Suite 2016,
Metairie, LA 70001
504-834-6600

Association of Mid-Continent Universities,
310 S. Peoria, Suite 210,
Chicago, IL 60607
312-829-9122

Atlantic Coast Conference,
P.O. Drawer ACC.,
Greensboro, NC 27419-6999
919-854-8787

Atlantic-10 Conference,
10 Woodbridge Center Drive,
Woodbridge, NJ 07095
201-634-6900

Big East Conference,
321 South Main Street,
Providence, RI 02903
401-272-9108

Big Eight Conference,
104 West Ninth., Suite 408,
Kansas City, MO 64105-1713
816-471-5088

Big Sky Athletic Conference,
P.O. Box 1736, Boise, ID 83701
208-345-5393

Big South Conference,
1551 21st Ave., Suite 13,
Myrtle Beach, SC 29577
803-448-9998

Big Ten Conference,
1500 West Higgons Rd.
Park Ridge, IL 60068
708-696-1010

Big West Conference,
1700 East Dyer Rd.
Santa Ana, CA 92705
714-261-2525

Central Collegiate Conference,
1705 Evanston St.,
Kalamazoo, MI 49008
616-349-1009

Dixie Intercollegiate Athletic Conference,
50 Shoe Ln.,
Newport News, VA 23606
804-599-5412

East Coast Conference,
946 Farnsworth Ave.,
Bordentown, NJ 08505
609-298-4009

Eastern College Athletic Conference,
P.O. Box 3, 1311 Craigville Beach Rd.,
Centerville, MA 02632
508-771-5060

Eastern Intercollegiate Athletic Association,
Amherst College,
Amherst, MA 01002
414-542-2316

Frontier Conference,
Huffman Bldg.,
Missouri State U.,
Bozeman, MT 59717
406-994-2401

Gateway Collegiate Athletic Conference,
7750 Clayton Rd., Suite 204, St. Louis, MO 63117-1342
314-645-8760

Great Lakes Intercollegiate Conference,
5015 Tressa Dr.,
Lansing, MI 48910
517-394-5015

Great Lakes Valley Conference, Box 1012, College Station, Rensselaer, IN 47978
219-866-5217

Great Northwest Conference,
P.O. Box 2002, Billings, MT 59103
406-656-4369

Gulf Coast Athletic Conference, 216 Myrtle St., Pineville, LA 71360
318-487-7102

Gulf South Conference,
4 Office Park Circle, Suite 218,
Birmingham, AL 35223
205-870-9750

Heart of America Athletic Conference,
3426 Craig Lane,
St. Joseph, MO 64506
816-279-1948

Heart of Texas Conference,
527 Dale, Waco, TX 76706
817-776-2060

Intercollegiate Association of Amateur Athletes of America,
P.O. Box 3, Centerville, MA 02632
508-771-5060

Independent College Athletic Conference,
Alfred U., Main St., Alfred, NY 14802
607-871-2193

Ivy League Conference,
70 Washington Rd.,
Princeton, NJ 08540
609-258-6426

Little East Conference,
Eastern Connecticut State U.,
Willimantic, CT 06226
203-456-5483

Metro Atlantic Athletic Conference,
1099 Wall St. West, Suite 242,
Lyndhurst, NJ 07071
201-896-8443

Metropolitan Collegiate Athletic Conference,
Two Ravinia Drive., Suite 210, Atlanta, GA 30346
404-395-6444

CONTINUED ON PAGE 213

New Jersey

According to long-standing, local legend, if you stop by a particular Jersey Shore bar on the right night, you might catch a glimpse of Bruce Springsteen. But if you miss the Boss, there's always the adjacent Asbury Park 10K Classic (August). ◆ There's also great fishing on the northern coast, as well as at Shrewsbury Rocks and the Barnegat Ridge. In South Jersey, there are surfing tournaments throughout the summer at Ocean City, and the Lifeguard Championships and Atlantic City Swim in August. ◆ The massive Meadowlands complex hosts the NFL Giants and Jets (Giants Stadium), and the NBA Nets and NHL Devils (Byrne Meadowlands Arena). Indy cars roll in for the Marlboro Grand Prix in mid-July. ◆ And for two-wheel competition, some of the world's best cycling talent shows up for The Tour of Somerville, over Memorial Day weekend.

STATBOX

POPULATION: 7,515,000
SQUARE MILES: 8,204
TIME ZONE: Eastern
MOTTO: Liberty and Prosperity
BIRD: Eastern Goldfinch
TREE: Red Oak
CAPITAL: Trenton
AVERAGE ANNUAL RAINFALL: 40-51"
MEAN TEMP: 24/38 (Jan.); 68/86 (July)
MAJOR LEAGUE TEAMS: 4
NATIONAL PARK/FOREST ACREAGE: 40,703
STATE PARK ACREAGE: 325,472
HIGHEST ELEVATION: 1,803'
LOWEST ELEVATION: sea level
WATERWAYS: 8,600 miles of rivers and streams

► SPECTATOR VENUES

Auto Racing

ATCO RACEWAY
NJ 534 (Jackson Road), 3 mi. E of NJ 73, Atco **[P. 77, J-5]**; (609) 768-2167. Track is 1/4-mile asphalt-conrete pad.
Eastern Nitrous Nationals (IHRA), August.

MEADOWLANDS SPORTS RACING COMPLEX
50 NJ 120, The Meadowlands, East Rutherford **[P. 80, G-4]**; (201) 507-9229. Track is 1.217-mile temporary road.
Marlboro Grand Prix at the Meadowlands (CART PPG Indy Car World Series), July.

OLD BRIDGE RACEWAY PARK
230 Pension Road, Englishtown **[P. 76, G-7]**; (908) 446-6331. Track is quarter-mile strip (for NHRA races).
Mopar Parts Summernationals (NHRA), early July.

Basketball

BRENDAN BYRNE MEADOWLANDS ARENA
The Meadowlands, NJ Turnpike & Rt. 3, East Rutherford **[P. 80, G-4]**. Built in 1981. Capacity: 20,039.
◆Moved from ABA to NBA in 1976.
New Jersey Nets (NBA Eastern Conf., Atlantic Div.); (201) 935-8888. Franchise began in 1967. Broadcasts by WNEW 1130 AM, WWOR Channel 9.

Bowling

CAROLIER LANES
790 Route 1, N. Brunswick; **[P. 76, E-6]**; (908) 846-2424.
Johnny Petragha Open (PBA), March.

College Sports

FAIRLEIGH DICKINSON UNIVERSITY KNIGHTS
1000 River Road, Teaneck **[P. 80, G-3]**; (201) 692-2229. FDU, capacity 5,000. Rothman Center, capacity 5,000.

MONMOUTH COLLEGE HAWKS
Cedar Avenue, West Long Branch **[P. 76, G-8]**; (908) 571-3415. Alumni Memorial Gym, capacity 2,800.

PRINCETON UNIVERSITY TIGERS
Princeton **[P. 76, F-5]**; (609) 258-3535. Palmer, capacity 45,725. Jadwin Gym, capacity 7,550.
◆Basketball coach Pete Carril really does look like the Star Wars character Yoda. But he also gets more out of less talent than any coach in the country.

RIDER COLLEGE BRONCS
2083 Lawrenceville Road, Lawrenceville **[P. 76, G-5]**; (609) 896-5054. Alumni, capacity 2,200.

RUTGERS UNIVERSITY PIONEERS
3rd & Linden Streets, Camden **[P. 100, D-5]**; (609) 757-6193. Rutgers Gym, capacity 2,100.

SETON HALL UNIVERSITY PIRATES
400 S. Orange Avenue, South Orange **[P. 81, H-1]**; (201) 761-9497. Owen T. Carroll. Walsh Auditorium, capacity 3,200.

ST. PETER'S COLLEGE PEACOCKS
2641 Kennedy Boulevard, Jersey City **[P. 81, J-4]**; (201) 915-9100. Yanitelli, capacity 3,600.

THE STATE UNIVERSITY OF N.J. RUTGERS SCARLET KNIGHTS
College Avenue, New Brunswick **[P. 76, F-6]**; (908) 932-8610. Rutgers, capacity 23,000.

Football

GIANTS STADIUM
The Meadowlands, East Rutherford **[P. 80, G-4]**. Built in 1976. Capacity: 76,891.
New York Jets (AFC Eastern Division); (516) 538-6600. Franchise began in 1960. Broadcasts by WCBS.
New York Giants (NFC Eastern Division); (201) 935-8111. Franchise began in 1925. Broadcasts by WNEW.

New York Knights (World League of American Football, North American East Division); (212) 644-1991. Franchise began in 1991. Broadcasts by WNEW 1130 AM.

Hockey

BRENDAN BYRNE MEADOWLANDS ARENA
The Meadowlands, East Rutherford **[P. 80, G-4]**. Built in 1981. Capacity: 19,040.
◆Kansas City Scouts from 1974 to 1976, then Colorado Rockies from 1976 until move to New Jersey.
New Jersey Devils (NHL, Wales Conference, Patrick Division); (201) 935-6050. Franchise began in 1982. Broadcasts by WABC (770 AM), SportsChannel.

Horse Racing

ATLANTIC CITY
US 40 & Black Horse Pike, McKee City **[P. 77, L-6]**; (609) 641-2190. Opened in 1946. Total capacity: 16,000.
Thoroughbred season from June to August. Quarterhorse racing May to July.

FREEHOLD RACEWAY
Routes 9 & 33, Freehold **[P. 76, G-7]**; (908) 462-3800. Opened in 1853. Clubhouse capacity: 3,000.
Harness season from Aug. to May.
◆Reopened in 1987 (after 1984 fire) with new grandstand and dining room.

GARDEN STATE PARK
Route 70 & Haddonfield Road, Cherry Hill **[P. 100, D-6]**; (609) 488-8400. Opened in 1985. Clubhouse capacity: 3,500. Grandstand capacity: 6,000.
Harness season from Sep. to Dec.
Thoroughbred season from Feb. to June.

MONMOUTH PARK
Route 36 & Oceanport Avenue, Oceanport **[P. 76, G-8]**; (908) 222-5100. Opened in 1870. Clubhouse capacity: 5,316. Grandstand capacity: 15,290.
Thoroughbred season from May to Sep.

THE MEADOWLANDS
50 Paterson Plank Road, East Rutherford **[P. 80, G-4]**; (201) 935-8500. Opened in 1977. Clubhouse capacity: 1,800. Grandstand capacity: 6,000. Total capacity: 40,000.
Harness season from Jan. to Aug.
Thoroughbred season from Sep. to Dec.
◆Harness racing's premier event, the Hambletonian, inaugurated in 1926, has been run here since 1981. It's the second race in the Trotting Triple Crown.

Museums & Halls of Fame

SPORTS CARD HALL OF FAME
124 Park Ave., East Rutherford; **[P. 80, G-4]**; (201) 930-0836.

UNITED STATES GOLF ASSOCIATION GOLF MUSEUM
Golf House, Liberty Corner Road, Far Hills **[P. 76, D-6]**; (908) 234-2300.

PGA/LPGA

SANDS COUNTRY CLUB
901 Mays Landing Rd., Somers Point **[P. 77, M-6]**; (609) 927-5071.
Atlantic City Classic (LPGA), June. Number of holes: 72.

Soccer

COCHRANE STADIUM
Chapel Avenue and Caven Point Road, Jersey City **[P. 81, J-4]**. Capacity: 5,000.
New Jersey Eagles (American Professional Soccer League); (201) 438-8920.
◆To resume league play in 1992. May not stay at Cochrane Stadium. Venue to be announced.

LIONS STADIUM
Trenton State College, Trenton **[P. 76, G-5]**. Capacity: 5,000.
Penn-Jersey Spirit (American Professional Soccer League, American Conference); (609) 394-2254.

Tennis

HAMILTON PARK CONFERENCE CENTER & STADIUM
175 Park Ave., Florham Park **[P. 76, D-6]**; (201) 377-2424. Surface is hard.
New Jersey Stars (TT), July to August.

Track & Field

BYRNE MEADOWLANDS ARENA
The Meadowlands, East Rutherford **[P. 80, G-4]**; (516) 742-5202.
Vitalis Invitational (USA/Mobil Grand Prix Event), Feb.

► OUTDOOR VENUES

National Parks

DELAWARE WATER GAP NATIONAL RECREATION AREA
Off I-80, at Kittatinny Point Visitors Center **[P. 76, B-4]**. Contains 70,000 acres.
C HK BT F S W HT

CONTINUED ON PAGE 184

USA SNAPSHOTS®

A look at statistics that shape the sports world

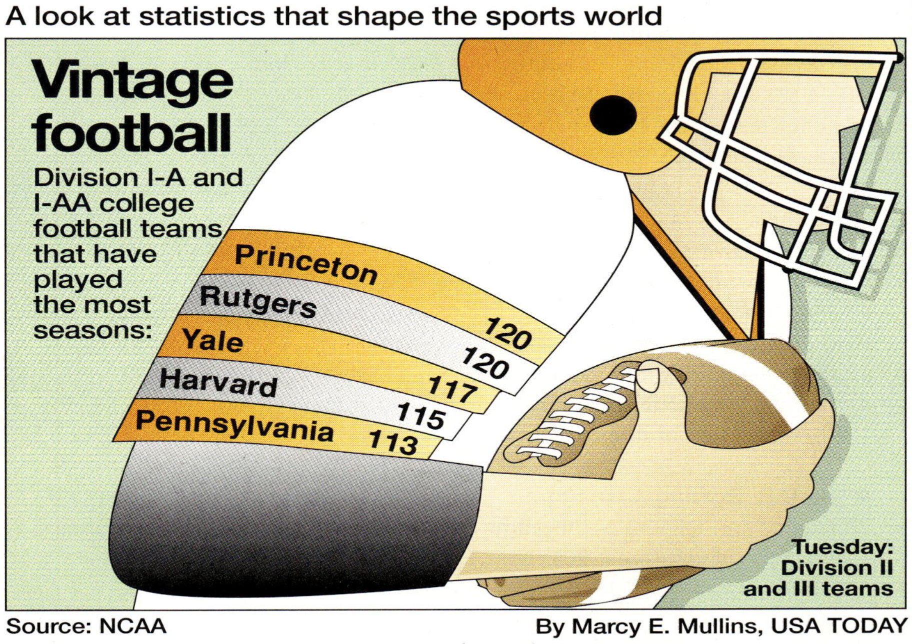

Vintage football
Division I-A and I-AA college football teams that have played the most seasons:
Princeton 120
Rutgers 120
Yale 117
Harvard 115
Pennsylvania 113
Tuesday: Division II and III teams

Source: NCAA

By Marcy E. Mullins, USA TODAY

New Jersey

CONTINUED FROM PAGE 183

GATEWAY NATIONAL RECREATION AREA/SANDY HOOK UNIT
NJ 36 at Highlands [P. 76, F-8]. Contains 4,675 acres. HK BT F S

State Parks

- Bike Trails: BK
- Boating: BT
- Camping: C
- Climbing: CL
- Diving: DV
- Fishing: F
- Golfing: G
- Hiking: HK
- Hunting: HT
- Riding: R
- Surfing: SU
- Swimming: S
- Tennis: TE
- Whitewater: WW
- Winter Sports: W

BASS RIVER STATE FOREST
3 mi. W. of Tuckerton on CR 592 [P. 77, K-6]. Contains 23,476 acres. C HK BT F S R HT

BELLEPLAIN STATE FOREST
On CR 550 at Belleplain [P. 77, M-5]. Contains 11,780 acres. C HK BT F S R HT

DELAWARE AND RARITAN CANAL STATE PARK
7 mi. W of New Brunswick on CR 514 [P. 76, F-4]. Contains 3,723 acres. C HK BT F R BK

HIGH POINT STATE PARK
8 mi. NW of Sussex on NJ 23 [P. 76, A-5]. Contains 14,192 acres. C HK BT F S W

HOPATCONG STATE PARK
2 mi. N of Landing off I-80 [P. 76, C-5]. Contains 113 acres. BT F S W

ISLAND BEACH STATE PARK
10-mile strip from Seaside Park to Barnegat Inlet [P. 77, J-8]. Contains 3,002 acres. HK F S

LEBANON STATE FOREST
Off NJ 70 and NJ 72, S of Fort Dix [P. 77, H-6]. Contains 31,879 acres. C HK S HT

PARVIN STATE PARK
6 mi. W of Vineland on CR 540 [P. 77, L-4]. Contains 1,125 acres. C HK BT F S

ROUND VALLEY RECREATION AREA
S of Lebanon off US 22 [P. 76, E-5]. Contains 3,639 acres. C HK BT F S R W

SPRUCE RUN RECREATION AREA
3 mi. N of Clinton on NJ 31 [P. 76, E-5]. Contains 1,910 acres. C HK BT F S W

STOKES STATE FOREST
3 mi. N of Branchville on US 206 [P. 76, B-5]. Contains 15,482 acres. C HK BT F S R W HT

SWARTSWOOD STATE PARK
3 mi. W of Newton [P. 76, C-5]. Contains 1,718 acres. HK BT F S R W HT

WAYAYANDA STATE PARKS
3 mi. E of Vernon [P. 76, B-6]. Contains 11,332 acres. HK BT F S W

WHARTON STATE FOREST
NE of Hammonton on US 206 or E of Pleasant Mills on CR 542 [P. 77, K-5]. Contains 109,328 acres. C HK BT F S W HT

WORTHINGTON STATE FOREST
N of I-80 at Millbrook exit, just E of PA state line [P. 76, C-4]. Contains 5,770 acres. C HK BT F W x

Skiing

ALPINE SKIING

HIDDEN VALLEY
Breakneck Road, Vernon [P. 76, B-6]; (201) 764-6161.
Vertical drop is 620 feet. Has three chairs.

VERNON VALLEY/GREAT GORGE
Route 94, Vernon [P. 76, B-6]; (201) 827-2000.
Vertical drop is 1,040 feet. Has three tows and fourteen chairs.

NORDIC SKIING

CAMP GORE MOUNTAIN SKI AREA
Camp Gore Road, Mahwah [P. 80, A-3]; (201) 327-7800.

CRAIGMEUR SKI AREA
Green Pond Road, Newfoundland [P. 76, C-6]; (201) 697-4500.

FAIRVIEW LAKE CROSS COUNTRY
Newton [P. 76, C-5]; (201) 383-9282.

HIDDEN VALLEY SKI AREA
Breckneck Road, Vernon [P. 76, B-6]; (201) 764-6161.

WILD WEST CITY
50 Lackawanna, Netcong [P. 76, D-5]; (201) 347-8900.

ACTIVE SPORTS

AEROBICS: AFAA, 16 Donny Brook Rd., Montvale; (201) 930-0508.

BASEBALL: Little League Baseball Eastern Region HQ, PO Box 3485, Williamsport, PA; (717) 326-1921. • **Pony Baseball-Softball,** 2 Byrnes Lane E., Sayreville; (718) 692-0444. • **American Legion Baseball,** 153 Trimble Ave., Clifton; (201) 340-3339. • **Babe Ruth Baseball,** Raymond P. Jones, 300 Lodge St., Piscataway, NJ; (908) 469-5841. • **Men's Senior Baseball League - Central Jersey,** 256 Luton Way, Somerset; (908) 873-1064. • **Men's Senior Baseball League - Bergen County,** 328 Monroe St., Hoboken; (201) 656-2138. • **Men's Senior Baseball League - Tri-state,** RD 5, Box 346, Sussex; (201) 875-4600.

BILLIARDS: Loree Jon Billiards, 229 Rt. 22, Green Brook; (908) 968-8228. • **The Billiard Club,** 62 Rt. 4 East, Englewood; (201) 568-0621.

BOARDSAILING: Heino's Sailboard School, Inc. , Bloomingdale; (201) 492-9181. • **Island Surf & Sail,** Brant Beach; (609) 494-5553. • **USWA Regional Director,** 1912 MacCumber Ln., Wilmington, NC; (919) 256-3553.

BOWLING: American Bowling Congress, 5301 S. 76th St., Greendale, WI; (414) 421-6400.

CANOEING & KAYAKING: ACA Atlantic Vice Commodore, 4 Russell Dr., RD 2, Wading River, NY; (516) 929-3177. • **ACA Middle States Vice Commodore,** 10236 Raider Ln., Fairfax, VA; (703) 359-2594.

CYCLING: LAW Mid-Atlantic Regional Director, 14 Gould Place, #2, Caldwell; (201) 228-7208. • **USCF New Jersey Representative,** 416 Catherine Street, Somerville; (908) 725-8245.

FITNESS: Governor's Council on Physical Fitness and Sports, 101 South Broad Street, CN 005, Trenton; (609) 633-7100.

FOOTBALL: Pop Warner Football, 1315 Walnut Street, Suite 1632, Philadelphia, PA; (215) 735-1450. • **U.S. Flag Football League,** 5834 Pine Tree Dr., Sanibel, FL; (813) 472-0544.

GOLF: New Jersey State Golf Association, 1000 BRd. Street, Bloomfield; (201) 338-8334. • **PGA New Jersey Section,** 128 Sussex Way, PO Box 200, Jamesburg; (908) 521-4000. • **PGA Philadelphia Section,** Plymouth Green Office Campus, 801 E. Germantown Pike, Suite F-6, Norristown, PA; (215) 277-5777. • **Southern Jersey State Golf Association,** 277 Mayflower Dr., Buena; (609) 697-9318. • **Trenton District Golf Association,** 7 High Acres Rd., West Trenton; (609) 771-2191.

HIKING & CLIMBING: Adirondack Mountain Club, RR #3, Box 3055, Lake George, NY; (518) 668-4447. • **Adventures for Women (AHS),** PO Box 515, Montvale; (201) 930-0557. • **New Jersey Sierra Club Chapter,** 57 Mountain Ave., Princeton; (609) 924-3141. • **The Appalachian Mountain Club** , 5 Joy St., Boston, MA; (617) 523-0636.

HOCKEY: USA Hockey Atlantic Registrar, 3 Pendleton Dr., Cherry Hill; (609) 424-8343.

HUNTING & FISHING: Department of Environmental Protection, 501 E. State St., CN 400, Trenton; (609) 292-9410. • **Olivers' Orvis Shop,** 44 Main St., Clinton; (908) 735-5959. • **Sportsmans Sanctuary (Orvis),** 770 River Rd., Fair Haven; (908) 747-6060. • **Trout Unlimited,** 1007 Coolidge Rd., Elizabeth; (201) 791-2176.

LACROSSE: Lacrosse Foundation Chapter, 9 Icemeadow Ln., Aberdeen; (908) 888-5419.

RIDING: New Jersey Horse Council, Box 538, Quakertown; (908) 735-2682.

RODEO: PRCA First Frontier Circuit, 5982 Summit Bridge Rd., Townsend, DE; (302) 378-4551.

RUNNING: RRCA NJ State Rep., PO Box 435, Keyport; (201) 290-1182.

SCUBA: Diver's Two, Inc., 1 Main Street, Avon By The Sea; (908) 776-7755. • **Dosil's Sport Centers,** 261 Highway 36, North Middletown; (908) 787-0508. • **Princeton Aqua Sports, Inc.,** 306 Alexander Street, Princeton; (609) 924-4240.

SHOOTING: West Creek Sporting Clays, RD 1, Stipson Island Rd., Eldora; (609) 861-2760.

SKATING: Middle Atlantic Skating Association, 3419 Irwin Ave., Bronx, NY; (212) 549-4290. • **USFSA,** 20 First Street, Colorado Springs, CO; (719) 635-5200.

SOCCER: New Jersey Soccer Ass'n, 588 Ave. A, Bayonne; (201) 436-9284. • **New Jersey State YSA,** PO Box 763, Clark; (908) 382-4031. • **AYSO Regional Director,** 4014 Oneida St., New Hartford, NY; (315) 737-5610.

SOFTBALL: ASA, 62 Main Street, PO Box 617, Lebanon; (908) 352-1653. • **Newark ASA,** 5 Fairfax Court, Nutley; (201) 667-5172.

SQUASH: Ricochet Racquet Club (USSRA), S. Plainfield; (908) 753-2300. • **Trenton Club (USSRA),** Trenton; (609) 393-4882. • **Watertower Racquet Club (USSRA),** Cherry Hill; (609) 795-2255.

SWIMMING: LMSC New Jersey Registrar, 126 Fourth St., Ridgefield Park; (201) 440-3469.

TENNIS: Recreational TEAMTENNIS East Region, National Program Coordinator, 246 N. Reservoir St., Lancaster, PA; (800) 633-6122. • **Eastern USTA,** 550 Mamaroneck Ave., Suite 505, Harrison, NY; (914) 698-0414. • **Middle States USTA,** 580 Shoemaker Rd., King of Prussia, PA; (215) 768-4040. • **New England USTA,** PO Box 587, Needham Heights, MA; (617) 964-2030.

TRIATHLON: Sandy Hooker Tri-Club, PO Box 186, Redbank; (908) 747-9255.

VOLLEYBALL: USVBA Garden Empire Commissioner, 891 Maple Ave., PO Box 627, Ridgefield; (201) 943-7694.

Tip Offs

Row, Row, Row

While many tend to associate competitive rowing with pain, strain and young, muscular Ivy Leaguers, that picture has shifted as the sport has grown. Increasingly, rowers are men and women who've come to the sport late in life and who do it for the fun—and the health—of it.

The masters membership category—27 and older—in the U.S. Rowing Association has grown 250 percent during the last three years. And new clubs are springing up in places far from the traditional training grounds of Philadelphia, Boston, San Diego and Seattle.

"I had been a competitive squash player, and I gave it up completely for rowing because it's kind of the whole answer," says Bill Killhour, 64 and chairman of the USRA's masters committee.

There's certainly little doubt about the answers it provides for the body. Rowers are lean machines, with powerfully developed legs and upper bodies. Workouts devour calories and build a cardiovascular system equivalent to that of a long distance runner.

Where to find out more:

- **The U.S. Rowing Association**
  Officials can tell you of programs and clubs in your area. 201 Capitol Ave., Suite 400, Indianapolis, IN 46225
- **Audi of America**
  The principal corporate sponsor of rowing in the USA provides a toll-free number for information about rowing and competitive schedules.
  1-800-OAR-AUDI.
- **Concept II Inc.**
  Makers of indoor rowers and ergometers. Indoor rowing regattas are becoming increasingly popular, with the annual, winter-time CRASH-B Sprints World Indoor Rowing Championships in Cambridge, Massachusetts the seminal event—the world record for 2,500 meters is 7 minutes, 15.5 seconds. RR1, Box 1100, Morrisville, VT 05661.
- **Martin Marine Co. Inc.**
  Makers of the Alden Ocean Shell. Box 251, Goodwin Road, Kitey Point, ME 03905.

New Mexico

The Mount Taylor Winter Quadrathlon—cycling, running, cross-country skiing and snowshoeing—was rated by *Runner's World* magazine as one of the top events in America (mid-February). ◆ Skiers travel from around the world for the famous dry powder at Taos Ski Valley. ◆ The President's Day weekend Chama Chile Classic is a cross-country ski race that draws hundreds of entrants from all over the nation. ◆ Two popular river races are the Rio Grande Whitewater Raft Race in Pilar (mid-May) and the Great Rio Grande Raft Race a week later, featuring 10-person rafts, canoes and kayaks. ◆ Albuquerque's Rio Grande Valley Bicycle Tour is an interesting journey, covering over 100 miles (April). ◆ Also in Albuquerque: Triple-A baseball (Los Angeles Dodgers) and the New Mexico State Fair Rodeo (early September).

STATBOX

POPULATION: 1,500,00
SQUARE MILES: 127,000
TIME ZONE: Mountain
MOTTO: It grows as it goes.
BIRD: Roadrunner
CAPITAL: Santa Fe
TREE: Piñon Pine
AVERAGE ANNUAL RAINFALL: 8"
MEAN TEMP: 50
MAJOR LEAGUE TEAMS: 0
NATIONAL PARK/FOREST ACREAGE: 391,795
STATE PARK ACREAGE: 115,789
HIGHEST ELEVATION: 14,000'
LOWEST ELEVATION: 3,505'
WATERWAYS: 85 fishable lakes

► SPECTATOR VENUES

Baseball

ALBUQUERQUE SPORTS STADIUM
1601 Stadium Blvd. SE, Albuquerque **[P. 79, N-6]**. Capacity: 10,510
Albuquerque Dukes (Pacific Coast League, Class AAA); (505) 243-1791. Entered League in 1972. Broadcasts by KOB 770-AM. MLB affiliation, Los Angeles Dodgers.

Bowling

LEISURE BOWL
7400 Lomas Blvd., NE, Albuquerque **[P. 79, N-7]**; (505) 268-4371.
Hammer Western Open (LPBT), October to November.

College Sports

NEW MEXICO STATE UNIVERSITY AGGIES
Las Cruces **[P. 79, J-4]**; (505) 646-4126. Memorial, capacity 30,000. Pan American Center, capacity 13,222.
◆The students are the show here. Their favorite gimmick: Making up a dummy of the opposing team's mascot, roughing it up on the floor and then hanging it from the rafters.

UNIVERSITY OF NEW MEXICO LOBOS
Albuquerque **[P. 79, N-6]**; (505) 277-6375. University, capacity 30,646. University Arena, capacity 17,126.
◆One of the most famous basketball gyms in the land. It's called "The Pit." They dug a big hole and put the gym floor at the bottom. Much of the gym is below ground. It's the pits for most visiting teams as well.

Horse Racing

LA MESA PARK
South Highway, S of Raton **[P. 78, B-6]**; (505) 445-2301. Opened in 1945. Clubhouse capacity: 586. Grandstand capacity: 1,500.
Thoroughbred season from June to Sep.

RUIDOSO DOWNS
Hwy. 70 E, 1 mi. past jct. Hwy. 48, Ruidoso Downs **[P. 79, H-5]**; (505) 378-4431 or (800) 622-6023. Opened in 1947. Grandstand capacity: 3,185. Total capacity: 5,948.
Thoroughbred season from May to Sep.

SAN JUAN DOWNS
Hwy. 64, btwn. Farmington & Bloomfield, Farmington **[P. 78, B-2]**; (505) 326-4551. Opened in 1984. Total capacity: 7,000.
Thoroughbred season from Apr. to Sep.
◆Mixed meet with quarterhorses.

SUNLAND PARK RACE TRACK
101 Futurity Dr., near El Paso, TX **[P. 79, K-4]**; (505) 589-1131. Opened in 1959. Clubhouse capacity: 1,210. Grandstand capacity: 4,000.
Thoroughbred season from Oct. to May.

THE DOWNS AT ALBUQUERQUE (at NEW MEXICO STATE FAIR RACE TRACK)
201 California, NE, on the New Mexico State Fair Grounds, Albuquerque **[P. 79, N-7]**; (505) 262-1188. Opened in 1938. Grandstand capacity: 15,000.
Thoroughbred season from Jan. to June.
◆The Downs at Albuquerque also features quarterhorse racing. The State Fair runs a fall meet in September and October (entrance at Gate 3, Central Ave. NE).

THE DOWNS AT SANTA FE
Off I-25, S of Santa Fe **[P. 78, D-4]**; (505) 471-3311. Opened in 1971. Clubhouse capacity: 2,500. Grandstand capacity: 10,000. Total capacity: 13,200.
Thoroughbred season from June to Sep.

PGA/LPGA

FOUR HILLS COUNTRY CLUB
911 Four Hills Rd. S.E., Albuquerque **[P. 79, N-8]**; (505) 299-9555.
Sunwest Bank/Charley Pride Senior Golf Classic (Senior PGA), Aug. Number of holes: 54.

Rodeo

TINGLEY COLISEUM
900 San Pedro, on the New Mexico State Fairgrounds, Albuquerque **[P. 79, N-7]**; (505) 265-1791.
New Mexico State Fair, September.

Tennis

ALBUQUERQUE TENNIS COMPLEX
1903 Stadium Blvd., SE, Albuquerque **[P. 79, N-6]**; (505) 848-1381. Surface is hard.
Virginia Slims of Albuquerque (WTA), August.

USA SNAPSHOTS®

A look at statistics that shape the sports world

You have to pay to play
The average cost of equipping athletes for a particular sport:
Golf $400
Racquetball $60
Bowling $100
Tennis $75
Skiing $500
Source: National Sporting Goods Assn., Sporting Goods Manufacturers Assn.

By Bob Laird, USA TODAY

► OUTDOOR VENUES

National Parks

CARLSBAD CAVERNS NATIONAL PARK
27 mi. S of Carlsbad on US 62/180 **[P. 79, J-6]**. Contains 46,765 acres. **HK**

CARSON NATIONAL FOREST
North central area of state **[P. 78, B-3,4,5]**. Contains 1,591,121 acres.
C HK BT F R BK W HT

CIBOLA NATIONAL FOREST
NM 14 and 536 **[P. 78, D-2, E-4, F-2 & 5, G-3]**. Contains 1,625,542 acres. **C HK F S R BK W CL**

EL MALPAIS NATIONAL MONUMENT
Off I-40, Grants **[P. 78, E-2]**. Contains 114,716 acres. **HK BK**

GILA NATIONAL FOREST
SW area of state **[P. 78, G-1; P. 79, H-1]**. Contains 3,321,101 acres. **C HK BT F R BK W CL**

LINCOLN NATIONAL FOREST
Southeastern NM **[P. 78, G-5; P. 79, H-5, J-6]**. Contains 1,103,441 acres. **C HK F R BK W CL**

SANTA FE NATIONAL FOREST
Santa Fe **[P. 78, C-4, D-5]**. Contains 1,568,820 acres. **C HK F R BK W HT**

State Parks

Bike Trails: BK
Boating: BT
Camping: C
Climbing: CL
Diving: DV
Fishing: F
Golfing: G
Hiking: HK
Hunting: HT
Riding: R
Surfing: SU
Swimming: S
Tennis: TE
Whitewater: WW
Winter Sports: W

BLUEWATER LAKE STATE PARK
28 mi. W of Grants off I-40 & NM 412 **[P. 78, D-2]**. Contains 3,000 acres. **C HK BT F S W**

CABALLO LAKE STATE PARK
S of Truth or Consequences off I-25 **[P. 79, H-3]**. Contains 16,300 acres. **C HK BT F S**

CLAYTON LAKE STATE PARK
15 mi. N of Clayton on NM 370 **[P. 78, B-8]**. Contains 417 acres. **C HK BT F**

CONCHAS LAKE STATE PARK
32 mi. NW of Tucumcari via NM 104 **[P. 78, D-7]**. Contains 10,000 acres. **C HK BT F S G**

ELEPHANT BUTTE LAKE STATE PARK
7 mi. N of Truth or Consequences off I-25 **[P. 79, H-3]**. Contains 50,000 acres. **C HK BT F S**

HERON LAKE STATE PARK
11 mi. W of Tierra Amarilla via US 64 & NM 95 **[P. 78, B-4]**. Contains 13,000 acres. **C HK BT F S W**

NAVAJO LAKE STATE PARK
25 mi. E of Bloomfield on US 64 & NM 511 **[P. 78, B-3]**. Contains 21,000 acres. **C HK BT F S W**

SANTA ROSA LAKE STATE PARK
7 mi. N of Santa Rosa on access road **[P. 78, E-6]**. Contains 4,300 acres. **C HK BT F S R BK**

UTE LAKE STATE PARK
3 mi. SW of Logan on NM 540 **[P. 78, D-8]**. Contains 9,500 acres. **C HK BT F S**

Skiing

ALPINE SKIING

ANGEL FIRE
North Angel Fire Road, Angel Fire **[P. 78, C-5]**; (800) 633-7463.
Vertical drop is 2,180 feet. Has six chairs.

SANTA FE SKI AREA
End of Hwy. 475 (Hyde Park Road), Santa Fe **[P. 78, C-5]**; (505) 982-4429.
Vertical drop is 1,650 feet. Has two tows, one bar and four chairs.

SKI APACHE
Ruidoso **[P. 78, G-5]**; (505) 336-4356.

CONTINUED ON PAGE 186

New Mexico

CONTINUED FROM PAGE 185

> **"There's a lot of different mountain ranges between Albuquerque and Taos and the environment changes drastically, from mountain scrub to miniature oaks. . . triathletes train here, also cyclists. . . It's the kind of area you see in the Road Runner films - really colorful. . . It's kind of two different states, because the north and south are so different. It's real fertile around the Rio Grande, but once you get away from it, it's desert again."**
>
> **Road racing champion cyclist *Janelle Parks***

Vertical drop is 1,800 feet. Has one tow, seven chairs and one gondola.

TAOS SKI VALLEY
End of Hwy. 150, Taos Ski Valley **[P. 78, B-5]**; (505) 776-2291.
Vertical drop is 2,612 feet. Has two surface lifts and seven chairs.
◆A European scene. Features a renowned ski school.

NORDIC SKIING

ENCHANTED FOREST XC
Bobcat Pass, Red River **[P. 78, B-5]**; (505) 754-2374.

▶ ACTIVE SPORTS

AEROBICS: AFAA, 369 Montezuma Street, #180, Santa Fe; (505) 982-8485.

BASEBALL: Little League Baseball Western Region HQ, 6707 Little League Dr., San Bernadino, CA; (714) 887-6444. • **Pony Baseball-Softball,** 7820 Pebbleford Dr., Ft. Worth, TX; (817) 293-1664. • **American Legion Baseball,** 10317 San Gabriel, Albuquerque; (505) 298-4562. • **Babe Ruth Baseball,** James Wagoner, 2930 Jenny Lind, Fort Smith, AR; (501) 646-3065.

BILLIARDS: The Corner Pocket, 9603 Lomas Blvd. NE, Albuquerque; (505) 294-8853.

BOARDSAILING: Four Corners Windsurfing , Fruitland; (505) 598-6688. • **USWA Regional Director,** 18354 W. 58th Pl. #62, Golden, CO; (303) 279-3185.

BOWLING: American Bowling Congress, 5301 S. 76th St., Greendale, WI; (414) 421-6400.

CANOEING & KAYAKING: ACA Rocky Mountain Vice Commodore, c/o Four Corners Marine, Box 379, Durango, CO; (303) 259-3893.

CYCLING: New Mexico AYH Council, 101 N. Cooper St., Silver City; (505) 388-5485.

FITNESS: Governor's Council on Physical Fitness and Health, c/o City of Albuquerque Office of Senior Affairs, 714 7th S.W., Albuquerque; (505) 764-6448. • **National Strength and Conditioning Ass'n State Director,** Dept. of Physical Education, NMSU, Box 30001, Dept. 3M, Las Cruces; (505) 646-1196.

FOOTBALL: Pop Warner Football, 1315 Walnut Street, Suite 1632, Philadelphia, PA; (215) 735-1450.

GOLF: PGA Sun Country Section, 111 Cardenas NE, Albuquerque; (505) 260-0167. • **Sun Amateur Country Golf Association,** 10035 Country Club Ln. N.W., Suite 5, Albuquerque; (505) 897-0864.

HIKING & CLIMBING: New Mexico Mountain Club (AHS), 119 40th St NW, Albuquerque. • **Rio Grande Sierra Club Chapter,** 207 San Pedro NE, Albuquerque; (505) 265-5506.

HOCKEY: USA Hockey Rocky Mountain Registrar, 7335 S. Garfield Ct., Littleton, CO; (303) 721-0936. • **USA Hockey Rocky Mountain Registrar,** 7335 S. Garfield Ct., Littleton, CO; (303) 721-0936.

HUNTING & FISHING: Department of Game & Fish, Villagra Building, 408 Galistea Street, Santa Fe; (505) 827-7899.

RACQUETBALL: AARA, PO Box 36179, Albuquerque; (505) 266-9213.

RIDING: New Mexico Horse Council, Box 10206, Alameda; (505) 344-8548.

RODEO: PRCA Turquoise Circuit, 4010 W. Palo Seco, Tucson, AZ; (602) 744-2304.

RUNNING: RRCA NM State Rep., PO Box 6045, Quintaro Station, Santa Fe; (505) 471-5007.

SCUBA: Watersports, Inc., 4927 Prospect NE, Albuquerque; (505) 883-0633.

SKATING: USFSA, 20 First Street, Colorado Springs, CO; (719) 635-5200.

SOCCER: AYSO Regional Director, 2971 N. Coronado St., Chandler; (602) 839-2114.

SOFTBALL: ASA, 1017 North Armijo, Las Cruces; (505) 523-4336.

SQUASH: Kiva Club (USSRA), Santa Fe; (505) 983-9654.

SWIMMING: LMSC New Mexico Registrar, 2600 Casa del Norte Ct. NE, Albuquerque; (505) 296-3190.

TENNIS: Recreational TEAMTENNIS Central-West Region, National Program Coordinator, 2105 Grant Ave., #4, Redondo Beach, CA; (800) 992-9042. • **Southwestern USTA,** 2164 E. Broadway Rd., Suite 235, Tempe, AZ; (602) 921-8964.

WHITEWATER RAFTING: Artemis Wilderness Tours, PO Box 1178, Taos; (505) 758-2203. • **New Wave Rafting,** Rt. 5, Box 302-A, Santa Fe; (505) 984-1444. • **Southwest Wilderness Center,** Box 9380, Santa Fe; (505) 982-7262.

Tip Offs

National Trails System

Winding through some of the most striking natural beauty in the country, the Appalachian National Scenic Trail and the Pacific Crest National Scenic Trail were, in 1968, the first federally designated long-distance trails. Since then, 16 other trails of all makes and sizes — 8 scenic and 8 historic — have been set aside for public use.

While the Iditarod, an old Gold Rush trail in Alaska, is today the site of a famous dog-mushing race, the Trail of Tears, running from North Carolina and Georgia to Oklahoma, marks the routes of the Cherokee Indians' forced removal from their ancestral homelands.

Appalachian National Scenic Trail, National Park Service, Harpers Ferry, WV 25425.
Drops south from Maine [P. 50 & 51, E-5 through D-1] to Georgia [P. 30, B-3], via New Hampshire [PP. 74-5], Vermont [P. 75], Massachusetts [P. 56], Connecticut [P. 24], New York [P. 85], New Jersey [P. 76], Pennsylvania [P. 99], Maryland [P. 52], Virginia [PP. 114-15], Tennessee [P. 107] and North Carolina [PP. 86-7].

Continental Divide National Scenic Trail, Director, Recreation Management, U.S. Forest Service, PO Box 2417, Washington, DC 20013.
Montana [P. 68, B-5 to G-7 and F-2 to H-4], Idaho [P. 35, H-5 to J-7], Wyoming [PP. 124-5, B-1 to F-9], Colorado [PP. 20-1, A-6 to H-6] and New Mexico [PP. 78-9, A-4 to L-1].

Florida National Scenic Trail, Director, Recreation Management, U.S. Forest Service, PO Box 2417, Washington, DC 20013. Florida [PP. 26-7, C-1, C-4, D-6 and H-7].

Ice Age National Scenic Trail, National Park Service, 7818 Big Sky Dr., Madison, WI 53719.
Wisconsin [PP. 122-23, E-1 to L-6]

Iditarod National Historic Trail, Alaska Region, National Park Service, 2525 Gambell St., Anchorage, AK 99503. Alaska [P. 8, C-2 to E-3].

Lewis and Clark National Historic Trail, Midwest Region, National Park Service, 1709 Jackson St., Omaha, NE 68102.
Winds from Illinois [P. 37, K-3] to the Pacific and back, via Missouri [PP. 66-7], Kansas [P. 45], Iowa [P. 42], Nebraska [P. 71], South Dakota [P. 105], North Dakota [P. 89], Montana [PP. 68-9], Idaho [P. 34], Washington [PP. 118-19] and Oregon [PP. 96-7].

Mormon Pioneer National Historic Trail, Rocky Mountain Region, National Park Service, P.O. Box 25287, Denver, CO 80225.
From Illinois [P. 36, F-2] to what is today called Salt Lake City, Utah [P. 112, C-5 to D-4], via Iowa [PP. 42-3], Nebraska [PP. 70-1] and Wyoming [PP. 124-5].

Natchez Trace National Scenic Trail, Southeast Region, National Park Service, Richard B. Russell Building, 75 Spring St., SW, Atlanta, GA 30303.
Travels across Mississippi [PP. 64-5, B-8 to M-2] to Alabama [P. 6, A-2 to B-1] and Tennessee [P. 106, B-7 to D-5].

Nez Perce National Historic Trail, Nez Perce National Forest, 319 E. Main St., Grangeville, ID 93530. In Oregon, Idaho, Montana and Wyoming. Not developed for public use.

North Country National Scenic Trail, Midwest Region, National Park Service, 1709 Jackson St., Omaha, NE 68102.
New York [PP. 84-5, E-13 to H-7], Pennsylvania [P. 98, B-5 to E-1], Ohio [PP. 90-1, C-2 to G-7], Michigan [PP. 58-9, C-6 to O-5], Wisconsin [PP. 122-3, C-1 to C-5], Minnesota [PP. 62-3, H-2, G-3 to J-7], North Dakota [P. 89, D-4 to G-8].

Oregon National Historic Trail, Pacific Northwest Region, National Park Service, 83 S. King St., Suite 212, Seattle, WA 98104.
A pioneer trail, running from Missouri, through Kansas, Nebraska, Wyoming and Idaho to Oregon. Not developed for public use.

Overmountain Victory National Historic Trail, Southeast Region, National Park Service, 75 Spring St., SW, Atlanta, GA 30303.
Revolutionary War trail in Virginia [P. 114], Tennessee [P. 107], North Carolina [P. 86, C-2 to F-2], South Carolina [P. 102, A-5 & 6]

Pacific Crest Trail, Director, Recreation Management, U.S. Forest Service, P.O. Box 2417, Washington, DC 20013.
Runs the length of California [PP. 14-5, A-4 to H-9; PP. 16-17, J-8 to Q-12] through Oregon [P. 96, B-6 to H-4] into Washington [PP. 118-19, A-8 to G-7].

Potomac Heritage National Scenic Trail, National Capital Region, 1100 Ohio Dr., SW, Washington, DC 20242. Washington, DC [P. 54, D-1 to F-4], Maryland [PP. 52-3, B-3 to H-10] and Pennsylvania [P. 98, F-4 to G-3].

Santa Fe National Historic Trail, Southwest Region, National Park Service, P.O. Box 728, Santa Fe, NM 87504. Extends from a point near Arrow Rock, Missouri through Kansas, Oklahoma and Colorado to Santa Fe, New Mexico. Not developed for public use.

Trail of Tears National Historic Trail, Southeast Region, National Park Service, 75 Spring St., SW, Atlanta, GA 30303.
Journies from North Carolina [P. 86], Tennessee [P. 106], and Kentucky [P. 46] across Georgia [P. 30], Alabama [P. 6] and Missouri [PP. 66-7] to Arkansas [PP. 12-13] and Oklahoma [P. 95].

New York

The Empire State has it all: a wonderland of winter activities, 13 National Parks Service areas, and the Big Apple of professional sports in New York City. ◆ The 11 Finger Lakes feature cool, clear waters formed by glaciers, good for windsurfing, boating, water skiing and sailing. ◆ Babe Ruth's locker and much else is preserved at the National Baseball Hall of Fame and Museum in Cooperstown. ◆ Buffalo has the NFL Bills, NHL Sabres and Triple-A baseball (Pittsburgh Pirates). ◆ Saratoga Raceway is a must for summertime horse racing, especially at The Travers Stakes. ◆ Long Island's white sand beaches—on both the sound and ocean sides—are ideal for sunning and bathing. ◆ And Madison Square Garden is the sports mecca in Manhattan, where the NBA Knicks and NHL Rangers compete for time with boxing, tennis, track and field and Menudo concerts.

STATBOX

POPULATION: 17,950,000
SQUARE MILES: 47,377
TIME ZONE: Eastern
MOTTO: Excelsior
BIRD: Red Breasted Bluebird
TREE: Sugar Maple
CAPITAL: Albany
AVERAGE ANNUAL RAINFALL: 40"
MEAN TEMP: 47/62
MAJOR LEAGUE TEAMS: 7
NATIONAL PARK ACREAGE: 80,177
STATE PARK ACREAGE: 259,321
HIGHEST ELEVATION: 5,344'
LOWEST ELEVATION: sea level
WATERWAYS: 1,632 square miles of water

► SPECTATOR VENUES

Auto Racing

NEW YORK INTERNATIONAL RACEWAY
2 mi. N of Leicester on NY 36, Leicaster **[P. 84, G-5]**; (716) 382-3030. Track is 1/4-mile asphalt-concrete pad.
Empire Nationals (IHRA), June.

WATKINS GLEN INTERNATIONAL
Country Route 16, 2 miles from Route 414, Watkins Glen **[P. 84, H-7]**; (607) 535-2481. Track is 2.428-mile, 7-turn road.
◆More Formula One Grand Prixs have taken place here than at any other spot in the country; the glamorous circuit made its USA home here from 1961 to 1980.
Camel Continental (IMSA Camel GT), June (on 3.377-mile road course).
The Budweiser at the Glen (NASCAR Winston Cup and SCCA Trans-Am Championship), August.

Baseball

ALEX T. DUFFY FAIRGROUNDS
900 Coffeen Street, Watertown **[P. 85, E-9]**. Capacity: 3,500
Watertown Indians (New York-Penn League, Class A); (315) 788-8747. Entered League in 1989. Broadcasts by WTNY 790 AM. MLB affiliation, Cleveland Indians.

COLLEGE STADIUM
485 Falconer Street, Jamestown **[P. 84, J-3]**. Capacity: 3,328
Jamestown Expos (New York-Penn League, Class A); (716) 665-4092. Entered League in 1939. Broadcasts by WJTN 1240 AM. MLB affiliation, Montreal Expos.

DAMASCHKE FIELD
95 River Street, Oneonta **[P. 85, H-10]**. Capacity: 3,200
Oneonta Yankees (New York-Penn League, Class A); (607) 432-6326. Entered League in 1966. MLB affiliation, New York Yankees.

DONOVAN FIELD
1700 Sunset Avenue, Utica **[P. 82, H-2]**. Capacity: 5,000
Utica Blue Sox (New York-Penn League, Class A); (315) 738-0999. Entered League in 1977. Broadcasts by WTOB 1310 AM. MLB affiliation, Chicago White Sox.

DUNN FIELD
Luce Street at Maple Street, Elmira **[P. 84, J-7]**. Capacity: 5,100
Elmira Pioneers (New York-Penn League, Class A); (607) 734-1811. Entered League in 1968. MLB affiliation, Boston Red Sox.

DWYER STADIUM
Corner of Denio & Bank St., Batavia **[P. 84, G-5]**. Capacity: 3,000
Batavia Clippers (New York-Penn League, Class A); (716) 343-7531. Entered League in 1939. Broadcasts by WBTA 1490-AM. MLB affiliation, Philadelphia Phillies.

FALCON PARK STADIUM
108 N. Division Street, Auburn **[P. 85, G-8]**. Capacity: 3,575
Auburn Astros (New York-Penn League, Class A); (315) 255-2489. Entered League in 1958. Broadcasts by WMBO 1340-AM. MLB affiliation, Houston Astros.

HERITAGE PARK
Albany Shaker Rd.,(near airport), Albany **[P. 82, E-4]**. Capacity: 5,700
Albany-Colonie Yankees (Eastern League, Class AA); (518) 869-9236. Entered League in 1983. Broadcasts by WGNA 1460-AM. MLB affiliation, New York Yankees.

MACARTHUR STADIUM
Hiawatha Blvd. and 2nd North St., Syracuse **[P. 82, A-6]**. Capacity: 10,500
Syracuse Chiefs (International League, Class AAA); (315) 474-7833. Entered League in 1986. Broadcasts by WNDR 1260-AM. MLB affiliation, Toronto Blue Jays.The Chiefs started in 1885, left the International League in 1956 and have been in and out through 1986.

MCDONOUGH PARK
Lyceum St. & Nursery St., Geneva **[P. 84, G-7]**. Capacity: 2,200
Geneva Cubs (New York-Penn League, Class A); (315) 789-2827. Entered League in 1958. Broadcasts by WEOS 89.7. MLB affiliation, Chicago Cubs since 1977.

PILOT FIELD
275 Washington St., Buffalo **[P. 84, F-1]**. Capacity: 20,900
Buffalo Bisons (American Association, Class AAA); (716) 846-2000. Entered League in 1985. Broadcasts by WGR 550-AM. MLB affiliation, Pittsburgh Pirates.

SAL MAGLIE STADIUM
1201 Hyde Park Boulevard, Niagara Falls **[P. 84, E-4]**. Capacity: 1,800
Niagara Falls Rapids (New York-Penn League, Class A); (716) 298-5400. Entered League in 1989. Broadcasts by WJJL 1440-AM. MLB affiliation, Detroit Tigers.

SHEA STADIUM
126th and Roosevelt Ave., Flushing **[P. 81, H-7]**. Built in 1964. Capacity: 55,601
◆They blare New York-themed music and other noise over a PA at heavy-metal concert levels. Right on the La Guardia flight path, enough to drown out the bad music most days.
New York Mets (NL East); (718) 507-6387. Franchise began in 1962. Broadcasts by WFAN 660 AM, WWOR Channel 9, Sportschannel America. Affiliates: Tidewater, VA (AAA); Williamsport, PA (AA); St. Lucie, FL (A); Columbia, SC (A); Pittsfield, MA (A); Kingsport, IN (Rookie); Sarasota, FL (Rookie). Spring training held in Port St. Lucie, FL.

SILVER STADIUM
500 Norton St., Rochester **[P. 82, A-2]**. Capacity: 12,503
Rochester Red Wings (International League, Class AAA); (716) 467-3000. Entered League in 1888. Broadcasts by WKQG 1280-AM. MLB affiliation, Baltimore Orioles.

YANKEE STADIUM
E. 161st St. and River Ave., Bronx **[P. 80, G-6]**. Built in 1923. Capacity: 57,545
◆Remodeled in the mid-Seventies, the House that Ruth Built updated its seating design (it's no longer possible to get stuck behind a girder), while retaining its eccentric outfield dimensions and wedding-cake exterior. A must-see is the pre-game tour of the monuments to past Yankee greats in the New York bullpen.
New York Yankees (AL East); (212) 293-4300. Franchise began in 1901. Broadcasts by WABC 770 AM, WPIX Channel 11, MSG Network. Affiliates: Columbus, OH (AAA); Albany-Colonie, NY (AA); Ft. Lauderdale, FL (A); Woodbridge, VA (A); Greensboro, NC (A); Oneonta, NY (short A); Tampa, FL (Rookie). Spring training held in Ft. Lauderdale, Fl.

Basketball

KNICKERBOCKER ARENA
51 South Pearl Street, Albany **[P. 82, G-5]**. Capacity: 17,000.
Albany Patroons (Continental Basketball Association, National Conference, Eastern Division); (518) 487-2222. Entered League in 1982.

MADISON SQUARE GARDEN
4 Pennsylvania Plaza, New York **[P. 81, J-5]**. Built in 1968. Capacity: 19,081.
◆One can get goose bumps walking into the mecca of New York sports. The basketball fans here are so persnickety they stayed away in droves from the final Knicks-Bulls playoff game after a disappointing season in 1991 — even though other arenas across the country regularly sell out when Michael Jordan flies into town. Woody Allen and Spike Lee are some of the Knicks' regular boosters. St. John's plays Big East games here.
New York Knickerbockers (NBA Eastern Conf., Atlantic Div.); (212) 465-6000. Franchise began in 1946. Broadcasts by WFAN 660 AM, MSG Network.

Bowling

MARCEL'S OLYMPIC BOWL
1350 Scottsville Road, Rochester **[P. 82, C-1]**; (716) 235-5341.
Chevy Truck Classic (PBA), October.

SAYVILLE BOWL
5660 Sunrise Highway, Sayville **[P. 89, M-5]**; (516) 567-8900.
Leisure Long Island Open (PBA), March.

THRUWAY LANES
1550 N. Walden Avenue, Cheektowaga **[P. 84, F-2]**; (716) 896-8507.
PBA Senior/Touring Pro Doubles, August.

College Sports

ADELPHI UNIVERSITY PANTHERS
South Avenue, Garden City **[P. 84, M-3]**; (516) 663-1155. Stiles Field, capacity 2,500. Woodruff Hall, capacity 1,400.

BROOKLYN COLLEGE KINGSMEN
Bedford Avenue & Avenue H, Brooklyn **[P. 81, L-5]**; (718) 780-5366.

C.W. POST PIONEERS
Greenvale **[P. 84, L-3]**; (516) 299-2289. Hickox, capacity 6,000.

CANISIUS COLLEGE GOLDEN GRIFFINS

CONTINUED ON PAGE 188

USA SNAPSHOTS®

A look at statistics that shape the sports world

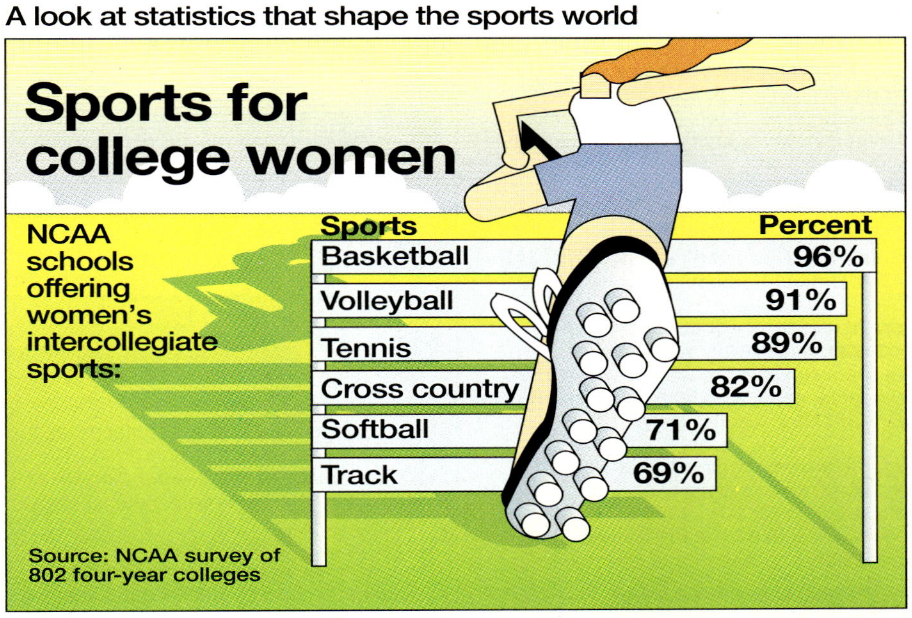

By Rod Little, USA TODAY

New York

CONTINUED FROM PAGE 187

2001 Main Street, Buffalo **[P. 84, F-2]**; (716) 888-2970. Demske Athletic Complex, capacity 1,000. Koessler Athletic Center, capacity 1,800.

COLGATE UNIVERSITY RED RAIDERS
13 Oak Drive, Hamilton **[P. 85, G-10]**; (315) 824-1000. Andy Kerr, capacity 12,500. Reid Center, capacity 3,000.

COLUMBIA UNIVERSITY LIONS
Dodge Physical Fitness Center, New York **[P. 80, G-5]**; (212) 854-2548. Wien Stadium at Baker Field.

CORNELL UNIVERSITY BIG RED
Ithaca **[P. 85, H-8]**; (607) 255-5220. Schoelkopf, capacity 27,000. Multi-Purpose, capacity 4,400.

FORDHAM UNIVERSITY RAMS
Bronx **[P. 80, F-6]**; (212) 579-2447. Jack Coffey Field, capacity 7,000. Rose Hill, capacity 3,500.

HAMILTON COLLEGE CONTINENTALS
Clinton **[P. 85, G-10]**; (315) 859-4114. Steuben Field, capacity 4,000.

HARTWICK COLLEGE WARRIORS
Oneonta **[P. 85, H-10]**; (607) 431-4700. Elmore Field, capacity 3,500. Binder PE Center, capacity 1,800.

HOBART COLLEGE STATESMEN
Geneva **[P. 84, G-7]**; (315) 781-3565. Boswell Field, capacity 4,500. Bristol Gym, capacity 1,300.

HOFSTRA UNIVERSITY FLYING DUTCHMEN
Physical Fitness Center, Hempstead **[P. 84, M-3]**; (516) 560-6750. Hofstra, capacity 7,000. PE Center, capacity 4,200.

IONA COLLEGE GAELS
715 North Avenue, New Rochelle **[P. 80, E-8]**; (914) 633-2304. Mulcahy, capacity 3,000.

LE MOYNE COLLEGE DOLPHINS
Le Moyne Heights, Syracuse **[P. 82, B-7]**; (315) 445-4410. Athletic Center, capacity 3,000.

LONG ISLAND UNIVERSITY BLACKBIRDS
University Plaza, Brooklyn **[P. 81, K-5]**; (718) 403-1030. Picariello Field, capacity 1,000. A&M Schwartz Athletic Center, capacity 1,750.

MANHATTAN COLLEGE JASPERS
Manhattan College Parkway, Bronx **[P. 80, E-6]**; (212) 920-0227.

MARIST COLLEGE RED FOXES
North Road, Poughkeepsie **[P. 85, K-13]**; (914) 471-3240. Leonidoff Field, capacity 2,500. McCann Center, capacity 3,944.

NIAGARA UNIVERSITY PURPLE EAGLES
Niagara University **[P. 84, E-4]**; (716) 285-1212. Niagara Falls Convention and Civic Center, capacity 6,000. NU Student Center, capacity 3,700.

RENSSELAER POLYTECHNIC INSTITUTE ENGINEERS
Troy **[P. 82, F-7]**; (518) 276-6685. '86 Field, capacity 3,000. Houston, capacity 5,400.
◆Great for hockey, very vocal crowd.

SIENA COLLEGE
Route 9, Loudonville **[P. 82, F-6]**; (518) 783-2528. Alumni Recreation Center. ARC, capacity 4,000.

SKIDMORE COLLEGE THOROUGHBREDS
No. Broadway, Saratoga **[P. 85, G-12]**; (518) 584-3023. Wagner Memorial, capacity 1,000.

ST. BONAVENTURE UNIVERSITY BONNIES
St. Bonaventure **[P. 84, J-4]**; (716) 375-2538. Reilly Center, capacity 6,000.

ST. FRANCIS COLLEGE TERRIERS
180 Remsen Street, Brooklyn Heights **[P. 81, K-5]**; (718) 522-2300. PE Center, capacity 2,000.

> **"People are really excited about the World Games, coming [to Buffalo] in '93. They're building an all-around stadium where the old football field used to be."**
>
> **Buffalo Bills football star *Cornelius Bennett***

ST. JOHN'S UNIVERSITY REDMEN
Jamaica **[P. 81, J-8]**; (718) 990-6217. St. John's, capacity 3,000. Alumni Hall, capacity 6,000.
◆The school is in Jamaica, but the Redmen play most of their games in Madison Square Garden. Nonetheless, they hold their annual Christmas tournament in cozy Alumni Hall; they've never lost it.

ST. LAWRENCE UNIVERSITY SAINTS
Canton **[P. 83, C-10]**; (315) 379-5421. Weeks Field, capacity 3,500. Augsbury, capacity 1,100.

STATE UNIVERSITY OF NEW YORK (AT ALBANY) GREAT DANES
1400 Washington Avenue, Albany **[P. 82, G-4]**; (518) 442-3076. University Gym, capacity 2,800.

STATE UNIVERSITY OF NEW YORK (AT BINGHAMTON) COLONIALS
Vestal Parkway East, Binghamton **[P. 85, M-9]**; (607) 777-4255. University, capacity 3,000.

STATE UNIVERSITY OF NEW YORK (AT STONY BROOK) PATRIOTS
Nicolls Road, Stony Brook **[P. 84, L-4]**; (516) 632-7210. Fieldhouse capacity 1,900.

STATE UNIVERSITY COLLEGE OF NEW YORK/BROCKPORT GOLDEN EAGLES
Brockport **[P. 84, G-5]**; (716) 395-2763. Special Olympics, capacity 9,500.

STATE UNIVERSITY COLLEGE OF NEW YORK/CORTLAND RED DRAGONS
Cortland **[P. 85, H-8]**; (607) 753-4953. Davis Field, capacity 4,000. Lusk Gym, capacity 1,000.

STATE UNIVERSITY COLLEGE OF NEW YORK/FREDONIA BLUE DEVILS
Fredonia **[P. 84, H-3]**; (716) 673-3102. Athletic Field, capacity 1,700. Fieldhouse capacity 4,000.

STATE UNIVERSITY COLLEGE OF NEW YORK/GENESEO KNIGHTS
Geneseo **[P. 84, G-5]**; (716) 245-5345. Schrader, capacity 1,440. Kuhl Gym, capacity 3,000.

STATE UNIVERSITY COLLEGE OF NEW YORK/ONEONTA RED DRAGONS
Oneonta **[P. 85, H-10]**; (607) 431-3594. Dragon Field, capacity 2,500. Dragon Gym, capacity 1,500.

STATE UNIVERSITY COLLEGE OF NEW YORK/OSWEGO LAKERS
Route 104, Oswego **[P. 85, F-8]**; (315) 341-4280. Golden Romney, capacity 2,000.

STATE UNIVERSITY COLLEGE OF NEW YORK/PLATTSBURGH CARDINALS
Plattsburgh **[P. 83, B-13]**; (518) 564-3140. Cardinal, capacity 3,500. ICC Arena-Ronald B. Stafford, capacity 3,500.

STATE UNIVERSITY COLLEGE OF NEW YORK/POTSDAM BEARS
Potsdam **[P. 83, B-11]**; (315) 267-2308. Molnar, capacity 2,000. Maxcy Hall, capacity 3,600.

STATE UNIVERSITY OF NEW YORK AT BUFFALO BULLS
Alumni Arena, Buffalo **[P. 84, F-1]**; (716) 636-3142. University at Buffalo, capacity 4,000. Alumni Arena, capacity 10,000.

SYRACUSE UNIVERSITY ORANGEMEN
Syracuse **[P. 82, B-6]**; (315) 443-2385. Carrier Dome, capacity 50,000. Manley, capacity 9,500.
◆The largest on-campus facility used for basketball in the country, Carrier Dome is a signature of the Big East. And if you get bored with the basketball game or the Dome Ranger romping through the building, you can always go behind the curtain where the other half of the football field is and party.

U.S. MILITARY ACADEMY
West Point **[P. 85, K-12]**; (914) 938-3701. Michie, capacity 40,000. Holleder Center, capacity 5,000.

UNION COLLEGE DUTCHMEN
Schenectady **[P. 82, D-3]**; (518) 370-6284. Bailey, capacity 5,000. Memorial, capacity 3,000.

UNIVERSITY OF ROCHESTER YELLOWJACKETS
Rochester **[P. 82, B-2]**; (716) 275-4301. Fauver, capacity 5,000. Louis Alexander Palestra, capacity 3,000.

WAGNER COLLEGE
Staten Island **[P. 81, L-3]**; (718) 390-3433. Fischer Field, capacity 8,000. Sutter, capacity 2,000.

Football

GIANTS STADIUM
The Meadowlands, East Rutherford **[P. 80, G-4]**. Built in 1976. Capacity: 76,891.
New York Jets (AFC Eastern Division); (516) 538-6600. Franchise began in 1960. Broadcasts by WCBS.
New York Giants (NFC Eastern Division); (201) 935-8111. Franchise began in 1925. Broadcasts by WNEW.

New York Knights (World League of American Football, North American East Division); (212) 644-1991. Franchise began in 1991. Broadcasts by WNEW 1130 AM.

RICH STADIUM
One Bills Drive, Orchard Park **[P. 84, G-4]**. Built in 1973. Capacity: 80,290.
◆In the snowbelt.
Buffalo Bills (AFC Eastern Division); (716) 648-1800. Franchise began in 1960. Broadcasts by WBEN-AM Buffalo.

Hockey

BROOME COUNTY VETERANS MEMORIAL ARENA
One Stuart Street, Binghamton **[P. 85, L-9]**. Capacity: 4,849.
◆A good, minor league facility.
Binghamton Rangers (American Hockey League); (607) 723-8937. Franchise began in 1977. Broadcasts by WRSG 1360, Channel 6.

GLENS FALLS CIVIC CENTER
1 Civic Center Plaza, Glenns Falls **[P. 85, F-13]**. Capacity: 4,804.
◆About one-and-a-half hours north of Albany in the beautiful Lake George vacation area.
Adirondack Red Wings (American Hockey League); (518) 798-0366. Franchise began in 1979. Broadcasts by WROW 590 AM (Albany), WBZA 1230 AM (Glens Falls), WSCG 935 FM (Corinth).

MADISON SQUARE GARDEN
4 Pennsylvania Plaza, New York **[P. 81, J-5]**. Built in 1968. Capacity: 16,792.
New York Rangers (NHL, Wales Conference, Patrick Divsion); (212) 465-6000. Franchise began in 1926. Broadcasts by WFAN (66 AM), Madison Square Garden Garden Cable Network.

MEMORIAL AUDITORIUM
140 Main, Buffalo **[P. 84, G-1]**. Built in 1940. Capacity: 16,325.
Buffalo Sabres (NHL, Wales Conference, Adams Division); (716) 856-7300. Franchise began in 1970.

NASSAU VETERANS' MEMORIAL COLISEUM
Hempstead Turnpike, Uniondale **[P. 84, M-3]**. Built in 1972. Capacity: 16,297.
New York Islanders (NHL, Wales Conference, Patrick Division); (516) 794-4100. Franchise began in 1972. Broadcasts by WEVD (1050 AM), WBAB (1240 AM), SportsChannel.

R.P.I. HOUSTON FIELD HOUSE
Peoples Avenue, Troy **[P. 82 F-7]**. Capacity: 5,203.
Capital District Islanders (American Hockey League); (518) 276-8375. Franchise began in 1990. Broadcasts by WABY 1400 AM.

UTICA MEMORIAL AUDITORIUM
400 Oriskany Street West, Utica **[P. 82, G-2]**. Capacity: 3,971.
Utica Devils (American Hockey League); (315) 724-2126. Franchise began in 1987. Broadcasts by WTLB Radio.

WAR MEMORIAL AUDITORIUM
100 Exchange St., Rochester **[P. 82, B-2]**. Capacity: 6,973.
Rochester Americans (American Hockey League); (716) 454-5335. Franchise began in 1956. Broadcasts by WBBF 950 AM, WGMC 90.1 FM, WBER 90.5 FM, WBTF 101.7 FM, WOKR TV-13.

Horse Racing

AQUEDUCT RACE TRACK
Rockaway Blvd. & 108th St., Ozone Park, Queens **[P. 81, K-7]**; (718) 641-4700. Opened in 1894. Clubhouse capacity: 1,200. Total capacity: 27,000.
Thoroughbred season from Oct. to May.
◆Hosted the 1985 Breeder's Cup. Site of the first, and only, triple dead heat in a stakes race when Brownie, Bossuet and Wait a Bit tied for first at the 1944 Carter Handicap. Better get here quickly; the New York Racing Association is evidently considering selling it to consolidate racing in the New York area at Belmont Park.

BATAVIA DOWNS
8315 Park Road, Batavia **[P. 84, G-5]**; (716) 343-3750. Opened in 1940. Clubhouse capacity: 600. Grandstand capacity: 9,000. Harness season from Feb. to Apr. and July to Dec.

BELMONT PARK
Hempstead Turnpike & Cross Island Pkwy., Elmont, Long Island **[P. 84, M-3]**; (718) 641-4700. Opened in 1905. Grandstand capacity: 30,000.
Thoroughbred season from May to Oct.
◆The Triple Crown's finale, the Belmont Stakes, has been run here since 1905. Held three weeks after the Preakness, it was inaugurated at Jerome Park in 1867 and moved to Morris Park in 1890, before coming to Belmont fifteen years later. You won't find a better after-race establishment than Esposito's Tavern. Short of the back stretch, this is the best spot for information. Be prepared to voice strong opinions or be shuttled to the background. Owners John and his brother Junior make it worthwhile if only to hear their stories.

CONTINUED ON PAGE 189

New York

CONTINUED FROM PAGE 188

BUFFALO RACEWAY
5600 McKinley Parkway, Hamburg **[P. 84, H-4]**; (716) 649-1280. Opened in 1942. Clubhouse capacity: 700. Grandstand capacity: 6,000.
Harness season from Apr. to July and in December, January & February.

FINGER LAKES
Route 96 & Beaver Creek Road, Farmington **[P. 84, G-6]**; (716) 924-3232. Opened in 1962. Clubhouse capacity: 2,000. Grandstand capacity: 4,000.
Thoroughbred season from Mar. to Dec.

MONTICELLO RACEWAY
Raceway Road, Monticello **[P. 85, K-11]**; (914) 794-4100. Opened in 1958. Clubhouse capacity: 500. Grandstand capacity: 4,500.
Harness season from Jan. to Dec.

SARATOGA RACE COURSE
Union Avenue, Saratoga Springs **[P. 85, G-13]**; (518) 584-6200. Opened in 1864. Clubhouse capacity: 465. Grandstand capacity: 6,214.
Thoroughbred season from July to Aug.
◆The oldest track in the nation offers great racing, great weather, great atmosphere. The town revolves around racing in August. Everything is within walking distance. Siro's is the after-race favorite. Up north is Lake George, an excellent resort; however, many never want to leave the Saratoga atmosphere.

SARATOGA HARNESS RACING (SARATOGA RACEWAY)
Nelson Avenue, at corner of Crescent Ave., Saratoga Springs **[P. 85, G-13]**; (518) 584-2110. Opened in 1941. Clubhouse capacity: 1,700. Grandstand capacity: 2,000.
Harness season from Jan. to Nov.

VERNON DOWNS
Ruth Street, Vernon **[P. 85, G-9]**; (315) 829-2201. Opened in 1953. Clubhouse capacity: 2,500. Grandstand capacity: 3,500.
Harness season from Apr. to Nov.

YONKERS RACEWAY
810 Central Avenue, Yonkers **[P. 80, E-7]**; (914) 968-4200. Opened in 1899. Clubhouse capacity: 15,000. Grandstand capacity: 15,000.
Harness season from Jan. to Dec.
◆Both the Trotting and Pacing Triple Crowns begin here, with, respectively, the Yonkers Trot and the Cane Pace.

Museums & Halls of Fame

AMATEUR SKATING UNION HALL OF FAME
371 Washington Street, Newburgh **[P. 85, K-12]**; (914) 561-6600.

BASEBALL HALL OF FAME
Main St., Cooperstown **[P. 85, H-10]**; (607) 547-9988.
◆A ballpark-styled theater presents a history of the national pastime. Visitors are greeted with a recording of Abbott and Costello's "Who's on First?" routine. The surrounding countryside is a sight in itself, and local Little Leaguers and baseball greats still play at Abner Doubleday Field.

CATSKILL FLY FISHING CENTER
RD 1, Old Route 17, Livingston Manor **[P. 85, J-11]**; (914) 439-4810.

INTERNATIONAL BOXING HALL OF FAME
N.Y. State Thruway & State Route 13, Canastota **[P. 85, G-9]**; (315) 697-7095.
◆Features fist impressions from Tyson, boxing gloves, trunks. A small museum.

INTERNATIONAL WOMEN'S SPORTS HALL OF FAME
342 Madison Ave., New York **[P. 81, J-5]**; (212) 972-9170.
◆No exhibitions. Library only; call first for appointment.

NATIONAL MUSEUM OF RACING AND HALL OF FAME
Union Ave. & Nelson Ave., Saratoga Springs **[P. 85, G-13]**; (518) 584-0400.
◆Across the street from the Saratoga track, it's a stately, homey museum.

NATIONAL SOCCER HALL OF FAME
5-11 Ford Ave., Oneonta **[P. 85, H-11]**; (607) 432-3351.
◆Commercially oriented. The exhibit is small.

THE TROTTING HORSE MUSEUM
240 Main Street, Goshen **[P. 85, K-12]**; (914) 294-6330.
◆A great surprise. Interesting exhibits, terrific art work, nifty gift shop.

PGA/LPGA

CORNING COUNTRY CLUB
E. Corning Rd., Corning **[P. 84, J-7]**; (607) 936-3711.
LPGA Corning Classic, May. Number of holes: 72.

EN-JOIE GOLF CLUB
722 W. Main St., Endicott **[P. 85, J-9]**; (607) 785-1661.
B.C. Open (PGA), Sept. Number of holes: 72.

LAFAYETTE COUNTRY CLUB
4480 Lafayette Rd., Jamesville **[P. 82, C-7]**; (315) 469-3296.
Mony Syracuse Senior Classic (Senior PGA), June. Number of holes: 54.

LOCUST HILL COUNTRY CLUB
2000 Jefferson Rd., Pittsford **[P. 84, G-6]**; (716) 427-7010.
Rochester International (LPGA), June. Number of holes: 72.

MEADOW BROOK CLUB
Rt. 107, Cedar Swamp Rd., Jericho **[P. 84, L-3]**; (516) 935-6500.
Northville Long Island Classic (Senior PGA), July. Number of holes: 54.

SLEEPY HOLLOW COUNTRY CLUB
Route 9, Scarborough-on-Hudson **[P. 80, A-7]**; (914) 941-8070.
NYNEX Commemorative (Senior PGA), May. Number of holes: 54.

WESTCHESTER COUNTRY CLUB
North St., off Hutchinson River Pkwy., Rye **[P. 84, L-3]**; (914) 967-6000.
Buick Classic (PGA), June. Number of holes: 72.

WYKAGYL COUNTRY CLUB
1195 North Ave., New Rochelle **[P. 80, E-8]**; (914) 636-8700.
JAL Big Apple Classic (LPGA), July. Number of holes: 72.

Polo

MEADOWBROOK POLO CLUB, INC.
Bethpage State Park, Jericho, L.I. **[P. 84, L-3]**; (516) 681-5300.

SKANEATELES POLO CLUB
W. Lake & Andrews Rd., Skaneateles **[P. 85, G-8]**; (315) 685-5715.

Soccer

BLEECKER STADIUM
Clinton Avenue, Albany **[P. 82, G-6]**. Capacity: 6,000.
Albany Capitals (American Professional Soccer League, American Conference); (518) 456-1015.

Tennis

CENTRAL PARK TENNIS COMPLEX
Central Park, just NW of Iroquois Lake, Schenectady **[P. 82, D-3]**; (518) 370-5151. Surface is hard.
OTB International Tennis Open (ATP, WTA), August.

MADISON SQUARE GARDEN
4 Penn Plaza, New York **[P. 81, J-5]**; (212) 465-6000. Surface is Supreme.
Pricey tickets.
Virginia Slims Championships (WTA), November.

MANHATTANVILLE COLLEGE
125 Purchase Street, Purchase; (203) 532-0400. Surface is hard.
Westchester Ladies Cup (WTA), July.

NATIONAL TENNIS CENTER
Flushing Meadow Park, Queens **[P. 81, H-7]**; (718) 592-8000. Surface is hard.
◆Adjacent to the Mets' Shea Stadium. A cornucopia of sights and smells, with a great variety of pricey food. Watch the free qualifiers beforehand, and roam the outer courts to see the stars of tomorrow. Parking is reserved, but subway and Long Island Rail Road are both fine from Manhattan.
US Open (ATP, WTA, USTA), Aug. and Sept.

THE HAMLET GOLF & COUNTRY CLUB
Hauppauge Road, Commack **[P. 84, M-3]**; (516) 385-1000. Surface is hard.
Norstar Bank Hamlet Challenge Cup (ATP), August.

Track & Field

CARRIER DOME
Syracuse University, Syracuse **[P. 82, B-6]**; (212) 227-0071.
National Scholastic Championships, March.

DOWNING STADIUM
Randall's Island, New York **[P. 79, H-6]**; (212) 227-0071.
USA/Mobil Outdoor Track & Field Championships, June, 1991.

MADISON SQUARE GARDEN
4 Penn Plaza, New York **[P. 81, J-5]**; (212) 465-6000.
USA/Mobil Championships, Feb.
Snickers Millrose Games (USA/Mobil Grand Prix Event), Feb.

STREETS OF NEW YORK
Base of Verrazano Bridge, Staten Bridge, New York **[P. 81, L-4]**; (212) 860-4455.
New York Marathon, November.

STREETS OF SUFFOLK COUNTY
Eisenhower Park, East Meadow **[P. 84, M-3]**; (516) 542-4439.
Long Island Marathon, May.

Yachting

MANHASSET BAY YACHT CLUB
455 Main St., Port Washington **[P. 84, L-3]**; (516) 767-2150.
Hinman Trophy (U.S. Team Race Championship), Sept.

► OUTDOOR VENUES

National Parks

FINGER LAKES NATIONAL FOREST
Between Rochester & Syracuse, Lake Ontario to PA border, off I-90, I-81 or NY 17 **[P. 85, H-9]**. Contains 13,000 acres.
C HK F R BK HT

FIRE ISLAND NATIONAL SEASHORE
Off the S shore of Long Island **[P. 84, M-5]**. Contains 6,095 acres.
C HK BT F S SU

GATEWAY NATIONAL RECREATION AREA/BREEZY POINT DISTRICT
Rockaway Peninsula **[P. 81, M-6]**. Contains 1,059 acres.
HK F S

GATEWAY NATIONAL RECREATION AREA/JAMAICA BAY DISTRICT
Brooklyn **[P. 81, L-7]**. Contains 4,450 acres.
HK BT F R TE

GATEWAY NATIONAL RECREATION AREA/STATEN ISLAND UNIT
New York **[P. 81, N-3 & 4]**. Contains 1,210 acres. **HK BT F S BK**

Bike Trails: BK
Boating: BT
Camping: C
Climbing: CL
Diving: DV
Fishing: F
Golfing: G
Hiking: HK
Hunting: HT
Riding: R
Surfing: SU
Swimming: S
Tennis: TE
Whitewater: WW
Winter Sports: W

State Parks

ALLEGANY STATE PARK
S of Salamanca on State Park Rd. 1 **[P. 84, J-4]**. Contains 62,000 acres.
C HK BT F S R BK W HT

BEAR MOUNTAIN STATE PARK
5 mi. S of West Point off US 9W **[P. 85, L-12]**. Contains 5,067 acres.
HK BT F S BK W

BOWMAN LAKE STATE PARK
8 mi. NW of Oxford off NY 220 **[P. 85, H-9]**. Contains 653 acres.
C HK BT F S BK W

CLARENCE FAHNESTOCK MEMORIAL STATE PARK
11 mi. W of Carmel on NY 301 **[P. 85, K-13]**. Contains 6,800 acres.
C HK BT F S R BK W

DELTA LAKE STATE PARK
6 mi. NE of Rome on NY 46 **[P. 85, F-10]**. Contains 400 acres.
C HK BT F S BK W

GRAFTON LAKES STATE PARK
0.5 mi. S of Grafton off NY 2 **[P. 85, G-13]**. Contains 2,357 acres.
HK BT F S R W HT

HARRIMAN STATE PARK
5 mi. W of Stony Point on NY 210 **[P. 84, K-1]**. Contains 46,613 acres.
C HK BT F S W G

JACQUES CARTIER STATE PARK
2 mi. W of Morristown off NY 12 **[P. 83, C-9]**. Contains 461 acres.
C HK BT F S BK W HT

Skiing

BELLEAYRE MOUNTAIN
Off Route 28, Highmount **[P. 85, J-11]**; (914) 254-5600.
Vertical drop is 1,340 feet. Has three bars and four chairs.

BIG TUPPER SKI AREAÏ
Tupper Lake **[P. 83, C-11]**; (518) 359-3651.
Vertical drop is 1,152 feet. Has one tow, one bar and three chairs.

BRISTOL MOUNTAIN
5658 Route 64, Canandaigua **[P. 84, G-6]**; (716) 374-6000.
Vertical drop is 1,200 feet. Has one tow and four chairs.

CATAMOUNT SKI AREA
Route 23, Hillsdale **[P. 85, J-13]**; (518) 325-3200.
Vertical drop is 1,000 feet. Has two bars and four chairs.

GORE MOUNTAIN SKI AREA
Peaceful Valley Road, North Creek **[P. 85, F-12]**; (518) 251-2411.

CONTINUED ON PAGE 190

New York

CONTINUED FROM PAGE 189

Vertical drop is 2,100 feet. Has one bar, six chairs and one gondola.

GREEK PEAK SKI RESORT
2000 NYS Route 392, Cortland **[P. 85, H-8]**; (607) 835-6111.
Vertical drop is 900 feet. Has two bars and five chairs.

HUNTER MOUNTAIN SKI BOWL
On Rt. 23A, Hunter **[P. 85, J-12]**; (518) 263-4223.
Vertical drop is 1,600 feet. Has five tows, one bar and eleven chairs.

SKI WINDHAM
C.D. Lane Road, Windham **[P. 85, J-12]**; (518) 734-4300.
Vertical drop is 1,600 feet. Has one bar and six chairs.

WEST MOUNTAIN SKI AREA
RD #2, West Mountain Road, Glens Falls **[P. 85, F-13]**; (518) 793-6606.
Vertical drop is 1,010 feet. Has two tows, one bar and three chairs.

WHITEFACE MOUNTAIN SKI CENTER
Route 86, Wilmington **[P. 83, C-12]**; (800) 462-6236.
Vertical drop is 3,216 feet. Has nine chairs.

NORDIC SKIING

BEAVERKILL VALLEY INN
Lew Beach **[P. 85, J-11]**; (914) 439-4844.

BIG TUPPER CROSS COUNTRY
c/o Cunningham's Ski Barn, Tupper Lake **[P. 83, C-11]**; (518) 359-3615.

CHAUTAUQUA COUNTY PARK
100 East 2nd Street, Jamestown **[P. 84, J-3]**; (716) 664-5602.

CUNNINGHAM'S SKI BARN
No. 1 Main Street, Northcreek **[P. 85, E-12]**; (518) 251-3215.

FROST VALLEY XC SKI
County Road 47, Oliverea **[P. 85, J-12]**; (914) 985-2291.

GARNET HILL
13th Lake Road, North River **[P. 85, E-12]**; (518) 251-2821.

LAKE PLACID CLUB-XC
c/o Cunningham's Ski Barn, Lake Placid **[P. 83, C-12]**; (518) 523-4460.

LAPLAND LAKE CROSS COUNTRY
RD 2, Northville **[P. 85, K-12]**; (518) 863-4974.

MOHONK MOUNTAIN HOUSE
Lake Mohonk, New Paltz **[P. 85, K-12]**; (914) 255-1000.

PECHLER'S XC SKI
2191 Shilling Road, Palmyra **[P. 84, G-6]**; (315) 597-4210.

PINERIDGE CROSS COUNTRY
E. Poestenkill, Petersburg **[P. 85, G-14]**; (518) 283-5509.

SAGAMORE RESORT
Sagamore Road, Bolton Landing **[P. 85, F-13]**; (518) 644-9400.

SARATOGA SPRINGS XC
Cunningham's Ski Barn/Saratoga Spa, Saratoga Springs **[P. 85, G-13]**; (518) 587-3116.

SPACE MOUNTAIN XC
Deposit Motel, Deposit **[P. 85, J-10]**; (607) 467-2998.

TACONIC OUTDOOR EDUCATION
12 Dennytown Road, Cold Spring **[P. 85, K-12]**; (914) 265-3773.

THE BARK EATER INN
Alstead Mill Road, Keene **[P. 83, C-13]**; (518) 576-2221.

TOP OF THE WORLD
Lockhart Mountain Road, Lake George **[P. 85, F-13]**; (518) 668-2062.

TREE HAVEN TRAILS
West Galway Road, Hagaman **[P. 85, G-12]**; (518) 882-9455.

WILLIAMS LAKE HOTEL XC
Binnewater Road, Rosendale **[P. 85, J-12]**; (914) 658-3101.

WINTER CLOVE
Winter Clove Road, Round Top **[P. 85, J-12]**; (518) 622-3267.

WIPPENOSE NORDIC SKI
800 Nottingham Road, Dewitt; (315) 446-3183.

ACTIVE SPORTS

ADVENTURE: New York City Outward Bound Center, 450 Park Ave. S., New York; (212) 481-8980.

AEROBICS: AFAA, 21 High St., Fairport; (716) 377-1690.

BASEBALL: Little League Baseball Eastern Region HQ, PO Box 3485, Williamsport, PA; (717) 326-1921. • **Pony Baseball-Softball,** 2 Byrnes Lane E., Sayreville, NJ; (718) 692-0444. • **American Legion Baseball,** 245 Oxford Rd., #29D, New Hartford; (315) 737-7555. • **Babe Ruth Baseball,** Raymond P. Jones, 300 Lodge St., Piscataway, NJ; (201) 469-5841. • **Men's Senior Baseball League - Long Island,** 8 Sutton Terrace, Jericho; (516) 931-2615. • **Men's Senior Baseball League - Rochester,** 103 Selbourne, Rochester; (716) 223-8895.

BILLIARDS: Chelsea Billiards, 54 W. 21st St., New York; (212) 989-0096. • **Julian Billiard Academy,** 138 E. 14th St., New York; (212) 475-9338. • **Le Q,** 36 E. 12th St., New York; (212) 995-8512. • **The Billiard Club,** 220 W. 19th St., New York; (212) 206-7665.

BOARDSAILING: Finger Lakes Aquatics , Canandaigua; (716) 394-8150. • **Island Windsurfing Corp. ,** New York; (212) 744-2000. • **Island Windsurfing Corp. ,** Southampton; (516) 283-1198. • **USWA Regional Director,** Bayview Bus Park Unit 10, Gilford, NH; (603) 293-2727.

BOWLING: American Bowling Congress, 5301 S. 76th St., Greendale, WI; (414) 421-6400.

CANOEING & KAYAKING: ACA Atlantic Vice Commodore, 4 Russell Dr., RD 2, Wading River; (516) 929-3177. • **ACA Northern New York Vice Commodore,** PO Box 163, Davenport; (607) 278-5990.

CYCLING: Hudson-Mohawk AYH Council, PO Box 6343, Albany; (518) 449-8261. • **LAW Mid-Atlantic Regional Director,** 14 Gould Place, #2, Caldwell, NJ; (201) 228-7208. • **Niagara Frontier AYH Council,** PO Box 1110, Ellicott Station, Buffalo; (716) 852-5222. • **Syracuse AYH Council,** 535 Oak Street, Syracuse; (315) 472-5788. • **USCF New York N. Representative,** 1128 Ardsley Rd., Schenectady; (518) 370-2011. • **USCF New York S. Representative,** 30 Clermont Ave., Port Chester; (914) 934-1327.

FITNESS: National Strength and Conditioning Ass'n State Director, #6 Henderson Rd., Massapequa Park; (516) 795-8524.

FOOTBALL: Pop Warner Football, 1315 Walnut Street, Suite 1632, Philadelphia, PA; (215) 735-1450. • **U.S. Flag Football League,** 5834 Pine Tree Drive, Sanibel, FL; (813) 472-0544.

GOLF: Buffalo District Golf Association, PO Box 19, Cheektowaga; (716) 632-1936. • **Metropolitan Golf Association,** 125 Spencer Place, FO Box 219, Mamaroneck; (914) 698-0390. • **New York State Golf Association,** PO Box 3459, Elmira; (607) 733-0007. • **PGA Central New York Section,** PO Box 216, Syracuse; (315) 468-6812. • **PGA Metropolitan Section,** Box 268, Wykagyl Station, New Rochelle; (914) 235-7277. • **PGA Northern New York Section,** 1500 Central Ave., Albany; (518) 869-2914. • **PGA Western New York Section,** PO Box 1728, Williamsville; (716) 626-0603. • **Rochester District Golf Association,** 9 Evanwood Dr., Rochester; (716) 253-2667. • **Syracuse District Golf Association,** 636 W. Onondaga Street, Syracuse; (315) 456-1000. • **Westchester Golf Association,** 1875 Palmer Ave., Suite 204, Larchmont; (914) 834-5869.

HIKING & CLIMBING: Adirondack Mountain Club , RR #3, Box 3055, Lake George; (518) 668-4447. • **Adirondak 46er's Inc. (AHS),** RFD 1, Box 390, Morrisonville; (518) 563-2973. • **Atlantic Sierra Club Chapter,** Empire State Plaza, Box 2112, Albany; (518) 472-1534. • **Finger Lake Trail Conference (AHS),** PO Box 18048, Rochester; (716) 288-7191. • **Genesee Valley Hiking Club (AHS),** 94 Sunset Trail W, Fairport; (716) 377-7575. • **NY/NJ Trail Conference (AHS),** 232 Madison Ave., Room 908, New York; (212) 685-9699. • **The Appalachian Mountain Club ,** 5 Joy St., Boston, MA; (617) 523-0636.

HOCKEY: USA Hockey New York Registrar, PO Box 307, Lewiston; (716) 754-8557.

HUNTING & FISHING: Beaverkill Angler (Orvis), Broad St., PO Box 198, Roscoe; (607) 498-5194. • **Department of Environmental Conservation,** 50 Wolf Rd., Room 524, Albany; (518) 457-5691. • **J. Patrick's Outfitters (Orvis),** 304 Factory St., Watertown; (315) 788-3519. • **Jones Outfitters, Ltd. (Orvis),** 37 Main St., Lake Placid; (518) 523-3468. • **Leisure Sports Outfitters (Orvis),** 97-H Main St., Stony Brook; (516) 689-9011. • **Orvis New York,** East 45th St., New York; (697) 313-3133. • **Panorama Outfitters (Orvis),** 900 Panorama Trail, Rochester; (716) 248-8390. • **The Orvis Shop,** 5655 Main St., Williamsville; (716) 631-5131. • **Trout Unlimited,** 2 Clyde Grover Road, Binghamton; (607) 648-3375. • **The Royal Coachman Ltd.,** 9 E. Genesee St., Skaneateles; (315) 685-0005.

LACROSSE: Lacrosse Foundation Chapter, 43 Willow Street, Floral Park; (516) 437-1175. • **Lacrosse Foundation Chapter,** 12 Thompson Ave., Croton; (914) 271-4574. • **Lacrosse Foundation Chapter,** 6430 Terese Terrace, Jamesville; (315) 474-6811.

RACQUETBALL: AARA, 142 Landing Ave., Smithtown; (516) 360-0979.

RIDING: Nassau-Suffolk Horsemen's Association, 274 Bedell Terrace, W. Hempstead; (516) 489-4555. • **New York State Horse Council,** 875 King St., Chappaqua; (914) 769-6732.

RODEO: PRCA First Frontier Circuit, 5982 Summit Bridge Rd., Townsend, DE; (302) 378-4551.

RUNNING: RRCA NY State Rep., 34 County Line Rd., Massapequa; (516) 799-3058.

SCUBA: East Coast Diving, Inc., 1500 Hylan Blvd., Staten Island; (718) 979-6056. • **Martini Scuba,** 2037 Central Park Avenue, Yonkers; (914) 779-9786. • **Pan Aqua Diving, Inc.,** 166 West 75th Street, New York; (212) 496-2267. • **Scuba Network,** 290 Atlantic Avenue, Brooklyn; (718) 802-0700. • **Sea Horse Divers,** 95-58 Queens Blvd., Queens; (718) 897 -2885.

SHOOTING: Mid Hudson Trap & Skeet, 411 N. Ohioville Rd., New Paltz; (914) 255-7460. • **Morris Creek Fish & Game Preserve,** Rd. 1, Box 122, S. New Berlin; (607) 263-5238. • **Sandanona Sporting Club,** Sharon Tpke. Rt. 44A, PO Box 800, Millbrook; (914) 677-9701. • **Taconic Trap Club, Inc.,** Rt. 82, Salt Point; (914) 266-3788.

SKATING: Middle Atlantic Skating Association, 3419 Irwin Ave., Bronx; (212) 549-4290. • **USFSA,** 20 First Street, Colorado Springs, CO; (719) 635-5200.

SOCCER: New York State West YSA, 37 Bryn Mawr, Rochester; (716) 426-1505. • **Eastern New York YSA,** 49 Front Street, Suite No. 2, Rockville Centre; (516) 766-0849. • **AYSO Regional Director,** 4014 Oneida St., New Hartford, NY; (315) 737-5610.

SOFTBALL: ASA, 186 E. Albany Street, Oswego; (315) 343-1928. • **Buffalo ASA,** 987 Fillmore Ave., Buffalo; (716) 891-8373. • **Long Island ASA,** 766 Grand Terrace, Baldwin; (516) 868-5280. • **New York City ASA,** 250 Waters Ave., Staten Island; (718) 816-8934.

SQUASH: Cobble Hill Racquet & Fitness Center (USSRA), Brooklyn; (718) 643-4400. • **Doral Inn Squash Club (USSRA),** New York; (212) 838-2102. • **Lincoln Squash Club (USSRA),** New York; (212) 265-0995. • **New York Athletic Club (USSRA),** New York; (212) 247-3470. • **Nichols School (USSRA),** Buffalo; (716) 875-8212. • **Poughkeepsie Squash Club (USSRA),** Poughkeepsie; (914) 471-9242.

SWIMMING: LMSC Adirondack Registrar, PO Box 232, Nassau; (518) 479-3739. • **LMSC Metropolitan Registrar,** 229 E. 25th St., #1C, New York; (212) 532-0730. • **LMSC Niagara Registrar,** 477 Antlers Dr., Rochester; (716) 271-2323

TABLE TENNIS: USTTA State Coordinator (Upstate NY), 5046 Bowen Dr., Nedrow; (315) 492-0325.

TENNIS: Recreational TEAMTENNIS East Region, National Program Coordinator, 246 N. Reservoir St., Lancaster, PA; (800) 633-6122. • **Eastern USTA,** 550 Mamaroneck Ave., Suite 505, Harrison; (914) 698-0414.

TRIATHLON: Big Apple Tri Club, Box 20427 Cherokee Station, New York; (212) 289-4113. • **New York Tri Association,** 3 Watch Hill Rd., New Paltz; (914) 255-8251. • **RATS,** 29 Westmoreland, Rochester; (716) 477-9530. • **Team Atomic,** 477 Connecticut, Buffalo; (716) 884-8204. • **Team Redline,** 55 W. 95th Street, #91, New York; (212) 502-1140.

VOLLEYBALL: USVBA Iroquois Empire Commissioner, 301 Ripplebrook Ln., Minoa; (315) 656-9489. • **USVBA Western Empire Commissioner,** 59 Hampshire Dr., Rochester; (716) 244-7108.

WHITEWATER RAFTING: Adirondack River Outfitters , PO Box 649, Old Forge; (315) 369-3536.

◆ ◆ ◆

North Carolina

Every year, more than 700,000 fans flock to see races at the Charlotte Motor Speedway, including the NASCAR Coca-Cola 600, which features the second-largest crowd in U.S. sports (118,000). ◆ Basketball fever has reached epic proportions in the state, both on the college level (North Carolina, N.C. State, and Duke) and in the NBA (Charlotte Hornets). Expect sellout crowds at either. ◆ North Carolina's minor league baseball has become the stuff of legend since the movie "Bull Durham" was released. Seven Single-A and two Double-A teams dot the state. And, yes, there is a team in Durham (Atlanta Braves). ◆ Great Smoky is the most visited national park in the country. The Appalachian Trail offers skiing, mountain biking, trout fishing, whitewater kayaking, and rafting. ◆ Pinehurst is a double-must for golf nuts: the PGA World Golf Hall of Fame and the LPGA Hall of Fame are located there.

▶ SPECTATOR VENUES

Auto Racing

CHARLOTTE MOTOR SPEEDWAY
US Highway 29, 12 miles north of Charlotte, in Concord **[P. 86, E-5]**; (704) 455-2121. Track is 1.5 miles.
◆The premiere motorsports facility in the USA. It holds over 100,000 spectators, has luxury sky boxes, condominiums and The Speedway Club for dining and entertainment.
Coca Cola 600 (NASCAR Winston Cup), May.
Mello Yello 500 (NASCAR Winston Cup), October.

NORTH CAROLINA MOTOR SPEEDWAY
Highway 1, 10 miles north of Rockingham **[P. 86, F-6]**; (919) 582-2861. Track is 1.017 miles.
◆Home of Buck Baker's High Performance Driving School.
Goodwrench 500 (NASCAR Winston Cup), March.
Winston Invitational (NHRA), early April at the Rockingham Dragway.
AC-Delco 500 (NASCAR Winston Cup), October.

NORTH WILKESBORO SPEEDWAY
Speedway Road, off Highway 421, 14 mi. from I-77, 45 mi. W of Winston-Salem **[P. 86, D-4]**; (919) 667-6663. Track is 0.625 miles.
First Union 400 (NASCAR Winston Cup), April.
Tyson Holly Farms 400 (NASCAR Winston Cup), Sept.

NORTH WILKESBORO DRAGWAY
6 mi. W of N. Wilkesboro on US 421, then S, in Lenoir **[P. 86, D-6]**; (704) 754-6433. Track is 1/4 mile asphalt-concrete pad.
Carolina Nitrous Nationals (IHRA), July.

Baseball

BURLINGTON ATHLETIC FIELD
1450 Graham Street, Burlington **[P. 86, D-7]**. Capacity: 3,500
Burlington Indians (Appalachian League, Rookie Class); (919) 222-0223. Entered League in 1986. Broadcasts by WBBB 920-AM. MLB affiliation, Cleveland Indians.

DURHAM ATHLETIC PARK
428 Morris St., Durham **[P. 88, E-4]**. Capacity: 5,000
Durham Bulls (Carolina League, Class A); (919) 688-8211. Entered League in 1980. Broadcasts by WDNC 620AM. MLB affiliation, Atlanta Braves.

ERNIE SHORE FIELD
401 W. 30th St., Winston-Salem **[P. 88, A-2]**. Capacity: 4,280
Winston-Salem Spirits (Carolina League, Class A); (919) 759-2233. Entered League in 1945. Broadcasts by WSJS 600AM. MLB affiliation, Chicago Cubs.

FIVE COUNTY STADIUM
US 264 and Hwy. 39, Cebulon **[P. 87, D-9]**. Capacity: 6,000
Carolina Mudcats (Southern League, Class AA); (919) 269-2287. Entered League in 1989. Broadcasts by WKIX 850 AM. MLB affiliation, Pittsburgh Pirates.

GRAINGER STADIUM
400 East Grainger Ave., Kinston **[P. 87, F-10]**. Capacity: 4,100
Kinston Indians (Carolina League, Class A); (919) 527-9111. Entered League in 1964. Broadcasts by WRNS 960AM. MLB affiliation, Cleveland Indians.

J.P. RIDDLE STADIUM
2823 Legion Road, Fayetteville **[P. 87, F-10]**. Capacity: 3,200
Fayetteville Generals (South Atlantic League, Class A); (919) 424-6500. Entered League in 1987. Broadcasts by WFNC 640 AM. MLB affiliation, Detroit Tigers.

MCCORMICK FIELD
30 Buchanan Avenue, Asheville **[P. 87, B-11]**. Capacity: 3,500
Asheville Tourists (South Atlantic League, Class A); (704) 258-0428. Entered League in 1977. MLB affiliation, Houston Astros.

SIMS LEGION PARK
1001 N. Marietta Street, Gastonia **[P. 86, F-4]**. Capacity: 3,200
Gastonia Rangers (South Atlantic League, Class A); (704) 867-3721. Entered League in 1977. Broadcasts by WGNC 1450-AM. MLB affiliation, Texas Rangers.

WAR MEMORIAL STADIUM
510 Yanceyville Street, Greensboro **[P. 88, B-7]**. Capacity: 7,500
Greensboro Hornets (South Atlantic League, Class A); (919) 275-1641. Entered League in 1980. Broadcasts by WTHP-FM 98.3. MLB affiliation, New York Yankees.

Basketball

CHARLOTTE COLISEUM
100 Paul Buck Blvd., Hive Drive, Charlotte **[P. 86, G-2]**. Built in 1988. Capacity: 23,901.
Charlotte Hornets (NBA Eastern Conf., Central Div.); (704) 357-0252. Franchise began in 1988. Broadcasts by WBT 1110 AM, WCCB Channel 18.

College Sports

APPALACHIAN STATE UNIVERSITY MOUNTAINEERS
Boone **[P. 86, D-3]**; (704) 262-4010. Kidd Brewer, capacity 18,000. Varsity Gym, capacity 8,000.

CAMPBELL UNIVERSITY FIGHTING CAMELS
Buies Creek **[P. 87, E-8]**; (919) 893-4111. Taylor Field, capacity 3,000. Carter Gym, capacity 1,000.

DAVIDSON COLLEGE WILDCATS
Davidson **[P. 86, E-5]**; (704) 892-2000. Richardson Field, capacity 8,000. Belk Arena, capacity 5,700.

DUKE UNIVERSITY BLUE DEVILS
Durham **[P. 88, F-3]**; (919) 684-2489. Wallace Wade, capacity 33,941. Cameron, capacity 8,564.
◆Cameron is one of college basketball's chapels. Cozy and cramped, it is generally acknowledged as being home to the zaniest group of college basketball fans in the country. The students get all the best seats and make it special with inventive and often funny cheers. They also know almost all the refs by their first name.

EAST CAROLINA UNIVERSITY PIRATES
Greenville **[P. 87, E-10]**; (919) 757-4600. Ficklen, capacity 35,000. Minges Coliseum, capacity 6,500.

FAYETTEVILLE STATE UNIVERSITY BRONCOS
Newbold Station, Fayetteville **[P. 87, F-8]**; (919) 486-1314. FSU Athletic, capacity 5,000.

LENOIR-RHYNE COLLEGE BEARS
Hickory **[P. 86, E-4]**; (704) 328-7115. CollegeField, capacity 8,500. Shuford Memorial Gym, capacity 3,200.

NORTH CAROLINA A&T STATE UNIVERSITY AGGIES
Greensboro **[P. 88, B-7]**; (919) 334-7686. Stadium capacity 16,500. Corbett Sports Center, capacity 6,500.

NORTH CAROLINA STATE UNIVERSITY WOLFPACK
Raleigh **[P. 88, H-5]**; (919) 737-2101. Carter-Finley, capacity 51,500. Reynolds Coliseum, capacity 12,400.
◆Reynolds is one of the sport's venerable buildings. It's odd shape, like an aircraft hangar's, gives it a special feel. The Wolfpack cheerleaders contend for the national title every year.

PFEIFFER COLLEGE FALCONS
Misenheimer **[P. 86, E-5]**; (704) 463-1360. Merner Gym, capacity 2,500.

UNIVERSITY OF NORTH CAROLINA TAR HEELS
Chapel Hill **[P. 88, F-2]**; (919) 962-6000. Kenan, capacity 52,000. Smith Center, capacity 21,444.
◆If anyone is ever going to pass Kentucky coach Adolph Rupp's win-loss record, it will be the Tar Heels' Dean Smith. He's at 600-plus and counting. Just how big is he in this state? The building where his team plays is already named after him.

UNIVERSITY OF NORTH CAROLINA 49ERS
Charlotte **[P. 86, F-3]**; (704) 547-4937. Coliseum, capacity 23,500.

UNIVERSITY OF NORTH CAROLINA SPARTANS
1000 Spring Garden, Greensboro **[P. 88, B-6]**; (919) 334-5213. Physical Activities Complex.

UNIVERSITY OF NORTH CAROLINA SEAHAWKS
601 S. College Road, Wilmington **[P. 87, G-10]**; (919) 395-3232. Trask Coliseum, capacity 6,100.

WAKE FOREST UNIVERSITY DEMON DEACONS
Winston-Salem **[P. 88, A-2]**; (919) 759-5616. Groves, capacity 31,000. Coliseum, capacity 8,200.

WESTERN CAROLINA UNIVERSITY CATAMOUNTS
Cullowhee **[P. 86, B-3]**; (704) 227-7338. Whitmire, capacity 12,000. Ramsey Center, capacity 8,000.

WINSTON-SALEM STATE UNIVERSITY RAMS
Winston-Salem **[P. 88, B-3]**; (919) 750-2140. Bowman Gray, capacity 18,000. Lawrence Joel Coliseum, capacity 14,000.

Football

CARTER-FINLEY STADIUM
State Fairgrounds, Raleigh **[P. 88, G-5]**. Capacity: 45,000.
Raleigh-Durham Skyhawks (World League of American Football, North American East Division); (919) 872-4311. Franchise began in 1991. Broadcasts by WPTF 680 AM, ABC Sports, USA Cable.

CONTINUED ON PAGE 192

STATBOX

POPULATION: 6,600,000
SQUARE MILES: 52,669
TIME ZONE: Eastern
MOTTO: Esse Quam Videri (To be, rather than to seem)
BIRD: Cardinal
CAPITAL: Raleigh
TREE: Dogwood
AVERAGE ANNUAL RAINFALL: 44"
MEAN TEMP: 58
MAJOR LEAGUE TEAMS: 1
NATIONAL PARK/FOREST ACREAGE: 1,785,000
STATE PARK ACREAGE: 2,327,903
HIGHEST ELEVATION: 6,684'
LOWEST ELEVATION: sea level
WATERWAYS: 3,615 square miles of water

USA SNAPSHOTS®

A look at statistics that shape the sports world

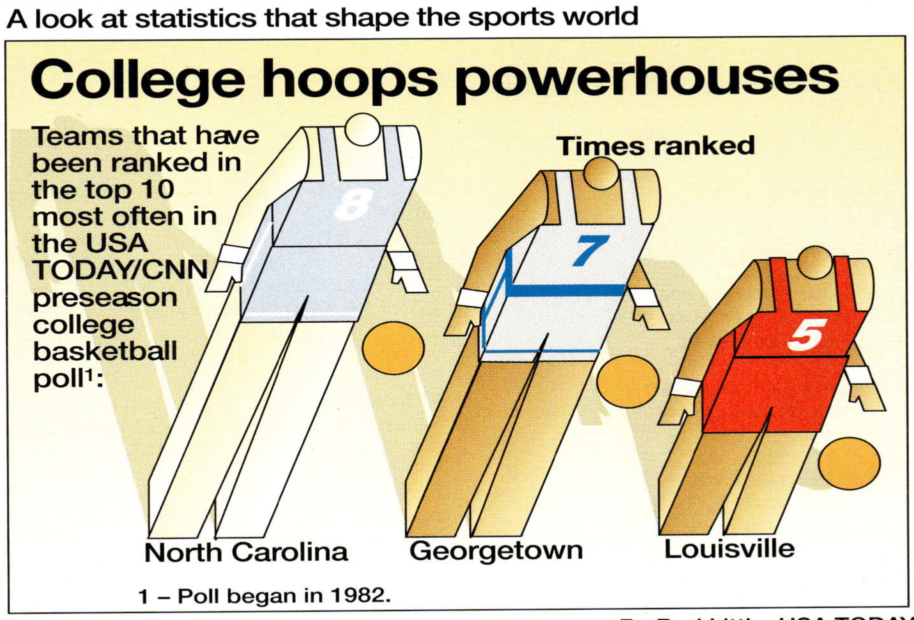
College hoops powerhouses
Teams that have been ranked in the top 10 most often in the USA TODAY/CNN preseason college basketball poll¹:
Times ranked
8
7
5
North Carolina
Georgetown
Louisville
1 – Poll began in 1982.

Source: USA TODAY research

By Rod Little, USA TODAY

North Carolina

CONTINUED FROM PAGE 191

Hockey

GREENSBORO COLISEUM
1921 W. Lee St., Greensboro **[P. 88, B-6]**. Capacity: 13,400.
Greensboro Monarchs (East Coast Hockey League); (919) 852-6170. Franchise began in 1989.

J.S. DORTON ARENA
1025 Blue Ridge Blvd., Raleigh **[P. 88, G-5]**. Capacity: 6,970.
Raleigh IceCaps (East Coast Hockey League); (919) 755-0022. Franchise began in 1991.

LAWRENCE JOEL VETERANS MEMORIAL COLISEUM ANNEX
300 Deacon Blvd., Winston Salem **[P. 88, A-2]**. Capacity: 3,500.
Winston Salem Thunderbirds (East Coast Hockey League); (919) 748-0919. Franchise began in 1988.

Museums & Halls of Fame

NORTH CAROLINA SPORTS HALL OF FAME
3316 Julian Dr., Raleigh **[P. 88, G-6]**; (919) 872-9289.

PGA/WORLD GOLF HALL OF FAME
PGA Blvd., off Midland Road, Pinehurst **[P. 86, F-7]**; (919) 295-6651.

PGA/LPGA

FOREST OAKS COUNTRY CLUB
4600 Forest Oaks Dr., Greensboro **[P. 88, C-7]**; (919) 674-2241.
K-Mart Greater Greensboro Open (PGA), April. Number of holes: 72.

TANGLEWOOD PARK
Highway Park, Clemmons **[P. 88, B-1]**; (919) 766-5082.
Vantage Championship (Senior PGA), Oct. Number of holes: 54.

TPC AT PIPER GLEN
4300 Piper Glen Dr., Charlotte **[P. 86, H-3]**; (704) 846-1515.
Painewebber Invitational (Senior PGA), June. Number of holes: 54.

Polo

PINEHURST POLO CLUB
At Pinehurst Track, Hwy. 5, Southern Pine **[P. 86, F-7]**; (919) 949-2106.

Soccer

VENUE TO BE ANNOUNCED
Raleigh-Durham.
Team name to be announced (American Professional Soccer League).
◆Expansion team. To begin league play in 1992.

Tennis

CHARLOTTE COLISEUM
100 Paul Buck Blvd., Charlotte **[P. 86, G-2]**; (704) 357-4700. Surface is Supreme.
Charlotte Heat (TT), July to August.

OLDE PROVIDENCE RACQUET CLUB
5952 Sharon View Road, Charlotte **[P. 86, H-2]**; (704) 366-9817. Surface is Har-Tru.
U.S. Men's Clay Court Championships (ATP), May.

RALEIGH CIVIC CENTER
500 Fayetteville Street Mall, Raleigh; **[P. 88, G-6]**; (919) 831-6011. Surface is Supreme.
Raleigh Edge (TT), July to August.

> **"The climate is. . . not overbearing, which is great, because the hotter it is, the less biting the fish do. . . the streams in the Great Smoky Mountains are extremely clean, which makes healthier, bigger fish. . . ideal for trout."**
>
> NBA star *Brad Daugherty*

OUTDOOR VENUES

National Parks

Bike Trails: BK
Boating: BT
Camping: C
Climbing: CL
Diving: DV
Fishing: F
Golfing: G
Hiking: HK
Hunting: HT
Riding: R
Surfing: SU
Swimming: S
Tennis: TE
Whitewater: WW
Winter Sports: W

CROATAN NATIONAL FOREST
S of New Bern **[P. 87, F-11]**. Contains 157,724 acres. C HK BT F S HT

GREAT SMOKY MOUNTAINS NATIONAL PARK
Bisected by US 441 **[P. 86, B-6]**. Contains 20,000 acres.
C HK F R BK

NANTAHALA NATIONAL FOREST
W of Waynesville & S of Great Smoky Mountains National Park **[P. 87, B-8, C-9]**. Contains 518,560 acres. C HK BT F S R BK W HT

PISGAH NATIONAL FOREST
N & S of I-40 **[P. 87, B-9]**. Contains 498,825 acres. C HK BT F S R BK W CL

UWHARRIE NATIONAL FOREST
2 mi. E of Troy on NC 27 **[P. 86, E-6]**. Contains 46,977 acres. C HK BT F S BK HT

State Parks

CAROLINA BEACH STATE PARK
1 mi. NW of Carolina Beach off US 421 **[P. 87, H-10]**. Contains 1,720 acres. C HK BT F

DUKE POWER STATE PARK
10 mi. S of Statesville via US 77 and US 21 **[P. 86, E-4]**. Contains 1,458 acres. C HK BT F S

FALLS LAKE STATE RECREATION AREA (AC)
7 mi. N of Raleigh, then Six Forks Rd. to CR 2003 **[P. 88, E-5]**. Contains 13,440 acres.
HK BT F S BK

HANGING ROCK STATE PARK
Danbury **[P. 86, C-5]**. Contains 6,142 acres.
C HK BT F S R

JOHN H. KERR RESERVOIR STATE RECREATION AREA (AC)
N of Henderson on the Virginia border **[P. 87, D-9]**. Contains 106,860 acres. C HK BT F S

JONES LAKE STATE PARK
4 mi. N of Elizabethtown off NC 242 **[P. 86, G-8]**. Contains 1,669 acres. C HK BT F S

JORDAN LAKE STATE RECREATION AREA (AC)
W of Apex off US 64.**[P. 86, E-7]**; Contains 15,825 acres. C HK BT F S

MORROW MOUNTAIN STATE PARK
Albemarle **[P. 86, E-6]**. Contains 4,693 acres.
C HK BT F S

PETTIGREW STATE PARK
Creswell **[P. 87, D-12]**. Contains 17,453 acres.
C HK BT F

STONE MOUNTAIN STATE PARK
5 mi. W of Roaring Gap on US 21 **[P. 86, D-4]**. Contains 13,434 acres. C HK F R

WILLIAM B. UMSTEAD STATE PARK
12 mi. NW of Raleigh off US 70 **[P. 88, G-5]**. Contains 5,637 acres. C HK BT F S

Skiing

ALPINE SKIING

SKI BEECH MOUNTAIN
Beech Mountain Parkway, Banner Elk **[P. 86, D-2]**; (704) 387-2011.
Vertical drop is 830 feet. Has one tow, one bar and seven chairs.

SUGAR MOUNTAIN RESORT
Highway 184, Banner Elk **[P. 86, D-2]**; (704) 898-4520.
Vertical drop is 1,200 feet. Has one tow, two bars and five chairs.

ACTIVE SPORTS

ADVENTURE: North Carolina Outward Bound School, 121 N. Sterling Street, Morganton; (800) 627-5971.

AEROBICS: AFAA, PO Box 9108, Wrightsville Beach; (919) 256-5937.

BASEBALL: Little League Baseball Southern Region HQ, PO Box 13366, St. Petersburg, FL; (813) 344-2661. • **American Legion Baseball,** 214 N. Mountain, Cherryville; (704) 435-9315. • **Babe Ruth Baseball,** William E. Whitehurst, Rt. 2, Box 56, Grifton, NC; (919) 524-5525. • **Men's Senior Baseball League - North Carolina,** PO Box 686, Bunn; (716) 223-8895.

BILLIARDS: Mother's Billiard Parlor & Grille, 6136 South Blvd., Charlotte; (704) 553-7457.

BOARDSAILING: The Old Post Office and B.W.'s Surf Shop , Ocracoke Island; (919) 928-6141. • **Sunsplash Ocean Sports ,** Atlantic Beach; (919) 247-6124. • **USWA Regional Director,** 1912 MacCumber Ln., Wilmington; (919) 256-3553.

BOWLING: American Bowling Congress, 5301 S. 76th St., Greendale, WI; (414) 421-6400

CANOEING & KAYAKING: ACA Dixie Vice Commodore, 2320 Salcedo Street, Savannah, GA; (912) 352-0717.

CYCLING: Coastal Carolina AYH Council, 173 Northeast Broad St., Southern Pines; (919) 692-9367. • **LAW Coastal Regional Director,** 205 E. Joppa Road, Baltimore, MD; (301) 828-8604. • **Research Triangle AYH Council,** RR 7, Box 115, Durham; (919) 968-3531. • **USCF North Carolina Representative,** 260 Brookwood Ave., #1D, Concord; (704) 788-2972.

FITNESS: Governor's Council on Physical Fitness and Health, Department of Health and Natural Resources, PO Box 27687, Raleigh; (919) 733-9615.

FOOTBALL: Pop Warner Football, 1315 Walnut Street, Suite 1632, Philadelphia, PA; (215) 735-1450. • **U.S. Flag Football League,** 5834 Pine Tree Drive, Sanibel, FL; (813) 472-0544.

GOLF: Carolinas Golf Association, PO Box 844, Clemmons; (919) 766-5992. • **Carolina Golf Promotion Association, Inc.,** Chinquapin Rd., Box 3986, McIntyre Station, Pinehurst; (800) 225-1521. • **PGA Carolinas Section,** 3852 Hwy. 9 East, SC; (803) 249-3496. • **Tarheel State Seniors Golf Association,** PO Box 2223, Charlotte; (704) 542-9161.

HIKING & CLIMBING: North Carolina Sierra Club Chapter, PO Box 272, Cedar Mtn.; (704) 885-8229.

HOCKEY: USA Hockey Southeastern Registrar, PO Box 5208, Takoma Park, MD; (301) 622-0032.

HUNTING & FISHING: Brookstown Angler, Inc. (Orvis), Coliseum Park Plaza, 710-C Coliseum Dr., Winston-Salem; (919) 722-4398. • **High Country Fly Fishing (Orvis),** Highway 105 Foscoe, PO Box 2956, Boone; (704) 963-7431. • **Trout Unlimited,** 33 Grovewood Rd., Asheville; (704) 253-7152. • **Wildlife Resources Commission,** Archdale Building, 512 N. Salisbury St., Raleigh; (919) 733-3391.

LACROSSE: Lacrosse Foundation Chapter, 206 W. Bedford, Wilmington; (919) 686-1962.

RACQUETBALL: AARA, 1409 B Whilden Place, Greensboro; (919) 379-0550.

RIDING: North Carolina Horse Council, Rt. 3, Box 80, Fuquay-Varina; (919) 552-3536.

RODEO: PRCA Southeastern Circuit, 1111 S. McGee Rd., Bonifay, FL; (904) 547-2534.

RUNNING: RRCA NC State Rep., 729 Berkley Ave., Charlotte; (704) 377-3679.

SCUBA: Blue Dolphin Dive Shop, Inc., 3010 South Straford Road, Winston Salem; (919) 760-9226. • **Charlotte Dive Center, Inc.,** 8510 Park Road, Charlotte; (704) 334-DIVE. • **Water World, Inc.,** 135 South Miami Blvd., Durham; (919) 596-8185.

SHOOTING: Adams Creek Sporting Clays, Inc., 6240 Adams Creek Road, Havelock; (919) 447-6808. • **Beaver Dam Sporting Clays Range,** Rt. 4, Box 97-M, Greenville; (919) 758-2266. • **Deep River Sporting Clays, Inc.,** PO Box 18066, Raleigh; (919) 774-7080. • **Shane's Sporting Clays,** 6319A Hwy. 158, Summerfield; (919) 643-7168.

SKATING: USFSA, 20 First Street, Colorado Springs, CO; (719) 635-5200.

SOCCER: North Carolina Soccer Ass'n, PO Box 37086, Raleigh; (919) 231-7459. • **North Carolina YSA,** 1834 Banking St., Greensboro; (919) 273-1722. • **AYSO Regional Director,** 1405 Inman Dr., Huntsville, AL; (205) 881-3138.

SOFTBALL: ASA, 5040 Mountain View Rd., Winston-Salem; (919) 768-3389.

SQUASH: Charlotte Country Club, Charlotte; (704) 334-7361.

SWIMMING: LMSC North Carolina Registrar, 304-B Ashland Dr., Greensboro; (919) 855-8715.

TABLE TENNIS: USTTA State Coordinator, PO Box 157, Wilson; (919) 237-3096.

TENNIS: Recreational TEAMTENNIS East Region, National Program Coordinator, 246 N. Reservoir St., Lancaster, PA; (800) 633-6122. • **Southern USTA,** 200 Sandy Springs Place, Suite 200, Atlanta, GA; (404) 257-1297.

TRIATHLON: Disciplined Tri Club, 1015 Carolina Beach Ave. North, Carolina Beach; (919) 458-7560.

VOLLEYBALL: USVBA Carolina Commissioner, 4240 Briar Creek Rd., Clemmons; (919) 766-5075.

WHITEWATER RAFTING: Edge of the World Outfitters , Box 1137, Hwy. 184, Banner Elk; (704) 898-9550. • **Rolling Thunder River Co. ,** Box 88, Almond; (704) 488-2030. • **Wahoo's Adventures ,** PO Box 1915, Hwy. 321 South, Boone; (800) 444-RAFT.

North Dakota

More perch are pulled out of ice-covered Devil's Lake every winter than from any other lake in the world; Lake Sakakawea—a 200-mile-long reservoir on the Missouri River—yields more ten-pound walleyes than anywhere in the USA. ◆ North Dakota also has more wildlife refuges and produces more ducks and geese than any other state in the nation. Also abundant for hunting are pheasant, grouse, and partridge. ◆ The most popular winter spectator sport is college hockey. The University of North Dakota's Fighting Sioux have won five Division I national championships. ◆ In the fall, fans follow college football. The North Dakota State Bison have had the most successful program in the country during the past 27 years, with a 251-54 record and seven national titles. ◆ The National Curling Championships are slated for March, 1992, in Grafton (701-248-3482).

STATBOX

POPULATION: 652,695
SQUARE MILES: 70,702
TIME ZONE: Mountain and Central
MOTTO: Liberty and Union, Now and Forever, One and Inseparable
BIRD: Western Meadowlark
TREE: American Elm
CAPITAL: Bismarck
AVERAGE ANNUAL RAINFALL: 13-20"
MEAN TEMP: 40
MAJOR LEAGUE TEAMS: 0
NATIONAL PARK/FOREST ACREAGE: 2,000,000
STATE PARK ACREAGE: 17,224
HIGHEST ELEVATION: 3,506'
LOWEST ELEVATION: 750'
WATERWAYS: 608 square miles of water

SPECTATOR VENUES

College Sports

NORTH DAKOTA STATE UNIVERSITY BISON
Fargo **[P. 89, A-6]**; (701) 237-8981. Dacotah Field, capacity 14,000. Bison Sports Arena, capacity 7,500.

UNIVERSITY OF NORTH DAKOTA FIGHTING SIOUX
Grand Forks **[P. 89, A-5]**; (701) 777-2234. Memorial, capacity 15,000. Hyslop Sports Center, capacity 9,708.

OUTDOOR VENUES

National Parks

THEODORE ROOSEVELT NATIONAL PARK
Off I-94 or ND 85 **[P. 89, E-2]**. Contains 70,416 acres. **C HK R W**

State Parks

Bike Trails: BK
Boating: BT
Camping: C
Climbing: CL
Diving: DV
Fishing: F
Golfing: G
Hiking: HK
Hunting: HT
Riding: R
Surfing: SU
Swimming: S
Tennis: TE
Whitewater: WW
Winter Sports: W

BEAVER LAKE STATE PARK
3 mi. NE of Burnstad **[P. 89, F-5]**. Contains 93 acres. **C HK BT F S W**

CROSS RANCH STATE PARK
5 mi. S of Hensler **[P. 89, E-4]**. Contains 560 acres. **C HK BT F W**

FORT ABRAHAM LINCOLN STATE PARK
4 mi. S of Mandan **[P. 88, H-1]**. Contains 1,006 acres. **C HK F W**

FORT RANSOM STATE PARK
2 mi. N of Fort Ransom **[P. 89, F-7]**. Contains 890 acres. **C HK F R W**

FORT STEVENSON STATE PARK
3 mi. S of Garrison **[P. 89, E-4]**. Contains 438 acres. **C HK BT F S W**

GRAHAM'S ISLAND STATE PARK
14 mi. SW of Devils Lake **[P. 89, D-6]**. Contains 1,200 acres. **C HK BT F**

LAKE METIGOSHE STATE PARK
12 mi. N of Bottineau **[P. 89, C-5]**. Contains 1,141 acres. **C HK BT F S W**

LAKE SAKAKAWEA STATE PARK
3 mi. W of Riverdale on ND 200 **[P. 89, E-4]**. Contains 822 acres. **C HK BT F S W**

LAKE SAKAKAWEA (AC)
12 mi. W of US Highway 83, off ND 200 **[P. 89, E-3]**. Contains 368,000 acres. **C HK BT F S R**

LEWIS AND CLARK STATE PARK
On Lake Sakakawea, 18 mi. E of Williston on ND 1804 **[P. 89, D-2]**. Contains 490 acres. **C HK BT F S W**

LITTLE MISSOURI STATE PARK
17 mi. N of Killdeer on ND 22 **[P. 89, E-3]**. Contains 6,000 acres. **C HK R**

TURTLE RIVER STATE PARK
22 mi. W of Grand Forks off US 2 **[P. 89, D-7]**. Contains 682 acres. **C HK S R BK W**

Skiing

NORDIC SKIING

BOIS DE SIOUX GOLF COURSE
Wahpeton **[P. 89, G-8]**; (701) 642-2811.

BOTTINEAU WINTER PARK
Bottineau **[P. 89, C-5]**; (701) 263-4556.

> **"Nearly every weekend from May to October, you can find a rodeo in this state. . . They grew out of all the ranches here. . . . It's a way of keeping traditions alive, family oriented, too."**
>
> **Champion bareback rider**
> ***Wayne Herman***

ACTIVE SPORTS

BASEBALL: Little League Baseball Central Region HQ, 4360 N. Mitthoeffer Rd., Indianapolis, IN; (317) 897-6127. • **American Legion Baseball,** Box 1615, Bismark; (701) 223-0514. • **Babe Ruth Baseball,** Norman Travis, Box 339, Burlington, CO; (719) 346-8803.

BOARDSAILING: Sailaway, Hazen; (701) 487-3447. • **USWA Regional Director,** 2625 S.46th, Lincoln, NE; (402)489-1002

BOWLING: American Bowling Congress, 5301 S. 76th St., Greendale, WI; (414) 421-6400.

CANOEING & KAYAKING: ACA Central Vice Commodore, 3410 Ridge Rd., N. Little Rock, AR; (501) 758-4716.

CYCLING: USCF Minnesota/Dakota-East Representative, 3135 Quebec Ave. S, St. Louis Park, MN; (612) 926-2213.

FITNESS: National Strength and Conditioning Ass'n State Director, Univ. of ND Athletic Dept., Box 8175, University Station, Grand Forks; (701) 777-4485.

FOOTBALL: Pop Warner Football, 1315 Walnut Street, Suite 1632, Philadelphia, PA; (215) 735-1450.

GOLF: North Dakota Golf Association, 930 Arthur Dr., Bismark; (701) 255-0242. • **PGA Minnesota Section,** Bunker Hills Golf Club, Hwy. 242 & Foley Blvd., Coon Rapids, MN; (612) 754-0820.

HOCKEY: USA Hockey Minnkota Registrar, PO Box 34340, Blaine, MN; (612) 755-3753.

HUNTING & FISHING: Game & Fish Department, 100 N. Bismark Expressway, Bismark; (701) 221-6300.

RACQUETBALL: AARA, 1522 35th Ave. S., Fargo; (701) 293-6193.

RODEO: PRCA Badlands Circuit, 400 S. Potter, Gettysburg, SD; (605) 765-9636.

RUNNING: RRCA ND & SD State Rep., Box 267, Brookings, SD; (605) 692-2414.

SHOOTING: Dakota Hunting Club & Kennels, Box 1643, Grand Forks; (701) 775-2074.

SKATING: USFSA, 20 First Street, Colorado Springs, CO; (719) 635-5200.

SOCCER: North Dakota Soccer Ass'n, PO Box 0147, Jamestown; (701) 252-8093. • **AYSO Regional Director,** 1720 Carmel Dr., Idaho Falls, ID; (208) 526-4485.

SOFTBALL: ASA, PO Box 2155, Jamestown; (701) 252-3666.

SQUASH: Southgate Racquet Club, Fargo; (701) 237-4805.

SWIMMING: LMSC North Dakota Registrar, Box 1038, Grand Forks; (701) 696-2224.

TENNIS: Recreational TEAMTENNIS Central-West Region, National Program Coordinator, 2105 Grant Ave., #4, Redondo Beach, CA; (800) 992-9042. • **Northwestern USTA,** 5525 Cedar Lake Rd., St. Louis Park, MN; (612) 546-0709.

Tip Offs: Where to Trade Cards

Sports trading cards have turned into the collectible of the 90s and a billion dollar business. All of the major sports have several competing sets of cards aimed at different market niches (Topps, Fleer, Upper Deck, Score, and Pro Set are brand names that have been working either to carve out, preserve or expand their pieces of the market). According to an editor at the hobby's weekly bible, *Sports Collectors Digest*, "We're seeing a lot more basketball, football and hockey cards in the last few years." And an editor at *Baseball Hobby News* states, "The quality, upscale baseball card has been extremely popular the last two years and will continue to grow in popularity."

In addition, cards are emerging for such sports as fishing (Big League Bass cards feature the country's top professional fishermen) and golf, to name just a few. There is even a braille card, for the sightless collector. The most valuable card on record (a vintage Honus Wagner) was sold at a Sotheby's auction to hockey star Wayne Gretzky and team owner Bruce McNall for $451,000.

Vendors and customers turn out for shows all over the country to buy and sell cards, autographs, uniforms and any other piece of memorabilia that can command a market. Some 30,000 attend the National Convention alone, an event which takes place in a different city each July.

Keep an eye on such specialty publications as *Sports Collectors Digest* (which, with its sport-specific, sister publications, has a circulation of over a million) and *Becketts*, for changing show information. The following are a half-dozen of the most established trading card shows in the USA.

15th Annual Cleveland Area Sports Collectors' Show
Holiday Inn
Strongsville, OH, April

St. Louis Sports Collectors' Annual Spring Convention
Holiday Inn North
St. Louis, MO, May

Madison Square Garden Baseball Card and Sports Collectors Show
Madison Square Garden
NY, NY, June

22nd Annual Plymouth Sports Collectors' Convention
Radisson Hotel
Plymouth, MI, July

12th National Sports Collectors' Convention,
Venue TBA for '92, July

East Coast National
Westchester Marriott
White Plains, NY, August

Ohio

Sports heroes are honored in three halls of fame: Canton's Pro Football Hall of Fame, Toledo's Ohio Baseball Hall of Fame, and the College Football Hall of Fame just outside Cincinnati. ◆ Five major pro teams wear home whites in Cincinnati and Cleveland, with minor league baseball, basketball and hockey sprinkled around the state. ◆ Annual golf and tennis events include the PGA Memorial Golf Tournament in Columbus, the World Series of Golf in Akron, the ATP Tennis Championships, and a PGA Seniors tournament outside Cincinnati. ◆ The Brown Jug—one of harness racing's Triple Crown events—is run in the town of Delaware. ◆ Other kinds of races? Try the Cleveland Grand Prix (July), the Hot Rod Spring Nationals in Hebron, and the National Hydrofoil Championships in Dayton. ◆ For a change of pace, stop by Akron's All-American Soap Box Derby (July)

▶ SPECTATOR VENUES

Auto Racing

BURKE LAKEFRONT AIRPORT
N. Marginal Road, E of Cleveland Stadium, Cleveland **[P. 93, B-10]**; (216) 781-3500. Track is 2.37 or 2.48-mile temporary road course.
Budweiser Cleveland Grand Prix (CART PPG Indy Car World Series and SCCA Trans-Am Championship), July.

ELDORA SPEEDWAY
State Route 118, 2.5 miles north of Rossburg **[P. 90, G-1]**; (513) 338-8511. Track is 0.5-mile dirt oval.
4-Crown Nationals (USAC Silver Crown), September.

MARION COUNTY INTERNATIONAL RACEWAY
2454 Richwood-LaRue Rd., 3 mi. S of LaRue on OH 37, LaRue **[P. 90, F-3]**; (614) 499-3666. Track is 1/4-mile asphalt-concrete pad.
Sports Nationals (IHRA), July.

MID-OHIO SPORTS CAR COURSE
Steam Corners Road, Lexington **[P. 90, F-5]**; (419) 884-4000. Track is 2.24 miles for CART/2.4-mile, 15-turn road course for IMSA & SCCA.
Pioneer 200 (CART PPG Indy Car World Series), Sept.
Mid-Ohio Trans-Am (SCCA), Sept.
Nissan Grand Prix of Ohio (IMSA Camel GT), June.

NATIONAL TRAIL RACEWAY
Interstate 70 at Kirkersville exit, Kirkersville **[P. 91, H-5]**; (614) 587-1005. Track is quarter-mile strip (for NHRA races).
Oldsmobile Springnationals (NHRA), mid-June.

NORWALK RACEWAY PARK
5 mi. S of OH Turnpike (exit 7) on US 250, then 3 mi. E of OH 18, Norwalk **[P. 90, D-5]**; (419) 668-5555. Track is 1/4-mile asphalt-concrete pad.
World Nationals (IHRA), August.

Baseball

CLEVELAND STADIUM
Boudreau Blvd., Cleveland **[P. 93, B-10]**. Built in 1932. Capacity: 74,483
◆Nicknamed "The Mistake on the Lake."
Cleveland Indians (AL East); (216) 861-1200. Franchise began in 1901. Broadcasts by WWWE 1100 AM, WUAB Channel 43, SportsChannel Ohio. Affiliates: Colorado Springs, CO (AAA); Canton-Akron, OH (AA); Columbus, GA (A); Kinston, NC (A); Watertown, NY (A); Burlington, NC (Rookie); Winter Haven, FL (Rookie). Spring training held in Tucson, AZ.

COOPER STADIUM
1155 W. Mound St., Columbus **[P. 92, C-3]**. Capacity: 15,000
Columbus Clippers (International League, Class AAA); (614) 462-5250. Entered League in 1977. Broadcasts by WBNS 1460-AM. MLB affiliation, New York Yankees.

NED SKELDON STADIUM
2901 Key St., Maumee **[P. 90, D-3]**. Capacity: 10,025
Toledo Mud Hens (International League, Class AAA); (419) 893-9483. Entered League in 1965. Broadcasts by WMTR 96.1 FM. MLB affiliation, Detroit Tigers.

RIVERFRONT STADIUM
100 Riverfront Stadium, Cincinnati **[P. 92, H-4]**. Built in 1970. Capacity: 52,952
◆Marge Schott, colorful and controversial owner of the Reds, always sits adjacent to the home dugout and is receptive to visits. When in town, make sure you try Skyline's Cincinnati chili.
Cincinnati Reds (NL West); (513) 421-4510. Franchise began in 1869. Broadcasts by WLW 700 AM, WLWT Channel 5. Affiliates: Nashville, TN (AAA); Chattanooga, TN (AA); Cedar Rapids, IA (A); Charleston, WV (A); Billings, MT (Short A); Princeton, WV (Rookie). Spring training held in Plant City, FL.

THURMAN MUNSON MEMORIAL STADIUM
2501 Allen Ave., SE, Canton **[P. 90, B-3]**. Capacity: 5,700
Canton-Akron Indians (Eastern League, Class AA); (216) 456-5100. Entered League in 1989. MLB affiliation, Cleveland Indians.

Basketball

BEEGHLY CENTER
410 Wick, Youngstown **[P. 90, B-6]**. Capacity: 6,896.
Youngstown Pride (World Basketball League); (216) 743-8111. Entered League in 1988. Broadcasts by WKBN 570 AM.

ERVIN J. NUTTER CENTER
Wright State University, 3640 Colonel Glenn Hwy., Dayton **[P. 93, B-3]**. Capacity: 10,464.
Dayton Wings (World Basketball League); (513) 429-4000. Entered League in 1991. Broadcasts by WONE 980 AM.

FAIRGROUNDS COLISEUM AT THE OHIO EXPOSITION CENTER
632 East 11th Avenue, Columbus **[P. 92, B-3]**. Capacity: 5,750.
Columbus Horizon (Continental Basketball Association, National Conference, Eastern Division); (614) 299-2100. Entered League in 1983. Broadcasts by WCOL 1230 FM; Cable Companies of Columbus.

THE COLISEUM
2923 Streetsboro Road, Richfield **[P. 90, D-6]**. Built in 1974. Capacity: 20,273.
◆In the snowbelt. Snows all winter.
Cleveland Cavaliers (NBA Eastern Conf., Central Div.); (216) 659-9100. Franchise began in 1970. Broadcasts by WOIO Channel 19, SportsChannel Ohio.

Bowling

IMPERIAL LANES
5505 West Central, Toledo **[P. 93, G-11]**; (419) 531-5338.
PBA National Championship, March.

RIVIERA LANES
20 South Miller Road, Akron **[P. 93, F-8]**; (216) 836-7985.
Firestone Tournament of Champions (PBA), April.

YORKTOWN LANES
6218 Pearl Road, Parma Heights **[P. 93, D-9]**; (216) 886-5300.
Bud Light Open (PBA), March.

USA SNAPSHOTS®

A look at statistics that shape the sports world

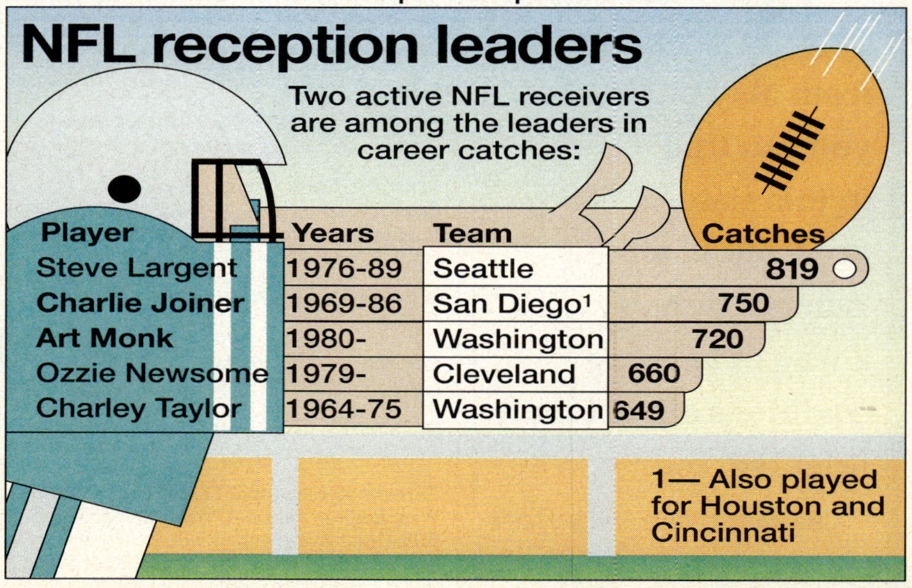

NFL reception leaders
Two active NFL receivers are among the leaders in career catches:
Player
Years
Team
Catches
Steve Largent
1976-89
Seattle
819
Charlie Joiner
1969-86
San Diego¹
750
Art Monk
1980-
Washington
720
Ozzie Newsome
1979-
Cleveland
660
Charley Taylor
1964-75
Washington
649
1— Also played for Houston and Cincinnati

Source: USA TODAY research

By Marcia Staimer, USA TODAY

STATBOX

POPULATION: 10,907,000
SQUARE MILES: 41,330
TIME ZONE: Eastern
MOTTO: With God All Things Are Possible
BIRD: Cardinal
TREE: Buckeye
CAPITAL: Columbus
AVERAGE ANNUAL RAINFALL: 37"
MEAN TEMP: 27 (Jan.); 74 (July)
MAJOR LEAGUE TEAMS: 5
NATIONAL PARK/FOREST ACREAGE: 4,146,000
STATE PARK ACREAGE: 208,069
HIGHEST ELEVATION: 1,549'
LOWEST ELEVATION: 455'
WATERWAYS: 247 square miles of inland water

College Sports

BOWLING GREEN STATE UNIVERSITY FALCONS
Bowling Green **[P. 90, D-3]**; (419) 372-2401. Doyt L. Perry Field, capacity 30,500. Anderson Arena, capacity 5,200.

CASE WESTERN RESERVE UNIVERSITY SPARTANS
10900 Euclid Avenue, Cleveland **[P. 93, B-11]**; (216) 368-2867. Edward L. Finnigan, capacity 3,000. Sam W. Emerson, capacity 3,000.

CLEVELAND STATE UNIVERSITY VIKINGS
2451 Euclid Avenue, Cleveland **[P. 93, B-10]**; (216) 687-4800. PE Center, capacity 3,000.

KENT STATE UNIVERSITY GOLDEN FLASHES
Kent **[P. 90, E-7]**; (216) 672-3120. Dix, capacity 30,520. Memorial, capacity 6,034.

MIAMI UNIVERSITY REDSKINS
Millett Hall, Oxford **[P. 91, J-1]**; (513) 529-3113. Yager, capacity 25,500. Millett Hall, capacity 9,200.

OHIO STATE UNIVERSITY BUCKEYES
410 Woody Haynes Drive, Columbus **[P. 92, B-3]**; (614) 292-7572. Ohio, capacity 87,031. St. John Arena, capacity 13,276.

OHIO UNIVERSITY BOBCATS
Athens **[P. 91, J-6]**; (614) 593-1174. Don Peden, capacity 20,000. Convocation Center, capacity 13,000.

THE UNIVERSITY OF AKRON ZIPS
Akron **[P. 93, G-9]**; (216) 972-7080. Rubber Bowl, capacity 35,482. JAR Arena, capacity 7,000.

UNIVERSITY OF CINCINNATI BEARCATS
Cincinnati **[P. 92, G-4]**; (513) 556-5601. Riverfront, capacity 59,754. Myrl Shoemaker Center, capacity 13,176.

UNIVERSITY OF DAYTON FLYERS
300 College Park, Dayton **[P. 90, B-2]**; (513) 229-4421. Welcome, capacity 11,000. UD Arena, capacity 13,458.

UNIVERSITY OF TOLEDO ROCKETS
2801 W. Bancroft Street, Toledo **[P. 93, G-12]**; (419) 537-4184. Glass Bowl, capacity 26,248. Savage Hall, capacity 9,200.

WRIGHT STATE UNIVERSITY RAIDERS
Dayton **[P. 90, B-2]**; (513) 873-2771. Erwin J. Nutter Center, capacity 10,300.

XAVIER UNIVERSITY MUSKATEERS
Victory Parkway, Cincinnati **[P. 92, G-4]**; (513) 745-3413. Corcoran Field, capacity 1,000. Schmidt, capacity 3,000.Cincinnati Gardens, capacity 10,400.

YOUNGSTOWN STATE UNIVERSITY PENGUINS
410 Wicks Avenue, Youngstown **[P. 90, B-6]**; (216) 742-3478. Stambaugh, capacity 16,000. Beeghly, capacity 7,200.

CONTINUED ON PAGE 195

Ohio

CONTINUED FROM PAGE 194

Football

CLEVELAND STADIUM
West 3rd Street, Cleveland **[P. 93, B-10]**. Built in 1931. Capacity: 80,098.
◆An old stadium, could be more comfortable. Often cold.
Cleveland Browns (AFC Central Division); (216) 696-5555. Franchise began in 1946. Broadcasts by WDOK-FM, WWWE-AM, Cleveland.

RIVERFRONT STADIUM
200 Riverfront Stadium, Cincinnati **[P. 92, H-4]**. Built in 1970. Capacity: 59,755.
Cincinnati Bengals (AFC Central Division); (513) 621-3550. Franchise began in 1968. Broadcasts by WKRC.

Hockey

CINCINNATI GARDENS
2250 Seymour Ave., Cincinnati **[P. 92, H-4]**. Capacity: 10,106.
Cincinnati Cyclones (East Coast Hockey League); (513) 531-7825. Franchise began in 1990.

HARA ARENA CONFERENCE & EXHIBITION CENTER
1001 Shiloh Springs Road, Dayton **[P. 90, A-1]**. Capacity: 5,943.
Dayton Bombers (East Coast Hockey League); (513) 277-3765. Franchise began in 1991.

TOLEDO SPORTS ARENA
1 Main Street, Toledo **[P. 93, G-12]**. Capacity: 5,234.
Toledo Storm (East Coast Hockey League); (419) 698-8998. Franchise began in 1991.

Horse Racing

BEULAH PARK
3664 Grant Avenue, Grove City **[P. 92, D-2]**; (614) 871-9600. Opened in 1980. Clubhouse capacity: 1,000. Grandstand capacity: 6,000.
Thoroughbred season from Sep. to May.

LEBANON RACEWAY
665 N. Broadway, Lebanon **[P. 91, J-2]**; (513) 932-4936. Opened in 1948. Grandstand capacity: 3,000.
Harness season from Sep. to May.

NORTHFIELD PARK HARNESS
10705 Northfield Road, Northfield **[P. 93, E-12]**; (216) 467-4101. Opened in 1957. Clubhouse capacity: 1,500. Grandstand capacity: 4,300.
Harness season from Jan. to Dec.

RACEWAY PARK
5700 Telegraph Road, Toledo **[P. 93, F-13]**; (419) 476-7751. Opened in 1962. Clubhouse capacity: 700. Grandstand capacity: 5,000.
Harness season from Mar. to Dec.

RIVER DOWNS
6301 Kellogg Avenue, Cincinnati **[P. 91, K-1]**; (513) 232-8000. Opened in 1925. Clubhouse capacity: 2,500. Grandstand capacity: 8,500.
Thoroughbred season from Apr. to early Nov.

SCIOTO DOWNS
6000 South High Street, Columbus **[P. 92, H-4]**; (614) 491-2515. Opened in 1959. Clubhouse capacity: 2,000. Grandstand capacity: 10,000.
Harness season from May to Sep.

THISTLEDOWN
21501 Emery Road, North Randall **[P. 93, C-12]**; (216) 662-8600. Opened in 1925. Clubhouse capacity: 1,125. Grandstand capacity: 5,000.
Thoroughbred season from Mar. to Dec.

> **"We have the Bengals, the Reds . . . The Cincinnati Bearcats basketball program is making a comeback, Xavier has always had a good program. . . And Cincinnati has some of the nicest public golf courses around. Go up north a little bit, Ohio State has a good football program, and another outstanding basketball program. Cleveland has the Browns, the Indians. For somebody who really enjoys sports, Ohio just offers a lot at both ends of the state."**
>
> **Former Cincinnati Bengals football star *Isaac Curtis***

Yachting

CLEVELAND YACHT CLUB
200 Yacht Club Dr., Rocky River **[P. 93, C-8]**; (216) 333-1155.
Mallory Cup (U.S. Men's Sailing Championship/USYRU), Sept.

MENTOR HARBOR YACHTING CLUB
5330 Coronado Dr., Mentor **[P. 90, C-7]**; (216) 257-7214.
Sears, Bemis, Smythe (USYRU/Rolex Jr. Sailing Championships), August, 1991.

Museums & Halls of Fame

NATIONAL FOOTBALL FOUNDATION'S COLLEGE FOOTBALL HALL OF FAME
5440 Kings Island Dr., Kings Island **[P. 91, J-2]**; (513) 398-5410.

PRO FOOTBALL HALL OF FAME
2121 George Halas Dr., N.W., Canton **[P. 90, B-3]**; (216) 456-8207.

TRAPSHOOTING HALL OF FAME
601 W. National Rd, Vandalia **[P. 91, H-2]**; (513) 898-1945.

PGA/LPGA

FIRESTONE COUNTRY CLUB
452 E. Warner Rd., Akron **[P. 90, E-6]**; (216) 644-8441.
NEC World Series of Golf (PGA), Aug.
Number of holes: 72.

HIGHLAND MEADOWS GOLF CLUB
7455 Erie St., Sylvania **[P. 90, C-3]**; (419) 882-4040.
Jamie Farr Toledo Classic (LPGA), July.
Number of holes: 54.

MUIRFIELD VILLAGE GOLF CLUB
5750 Memorial Dr., Dublin **[P. 90, G-4]**; (614) 889-6700.
Memorial Tournament (PGA), May. Number of holes: 72.

SQUAW CREEK COUNTRY CLUB
761 Youngstown-Kingsville Road, Vienna **[P. 90, D-8]**; (216) 539-5008.
Phar-Mor in Youngstown (LPGA), August.
Number of holes: 54.

THE GRIZZLEY COURSE
Jack Nicklaus Sports Center, 3565 Kingsmail Road, Kings Island **[P. 91, J-2]**; (513) 398-5200.
Kroger Senior Classic (Senior PGA), July.
Number of holes: 54.

Polo

CINCINNATI POLO CLUB
5255 Irwin Rd., Mason **[P. 91, J-2]**; (513) 398-0278.

CLEVELAND POLO CLUB
Route 87 & River Rd., Moreland Hills **[P. 93, B-10]**; (216) 338-4383.

Soccer

RICHFIELD COLISEUM
2923 Streetsboro Road, Richfield **[P. 90, D-6]**. Capacity: 17,213.
Cleveland Crunch (Major Soccer League); (216) 349-2090.

Tennis

ATP STADIUM
Jack Nicklaus Sports Center, Kings Island **[P. 91, J-2]**; (513) 398-2872. Surface is Deco Turf II.
Thriftway ATP Championship, August.

Track & Field

STREETS OF COLUMBUS
Columbus **[P. 92, C-3]**; (614) 433-0395.
Columbus Marathon (US National Championship) , November.

▶ OUTDOOR VENUES

National Parks

CUYAHOGA VALLEY NATIONAL RECREATION AREA
I-80, btwn. Cleveland & Akron **[P. 93, E-11]**. Contains 32,460 acres. **HK F S R BK W G**

WAYNE NATIONAL FOREST
Off OH 93 **[P. 91, L-5, H-5, J-7]**. Contains 200,000 acres. **C HK BT F S R BK HT**

State Parks

Bike Trails: BK
Boating: BT
Camping: C
Climbing: CL
Diving: DV
Fishing: F
Golfing: G
Hiking: HK
Hunting: HT
Riding: R
Surfing: SU
Swimming: S
Tennis: TE
Whitewater: WW
Winter Sports: W

ALUM CREEK STATE PARK
7 mi. SE of Delaware off OH 36 and 37, 1 mi. W of jct. I-71 **[P. 90, G-4]**. Contains 8,600 acres.
C HK BT F S R W HT

BARKCAMP STATE PARK
1 mi. E of Belmont off OH 149 **[P. 90, G-7]**. Contains 1,232 acres.
C HK BT F S R W HT

BLUE ROCK STATE PARK
12 mi. SE of Zanesville off OH 60 and CR 45 **[P. 91, H-6]**. Contains 350 acres. **C HK BT F S R W HT**

CAESAR CREEK STATE PARK
OH 63, 6 mi. W of Jct. I-71 **[P. 91, J-2]**. Contains 10,771 acres. **C HK BT F S R W HT**

FORKED RUN STATE PARK
3 mi. SW of Reedsville off OH 124 **[P. 91, K-6]**. Contains 817 acres. **C HK BT F S W HT**

GRAND LAKE ST. MARYS STATE PARK
2 mi. W of St. Marys on OH 703 **[P. 90, F-1]**. Contains 14,000 acres. **C HK BT F S W HT**

HUESTON WOODS STATE PARK
5 mi. N of Oxford off OH 732 **[P. 91, J-1]**. Contains 3,596 acres. **C HK BT F S R W G**

INDIAN LAKE STATE PARK
2 mi. N of Lakeview on OH 235 **[P. 90, F-2]**. Contains 6,448 acres. **C HK BT F S W HT**

MAUMEE BAY STATE PARK
On Lake Erie, near Toledo, off Route 2 **[P. 90, C-3]**. Contains 1,845 acres.
C HK BT F S BK W TE

MOSQUITO CREEK STATE PARK
10 mi. N of Warren off OH 305 **[P. 90, D-8]**. Contains 11,811 acres. **C HK BT F S R W HT**

PAINT CREEK STATE PARK
17 mi. E of Hillsboro on US 50 **[P. 91, K-3]**. Contains 10,200 acres. **C HK BT F S R W HT**

PYMATUNING STATE PARK
6 mi. SE of Andover off US 85 **[P. 90, C-8]**. Contains 17,500 acres. **C HK BT F S W**

SALT FORK STATE PARK
7 mi. NE of Cambridge on US 22 **[P. 90, G-7]**. Contains 20,181 acres. **C HK BT F S R W HT**

SHAWNEE STATE PARK
8 mi. W of Portsmouth on OH 125 **[P. 91, L-4]**. Contains 1,168 acres. **C HK BT F S R W HT**

STROUDS RUN STATE PARK
8 mi. NE of Athens off US 50A on CR 20 **[P. 91, J-6]**. Contains 2,767 acres. **C HK BT F S W HT**

TAR HOLLOW STATE PARK
10 mi. S of Adelphi off OH 540 **[P. 91, J-4]**. Contains 634 acres. **C HK BT F S R HT**

WEST BRANCH STATE PARK
5 mi. E of Ravenna off OH 5 **[P. 90, E-7]**. Contains 8,002 acres. **C HK BT F S R W HT**

Skiing

ALPINE SKIING

BRANDYWINE SKI RESORT
Northfield **[P. 93, F-12]**; (216) 467-8197.
Vertical drop is 241 feet. Has ten tows and six chairs.

SNOW TRAILS SKI RESORT
Possum Run Road, Mansfield **[P. 90, F-5]**; (419) 522-7393.
Vertical drop is 300 feet. Has six chairs.

NORDIC SKIING

CROSS COUNTRY SKI CENTER
Dayton Community Golf Course, Kettering **[P. 90, C-2]**; (513) 294-0230.

NORDIC SPORTS (AT HOLDEN ARBORETUM)
9500 Sperry Road, Mentor **[P. 90, C-7]**; (216) 238-2181.

NORDIC SPORTS (AT SLEEPY HOLLOW GOLF COURSE)
Cleveland Metro Parks, Route 21, Brecksville **[P. 93, E-11]**; (216) 238-2181.

▶ ACTIVE SPORTS

AEROBICS: AFAA, 1593 Roxbury Rd., Apt. G, Columbus; (614) 488-5802.

CONTINUED ON PAGE 196

Ohio

CONTINUED FROM PAGE 195

BASEBALL: Little League Baseball Central Region HQ, 4360 N. Mitthoeffer Rd., Indianapolis, IN; (317) 897-6127. • **American Legion Baseball,** PO Box 14348, Columbus; (614) 268-7072. • **Babe Ruth Baseball,** Robert Dickson, RR 4, Box 332F, Alexandria, IN; (317) 724-4883. • **Men's Senior Baseball League - Cincinnati,** 12117 Heathertree, Cincinnati; (513) 489-8658. • **Men's Senior Baseball League - Columbus,** 2423 Dover Road, Columbus.

BILLIARDS: Royal Family Billiards, 5270 Cruickshark Rd., Cincinnati; (513) 922-2220.

BOARDSAILING: Gale Force Sports , Wickliffe; (216) 944-0905. • **North Coast Windsurfing ,** Vermillion; (216) 967-3493. • **USWA Regional Director,** N7315 Winnebago Dr., Fond du Lac, WI; (414) 922-2550.

BOWLING: American Bowling Congress, 5301 S. 76th St., Greendale, WI; (414) 421-6400.

CANOEING & KAYAKING: ACA Ohio/Penn Vice Commodore, 38277 Wilson Avenue, Willoughby; (216) 942-5376.

CYCLING: Columbus AYH Council, PO Box 14384, Columbus; (614) 447-1006. • **LAW East Central Regional Director,** 4724 Bokay Drive, Dayton; (513) 435-9366. • **Lima AYH Council,** PO Box 173, Lima; (419) 339-4751. • **N.E. Ohio AYH Council,** 6093 Stanford Rd., Peninsula; (216) 467-8711. • **Toledo Area AYH Council,** 6206 Pembridge Drive, Toledo; (419) 841-4510. • **Tri-state AYH Council,** PO Box 141015, Cincinnati; (513) 488-3755. • **USCF Ohio/West Virginia Representative,** 25 Parkwood Boulevard, Mansfield; (419) 526-3787.

FITNESS: Governor's Council on Physical Fitness and Sports, The Davis Building, Suite 320, 151 N. Michigan Street, Toledo; (419) 255-1220.

FOOTBALL: Pop Warner Football, 1315 Walnut Street, Suite 1632, Philadelphia, PA; (215) 735-1450. • **U.S. Flag Football League,** 5834 Pine Tree Drive, Sanibel, FL; (813) 472-0544.

GOLF: Columbus District Golf Association, 437 Pamlico, Columbus; (614) 274-5441. • **Greater Cincinnati Golf Association,** PO Box 317825, Cincinnati; (513) 522-5780. • **Northern Ohio Golf Association,** 17800 Chillicothe Rd., Suite 210, Chagrin Falls; (216) 543-6320. • **Ohio Golf Association,** 6175 Shamrock Ct., Suite N, Dublin; (614) 792-3101. • **PGA Northern Ohio Section,** 38121 Euclid Ave., Willoughby; (216) 951-4546. • **PGA Southern Ohio Section,** 17 South High Street, 12th Floor, Columbus; (614) 221-1900. • **Toledo District Golf Association,** PO Box 6313, Toledo; (419) 866-4771.

HIKING & CLIMBING: Buckeye Trail Association (AHS), 6502 Olde York Rd., Parma Heights; (513) 275-8972. • **Cleveland Hiking Club (AHS),** 2508 Portman Ave., Cleveland; (216) 398-5852. • **Cuyahoga Trails Council (AHS),** 1607 Delta Ave., Akron; (216) 864-6033. • **Ohio Sierra Club Chapter,** 145 N. High St., Columbus; (614) 461-0734.

HOCKEY: USA Hockey Mid-American Registrar, 647 Stacey Ln., Maumee; (419) 893-9665.

HUNTING & FISHING: Department of Natural Resources, 1840 Belcher Drive, Building G-3, Columbus; (614) 265-6300. • **Streamside Outfitters (Orvis),** 7791 Cooper Rd., Montgomery; (513) 891-0020.

LACROSSE: Lacrosse Foundation Chapter, 1615 Lafayette Dr., Columbus; (614) 228-6161.

RACQUETBALL: AARA, 374 Slate Run Rd., Powell; (614) 548-4955.

RIDING: Ohio Horsemen's Council, 8677 Oregon Rd., Canal Winchester; (614) 833-1211.

RODEO: PRCA Great Lakes Circuit, Rt. 1, Box 54, Clayton, IN; (317) 539-5039.

RUNNING: RRCA OH State Rep., 2523 Helva Ct., Toledo; (419) 241-1261.

SCUBA: Anchor Dive Center of North Olmsted, Inc., 28669 Lorain Road, North Olmsted; (216) 779-9660. • **C & J Scuba Supply,** 5825 North Dixie Drive, Dayton; (513) 890-6900. • **Miami Valley School of Diving,** 871 East Franklin, Dayton; (513) 434-3483.

SHOOTING: Elkhorn Lake Hunt Club, 4154 Klopfenstein Rd., Bucyrus; (419) 562-1471. • **Hill-N-Dale Club,** 3605 Poe Rd., Medina; (216) 725-2097. • **Pheasant View Farm, Inc.,** 11625 Beloit Snodes Rd., Beloit; (216) 584-6828.

SKATING: Ohio Skating Association, 1495 Wayne Ave., Lakewood; (216) 521-1582. • **USFSA,** 20 First Street, Colorado Springs, CO; (719) 635-5200.

SOCCER: North Ohio Soccer Ass'n, 4821 W. 228th St., Fairview Park. • **South Ohio Soccer Ass'n,** 6131 Campus Lane, Cincinnati. • **Ohio South YSA, Inc.,** 4821 W. 228th St., Fairview Park; (216) 734-5138 • **AYSO Regional Director,** 5403 W. 138th Street, Hawthorne, CA; (800) 421-5700.

SOFTBALL: ASA, 1350 Center Ln. Dr., Ashland; (419) 289-6103. • **Cincinnati ASA,** 4461 Perin Ln., Harrison; (513) 738-1850. • **Cleveland ASA,** 4302 W. 30th St., Cleveland; (216) 741-9037. • **Columbus ASA,** 943 South Warren Ave., Columbus; (614) 279-1161. • **Dayton ASA,** 2345 Grange Hall Rd., Beavercreek; (513) 426-7761.

SQUASH: Thirteenth Street Racquet Club (USSRA), Cleveland; (216) 696-1365.

SWIMMING: LMSC Lake Erie Registrar, PO Box 8005, Canton; (216) 455-4176. • **LMSC Ohio Registrar,** 24 E. Sharon Rd., Cincinnati; (513) 771-6565.

TABLE TENNIS: USTTA State Coordinator, 797 Babitt Rd. #29, Euclid; (216) 731-7337.

TENNIS: Recreational TEAMTENNIS Midwest-Southeast Region, National Program Coordinator, 445 N. Wells, Ste. #404, Chicago, IL; (800) TEAMTEN. • **Western USTA,** 2242 Olympic Street, Springfield; (513) 390-2740.

TRIATHLON: Team Toledo Tri Club, 4718 Charlesagate, Sylvania; (419) 885-2089.

VOLLEYBALL: USVBA Ohio Valley Commissioner, 315 Johnson Rd., Kent; (216) 678-4601.

Tip Offs

Olympic Organizing Bodies: Part II

CONTINUED FROM PAGE 176

U.S. Luge Association (USLA), P.O. Box 651, Lake Placid, NY 12946
518-523-2071

U.S. Modern Pentathlon Association (USMPA), P.O. Box 8178, San Antonio, TX 78208
512-246-3000

National Archery Association (NAA), 1750 East Boulder Street, Colorado Springs, CO 80909
719-578-4576

Olympic House, 1750 East Boulder Street, Colorado Springs, CO 80909
719-632-5551

U.S. Olympic Training Centers, 1776 East Boulder Street, Colorado Springs, CO 80909
719-578-4500

U.S. Orienteering Federation, P.O. Box 1444, Forest Park, GA 30051 404-363-2110

U.S. Rowing Association (US Rowing), Pan American Plaza, Suite 400, 201 South Capitol Avenue, Indianapolis, IN 46225
317-237-5656

U.S. Ski Association (USSA), U.S. Ski Team (USST), P.O. Box 100, Park City, UT 84060
801-649-9090

U.S. Soccer Federation (USSF),1750 East Boulder Street, Colorado Springs, CO 80909
719-578-4678

U. S. Sports Acrobatics Federation, 1434 Country Park Drive, Katy, TX 77450
713-952-8334/713-578-8671

U.S. Squash Racquets Association, 23 Cynwyd Road, P.O. Box 1216, Bala Cynwyd, PA 19004
215-667-4006

U.S. Swimming, Inc. (USS), 1750 East Boulder Street, Colorado Springs, CO 80909
719-578-4578

U.S. Synchronized Swimming, Inc. (USSS), Pan American Plaza, Suite 510, 201 South Capitol Avenue, Indianapolis, IN 46225
317-237-5700

U.S. Table Tennis Association (USTTA), 1750 East Boulder Street, Colorado Springs, CO 80909
719-578-4583

U.S. Taekwondo Union (USTU), 1750 East Boulder Street, Colorado Springs, CO 80909
719-578-4632

U.S. Team Handball Federation (USTHF), 1750 East Boulder Street, Colorado Springs, CO 80909
719-578-4582

U.S. Tennis Association (USTA), 1212 Avenue of the Americas, 12th Floor, New York, NY 10036
212-302-3322

U.S. Tenpin Bowling Federation, 5301 South 76th Street, Greendale, WI 53129
414-421-9008

U.S. Volleyball Association (USVBA), 1750 East Boulder Street, Colorado Springs, CO 80909
719-578-4750

United States Water Polo (USWP), 1750 East Boulder Street, Colorado Springs, CO 80909
719-578-4549

U.S. Weightlifting Federation (USWF), 1750 East Boulder Street, Colorado Springs, CO 80909 719-578-4508

USA Wrestling, 225 South Academy Boulevard, Colorado Springs, CO 80910 719-597-8333

U.S. Yacht Racing Union (USYRU), P.O. Box 209, Newport, RI 02840
401-849-520

AFFILIATED ORGANIZATIONS

American Water Ski Association, 799 Overlook Drive, Winter Haven, FL 33884 813-324-4341

Amateur Athletic Union (AAU), 3400 West 86th Street, P.O. Box 68207, Indianapolis, IN 46268
317-872-2900

American Alliance for Health, Physical Education, Recreation and Dance (AAHPERD), 1900 Association Drive, Reston, VA 22091
703-476-3461

Boys Clubs of America, 771 First Avenue, New York, NY 10017
212-351-5900

Catholic Youth Organization (CYO), 1011 First Avenue, New York, NY 10022 212-371-1000

JWB, 15 East 26th Street, New York, NY 10010
212-532-4949

National Association of Intercollegiate Athletics (NAIA), 1221 Baltimore, Kansas City, MO 64105
816-842-5050

National Collegiate Athletic Association (NCAA), P.O. Box 1906, Mission, KS 66201
913-384-3220

National Exploring Division, Boy Scouts of America, 1325 Walnut Hill Lane, P.O. Box 152079 (S210), Irving, TX 75015
214-580-2423

National Federation of State High School Associations (NFSHSA), P.O. Box 20626, Kansas City, MO 64195
816-464-5400

National Junior College Athletic Association (NJCAA), P.O. Box 7305, Colorado Springs, CO 80933
719-590-9788

National Association of Police Athletic Leagues, 200 Castlewood Drive, North Palm, Beach, FL 33408
407-844-1823

Underwater Society of America, 849 West Orange Avenue, No. 1002, South San Francisco, CA 94080
415-583-8492

U.S. Armed Forces Sports, Hoffman Building #1, Room 1416, 2461 Eisenhower Avenue, Alexandria, VA 22331
202-325-8871

YMCA of the USA, 101 North Wacker Drive, Chicago, IL 60606
312-977-0031

YWCA of the USA, 726 Broadway, New York, NY 10001
212-614-2700

Oklahoma

Parts of the state were initially staked out by settlers in the famous Oklahoma Run. Today, watching the Sooners run with a football is probably the state's biggest attraction. ◆ The Texas Rangers raise their best players on teams in Oklahoma City and Tulsa. ◆ The National Cowboy Hall of Fame in Oklahoma City attests to the popularity of rodeos; the International Finals (January) are the major draw. ◆ Motor racing is also popular throughout the state, with the Hallett Motor Racing Circuit providing the biggest events. ◆ There are over 200 man-made lakes in the state, with loads of water sports and fishing. ◆ Some of the prime hunting destinations: the Black Kettle National Grassland Ouachita National Forest, and the lakes region in northeast Oklahoma. ◆ And don't forget Oklahoma City's National Softball Hall of Fame and Stillwater's National Wrestling Hall of Fame.

▶ SPECTATOR VENUES

Baseball

ALL SPORTS STADIUM
89er Drive, State Fairgrounds, Oklahoma City **[P. 94, G-4]**. Capacity: 12,000
Oklahoma City 89ers (American Association, Class AAA); (405) 946-8989. Entered League in 1969. Broadcasts by KXY 1340-AM. MLB affiliation, Texas Rangers.

DRILLERS STADIUM
4802 E. 15th St., Tulsa **[P. 94, D-4]**. Capacity: 10,810
Tulsa Drillers (Texas League, Class AA); (918) 744-5901. Entered League in 1977. Broadcasts by KAKC 1300AM. MLB affiliation, Texas Rangers.

Basketball

EXPO SQUARE PAVILION
17th & New Haven, Tulsa **[P. 94, D-4]**. Capacity: 6,141.
Tulsa Fast Breakers (Continental Basketball Association, National Conference, Western Division); (918) 665-6111. Entered League in 1982. Broadcasts by "KAKC 1300 AM".

MYRIAD CONVENTION CENTER
1 Myriad Gardens, Oklahoma City **[P. 94, G4]**. Capacity: 13,475.
Oklahoma City Cavalry (Continental Basketball Association, National Conference, Western Div.); (405) 232-3865. Entered League in 1990. Broadcasts by KXY 96.1 FM, 1230 AM.

Bowling

BOULEVARD BOWL
3501 South Boulevard, Edmond **[P. 95, C9]**; (405) 348-3210.
Choice Hotels Summer Classic (PBA), July to Aug.

College Sports

OKLAHOMA STATE UNIVERSITY COWBOYS
Stillwater **[P. 95, B-10]**; (405) 744-5733. Lewis Field, capacity 50, 440. Gallagher Hall, capacity 6,381.

THE UNIVERSITY OF TULSA GOLDEN HURRICANE
600 S. College, Tulsa **[P. 94, D-4]**; (918) 592-6000. Skelly, capacity 40,235.

UNIVERSITY OF OKLAHOMA SOONERS
180 West Brooks, Norman **[P. 95, D-9]**; (405) 325-8200. Owen Field, capacity 75,004. Noble Center, capacity 10,854.
◆Another place where the color red is in. The "Boomer Schooner," a covered wagon, races all over the field when the Sooners score — which usually is often.

Horse Racing

BLUE RIBBON DOWNS
US 64 West, Sallisaw **[P. 95, C-13]**; (918) 775-7771. Opened in 1962. Total capacity: 3,500. Thoroughbred season from Jan. to Dec.
◆Went parimutuel in 1984.

REMINGTON PARK
1 Remington Place, Oklahoma City **[P. 94, F-4]**; (405) 424-1000. Opened in 1988. Clubhouse capacity: 1,058. Grandstand capacity: 3,318.
Thoroughbred season from Sep. to May. Quarterhorse season mid-May to mid-July.

Museums & Halls of Fame

NATIONAL SOFTBALL HALL OF FAME AND MUSEUM
2801 N.E. 50th St., Oklahoma City **[P. 94, G-4]**; (405) 424-5266.

NATIONAL WRESTLING HALL OF FAME
405 W. Hall of Fame, Stillwater **[P. 95, B-10]**; (405) 377-5243.

NATIONAL COWBOY HALL OF FAME
1700 NE 63rd Street, Oklahoma City **[P. 94, F-4]**; (405) 478-2250.

Polo

TULSA POLO CLUB
N. 36th St., Mohawk Park **[P. 94, D-4]**; (918) 341-7656.

Tennis

THE GREENS COUNTRY CLUB
13100 Green Valley Dr., Oklahoma City **[P. 94, F-3]**; (405) 751-6266. Surface is hard.
Virginia Slims of Oklahoma (WTA), February.

Rodeo

STATE FAIR ARENA
Gordon Cooper Blvd., Oklahoma City **[P. 94, G-4]**; (405) 948-6700.
State Fair Championship PRCA Rodeo, September

▶ OUTDOOR VENUES

National Parks

CHICKASAW NATIONAL RECREATION AREA
Near Sulphur **[P. 95, E-10]**. Contains 9,821 acres. C HK BT F S HT

State Parks

ARROWHEAD STATE PARK
15 mi. NE of McAlester off US 69 **[P. 95, D-12]**. Contains 2,459 acres. C HK BT F S R

BEAVERS BEND STATE PARK
11 mi. NE of Broken Bow on OK 259A **[P. 95, F-14]**. Contains 3,522 acres.
C HK BT F S R BK

CHEROKEE STATE PARK
SE of Langley on OK 20 **[P. 95, B-13]**. Contains 43 acres.
C BT F S BK

FORT COBB STATE PARK
5 mi. NW of Fort Cobb off OK 9 **[P. 95, D-8]**. Contains 1,872 acres. C BT F S BK

FOUNTAINHEAD STATE PARK
14 mi. SW of Checotah via I-40 and OK 150 **[P. 95, D-12]**. Contains 3,401 acres.
C HK BT F S R BK

HOCHATOWN STATE PARK
7 mi. N of Broken Bow on OK 259A **[P. 95, E-14]**. Contains 1,713 acres. C HK BT F S

LAKE EUFAULA (AC)
OK 69, 10 mi. N of McAlester **[P. 95, D-12]**. Contains 102,800 acres. C HK BT F S R BK

LAKE MURRAY STATE PARK
6 mi. SE of Ardmore off US 77 **[P. 95, F-10]**. Contains 12,496 acres. C HK BT F S R BK

LAKE TEXOMA STATE PARK
5 mi. E of Kingston on US 70 **[P. 95, F-11]**. Contains 1,882 acres. C HK BT F S R

LAKE WISTER STATE PARK
2 mi. S of Wister on US 270 **[P. 95, D-14]**. Contains 3,040 acres. C BT F S

PINE CREEK STATE PARK
16 mi. E of Oleta off OK 3 **[P. 95, E-13]**. Contains 2,050 acres. C BT F

QUARTZ MOUNTAIN STATE PARK
18 mi. N of Altus off OK 44A **[P. 94, D-7]**. Contains 4,284 acres. C HK BT F S

ROMAN NOSE STATE PARK
7 mi. NW of Watonga via OK 8 and 8A **[P. 95, C8]**. Contains 515 acres. C HK BT F S

SEQUOYAH WESTERN HILLS STATE PARK
6 mi. E of Wagoner on OK 51 **[P. 95, C-13]**. Contains 2,876 acres. C HK BT F S R

SEQUOYAH BAY STATE PARK
9 mi. SE of Wagoner on US 69 **[P. 95, C-13]**. Contains 303 acres. C BT F S

Bike Trails: BK
Boating: BT
Camping: C
Climbing: CL
Diving: DV
Fishing: F
Golfing: G
Hiking: HK
Hunting: HT
Riding: R
Surfing: SU
Swimming: S
Tennis: TE
Whitewater: WW
Winter Sports: W

STATBOX

POPULATION: 3,240,000
SQUARE MILES: 1,137
TIME ZONE: Central
MOTTO: Labor Omnia Vincit (Labor conquers all)
BIRD: Scissor-Tailed Fly Catcher
TREE: Redbud
CAPITAL: Oklahoma City
AVERAGE ANNUAL RAINFALL: 31"
MEAN TEMP: 60
MAJOR LEAGUE TEAMS: 0
NATIONAL PARK/FOREST ACREAGE: 249,500
STATE PARK ACREAGE: 94,150
HIGHEST ELEVATION: 4,873'
LOWEST ELEVATION: 300'
WATERWAYS: 2 large rivers; 9 smaller rivers

USA SNAPSHOTS®

A look at statistics that shape the sports world

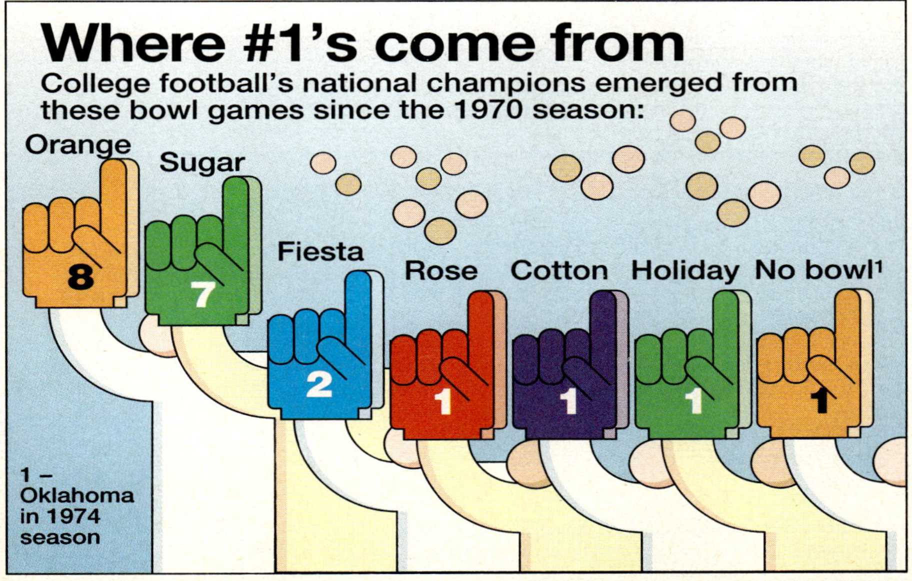

Source: USA TODAY research — By Marty Baumann, USA TODAY

▶ ACTIVE SPORTS

BASEBALL: Little League Baseball Central Region HQ, 4360 N. Mitthoeffer Rd., Indianapolis, IN; (317) 897-6127. • **Pony Baseball-Softball,** 7820 Pebbleford Dr., Ft. Worth, TX; (817) 293-1664. • **American Legion Baseball,** Box 128, Stillwater; (405)

CONTINUED ON PAGE 198

Oregon

Don't ask Oregonians about the state's possibilities for play—they like to keep it a secret. Oregon's rainy, but spectacular coastline, the fertile Willamette Valley, and arid terrain east of the Cascade Mountain range offer excellent skiing, fishing, kayaking, hiking, windsurfing, and running in an uncrowded setting. ◆ Less than one hour from Portland, the Columbia Gorge offers superior windsurfing, and Mount Hood has skiing nearly year round. ◆ Mount Bachelor, near Bend, is a haven for skiers who want the same light, dry powder you find in Utah, without the long lift lines. ◆ Spectacular scenery for hikers is to be found in Crater Lake National Park. ◆ And in Portland you can catch some Triple-A baseball. But don't even think about going to an NBA Trailblazers game unless you know somebody on the team; they have sold out every home date since 1978.

► SPECTATOR VENUES

Auto Racing

PORTLAND INTERNATIONAL RACEWAY
1940 North Victory Blvd., Portland **[P. 96, A-2]**; (503) 232-3000 or (503) 236-8006 (for CART). Track is 1.922-mile, nine-turn road course.
Budweiser/G.I. Joe's 200 (CART PPG Indy Car World Series and SCCA Trans-Am Championship), June.
G.I. Joe's Camel Gran Prix (IMSA Camel GT), July.

Baseball

CIVIC STADIUM
1844 SW Morrison Ave., Portland **[P. 96, E-2]**. Capacity: 23,000
Portland Beavers (Pacific Coast League, Class AAA); (503) 223-2837. Entered League in 1977. Broadcasts by KFXX 1520 AM. MLB affiliation, Minnesota Twins.

CIVIC STADIUM
2077 Willamette Drive, Eugene **[P. 96, B-2]**. Capacity: 7,200
Eugene Emeralds (Northwest League, Class A); (503) 342-5367. Entered League in 1974. Broadcasts by KUGN 590-AM. MLB affiliation, Kansas City Royals.

MILES FIELD
South Pacific Highway, Medford **[P. 96, H-5]**. Capacity: 2,900
Southern Oregon Athletics (Northwest League, Class A); (503) 770-5364. Entered League in 1979. Broadcasts by KMFR 880-FM. MLB affiliation, Oakland Athletics.

VINCE GENNA STADIUM
401 S.E. Roosevelt, Bend **[P. 96, E-6]**. Capacity: 2,850
Bend Bucks (Northwest League, Class A); (503) 382-8011. Entered League in 1971. Broadcasts by KGRL 940-AM. MLB affiliation, Co-op.

Basketball

MEMORIAL COLISEUM
1401 N. Wheeler Avenue, Portland **[P. 96, B-2]**. Built in 1960. Capacity: 12,884.
Portland Trail Blazers (NBA Western Conf., Pacific Div.); (503) 234-9291. Franchise began in 1970. Broadcasts by KEX 1190 AM, KOIN Channel 6.

Bowling

HOLLYWOOD BOWL
4030 N.E. Halsey St., Portland **[P. 96, B-2]**; (503) 288-9237.
Oregon Open (PBA), June.

College Sports

COLUMBIA CHRISTIAN COLLEGE CLIPPERS
9101 E. Burnside, Portland **[P. 96, B-3]**; (503) 255-7060.

OREGON STATE UNIVERSITY BEAVERS
Corvallis **[P. 96, C-4]**; (503) 737-2547. Parker, capacity 40,593. Gill Coliseum, capacity 10,400.

UNIVERSITY OF OREGON DUCKS
McArthur Court, Eugene **[P. 96, E-2]**; (503) 346-4481. Autzen, capacity 42,000. McArthur Court, capacity 10,000.

UNIVERSITY OF PORTLAND PILOTS
5000 N. Williamette Blvd., Portland **[P. 96, A-1]**; (503) 283-7117. Earle Chiles Center.

Horse Racing

GRANTS PASS DOWNS
1451 Fairgrounds, Grants Pass **[P. 96, G-4]**; (503) 476-3215. Opened in 1979. Total capacity: 3,500.
Thoroughbred season from May to July.

OREGON STATE FAIR & EXPO CENTER
2330 17th Street N.E., Salem **[P. 96, C-2]**; (503) 378-3247. Opened in 1929. Total capacity: 4,500.
Thoroughbred season from Aug. to Oct.
◆Some quarterhorse racing.

PORTLAND MEADOWS
1001 North Schmeer Road, Portland **[P. 96, A-2]**; (503) 285-9144. Opened in 1946. Clubhouse capacity: 1,000. Grandstand capacity: 4,900.
Thoroughbred season from Oct. to Apr.

Museums & Halls of Fame

THE STATE OF OREGON SPORTS HALL OF FAME AND MUSEUM
900 S.W. Fourth Ave., Portland **[P. 96, B-2]**; (503) 227-7466.

STATBOX

POPULATION: 2,791,000
SQUARE MILES: 95,910
TIME ZONE: Pacific
MOTTO: The Union
BIRD: Western Meadowlark
TREE: Douglas Fir
CAPITAL: Salem
AVERAGE ANNUAL RAINFALL: 37"
MEAN TEMP: 60
MAJOR LEAGUE TEAMS: 1
NATIONAL PARK/FOREST ACREAGE: 30,000,000
STATE PARK ACREAGE: 89,935
HIGHEST ELEVATION: 11,237'
LOWEST ELEVATION: sea level
WATERWAYS: 62,000 miles of rivers and streams; 1,600 lakes

PGA/LPGA

COLUMBIA EDGEWATER COUNTRY CLUB
2318 N.E. Marine Dr., Portland **[P. 96, A-2]**; (503) 285-3676.
Ping-Cellular One LPGA Golf Championship, September. Number of holes: 54.

Rodeo

PENDLETON ROUND-UP GROUNDS
1205 S.W. Court, Pendleton **[P. 97, B-10]**; (503) 276-2553.
Pendleton Round-Up Rodeo, September.

Track & Field

MEMORIAL COLISEUM
1401 N. Wheeler Ave., Portland **[P. 96, B-2]**; (503) 683-5635.
Oregon Indoor Track Meet (USA/Mobil Grand Prix Event), Jan.

STREETS OF PORTLAND
City Hall, S.W. 4th Ave. & S.W. Madison Ave., Portland **[P. 96, B-2]**; (503) 226-1111.
Portland Marathon, September.

► OUTDOOR VENUES

National Parks

CRATER LAKE NATIONAL PARK

CONTINUED ON PAGE 199

Oklahoma

CONTINUED FROM PAGE 197

372-7366. • **Babe Ruth Baseball,** James Wagoner, 2930 Jenny Lind, Fort Smith, AR; (501) 646-3065. • **Men's Senior Baseball League - Oklahoma City,** 2800 Northampton, Oklahoma City; (405) 755-6966.

BILLIARDS: Tulsa Billiards Palace, 1134 S. Harvard, Tulsa; (918) 582-3486.

BOARDSAILING: Grand Lake Windsurfing, Bartlesville; (918) 336-1941. • **USWA Regional Director,** 244 Spring Rd. Argyle,TX (817)455-2819

BOWLING: American Bowling Congress, 5301 S. 76th St., Greendale, WI; (414) 421-6400.

CANOEING & KAYAKING: ACA Central Vice Commodore, 3410 Ridge Rd., N. Little Rock, AR; (501) 758-4716.

CYCLING: LAW South Central Regional Director, 1618 7th S., New Orleans, LA; (504) 899-8575. • **USCF Oklahoma Representative,** 6547 E. 25th Place, Tulsa; (918) 832-9086.

FITNESS: Governor's Council on Physical Fitness & Sports, 2801 N.E. 50th St., Oklahoma City; (405) 424-6937. • **National Strength and Conditioning Ass'n State Director,** Reese Bridgeman, Assistant Football Coach, Dept. of HPER & Athletics, Southeastern OK State University; (405) 924-0121.

FOOTBALL: Pop Warner Football, 1315 Walnut Street, Suite 1632, Philadelphia, PA; (215) 735-1450.

GOLF: Oklahoma Golf Association, PO Box 449, Edmond; (405) 340-6333. • **PGA South Central Section,** 2745 E. Skelly Dr., Ste. 103, Tulsa; (918) 742-5672.

HIKING & CLIMBING: Oklahoma Sierra Club Chapter, 312 Keith, Norman; (405) 360-6445.

HOCKEY: USA Hockey Rocky Mountain Registrar, 7335 S. Garfield Ct., Littleton, CO; (303) 721-0936.

HUNTING & FISHING: Department of Wildlife Conservation, 1801 N. Lincoln Blvd., Oklahoma City; (405) 521-3851.

RACQUETBALL: AARA, 7344 Edenborough, Oklahoma City; (405) 722-3679.

RODEO: PRCA Prairie Circuit, RR 2, Box 20, Abbyville, KS; (316) 286-5319.

RUNNING: RRCA OK State Rep., Route 1, Box 595, Noble; (405) 872-9885.

SCUBA: Poseidon Adventures, 3916 South Peoria, Tulsa; (918) 749-3483. • **Scuba World, Inc.,** 1710 Midwest Blvd., Midwest City; (405) 737-4433.

SHOOTING: Southern Ranch Hunting Club, Rt. 2, Box 75, Chandler; (405) 258-0000.

SKATING: USFSA, 20 First Street, Colorado Springs, CO; (719) 635-5200.

SOCCER: Oklahoma Soccer Ass'n, 4833 S. Sheridan, Suite 409, Tulsa; (918) 627-2663. • **AYSO Regional Director,** 2971 N. Coronado St., Chandler; (602) 839-2114.

SOFTBALL: ASA, R.R. #1, Box 332-B, Tonkawa; (405) 628-5185. • **Oklahoma City ASA,** 1323 SW 28th Street, Oklahoma City; (405) 632-9865. • **Tulsa ASA,** 10303 E. 23rd Place, Tulsa; (918) 663-3773

SQUASH: Tulsa Racquetball & Aerobics (USSRA), Tulsa; (918) 749-9347.

SWIMMING: LMSC Oklahoma Registrar, 6506 S. Lewis, Suite 108, Tulsa; (918) 492-6917.

TENNIS: Recreational TEAMTENNIS Central-West Region, National Program Coordinator, 2105 Grant Ave., #4, Redondo Beach, CA; (800) 992-9042. • **Missouri Valley USTA,** 722 Walnut St., Suite #1, Kansas City, MO; (816) 556-0777.

TRIATHLON: Oklahoma Triathlon Federation, 8416 NW 90th, Oklahoma City; (405) 425-2560. • **SW Oklahoma Tri Club,** 2305 Redwood Ln., Lawton; (405) 357-2344.

VOLLEYBALL: USVBA Oklahoma Commissioner, 3471 E. 75th Place, Tulsa; (918) 492-0307.

Oregon

CONTINUED FROM PAGE 198

Bike Trails: BK
Boating: BT
Camping: C
Climbing: CL
Diving: DV
Fishing: F
Golfing: G
Hiking: HK
Hunting: HT
Riding: R
Surfing: SU
Swimming: S
Tennis: TE
Whitewater: WW
Winter Sports: W

N of Medford on OR 62 **[P. 96, H-1]**. Contains 183,224 acres. C HK F S W CL

DESCHUTES NATIONAL FOREST
Central area of state **[P. 96, D-6]**. Contains 1,602,609 acres. C HK BT F S R BK W WW

FREMONT NATIONAL FOREST
South central area of state **[P. 96, F-7; P. 97, H-8]**. Contains 1,198,308 acres. C HK BT F R BK W HT

HELLS CANYON NATIONAL RECREATION AREA
via US 95 in ID, or OR 82 and 86 in OR **[P. 97, B-13]**. Contains 652,488 acres. C HK BT F R W CL

MALHEUR NATIONAL FOREST
SW Blue Mountains in north central area of state **[P. 97, D-10]**. Contains 1,461,805 acres. C HK BT F S R W HT

MOUNT HOOD NATIONAL FOREST
Northwest Oregon **[P. 96, B-6]**. Contains 1,059,240 acres. C HK BT F S R BK W HT

OCHOCO NATIONAL FOREST
W of Malheur, central Oregon **[P. 96, D-7; P. 97, D-8, E-9]**. Contains 843,694 acres. C HK BT F S R BK W HT

OREGON DUNES NATIONAL RECREATION AREA
Near Reedsport on OR 38 **[P. 96, E-3]**. Contains 32,000 acres. C HK BT F S R HT

ROGUE RIVER NATIONAL FOREST
SW Oregon **[P. 96, G-5, H-4]**. Contains 629,088 acres. C HK BT F S R BK W HT

SISKIYOU NATIONAL FOREST
South coast, I-5 on the east or US 101 on the west **[P. 96, G-3]**. Contains 1,091,498 acres. C HK BT F S R WW

SIUSLAW NATIONAL FOREST
Tillamook to Coos Bay, west central coast **[P. 96, C-3, D-3]**. Contains 629,460 acres. C HK BT F S HT

UMATILLA NATIONAL FOREST
NE Oregon **[P. 97, A-11, C-9]**. Contains 1,402,475 acres. C HK BT F S R BK W HT

UMPQUA NATIONAL FOREST
SW Oregon **[P. 96, F-5]**. Contains 984,797 acres. C HK BT F R W HT

WALLOWA-WHITMAN NATIONAL FOREST
NE Oregon **[P. 97, B-12, C-11]**. Contains 2,253,420 acres. C HK BT F S R BK W WW

WILLAMETTE NATIONAL FOREST
West Oregon **[P. 96, D-5]**. Contains 1,675,407 acres. C HK BT F S R BK W CL

WINEMA NATIONAL FOREST
South central Oregon **[P. 96, F-6, G-5]**. Contains 1,042,810 acres. C HK BT F S R W HT

State Parks

BULLARDS BEACH STATE PARK
2 mi. N of Bandon **[P. 96, F-2]**. Contains 1,226 acres. C HK BT F S R BK

CHAMPOEG STATE PARK
7 mi. E of Newberg **[P. 96, F-2]**. Contains 568 acres. C HK BT F BK

DESCHUTES RIVER STATE RECREATION AREA
Off I-84, 17 mi. E. of The Dalles **[P. 96, B-7]**. Contains 80 acres. C HK BT F

DETROIT LAKE STATE PARK
OR 22, 2 mi. W of Detroit **[P. 96, C-5]**. Contains 104 acres. C BT F S

FORT STEVENS STATE PARK
10 mi. W of Astoria **[P. 96, A-3]**. Contains 3,763 acres. C HK BT F S BK

LOOKOUT POINT LAKE (AC)
Off SR 58, NE of Dexter **[P. 96, E-5]**. Contains 4,360 acres. C HK BT F S BK DV

LOST CREEK LAKE (AC)
OR 62, 30 mi. NE of Medford **[P. 96, G-5]**. Contains 3,430 acres. C HK BT F S BK

SILVER FALLS STATE PARK
26 mi. E of Salem **[P. 96, C-5]**. Contains 8,502 acres. C HK F S R BK

THE COVE PALISADES STATE PARK
15 mi. SW of Madras **[P. 96, D-7]**. Contains 4,119 acres. C HK BT F S

TILLAMOOK STATE FOREST
OR 6, 5 mi. E of Tillamook **[P. 96, B-4]**. Contains 250,000 acres. C HK F S BK HT

WALLOWA LAKE STATE PARK
OR 82, 6 mi. S of Joseph **[P. 97, C-12]**. Contains 166 acres. C HK BT F S R

Skiing

ALPINE SKIING

MT. ASHLAND SKI AREA
Off I-5, Ashland **[P. 96, H-5]**; (503) 482-2897. Vertical drop is 1,150 feet. Has four chairs.

MT. BACHELOR SKI AND SUMMER RESORT
335 S.W. Century Drive, Bend **[P. 96, E-6]**; (503) 382-2607.
Vertical drop is 3,100 feet. Has two tows and nine chairs.
◆Dry, light powder, like the kind found at Park City and Sun Valley, makes for excellent skiing — without the lines and hoopla found at other western resorts.

MT. HOOD MEADOWS SKI AREA
20 mi. S of Parkdale on Hwy. 35, Mt. Hood **[P. 96, B-6]**; (503) 337-2222.
Vertical drop is 2,777 feet. Has one tow and nine chairs.

NORDIC SKIING

BLUE LAKE NORDIC CENTER
Star Route, Sisters **[P. 96, D-6]**; (503) 595-6675.

DIAMOND LAKE NORDIC CENTER
Diamond Lake **[P. 96, F-5]**; (503) 793-3333.

HOODOO XC SKI BOWL
Highway 20, Sisters **[P. 96, D-6]**; (503) 342-5540.

MIRROR MOUNTAIN SKI AREA
Government Camp **[P. 96, C-6]**; (503) 272-3522.

MT. BACHELOR XC CENTER
335 South West Century Drive, Bend **[P. 96, E-7]**; (503) 382-2442.
◆The Bend area is the ski touring gem of the Pacific Northwest, and Mt. Bachelor is noted for its grooming.

WILLAMETTE PASS SKI AREA
Mile Post 62, Highway 58, Cresent Lake Jct. **[P. 96, E-6]**; (503) 484-5030.

ACTIVE SPORTS

ADVENTURE: Pacific Crest Outward Bound School, 0110 SW Bancroft Street, Portland; (800) 547-3312.

AEROBICS: AFAA, 3608 SE Milwaukee, Portland; (503) 234-1083.

BASEBALL: Little League Baseball Western Region HQ, 6707 Little League Drive, San Bernardino, CA; (714) 887-6444. • **Pony Baseball-Softball,** 908 Redbird Drive , San Jose, CA; (408) 265-3309. • **American Legion Baseball,** 816 Davis Street ., Milton-Freewater; (503) 938-7267. • **Babe Ruth Baseball,** Jim Lemp, 1911 Oxford Dr., Cheyenne, WY; (307) 638-6023. • **Men's Senior Baseball League - Oregon,** 733 Caroline Way, Monmouth; (503) 838-6082.

BILLIARDS: Classic Billiards, 3636 SE 122nd Ave., Portland; (503) 761-2622.

BOARDSAILING: Gorge Performance , Portland; (503) 246-6646. • **Gorge Windsurfing ,** The Dalles; (503) 298-8796. • **High-Tech Ski & Surf ,** Medford; (503) 779-9623. • **USWA Regional Director,** 9889 NW Hoge, Portland; (503) 286-6100.

BOWLING: American Bowling Congress, 5301 S. 76th St., Greendale, WI; (414) 421-6400.

CANOEING & KAYAKING: ACA Northwest Vice Commodore, 550 Shoup Avenue, Idaho Falls, ID; (208) 524-0282.

CYCLING: Oregon AYH Council, 3031 Southeast Hawthorne Blvd., Portland; (503) 236-3380. • **USCF Oregon Representative,** 4318 SE 8th Ct., Gresham; (503) 667-6220.

FOOTBALL: Pop Warner Football, 1315 Walnut Street, Suite 1632, Philadelphia, PA; (215) 735-1450.

GOLF: Oregon Golf Association, 520 Southwest Sixth Street , 1003 Cascade Building, Portland; (503) 222-1139. • **PGA Pacific Northwest Section,** 1201 M Street Southeast, Auburn, WA; (503) 222-1139.

HIKING & CLIMBING: Desert Trail Association (AHS), Box 589, Burns; (503) 573-2932. • **Mazamas ,** 909 Northwest 19th Avenue, Portland; (503) 227-2345. • **Oregon Sierra Club Chapter,** 3550 Willamette Street , Eugene; (503) 343-5902. • **Pacific Crest Trail Conference (AHS),** 365 West 29th Avenue, Eugene; (503) 485-5550.

HOCKEY: USA Hockey Pacific Registrar, 5703 Sun Ridge Ct., Castro Valley, CA; (415) 886-0706.

HUNTING & FISHING: Department of Fish & Wildlife, P.O. Box 59, Portland; (503) 229-5406. • **The Fly Fisher's Place (Orvis),** 230 Main St., P.O. Box 1179, Sisters; (503) 549-3474. • **Trout Unlimited,** P.O. Box 2, Prineville; (503) 447-4066.

RACQUETBALL: AARA, 8495 Southwest Mapleridge Drive , Portland; (503) 297-4947.

RIDING: Hourse Council of Oregon, P.O. Box 234, Cheshire; (503) 998-2803.

RODEO: PRCA Columbia River Circuit, Rt. 2, Box 286, Walla Walla, WA; (509) 529-0819.

SCUBA: Salem Scuba & Travel Inc., 1170 Vista SE, Salem; (503) 588-3483. • **Streed's Scuba Unlimited,** 8450 SE 82nd Avenue, Portland; (503) 777-3347.

SKATING: USFSA, 20 First Street, Colorado Springs, CO; (719) 635-5200.

SOCCER: Oregon YSA, 1750 SW Skyline Boulevard., No. 25, Portland; (503) 292-5542 • **AYSO Regional Director,** 1720 Carmel Drive, Idaho Falls, ID; (208) 526-4485.

SOFTBALL: ASA, 111 Allendale Dr., St. Helens; (503) 397-0428. • **Portland ASA,** 1120 SW 5th, Room 502, Portland; (503) 654-9406.

SQUASH: Hot Springs Squash Club (USSRA), Klamath Falls; (503) 882-9907. • **Multnomah Metro-YMCA,** Portland; (503) 294-3366.

SWIMMING: LMSC Oregon Registrar, 8120 Southwest. 68th Place, Portland; (503) 244-5217.

TABLE TENNIS: USTTA State Coordinator, 10380 SE Charlotte Dr., Portland; (503) 239-4116.

TENNIS: Recreational TEAMTENNIS Central-West Region, National Program Coordinator, 2105 Grant Ave., #4, Redondo Beach, CA; (800) 992-9042. • **Pacific Northwest USTA,** 10175 SW Barbur Blvd., 306B, Portland; (503) 245-3048.

VOLLEYBALL: USVBA Columbia Empire Commissioner, 10514 N.E. Halsey, Portland; (503) 255-4955. • **USVBA Southern California Commissioner,** HC 64, Box 640, Lakeview; (503) 947-2831.

WHITEWATER RAFTING: Dave Helfrich River Outfitter , 47555 McKenzie Hwy., Vida; (503) 896-3786. • **River Trips Unlimited, Inc.,** 4140 Dry Creek Rd., Medford; (503) 779-3798.

USA SNAPSHOTS®

A look at statistics that shape the sports world

Source: USA TODAY research — By Julie Stacey, USA TODAY

Pennsylvania

Pennsylvania is the only state that can say it hosts baseball's World Series every year—the Little League World Series, that is. It happens every August in Williamsport. ◆ If you want major-league teams, Philadelphia has four; Pittsburgh has three. And then there are the major college squads (Pitt, Penn State). ◆ Skiers can find slopes just a short drive away from virtually any point. The 31 ski areas extend from the Laurel Highlands in the southwest to the Poconos in the northeast. ◆ Anglers say some of the best trout fishing in the eastern USA is found in central Pennsylvania. The spot of spots: Letort Spring Run, near Carlisle. ◆ For hunters, Pennsylvania claims to have more deer (1.1 million) than any other state in the union. In 1989, hunters took 388,601 deer. And you can hunt virtually anywhere in the state, even in the Philadelphia area.

STATBOX

POPULATION: 11,863,395
SQUARE MILES: 45,888
TIME ZONE: Eastern
MOTTO: Virtue, Liberty and Independence
BIRD: Ruffled Grouse
TREE: Hemlock
CAPITAL: Harrisburg
AVERAGE ANNUAL RAINFALL: 39"
MEAN TEMP: 16/81 (Pitts.); 20/85 (Phila.)
MAJOR LEAGUE TEAMS: 7
NATIONAL PARK/FOREST ACREAGE: 10,040
STATE PARK ACREAGE: 3,678,411
HIGHEST ELEVATION: 3,213'
LOWEST ELEVATION: sea level
WATERWAYS: 45,000 miles of rivers and streams; 2,550 lakes

▶ SPECTATOR VENUES

Auto Racing

MAPLE GROVE RACEWAY
Route 10, between Reading & PA Turnpike 22, Maple Grove **[P. 99, G-11]**; (215) 856-7812. Track is quarter-mile strip (for NHRA races). Sunoco Keystone Nationals (NHRA), mid-Sept.

PENNSYLVANIA INTERNATIONAL RACEWAY
Highway 191, Nazareth **[P. 99, F-12]**; (215) 759-8000. Track is 1-mile oval.
Bosch Spark Plug Grand Prix (CART PPG Indy Car World Series), Oct.

POCONO INTERNATIONAL RACEWAY
Pennsylvania Route 115, 3 miles south of I-80 exit 43, Long Pond **[P. 99, E-12]**; (717) 646-2300. Track is 2.5 miles.
Champion Spark Plug 500 (NASCAR Winston Cup), June.
Miller Genuine Draft 500 (NASCAR Winston Cup), July.

Baseball

AINSWORTH FIELD
23rd & Washington Place, Erie **[P. 101, G-8]**. Capacity: 3,500
Erie Sailors (New York-Penn League, Class A); (814) 453-3900. Entered League in 1980. Broadcasts by WERG 89.9 FM. MLB affiliation, Independent.

BOWMAN FIELD
W. Fourth St., Williamsport **[P. 99, D-9]**. Capacity: 4,200
Williamsport Bills (Eastern League, Class AA); (717) 321-1210. Entered League in 1987. Broadcasts by WGBE 107.9 FM. MLB affiliation, New York Mets.

LACKAWANNA COUNTY MULTI-PURPOSE STADIUM
235 Montage Mountain Rd., Moosic **[P. 101, B-14]**. Capacity: 10,004
Scranton Red Barons (International League, Class AAA); (717) 963-6556. Entered League in 1989. Broadcasts by WICK 1400-AM. MLB affiliation, Philadelphia Phillies.

READING MUNICIPAL MEMORIAL STADIUM
Rt. 61 South/Centre Ave., Reading **[P. 101, C-13]**. Capacity: 7,000
Reading Phillies (Eastern League, Class AA); (215) 375-8469. Entered League in 1967. Broadcasts by WEEU 850 AM. MLB affiliation, Philadelphia Phillies.

RIVERSIDE STADIUM
City Island, Harrisburg **[P. 101, D-10]**. Capacity: 5,600
Harisburg Senators (Eastern League, Class AA); (717) 231-4444. Entered League in 1987. Broadcasts by WCMB 1460AM. MLB affiliation, Montreal Expos.

THREE RIVERS STADIUM
600 Stadium Circle, Pittsburgh **[P. 100, G-4]**. Built in 1970. Capacity: 58,729
Pittsburgh Pirates (NL East); (412) 323-5000. Franchise began in 1876. Broadcasts by KDKA 1020 AM, KDKA Channel 2, TCI Cable. Affiliates: Buffalo, NY (AAA); Zebulon, NC (AA); Salem, VA (A); Augusta, GA (A); Welland, Ontario (Short A); Bradenton, FL (Rookie). Spring training held in Bradenton, FL.

VETERANS STADIUM
Broad and Pattison Streets, Philadelphia **[P. 100, D-5]**. Built in 1971. Capacity: 62,382
◆Right in the heart of South Philly, Veterans Stadium is the home of the Philly Phanatic, generally regarded as the one (and perhaps only) truly entertaining mascot in the majors. Be sure to go to Pats Steaks in town for an authentic Philly cheesesteak.
Philadelphia Phillies (NL East); (215) 463-6000. Franchise began in 1883. Broadcasts by WOGL 1210 AM, WTXF-TV Channel 29. Affiliates: Scranton/Wilkes-Barre, PA (AAA); Reading, PA (AA); Clearwater, FL (A); Spartanburg, SC (A); Batavia, NY (A); Martinsville, VA (Rookie); Princeton, WV (Rookie). Spring training held in Clearwater, FL.

Basketball

LOUIS J. TULLIO CONVENTION CENTER
809 French Street, Erie **[P. 101, G-9]**. Capacity: 6,089.
Erie Wave (World Basketball League); (814) 456-9283. Entered League in 1990. Broadcasts by WLKK 1400 AM.

THE SPECTRUM
◆Pattison Place, Philadelphia **[P. 100, E-5]**. Built in 1967. Capacity: 18,168.
The 76ers originated in Syracuse, New York and moved out of state in 1963.
Philadelphia 76ers (NBA Eastern Conf., Atlantic Div.); (215) 339-7600. Franchise began in 1949. Broadcasts by WIP 610 AM, WPHL Channel 17, PRISM.

Bowling

EASTWAY LANES
4110 Buffalo Road, Erie **[P. 101, G-9]**; (814) 899-9855.
Flagship City Open (PBA).

College Sports

BUCKNELL UNIVERSITY BISON
Lewisburg **[P. 99, E-9]**; (717) 524-1232. Christy Mathewson Memorial Stadium, capacity 14,500. Davis Gym, capacity 2,400.

DREXEL UNIVERSITY DRAGONS
32nd & Chestnut Streets, Philadelphia **[P. 100, D-5]**; (215) 590-8930. Drexel Field, capacity 5,000. PE Center, capacity 2,000.

DUQUESNE UNIVERSITY DUKES
600 Forbes Avenue, Pittsburgh **[P. 100, G-5]**; (412) 434-6565. South Stadium, capacity 7,000. A.J. Palumbo Center, capacity 6,300.

LA SALLE UNIVERSITY EXPLORERS
20th and Olney Avenue, Philadelphia **[P. 100, C-5]**; (215) 951-1516. McCarthy, capacity 10,000. Hayman Hall, capacity 2,000. Philadelphia Civic Center, capacity 10,000.

LAFAYETTE COLLEGE LEOPARDS
Easton **[P. 99, F-12]**; (215) 250-5470. Fisher Field, capacity 13,500. Allan P. Kirby, capacity 3,500.

LEHEIGH UNIVERSITY ENGINEERS
Bethlehem **[P. 101, G-13]**; (215) 758-4320. Goodman, capacity 16,000. Grace Hall, capacity 3,000.

PENN STATE UNIVERSITY NITTANY LIONS
University Park **[P. 101, A-13]**; (814) 863-0351. Beaver, capacity 83,370. Recreation Hall, capacity 7,200.
◆They call this place "Happy Valley." It's not the easiest place to get to, but you'll see 90,000 on a fall Saturday afternoon. And coach Joe Paterno's team usually keeps everybody in the valley happy.

PHILADELPHIA COLLEGE OF TEXTILES & SCIENCE RAMS
School House Lake & Henry Avenue, Philadelphia **[P. 100, C-4]**; (215) 951-2720. Althouse Hall, capacity 1,100.

ROBERT MORRIS COLLEGE
Narrows Run Road, Coraopolis **[P. 98, F-2]**; (412) 262-8295., Charles L. Sewall Center, capacity 3,056.

ST. FRANCIS COLLEGE OF PA RED FLASH
Loretto **[P. 98, F-5]**; (814) 472-3018. Pine Bowl. Stokes Athletic Center, capacity 4,000.

ST. JOSEPH'S UNIVERSITY HAWKS
54th Street and City Avenue, Philadelphia **[P. 100, C-4]**; (215) 660-1707. Alumni Memorial, capacity 3,200.

SWARTHMORE COLLEGE GARNET
Swarthmore **[P. 100, E-2]**; (215) 328-8218. Isaac H. Clothier, capacity 2,000. Lamb-Miller, capacity 1,200.

TEMPLE UNIVERSITY OWLS
Philadelphia **[P. 100, D-5]**; (215) 787-7447. Veterans, capacity 66,592. McGonigle Hall, capacity 3,999.

UNIVERSITY OF PENNSYLVANIA RED & BLUE QUAKERS
Weighman Hall-North, Philadelphia **[P. 100, D-4]**; (215) 898-6121. Franklin Field, capacity 60,546. Palestra, capacity 8,700.
◆Perhaps the best old gym in the country, the true birthplace of college basketball in the East. It even has stained glass windows. Tripleheaders on a Saturday afternoon were a Philadelphia tradition.

UNIVERSITY OF PITTSBURGH PANTHERS
Pittsburgh **[P. 100, G-5]**; (412) 648-8200. Pittsburgh, capacity 56,500. Fitzgerald, capacity 6,798.

VILLANOVA UNIVERSITY WILDCATS
Villanova **[P. 100, C-2]**; (215) 645-4110. Villanova, capacity 13,500. John E. duPont Pavilion, capacity 6,500.

WEST CHESTER UNIVERSITY RAMS
West Chester **[P. 99, G-12]**; (215) 436-3555. Farrell, capacity 8,000. Hollinger, capacity 2,400.

Football

THREE RIVERS STADIUM
300 Stadium Circle, Pittsburgh **[P. 100, G-4]**. Built in 1970. Capacity: 59,000.
◆Cold, occasionally dreary weather.
Pittsburgh Steelers (AFC Central Division); (412) 323-1200. Franchise began in 1933. Broadcasts by WTAE-AM, WHTX-FM.

VETERANS STADIUM
Broad Street and Pattison Avenue,

CONTINUED ON PAGE 201

USA SNAPSHOTS®

A look at statistics that shape your finances

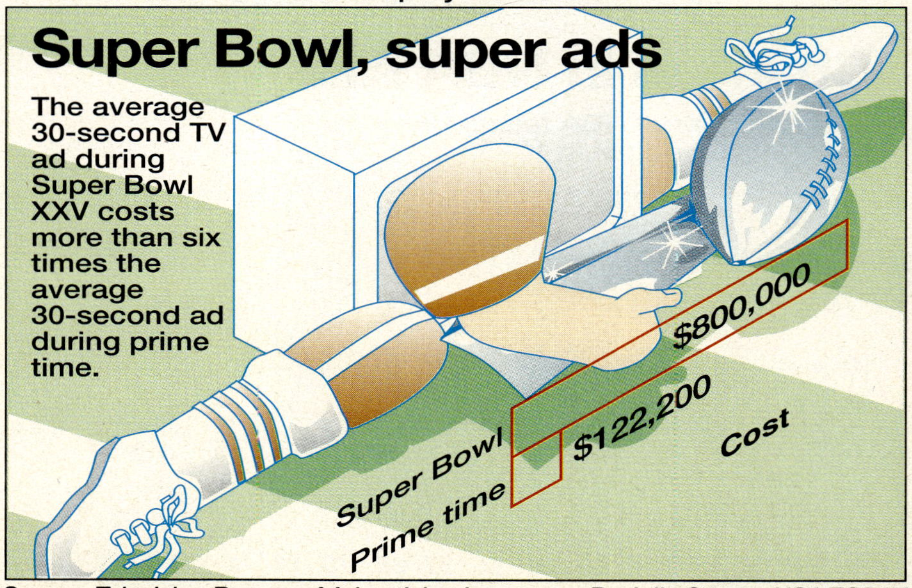
Super Bowl, super ads
The average 30-second TV ad during Super Bowl XXV costs more than six times the average 30-second ad during prime time.
$800,000
$122,200
Cost
Super Bowl
Prime time

Source: Television Bureau of Advertising Inc. By Julie Stacey, USA TODAY

Pennsylvania

CONTINUED FROM PAGE 200

Philadelphia **[P. 100, D-4]**. Built in 1971. Capacity: 65,356.

Philadelphia Eagles (NFC Eastern Division); (215) 463-2500. Franchise began in 1933. Broadcasts by WIP.

Hockey

CIVIC ARENA
300 Auditorium Place, Pittsburgh **[P. 100, G-5]**. Built in 1961. Capacity: 16,164.
◆Nicknamed "The Igloo."
Pittsburgh Penguins (NHL, Wales Conf., Patrick Div.); (412) 642-1800. Franchise began in 1967. Broadcasts by KDKA 1020 AM, KDKA TV, KBL Sports Network (Cable).

ERIE CIVIC CENTER
809 French St., Erie **[P. 101, G-9]**. Capacity: 5,680.
Erie Panthers (East Coast Hockey League); (814) 455-3936. Franchise began in 1988.

HERSHEYPARK ARENA
100 West Hersheypark Drive, Hershey **[P. 99, G-9]**. Capacity: 7,256.
◆Great area to take the family. Smell of chocolate is in the air. Includes an amusement park.
Hershey Bears (American Hockey League); (717) 534-3380. Franchise began in 1938. Broadcasts by WCMB 1460 AM.

THE SPECTRUM
Pattison Place, Philadelphia **[P. 100, D-5]**. Built in 1967. Capacity: 17,382.
Philadelphia Flyers (NHL, Wales Conference, Patrick Division); (215) 465-4500. Franchise began in 1967. Broadcasts by 610 WIP All Sports Radio, WGBS-TV (Channel 57), PRISM (Cable).

WAR MEMORIAL AUDITORIUM
326 Napoleon St., Johnstown **[P. 98, G-4]**. Capacity: 4,031.
Johnstown Chiefs (East Coast Hockey League); (814) 539-1799. Franchise began in 1988.

Museums & Halls of Fame

AMATEUR SPORTS HALL OF FAME
301 Central Avenue, Johnstown **[P. 98, G-4]**; (814) 536-7881.
◆Temporarily closed for relocation.

DELAWARE COUNTY ATHLETES HALL OF FAME
Widener University, Chester **[P. 100, E-2]**; (215) 586-8074.
◆Plaques only.

PENNSYLVANIA SPORTS HALL OF FAME
937 Willow St., Lebanon **[P. 99, G-10]**; (717) 274-3644.

PETER J. McGOVERN LITTLE LEAGUE BASEBALL MUSEUM
Route 15, South Williamsport **[P. 99, D-9]**; (717) 326-3607.
◆Batting and pitching cages with instant video replays of your performance.

PGA/LPGA

HERSHEY COUNTRY CLUB
Derry Rd., Hershey **[P. 99, G-9]**; (717) 533-2350.
Lady Keystone Open (LPGA), June. Number of holes: 54.

WHITE MANOR COUNTRY CLUB
831 Providence Road, Malvern **[P. 99, G-12]**; (215) 647-1707.
Bell Atlantic Classic (Senior PGA), May. Number of holes: 54.

> **"The eastern part of the state probably has some of the best basketball in the nation. . . the western part [is] known for great football. Western Pennsylvania has put out some of the greatest football players. Quarterbacks Joe Montana, Jim Kelly and Dan Marino, and that's just the active ones. It doesn't include Joe Namath and others."**
>
> **NFL Hall of Famer *Franco Harris***

Tennis

PHILADELPHIA CIVIC CENTER
34th & Civic Center Blvd., Philadelphia **[P. 100, D-4]**; (215) 823-5600. Surface is hard.
Virginia Slims of Philadelphia (WTA), August.

THE SPECTRUM
Broad Street & Pattison Avenue, Philadelphia; (215) 463-6300. Surface is Supreme.
Ebel U.S. Pro Indoor Tennis (ATP) Championships, February.

Horse Racing

LADBROKE AT THE MEADOWS
Race Track Road, Meadow Lands **[P. 98, G-1]**; (412) 225-9300 or 563-1224. Opened in 1963. Clubhouse capacity: 1,150. Grandstand capacity: 4,500.
Harness season from Jan. to Dec.

PENN NATIONAL RACE COURSE
I-81, exit 28, Grantville **[P. 99, F-9]**; (717) 469-2211. Opened in 1972. Clubhouse capacity: 3,570. Grandstand capacity: 6,000.
Thoroughbred season from Jan. to Dec.

PHILADELPHIA PARK
Street & Richlieu Roads, Bensalem **[P. 100, B-7]**; (215) 639-9000. Opened in 1974. Clubhouse capacity: 2,000. Grandstand capacity: 6,400.
Thoroughbred season from Jan. to Dec.

POCONO DOWNS
Route 315, Wilkes-Barre **[P. 101, A-12]**; (717) 825-6681. Opened in 1965. Clubhouse capacity: 1,000. Grandstand capacity: 5,000.
Harness season from Mar. to Nov.

▶ OUTDOOR VENUES

National Parks

ALLEGHENY NATIONAL FOREST
40 mi. S from NY-PA border, through Warren, Forest, Elk & McKean counties **[P. 98, C-4]**. Contains approx. 512,000 acres.
C HK BT F S R BK W HT

State Parks

Bike Trails: BK
Boating: BT
Camping: C
Climbing: CL
Diving: DV
Fishing: F
Golfing: G
Hiking: HK
Hunting: HT
Riding: R
Surfing: SU
Swimming: S
Tennis: TE
Whitewater: WW
Winter Sports: W

BALD EAGLE STATE PARK
Off PA 150 between Milesburg and Lock Haven **[P. 98, E-7]**. Contains 5,900 acres.
C HK BT F S W HT

BLACK MOSHANNON STATE PARK
9 mi. E of Philipsburg on PA 504 **[P. 98, E-6]**. Contains 3,394 acres. **C HK BT F S W HT**

CALEDONIA STATE PARK
Midway between Chambersburg & Gettysburg on US 30 **[P. 99, H-8]**. Contains 1,130 acres. **C HK F S BK G**

CANOE CREEK STATE PARK
7.5 mi. NE of Hollidaysburg off US 22 **[P. 98, F-6]**. Contains 959 acres. **HK BT F S R BK W HT**

CLEAR CREEK STATE PARK
5 mi. N of Sigel off PA 949 **[P. 98, D-4]**. Contains 1,209 acres.
C HK F S W HT

CODORUS STATE PARK
3 mi. SE of Hanover off PA 216 **[P. 99, H-9]**. Contains 3,324 acres. **C HK BT F S R W HT**

COOK FOREST STATE PARK
1 mi. N of Cooksburg off PA 36 **[P. 98, D-4]**. Contains 6,422 acres. **C HK F S R BK W HT**

FRANCES SLOCUM STATE PARK
4 mi. E of Dallas off PA 309 **[P. 99, D-11]**. Contains 1,034 acres. **C HK BT F W HT**

FRENCH CREEK STATE PARK
7 mi. NE of Pennsylvania Turnpike, exit 22 off PA 345 **[P. 99, G-11]**. Contains 7,344 acres.
C HK BT F S R W HT

GIFFORD PINCHOT STATE PARK
E of Rossville off PA 74 **[P. 99, G-9]**. Contains 2,337 acres. **C HK BT F S R W HT**

HILLS CREEK STATE PARK
Just N of US 6, between Wellsboro and Mansfield **[P. 99, C-8]**. Contains 407 acres.
C HK BT F S W

KETTLE CREEK STATE PARK
Off PA 4001, 7 mi. N of Westport and PA 120 **[P. 98, D-7]**. Contains 1,626 acres. **C HK BT F S W HT**

LAKE WALLENPAUPACK
15 mi. E of Hamlin off SR 590 **[P. 99, D-12]**. Contains 5,700 acres. **C HK BT F S R HT**

LAUREL HILL STATE PARK
10 mi. W of Somerset off PA 31 near Trent **[P. 98, G-4]**. Contains 3,934 acres.
C HK BT F S R W HT

MAUCH CHUNK LAKE PARK
3.5 mi. W of Jim Thorpe **[P. 99, E-11]**. Contains 2,445 acres. **C HK BT F S BK W HT**

MORAINE STATE PARK
8 mi. NW of Butler off US 422 **[P. 98, E-2]**. Contains 15,848 acres. **HK BT F S R BK W HT**

OHIOPYLE STATE PARK
14 mi. NW of Uniont, SE on US 40, then NW on PA 381 **[P. 98, H-3]**. Contains 18,719 acres.
C HK F BK W WW

PRESQUE ISLE STATE PARK
By PA 832, on Lake Erie **[P. 101, F & G - 8 & 9]**. Contains 3,202 acres. **HK BT F S BK W HT**

PYMATUNING STATE PARK
1.5 mi. N of Jamestown off US 322 **[P. 98, C-1]**. Contains 21,122 acres. **C HK BT F S W HT**

RAYSTOWN LAKE PROJECT (AC)
Off SR 26, SW of Huntington **[P. 98, G-6]**. Contains 29,300 acres. **C HK BT F S BK DV**

RICKETTS GLEN STATE PARK
PA 487 from Red Rock **[P. 99, D-10]**. Contains 13,050 acres. **C HK BT F S R W HT**

TOBYHANNA STATE PARK
2 mi. N of Tobyhanna on PA 423 **[P. 99, D-12]**. Contains 5,440 acres. **C HK BT F S BK W HT**

YELLOW CREEK STATE PARK
18 mi. NW of Ebensburg on US 422 **[P. 98, F-5]**. Contains 2,981 acres. **HK BT F S W HT**

Skiing

ALPINE SKIING

BLUE KNOB SKI AREA
Claysburg **[P. 98, G-5]**; (814) 239-5111.
Vertical drop is 1,052 feet. Has three pulls and four chairs.

BLUE MOUNTAIN SKI AREA
5 mi. E of Palmerton, Palmerton **[P. 99, E-12]**; (215) 826-7700.
Vertical drop is 931 feet. Has one tow, one bar and four chairs.

SEVEN SPRINGS MOUNTAIN RESORT
RD #1, Champion **[P. 98, G-4]**; (814) 352-7777.
Vertical drop is 750 feet. Has seven tows and eleven chairs.

NORDIC SKIING

BLACK MOSHANNON XC
Black Moshannon State Park, Phillipsburg **[P. 98, E-6]**; (814) 342-1410.

CALLENDER'S WINDY ACRES FARM
Wrighter Lake Road, Thompson **[P. 99, C-12]**; (717) 727-2982.

CHERRY RIDGE FARM
Gallagher Road, Tobyhanna **[P. 99, D-12]**; (717) 676-4904.

CRYSTAL LAKE SKI CENTER
Highland Park Road, Tivoli **[P. 99, D-9]**; (717) 584-4209.

EVERGREEN PARK XC AREA
Cherry Lane Road, Analomink **[P. 99, E-12]**; (717) 421-7721.

HANLEY'S HAPPY HILL
Route 42, Eagles Mere **[P. 99, D-9]**; (717) 525-3461.

HICKORY RIDGE XC SKI AREA
Route 191, Honesdale **[P. 99, D-12]**; (717) 253-0980.

STONE VALLEY RECREATION AREA
304 Old Maine, University Park **[P. 98, E-7]**; (814) 863-2000.

THE INN AT STARLIGHT LAKE
Starlight **[P. 99, C-10]**; (717) 798-2519.

WHITE DEER GOLF COURSE
US Route 15, Blind Road, Montgomery **[P. 99, D-9]**; (717) 547-2826.

▶ ACTIVE SPORTS

AEROBICS: AFAA, StarRoute, Box 113, Saylorsburg; (717) 992-7684.

BASEBALL: Little League Baseball Eastern Region HQ, PO Box 3485, Williamsport, PA; (717) 326-1921. • **American Legion Baseball,** PO Box 2324, Harrisburg; (717) 763-7801. • **Babe Ruth Baseball,** Raymond P. Jones, 300 Lodge St., Piscataway, NJ; (201) 469-5841. • **Men's Senior Baseball League - Lehigh Valley,** 4402 S. Fifth Street,

CONTINUED ON PAGE 202

Pennsylvania

CONTINUED FROM PAGE 201

Emmaus; (215) 967-6540. • **Men's Senior Baseball League - Philadelphia,** 6314 Arlingham Road, Flowertown; (215) 233-2868.

BILLIARDS: Willie Mosconi's Golden Cue Billiard & Amusement Center, 2027 Oregon Ave., Philadelphia; (215) 462-0194

BOARDSAILING: Hooked on Windsurfing at Nestor's , Whitehall; (215) 432-2323. • **USWA Regional Director,** 1912 MacCumber Ln., Wilmington, NC; (919) 256-3553. • **Wind & Water Boat Works ,** Butler; (412) 586-2030.

BOWLING: American Bowling Congress, 5301 S. 76th St., Greendale, WI; (414) 421-6400.

CANOEING & KAYAKING: ACA Middle States Vice Commodore, 10236 Raider Ln., Fairfax, VA; (703) 359-2594. • **ACA Ohio/Penn Vice Commodore,** 38277 Wilson Avenue, Willoughby, OH; (216) 942-5376.

CYCLING: Delaware Valley AYH Council, 38 S. Third St., Philadelphia; (215) 925-6004. • **LAW Eastern Regional Director,** 303 South Washington, Gettysburg; (717) 334-0742. • **Pittsburgh AYH Council,** 6300 Fifth Ave., Pittsburgh; (412) 362-8181. • **USCF Pennsylvania Representative,** 1605 Cardinal Drive, Bethlehem; (215) 866-4051.

FITNESS: Governor's Council on Physical Fitness & Sports, PO Box 90, Harrisburg; (717) 783-1984. • **National Strength and Conditioning Ass'n State Director,** Fieldhouse, Wrestling Office, Bucknell University, Lewisburg; (717) 524-3594.

FOOTBALL: Pop Warner Football, 1315 Walnut Street, Suite 1632, Philadelphia; (215) 735-1450. • **U.S. Flag Football League,** 5834 Pine Tree Drive, Sanibel, FL; (813) 472-0544.

GOLF: Erie District Golf Association, 4058 Zimmermann Rd., Erie; (814) 838-8524. • **Golf Association of Philadelphia (Also Pennsylvania Golf Association),** Drawer 808, Southeastern; (215) 687-2340. • **PGA Philadelphia Section,** Plymouth Green Office Campus, 801 E. Germantown Pike, Suite F-6, Norristown; (215) 277-5777. • **PGA Tri-State Section,** 221 Sherwood Dr., Monaca; (412) 774-2224. • **Western Pennsylvania Golf Association,** 1378 Freeport Rd., Suite 1-D, Pittsburgh; (412) 963-9806.

HIKING & CLIMBING: Adirondack Mountain Club , RR #3, Box 3055, Lake George, NY; (518) 668-4447. • **Allentown Hiking Club (AHS),** PO Box 1542, Allentown; (215) 257-2101. • **Blue Mountain Eagle Climb Club (AHS),** PO Box 149B2, Reading; (215) 775-3482. • **Lancaster Hiking Club (AHS),** PO Box 6037, Lancaster; (717) 397-3039. • **Penn State Outing Club/Hiking Division (AHS),** Room 4, Intramural Bldg., University Park; (814) 865-2472. • **Pennsylvania Sierra Club Chapter,** 600 N. Second St., PO Box 663, Harrisburg; (717) 232-0101. • **Shenango Outing Club (AHS),** PO Box 244, Greenville; (412) 588-6164. • **Susquehanna Appalachian Trail Club, Inc. (AHS),** PO Box 215, Harrisburg; (717) 564-1447. • **The Appalachian Mountain Club ,** 5 Joy St., Boston, MA; (617) 523-0636.

HOCKEY: USA Hockey Atlantic Registrar, 3 Pendleton Dr., Cherry Hill, NJ; (609) 424-8343. • **USA Hockey Mid-American Registrar,** 647 Stacey Ln., Maumee, OH; (419) 893-9665.

HUNTING & FISHING: Forest County Sports Center (Orvis), 311 Elm St., Tionesta; (800) 458-6093. • **Game Commission,** 2001 Elmerton Ave., Harrisburg; (717) 787-6286. • **Harts Sporting Center (Orvis),** Rt. 403 South, Tire Hill, RR 7, Box 170, Johnstown; (814) 288-5099. • **Orvis Philadelphia,** 1423 Walnut St., Philadelphia; (215) 567-6207. • **Orvis Philadelphia,** 8605 Germantown Ave., Chestnut Hill; (215) 242-9332. • **Slate Run Tackle Shop (Orvis),** Box 1, Rt. 414, Slate Run; (717) 753-8551. • **The Sporting Gentleman, Inc. (Orvis),** 306 E. Baltimore Pike, Media; (215) 565-6140. • **Trout Unlimited,** Rt. #1, Fairmount City; (814) 275-2531. • **Fish Commission ,** PO Box 1673, 3532 Walnut St., Harrisburg; (717) 657-4518

LACROSSE: Lacrosse Foundation Chapter, 2250 Hickory Rd., Box 638, Plymouth Mtg.; (215) 834-8340.

RACQUETBALL: AARA, 1802 Town Hall Rd., Erie; (814) 868-0072.

RIDING: Pennsylvania Equine Council, PO Box 339, Grantville; (717) 469-7517.

RODEO: PRCA First Frontier Circuit, 5982 Summit Bridge Rd., Townsend, DE; (302) 378-4551.

RUNNING: RRCA PA State Rep., 566 Fairfield Rd., Lewisburg; (717) 524-9713.

SCUBA: Bainbridge Sportsmen's Club, Inc., RD 1, Box 23-1, Bainbridge; (717) 426-2114. • **Mid-Atlantic Scuba Center,** 3600 Street Rd., Bensalem; (215) 628-4935. • **Sea-World Divers, Inc.,** 1820 Union Blvd., Allentown; (215) 432-6866. • **Scuba South,** 2727 Banksville Road, Pittsburgh; (412) 531-5577.

SHOOTING: Chestnut Ridge Sporting Clays, PO Box 547, Youngstown; (412) 539-2070. • **Gap View Sporting Clays,** RD #1, Box 85, Dalmation; (717) 758-1535. • **Hillside Hunting Preserve,** PO Box 128, Berlin; (814) 267-3945. • **The Busted Flush,** Rt. 3, Shreve Rd., Box 57, Titusville; (814) 827-4030.

SKATING: Middle Atlantic Skating Association, 3419 Irwin Ave., Bronx, NY; (212) 549-4290. • **USFSA,** 20 First Street, Colorado Springs, CO; (719) 635-5200. • **Western New York Skating Association,** 140 Carnella Dr., Irwin; (412) 744-0037.

SOCCER: Pennsylvania Soccer Ass'n, EPSA Office, Two Village Rd., Suite 7, Horsham; (215) 659-1393. • **Eastern Pennsylvania YSA,** 2 Village Rd, Ste. 7, Horsham; (215) 657-7727. • **AYSO Regional Director,** 4014 Oneida St., New Hartford, NY; (315) 737-5610.

SOFTBALL: ASA, 321 North W. End Ave., Lancaster; (717) 394-6552. • **ASA,** 102 Village Dr., Feusterville; (215) 355-8245.

SQUASH: City Club (USSRA), Pittsburgh; (412) 391-3300. • **University of Pennsylvania (USSRA),** Philadelphia; (215) 243-6146. • **University Club of Pittsburgh (USSRA),** Pittsburgh; (412) 621-1890.

SWIMMING: LMSC Allegheny Mountain Registrar, 3805 Myrtle St., Erie; (814) 868-6904.

TABLE TENNIS: USTTA State Coordinator, 4200 Wolf Hollow Rd., Bloomsburg; (717) 784-5934.

TENNIS: Recreational TEAMTENNIS East Region, National Program Coordinator, 246 N. Reservoir St., Lancaster; (800) 633-6122. • **Middle States USTA,** 580 Shoemaker Rd., King of Prussia; (215) 768-4040.

TRIATHLON: Endurefiends, 520 Washington Ave., #3, Carnegie; (800) 245-0660. • **Lehigh Valley Tri Club,** 941 Hamilton Street, Bath; (213) 837-7759.

VOLLEYBALL: USVBA Keystone Commissioner, 128-130 Plant Ave., Wayne; (215) 688-3620.

WHITEWATER RAFTING: Kittatinny Canoes, SR Box 360, Silver Lake Rd., Dingmans Ferry; (717) 828-2338. • **Mountain Streams and Trails Outfitters, Inc.,** PO Box 106, Rt. 381 Main St., Ohiopyle; (800) 245-4090. • **White Water Adventures, Inc.,** PO Box 31, Ohiopyle; (412) 329-8850. • **Whitewater Rafting Adventures,** Box 88, Rt. 534, Albrightsville; (717) 722-0285. • **Wilderness Voyageurs, Inc.,** PO Box 97, Ohiopyle; (412) 329-4752.

Tip Offs

National Wild, Scenic and Recreational Rivers

From the Mississippi navigated by Huck Finn to the rapids of the Grand Canyon braved by today's helmeted kayakers, rivers are a cornerstone of our national character — for recreation as well as agriculture and wildlife.

A handful of the country's free-flowing waterways have been set aside for public enjoyment and preservation by the federal government. The Wild and Scenic Rivers System includes three types of waterways.

Wild rivers are far-removed from human presence, free of dams and generally inaccessible except by trail. Scenic rivers are largely undeveloped, with limited access, sometimes by road, while recreational rivers usually have facilities, are easy to access and are often dammed.

Surprisingly, some of the country's greatest waterways, such as the Colorado and the Mississippi, are not protected and are threatened, respectively, by dam-controlled water-flows and by pollution. The conservation agency, American Rivers, (see Conservation Contacts on p.208) annually updates a list of the ten most endangered rivers in the nation. The 1991 list includes North Carolina's New River, which is the second-oldest river in the world, and Idaho's Snake — both designated National Wild and Scenic Rivers.

A selection of those Wild and Scenic Rivers administered by the National Park Service follows, arranged alphabetically.

These rivers have been specially highlighted on our mapping; grid coordinates are provided after each listing.

Alagnak Wild River [P. 8, E-2], Katmai National Park and Preserve, PO Box 7, King Salmon, AK 99613

Alatna Wild River [P. 8, B-3], Gates of the Arctic National Park and Preserve, PO Box 74680, Fairbanks, AK 99707

Aniakchak Wild River [P. 8, E-2], Katmai National Park and Preserve, PO Box 7, King Salmon, AK 99613

Bluestone National Scenic River [P. 116, F-6 through G-7], c/o New River Gorge National River, PO Box 246, Glen Jean, WV 25846

Charley Wild River [P. 8, C-4], Yukon-Charley Rivers National Preserve, PO Box 64, Eagle, AK 99738

Chilikadrotna Wild River [P. 8, C-4], Lake Clark National Park and Preserve, 701 C Street, Box 61, Anchorage, AK 99513

Delaware National Scenic River [P. 99, D-13 through E-13 and P. 76, A-5 through C-6], c/o Delaware Water Gap National Recreation Area, Bushkill, PA 18324

John Wild River [P. 8, B-3], Gates of the Arctic National Park and Preserve, PO Box 74680, Fairbanks, AK 99707

Kern Recreational River [P. 17, L-9], Sequoia National Park , Three Rivers, CA 93271

Kings Recreational River [P. 17, K-13 through 15], Kings Canyon National Park, Three Rivers, CA 93271

Kobuk Wild River [P. 8, B-3], Gates of the Arctic National Park and Preserve, PO Box 74680, Fairbanks, AK 99707

Lower Saint Croix National Scenic Riverway [P. 122 & 123, F-1 through H-3 and P. 63, K-6 through L-6], PO Box 708, St. Croix Falls, WI 54024

Merced River [P. 15, D-8 & 9], Yosemite National Park, PO Box 577, Yosemite National Park, CA 95389

Missouri National Recreational River [P. 71, A-11 through B-12 and P. 105, M-7 through M-8], c/o Midwest Region National Park Service, 1709 Jackson Street, Omaha, NE 68102

Mulchatna Wild River [P. 8, D-3], Lake Clark National Park and Preserve, 701 C Street, Box 61, Anchorage, AK 99513

Noatak Wild River [P. 8, B-2 & 3], Gates of the Arctic National Park and Preserve, PO Box 74680, Fairbanks, AK 99707

North Fork of the Koyukuk Wild River [P. 8, B-3], Gates of the Arctic National Park and Preserve, PO Box 74680, Fairbanks, AK 99707

Obed Wild and Scenic River [P. 107, B-10 & 11], PO Drawer 630, Oneida, TN 37841

Rio Grande Wild and Scenic River [P. 109, L-5], Big Bend National Park, TX 79834.

Saint Croix National Scenic Riverway [P. 122, C-3 through F-1 and P. 63, J-7 through L-6], PO Box 708, St. Croix Falls, WI 54024

Salmon Wild River [P. 8, B-3], Kobuk Valley National Park, PO Box 1029, Kotzebue, AK 99752

Tuolumne Recreational River [P. 14, G-7 and P. 15, C-8 & 9], Stanislaus National Forest, 19777 Greenley Road, Sonora, CA 95370

Upper Delaware River [P. 99, B-12 through D-14], Delaware Water Gap National Recreation Area, Bushkill, PA 18324

(For a list of the preserved rivers administered by other agencies see the Rivers II Tip-Off on P. 205.)

Rhode Island

No matter where you are in the Ocean State, you're never more than an hour's drive from a beach. More than 400 miles of shoreline include 69 saltwater beaches. Surf varies from gentle (Roger W. Wheeler Memorial) to challenging (Misquamicut). February's New England Midwinter Surfing Championships are held at Narragansett Pier. ◆ Anglers can catch the Rhode Island Tuna Tournament (Galilee) during Labor Day weekend, or the Snug Harbor Shark Tournament in July. ◆ Newport hosts the annual Volvo Newport Regatta (July) and the Newport to Bermuda Yacht Race (held on even years in June). ◆ There are fine grass courts at Newport's International Tennis Hall of Fame. ◆ You can pedal in the Flattest Century in the East, a 100-mile bike tour starting in Triverton (September). ◆ And catch the venerable "Paw Sox", Boston's Triple-A talent, in Pawtucket.

STATBOX

POPULATION: 47,154
SQUARE MILES: 1,214 (land and inland water)
TIME ZONE: Eastern
MOTTO: Hope
BIRD: Rhode Island Red
TREE: Red Maple
CAPITAL: Providence
AVERAGE ANNUAL RAINFALL: 45.32"
MEAN TEMP: 28 (Jan.); 72 (July)
MAJOR LEAGUE TEAMS: 0
NATIONAL PARK/FOREST ACREAGE: 1,200
STATE PARK ACREAGE: 55,300
HIGHEST ELEVATION: 812'
LOWEST ELAVATION: sea level
WATERWAYS: 724 miles of rivers and streams; 385 lakes

▶ SPECTATOR VENUES

Baseball

MCCOY STADIUM
1 Columbus Ave., Pawtucket **[P. 23, E-6]**. Capacity: 6,010
Pawtucket Red Sox (International League, Class AAA); (401) 724-7300. Entered League in 1973. Broadcasts by WARA 1320-AM. MLB affiliation, Boston Red Sox.

College Sports

BROWN UNIVERSITY BEARS
Hope Street, Providence **[P. 23, F-5]**; (401) 863-2211. Brown, capacity 20,000. Paul Bailey Pizzitola Memorial Sports Center, capacity 2,500.

PROVIDENCE COLLEGE FRIARS
River Avenue, Providence **[P. 23, F-5]**; (401) 865-2500. Hendricken Field, capacity 6,500. Peterson Rec. Center, capacity 3,000. Civic Center, capacity 13,106.
◆Legend has it that long ago, then-Senator John F. Kennedy happened to be in Rhode Island to make a banquet speech on the same night the Friars were playing in the NCAA tournament. When the score was tied during the game's final minutes, a banquet guest, who had been surreptitously listening to the broadcast on a transistor radio, called out the score from the rear of the room. Kennedy graciously paused while the audience gathered around the radio to finish out the match.

RHODE ISLAND COLLEGE ANCHORMEN
600 Mount Pleasant Avenue, Providence **[P. 23, F-5]**; (401) 456-8007. Walsh Gym, capacity 2,600.

ROGER WILLIAMS COLLEGE HAWKS
Old Ferry Road, Bristol **[P. 23, B-10]**; (401) 253-1040.

SALVE REGINA COLLEGE NEWPORTERS
Ochre Point Avenue, Newport **[P. 23, B-7]**; (401) 849-6920. Wetmore Field.

UNIVERSITY OF RHODE ISLAND RAMS
Kingston **[P. 25, C-9]**; (401) 792-2233. Meade, capacity 12,000. Providence Civic, capacity 11,500.

Museums & Halls of Fame

MUSEUM OF YACHTING
Fort Adams State Park, Newport **[P. 23, B-6]**; (401) 847-1018.

THE INTERNATIONAL TENNIS HALL OF FAME
at Newport Casino, 194 Bellevue Ave., Newport **[P. 23, B-7]**; (401) 846-4567.
◆A must-see in touristy Newport. In 1881, Newport Casino hosted the country's first national tennis championship, which stayed there until 1905 and today is known as the US Open. With its latticed porches, shingled roofs, indoor theater, circular courtyard playing area, and thirteen grass courts available to the public for play, the Casino (where gambling has never been allowed) is an architectural landmark. The only professional tournaments in the USA still played on grass courts are held here. Includes a museum of tennis history and an extensive tennis library.

PGA/LPGA

NEWPORT COUNTRY CLUB
Harrison Ave., Newport **[P. 23, C-5]**; (401) 846-0461.
Newport Cup (Senior PGA), July. Number of holes: 54.

Tennis

NEWPORT CASINO
194 Bellevue Avenue, Newport **[P. 23, B-7]**; (401) 849-3990. Surface is Grass.
◆See International Tennis Hall of Fame above.
Volvo Tennis/Hall of Fame Championships (ATP), July.

Yachting

IDA LEWIS YACHT CLUB
Wellington Ave., Newport **[P. 23, B-7]**; (401) 846-1969.
Rolex International Women's Keelboat Championship (USYRU), Sept.

SAIL NEWPORT SAILING CENTER
Fort Adams State Park, Newport **[P. 23, B-6]**; **(401) 846-1983.**
U.S. Independence Cup, Aug, 1991.

▶ OUTDOOR VENUES

State Parks

Bike Trails:BK
Boating: BT
Camping: C
Climbing: CL
Diving: DV
Fishing: F
Golfing: G
Hiking: HK
Hunting: HT
Riding: R
Surfing: SU
Swimming: S
Tennis: TE
Whitewater: WW
Winter Sports: W

ARCADIA MANAGEMENT AREA (STATE FOREST)
Arcadia off RI 165 **[P. 23, C-8]**. Contains 14,000 acres.
HK BT F S W

BLOCK ISLAND STATE BEACH
Block Island, on Corn Neck Road **[P. 23, E-9]**. Contains 18 acres.
C BT F S W

BURLINGAME STATE PARK
5 mi. W of Charlestown off US 1 **[P. 23, D-8]**. Contains 2,100 acres. **C HK BT F S**

COLT STATE PARK
2 mi. W of Narragansett Pier **[P. 25, F-8]**. Contains 455 acres. **HK BT F R BK**

EAST MATUNUCK STATE BEACH
S of US 1, off Succotash Rd., S. Kingston **[P. 25, D-9]**. Contains 102 acres. **F S**

FORT ADAMS STATE PARK
Newport Harbor, Newport **[P. 23, B-6]**. Contains 132 acres. **BT F S**

GODDARD STATE PARK
Off US 1 in Warwick, on Ives Rd. **[P. 25, E-9]**. Contains 472 acres. **HK BT F S R G**

LINCOLN WOODS STATE PARK
5 mi. N of Providence on RI 146 **[P. 23, E-5]**. Contains 627 acres. **HK BT F S R W**

MISQUAMICUT STATE BEACH
Atlantic Avenue in Westerly, off RI 1A **[P. 23, D-8]**. Contains 151 acres. **F S**

PULASKI MEMORIAL PARK
6 mi. W of Chepacheton **[P. 23, B-8]**. Contains 100 acres. **HK F S W**

SCARBOROUGH STATE BEACH
In Point Judith on Ocean Road **[P. 23, D-9]**. Contains 60 acres. **F S**

▶ ACTIVE SPORTS

AEROBICS: AFAA, RR 6, Box 5185, West Greenwich; (401) 397-3910.

BASEBALL: Little League Baseball Eastern Region HQ, PO Box 3485, Williamsport, PA; (717) 326-1921. • **American Legion Baseball,** PO Box 501, Providence; (401) 467-7241. • **Babe Ruth Baseball,** Ernest P. Papazoglou, 71 Tracy Ave., Lynn, MA; (617) 595-7603. • **Men's Senior Baseball League - Rhode Island,** 6 Apple Tree Ln., Barrington; (401) 245-5856.

BOARDSAILING: USWA Regional Director, Bayview Bus Park Unit 10, Gilford, NH; (603) 293-2727. • **Westerly Winds Windsurfing** , Wakefield; (401) 789-8731.

BOWLING: American Bowling Congress, 5301 S. 76th St., Greendale, WI; (414) 421-6400.

CANOEING & KAYAKING: ACA New England Vice Commodore, 785 Bow Ln., Middleton, CT

CYCLING: LAW New England Regional Director, PO Box 305, Atkinson, NH; (603) 362-4572. • **USCF Massachusetts/Rhode Island Representative,** 98 Franklin Ave., Wollaston, MA; (617) 328-8704.

FITNESS: National Strength and Conditioning Ass'n State Director, Kearney Gym, University of Rhode Island, Kingston; (401) 792-5230.

FOOTBALL: Pop Warner Football, 1315 Walnut Street, Suite 1632, Philadelphia, PA; (215) 735-1450. • **U.S. Flag Football League,** 5834 Pine Tree Drive, Sanibel, FL; (813) 472-0544.

GOLF: PGA New England Section, 1 Audubon Rd., Wakefield, MA; (617) 246-4653. • **Rhode Island Golf Association,** Charles Orms Building, 10 Orms Street, Providence; (401) 272-1350.

HIKING & CLIMBING: The Appalachian Mountain Club , 5 Joy St., Boston, MA; (617) 523-0636.

HOCKEY: USA Hockey New England Registrar, 15 Orange Street, Rumford; (401) 438-2954.

HUNTING & FISHING: Division of Fish and Wildlife, Oliver Stedman Government Center, 4808 Tower Hill Road, Wakefield; (401) 789-3094. • **Oceans & Ponds (Orvis),** 217 Ocean Ave., PO Box 136, Block Island; (401) 466-5131. • **Trout Unlimited,** 33 Jericho Path, Falmouth, MA; (508) 548-4087.

RODEO: PRCA First Frontier Circuit, 5982 Summit Bridge Rd., Townsend, DE; (302) 378-4551.

SCUBA: Alpine Ski Sports, Inc.,/Divers World, 50 Maple Street, Warwick; (401) 941-4000.

SHOOTING: Addieville East Farm, Box 248, 200 Pheasant Dr., Mapleville; (401) 568-3185.

SKATING: Northeastern Skating Association, 1477 Beacon Street, #69, Brookline, MA; (617) 731-9411. • **USFSA,** 20 First Street, Colorado Springs, CO; (719) 635-5200.

SOCCER: Rhode Island Soccer Ass'n, 18 Scott Street, Cranston; (401) 942-5929. • **Rhode Island YSA, Inc.,** 116 Eileen Dr., N. Kingstown; (401) 885-0379. • **AYSO Regional Director,** 5403 W. 138th Street, Hawthorne, CA; (800) 421-5700.

SOFTBALL: ASA, 89 Michael Dr., Cranston; (401) 942-0061.

SQUASH: Newport Squash Racquets (USSRA), Newport; (401) 846-1011.

TENNIS: Recreational TEAMTENNIS East Region, National Program Coordinator, 246 N. Reservoir St., Lancaster, PA; (800) 633-6122. • **New England USTA,** PO Box 587, Needham Heights, MA; (617) 964-2030.

South Carolina

More than 90 golf courses adorn the Grand Strand, a 60-mile stretch of beach along the state's northern coast. World-class links can also be found further south on such resort islands as Seabrook, the Isle of Palms, Kiaweh (the Ryder Cup Classic), Edisto, Fripp, and Hilton Head (the Heritage Classic). ◆ If you get a hankering for burning rubber and ice-cold beer, head to Darlington for NASCAR's TranSouth 500 (April) or the Heinz Southern 500 (September). ◆ Thoroughbred fans can catch steeplechase competition: the Carolina Cup (March) and Colonial Cup (November). ◆ Try the oft-crowded Chattanooga River (the setting of "Deliverance") for whitewater rafting, Lake Murray for sailing, and the Edisto River for scenic canoeing and kayaking. ◆ Lake Moultrie and Lake Marion provide top sports fishing.

▶ SPECTATOR VENUES

Auto Racing

CAROLINA DRAGWAY
1.5 mi. N of Jackson on SC 125 (SE of Augusta, GA), Williston **[P. 102, E-4]**; (803) 471-2285. Track is 1/4-mile asphalt-concrete pad.
Dixie Nitrous Nationals (IHRA), March.

DARLINGTON RACEWAY
Highway 151-34, 2 miles west of Darlington **[P. 103, C-9]**; (803) 393-4041. Track is 1.366 miles.
◆The first superspeedway, it was built in 1950 and is home of the Southern 500. It is a unique, egg-shaped track called "too tough to tame."
TranSouth 500 (NASCAR Winston Cup), April.
Heinz Southern 500 (NASCAR Winston Cup), September.

DARLINGTON INTERNATIONAL DRAGWAY
Hwy. 151, btwn. Darlington and Hartsville **[P. 103, C-8]**; (803) 332-0123. Track is 1/4-mile asphalt-concrete pad.
Winter Nationals (IHRA), March.
U.S. Open Nationals (IHRA), September.

Baseball

CAPITAL CITY STADIUM
301 S. Assembly Street, Columbia **[P. 104, F-6]**. Capacity: 6,000
Columbia Mets (South Atlantic League, Class A); (803) 256-4110. Entered League in 1983. Broadcasts by WVOC 560 AM. MLB affiliation, New York Mets.

COASTAL CAROLINA STADIUM
Hwy. 501, Connay **[P. 103, D-10]**. Capacity: 3,500
Myrtle Beach Hurricanes (South Atlantic League, Class A); (803) 626-1987. Entered League in 1987. Broadcasts by WGSN AM 900, WYAK 1270 AM. MLB affiliation, Toronto Blue Jays.

COLLEGE PARK STADIUM
701 Rutledge Avenue, Charleston **[P. 102, F-2]**. Capacity: 4,300
Charleston Rainbows (South Atlantic League, Class A); (803) 723-7241. Entered League in 1983. MLB affiliation, San Diego Padres.

DUNCAN PARK STADIUM
1000 Duncan Park Drive, Spartanburg **[P. 104, C-6]**. Capacity: 3,500
Spartanburg Phillies (South Atlantic League, Class A); (803) 585-6279. Entered League in 1913. MLB affiliation, Philadelphia Phillies.

GREENVILLE MUNICIPAL STADIUM
One Braves Ave., Greenville **[P. 104, B-3]**. Capacity: 7,023
Greenville Braves (Southern League, Class AA); (803) 299-3456. Entered League in 1984. Broadcasts by WPJM 800 AM. MLB affiliation, Atlanta Braves.

KNIGHTS CASTLE STADIUM
2280 Deerfield Drive, Fort Mill **[P. 102, A-6]**. Capacity: 10,917
Charlotte Knights (Southern League, Class AA); (704) 332-3746. Entered League in 1976. Broadcasts by WSOC AM 930. MLB affiliation, Chicago Cubs.

RILEY PARK
615 Church Street, Sumter **[P. 103, D-8]**. Capacity: 4,000
Sumter Flyers (South Atlantic League, Class A); (803) 775-4867. Entered League in 1991. Broadcasts by WDXY 1240 AM. MLB affiliation, Montreal Expos.

Bowling

MAIN STREET LANES
2600 Main St., Hilton Head Island **[P. 103, G-14]**; (803) 681-7750.
Carolina Classic (LPBT), April.

College Sports

BAPTIST COLLEGE BUCCANEERS
Charleston **[P. 102, D-2]**; (803) 797-4117. Baptist College Gym, capacity 2,500.

CLEMSON UNIVERSITY TIGERS
Clemson **[P. 104, D-2]**; (803) 656-2101. Memorial, capacity 79,854. Littlejohn, capacity 11,020.
◆It's a long way from anywhere, but don't worry about finding the football stadium. Just follow the orange tiger paws painted on the road as you enter the city. Once you get inside, watch the one hundred-strong Tiger team rush down the entrance way from the locker room and touch the lucky rock.

COLLEGE OF CHARLESTON COUGARS
Charleston **[P. 102 F-2]**; (803) 792-5556. F.M. Johnson Center, capacity 3,400.

FURMAN UNIVERSITY PALADINS
Poinsett Highway, Greenville **[P. 104, A-3]**; (803) 294-2150. Furman, capacity 15,900. Memorial Auditorium, capacity 6,000.

SOUTH CAROLINA STATE COLLEGE BULLDOGS
Orangeburg **[P. 102, E-6]**; (803) 536-7243. Bulldog, capacity 14,000. SHM Memorial, capacity 3,200.

THE CITADEL BULLDOGS
Citadel Station, Charleston **[P. 102, G-2]**; (803) 792-5030. Johnson Hagood, capacity 22,500. McAlister, capacity 6,000.

UNIVERSITY OF SOUTH CAROLINA FIGHTING GAMECOCKS
Columbia **[P. 104, E-6]**; (803) 777-4202. Williams-Brice, capacity 72,400. Carolina Coliseum, capacity 12,401.
◆One of the great pregame introductions in all of college football. The lights go dim, the fireworks and light show start, the music grows louder and then the black-clad Gamecocks storm the field.

UNIVERSITY OF SOUTH CAROLINA RIFLES
800 University Way, Spartanburg **[P. 104, C-6]**; (803) 599-2141. Hodge Center, capacity 1,650.

WINTHROP COLLEGE EAGLES
Rock Hill **[P. 104, B-6]**; (803) 329-2140. Winthrop Coliseum, capacity 6,100.

Museums & Halls of Fame

NATIONAL MOTORSPORTS PRESS ASSOCIATION HALL OF FAME
Routes 151 & 34, Darlington **[P. 103, C-9]**; (803) 393-2103.
◆Projected opening in summer, 1991.

USA SNAPSHOTS®

A look at statistics that shape the sports world

Senior shines

Lee Trevino Sunday surpassed the earnings of Greg Norman and became the first Senior PGA Tour player to win more than the money-winning leader of the more lucrative PGA Tour.

Annual earnings of each tour's top money winners (in millions):

Year	PGA Tour	Senior PGA Tour
1990	$1.17	$1.19
1989	$1.40	$0.73
1988	$1.15	$0.53
1987	$0.93	$0.51
1986	$0.65	$0.45
1985	$0.54	$0.39

Source: Senior PGA Tour Book 1990 — By Marty Baumann, USA TODAY

STATBOX

POPULATION: 3,500,000
SQUARE MILES: 31,000
TIME ZONE: Eastern
MOTTO: Dum Spiro Spero (Where I breathe, I hope)
BIRD: Carolina Wren
TREE: Palmetto
CAPITAL: Columbia
AVERAGE ANNUAL RAINFALL: 50"
MEAN TEMP: 71
MAJOR LEAGUE TEAMS: 0
NATIONAL PARK/FOREST ACREAGE: 630,135
STATE PARK ACREAGE: 80,000
HIGHEST ELEVATION: 3,580'
LOWEST ELEVATION: sea level
WATERWAYS: 750 square miles of inland water

PGA/LPGA

HARBOUR TOWN GOLF LINKS
11 Lighthouse Lane, Hilton Head Island **[P. 103, H-13]**; (803) 671-2446.
MCI Heritage (PGA), April. Number of holes: 72.
◆Beware of the beautiful 16th hole, overlooking the sea, especially anyone with a slice. The million dollar condos on the right are 80% glass.

Tennis

SEA PINES RACQUET CLUB
11 Lighthouse Lane, Hilton Head Island **[P. 103, H-13]**; (808) 671-2494. Surface is Clay. Family Circle Magazine Cup (WTA), April.

▶ OUTDOOR VENUES

National Parks

FRANCIS MARION NATIONAL FOREST
Coastal Plain, N of Charleston **[P. 103, F-9]**. Contains 250,000 acres. **C HK BT F R**

SUMTER NATIONAL FORESTS
Sumter **[P. 104, A-2, C-5, D-4]**. Contains 360,000 acres. **C HK BT F S R**

State Parks

Bike Trails:BK
Boating: BT
Camping: C
Climbing: CL
Diving: DV
Fishing: F
Golfing: G
Hiking: HK
Hunting: HT
Riding: R
Surfing: SU
Swimming: S
Tennis: TE
Whitewater: WW
Winter Sports: W

AIKEN STATE PARK
16 mi. E of Aiken off SC 302 **[P. 102, E-5]**. Contains 1,067 acres. **C HK BT F S**

BAKER CREEK
3 mi. W of McCormick on US 378 **[P. 102, D-3]**. Contains 1,305 acres. **C HK BT F S**

CAESARS HEAD
16 mi. N of Greenville on US 276 at NC state line **[P. 102, A-3]**. Contains 7,467 acres. **HK BK**

CHERAW STATE PARK
4 mi. SW of Cheraw on US 1 **[P. 103, B-9]**. Contains 7,361 acres. **C HK BT F S BK**

CHESTER STATE PARK
3 mi. SW of Chester on SC 72 **[P. 102, B-6]**. Contains 523 acres. **C HK BT F**

DREHER ISLAND STATE PARK
6 mi. SW of Chapin off US 76 **[P. 102, C-5]**. Contains 348 acres. **C HK BT F S**

EDISTO BEACH STATE PARK
50 mi. SE of Charleston on SC 174 **[P. 103, G-8]**. Contains 1,255 acres. **C HK F S SU**

CONTINUED ON PAGE 205

South Carolina

CONTINUED FROM PAGE 204

HICKORY KNOB STATE RESORT PARK
8 mi. W of McCormick off US 378 **[P. 102, D-3].** Contains 1,090 acres. **C HK BT F S R TE**

HUNTING ISLAND STATE PARK
16 mi. SE of Beaufort on US 21 **[P. 102, H-7].** Contains 5,000 acres. **C HK BT F S SU**

HUNTINGTON BEACH STATE PARK
3 mi. S of Murrells Inlet on US 17 **[P. 103, E-11].** Contains 2,500 acres. **C HK F S SU**

KINGS MOUNTAIN STATE PARK
14 mi. NW of York on SC 161 **[P. 102, B-6].** Contains 6,141 acres. **C HK BT F S R**

LAKE GREENWOOD STATE PARK
17 mi. E of Greenwood on SC 702 **[P. 102 C-4].** Contains 914 acres. **C HK BT F**

LEE STATE PARK
7 mi. E of Bishopville off I-20 **[P. 103, C-8].** Contains 2,839 acres. **C HK BT F S**

LITTLE PEE DEE STATE PARK
11 mi. SE of Dillon off SC 57 **[P. 103, C-10].** Contains 835 acres. **C HK BT F S**

MYRTLE BEACH STATE PARK
3 mi. S of Myrtle Beach on US 17 **[P. 103, F-13].** Contains 312 acres. **C HK F S SU**

PARIS MOUNTAIN STATE PARK
9 mi. N of Greenville off US 25 **[P. 104, A-3].** Contains 1,275 acres. **C HK BT F S**

SANTEE STATE PARK
3 mi. NW of Santee off US 301 **[P. 102, E-7].** Contains 2,495 acres. **C HK BT F S BK**

TABLE ROCK
16 mi. N of Pickens off SC 11 **[P. 102, A-3].** Contains 2,860 acres. **C HK BT F S CL**

► ACTIVE SPORTS

AEROBICS: AFAA, 1237 Llewellyn Rd., Mt. Pleasant; (803) 884-6337.

BASEBALL: Little League Baseball Southern Region HQ, P.O. Box 13366, St. Petersburg, FL; (813) 344-2661. • **Pony Baseball-Softball,** 109 Green Valley Rd., Greensboro, NC; (919) 299-3965. • **American Legion Baseball,** 1719 Brantley Dr., Charleston; (803) 795-0208. • **Babe Ruth Baseball,** William E. Whitehurst, Rt. 2, Box 56, Grifton, NC; (919) 524-5525.

BILLIARDS: A & R Player's, 9600 Kinap Hwy., Myrtle Beach; (803) 449-8660.

BOARDSAILING: Sail & Ski Connection , Myrtle Beach; (803) 626-7245. • **USWA Regional Director,** 2580 Prosperity Oaks Ct., Palm Beach Gdns, FL; (407) 881-0001. • **Windsurfing Hilton Head Island,** Hilton Head; (803) 686-6996.

BOWLING: American Bowling Congress, 5301 S. 76th St., Greendale, WI; (414) 421-6400.

CANOEING & KAYAKING: ACA Dixie Vice Commodore, 2320 Salcedo Street, Savannah, GA; (912) 352-0717.

CYCLING: LAW Southeastern Regional Director, 201 1st Ave., PO Box 2549, High Springs, FL; (904) 454-5000. • **USCF South Carolina Representative,** P.O. Box 2860, Greenville; (803) 239-1404.

FITNESS: Governor's Council on Physical Fitness, 2600 Bull Street, Columbia; (803) 737-4137.

FOOTBALL: Pop Warner Football, 1315 Walnut Street, Suite 1632, Philadelphia, PA; (215) 735-1450.

> **"I've traveled all over the world and not found a better spot. We have mountains for skiing, lakes for water sports and a great coastline. . . And they have good motorsports in South Carolina. Darlington was the first stock car superspeedway ever built. It's a great sports state. We don't take a back seat to anybody."**
>
> **Racecar driver and team owner *Cale Yarbrough***

GOLF: PGA Carolinas Section, 3852 Hwy. 9 East; (803) 249-3496. • **South Carolina Golf Association,** 145 Birdsong Trail, Chapin; (803) 781-6992.

HIKING & CLIMBING: South Carolina Sierra Club Chapter, P.O. Box 12112, Columbia; (803) 256-8487.

HOCKEY: USA Hockey Southeastern Registrar, P.O. Box 5208, Takoma Park, MD; (301) 622-0032.

HUNTING & FISHING: Penn Branch Outfitters (Orvis), Columbia Mall, Columbia; (803) 736-2900. • **Trout Unlimited,** 22 Beacon Ridge Cir., Salem; (803) 944-1230. • **Wildlife & Marine Resources Department,** PO Box 167, Rembert C. Dennis Building, Columbia; (803) 734-4007.

RACQUETBALL: AARA, 15 Wellington Ave., Greenville; (803) 242-1648

RODEO: PRCA Southeastern Circuit, 1111 S. McGee Rd., Bonifay, FL; (904) 547-2534.

RUNNING: RRCA SC State Rep., 123 Burlington Ave., Greer; (803) 244-0224.

SCUBA: Hilton Head Divers, Inc., 1-B Port Royal Plaza, Hilton Head Island; (803) 681-3483. • **South Carolina Scuba,** 1514 Highway 501, Myrtle Beach; (803) 626-3265.

SHOOTING: Broxton Bridge Plantation, P.O. Box 97, Ehrhardt; (803) 866-2218. • **Cedar Branch Shooting Club,** PO Drawer 418, Aiken; (803) 648-0067. • **Okatie Gun Club,** Rt. 1, Box 67A, Bluffton; (803) 757-5180. • **River Bend Sportsman's Resort,** P.O. Box 625, Inmans; (803) 592-1348.

SKATING: USFSA, 20 First Street, Colorado Springs, CO; (719) 635-5200.

SOCCER: South Carolina YSA, 304 Rosemary Lane, Greenville; (803) 288-3490. • **AYSO Regional Director,** 1405 Inman Dr., Huntsville, AL; (205) 881-3138.

SOFTBALL: ASA, 429 Royal Oak Dr., Spartansburg; (803) 542-8313.

SQUASH: Washington Park Squash Club (USSRA), Easley; (803) 288-1302.

SWIMMING: LMSC South Carolina Registrar, 100 Oxford Dr., Anderson; (803) 225-3191.

TABLE TENNIS: USTTA State Coordinator, 105 Cherrywood Circle, West Columbia; (803) 877-3341.

TENNIS: Recreational TEAMTENNIS East Region, National Program Coordinator, 246 N. Reservoir St., Lancaster, PA; (800) 633-6122. • **Southern USTA,** 200 Sandy Springs Place, Suite 200, Atlanta, GA; (404) 257-1297.

TRIATHLON: Charleston Tri Club, 900 Bowman Rd., Suite 300, Mount Pleasant; (803) 884-1011.

VOLLEYBALL: USVBA Palmetto Commissioner, 123 Sunset Ct., Easley; (803) 859-1849.

WHITEWATER RAFTING: Wildwater Ltd. , P.O. Box 100, Long Creek; (803) 647-5361.

Tip Offs

National Wild and Scenic Rivers: Part II

The National Wild and Scenic Rivers System includes many rivers overseen by agencies other than the National Park Service; here is a selection of them, organized by state. Since these rivers are marked on our mapping, grid coordinates have been provided.

ALABAMA
Sipsey Fork, West Fork River [P. 6, C-3]

ALASKA
Andreafsky River [P. 8, C-2]
Beaver Creek [P. 8, C-4]
Birch Creek [P. 8, C-4]
Delta River [P. 8, D-4]
Fortymile River [P. 8, C-4]
Gulkana River [P. 8, D-4]
Nowitna River [P. 8, C-3]
Selawick River [P. 8, B-2]
Sheenjek River [P. 8, B-4]
Unalakleet River [P. 8, B-4]
Wind River [P. 8, B-4]

ARIZONA
Verde River [P. 10, E-4 through G-5]

CALIFORNIA
American River, North Fork [P. 14, E-6]
Eel River [P. 14, C-2 through E-3]
Feather River, Middle Fork [P. 14, F-5 & 6]
Klamath River [P. 14, A-2 through A-4]
Lower American River [P. 14, A-2 through A-4]
Smith River [P. 14, A-2 & 3]
Trinity River [P. 14, B & C-3]

COLORADO
Cache la Poudre River [P. 21, A-8]

FLORIDA
Loxahatchee River [P. 28, D-7 & 8]

GEORGIA
Chattooga River [P. 30, C-1]

IDAHO
Clearwater River, Middle Fork [P. 34, F-2 through G-3]
Saint Joe River [P. 34, D-2 through E-3]
Salmon River (permit required depending on season) [P. 34, G-2 through 4]
Salmon River, Middle Fork (permit required at all times) [P. 35, J-3, H-3 & 4]

ILLINOIS
Middle Fork of the Vermilion River [P. 36, F-7 through G-8]

LOUISIANA
Saline Bayou [P. 48, B & C-6]

MICHIGAN
Au Sable River [P. 58 & 59, G-5 through H-9]
Pere Marquette River [P. 59, J-3 & 4]

MISSISSIPPI
Black Creek [P. 65, L-6 through M-7]

MONTANA
Flathead River [P. 68, B-4 through C-5]
Missouri River [P. 69, C-6 through C-9]

NEW HAMPSHIRE
Wildcat Creek [P. 74, F-7]

NEW MEXICO
Rio Chama [P. 78, C-4]
Rio Grande [P. 78, B-5]

NORTH CAROLINA
Horsepasture River [P. 86, C-3 & 4]
New River, South Fork [P. 86, C & D-3]

OHIO
Little Beaver Creek [P. 90, F-8]
Little Miami River [P. 91, J-2]

OREGON
Big Marsh Creek [P. 96, F-6]
Chetco River [P. 96, H-3]
Clackmas River [P. 96, H-3]
Crescent Creek [P. 96, F-6]
Crooked River [P. 96, D-7]
Crooked River, North Fork [P. 96, D-7]
Deschutes River [P. 96, C, D & E-7]
Donner Und Blitzen River [P. 97, G-10]
Eagle Creek [P. 97, C-12]
Elk River [P. 96, G-3]
Grande Ronde River [P. 97, B-11]
Illinois River [P. 96, H-3]
Imnaha River [P. 97, B-12]
John Day River [P. 97, B-8, C-10, D-9]
Joseph Creek [P. 97, B-12]
Little Deschutes River [P. 96, F-6]
Lostine River [P. 97, B-12]
McKenzie River [P. 96, D-6]
Malheur River [P. 97, E-10]
Malheur River, North Fork [P. 97, D-10]
Metolius River [P. 96, D-6]
Minam River [P. 97, B-11]
North Powder River [P. 97, C-11]
North Umpqua River [P. 96, F-4]
Owyhee River [P. 97, F-11, G-12, H-12[P.
Powder River [P. 97, C-11]
Quartzville Creek [P. 96, D-5]
Roaring River [P. 96, C-6]
Rogue River [P. 96, G-3]
Salmon River [P. 96, C-6]
Sandy River [P. 96, B-5 & 6]
Smith River, North Fork [P. 96, H-3]
Snake River [P. 97, B-13]
Sprague River, North Fork [P. 96, G-7]
Squaw Creek [P. 96, D-6]
Sycan River [P. 96, G-7]
Upper Rogue River [P. 96, F-5]
Wenaha River [P. 97, A-11]
White River [P. 96, C-6]
Willamette River, North Fork of Middle Fork [P. 96, E-5]

WASHINGTON
Klickitat River [P. 119, F & G-8]
Skagit River [P. 118 & 119, C-7 & 8]
White Salmon River [P. 118, G-7]

South Dakota

A few buffalo still roam in Custer State Park. ◆ The Black Hills in the western part of the state cover 1.6 million acres of national forest. Hike, fish, camp, ride a mountain bike, zoom around in a snowmobile, and ski downhill or cross-country. Skiing is best in the Lead-Deadwood area at Terry Peak (605-584-2165) and Deer Mountain (605-584-3230). ◆ Hearty mountaineers can climb Harney Peak, the highest mountain east of the Rockies (7,200 feet). ◆ The Governor's Cup Walleye Fishing Tournament is usually held in August in conjunction with the Hobie Sailboat Regatta in Pierre (605-224-6426). ◆ Try the Great Lakes Escape Biathlon in Yankton (May, 605-847-4256). ◆ And don't forget the Boss Cowman Rodeo in Lemmon or the Corn Palace Stampede Rodeo in Mitchell. ◆ The state amateur baseball tournament—also in Mitchell—draws more than 50,000 fans each year (August).

▶ SPECTATOR VENUES

Basketball

RUSHMORE PLAZA CIVIC CENTER
444 Mt. Rushmore Road, North, Rapid City **[P. 105, N-2]**. Capacity: 8,200.
Rapid City Thrillers (Continental Basketball Association, American Conference, Midwest Division); (605) 342-2255. Entered League in 1984. Broadcasts by KOTA 1380 AM.

SIOUX FALLS ARENA
1201 West Avenue, North Sioux Falls **[P. 104, F-3]**. Capacity: 6,500.
Sioux Falls Skyforce (Continental Basketball Association, American Conference, Midwest Division); (605) 332-0605. Entered League in 1989. Broadcasts by KSOO 1140 AM.

College Sports

SOUTH DAKOTA STATE UNIVERSITY JACKRABBITS
Brookings **[P. 105, K-7]**; (605) 688-5625. Coughlin Alumni, capacity 16,800. Frost Arena, capacity 9,000.

UNIVERSITY OF SOUTH DAKOTA COYOTES
414 E. Clark Street, Vermillion **[P. 105, M-7]**; (605) 677-5309. Dakota Dome, capacity 10,000.

Track & Field

DAKOTA DOME
University of South Dakota, Vermillion **[P. 105, M-7]**; (605) 677-5958.
NCAA II (Collegiate National Championship), March, 1991.

▶ OUTDOOR VENUES

National Parks

BADLANDS NATIONAL PARK
Badlands Loop, SR 240 **[P. 105, K-2]**. Contains 244,000 acres. **C HK R BK**

BLACK HILLS NATIONAL FOREST
Adjacent to I-90 **[P. 105, K-1]**. Contains 1,235,917 acres. **C HK BT F S R W**

CUSTER NATIONAL FOREST
NW corner of state, near Buffalo **[P. 105, H-1]**. **C HK F R**

WIND CAVE NATIONAL PARK
10 mi. N of Hot Springs on US 385 **[P. 105, L-1]**. Contains 28,292 acres. **C HK BK**

State Parks

- Bike Trails: BK
- Boating: BT
- Camping: C
- Climbing: CL
- Diving: DV
- Fishing: F
- Golfing: G
- Hiking: HK
- Hunting: HT
- Riding: R
- Surfing: SU
- Swimming: S
- Tennis: TE
- Whitewater: WW
- Winter Sports: W

ANGOSTURA RECREATION AREA
10 mi. SE of Hot Springs off US 18 **[P. 105, L-1]**. Contains 1,125 acres. **C HK BT F S BK**

BEAR BUTTE STATE PARK
6 mi. NE of Sturgis **[P. 105, K-1]**. Contains 1,931 acres. **C HK F S R**

CUSTER STATE PARK
5 mi. E of Custer on US 16A **[P. 105, L-1]**. Contains 73,000 acres. **C HK BT F S R W CL**

FARM ISLAND RECREATION AREA
4 mi. E of Pierre on SD 34 **[P. 104, G-2]**. Contains 1,225 acres. **C HK BT F S W**

LEWIS AND CLARK RECREATION AREA
5 mi. W of Yankton on SD 52 **[P. 105, M-6]**. Contains 855 acres. **C HK BT F S R BK W**

LEWIS AND CLARK (AC)
Off SR 52, S.W. of Yankton **[P. 105, M-6]**. Contains 825 acres. **C HK BT F S R BK W**

OAKWOOD LAKES STATE PARK
7 mi. N & 3 mi. W of Volga, off US 14 **[P. 105, K-7]**. Contains 255 acres. **C HK BT F S R W**

PALISADES STATE PARK
10 mi. N of Carson, off I-90 **[P. 105, L-7]**. Contains 155 acres. **C HK F S CL**

PELICAN LAKE RECREATION AREA
8 mi. SW of Watertown on US 212 **[P. 105, J-7]**. Contains 539 acres. **C HK BT F S**

RICHMOND LAKE RECREATION AREA
10 mi. NW of Aberdeen off US 281 **[P. 105, H-6]**. Contains 368 acres. **C HK BT F S**

SANDY SHORE RECREATION AREA
5 mi. W of Watertown on US 212 **[P. 105, J-7]**. Contains 8 acres. **C BT F S**

SNAKE CREEK RECREATION AREA
16 mi. W of Platte on SR 44 **[P. 105, L-5]**. Contains 735 acres. **C HK BT F S**

UNION COUNTY STATE PARK
11 mi. S of Beresford via I-29 **[P. 105, M-7]**. Contains 499 acres. **C HK R**

WEST WHITLOCK RECREATION AREA
18 mi. W of Gettysburg on US 212 **[P. 105, J-4]**. Contains 175 acres. **C HK BT F S**

Skiing

ALPINE SKIING

TERRY PEAK SKI AREA
Nevada Gulch, Lead **[P. 105, K-1]**; (605) 584-2165.
Vertical drop is 1,052 feet. Has one tow and five chairs.

NORDIC SKIING

DEER MOUNTAIN SKI AREA
Deadwood **[P. 105, K-1]**; (605) 584-3230.

PLEASANT VALLEY SKI AREA
Route 1, Gary **[P. 105, J-7]**; (605) 272-5614.

SKI CROSS COUNTRY
Spearfish **[P. 105, K-1]**; (605) 642-3851.

▶ ACTIVE SPORTS

BASEBALL: Little League Baseball Central Region HQ, 4360 N. Mitthoeffer Rd., Indianapolis, IN; (317) 897-6127. • **American Legion Baseball**, P.O. Box 67, Watertown; (605) 886-3604. • **Babe Ruth Baseball**, Norman Travis, Box 339, Burlington, CO; (719) 346-8803.

BOARDSAILING: Sea Gull's Sailboards, Brookings; (605) 693-4441.

BOWLING: American Bowling Congress, 5301 S. 76th St., Greendale, WI; (414) 421-6400.

CANOEING & KAYAKING: ACA Central Vice Comodore, 3410 Ridge Rd., N. Little Rock, AR; (501) 758-4716.

CYCLING: USCF Minnesota/Dakota-East Representative, 3135 Quebec Ave. S, St. Louis Park, MN; (612) 926-2213.

FITNESS: National Strength and Conditioning Ass'n State Director, Dakota Wesleyan University, Box 385-DWU, Mitchell; (605) 996-6511.

FOOTBALL: Pop Warner Football, 1315 Walnut Street, Suite 1632, Philadelphia, PA; (215) 735-1450.

GOLF: PGA Minnesota Section, Bunker Hills Golf Club, Hwy. 242 & Foley Blvd., Coon Rapids, MN; (612) 754-0820. • **South Dakota Golf Association**, 509 Holt Ave., Sioux Falls; (605) 338-7499.

HIKING & CLIMBING: Dacotah Sierra Club Chapter, P.O. Box 1624, Rapid City; (605) 348-1351.

HOCKEY: USA Hockey Minnkota Registrar, P.O. Box 34340, Blaine, MN; (612) 755-3753.

HUNTING & FISHING: Game, Fish & Parks Department, 445 E. Capitol, Pierre; (605) 773-3718.

RACQUETBALL: AARA, 1128 N. Dakota Ave., Sioux Falls; (605) 338-3832.

RIDING: South Dakota Horse Council, Box 272, Brookings; (605) 693-3820.

RODEO: PRCA Badlands Circuit, 400 S. Potter, Gettysburg; (605) 765-9636.

RUNNING: RRCA ND & SD State Rep., Box 267, Brookings; (605) 692-2414.

SCUBA: Scuba Supply, 1607 West St. Joe, Rapid City; (605) 342-1038.

SHOOTING: Dakota Sharpshooter, RR3, Box 167, Madison; (605) 256-3636.

SKATING: USFSA, 20 First Street, Colorado Springs, CO; (719) 635-5200.

SOCCER: South Dakota State YSA, 2308 Royal Ct., Sioux Falls; (605) 361-2308. • **AYSO Regional Director**, 5403 W. 138th Street, Hawthorne, CA; (800) 421-5700.

SOFTBALL: ASA, 1806 Meadowlark, P.O. Box 86, Sturgis; (605) 347-3109.

SWIMMING: LMSC South Dakota Registrar, P.O. Box 138, Sioux Falls; (605) 334-7859.

TENNIS: Recreational TEAMTENNIS Central-West Region, National Program Coordinator, 2105 Grant Ave., #4, Redondo Beach, CA; (800) 992-9042. • **Northwestern USTA**, 5525 Cedar Lake Rd., St. Louis Park, MN; (612) 546-0709.

STATBOX

POPULATION: 715,000
SQUARE MILES: 77,615
TIME ZONE: Central and Mountain
MOTTO: Under God the People Rule
BIRD: Chinese Ring-Necked Pheasant
TREE: Black Hills Spruce
CAPITAL: Pierre
AVERAGE ANNUAL RAINFALL: 16"
MEAN TEMP: 14 (Jan.); 73 (July)
MAJOR LEAGUE TEAMS: 0
NATIONAL PARK/FOREST ACREAGE: 2,416,053
STATE PARK ACREAGE: 90,247
HIGHEST ELEVATION: 7,242'
LOWEST ELEVATION: 960'
WATERWAYS: 9,937 miles of rivers; 799 lakes and reservoirs

USA SNAPSHOTS®

A look at statistics that shape the sports world

NFL roster review

NFL teams are allowed to have 45 active players, down from a high of 49 in the mid-'80s. But the roster limit has more than doubled since the league's early days:

Source: National Football League

By Sam Ward, USA TODAY

Tennessee

The University of Tennessee in Knoxville boasts the USA's second-largest college football stadium (91,110-seat Neyland Stadium) and the nation's largest on-campus basketball arena (24,985-seat Thompson-Boling arena). ◆ The unique gait of the Tennessee Walking Horse is celebrated at August competitions in Shelbyville and Murfreesboro. ◆ The high school girls' basketball tournament held in March at Middle Tennessee State (Murfreesboro) has been called the best in the USA. ◆ Some 50,000 fans show up at Nashville's Percy Warner Park for the Iroquois Steeplechase (May), which has the richest purse of its kind ($100,000 in 1990). ◆ And for the restless, the Ocoee River has some of the top whitewater rapids east of the Mississippi, Lookout Mountain near Chattanooga is a popular rock climbing site, and the Great Smoky Mountains are criss-crossed with hiking trails.

► SPECTATOR VENUES

Auto Racing

BRISTOL INTERNATIONAL RACEWAY
Off I-81 on US 19/11E, S of Bristol **[P. 107, D-13]**; (615) 764-1161. Track is 0.533 miles.
◆With 36 degree banking in the turns, Bristol is truly unique. It's the toughest track in NASCAR on drivers and equipment. One driver once said racing at Bristol was "like racing in a barrel."
Valleydale Meats 500 (NASCAR Winston Cup), April.
Bud 500 (NASCAR Winston Cup), August.

BRISTOL INTERNATIONAL DRAGWAY
7 mi. SW of Bristol on US 19/11E, Bristol **[P. 107, D13]**; (615) 764-1164. Track is 1/4-mile asphalt-concrete pad.
◆Directly adjacent to the Bristol International Raceway. The two tracks share a common entrance but are under separate ownership.
Spring Nationals (IHRA), May.
Fall Nationals, October.

MEMPHIS INTERNATIONAL MOTORSPORTS PARK
5500 Taylor-Forge Road, Memphis **[P. 106, F-3]**; (901) 358-7223. Track is quarter-mile strip (for NHRA races).
Goody's Mid-South Nationals (NHRA), Early May.

Baseball

BILL MEYER STADIUM
633 Jessamine St., Knoxville **[P. 107, G-13]**. Capacity: 6,412
Knoxville Blue Jays (Southern League, Class AA); (615) 525-3809. Entered League in 1971. Broadcasts by WIVK 990 AM. MLB affiliation, Toronto Blue Jays.

HERSCHEL GREER STADIUM
534 Chestnut St., Nashville **[P. 106, G-6]**. Capacity: 18,000
Nashville Sounds (American Association, Class AAA); (615) 242-4371. Entered League in 1985. Broadcasts by WWTN 99.7 FM. MLB affiliation, Cincinnati Reds.

HISTORIC ENGEL STADIUM
1131 East Third St., Chattanooga **[P. 107, G-9]**. Capacity: 7,500
Chattanooga Lookouts (Southern League, Class AA); (615) 267-2208. Entered League in 1976. Broadcasts by WDEF 1370 AM. MLB affiliation, Cincinnati Reds.

HOWARD JOHNSON FIELD
111 Legion Street, Johnson City **[P. 107, E-13]**. Capacity: 3,500
Johnson City Cardinals (Appalachian League, Rookie Class); (615) 926-7109. Entered League in 1959. Broadcasts by WJCW 910-AM. MLB affiliation, St. Louis Cardinals.

J. FRED JOHNSON STADIUM
1800 Fort Henry Drive, Kingsport **[P. 107, D-12]**. Capacity: 8,000
Kingsport Mets (Appalachian League, Rookie Class); (615) 245-1973. Entered League in 1959. Broadcasts by WKPT 1400 AM. MLB affiliation, New York Mets.

JOE O'BRIEN FIELD
Holly Lane, Elizabethton **[P. 107, D-12]**. Capacity: 1,500
Elizabethton Twins (Appalachian, Rookie Class); (615) 543-4395. Entered League in 1974. MLB affiliation, Minnesota Twins.

TIM McCARVER STADIUM
800 Home Run Lane, Memphis **[P. 106, G-2]**. Capacity: 10,000
Memphis Chicks (Southern League, Class AA); (901) 272-1687. Entered League in 1978. Broadcasts by WREC 600 AM. MLB affiliation, Kansas City Royals.

Basketball

MID-SOUTH COLISEUM
996 Early Maxwell Blvd., Memphis **[P. 106, G-2]**. Capacity: 11,200.
Memphis Rockers (World Basketball League); (901) 726-6400. Entered League in 1990. Broadcasts by WMC 790 AM.

NASHVILLE MUNICIPAL AUDITORIUM
417 Fourth Avenue North, Nashville **[P. 106, G-6]**. Capacity: 8,600.
Nashville Stars (World Basketball League); (615) 242-9334. Entered League in 1991. Broadcasts by WAMB 1160 AM & 106.7 FM.

Bowling

PIN CHASE CENTER
322 E. Campbell Blvd., Columbia **[P. 106, C-7]**; (615) 381-2695.
Lady Ebonite Classic (LPBT), April.

College Sports

AUSTIN PEAY STATE UNIVERSITY GOVERNORS
Clarksville **[P. 106, A-6]**; (615) 648-7903. Municipal, capacity 10,000. Winfield Dunn, capacity 9,000.
◆Home of one of the more off-color cheers in college sports — "Let's Go Peay."

EAST TENNESSEE STATE UNIVERSITY BUCS
Johnson City **[P. 107, E-13]**; (615) 929-4343.
◆A great four years by one group of recruits has caused the basketball world to find out just where Johnson City is.

MEMPHIS STATE UNIVERSITY TIGERS
Memphis **[P. 106, G-2]**; (901) 678-2331. Liberty Bowl Memorial/Rex Dockery Field, capacity 63,000. Mid-South, capacity 11,200.
◆The basketball team generally is good. The dance team is spectacular.

MIDDLE TENNESSEE STATE UNIVERSITY BLUE RAIDERS
Murfreesboro **[P. 107, B-8]**; (615) 898-2450. Johnny "Red" Floyd, capacity 15,000. Murphy Center, capacity 11,520.

TENNESSEE STATE UNIVERSITY TIGERS
3500 John A. Merritt Boulevard, Nashville **[P. 106, G-5]**; (615) 320-3597. W.J. Hale, capacity 16,000. Howard C. Gentry Complex, capacity 10,000.

TENNESSEE TECH UNIVERSITY GOLDEN EAGLES
Cookeville **[P. 107, B-9]**; (615) 372-3940. Wilburn Tucker, Iverall Field, capacity 16,000. Hooper Eblen, capacity 10,200.

UNIVERSITY OF THE SOUTH TIGERS
Sewanee **[P. 107, D-9]**; (615) 598-1284. McGee Field, capacity 3,500. Juhan Gym, capacity 1,500.

UNIVERSITY OF TENNESSEE MOCCASINS
615 McCallie Avenue, Chattanooga **[P. 107, G-9]**; (615) 755-4495. Chamberlain, capacity 10,500. UTC Sports Arena, capacity 11,200.

UNIVERSITY OF TENNESSEE VOLUNTEERS
1720 Volunteer Blvd., Knoxville **[P. 107, H-13]**; (615) 974-1224. Neyland, capacity 91,110. Thompson-Boling Assem. Center & Arena, capacity 25,000.
◆Football coach Johnny Majors is a familiar name in the Volunteer State. He was a prep star in the state, an All-American at Tennessee — finishing second in the Heisman balloting — and now must keep a hard-to-please throng of 90,000 on Saturdays satisfied by winning often.

UNIVERSITY OF TENNESSEE PACERS
Martin **[P. 106, A-4]**; (901) 587-7660. Pacer, capacity 7,500. PE Complex, capacity 7,000.

VANDERBILT UNIVERSITY COMMODORES
2601 Jess Neely Drive, Nashville **[P. 106, G-5]**; (615) 322-4727. Vanderbilt, capacity 41,000. Memorial Gym, capacity 15,626.
◆The oddest basketball court in college basketball. The teams' benches are behind the two baskets.

Hockey

CIVIC COLISEUM
500 E. Church St., Knoxville **[P. 107, G-13]**. Capacity: 4,600.
Knoxville Cherokees (East Coast Hockey League); (615) 546-6707. Franchise began in 1988.

MUNICIPAL AUDITORIUM
417 4th Ave. N., Nashville **[P. 106, G-6]**. Capacity: 8,400.
Nashville Knights (East Coast Hockey League); (615) 255-7825. Franchise began in 1989.

Museums & Halls of Fame

UNITED STATES BASEBALL FEDERATION HALL OF FAME
4880 Navy Road, Millington **[P. 106, C-2]**; (901) 872-3311.

PGA/LPGA

HERMITAGE GOLF COURSE
3939 Old Hickory Blvd., Old Hickory **[P. 106, B-7]**; (615) 847-4001.
Sara Lee Classic (LPGA), May. Number of holes: 72.

TPC AT SOUTHWIND
3325 Club at Southwind, Memphis **[P. 106, H-4]**; (901) 748-0534. Federal Express St. Jude Classic (PGA), Aug. Number of holes: 72.

VALLEYBROOK GOLF & COUNTRY CLUB
180 Valleybrook Rd., Hixson **[P. 107, D-10]**; (615) 842-4646.

CONTINUED ON PAGE 208

STATBOX

POPULATION: 4,855,651
SQUARE MILES: 42,244
TIME ZONE: Eastern and Central
MOTTO: Agriculture and Commerce
BIRD: Mockingbird
TREE: Tulip Poplar
CAPITAL: Nashville
AVERAGE ANNUAL RAINFALL: 50"
MEAN TEMP: 30/49 (winter); 67/89 (summer)
MAJOR LEAGUE TEAMS: 0
NATIONAL PARK/FOREST ACREAGE: 1,000,000
STATE PARK ACREAGE: 134,000
HIGHEST ELEVATION: 6,643'
LOWEST ELEVATION: 143'
WATERWAYS: 19,000 miles of rivers and streams; 29 major lakes

USA SNAPSHOTS®

A look at statistics that shape the sports world

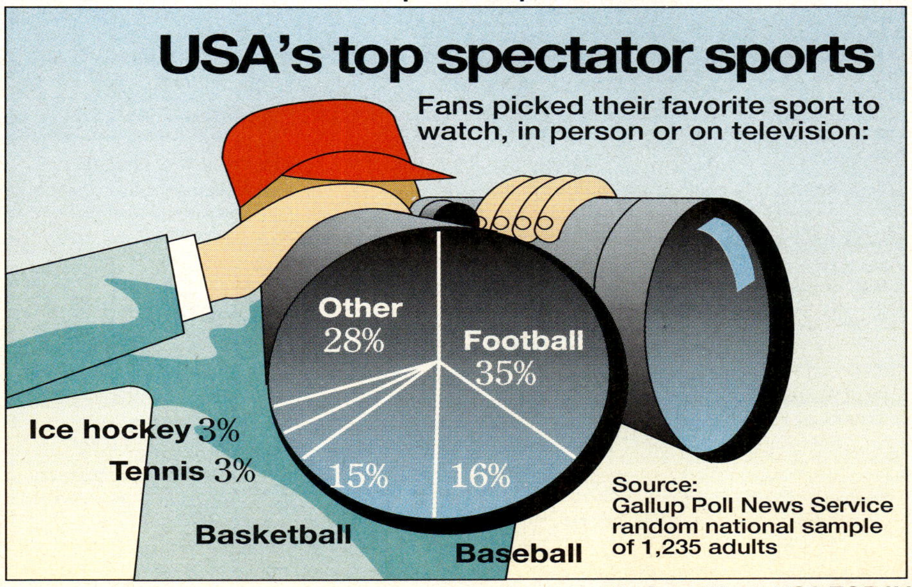

By Sam Ward, USA TODAY

Tennessee

CONTINUED FROM PAGE 207

Chattanooga Classic (PGA), July. Number of holes: 72.

Polo

NASHVILLE POLO CLUB
Hwy 100 & Old Hickory Blvd., Nashville [**P. 106, B-7**]; (615) 244-2230.

Tennis

MARYLAND FARMS RACQUET & COUNTRY CLUB
5101 Maryland Way, Brentwood [**P. 106, B-7**]; (615) 373-5120. Surface is hard, Clay. Virginia Slims of Nashville (WTA), November.

RACQUET CLUB OF MEMPHIS
5111 Sanderlin Road, Memphis [**P. 106, G-3**]; (901) 765-4400. Surface is hard. Volvo Tennis Indoor (ATP), Feb. to Mar.

Track & Field

MEMORIAL CENTER
State of Franklin Rd., East Tennessee State University, Johnson City [**P. 107, E-13**]; (615) 929-5372.
US Air Invitational (USA/Mobil Grand Prix Event), Jan.

OUTDOOR VENUES

National Parks

- Bike Trails: BK
- Boating: BT
- Camping: C
- Climbing: CL
- Diving: DV
- Fishing: F
- Golfing: G
- Hiking: HK
- Hunting: HT
- Riding: R
- Surfing: SU
- Swimming: S
- Tennis: TE
- Whitewater: WW
- Winter Sports: W

BIG SOUTH FORK NATIONAL RIVER AND RECREATION AREA
15 mi. W of Oneida & 24 mi. E of Jamestown, at the Bandy Creek Campground off Leatherwood Ford Road (TN 297) [**P. 107, A-11**]. Contains 105,000 acres.
C HK BT F S R WW

CHEROKEE NATIONAL FOREST
Cleveland [**P. 107, D-11, E-12**]. Contains 625,000 acres. **C HK BT F S R BK WW**

GREAT SMOKY MOUNTAINS NATIONAL PARK
2 mi. S of Gatlinburg [**P. 86, A-5**]. Contains 520,000 acres. **C HK F S R W**

State Parks

BIG RIDGE STATE RUSTIC PARK
On Norris Lake, 14 mi. NE of Norris on TN 61, Route 1, Maynardville [**P. 107, B-12**]. Contains 3,600 acres. **C HK BT F S**

BOOKER T. WASHINGTON STATE RECREATIONAL PARK
On Chickamauga Lake, 6 mi. NE of Chattanooga off TN 58 [**P. 107, F-10**]. Contains 350 acres. **C HK BT F S**

CHICKASAW STATE RUSTIC PARK
7 mi. W of Henderson on TN 100 [**P. 106, C-4**]. Contains 11,215 acres. **C HK BT F S**

CORDELL HULL LAKE (AC)
Off SR 85, 50 mi. E of Nashville [**P. 107, B-9**]. Contains 32,705 acres. **C HK BT F S R BK**

DALE HOLLOW DAM PARK (AC)
TN 53, 2 mi. E of Celina [**P. 107, A-10**]. Contains 52,542 acres. **C HK BT F S R BK**

EDGAR EVINS STATE RUSTIC PARK
N of Smithville, off I-40 on Center Hill Lake [**P. 107, B-9**]. Contains 6,000 acres. **C HK BT F S**

FALL CREEK FALLS STATE RESORT PARK
Hwy. 111, 7 mi. S of Spencer [**P. 107, C-10**]. Contains 16,000 acres. **C HK BT F S R BK TE**

FROZEN HEAD STATE NATURAL AREA
6 mi. E of Wartburg on TN 62 [**P. 107, B-11**]. Contains 10,000 acres. **C HK**

J. PERCY PRIEST LAKE (AC)
Off I-40, 11 mi. E of Nashville [**P. 107, B-8**]. Contains 33,662 acres. **C HK BT F S R BK**

MEEMAN-SHELBY FOREST STATE RECREATIONAL PARK
16 mi. N of Memphis off US 51 [**P. 106, F-2**]. Contains 12,512 acres. **C HK BT F S R BK**

MONTGOMERY BELL STATE RESORT PARK
8 mi. E of Dickson on US 70 [**P. 106, B-6**]. Contains 4,600 acres. **C HK BT F S G**

NATCHEZ TRACE STATE RESORT PARK AND FOREST
Off I-40 westbound, between Memphis & Nashville [**P. 106, B-5**]. Contains 43,000 acres. **C HK BT F S x**

NORRIS DAM STATE RESORT DAM
On Norris Lake, off I-75 north at Lake City, 14 mi. N of Knoxville [**P. 107, B-12**]. Contains 2,321 acres. **C HK BT F S TE**

PARIS LANDING STATE RESORT PARK
On Kentucky Lake, 17 mi. NE of Paris on US 79 [**P. 106, A-5**]. Contains 1,200 acres. **C BT F S G**

PICKETT STATE RUSTIC PARK
13 mi. NE of Jamestown on TN 154 [**P. 107, A-5**]. Contains 14,000 acres. **C HK BT F S**

REELFOOT LAKE STATE RESORT PARK
5 mi. E of Tiptonville on TN 21 [**P. 106, A-3**]. Contains 250 acres. **C HK BT F S**

WARRIOR'S PATH STATE RECREATIONAL PARK
On Fort Patrick Henry Lake, 5 mi. SE of Kingsport on US 23 [**P. 107, E-12**]. Contains 1,500 acres. **C HK BT F S R G**

Skiing

ALPINE SKIING

OBER GATLINBURG
1001 Park Way, Gatlinburg [**P. 86, A-7**]; (615) 436-5423.
Vertical drop is 600 feet. Has one tow, four chairs and one tram.

TERRY PEAK SKI AREA
Nevada Gulch, Lead [**P. 105, K-1**]; (605) 584-2165. Vertical drop is 1,052 feet. Has one tow and five chairs.

NORDIC SKIING

DEER MOUNTAIN SKI AREA
Deadwood [**P. 105, K-1**]; (605) 584-3230.

PLEASANT VALLEY SKI AREA
Route 1, Gary [**P. 105, J-7**]; (605) 272-5614.

SKI CROSS COUNTRY
Spearfish [**P. 105, K-1**]; (605) 642-3851.

ACTIVE SPORTS

AEROBICS: AFAA, 3110 West End Cir., #12, Nashville; (615) 383-8796.

BASEBALL: Little League Baseball Southern Region HQ, PO Box 13366, St. Petersburg, FL; (813) 344-2661. • **American Legion Baseball,** 906 Belvoir Hill Dr., Chattanooga; (615) 698-1034. • **Babe Ruth Baseball,** William E. Whitehurst, Rt. 2, Box 56, Grifton, NC; (919) 524-5525. • **Men's Senior Baseball League - Nashville,** 3880 Priest Lake Dr. #4, Nashville; (615) 367-4748.

BILLIARDS: Highpockets, 5099 Old Summer, Memphis; (901) 761-1583.

BOARDSAILING: Interwheel Sports, Knoxville; (615) 525-4606. • **USWA Regional Director,** 2580 Prosperity Oaks Ct., Palm Beach Gdns, FL; (407) 881-0001.

BOWLING: American Bowling Congress, 5301 S. 76th St., Greendale, WI; (414) 421-6400.

CANOEING & KAYAKING: ACA Dixie Vice Commodore, 2320 Salcedo Street, Savannah, GA; (912) 352-0717.

CYCLING: LAW East Central Regional Director, 4724 Bokay Drive, Dayton, OH; (513) 435-9366. • **USCF Tennessee Representative,** 644 Walnut Bend, Cordova; (901) 756-5341.

FITNESS: Governor's Council on Physical Fitness and Health, c/o Tennessee Department of Health and Environment, 5th Floor, Cordell Hall Building, Nashville; (615) 741-7366. • **National Strength and Conditioning Ass'n State Director,** Football Office, East Tennessee State University, Johnson City; (615) 929-4261.

FOOTBALL: Pop Warner Football, 1315 Walnut Street, Suite 1632, Philadelphia, PA; (215) 735-1450.

GOLF: PGA Tennessee Section, 4711 Trousdale Dr., Nashville; (615) 833-9689. • **Tennessee Golf Association,** 4711 Trousdale Dr., Nashville; (615) 833-9689.

HIKING & CLIMBING: Greeneville Hiking Club (AHS), Rt. 3 Box 274, Chuckey; (615) 257-5082. • **Tennessee Sierra Club Chapter,** 871 Kensington Pl., Memphis; (901) 274-1510

HOCKEY: USA Hockey Southeastern Registrar, PO Box 5208, Takoma Park, MD; (301) 622-0032.

HUNTING & FISHING: Cumberland Transit (Orvis), 2807 West End Ave., Nashville; (615) 321-4069 .• **The Sporting Life (Orvis),** 3092 Poplar Ave., Memphis; (901) 324-2383. • **Trout Unlimited,** c/o Wagner, Nelson & Weeks, 1418 First Tennessee Building, Chattanooga; (615) 266-8816. • **Wildlife Resources Agency ,** PO Box 40747, Ellington Agricultural Center, Nashville; (615) 781-6552

RACQUETBALL: AARA, 6167 S. Mt. Juliet Rd., Hermitage; (615) 391-0905.

RIDING: Tennessee Horse Council, 701 4th Ave. South, Nashville; (615) 255-6304.

RODEO: PRCA Southeastern Circuit, 1111 S. McGee Rd., Bonifay, FL; (904) 547-2534.

SCUBA: Adventure Swim & Scuba, 7664 Northshore Drive, Knoxville; (615) 690-3483. • **Ski/Scuba Center,** 2543 Sutherland Avenue, Knoxville; (615) 673-8733.

SKATING: USFSA, 20 First Street, Colorado Springs, CO; (719) 635-5200.

SOCCER: Tennessee Soccer Ass'n, 141 Highway 72 East, Suite No. 8, Collierville; (901) 853-5051. • **AYSO Regional Director,** 1405 Inman Dr., Huntsville, AL; (205) 881-3138.

SOFTBALL: Tennessee ASA, 805 Sunset Ave. NW, Cleveland; (615) 472-2046. • **Memphis ASA,** 4233 Crafton Ave., Memphis; (901) 683-6108.

SWIMMING: LMSC Southeastern Registrar, 932 West Outer Dr., Oak Ridge; (615) 482-2575.

TENNIS: Recreational TEAMTENNIS Midwest-Southeast Region, National Program Coordinator, 445 N. Wells, Ste. #404, Chicago, IL; (800) TEAMTEN. • **Southern USTA,** 200 Sandy Springs Place, Suite 200, Atlanta, GA; (404) 257-1297.

WHITEWATER RAFTING: Ocoee Outdoors, Box 72, Ocoee; (615) 338-2438. • **Pigeon River Outdoors, Inc./Rafting in the Smokies,** PO Box 592, Gatlinburg; (615) 436-5008.

Tip Offs: Conservation Organizations

From Ducks Unlimited's participation in the preservation of wetlands to the long-term, broad-based efforts of the Sierra Club, conservation organizations have been pivotal in protecting our backcountries and shorelines for hunters and hikers alike. A selection of major groups involved in conserving wilderness and wildlife follows.

American Rivers,
801 Pennsylvania Ave., SE, Suite 400, Washington, DC; (202) 547-6900.

Defenders of Wildlife,
1244 19th Street, NW, Washington, DC 20036.

Ducks Unlimited, 1 Waterfowl Way, Long Grove, IL; (708) 438-4300.

National Audubon Society,
950 Third Avenue, New York, NY 10022.

National Association of Conservation Districts,
509 Capitol Ct., NE, Washington, DC 20005.

National Recreation and Park Ass'n,
3101 Park Center Drive, Alexandria, VA 22302.

National Wildlife Federation Endowment, Inc.,
1400 16th St., NW, Washington, DC 20036.

Pheasants Forever,
PO Box 75473, St. Paul, MN; (612) 481-7142.

Quail Unlimited, PO Box 10041, Augusta, GA; (803) 637-5731.

Rails-To-Trails Conservancy,
1400 16th St., NW, Washington, DC; (202) 797-5400.

Rocky Mountain Elk Foundation, 2291 W. Broadway, Missoula, MT; (406) 721-0010.

Sierra Club, Office of Volunteer Development, 730 Polk Street, San Francisco, CA; (415) 923-5576.

The Conservation Foundation, 1250 24th St., NW, Washington, DC 20036.

The Friends of the Earth,
218 D Street, SE, Washington, DC 20003.

The Humane Society of the United States,
2100 L Street, NW, Washington, DC 20037.

The Nature Conservancy,
1815 North Lynn, Arlington, VA 22209.

The Wildlife Society,
5410 Grosvenor Lane, Bethesda, MD; (301) 897-9770.

The Wildlife Legislative Fund of America,
801 Kingsmill Pkwy., Columbus, OH; (614) 888-4868.

Waterfowl USA Ltd.
PO Box 50, Edgefield, SC; (803) 637-5767.

Wildlife Management Institute, 1101 14th St., NW, Suite 725, Washington, DC; (202) 371-1808.

Texas

Nolan Ryan's Rangers play ball at Arlington Stadium. Texans have named a freeway after their native pitching ace. ◆ Further south, the Houston Astrodome—first of its breed—has been home to the strange and wonderful: cult movies ("Brewster McCloud"), Evel Knievel's first indoor motorcycle jump, Bobby Riggs vs. Billie Jean King and, of course, the Astros and Oilers. ◆ Seven major league teams draw more than six million fans a year here. ◆ The Houston Livestock Show and Rodeo features the nation's best calf-ropers, steer-wrestlers, and barrel-racers. ◆ Austin's hill country offers a bounty of PGA golf courses, as well as residents Tom Kite, Ben Crenshaw, and Willie Nelson, who, until tax troubles, played on his own links. ◆ Ride, hike, fish and camp at Big Bend in the Southwest corner of the state, one of the USA's least known and most stunning national parks.

STATBOX

POPULATION: 16,841,000
SQUARE MILES: 275,416
TIME ZONE: Central and Mountain
MOTTO: Friendship
BIRD: Mockingbird
TREE: Pecan
CAPITAL: Austin
AVERAGE ANNUAL RAINFALL: 28"
MEAN TEMP: 78-84
MAJOR LEAGUE TEAMS: 7
NATIONAL PARK/FOREST ACREAGE: 1,201,479
STATE PARK ACREAGE: 447,068
HIGHEST ELEVATION: 8,749'
LOWEST ELEVATION: sea level
WATERWAYS: 80,000 miles of rivers and streams; 5,700 reservoirs

► SPECTATOR VENUES

Auto Racing

ADDISON AIRPORT
15404 Addison Rd., Dallas **[P. 111, O-15]**; (214) 701-9091. Track is 1.6-mile temporary road.
Grand Prix of Dallas in Addison (SCCA Trans-Am Championship), June.

HOUSTON RACEWAY PARK
FM 565, Baytown **[P. 111, K-14]**; (713) 383-2666. Track is quarter-mile strip (for NHRA races).
Fram Supernationals (NHRA), early March.

TEXAS MOTORPLEX
US Highway 287, 2 miles west of Ennis **[P. 110, G-13]**; (214) 875-2641. Track is quarter-mile strip (for NHRA races).
Chief Auto Parts Nationals (NHRA), early Oct.

Baseball

ANGELS STADIUM
4300 N. Lamesa Rd., Midland **[P. 108, E-4]**. Capacity: 4,000
Midland Angels (Texas League, Class AA); (915) 683-4251. Entered League in 1972. Broadcasts by KCRS 550AM. MLB affiliation, California Angels.

ARLINGTON STADIUM
1700 Copeland Rd., Arlington **[P. 111, P-14]**. Built in 1972. Capacity: 43,508
Texas Rangers (AL West); (817) 273-5000. Franchise began in 1961. Broadcasts by WBAP-AM 820, KTVT-TV 11, Home Sports Entertainment. Affiliates: Oklahoma City, OK (AAA); Tulsa, OK (AA); Port Charlotte, FL (A); Gastonia, NC (A); Butte, MT (Rookie); Port Charlotte, FL (Rookie). Spring training held in Port Charlotte, FL.

COHEN STADIUM
9700 Gateway North Blvd., El Paso **[P. 108, E-2]**. Capacity: 10,000
El Paso Diablos (Texas League, Class AA); (915) 755-2000. Entered League in 1972. Broadcasts by KHEY 690AM. MLB affiliation, Milwaukee Brewers.

THE ASTRODOME
8400 Kirby Dr., Houston **[P. 111, N-14]**. Built in 1965. Capacity: 54,816
◆When it debuted in 1964, it was called "The Eighth Wonder of the World," a reference to its status as the first domed stadium. The luster is gone. The ballpark is old and worn and getting renovated. The exploding scoreboard has been toned down. Ballplayers love to eat at Cap'n Benny's seafood stand on nearby South Main, and also opt for the best barbeque in baseball, at Goode Company on Kirby.
Houston Astros (NL West); (713) 799-9500. Franchise began in 1962. Broadcasts by KPRC 950 AM, KTXH Channel 20, Home Sports Entertainment Cable. Affiliates: Tucson, AZ (AAA); Jackson, MS (AA); Burlington, IA (A); Osceola, Kissimmee, FL (A); Asheville, NC (A); Auburn, NY (A); Osceola, FL (Rookie). Spring training held in Kissimmee, FL.

V.J. KEEFE MEMORIAL STADIUM
36th at Culebra, San Antonio **[P. 111, P-9]**. Capacity: 3,500
San Antonio Missions (Texas League, Class AA); (512) 434-9311. Entered League in 1888. Broadcasts by KCHL 1480 AM. MLB affiliation, Los Angeles Dodgers.

Basketball

D.L. LIGON COLISEUM
3400 Taft Blvd., Wichita Falls **[P. 108, B-4]**. Capacity: 4,738.
Wichita Falls Texans (Continental Basketball Association, National Conference, Western Division); (817) 691-2204. Entered League in 1983. Broadcasts by KTLT FM 106.

HEMISFAIR ARENA
600 Convention Way, San Antonio **[P. 111, Q-9]**. Built in 1968. Capacity: 15,910.
◆The Spurs moved from Dallas to Ft. Worth and Lubbock before coming here. Started in ABA, joined NBA in 1976.
San Antonio Spurs (NBA Western Conf., Midwest Div.); (512) 554-7787. Franchise began in 1967. Broadcasts by WOAI 1200 AM, KSAH 720 AM (Spanish), KSAT Channel 12 (13 on cable), HSE Cable 23.

REUNION ARENA
777 Sports Street, Dallas **[P. 111, P-15]**. Built in 1980. Capacity: 17,007.
Dallas Mavericks (NBA Western Conf., Midwest Div.); (214) 748-1808. Franchise began in 1980. Broadcasts by WBAP 820 AM, KRLD 1080 AM (Playoffs only), KTVT Channel 11, Home Sports Entertainment.

THE SUMMIT
10 Greenway Plaza, Houston **[P. 111, N-14]**. Built in 1975. Capacity: 16,279.
◆The Rockets were a San Diego team from 1967 to 1971.
Houston Rockets (NBA Western Conf., Midwest Div.); (713) 627-0600. Franchise began in 1967. Broadcasts by KTRH 740 AM, KXYZ 1320 AM (Spanish), KTXH TV-20, Home Sports Entertainment.

Bowling

BOWL EL PASO
11144 Pellicano, El Paso **[P. 108, G-1]**; (915) 593-7777.
El Paso Open (PBA), July.

CROSSROADS LANES
4370 Dowlen, Beaumont **[P. 110, D-15]**; (409) 899-2695.
Beaumont PBA Doubles Classic, May.

FAIR LANES SOUTHWAY
8180 S. Gessner, Houston **[P. 111, N-14]**; (713) 771-2353.
Lady Ebonite Classic (LPBT), October.

FORUM BOWLING LANES
2001 Great Southwest Parkway, Grand Prairie **[P. 111, Q-14]**; (214) 641-4406.
Quaker State Open (PBA), January to February.

HIGHLAND LANES
8909 Burnet Road, Austin **[P. 108, C-4]**; (512) 458-1215.
Columbia 300 Open (PBA), July.

SHOWPLACE LANES
1950 Plaza Drive, Garland **[P. 111, P-15]**; (214) 613-8100.
Garland Open (LPBT), February.

USA SNAPSHOTS®

A look at statistics that shape the sports world

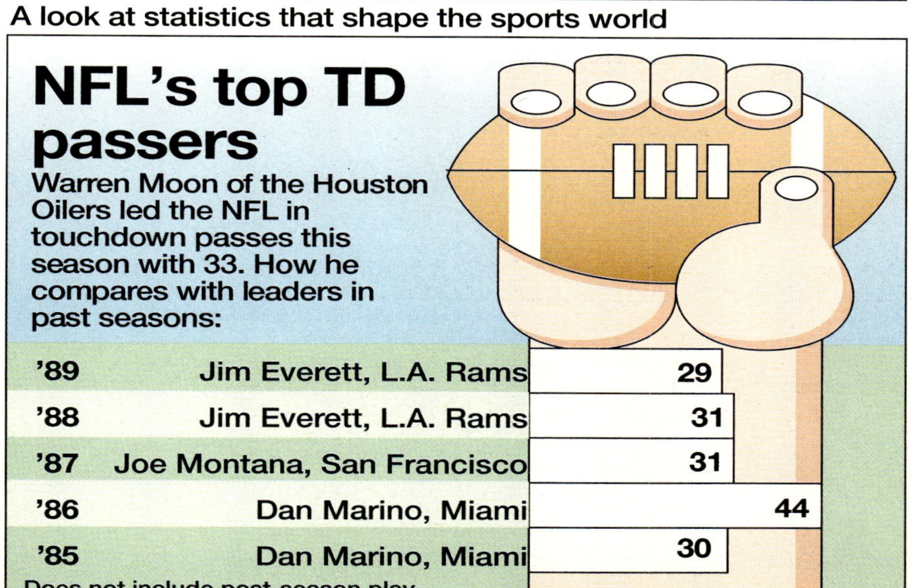

NFL's top TD passers
Warren Moon of the Houston Oilers led the NFL in touchdown passes this season with 33. How he compares with leaders in past seasons:
'89 Jim Everett, L.A. Rams 29
'88 Jim Everett, L.A. Rams 31
'87 Joe Montana, San Francisco 31
'86 Dan Marino, Miami 44
'85 Dan Marino, Miami 30
Does not include post-season play

Source: Elias Sports Bureau — By Marty Baumann, USA TODAY

College Sports

BAYLOR UNIVERSITY BEARS
3031 Dutton, Waco **[P. 110, H-12]**; (817) 754-4648. Floyd Casey, capacity 48,500. Ferrell Center, capacity 10,080.

HARDIN-SIMMONS UNIVERSITY COWBOYS
Abilene **[P. 110, G-9]**; (915) 670-1473. Mabee Complex, capacity 2,500.

LAMAR UNIVERSITY CARDINALS
Beaumont **[P. 110, D-15]**; (409) 880-8323. Cardinal, capacity 17,150. Montagne Center, capacity 10,500.

PRAIRIE VIEW A&M UNIVERSITY PANTHERS
Prairie View **[P. 111, K-13]**; (409) 857-2114. Blackshear, capacity 6,600. Little Dome, capacity 6,600.

RICE UNIVERSITY OWLS
Houston **[P. 111, N-14]**; (713) 527-4077. Rice, capacity 70,000. Autry Court, capacity 5,000.

SAM HOUSTON STATE UNIVERSITY BEARKATS
Huntsville **[P. 110, J-14]**; (409) 294-1726. Bearkat, capacity 14,000. University Coliseum, capacity 6,200.

SOUTHERN METHODIST UNIVERSITY MUSTANGS
Dallas **[P. 111, P-15]**; (214) 692-2864. Ownby, capacity 23,783. Moody Coliseum, capacity 9,007.

SOUTHWEST TEXAS STATE UNIVERSITY BOBCATS
San Marcos **[P. 111, K-11]**; (512) 245-2114. Bobcat, capacity 14,104. Strahan coliseum, capacity 7,200.

STEPHEN F. AUSTIN STATE UNIVERSITY LUMBERJACKS
Nacogdoches **[P. 110, H-15]**; (409) 568-3501. Homer Bryce, capacity 14,575. SFA Coliseum, capacity 7,007.

TEXAS A&M UNIVERSITY AGGIES
College Station **[P. 110, J-13]**; (409) 845-0564. Kyle Field, capacity 72,367. G. Rollie White, capacity 7,500.

TEXAS CHRISTIAN UNIVERSITY HORNED FROGS
Fort Worth **[P. 111, Q-13]**; (817) 921-7969. Amon G. Carter, capacity 46,000. Daniel-Meyer, capacity 7,200.

TEXAS SOUTHERN UNIVERSITY TIGERS
3100 Cleburne, Houston **[P. 111, N-15]**; (713) 527-7273. Robertson, capacity 24,000.

TEXAS TECH UNIVERSITY RED RAIDERS
6th & Akron, Lubbock **[P. 108, D-2]**; (806) 742-3355. Jones, capacity 47,500. Coliseum, capacity 8,174.
◆The problem is getting to Lubbock. Once you're there, the friendly folks know how to throw a football weekend.

UNIVERSITY OF HOUSTON COUGARS
Houston **[P. 111, N-15]**; (713) 749-3722. Astrodome, capacity 65,000. Hofheinz, capacity 10,060.

CONTINUED ON PAGE 210

Texas

CONTINUED FROM PAGE 209

UNIVERSITY OF NORTH TEXAS MEAN GREEN EAGLES
Denton **[P. 110, E-12]**; (817) 565-2662. Fouts Field, capacity 20,000. NTSU Coliseum, capacity 10,000.

UNIVERSITY OF TEXAS LONGHORNS
Austin **[P. 108, D-3]**; (512) 471-4602. Texas Memorial, capacity 75,524. Erwin Special Events, capacity 16,231.
◆Football is a Texas religion, and the Horns are the state's passion. Austin also happens to be a great college party town.

UNIVERSITY OF TEXAS MINERS
El Paso **[P. 108, F-1]**; (915) 747-5347. Sun Bowl, capacity 53,000. Special Events, capacity 12,000.

UNIVERSITY OF TEXAS BRONCS
1201 W. University Drive, Edinburg **[P. 111, D-11]**; (512) 381-2221. PAU, capacity 5,000.

UNIVERSITY OF TEXAS ROADRUNNERS
San Antonio **[P. 111, D-9]**; (512) 691-4161. Convocation, capacity 4,500.

Football

ALAMO STADIUM
110 Tuleta, San Antonio **[P. 111, P-9]**. Capacity: 25,000.
San Antonio Riders (World League of American Football, North American West Division); (512) 496-5401. Franchise began in 1991. Broadcasts by WOAI 1200 AM.

ASTRODOME
Loop 610, Kirby and Fannin Streets, Houston **[P. 111, N-14]**. Built in 1965. Capacity: 60,502.
Houston Oilers (AFC Central Division); (713) 797-9111. Franchise began in 1960. Broadcasts by KODA-FM, Houston.

TEXAS STADIUM
Jct. of Hwy. 183, Hwy. 114, & Loop 12, at 2401 E. Airport Freeway, Irving **[P. 111, D-15]**. Built in 1971. Capacity: 65,024.
Dallas Cowboys (NFC Eastern Division); (214) 556-9900. Franchise began in 1960. Broadcasts by KRLD.

Polo

HOUSTON POLO CLUB
8552 Memorial Dr., Houston **[P. 111, N-14]**; (713) 681-8571.

MIDLAND POLO CLUB
5505 Polo Club Rd., Midland **[P. 108, E-4]**; (915) 684-6493.

OAK GROVE POLO CLUB
Decatur **[P. 110, E-11]**; (817) 627-6400.

SAN ANTONIO POLO CLUB
16315 Lookout Rd., San Antonio **[P. 111, P-9]**; (512) 651-5217.

WILLOW BEND POLO CLUB
5845 W. Park Blvd., Plano **[P. 110, F-2]**; (214) 248-6298

Museums & Halls of Fame

TEXAS SPORTS HALL OF CHAMPIONS AND TEXAS TENNIS MUSEUM
14th at Jefferson, Waco **[P. 110, H-12]**; (817) 756-2307.

PGA/LPGA

BARTON CREEK COUNTRY CLUB
8212 Barton Club Dr., Austin **[P. 108, D-3]**; (512) 282-0129.
◆Gorgeous green vistas.
Liberty Mutual Legends of Golf (Senior PGA), April. Number of holes: 72.

CHAMPIONS GOLF CLUB
13722 Champion Dr., Houston **[P. 111, K-14]**; (713) 444-6262.
Former host of Nabisco Champions (PGA), Oct. Number of holes: 72.

COLONIAL COUNTRY CLUB
3735 Country Club Circle, Ft. Worth **[P. 111, P-13]**; (817) 927-4221.
Southwestern Bell Colonial (PGA), May.
US Women's Open (LPGA), July. Number of holes: 72.

DEERWOOD CLUB
1717 Forest Garden, Kingwood **[P. 111, K-14]**; (713) 360-1060.
Doug Sanders Kingwood Celebrity Classic (Senior PGA), May. Number of holes: 54.

OAK HILLS COUNTRY CLUB
5403 Fredericksburg Rd., San Antonio **[P. 111, P-9]**; (512) 349-5151.
Texas Open (PGA), September. Number of holes: 72.

STONEBRIAR COUNTRY CLUB
5050 Country Club Dr., Frisco **[P. 110, F-12]**; (214) 625-5050.
Murata Reunion Pro-Am (Senior PGA), May. Number of holes: 54.

THE DOMINION COUNTRY CLUB
1 Dominion Dr., San Antonio **[P. 111, D-9]**; (512) 698-1146.
Vantage at the Dominion (Senior PGA), March. Number of holes: 54.

TPC AT THE WOODLANDS
1730 S. Millbend Dr., The Woodlands **[P. 111, K-14]**; (713) 367-7285.
Houston Open (PGA), April. Number of holes: 72.

TPC AT LAS COLINAS
4200 N. McArthur Blvd., Irving **[P. 111, P-14]**; (214) 717-2500.
GTE Byron Nelson Golf Classic (PGA), May. Number of holes: 72.

Tennis

McFARLIN TENNIS CENTER
1503 San Pedro, San Antonio **[P. 111, Q-9]**; (512) 734-4781. Surface is hard.
San Antonio Racquets (TT), July to August, (512) 821-5811.
U.S. Women's hards **Championships** (WTA), March.

WESTSIDE TENNIS CLUB
1200 Wilcrest Ave., Houston **[P. 111, N-14]**; (713) 783-1620. Surface is Clay.
Virginia Slims of Houston (WTA), April.

Rodeo

ASTRODOME
610 Loop & Kirby, Houston **[P. 111, N-14]**; (713) 791-9000.
Houston Livestock Show & Rodeo, Feb.

EL PASO COUNTY ARENA
4100 E. Paisano, El Paso **[P. 108, F-2]**; (915) 532-1401.
Southwestern International Livestock Show & Rodeo, Feb.

JOE & HARRY FREEMAN COLISEUM
3201 E. Houston, San Antonio **[P. 111, Q-9]**; (512) 225-5851.
San Antonio Livestock Exposition Rodeo, Feb.

WEST OF THE PECOS RODEO ARENA
TX Highway 285 West, Pecos **[P. 109, H-4]**; (915) 447-2251.
West of the Pecos Rodeo, July.

WILL ROGERS MEMORIAL COLISEUM
3400 West Crestline Road, Fort Worth **[P. 111, P-13]**; (817) 877-2400.
Southwestern Exposition & Livestock Show & Rodeo, Jan. to Feb.

Soccer

REUNION ARENA
7777 Sports Street, Dallas **[P. 111, P-15]**. Capacity: 16,824.
Dallas Sidekicks (Major Soccer League); (214) 361-5425.

Yachting

HOUSTON YACHT CLUB
3620 Miramar Dr., La Porte **[P. 111, L-14]**; (713) 471-1255.
◆Host of U.S. Women's Sailing Championship (Adams Cup) in 1990.

OUTDOOR VENUES

National Parks

- Bike Trails: BK
- Boating: BT
- Camping: C
- Climbing: CL
- Diving: DV
- Fishing: F
- Golfing: G
- Hiking: HK
- Hunting: HT
- Riding: R
- Surfing: SU
- Swimming: S
- Tennis: TE
- Whitewater: WW
- Winter Sports: W

AMISTAD NATIONAL RECREATION AREA
NW of Del Rio via US 90 **[P. 109, K-7]**. Contains 67,000 acres. **C HK BT F S R**

ANGELINA NATIONAL FOREST
Lufkin **[P. 110, H-15]**. Contains 152,883 acres. **C HK BT F S HT**

BIG BEND NATIONAL PARK
SE of Alpine on TX 118 and US 385 **[P. 109, L-4]**. Contains 775,243 acres. **C HK BT F R HT**

BIG THICKET NATIONAL PRESERVE
Six separate areas, information center is 2.5 mi. E of US 69 **[P. 110, J-15]**. Contains 84,550 acres. **C HK BT F S R HT**

DAVY CROCKETT NATIONAL FOREST
Crockett and Apple Springs **[P. 110, H-14]**. Contains 163,120 acres. **C HK BT F S HT**

GUADALUPE MOUNTAINS NATIONAL PARK
110 mi. E of El Paso on US 62/180 **[P. 108, G-3]**. Contains 76,293 acres. **C HK R HT**

LAKE MEREDITH NATIONAL RECREATION AREA
45 mi. NE of Amarillo and 9 mi. W of Borger, via TX 136 **[P. 108, B-6]**. Contains 45,000 acres. **C BT F S HT**

PADRE ISLAND NATIONAL SEASHORE
Between Port Isabel and Corpus Christi **[P. 111, O-12]**. Contains 130,697 acres. **C HK BT F S R**

SABINE NATIONAL FOREST
Hemphill & San Augustine **[P. 110, G-15]**. Contains 158,503 acres. **C HK BT F S HT**

SAM HOUSTON NATIONAL FOREST
Cleveland and New Waverly **[P. 110, J-7]**. Contains 161,320 acres. **C HK BT F S HT**

State Parks

ATLANTA STATE PARK
12 mi. NW of Atlanta off US 59 **[P. 110, E-15]**. Contains 1,475 acres. **C HK BT F S**

BONHAM STATE PARK
3.5 mi. SE of Bonham on FM 271 **[P. 110, E-13]**. Contains 261 acres. **C BT F S**

CADDO LAKE STATE PARK
15 mi. NE of Marshall off TX 43 **[P. 110, F-15]**. Contains 484 acres. **C HK BT F S**

CAPROCK CANYONS STATE PARK
3.5 mi. N of Quitaque off TX 86 **[P. 108, D-7]**. Contains 13,960 acres. **C HK BT F S R**

CLEBURNE STATE PARK
14 mi. SW of Cleburne via US 67 and Park Rd. 21 **[P. 110, G-11]**. Contains 529 acres. **C HK BT F S**

DAINGERFIELD STATE PARK
2 mi. SE of Daingerfield on TX 49 **[P. 110, F-15]**. Contains 551 acres. **C HK BT F S**

EISENHOWER STATE PARK
7 mi. NW of Denison off TX 75A **[P. 110, E-12]**. Contains 457 acres. **C HK BT F S**

FAIRFIELD LAKE STATE PARK
6 mi. N of Fairfield off TX 1124 **[P. 110, G-13]**. Contains 1,460 acres. **C HK BT F S**

FALCON STATE PARK
On Falcon Reservoir, 29 mi. NW of Rio Grande City, in Starr and Zapata Counties **[P. 111, P-10]**. Contains 573 acres. **C HK BT F S**

FORT PARKER STATE PARK
7 mi. S of Mexia on TX 14 **[P. 110, H-13]**. Contains 1,459 acres. **C HK BT F S**

GARNER STATE PARK
7 mi. N of Concan off US 83 in Uvalde County **[P. 111, L-9]**. Contains 1,419 acres. **C HK BT F S**

HUNTSVILLE STATE PARK
10 mi. S of Huntsville off I-45 **[P. 110, J-14]**. Contains 2,083 acres. **C HK BT F S**

LAKE BROWNWOOD STATE PARK
22 mi. NW of Brownwood off TX 279 **[P. 110, G-10]**. Contains 537 acres. **C HK BT F S**

LAKE LIVINGSTON STATE PARK
5 mi. SW of Livingston off FM 1988 **[P. 110, J-14]**. Contains 635 acres. **C HK BT F S BK**

LAKE MINERAL WELLS STATE PARK
4 mi. E of Mineral Wells on US 180 **[P. 110, F-11]**. Contains 2,905 acres. **C HK BT F S R CL**

LAKE SOMERVILLE STATE PARK/BIRCH CREEK UNIT
W of Lyons, off Hwy. 60W on Park Rd. 57, in Burleson County **[P. 110, J-13]**. Contains 3,140 acres. **C HK BT F S R BK**

LAKE SOMERVILLE STATE PARK/NAILS CREEK UNIT
NE of Giddings, 11 mi. N of US 290, in Lee County **[P. 110, J-13]**. Contains 2,630 acres. **C HK BT F S R BK**

LAKE TEXOMA (AC)
N of Denison **[P. 110, E-12]**. Contains 195,326 acres. **C HK BT F S R**

PALO DURO CANYON STATE PARK
Canyon **[P. 108, C-6]**. Contains 16,402 acres. **C HK F R**

SAM RAYBURN DAM & RESERVOIR (AC)
Near Jasper, in Jasper, Sabine, St. Augustine, Angelina & Nacogdoches Counties **[P. 110, H-15]**. Contains 114,500 acres. **C BT F S**

ACTIVE SPORTS

ADVENTURE: Voyageur Outward Bound School, 10900 Cedar Lake Rd., Minnetonka, MN; (800) 328-2943

AEROBICS: AFAA, 8201 Fair Oaks Cross, #1091, Dallas; (214) 503-9034.

BASEBALL: Little League Baseball Texas State HQ, 1612 S. University-Parks Dr., Waco; (817) 756-1816. • **Pony Baseball-Softball,** 7820 Pebbleford Dr., Ft. Worth; (817) 293-1664. • **American Legion Baseball,** Box 821, South Houston; (713) 944-6980. • **Babe Ruth Baseball,** James Wagoner, 2930 Jenny Lind, Fort Smith, AR; (501) 646-3065. • **Men's Senior Baseball League - Dallas,** 7726 El Pastel Dr., Dallas; (214) 991-6294.

BILLIARDS: Royal Rack, 1906 Greenville, Dallas; (214) 824-9733.

BOARDSAILING: M.D. Surf and Skate, Corpus Christi; (512) 854-7873. • **USWA Regional Director,** 244 Spring Rd.,

CONTINUED ON PAGE 211

Texas

CONTINUED FROM PAGE 210

Argyle; (817) 455-2819 • **Windsurfing Gale,** Houston; (713) 529-9002

BOWLING: American Bowling Congress, 5301 S. 76th St., Greendale, WI; (414) 421-6400.

CANOEING & KAYAKING: ACA Central Vice Commodore, 3410 Ridge Rd., N. Little Rock, AR; (501) 758-4716.

CYCLING: Bluebonnet AYH Council, 5302 Crawford Street, Houston; (713) 523-1009. • **LAW South Central Regional Director,** 1618 7th Street South., New Orleans, LA; (504) 899-8575. • **North Texas AYH Council,** 3530 Forest Lane, #127, Dallas; (214) 350-4294. • **Southwest Texas AYH Council,** 2200 South Lakeshore Boulevard., Austin; (512) 444-2294. • **USCF Texas Representative,** 1819 Eagle Meadow Street, San Antonio; (512) 493-8723.

FITNESS: National Strength and Conditioning Ass'n State Director, 2616 W. Beauregard, San Angelo; (915) 658-2702.

FOOTBALL: Pop Warner Football, 1315 Walnut Street, Suite 1632, Philadelphia, PA; (215) 735-1450.

GOLF: Dallas District Golf Association, 4321 Live Oak, Dallas; (214) 823-6004. • **Houston Golf Association,** 1830 S. Millbend Dr., The Woodlands; (713) 367-7999. • **PGA Northern Texas Section,** 500 N. Central Expressway, Suite 272, Plano; (214) 881-4653. • **PGA Southern Texas Section,** 1830 S. Millbend Dr., The Woodlands; (713) 363-0511. • **San Antonio Golf Association,** 10715 Gulfdale, Suite 265, San Antonio; (512) 341-0823. • **Texas Golf Association,** 1000 Westbank Dr., Suite 2B, Austin; (512) 328-4653.

HIKING & CLIMBING: Lone Star Sierra Club Chapter, PO Box 1931, Austin; (512) 477-1729. • **West Texas Trail Walkers, Inc. (AHS),** 1100 Wayland Drive, Arlington; (817) 460-4889.

HOCKEY: USA Hockey Rocky Mountain Registrar, 7335 S. Garfield Ct., Littleton, CO; (303) 721-0936.

HUNTING & FISHING: Hunter Bradlee Co. (Orvis), 4025 Northwest Parkway, Dallas; (214) 363-9213. • **Orvis Houston,** 5848 Westheimer Road, Houston; (713) 783-2111. • **Parks & Wildlife Department,** 4200 Smith School Road, Austin; (512) 389-4800. • **The Tackle Box Outfitters (Orvis),** 6330 North New Braunfels Street, San Antonio; (512) 821-5806.

LACROSSE: Lacrosse Foundation Chapter, 2214 Euclid Ave., Austin; (512) 443-7582. • **Lacrosse Foundation Chapter,** 1851 Bethlehem, Houston; (713) 688-8766.

RACQUETBALL: AARA, 5608 White Haven, Bellaire; (713) 664-4153.

RIDING: Texas Horse Council, PO Box 974, Lancaster; (214) 227-7372

RODEO: PRCA Texas Circuit, Rt. 2, Box 2394, Belton; (817) 939-8758.

RUNNING: RRCA North TX State Rep., 3202 88th St., Lubbock; (806) 793-4664.

SCUBA: Aqua Adventures, Inc., 5418 Broadway Boulevard., Garland; (214) 240-8000. • **Austin Scuba Center,** 1004-B Romeria Drive, Austin; (512) 452-2216. • **Diver's Depot,** PO Box 632687, Macogdoches; (409) 564-3483. • **Divetech, Inc.,** 8713-A Katy Freeway, Houston; (713) 973-2946. • **Scuba Training Center,** 2600 Paramount Street, #B-5, PO Box 19335, Amarillo; (806) 358-0727. • **Sport Divers of Houston, Inc.,** 125 West Bay Area Boulevard , Webster; (713) 338-1611. • **Tropical Divers,** 2250 Thousand Oaks, Suite 212, San Antonio; (512) 490-3483.

SHOOTING: Amarillo Gun Club, PO Box 30064, Amarillo; (806) 372-0678. • **Champion Lake Gun Club, Inc.,** 5615 Hilton View, Houston; (713) 893-5868. • **Clear Creek Gun Range,** 306 Crystal Street, League City; (713) 337-1722 • **Cypress Valley Preserve, Inc.,** PO Box 5783, Austin; (512) 825-3396. • **Honey Creek Sporting Clays,** Rt. 3, Box 174, Hico; (817) 796-2148. • **La Paloma Sporting Club,** PO Box 160516, San Antonio; (512) 980-4424. • **NSCA National Gun Club,** PO Box 680007, San Antonio; (800) 877-5338. • **One In One Hundred Gun Club,** Rt. 1, Box 1021, Kountze; (409) 755-9903. • **San Angelo Claybird Association,** PO Box 61211, San Angelo; (915) 658-1986. • **West Texas Sportsman's Club,** PO Box 14214, Odessa; (915) 561-9379.

SKATING: USFSA, 20 First Street, Colorado Springs, CO; (719) 635-5200.

SOCCER: North Texas Soccer Ass'n, 1740 S. I-35, Suite 112, Carrolton; (214) 323-1323. • **South Texas Soccer Ass'n,** PO Box 35964, Houston; (713) 723-8527 • **South Texas YSA,** PO Box 1370, Georgetown; (512) 863-4969. • **AYSO Regional Director,** 2971 North Coronado Street, Chandler; (602) 839-2114.

SOFTBALL: Houston ASA, 6122 Jessamime Street, Houston; (713) 981-6420. • **Texas ASA,** 1925 Marshall Street, Waco; (817) 836-4274. • **Austin ASA,** 8907 Ravello Pass, PO Box 56, Austin; (512) 280-9107. • **Dallas ASA,** 407 Tanglewood Street, Duncanville; (214) 296-5646. • **Fort Worth ASA,** 600 Congress Street, Fort Worth; (817) 551-7631. • **San Antonio ASA,** 905 E. Hildebrand Avenue., San Antonio; (512) 821-3020.

SQUASH: Concord Athletic Club (USSRA), San Antonio; (512) 828-8880. • **Premier Club (USSRA),** Dallas; (214) 891-6600. • **Texas Club - Dallas (USSRA),** Dallas; (214) 744-2582. • **Texas Club (USSRA),** Houston; (713) 227-7000. • **University of Texas - Austin (USSRA),** Austin; (512) 471-5757.

SWIMMING: LMSC Border Registrar, 600 Willow Glen Drive, El Paso; (915) 571-5626. • **LMSC Gulf Registrar,** 7622 Alcomita Street, Houston; (713) 498-4252. • **LMSC North Texas Registrar,** 1920 Webster Street, Plano; (214) 596-0887. • **LMSC South Texas Registrar,** 2600 Tracy Trail, Austin; (512) 251-0110. • **LMSC West Texas Registrar,** 900 W. Kansas, Midland; (915) 682-7126.

TENNIS: Recreational TEAMTENNIS Central-West Region, National Program Coordinator, 2105 Grant Avnue, #4, Redondo Beach, CA; (800) 992-9042. • **Southern USTA,** 200 Sandy Springs Place, Suite 200, Atlanta, GA; (404) 257-1297. • **Southwestern USTA,** 2164 East Broadway Road, Suite 235, Tempe, AZ; (602) 921-8964. (El Paso County.) • **Texas USTA,** 2111 Dickson Street , Suite 33, Austin; (512) 443-1334.

TRIATHLON: Austin Triathletes, 1806A Ford Street, Austin; (512) 441-5047. • **Bay Area Triathletes,** 416 Deer Fern Drive, League City; (713) 488-1703. • **Finish Line Sports,** 13895 Southwest Freeway, Sugar Lane.; (713) 242-7700. • **Houston Racing,** 7402 Benwich Circle., Houston; (713) 550-1568. • **Sabar,** 6146 Vanderbilt, Dallas; (214) 783-8881. • **Team Northlake,** 8439 Foxhaven, Dalls; (214) 298-9054. • **Team Plano,** 605 E. 18th Street, Plano; (214) 423-4130. • **Tri Dallas,** 3513 Lily Ln., Rowlett; (214) 387-2929.

VOLLEYBALL: USVBA Lone Star Commissioner, Route 3, Box 559, Seguin; (512) 372-3909. • **USVBA North Texas Commissioner,** 3211 S. Houston School Rd., Lancaster; (214) 223-1143. • **USVBA Sun Country Commissioner,** 7818 Cervin Dr., Amarillo; (806) 359-8225.

WHITEWATER RAFTING: Big Bend River Tours, PO Box 317, Lajitas; (915) 424-3219. • **Far Flung Adventures,** PO Box 31, Terlingua; (915) 371-2489. • **Texas River Expeditions, Inc.,** PO Box 301152, Houston; (713) 242-1525.

Tip Offs

Going Back to Camp

On the heels of the fitness boom came an increased demand from adults eager for tutoring in athletic skills they had never quite mastered or had long ago forgotten. Given that gym had suddenly become everyone's favorite class, a return to camp couldn't be far behind.

Adult sports camps tailored to every conceivable athletic pursuit have become a thriving business in the USA. Golf and tennis are among the most popular, with one recent study showing some 60,000 people attending USA golf schools annually, a figure that has more than doubled over the past five years.

Whatever your sport of choice, be prepared for an intensive immersion, replete with video replays, computers and specialized props—and a marked improvement in your skills. The concept wouldn't be so popular if it didn't work.

The following is a sampling of top examples from several sports.

BICYCLING

United States Cycling Federation Development Camp, 5 days, category 3 and 4 (first and second year competitive) senior riders, September-October, Lake Placid, NY and Colorado Springs, CO, (719) 578-4581.

GOLF

John Jacobs Practical Golf School, Scottsdale, AZ (also Palm Springs, CA, Ft. Lauderdale and Orlando, FL, Atlantic City, NJ and Long Island, NY), year-round, two to five-day sessions, (800) 472-5007.

Mt. Snow Golf School, Mt. Snow, VT, (also Crystal River, FL in the winter), two to five-day sessions, adults, juniors, May-October, (800) 451-4211.

Pinehurst Golf Advantage School, Pinehurst, NC, two or five-day sessions, March-October, (800) 634-9297.

The Roland Stafford Golf School, Hanah Country Resort, Margaretville, NY, (also in Stowe, VT, Clymer, NY and Miami Beach, FL). Two or five-day sessions, April-October, (800) 447-8894.

RUNNING AND FITNESS

Craftsbury Center Running Camp, Craftbury Common, VT, June-September, running clinics (plus instruction and activities available in sculling, race walking, horseback riding, triathlon, fitness, orienteering, canoe racing, and cross-country skiing in the winter), (802) 586-7767.

Jeff Galloway's Running and Fitness Vacations, July-August, Lake Tahoe, CA, Atlanta, GA and Blue Ridge Mts, NC, (404) 875-4268.

SKIING

While almost every resort has instruction packages, and most have put more and more effort into this area, the following camps are for racing:

Don Lyon International Racing Development Camp, Mt. Hood, OR, June-July, (613) 236-3904.

Red Lodge International Summer Ski Racing Camp, Red Lodge, MT, June. Contact Mrs. Larkin at (406) 446-1878.

TENNIS

Nick Bollettieri Tennis Camp, Bradenton FL. In addition to his famed, multi-year junior program that boasts such graduates as Andre Agassi, Bollettieri holds week-long sessions for adults year-round, plus similar golf instruction, (813) 755-1000, or (800) USA-NICK.

The Vic Braden Tennis College, Coto de Caza, CA and St. George, UT. Maybe the granddaddy of hi-tech, new age instruction, with two, three or five-day sessions year round, (800) 237-1068.

4 Star Tennis Academy, University of Virginia, Charlottesville, VA, May-August, three, four or seven-day sessions, adults, juniors, (800) 334-STAR.

Van de Meer University, Hilton Head, SC, year round, (also Sweetbriar, VA, June-August), three to five-day sessions, adults, juniors, (803) 785-8388.

GENERAL

Club Getaway, Kent, CT; two to seven day sessions, May-Oct., for adults and families; hiking, rock climbing, basketball, softball, water skiing, and board sailing; (212) 935-0222.

FANTASY CAMPS

Dream Week Inc., Philadelphia, PA, November-April; one week sessions in which grown-up wannabes can rub shoulders, learn from and play with National Football League players, Association of Tennis Professionals touring pros, Major League Baseball All-Stars and nostalgia squads repesenting such MLB teams as the Pirates, Phillies and Royals; (800) 888-4376.

Sportsworld, Pepperdine University, Malibu, CA, January-July and June-August (kids); a similiar concept including a basketball camp with famed former UCLA coach John Wooden, and baseball camps with squads representing the Oakland A's, Minnesota Twins, San Francisco Giants, Cleveland Indians and Milwaukee Brewers; kids camps include golf in San Diego, and volleyball; (415) 215-1000.

Utah

While Brigham Young University and the NBA Jazz have put Utah on the national sports map, some of the state's top attractions can be found outdoors. Whitewater rafting as we know it originated here in 1932. Canyons on the Colorado, Green, San Juan and other Utah rivers feature rapids from the most placid to the wildest. ◆ Light, dry powder at Alta, Sundance, and 13 other ski resorts have made Salt Lake a longtime frontrunner to host the Winter Olympics. ◆ Camping and hiking are an adventure at Dinosaur National Monument, where you'll see petroglyphs carved into the sides of mountains and giant fossils preserved in rock. The Arches' desert formations and Bryce Canyon's limestone pinnacles are hikers' favorites. ◆ For mountain biking, try Slick Rock Trail. Also in the Moab area: the Canyonlands Fat Tire Festival (October) and the Jeep Safari (Easter weekend).

▶ SPECTATOR VENUES

Baseball

DERKS FIELD
1301 South West Temple, Salt Lake City **[P. 112, B-8]**. Capacity: 10,200
Salt Lake Trappers (Pioneer League, Rookie Class); (801) 484-9900. Entered League in 1985. Broadcasts by KALL 910 AM. MLB affiliation, Independent.

Basketball

THE SALT PALACE
100 South West Temple, Salt Lake City **[P. 112, B-7]**. Built in 1969. Capacity: 12,616.
Utah Jazz (NBA Western Conf., Midwest Div.); (801) 575-7800. Franchise began in 1974. Broadcasts by KISN 570 AM, KSTU Channel 13.

College Sports

BRIGHAM YOUNG UNIVERSITY
Provo **[P. 112, E-4]**; (801) 378-2096. Cougar, capacity 65,000. Marriott Center, capacity 22,700.

SOUTHERN UTAH STATE THUNDERBIRDS
Cedar City **[P. 113, K-2]**; (801) 586-1937. Thunderbird, capacity 5,000. Centrum, capacity 5,300.

UNIVERSITY OF UTAH
Salt Lake City **[P. 112, B-8]**; (801) 581-8171. Rice, capacity 35,000. Jon M. Huntsman Center, capacity 15,000.

UTAH STATE UNIVERSITY AGGIES
Logan **[P. 112, B-4]**; (801) 750-1850. Romney, capacity 30,000. Spectrum, capacity 10,200.

WEBER STATE COLLEGE WILDCATS
3750 Harrison Blvd., Ogden **[P. 112, C-4]**; (801) 626-6500. Wildcat, capacity 17,500. Dee Center, capacity 12,000.

Hockey

SALT PALACE
100 South West Temple, Salt Lake City **[P. 112, B-7]**. Capacity: 10,700.
Salt Lake Golden Eagles (International Hockey League); (801) 534-4777. Franchise began in 1984. Broadcasts by KRSP 1230 AM.

PGA/LPGA

JEREMY RANCH GOLF CLUB
8770 N. Jeremy Rd., Park City **[P. 112, D-5]**; (801) 649-2700.
Showdown Classic (Senior PGA), Aug.
Number of holes: 54.

Rodeo

SALT PALACE
101 S West Temple, Salt Lake City **[P. 112, B-7]**; (801) 538-8443.
Day of the Forty Seven Rodeo, September.

Soccer

DERKS FIELD
1301 S. West Temple Ave., Salt Lake City **[P. 112, B-8]**. Capacity: 10,185.
Salt Lake Sting (American Professional Soccer League, Western Conference); (801) 487-8464.
◆The Sting is a local favorite. Fans sat through a downpour and lightening storm during the team's first game at this stadium.

▶ OUTDOOR VENUES

National Parks

Bike Trails: BK
Boating: BT
Camping: C
Climbing: CL
Diving: DV
Fishing: F
Golfing: G
Hiking: HK
Hunting: HT
Riding: R
Surfing: SU
Swimming: S
Tennis: TE
Whitewater: WW
Winter Sports: W

ARCHES NATIONAL PARK
Moab **[P. 113, H-7]**. Contains 73,379 acres. **C HK**

ASHLEY NATIONAL FOREST
Vernal **[P. 112, D-6, F-5]**. Contains 1,384,133 acres. **C HK BT F S R**

BRYCE CANYON NATIONAL PARK
SE of Panguitch **[P. 113, L-4]**. Contains 35,835 acres. **C HK R W**

CANYONLANDS NATIONAL PARK
Moab **[P. 113, J-7]**. Contains 337,570 acres. **C HK R WW**

CAPITOL REEF NATIONAL PARK
Torrey **[P. 113, J-5]**. Contains 241,904 acres. **C HK CL**

DINOSAUR NATIONAL MONUMENT
E of Vernal **[P. 112, E-7]**. Contains 211,141 acres. **C HK F CL**

DIXIE NATIONAL FOREST
Cedar City **[P. 113, K-4, L-1]**. Contains 1,883,846 acres. **C HK BT F S R BK W**

FISHLAKE NATIONAL FOREST
Richfield **[P. 112 & 113, G-4, H-4, J-4]**. Contains 1,424,913 acres. **C HK BT F R BK W**

FLAMING GORGE NATIONAL RECREATION AREA
UT 191, NE Utah, in Ashley National Forest **[P. 112, D-8]**. **C HK BT F S W**

GLEN CANYON NATIONAL RECREATION AREA
UT 95 or US 89, Lake Powell, south central **[P. 113, L-5]**. Contains 1,236,880 acres. **C HK BT F S**

MANTI-LA SAL NATIONAL FOREST
Price **[P. 112 & 113, F-5, J-8, K-7]**. Contains 1,238,410 acres. **C HK BT F R W**

UINTA NATIONAL FOREST
Provo **[P. 112, E-5, F-3 & 4]**. Contains 813,445 acres. **C HK BT F S R BK W**

WASATCH-CACHE NATIONAL FOREST
Northcentral & Northeastern Utah **[P. 112, C-4, D-5, E-3, F-3]**. Contains 560,643 acres. **C HK BT F S R BK W**

ZION NATIONAL PARK
Springdale **[P. 113, L-2]**. Contains 146,597 acres. **C HK R W CL**

USA SNAPSHOTS®

A look at statistics that shape the sports world

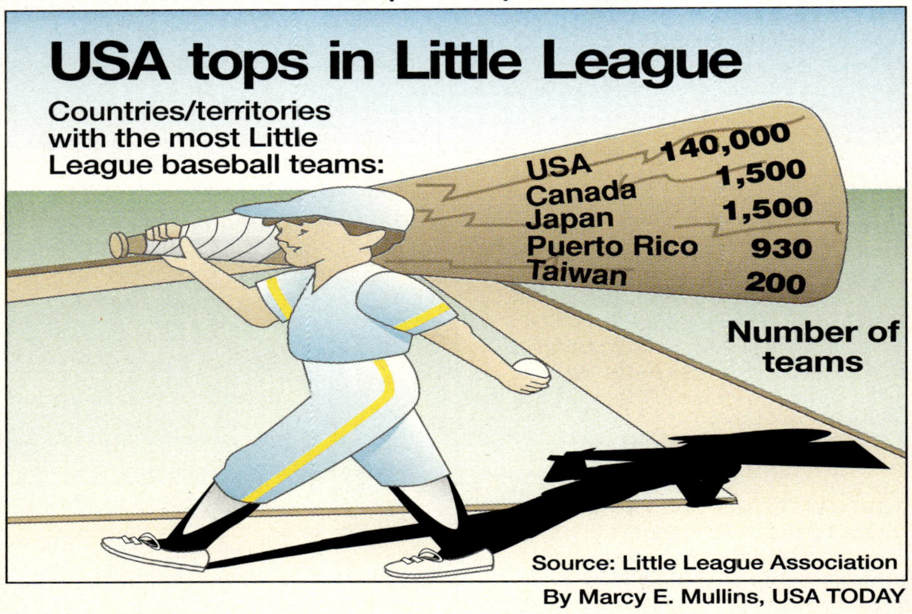

USA tops in Little League
Countries/territories with the most Little League baseball teams:
USA 140,000
Canada 1,500
Japan 1,500
Puerto Rico 930
Taiwan 200
Number of teams
Source: Little League Association

By Marcy E. Mullins, USA TODAY

STATBOX

POPULATION: 1,715,000
SQUARE MILES: 84,990
TIME ZONE: Mountain
MOTTO: None
BIRD: California Gull
TREE: Blue Spruce
CAPITAL: Salt Lake City
AVERAGE ANNUAL RAINFALL: 13"
MEAN TEMP: 50
MAJOR LEAGUE TEAMS: 1
NATIONAL PARK/FOREST ACREAGE: 10,716,021
STATE PARK ACREAGE: 94,893
HIGHEST ELEVATION: 13,528'
LOWEST ELEVATION: 2,200'
WATERWAYS: 400 miles of raftable rivers; 1,000 fishable lakes

State Parks

CORAL PINK SAND DUNES STATE PARK
35 mi. NW of Kanab **[P. 113, M-3]**. Contains 3,730 acres. **C HK**

DEER CREEK STATE PARK
US 189, 8 mi. SW of Heber City **[P. 112, E-5]**. Contains 3,260 acres. **C BT F S W**

EAST CANYON STATE PARK
UT 65, 25 mi. NE of Salt Lake City **[P. 112, D-4]**. Contains 267 acres. **C HK BT F S BK**

HUNTINGTON STATE PARK
Off UT 10, 2 mi. NW of Huntington **[P. 112, D-4]**. Contains 111 acres. **C HK BT F S**

MILLSITE STATE PARK
Off UT 10, 4 mi. W of Ferron **[P. 113, H-5]**. Contains 111 acres. **C BT F S W**

OTTER CREEK STATE PARK
4 mi. N of Antimona **[P. 113, J-4]**. Contains 80 acres. **C BT F S W**

ROCKPORT STATE PARK
Off I-80, 30 mi. E of Salt Lake City & 4 mi. S of Wanship **[P. 112, D-5]**. Contains 550 acres. **C BT F S W**

STARVATION STATE PARK
4 mi. NW of Duchesne **[P. 112, E-6]**. Contains 3,310 acres. **C BT F**

WASATCH MOUNTAIN STATE PARK
2 mi. NW of Midway **[P. 112, E-5]**. Contains 21,592 acres. **C HK F R W G**

WILLARD BAY STATE PARK
15 mi. N of Ogden **[P. 112, C-4]**. Contains 2,673 acres. **C BT F S W**

Skiing

ALPINE SKIING

ALTA
Highway 210, Little Cottonwood Canyon, Alta **[P. 112, E-4]**; (801) 742-3333.
Vertical drop is 2,050 feet. Has three tows and eight chairs.
◆Utah's deep, dry powder and the steep runs make Alta and nearby Snowbird premier areas.

BRIAN HEAD SKI RESORT
Highway 143, Brian Head **[P. 113, K-3]**; (801) 677-2035.
Vertical drop is 1,200 feet. Has seven chairs.

DEER VALLEY
2250 Deer Valley Drive South, Park City **[P.**

CONTINUED ON PAGE 213

Utah

CONTINUED FROM PAGE 212

112, D-5]; (801) 649-1000.
Vertical drop is 2,200 feet. Has eleven chairs.

PARK CITY SKI AREA
1345 Lowell Avenue, Park City **[P. 112, D-4]**; (801) 649-8111.
Vertical drop is 3,100 feet. Has twelve chairs and one gondola.
◆Remnants of what was the country's largest silver mining camp are still visible from some of the trails here.

SNOWBIRD SKI & SUMMER RESORT
Little Cottonwood Canyon, Snowbird **[P. 112, E-4]**; (801) 742-2222.
Vertical drop is 3,100 feet. Has seven chairs and one tram.

SOLITUDE SKI RESORT
Big Cottonwood Canyon, Salt Lake City **[P. 112, E-4]**; (801) 534-1400.
Vertical drop is 2,030 feet. Has seven chairs.

SUNDANCE
North Fork, Provo Canyon, Provo **[P. 112, E-4]**; (801) 225-4107.
Vertical drop is 2,150 feet. Has four chairs.

NORDIC SKIING

HOMESTEAD RESORT
975 West Golf Course Drive, Midway **[P. 112, E-5]**; (801) 654-5810.

MOUNTAIN DELL
Parley's Canyon, Salt Lake City **[P. 112, D-4]**; (801) 582-3812.

SOLITUDE NORDIC CENTER
Big Cottonwood Canyon, Highway 190, Salt Lake City **[P. 112, E-4]**; (801) 272-7613.

WHITE PINE TOURING
Payne's Canyon Drive, Park City **[P. 112, D-5]**; (801) 649-8701.

ACTIVE SPORTS

ADVENTURE: Colorado Outward Bound School, 945 Pennsylvania Street, Denver, CO; (800) 477-2627.

AEROBICS: AFAA, 7724 S. Silver Lake Dr., Salt Lake City; (801) 942-8437.

BASEBALL: Little League Baseball Western Region HQ, 6707 Little League Dr., San Bernadino, CA; (714) 887-6444. • **American Legion Baseball,** 9321 S. 3400 W., W. Jordan; (801) 255-3081. • **Babe Ruth Baseball,** Dennis R. Poarch, 809 W. Gibson Rd., Woodland, CA; (415) 581-6879. • **Men's Senior Baseball League - Salt Lake City,** 9204 Winter Wren Dr., Sandy; (801) 943-2250.

BOARDSAILING: BYU Outdoors Unlimited, Provo; (801) 378-3390. • **FreeSailing ,** Salt Lake City; (801) 521-0167. • **USWA Regional Director,** PO Box 6272, Laguna Niguel, CA; (714) 495-0368.

BOWLING: American Bowling Congress, 5301 S. 76th St., Greendale, WI; (414) 421-6400.

CANOEING & KAYAKING: ACA Rocky Mountain Vice Commodore, c/o Four Corners Marine, Box 379, Durango, CO; (303) 259-3893.

CYCLING: USCF Utah Representative, 1591 Canyon Rd., Ogden; (801) 392-4019.

FITNESS: Governor's Council on Health & Physical Fitness, 496 East Pioneer Avenue , Sandy; (801) 485-1852. • **National Strength and Conditioning Association State Director,** University of Utah, JH Center, Salt Lake City; (801) 581-4548.

FOOTBALL: Pop Warner Football, 1315 Walnut Street, Suite 1632, Philadelphia, PA; (215) 735-1450.

GOLF: PGA Utah Section, 419 E., 100 South, Salt Lake City; (801) 532-7421. • **Utah Golf Association,** 1512 South 1100 E., Salt Lake City; (801) 466-1132.

HIKING & CLIMBING: Utah Sierra Club Chapter, 177 East 900 South, Suite 102, Salt Lake City; (801) 363-9621.

HOCKEY: USA Hockey Rocky Mountain Registrar, 7335 S. Garfield Ct., Littleton, CO; (303) 721-0936.

HUNTING & FISHING: Department of Natural Resource, 1636 W. North Temple, Salt Lake City; (801) 533-9333. • **Trout Unlimited,** 5968 S. 400 West, Westvalley; (801) 957-2834.

RACQUETBALL: AARA, 88 N. 600E, Orem; (801) 225-4943.

RODEO: PRCA Wilderness Circuit, 254 Clinton Drive, Twin Falls, ID; (208) 536-2772.

SCUBA: Thunder Island Divers, 2465 North Main, Sunset; (801) 776-6316. • **Thunder Island Divers, Inc.,** 2520 West 4700 South, Salt Lake City; (801) 968-9600.

SKATING: USFSA, 20 First Street, Colorado Springs, CO; (719) 635-5200.

SOCCER: Utah YSA, 42 E. Claybourne Avenue, Salt Lake City; (801) 467-0451. • **AYSO Regional Director,** 1720 Carmel Dr., Idaho Falls, ID; (208) 526-4485.

SOFTBALL: Utah ASA, 6002 South 1300 East, Salt Lake City; (801) 262-2856.

SQUASH: Desert Gymnasium, Salt Lake City; (801) 359-3911.

SWIMMING: LMSC Utah Registrar, 2676 S. 1900 E., Salt Lake City; (801) 486-8525.

TABLE TENNIS: USTTA State Coordinator, 573 North Sir Michael Dr., Salt Lake City; (801) 877-3341.

TENNIS: Recreational TEAMTENNIS Central-West Region, National Program Coordinator, 2105 Grant Ave., #4, Redondo Beach, CA; (800) 992-9042. • **Intermountain USTA,** 1201 South Parker Rd., #102, Denver, CO; (303) 695-4117.

VOLLEYBALL: USVBA Inter-Mountain Commissioner, 945 Pheasant Creek, Logan; (801) 752-4084.

WHITEWATER RAFTING: Don Hatch River Expeditions , Box 1150, Vernal; (801) 789-4316. • **Holiday River Expeditions ,** 544 East 3900 South, Salt Lake City; (801) 266-2087. • **Land Escape Expeditions ,** 112 East Covecrest Dr., Price; (801) 637-0842. • **Sheri Griffith River Expeditions ,** PO Box 1324, Moab; (800) 332-3200. • **Western River Expeditions ,** 7258 Racquet Club Dr., Salt Lake City; (801) 942-6669. • **Wild Rivers Expeditions ,** PO Box 118, 101 Main Bluff; (801) 672-2244.

◆ ◆ ◆

Tip Offs: College Conferences: Part II

CONTINUED FROM PAGE 182

Mid-American Conference,
Four SeaGate, Suite 102,
Toledo, OH 43604
419-249-7177

Mid-Eastern Athletic Conference,
P.O. Box 21205,
Greensboro, NC 27420-1205
919-275-9961

Middle Atlantic States Collegiate Athletic Conference,
Widener U., Chester, PA 19013
215-499-4525

Midwest Collegiate Athletic Conference,
Lake Forest College,
Lake Forest, IL 60045
312-234-3100

Midwestern Collegiate Conference,
One Pan American Plaza,
201 S. Capitol, Suite 500,
Indianapolis, IN 46225
317-237-5622

Missouri Valley Conference,
100 N. Broadway, Suite 1135, St. Louis, MO 63102
314-421-0339

National Collegiate Athletic Association
6201 College Blvd.
Overland Park, KS 66211
913-339-1906

New England Collegiate Conference,
Keene State College, 229 Main Street,
Keene, NH 03431
603-352-1909

North Atlantic Conference,
P.O. Box 69, Orono, ME 04469
207-866-2383

North Central Intercollegiate Athletic Conference,
2400 N. Louise, Ramkota Inn,
Sioux Falls, SD 57107
605-338-0907

North Coast Athletic Conference,
P.O. Box 16679,
Cleveland, OH 44116
216-871-8100

Northeast Conference,
900 Route 9, Suite 120,
Woodbridge, NJ 07095
201-636-9119

Northeast-10 Conference,
American International College, 1000 State Street, Springfield, MA 01109
413-736-8245

Northern Intercollegiate Conference,
Winona State U., Winona, MN 55987
507-457-5295

Northwest Conference of Independent Colleges,
P.O. Box 328,
Gig Harbor, WA 98335
206-858-9404

Ohio Valley Conference,
278 Franklin Rd., Suite 103,
Brentwood, TN 37027
615-371-1698

Old Dominion Athletic Conference,
P.O.Box 971, Salem, VA 24153
703-389-7373

Pacific-10 Conference,
800 S. Broadway,
Walnut Creek, CA 94596
415-932-4411

Patriot League,
3897 Adler Place, Bldg. C., Suite 310,
Bethlehem, PA 18017
215-691-2414

Rocky Mountain Athletic Conference,
2940 E. Bates Ave.,
Denver, CO 80210
303-753-0600

South Atlantic Conference,
5250 77 Center Dr., Suite 350,
Charlotte, NC 28217
704-522-0011

Southeastern Athletic Conference,
3000 Galleria Tower, Suite 990,
Birmingham, AL 35244
205-985-3685

Southern Conference,
Ten Woodfin St., Suite 206, Asheville, NC 28801
704-255-7872

Southland Conference,
1309 West 15th, Suite 303,
Plano, TX 75075
214-424-4833

Southwest Athletic Conference,
1300 West Mockingbird, Suite 444,
Dallas, TX 75247
214-634-7353

Southwestern Athletic Conference,
Louisiana Superdome,
New Orleans, LA 70112
504-523-7574

Sun Belt Conference,
1408 N. Westshore Blvd., Suite 1010,
Tampa, FL 33607
813-872-1511

Trans America Athletic Conference,
337 S. Milledge Ave., Suite 200,
Athens, GA 30605
404-548-3369

University Athletic Association, 668 Mt. Hope Avenue,
Rochester, NY 14620
716-275-3814

West Coast Conference,
400 Oyster Point Blvd., Suite 221,
South San Francisco, CA 94080
415-873-8622

Western Athletic Conference,
14 West Dry Creek Circle,
Littleton, CO 80120-4478
303-795-1962

Yankee Conference,
U. of Delaware, Newark, DE 19716
302-451-1818

Vermont

The first chairlift in the USA was opened on Mt. Mansfield in 1940, appropriate since Vermont's 29 ski resorts average nearly 50 percent more vertical drop and more skiing (900 downhill trails) than anywhere else in the East. ◆ You can sample the vivid green of the summers by heading out onto the Long Trail, a 272-mile trek from Massachusetts to Quebec. The oldest formal hiking trail in America, it is easily accessible in the Green Mountains. ◆ Canoeing is popular in the West River area, the Upper Connecticut River and major tributaries of Lake Champlain. ◆ The Bud Light Triathlon circuit makes a stop in Shelburne (July). ◆ Malletts Bay (Colchester) is a nice spot for sailing. ◆ Hunters take more white-tailed deer in Vermont than anywhere else in New England. ◆ The Battenkill River is one of the top trout fishing streams in the northeast.

STATBOX

POPULATION: 567,000
SQUARE MILES: 9,606
TIME ZONE: Eastern
MOTTO: Freedom and Unity
BIRD: Hermit Thrush
TREE: Sugar Maple
CAPITAL: Montpelier
AVERAGE ANNUAL RAINFALL: 34"
MEAN TEMP: 44
MAJOR LEAGUE TEAMS: 0
NATIONAL PARK/FOREST ACREAGE: 324,119
STATE PARK ACREAGE: 34,812
HIGHEST ELEVATION: 4,393'
LOWEST ELEVATION: 95'
WATERWAYS: 5,000 miles of rivers and streams, 288 public lakes (20 acres plus)

▶ SPECTATOR VENUES

College Sports

MIDDLEBURY COLLEGE PANTHERS
Middlebury **[P. 74, G-2]**; (802) 388-0259. Porter, capacity 5,000. Memorial, capacity 2,000.

NORWICH UNIVERSITY CADETS
Northfield **[P. 74, G-3]**; (802) 485-2230. Sabine Field, capacity 6,000. Andrew Hall, capacity 1,500.

ST. MICHAEL'S COLLEGE PURPLE KNIGHTS
Winooski Park, Colchester **[P. 74, E-2]**; (802) 655-2000. "Doc" Jacobs Field. Ross Center.

UNIVERSITY OF VERMONT CATAMOUNTS
Burlington **[P. 74, B-2]**; (802) 656-3074. Gutterson, capacity 3,180.

Museums & Halls of Fame

AMERICAN MUSEUM OF FLY FISHING
Historic Route 7A & Seminary Ave., Manchester **[P. 75, L-2]**; (802) 362-3300.

PGA/LPGA

STRATTON MOUNTAIN COUNTRY CLUB
Stratton Mountain Road, Stratton Mountain **[P. 75, L-2]**; (802) 297-2200.
Stratton Mountain LPGA Classic, Aug.
Number of holes: 90.

Tennis

STOWE POLO CLUB
616 West Hill Road, Stowe **[P. 74, F-3]**; (802) 888-7685.
◆Summer, outdoor games from May 15 to Oct. 15 at above address. Winter, indoor games rest of year, 5.4 mi. N of Stowe on Route 100. Polo school for all levels of skill.

▶ OUTDOOR VENUES

National Parks

GREEN MOUNTAIN NATIONAL FOREST
On Route 7 North, Rutland **[P. 75, G-2; P. 75, K-2]**. Contains 363,000 acres.
C HK BT F S W HT

State Parks

Bike Trails: BK
Boating: BT
Camping: C
Climbing: CL
Diving: DV
Fishing: F
Golfing: G
Hiking: HK
Hunting: HT
Riding: R
Surfing: SU
Swimming: S
Tennis: TE
Whitewater: WW
Winter Sports: W

ASCUTNEY STATE PARK
3 mi. NW of Ascutney off US 5 **[P. 75, K-3]**. Contains 1,984 acres.
C HK W HT

BOMOSEEN STATE PARK
4 mi. N of Hydeville on Route 4 **[P. 75, J-2]**. Contains 2,739 acres.
C HK BT F S

BRANBURY STATE PARK
11 mi. S of Middlebury **[P. 75, H-2]**. Contains 96 acres.
C HK BT F S

BURTON ISLAND STATE PARK
3.5 mi. SW of St. Albans Bay for Ferry **[P. 74, D-2]**. Contains 253 acres. **C HK BT F S HT**

COOLIDGE FOREST STATE PARK
2 mi. N of Plymouth via VT 100A **[P. 75, J-3]**. Contains 16,165 acres. **C HK F W HT**

EMERALD LAKE STATE PARK
North Dorset on US 7 **[P. 75, K-2]**. Contains 430 acres. **C HK BT F S HT**

GRANVILLE GULF STATE PARK
In Granville and Warren **[P. 74, G-2]**. Contains 1,171 acres. **HK F W**

GROTON STATE FOREST
Midway between Montpelier and St. Johnsbury **[P. 74, F-4]**. Contains 25,625 acres.
C HK BT F S W HT

LAKE CARMI STATE PARK
6 mi. NW of Enosburg Falls **[P. 74, C-2]**. Contains 482 acres. **C HK BT F S HT**

LAKE ST. CATHERINE STATE PARK
3 mi. S of Poultney **[P. 75, K-1]**. Contains 117 acres. **C HK BT F S**

MOUNT MANSFIELD STATE FOREST
Mount Mansfield **[P. 74, E-3]**. Contains 27,613 acres. **C HK BT F S W HT**

SAND BAR STATE PARK
I-89, exit 17 **[P. 74, E-1]**. Contains 20 acres.
BT S

SILVER LAKE STATE FOREST
0.25 mi. N of Barnard on Town Road **[P. 75, H-3]**. Contains 34 acres. **C BT F S HT**

WOODFORD STATE PARK
10 mi. E of Bennington on Highway 9 **[P. 75, M-2]**. Contains 400 acres. **C HK BT F S HT**

Skiing

ALPINE SKIING

ASCUTNEY MTN RESORT
Route 44, Brownsville **[P. 75, K-3]**; (802) 484-7711.
Vertical drop is 1,530 feet. Has four chairs.

BOLTON VALLEY RESORT
Bolton **[P. 74, F-3]**; (802) 434-2131.
Vertical drop is 1,625 feet. Has one bar and five chairs.

JAY PEAK RESORT
Route 242, Jay **[P. 74, D-3]**; (802) 988-2611.
Vertical drop is 2,153 feet. Has two bars, three chairs and one tram.

KILLINGTON SKI RESORT
Killington **[P. 75, J-3]**; (802) 422-3333.
Vertical drop is 3,175 feet. Has two bars, fifteen chairs and one gondola.
◆Extensive snow making, and the longest lift in North America. Six mountains offer abundant, lengthy, intermediate trails.

MAD RIVER GLEN
Route 17, Waitsfield **[P. 74, G-2]**; (802) 496-3551.
Vertical drop is 2,000 feet. Has four chairs.

MOUNT SNOW RESORT
Route 100, Mount Snow **[P. 75, M-2]**; (802) 464-3333.
Vertical drop is 1,700 feet. Has two tows and sixteen chairs.
◆The biggest mountain in southern New England.

OKEMO MOUNTAIN
RR #1, Ludlow **[P. 75, K-3]**; (802) 228-4041.
Vertical drop is 2,150 feet. Has two bars and eight chairs.

PICO SKI RESORT
H.C.R. 34, Rutland **[P. 75, J-3]**; (802) 775-4345.
Vertical drop is 1,967 feet. Has two bars and seven chairs.

SMUGGLERS' NOTCH SKI RESORT
Route 108, Smugglers' Notch **[P. 74, E-3]**; (802) 644-8851 or (800) 451 8752.
Vertical drop is 2,610 feet. Has two tows and four chairs.

STOWE SKI RESORT
RR # 108, Stowe **[P. 74, E-3]**; (802) 253-7311.
Vertical drop is 2,350 feet. Has nine chairs and one gondola.
◆Vermont's highest mountain offers the top expert runs in the East. A complete resort with an international reputation.

STRATTON MOUNTAIN
Off Route 30, Stratton Mountain **[P. 75, L-2]**; (802) 297-2200.
Vertical drop is 2,003 feet. Has eleven chairs and one gondola.

SUGARBUSH RESORT
Off Route 100, Warren **[P. 74, G-2]**; (802) 583-2381.
Vertical drop is 2,600 feet. Has one tow, three bars and twelve chairs.

SUICIDE SIX SKI AREA
4 mi. N of Woodstock, Woodstock **[P. 75, J-3]**; (802) 457-1666.
Vertical drop is 650 feet. Has one bar and two chairs.

NORDIC SKIING

BLUEBERRY HILL
RD 3, Goshen **[P. 75, H-2]**; (802) 247-6735.

BLUEBERRY LAKE XC
Warren **[P. 74, G-2]**; (802) 496-6687.

BRATTLEBORO OUTING CLUB SKI HUT
Upper Drummerston Road, Brattleboro **[P. 75, M-3]**; (802) 254-4081.

BURKE MOUNTAIN XC
Mountain Road, East Burke **[P. 74, E-5]**; (802) 626-8338.

CAMEL'S HUMP NORDIC CENTER
East Street, Huntington **[P. 74, F-2]**; (802) 434-2704.

CATAMOUNT FAMILY CENTER
421 Governor Chittenden Road, Williston **[P. 74, F-2]**; (802) 879-6001.

CONTINUED ON PAGE 215

USA SNAPSHOTS®

A look at statistics that shape the sports world

Burning up the lanes

Professional bowlers with the most 300 games in PBA national tournaments:

1 – since record keeping began in 1959

Source: Professional Bowlers Association

By Julie Stacey, USA TODAY

Vermont

CONTINUED FROM PAGE 214

CRAFTSBURY NORDIC CENTER
Craftsbury Common **[P. 74, E-4]**; (802) 586-7767.

FOX RUN
Fox Lane, Route 100 & 103, Ludlow **[P. 75, K-3]**; (802) 228-8871.

GRAFTON PONDS XC CENTER
Route 121, Main Street, Grafton **[P. 75, L-3]**; (802) 843-2231.

HAZEN'S NOTCH XC CENTER
Route 58, Montgomery Center **[P. 74, D-3]**; (802) 326-4708.

HERMITAGE XC SKI AREA
Coldbrook Road, Wilmington **[P. 75, M-2]**; (802) 464-3511.

HIGHLAND LODGE
Craftsbury Road, Greensboro **[P. 74, E-4]**; (802) 533-2647.

MOUNTAIN MEADOWS XC
Thundering Brook Road, Killington **[P. 75, J-3]**; (802) 775-7077.

MOUNTAIN TOP CROSS COUNTRY
Mountain Top Road, Chittenden **[P. 75, J-2]**; (800) 445-2100.

PROSPECT MOUNTAIN XC
Route 9, Woodford **[P. 75, M-2]**; (802) 442-2575.

SITZMARK SKI CENTER
East Dover Road, Wilmington **[P. 75, M-2]**; (802) 464-5498.

STERLING RIDGE INN
Junction Hill Road, Jeffersonville **[P. 74, E-2]**; (802) 644-8265.

STRATTON XC CENTER
Stratton Access Road, Stratton **[P. 75, L-2]**; (802) 297-1880.

SUGAR SHACK NORDIC CENTER
The Village at Smugglers' Notch, Jeffersonville **[P. 74,E-3]**; (802) 644-8851. ext. 173.

SUGARBUSH XC SKI CENTER
Sugarbush Golf Course, Warren **[P. 74, G-2]**; (802) 583-2301.

TIMBER CREEK XC SKI CENTER
Route 100, Mount Snow **[P. 75, M-2]**; (802) 464-0999.

TRAPP FAMILY LODGE XC
Luce Hill Road, Stowe **[P. 74, E-3]**; (802) 253-8511.
◆Most closely approximates the European ski touring experience. Trapp's was the first and has set the standard for New England touring centers.

VIKING XC SKI CENTRE
Little Pond Road, Londonderry **[P. 75, L-3]**; (802) 824-3933.

WILD WINGS XC CENTER
North Road, Peru **[P. 75, L-2]**; (802) 824-6793.

WOLF RUN RESORT
Boston Post Road, Bakersfield **[P. 74, D-3]**; (802) 933-4007.

WOODSTOCK SKI CENTER
Route 106, Woodstock **[P. 75, J-3]**; (802) 457-2114.

▶ ACTIVE SPORTS

BASEBALL: Little League Baseball Eastern Region HQ, PO Box 3485, Williamsport, PA; (717) 326-1921 • **American Legion Baseball,** 18 E. Center St., Rutland; (802) 775-5721. • **Babe Ruth Baseball,** Ernest P. Papazoglou, 71 Tracy Ave., Lynn, MA; (617) 595-7603. • **Men's Senior Baseball League - Vermont,** Box 233, Mt. Holly; (802) 259-2637.

BOARDSAILING: New England Sailboard Academy , Jamaica; (802) 874-4178. • **USWA Regional Director,** 18354 W. 58th Pl. #62, Golden, CO; (303)279-3185.

BOWLING: American Bowling Congress, 5301 S. 76th St., Greendale, WI; (414) 421-6400.

CANOEING & KAYAKING: ACA New England Vice Commodore, 785 Bow Ln., Middleton, CT.

CYCLING: LAW New England Regional Director, PO Box 305, Atkinson, NH, (603) 362-4572. • **USCF Vermont Representative,** PO Box 214, Hillview Rd., Richmond; (802) 434-3305.

FITNESS: Governor's Council on Physical Fitness & Sports, c/o Vermont Recreation Division, 103 S. Main, Waterbury; (802) 244-8713. • **National Strength and Conditioning Ass'n State Director,** c/o RFD 1, Box 5940, Montpelier.

FOOTBALL: Pop Warner Football, 1315 Walnut Street, Suite 1632, Philadelphia, PA; (215) 735-1450.

GOLF: PGA New England Section, 1 Audubon Rd., Wakefield, MA; (617) 246-4653. • **Vermont Golf Association,** 117 Crescent Street, Rutland; (802) 773-7693.

HOCKEY: USA Hockey New England Registrar, 15 Orange Street, Rumford, RI; (401) 438-2954.

HUNTING & FISHING: Fish and Game Department, Waterbury Complex, 103 South Main St., Waterbury; (802) 244-7331. • **Orvis Manchester,** Historic Rt. 7A, Manchester; (802) 362-3750. • **The Classic Outfitters & Fly Fishing Shop (Orvis),** Champlain Mill, Winooski; (802) 655-7999. • **Trout Unlimited,** Box 308, Jonesville; (802) 434-3915.

LACROSSE: Lacrosse Foundation Chapter, c/o Vermont Systems, 12 Market Place, Essex Junction; (802) 879-6993.

RACQUETBALL: AARA, 5 Stanton Drive, Essex Junction; (802) 875-4966.

RIDING: Vermont Horse Council, RD 1, Box 344, Perkinsville; (802) 263-9398.

RODEO: PRCA First Frontier Circuit, 5982 Summit Bridge Rd., Townsend, DE; (302) 378-4551.

RUNNING: RRCA VT State Rep., Upper North St., Box 170, Montpelier; (802) 223-2080.

SCUBA: Great Outdoors Trading Co., 41 Center Street, Rutland; (802) 775-6531.

SHOOTING: Tinmouth Hunting Preserve, Ltd., RR 1, Box 556, Wallingford; (802) 446-2337.

SKATING: Northern New York Skating Association, 116 Shore Dr., Pittsfield, MA; (413) 443-3466. • **USFSA,** 20 First Street, Colorado Springs, CO; (719) 635-5200.

SOCCER: Vermont Soccer Ass'n, RR 1, Box 1128E, Charlotte; (802) 425-3832.

SOFTBALL: Vermont ASA, 80 Airport Parkway, South Burlington; (802) 863-2761.

SQUASH: Twin Oaks Tennis & Fitness Center (USSRA), South Burlington; (802) 658-0001.

TENNIS: Recreational TEAMTENNIS East Region, National Program Coordinator, 246 N. Reservoir St., Lancaster, PA; (800) 633-6122. • **New England USTA,** PO Box 587, Needham Heights, MA; (617) 964-2030.

Tip Offs: Canada

The nation to our north is still the spiritual home of North American hockey with seven NHL franchises, and one more to start play in Ottawa in 1992 (see below). In the meantime, the Expos try to keep baseball alive in Montreal's cavernous Olympic Stadium, and the perennially second-place Blue Jays draw more than any other team in the Major Leagues up in Toronto's SkyDome.

Baseball

OLYMPIC STADIUM
4549 Pierre De Coubertin St., Montreal, Quebec **[P. 127]**. Built in 1976. Capacity: 43,739
◆The ballpark is accessed by one of the finest subway systems in the world. Use the Pie-IX Stop (pronounced pee-nuff). The hot dog is first rate at the park, as is the corned beef-like sandwich called a smoked meat ("viande fume"). All announcements in French first, then in English. Great French dining in town. Try Les Halles first.
Montreal Expos (NL East); (514) 253-3434. Franchise began in 1969. Broadcasts by CFCF 600 AM, CTV, TSN (all English), CKAC 730 AM, CBFT-TV, RDS (French). Affiliates: Indianapolis, IN (AAA); Harrisburg, PA (AA); West Palm Beach, FL (A); Jamestown, NY (A); Rockford, IL (A); Bradenton, FL (Rookie). Spring training held in West Palm Beach, FL.

SKYDOME
300 The Esplanade West, Toronto, Ontario **[P. 127]**. Built in 1989. Capacity: 49,500
◆The Blue Jays moved into this space age, giant, retractable dome building when they abandoned the old Exhibition Stadium. Some think this one could still be called "exhibition stadium," because built-in hotel rooms overlook the field, and on at least two occassions in 1990, hotel guests got overenthusiastic and, visible to almost all, put on a show more heated than anything happening on the field.
Toronto Blue Jays (AL East); (416) 341-1000. Franchise began in 1977. Broadcasts by CJCL-AM 1430, CFTO-TV 9, TSN Cable TV. Affiliates: Syracuse, NY (AAA); Knoxville, TN (AA); Dunedin, FL (A); Myrtle Beach, SC (A); St. Catharines, Ont. (A); Medicine Hat. Alberta (Rookie). Spring training held in Dunedin, FL.

Hockey

COLISEE DE QUEBEC
2205 Ave du Colisee, Quebec City, Quebec **[P. 127]**. Built in 1949. Capacity: 15,399.
◆Began in World Hockey League, 1972. Moved to NHL in 1979.
Quebec Nordiques (NHL, Wales Conf., Adams Div.); (418) 529-8441. Franchise began in 1979. Broadcasts by CJRP 1060 AM (40 station network), CFAP 2 Quarte-Saisons.

FORUM DE MONTREAL
2313 St. Catherine St.,West, Montreal, Quebec **[P. 127]**. Built in 1924. Capacity: 16,197.
◆Resonates hockey with a great tradition. Fans here are very vocal (in French, no less).
Montreal Canadiens (NHL, Wales Conference, Adams Division); (514) 932-2582. Franchise began in 1916. Broadcasts by CBF (690 AM), CFCF (600 AM), CBMT (6), CFTM (10), CBFT (2).

MAPLE LEAF GARDENS
60 Carlton St., Toronto, Ontario **[P. 127]**. Built in 1931. Capacity: 16,182.
Toronto Maple Leafs (NHL, Campbell Conference, Norris Division); (416) 977-1641. Franchise began in 1917. Broadcasts by TBS (CJCL 1430 AM), CBC-TV 5 and Global TV.

NORTHLANDS COLISEUM
7424 118th Ave., Edmonton, Alberta **[P. 126]**. Built in 1974. Capacity: 17,503.
◆Initially a World Hockey League franchise, the Oilers moved to the NHL in 1979.
Edmonton Oilers (NHL, Campbell Conference, Smythe Division); (403) 474-8561. Franchise began in 1972. Broadcasts by CFRN 1260 AM, CITV Channel 13/Cable 8, CBXT TV Channel 5/Cable 4.

OLYMPIC SADDLEDOME
Olympic Way & 14th Ave., Calgary, Alberta **[P. 126]**. Built in 1983. Capacity: 20,132.
◆The Flames started out in Atlanta in 1972 and moved to Calgary in 1980.
Calgary Flames (NHL, Campbell Conference, Smythe Division); (403) 261-0475. Franchise began in 1980. Broadcasts by CFR Radio (660 AM), CKKX-TV (Channels 2 & 7), CBC-TV (Channels 6 & 9).

PACIFIC COLISEUM
100 North Renfrew St., Vancouver, British Columbia **[P. 126]**. Built in 1968. Capacity: 16,123.
Vancouver Canucks (NHL, Campbell Conference, Smythe Division); (604) 254-5141. Franchise began in 1970. Broadcasts by CKNW (980 AM), CBC Channel 2, BCTV Channel 8.

VENUE TO BE ANNOUNCED
Ottawa, Ontario.
◆An NHL expansion team is scheduled to begin play here in October, 1992.
Ottawa Senators (NHL, Conference & Division TBA); (613) 726-0540. Franchise will begin in 1992.

WINNIPEG ARENA
15-1430 Maroons Road, Winnipeg, Manitoba **[P. 126]**. Built in 1956. Capacity: 15,393. Member of World Hockey League from 1972 - 1979.
Winnipeg Jets (NHL, Campbell Conference, Smythe Division); (204) 783-5387. Franchise began in 1979. Broadcasts by CKY AM 580, CKY-TV.

Virginia

Virginia offers a little bit of everything: the Blue Ridge Mountains, Shenandoah National Park and Virginia Beach for outdoor recreation; major stock car racing; lots of minor league baseball and hockey; and major college sports at the University of Virginia and Virginia Tech. ◆ Auto racing is popular with the NASCAR Winston Cup circuit making four stops at Virginia's two tracks: Richmond International Raceway and Martinsville Speedway. ◆ The annual Virginia Gold Cup steeplechase competition at the Great Meadow (May) is the state's top equestrian event. ◆ A hike on the Appalachian Trail is a lesson in history as well as nature. ◆ Visit the Potomac and Chesapeake Bay for boating and fishing. Or try your luck on the James River, where you'll find some of the best small-mouth and large-mouth fishing in the USA.

STATBOX

POPULATION: 6,098,000
SQUARE MILES: 40,815
TIME ZONE: Eastern
MOTTO: Sic Temper Tyranni
BIRD: Cardinal
TREE: Dogwood
CAPITAL: Richmond
AVERAGE ANNUAL RAINFALL: 38-44"
MEAN TEMP: 53-59
MAJOR LEAGUE TEAMS: 0
NATIONAL PARK/FOREST ACREAGE: 3,403,000
STATE PARK ACREAGE: 52,609
HIGHEST ELEVATION: 5,729'
LOWEST ELEVATION: sea level
WATERWAYS: 4,500 miles of rivers and streams; 50,000 ponds and lakes

▶ SPECTATOR VENUES

Auto Racing

MARTINSVILLE SPEEDWAY
220 South, near NC border, Martinsville **[P. 114, H-7]**; (703) 956-3151. Track is 0.526 miles.
Hanes Activewear 500 (NASCAR Winston Cup), April.
Goody's 500 (NASCAR Winston Cup), September.

RICHMOND INTERNATIONAL RACEWAY
Laburnam Ave. at the Atlantic Rural Expostion Grounds, Richmond **[P. 117, F-13]**; (804) 329-6796. Track is 0.750 miles.
Pontiac Excitement 400 (NASCAR Winston Cup), Feb.
Miller 400 (NASCAR Winston Cup), Sep.

Baseball

CALFEE PARK
Fifth & Pierce Ave., Pulaski **[P. 114, G-5]**. Capacity: 2,000
Pulaski Braves (Appalachian League); (703) 980-8200. Entered League in 1982. Broadcasts by WBLB 1340 AM. MLB affiliation, Atlanta Braves.

CITY STADIUM
Fort Ave. & Wythe Rd., Lynchburg **[P. 115, B-9]**. Capacity: 4,000
Lynchburg Red Sox (Carolina League, Class A); (804) 528-1144. Entered League in 1966. Broadcasts by WLLL 930 AM & WAMV 1420 AM. MLB affiliation, Boston Red Sox.

DEVAULT MEMORIAL STADIUM
1501 Euclid Avenue, Bristol **[P. 114, H-3]**. Capacity: 1,200
Bristol Tigers (Appalachian League, Rookie Class); (703) 466-8310. Entered League in 1943. Broadcasts by WBBI AM 1250. MLB affiliation, Detroit Tigers.

ENGLISH FIELD
Commonwealth Blvd. & Chatham Heights, Martinsville **[P. 114, H-7]**. Capacity: 3,200
Martinsville Phillies (Appalachian League, Rookie Class); (703) 666-2000. Entered League in 1988. MLB affiliation, Philadelphia Phillies.

METROPOLITAN PARK
6000 Northhampton Blvd., Norfolk **[P. 114, C-5]**. Capacity: 6,162
Tidewater Tides (International League, Class AAA); (804) 461-5600. Entered League in 1969. Broadcasts by WTAR 790-AM. MLB affiliation, New York Mets.

PRINCE WILLIAM COUNTY STADIUM
7 County Complex Ct., Woodbridge **[P. 115, D-11]**. Capacity: 6,000
Prince William Cannons (Carolina League, Class A); (703) 590-2311. Entered League in 1984. Broadcasts by WQRA 94.3 FM. MLB affiliation, New York Yankees.

SALEM MUNICIPAL FIELD
620 Florida St., Salem **[P. 114, B-5]**. Capacity: 5,000
Salem Buccaneers (Carolina League, Class A); (703) 389-3333. Entered League in 1968. Broadcasts by WROV 1240AM. MLB affiliation, Pittsburgh Pirates.

THE DIAMOND
3001 North Blvd., Richmond **[P. 117, F-12]**. Capacity: 12,000
◆Has superboxes, just like most major league parks. Great BBQ across the street.
Richmond Braves (International League, Class AAA); (804) 359-4444. Entered League in 1966. Broadcasts by WRNL 910-AM. MLB affiliation, Atlanta Braves.

WAR MEMORIAL STADIUM
1889 West Pembroke Ave., Hampton **[P. 114, C-4]**. Capacity: 4,330
Peninsula Pilots (Carolina League, Class A); (804) 244-2255. Entered League in 1976. Broadcasts by WHOV 88.3 FM. MLB affiliation, Seattle Mariners.

Bowling

PINBOYS OF CHESAPEAKE
112 Medical Parkway, Chesapeake **[P. 114, D-4]**; (804) 436-4444.
AMF Cobra Classic (LPBT), September.

College Sports

COLLEGE OF WILLIAM & MARY TRIBE
Williamsburg **[P. 114, A-1]**; (804) 221-3400. Cary Field, capacity 15,000. W&M Hall, capacity 10,700.

GEORGE MASON UNIVERSITY PATRIOTS
4400 University Drive, Fairfax **[P. 115, D-14]**; (703) 323-2320. PE Building, capacity 3,000.

JAMES MADISON UNIVERSITY DUKES
South Main Street, Harrisonburg **[P. 115, E-9]**; (703) 568-6164. Madison, capacity 15,000. Convocation Center, capacity 7,600.
◆A little school with big basketball ambitions. The Dukes also have one of the true characters of the game in coach Lefty Driesell. The lefthander's favorite way to preface any statement is "Well, ya know, I don't know."

LIBERTY UNIVERSITY FLAMES
Lynchburg **[P. 115, B-9]**; (804) 582-2100. Liberty, capacity 12,000. Vines Center, capacity 9,000.

OLD DOMINION UNIVERSITY MONARCHS
Norfolk **[P. 114, C-4]**; (804) 683-3375. Foreman Field, capacity 26,000. N&PE Building, capacity 5,200.

RADFORD UNIVERSITY HIGHLANDERS
Radford **[P. 114, G-4]**; (703) 831-5228. Dedmon Center, capacity 5,000.

ST. PAUL'S COLLEGE TIGERS
Lawrenceville **[P. 115, H-10]**; (804) 848-4189. Russell Field, capacity 3,000. T.W. Gym, capacity 2,000.

U.S. MARINE CORPS ACADEMY
Quantico **[P. 115, E-11]**; (703) 640-2174. Butler, capacity 15,000. Larson, capacity 2,000.

UNIVERSITY OF RICHMOND SPIDERS
Richmond **[P. 117, F-11]**; (804) 289-8371. Richmond, capacity 22,000. Robins Center, capacity 10,000.

UNIVERSITY OF VIRGINIA WAHOOS & CAVALIERS
Charlottesville **[P. 115, B-13]**; (804) 982-5100. Scott, capacity 42,000. University Hall, capacity 8,200.

VIRGINIA COMMONWEALTH UNIVERSITY RAMS
Richmond **[P. 117, F-12]**; (804) 367-1277. Coliseum, capacity 10,716.

VIRGINIA MILITARY INSTITUTE KEYDETS
Route 11 North, Lexington **[P. 115, F-8]**; (703) 464-7251. Alumni Memorial, capacity 10,000. Cameron Hall, capacity 5,000.

VIRGINIA POLYTECHNIC INSTITUTE & STATE U. GOBBLERS & HOKIES
Blacksburg **[P. 114, G-6]**; (703) 231-6796. Lane, capacity 51,000. Cassell Coliseum, capacity 9,971.

VIRGINIA STATE UNIVERSITY TROJANS
Petersburg **[P. 115, G-11]**; (804) 524-5000. Rogers, capacity 5,000. Daniel Gym, capacity 3,454.

WASHINGTON & LEE UNIVERSITY GENERALS
Lexington **[P. 115, F-8]**; (703) 463-8670. Wilson Field, capacity 7,000. Warner Center, capacity 2,500.

Hockey

LANCERLOT SPORTS COMPLEX
1111 Vineyard Rd., Vinton **[P. 114, B-7]**. Capacity: 4,006.
Roanoke Valley Rebels (East Coast Hockey League); (703) 345-3557. Franchise began in 1988.

RICHMOND COLISEUM
601 E. Leigh St., Richmond **[P. 117, F-13]**. Capacity: 9,200.
Richmond Renegades (East Coast Hockey League); (804) 643-7825. Franchise began in 1990.

SCOPE PLAZA
201 Brambleton Ave., Norfolk **[P. 114, D-4]**. Capacity: 8,800.
Hampton Roads Admirals (East Coast Hockey League); (804) 640-8447. Franchise began in 1989.

Museums & Halls of Fame

UNITED STATES SLO-PITCH SOFTBALL ASSOCIATION HALL OF FAME MUSEUM
3935 South Crater Rd., Petersburg **[P. 115, G-11]**; (804) 732-4099.

PGA/LPGA

GREENBRIER COUNTRY CLUB
1301 Volvo Parkway, Chesapeake **[P. 114, D-4]**; (804) 547-7375.
Crestar-Farm Fresh Classic (LPGA), May. Number of holes: 54.

KINGSMILL GOLF CLUB
100 Golf Club Rd., Williamsburg **[P. 114, A-2]**; (804) 253-3941. Anheuser-Busch Golf

CONTINUED ON PAGE 217

USA SNAPSHOTS®

A look at statistics that shape the sports world

Major turnout at minor leagues

Minor league baseball teams with the highest average home attendance this year:

Team	League	Avg. attendance/ game
Buffalo Bisons	Amer. Assn. (AAA)	16,147
Louisville Redbirds	Amer. Assn.	8,210
Scranton W. B. Red Barons	Intl. (AAA)	7,885
Nashville Sounds	Amer. Assn.	7,227
Richmond Braves	Intl.	6,210

Source: Howe Sports Data International

By Bob Laird, USA TODAY

Virginia

CONTINUED FROM PAGE 216

Classic (PGA), June. Number of holes: 72.

Polo

BULL RUN POLO CLUB
Clifton **[P. 115, D-11]**; (703) 385-3888.

MIDDLEBURG POLO CLUB
16 Wirt St. SW, Lees **[P. 115, D-10]**; (703) 777-1403.

Track & Field

ARTHUR ASHE JR. ATHLETIC CENTER
3001 North Blvd., Richmond **[P. 117, F-12]**; (804) 780-6131.
East Coast Invitational, Jan.

SPORTS RECREATION COMPLEX
Route 123 & University Drive, George Mason University, Fairfax **[P. 115, D-11]**; (703) 323-2325.
Mobil 1 Invitational (USA/Mobil Grand Prix Event), Feb.

STREETS OF ARLINGTON, VIRGINIA AND WASHINGTON, D.C.
Iwo Jima Memorial, Arlington **[P. 54, F-3]**; (703) 640-2225.
Marine Corps Marathon, November.

▶ OUTDOOR VENUES

National Parks

- Bike Trails: BK
- Boating: BT
- Camping: C
- Climbing: CL
- Diving: DV
- Fishing: F
- Golfing: G
- Hiking: HK
- Hunting: HT
- Riding: R
- Surfing: SU
- Swimming: S
- Tennis: TE
- Whitewater: WW
- Winter Sports: W

GEORGE WASHINGTON NATIONAL FOREST
Along western border of VA, Winchester to Covington **[P. 115, G-11]**. Contains 1,100,000 acres.
C HK BT F S R BK WW

EFFERSON NATIONAL OREST
rom Natural Bridge Big Stone Gap **[P. 4, G-2, F-6 & 7]**. ntains 704,000 res.
HK BT F S R BK W WW

MOUNT ROGERS NATIONAL RECREATION AREA
In Jefferson National Forest, S of Marion off I-81, or SW of Wytheville **[P. 114, H-5]**. Contains 116,000 acres. **C HK F S R BK W CL**

SHENANDOAH NATIONAL PARK
Btwn. Front Royal & Charlottesville, off I-66 & 64 **[P. 115, E-9]**. Contains 196,000 acres. **C HK F R BK W CL**

State Parks

BREAKS INTERSTATE PARK
On VA 80 in Breaks **[P. 114, G-3]**. Contains 4,200 acres. **C HK BT F S**

BURKE LAKE PARK
6 mi. SW of I-495 exit 5W via CR 620, CR 645 and SR 123 **[P. 115, D-11]**. Contains 888 acres. **C HK F BK**

CLAYTON LAKE STATE STATE PARK
4 mi. S of Radford via I-81, then 2 mi. on VA 660 **[P. 114, G-6]**. Contains 472 acres.
C HK BT F S R

DOUTHAT STATE PARK
6 mi. N of Clifton Forge on VA 629 **[P. 114, F-7]**. Contains 4,493 acres. **C HK BT F S**

> **"You have access to one of the best beaches in the country. . . you're not that far from the mountains, and the weather is good."**
>
> **Buffalo Bills football star *Bruce Smith***

FAIRY STONE STATE PARK
8 mi. W of Bassett on SR 57 **[P. 114, H-7]**. Contains 4,570 acres. **C HK BT F S BK**

HOLLIDAY LAKE STATE PARK
6 mi. NE of Appomatox on VA 24, then 4 mi. E via VA 626/629 **[P. 115, G-9]**. Contains 250 acres. **C HK BT F S**

HUNGRY MOTHER STATE PARK
3 mi. NE of Marion on VA 16 **[P. 114, H-4]**. Contains 2,180 acres. **C HK BT F S R**

LAKE FAIRFAX PARK
7 mi. W of I-495 exit 10W via VA 7 and CR 606 **[P. 115, D-11]**. Contains 376 acres. **C HK BT F S**

POCAHONTAS STATE PARK
4 mi. SW of Chesterfield off VA 655 **[P. 117, H-11]**. Contains 7,604 acres. **C HK BT F S BK W HT**

POHICK BAY REGIONAL PARK
I-95 to Lorton exit, S on US 1 to Gunston Rd. and 3 mi. E **[P. 115, D-11]**. Contains 1,000 acres. **C HK BT F S R G**

RIVERBEND PARK
10 mi. W of I-495 exit 13, via VA 193, CR 603 and Jeffrey Rd. (CR 1268) **[P. 115, D-11]**. Contains 409 acres. **HK BT F WW**

SEASHORE STATE PARK
Cape Henry on US 60 **[P. 114, C-6]**. Contains 2,670 acres. **C HK BT F BK**

SMITH MOUNTAIN LAKE STATE PARK
From US 460, VA 43 to Route 626 south **[P. 114, G-7]**. Contains 1,506 acres. **C HK BT F S**

STAUNTON RIVER STATE PARK
9 mi. SE of Scottsburg on VA 344 **[P. 115, H-9]**. Contains 1,287 acres. **C HK BT F S**

WESTMORELAND STATE PARK
5 mi. NW of Montross on VA 3 **[P. 115, E-12]**. Contains 1,295 acres. **C HK BT F S BK W**

Skiing

ALPINE SKIING

MASSANUTTEN VILLAGE SKI AREA
Route 644, Harrisonburg **[P. 115, E-9]**; (703) 289-9441.
Vertical drop is 1,153 feet. Has one bar and four chairs.

THE HOMESTEAD SKI AREA
On VA 220, Hot Springs **[P. 114, F-7]**; (703) 839-7721.
Vertical drop is 700 feet. Has one tow, two bars and one chair.

NORDIC SKIING

MOUNTAIN LAKE RESORT
Route 700, Mountain Lake **[P. 114, G-6]**; (800) 346-3334.

▶ ACTIVE SPORTS

AEROBICS: AFAA, 203 Yoakum Parkway, Unit 217, Alexandria; (703) 370-3354.

BASEBALL: Little League Baseball Southern Region HQ, PO Box 13366, St. Petersburg, FL; (813) 344-2661. • **American Legion Baseball,** 114 Darden Dr., Poquoson; (804) 868-6858. • **Babe Ruth Baseball,** William E. Whitehurst, Rt. 2, Box 56, Grifton, NC; (919) 524-5525.

BILLIARDS: Obelisk Billiard Club, 14346 Warwick Blvd., Newport News; (804) 874-8588.

BOARDSAILING: Buckroe Water Sports, Hampton; (804) 827-6260. • **Chick's Beach Sailing Center,** Virginia Beach; (804) 481-3067. • **USWA Regional Director,** 1912 MacCumber Ln., Wilmington, NC; (919) 256-3553.

BOWLING: American Bowling Congress, 5301 S. 76th St., Greendale, WI; (414) 421-6400.

CANOEING & KAYAKING: ACA Middle States Vice Commodore, 10236 Raider Ln., Fairfax; (703) 359-2594.

CYCLING: LAW Coastal Regional Director, 205 E. Joppa Road, Baltimore, MD; (301) 828-8604. • **USCF Virginia/Washington DC Representative,** 946 Shillelagh Rd., Chesapeake; (804) 547-7905.

FITNESS: Governor's Commission on Physical Fitness & Sports, c/o Lloyd Bird High School, 1301 Court House Rd., Chesterfield; (804) 796-5987.

FOOTBALL: Pop Warner Football, 1315 Walnut Street, Suite 1632, Philadelphia, PA; (215) 735-1450. • **U.S. Flag Football League,** 5834 Pine Tree Drive, Sanibel, FL; (813) 472-0544.

GOLF: PGA Middle Atlantic Section, 7270 Cradlerock Way, Columbia, MD; (301) 621-8320. • **Virginia State Golf Association,** 6952 Forest Hill Ave., Suite B, Richmond; (804)378-2300.• **Washington Metropolitan Golf Association,** 8012 Colorado Springs Dr., Springfield; (703) 569-6311.

HIKING & CLIMBING: Appalachian Long Distance Hikers (AHS), 13220 Yates Ford Rd., Clifton; (215) 756-6995. • **Natural Bridge Appalachian Trail Club (AHS),** Box 3012, Lynchburg; (804) 239-6557. • **Old Dominion ATC (AHS),** PO Box 25283, Richmond; (804) 796-6763. • **Potomac Appalachian Trail Club,** 1718 N St. Northwest, Washington, DC; (202) 638-5306. • **Roanoke ATC (AHS),** PO Box 12282, Roanoke; (703) 366-7784. • **The Appalachian Mountain Club ,** 5 Joy St., Boston, MA; (617) 523-0636. • **Tidewater ATC (AHS),** Box 8246, Norfolk; (804) 898-5157. • **Virginia Sierra Club Chapter,** PO Box 14648, Richmond; (703) 978-4782. • **Virginia Tech Outing Club (AHS),** PO Box 538, Blacksburg; (703) 552-8587. • **Virginia Trails Association (AHS),** 13 Maple St., Alexandria; (703) 548-7490.

HOCKEY: USA Hockey Southeastern District, PO Box 5208, Takoma Park, MD; (301) 622-0032.

HUNTING & FISHING: Department of Game & Inland Fisheries, 4010 W. Broad St., Richmond; (804) 367-1000. • **Orvis Roanoke,** Market Square, 19 Campbell Ave., Roanoke; (703) 345-3635. • **Stoney Creek Tackle Co. (Orvis),** Valley Green Center, Box 452, Wintergreen; (804) 361-2424. • **The Classic Sportsman (Orvis),** The Marketplace at Kingsmill, Rt. 60 East, Williamsburg; (804) 220-4911. • **Trout Unlimited,** PO Box 838, Waynesboro; (703) 943-2336.

LACROSSE: Lacrosse Foundation Chapter, 5757 University Place, Apt. 102, Virginia Beach; (804) 456-5684.

RACQUETBALL: AARA, 308 Glenn Dr., Sterling; (703) 430-0666.

RIDING: Virginia Horse Council, Rt. 2, Box 273, Newport (703) 552-9010.

RODEO: PRCA First Frontier Circuit, 5982 Summit Bridge Rd., Townsend, DE; (302) 378-4551.

SCUBA: Cassidy's Great Adventures, Inc., 7229 Nathan Court, Manassas; (703) 361-3483. • **Chesapeake Diving Center,** 1815 West Queen Street, Hampton; (804) 838-2218. • **The Ocean Window,** 6715-K Backlick Road, Springfield; (703) 440-9771.

SHOOTING: Eastern Shore Safaris, Box 37, Rt. 183, Jamesville; (804) 442-6035.

SKATING: USFSA, 20 First Street, Colorado Springs, CO; (719) 635-5200.

SOCCER: Virginia YSA, 1614 Rosemont Court, McLean; (703) 356-3252. • **AYSO Regional Director,** 4014 Oneida St., New Hartford, NY; (315) 737-5610.

SOFTBALL: Central Virginia ASA, 6924 Lakeside Ave., Richmond; (804) 262-0142. • **Piedmont ASA,** 101 Lupine Ln., Charlottesville; (804) 973-5925. • **Tidewater Virginia ASA,** 9460 Granby Street, Norfolk; (804) 583-0379.

SQUASH: Sentara Athletic Club (USSRA), Norfolk; (804) 625-2222.

SWIMMING: LMSC Potomac Valley Registrar, 4913 Kingston Dr., Annandale; (703) 354-2130. • **LMSC Virginia Registrar,** 211 - 66th Street, Virginia Beach; (804) 422-6811.

TENNIS: Recreational TEAMTENNIS East Region, National Program Coordinator, 246 N. Reservoir St., Lancaster, PA; (800) 633-6122. • **Mid-Atlantic USTA,** PO Drawer F, Springfield; (703) 321-9045.

TRIATHLON: Northern VA Tri Club, PO Box 1611, Winchester; (703) 667-6431.

VOLLEYBALL: USVBA Chesapeake Commissioner, 10139 Grist Mill Ct., Manassas; (703) 361-3815. • **USVBA Old Dominion Commissioner,** 1304 Grey Ct. Ave., Richmond; (804) 264-3692.

WHITEWATER RAFTING: Richmond Raft Company , 4400 E. Main Street, Richmond; (804) 222-RAFT.

Tip Offs: East Coast Bluefish Regulations

Federal Waters (three to 200 miles) have a ten fish limit. Otherwise, in almost every coastal state, some form of local bluefish regulation is either proposed or already in effect. Here is where they stood a year ago:

Maine	No regulation
New Hampshire	10-fish limit
Massachusetts	10-fish limit
Rhode Island	10-fish limit
Connecticut	10-fish limit,(pending legislative approval)
New York	No regulation
New Jersey	No regulation
Delaware	10-fish limit
Maryland	8-inch minimum
Virginia	10-fish limit
North Carolina	No regulation
South Carolina	No regulation
Georgia	15-fish limit, 12 inches or longer
Florida	10-inch minimum

Washington

Washington has 2,600 miles of shoreline, 8,000 lakes and Seattle is among the nation's leaders in per-capita boat ownership. The city was also chosen as the most "bicycle-friendly" metro area in the USA by Cycling magazine (1990). ◆ For an unforgettable two-wheel tour, ride around the San Juan Islands (Puget Sound) during berry-picking season in the fall. ◆ The NBA SuperSonics are Washington's oldest big-league franchise (1967-68) and the only one with a league title. The NFL Seahawks and American League baseball Mariners share the Kingdome in Seattle, a city which actually averages less annual rainfall than New York. ◆ Fish the Pacific Ocean and the Sound for salmon, inland waters for trout. ◆ Much of the state's recreational bounty is showcased in the Sea to Ski Race (Washingon has 13 alpine resorts) from Mt. Baker to Bellingham, Memorial Day weekend.

► SPECTATOR VENUES

Auto Racing

SEATTLE INTERNATIONAL RACEWAY
Highway 18, Kent **[P. 120, F-5]**; (206) 631-1550. Track is quarter-mile strip (for NHRA races).
Jolly Rancher Northwest Nationals (NHRA), early Aug.

Baseball

CHENEY STADIUM
2525 Bantz Blvd., Tacoma **[P. 120, G-2]**. Capacity: 8,500
Tacoma Tigers (Pacific Coast League, Class AAA); (206) 752-7707. Entered League in 1960. Broadcasts by KLAY 1180 AM. MLB affiliation, Oakland Athletics.

EVERETT MEMORIAL STADIUM
39th & Broadway, Everett **[P. 118, A-4]**. Capacity: 2,400
Everett Giants (Northwest League, Class A); (206) 258-3673. Entered League in 1984. Broadcasts by KWYZ 1230 AM. MLB affiliation, San Francisco Giants.

INTERSTATE FAIRGROUNDS STADIUM
N. 602 Havana, Spokane **[P. 120, B-7]**. Capacity: 8,314
Spokane Indians (Northwest League, Class A); (509) 535-2922. Entered League in 1983. MLB affiliation, San Diego Padres.

JOE MARTIN STADIUM
1500 Orleans Street, Bellingham **[P. 118, B-6]**. Capacity: 2,200
Bellingham Mariners (Northwest League, Class A); (206) 671-6347. Entered League in 1973. Broadcasts by KGMI 790 AM. MLB affiliation, Seattle Mariners.

PARKER FIELD
1015 South 16th Ave., Yakima **[P. 118, H-4]**. Capacity: 3,148
Yakima Bears (Northwest League, Class A); (509) 457-5151. Entered League in 1990. Broadcasts by KUTI 980 AM. MLB affiliation, Los Angeles Dodgers.

THE KINGDOME
201 S. King Street, Seattle **[P. 120, C-3]**. Built in 1976. Capacity: 57,748
Seattle Mariners (AL West); (206) 628-3555. Franchise began in 1977. Broadcasts by KIRO-AM 710, KSTW-TV Channel 11. Affiliates: Calgary, Alberta (AAA); Jacksonville, FL (AA); San Bernardino, CA (A); Hampton, VA (A); Bellingham, WA (Rookie); Tempe, AZ (Rookie). Spring training held in Tempe, Az.

Basketball

THE SEATTLE CENTER COLISEUM
305 Harrison St., Seattle **[P. 120, C-3]**. Built in 1962. Capacity: 14,132.
Seattle Supersonics (NBA Western Conf., Pacific Div.); (206) 281-5800. Franchise began in 1967. Broadcasts by KJR 950 AM, Prime Sports Northwest Channel 6, KING Channel 5.

YAKIMA SUNDOME
at the Washington State Fairgrounds, 1301 South Tenth St., Yakima **[P. 120, C-3]**. Capacity: 6,006.
Yakima Sun Kings (Continental Basketball Association, American Conf., Midwest Div.); (509) 248-1222. Entered League in 1990. Broadcasts by KUTI 980 AM.

Bowling

SKYWAY PARK BOWL
11819 Renton Ave. South, Seattle **[P. 120, D-4]**; (206) 772-1220.

Seattle Open (PBA), June.

College Sports

EASTERN WASHINGTON UNIVERSITY EAGLES
Cheney **[P. 119, D-13]**; (509) 359-2463. Woodward, capacity 9,000. Reese Court, capacity 5,000.

GONZAGA UNIVERSITY BULLDOGS & ZAGS
E. 502 Boone Avenue, Spokane **[P. 120, B-7]**; (509) 328-4220. Martin Center, capacity 2,900.

UNIVERSITY OF WASHINGTON HUSKIES
Seattle **[P. 120, B-3]**; (206) 543-2210. Husky, capacity 72,400. Hec Edhundson Pavilion, capacity 8,000.

WASHINGTON STATE UNIVERSITY COUGARS
107 Bohler Gym, Pullman **[P. 119, E-14]**; (509) 335-0311. Clarence Martin, capacity 40,000. Friel Court, capacity 12,058.

Football

KINGDOME
201 South King Street, Seattle **[P. 120, C-3]**. Built in 1976. Capacity: 64,984.
Seattle Seahawks (AFC Western Division); (206) 827-9777. Franchise began in 1976. Broadcasts by KIRO AM 710.

Horse Racing

LONGACRES PARK
1621 S.W. 16th, Renton **[P. 120, E-4]**; (206) 226-3131. Opened in 1933. Clubhouse capacity: 2,850. Grandstand capacity: 9,000. Total capacity: 17,500.
Thoroughbred season from Apr. to Sep.
◆Recently purchased by Boeing and subleased for racing, the land may be redeveloped before 1992 season.

PLAYFAIR RACE COURSE
N. Altamont & E. Main St., Spokane **[P. 120, B-7]**; (509) 534-0505. Opened in 1905. Clubhouse capacity: 400. Grandstand capacity: 4,000. Total capacity: 5,350.
Thoroughbred season from July to Nov.
◆Revival in 1935.

SUN DOWNS
Off Tenth & S. Oak Sts., Benton-Franklin County Fair Grounds, Kennewick **[P. 119, G-11]**; (509) 582-5434. Opened in 1963. Total capacity: 3,800.
Thoroughbred season from Apr. to May.
◆Mixed meet with quarterhorses. Races also in September.

YAKIMA MEADOWS
at Washington State Fairgrounds, 1301 S. 10th St., Yakima **[P. 118, H-4]**; (509) 248-3920. Opened in 1961. Clubhouse capacity: 1,200. Grandstard capacity: 2,200. Total capacity: 4,900.
Thoroughbred season from Nov. to March.

PGA/LPGA

INGLEWOOD COUNTRY CLUB
6505 Inglewood Rd. N.E., Kenmore **[P. 120, A-4]**; (206) 488-8800.
GTE Northwest Classic (Senior PGA), Aug. Number of holes: 54.

MERIDIAN VALLEY COUNTRY CLUB
24830 136th Ave. S.E., Kent **[P. 120, F-4]**; (206) 631-3131.
Safeco Classic (LPGA), Sep. Number of holes: 72.

Polo

BELLINGHAM POLO CLUB
Dahlberg Rd., Bellingham **[P. 118, B-6]**; (206) 733-8190.

SPOKANE POLO CLUB
8100 W. Sunset Hwy. (U.S. 2), Spokane **[P. 120, B-5]**; (509) 353-4700.

Rodeo

ELLENSBURG RODEO ARENA
Kittatas City Fairgrounds, off Chestnut St Ellensburg **[P. 119, E-9]**; (509) 925-2833. Ellensburg Rodeo, August.

Soccer

MEMORIAL STADIUM (SEATTLE CENTER)
815 Fourth Ave. North, Seattle **[P. 120, C-3]**. Capacity: 11,500.
Seattle Storm (American Professional Soccer League); (206) 441-3390.
◆To resume league play in 1992.

TACOMA DOME
2727 East D Street, Tacoma **[P. 120, G-2]**. Capacity: 19,500.
Tacoma Stars (Major Soccer League); (206) 572-7827.

USA SNAPSHOTS®

A look at statistics that shape the sports world

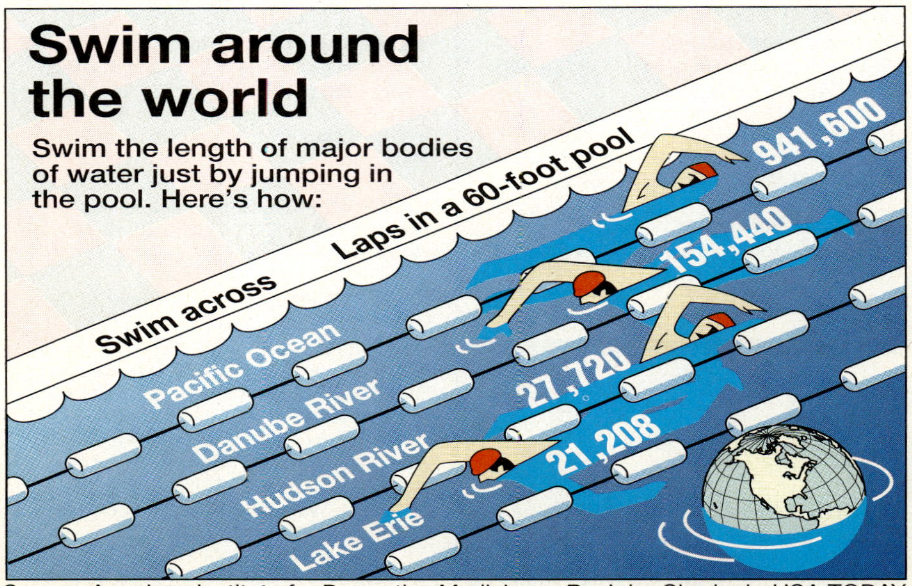

Source: American Institute for Preventive Medicine By John Sherlock, USA TODAY

STATBOX

POPULATION: 4,500,000
SQUARE MILES: 68,192
TIME ZONE: Pacific
MOTTO: AL-ki (By and By)
BIRD: Willow Goldfinch
TREE: Western Hemlock
CAPITAL: Olympia
AVERAGE ANNUAL RAINFALL: 30"
MEAN TEMP: 37 (Jan.); 63 (July)
MAJOR LEAGUE TEAMS: 3
NATIONAL PARK/FOREST ACREAGE: 1,657,463
STATE PARK ACREAGE: 279,845
HIGHEST ELEVATION: 14,411'
LOWEST ELEVATION: sea level
WATERWAYS: 2,656 miles of marine shoreline; 7,938 lakes

► OUTDOOR VENUES

National Parks

COLVILLE NATIONAL FOREST

CONTINUED ON PAGE 219

Washington

CONTINUED FROM PAGE 218

Bike Trails: BK
Boating: BT
Camping: C
Climbing: CL
Diving: DV
Fishing: F
Golfing: G
Hiking: HK
Hunting: HT
Riding: R
Surfing: SU
Swimming: S
Tennis: TE
Whitewater: WW
Winter Sports: W

Colville **[P. 119, B-11 & 12]**. Contains 1,028,162 acres. **C HK BT F S W**

COULEE DAM NATIONAL RECREATION AREA
North central Washington **[P. 119, C-12]**. Contains 100,390 acres. **C BT F S HT**

GIFFORD PINCHOT NATIONAL FOREST
Vancouver **[P. 118, F-7]**. Contains 1,388,689 acres. **C HK BT F S R W**

LAKE CHELAN NATIONAL RECREATION AREA
Stehekin **[P. 119, B-9]**. Contains 61,882 acres. **C HK BT F R W HT**

MOUNT BAKER-SNOQUALMIE NATIONAL FORESTS
I-90; US 2, WA 20 and WA 410 in NW WA **[P. 118, B-7, C-7; P. E-8]**. Contains 2,872,066 total acres.
C HK BT F S R W

MOUNT RAINIER NATIONAL PARK
Off WA 706 at Ashford; off WA 165 at Carbon River Road; or off WA 410 at White River Road **[P. 118, E-7]**. Contains 235,612 acres.
C HK F W CL

NORTH CASCADES NATIONAL PARK
Sedro Woolley, WA 20 **[P. 119, B-8]**. Contains 504,780 acres. **C HK F R**

OKANOGAN NATIONAL FOREST
US 2 and US 97, N & S, and WA 20, E & W **[P. 119, B-9]**. Contains 1,536,958 acres.
C HK BT F S R W

OLYMPIC NATIONAL PARK
Port Angeles **[P. 118, C-4]**. Contains 922,653 acres. **C HK BT F S R W CL**

OLYMPIC NATIONAL FOREST
US 101, NW WA **[P. 118, C-4]**. Contains 692,688 acres. **C HK BT F S R W HT**

ROSS LAKE NATIONAL RECREATION AREA
VA 20 **[P. 119, A-8]**. Contains 117,574 acres.
HK BT F R HT

VENATCHEE NATIONAL FOREST
Venatchee **[P. 119, C-9, D-9]**. Contains 908,006 acres. **C HK BT F S R BK W**

State Parks

BATTLE GROUND LAKE STATE PARK
21 mi. NE of Vancouver **[P. 118, G-6]**. Contains 279 acres. **C HK BT S R BK**

BLAKE ISLAND STATE PARK
In Puget Sound, 3 mi. W of Seattle (boat access only) **[P. 120, D-1]**. Contains 476 acres. **C HK**

CHIEF TIMOTHY
US 12, 8 mi. W of Clarkston **[P. 119, F-14]**. Contains 282 acres. **C HK BT F S BK**

DECEPTION PASS STATE PARK
10 mi. N of Oak Harbor on Hwy **[P. 118, B-6]**. 20. Contains 2,477 acres. **C HK BT F S**

FORT WORDEN STATE PARK
N limits of Fort Townsend **[P. 118, C-6]**. Contains 433 acres. **C HK BT F S BK**

ILLAHEE STATE PARK
WA 306, 3 mi. NE of Bremerton **[P. 118, D-6]**. Contains 75 acres. **C HK BT F S**

LAKE CHELAN STATE PARK
9 mi. W of Chelan, off Hwy. 97 **[P. 119, C-9]**. Contains 127 acres. **C HK BT F S**

LAKE SYLVIA STATE PARK
Off US 12, 1 mi. N of Montesano **[P. 118, E-4]**. Contains 233 acres. **C HK BT F S**

LAKE WENATCHEE STATE PARK
Off WA 207, 22 mi. N of Leavenworth **[P. 119, D-9]**. Contains 474 acres.
C HK BT F S R W

LARRABEE STATE PARK
WA 11, 7 mi. S of Bellingham **[P. 118, B-6]**. Contains 1,984 acres. **C HK BT F**

MORAN STATE PARK
Orcas Island, near Eastsound **[P. 118, B-6]**. Contains 4,605 acres. **C HK BT F S BK**

SILVER LAKE COUNTY PARK
Off WA 542, 3 mi. N of Maple Falls **[P. 118, B-7]**. Contains 411 acres. **C HK BT F S R W**

SUN LAKES STATE PARK
7 mi. SW of Coulee City, off WA 17 **[P. 119, D-11]**. Contains 4,023 acres. **C BT F S R**

TWENTY-FIVE MILE CREEK STATE PARK
18 mi. N of Chelan **[P. 119, C-9]**. Contains 235 acres. **C BT F S**

Skiing

ALPINE SKIING

ALPENTAL/SKI ACRES/SNOQUALMIE
Snoqualmie Pass **[P. 119, D-8]**; (206) 434-6112.
Vertical drop is 2,200 feet. Has twelve tows, one bar and 21 chairs.

CRYSTAL MOUNTAIN RESORT
Crystal Mountain Lane, Crystal Mountain **[P. 120, E-7]**; (206) 663-2265.
Vertical drop is 3,100 feet. Has ten chairs.

MISSION RIDGE
Wenatchee **[P. 119, E-9]**; (509) 663-7631.
Vertical drop is 2,140 feet. Has two tows and four chairs.

NORDIC SKIING

BEAR MOUNTAIN RANCH
Route 1, Chelan **[P. 119, C-10]**; (509) 682-5444.

METHOW VALLEY SKI TOURING ASSOCIATION
Winthrop **[P. 119, B-9]**; (509) 996-3287.

MOUNTAINHOLM LODGE
Airport Road, Easton **[P. 119, E-8]**; (509) 656-2346.

NORDIC WAY
70 E. Sunset Way, Issaquah **[P. 118, D-7]**; (206) 996-2873.

RENDEZVOUS OUTFITTERS INC.
Winthrop **[P. 119, B-9]**; (509) 996-2873.

SALMON RIDGE XC
9308 Mt. Baker Highway, Glacier **[P. 118, B-7]**; (206) 671-4615.

SKI ACRES XC CENTER
Snoqualmie Pass **[P. 119, D-8]**; (206) 434-6646.

SUN MOUNTAIN LODGE
Winthrop **[P. 119, B-9]**; (509) 996-2211.

> **"Because of where we live, on Puget Sound, when family and friends come, I say, 'Let's take the ferry and go whale watching.' The next thing is riding bicycles. Seattle is the biking capital of the world. We ride around [Green Lake], on the waterfront in the parks and on Burke Gilman Trail. . . You can go for hours without ever seeing an automobile."**
>
> **Former NFL Seattle Seahawks star *Sam McCullum***

► ACTIVE SPORTS

ADVENTURE: Pacific Crest Outward Bound School, 0110 SW Bancroft Street, Portland, OR; (800) 547-3312.

AEROBICS: AFAA, 1916 Pike Pl., #57, Seattle; (206) 526-5518.

BASEBALL: Little League Baseball Western Region HQ, 6707 Little League Dr., San Bernadino, CA; (714) 887-6444. • **Pony Baseball-Softball,** 908 Redbird Dr., San Jose, CA; (408) 265-3309. • **American Legion Baseball,** 1211 Fremont Hills Dr., Selah; (509) 697-6915. • **Babe Ruth Baseball,** Jim Lemp, 1911 Oxford Dr., Cheyenne, WY; (307) 638-6023. • **Men's Senior Baseball League - Seattle,** 311 W. Smith Street, Seattle; (206) 285-5397.

BILLIARDS: 211 Billiard Club, 2304 Second, Seattle; (206) 443-1211.

BOARDSAILING: Bavarian Surf , Seattle; (206) 545-9463. • **Columbia Windsurfing Academy,** Vancouver; (206) 573-1212. • **USWA Regional Director,** 9889 N.W. Hoge, Portland, OR; (503) 286-6100.

BOWLING: American Bowling Congress, 5301 S. 76th St., Greendale, WI; (414) 421-6400.

CANOEING & KAYAKING: ACA Northwest Vice Commodore, 550 Shoup Avenue, Idaho Falls, ID; (208) 524-0282.

CYCLING: USCF Washington Representative, West 1012 23rd Ave., Spokane; (509) 838-3707. • **Washington State AYH Council,** 419 Queen Anne Ave. N. #108, Seattle; (206) 281-7306.

FITNESS: State Governor's Council on Physical Fitness, Health & Sports, H1-53 PO Box 100, Richland; (509) 376-9580

FOOTBALL: Pop Warner Football, 1315 Walnut Street, Suite 1632, Philadelphia, PA; (215) 735-1450.

GOLF: PGA Pacific Northwest Section, 1201 M St. Southeast, Auburn; (503) 222-1139. • **Washington Junior Golf Association,** 4423 Merry Ln., Tacoma; (206) 564-0348. • **Washington State Golf Association,** 2100 W. Commodore Way, Seattle; (206) 282-5555.

HIKING & CLIMBING: Cascade Sierra Club Chapter, 1516 Melrose, Seattle; (206) 621-1696. • **Chinook Trail Association (AHS),** POBox 997, Vancouver; (206) 696-1693. • **Mazamas,** 909 Northwest 19th Ave., Portland, OR; (503) 227-2345. • **The Cascadians (AHS),** PO Box 2201, Yakima. • **The Mountaineers (AHS),** 300 Third Ave. W., Seattle; (206) 284-6310. • **Washington Trails Association (AHS),** 1305 Fourth Ave. #512, Seattle; (206) 625-1367.

HOCKEY: USA Hockey Pacific Registrar, 5703 Sun Ridge Ct., Castro Valley, CA; (415) 886-0706.

HUNTING & FISHING: Department of Wildlife, 600 N. Capitol Way, Olympia; (206) 753-5700. • **Trout Unlimited,** 4600 SW Graham, Seattle; (206) 932-6959. • **Department of Fisheries,** 115 General Administration Building, Olympia; (206) 753-6000

LACROSSE: Lacrosse Foundation Chapter, 7053 26th Ave., N.W., Seattle; (206) 682-7386.

RACQUETBALL: AARA, 14326 Interlake North, Seattle; (206) 367-6440.

RIDING: Washington State Horse Council, Box 88601, Seattle; (206) 255-5892.

RODEO: PRCA Columbia River Circuit, Rt. 2, Box 286, Walla Walla; (509) 529-0819.

RUNNING: RRCA WA State Rep., 2307 W. Bonne, Spokane; (509) 327-5142.

SCUBA: Pacific Reef, 7516 27th Street West, Tacoma; (206) 564-0356. • **Puget Sound Dive Enterprises,** 1921 Wheaton Way, Bremerton; (206) 377-0554. • **Thunder Reef Divers, Inc.,** 12104 NE Highway 99, Vancouver; (206) 573-8507.

SHOOTING: R & M Game Birds Sporting Clays, 495 Fisher Hill Rd., Lyle; (509) 365-3245.

SKATING: USFSA, 20 First Street, Colorado Springs, CO; (719) 635-5200.

SOCCER: Washington Soccer Ass'n, 317 N. 148th St., Seattle; (206) 367-3675. • **Washington State YSA, Inc.,** 6720 Southcenter Blvd., Suite 210, Seattle; (206) 246-5161. • **AYSO Regional Director,** 1720 Carmel Dr., Idaho Falls, ID; (208) 526-4485.

SOFTBALL: Washington ASA, 427 W. 19th, Kennewick; (509) 586-1252. • **Seattle ASA,** 11729 Bartlett NE, Seattle; (206) 362-7937. • **Spokane ASA,** 6920 North Country Homes Blvd., Spokane; (509) 328-9856. • **Tacoma ASA,** 6120 Milwaukee Avenue E., Puyallup; (206) 841-4420.

SQUASH: Seattle Downtown YMCA, Seattle; (206) 382-5010. • **Tacoma Family YMCA (USSRA),** Tacoma; (206) 564-9622.

SWIMMING: LMSC Inland Empire Registrar, South 13927 Traver Lane, Valleyford; (509) 448-5250.

TABLE TENNIS: USTTA State Coordinator, 533 Medical/Dental Building, Seattle; (206) 622-9215.

TENNIS: Recreational TEAMTENNIS Central-West Region, National Program Coordinator, 2105 Grant Ave., #4, Redondo Beach, CA; (800) 992-9042. • **Pacific Northwest USTA,** 10175 SW Barbur Blvd., 306B, Portland, OR; (503) 245-3048.

VOLLEYBALL: USVBA Evergreen Office, 11049 NE 12th Street, #7, Bellevue; (206) 455-5698.

◆ ◆ ◆

West Virginia

Arguably, for accessibility and excitement, the best whitewater in the USA can be found in West Virginia. The New River is called the Grand Canyon of the East, the Cheat has rapids with names like "Even Nastier", and the Gauley drops 668 feet over 28 miles. Dozens of outfitters are available (800-Call-WVA). ◆ If you like tamer aqua activities, try angling on any of the state's rivers, or such public fishing and hunting spots as Bear Rock Lake in the Wheeling area, Stonewall Jackson in Weston, and Louis Wetzel in the Wetzel area. ◆ For hikers and backpackers, Monongahela National Forest has 850 miles of trails while Cranberry Glades and Dolly Sods both offer plenty of backcountry adventures year-round. ◆ Both cross-country and downhill skiers will enjoy Canaan Valley and Snowshoe. ◆ The Orioles, Cubs and Reds all groom their prospects on minor league teams in the state.

▶ SPECTATOR VENUES

Baseball

BOWEN FIELD
In City Park, Bluefield **[P. 116, H-6]**. Capacity: 3,000
Bluefield Orioles (Appalachian League, Rookie Class); (703) 326-1326. Entered League in 1958. MLB affiliation, Baltimore Orioles.

HUNNICUTT FIELD
On Old Bluefield Road, Princeton **[P. 116, H-6]**. Capacity: 1,500
Princeton Reds (Appalachian League, Rookie Class); (304) 487-2000. Entered League in 1988. MLB affiliation, Cincinatti Reds.

ST. CLOUD COMMONS
1901 Jackson Avenue, Huntington **[P. 116, B-1]**. Capacity: 3,200
Huntington Cubs (Appalachian League, Rookie Class); (304) 429-1700. Entered League in 1990. Broadcasts by WKEE 800 AM. MLB affiliation, Chicago Cubs.

WATT POWELL PARK
3403 MacCorkle Avenue SE, Charleston **[P. 117, B-10]**. Capacity: 6,800
Charleston Wheelers (South Atlantic League, Class A); (304) 925-8222. Entered League in 1987. Broadcasts by WCHS 580-AM. MLB affiliation, Cincinnati Reds.

College Sports

MARSHALL UNIVERSITY THUNDERING HERD
Huntington **[P. 116, A-4]**; (304) 696-5409. Fairfield, capacity 17,312. Henderson Center, capacity 10,250.

SHEPHERD COLLEGE RAMS
Shepherdstown **[P. 117, C-13]**; (304) 876-2511. HPER Center, capacity 3,500.

WEST VIRGINIA UNIVERSITY MOUNTAINEERS
Morgantown **[P. 117, C-8]**; (304) 293-5621. Mountaineer Field, capacity 63,500. WVU Coliseum, capacity 14,000.

Horse Racing

CHARLES TOWN RACES
Race Track Road, Charles Town **[P. 117, D-13]**; (304) 725-7001. Opened in 1933. Clubhouse capacity: 2,500. Grandstand capacity: 4,000.
Thoroughbred season from Jan. to Dec.
◆This small track, located near historic Harper's Ferry, is a good place to bring the whole family.

MOUNTAINEER PARK
WV Route 2, Chester **[P. 116, A-7]**; (304) 387-2400. Opened in 1951. Clubhouse capacity: 1,600. Grandstand capacity: 5,800.
Thoroughbred season from Jan. to Dec.
◆Formerly Waterford Park.

▶ OUTDOOR VENUES

National Parks

Key
Bike Trails: BK
Boating: BT
Camping: C
Climbing: CL
Diving: DV
Fishing: F
Golfing: G
Hiking: HK
Hunting: HT
Riding: R
Surfing: SU
Swimming: S
Tennis: TE
Whitewater: WW
Winter Sports: W

MONONGAHELA NATIONAL FOREST
Accessible via I-81, I-64, I-79 **[P. 117, D-9]**. Contains 901,000 acres. **C HK BT F S CL**

NEW RIVER GORGE NATIONAL RIVER
Between Fayetteville & Hinton **[P. 116, F-6, G-7]**. Contains 62,000 acres. **HK BT F S R WW**

SPRUCE KNOB-SENECA ROCKS NATIONAL RECREATION AREA
NE area of Monongahela National Forest, off I-81 **[P. 117, E-9]**. Contains 56,000 acres. **C HK BT F S CL**

State Parks

BABCOCK STATE PARK
4 mi. SW of Clifftop on WV 41 **[P. 116, G-6]**. Contains 4,127 acres. **C HK BT F S R W TE**

BEECH FORK STATE PARK
15 mi. SE of Huntington on WV 152 **[P. 116, F-4]**. Contains 3,981 acres. **C HK BT F S BK W DV**

BLACKWATER FALLS STATE PARK
Davis **[P. 117, D-9]**. Contains 1,688 acres. **C HK BT S R W TE**

BLUESTONE STATE PARK
4 mi. S of Hinton on WV 20 **[P. 116, G-6]**. Contains 2,155 acres. **C HK BT F S DV**

BURNSVILLE LAKE
off I-79 at Burnsville exit **[P. 116, E-7]**. Contains 970 acres. **C HK BT F S R BK**

CACAPON STATE PARK
10 mi. S of Berkeley Springs on US 522 **[P. 117, C-12]**. Contains 6,115 acres.
HK BT F S R BK G

CANAAN VALLEY STATE PARK
10 mi. S of Davis on WV 32 **[P. 117, D-9]**. Contains 6,015 acres. **C HK F S BK W**

HAWK'S NEST STATE PARK
Ansted **[P. 116, F-6]**. Contains 276 acres.
HK BT F S

LOST RIVER STATE PARK
Mathias **[P. 117, E-10]**. Contains 3,712 acres.
HK S R BK TE

NORTH BEND STATE PARK
2 mi. E of Cairo off WV 31 **[P. 116, D-6]**. Contains 1,405 acres. **C HK F S TE**

OGLEBAY PARK
Wheeling **[P. 117, B-7]**. Contains 1,500 acres.
HK BT F S R W G

PIPESTEM STATE PARK
9 mi. N of Athens on WV 20 **[P. 116, H-6]**. Contains 4,023 acres. **C HK BT F S R W G**

SUMMERSVILLE LAKE (AC)
4 mi. S of Summersville off US 19 on WV 129 **[P. 116, F-7]**. Contains 2,700 acres. **C BT F S DV**

SUTTON LAKE (AC)
Sutton. Contains 1,440 acres **[P. 116, E-7]**.
C HK BT F S DV

TYGART LAKE STATE PARK
2 mi. S of Grafton **[P. 117, D-9]**. Contains 2,134 acres. **C HK BT F S DV**

WATOGA STATE PARK
10 mi. S of Huntersville **[P. 117, F-8]**. Contains 10,106 acres. **C HK BT F S R BK W**

Skiing

ALPINE SKIING

CANAAN VALLEY RESORT
Off of Route 32, Davis **[P. 117, D-9]**; (304) 866-4121.
Vertical drop is 850 feet. Has one bar and three chairs.

SNOWSHOE MOUNTAIN RESORT
Snowshoe Drive, Snowshoe **[P. 117, F-8]**; (304) 572-1000.
Vertical drop is 1,500 feet. Has seven chairs.

TIMBERLINE FOUR SEASONS RESORT
Timberline Road, Route 32, Canaan Valley **[P. 117, D-10]**; (304) 866-4801.
Vertical drop is 1,000 feet. Has one tow, one bar and one chair.

NORDIC SKIING

WHITE GRASS SKI AREA
Canaan Valley, Davis **[P. 117, D-9]**; (304) 866-4114.

▶ ACTIVE SPORTS

BASEBALL: Little League Baseball Southern Region HQ, PO Box 13366, St. Petersburg, FL; (813) 344-2661. • **American Legion Baseball,** 816 Ridgeway Ave., Morgantown; (304) 296-4678. • **Babe Ruth Baseball,** Robert Dickson, RR 4, Box 332F, Alexandria, IN; (317) 724-4883.

BOARDSAILING: USWA Regional Director, 1912 MacCumber Ln., Wilmington, NC; (919) 256-3553.

BOWLING: American Bowling Congress, 5301 S. 76th St., Greendale, WI; (414) 421-6400.

CANOEING & KAYAKING: ACA Middle States Vice Commodore, 10236 Raider Ln., Fairfax, VA; (703) 359-2594.

CYCLING: LAW Coastal Regional Director, 205 E. Joppa Road, Baltimore, MD; (301) 828-8604. • **USCF Ohio/West Virginia Representative,** 25 Parkwood Boulevard, Mansfield, OH; (419) 526-3787.

STATBOX

POPULATION: 1,949,644
SQUARE MILES: 24,282
TIME ZONE: Eastern
MOTTO: Montani Semper Liberi (Mountaineers are always free)
BIRD: Cardinal
TREE: Sugar Maple
CAPITAL: Charleston
AVERAGE ANNUAL RAINFALL: 40.97"
MEAN TEMP: 66
MAJOR LEAGUE TEAMS: 0
NATIONAL PARK/FOREST ACREAGE: 76,735
STATE PARK ACREAGE: 151,617
HIGHEST ELEVATION: 4,861'
LOWEST ELEVATION: 247'
WATERWAYS: 2,163 miles of rivers and streams; 14,700 acres of lakes

FOOTBALL: Pop Warner Football, 1315 Walnut Street, Suite 1632, Philadelphia, PA; (215) 735-1450. • **U.S. Flag Football League,** 5834 Pine Tree Drive, Sanibel, FL; (813) 472-0544.

GOLF: PGA Middle Atlantic Section, 7270 Cradlerock Way, Columbia, MD; (301) 621-8320. • **PGA Northern Ohio Section,** 38121 Euclid Ave., Willoughby, OH; (216) 951-4546. • **PGA Tri-State Section,** 221 Sherwood Dr., Monaca, PA; (412) 774-2224. • **West Virginia Golf Association,** PO Box 8133, Huntington; (304) 525-0000.

HIKING & CLIMBING: Appalachian Trail Conference (AHS), PO Box 807, Harpers Ferry; (304) 535-6331. • **Potomac Appalachian Trail Club ,** 1718 N St. Northwest, Washington, DC; (202) 638-5306. • **West Virginia Sierra Club Chapter,** PO Box 4142, Morgantown; (304) 274-1130.

HOCKEY: USA Hockey Mid-American Registrar, 647 Stacey Ln., Maumee, OH; (419) 893-9665.

HUNTING & FISHING: Department of Natural Resources, 1900 Kanawha Blvd East, Charleston; (304) 348-2771. • **Trout Unlimited,** Route 1, Box 109A, Bristol; (304) 783-5345.

RACQUETBALL: AARA, 118 Locust Street, Huntington; (304) 525-7639.

RODEO: PRCA First Frontier Circuit, 5982 Summit Bridge Rd., Townsend, DE; (302) 378-4551.

RUNNING: RRCA WV State Rep., PO Box 69, St. Marys; (304) 684-3673.

SCUBA: Mountaineer II Dive Shop, 505 Dunbar Avenue, Dunbar; (304) 768-7753.

SKATING: USFSA, 20 First Street, Colorado Springs, CO; (719) 635-5200.

SOCCER: West Virginia Soccer Ass'n, PO Box 3360, Beckley; (304) 253-1688. • **AYSO Regional Director,** 4014 Oneida St., New Hartford, NY; (315) 737-5610.

SOFTBALL: West Virginia ASA, 5 Lynn Ln., Scott Depot; (304) 757-9103.

SQUASH: Charleston Family YMCA, Charleston; (304) 340-3527.

TENNIS: Recreational TEAMTENNIS Midwest-Southeast Region, National Program Coordinator, 445 N. Wells, Ste. #404, Chicago, IL; (800) TEAMTEN. • **Mid-Atlantic USTA,** PO Drawer F, Springfield, VA; (703) 321-9045. • **Middle States USTA,** 580 Shoemaker Rd., King of Prussia, PA; (215) 768-4040. • **Western USTA,** 8720 Castle Creek Parkway, Ste. 329, Indianapolis, IN; (513) 390-2740

WHITEWATER RAFTING: American-Canadian Expeditions, Ltd. , PO Box 249, Glen Jean; (304) 469-2651. • **Cheat River Outfitters, Inc. ,** PO Box 134, Albright; (304) 329-2024. • **New River Scenic Whitewater Tours, Inc. ,** Box 637, Hinton; (304) 466-2288. • **North American River Runners, Inc. ,** PO Box 81, U.S. Rt. 60, Hico; (304) 658-5276. • **Rivers II, Inc. ,** PO Drawer 39, Lansing; (304) 574-3834. • **Wildwater Expeditions Unlimited ,** PO Box 55, Dept. E, Thurmond; (304) 465-5551.

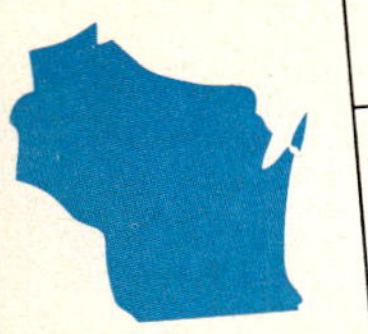

Wisconsin

Oshkosh and Neenah have two of the highest ratios of bowling alleys per capita in the USA. ◆ The National Freshwater Fishing Hall of Fame is located in Hayward; The northern part of the state is great for bass and muskie. ◆ In addition to the NBA Bucks, NFL Packers, and MLB Brewers, you'll find plenty of minor league sports here, plus Indy car racing. ◆ Wisconsin is home to fast-moving, flat-bottomed lake boats known as "Scows." Lake Michigan and Lake Geneva usually host the Scow nationals; The University of Wisconsin (between Lake Monona and Lake Mendota) offers excellent lake sailing. ◆ More than 1,400 participants enter Janesville's National Show Ski Championships each year, the largest water skiing event in the USA. ◆ And there's always the internationally known Birkebeiner nordic ski race near the Telemark Ski Area in winter.

► SPECTATOR VENUES

Auto Racing

ROAD AMERICA
Off Highway 67, S of Elkhart Lake **[P. 123, H-8]**; (414) 876-3366. Track is 4-mile, 11-turn road course.
Texaco/Havoline 200 (CART PPG Indy Car World Series), September.
Road America Trans-Am (SCCA).
Nissan Grand Prix of Road America (IMSA Camel GT), August.

WISCONSIN STATE FAIR PARK SPEEDWAY
8200 W. Greenfield Ave., State Park Fair, West Allis **[P. 121, D-11]**; (414) 453-5514.
Track is 1-mile paved oval.
Miller Genuine Draft 100 (USAC Silver Crown).
Miller Genuine Draft 200 (CART PPG Indy Car World Series), June.

Baseball

[GO]ODLAND FIELD
[20]22 W. 4th St., Appleton **[P. 122, G-7]**.
[Ca]pacity: 4,300
Appleton Foxes (Midwest League, Class [A]); (414) 733-4152. Entered League in 1958. MLB affiliation, Kansas City Royals.

[H]ARRY C. POHLMAN FIELD
[1]2301 Skyline Dr., Beloit **[P. 123, L-6]**. Capacity: 3,200
Beloit Brewers (Midwest League, Class A); (608) 362-2272. Entered League in 1982. Broadcasts by WBEL 1380 AM, WCLO 1230 AM. MLB affiliation, Milwaukee Brewers.

MILWAUKEE COUNTY STADIUM
201 South 46th St., Milwaukee **[P. 121, D-12]**. Built in 1953. Capacity: 53,192
◆The Stadium hosts several Green Bay Packers' games every year. Serves what is generally regarded as the best Bratwurst in sports. The Brewers' franchise began in 1969 as the notorious Seattle Pilots of Jim Bouton's *Ball Four.* Moved to Milwaukee the next season.
Milwaukee Brewers (AL East); (414) 933-1818. Franchise began in 1969. Broadcasts by WTMJ 620 AM, WCGV-TV 24. Affiliates: Denver, CO (AAA); El Paso, TX (AA); Stockton, CA (A); Beloit, WI (A); Helena, MT (Rookie); Peoria, AZ (Rookie). Spring training held in Chandler, AZ.

SIMMONS FIELD
7817 Sheridan Road, Kenosha **[P. 121, H-12]**. Capacity: 3,500
Kenosha Twins (Midwest League, Class A); (414) 657-7997. Entered League in 1984. Broadcasts by WKRS 1220 AM, WLIP 1050 AM. MLB affiliation, Minnesota Twins.

WARNER PARK
1617 Northport Drive, Madison **[P. 123, M-6]**. Capacity: 3,923
Madison Muskies (Midwest League, Class A); (608) 241-0010. Entered League in 1982. MLB affiliation, Oakland Athletics.

Basketball

BRADLEY CENTER
1001 N. Fourth Street, Milwaukee **[P. 121, C-12]**. Built in 1988. Capacity: 18,633.
Milwaukee Bucks (NBA Eastern Conf., Central Div.); (414) 227-0500. Franchise began in 1968. Broadcasts by WTMJ 620 AM, WCGV Channel 24.

LA CROSSE CENTER
300 Harborview Plaza, La Crosse **[P. 121, H-8]**. Capacity: 6,090.
La Crosse Catbirds (Continental Basketball Association, American Conference, Central Division); (608) 782-4700. Entered League in 1983. Broadcasts by WIZM 1410 AM.

Bowling

RED CARPET CELEBRITY LANES
5757 South 27th Street, Milwaukee **[P. 121, E-12]**; (414) 282-0100.
American Bowling Congress Fall (PBA), November.

RED CARPET LANES
2650 S. Ashland Ave., Green Bay **[P. 123, O-7]**; (414) 499-0281.
La Mode Classic (PBA), August.

College Sports

MARQUETTE UNIVERSITY WARRIORS
1212 West Wisconsin Avenue, Milwaukee **[P. 121, D-12]**; (414) 288-6303. Bradley Center, capacity 18,000.

UNIVERSITY OF WISCONSIN PHOENIX
2420 Nicolet Drive, Green Bay **[P. 121, N-8]**; (414) 465-2145. Phoenix Field, capacity 5,000. Brown Co. Arena, capacity 6,000.

UNIVERSITY OF WISCONSIN EAGLES
La Crosse **[P. 123, H-8]**; (608) 785-8616. Memorial Field, capacity 6,000. Mitchell Hall, capacity 3,600.

UNIVERSITY OF WISCONSIN BADGERS
1440 Monroe Street, Madison **[P. 123, N-5]**; (608) 262-1866. Camp Randall, capacity 77,280. U. of Wisconsin, capacity 12,868.

UNIVERSITY OF WISCONSIN PANTHERS
Milwaukee **[P. 121, C-13]**; (414) 229-5151. UWM, Klotsche, capacity 3,000.

UNIVERSITY OF WISCONSIN TITANS
800 Algoma Boulevard, Oshkosh **[P. 123, H-7]**; (414) 424-1034. Titan, capacity 10,000. Kolf, capacity 6,300.

UNIVERSITY OF WISCONSIN RANGERS
Kenosha **[P. 123, L-8]**; (414) 553-2245. Stadium capacity 1,500. PE Building, capacity 2,400.

UNIVERSITY OF WISCONSIN FALCONS
Cascade Street, River Falls **[P. 122, F-1]**; (715) 425-3900. Ramer, capacity 4,000. Karges Center, capacity 2,600.

UNIVERSITY OF WISCONSIN POINTERS
4th Avenue, Stevens Point **[P. 122, G-5]**; (715) 346-3888. Georke Field, capacity 5,000. Quandt, capacity 4,200.

UNIVERSITY OF WISCONSIN YELLOWJACKETS
Superior **[P. 123, O-4]**; (715) 394-8193. Haugsrud Field, capacity 400. Gates PE Building, capacity 3,000.

UNIVERSITY OF WISCONSIN WARHAWKS
Whitewater **[P. 123, L-7]**; (414) 472-4661. Warhawk, capacity 13,500.

USA SNAPSHOTS®

A look at statistics that shape the sports world

Showing the team colors

Projected retail sales of licensed, professional-sports merchandise for 1990-91 seasons:

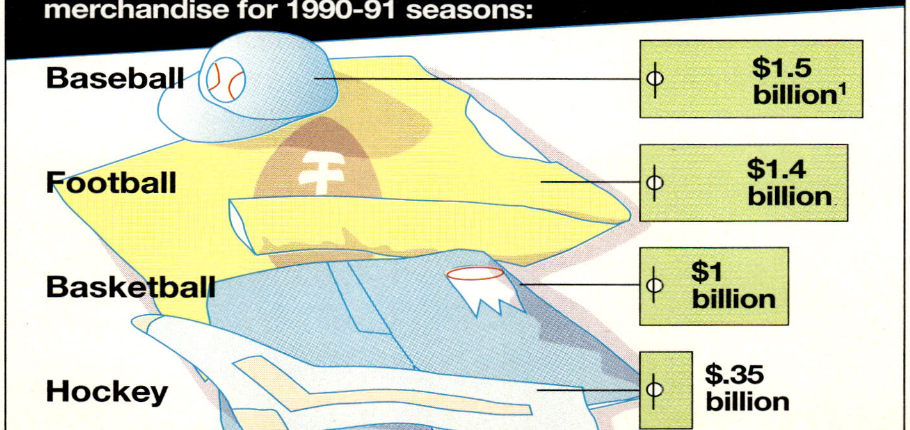

1 — for 1990 only

Source: *Amusement Business* magazine By Elys McLean-Ibrahim, USA TODAY

STATBOX

POPULATION: 5,000,000
SQUARE MILES: 56,153
TIME ZONE: Central
MOTTO: Forward
BIRD: Robin
TREE: Sugar Maple
CAPITAL: Madison
AVERAGE ANNUAL RAINFALL: 31"
MEAN TEMP: 44
MAJOR LEAGUE TEAMS: 3
NATIONAL PARK/FOREST ACREAGE: 1,500,000
STATE PARK ACREAGE: 500,000
HIGHEST ELEVATION: 1,952
LOWEST ELEVATION: sea level
WATERWAYS: 17,770 miles of rivers and steams; 15,000 lakes

Football

LAMBEAU FIELD
1265 Lombardi Avenue, Green Bay **[P. 123, N-7]**. Built in 1957. Capacity: 59,543.
The Packers also play three regular season games every year at MILWAUKEE COUNTY STADIUM (see listing above, under Baseball).
Green Bay Packers (NFC Central Division); (414) 496-5700. Franchise began in 1921. Broadcasts by WTMJ.

Hockey

BRADLEY CENTER
1001 North 4th Street, Milwaukee **[P. 121, C-12]**. Capacity: 17,809.
◆Most hockey teams play in arenas built for basketball audiences. Bradley Center is one of the few buildings in the country designed specifically for hockey. The scoreboard clock has spaces for shots and saves, and all seats have good sightlines to the goals. Since the sumptuous arena was built several years ago, the Admirals have consistently drawn the largest crowds in the IHL, averaging 8,723 per game in the 1989-90 and '90-91 seasons.
Milwaukee Admirals (International Hockey League); (414) 227-0400. Franchise began in 1977. Broadcasts by WISN 1130 AM.

Museums & Halls of Fame

GREEN BAY PACKER HALL OF FAME
855 Lombardi Ave., Green Bay **[P. 123, N-7]**; (414) 499-4281.

INTERNATIONAL SNOWMOBILE RACING HALL OF FAME
Hwy. 45 & Hwy. 70W, Eagle River **[P. 122, D-6]**; (608) 825-6373.

NATIONAL FRESH WATER FISHING HALL OF FAME
1 Hall of Fame Dr., Hayward **[P. 122, C-3]**; (715) 634-4440.
◆The museum is housed in a four-and-a-half stories high muskie.

LPGA/PGA

TUCKAWAY COUNTRY CLUB
6901 W. Drexel Ave., Franklin **[P. 121, F-11]**; (414) 425-4280.
Greater Milwaukee Open (PGA), end of Aug.
Number of holes: 72.

Polo

JOY FARM POLO CLUB
7007 N. 115th St., Milwaukee **[P. 121, B-11]**; (414) 353-9200.

OLYMPIA POLO CLUB
65th St. & Good Hope Rd., Milwaukee **[P. 123,**

CONTINUED ON PAGE 222

Wisconsin

CONTINUED FROM PAGE 221

K-7]; (414) 289-3508.

Yachting

LAKE GENEVA YACHT CLUB
South Shore Dr., Fontana [P. 123, L-7]; (414) 275-2727.
O'Day Trophy (U.S. Singlehanded Championship, USYRU), August, 1991.

MILWAUKEE YACHT CLUB
1700 N. Lincoln Memorial Dr., Milwaukee [P. 121, C-13]; (414) 271-4455.
USYRU/Nautica U.S. Youth Sailing Championship, June, 1991.

▶ OUTDOOR VENUES

National Parks

Bike Trails: BK
Boating: BT
Camping: C
Climbing: CL
Diving: DV
Fishing: F
Golfing: G
Hiking: HK
Hunting: HT
Riding: R
Surfing: SU
Swimming: S
Tennis: TE
Whitewater: WW
Winter Sports: W

APOSTLE ISLANDS NATIONAL LAKESHORE
Off northern Wisconsin's Bayfield Peninsula in Lake Superior [P. 122, A-3]. Contains 69,000 acres.
C HK BT F S W DV

CHEQUAMEGON NATIONAL FOREST
North central area of state [P. 122, B-3, C-3, D-4, E-4]. Contains 845,000 acres. C HK BT F S R BK W HT

NICOLET NATIONAL FOREST
Off US 8 or WI 70 [P. 122, D-6]. Contains 661,025 acres. C HK BT F S R BK W HT

ST. CROIX NATIONAL SCENIC RIVERWAY
From Hayward to Prescott, on US 63 or WI 35 [P. 122]. Contains 76,909 acres.
C HK BT F S W HT

State Parks

BLACK RIVER STATE FOREST
Black River Falls [P. 122, G-4]. Contains 65,782 acres. C HK BT F S W HT

BONG STATE RECREATION AREA
8 mi. E of Burlington on WI 142 [P. 123, L-8]. Contains 4,515 acres. C HK BT F S R W HT

BRUNET ISLAND STATE PARK
Off WI 27, 1 mi. N of Cornell [P. 122, E-3]. Contains 1,032 acres. C HK BT F S W

COUNCIL GROUNDS STATE PARK
WI 107, 2 mi. NW of Merrill [P. 122, E-5]. Contains 427 acres. C HK BT F S W

DEVIL'S LAKE STATE PARK
2 mi. S of Baraboo on WI 123 [P. 123, J-5]. Contains 8,359 acres. C HK F S W HT

FLAMBEAU RIVER STATE FOREST
22 mi. W of Phillips on County Highway W [P. 122, D-4]. Contains 89,807 acres.
C HK BT F S W HT

HARRINGTON BEACH STATE PARK
County D, 2 mi. E of Belgium [P. 123, J-8]. Contains 636 acres. HK F S W

INTERSTATE STATE PARK
S of St. Croix Falls on WI 35 [P. 122, E-1]. Contains 1,368 acres. C HK BT F S W HT

KETTLE MORAINE NORTH STATE FOREST
7 mi. N of Kewaskum on County G [P. 123, J-7]. Contains 27,725 acres. C HK BT F S R W HT

> **"You'll come across more loyal fans. . . there are tailgating parties. . . It's people who make the difference here."**
>
> Track star *Suzy Favor*

KETTLE MORAINE SOUTH STATE FOREST
3 mi. W of Eagle on WI 59 [P. 123, K-7]. Contains 17,987 acres. C HK BT F S R W HT

LAKE WISSOTA STATE PARK
5 mi. E of Chippewa Falls on County O [P. 122, F-3]. Contains 1,062 acres.
C HK BT F S R W

MIRROR LAKE STATE PARK
WI 23, 4 mi. SW of Lake Delton [P. 123, J-5]. Contains 2,057 acres. C HK BT F S W HT

NORTHERN HIGHLAND-AMERICAN LEGION STATE FOREST
WI 70, 3 mi. W of Eagle River [P. 122, C-5]. Contains 218,021 acres. C HK BT F S W HT

PENINSULA STATE PARK
NE of Fish Creek on WI 42 [P. 122, B-8]. Contains 3,763 acres. C HK BT F S BK W G

POTAWATOMI STATE PARK
1 mi. NW of Surgeon Bay on Park Drive [P. 122, B-7]. Contains 1,126 acres. C HK BT F W

ROCK ISLAND STATE PARK
Rock Island [P. 122, A-8]. Contains 912 acres.
C HK BT F S W HT

WILLOW RIVER STATE PARK
7 mi. NE of Hudson on County Highway A [P. 122, F-1]. Contains 2,843 acres. C HK BT F S W HT

YELLOWSTONE LAKE STATE PARK
County N, 7 mi. NW of Argyle [P. 123, L-5]. Contains 771 acres. C HK BT F S W HT

Skiing

ALPINE SKIING

MT. LA CROSSE
Route 3, Old Town Hall Road, La Crosse [P. 123, J-3]; (608) 788-0044.
Vertical drop is 516 feet. Has one tow and three chairs.

RIB MOUNTAIN SKI AREA
3605 N. Mountain Road, Wausau [P. 122, F-5]; (715) 845-2846.
Vertical drop is 624 feet. Has one tow and three chairs.

NORDIC SKIING

DANE COUNTY PARKS
4318 Robertson Road, Madison [P. 123, K-5]; (608) 246-3896.

MINOCQUA WINTER PARK
12375 Scotchman Lake Road, Minocqua [P. 122, D-5]; (715) 356-3309.

▶ ACTIVE SPORTS

AEROBICS: AFAA, 5136 N. 65th Street, Milwaukee; (414) 464-3297.

BASEBALL: Little League Baseball Central Region HQ, 4360 N. Mitthoeffer Rd., Indianapolis, IN; (317) 897-6127. • **Pony Baseball-Softball,** 531 Parkshore Dr., Shorewood, IL; (815) 725-3047. • **American Legion Baseball,** 6 New Berm Ct., Madison; (608) 274-3405. • **Babe Ruth Baseball,** Robert Dickson, RR 4, Box 332F, Alexandria, IN; (317) 724-4883. • **Men's Senior Baseball League,** 112 Cedar, Nekoosa; (715) 886-4679.

BILLIARDS: Cue-Nique Billiards, 317 W. Gorham, Madison; (608) 251-1134. • **Romine's High Pockets,** 2715 W. Wisconsin, Milwaukee; (414) 344-5666.

BOARDSAILING: Aquatic World II , Oconomowoc; (414) 567-7245. • **Flying Fish Sailboards ,** Madison; (608) 251-4500. • **USWA Regional Director,** N7315 Winnebago Dr., Fond du Lac; (414) 922-2550. • **Wind Power Windsurfing Center ,** Fond du Lac; (414) 922-2550.

BOWLING: American Bowling Congress, 5301 S. 76th St., Greendale; (414) 421-6400.

CANOEING & KAYAKING: ACA Midwest Vice Commodore, 1343 N. Portage, Palatine, IL; (708) 359-5047.

CYCLING: LAW North Central Regional Director, Route 1, Box 99, Cushing; (715) 648-5519. • **USCF Wisconsin Representative,** 1505 Coachlight Drive, #14, New Berlin; (414) 786-0623. • **Wisconsin AYH Council,** 2224 W. Wisconsin, Milwaukee; (414) 933-1155.

FITNESS: Governor's Council on Physical Fitness and Health, Department of Public Instruction, 125 S. Webster St., PO Box 7841, Madison; (608) 266-7032.

FOOTBALL: Pop Warner Football, 1315 Walnut Street, Suite 1632, Philadelphia, PA; (215) 735-1450.

GOLF: PGA Wisconsin Section, PO Box 885, Brookfield; (414) 785-9742. • **Wisconsin State Golf Association,** PO Box 35, Elm Grove; (414) 786-4301.

HIKING & CLIMBING: John Muir Sierra Club Chapter, 111 King St., Madison; (608) 256-0565. • **Wisconsin Go Hiking Club (AHS),** 3672 S. 21st St., Milwaukee; (414) 463-0792.

HOCKEY: USA Hockey Central Registrar, PO Box 1738, Lisle, IL; (708) 963-1098.

HUNTING & FISHING: Department of Natural Resources, Box 7921, Madison; (608) 266-2121. • **Trout Unlimited,** 174 Ripon Rd., Berlin; (414) 361-3823.

RACQUETBALL: AARA, N85 W15960 Appleton Ave., Menomonee Falls; (414) 255-7751.

RIDING: Wisconsin State Horse Council, 1675 Observatory Dr., Madison; (608) 263-4303.

RODEO: PRCA Great Lakes Circuit, Rt. 1, Box 54, Clayton, IN; (317) 539-5039.

RUNNING: RRCA WI State Rep., 2300 Rugby Rd., Madison; (608) 238-1323.

SCUBA: 3 Little Devil's Inc., South 5780-A Highway 123, Baraboo; (608) 356-5866. • **Down Under Diving,** 3405 Douglas Avenue, Racine; (414) 639-9344. • **Underwater Ventures, Inc.,** 1724 North Clairemont Avenue, Eau Claire; (715) 834-0002.

SHOOTING: Hartland Sportsmen Club, 1701 Pewaukee Rd., Waukesha; (414) 548-9536. • **Top Gun Sporting Clays,** N3249 River View Rd., Juneau; (414) 349-8128. • **Trout and Grouse Shooting Grounds,** 11110 110th St., Kenosha; (414) 857-7232. • **Woodhollow Sporting Clays,** 517 Copelan[illegible] Avenue, La Crosse; (608) 784-0482.

SKATING: USFSA, 20 First Street, Colorado Springs, CO; (719) 635-5200. • **Wisconsin Skating Association,** 1969 South 73rd Street, West Allis; (414) 321-9372

SOCCER: Wisconsin Soccer Ass'n, 112255 W. Bluemound Road, Milwaukee; (414) 476-9972. • **AYSO Regional Director,** 1918 Springside Dr., Naperville, IL; (807) 416-8520.

SOFTBALL: Wisconsin ASA, 3161 Runway Ave., Eau Claire; (715) 839-0420.

SQUASH: Milwaukee Central YMCA, Milwaukee; (414) 291-5960. • **University of Wisconsin (USSRA),** Madison; (608) 262-0465.

SWIMMING: LMSC Wisconsin Registrar, 10251 York Ct., Wauawtosa; (414) 463-4466.

TENNIS: Recreational TEAMTENNIS Midwest-Southeast Region, National Program Coordinator, 445 N. Wells, Ste. #404, Chicago, IL; (800) TEAMTEN. • **Northwestern USTA,** 5525 Cedar Lake Rd., St. Louis Park, MN; (612) 546-0709. • **Western USTA,** 8720 Castle Creek Parkway, Ste. 329, Indianapolis, IN; (513) 390-2740.

Tip Offs: Bike Commuters' Favorite Cities

In 1980, some 550,000 commuters in the USA bicycled to work. By the end of the decade that number had increased to 3.5 million. With federal biking transportation studies in the works, more and more states with official cycling coordinators in place, and bike lanes and parking fighting for space, the National Congress of Bicyclists predicts the figure will reach 5.5 million by 1994.

According to a recent survey by *Bicycling* magazine, the 10 best cities in the USA and Canada to be a cyclist are as follows:

1. **Seattle, WA**
2. **Palo Alto, CA**
3. **San Diego, CA**
4. **Boulder, CO**
5. **Davis, CA**
6. **Gainesville, FL**
7. **Eugene, OR**
8. **Montreal**
9. **Madison, WI**
10. **Missoula, MT**

Wyoming

Ninety-one percent of Yellowstone National Park is in Wyoming. Boat rentals and horseback riding are available all summer; fishing is permitted (with a permit) from Memorial Day weekend through October. Overnight backpacking is also allowed with a permit. ◆ The National Outdoor Leadership School in Lander offers basic wilderness skills, including mountain climbing, backpacking and skiing (307-332-6973). ◆ Frontier Days (July) in Cheyenne is one of the biggest rodeos in the USA. Or catch Casper's Central Wyoming Fair and Rodeo just days later. Special summer treat: night rodeos in Cheyenne. ◆ Expert skiers hail Wyoming's pristine ski areas (Jackson Hole, Grand Targhee, Snow King) as some of the most beautiful and challenging in the USA. ◆ The University of Wyoming (Laramie) holds the state's only Division I football and basketball games (see below).

SPECTATOR VENUES

College Sports

UNIVERSITY OF WYOMING COWBOYS
Laramie **[P. 125, E-14]**; (307) 766-2292. War Memorial, capacity 33,500. Auditorium, capacity 15,000.

Horse Racing

WYOMING DOWNS
Highway 89, N of, Evanston **[P. 124, F-4]**; (800) 842-8722 or (307) 789-0511. Opened in 1985. Grandstand capacity: 2,100. Total capacity: 22,000.
Thoroughbred season from May to Sep.
◆Thoroughbred and quarterhorse racing.

Rodeo

RONTIER PARK
arey Ave., Cheyenne **[P. 125, A-8]**; (307) 778-200.
heyenne Frontier Days, last full week of ly.

OUTDOOR VENUES

National Parks

Key	
Bike Trails:	BK
Boating:	BT
Camping:	C
Climbing:	CL
Diving:	DV
Fishing:	F
Golfing:	G
Hiking:	HK
Hunting:	HT
Riding:	R
Surfing:	SU
Swimming:	S
Tennis:	TE
Whitewater:	WW
Winter Sports:	W

BIGHORN NATIONAL FOREST
Off US 14 & 16, north central **[P. 125, A-8]**. Contains 1,115,171 acres. **C HK BT F R W HT**

BIGHORN CANYON NATIONAL RECREATION AREA
On MT border, US Alt. 14 **[P. 124, A-7]**. Contains 120,296 acres. **C HK BT F S W CL**

BRIDGER-TETON NATIONAL FOREST
Pinedale and Jackson **[P. 124, C-2, C-5]**. Contains 3,399,767 acres. **C HK BT F S R BK W HT**

DEVILS TOWERS NATIONAL MONUMENT
Northeast corner of state **[P. 125, A-11]**. Contains 1,346 acres. **C HK F CL**

FLAMING GORGE NATIONAL RECREATION AREA
WY 530 or US 191 from I-80 in WY or US 191 from UT **[P. 124, F-6]**. Contains 285,000 acres. **C HK BT F S R BK W WW**

GRAND TETON NATIONAL PARK
N of Jackson on US 26/89/191 **[P. 124, C-1]**. Contains 309,993 acres. **C HK BT F S R BK W CL**

MEDICINE BOW NATIONAL FOREST
Off I-80 or US 287, south central **[P. 125, D-10, F-8, F-11]**. Contains 1,665,000 acres. **C HK BT F S R W HT**

SHOSHONE NATIONAL FOREST
NW WY, US 14/20 & US 287, adjacent to Yellowstone National Park **[P. 124, A-5, D-6]**. Contains 2,433,125 acres. **C HK F S R W HT**

THUNDER BASIN NATIONAL GRASSLAND
US 16, just off I-90, northeastern area of state **[P. 125, A, B & C-10 & 11]**. Contains 572,223 acres. **HK F BK HT**

YELLOWSTONE NATIONAL PARK
NW corner of state, N of Jackson & W of Cody **[P. 124, A-3]**. Contains 2,219,791 acres. **C HK BT F S R W**

State Parks

ALCOVA RESERVOIR
S of Alcova **[P. 125, D-9]**. Contains 5,872 acres. **C HK BT F S R BK**

BIG SANDY STATE RECREATION AREA
8 mi. N of Farson on US 191 **[P. 124, E-6]**. Contains 6,190 acres. **C BT F S**

BOYSEN STATE PARK
14 mi. NW of Shoshoni off US 20 **[P. 124, C-7]**. Contains 39,545 acres. **C BT F S W HT**

BUFFALO BILL STATE PARK
6 mi. W of Cody off US 20 **[P. 124, B-6]**. Contains 11,498 acres. **C BT F W HT**

CURT GOWDY STATE PARK
26 mi. W of Cheyenne **[P. 125, F-11]**. Contains 1,960 acres. **C HK BT F HT**

EDNESS KIMBALL WILKINS STATE PARK
6 mi. E of Casper **[P. 125, D-9]**. Contains 318 acres. **HK F S BK W**

GLENDO STATE PARK
4 mi. E of Glendo off US 87 **[P. 125, D-11]**. Contains 22,430 acres. **C HK BT F S W**

GUERNSEY STATE PARK
3 mi. W of Guernsey, off US 26 **[P. 125, E-11]**. Contains 8,638 acres. **C HK BT S**

KEYHOLE STATE PARK
7 mi. N of I-90 between Moorcroft and Sundance **[P. 125, B-11]**. Contains 15,674 acres. **C BT F S W**

SINKS CANYON STATE PARK
6 mi. SE of Lander **[P. 124, D-6]**. Contains 600 acres. **C F HT**

Skiing

ALPINE SKIING

GRAND TARGHEE RESORT
Ski Hill Road, Alta **[P. 124, D-1]**; (307) 353-2304.
Vertical drop is 2,200 feet. Has one tow and three chairs.

JACKSON HOLE SKI RESORT
7658 N. Teewinot Rd., Teton Village **[P. 124, D-1]**; (307) 733-2292.
Vertical drop is 4,139 feet. Has two surface lifts, seven chairs and one tram.
◆One of the best resorts in the USA for serious, expert skiing.

SNOW KING RESORT
400 E. Snow King Ave., Jackson **[P. 124, C-4]**; (307) 733-5200.
Vertical drop is 1,571 feet. Has one tow and two chairs.

NORDIC SKIING

GRAND TARGHEE NORDIC CENTER
Alta **[P. 124, D-1]**; (307) 353-2304.

ROSSIGNOL NORDIC CENTER
Jackson Hole Ski Area, Teton Village **[P. 124, D-1]**; (307) 733-2292.

TOGWOTEE MOUNTAIN LODGE
US Highway 26, Moran **[P. 124, D-2]**; (307) 543-2847.

YELLOWSTONE NATIONAL PARK T.W. SERVICES
Mammoth Hot Springs in Yellowstone Park **[P. 124, E-2]**; (800) 421-3401.

ACTIVE SPORTS

BASEBALL: Little League Baseball Western Region HQ, 6707 Little League Dr., San Bernadino, CA; (714) 887-6444. • **American Legion Baseball,** 240 S. Walcott, Midwest Building, Suite 200, Casper; (307) 473-9024. • **Babe Ruth Baseball,** Jim Lemp, 1911 Oxford Dr., Cheyenne; (307) 638-6023.

CANOEING & KAYAKING: ACA Rocky Mountain Vice Commodore, c/o Four Corners Marine, Box 379, Durango, CO; (303) 259-3893.

CYCLING: USCF Wyoming/Dakota-West Representative, 225 Johnson, Laramie; (307) 742-4763.

FOOTBALL: Pop Warner Football, 1315 Walnut Street, Suite 1632, Philadelphia, PA; (215) 735-1450

GOLF: PGA Colorado Section, 12323 E. Cornell, Suite 21, Aurora, CO; (303) 745-3697. • **PGA Rocky Mountain Section,** 595 E. State St., Eagle, ID; (208) 939-6028. • **Wyoming Golf Association,** 501 First Ave. South, Greybull; (307) 568-3304

HIKING & CLIMBING: Wyoming Sierra Club Chapter, RR 31, Box 807, Dubois; (307) 455-2161

HOCKEY: USA Hockey Rocky Mountain Registrar, 7335 S. Garfield Ct., Littleton, CO; (303) 721-0936.

HUNTING & FISHING: Game & Fish Department, 5400 Bishop Blvd., Cheyenne; (307) 777-7735. • **Trout Unlimited,** 1250 W. Foothill Blvd., Rock Springs; (307) 382-4857.

RACQUETBALL: AARA, 121 1st Street, PO Box 6075, Rock Springs; (307) 382-5803.

RODEO: PRCA Mountain States Circuit, 23459 WCR 58, Greeley, CO; (303) 352-6638.

RUNNING: RRCA WY State Rep., 3204 Reed Ave., Cheyenne; (307) 632-2602.

SCUBA: Teton Aquatic Supplies, 145 West Gill, PO Box 3482, Jackson; (307) 733-3127. • **Western Divers, Ltd.,** 323 Thelma Drive, Casper; (307) 472-0230.

SHOOTING: HF Bar Ranch, Saddlestring; (307) 684-2487.

SKATING: USFSA, 20 First Street, Colorado Springs, CO; (719) 635-5200.

SOCCER: Wyoming State Soccer Ass'n, 352 Indian Paintbrush, Casper. • **AYSO Regional Director,** 1720 Carmel Dr., Idaho Falls, ID; (208) 526-4485.

SOFTBALL: Wyoming ASA, 275 Saddle Ridge Rd., Evanston; (307) 789-3995.

SQUASH: Casper YMCA, Casper; (307) 234-9187.

SWIMMING: LMSC Wyoming Registrar, 1203 Reynolds, Laramie; (307) 745-5010

TENNIS: Recreational TEAMTENNIS Central-West Region, National Program Coordinator, 2105 Grant Ave., #4, Redondo Beach, CA; (800) 992-9042. • **Intermountain USTA,** 1201 South Parker Rd., #102, Denver, CO; (303) 695-4117.

STATBOX

POPULATION: 470,000
SQUARE MILES: 100,375
TIME ZONE: Mountain
MOTTO: Equal Rights
BIRD: Meadowlark
TREE: Cottonwood
CAPITAL: Cheyenne
AVERAGE ANNUAL RAINFALL: 5" to 45"
MEAN TEMP: 85/95 (summer); 14/25 (winter)
MAJOR LEAGUE TEAMS: 0
NATIONAL PARK/FORESTS: 3,572 square miles
STATE PARK ACREAGE: 112,078
HIGHEST ELEVATION: 13,804'
LOWEST ELEVATION: 3,100'
WATERWAYS: 15,846 miles of rivers and streams; 297,632 acres of lakes

> **"I was very lucky growing up [in Wyoming]. Everything I loved was there. . . Yellowstone Park, Jackson Hole, which I think is the prettiest place in the U.S. . . . [And] Wyoming has an excellent wildlife management program. The state is probably one of the best in America for offering fishing, hunting, skiing. That's a way of life out there."**
>
> Television sportscaster *Curt Gowdy*

District of Columbia

The District of Columbia may have the House, the Senate, and the Supreme Court, but those who live there can get more excited about the NFL's Redskins, the NBA's Bullets, and the NHL's Capitals. (The latter two are located just across the border in Landover, Maryland, but "belong" to Washington.) ◆ Outdoor enthusiasts will love Rock Creek Park. It has 1,700 acres with golf courses, tennis courts, horse stables and bike trails. (The top-flight Sovran Bank Tennis Classic in July is the nation's only pro tournament held at a public tennis facility—Rock Creek Tennis Stadium.) ◆ The Marine Corps Marathon, which has often been scheduled against its New York sister race, is considered one of the USA's quality 26-milers. ◆ And college basketball fans across the nation avidly follow Georgetown's Big East powerhouse, the Hoyas.

▶ SPECTATOR VENUES

College Sports

AMERICAN UNIVERSITY EAGLES
4400 Massachusetts Avenue NW, Washington **[P. 54, E-3]**; (202) 885-3000. Reeves Field, capacity 5,000. Bender Arena, capacity 5,000.
◆New on-campus arena.

GEORGE WASHINGTON UNIVERSITY COLONIALS
600 22nd Street NW, Washington **[P. 54, F-4]**; (202) 994-6650. Smith Center, capacity 5,000.
◆Small arena, relatively expensive tickets.

GEORGETOWN UNIVERSITY HOYAS
37th & "O" Streets NW, Washington **[P. 54, F-3]**; (202) 687-2435. Kehoe Field, capacity 4,000. McDonough Arena, capacity 4,000.
◆McDonough very small and cramped. The Hoyas play most of their games at Capital Centre in Landover (see Maryland, below), so it's not exactly a college atmosphere. But you do get to watch big John Thompson stalk the sideline.

HOWARD UNIVERSITY BISON
6th and Girard Streets NW, Washington **[P. 54, F-4]**; (202) 806-7140. Howard, capacity 8,000. Burr Gym, capacity 3,000.
Robert F. Kennedy Stadium, capacity 56,000.

Football

ROBERT F. KENNEDY STADIUM
East Capitol Street, Washington **[P. 54, F-5]**. Built in 1961. Capacity: 55,672.
◆Access via Metrorail. Redskins games are usually sold out. The food could use improvement.
Washington Redskins (NFC Eastern Division); (703) 471-9100. Franchise began in 1932. Broadcasts by WMAL.

Polo

NATIONAL CAPITAL POLO CLUB
Ohio Dr. & Independence Dr., Washington **[P. 54, F-4]**; (703) 494-5422.

Tennis

THE GEORGE WASHINGTON UNIVERSITY'S SMITH CENTER
600 22nd St. NW, Washington **[P. 54, F-4]**; (202) 994-6650. Surface is Supreme.
◆Small arena, close-to-the-action seating. Former host of WTA's Virginia Slims of Washington.

WILLIAM H.G. FITZGERALD TENNIS CENTER
16th and Kennedy Streets, NW, Washington **[P. 54, E-4]**; (202) 291-9763. Surface is hard.
◆Virginia Slims of Washington (WTA), August, (202) 291-9888.American Tennis Association National Championship, August.
Sovran Bank Classic (ATP), July.

▶ ACTIVE SPORTS

AEROBICS: AFAA, 3441 B March Cir., Washington; (202) 561-9190.

BASEBALL: Little League Baseball Eastern Region HQ, PO Box 3485, Williamsport, PA; (717) 326-1921. • **Men's Senior Baseball League - Washington, DC,** 11001 Cross Laurel Dr., Germantown, MD; (301) 540-0216.

BOARDSAILING: USWA Regional Director, 1912 MacCumber Ln., Wilmington, NC; (919) 256-3553.

BOWLING: American Bowling Congress, 5301 S. 76th St., Greendale, WI; (414) 421-6400.

CANOEING & KAYAKING: ACA Middle States Vice Commodore, 10236 Raider Ln., Fairfax, VA; (703) 359-2594.

CYCLING: LAW Coastal Regional Director, 205 E. Joppa Road, Baltimore, MD; (301) 828-8604. • **Potomac Area AYH Council,** PO Box 28607, Central Station, Washington; (202) 783-4943. • **USCF Virginia/Washington DC Representative,** 946 Shillelagh Rd., Chesapeake, VA; (804) 547-7905.

FOOTBALL: Pop Warner Football, 1315 Walnut Street, Suite 1632, Philadelphia, PA; (215) 735-1450. • **U.S. Flag Football League,** 5834 Pine Tree Drive, Sanibel, FL; (813) 472-0544.

GOLF: PGA Middle Atlantic Section, 7270 Cradlerock Way, Columbia, MD; (301) 621-8320.

HIKING & CLIMBING: Potomac Appalachian Trail Club, 1718 N St. Northwest, Washington; (202) 638-5306. • **Rails-To-Trails Conservancy (AHS),** 1400 16th St. NW, Washington; (202) 797-5400.

HOCKEY: USA Hockey Southeastern Registrar, PO Box 5208, Takoma Park, MD; (301) 622-0032.

SCUBA: National Diving Center, 4932 Wisconsin Avenue NW, Washington; (202) 363-6123.

SKATING: USFSA, 20 First Street, Colorado Springs, CO; (719) 635-5200.

SOCCER: AYSO Regional Director, 4014 Oneida St., New Hartford, NY; (315) 737-5610.

SQUASH: Capitol Hill Squash Club (USSRA), Washington; (202) 547-2255. • **Washington Squash & Nautilus (USSRA),** Washington; (202) 659-9570.

TENNIS: Recreational TEAMTENNIS East Region, National Program Coordinator, 246 N. Reservoir St., Lancaster, PA; (800) 633-6122. • **Mid-Atlantic USTA,** PO Drawer F, Springfield, VA; (703) 321-9045.

USA SNAPSHOTS®

A look at statistics that shape the sports world

LPGA's winning underdogs

Source: LPGA

By Keith Carter, USA TODAY

STATBOX

POPULATION: 636,000
SQUARE MILES: 69
TIME ZONE: Eastern
MOTTO: Celebrate the city; discover the world
BIRD: Wood Thrush
TREE: Scarlet Oak
AVERAGE ANNUAL RAINFALL: 39"
MEAN TEMP: 58
MAJOR LEAGUE TEAMS: 3
NATIONAL PARK/FOREST ACREAGE: 8,559
HIGHEST ELEVATION: 410
LOWEST ELEVATION: sea level
WATERWAYS: 19 miles of rivers

Tip Offs — The Pick of Pick-up Games

If you're looking for action which is flashy and furious — either as a spectator or as a player — every city has its hot spots where the cream of the local talent comes to showcase its moves. Magic Johnson, Byron Scott and other NBA stars have been known to drop by the wood court gym at UCLA for off-season refreshers. So, if you have a student ID or a friend who can get you in, its always worth checking out local colleges or YMCAs. Meanwhile, to get you off on the right foot, here's a sampling of parks, playgrounds and programs noted for intense play.

West 4th Street, New York City: Just one block from Washington Square Park in Greenwich Village, there's always some lively action here — if not on the cramped full court or the always-crowded handball courts, then on the surrounding streets. Bleachers are set up during summer for sponsored five-on-five tournaments, where teams put together professional-looking fast-break ball.

Central Park, New York City: Home of summer softball; it seems to go on around the clock. Ball fields are located in three separate areas — Hecksher Playground at 62nd St., the Great Lawn at 84th St. and the North Meadow at 98th St. Call (212) 480-0205.

Hammond Park, Atlanta: The basketball courts feature serious playing, worth stopping to watch. . . or join if you dare.

Grant Park, Chicago: With Michigan Boulevard's distinct skyline on one side and the lake on the other, Grant Park is a hub of activity, replete with summer softball leagues and pick-up soccer.

Lincoln Park, Chicago: With drop-ins such as former Bears back-up QB Mike Tomczak and line men from the Big Ten — known to play here on weekends — the touch football games stand out.

Venice Beach, Los Angeles: Two blocks south of Windward Ave. on the boardwalk, the basketball games are always fun to watch, or, with three full-length courts, to play in.

Pizza Hut/Pepsi Hoop-It-Up: With playground rules, where players call their own fouls, the travelling Hoop-It-Up tournament has transformed pick-up street ball. In its birthplace city, Dallas, Hoop-It-Up attracts 15,000 players and more than 100,000 spectators; and the high-skill division finals will be televised this year by NBC immediately after the USC-Notre Dame football game. As it tours 34 cities from April to November, Hoop-It-Up holds an estimated 26,000 games on closed-off streets lined with its portable goals. With multiple 16-team divisions, grouped by prior playing experience (varsity, intramural, college, semi-pro, pro, etc.), everybody's gauranteed to play in at least three games — whether you're former NBAer Wes Matthews or pushing sixty and shoot from the hip. For more information call (800) 733-HOOP or (214) 954-0200. — Duncan Bock